ROUTLEDGE

STUDENT STATUTE

European Union Legislation

2012–2013

'Focused content, layout and price – Routledge competes and wins in relation to all of these factors' – Craig Lind, University of Sussex, UK

'The best value and best format books on the market' – Ed Bates, Southampton University, UK

Routledge Student Statutes present all the legislation students need in one easy-to-use volume. Developed in response to feedback from lecturers and students, this book offers a fully up-to-date, comprehensive, and clearly presented collection of legislation – ideal for LLB and GDL course and exam use.

Routledge Student Statutes are:

- **Exam Friendly:** un-annotated and conforming to exam regulations

- **Tailored to fit your course:** 80% of lecturers we surveyed agree that *Routledge Student Statutes* match their course and cover the relevant legislation

- **Trustworthy:** *Routledge Student Statutes* are compiled by subject experts, updated annually and have been developed to meet student needs through extensive market research

- **Easy to use:** a clear text design, comprehensive table of contents, multiple indexes and highlighted amendments to the law make these books the more student-friendly Statutes on the market

- **Competitively Priced:** *Routledge Student Statutes* offer content and usability rated as good or better than our major competitor, but at a more competitive price

- **Supported by a Companion Website:** presenting scenario questions for interpreting Statutes, annotated web links, and multiple-choice questions, these resources are designed to help students to be confident and prepared.

Jeffrey Kenner is Professor of European Law at the University of Nottingham.

ROUTLEDGE STUDENT STATUTES

www.routledge.com/cw/statutes

Praise for Routledge Student Statutes

'The best value and best format books on the market' – Ed Bates, University of Southampton, UK

'Focused content, layout and price – Routledge competes and wins in relation to all of these factors' – Craig Lind, University of Sussex, UK

'comprehensive and reliable' – Andromachi Georgosouli, University of Leicester, UK

'user friendly and sensibly laid out' – John Stanton, Kingston University, UK

'An exciting and valuable selection of the key legislative material' – David Radlett, University of Kent, UK

'I prefer the layout of the Routledge statute book to other statute books that I have seen' – Nicola Haralambous, University of Hertfordshire, UK

'Well-presented and has thorough content [. . .] clearly a good competitor' – Brian Coggon, University of Lincoln, UK

'. . . given the addition of the useful web resource and the easy to read section headings, I would be more inclined to recommend this book than other statute texts' – Emma Warner-Reed, Leeds Metropolitan University, UK

'excellent and relevant' – Sarwan Singh, City University London, UK

'I personally prefer the Routledge series as it is better laid out and more accessible' – Jonathan Doak, University of Nottingham, UK

'Routledge Student Statutes are practical and carefully designed for the needs of the students' – Stelios Andreadakis, Oxford Brookes University, UK

'an excellent statute text' – Fang Ma, University of Hertfordshire, UK

'Other statute books are not as attractive in look or feel, not as easy to navigate, more expensive and amendments are less clear' – Jason Lowther, University of Plymouth, UK

'Gives good coverage and certainly includes all elements addressed on our current syllabus. I personally think this statute is more clearly set out than other statute books and is more user friendly for it' – Samantha Pegg, Nottingham Trent University, UK

'This statute book is a student friendly material. Index features as well as the overall content make this book a valuable contribution to student reading lists' – Orkun Akseli, Newcastle University, UK

'A very welcome publication' – Simon Barnett, University of Hertfordshire, UK

'I am sticking with *Routledge Student Statutes*' – Francis Tansinda, Manchester Metropolitan University, UK

ROUTLEDGE
STUDENT STATUTES

....

European Union Legislation
2012–2013

JEFFREY KENNER
Professor of European Law at the University of Nottingham

LONDON AND NEW YORK

First published 2013
by Routledge
2 Park Square, Milton Park, Abingdon, Oxon OX14 4RN

Simultaneously published in the USA and Canada
by Routledge
711 Third Avenue, New York, NY 10017

Routledge is an imprint of the Taylor & Francis Group, an informa business

British Library Cataloguing in Publication Data
A catalogue record for this book is available from the British Library

Library of Congress Cataloging in Publication Data
A catalog record for this book has been requested

Parliamentary material is reproduced with the permission
of the Controller of HMSO on behalf of Parliament.

ISBN: 978–0–415–63386–4 (pbk)

Typeset in Sabon
by RefineCatch Limited, Bungay, Suffolk

Printed and bound in Great Britain by
TJ International Ltd, Padstow, Cornwall

Contents

Preface

The purpose of this book is to compile and present in an accessible form the essential European Union legislation that all law students need to have to hand in tutorials, in private study and in the examination hall. EU Treaty and legislation books are the principal tool for instant reference for students on a regular basis throughout the year. My aim has been to produce a book that students can use quickly and effectively whenever and wherever the need arises, whether in parallel to reading from text books, the internet, or lecture notes, or when seeking to intervene in class, or, ultimately, to search for and speedily identify an elusive point of law in the examination. It is also ideal to use in conjunction with further research into the sources of the law from EUR-Lex, the EU's wonderful online depository of the *acquis communautaire* and the essential source for the material contained within this book.

For an EU legislation book to be effective in the contexts in which it is most needed by students, the selection of laws must be relevant and up to date, the editing concise, and the presentation clear. I have sought to ensure that every editorial decision I make is tested against these criteria. In the previous edition I added several new governance measures. These included a Regulation on the Citizens' initiative and an amending Regulation on the control of the Commission's implementing powers. Also featured were a new Directive on patients' rights to cross-border healthcare, a codification of the Free Movement of Workers Regulation and a revised Directive on parental leave. I introduced two innovations in response to student demand and helpful advice from reviewers. Firstly, Part II on Fundamental Rights now includes not only the Charter of Fundamental Rights but also the Charter's essential sources – or explanations – for interpretation of each of its provisions. Secondly, I reorganised Part VI on Competition Law into two sections, one containing an expanded selection of notices or guidance from the European Commission, which provide a reference point for the law in this area, and the other containing the core Regulations.

By contrast, the 2012–2013 edition contains only minor changes. In Part IV there are amended versions of the Court of Justice's Rules of Procedure and its Information Note on references from national courts for a preliminary ruling. On the advice of reviewers, the old Directive 70/50/EEC has been left out of Part V, as it is only of historic interest, along with Directive 77/486/EEC on the education of children of migrant workers. The relatively unheralded Directive 94/33/EC on young workers has been omitted from Part VII.

As with previous editions, I have started with the Treaties followed by the tables of equivalences for converting Treaty numbers. In addition to selected Treaty protocols, I have also included the most important of the declarations annexed to the Final Act of the Intergovernmental Conference which adopted the Treaty of Lisbon. I have not included the draft Treaty on Stability, Coordination and Governance in the Economic and Monetary Union, the so-called Fiscal Union Treaty, because, although it will create a new set of binding rules for Eurozone countries, it is not intended to amend the Treaties, will not apply to all Member States, and faces considerable political hurdles (and possible legal challenges) before it can enter into legal force.

For secondary legislation, I have included, firstly, the essential supplementary rules governing the institutions, law-making and the judicial process – the core governance elements of EU law courses – and, secondly, implementing legislation in the substantive areas of internal market, competition law and social policy, normally taught in the second semester of whole year EU law courses or as separate subjects.

I have sought to cover these areas as fully as possible in preference to extending the book thinly into other areas. In order to ensure that the book has a readable font size I have sought to eliminate superfluous material by omitting unnecessary footnotes and, in some cases, dispensing with preambles.

For more guidance on how to use this book why not access the additional learning resources online at www.routledgelaw.com/statutes. Here you can practice your application of EU legislation in a series of exam-type scenarios. You will find a set of multiple choice questions to test you on your knowledge of both primary and secondary legislation. Finally, there is a guide on how to gain the maximum benefit from an EU legislation book.

The legislation in this book is up-to-date as of 1 May 2012. I am grateful to the Publications Office of the European Union for their kind permission to reproduce the materials from EUR-Lex (© European Union, http://eur-lex.europa.eu) and Europa used in this volume. In some cases the consolidated form of legislation published in EUR-Lex has been reproduced and, although wholly accurate, it is not strictly authentic as it is not reproduced in the form published in the *Official Journal of the European Union*.

I have been immensely helped in this task by the smooth operation at Routledge, especially from Rebecca Slorach, Damian Mitchell, Emma Nugent and Fiona Kinnear. I am also hugely in debt, as ever, to Jacqueline Abbott for her encouragement and support throughout this project.

Jeff Kenner
Nottingham
May 2012

Guide to the Companion Website

....

www.routledge.com/cw/statutes

Visit the Companion Website for *Routledge Student Statutes* in order to:

- Understand how to use a statute book in tutorials and exams;

- Learn how to interpret statutes and other legislation to maximum effect;

- Gain essential practice in statute interpretation prior to your exams, through unique problem-based scenarios;

- Test your understanding of statutes through a set of Multiple Choice Questions for revision or to check your own progress;

- Understand how the law is developing with updates, additional information and links to useful websites.

Chronological Index*

---

* Ordered by publication date in the *Official Journal of the European Union* unless otherwise stated

I Treaties

NOTE TO THE READER ACCOMPANYING THE CONSOLIDATED VERSIONS OF THE TREATY ON EUROPEAN UNION AND THE TREATY ON THE FUNCTIONING OF THE EUROPEAN UNION
OJ C 83, 30.3.2010*

This publication contains the consolidated versions of the Treaty on European Union and of the Treaty on the Functioning of the European Union, together with the annexes and protocols thereto, as they result from the amendments introduced by the Treaty of Lisbon, which was signed on 13 December 2007 in Lisbon and which entered into force on 1 December 2009. It also contains the declarations annexed to the Final Act of the Intergovernmental Conference which adopted the Treaty of Lisbon.

As indicated in the Note to the Reader accompanying the previous issue of the consolidated Treaties (OJ C 115, 9.5.2008, p. 1), the current issue includes those rectifications which were adopted up to the time of publication.

This publication also contains the Charter of Fundamental Rights of the European Union which was proclaimed at Strasbourg on 12 December 2007 by the European Parliament, the Council and the Commission (OJ C 303, 14.12.2007, p. 1). This text repeats and adapts the Charter proclaimed on 7 December 2000, and replaces it with effect from 1 December 2009, the date of entry into force of the Treaty of Lisbon. By virtue of the first subparagraph of Article 6(1) of the Treaty on European Union, the Charter proclaimed in 2007 has the same legal value as the Treaties.

Final paragraph omitted

---

* EDITOR'S NOTE: This book reproduces essentially the bulk of the material referred to in the above Note to the Reader accompanying the consolidated Treaties in the edition of the *Official Journal of the European Union* of 30 March 2010, C 83. However, a number of the protocols and declarations have been omitted as have the annexess. For a full set of the Treaties, past and present, including the Treaties of Accession, refer to EUR-Lex at: http://eur-lex.europa.eu/en/treaties/index.htm.

CONSOLIDATED VERSION OF THE TREATY ON EUROPEAN UNION
OJ C 83, 30.3.2010, P. 13*

PREAMBLE

His Majesty the King of the Belgians, Her Majesty the Queen of Denmark, the President of the Federal Republic of Germany, the President of Ireland, the President of the Hellenic Republic, His Majesty the King of Spain, the President of the French Republic, the President of the Italian Republic, his Royal Highness the Grand Duke of Luxembourg, Her Majesty the Queen of the Netherlands, the President of the Portuguese Republic, her Majesty the Queen of the United Kingdom of Great Britain and Northern Ireland, [1]

RESOLVED to mark a new stage in the process of European integration undertaken with the establishment of the European Communities,

DRAWING INSPIRATION from the cultural, religious and humanist inheritance of Europe, from which have developed the universal values of the inviolable and inalienable rights of the human person, freedom, democracy, equality and the rule of law,

RECALLING the historic importance of the ending of the division of the European continent and the need to create firm bases for the construction of the future Europe,

CONFIRMING their attachment to the principles of liberty, democracy and respect for human rights and fundamental freedoms and of the rule of law,

CONFIRMING their attachment to fundamental social rights as defined in the European Social Charter signed at Turin on 18 October 1961 and in the 1989 Community Charter of the Fundamental Social Rights of Workers,

---

* EDITOR'S NOTE: Where articles in the Treaty on European Union replace previous Treaty articles, the old article numbers from the previous version of the Treaty on European Union (TEU) and/or the now replaced Treaty establishing the European Community (TEC) are shown in brackets. See the Table of Equivalences for the Treaty on European Union reproduced in Part II of this edition for a complete conversion table from the old to the new article numbers and vice versa.

[1] The Republic of Bulgaria, the Czech Republic, the Republic of Estonia, the Republic of Cyprus, the Republic of Latvia, the Republic of Lithuania, the Republic of Hungary, the Republic of Malta, the Republic of Austria, the Republic of Poland, Romania, the Republic of Slovenia, the Slovak Republic, the Republic of Finland and the Kingdom of Sweden have since become members of the European Union.

DESIRING to deepen the solidarity between their peoples while respecting their history, their culture and their traditions,

DESIRING to enhance further the democratic and efficient functioning of the institutions so as to enable them better to carry out, within a single institutional framework, the tasks entrusted to them,

RESOLVED to achieve the strengthening and the convergence of their economies and to establish an economic and monetary union including, in accordance with the provisions of this Treaty and of the Treaty on the Functioning of the European Union, a single and stable currency,

DETERMINED to promote economic and social progress for their peoples, taking into account the principle of sustainable development and within the context of the accomplishment of the internal market and of reinforced cohesion and environmental protection, and to implement policies ensuring that advances in economic integration are accompanied by parallel progress in other fields,

RESOLVED to establish a citizenship common to nationals of their countries,

RESOLVED to implement a common foreign and security policy including the progressive framing of a common defence policy, which might lead to a common defence in accordance with the provisions of Article 42, thereby reinforcing the European identity and its independence in order to promote peace, security and progress in Europe and in the world,

RESOLVED to facilitate the free movement of persons, while ensuring the safety and security of their peoples, by establishing an area of freedom, security and justice, in accordance with the provisions of this Treaty and of the Treaty on the Functioning of the European Union,

RESOLVED to continue the process of creating an ever closer union among the peoples of Europe, in which decisions are taken as closely as possible to the citizen in accordance with the principle of subsidiarity,

IN VIEW of further steps to be taken in order to advance European integration,

HAVE DECIDED to establish a European Union and to this end have designated as their Plenipotentiaries: *(list of plenipotentiaries not reproduced)*

WHO, having exchanged their full powers, found in good and due form, have agreed as follows:

TITLE I
COMMON PROVISIONS

Article 1 (ex Article 1 TEU)
By this Treaty, the HIGH CONTRACTING PARTIES establish among themselves a EUROPEAN UNION, hereinafter called 'the Union', on which the Member States confer competences to attain objectives they have in common.

This Treaty marks a new stage in the process of creating an ever closer union among the peoples of Europe, in which decisions are taken as openly as possible and as closely as possible to the citizen.

The Union shall be founded on the present Treaty and on the Treaty on the Functioning of the European Union (hereinafter referred to as 'the Treaties'). Those two Treaties shall have the same legal value. The Union shall replace and succeed the European Community.

Article 2
The Union is founded on the values of respect for human dignity, freedom, democracy, equality, the rule of law and respect for human rights, including the rights of persons belonging to

minorities. These values are common to the Member States in a society in which pluralism, non-discrimination, tolerance, justice, solidarity and equality between women and men prevail.

Article 3 (ex Article 2 TEU)

1. The Union's aim is to promote peace, its values and the well-being of its peoples.

2. The Union shall offer its citizens an area of freedom, security and justice without internal frontiers, in which the free movement of persons is ensured in conjunction with appropriate measures with respect to external border controls, asylum, immigration and the prevention and combating of crime.

3. The Union shall establish an internal market. It shall work for the sustainable development of Europe based on balanced economic growth and price stability, a highly competitive social market economy, aiming at full employment and social progress, and a high level of protection and improvement of the quality of the environment. It shall promote scientific and technological advance.

   It shall combat social exclusion and discrimination, and shall promote social justice and protection, equality between women and men, solidarity between generations and protection of the rights of the child.

   It shall promote economic, social and territorial cohesion, and solidarity among Member States.

   It shall respect its rich cultural and linguistic diversity, and shall ensure that Europe's cultural heritage is safeguarded and enhanced.

4. The Union shall establish an economic and monetary union whose currency is the euro.

5. In its relations with the wider world, the Union shall uphold and promote its values and interests and contribute to the protection of its citizens. It shall contribute to peace, security, the sustainable development of the Earth, solidarity and mutual respect among peoples, free and fair trade, eradication of poverty and the protection of human rights, in particular the rights of the child, as well as to the strict observance and the development of international law, including respect for the principles of the United Nations Charter.

6. The Union shall pursue its objectives by appropriate means commensurate with the competences which are conferred upon it in the Treaties.

Article 4

1. In accordance with Article 5, competences not conferred upon the Union in the Treaties remain with the Member States.

2. The Union shall respect the equality of Member States before the Treaties as well as their national identities, inherent in their fundamental structures, political and constitutional, inclusive of regional and local self-government. It shall respect their essential State functions, including ensuring the territorial integrity of the State, maintaining law and order and safeguarding national security. In particular, national security remains the sole responsibility of each Member State.

3. Pursuant to the principle of sincere cooperation, the Union and the Member States shall, in full mutual respect, assist each other in carrying out tasks which flow from the Treaties.

   The Member States shall take any appropriate measure, general or particular, to ensure fulfilment of the obligations arising out of the Treaties or resulting from the acts of the institutions of the Union.

The Member States shall facilitate the achievement of the Union's tasks and refrain from any measure which could jeopardise the attainment of the Union's objectives.

Article 5 (ex Article 5 TEC)

1. The limits of Union competences are governed by the principle of conferral. The use of Union competences is governed by the principles of subsidiarity and proportionality.

2. Under the principle of conferral, the Union shall act only within the limits of the competences conferred upon it by the Member States in the Treaties to attain the objectives set out therein. Competences not conferred upon the Union in the Treaties remain with the Member States.

3. Under the principle of subsidiarity, in areas which do not fall within its exclusive competence, the Union shall act only if and in so far as the objectives of the proposed action cannot be sufficiently achieved by the Member States, either at central level or at regional and local level, but can rather, by reason of the scale or effects of the proposed action, be better achieved at Union level.

   The institutions of the Union shall apply the principle of subsidiarity as laid down in the Protocol on the application of the principles of subsidiarity and proportionality.

   National Parliaments ensure compliance with the principle of subsidiarity in accordance with the procedure set out in that Protocol.

4. Under the principle of proportionality, the content and form of Union action shall not exceed what is necessary to achieve the objectives of the Treaties.

   The institutions of the Union shall apply the principle of proportionality as laid down in the Protocol on the application of the principles of subsidiarity and proportionality.

Article 6 (ex Article 6 TEU)

1. The Union recognises the rights, freedoms and principles set out in the Charter of Fundamental Rights of the European Union of 7 December 2000, as adapted at Strasbourg, on 12 December 2007, which shall have the same legal value as the Treaties.

   The provisions of the Charter shall not extend in any way the competences of the Union as defined in the Treaties.

   The rights, freedoms and principles in the Charter shall be interpreted in accordance with the general provisions in Title VII of the Charter governing its interpretation and application and with due regard to the explanations referred to in the Charter, that set out the sources of those provisions.

2. The Union shall accede to the European Convention for the Protection of Human Rights and Fundamental Freedoms. Such accession shall not affect the Union's competences as defined in the Treaties.

3. Fundamental rights, as guaranteed by the European Convention for the Protection of Human Rights and Fundamental Freedoms and as they result from the constitutional traditions common to the Member States, shall constitute general principles of the Union's law.

Article 7 (ex Article 7 TEU)

1. On a reasoned proposal by one third of the Member States, by the European Parliament or by the European Commission, the Council, acting by a majority of four fifths of its members after obtaining the consent of the European Parliament, may determine that there is a clear risk of a serious breach by a Member State of the values referred to in

Article 2. Before making such a determination, the Council shall hear the Member State in question and may address recommendations to it, acting in accordance with the same procedure.

The Council shall regularly verify that the grounds on which such a determination was made continue to apply.

2.   The European Council, acting by unanimity on a proposal by one third of the Member States or by the Commission and after obtaining the consent of the European Parliament, may determine the existence of a serious and persistent breach by a Member State of the values referred to in Article 2, after inviting the Member State in question to submit its observations.

3.   Where a determination under paragraph 2 has been made, the Council, acting by a qualified majority, may decide to suspend certain of the rights deriving from the application of the Treaties to the Member State in question, including the voting rights of the representative of the government of that Member State in the Council. In doing so, the Council shall take into account the possible consequences of such a suspension on the rights and obligations of natural and legal persons.

The obligations of the Member State in question under this Treaty shall in any case continue to be binding on that State.

4.   The Council, acting by a qualified majority, may decide subsequently to vary or revoke measures taken under paragraph 3 in response to changes in the situation which led to their being imposed.

5.   The voting arrangements applying to the European Parliament, the European Council and the Council for the purposes of this Article are laid down in Article 354 of the Treaty on the Functioning of the European Union.

Article 8
1.   The Union shall develop a special relationship with neighbouring countries, aiming to establish an area of prosperity and good neighbourliness, founded on the values of the Union and characterised by close and peaceful relations based on cooperation.

2.   For the purposes of paragraph 1, the Union may conclude specific agreements with the countries concerned. These agreements may contain reciprocal rights and obligations as well as the possibility of undertaking activities jointly. Their implementation shall be the subject of periodic consultation.

TITLE II
PROVISIONS ON DEMOCRATIC PRINCIPLES

Article 9
In all its activities, the Union shall observe the principle of the equality of its citizens, who shall receive equal attention from its institutions, bodies, offices and agencies. Every national of a Member State shall be a citizen of the Union. Citizenship of the Union shall be additional to and not replace national citizenship.

Article 10
1.   The functioning of the Union shall be founded on representative democracy.

2.   Citizens are directly represented at Union level in the European Parliament.

Member States are represented in the European Council by their Heads of State or Government and in the Council by their governments, themselves democratically accountable either to their national Parliaments, or to their citizens.

3. Every citizen shall have the right to participate in the democratic life of the Union. Decisions shall be taken as openly and as closely as possible to the citizen.

4. Political parties at European level contribute to forming European political awareness and to expressing the will of citizens of the Union.

Article 11

1. The institutions shall, by appropriate means, give citizens and representative associations the opportunity to make known and publicly exchange their views in all areas of Union action.

2. The institutions shall maintain an open, transparent and regular dialogue with representative associations and civil society.

3. The European Commission shall carry out broad consultations with parties concerned in order to ensure that the Union's actions are coherent and transparent.

4. Not less than one million citizens who are nationals of a significant number of Member States may take the initiative of inviting the European Commission, within the framework of its powers, to submit any appropriate proposal on matters where citizens consider that a legal act of the Union is required for the purpose of implementing the Treaties.

    The procedures and conditions required for such a citizens' initiative shall be determined in accordance with the first paragraph of Article 24 of the Treaty on the Functioning of the European Union.

Article 12

National Parliaments contribute actively to the good functioning of the Union:

(a) through being informed by the institutions of the Union and having draft legislative acts of the Union forwarded to them in accordance with the Protocol on the role of national Parliaments in the European Union;

(b) by seeing to it that the principle of subsidiarity is respected in accordance with the procedures provided for in the Protocol on the application of the principles of subsidiarity and proportionality;

(c) by taking part, within the framework of the area of freedom, security and justice, in the evaluation mechanisms for the implementation of the Union policies in that area, in accordance with Article 70 of the Treaty on the Functioning of the European Union, and through being involved in the political monitoring of Europol and the evaluation of Eurojust's activities in accordance with Articles 88 and 85 of that Treaty;

(d) by taking part in the revision procedures of the Treaties, in accordance with Article 48 of this Treaty;

(e) by being notified of applications for accession to the Union, in accordance with Article 49 of this Treaty;

(f) by taking part in the inter-parliamentary cooperation between national Parliaments and with the European Parliament, in accordance with the Protocol on the role of national Parliaments in the European Union.

TITLE III
PROVISIONS ON THE INSTITUTIONS

Article 13

1. The Union shall have an institutional framework which shall aim to promote its values, advance its objectives, serve its interests, those of its citizens and those of the Member States, and ensure the consistency, effectiveness and continuity of its policies and actions.

   The Union's institutions shall be:
   — the European Parliament,
   — the European Council,
   — the Council,
   — the European Commission (hereinafter referred to as 'the Commission'),
   — the Court of Justice of the European Union,
   — the European Central Bank,
   — the Court of Auditors.

2. Each institution shall act within the limits of the powers conferred on it in the Treaties, and in conformity with the procedures, conditions and objectives set out in them. The institutions shall practice mutual sincere cooperation.

3. The provisions relating to the European Central Bank and the Court of Auditors and detailed provisions on the other institutions are set out in the Treaty on the Functioning of the European Union.

4. The European Parliament, the Council and the Commission shall be assisted by an Economic and Social Committee and a Committee of the Regions acting in an advisory capacity.

Article 14

1. The European Parliament shall, jointly with the Council, exercise legislative and budgetary functions. It shall exercise functions of political control and consultation as laid down in the Treaties. It shall elect the President of the Commission.

2. The European Parliament shall be composed of representatives of the Union's citizens. They shall not exceed seven hundred and fifty in number, plus the President. Representation of citizens shall be degressively proportional, with a minimum threshold of six members per Member State. No Member State shall be allocated more than ninety-six seats.

   The European Council shall adopt by unanimity, on the initiative of the European Parliament and with its consent, a decision establishing the composition of the European Parliament, respecting the principles referred to in the first subparagraph.

3. The members of the European Parliament shall be elected for a term of five years by direct universal suffrage in a free and secret ballot.

4. The European Parliament shall elect its President and its officers from among its members.

Article 15

1. The European Council shall provide the Union with the necessary impetus for its development and shall define the general political directions and priorities thereof. It shall not exercise legislative functions.

2. The European Council shall consist of the Heads of State or Government of the Member States, together with its President and the President of the Commission. The High

Representative of the Union for Foreign Affairs and Security Policy shall take part in its work.

3. The European Council shall meet twice every six months, convened by its President. When the agenda so requires, the members of the European Council may decide each to be assisted by a minister and, in the case of the President of the Commission, by a member of the Commission. When the situation so requires, the President shall convene a special meeting of the European Council.

4. Except where the Treaties provide otherwise, decisions of the European Council shall be taken by consensus.

5. The European Council shall elect its President, by a qualified majority, for a term of two and a half years, renewable once. In the event of an impediment or serious misconduct, the European Council can end the President's term of office in accordance with the same procedure.

6. The President of the European Council:
   (a) shall chair it and drive forward its work;
   (b) shall ensure the preparation and continuity of the work of the European Council in cooperation with the President of the Commission, and on the basis of the work of the General Affairs Council;
   (c) shall endeavour to facilitate cohesion and consensus within the European Council;
   (d) shall present a report to the European Parliament after each of the meetings of the European Council.
   The President of the European Council shall, at his level and in that capacity, ensure the external representation of the Union on issues concerning its common foreign and security policy, without prejudice to the powers of the High Representative of the Union for Foreign Affairs and Security Policy.

   The President of the European Council shall not hold a national office.

Article 16

1. The Council shall, jointly with the European Parliament, exercise legislative and budgetary functions. It shall carry out policy-making and coordinating functions as laid down in the Treaties.

2. The Council shall consist of a representative of each Member State at ministerial level, who may commit the government of the Member State in question and cast its vote.

3. The Council shall act by a qualified majority except where the Treaties provide otherwise.

4. As from 1 November 2014, a qualified majority shall be defined as at least 55% of the members of the Council, comprising at least fifteen of them and representing Member States comprising at least 65% of the population of the Union.

   A blocking minority must include at least four Council members, failing which the qualified majority shall be deemed attained.

   The other arrangements governing the qualified majority are laid down in Article 238(2) of the Treaty on the Functioning of the European Union.

5. The transitional provisions relating to the definition of the qualified majority which shall be applicable until 31 October 2014 and those which shall be applicable from 1 November 2014 to 31 March 2017 are laid down in the Protocol on transitional provisions.

6.   The Council shall meet in different configurations, the list of which shall be adopted in accordance with Article 236 of the Treaty on the Functioning of the European Union.

The General Affairs Council shall ensure consistency in the work of the different Council configurations. It shall prepare and ensure the follow-up to meetings of the European Council, in liaison with the President of the European Council and the Commission.

The Foreign Affairs Council shall elaborate the Union's external action on the basis of strategic guidelines laid down by the European Council and ensure that the Union's action is consistent.

7.   A Committee of Permanent Representatives of the Governments of the Member States shall be responsible for preparing the work of the Council.

8.   The Council shall meet in public when it deliberates and votes on a draft legislative act. To this end, each Council meeting shall be divided into two parts, dealing respectively with deliberations on Union legislative acts and non-legislative activities.

9.   The Presidency of Council configurations, other than that of Foreign Affairs, shall be held by Member State representatives in the Council on the basis of equal rotation, in accordance with the conditions established in accordance with Article 236 of the Treaty on the Functioning of the European Union.

Article 17

1.   The Commission shall promote the general interest of the Union and take appropriate initiatives to that end. It shall ensure the application of the Treaties, and of measures adopted by the institutions pursuant to them. It shall oversee the application of Union law under the control of the Court of Justice of the European Union. It shall execute the budget and manage programmes. It shall exercise coordinating, executive and management functions, as laid down in the Treaties. With the exception of the common foreign and security policy, and other cases provided for in the Treaties, it shall ensure the Union's external representation. It shall initiate the Union's annual and multiannual programming with a view to achieving interinstitutional agreements.

2.   Union legislative acts may only be adopted on the basis of a Commission proposal, except where the Treaties provide otherwise. Other acts shall be adopted on the basis of a Commission proposal where the Treaties so provide.

3.   The Commission's term of office shall be five years.

The members of the Commission shall be chosen on the ground of their general competence and European commitment from persons whose independence is beyond doubt.

In carrying out its responsibilities, the Commission shall be completely independent. Without prejudice to Article 18(2), the members of the Commission shall neither seek nor take instructions from any Government or other institution, body, office or entity. They shall refrain from any action incompatible with their duties or the performance of their tasks.

4.   The Commission appointed between the date of entry into force of the Treaty of Lisbon and 31 October 2014, shall consist of one national of each Member State, including its President and the High Representative of the Union for Foreign Affairs and Security Policy who shall be one of its Vice- Presidents.

5.   As from 1 November 2014, the Commission shall consist of a number of members, including its President and the High Representative of the Union for Foreign Affairs and Security Policy, corresponding to two thirds of the number of Member States, unless the European Council, acting unanimously, decides to alter this number.

The members of the Commission shall be chosen from among the nationals of the Member States on the basis of a system of strictly equal rotation between the Member States, reflecting the demographic and geographical range of all the Member States. This system shall be established unanimously by the European Council in accordance with Article 244 of the Treaty on the Functioning of the European Union.

6.   The President of the Commission shall:
(a) lay down guidelines within which the Commission is to work;
(b) decide on the internal organisation of the Commission, ensuring that it acts consistently, efficiently and as a collegiate body;
(c) appoint Vice-Presidents, other than the High Representative of the Union for Foreign Affairs and Security Policy, from among the members of the Commission.
A member of the Commission shall resign if the President so requests. The High Representative of the Union for Foreign Affairs and Security Policy shall resign, in accordance with the procedure set out in Article 18(1), if the President so requests.

7.   Taking into account the elections to the European Parliament and after having held the appropriate consultations, the European Council, acting by a qualified majority, shall propose to the European Parliament a candidate for President of the Commission. This candidate shall be elected by the European Parliament by a majority of its component members. If he does not obtain the required majority, the European Council, acting by a qualified majority, shall within one month propose a new candidate who shall be elected by the European Parliament following the same procedure.

The Council, by common accord with the President-elect, shall adopt the list of the other persons whom it proposes for appointment as members of the Commission. They shall be selected, on the basis of the suggestions made by Member States, in accordance with the criteria set out in paragraph 3, second subparagraph, and paragraph 5, second subparagraph.

The President, the High Representative of the Union for Foreign Affairs and Security Policy and the other members of the Commission shall be subject as a body to a vote of consent by the European Parliament. On the basis of this consent the Commission shall be appointed by the European Council, acting by a qualified majority.

8.   The Commission, as a body, shall be responsible to the European Parliament. In accordance with Article 234 of the Treaty on the Functioning of the European Union, the European Parliament may vote on a motion of censure of the Commission. If such a motion is carried, the members of the Commission shall resign as a body and the High Representative of the Union for Foreign Affairs and Security Policy shall resign from the duties that he carries out in the Commission.

Article 18
1.   The European Council, acting by a qualified majority, with the agreement of the President of the Commission, shall appoint the High Representative of the Union for Foreign Affairs and Security Policy. The European Council may end his term of office by the same procedure.

2.   The High Representative shall conduct the Union's common foreign and security policy. He shall contribute by his proposals to the development of that policy, which he shall carry out as mandated by the Council. The same shall apply to the common security and defence policy.

3.   The High Representative shall preside over the Foreign Affairs Council.

4.   The High Representative shall be one of the Vice-Presidents of the Commission. He shall ensure the consistency of the Union's external action. He shall be responsible within the

Commission for responsibilities incumbent on it in external relations and for coordinating other aspects of the Union's external action. In exercising these responsibilities within the Commission, and only for these responsibilities, the High Representative shall be bound by Commission procedures to the extent that this is consistent with paragraphs 2 and 3.

Article 19

1.   The Court of Justice of the European Union shall include the Court of Justice, the General Court and specialised courts. It shall ensure that in the interpretation and application of the Treaties the law is observed.

Member States shall provide remedies sufficient to ensure effective legal protection in the fields covered by Union law.

2.   The Court of Justice shall consist of one judge from each Member State. It shall be assisted by Advocates-General.

The General Court shall include at least one judge per Member State.

The Judges and the Advocates-General of the Court of Justice and the Judges of the General Court shall be chosen from persons whose independence is beyond doubt and who satisfy the conditions set out in Articles 253 and 254 of the Treaty on the Functioning of the European Union. They shall be appointed by common accord of the governments of the Member States for six years. Retiring Judges and Advocates-General may be reappointed.

3.   The Court of Justice of the European Union shall, in accordance with the Treaties:
(a) rule on actions brought by a Member State, an institution or a natural or legal person;
(b) give preliminary rulings, at the request of courts or tribunals of the Member States, on the interpretation of Union law or the validity of acts adopted by the institutions;
(c) rule in other cases provided for in the Treaties.

TITLE IV
PROVISIONS ON ENHANCED COOPERATION

Article 20 (ex Articles 27a to 27e, 40 to 40b and 43 to 45 TEU and ex Articles 11 and 11a TEC)

1.   Member States which wish to establish enhanced cooperation between themselves within the framework of the Union's non-exclusive competences may make use of its institutions and exercise those competences by applying the relevant provisions of the Treaties, subject to the limits and in accordance with the detailed arrangements laid down in this Article and in Articles 326 to 334 of the Treaty on the Functioning of the European Union.

Enhanced cooperation shall aim to further the objectives of the Union, protect its interests and reinforce its integration process. Such cooperation shall be open at any time to all Member States, in accordance with Article 328 of the Treaty on the Functioning of the European Union.

2.   The decision authorising enhanced cooperation shall be adopted by the Council as a last resort, when it has established that the objectives of such cooperation cannot be attained within a reasonable period by the Union as a whole, and provided that at least nine Member States participate in it. The Council shall act in accordance with the procedure laid down in Article 329 of the Treaty on the Functioning of the European Union.

3.   All members of the Council may participate in its deliberations, but only members of the Council representing the Member States participating in enhanced cooperation shall take

part in the vote. The voting rules are set out in Article 330 of the Treaty on the Functioning of the European Union.

4.   Acts adopted in the framework of enhanced cooperation shall bind only participating Member States. They shall not be regarded as part of the *acquis* which has to be accepted by candidate States for accession to the Union.

TITLE V
GENERAL PROVISIONS ON THE UNION'S EXTERNAL ACTION AND SPECIFIC PROVISIONS ON THE COMMON FOREIGN AND SECURITY POLICY

Chapter 1 GENERAL PROVISIONS ON THE UNION'S EXTERNAL ACTION

Article 21

1.   The Union's action on the international scene shall be guided by the principles which have inspired its own creation, development and enlargement, and which it seeks to advance in the wider world: democracy, the rule of law, the universality and indivisibility of human rights and fundamental freedoms, respect for human dignity, the principles of equality and solidarity, and respect for the principles of the United Nations Charter and international law.

The Union shall seek to develop relations and build partnerships with third countries, and international, regional or global organisations which share the principles referred to in the first subparagraph. It shall promote multilateral solutions to common problems, in particular in the framework of the United Nations.

2.   The Union shall define and pursue common policies and actions, and shall work for a high degree of cooperation in all fields of international relations, in order to:
(a)   safeguard its values, fundamental interests, security, independence and integrity;
(b)   consolidate and support democracy, the rule of law, human rights and the principles of international law;
(c)   preserve peace, prevent conflicts and strengthen international security, in accordance with the purposes and principles of the United Nations Charter, with the principles of the Helsinki Final Act and with the aims of the Charter of Paris, including those relating to external borders;
(d)   foster the sustainable economic, social and environmental development of developing countries, with the primary aim of eradicating poverty;
(e)   encourage the integration of all countries into the world economy, including through the progressive abolition of restrictions on international trade;
(f)   help develop international measures to preserve and improve the quality of the environment and the sustainable management of global natural resources, in order to ensure sustainable development;
(g)   assist populations, countries and regions confronting natural or man-made disasters; and
(h)   promote an international system based on stronger multilateral cooperation and good global governance.

3.   The Union shall respect the principles and pursue the objectives set out in paragraphs 1 and 2 in the development and implementation of the different areas of the Union's external action covered by this Title and by Part Five of the Treaty on the Functioning of the European Union, and of the external aspects of its other policies.

The Union shall ensure consistency between the different areas of its external action and between these and its other policies. The Council and the Commission, assisted by the

High Representative of the Union for Foreign Affairs and Security Policy, shall ensure that consistency and shall cooperate to that effect.

Article 22
1.   On the basis of the principles and objectives set out in Article 21, the European Council shall identify the strategic interests and objectives of the Union.

Decisions of the European Council on the strategic interests and objectives of the Union shall relate to the common foreign and security policy and to other areas of the external action of the Union. Such decisions may concern the relations of the Union with a specific country or region or may be thematic in approach. They shall define their duration, and the means to be made available by the Union and the Member States.

The European Council shall act unanimously on a recommendation from the Council, adopted by the latter under the arrangements laid down for each area. Decisions of the European Council shall be implemented in accordance with the procedures provided for in the Treaties.

2.   The High Representative of the Union for Foreign Affairs and Security Policy, for the area of common foreign and security policy, and the Commission, for other areas of external action, may submit joint proposals to the Council.

Chapter 2 SPECIFIC PROVISIONS ON THE COMMON FOREIGN AND SECURITY POLICY

SECTION 1 COMMON PROVISIONS

Article 23
The Union's action on the international scene, pursuant to this Chapter, shall be guided by the principles, shall pursue the objectives of, and be conducted in accordance with, the general provisions laid down in Chapter 1.

Article 24 (ex Article 11 TEU)
1.   The Union's competence in matters of common foreign and security policy shall cover all areas of foreign policy and all questions relating to the Union's security, including the progressive framing of a common defence policy that might lead to a common defence.

The common foreign and security policy is subject to specific rules and procedures. It shall be defined and implemented by the European Council and the Council acting unanimously, except where the Treaties provide otherwise. The adoption of legislative acts shall be excluded. The common foreign and security policy shall be put into effect by the High Representative of the Union for Foreign Affairs and Security Policy and by Member States, in accordance with the Treaties. The specific role of the European Parliament and of the Commission in this area is defined by the Treaties. The Court of Justice of the European Union shall not have jurisdiction with respect to these provisions, with the exception of its jurisdiction to monitor compliance with Article 40 of this Treaty and to review the legality of certain decisions as provided for by the second paragraph of Article 275 of the Treaty on the Functioning of the European Union.

2.   Within the framework of the principles and objectives of its external action, the Union shall conduct, define and implement a common foreign and security policy, based on the development of mutual political solidarity among Member States, the identification of questions of general interest and the achievement of an ever-increasing degree of convergence of Member States' actions.

3.   The Member States shall support the Union's external and security policy actively and
unreservedly in a spirit of loyalty and mutual solidarity and shall comply with the Union's
action in this area.

The Member States shall work together to enhance and develop their mutual political
solidarity. They shall refrain from any action which is contrary to the interests of the
Union or likely to impair its effectiveness as a cohesive force in international relations.

The Council and the High Representative shall ensure compliance with these principles.

Article 25 (ex Article 12 TEU)
The Union shall conduct the common foreign and security policy by:
(a)   defining the general guidelines;

(b)   adopting decisions defining:
       (i)   actions to be undertaken by the Union;
       (ii) positions to be taken by the Union;
       (iii) arrangements for the implementation of the decisions referred to in points (i) and (ii);
             and by

(c)   strengthening systematic cooperation between Member States in the conduct of policy.

Article 26 (ex Article 13 TEU)
1.   The European Council shall identify the Union's strategic interests, determine the
objectives of and define general guidelines for the common foreign and security policy,
including for matters with defence implications. It shall adopt the necessary decisions.

If international developments so require, the President of the European Council shall
convene an extraordinary meeting of the European Council in order to define the strategic
lines of the Union's policy in the face of such developments.

2.   The Council shall frame the common foreign and security policy and take the decisions
necessary for defining and implementing it on the basis of the general guidelines and
strategic lines defined by the European Council.

The Council and the High Representative of the Union for Foreign Affairs and Security
Policy shall ensure the unity, consistency and effectiveness of action by the Union.

3.   The common foreign and security policy shall be put into effect by the High
Representative and by the Member States, using national and Union resources.

Article 27
1.   The High Representative of the Union for Foreign Affairs and Security Policy, who shall
chair the Foreign Affairs Council, shall contribute through his proposals to the
development of the common foreign and security policy and shall ensure implementation
of the decisions adopted by the European Council and the Council.

2.   The High Representative shall represent the Union for matters relating to the common
foreign and security policy. He shall conduct political dialogue with third parties on the
Union's behalf and shall express the Union's position in international organisations and at
international conferences.

3.   In fulfilling his mandate, the High Representative shall be assisted by a European External
Action Service. This service shall work in cooperation with the diplomatic services of the
Member States and shall comprise officials from relevant departments of the General
Secretariat of the Council and of the Commission as well as staff seconded from national

diplomatic services of the Member States. The organisation and functioning of the European External Action Service shall be established by a decision of the Council. The Council shall act on a proposal from the High Representative after consulting the European Parliament and after obtaining the consent of the Commission.

Article 28 (ex Article 14 TEU)

1.   Where the international situation requires operational action by the Union, the Council shall adopt the necessary decisions. They shall lay down their objectives, scope, the means to be made available to the Union, if necessary their duration, and the conditions for their implementation.

If there is a change in circumstances having a substantial effect on a question subject to such a decision, the Council shall review the principles and objectives of that decision and take the necessary decisions.

2.   Decisions referred to in paragraph 1 shall commit the Member States in the positions they adopt and in the conduct of their activity.

3.   Whenever there is any plan to adopt a national position or take national action pursuant to a decision as referred to in paragraph 1, information shall be provided by the Member State concerned in time to allow, if necessary, for prior consultations within the Council. The obligation to provide prior information shall not apply to measures which are merely a national transposition of Council decisions.

4.   In cases of imperative need arising from changes in the situation and failing a review of the Council decision as referred to in paragraph 1, Member States may take the necessary measures as a matter of urgency having regard to the general objectives of that decision. The Member State concerned shall inform the Council immediately of any such measures.

5.   Should there be any major difficulties in implementing a decision as referred to in this Article, a Member State shall refer them to the Council which shall discuss them and seek appropriate solutions. Such solutions shall not run counter to the objectives of the decision referred to in paragraph 1 or impair its effectiveness.

Article 29 (ex Article 15 TEU)

The Council shall adopt decisions which shall define the approach of the Union to a particular matter of a geographical or thematic nature. Member States shall ensure that their national policies conform to the Union positions.

Article 30 (ex Article 22 TEU)

1.   Any Member State, the High Representative of the Union for Foreign Affairs and Security Policy, or the High Representative with the Commission's support, may refer any question relating to the common foreign and security policy to the Council and may submit to it, respectively, initiatives or proposals.

2.   In cases requiring a rapid decision, the High Representative, of his own motion, or at the request of a Member State, shall convene an extraordinary Council meeting within 48 hours or, in an emergency, within a shorter period.

Article 31 (ex Article 23 TEU)

1.   Decisions under this Chapter shall be taken by the European Council and the Council acting unanimously, except where this Chapter provides otherwise. The adoption of legislative acts shall be excluded.

When abstaining in a vote, any member of the Council may qualify its abstention by making a formal declaration under the present subparagraph. In that case, it shall not be obliged to apply the decision, but shall accept that the decision commits the Union. In a spirit of mutual solidarity, the Member State concerned shall refrain from any action likely to conflict with or impede Union action based on that decision and the other Member States shall respect its position. If the members of the Council qualifying their abstention in this way represent at least one third of the Member States comprising at least one third of the population of the Union, the decision shall not be adopted.

2. By derogation from the provisions of paragraph 1, the Council shall act by qualified majority:
— when adopting a decision defining a Union action or position on the basis of a decision of the European Council relating to the Union's strategic interests and objectives, as referred to in Article 22(1),
— when adopting a decision defining a Union action or position, on a proposal which the High Representative of the Union for Foreign Affairs and Security Policy has presented following a specific request from the European Council, made on its own initiative or that of the High Representative,
— when adopting any decision implementing a decision defining a Union action or position,
— when appointing a special representative in accordance with Article 33.
If a member of the Council declares that, for vital and stated reasons of national policy, it intends to oppose the adoption of a decision to be taken by qualified majority, a vote shall not be taken. The High Representative will, in close consultation with the Member State involved, search for a solution acceptable to it. If he does not succeed, the Council may, acting by a qualified majority, request that the matter be referred to the European Council for a decision by unanimity.

3. The European Council may unanimously adopt a decision stipulating that the Council shall act by a qualified majority in cases other than those referred to in paragraph 2.

4. Paragraphs 2 and 3 shall not apply to decisions having military or defence implications.

5. For procedural questions, the Council shall act by a majority of its members.

Article 32 (ex Article 16 TEU)
Member States shall consult one another within the European Council and the Council on any matter of foreign and security policy of general interest in order to determine a common approach. Before undertaking any action on the international scene or entering into any commitment which could affect the Union's interests, each Member State shall consult the others within the European Council or the Council. Member States shall ensure, through the convergence of their actions, that the Union is able to assert its interests and values on the international scene. Member States shall show mutual solidarity.

When the European Council or the Council has defined a common approach of the Union within the meaning of the first paragraph, the High Representative of the Union for Foreign Affairs and Security Policy and the Ministers for Foreign Affairs of the Member States shall coordinate their activities within the Council.

The diplomatic missions of the Member States and the Union delegations in third countries and at international organisations shall cooperate and shall contribute to formulating and implementing the common approach.

Article 33 (ex Article 18 TEU)
The Council may, on a proposal from the High Representative of the Union for Foreign Affairs and Security Policy, appoint a special representative with a mandate in relation to particular policy issues. The special representative shall carry out his mandate under the authority of the High Representative.

Article 34 (ex Article 19 TEU)

1.   Member States shall coordinate their action in international organisations and at international conferences. They shall uphold the Union's positions in such forums. The High Representative of the Union for Foreign Affairs and Security Policy shall organise this coordination.

In international organisations and at international conferences where not all the Member States participate, those which do take part shall uphold the Union's positions.

2.   In accordance with Article 24(3), Member States represented in international organisations or international conferences where not all the Member States participate shall keep the other Member States and the High Representative informed of any matter of common interest.

Member States which are also members of the United Nations Security Council will concert and keep the other Member States and the High Representative fully informed. Member States which are members of the Security Council will, in the execution of their functions, defend the positions and the interests of the Union, without prejudice to their responsibilities under the provisions of the United Nations Charter.

When the Union has defined a position on a subject which is on the United Nations Security Council agenda, those Member States which sit on the Security Council shall request that the High Representative be invited to present the Union's position.

Article 35 (ex Article 20 TEU)

The diplomatic and consular missions of the Member States and the Union delegations in third countries and international conferences, and their representations to international organisations, shall cooperate in ensuring that decisions defining Union positions and actions adopted pursuant to this Chapter are complied with and implemented.

They shall step up cooperation by exchanging information and carrying out joint assessments.

They shall contribute to the implementation of the right of citizens of the Union to protection in the territory of third countries as referred to in Article 20(2)(c) of the Treaty on the Functioning of the European Union and of the measures adopted pursuant to Article 23 of that Treaty.

Article 36 (ex Article 21 TEU)

The High Representative of the Union for Foreign Affairs and Security Policy shall regularly consult the European Parliament on the main aspects and the basic choices of the common foreign and security policy and the common security and defence policy and inform it of how those policies evolve. He shall ensure that the views of the European Parliament are duly taken into consideration. Special representatives may be involved in briefing the European Parliament.

The European Parliament may address questions or make recommendations to the Council or the High Representative. Twice a year it shall hold a debate on progress in implementing the common foreign and security policy, including the common security and defence policy.

Article 37 (ex Article 24 TEU)

The Union may conclude agreements with one or more States or international organisations in areas covered by this Chapter.

Article 38 (ex Article 25 TEU)

Without prejudice to Article 240 of the Treaty on the Functioning of the European Union, a Political and Security Committee shall monitor the international situation in the areas covered by the common foreign and security policy and contribute to the definition of policies by delivering opinions to the Council at the request of the Council or of the High Representative of the Union for Foreign Affairs and Security Policy or on its own initiative. It shall also monitor the implementation of agreed policies, without prejudice to the powers of the High Representative.

Within the scope of this Chapter, the Political and Security Committee shall exercise, under the responsibility of the Council and of the High Representative, the political control and strategic direction of the crisis management operations referred to in Article 43.

The Council may authorise the Committee, for the purpose and for the duration of a crisis management operation, as determined by the Council, to take the relevant decisions concerning the political control and strategic direction of the operation.

Article 39

In accordance with Article 16 of the Treaty on the Functioning of the European Union and by way of derogation from paragraph 2 thereof, the Council shall adopt a decision laying down the rules relating to the protection of individuals with regard to the processing of personal data by the Member States when carrying out activities which fall within the scope of this Chapter, and the rules relating to the free movement of such data. Compliance with these rules shall be subject to the control of independent authorities.

Article 40 (ex Article 47 TEU)

The implementation of the common foreign and security policy shall not affect the application of the procedures and the extent of the powers of the institutions laid down by the Treaties for the exercise of the Union competences referred to in Articles 3 to 6 of the Treaty on the Functioning of the European Union.

Similarly, the implementation of the policies listed in those Articles shall not affect the application of the procedures and the extent of the powers of the institutions laid down by the Treaties for the exercise of the Union competences under this Chapter.

Article 41 (ex Article 28 TEU)

1. Administrative expenditure to which the implementation of this Chapter gives rise for the institutions shall be charged to the Union budget.

2. Operating expenditure to which the implementation of this Chapter gives rise shall also be charged to the Union budget, except for such expenditure arising from operations having military or defence implications and cases where the Council acting unanimously decides otherwise.

   In cases where expenditure is not charged to the Union budget, it shall be charged to the Member States in accordance with the gross national product scale, unless the Council acting unanimously decides otherwise. As for expenditure arising from operations having military or defence implications, Member States whose representatives in the Council have made a formal declaration under Article 31(1), second subparagraph, shall not be obliged to contribute to the financing thereof.

3. The Council shall adopt a decision establishing the specific procedures for guaranteeing rapid access to appropriations in the Union budget for urgent financing of initiatives in the framework of the common foreign and security policy, and in particular for preparatory activities for the tasks referred to in Article 42(1) and Article 43. It shall act after consulting the European Parliament.

   Preparatory activities for the tasks referred to in Article 42(1) and Article 43 which are not charged to the Union budget shall be financed by a start-up fund made up of Member States' contributions.

   The Council shall adopt by a qualified majority, on a proposal from the High Representative of the Union for Foreign Affairs and Security Policy, decisions establishing:

(a) the procedures for setting up and financing the start-up fund, in particular the amounts allocated to the fund;

(b) the procedures for administering the start-up fund;

(c) the financial control procedures.

When the task planned in accordance with Article 42(1) and Article 43 cannot be charged to the Union budget, the Council shall authorise the High Representative to use the fund. The High Representative shall report to the Council on the implementation of this remit.

SECTION 2 PROVISIONS ON THE COMMON SECURITY AND DEFENCE POLICY

Article 42 (ex Article 17 TEU)

1. The common security and defence policy shall be an integral part of the common foreign and security policy. It shall provide the Union with an operational capacity drawing on civilian and military assets. The Union may use them on missions outside the Union for peace-keeping, conflict prevention and strengthening international security in accordance with the principles of the United Nations Charter. The performance of these tasks shall be undertaken using capabilities provided by the Member States.

2. The common security and defence policy shall include the progressive framing of a common Union defence policy. This will lead to a common defence, when the European Council, acting unanimously, so decides. It shall in that case recommend to the Member States the adoption of such a decision in accordance with their respective constitutional requirements.

    The policy of the Union in accordance with this Section shall not prejudice the specific character of the security and defence policy of certain Member States and shall respect the obligations of certain Member States, which see their common defence realised in the North Atlantic Treaty Organisation (NATO), under the North Atlantic Treaty and be compatible with the common security and defence policy established within that framework.

3. Member States shall make civilian and military capabilities available to the Union for the implementation of the common security and defence policy, to contribute to the objectives defined by the Council. Those Member States which together establish multinational forces may also make them available to the common security and defence policy.

    Member States shall undertake progressively to improve their military capabilities. The Agency in the field of defence capabilities development, research, acquisition and armaments (hereinafter referred to as 'the European Defence Agency') shall identify operational requirements, shall promote measures to satisfy those requirements, shall contribute to identifying and, where appropriate, implementing any measure needed to strengthen the industrial and technological base of the defence sector, shall participate in defining a European capabilities and armaments policy, and shall assist the Council in evaluating the improvement of military capabilities.

4. Decisions relating to the common security and defence policy, including those initiating a mission as referred to in this Article, shall be adopted by the Council acting unanimously on a proposal from the High Representative of the Union for Foreign Affairs and Security Policy or an initiative from a Member State. The High Representative may propose the use of both national resources and Union instruments, together with the Commission where appropriate.

5. The Council may entrust the execution of a task, within the Union framework, to a group of Member States in order to protect the Union's values and serve its interests. The execution of such a task shall be governed by Article 44.

6.   Those Member States whose military capabilities fulfil higher criteria and which have made more binding commitments to one another in this area with a view to the most demanding missions shall establish permanent structured cooperation within the Union framework. Such cooperation shall be governed by Article 46. It shall not affect the provisions of Article 43.

7.   If a Member State is the victim of armed aggression on its territory, the other Member States shall have towards it an obligation of aid and assistance by all the means in their power, in accordance with Article 51 of the United Nations Charter. This shall not prejudice the specific character of the security and defence policy of certain Member States.

Commitments and cooperation in this area shall be consistent with commitments under the North Atlantic Treaty Organisation, which, for those States which are members of it, remains the foundation of their collective defence and the forum for its implementation.

Article 43

1.   The tasks referred to in Article 42(1), in the course of which the Union may use civilian and military means, shall include joint disarmament operations, humanitarian and rescue tasks, military advice and assistance tasks, conflict prevention and peace-keeping tasks, tasks of combat forces in crisis management, including peace-making and post-conflict stabilisation. All these tasks may contribute to the fight against terrorism, including by supporting third countries in combating terrorism in their territories.

2.   The Council shall adopt decisions relating to the tasks referred to in paragraph 1, defining their objectives and scope and the general conditions for their implementation. The High Representative of the Union for Foreign Affairs and Security Policy, acting under the authority of the Council and in close and constant contact with the Political and Security Committee, shall ensure coordination of the civilian and military aspects of such tasks.

Article 44

1.   Within the framework of the decisions adopted in accordance with Article 43, the Council may entrust the implementation of a task to a group of Member States which are willing and have the necessary capability for such a task. Those Member States, in association with the High Representative of the Union for Foreign Affairs and Security Policy, shall agree among themselves on the management of the task.

2.   Member States participating in the task shall keep the Council regularly informed of its progress on their own initiative or at the request of another Member State. Those States shall inform the Council immediately should the completion of the task entail major consequences or require amendment of the objective, scope and conditions determined for the task in the decisions referred to in paragraph 1. In such cases, the Council shall adopt the necessary decisions.

Article 45

1.   The European Defence Agency referred to in Article 42(3), subject to the authority of the Council, shall have as its task to:
(a)   contribute to identifying the Member States' military capability objectives and evaluating observance of the capability commitments given by the Member States;
(b)   promote harmonisation of operational needs and adoption of effective, compatible procurement methods;
(c)   propose multilateral projects to fulfil the objectives in terms of military capabilities, ensure coordination of the programmes implemented by the Member States and management of specific cooperation programmes;

(d) support defence technology research, and coordinate and plan joint research activities and the study of technical solutions meeting future operational needs;

(e) contribute to identifying and, if necessary, implementing any useful measure for strengthening the industrial and technological base of the defence sector and for improving the effectiveness of military expenditure.

2. The European Defence Agency shall be open to all Member States wishing to be part of it. The Council, acting by a qualified majority, shall adopt a decision defining the Agency's statute, seat and operational rules. That decision should take account of the level of effective participation in the Agency's activities. Specific groups shall be set up within the Agency bringing together Member States engaged in joint projects. The Agency shall carry out its tasks in liaison with the Commission where necessary.

Article 46

1. Those Member States which wish to participate in the permanent structured cooperation referred to in Article 42(6), which fulfil the criteria and have made the commitments on military capabilities set out in the Protocol on permanent structured cooperation, shall notify their intention to the Council and to the High Representative of the Union for Foreign Affairs and Security Policy.

2. Within three months following the notification referred to in paragraph 1 the Council shall adopt a decision establishing permanent structured cooperation and determining the list of participating Member States. The Council shall act by a qualified majority after consulting the High Representative.

3. Any Member State which, at a later stage, wishes to participate in the permanent structured cooperation shall notify its intention to the Council and to the High Representative.

    The Council shall adopt a decision confirming the participation of the Member State concerned which fulfils the criteria and makes the commitments referred to in Articles 1 and 2 of the Protocol on permanent structured cooperation. The Council shall act by a qualified majority after consulting the High Representative. Only members of the Council representing the participating Member States shall take part in the vote.

    A qualified majority shall be defined in accordance with Article 238(3)(a) of the Treaty on the Functioning of the European Union.

4. If a participating Member State no longer fulfils the criteria or is no longer able to meet the commitments referred to in Articles 1 and 2 of the Protocol on permanent structured cooperation, the Council may adopt a decision suspending the participation of the Member State concerned.

    The Council shall act by a qualified majority. Only members of the Council representing the participating Member States, with the exception of the Member State in question, shall take part in the vote.

    A qualified majority shall be defined in accordance with Article 238(3)(a) of the Treaty on the Functioning of the European Union.

5. Any participating Member State which wishes to withdraw from permanent structured cooperation shall notify its intention to the Council, which shall take note that the Member State in question has ceased to participate.

6. The decisions and recommendations of the Council within the framework of permanent structured cooperation, other than those provided for in paragraphs 2 to 5, shall be adopted by unanimity. For the purposes of this paragraph, unanimity shall be constituted by the votes of the representatives of the participating Member States only.

TITLE VI
FINAL PROVISIONS

Article 47
The Union shall have legal personality.

Article 48 (ex Article 48 TEU)
1.   The Treaties may be amended in accordance with an ordinary revision procedure. They may also be amended in accordance with simplified revision procedures.

Ordinary revision procedure
2.   The Government of any Member State, the European Parliament or the Commission may submit to the Council proposals for the amendment of the Treaties. These proposals may, inter alia, serve either to increase or to reduce the competences conferred on the Union in the Treaties. These proposals shall be submitted to the European Council by the Council and the national Parliaments shall be notified.

3.   If the European Council, after consulting the European Parliament and the Commission, adopts by a simple majority a decision in favour of examining the proposed amendments, the President of the European Council shall convene a Convention composed of representatives of the national Parliaments, of the Heads of State or Government of the Member States, of the European Parliament and of the Commission. The European Central Bank shall also be consulted in the case of institutional changes in the monetary area. The Convention shall examine the proposals for amendments and shall adopt by consensus a recommendation to a conference of representatives of the governments of the Member States as provided for in paragraph 4.

The European Council may decide by a simple majority, after obtaining the consent of the European Parliament, not to convene a Convention should this not be justified by the extent of the proposed amendments. In the latter case, the European Council shall define the terms of reference for a conference of representatives of the governments of the Member States.

4.   A conference of representatives of the governments of the Member States shall be convened by the President of the Council for the purpose of determining by common accord the amendments to be made to the Treaties.

The amendments shall enter into force after being ratified by all the Member States in accordance with their respective constitutional requirements.

5.   If, two years after the signature of a treaty amending the Treaties, four fifths of the Member States have ratified it and one or more Member States have encountered difficulties in proceeding with ratification, the matter shall be referred to the European Council.

Simplified revision procedures
6.   The Government of any Member State, the European Parliament or the Commission may submit to the European Council proposals for revising all or part of the provisions of Part Three of the Treaty on the Functioning of the European Union relating to the internal policies and action of the Union.

The European Council may adopt a decision amending all or part of the provisions of Part Three of the Treaty on the Functioning of the European Union. The European Council shall act by unanimity after consulting the European Parliament and the Commission, and the European Central Bank in the case of institutional changes in the monetary area. That decision shall not enter into force until it is approved by the Member States in accordance with their respective constitutional requirements.

The decision referred to in the second subparagraph shall not increase the competences conferred on the Union in the Treaties.

7.   Where the Treaty on the Functioning of the European Union or Title V of this Treaty provides for the Council to act by unanimity in a given area or case, the European Council may adopt a decision authorising the Council to act by a qualified majority in that area or in that case. This subparagraph shall not apply to decisions with military implications or those in the area of defence.

Where the Treaty on the Functioning of the European Union provides for legislative acts to be adopted by the Council in accordance with a special legislative procedure, the European Council may adopt a decision allowing for the adoption of such acts in accordance with the ordinary legislative procedure.

Any initiative taken by the European Council on the basis of the first or the second subparagraph shall be notified to the national Parliaments. If a national Parliament makes known its opposition within six months of the date of such notification, the decision referred to in the first or the second subparagraph shall not be adopted. In the absence of opposition, the European Council may adopt the decision.

For the adoption of the decisions referred to in the first and second subparagraphs, the European Council shall act by unanimity after obtaining the consent of the European Parliament, which shall be given by a majority of its component members.

Article 49 (ex Article 49 TEU)

Any European State which respects the values referred to in Article 2 and is committed to promoting them may apply to become a member of the Union. The European Parliament and national Parliaments shall be notified of this application. The applicant State shall address its application to the Council, which shall act unanimously after consulting the Commission and after receiving the consent of the European Parliament, which shall act by a majority of its component members. The conditions of eligibility agreed upon by the European Council shall be taken into account.

The conditions of admission and the adjustments to the Treaties on which the Union is founded, which such admission entails, shall be the subject of an agreement between the Member States and the applicant State. This agreement shall be submitted for ratification by all the contracting States in accordance with their respective constitutional requirements.

Article 50

1.   Any Member State may decide to withdraw from the Union in accordance with its own constitutional requirements.

2.   A Member State which decides to withdraw shall notify the European Council of its intention. In the light of the guidelines provided by the European Council, the Union shall negotiate and conclude an agreement with that State, setting out the arrangements for its withdrawal, taking account of the framework for its future relationship with the Union. That agreement shall be negotiated in accordance with Article 218(3) of the Treaty on the Functioning of the European Union. It shall be concluded on behalf of the Union by the Council, acting by a qualified majority, after obtaining the consent of the European Parliament.

3.   The Treaties shall cease to apply to the State in question from the date of entry into force of the withdrawal agreement or, failing that, two years after the notification referred to in paragraph 2, unless the European Council, in agreement with the Member State concerned, unanimously decides to extend this period.

4.   For the purposes of paragraphs 2 and 3, the member of the European Council or of the Council representing the withdrawing Member State shall not participate in the discussions of the European Council or Council or in decisions concerning it.

A qualified majority shall be defined in accordance with Article 238(3)(b) of the Treaty on the Functioning of the European Union.

5.   If a State which has withdrawn from the Union asks to rejoin, its request shall be subject to the procedure referred to in Article 49.

Article 51
The Protocols and Annexes to the Treaties shall form an integral part thereof.

Article 52
1.   The Treaties shall apply to the Kingdom of Belgium, the Republic of Bulgaria, the Czech Republic, the Kingdom of Denmark, the Federal Republic of Germany, the Republic of Estonia, Ireland, the Hellenic Republic, the Kingdom of Spain, the French Republic, the Italian Republic, the Republic of Cyprus, the Republic of Latvia, the Republic of Lithuania, the Grand Duchy of Luxembourg, the Republic of Hungary, the Republic of Malta, the Kingdom of the Netherlands, the Republic of Austria, the Republic of Poland, the Portuguese Republic, Romania, the Republic of Slovenia, the Slovak Republic, the Republic of Finland, the Kingdom of Sweden and the United Kingdom of Great Britain and Northern Ireland.

2.   The territorial scope of the Treaties is specified in Article 355 of the Treaty on the Functioning of the European Union.

Article 53 (ex Article 51 TEU)
This Treaty is concluded for an unlimited period.

Article 54 (ex Article 52 TEU)
1.   This Treaty shall be ratified by the High Contracting Parties in accordance with their respective constitutional requirements. The instruments of ratification shall be deposited with the Government of the Italian Republic.

2.   This Treaty shall enter into force on 1 January 1993, provided that all the Instruments of ratification have been deposited, or, failing that, on the first day of the month following the deposit of the Instrument of ratification by the last signatory State to take this step.

Article 55 (ex Article 53 TEU)
1.   This Treaty, drawn up in a single original in the Bulgarian, Czech, Danish, Dutch, English, Estonian, Finnish, French, German, Greek, Hungarian, Irish, Italian, Latvian, Lithuanian, Maltese, Polish, Portuguese, Romanian, Slovak, Slovenian, Spanish and Swedish languages, the texts in each of these languages being equally authentic, shall be deposited in the archives of the Government of the Italian Republic, which will transmit a certified copy to each of the governments of the other signatory States.

2.   This Treaty may also be translated into any other languages as determined by Member States among those which, in accordance with their constitutional order, enjoy official status in all or part of their territory. A certified copy of such translations shall be provided by the Member States concerned to be deposited in the archives of the Council.

IN WITNESS WHEREOF the undersigned Plenipotentiaries have signed this Treaty.

Done at Maastricht on the seventh day of February in the year one thousand nine hundred and ninety-two.

(List of signatories not reproduced)

CONSOLIDATED VERSION OF THE TREATY ON THE FUNCTIONING OF THE EUROPEAN UNION
OJ C 83, 30.3.2010, P. 47*

---

* EDITOR'S NOTE: Where articles in the Treaty on the Functioning of the European Union (TFEU) replace previous Treaty articles, the old article numbers from the previous version of the Treaty on European Union (TEU) and/or the now replaced Treaty establishing the European Community (TEC) are shown in brackets. See the Table of Equivalences for the TFEU reproduced in Part II of this edition for a complete conversion table from the old to the new article numbers and vice versa.

Preamble

His Majesty the King of the Belgians, The President of the Federal Republic of Germany, The President of the French Republic, The President of the Italian Republic, Her Royal Highness the Grand Duchess of Luxembourg, Her Majesty the Queen of the Netherlands,[1]

DETERMINED to lay the foundations of an ever closer union among the peoples of Europe,

RESOLVED to ensure the economic and social progress of their States by common action to eliminate the barriers which divide Europe,

AFFIRMING as the essential objective of their efforts the constant improvements of the living and working conditions of their peoples,

---

[1] The Republic of Bulgaria, the Czech Republic, the Kingdom of Denmark, the Republic of Estonia, Ireland, the Hellenic Republic, the Kingdom of Spain, the Republic of Cyprus, the Republic of Latvia, the Republic of Lithuania, the Republic of Hungary, the Republic of Malta, the Republic of Austria, the Republic of Poland, the Portuguese Republic, Romania, the Republic of Slovenia, the Slovak Republic, the Republic of Finland, the Kingdom of Sweden and the United Kingdom of Great Britain and Northern Ireland have since become members of the European Union.

RECOGNISING that the removal of existing obstacles calls for concerted action in order to guarantee steady expansion, balanced trade and fair competition,

ANXIOUS to strengthen the unity of their economies and to ensure their harmonious development by reducing the differences existing between the various regions and the backwardness of the less favoured regions,

DESIRING to contribute, by means of a common commercial policy, to the progressive abolition of restrictions on international trade,

INTENDING to confirm the solidarity which binds Europe and the overseas countries and desiring to ensure the development of their prosperity, in accordance with the principles of the Charter of the United Nations,

RESOLVED by thus pooling their resources to preserve and strengthen peace and liberty, and calling upon the other peoples of Europe who share their ideal to join in their efforts,

DETERMINED to promote the development of the highest possible level of knowledge for their peoples through a wide access to education and through its continuous updating, and to this end HAVE DESIGNATED as their Plenipotentiaries:

(List of plenipotentiaries not reproduced)

WHO, having exchanged their full powers, found in good and due form, have agreed as follows.

Part One PRINCIPLES

Article 1

1.   This Treaty organises the functioning of the Union and determines the areas of, delimitation of, and arrangements for exercising its competences.

2.   This Treaty and the Treaty on European Union constitute the Treaties on which the Union is founded. These two Treaties, which have the same legal value, shall be referred to as 'the Treaties'.

TITLE I
CATEGORIES AND AREAS OF UNION COMPETENCE

Article 2

1.   When the Treaties confer on the Union exclusive competence in a specific area, only the Union may legislate and adopt legally binding acts, the Member States being able to do so themselves only if so empowered by the Union or for the implementation of Union acts.

2.   When the Treaties confer on the Union a competence shared with the Member States in a specific area, the Union and the Member States may legislate and adopt legally binding acts in that area. The Member States shall exercise their competence to the extent that the Union has not exercised its competence. The Member States shall again exercise their competence to the extent that the Union has decided to cease exercising its competence.

3.   The Member States shall coordinate their economic and employment policies within arrangements as determined by this Treaty, which the Union shall have competence to provide.

4.   The Union shall have competence, in accordance with the provisions of the Treaty on European Union, to define and implement a common foreign and security policy, including the progressive framing of a common defence policy.

5. In certain areas and under the conditions laid down in the Treaties, the Union shall have competence to carry out actions to support, coordinate or supplement the actions of the Member States, without thereby superseding their competence in these areas.

   Legally binding acts of the Union adopted on the basis of the provisions of the Treaties relating to these areas shall not entail harmonisation of Member States' laws or regulations.

6. The scope of and arrangements for exercising the Union's competences shall be determined by the provisions of the Treaties relating to each area.

Article 3

1. The Union shall have exclusive competence in the following areas:
   (a) customs union;
   (b) the establishing of the competition rules necessary for the functioning of the internal market;
   (c) monetary policy for the Member States whose currency is the euro;
   (d) the conservation of marine biological resources under the common fisheries policy;
   (e) common commercial policy.

2. The Union shall also have exclusive competence for the conclusion of an international agreement when its conclusion is provided for in a legislative act of the Union or is necessary to enable the Union to exercise its internal competence, or in so far as its conclusion may affect common rules or alter their scope.

Article 4

1. The Union shall share competence with the Member States where the Treaties confer on it a competence which does not relate to the areas referred to in Articles 3 and 6.

2. Shared competence between the Union and the Member States applies in the following principal areas:
   (a) internal market;
   (b) social policy, for the aspects defined in this Treaty;
   (c) economic, social and territorial cohesion;
   (d) agriculture and fisheries, excluding the conservation of marine biological resources;
   (e) environment;
   (f) consumer protection;
   (g) transport;
   (h) trans-European networks;
   (i) energy;
   (j) area of freedom, security and justice;
   (k) common safety concerns in public health matters, for the aspects defined in this Treaty.

3. In the areas of research, technological development and space, the Union shall have competence to carry out activities, in particular to define and implement programmes; however, the exercise of that competence shall not result in Member States being prevented from exercising theirs.

4. In the areas of development cooperation and humanitarian aid, the Union shall have competence to carry out activities and conduct a common policy; however, the exercise of that competence shall not result in Member States being prevented from exercising theirs.

Article 5

1. The Member States shall coordinate their economic policies within the Union. To this end, the Council shall adopt measures, in particular broad guidelines for these policies.

Specific provisions shall apply to those Member States whose currency is the euro.

2.   The Union shall take measures to ensure coordination of the employment policies of the Member States, in particular by defining guidelines for these policies.

3.   The Union may take initiatives to ensure coordination of Member States' social policies.

Article 6
The Union shall have competence to carry out actions to support, coordinate or supplement the actions of the Member States. The areas of such action shall, at European level, be:
(a)   protection and improvement of human health;

(b)   industry;

(c)   culture;

(d)   tourism;

(e)   education, vocational training, youth and sport;

(f)   civil protection;

(g)   administrative cooperation.

TITLE II
PROVISIONS HAVING GENERAL APPLICATION

Article 7
The Union shall ensure consistency between its policies and activities, taking all of its objectives into account and in accordance with the principle of conferral of powers.

Article 8 (ex Article 3(2) TEC)
In all its activities, the Union shall aim to eliminate inequalities, and to promote equality, between men and women.

Article 9
In defining and implementing its policies and activities, the Union shall take into account requirements linked to the promotion of a high level of employment, the guarantee of adequate social protection, the fight against social exclusion, and a high level of education, training and protection of human health.

Article 10
In defining and implementing its policies and activities, the Union shall aim to combat discrimination based on sex, racial or ethnic origin, religion or belief, disability, age or sexual orientation.

Article 11 (ex Article 6 TEC)
Environmental protection requirements must be integrated into the definition and implementation of the Union's policies and activities, in particular with a view to promoting sustainable development.

Article 12 (ex Article 153(2) TEC)
Consumer protection requirements shall be taken into account in defining and implementing other Union policies and activities.

Article 13
In formulating and implementing the Union's agriculture, fisheries, transport, internal market, research and technological development and space policies, the Union and the Member States

shall, since animals are sentient beings, pay full regard to the welfare requirements of animals, while respecting the legislative or administrative provisions and customs of the Member States relating in particular to religious rites, cultural traditions and regional heritage.

Article 14 (ex Article 16 TEC)

Without prejudice to Article 4 of the Treaty on European Union or to Articles 93, 106 and 107 of this Treaty, and given the place occupied by services of general economic interest in the shared values of the Union as well as their role in promoting social and territorial cohesion, the Union and the Member States, each within their respective powers and within the scope of application of the Treaties, shall take care that such services operate on the basis of principles and conditions, particularly economic and financial conditions, which enable them to fulfil their missions. The European Parliament and the Council, acting by means of regulations in accordance with the ordinary legislative procedure, shall establish these principles and set these conditions without prejudice to the competence of Member States, in compliance with the Treaties, to provide, to commission and to fund such services.

Article 15 (ex Article 255 TEC)

1. In order to promote good governance and ensure the participation of civil society, the Union's institutions, bodies, offices and agencies shall conduct their work as openly as possible.

2. The European Parliament shall meet in public, as shall the Council when considering and voting on a draft legislative act.

3. Any citizen of the Union, and any natural or legal person residing or having its registered office in a Member State, shall have a right of access to documents of the Union's institutions, bodies, offices and agencies, whatever their medium, subject to the principles and the conditions to be defined in accordance with this paragraph. General principles and limits on grounds of public or private interest governing this right of access to documents shall be determined by the European Parliament and the Council, by means of regulations, acting in accordance with the ordinary legislative procedure.

   Each institution, body, office or agency shall ensure that its proceedings are transparent and shall elaborate in its own Rules of Procedure specific provisions regarding access to its documents, in accordance with the regulations referred to in the second subparagraph.

   The Court of Justice of the European Union, the European Central Bank and the European Investment Bank shall be subject to this paragraph only when exercising their administrative tasks.

   The European Parliament and the Council shall ensure publication of the documents relating to the legislative procedures under the terms laid down by the regulations referred to in the second subparagraph.

Article 16 (ex Article 286 TEC)

1. Everyone has the right to the protection of personal data concerning them.

2. The European Parliament and the Council, acting in accordance with the ordinary legislative procedure, shall lay down the rules relating to the protection of individuals with regard to the processing of personal data by Union institutions, bodies, offices and agencies, and by the Member States when carrying out activities which fall within the scope of Union law, and the rules relating to the free movement of such data. Compliance with these rules shall be subject to the control of independent authorities.

   The rules adopted on the basis of this Article shall be without prejudice to the specific rules laid down in Article 39 of the Treaty on European Union.

Article 17
1.   The Union respects and does not prejudice the status under national law of churches and religious associations or communities in the Member States.

2.   The Union equally respects the status under national law of philosophical and non-confessional organisations.

3.   Recognising their identity and their specific contribution, the Union shall maintain an open, transparent and regular dialogue with these churches and organisations.

Part Two NON-DISCRIMINATION AND CITIZENSHIP OF THE UNION

Article 18 (ex Article 12 TEC)
Within the scope of application of the Treaties, and without prejudice to any special provisions contained therein, any discrimination on grounds of nationality shall be prohibited.
The European Parliament and the Council, acting in accordance with the ordinary legislative procedure, may adopt rules designed to prohibit such discrimination.

Article 19 (ex Article 13 TEC)
1.   Without prejudice to the other provisions of the Treaties and within the limits of the powers conferred by them upon the Union, the Council, acting unanimously in accordance with a special legislative procedure and after obtaining the consent of the European Parliament, may take appropriate action to combat discrimination based on sex, racial or ethnic origin, religion or belief, disability, age or sexual orientation.

2.   By way of derogation from paragraph 1, the European Parliament and the Council, acting in accordance with the ordinary legislative procedure, may adopt the basic principles of Union incentive measures, excluding any harmonisation of the laws and regulations of the Member States, to support action taken by the Member States in order to contribute to the achievement of the objectives referred to in paragraph 1.

Article 20 (ex Article 17 TEC)
1.   Citizenship of the Union is hereby established. Every person holding the nationality of a Member State shall be a citizen of the Union. Citizenship of the Union shall be additional to and not replace national citizenship.

2.   Citizens of the Union shall enjoy the rights and be subject to the duties provided for in the Treaties. They shall have, inter alia:
   (a) the right to move and reside freely within the territory of the Member States;
   (b) the right to vote and to stand as candidates in elections to the European Parliament and in municipal elections in their Member State of residence, under the same conditions as nationals of that State;
   (c) the right to enjoy, in the territory of a third country in which the Member State of which they are nationals is not represented, the protection of the diplomatic and consular authorities of any Member State on the same conditions as the nationals of that State;
   (d) the right to petition the European Parliament, to apply to the European Ombudsman, and to address the institutions and advisory bodies of the Union in any of the Treaty languages and to obtain a reply in the same language.
   These rights shall be exercised in accordance with the conditions and limits defined by the Treaties and by the measures adopted thereunder.

Article 21 (ex Article 18 TEC)
1.   Every citizen of the Union shall have the right to move and reside freely within the territory of the Member States, subject to the limitations and conditions laid down in the Treaties and by the measures adopted to give them effect.

2.   If action by the Union should prove necessary to attain this objective and the Treaties have not provided the necessary powers, the European Parliament and the Council, acting in accordance with the ordinary legislative procedure, may adopt provisions with a view to facilitating the exercise of the rights referred to in paragraph 1.

3.   For the same purposes as those referred to in paragraph 1 and if the Treaties have not provided the necessary powers, the Council, acting in accordance with a special legislative procedure, may adopt measures concerning social security or social protection. The Council shall act unanimously after consulting the European Parliament.

Article 22 (ex Article 19 TEC)

1.   Every citizen of the Union residing in a Member State of which he is not a national shall have the right to vote and to stand as a candidate at municipal elections in the Member State in which he resides, under the same conditions as nationals of that State. This right shall be exercised subject to detailed arrangements adopted by the Council, acting unanimously in accordance with a special legislative procedure and after consulting the European Parliament; these arrangements may provide for derogations where warranted by problems specific to a Member State.

2.   Without prejudice to Article 223(1) and to the provisions adopted for its implementation, every citizen of the Union residing in a Member State of which he is not a national shall have the right to vote and to stand as a candidate in elections to the European Parliament in the Member State in which he resides, under the same conditions as nationals of that State. This right shall be exercised subject to detailed arrangements adopted by the Council, acting unanimously in accordance with a special legislative procedure and after consulting the European Parliament; these arrangements may provide for derogations where warranted by problems specific to a Member State.

Article 23 (ex Article 20 TEC)

Every citizen of the Union shall, in the territory of a third country in which the Member State of which he is a national is not represented, be entitled to protection by the diplomatic or consular authorities of any Member State, on the same conditions as the nationals of that State. Member States shall adopt the necessary provisions and start the international negotiations required to secure this protection.

The Council, acting in accordance with a special legislative procedure and after consulting the European Parliament, may adopt directives establishing the coordination and cooperation measures necessary to facilitate such protection.

Article 24 (ex Article 21 TEC)

The European Parliament and the Council, acting by means of regulations in accordance with the ordinary legislative procedure, shall adopt the provisions for the procedures and conditions required for a citizens' initiative within the meaning of Article 11 of the Treaty on European Union, including the minimum number of Member States from which such citizens must come.

Every citizen of the Union shall have the right to petition the European Parliament in accordance with Article 227.

Every citizen of the Union may apply to the Ombudsman established in accordance with Article 228.

Every citizen of the Union may write to any of the institutions or bodies referred to in this Article or in Article 13 of the Treaty on European Union in one of the languages mentioned in Article 55(1) of the Treaty on European Union and have an answer in the same language.

Article 25 (ex Article 22 TEC)

The Commission shall report to the European Parliament, to the Council and to the Economic and Social Committee every three years on the application of the provisions of this Part. This report shall take account of the development of the Union.

On this basis, and without prejudice to the other provisions of the Treaties, the Council, acting unanimously in accordance with a special legislative procedure and after obtaining the consent of the European Parliament, may adopt provisions to strengthen or to add to the rights listed in Article 20(2). These provisions shall enter into force after their approval by the Member States in accordance with their respective constitutional requirements.

Part Three UNION POLICIES AND INTERNAL ACTIONS

TITLE I
THE INTERNAL MARKET

Article 26 (ex Article 14 TEC)

1. The Union shall adopt measures with the aim of establishing or ensuring the functioning of the internal market, in accordance with the relevant provisions of the Treaties.

2. The internal market shall comprise an area without internal frontiers in which the free movement of goods, persons, services and capital is ensured in accordance with the provisions of the Treaties.

3. The Council, on a proposal from the Commission, shall determine the guidelines and conditions necessary to ensure balanced progress in all the sectors concerned.

Article 27 (ex Article 15 TEC)

When drawing up its proposals with a view to achieving the objectives set out in Article 26, the Commission shall take into account the extent of the effort that certain economies showing differences in development will have to sustain for the establishment of the internal market and it may propose appropriate provisions.

If these provisions take the form of derogations, they must be of a temporary nature and must cause the least possible disturbance to the functioning of the internal market.

TITLE II
FREE MOVEMENT OF GOODS

Article 28 (ex Article 23 TEC)

1. The Union shall comprise a customs union which shall cover all trade in goods and which shall involve the prohibition between Member States of customs duties on imports and exports and of all charges having equivalent effect, and the adoption of a common customs tariff in their relations with third countries.

2. The provisions of Article 30 and of Chapter 2 of this Title shall apply to products originating in Member States and to products coming from third countries which are in free circulation in Member States.

Article 29 (ex Article 24 TEC)

Products coming from a third country shall be considered to be in free circulation in a Member State if the import formalities have been complied with and any customs duties or charges having equivalent effect which are payable have been levied in that Member State, and if they have not benefited from a total or partial drawback of such duties or charges.

Chapter 1 THE CUSTOMS UNION

Article 30 (ex Article 25 TEC)
Customs duties on imports and exports and charges having equivalent effect shall be prohibited between Member States. This prohibition shall also apply to customs duties of a fiscal nature.

Article 31 (ex Article 26 TEC)
Common Customs Tariff duties shall be fixed by the Council on a proposal from the Commission.

Article 32 (ex Article 27 TEC)
In carrying out the tasks entrusted to it under this Chapter the Commission shall be guided by:
(a)   the need to promote trade between Member States and third countries;

(b)   developments in conditions of competition within the Union in so far as they lead to an improvement in the competitive capacity of undertakings;

(c)   the requirements of the Union as regards the supply of raw materials and semi-finished goods; in this connection the Commission shall take care to avoid distorting conditions of competition between Member States in respect of finished goods;

(d)   the need to avoid serious disturbances in the economies of Member States and to ensure rational development of production and an expansion of consumption within the Union.

Chapter 2 CUSTOMS COOPERATION

Article 33 (ex Article 135 TEC)
Within the scope of application of the Treaties, the European Parliament and the Council, acting in accordance with the ordinary legislative procedure, shall take measures in order to strengthen customs cooperation between Member States and between the latter and the Commission.

Chapter 3 PROHIBITION OF QUANTITATIVE RESTRICTIONS BETWEEN MEMBER STATES

Article 34 (ex Article 28 TEC)
Quantitative restrictions on imports and all measures having equivalent effect shall be prohibited between Member States.

Article 35 (ex Article 29 TEC)
Quantitative restrictions on exports, and all measures having equivalent effect, shall be prohibited between Member States.

Article 36 (ex Article 30 TEC)
The provisions of Articles 34 and 35 shall not preclude prohibitions or restrictions on imports, exports or goods in transit justified on grounds of public morality, public policy or public security; the protection of health and life of humans, animals or plants; the protection of national treasures possessing artistic, historic or archaeological value; or the protection of industrial and commercial property. Such prohibitions or restrictions shall not, however, constitute a means of arbitrary discrimination or a disguised restriction on trade between Member States.

Article 37 (ex Article 31 TEC)
1.   Member States shall adjust any State monopolies of a commercial character so as to ensure that no discrimination regarding the conditions under which goods are procured and marketed exists between nationals of Member States.

The provisions of this Article shall apply to any body through which a Member State, in law or in fact, either directly or indirectly supervises, determines or appreciably influences imports or exports between Member States. These provisions shall likewise apply to monopolies delegated by the State to others.

2.   Member States shall refrain from introducing any new measure which is contrary to the principles laid down in paragraph 1 or which restricts the scope of the articles dealing with the prohibition of customs duties and quantitative restrictions between Member States.

3.   If a State monopoly of a commercial character has rules which are designed to make it easier to dispose of agricultural products or obtain for them the best return, steps should be taken in applying the rules contained in this Article to ensure equivalent safeguards for the employment and standard of living of the producers concerned.

TITLE III
AGRICULTURE AND FISHERIES

Article 38 (ex Article 32 TEC)
1.   The Union shall define and implement a common agriculture and fisheries policy.

The internal market shall extend to agriculture, fisheries and trade in agricultural products. 'Agricultural products' means the products of the soil, of stockfarming and of fisheries and products of first-stage processing directly related to these products. References to the common agricultural policy or to agriculture, and the use of the term 'agricultural', shall be understood as also referring to fisheries, having regard to the specific characteristics of this sector.

2.   Save as otherwise provided in Articles 39 to 44, the rules laid down for the establishment and functioning of the internal market shall apply to agricultural products.

3.   The products subject to the provisions of Articles 39 to 44 are listed in Annex I.

4.   The operation and development of the internal market for agricultural products must be accompanied by the establishment of a common agricultural policy.

Article 39 (ex Article 33 TEC)
1.   The objectives of the common agricultural policy shall be:
(a) to increase agricultural productivity by promoting technical progress and by ensuring the rational development of agricultural production and the optimum utilisation of the factors of production, in particular labour;
(b) thus to ensure a fair standard of living for the agricultural community, in particular by increasing the individual earnings of persons engaged in agriculture;
(c) to stabilise markets;
(d) to assure the availability of supplies;
(e) to ensure that supplies reach consumers at reasonable prices.

2.   In working out the common agricultural policy and the special methods for its application, account shall be taken of:
(a) the particular nature of agricultural activity, which results from the social structure of agriculture and from structural and natural disparities between the various agricultural regions;
(b) the need to effect the appropriate adjustments by degrees;
(c) the fact that in the Member States agriculture constitutes a sector closely linked with the economy as a whole.

Article 40 (ex Article 34 TEC)
1.   In order to attain the objectives set out in Article 39, a common organisation of agricultural markets shall be established.

This organisation shall take one of the following forms, depending on the product concerned:
(a)   common rules on competition;
(b)   compulsory coordination of the various national market organisations;
(c)   a European market organisation.

2.   The common organisation established in accordance with paragraph 1 may include all measures required to attain the objectives set out in Article 39, in particular regulation of prices, aids for the production and marketing of the various products, storage and carryover arrangements and common machinery for stabilising imports or exports.

The common organisation shall be limited to pursuit of the objectives set out in Article 39 and shall exclude any discrimination between producers or consumers within the Union.

Any common price policy shall be based on common criteria and uniform methods of calculation.

3.   In order to enable the common organisation referred to in paragraph 1 to attain its objectives, one or more agricultural guidance and guarantee funds may be set up.

Article 41 (ex Article 35 TEC)
To enable the objectives set out in Article 39 to be attained, provision may be made within the framework of the common agricultural policy for measures such as:
(a)   an effective coordination of efforts in the spheres of vocational training, of research and of the dissemination of agricultural knowledge; this may include joint financing of projects or institutions;

(b)   joint measures to promote consumption of certain products.

Article 42 (ex Article 36 TEC)
The provisions of the Chapter relating to rules on competition shall apply to production of and trade in agricultural products only to the extent determined by the European Parliament and the Council within the framework of Article 43(2) and in accordance with the procedure laid down therein, account being taken of the objectives set out in Article 39.

The Council, on a proposal from the Commission, may authorise the granting of aid:
(a)   for the protection of enterprises handicapped by structural or natural conditions;

(b)   within the framework of economic development programmes.

Article 43 (ex Article 37 TEC)
1.   The Commission shall submit proposals for working out and implementing the common agricultural policy, including the replacement of the national organisations by one of the forms of common organisation provided for in Article 40(1), and for implementing the measures specified in this Title.

These proposals shall take account of the interdependence of the agricultural matters mentioned in this Title.

2.   The European Parliament and the Council, acting in accordance with the ordinary legislative procedure and after consulting the Economic and Social Committee, shall establish the common organisation of agricultural markets provided for in Article 40(1) and the other provisions necessary for the pursuit of the objectives of the common agricultural policy and the common fisheries policy.

3.   The Council, on a proposal from the Commission, shall adopt measures on fixing prices, levies, aid and quantitative limitations and on the fixing and allocation of fishing opportunities.

4.   In accordance with paragraph 2, the national market organisations may be replaced by the common organisation provided for in Article 40(1) if:
    (a) the common organisation offers Member States which are opposed to this measure and which have an organisation of their own for the production in question equivalent safeguards for the employment and standard of living of the producers concerned, account being taken of the adjustments that will be possible and the specialisation that will be needed with the passage of time;
    (b) such an organisation ensures conditions for trade within the Union similar to those existing in a national market.

5.   If a common organisation for certain raw materials is established before a common organisation exists for the corresponding processed products, such raw materials as are used for processed products intended for export to third countries may be imported from outside the Union.

Article 44 (ex Article 38 TEC)

Where in a Member State a product is subject to a national market organisation or to internal rules having equivalent effect which affect the competitive position of similar production in another Member State, a countervailing charge shall be applied by Member States to imports of this product coming from the Member State where such organisation or rules exist, unless that State applies a countervailing charge on export.

The Commission shall fix the amount of these charges at the level required to redress the balance; it may also authorise other measures, the conditions and details of which it shall determine.

TITLE IV
FREE MOVEMENT OF PERSONS, SERVICES AND CAPITAL

Chapter 1 WORKERS

Article 45 (ex Article 39 TEC)

1.   Freedom of movement for workers shall be secured within the Union.

2.   Such freedom of movement shall entail the abolition of any discrimination based on nationality between workers of the Member States as regards employment, remuneration and other conditions of work and employment.

3.   It shall entail the right, subject to limitations justified on grounds of public policy, public security or public health:
    (a) to accept offers of employment actually made;
    (b) to move freely within the territory of Member States for this purpose;
    (c) to stay in a Member State for the purpose of employment in accordance with the provisions governing the employment of nationals of that State laid down by law, regulation or administrative action;
    (d) to remain in the territory of a Member State after having been employed in that State, subject to conditions which shall be embodied in regulations to be drawn up by the Commission.

4.   The provisions of this Article shall not apply to employment in the public service.

Article 46 (ex Article 40 TEC)
The European Parliament and the Council shall, acting in accordance with the ordinary legislative procedure and after consulting the Economic and Social Committee, issue directives or make regulations setting out the measures required to bring about freedom of movement for workers, as defined in Article 45, in particular:

(a)   by ensuring close cooperation between national employment services;

(b)   by abolishing those administrative procedures and practices and those qualifying periods in respect of eligibility for available employment, whether resulting from national legislation or from agreements previously concluded between Member States, the maintenance of which would form an obstacle to liberalisation of the movement of workers;

(c)   by abolishing all such qualifying periods and other restrictions provided for either under national legislation or under agreements previously concluded between Member States as imposed on workers of other Member States conditions regarding the free choice of employment other than those imposed on workers of the State concerned;

(d)   by setting up appropriate machinery to bring offers of employment into touch with applications for employment and to facilitate the achievement of a balance between supply and demand in the employment market in such a way as to avoid serious threats to the standard of living and level of employment in the various regions and industries.

Article 47 (ex Article 41 TEC)
Member States shall, within the framework of a joint programme, encourage the exchange of young workers.

Article 48 (ex Article 42 TEC)
The European Parliament and the Council shall, acting in accordance with the ordinary legislative procedure, adopt such measures in the field of social security as are necessary to provide freedom of movement for workers; to this end, they shall make arrangements to secure for employed and self- employed migrant workers and their dependants:

(a)   aggregation, for the purpose of acquiring and retaining the right to benefit and of calculating the amount of benefit, of all periods taken into account under the laws of the several countries;

(b)   payment of benefits to persons resident in the territories of Member States.

Where a member of the Council declares that a draft legislative act referred to in the first subparagraph would affect important aspects of its social security system, including its scope, cost or financial structure, or would affect the financial balance of that system, it may request that the matter be referred to the European Council. In that case, the ordinary legislative procedure shall be suspended. After discussion, the European Council shall, within four months of this suspension, either:

(a)   refer the draft back to the Council, which shall terminate the suspension of the ordinary legislative procedure; or

(b)   take no action or request the Commission to submit a new proposal; in that case, the act originally proposed shall be deemed not to have been adopted.

Chapter 2 RIGHT OF ESTABLISHMENT

Article 49 (ex Article 43 TEC)
Within the framework of the provisions set out below, restrictions on the freedom of establishment of nationals of a Member State in the territory of another Member State shall be prohibited. Such prohibition shall also apply to restrictions on the setting-up of agencies, branches or subsidiaries by nationals of any Member State established in the territory of any Member State.

Freedom of establishment shall include the right to take up and pursue activities as self-employed persons and to set up and manage undertakings, in particular companies or firms within the meaning of the second paragraph of Article 54, under the conditions laid down for its own nationals by the law of the country where such establishment is effected, subject to the provisions of the Chapter relating to capital.

Article 50 (ex Article 44 TEC)

1.   In order to attain freedom of establishment as regards a particular activity, the European Parliament and the Council, acting in accordance with the ordinary legislative procedure and after consulting the Economic and Social Committee, shall act by means of directives.

2.   The European Parliament, the Council and the Commission shall carry out the duties devolving upon them under the preceding provisions, in particular:

(a)   by according, as a general rule, priority treatment to activities where freedom of establishment makes a particularly valuable contribution to the development of production and trade;

(b)   by ensuring close cooperation between the competent authorities in the Member States in order to ascertain the particular situation within the Union of the various activities concerned;

(c)   by abolishing those administrative procedures and practices, whether resulting from national legislation or from agreements previously concluded between Member States, the maintenance of which would form an obstacle to freedom of establishment;

(d)   by ensuring that workers of one Member State employed in the territory of another Member State may remain in that territory for the purpose of taking up activities therein as self-employed persons, where they satisfy the conditions which they would be required to satisfy if they were entering that State at the time when they intended to take up such activities;

(e)   by enabling a national of one Member State to acquire and use land and buildings situated in the territory of another Member State, in so far as this does not conflict with the principles laid down in Article 39(2);

(f)   by effecting the progressive abolition of restrictions on freedom of establishment in every branch of activity under consideration, both as regards the conditions for setting up agencies, branches or subsidiaries in the territory of a Member State and as regards the subsidiaries in the territory of a Member State and as regards the conditions governing the entry of personnel belonging to the main establishment into managerial or supervisory posts in such agencies, branches or subsidiaries;

(g)   by coordinating to the necessary extent the safeguards which, for the protection of the interests of members and others, are required by Member States of companies or firms within the meaning of the second paragraph of Article 54 with a view to making such safeguards equivalent throughout the Union;

(h)   by satisfying themselves that the conditions of establishment are not distorted by aids granted by Member States.

Article 51 (ex Article 45 TEC)

The provisions of this Chapter shall not apply, so far as any given Member State is concerned, to activities which in that State are connected, even occasionally, with the exercise of official authority.

The European Parliament and the Council, acting in accordance with the ordinary legislative procedure, may rule that the provisions of this Chapter shall not apply to certain activities.

Article 52 (ex Article 46 TEC)

1.   The provisions of this Chapter and measures taken in pursuance thereof shall not prejudice the applicability of provisions laid down by law, regulation or administrative action providing for special treatment for foreign nationals on grounds of public policy, public security or public health.

2.   The European Parliament and the Council shall, acting in accordance with the ordinary legislative procedure, issue directives for the coordination of the abovementioned provisions.

Article 53 (ex Article 47 TEC)

1.   In order to make it easier for persons to take up and pursue activities as self-employed persons, the European Parliament and the Council shall, acting in accordance with the ordinary legislative procedure, issue directives for the mutual recognition of diplomas, certificates and other evidence of formal qualifications and for the coordination of the provisions laid down by law, regulation or administrative action in Member States concerning the taking-up and pursuit of activities as self-employed persons.

2.   In the case of the medical and allied and pharmaceutical professions, the progressive abolition of restrictions shall be dependent upon coordination of the conditions for their exercise in the various Member States.

Article 54 (ex Article 48 TEC)

Companies or firms formed in accordance with the law of a Member State and having their registered office, central administration or principal place of business within the Union shall, for the purposes of this Chapter, be treated in the same way as natural persons who are nationals of Member States.

'Companies or firms' means companies or firms constituted under civil or commercial law, including cooperative societies, and other legal persons governed by public or private law, save for those which are non-profit-making.

Article 55 (ex Article 294 TEC)

Member States shall accord nationals of the other Member States the same treatment as their own nationals as regards participation in the capital of companies or firms within the meaning of Article 54, without prejudice to the application of the other provisions of the Treaties.

Chapter 3 SERVICES

Article 56 (ex Article 49 TEC)

Within the framework of the provisions set out below, restrictions on freedom to provide services within the Union shall be prohibited in respect of nationals of Member States who are established in a Member State other than that of the person for whom the services are intended.

The European Parliament and the Council, acting in accordance with the ordinary legislative procedure, may extend the provisions of the Chapter to nationals of a third country who provide services and who are established within the Union.

Article 57 (ex Article 50 TEC)

Services shall be considered to be 'services' within the meaning of the Treaties where they are normally provided for remuneration, in so far as they are not governed by the provisions relating to freedom of movement for goods, capital and persons.
'Services' shall in particular include:

(a)   activities of an industrial character;

(b)   activities of a commercial character;

(c)   activities of craftsmen;

(d)   activities of the professions.

Without prejudice to the provisions of the Chapter relating to the right of establishment, the person providing a service may, in order to do so, temporarily pursue his activity in the Member

State where the service is provided, under the same conditions as are imposed by that State on its own nationals.

Article 58 (ex Article 51 TEC)

1.   Freedom to provide services in the field of transport shall be governed by the provisions of the Title relating to transport.

2.   The liberalisation of banking and insurance services connected with movements of capital shall be effected in step with the liberalisation of movement of capital.

Article 59 (ex Article 52 TEC)

1.   In order to achieve the liberalisation of a specific service, the European Parliament and the Council, acting in accordance with the ordinary legislative procedure and after consulting the Economic and Social Committee, shall issue directives.

2.   As regards the directives referred to in paragraph 1, priority shall as a general rule be given to those services which directly affect production costs or the liberalisation of which helps to promote trade in goods.

Article 60 (ex Article 53 TEC)

The Member States shall endeavour to undertake the liberalisation of services beyond the extent required by the directives issued pursuant to Article 59(1), if their general economic situation and the situation of the economic sector concerned so permit.

To this end, the Commission shall make recommendations to the Member States concerned.

Article 61 (ex Article 54 TEC)

As long as restrictions on freedom to provide services have not been abolished, each Member State shall apply such restrictions without distinction on grounds of nationality or residence to all persons providing services within the meaning of the first paragraph of Article 56.

Article 62 (ex Article 55 TEC)

The provisions of Articles 51 to 54 shall apply to the matters covered by this Chapter.

Chapter 4 CAPITAL AND PAYMENTS

Article 63 (ex Article 56 TEC)

1.   Within the framework of the provisions set out in this Chapter, all restrictions on the movement of capital between Member States and between Member States and third countries shall be prohibited.

2.   Within the framework of the provisions set out in this Chapter, all restrictions on payments between Member States and between Member States and third countries shall be prohibited.

Article 64 (ex Article 57 TEC)

1.   The provisions of Article 63 shall be without prejudice to the application to third countries of any restrictions which exist on 31 December 1993 under national or Union law adopted in respect of the movement of capital to or from third countries involving direct investment — including in real estate — establishment, the provision of financial services or the admission of securities to capital markets. In respect of restrictions existing under national law in Bulgaria, Estonia and Hungary, the relevant date shall be 31 December 1999.

2.   Whilst endeavouring to achieve the objective of free movement of capital between Member States and third countries to the greatest extent possible and without prejudice to the other Chapters of the Treaties, the European Parliament and the Council, acting in

accordance with the ordinary legislative procedure, shall adopt the measures on the movement of capital to or from third countries involving direct investment — including investment in real estate — establishment, the provision of financial services or the admission of securities to capital markets.

3. Notwithstanding paragraph 2, only the Council, acting in accordance with a special legislative procedure, may unanimously, and after consulting the European Parliament, adopt measures which constitute a step backwards in Union law as regards the liberalisation of the movement of capital to or from third countries.

Article 65 (ex Article 58 TEC)
1. The provisions of Article 63 shall be without prejudice to the right of Member States:
    (a) to apply the relevant provisions of their tax law which distinguish between taxpayers who are not in the same situation with regard to their place of residence or with regard to the place where their capital is invested;
    (b) to take all requisite measures to prevent infringements of national law and regulations, in particular in the field of taxation and the prudential supervision of financial institutions, or to lay down procedures for the declaration of capital movements for purposes of administrative or statistical information, or to take measures which are justified on grounds of public policy or public security.

2. The provisions of this Chapter shall be without prejudice to the applicability of restrictions on the right of establishment which are compatible with the Treaties.

3. The measures and procedures referred to in paragraphs 1 and 2 shall not constitute a means of arbitrary discrimination or a disguised restriction on the free movement of capital and payments as defined in Article 63.

4. In the absence of measures pursuant to Article 64(3), the Commission or, in the absence of a Commission decision within three months from the request of the Member State concerned, the Council, may adopt a decision stating that restrictive tax measures adopted by a Member State concerning one or more third countries are to be considered compatible with the Treaties in so far as they are justified by one of the objectives of the Union and compatible with the proper functioning of the internal market. The Council shall act unanimously on application by a Member State.

Article 66 (ex Article 59 TEC)
Where, in exceptional circumstances, movements of capital to or from third countries cause, or threaten to cause, serious difficulties for the operation of economic and monetary union, the Council, on a proposal from the Commission and after consulting the European Central Bank, may take safeguard measures with regard to third countries for a period not exceeding six months if such measures are strictly necessary.

TITLE V
AREA OF FREEDOM, SECURITY AND JUSTICE

Chapter 1 GENERAL PROVISIONS

Article 67 (ex Article 61 TEC and ex Article 29 TEU)
1. The Union shall constitute an area of freedom, security and justice with respect for fundamental rights and the different legal systems and traditions of the Member States.

2. It shall ensure the absence of internal border controls for persons and shall frame a common policy on asylum, immigration and external border control, based on solidarity between Member States, which is fair towards third-country nationals. For the purpose of this Title, stateless persons shall be treated as third-country nationals.

3.   The Union shall endeavour to ensure a high level of security through measures to prevent and combat crime, racism and xenophobia, and through measures for coordination and cooperation between police and judicial authorities and other competent authorities, as well as through the mutual recognition of judgments in criminal matters and, if necessary, through the approximation of criminal laws.

4.   The Union shall facilitate access to justice, in particular through the principle of mutual recognition of judicial and extrajudicial decisions in civil matters.

Article 68
The European Council shall define the strategic guidelines for legislative and operational planning within the area of freedom, security and justice.

Article 69
National Parliaments ensure that the proposals and legislative initiatives submitted under Chapters 4 and 5 comply with the principle of subsidiarity, in accordance with the arrangements laid down by the Protocol on the application of the principles of subsidiarity and proportionality.

Article 70
Without prejudice to Articles 258, 259 and 260, the Council may, on a proposal from the Commission, adopt measures laying down the arrangements whereby Member States, in collaboration with the Commission, conduct objective and impartial evaluation of the implementation of the Union policies referred to in this Title by Member States' authorities, in particular in order to facilitate full application of the principle of mutual recognition. The European Parliament and national Parliaments shall be informed of the content and results of the evaluation.

Article 71 (ex Article 36 TEU)
A standing committee shall be set up within the Council in order to ensure that operational cooperation on internal security is promoted and strengthened within the Union. Without prejudice to Article 240, it shall facilitate coordination of the action of Member States' competent authorities. Representatives of the Union bodies, offices and agencies concerned may be involved in the proceedings of this committee. The European Parliament and national Parliaments shall be kept informed of the proceedings.

Article 72 (ex Article 64(1) TEC and ex Article 33 TEU)
This Title shall not affect the exercise of the responsibilities incumbent upon Member States with regard to the maintenance of law and order and the safeguarding of internal security.

Article 73
It shall be open to Member States to organise between themselves and under their responsibility such forms of cooperation and coordination as they deem appropriate between the competent departments of their administrations responsible for safeguarding national security.

Article 74 (ex Article 66 TEC)
The Council shall adopt measures to ensure administrative cooperation between the relevant departments of the Member States in the areas covered by this Title, as well as between those departments and the Commission. It shall act on a Commission proposal, subject to Article 76, and after consulting the European Parliament.

Article 75 (ex Article 60 TEC)
Where necessary to achieve the objectives set out in Article 67, as regards preventing and combating terrorism and related activities, the European Parliament and the Council, acting by means of regulations in accordance with the ordinary legislative procedure, shall define a framework for administrative measures with regard to capital movements and payments, such as the freezing of funds, financial assets or economic gains belonging to, or owned or held by, natural or legal persons, groups or non-State entities.

The Council, on a proposal from the Commission, shall adopt measures to implement the framework referred to in the first paragraph.

The acts referred to in this Article shall include necessary provisions on legal safeguards.

Article 76
The acts referred to in Chapters 4 and 5, together with the measures referred to in Article 74 which ensure administrative cooperation in the areas covered by these Chapters, shall be adopted:

(a)   on a proposal from the Commission, or

(b)   on the initiative of a quarter of the Member States.

Chapter 2 POLICIES ON BORDER CHECKS, ASYLUM AND IMMIGRATION

Article 77 (ex Article 62 TEC)
1.   The Union shall develop a policy with a view to:
   (a) ensuring the absence of any controls on persons, whatever their nationality, when crossing internal borders;
   (b) carrying out checks on persons and efficient monitoring of the crossing of external borders;
   (c) the gradual introduction of an integrated management system for external borders.

2.   For the purposes of paragraph 1, the European Parliament and the Council, acting in accordance with the ordinary legislative procedure, shall adopt measures concerning:
   (a) the common policy on visas and other short-stay residence permits;
   (b) the checks to which persons crossing external borders are subject;
   (c) the conditions under which nationals of third countries shall have the freedom to travel within the Union for a short period;
   (d) any measure necessary for the gradual establishment of an integrated management system for external borders;
   (e) the absence of any controls on persons, whatever their nationality, when crossing internal borders.

3.   If action by the Union should prove necessary to facilitate the exercise of the right referred to in Article 20(2)(a), and if the Treaties have not provided the necessary powers, the Council, acting in accordance with a special legislative procedure, may adopt provisions concerning passports, identity cards, residence permits or any other such document. The Council shall act unanimously after consulting the European Parliament.

4.   This Article shall not affect the competence of the Member States concerning the geographical demarcation of their borders, in accordance with international law.

Article 78 (ex Articles 63, points 1 and 2, and 64(2) TEC)
1.   The Union shall develop a common policy on asylum, subsidiary protection and temporary protection with a view to offering appropriate status to any third-country national requiring international protection and ensuring compliance with the principle of non-refoulement. This policy must be in accordance with the Geneva Convention of 28 July 1951 and the Protocol of 31 January 1967 relating to the status of refugees, and other relevant treaties.

2.   For the purposes of paragraph 1, the European Parliament and the Council, acting in accordance with the ordinary legislative procedure, shall adopt measures for a common European asylum system comprising:
   (a) a uniform status of asylum for nationals of third countries, valid throughout the Union;
   (b) a uniform status of subsidiary protection for nationals of third countries who, without obtaining European asylum, are in need of international protection;

(c) a common system of temporary protection for displaced persons in the event of a massive inflow;

(d) common procedures for the granting and withdrawing of uniform asylum or subsidiary protection status;

(e) criteria and mechanisms for determining which Member State is responsible for considering an application for asylum or subsidiary protection;

(f) standards concerning the conditions for the reception of applicants for asylum or subsidiary protection;

(g) partnership and cooperation with third countries for the purpose of managing inflows of people applying for asylum or subsidiary or temporary protection.

3. In the event of one or more Member States being confronted by an emergency situation characterised by a sudden inflow of nationals of third countries, the Council, on a proposal from the Commission, may adopt provisional measures for the benefit of the Member State(s) concerned. It shall act after consulting the European Parliament.

Article 79 (ex Article 63, points 3 and 4, TEC)

1. The Union shall develop a common immigration policy aimed at ensuring, at all stages, the efficient management of migration flows, fair treatment of third-country nationals residing legally in Member States, and the prevention of, and enhanced measures to combat, illegal immigration and trafficking in human beings.

2. For the purposes of paragraph 1, the European Parliament and the Council, acting in accordance with the ordinary legislative procedure, shall adopt measures in the following areas:

(a) the conditions of entry and residence, and standards on the issue by Member States of long-term visas and residence permits, including those for the purpose of family reunification;

(b) the definition of the rights of third-country nationals residing legally in a Member State, including the conditions governing freedom of movement and of residence in other Member States;

(c) illegal immigration and unauthorised residence, including removal and repatriation of persons residing without authorisation;

(d) combating trafficking in persons, in particular women and children.

3. The Union may conclude agreements with third countries for the readmission to their countries of origin or provenance of third-country nationals who do not or who no longer fulfil the conditions for entry, presence or residence in the territory of one of the Member States.

4. The European Parliament and the Council, acting in accordance with the ordinary legislative procedure, may establish measures to provide incentives and support for the action of Member States with a view to promoting the integration of third-country nationals residing legally in their territories, excluding any harmonisation of the laws and regulations of the Member States.

5. This Article shall not affect the right of Member States to determine volumes of admission of third-country nationals coming from third countries to their territory in order to seek work, whether employed or self-employed.

Article 80

The policies of the Union set out in this Chapter and their implementation shall be governed by the principle of solidarity and fair sharing of responsibility, including its financial implications, between the Member States. Whenever necessary, the Union acts adopted pursuant to this Chapter shall contain appropriate measures to give effect to this principle.

Chapter 3 JUDICIAL COOPERATION IN CIVIL MATTERS

Article 81 (ex Article 65 TEC)

1.   The Union shall develop judicial cooperation in civil matters having cross-border implications, based on the principle of mutual recognition of judgments and of decisions in extrajudicial cases. Such cooperation may include the adoption of measures for the approximation of the laws and regulations of the Member States.

2.   For the purposes of paragraph 1, the European Parliament and the Council, acting in accordance with the ordinary legislative procedure, shall adopt measures, particularly when necessary for the proper functioning of the internal market, aimed at ensuring:
      (a) the mutual recognition and enforcement between Member States of judgments and of decisions in extrajudicial cases;
      (b) the cross-border service of judicial and extrajudicial documents;
      (c) the compatibility of the rules applicable in the Member States concerning conflict of laws and of jurisdiction;
      (d) cooperation in the taking of evidence;
      (e) effective access to justice;
      (f) the elimination of obstacles to the proper functioning of civil proceedings, if necessary by promoting the compatibility of the rules on civil procedure applicable in the Member States;
      (g) the development of alternative methods of dispute settlement;
      (h) support for the training of the judiciary and judicial staff.

3.   Notwithstanding paragraph 2, measures concerning family law with cross-border implications shall be established by the Council, acting in accordance with a special legislative procedure. The Council shall act unanimously after consulting the European Parliament.

      The Council, on a proposal from the Commission, may adopt a decision determining those aspects of family law with cross-border implications which may be the subject of acts adopted by the ordinary legislative procedure. The Council shall act unanimously after consulting the European Parliament.

      The proposal referred to in the second subparagraph shall be notified to the national Parliaments. If a national Parliament makes known its opposition within six months of the date of such notification, the decision shall not be adopted. In the absence of opposition, the Council may adopt the decision.

Chapter 4 JUDICIAL COOPERATION IN CRIMINAL MATTERS

Article 82 (ex Article 31 TEU)

1.   Judicial cooperation in criminal matters in the Union shall be based on the principle of mutual recognition of judgments and judicial decisions and shall include the approximation of the laws and regulations of the Member States in the areas referred to in paragraph 2 and in Article 83.

      The European Parliament and the Council, acting in accordance with the ordinary legislative procedure, shall adopt measures to:
      (a) lay down rules and procedures for ensuring recognition throughout the Union of all forms of judgments and judicial decisions;
      (b) prevent and settle conflicts of jurisdiction between Member States;
      (c) support the training of the judiciary and judicial staff;
      (d) facilitate cooperation between judicial or equivalent authorities of the Member States in relation to proceedings in criminal matters and the enforcement of decisions.

2.   To the extent necessary to facilitate mutual recognition of judgments and judicial decisions and police and judicial cooperation in criminal matters having a cross-border dimension, the European Parliament and the Council may, by means of directives adopted in accordance with the ordinary legislative procedure, establish minimum rules. Such rules shall take into account the differences between the legal traditions and systems of the Member States.

They shall concern:
(a) mutual admissibility of evidence between Member States;
(b) the rights of individuals in criminal procedure;
(c) the rights of victims of crime;
(d) any other specific aspects of criminal procedure which the Council has identified in advance by a decision; for the adoption of such a decision, the Council shall act unanimously after obtaining the consent of the European Parliament.
Adoption of the minimum rules referred to in this paragraph shall not prevent Member States from maintaining or introducing a higher level of protection for individuals.

3.   Where a member of the Council considers that a draft directive as referred to in paragraph 2 would affect fundamental aspects of its criminal justice system, it may request that the draft directive be referred to the European Council. In that case, the ordinary legislative procedure shall be suspended. After discussion, and in case of a consensus, the European Council shall, within four months of this suspension, refer the draft back to the Council, which shall terminate the suspension of the ordinary legislative procedure.

Within the same timeframe, in case of disagreement, and if at least nine Member States wish to establish enhanced cooperation on the basis of the draft directive concerned, they shall notify the European Parliament, the Council and the Commission accordingly. In such a case, the authorisation to proceed with enhanced cooperation referred to in Article 20(2) of the Treaty on European Union and Article 329(1) of this Treaty shall be deemed to be granted and the provisions on enhanced cooperation shall apply.

Article 83 (ex Article 31 TEU)

1.   The European Parliament and the Council may, by means of directives adopted in accordance with the ordinary legislative procedure, establish minimum rules concerning the definition of criminal offences and sanctions in the areas of particularly serious crime with a cross-border dimension resulting from the nature or impact of such offences or from a special need to combat them on a common basis. These areas of crime are the following: terrorism, trafficking in human beings and sexual exploitation of women and children, illicit drug trafficking, illicit arms trafficking, money laundering, corruption, counterfeiting of means of payment, computer crime and organised crime.

On the basis of developments in crime, the Council may adopt a decision identifying other areas of crime that meet the criteria specified in this paragraph. It shall act unanimously after obtaining the consent of the European Parliament.

2.   If the approximation of criminal laws and regulations of the Member States proves essential to ensure the effective implementation of a Union policy in an area which has been subject to harmonisation measures, directives may establish minimum rules with regard to the definition of criminal offences and sanctions in the area concerned. Such directives shall be adopted by the same ordinary or special legislative procedure as was followed for the adoption of the harmonisation measures in question, without prejudice to Article 76.

3.   Where a member of the Council considers that a draft directive as referred to in paragraph 1 or 2 would affect fundamental aspects of its criminal justice system, it may request that the

draft directive be referred to the European Council. In that case, the ordinary legislative procedure shall be suspended. After discussion, and in case of a consensus, the European Council shall, within four months of this suspension, refer the draft back to the Council, which shall terminate the suspension of the ordinary legislative procedure.

Within the same timeframe, in case of disagreement, and if at least nine Member States wish to establish enhanced cooperation on the basis of the draft directive concerned, they shall notify the European Parliament, the Council and the Commission accordingly. In such a case, the authorisation to proceed with enhanced cooperation referred to in Article 20(2) of the Treaty on European Union and Article 329(1) of this Treaty shall be deemed to be granted and the provisions on enhanced cooperation shall apply.

Article 84

The European Parliament and the Council, acting in accordance with the ordinary legislative procedure, may establish measures to promote and support the action of Member States in the field of crime prevention, excluding any harmonisation of the laws and regulations of the Member States.

Article 85 (ex Article 31 TEU)

1. Eurojust's mission shall be to support and strengthen coordination and cooperation between national investigating and prosecuting authorities in relation to serious crime affecting two or more Member States or requiring a prosecution on common bases, on the basis of operations conducted and information supplied by the Member States' authorities and by Europol.

In this context, the European Parliament and the Council, by means of regulations adopted in accordance with the ordinary legislative procedure, shall determine Eurojust's structure, operation, field of action and tasks. These tasks may include:
(a) the initiation of criminal investigations, as well as proposing the initiation of prosecutions conducted by competent national authorities, particularly those relating to offences against the financial interests of the Union;
(b) the coordination of investigations and prosecutions referred to in point (a);
(c) the strengthening of judicial cooperation, including by resolution of conflicts of jurisdiction and by close cooperation with the European Judicial Network.
These regulations shall also determine arrangements for involving the European Parliament and national Parliaments in the evaluation of Eurojust's activities.

2. In the prosecutions referred to in paragraph 1, and without prejudice to Article 86, formal acts of judicial procedure shall be carried out by the competent national officials.

Article 86

1. In order to combat crimes affecting the financial interests of the Union, the Council, by means of regulations adopted in accordance with a special legislative procedure, may establish a European Public Prosecutor's Office from Eurojust. The Council shall act unanimously after obtaining the consent of the European Parliament.

In the absence of unanimity in the Council, a group of at least nine Member States may request that the draft regulation be referred to the European Council. In that case, the procedure in the Council shall be suspended. After discussion, and in case of a consensus, the European Council shall, within four months of this suspension, refer the draft back to the Council for adoption.

Within the same timeframe, in case of disagreement, and if at least nine Member States wish to establish enhanced cooperation on the basis of the draft regulation concerned, they shall notify the European Parliament, the Council and the Commission accordingly. In such a case, the authorisation to proceed with enhanced cooperation referred to in Article 20(2) of the Treaty on European Union and Article 329(1) of this Treaty shall be deemed to be granted and the provisions on enhanced cooperation shall apply.

2.   The European Public Prosecutor's Office shall be responsible for investigating, prosecuting and bringing to judgment, where appropriate in liaison with Europol, the perpetrators of, and accomplices in, offences against the Union's financial interests, as determined by the regulation provided for in paragraph 1. It shall exercise the functions of prosecutor in the competent courts of the Member States in relation to such offences.

3.   The regulations referred to in paragraph 1 shall determine the general rules applicable to the European Public Prosecutor's Office, the conditions governing the performance of its functions, the rules of procedure applicable to its activities, as well as those governing the admissibility of evidence, and the rules applicable to the judicial review of procedural measures taken by it in the performance of its functions.

4.   The European Council may, at the same time or subsequently, adopt a decision amending paragraph 1 in order to extend the powers of the European Public Prosecutor's Office to include serious crime having a cross-border dimension and amending accordingly paragraph 2 as regards the perpetrators of, and accomplices in, serious crimes affecting more than one Member State. The European Council shall act unanimously after obtaining the consent of the European Parliament and after consulting the Commission.

Chapter 5 POLICE COOPERATION

Article 87 (ex Article 30 TEU)

1.   The Union shall establish police cooperation involving all the Member States' competent authorities, including police, customs and other specialised law enforcement services in relation to the prevention, detection and investigation of criminal offences.

2.   For the purposes of paragraph 1, the European Parliament and the Council, acting in accordance with the ordinary legislative procedure, may establish measures concerning:
(a) the collection, storage, processing, analysis and exchange of relevant information;
(b) support for the training of staff, and cooperation on the exchange of staff, on equipment and on research into crime-detection;
(c) common investigative techniques in relation to the detection of serious forms of organised crime.

3.   The Council, acting in accordance with a special legislative procedure, may establish measures concerning operational cooperation between the authorities referred to in this Article. The Council shall act unanimously after consulting the European Parliament.

In case of the absence of unanimity in the Council, a group of at least nine Member States may request that the draft measures be referred to the European Council. In that case, the procedure in the Council shall be suspended. After discussion, and in case of a consensus, the European Council shall, within four months of this suspension, refer the draft back to the Council for adoption.

Within the same timeframe, in case of disagreement, and if at least nine Member States wish to establish enhanced cooperation on the basis of the draft measures concerned, they shall notify the European Parliament, the Council and the Commission accordingly. In such a case, the authorisation to proceed with enhanced cooperation referred to in Article 20(2) of the Treaty on European Union and Article 329(1) of this Treaty shall be deemed to be granted and the provisions on enhanced cooperation shall apply.

The specific procedure provided for in the second and third subparagraphs shall not apply to acts which constitute a development of the Schengen *acquis*.

Article 88 (ex Article 30 TEU)
1.   Europol's mission shall be to support and strengthen action by the Member States' police authorities and other law enforcement services and their mutual cooperation in preventing and combating serious crime affecting two or more Member States, terrorism and forms of crime which affect a common interest covered by a Union policy.

2.   The European Parliament and the Council, by means of regulations adopted in accordance with the ordinary legislative procedure, shall determine Europol's structure, operation, field of action and tasks. These tasks may include:
   (a)   the collection, storage, processing, analysis and exchange of information, in particular that forwarded by the authorities of the Member States or third countries or bodies;
   (b)   the coordination, organisation and implementation of investigative and operational action carried out jointly with the Member States' competent authorities or in the context of joint investigative teams, where appropriate in liaison with Eurojust.
   These regulations shall also lay down the procedures for scrutiny of Europol's activities by the European Parliament, together with national Parliaments.

3.   Any operational action by Europol must be carried out in liaison and in agreement with the authorities of the Member State or States whose territory is concerned. The application of coercive measures shall be the exclusive responsibility of the competent national authorities.

Article 89 (ex Article 32 TEU)
The Council, acting in accordance with a special legislative procedure, shall lay down the conditions and limitations under which the competent authorities of the Member States referred to in Articles 82 and 87 may operate in the territory of another Member State in liaison and in agreement with the authorities of that State. The Council shall act unanimously after consulting the European Parliament.

TITLE VI
TRANSPORT

Article 90 (ex Article 70 TEC)
The objectives of the Treaties shall, in matters governed by this Title, be pursued within the framework of a common transport policy.

Article 91 (ex Article 71 TEC)
1.   For the purpose of implementing Article 90, and taking into account the distinctive features of transport, the European Parliament and the Council shall, acting in accordance with the ordinary legislative procedure and after consulting the Economic and Social Committee and the Committee of the Regions, lay down:
   (a)   common rules applicable to international transport to or from the territory of a Member State or passing across the territory of one or more Member States;
   (b)   the conditions under which non-resident carriers may operate transport services within a Member State;
   (c)   measures to improve transport safety;
   (d)   any other appropriate provisions.

2.   When the measures referred to in paragraph 1 are adopted, account shall be taken of cases where their application might seriously affect the standard of living and level of employment in certain regions, and the operation of transport facilities.

Article 92 (ex Article 72 TEC)

Until the provisions referred to in Article 91(1) have been laid down, no Member State may, unless the Council has unanimously adopted a measure granting a derogation, make the various provisions governing the subject on 1 January 1958 or, for acceding States, the date of their accession less favourable in their direct or indirect effect on carriers of other Member States as compared with carriers who are nationals of that State.

Article 93 (ex Article 73 TEC)

Aids shall be compatible with the Treaties if they meet the needs of coordination of transport or if they represent reimbursement for the discharge of certain obligations inherent in the concept of a public service.

Article 94 (ex Article 74 TEC)

Any measures taken within the framework of the Treaties in respect of transport rates and conditions shall take account of the economic circumstances of carriers.

Article 95 (ex Article 75 TEC)

1.   In the case of transport within the Union, discrimination which takes the form of carriers charging different rates and imposing different conditions for the carriage of the same goods over the same transport links on grounds of the country of origin or of destination of the goods in question shall be prohibited.

2.   Paragraph 1 shall not prevent the European Parliament and the Council from adopting other measures pursuant to Article 91(1).

3.   The Council shall, on a proposal from the Commission and after consulting the European Parliament and the Economic and Social Committee, lay down rules for implementing the provisions of paragraph 1.

      The Council may in particular lay down the provisions needed to enable the institutions of the Union to secure compliance with the rule laid down in paragraph 1 and to ensure that users benefit from it to the full.

4.   The Commission shall, acting on its own initiative or on application by a Member State, investigate any cases of discrimination falling within paragraph 1 and, after consulting any Member State concerned, shall take the necessary decisions within the framework of the rules laid down in accordance with the provisions of paragraph 3.

Article 96 (ex Article 76 TEC)

1.   The imposition by a Member State, in respect of transport operations carried out within the Union, of rates and conditions involving any element of support or protection in the interest of one or more particular undertakings or industries shall be prohibited, unless authorised by the Commission.

2.   The Commission shall, acting on its own initiative or on application by a Member State, examine the rates and conditions referred to in paragraph 1, taking account in particular of the requirements of an appropriate regional economic policy, the needs of underdeveloped areas and the problems of areas seriously affected by political circumstances on the one hand, and of the effects of such rates and conditions on competition between the different modes of transport on the other.

      After consulting each Member State concerned, the Commission shall take the necessary decisions.

3.   The prohibition provided for in paragraph 1 shall not apply to tariffs fixed to meet competition.

Article 97 (ex Article 77 TEC)
Charges or dues in respect of the crossing of frontiers which are charged by a carrier in addition to the transport rates shall not exceed a reasonable level after taking the costs actually incurred thereby into account.

Member States shall endeavour to reduce these costs progressively.
The Commission may make recommendations to Member States for the application of this Article.

Article 98 (ex Article 78 TEC)
The provisions of this Title shall not form an obstacle to the application of measures taken in the Federal Republic of Germany to the extent that such measures are required in order to compensate for the economic disadvantages caused by the division of Germany to the economy of certain areas of the Federal Republic affected by that division. Five years after the entry into force of the Treaty of Lisbon, the Council, acting on a proposal from the Commission, may adopt a decision repealing this Article.

Article 99 (ex Article 79 TEC)
An Advisory Committee consisting of experts designated by the governments of Member States shall be attached to the Commission. The Commission, whenever it considers it desirable, shall consult the Committee on transport matters.

Article 100 (ex Article 80 TEC)
1.   The provisions of this Title shall apply to transport by rail, road and inland waterway.

2.   The European Parliament and the Council, acting in accordance with the ordinary legislative procedure, may lay down appropriate provisions for sea and air transport. They shall act after consulting the Economic and Social Committee and the Committee of the Regions.

TITLE VII
COMMON RULES ON COMPETITION, TAXATION AND APPROXIMATION OF LAWS

Chapter 1 RULES ON COMPETITION

SECTION 1 RULES APPLYING TO UNDERTAKINGS

Article 101 (ex Article 81 TEC)
1.   The following shall be prohibited as incompatible with the internal market: all agreements between undertakings, decisions by associations of undertakings and concerted practices which may affect trade between Member States and which have as their object or effect the prevention, restriction or distortion of competition within the internal market, and in particular those which:
   (a)   directly or indirectly fix purchase or selling prices or any other trading conditions;
   (b)   limit or control production, markets, technical development, or investment;
   (c)   share markets or sources of supply;
   (d)   apply dissimilar conditions to equivalent transactions with other trading parties, thereby placing them at a competitive disadvantage;
   (e)   make the conclusion of contracts subject to acceptance by the other parties of supplementary obligations which, by their nature or according to commercial usage, have no connection with the subject of such contracts.

2.   Any agreements or decisions prohibited pursuant to this Article shall be automatically void.

3.   The provisions of paragraph 1 may, however, be declared inapplicable in the case of:
— any agreement or category of agreements between undertakings,
— any decision or category of decisions by associations of undertakings,
— any concerted practice or category of concerted practices,

which contributes to improving the production or distribution of goods or to promoting technical or economic progress, while allowing consumers a fair share of the resulting benefit, and which does not:
(a) impose on the undertakings concerned restrictions which are not indispensable to the attainment of these objectives;
(b) afford such undertakings the possibility of eliminating competition in respect of a substantial part of the products in question.

Article 102 (ex Article 82 TEC)
Any abuse by one or more undertakings of a dominant position within the internal market or in a substantial part of it shall be prohibited as incompatible with the internal market in so far as it may affect trade between Member States.
Such abuse may, in particular, consist in:
(a)   directly or indirectly imposing unfair purchase or selling prices or other unfair trading conditions;

(b)   limiting production, markets or technical development to the prejudice of consumers;

(c)   applying dissimilar conditions to equivalent transactions with other trading parties, thereby placing them at a competitive disadvantage;

(d)   making the conclusion of contracts subject to acceptance by the other parties of supplementary obligations which, by their nature or according to commercial usage, have no connection with the subject of such contracts.

Article 103 (ex Article 83 TEC)
1.   The appropriate regulations or directives to give effect to the principles set out in Articles 101 and 102 shall be laid down by the Council, on a proposal from the Commission and after consulting the European Parliament.

2.   The regulations or directives referred to in paragraph 1 shall be designed in particular:
(a) to ensure compliance with the prohibitions laid down in Article 101(1) and in Article 102 by making provision for fines and periodic penalty payments;
(b) to lay down detailed rules for the application of Article 101(3), taking into account the need to ensure effective supervision on the one hand, and to simplify administration to the greatest possible extent on the other;
(c) to define, if need be, in the various branches of the economy, the scope of the provisions of Articles 101 and 102;
(d) to define the respective functions of the Commission and of the Court of Justice of the European Union in applying the provisions laid down in this paragraph;
(e) to determine the relationship between national laws and the provisions contained in this Section or adopted pursuant to this Article.

Article 104 (ex Article 84 TEC)
Until the entry into force of the provisions adopted in pursuance of Article 103, the authorities in Member States shall rule on the admissibility of agreements, decisions and concerted practices and on abuse of a dominant position in the internal market in accordance with the law of their country and with the provisions of Article 101, in particular paragraph 3, and of Article 102.

Article 105 (ex Article 85 TEC)

1.   Without prejudice to Article 104, the Commission shall ensure the application of the principles laid down in Articles 101 and 102. On application by a Member State or on its own initiative, and in cooperation with the competent authorities in the Member States, which shall give it their assistance, the Commission shall investigate cases of suspected infringement of these principles. If it finds that there has been an infringement, it shall propose appropriate measures to bring it to an end.

2.   If the infringement is not brought to an end, the Commission shall record such infringement of the principles in a reasoned decision. The Commission may publish its decision and authorise Member States to take the measures, the conditions and details of which it shall determine, needed to remedy the situation.

3.   The Commission may adopt regulations relating to the categories of agreement in respect of which the Council has adopted a regulation or a directive pursuant to Article 103(2)(b).

Article 106 (ex Article 86 TEC)

1.   In the case of public undertakings and undertakings to which Member States grant special or exclusive rights, Member States shall neither enact nor maintain in force any measure contrary to the rules contained in the Treaties, in particular to those rules provided for in Article 18 and Articles 101 to 109.

2.   Undertakings entrusted with the operation of services of general economic interest or having the character of a revenue-producing monopoly shall be subject to the rules contained in the Treaties, in particular to the rules on competition, in so far as the application of such rules does not obstruct the performance, in law or in fact, of the particular tasks assigned to them. The development of trade must not be affected to such an extent as would be contrary to the interests of the Union.

3.   The Commission shall ensure the application of the provisions of this Article and shall, where necessary, address appropriate directives or decisions to Member States.

SECTION 2 AIDS GRANTED BY STATES

Article 107 (ex Article 87 TEC)

1.   Save as otherwise provided in the Treaties, any aid granted by a Member State or through State resources in any form whatsoever which distorts or threatens to distort competition by favouring certain undertakings or the production of certain goods shall, in so far as it affects trade between Member States, be incompatible with the internal market.

2.   The following shall be compatible with the internal market:
    (a)   aid having a social character, granted to individual consumers, provided that such aid is granted without discrimination related to the origin of the products concerned;
    (b)   aid to make good the damage caused by natural disasters or exceptional occurrences;
    (c)   aid granted to the economy of certain areas of the Federal Republic of Germany affected by the division of Germany, in so far as such aid is required in order to compensate for the economic disadvantages caused by that division. Five years after the entry into force of the Treaty of Lisbon, the Council, acting on a proposal from the Commission, may adopt a decision repealing this point.

3.   The following may be considered to be compatible with the internal market:
    (a)   aid to promote the economic development of areas where the standard of living is abnormally low or where there is serious underemployment, and of the regions referred to in Article 349, in view of their structural, economic and social situation;

(b) aid to promote the execution of an important project of common European interest or to remedy a serious disturbance in the economy of a Member State;

(c) aid to facilitate the development of certain economic activities or of certain economic areas, where such aid does not adversely affect trading conditions to an extent contrary to the common interest;

(d) aid to promote culture and heritage conservation where such aid does not affect trading conditions and competition in the Union to an extent that is contrary to the common interest;

(e) such other categories of aid as may be specified by decision of the Council on a proposal from the Commission.

Article 108 (ex Article 88 TEC)

1. The Commission shall, in cooperation with Member States, keep under constant review all systems of aid existing in those States. It shall propose to the latter any appropriate measures required by the progressive development or by the functioning of the internal market.

2. If, after giving notice to the parties concerned to submit their comments, the Commission finds that aid granted by a State or through State resources is not compatible with the internal market having regard to Article 107, or that such aid is being misused, it shall decide that the State concerned shall abolish or alter such aid within a period of time to be determined by the Commission.

   If the State concerned does not comply with this decision within the prescribed time, the Commission or any other interested State may, in derogation from the provisions of Articles 258 and 259, refer the matter to the Court of Justice of the European Union direct.

   On application by a Member State, the Council may, acting unanimously, decide that aid which that State is granting or intends to grant shall be considered to be compatible with the internal market, in derogation from the provisions of Article 107 or from the regulations provided for in Article 109, if such a decision is justified by exceptional circumstances. If, as regards the aid in question, the Commission has already initiated the procedure provided for in the first subparagraph of this paragraph, the fact that the State concerned has made its application to the Council shall have the effect of suspending that procedure until the Council has made its attitude known.

   If, however, the Council has not made its attitude known within three months of the said application being made, the Commission shall give its decision on the case.

3. The Commission shall be informed, in sufficient time to enable it to submit its comments, of any plans to grant or alter aid. If it considers that any such plan is not compatible with the internal market having regard to Article 107, it shall without delay initiate the procedure provided for in paragraph 2. The Member State concerned shall not put its proposed measures into effect until this procedure has resulted in a final decision.

4. The Commission may adopt regulations relating to the categories of State aid that the Council has, pursuant to Article 109, determined may be exempted from the procedure provided for by paragraph 3 of this Article.

Article 109 (ex Article 89 TEC)

The Council, on a proposal from the Commission and after consulting the European Parliament, may make any appropriate regulations for the application of Articles 107 and 108 and may in particular determine the conditions in which Article 108(3) shall apply and the categories of aid exempted from this procedure.

Chapter 2 TAX PROVISIONS

Article 110 (ex Article 90 TEC)

No Member State shall impose, directly or indirectly, on the products of other Member States any internal taxation of any kind in excess of that imposed directly or indirectly on similar domestic products.

Furthermore, no Member State shall impose on the products of other Member States any internal taxation of such a nature as to afford indirect protection to other products.

Article 111 (ex Article 91 TEC)

Where products are exported to the territory of any Member State, any repayment of internal taxation shall not exceed the internal taxation imposed on them whether directly or indirectly.

Article 112 (ex Article 92 TEC)

In the case of charges other than turnover taxes, excise duties and other forms of indirect taxation, remissions and repayments in respect of exports to other Member States may not be granted and countervailing charges in respect of imports from Member States may not be imposed unless the measures contemplated have been previously approved for a limited period by the Council on a proposal from the Commission.

Article 113 (ex Article 93 TEC)

The Council shall, acting unanimously in accordance with a special legislative procedure and after consulting the European Parliament and the Economic and Social Committee, adopt provisions for the harmonisation of legislation concerning turnover taxes, excise duties and other forms of indirect taxation to the extent that such harmonisation is necessary to ensure the establishment and the functioning of the internal market and to avoid distortion of competition.

Chapter 3 APPROXIMATION OF LAWS

Article 114 (ex Article 95 TEC)

1.   Save where otherwise provided in the Treaties, the following provisions shall apply for the achievement of the objectives set out in Article 26. The European Parliament and the Council shall, acting in accordance with the ordinary legislative procedure and after consulting the Economic and Social Committee, adopt the measures for the approximation of the provisions laid down by law, regulation or administrative action in Member States which have as their object the establishment and functioning of the internal market.

2.   Paragraph 1 shall not apply to fiscal provisions, to those relating to the free movement of persons nor to those relating to the rights and interests of employed persons.

3.   The Commission, in its proposals envisaged in paragraph 1 concerning health, safety, environmental protection and consumer protection, will take as a base a high level of protection, taking account in particular of any new development based on scientific facts. Within their respective powers, the European Parliament and the Council will also seek to achieve this objective.

4.   If, after the adoption of a harmonisation measure by the European Parliament and the Council, by the Council or by the Commission, a Member State deems it necessary to maintain national provisions on grounds of major needs referred to in Article 36, or relating to the protection of the environment or the working environment, it shall notify the Commission of these provisions as well as the grounds for maintaining them.

5.   Moreover, without prejudice to paragraph 4, if, after the adoption of a harmonisation measure by the European Parliament and the Council, by the Council or by the Commission, a Member State deems it necessary to introduce national provisions based on new scientific evidence relating to the protection of the environment or the working environment on grounds of a problem specific to that Member State arising after the adoption of the harmonisation measure, it shall notify the Commission of the envisaged provisions as well as the grounds for introducing them.

6.   The Commission shall, within six months of the notifications as referred to in paragraphs 4 and 5, approve or reject the national provisions involved after having verified whether or not they are a means of arbitrary discrimination or a disguised restriction on trade between Member States and whether or not they shall constitute an obstacle to the functioning of the internal market.

     In the absence of a decision by the Commission within this period the national provisions referred to in paragraphs 4 and 5 shall be deemed to have been approved.

     When justified by the complexity of the matter and in the absence of danger for human health, the Commission may notify the Member State concerned that the period referred to in this paragraph may be extended for a further period of up to six months.

7.   When, pursuant to paragraph 6, a Member State is authorised to maintain or introduce national provisions derogating from a harmonisation measure, the Commission shall immediately examine whether to propose an adaptation to that measure.

8.   When a Member State raises a specific problem on public health in a field which has been the subject of prior harmonisation measures, it shall bring it to the attention of the Commission which shall immediately examine whether to propose appropriate measures to the Council.

9.   By way of derogation from the procedure laid down in Articles 258 and 259, the Commission and any Member State may bring the matter directly before the Court of Justice of the European Union if it considers that another Member State is making improper use of the powers provided for in this Article.

10.   The harmonisation measures referred to above shall, in appropriate cases, include a safeguard clause authorising the Member States to take, for one or more of the non-economic reasons referred to in Article 36, provisional measures subject to a Union control procedure.

Article 115 (ex Article 94 TEC)
Without prejudice to Article 114, the Council shall, acting unanimously in accordance with a special legislative procedure and after consulting the European Parliament and the Economic and Social Committee, issue directives for the approximation of such laws, regulations or administrative provisions of the Member States as directly affect the establishment or functioning of the internal market.

Article 116 (ex Article 96 TEC)
Where the Commission finds that a difference between the provisions laid down by law, regulation or administrative action in Member States is distorting the conditions of competition in the internal market and that the resultant distortion needs to be eliminated, it shall consult the Member States concerned.

If such consultation does not result in an agreement eliminating the distortion in question, the European, Parliament and the Council, acting in accordance with the ordinary legislative procedure, shall issue the necessary directives. Any other appropriate measures provided for in the Treaties may be adopted.

Article 117 (ex Article 97 TEC)

1. Where there is a reason to fear that the adoption or amendment of a provision laid down by law, regulation or administrative action may cause distortion within the meaning of Article 116, a Member State desiring to proceed therewith shall consult the Commission. After consulting the Member States, the Commission shall recommend to the States concerned such measures as may be appropriate to avoid the distortion in question.

2. If a State desiring to introduce or amend its own provisions does not comply with the recommendation addressed to it by the Commission, other Member States shall not be required, pursuant to Article 116, to amend their own provisions in order to eliminate such distortion. If the Member State which has ignored the recommendation of the Commission causes distortion detrimental only to itself, the provisions of Article 116 shall not apply.

Article 118

In the context of the establishment and functioning of the internal market, the European Parliament and the Council, acting in accordance with the ordinary legislative procedure, shall establish measures for the creation of European intellectual property rights to provide uniform protection of intellectual property rights throughout the Union and for the setting up of centralised Union-wide authorisation, coordination and supervision arrangements.
The Council, acting in accordance with a special legislative procedure, shall by means of regulations establish language arrangements for the European intellectual property rights. The Council shall act unanimously after consulting the European Parliament.

TITLE VIII
ECONOMIC AND MONETARY POLICY

Article 119 (ex Article 4 TEC)

1. For the purposes set out in Article 3 of the Treaty on European Union, the activities of the Member States and the Union shall include, as provided in the Treaties, the adoption of an economic policy which is based on the close coordination of Member States' economic policies, on the internal market and on the definition of common objectives, and conducted in accordance with the principle of an open market economy with free competition.

2. Concurrently with the foregoing, and as provided in the Treaties and in accordance with the procedures set out therein, these activities shall include a single currency, the euro, and the definition and conduct of a single monetary policy and exchange-rate policy the primary objective of both of which shall be to maintain price stability and, without prejudice to this objective, to support the general economic policies in the Union, in accordance with the principle of an open market economy with free competition.

3. These activities of the Member States and the Union shall entail compliance with the following guiding principles: stable prices, sound public finances and monetary conditions and a sustainable balance of payments.

Chapter 1 ECONOMIC POLICY

Article 120 (ex Article 98 TEC)

Member States shall conduct their economic policies with a view to contributing to the achievement of the objectives of the Union, as defined in Article 3 of the Treaty on European Union, and in the context of the broad guidelines referred to in Article 121(2). The Member States and the Union shall act in accordance with the principle of an open market economy with free competition, favouring an efficient allocation of resources, and in compliance with the principles set out in Article 119.

Article 121 (ex Article 99 TEC)

1.   Member States shall regard their economic policies as a matter of common concern and shall coordinate them within the Council, in accordance with the provisions of Article 120.

2.   The Council shall, on a recommendation from the Commission, formulate a draft for the broad guidelines of the economic policies of the Member States and of the Union, and shall report its findings to the European Council.

     The European Council shall, acting on the basis of the report from the Council, discuss a conclusion on the broad guidelines of the economic policies of the Member States and of the Union.

     On the basis of this conclusion, the Council shall adopt a recommendation setting out these broad guidelines. The Council shall inform the European Parliament of its recommendation.

3.   In order to ensure closer coordination of economic policies and sustained convergence of the economic performances of the Member States, the Council shall, on the basis of reports submitted by the Commission, monitor economic developments in each of the Member States and in the Union as well as the consistency of economic policies with the broad guidelines referred to in paragraph 2, and regularly carry out an overall assessment.

     For the purpose of this multilateral surveillance, Member States shall forward information to the Commission about important measures taken by them in the field of their economic policy and such other information as they deem necessary.

4.   Where it is established, under the procedure referred to in paragraph 3, that the economic policies of a Member State are not consistent with the broad guidelines referred to in paragraph 2 or that they risk jeopardising the proper functioning of economic and monetary union, the Commission may address a warning to the Member State concerned. The Council, on a recommendation from the Commission, may address the necessary recommendations to the Member State concerned. The Council may, on a proposal from the Commission, decide to make its recommendations public.

     Within the scope of this paragraph, the Council shall act without taking into account the vote of the member of the Council representing the Member State concerned.

     A qualified majority of the other members of the Council shall be defined in accordance with Article 238(3)(a).

5.   The President of the Council and the Commission shall report to the European Parliament on the results of multilateral surveillance. The President of the Council may be invited to appear before the competent committee of the European Parliament if the Council has made its recommendations public.

6.   The European Parliament and the Council, acting by means of regulations in accordance with the ordinary legislative procedure, may adopt detailed rules for the multilateral surveillance procedure referred to in paragraphs 3 and 4.

Article 122 (ex Article 100 TEC)

1.   Without prejudice to any other procedures provided for in the Treaties, the Council, on a proposal from the Commission, may decide, in a spirit of solidarity between Member States, upon the measures appropriate to the economic situation, in particular if severe difficulties arise in the supply of certain products, notably in the area of energy.

2.   Where a Member State is in difficulties or is seriously threatened with severe difficulties caused by natural disasters or exceptional occurrences beyond its control, the Council, on

a proposal from the Commission, may grant, under certain conditions, Union financial assistance to the Member State concerned. The President of the Council shall inform the European Parliament of the decision taken.

Article 123 (ex Article 101 TEC)

1.   Overdraft facilities or any other type of credit facility with the European Central Bank or with the central banks of the Member States (hereinafter referred to as 'national central banks') in favour of Union institutions, bodies, offices or agencies, central governments, regional, local or other public authorities, other bodies governed by public law, or public undertakings of Member States shall be prohibited, as shall the purchase directly from them by the European Central Bank or national central banks of debt instruments.

2.   Paragraph 1 shall not apply to publicly owned credit institutions which, in the context of the supply of reserves by central banks, shall be given the same treatment by national central banks and the European Central Bank as private credit institutions.

Article 124 (ex Article 102 TEC)

Any measure, not based on prudential considerations, establishing privileged access by Union institutions, bodies, offices or agencies, central governments, regional, local or other public authorities, other bodies governed by public law, or public undertakings of Member States to financial institutions, shall be prohibited.

Article 125 (ex Article 103 TEC)

1.   The Union shall not be liable for or assume the commitments of central governments, regional, local or other public authorities, other bodies governed by public law, or public undertakings of any Member State, without prejudice to mutual financial guarantees for the joint execution of a specific project. A Member State shall not be liable for or assume the commitments of central governments, regional, local or other public authorities, other bodies governed by public law, or public undertakings of another Member State, without prejudice to mutual financial guarantees for the joint execution of a specific project.

2.   The Council, on a proposal from the Commission and after consulting the European Parliament, may, as required, specify definitions for the application of the prohibitions referred to in Articles 123 and 124 and in this Article.

Article 126 (ex Article 104 TEC)

1.   Member States shall avoid excessive government deficits.

2.   The Commission shall monitor the development of the budgetary situation and of the stock of government debt in the Member States with a view to identifying gross errors. In particular it shall examine compliance with budgetary discipline on the basis of the following two criteria:
(a) whether the ratio of the planned or actual government deficit to gross domestic product exceeds a reference value, unless:
   — either the ratio has declined substantially and continuously and reached a level that comes close to the reference value,
   — or, alternatively, the excess over the reference value is only exceptional and temporary and the ratio remains close to the reference value;
(b) whether the ratio of government debt to gross domestic product exceeds a reference value, unless the ratio is sufficiently diminishing and approaching the reference value at a satisfactory pace.
The reference values are specified in the Protocol on the excessive deficit procedure annexed to the Treaties.

3.   If a Member State does not fulfil the requirements under one or both of these criteria, the Commission shall prepare a report. The report of the Commission shall also take into account whether the government deficit exceeds government investment expenditure and take into account all other relevant factors, including the medium-term economic and budgetary position of the Member State.

The Commission may also prepare a report if, notwithstanding the fulfilment of the requirements under the criteria, it is of the opinion that there is a risk of an excessive deficit in a Member State.

4.   The Economic and Financial Committee shall formulate an opinion on the report of the Commission.

5.   If the Commission considers that an excessive deficit in a Member State exists or may occur, it shall address an opinion to the Member State concerned and shall inform the Council accordingly.

6.   The Council shall, on a proposal from the Commission, and having considered any observations which the Member State concerned may wish to make, decide after an overall assessment whether an excessive deficit exists.

7.   Where the Council decides, in accordance with paragraph 6, that an excessive deficit exists, it shall adopt, without undue delay, on a recommendation from the Commission, recommendations addressed to the Member State concerned with a view to bringing that situation to an end within a given period. Subject to the provisions of paragraph 8, these recommendations shall not be made public.

8.   Where it establishes that there has been no effective action in response to its recommendations within the period laid down, the Council may make its recommendations public.

9.   If a Member State persists in failing to put into practice the recommendations of the Council, the Council may decide to give notice to the Member State to take, within a specified time limit, measures for the deficit reduction which is judged necessary by the Council in order to remedy the situation.

In such a case, the Council may request the Member State concerned to submit reports in accordance with a specific timetable in order to examine the adjustment efforts of that Member State.

10.   The rights to bring actions provided for in Articles 258 and 259 may not be exercised within the framework of paragraphs 1 to 9 of this Article.

11.   As long as a Member State fails to comply with a decision taken in accordance with paragraph 9, the Council may decide to apply or, as the case may be, intensify one or more of the following measures:
— to require the Member State concerned to publish additional information, to be specified by the Council, before issuing bonds and securities,
— to invite the European Investment Bank to reconsider its lending policy towards the Member State concerned,
— to require the Member State concerned to make a non-interest-bearing deposit of an appropriate size with the Union until the excessive deficit has, in the view of the Council, been corrected,
— to impose fines of an appropriate size.
The President of the Council shall inform the European Parliament of the decisions taken.

12. The Council shall abrogate some or all of its decisions or recommendations referred to in paragraphs 6 to 9 and 11 to the extent that the excessive deficit in the Member State concerned has, in the view of the Council, been corrected. If the Council has previously made public recommendations, it shall, as soon as the decision under paragraph 8 has been abrogated, make a public statement that an excessive deficit in the Member State concerned no longer exists.

13. When taking the decisions or recommendations referred to in paragraphs 8, 9, 11 and 12, the Council shall act on a recommendation from the Commission.

When the Council adopts the measures referred to in paragraphs 6 to 9, 11 and 12, it shall act without taking into account the vote of the member of the Council representing the Member State concerned.

A qualified majority of the other members of the Council shall be defined in accordance with Article 238(3)(a).

14. Further provisions relating to the implementation of the procedure described in this Article are set out in the Protocol on the excessive deficit procedure annexed to the Treaties.

The Council shall, acting unanimously in accordance with a special legislative procedure and after consulting the European Parliament and the European Central Bank, adopt the appropriate provisions which shall then replace the said Protocol.

Subject to the other provisions of this paragraph, the Council shall, on a proposal from the Commission and after consulting the European Parliament, lay down detailed rules and definitions for the application of the provisions of the said Protocol.

Chapter 2 MONETARY POLICY

Article 127 (ex Article 105 TEC)

1. The primary objective of the European System of Central Banks (hereinafter referred to as 'the ESCB') shall be to maintain price stability. Without prejudice to the objective of price stability, the ESCB shall support the general economic policies in the Union with a view to contributing to the achievement of the objectives of the Union as laid down in Article 3 of the Treaty on European Union. The ESCB shall act in accordance with the principle of an open market economy with free competition, favouring an efficient allocation of resources, and in compliance with the principles set out in Article 119.

2. The basic tasks to be carried out through the ESCB shall be:
     — to define and implement the monetary policy of the Union,
     — to conduct foreign-exchange operations consistent with the provisions of Article 219,
     — to hold and manage the official foreign reserves of the Member States,
     — to promote the smooth operation of payment systems.

3. The third indent of paragraph 2 shall be without prejudice to the holding and management by the governments of Member States of foreign-exchange working balances.

4. The European Central Bank shall be consulted:
     — on any proposed Union act in its fields of competence,
     — by national authorities regarding any draft legislative provision in its fields of competence, but within the limits and under the conditions set out by the Council in accordance with the procedure laid down in Article 129(4).
     The European Central Bank may submit opinions to the appropriate Union institutions, bodies, offices or agencies or to national authorities on matters in its fields of competence.

5.   The ESCB shall contribute to the smooth conduct of policies pursued by the competent authorities relating to the prudential supervision of credit institutions and the stability of the financial system.

6.   The Council, acting by means of regulations in accordance with a special legislative procedure, may unanimously, and after consulting the European Parliament and the European Central Bank, confer specific tasks upon the European Central Bank concerning policies relating to the prudential supervision of credit institutions and other financial institutions with the exception of insurance undertakings.

Article 128 (ex Article 106 TEC)

1.   The European Central Bank shall have the exclusive right to authorise the issue of euro banknotes within the Union. The European Central Bank and the national central banks may issue such notes. The banknotes issued by the European Central Bank and the national central banks shall be the only such notes to have the status of legal tender within the Union.

2.   Member States may issue euro coins subject to approval by the European Central Bank of the volume of the issue. The Council, on a proposal from the Commission and after consulting the European Parliament and the European Central Bank, may adopt measures to harmonise the denominations and technical specifications of all coins intended for circulation to the extent necessary to permit their smooth circulation within the Union.

Article 129 (ex Article 107 TEC)

1.   The ESCB shall be governed by the decision-making bodies of the European Central Bank which shall be the Governing Council and the Executive Board.

2.   The Statute of the European System of Central Banks and of the European Central Bank (hereinafter referred to as 'the Statute of the ESCB and of the ECB') is laid down in a Protocol annexed to the Treaties.

3.   Articles 5.1, 5.2, 5.3, 17, 18, 19.1, 22, 23, 24, 26, 32.2, 32.3, 32.4, 32.6, 33.1(a) and 36 of the Statute of the ESCB and of the ECB may be amended by the European Parliament and the Council, acting in accordance with the ordinary legislative procedure. They shall act either on a recommendation from the European Central Bank and after consulting the Commission or on a proposal from the Commission and after consulting the European Central Bank.

4.   The Council, either on a proposal from the Commission and after consulting the European Parliament and the European Central Bank or on a recommendation from the European Central Bank and after consulting the European Parliament and the Commission, shall adopt the provisions referred to in Articles 4, 5.4, 19.2, 20, 28.1, 29.2, 30.4 and 34.3 of the Statute of the ESCB and of the ECB.

Article 130 (ex Article 108 TEC)

When exercising the powers and carrying out the tasks and duties conferred upon them by the Treaties and the Statute of the ESCB and of the ECB, neither the European Central Bank, nor a national central bank, nor any member of their decision-making bodies shall seek or take instructions from Union institutions, bodies, offices or agencies, from any government of a Member State or from any other body. The Union institutions, bodies, offices or agencies and the governments of the Member States undertake to respect this principle and not to seek to influence the members of the decision-making bodies of the European Central Bank or of the national central banks in the performance of their tasks.

Article 131 (ex Article 109 TEC)
Each Member State shall ensure that its national legislation including the statutes of its national central bank is compatible with the Treaties and the Statute of the ESCB and of the ECB.

Article 132 (ex Article 110 TEC)
1.   In order to carry out the tasks entrusted to the ESCB, the European Central Bank shall, in accordance with the provisions of the Treaties and under the conditions laid down in the Statute of the ESCB and of the ECB:
      —   make regulations to the extent necessary to implement the tasks defined in Article 3.1, first indent, Articles 19.1, 22 and 25.2 of the Statute of the ESCB and of the ECB in cases which shall be laid down in the acts of the Council referred to in Article 129(4),
      —   take decisions necessary for carrying out the tasks entrusted to the ESCB under the Treaties and the Statute of the ESCB and of the ECB,
      —   make recommendations and deliver opinions.

2.   The European Central Bank may decide to publish its decisions, recommendations and opinions.

3.   Within the limits and under the conditions adopted by the Council under the procedure laid down in Article 129(4), the European Central Bank shall be entitled to impose fines or periodic penalty payments on undertakings for failure to comply with obligations under its regulations and decisions.

Article 133
Without prejudice to the powers of the European Central Bank, the European Parliament and the Council, acting in accordance with the ordinary legislative procedure, shall lay down the measures necessary for the use of the euro as the single currency. Such measures shall be adopted after consultation of the European Central Bank.

Chapter 3 INSTITUTIONAL PROVISIONS

Article 134 (ex Article 114 TEC)
1.   In order to promote coordination of the policies of Member States to the full extent needed for the functioning of the internal market, an Economic and Financial Committee is hereby set up.

2.   The Economic and Financial Committee shall have the following tasks:
      —   to deliver opinions at the request of the Council or of the Commission, or on its own initiative for submission to those institutions,
      —   to keep under review the economic and financial situation of the Member States and of the Union and to report regularly thereon to the Council and to the Commission, in particular on financial relations with third countries and international institutions,
      —   without prejudice to Article 240, to contribute to the preparation of the work of the Council referred to in Articles 66, 75, 121(2), (3), (4) and (6), 122, 124, 125, 126, 127(6), 128(2), 129(3) and (4), 138, 140(2) and (3), 143, 144(2) and (3), and in Article 219, and to carry out other advisory and preparatory tasks assigned to it by the Council,   .
      —   to examine, at least once a year, the situation regarding the movement of capital and the freedom of payments, as they result from the application of the Treaties and of measures adopted by the Council; the examination shall cover all measures relating to capital movements and payments; the Committee shall report to the Commission and to the Council on the outcome of this examination.
      The Member States, the Commission and the European Central Bank shall each appoint no more than two members of the Committee.

3.   The Council shall, on a proposal from the Commission and after consulting the European Central Bank and the Committee referred to in this Article, lay down detailed provisions concerning the composition of the Economic and Financial Committee. The President of the Council shall inform the European Parliament of such a decision.

4.   In addition to the tasks set out in paragraph 2, if and as long as there are Member States with a derogation as referred to in Article 139, the Committee shall keep under review the monetary and financial situation and the general payments system of those Member States and report regularly thereon to the Council and to the Commission.

Article 135 (ex Article 115 TEC)

For matters within the scope of Articles 121(4), 126 with the exception of paragraph 14, 138, 140(1), 140(2), first subparagraph, 140(3) and 219, the Council or a Member State may request the Commission to make a recommendation or a proposal, as appropriate. The Commission shall examine this request and submit its conclusions to the Council without delay.

Chapter 4 PROVISIONS SPECIFIC TO MEMBER STATES WHOSE CURRENCY IS THE EURO

Article 136

1.   In order to ensure the proper functioning of economic and monetary union, and in accordance with the relevant provisions of the Treaties, the Council shall, in accordance with the relevant procedure from among those referred to in Articles 121 and 126, with the exception of the procedure set out in Article 126(14), adopt measures specific to those Member States whose currency is the euro:
(a) to strengthen the coordination and surveillance of their budgetary discipline;
(b) to set out economic policy guidelines for them, while ensuring that they are compatible with those adopted for the whole of the Union and are kept under surveillance.

2.   For those measures set out in paragraph 1, only members of the Council representing Member States whose currency is the euro shall take part in the vote.

A qualified majority of the said members shall be defined in accordance with Article 238(3)(a).

Article 137

Arrangements for meetings between ministers of those Member States whose currency is the euro are laid down by the Protocol on the Euro Group.

Article 138 (ex Article 111(4), TEC)

1.   In order to secure the euro's place in the international monetary system, the Council, on a proposal from the Commission, shall adopt a decision establishing common positions on matters of particular interest for economic and monetary union within the competent international financial institutions and conferences. The Council shall act after consulting the European Central Bank.

2.   The Council, on a proposal from the Commission, may adopt appropriate measures to ensure unified representation within the international financial institutions and conferences. The Council shall act after consulting the European Central Bank.

3.   For the measures referred to in paragraphs 1 and 2, only members of the Council representing Member States whose currency is the euro shall take part in the vote.

A qualified majority of the said members shall be defined in accordance with Article 238(3)(a).

Chapter 5 TRANSITIONAL PROVISIONS

Article 139
1.   Member States in respect of which the Council has not decided that they fulfil the necessary conditions for the adoption of the euro shall hereinafter be referred to as 'Member States with a derogation'.

2.   The following provisions of the Treaties shall not apply to Member States with a derogation:
      (a) adoption of the parts of the broad economic policy guidelines which concern the euro area generally (Article 121(2));
      (b) coercive means of remedying excessive deficits (Article 126(9) and (11));
      (c) the objectives and tasks of the ESCB (Article 127(1) to (3) and (5));
      (d) issue of the euro (Article 128);
      (e) acts of the European Central Bank (Article 132);
      (f) measures governing the use of the euro (Article 133);
      (g) monetary agreements and other measures relating to exchange-rate policy (Article 219);
      (h) appointment of members of the Executive Board of the European Central Bank (Article 283(2));
      (i) decisions establishing common positions on issues of particular relevance for economic and monetary union within the competent international financial institutions and conferences (Article 138(1));
      (j) measures to ensure unified representation within the international financial institutions and conferences (Article 138(2)).
      In the Articles referred to in points (a) to (j), 'Member States' shall therefore mean Member States whose currency is the euro.

3.   Under Chapter IX of the Statute of the ESCB and of the ECB, Member States with a derogation and their national central banks are excluded from rights and obligations within the ESCB.

4.   The voting rights of members of the Council representing Member States with a derogation shall be suspended for the adoption by the Council of the measures referred to in the Articles listed in paragraph 2, and in the following instances:
      (a) recommendations made to those Member States whose currency is the euro in the framework of multilateral surveillance, including on stability programmes and warnings (Article 121(4));
      (b) measures relating to excessive deficits concerning those Member States whose currency is the euro (Article 126(6), (7), (8), (12) and (13)).
      A qualified majority of the other members of the Council shall be defined in accordance with Article 238(3)(a).

Article 140 (ex Articles 121(1), 122(2), second sentence, and 123(5) TEC)
1.   At least once every two years, or at the request of a Member State with a derogation, the Commission and the European Central Bank shall report to the Council on the progress made by the Member States with a derogation in fulfilling their obligations regarding the achievement of economic and monetary union. These reports shall include an examination of the compatibility between the national legislation of each of these Member States, including the statutes of its national central bank, and Articles 130 and 131 and the Statute of the ESCB and of the ECB. The reports shall also examine the achievement of a high degree of sustainable convergence by reference to the fulfilment by each Member State of the following criteria:
      — the achievement of a high degree of price stability; this will be apparent from a rate of inflation which is close to that of, at most, the three best performing Member States in terms of price stability,

— the sustainability of the government financial position; this will be apparent from having achieved a government budgetary position without a deficit that is excessive as determined in accordance with Article 126(6),

— the observance of the normal fluctuation margins provided for by the exchange-rate mechanism of the European Monetary System, for at least two years, without devaluing against the euro,

— the durability of convergence achieved by the Member State with a derogation and of its participation in the exchange-rate mechanism being reflected in the long-term interest-rate levels.

The four criteria mentioned in this paragraph and the relevant periods over which they are to be respected are developed further in a Protocol annexed to the Treaties. The reports of the Commission and the European Central Bank shall also take account of the results of the integration of markets, the situation and development of the balances of payments on current account and an examination of the development of unit labour costs and other price indices.

2.   After consulting the European Parliament and after discussion in the European Council, the Council shall, on a proposal from the Commission, decide which Member States with a derogation fulfil the necessary conditions on the basis of the criteria set out in paragraph 1, and abrogate the derogations of the Member States concerned.

The Council shall act having received a recommendation of a qualified majority of those among its members representing Member States whose currency is the euro. These members shall act within six months of the Council receiving the Commission's proposal.

The qualified majority of the said members, as referred to in the second subparagraph, shall be defined in accordance with Article 238(3)(a).

3.   If it is decided, in accordance with the procedure set out in paragraph 2, to abrogate a derogation, the Council shall, acting with the unanimity of the Member States whose currency is the euro and the Member State concerned, on a proposal from the Commission and after consulting the European Central Bank, irrevocably fix the rate at which the euro shall be substituted for the currency of the Member State concerned, and take the other measures necessary for the introduction of the euro as the single currency in the Member State concerned.

Article 141 (ex Articles 123(3) and 117(2) first five indents, TEC)

1.   If and as long as there are Member States with a derogation, and without prejudice to Article 129(1), the General Council of the European Central Bank referred to in Article 44 of the Statute of the ESCB and of the ECB shall be constituted as a third decision-making body of the European Central Bank.

2.   If and as long as there are Member States with a derogation, the European Central Bank shall, as regards those Member States:
— strengthen cooperation between the national central banks,
— strengthen the coordination of the monetary policies of the Member States, with the aim of ensuring price stability,
— monitor the functioning of the exchange-rate mechanism,
— hold consultations concerning issues falling within the competence of the national central banks and affecting the stability of financial institutions and markets,
— carry out the former tasks of the European Monetary Cooperation Fund which had subsequently been taken over by the European Monetary Institute.

Article 142 (ex Article 124(1) TEC)

Each Member State with a derogation shall treat its exchange-rate policy as a matter of common interest. In so doing, Member States shall take account of the experience acquired in cooperation within the framework of the exchange-rate mechanism.

Article 143 (ex Article 119 TEC)

1. Where a Member State with a derogation is in difficulties or is seriously threatened with difficulties as regards its balance of payments either as a result of an overall disequilibrium in its balance of payments, or as a result of the type of currency at its disposal, and where such difficulties are liable in particular to jeopardise the functioning of the internal market or the implementation of the common commercial policy, the Commission shall immediately investigate the position of the State in question and the action which, making use of all the means at its disposal, that State has taken or may take in accordance with the provisions of the Treaties. The Commission shall state what measures it recommends the State concerned to take.

   If the action taken by a Member State with a derogation and the measures suggested by the Commission do not prove sufficient to overcome the difficulties which have arisen or which threaten, the Commission shall, after consulting the Economic and Financial Committee, recommend to the Council the granting of mutual assistance and appropriate methods therefor.

   The Commission shall keep the Council regularly informed of the situation and of how it is developing.

2. The Council shall grant such mutual assistance; it shall adopt directives or decisions laying down the conditions and details of such assistance, which may take such forms as:
   (a) a concerted approach to or within any other international organisations to which Member States with a derogation may have recourse;
   (b) measures needed to avoid deflection of trade where the Member State with a derogation which is in difficulties maintains or reintroduces quantitative restrictions against third countries;
   (c) the granting of limited credits by other Member States, subject to their agreement.

3. If the mutual assistance recommended by the Commission is not granted by the Council or if the mutual assistance granted and the measures taken are insufficient, the Commission shall authorise the Member State with a derogation which is in difficulties to take protective measures, the conditions and details of which the Commission shall determine.

   Such authorisation may be revoked and such conditions and details may be changed by the Council.

Article 144 (ex Article 120 TEC)

1. Where a sudden crisis in the balance of payments occurs and a decision within the meaning of Article 143(2) is not immediately taken, a Member State with a derogation may, as a precaution, take the necessary protective measures. Such measures must cause the least possible disturbance in the functioning of the internal market and must not be wider in scope than is strictly necessary to remedy the sudden difficulties which have arisen.

2. The Commission and the other Member States shall be informed of such protective measures not later than when they enter into force. The Commission may recommend to the Council the granting of mutual assistance under Article 143.

3. After the Commission has delivered a recommendation and the Economic and Financial Committee has been consulted, the Council may decide that the Member State concerned shall amend, suspend or abolish the protective measures referred to above.

TITLE IX
EMPLOYMENT

Article 145 (ex Article 125 TEC)
Member States and the Union shall, in accordance with this Title, work towards developing a coordinated strategy for employment and particularly for promoting a skilled, trained and adaptable workforce and labour markets responsive to economic change with a view to achieving the objectives defined in Article 3 of the Treaty on European Union.

Article 146 (ex Article 126 TEC)
1.   Member States, through their employment policies, shall contribute to the achievement of the objectives referred to in Article 145 in a way consistent with the broad guidelines of the economic policies of the Member States and of the Union adopted pursuant to Article 121(2).

2.   Member States, having regard to national practices related to the responsibilities of management and labour, shall regard promoting employment as a matter of common concern and shall coordinate their action in this respect within the Council, in accordance with the provisions of Article 148.

Article 147 (ex Article 127 TEC)
1.   The Union shall contribute to a high level of employment by encouraging cooperation between Member States and by supporting and, if necessary, complementing their action. In doing so, the competences of the Member States shall be respected.

2.   The objective of a high level of employment shall be taken into consideration in the formulation and implementation of Union policies and activities.

Article 148 (ex Article 128 TEC)
1.   The European Council shall each year consider the employment situation in the Union and adopt conclusions thereon, on the basis of a joint annual report by the Council and the Commission.

2.   On the basis of the conclusions of the European Council, the Council, on a proposal from the Commission and after consulting the European Parliament, the Economic and Social Committee, the Committee of the Regions and the Employment Committee referred to in Article 150, shall each year draw up guidelines which the Member States shall take into account in their employment policies. These guidelines shall be consistent with the broad guidelines adopted pursuant to Article 121(2).

3.   Each Member State shall provide the Council and the Commission with an annual report on the principal measures taken to implement its employment policy in the light of the guidelines for employment as referred to in paragraph 2.

4.   The Council, on the basis of the reports referred to in paragraph 3 and having received the views of the Employment Committee, shall each year carry out an examination of the implementation of the employment policies of the Member States in the light of the guidelines for employment. The Council, on a recommendation from the Commission, may, if it considers it appropriate in the light of that examination, make recommendations to Member States.

5.   On the basis of the results of that examination, the Council and the Commission shall make a joint annual report to the European Council on the employment situation in the Union and on the implementation of the guidelines for employment.

Article 149 (ex Article 129 TEC)

The European Parliament and the Council, acting in accordance with the ordinary legislative procedure and after consulting the Economic and Social Committee and the Committee of the Regions, may adopt incentive measures designed to encourage cooperation between Member States and to support their action in the field of employment through initiatives aimed at developing exchanges of information and best practices, providing comparative analysis and advice as well as promoting innovative approaches and evaluating experiences, in particular by recourse to pilot projects.

Those measures shall not include harmonisation of the laws and regulations of the Member States.

Article 150 (ex Article 130 TEC)

The Council, acting by a simple majority after consulting the European Parliament, shall establish an Employment Committee with advisory status to promote coordination between Member States on employment and labour market policies. The tasks of the Committee shall be:

— to monitor the employment situation and employment policies in the Member States and the Union,

— without prejudice to Article 240, to formulate opinions at the request of either the Council or the Commission or on its own initiative, and to contribute to the preparation of the Council proceedings referred to in Article 148.

In fulfilling its mandate, the Committee shall consult management and labour.
Each Member State and the Commission shall appoint two members of the Committee.

TITLE X
SOCIAL POLICY

Article 151 (ex Article 136 TEC)

The Union and the Member States, having in mind fundamental social rights such as those set out in the European Social Charter signed at Turin on 18 October 1961 and in the 1989 Community Charter of the Fundamental Social Rights of Workers, shall have as their objectives the promotion of employment, improved living and working conditions, so as to make possible their harmonisation while the improvement is being maintained, proper social protection, dialogue between management and labour, the development of human resources with a view to lasting high employment and the combating of exclusion.

To this end the Union and the Member States shall implement measures which take account of the diverse forms of national practices, in particular in the field of contractual relations, and the need to maintain the competitiveness of the Union's economy.

They believe that such a development will ensue not only from the functioning of the internal market, which will favour the harmonisation of social systems, but also from the procedures provided for in the Treaties and from the approximation of provisions laid down by law, regulation or administrative action.

Article 152

The Union recognises and promotes the role of the social partners at its level, taking into account the diversity of national systems. It shall facilitate dialogue between the social partners, respecting their autonomy.

The Tripartite Social Summit for Growth and Employment shall contribute to social dialogue.

Article 153 (ex Article 137 TEC)

1.   With a view to achieving the objectives of Article 151, the Union shall support and complement the activities of the Member States in the following fields:
   (a) improvement in particular of the working environment to protect workers' health and safety;
   (b) working conditions;
   (c) social security and social protection of workers;
   (d) protection of workers where their employment contract is terminated;
   (e) the information and consultation of workers;
   (f) representation and collective defence of the interests of workers and employers, including co-determination, subject to paragraph 5;
   (g) conditions of employment for third-country nationals legally residing in Union territory;
   (h) the integration of persons excluded from the labour market, without prejudice to Article 166;
   (i) equality between men and women with regard to labour market opportunities and treatment at work;
   (j) the combating of social exclusion;
   (k) the modernisation of social protection systems without prejudice to point (c).

2.   To this end, the European Parliament and the Council:
   (a) may adopt measures designed to encourage cooperation between Member States through initiatives aimed at improving knowledge, developing exchanges of information and best practices, promoting innovative approaches and evaluating experiences, excluding any harmonisation of the laws and regulations of the Member States;
   (b) may adopt, in the fields referred to in paragraph 1(a) to (i), by means of directives, minimum requirements for gradual implementation, having regard to the conditions and technical rules obtaining in each of the Member States. Such directives shall avoid imposing administrative, financial and legal constraints in a way which would hold back the creation and development of small and medium-sized undertakings.

   The European Parliament and the Council shall act in accordance with the ordinary legislative procedure after consulting the Economic and Social Committee and the Committee of the Regions.

   In the fields referred to in paragraph 1(c), (d), (f) and (g), the Council shall act unanimously, in accordance with a special legislative procedure, after consulting the European Parliament and the said Committees.

   The Council, acting unanimously on a proposal from the Commission, after consulting the European Parliament, may decide to render the ordinary legislative procedure applicable to paragraph 1(d), (f) and (g).

3.   A Member State may entrust management and labour, at their joint request, with the implementation of directives adopted pursuant to paragraph 2, or, where appropriate, with the implementation of a Council decision adopted in accordance with Article 155.

   In this case, it shall ensure that, no later than the date on which a directive or a decision must be transposed or implemented, management and labour have introduced the necessary measures by agreement, the Member State concerned being required to take any necessary measure enabling it at any time to be in a position to guarantee the results imposed by that directive or that decision.

4.   The provisions adopted pursuant to this Article:
   — shall not affect the right of Member States to define the fundamental principles of their social security systems and must not significantly affect the financial equilibrium thereof,

— shall not prevent any Member State from maintaining or introducing more stringent protective measures compatible with the Treaties.

5. The provisions of this Article shall not apply to pay, the right of association, the right to strike or the right to impose lock-outs.

Article 154 (ex Article 138 TEC)

1. The Commission shall have the task of promoting the consultation of management and labour at Union level and shall take any relevant measure to facilitate their dialogue by ensuring balanced support for the parties.

2. To this end, before submitting proposals in the social policy field, the Commission shall consult management and labour on the possible direction of Union action.

3. If, after such consultation, the Commission considers Union action advisable, it shall consult management and labour on the content of the envisaged proposal. Management and labour shall forward to the Commission an opinion or, where appropriate, a recommendation.

4. On the occasion of the consultation referred to in paragraphs 2 and 3, management and labour may inform the Commission of their wish to initiate the process provided for in Article 155. The duration of this process shall not exceed nine months, unless the management and labour concerned and the Commission decide jointly to extend it.

Article 155 (ex Article 139 TEC)

1. Should management and labour so desire, the dialogue between them at Union level may lead to contractual relations, including agreements.

2. Agreements concluded at Union level shall be implemented either in accordance with the procedures and practices specific to management and labour and the Member States or, in matters covered by Article 153, at the joint request of the signatory parties, by a Council decision on a proposal from the Commission. The European Parliament shall be informed.

   The Council shall act unanimously where the agreement in question contains one or more provisions relating to one of the areas for which unanimity is required pursuant to Article 153(2).

Article 156 (ex Article 140 TEC)

With a view to achieving the objectives of Article 151 and without prejudice to the other provisions of the Treaties, the Commission shall encourage cooperation between the Member States and facilitate the coordination of their action in all social policy fields under this Chapter, particularly in matters relating to:

— employment,

— labour law and working conditions,

— basic and advanced vocational training,

— social security,

— prevention of occupational accidents and diseases,

— occupational hygiene,

— the right of association and collective bargaining between employers and workers.

To this end, the Commission shall act in close contact with Member States by making studies, delivering opinions and arranging consultations both on problems arising at national level and on those of concern to international organisations, in particular initiatives aiming at the establishment of guidelines and indicators, the organisation of exchange of best practice, and the preparation of the necessary elements for periodic monitoring and evaluation. The European Parliament shall be kept fully informed.

Before delivering the opinions provided for in this Article, the Commission shall consult the Economic and Social Committee.

Article 157 (ex Article 141 TEC)

1. Each Member State shall ensure that the principle of equal pay for male and female workers for equal work or work of equal value is applied.

2. For the purpose of this Article, 'pay' means the ordinary basic or minimum wage or salary and any other consideration, whether in cash or in kind, which the worker receives directly or indirectly, in respect of his employment, from his employer.

    Equal pay without discrimination based on sex means:
    (a) that pay for the same work at piece rates shall be calculated on the basis of the same unit of measurement;
    (b) that pay for work at time rates shall be the same for the same job.

3. The European Parliament and the Council, acting in accordance with the ordinary legislative procedure, and after consulting the Economic and Social Committee, shall adopt measures to ensure the application of the principle of equal opportunities and equal treatment of men and women in matters of employment and occupation, including the principle of equal pay for equal work or work of equal value.

4. With a view to ensuring full equality in practice between men and women in working life, the principle of equal treatment shall not prevent any Member State from maintaining or adopting measures providing for specific advantages in order to make it easier for the underrepresented sex to pursue a vocational activity or to prevent or compensate for disadvantages in professional careers.

Article 158 (ex Article 142 TEC)

Member States shall endeavour to maintain the existing equivalence between paid holiday schemes.

Article 159 (ex Article 143 TEC)

The Commission shall draw up a report each year on progress in achieving the objectives of Article 151, including the demographic situation in the Union. It shall forward the report to the European Parliament, the Council and the Economic and Social Committee.

Article 160 (ex Article 144 TEC)

The Council, acting by a simple majority after consulting the European Parliament, shall establish a Social Protection Committee with advisory status to promote cooperation on social protection policies between Member States and with the Commission. The tasks of the Committee shall be:

—   to monitor the social situation and the development of social protection policies in the Member States and the Union,

—   to promote exchanges of information, experience and good practice between Member States and with the Commission,

—   without prejudice to Article 240, to prepare reports, formulate opinions or undertake other work within its fields of competence, at the request of either the Council or the Commission or on its own initiative.

In fulfilling its mandate, the Committee shall establish appropriate contacts with management and labour.

Each Member State and the Commission shall appoint two members of the Committee.

Article 161 (ex Article 145 TEC)
The Commission shall include a separate chapter on social developments within the Union in its annual report to the European Parliament.

The European Parliament may invite the Commission to draw up reports on any particular problems concerning social conditions.

TITLE XI
THE EUROPEAN SOCIAL FUND

Article 162 (ex Article 146 TEC)
In order to improve employment opportunities for workers in the internal market and to contribute thereby to raising the standard of living, a European Social Fund is hereby established in accordance with the provisions set out below; it shall aim to render the employment of workers easier and to increase their geographical and occupational mobility within the Union, and to facilitate their adaptation to industrial changes and to changes in production systems, in particular through vocational training and retraining.

Article 163 (ex Article 147 TEC)
The Fund shall be administered by the Commission.

The Commission shall be assisted in this task by a Committee presided over by a Member of the Commission and composed of representatives of governments, trade unions and employers' organisations.

Article 164 (ex Article 148 TEC)
The European Parliament and the Council, acting in accordance with the ordinary legislative procedure and after consulting the Economic and Social Committee and the Committee of the Regions, shall adopt implementing regulations relating to the European Social Fund.

TITLE XII
EDUCATION, VOCATIONAL TRAINING, YOUTH AND SPORT

Article 165 (ex Article 149 TEC)
1.   The Union shall contribute to the development of quality education by encouraging cooperation between Member States and, if necessary, by supporting and supplementing their action, while fully respecting the responsibility of the Member States for the content of teaching and the organisation of education systems and their cultural and linguistic diversity.

The Union shall contribute to the promotion of European sporting issues, while taking account of the specific nature of sport, its structures based on voluntary activity and its social and educational function.

2.   Union action shall be aimed at:
   — developing the European dimension in education, particularly through the teaching and dissemination of the languages of the Member States,
   — encouraging mobility of students and teachers, by encouraging inter alia, the academic recognition of diplomas and periods of study,
   — promoting cooperation between educational establishments,

— developing exchanges of information and experience on issues common to the education systems of the Member States,
— encouraging the development of youth exchanges and of exchanges of socio-educational instructors, and encouraging the participation of young people in democratic life in Europe,
— encouraging the development of distance education,
— developing the European dimension in sport, by promoting fairness and openness in sporting competitions and cooperation between bodies responsible for sports, and by protecting the physical and moral integrity of sportsmen and sportswomen, especially the youngest sportsmen and sportswomen.

3.   The Union and the Member States shall foster cooperation with third countries and the competent international organisations in the field of education and sport, in particular the Council of Europe.

4.   In order to contribute to the achievement of the objectives referred to in this Article:
— the European Parliament and the Council, acting in accordance with the ordinary legislative procedure, after consulting the Economic and Social Committee and the Committee of the Regions, shall adopt incentive measures, excluding any harmonisation of the laws and regulations of the Member States,
— the Council, on a proposal from the Commission, shall adopt recommendations.

Article 166 (ex Article 150 TEC)
1.   The Union shall implement a vocational training policy which shall support and supplement the action of the Member States, while fully respecting the responsibility of the Member States for the content and organisation of vocational training.

2.   Union action shall aim to:
— facilitate adaptation to industrial changes, in particular through vocational training and retraining,
— improve initial and continuing vocational training in order to facilitate vocational integration and reintegration into the labour market,
— facilitate access to vocational training and encourage mobility of instructors and trainees and particularly young people,
— stimulate cooperation on training between educational or training establishments and firms,
— develop exchanges of information and experience on issues common to the training systems of the Member States.

3.   The Union and the Member States shall foster cooperation with third countries and the competent international organisations in the sphere of vocational training.

4.   The European Parliament and the Council, acting in accordance with the ordinary legislative procedure and after consulting the Economic and Social Committee and the Committee of the Regions, shall adopt measures to contribute to the achievement of the objectives referred to in this Article, excluding any harmonisation of the laws and regulations of the Member States, and the Council, on a proposal from the Commission, shall adopt recommendations.

TITLE XIII
CULTURE

Article 167 (ex Article 151 TEC)
1.   The Union shall contribute to the flowering of the cultures of the Member States, while respecting their national and regional diversity and at the same time bringing the common cultural heritage to the fore.

2.   Action by the Union shall be aimed at encouraging cooperation between Member States and, if necessary, supporting and supplementing their action in the following areas:
  — improvement of the knowledge and dissemination of the culture and history of the European peoples,
  — conservation and safeguarding of cultural heritage of European significance,
  — non-commercial cultural exchanges,
  — artistic and literary creation, including in the audiovisual sector.

3.   The Union and the Member States shall foster cooperation with third countries and the competent international organisations in the sphere of culture, in particular the Council of Europe.

4.   The Union shall take cultural aspects into account in its action under other provisions of the Treaties, in particular in order to respect and to promote the diversity of its cultures.

5.   In order to contribute to the achievement of the objectives referred to in this Article:
  — the European Parliament and the Council acting in accordance with the ordinary legislative procedure and after consulting the Committee of the Regions, shall adopt incentive measures, excluding any harmonisation of the laws and regulations of the Member States,
  — the Council, on a proposal from the Commission, shall adopt recommendations.

TITLE XIV
PUBLIC HEALTH

Article 168 (ex Article 152 TEC)
1.   A high level of human health protection shall be ensured in the definition and implementation of all Union policies and activities.

Union action, which shall complement national policies, shall be directed towards improving public health, preventing physical and mental illness and diseases, and obviating sources of danger to physical and mental health. Such action shall cover the fight against the major health scourges, by promoting research into their causes, their transmission and their prevention, as well as health information and education, and monitoring, early warning of and combating serious cross-border threats to health.

The Union shall complement the Member States' action in reducing drugs-related health damage, including information and prevention.

2.   The Union shall encourage cooperation between the Member States in the areas referred to in this Article and, if necessary, lend support to their action. It shall in particular encourage cooperation between the Member States to improve the complementarity of their health services in cross-border areas.

Member States shall, in liaison with the Commission, coordinate among themselves their policies and programmes in the areas referred to in paragraph 1. The Commission may, in close contact with the Member States, take any useful initiative to promote such coordination, in particular initiatives aiming at the establishment of guidelines and indicators, the organisation of exchange of best practice, and the preparation of the necessary elements for periodic monitoring and evaluation. The European Parliament shall be kept fully informed.

3.   The Union and the Member States shall foster cooperation with third countries and the competent international organisations in the sphere of public health.

4.   By way of derogation from Article 2(5) and Article 6(a) and in accordance with Article 4(2)(k) the European Parliament and the Council, acting in accordance with the

ordinary legislative procedure and after consulting the Economic and Social Committee and the Committee of the Regions, shall contribute to the achievement of the objectives referred to in this Article through adopting in order to meet common safety concerns:

(a) measures setting high standards of quality and safety of organs and substances of human origin, blood and blood derivatives; these measures shall not prevent any Member State from maintaining or introducing more stringent protective measures;

(b) measures in the veterinary and phytosanitary fields which have as their direct objective the protection of public health;

(c) measures setting high standards of quality and safety for medicinal products and devices for medical use.

5.   The European Parliament and the Council, acting in accordance with the ordinary legislative procedure and after consulting the Economic and Social Committee and the Committee of the Regions, may also adopt incentive measures designed to protect and improve human health and in particular to combat the major cross-border health scourges, measures concerning monitoring, early warning of and combating serious cross-border threats to health, and measures which have as their direct objective the protection of public health regarding tobacco and the abuse of alcohol, excluding any harmonisation of the laws and regulations of the Member States.

6.   The Council, on a proposal from the Commission, may also adopt recommendations for the purposes set out in this Article.

7.   Union action shall respect the responsibilities of the Member States for the definition of their health policy and for the organisation and delivery of health services and medical care. The responsibilities of the Member States shall include the management of health services and medical care and the allocation of the resources assigned to them. The measures referred to in paragraph 4(a) shall not affect national provisions on the donation or medical use of organs and blood.

TITLE XV
CONSUMER PROTECTION

Article 169 (ex Article 153 TEC)

1.   In order to promote the interests of consumers and to ensure a high level of consumer protection, the Union shall contribute to protecting the health, safety and economic interests of consumers, as well as to promoting their right to information, education and to organise themselves in order to safeguard their interests.

2.   The Union shall contribute to the attainment of the objectives referred to in paragraph 1 through:

(a) measures adopted pursuant to Article 114 in the context of the completion of the internal market;

(b) measures which support, supplement and monitor the policy pursued by the Member States.

3.   The European Parliament and the Council, acting in accordance with the ordinary legislative procedure and after consulting the Economic and Social Committee, shall adopt the measures referred to in paragraph 2(b).

4.   Measures adopted pursuant to paragraph 3 shall not prevent any Member State from maintaining or introducing more stringent protective measures. Such measures must be compatible with the Treaties. The Commission shall be notified of them.

TITLE XVI
TRANS-EUROPEAN NETWORKS

Article 170 (ex Article 154 TEC)
1.   To help achieve the objectives referred to in Articles 26 and 174 and to enable citizens of the Union, economic operators and regional and local communities to derive full benefit from the setting-up of an area without internal frontiers, the Union shall contribute to the establishment and development of trans-European networks in the areas of transport, telecommunications and energy infrastructures.

2.   Within the framework of a system of open and competitive markets, action by the Union shall aim at promoting the interconnection and interoperability of national networks as well as access to such networks. It shall take account in particular of the need to link island, landlocked and peripheral regions with the central regions of the Union.

Article 171 (ex Article 155 TEC)
1.   In order to achieve the objectives referred to in Article 170, the Union:
   — shall establish a series of guidelines covering the objectives, priorities and broad lines of measures envisaged in the sphere of trans-European networks; these guidelines shall identify projects of common interest,
   — shall implement any measures that may prove necessary to ensure the interoperability of the networks, in particular in the field of technical standardisation,
   — may support projects of common interest supported by Member States, which are identified in the framework of the guidelines referred to in the first indent, particularly through feasibility studies, loan guarantees or interest-rate subsidies; the Union may also contribute, through the Cohesion Fund set up pursuant to Article 177, to the financing of specific projects in Member States in the area of transport infrastructure.
   The Union's activities shall take into account the potential economic viability of the projects.

2.   Member States shall, in liaison with the Commission, coordinate among themselves the policies pursued at national level which may have a significant impact on the achievement of the objectives referred to in Article 170. The Commission may, in close cooperation with the Member State, take any useful initiative to promote such coordination.

3.   The Union may decide to cooperate with third countries to promote projects of mutual interest and to ensure the interoperability of networks.

Article 172 (ex Article 156 TEC)
The guidelines and other measures referred to in Article 171(1) shall be adopted by the European Parliament and the Council, acting in accordance with the ordinary legislative procedure and after consulting the Economic and Social Committee and the Committee of the Regions.

Guidelines and projects of common interest which relate to the territory of a Member State shall require the approval of the Member State concerned.

TITLE XVII
INDUSTRY

Article 173 (ex Article 157 TEC)
1.   The Union and the Member States shall ensure that the conditions necessary for the competitiveness of the Union's industry exist.

For that purpose, in accordance with a system of open and competitive markets, their action shall be aimed at:

— speeding up the adjustment of industry to structural changes,

— encouraging an environment favourable to initiative and to the development of undertakings throughout the Union, particularly small and medium-sized undertakings,

— encouraging an environment favourable to cooperation between undertakings,

— fostering better exploitation of the industrial potential of policies of innovation, research and technological development.

2. The Member States shall consult each other in liaison with the Commission and, where necessary, shall coordinate their action. The Commission may take any useful initiative to promote such coordination, in particular initiatives aiming at the establishment of guidelines and indicators, the organisation of exchange of best practice, and the preparation of the necessary elements for periodic monitoring and evaluation. The European Parliament shall be kept fully informed.

3. The Union shall contribute to the achievement of the objectives set out in paragraph 1 through the policies and activities it pursues under other provisions of the Treaties. The European Parliament and the Council, acting in accordance with the ordinary legislative procedure and after consulting the Economic and Social Committee, may decide on specific measures in support of action taken in the Member States to achieve the objectives set out in paragraph 1, excluding any harmonisation of the laws and regulations of the Member States.

This Title shall not provide a basis for the introduction by the Union of any measure which could lead to a distortion of competition or contains tax provisions or provisions relating to the rights and interests of employed persons.

TITLE XVIII
ECONOMIC, SOCIAL AND TERRITORIAL COHESION

Article 174 (ex Article 158 TEC)

In order to promote its overall harmonious development, the Union shall develop and pursue its actions leading to the strengthening of its economic, social and territorial cohesion.

In particular, the Union shall aim at reducing disparities between the levels of development of the various regions and the backwardness of the least favoured regions.

Among the regions concerned, particular attention shall be paid to rural areas, areas affected by industrial transition, and regions which suffer from severe and permanent natural or demographic handicaps such as the northernmost regions with very low population density and island, cross- border and mountain regions.

Article 175 (ex Article 159 TEC)

Member States shall conduct their economic policies and shall coordinate them in such a way as, in addition, to attain the objectives set out in Article 174. The formulation and implementation of the Union's policies and actions and the implementation of the internal market shall take into account the objectives set out in Article 174 and shall contribute to their achievement. The Union shall also support the achievement of these objectives by the action it takes through the Structural Funds (European Agricultural Guidance and Guarantee Fund, Guidance Section; European Social Fund; European Regional Development Fund), the European Investment Bank and the other existing Financial Instruments.

The Commission shall submit a report to the European Parliament, the Council, the Economic and Social Committee and the Committee of the Regions every three years on the progress made towards achieving economic, social and territorial cohesion and on the manner in which the various means provided for in this Article have contributed to it. This report shall, if necessary, be accompanied by appropriate proposals.

If specific actions prove necessary outside the Funds and without prejudice to the measures decided upon within the framework of the other Union policies, such actions may be adopted by the Council acting in accordance with the ordinary legislative procedure and after consulting the Economic and Social Committee and the Committee of the Regions.

Article 176 (ex Article 160 TEC)
The European Regional Development Fund is intended to help to redress the main regional imbalances in the Union through participation in the development and structural adjustment of regions whose development is lagging behind and in the conversion of declining industrial regions.

Article 177 (ex Article 161 TEC)
Without prejudice to Article 178, the European Parliament and the Council, acting by means of regulations in accordance with the ordinary legislative procedure and consulting the Economic and Social Committee and the Committee of the Regions, shall define the tasks, priority objectives and the organisation of the Structural Funds, which may involve grouping the Funds. The general rules applicable to them and the provisions necessary to ensure their effectiveness and the coordination of the Funds with one another and with the other existing Financial Instruments shall also be defined by the same procedure.

A Cohesion Fund set up in accordance with the same procedure shall provide a financial contribution to projects in the fields of environment and trans-European networks in the area of transport infrastructure.

Article 178 (ex Article 162 TEC)
Implementing regulations relating to the European Regional Development Fund shall be taken by the European Parliament and the Council, acting in accordance with the ordinary legislative procedure and after consulting the Economic and Social Committee and the Committee of the Regions.

With regard to the European Agricultural Guidance and Guarantee Fund, Guidance Section, and the European Social Fund, Articles 43 and 164 respectively shall continue to apply.

TITLE XIX
RESEARCH AND TECHNOLOGICAL DEVELOPMENT AND SPACE

Article 179 (ex Article 163 TEC)
1. The Union shall have the objective of strengthening its scientific and technological bases by achieving a European research area in which researchers, scientific knowledge and technology circulate freely, and encouraging it to become more competitive, including in its industry, while promoting all the research activities deemed necessary by virtue of other Chapters of the Treaties.

2. For this purpose the Union shall, throughout the Union, encourage undertakings, including small and medium-sized undertakings, research centres and universities in their research and technological development activities of high quality; it shall support their efforts to cooperate with one another, aiming, notably, at permitting researchers to cooperate freely across borders and at enabling undertakings to exploit the internal market potential to the full, in particular through the opening-up of national public contracts, the definition of common standards and the removal of legal and fiscal obstacles to that cooperation.

3. All Union activities under the Treaties in the area of research and technological development, including demonstration projects, shall be decided on and implemented in accordance with the provisions of this Title.

Article 180 (ex Article 164 TEC)

In pursuing these objectives, the Union shall carry out the following activities, complementing the activities carried out in the Member States:

(a)   implementation of research, technological development and demonstration programmes, by promoting cooperation with and between undertakings, research centres and universities;

(b)   promotion of cooperation in the field of Union research, technological development and demonstration with third countries and international organisations;

(c)   dissemination and optimisation of the results of activities in Union research, technological development and demonstration;

(d)   stimulation of the training and mobility of researchers in the Union.

Article 181 (ex Article 165 TEC)

1.   The Union and the Member States shall coordinate their research and technological development activities so as to ensure that national policies and Union policy are mutually consistent.

2.   In close cooperation with the Member State, the Commission may take any useful initiative to promote the coordination referred to in paragraph 1, in particular initiatives aiming at the establishment of guidelines and indicators, the organisation of exchange of best practice, and the preparation of the necessary elements for periodic monitoring and evaluation. The European Parliament shall be kept fully informed.

Article 182 (ex Article 166 TEC)

1.   A multiannual framework programme, setting out all the activities of the Union, shall be adopted by the European Parliament and the Council, acting in accordance with the ordinary legislative procedure after consulting the Economic and Social Committee.

The framework programme shall:
—   establish the scientific and technological objectives to be achieved by the activities provided for in Article 180 and fix the relevant priorities,
—   indicate the broad lines of such activities,
—   fix the maximum overall amount and the detailed rules for Union financial participation in the framework programme and the respective shares in each of the activities provided for.

2.   The framework programme shall be adapted or supplemented as the situation changes.

3.   The framework programme shall be implemented through specific programmes developed within each activity. Each specific programme shall define the detailed rules for implementing it, fix its duration and provide for the means deemed necessary. The sum of the amounts deemed necessary, fixed in the specific programmes, may not exceed the overall maximum amount fixed for the framework programme and each activity.

4.   The Council, acting in accordance with a special legislative procedure and after consulting the European Parliament and the Economic and Social Committee, shall adopt the specific programmes.

5.   As a complement to the activities planned in the multiannual framework programme, the European Parliament and the Council, acting in accordance with the ordinary legislative procedure and after consulting the Economic and Social Committee, shall establish the measures necessary for the implementation of the European research area.

Article 183 (ex Article 167 TEC)
For the implementation of the multiannual framework programme the Union shall:
—   determine the rules for the participation of undertakings, research centres and universities,

—   lay down the rules governing the dissemination of research results.

Article 184 (ex Article 168 TEC)
In implementing the multiannual framework programme, supplementary programmes may be decided on involving the participation of certain Member States only, which shall finance them subject to possible Union participation.

The Union shall adopt the rules applicable to supplementary programmes, particularly as regards the dissemination of knowledge and access by other Member States.

Article 185 (ex Article 169 TEC)
In implementing the multiannual framework programme, the Union may make provision, in agreement with the Member States concerned, for participation in research and development programmes undertaken by several Member States, including participation in the structures created for the execution of those programmes.

Article 186 (ex Article 170 TEC)
In implementing the multiannual framework programme the Union may make provision for cooperation in Union research, technological development and demonstration with third countries or international organisations.

The detailed arrangements for such cooperation may be the subject of agreements between the Union and the third parties concerned.

Article 187 (ex Article 171 TEC)
The Union may set up joint undertakings or any other structure necessary for the efficient execution of Union research, technological development and demonstration programmes.

Article 188 (ex Article 172 TEC)
The Council, on a proposal from the Commission and after consulting the European Parliament and the Economic and Social Committee, shall adopt the provisions referred to in Article 187.

The European Parliament and the Council, acting in accordance with the ordinary legislative procedure and after consulting the Economic and Social Committee, shall adopt the provisions referred to in Articles 183, 184 and 185. Adoption of the supplementary programmes shall require the agreement of the Member States concerned.

Article 189
1.   To promote scientific and technical progress, industrial competitiveness and the implementation of its policies, the Union shall draw up a European space policy. To this end, it may promote joint initiatives, support research and technological development and coordinate the efforts needed for the exploration and exploitation of space.

2.   To contribute to attaining the objectives referred to in paragraph 1, the European Parliament and the Council, acting in accordance with the ordinary legislative procedure, shall establish the necessary measures, which may take the form of a European space programme, excluding any harmonisation of the laws and regulations of the Member States.

3.   The Union shall establish any appropriate relations with the European Space Agency.

4.   This Article shall be without prejudice to the other provisions of this Title.

Article 190 (ex Article 173 TEC)

At the beginning of each year the Commission shall send a report to the European Parliament and to the Council. The report shall include information on research and technological development activities and the dissemination of results during the previous year, and the work programme for the current year.

TITLE XX
ENVIRONMENT

Article 191 (ex Article 174 TEC)

1.   Union policy on the environment shall contribute to pursuit of the following objectives:
      — preserving, protecting and improving the quality of the environment,
      — protecting human health,
      — prudent and rational utilisation of natural resources,
      — promoting measures at international level to deal with regional or worldwide environmental problems, and in particular combating climate change.

2.   Union policy on the environment shall aim at a high level of protection taking into account the diversity of situations in the various regions of the Union. It shall be based on the precautionary principle and on the principles that preventive action should be taken, that environmental damage should as a priority be rectified at source and that the polluter should pay.

      In this context, harmonisation measures answering environmental protection requirements shall include, where appropriate, a safeguard clause allowing Member States to take provisional measures, for non-economic environmental reasons, subject to a procedure of inspection by the Union.

3.   In preparing its policy on the environment, the Union shall take account of:
      — available scientific and technical data,
      — environmental conditions in the various regions of the Union,
      — the potential benefits and costs of action or lack of action,
      — the economic and social development of the Union as a whole and the balanced development of its regions.

4.   Within their respective spheres of competence, the Union and the Member States shall cooperate with third countries and with the competent international organisations. The arrangements for Union cooperation may be the subject of agreements between the Union and the third parties concerned.

      The previous subparagraph shall be without prejudice to Member States' competence to negotiate in international bodies and to conclude international agreements.

Article 192 (ex Article 175 TEC)

1.   The European Parliament and the Council, acting in accordance with the ordinary legislative procedure and after consulting the Economic and Social Committee and the Committee of the Regions, shall decide what action is to be taken by the Union in order to achieve the objectives referred to in Article 191.

2.   By way of derogation from the decision-making procedure provided for in paragraph 1 and without prejudice to Article 114, the Council acting unanimously in accordance with a special legislative procedure and after consulting the European Parliament, the

Economic and Social Committee and the Committee of the Regions, shall adopt:
(a) provisions primarily of a fiscal nature;
(b) measures affecting:
— town and country planning,
— quantitative management of water resources or affecting, directly or indirectly, the availability of those resources,
— land use, with the exception of waste management;
(c) measures significantly affecting a Member State's choice between different energy sources and the general structure of its energy supply.

The Council, acting unanimously on a proposal from the Commission and after consulting the European Parliament, the Economic and Social Committee and the Committee of the Regions, may make the ordinary legislative procedure applicable to the matters referred to in the first subparagraph.

3. General action programmes setting out priority objectives to be attained shall be adopted by the European Parliament and the Council, acting in accordance with the ordinary legislative procedure and after consulting the Economic and Social Committee and the Committee of the Regions.

The measures necessary for the implementation of these programmes shall be adopted under the terms of paragraph 1 or 2, as the case may be.

4. Without prejudice to certain measures adopted by the Union, the Member States shall finance and implement the environment policy.

5. Without prejudice to the principle that the polluter should pay, if a measure based on the provisions of paragraph 1 involves costs deemed disproportionate for the public authorities of a Member State, such measure shall lay down appropriate provisions in the form of:
— temporary derogations, and/or
— financial support from the Cohesion Fund set up pursuant to Article 177.

Article 193 (ex Article 176 TEC)
The protective measures adopted pursuant to Article 192 shall not prevent any Member State from maintaining or introducing more stringent protective measures. Such measures must be compatible with the Treaties. They shall be notified to the Commission.

TITLE XXI
ENERGY

Article 194
1. In the context of the establishment and functioning of the internal market and with regard for the need to preserve and improve the environment, Union policy on energy shall aim, in a spirit of solidarity between Member States, to:
(a) ensure the functioning of the energy market;
(b) ensure security of energy supply in the Union;
(c) promote energy efficiency and energy saving and the development of new and renewable forms of energy; and
(d) promote the interconnection of energy networks.

2. Without prejudice to the application of other provisions of the Treaties, the European Parliament and the Council, acting in accordance with the ordinary legislative procedure, shall establish the measures necessary to achieve the objectives in paragraph 1. Such measures shall be adopted after consultation of the Economic and Social Committee and the Committee of the Regions.

Such measures shall not affect a Member State's right to determine the conditions for exploiting its energy resources, its choice between different energy sources and the general structure of its energy supply, without prejudice to Article 192(2)(c).

3.   By way of derogation from paragraph 2, the Council, acting in accordance with a special legislative procedure, shall unanimously and after consulting the European Parliament, establish the measures referred to therein when they are primarily of a fiscal nature.

TITLE XXII
TOURISM

Article 195
1.   The Union shall complement the action of the Member States in the tourism sector, in particular by promoting the competitiveness of Union undertakings in that sector.

To that end, Union action shall be aimed at:
(a) encouraging the creation of a favourable environment for the development of undertakings in this sector;
(b) promoting cooperation between the Member States, particularly by the exchange of good practice.

2.   The European Parliament and the Council, acting in accordance with the ordinary legislative procedure, shall establish specific measures to complement actions within the Member States to achieve the objectives referred to in this Article, excluding any harmonisation of the laws and regulations of the Member States.

TITLE XXIII
CIVIL PROTECTION

Article 196
1.   The Union shall encourage cooperation between Member States in order to improve the effectiveness of systems for preventing and protecting against natural or man-made disasters.

Union action shall aim to:
(a) support and complement Member States' action at national, regional and local level in risk prevention, in preparing their civil-protection personnel and in responding to natural or man-made disasters within the Union;
(b) promote swift, effective operational cooperation within the Union between national civil-protection services;
(c) promote consistency in international civil-protection work.

2.   The European Parliament and the Council, acting in accordance with the ordinary legislative procedure shall establish the measures necessary to help achieve the objectives referred to in paragraph 1, excluding any harmonisation of the laws and regulations of the Member States.

TITLE XXIV
ADMINISTRATIVE COOPERATION

Article 197
1.   Effective implementation of Union law by the Member States, which is essential for the proper functioning of the Union, shall be regarded as a matter of common interest.

2.   The Union may support the efforts of Member States to improve their administrative
capacity to implement Union law. Such action may include facilitating the exchange of
information and of civil servants as well as supporting training schemes. No Member
State shall be obliged to avail itself of such support. The European Parliament and the
Council, acting by means of regulations in accordance with the ordinary legislative
procedure, shall establish the necessary measures to this end, excluding any harmonisation
of the laws and regulations of the Member States.

3.   This Article shall be without prejudice to the obligations of the Member States to
implement Union law or to the prerogatives and duties of the Commission. It shall also be
without prejudice to other provisions of the Treaties providing for administrative
cooperation among the Member States and between them and the Union.

Part Four ASSOCIATION OF THE OVERSEAS COUNTRIES AND TERRITORIES*

Article 198 (ex Article 182 TEC)
The Member States agree to associate with the Union the non-European countries and
territories which have special relations with Denmark, France, the Netherlands and the United
Kingdom. These countries and territories (hereinafter called the 'countries and territories') are
listed in Annex II.

The purpose of association shall be to promote the economic and social development of the
countries and territories and to establish close economic relations between them and the Union
as a whole.

In accordance with the principles set out in the preamble to this Treaty, association shall
serve primarily to further the interests and prosperity of the inhabitants of these countries and
territories in order to lead them to the economic, social and cultural development to which they
aspire.

Article 199 (ex Article 183 TEC)
Association shall have the following objectives.
1.   Member States shall apply to their trade with the countries and territories the same
treatment as they accord each other pursuant to the Treaties.

2.   Each country or territory shall apply to its trade with Member States and with the other
countries and territories the same treatment as that which it applies to the European State
with which is has special relations.

3.   The Member States shall contribute to the investments required for the progressive
development of these countries and territories.

4.   For investments financed by the Union, participation in tenders and supplies shall be open
on equal terms to all natural and legal persons who are nationals of a Member State or of
one of the countries and territories.

5.   In relations between Member States and the countries and territories the right of
establishment of nationals and companies or firms shall be regulated in accordance with

....

*   EDITOR'S NOTE; Annex II of the Treaties lists the overseas countries and territories to which the provisions of
Part Four apply. These are: Greenland, New Caledonia and Dependencies, French Polynesia, French Southern and
Antarctic Territories, Wallis and Futuna Islands, Mayotte, Saint Pierre and Miquelon, Aruba, Netherlands Antilles:
Bonaire, Curaçao, Saba, Sint Eustatius, Sint Maarten, Anguilla, Cayman Islands, Falkland Islands, South Georgia and
the South Sandwich Islands, Montserrat, Pitcairn, Saint Helena and Dependencies, British Antarctic Territory, British
Indian Ocean Territory, Turks and Caicos Islands, British Virgin Islands, and Bermuda.

the provisions and procedures laid down in the Chapter relating to the right of establishment and on a non-discriminatory basis, subject to any special provisions laid down pursuant to Article 203.

Article 200 (ex Article 184 TEC)

1. Customs duties on imports into the Member States of goods originating in the countries and territories shall be prohibited in conformity with the prohibition of customs duties between Member States in accordance with the provisions of the Treaties.

2. Customs duties on imports into each country or territory from Member States or from the other countries or territories shall be prohibited in accordance with the provisions of Article 30.

3. The countries and territories may, however, levy customs duties which meet the needs of their development and industrialisation or produce revenue for their budgets.

    The duties referred to in the preceding subparagraph may not exceed the level of those imposed on imports of products from the Member State with which each country or territory has special relations.

4. Paragraph 2 shall not apply to countries and territories which, by reason of the particular international obligations by which they are bound, already apply a non-discriminatory customs tariff.

5. The introduction of or any change in customs duties imposed on goods imported into the countries and territories shall not, either in law or in fact, give rise to any direct or indirect discrimination between imports from the various Member States.

Article 201 (ex Article 185 TEC)

If the level of the duties applicable to goods from a third country on entry into a country or territory is liable, when the provisions of Article 200(1) have been applied, to cause deflections of trade to the detriment of any Member State, the latter may request the Commission to propose to the other Member States the measures needed to remedy the situation.

Article 202 (ex Article 186 TEC)

Subject to the provisions relating to public health, public security or public policy, freedom of movement within Member States for workers from the countries and territories, and within the countries and territories for workers from Member States, shall be regulated by acts adopted in accordance with Article 203.

Article 203 (ex Article 187 TEC)

The Council, acting unanimously on a proposal from the Commission, shall, on the basis of the experience acquired under the association of the countries and territories with the Union and of the principles set out in the Treaties, lay down provisions as regards the detailed rules and the procedure for the association of the countries and territories with the Union. Where the provisions in question are adopted by the Council in accordance with a special legislative procedure, it shall act unanimously on a proposal from the Commission and after consulting the European Parliament.

Article 204 (ex Article 188 TEC)

The provisions of Articles 198 to 203 shall apply to Greenland, subject to the specific provisions for Greenland set out in the Protocol on special arrangements for Greenland, annexed to the Treaties.

Part Five **EXTERNAL ACTION BY THE UNION**

TITLE I
GENERAL PROVISIONS ON THE UNION'S EXTERNAL ACTION

Article 205
The Union's action on the international scene, pursuant to this Part, shall be guided by the principles, pursue the objectives and be conducted in accordance with the general provisions laid down in Chapter 1 of Title V of the Treaty on European Union.

TITLE II
COMMON COMMERCIAL POLICY

Article 206 (ex Article 131 TEC)
By establishing a customs union in accordance with Articles 28 to 32, the Union shall contribute, in the common interest, to the harmonious development of world trade, the progressive abolition of restrictions on international trade and on foreign direct investment, and the lowering of customs and other barriers.

Article 207 (ex Article 133 TEC)
1.   The common commercial policy shall be based on uniform principles, particularly with regard to changes in tariff rates, the conclusion of tariff and trade agreements relating to trade in goods and services, and the commercial aspects of intellectual property, foreign direct investment, the achievement of uniformity in measures of liberalisation, export policy and measures to protect trade such as those to be taken in the event of dumping or subsidies. The common commercial policy shall be conducted in the context of the principles and objectives of the Union's external action.

2.   The European Parliament and the Council, acting by means of regulations in accordance with the ordinary legislative procedure, shall adopt the measures defining the framework for implementing the common commercial policy.

3.   Where agreements with one or more third countries or international organisations need to be negotiated and concluded, Article 218 shall apply, subject to the special provisions of this Article.

   The Commission shall make recommendations to the Council, which shall authorise it to open the necessary negotiations. The Council and the Commission shall be responsible for ensuring that the agreements negotiated are compatible with internal Union policies and rules.

   The Commission shall conduct these negotiations in consultation with a special committee appointed by the Council to assist the Commission in this task and within the framework of such directives as the Council may issue to it. The Commission shall report regularly to the special committee and to the European Parliament on the progress of negotiations.

4.   For the negotiation and conclusion of the agreements referred to in paragraph 3, the Council shall act by a qualified majority.

   For the negotiation and conclusion of agreements in the fields of trade in services and the commercial aspects of intellectual property, as well as foreign direct investment, the Council shall act unanimously where such agreements include provisions for which unanimity is required for the adoption of internal rules.

   The Council shall also act unanimously for the negotiation and conclusion of agreements:

(a) in the field of trade in cultural and audiovisual services, where these agreements risk prejudicing the Union's cultural and linguistic diversity;

(b) in the field of trade in social, education and health services, where these agreements risk seriously disturbing the national organisation of such services and prejudicing the responsibility of Member States to deliver them.

5.   The negotiation and conclusion of international agreements in the field of transport shall be subject to Title VI of Part Three and to Article 218.

6.   The exercise of the competences conferred by this Article in the field of the common commercial policy shall not affect the delimitation of competences between the Union and the Member States, and shall not lead to harmonisation of legislative or regulatory provisions of the Member States in so far as the Treaties exclude such harmonisation.

TITLE III
COOPERATION WITH THIRD COUNTRIES AND HUMANITARIAN AID

Chapter 1 DEVELOPMENT COOPERATION

Article 208 (ex Article 177 TEC)

1.   Union policy in the field of development cooperation shall be conducted within the framework of the principles and objectives of the Union's external action. The Union's development cooperation policy and that of the Member States complement and reinforce each other.

Union development cooperation policy shall have as its primary objective the reduction and, in the long term, the eradication of poverty. The Union shall take account of the objectives of development cooperation in the policies that it implements which are likely to affect developing countries.

2.   The Union and the Member States shall comply with the commitments and take account of the objectives they have approved in the context of the United Nations and other competent international organisations.

Article 209 (ex Article 179 TEC)

1.   The European Parliament and the Council, acting in accordance with the ordinary legislative procedure, shall adopt the measures necessary for the implementation of development cooperation policy, which may relate to multiannual cooperation programmes with developing countries or programmes with a thematic approach.

2.   The Union may conclude with third countries and competent international organisations any agreement helping to achieve the objectives referred to in Article 21 of the Treaty on European Union and in Article 208 of this Treaty.

The first subparagraph shall be without prejudice to Member States' competence to negotiate in international bodies and to conclude agreements.

3.   The European Investment Bank shall contribute, under the terms laid down in its Statute, to the implementation of the measures referred to in paragraph 1.

Article 210 (ex Article 180 TEC)

1.   In order to promote the complementarity and efficiency of their action, the Union and the Member States shall coordinate their policies on development cooperation and shall consult each other on their aid programmes, including in international organisations and during international conferences. They may undertake joint action. Member States shall contribute if necessary to the implementation of Union aid programmes.

2.   The Commission may take any useful initiative to promote the coordination referred to in paragraph 1.

Article 211 (ex Article 181 TEC)

Within their respective spheres of competence, the Union and the Member States shall cooperate with third countries and with the competent international organisations.

Chapter 2 ECONOMIC, FINANCIAL AND TECHNICAL COOPERATION WITH THIRD COUNTRIES

Article 212 (ex Article 181a TEC)

1.   Without prejudice to the other provisions of the Treaties, and in particular Articles 208 to 211, the Union shall carry out economic, financial and technical cooperation measures, including assistance, in particular financial assistance, with third countries other than developing countries. Such measures shall be consistent with the development policy of the Union and shall be carried out within the framework of the principles and objectives of its external action. The Union's operations and those of the Member States shall complement and reinforce each other.

2.   The European Parliament and the Council, acting in accordance with the ordinary legislative procedure, shall adopt the measures necessary for the implementation of paragraph 1.

3.   Within their respective spheres of competence, the Union and the Member States shall cooperate with third countries and the competent international organisations. The arrangements for Union cooperation may be the subject of agreements between the Union and the third parties concerned.

The first subparagraph shall be without prejudice to the Member States' competence to negotiate in international bodies and to conclude international agreements.

Article 213

When the situation in a third country requires urgent financial assistance from the Union, the Council shall adopt the necessary decisions on a proposal from the Commission.

Chapter 3 HUMANITARIAN AID

Article 214

1.   The Union's operations in the field of humanitarian aid shall be conducted within the framework of the principles and objectives of the external action of the Union. Such operations shall be intended to provide ad hoc assistance and relief and protection for people in third countries who are victims of natural or man-made disasters, in order to meet the humanitarian needs resulting from these different situations. The Union's measures and those of the Member States shall complement and reinforce each other.

2.   Humanitarian aid operations shall be conducted in compliance with the principles of international law and with the principles of impartiality, neutrality and non-discrimination.

3.   The European Parliament and the Council, acting in accordance with the ordinary legislative procedure, shall establish the measures defining the framework within which the Union's humanitarian aid operations shall be implemented.

4.   The Union may conclude with third countries and competent international organisations any agreement helping to achieve the objectives referred to in paragraph 1 and in Article 21 of the Treaty on European Union.

The first subparagraph shall be without prejudice to Member States' competence to negotiate in international bodies and to conclude agreements.

5. In order to establish a framework for joint contributions from young Europeans to the humanitarian aid operations of the Union, a European Voluntary Humanitarian Aid Corps shall be set up. The European Parliament and the Council, acting by means of regulations in accordance with the ordinary legislative procedure, shall determine the rules and procedures for the operation of the Corps.

6. The Commission may take any useful initiative to promote coordination between actions of the Union and those of the Member States, in order to enhance the efficiency and complementarity of Union and national humanitarian aid measures.

7. The Union shall ensure that its humanitarian aid operations are coordinated and consistent with those of international organisations and bodies, in particular those forming part of the United Nations system.

TITLE IV
RESTRICTIVE MEASURES

Article 215 (ex Article 301 TEC)
1. Where a decision, adopted in accordance with Chapter 2 of Title V of the Treaty on European Union, provides for the interruption or reduction, in part or completely, of economic and financial relations with one or more third countries, the Council, acting by a qualified majority on a joint proposal from the High Representative of the Union for Foreign Affairs and Security Policy and the Commission, shall adopt the necessary measures. It shall inform the European Parliament thereof.

2. Where a decision adopted in accordance with Chapter 2 of Title V of the Treaty on European Union so provides, the Council may adopt restrictive measures under the procedure referred to in paragraph 1 against natural or legal persons and groups or non-State entities.

3. The acts referred to in this Article shall include necessary provisions on legal safeguards.

TITLE V
INTERNATIONAL AGREEMENTS

Article 216
1. The Union may conclude an agreement with one or more third countries or international organisations where the Treaties so provide or where the conclusion of an agreement is necessary in order to achieve, within the framework of the Union's policies, one of the objectives referred to in the Treaties, or is provided for in a legally binding Union act or is likely to affect common rules or alter their scope.

2. Agreements concluded by the Union are binding upon the institutions of the Union and on its Member States.

Article 217 (ex Article 310 TEC)
The Union may conclude with one or more third countries or international organisations agreements establishing an association involving reciprocal rights and obligations, common action and special procedure.

Article 218 (ex Article 300 TEC)

1. Without prejudice to the specific provisions laid down in Article 207, agreements between the Union and third countries or international organisations shall be negotiated and concluded in accordance with the following procedure.

2. The Council shall authorise the opening of negotiations, adopt negotiating directives, authorise the signing of agreements and conclude them.

3. The Commission, or the High Representative of the Union for Foreign Affairs and Security Policy where the agreement envisaged relates exclusively or principally to the common foreign and security policy, shall submit recommendations to the Council, which shall adopt a decision authorising the opening of negotiations and, depending on the subject of the agreement envisaged, nominating the Union negotiator or the head of the Union's negotiating team.

4. The Council may address directives to the negotiator and designate a special committee in consultation with which the negotiations must be conducted.

5. The Council, on a proposal by the negotiator, shall adopt a decision authorising the signing of the agreement and, if necessary, its provisional application before entry into force.

6. The Council, on a proposal by the negotiator, shall adopt a decision concluding the agreement.

   Except where agreements relate exclusively to the common foreign and security policy, the Council shall adopt the decision concluding the agreement:
   (a) after obtaining the consent of the European Parliament in the following cases:
       (i)   association agreements;
       (ii) agreement on Union accession to the European Convention for the Protection of Human Rights and Fundamental Freedoms;
       (iii) agreements establishing a specific institutional framework by organising cooperation procedures;
       (iv) agreements with important budgetary implications for the Union;
       (v)   agreements covering fields to which either the ordinary legislative procedure applies, or the special legislative procedure where consent by the European Parliament is required.
   The European Parliament and the Council may, in an urgent situation, agree upon a time-limit for consent.

   (b) after consulting the European Parliament in other cases. The European Parliament shall deliver its opinion within a time-limit which the Council may set depending on the urgency of the matter. In the absence of an opinion within that time-limit, the Council may act.

7. When concluding an agreement, the Council may, by way of derogation from paragraphs 5, 6 and 9, authorise the negotiator to approve on the Union's behalf modifications to the agreement where it provides for them to be adopted by a simplified procedure or by a body set up by the agreement. The Council may attach specific conditions to such authorisation.

8. The Council shall act by a qualified majority throughout the procedure.

   However, it shall act unanimously when the agreement covers a field for which unanimity is required for the adoption of a Union act as well as for association agreements and the agreements referred to in Article 212 with the States which are candidates for accession.

The Council shall also act unanimously for the agreement on accession of the Union to the European Convention for the Protection of Human Rights and Fundamental Freedoms; the decision concluding this agreement shall enter into force after it has been approved by the Member States in accordance with their respective constitutional requirements.

9.   The Council, on a proposal from the Commission or the High Representative of the Union for Foreign Affairs and Security Policy, shall adopt a decision suspending application of an agreement and establishing the positions to be adopted on the Union's behalf in a body set up by an agreement, when that body is called upon to adopt acts having legal effects, with the exception of acts supplementing or amending the institutional framework of the agreement.

10.   The European Parliament shall be immediately and fully informed at all stages of the procedure.

11.   A Member State, the European Parliament, the Council or the Commission may obtain the opinion of the Court of Justice as to whether an agreement envisaged is compatible with the Treaties. Where the opinion of the Court is adverse, the agreement envisaged may not enter into force unless it is amended or the Treaties are revised.

Article 219 (ex Article 111(1) to (3) and (5) TEC)

1.   By way of derogation from Article 218, the Council, either on a recommendation from the European Central Bank or on a recommendation from the Commission and after consulting the European Central Bank, in an endeavour to reach a consensus consistent with the objective of price stability, may conclude formal agreements on an exchange-rate system for the euro in relation to the currencies of third States. The Council shall act unanimously after consulting the European Parliament and in accordance with the procedure provided for in paragraph 3.

The Council may, either on a recommendation from the European Central Bank or on a recommendation from the Commission, and after consulting the European Central Bank, in an endeavour to reach a consensus consistent with the objective of price stability, adopt, adjust or abandon the central rates of the euro within the exchange-rate system. The President of the Council shall inform the European Parliament of the adoption, adjustment or abandonment of the euro central rates.

2.   In the absence of an exchange-rate system in relation to one or more currencies of third States as referred to in paragraph 1, the Council, either on a recommendation from the Commission and after consulting the European Central Bank or on a recommendation from the European Central Bank, may formulate general orientations for exchange-rate policy in relation to these currencies. These general orientations shall be without prejudice to the primary objective of the ESCB to maintain price stability.

3.   By way of derogation from Article 218, where agreements concerning monetary or foreign exchange regime matters need to be negotiated by the Union with one or more third States or international organisations, the Council, on a recommendation from the Commission and after consulting the European Central Bank, shall decide the arrangements for the negotiation and for the conclusion of such agreements. These arrangements shall ensure that the Union expresses a single position. The Commission shall be fully associated with the negotiations.

4.   Without prejudice to Union competence and Union agreements as regards economic and monetary union, Member States may negotiate in international bodies and conclude international agreements.

TITLE VI
THE UNION'S RELATIONS WITH INTERNATIONAL ORGANISATIONS AND THIRD COUNTRIES AND UNION DELEGATIONS

Article 220 (ex Articles 302 to 304 TEC)

1.   The Union shall establish all appropriate forms of cooperation with the organs of the United Nations and its specialised agencies, the Council of Europe, the Organisation for Security and Cooperation in Europe and the Organisation for Economic Cooperation and Development.

   The Union shall also maintain such relations as are appropriate with other international organisations.

2.   The High Representative of the Union for Foreign Affairs and Security Policy and the Commission shall implement this Article.

Article 221

1.   Union delegations in third countries and at international organisations shall represent the Union.

2.   Union delegations shall be placed under the authority of the High Representative of the Union for Foreign Affairs and Security Policy. They shall act in close cooperation with Member States' diplomatic and consular missions.

TITLE VII
SOLIDARITY CLAUSE

Article 222

1.   The Union and its Member States shall act jointly in a spirit of solidarity if a Member State is the object of a terrorist attack or the victim of a natural or man-made disaster. The Union shall mobilise all the instruments at its disposal, including the military resources made available by the Member States, to:
   (a) —   prevent the terrorist threat in the territory of the Member States;
       —   protect democratic institutions and the civilian population from any terrorist attack;
       —   assist a Member State in its territory, at the request of its political authorities, in the event of a terrorist attack;
   (b) assist a Member State in its territory, at the request of its political authorities, in the event of a natural or man-made disaster.

2.   Should a Member State be the object of a terrorist attack or the victim of a natural or man-made disaster, the other Member States shall assist it at the request of its political authorities. To that end, the Member States shall coordinate between themselves in the Council.

3.   The arrangements for the implementation by the Union of the solidarity clause shall be defined by a decision adopted by the Council acting on a joint proposal by the Commission and the High Representative of the Union for Foreign Affairs and Security Policy. The Council shall act in accordance with Article 31(1) of the Treaty on European Union where this decision has defence implications. The European Parliament shall be informed.

   For the purposes of this paragraph and without prejudice to Article 240, the Council shall be assisted by the Political and Security Committee with the support of the structures developed in the context of the common security and defence policy and by the Committee referred to in Article 71; the two committees shall, if necessary, submit joint opinions.

4.   The European Council shall regularly assess the threats facing the Union in order to enable the Union and its Member States to take effective action.

Part Six INSTITUTIONAL AND FINANCIAL PROVISIONS

TITLE I
INSTITUTIONAL PROVISIONS

Chapter 1 THE INSTITUTIONS

SECTION 1 THE EUROPEAN PARLIAMENT

Article 223 (ex Article 190(4) and (5) TEC)
1.   The European Parliament shall draw up a proposal to lay down the provisions necessary for the election of its Members by direct universal suffrage in accordance with a uniform procedure in all Member States or in accordance with principles common to all Member States.

The Council, acting unanimously in accordance with a special legislative procedure and after obtaining the consent of the European Parliament, which shall act by a majority of its component Members, shall lay down the necessary provisions. These provisions shall enter into force following their approval by the Member States in accordance with their respective constitutional requirements.

2.   The European Parliament, acting by means of regulations on its own initiative in accordance with a special legislative procedure after seeking an opinion from the Commission and with the consent of the Council, shall lay down the regulations and general conditions governing the performance of the duties of its Members. All rules or conditions relating to the taxation of Members or former Members shall require unanimity within the Council.

Article 224 (ex Article 191, second subparagraph, TEC)
The European Parliament and the Council, acting in accordance with the ordinary legislative procedure, by means of regulations, shall lay down the regulations governing political parties at European level referred to in Article 10(4) of the Treaty on European Union and in particular the rules regarding their funding.

Article 225 (ex Article 192, second subparagraph, TEC)
The European Parliament may, acting by a majority of its component Members, request the Commission to submit any appropriate proposal on matters on which it considers that a Union act is required for the purpose of implementing the Treaties. If the Commission does not submit a proposal, it shall inform the European Parliament of the reasons.

Article 226 (ex Article 193 TEC)
In the course of its duties, the European Parliament may, at the request of a quarter of its component Members, set up a temporary Committee of Inquiry to investigate, without prejudice to the powers conferred by the Treaties on other institutions or bodies, alleged contraventions or maladministration in the implementation of Union law, except where the alleged facts are being examined before a court and while the case is still subject to legal proceedings.

The temporary Committee of Inquiry shall cease to exist on the submission of its report.
The detailed provisions governing the exercise of the right of inquiry shall be determined by the European Parliament, acting by means of regulations on its own initiative in accordance with a special legislative procedure, after obtaining the consent of the Council and the Commission.

Article 227 (ex Article 194 TEC)
Any citizen of the Union, and any natural or legal person residing or having its registered office in a Member State, shall have the right to address, individually or in association with other citizens or persons, a petition to the European Parliament on a matter which comes within the Union's fields of activity and which affects him, her or it directly.

Article 228 (ex Article 195 TEC)
1.   A European Ombudsman, elected by the European Parliament, shall be empowered to receive complaints from any citizen of the Union or any natural or legal person residing or having its registered office in a Member State concerning instances of maladministration in the activities of the Union institutions, bodies, offices or agencies, with the exception of the Court of Justice of the European Union acting in its judicial role. He or she shall examine such complaints and report on them.

In accordance with his duties, the Ombudsman shall conduct inquiries for which he finds grounds, either on his own initiative or on the basis of complaints submitted to him direct or through a Member of the European Parliament, except where the alleged facts are or have been the subject of legal proceedings. Where the Ombudsman establishes an instance of maladministration, he shall refer the matter to the institution, body, office or agency concerned, which shall have a period of three months in which to inform him of its views. The Ombudsman shall then forward a report to the European Parliament and the institution, body, office or agency concerned. The person lodging the complaint shall be informed of the outcome of such inquiries.

The Ombudsman shall submit an annual report to the European Parliament on the outcome of his inquiries.

2.   The Ombudsman shall be elected after each election of the European Parliament for the duration of its term of office. The Ombudsman shall be eligible for reappointment.

The Ombudsman may be dismissed by the Court of Justice at the request of the European Parliament if he no longer fulfils the conditions required for the performance of his duties or if he is guilty of serious misconduct.

3.   The Ombudsman shall be completely independent in the performance of his duties. In the performance of those duties he shall neither seek nor take instructions from any Government, institution, body, office or entity. The Ombudsman may not, during his term of office, engage in any other occupation, whether gainful or not.

4.   The European Parliament acting by means of regulations on its own initiative in accordance with a special legislative procedure shall, after seeking an opinion from the Commission and with the consent of the Council, lay down the regulations and general conditions governing the performance of the Ombudsman's duties.

Article 229 (ex Article 196 TEC)
The European Parliament shall hold an annual session. It shall meet, without requiring to be convened, on the second Tuesday in March.

The European Parliament may meet in extraordinary part-session at the request of a majority of its component Members or at the request of the Council or of the Commission.

Article 230 (ex Article 197, second, third and fourth paragraph, TEC)
The Commission may attend all the meetings and shall, at its request, be heard.

The Commission shall reply orally or in writing to questions put to it by the European Parliament or by its Members.
The European Council and the Council shall be heard by the European Parliament in accordance with the conditions laid down in the Rules of Procedure of the European Council and those of the Council.

Article 231 (ex Article 198 TEC)
Save as otherwise provided in the Treaties, the European Parliament shall act by a majority of the votes cast.

The Rules of Procedure shall determine the quorum.

Article 232 (ex Article 199 TEC)
The European Parliament shall adopt its Rules of Procedure, acting by a majority of its Members.

The proceedings of the European Parliament shall be published in the manner laid down in the Treaties and in its Rules of Procedure.

Article 233 (ex Article 200 TEC)
The European Parliament shall discuss in open session the annual general report submitted to it by the Commission.

Article 234 (ex Article 201 TEC)
If a motion of censure on the activities of the Commission is tabled before it, the European Parliament shall not vote thereon until at least three days after the motion has been tabled and only by open vote.

If the motion of censure is carried by a two-thirds majority of the votes cast, representing a majority of the component Members of the European Parliament, the members of the Commission shall resign as a body and the High Representative of the Union for Foreign Affairs and Security Policy shall resign from duties that he or she carries out in the Commission. They shall remain in office and continue to deal with current business until they are replaced in accordance with Article 17 of the Treaty on European Union. In this case, the term of office of the members of the Commission appointed to replace them shall expire on the date on which the term of office of the members of the Commission obliged to resign as a body would have expired.

SECTION 2 THE EUROPEAN COUNCIL

Article 235
1.   Where a vote is taken, any member of the European Council may also act on behalf of not more than one other member.

Article 16(4) of the Treaty on European Union and Article 238(2) of this Treaty shall apply to the European Council when it is acting by a qualified majority. Where the European Council decides by vote, its President and the President of the Commission shall not take part in the vote.

Abstentions by members present in person or represented shall not prevent the adoption by the European Council of acts which require unanimity.

2.   The President of the European Parliament may be invited to be heard by the European Council.

3.   The European Council shall act by a simple majority for procedural questions and for the adoption of its Rules of Procedure.

4.   The European Council shall be assisted by the General Secretariat of the Council.

Article 236

The European Council shall adopt by a qualified majority:

(a)   a decision establishing the list of Council configurations, other than those of the General Affairs Council and of the Foreign Affairs Council, in accordance with Article 16(6) of the Treaty on European Union;

(b)   a decision on the Presidency of Council configurations, other than that of Foreign Affairs, in accordance with Article 16(9) of the Treaty on European Union.

SECTION 3 THE COUNCIL

Article 237 (ex Article 204 TEC)

The Council shall meet when convened by its President on his own initiative or at the request of one of its Members or of the Commission.

Article 238 (ex Article 205(1) and (2), TEC)

1.   Where it is required to act by a simple majority, the Council shall act by a majority of its component members.

2.   By way of derogation from Article 16(4) of the Treaty on European Union, as from 1 November 2014 and subject to the provisions laid down in the Protocol on transitional provisions, where the Council does not act on a proposal from the Commission or from the High Representative of the Union for Foreign Affairs and Security Policy, the qualified majority shall be defined as at least 72 % of the members of the Council, representing Member States comprising at least 65 % of the population of the Union.

3.   As from 1 November 2014 and subject to the provisions laid down in the Protocol on transitional provisions, in cases where, under the Treaties, not all the members of the Council participate in voting, a qualified majority shall be defined as follows:
   (a)   A qualified majority shall be defined as at least 55 % of the members of the Council representing the participating Member States, comprising at least 65 % of the population of these States.
   A blocking minority must include at least the minimum number of Council members representing more than 35 % of the population of the participating Member States, plus one member, failing which the qualified majority shall be deemed attained;
   (b)   By way of derogation from point (a), where the Council does not act on a proposal from the Commission or from the High Representative of the Union for Foreign Affairs and Security Policy, the qualified majority shall be defined as at least 72 % of the members of the Council representing the participating Member States, comprising at least 65 % of the population of these States.

4.   Abstentions by Members present in person or represented shall not prevent the adoption by the Council of acts which require unanimity.

Article 239 (ex Article 206 TEC)

Where a vote is taken, any Member of the Council may also act on behalf of not more than one other member.

Article 240 (ex Article 207 TEC)

1.   A committee consisting of the Permanent Representatives of the Governments of the Member States shall be responsible for preparing the work of the Council and for carrying out the tasks assigned to it by the latter. The Committee may adopt procedural decisions in cases provided for in the Council's Rules of Procedure.

2.   The Council shall be assisted by a General Secretariat, under the responsibility of a Secretary-General appointed by the Council.

      The Council shall decide on the organisation of the General Secretariat by a simple majority.

3.   The Council shall act by a simple majority regarding procedural matters and for the adoption of its Rules of Procedure.

Article 241 (ex Article 208 TEC)

The Council, acting by a simple majority, may request the Commission to undertake any studies the Council considers desirable for the attainment of the common objectives, and to submit to it any appropriate proposals. If the Commission does not submit a proposal, it shall inform the Council of the reasons.

Article 242 (ex Article 209 TEC)

The Council, acting by a simple majority shall, after consulting the Commission, determine the rules governing the committees provided for in the Treaties.

Article 243 (ex Article 210 TEC)

The Council shall determine the salaries, allowances and pensions of the President of the European Council, the President of the Commission, the High Representative of the Union for Foreign Affairs and Security Policy, the Members of the Commission, the Presidents, Members and Registrars of the Court of Justice of the European Union, and the Secretary-General of the Council. It shall also determine any payment to be made instead of remuneration.

SECTION 4 THE COMMISSION

Article 244

In accordance with Article 17(5) of the Treaty on European Union, the Members of the Commission shall be chosen on the basis of a system of rotation established unanimously by the European Council and on the basis of the following principles:

(a)   Member States shall be treated on a strictly equal footing as regards determination of the sequence of, and the time spent by, their nationals as members of the Commission; consequently, the difference between the total number of terms of office held by nationals of any given pair of Member States may never be more than one;

(b)   subject to point (a), each successive Commission shall be so composed as to reflect satisfactorily the demographic and geographical range of all the Member States.

Article 245 (ex Article 213 TEC)

The Members of the Commission shall refrain from any action incompatible with their duties. Member States shall respect their independence and shall not seek to influence them in the performance of their tasks.

The Members of the Commission may not, during their term of office, engage in any other occupation, whether gainful or not. When entering upon their duties they shall give a solemn undertaking that, both during and after their term of office, they will respect the obligations arising therefrom and in particular their duty to behave with integrity and discretion as regards the acceptance, after they have ceased to hold office, of certain appointments or benefits. In the event of any breach of these obligations, the Court of Justice may, on application by the Council acting by a simple majority or the Commission, rule that the Member concerned be, according to the circumstances, either compulsorily retired in accordance with Article 247 or deprived of his right to a pension or other benefits in its stead.

Article 246 (ex Article 215 TEC)
Apart from normal replacement, or death, the duties of a Member of the Commission shall end when he resigns or is compulsorily retired.

A vacancy caused by resignation, compulsory retirement or death shall be filled for the remainder of the Member's term of office by a new Member of the same nationality appointed by the Council, by common accord with the President of the Commission, after consulting the European Parliament and in accordance with the criteria set out in the second subparagraph of Article 17(3) of the Treaty on European Union.

The Council may, acting unanimously on a proposal from the President of the Commission, decide that such a vacancy need not be filled, in particular when the remainder of the Member's term of office is short.

In the event of resignation, compulsory retirement or death, the President shall be replaced for the remainder of his term of office. The procedure laid down in the first subparagraph of Article 17(7) of the Treaty on European Union shall be applicable for the replacement of the President.

In the event of resignation, compulsory retirement or death, the High Representative of the Union for Foreign Affairs and Security Policy shall be replaced, for the remainder of his or her term of office, in accordance with Article 18(1) of the Treaty on European Union.

In the case of the resignation of all the Members of the Commission, they shall remain in office and continue to deal with current business until they have been replaced, for the remainder of their term of office, in accordance with Article 17 of the Treaty on European Union.

Article 247 (ex Article 216 TEC)
If any Member of the Commission no longer fulfils the conditions required for the performance of his duties or if he has been guilty of serious misconduct, the Court of Justice may, on application by the Council acting by a simple majority or the Commission, compulsorily retire him.

Article 248 (ex Article 217(2) TEC)
Without prejudice to Article 18(4) of the Treaty on European Union, the responsibilities incumbent upon the Commission shall be structured and allocated among its members by its President, in accordance with Article 17(6) of that Treaty. The President may reshuffle the allocation of those responsibilities during the Commission's term of office. The Members of the Commission shall carry out the duties devolved upon them by the President under his authority.

Article 249 (ex Articles 218(2) and 212 TEC)
1.   The Commission shall adopt its Rules of Procedure so as to ensure that both it and its departments operate. It shall ensure that these Rules are published.

2.   The Commission shall publish annually, not later than one month before the opening of the session of the European Parliament, a general report on the activities of the Union.

Article 250 (ex Article 219 TEC)
The Commission shall act by a majority of its Members.

Its Rules of Procedure shall determine the quorum.

SECTION 5 THE COURT OF JUSTICE OF THE EUROPEAN UNION

Article 251 (ex Article 221 TEC)
The Court of Justice shall sit in chambers or in a Grand Chamber, in accordance with the rules laid down for that purpose in the Statute of the Court of Justice of the European Union.

When provided for in the Statute, the Court of Justice may also sit as a full Court.

Article 252 (ex Article 222 TEC)
The Court of Justice shall be assisted by eight Advocates-General. Should the Court of Justice so request, the Council, acting unanimously, may increase the number of Advocates-General.

It shall be the duty of the Advocate-General, acting with complete impartiality and independence, to make, in open court, reasoned submissions on cases which, in accordance with the Statute of the Court of Justice of the European Union, require his involvement.

Article 253 (ex Article 223 TEC)
The Judges and Advocates-General of the Court of Justice shall be chosen from persons whose independence is beyond doubt and who possess the qualifications required for appointment to the highest judicial offices in their respective countries or who are jurisconsults of recognised competence; they shall be appointed by common accord of the governments of the Member States for a term of six years, after consultation of the panel provided for in Article 255.

Every three years there shall be a partial replacement of the Judges and Advocates-General, in accordance with the conditions laid down in the Statute of the Court of Justice of the European Union.

The Judges shall elect the President of the Court of Justice from among their number for a term of three years. He may be re-elected.

Retiring Judges and Advocates-General may be reappointed.

The Court of Justice shall appoint its Registrar and lay down the rules governing his service.

The Court of Justice shall establish its Rules of Procedure. Those Rules shall require the approval of the Council.

Article 254 (ex Article 224 TEC)
The number of Judges of the General Court shall be determined by the Statute of the Court of Justice of the European Union. The Statute may provide for the General Court to be assisted by Advocates-General.

The members of the General Court shall be chosen from persons whose independence is beyond doubt and who possess the ability required for appointment to high judicial office. They shall be appointed by common accord of the governments of the Member States for a term of six years, after consultation of the panel provided for in Article 255. The membership shall be partially renewed every three years. Retiring members shall be eligible for reappointment.

The Judges shall elect the President of the General Court from among their number for a term of three years. He may be re-elected.

The General Court shall appoint its Registrar and lay down the rules governing his service.

The General Court shall establish its Rules of Procedure in agreement with the Court of Justice.

Those Rules shall require the approval of the Council.

Unless the Statute of the Court of Justice of the European Union provides otherwise, the provisions of the Treaties relating to the Court of Justice shall apply to the General Court.

Article 255

A panel shall be set up in order to give an opinion on candidates' suitability to perform the duties of Judge and Advocate-General of the Court of Justice and the General Court before the governments of the Member States make the appointments referred to in Articles 253 and 254.

The panel shall comprise seven persons chosen from among former members of the Court of Justice and the General Court, members of national supreme courts and lawyers of recognised competence, one of whom shall be proposed by the European Parliament. The Council shall adopt a decision establishing the panel's operating rules and a decision appointing its members. It shall act on the initiative of the President of the Court of Justice.

Article 256 (ex Article 225 TEC)

1. The General Court shall have jurisdiction to hear and determine at first instance actions or proceedings referred to in Articles 263, 265, 268, 270 and 272, with the exception of those assigned to a specialised court set up under Article 257 and those reserved in the Statute for the Court of Justice. The Statute may provide for the General Court to have jurisdiction for other classes of action or proceeding.

    Decisions given by the General Court under this paragraph may be subject to a right of appeal to the Court of Justice on points of law only, under the conditions and within the limits laid down by the Statute.

2. The General Court shall have jurisdiction to hear and determine actions or proceedings brought against decisions of the specialised courts.

    Decisions given by the General Court under this paragraph may exceptionally be subject to review by the Court of Justice, under the conditions and within the limits laid down by the Statute, where there is a serious risk of the unity or consistency of Union law being affected.

3. The General Court shall have jurisdiction to hear and determine questions referred for a preliminary ruling under Article 267, in specific areas laid down by the Statute.

    Where the General Court considers that the case requires a decision of principle likely to affect the unity or consistency of Union law, it may refer the case to the Court of Justice for a ruling.

    Decisions given by the General Court on questions referred for a preliminary ruling may exceptionally be subject to review by the Court of Justice, under the conditions and within the limits laid down by the Statute, where there is a serious risk of the unity or consistency of Union law being affected.

Article 257 (ex Article 225a TEC)

The European Parliament and the Council, acting in accordance with the ordinary legislative procedure, may establish specialised courts attached to the General Court to hear and determine at first instance certain classes of action or proceeding brought in specific areas. The European Parliament and the Council shall act by means of regulations either on a proposal from the Commission after consultation of the Court of Justice or at the request of the Court of Justice after consultation of the Commission.

The regulation establishing a specialised court shall lay down the rules on the organisation of the court and the extent of the jurisdiction conferred upon it.

Decisions given by specialised courts may be subject to a right of appeal on points of law only or, when provided for in the regulation establishing the specialised court, a right of appeal also on matters of fact, before the General Court.

The members of the specialised courts shall be chosen from persons whose independence is beyond doubt and who possess the ability required for appointment to judicial office. They shall be appointed by the Council, acting unanimously.

The specialised courts shall establish their Rules of Procedure in agreement with the Court of Justice. Those Rules shall require the approval of the Council.

Unless the regulation establishing the specialised court provides otherwise, the provisions of the Treaties relating to the Court of Justice of the European Union and the provisions of the Statute of the Court of Justice of the European Union shall apply to the specialised courts. Title I of the Statute and Article 64 thereof shall in any case apply to the specialised courts.

Article 258 (ex Article 226 TEC)

If the Commission considers that a Member State has failed to fulfil an obligation under the Treaties, it shall deliver a reasoned opinion on the matter after giving the State concerned the opportunity to submit its observations.

If the State concerned does not comply with the opinion within the period laid down by the Commission, the latter may bring the matter before the Court of Justice of the European Union.

Article 259 (ex Article 227 TEC)

A Member State which considers that another Member State has failed to fulfil an obligation under the Treaties may bring the matter before the Court of Justice of the European Union.

Before a Member State brings an action against another Member State for an alleged infringement of an obligation under the Treaties, it shall bring the matter before the Commission.

The Commission shall deliver a reasoned opinion after each of the States concerned has been given the opportunity to submit its own case and its observations on the other party's case both orally and in writing.

If the Commission has not delivered an opinion within three months of the date on which the matter was brought before it, the absence of such opinion shall not prevent the matter from being brought before the Court.

Article 260 (ex Article 228 TEC)

1. If the Court of Justice of the European Union finds that a Member State has failed to fulfil an obligation under the Treaties, the State shall be required to take the necessary measures to comply with the judgment of the Court.

2. If the Commission considers that the Member State concerned has not taken the necessary measures to comply with the judgment of the Court, it may bring the case before the Court after giving that State the opportunity to submit its observations. It shall specify the amount of the lump sum or penalty payment to be paid by the Member State concerned which it considers appropriate in the circumstances.

    If the Court finds that the Member State concerned has not complied with its judgment it may impose a lump sum or penalty payment on it.

    This procedure shall be without prejudice to Article 259.

3. When the Commission brings a case before the Court pursuant to Article 258 on the grounds that the Member State concerned has failed to fulfil its obligation to notify measures transposing a directive adopted under a legislative procedure, it may, when it deems appropriate, specify the amount of the lump sum or penalty payment to be paid by the Member State concerned which it considers appropriate in the circumstances.

If the Court finds that there is an infringement it may impose a lump sum or penalty payment on the Member State concerned not exceeding the amount specified by the Commission. The payment obligation shall take effect on the date set by the Court in its judgment.

Article 261 (ex Article 229 TEC)

Regulations adopted jointly by the European Parliament and the Council, and by the Council, pursuant to the provisions of the Treaties, may give the Court of Justice of the European Union unlimited jurisdiction with regard to the penalties provided for in such regulations.

Article 262 (ex Article 229a TEC)

Without prejudice to the other provisions of the Treaties, the Council, acting unanimously in accordance with a special legislative procedure and after consulting the European Parliament, may adopt provisions to confer jurisdiction, to the extent that it shall determine, on the Court of Justice of the European Union in disputes relating to the application of acts adopted on the basis of the Treaties which create European intellectual property rights. These provisions shall enter into force after their approval by the Member States in accordance with their respective constitutional requirements.

Article 263 (ex Article 230 TEC)

The Court of Justice of the European Union shall review the legality of legislative acts, of acts of the Council, of the Commission and of the European Central Bank, other than recommendations and opinions, and of acts of the European Parliament and of the European Council intended to produce legal effects vis-à-vis third parties. It shall also review the legality of acts of bodies, offices or agencies of the Union intended to produce legal effects vis-à-vis third parties.

It shall for this purpose have jurisdiction in actions brought by a Member State, the European Parliament, the Council or the Commission on grounds of lack of competence, infringement of an essential procedural requirement, infringement of the Treaties or of any rule of law relating to their application, or misuse of powers.

The Court shall have jurisdiction under the same conditions in actions brought by the Court of Auditors, by the European Central Bank and by the Committee of the Regions for the purpose of protecting their prerogatives.

Any natural or legal person may, under the conditions laid down in the first and second paragraphs, institute proceedings against an act addressed to that person or which is of direct and individual concern to them, and against a regulatory act which is of direct concern to them and does not entail implementing measures.

Acts setting up bodies, offices and agencies of the Union may lay down specific conditions and arrangements concerning actions brought by natural or legal persons against acts of these bodies, offices or agencies intended to produce legal effects in relation to them.

The proceedings provided for in this Article shall be instituted within two months of the publication of the measure, or of its notification to the plaintiff, or, in the absence thereof, of the day on which it came to the knowledge of the latter, as the case may be.

Article 264 (ex Article 231 TEC)

If the action is well founded, the Court of Justice of the European Union shall declare the act concerned to be void.

However, the Court shall, if it considers this necessary, state which of the effects of the act which it has declared void shall be considered as definitive.

Article 265 (ex Article 232 TEC)

Should the European Parliament, the European Council, the Council, the Commission or the European Central Bank, in infringement of the Treaties, fail to act, the Member States and the other institutions of the Union may bring an action before the Court of Justice of the European Union to have the infringement established. This Article shall apply, under the same conditions, to bodies, offices and agencies of the Union which fail to act.

The action shall be admissible only if the institution, body, office or agency concerned has first been called upon to act. If, within two months of being so called upon, the institution, body, office or agency concerned has not defined its position, the action may be brought within a further period of two months.

Any natural or legal person may, under the conditions laid down in the preceding paragraphs, complain to the Court that an institution, body, office or agency of the Union has failed to address to that person any act other than a recommendation or an opinion.

Article 266 (ex Article 233 TEC)

The institution whose act has been declared void or whose failure to act has been declared contrary to the Treaties shall be required to take the necessary measures to comply with the judgment of the Court of Justice of the European Union.

This obligation shall not affect any obligation which may result from the application of the second paragraph of Article 340.

Article 267 (ex Article 234 TEC)

The Court of Justice of the European Union shall have jurisdiction to give preliminary rulings concerning:
(a)   the interpretation of the Treaties;

(b)   the validity and interpretation of acts of the institutions, bodies, offices or agencies of the Union;

Where such a question is raised before any court or tribunal of a Member State, that court or tribunal may, if it considers that a decision on the question is necessary to enable it to give judgment, request the Court to give a ruling thereon.

Where any such question is raised in a case pending before a court or tribunal of a Member State against whose decisions there is no judicial remedy under national law, that court or tribunal shall bring the matter before the Court.

If such a question is raised in a case pending before a court or tribunal of a Member State with regard to a person in custody, the Court of Justice of the European Union shall act with the minimum of delay.

Article 268 (ex Article 235 TEC)

The Court of Justice of the European Union shall have jurisdiction in disputes relating to compensation for damage provided for in the second and third paragraphs of Article 340.

Article 269

The Court of Justice shall have jurisdiction to decide on the legality of an act adopted by the European Council or by the Council pursuant to Article 7 of the Treaty on European Union solely at the request of the Member State concerned by a determination of the European Council or of the Council and in respect solely of the procedural stipulations contained in that Article.

Such a request must be made within one month from the date of such determination. The Court shall rule within one month from the date of the request.

Article 270 (ex Article 236 TEC)
The Court of Justice of the European Union shall have jurisdiction in any dispute between the Union and its servants within the limits and under the conditions laid down in the Staff Regulations of Officials and the Conditions of Employment of other servants of the Union.

Article 271 (ex Article 237 TEC)
The Court of Justice of the European Union shall, within the limits hereinafter laid down, have jurisdiction in disputes concerning:

(a)   the fulfilment by Member States of obligations under the Statute of the European Investment Bank. In this connection, the Board of Directors of the Bank shall enjoy the powers conferred upon the Commission by Article 258;

(b)   measures adopted by the Board of Governors of the European Investment Bank. In this connection, any Member State, the Commission or the Board of Directors of the Bank may institute proceedings under the conditions laid down in Article 263;

(c)   measures adopted by the Board of Directors of the European Investment Bank. Proceedings against such measures may be instituted only by Member States or by the Commission, under the conditions laid down in Article 263, and solely on the grounds of non-compliance with the procedure provided for in Article 19(2), (5), (6) and (7) of the Statute of the Bank;

(d)   the fulfilment by national central banks of obligations under the Treaties and the Statute of the ESCB and of the ECB. In this connection the powers of the Governing Council of the European Central Bank in respect of national central banks shall be the same as those conferred upon the Commission in respect of Member States by Article 258. If the Court finds that a national central bank has failed to fulfil an obligation under the Treaties, that bank shall be required to take the necessary measures to comply with the judgment of the Court.

Article 272 (ex Article 238 TEC)
The Court of Justice of the European Union shall have jurisdiction to give judgment pursuant to any arbitration clause contained in a contract concluded by or on behalf of the Union, whether that contract be governed by public or private law.

Article 273 (ex Article 239 TEC)
The Court of Justice shall have jurisdiction in any dispute between Member States which relates to the subject matter of the Treaties if the dispute is submitted to it under a special agreement between the parties.

Article 274 (ex Article 240 TEC)
Save where jurisdiction is conferred on the Court of Justice of the European Union by the Treaties, disputes to which the Union is a party shall not on that ground be excluded from the jurisdiction of the courts or tribunals of the Member States.

Article 275
The Court of Justice of the European Union shall not have jurisdiction with respect to the provisions relating to the common foreign and security policy nor with respect to acts adopted on the basis of those provisions.

However, the Court shall have jurisdiction to monitor compliance with Article 40 of the Treaty on European Union and to rule on proceedings, brought in accordance with the conditions laid down in the fourth paragraph of Article 263 of this Treaty, reviewing the legality of decisions providing for restrictive measures against natural or legal persons adopted by the Council on the basis of Chapter 2 of Title V of the Treaty on European Union.

Article 276
In exercising its powers regarding the provisions of Chapters 4 and 5 of Title V of Part Three relating to the area of freedom, security and justice, the Court of Justice of the European Union shall have no jurisdiction to review the validity or proportionality of operations carried out by the police or other law-enforcement services of a Member State or the exercise of the responsibilities incumbent upon Member States with regard to the maintenance of law and order and the safeguarding of internal security.

Article 277 (ex Article 241 TEC)
Notwithstanding the expiry of the period laid down in Article 263, sixth paragraph, any party may, in proceedings in which an act of general application adopted by an institution, body, office or agency of the Union is at issue, plead the grounds specified in Article 263, second paragraph, in order to invoke before the Court of Justice of the European Union the inapplicability of that act.

Article 278 (ex Article 242 TEC)
Actions brought before the Court of Justice of the European Union shall not have suspensory effect. The Court may, however, if it considers that circumstances so require, order that application of the contested act be suspended.

Article 279 (ex Article 243 TEC)
The Court of Justice of the European Union may in any cases before it prescribe any necessary interim measures.

Article 280 (ex Article 244 TEC)
The judgments of the Court of Justice of the European Union shall be enforceable under the conditions laid down in Article 299.

Article 281 (ex Article 245 TEC)
The Statute of the Court of Justice of the European Union shall be laid down in a separate Protocol.

The European Parliament and the Council, acting in accordance with the ordinary legislative procedure, may amend the provisions of the Statute, with the exception of Title I and Article 64. The European Parliament and the Council shall act either at the request of the Court of Justice and after consultation of the Commission, or on a proposal from the Commission and after consultation of the Court of Justice.

SECTION 6 THE EUROPEAN CENTRAL BANK

Article 282
1.   The European Central Bank, together with the national central banks, shall constitute the European System of Central Banks (ESCB). The European Central Bank, together with the national central banks of the Member States whose currency is the euro, which constitute the Eurosystem, shall conduct the monetary policy of the Union.

2.   The ESCB shall be governed by the decision-making bodies of the European Central Bank. The primary objective of the ESCB shall be to maintain price stability. Without prejudice to that objective, it shall support the general economic policies in the Union in order to contribute to the achievement of the latter's objectives.

3.   The European Central Bank shall have legal personality. It alone may authorise the issue of the euro. It shall be independent in the exercise of its powers and in the management of its finances. Union institutions, bodies, offices and agencies and the governments of the Member States shall respect that independence.

4.   The European Central Bank shall adopt such measures as are necessary to carry out its tasks in accordance with Articles 127 to 133, with Article 138, and with the conditions laid down in the Statute of the ESCB and of the ECB. In accordance with these same Articles, those Member States whose currency is not the euro, and their central banks, shall retain their powers in monetary matters.

5.   Within the areas falling within its responsibilities, the European Central Bank shall be consulted on all proposed Union acts, and all proposals for regulation at national level, and may give an opinion.

Article 283 (ex Article 112 TEC)

1.   The Governing Council of the European Central Bank shall comprise the members of the Executive Board of the European Central Bank and the Governors of the national central banks of the Member States whose currency is the euro.

2.   The Executive Board shall comprise the President, the Vice-President and four other members.

The President, the Vice-President and the other members of the Executive Board shall be appointed by the European Council, acting by a qualified majority, from among persons of recognised standing and professional experience in monetary or banking matters, on a recommendation from the Council, after it has consulted the European Parliament and the Governing Council of the European Central Bank.

Their term of office shall be eight years and shall not be renewable.

Only nationals of Member States may be members of the Executive Board.

Article 284 (ex Article 113 TEC)

1.   The President of the Council and a Member of the Commission may participate, without having the right to vote, in meetings of the Governing Council of the European Central Bank.

The President of the Council may submit a motion for deliberation to the Governing Council of the European Central Bank.

2.   The President of the European Central Bank shall be invited to participate in Council meetings when the Council is discussing matters relating to the objectives and tasks of the ESCB.

3.   The European Central Bank shall address an annual report on the activities of the ESCB and on the monetary policy of both the previous and current year to the European Parliament, the Council and the Commission, and also to the European Council. The President of the European Central Bank shall present this report to the Council and to the European Parliament, which may hold a general debate on that basis.

The President of the European Central Bank and the other members of the Executive Board may, at the request of the European Parliament or on their own initiative, be heard by the competent committees of the European Parliament.

SECTION 7 THE COURT OF AUDITORS

Article 285 (ex Article 246 TEC)
The Court of Auditors shall carry out the Union's audit.
It shall consist of one national of each Member State. Its Members shall be completely independent in the performance of their duties, in the Union's general interest.

Article 286 (ex Article 247 TEC)
1.   The Members of the Court of Auditors shall be chosen from among persons who belong or have belonged in their respective States to external audit bodies or who are especially qualified for this office. Their independence must be beyond doubt.

2.   The Members of the Court of Auditors shall be appointed for a term of six years. The Council, after consulting the European Parliament, shall adopt the list of Members drawn up in accordance with the proposals made by each Member State. The term of office of the Members of the Court of Auditors shall be renewable.

      They shall elect the President of the Court of Auditors from among their number for a term of three years. The President may be re-elected.

3.   In the performance of these duties, the Members of the Court of Auditors shall neither seek nor take instructions from any government or from any other body. The Members of the Court of Auditors shall refrain from any action incompatible with their duties.

4.   The Members of the Court of Auditors may not, during their term of office, engage in any other occupation, whether gainful or not. When entering upon their duties they shall give a solemn undertaking that, both during and after their term of office, they will respect the obligations arising therefrom and in particular their duty to behave with integrity and discretion as regards the acceptance, after they have ceased to hold office, of certain appointments or benefits.

5.   Apart from normal replacement, or death, the duties of a Member of the Court of Auditors shall end when he resigns, or is compulsorily retired by a ruling of the Court of Justice pursuant to paragraph 6.

      The vacancy thus caused shall be filled for the remainder of the Member's term of office.

      Save in the case of compulsory retirement, Members of the Court of Auditors shall remain in office until they have been replaced.

6.   A Member of the Court of Auditors may be deprived of his office or of his right to a pension or other benefits in its stead only if the Court of Justice, at the request of the Court of Auditors, finds that he no longer fulfils the requisite conditions or meets the obligations arising from his office.

7.   The Council shall determine the conditions of employment of the President and the Members of the Court of Auditors and in particular their salaries, allowances and pensions. It shall also determine any payment to be made instead of remuneration.

8.   The provisions of the Protocol on the privileges and immunities of the European Union applicable to the Judges of the Court of Justice of the European Union shall also apply to the Members of the Court of Auditors.

Article 287 (ex Article 248 TEC)
1.   The Court of Auditors shall examine the accounts of all revenue and expenditure of the Union. It shall also examine the accounts of all revenue and expenditure of all bodies, offices or agencies set up by the Union in so far as the relevant constituent instrument does not preclude such examination.

The Court of Auditors shall provide the European Parliament and the Council with a statement of assurance as to the reliability of the accounts and the legality and regularity of the underlying transactions which shall be published in the *Official Journal of the European Union*. This statement may be supplemented by specific assessments for each major area of Union activity.

2. The Court of Auditors shall examine whether all revenue has been received and all expenditure incurred in a lawful and regular manner and whether the financial management has been sound. In doing so, it shall report in particular on any cases of irregularity.

The audit of revenue shall be carried out on the basis both of the amounts established as due and the amounts actually paid to the Union.

The audit of expenditure shall be carried out on the basis both of commitments undertaken and payments made.

These audits may be carried out before the closure of accounts for the financial year in question.

3. The audit shall be based on records and, if necessary, performed on the spot in the other institutions of the Union, on the premises of any body, office or agency which manages revenue or expenditure on behalf of the Union and in the Member States, including on the premises of any natural or legal person in receipt of payments from the budget. In the Member States the audit shall be carried out in liaison with national audit bodies or, if these do not have the necessary powers, with the competent national departments. The Court of Auditors and the national audit bodies of the Member States shall cooperate in a spirit of trust while maintaining their independence. These bodies or departments shall inform the Court of Auditors whether they intend to take part in the audit.

The other institutions of the Union, any bodies, offices or agencies managing revenue or expenditure on behalf of the Union, any natural or legal person in receipt of payments from the budget, and the national audit bodies or, if these do not have the necessary powers, the competent national departments, shall forward to the Court of Auditors, at its request, any document or information necessary to carry out its task.

In respect of the European Investment Bank's activity in managing Union expenditure and revenue, the Court's rights of access to information held by the Bank shall be governed by an agreement between the Court, the Bank and the Commission. In the absence of an agreement, the Court shall nevertheless have access to information necessary for the audit of Union expenditure and revenue managed by the Bank.

4. The Court of Auditors shall draw up an annual report after the close of each financial year. It shall be forwarded to the other institutions of the Union and shall be published, together with the replies of these institutions to the observations of the Court of Auditors, in the *Official Journal of the European Union*.

The Court of Auditors may also, at any time, submit observations, particularly in the form of special reports, on specific questions and deliver opinions at the request of one of the other institutions of the Union.

It shall adopt its annual reports, special reports or opinions by a majority of its Members. However, it may establish internal chambers in order to adopt certain categories of reports or opinions under the conditions laid down by its Rules of Procedure.

It shall assist the European Parliament and the Council in exercising their powers of control over the implementation of the budget.

The Court of Auditors shall draw up its Rules of Procedure. Those rules shall require the approval of the Council.

Chapter 2 LEGAL ACTS OF THE UNION, ADOPTION PROCEDURES AND OTHER PROVISIONS

SECTION 1 THE LEGAL ACTS OF THE UNION

Article 288 (ex Article 249 TEC)

To exercise the Union's competences, the institutions shall adopt regulations, directives, decisions, recommendations and opinions.

A regulation shall have general application. It shall be binding in its entirety and directly applicable in all Member States.

A directive shall be binding, as to the result to be achieved, upon each Member State to which it is addressed, but shall leave to the national authorities the choice of form and methods.

A decision shall be binding in its entirety. A decision which specifies those to whom it is addressed shall be binding only on them.

Recommendations and opinions shall have no binding force.

Article 289

1. The ordinary legislative procedure shall consist in the joint adoption by the European Parliament and the Council of a regulation, directive or decision on a proposal from the Commission. This procedure is defined in Article 294.

2. In the specific cases provided for by the Treaties, the adoption of a regulation, directive or decision by the European Parliament with the participation of the Council, or by the latter with the participation of the European Parliament, shall constitute a special legislative procedure.

3. Legal acts adopted by legislative procedure shall constitute legislative acts.

4. In the specific cases provided for by the Treaties, legislative acts may be adopted on the initiative of a group of Member States or of the European Parliament, on a recommendation from the European Central Bank or at the request of the Court of Justice or the European Investment Bank.

Article 290

1. A legislative act may delegate to the Commission the power to adopt non-legislative acts of general application to supplement or amend certain non-essential elements of the legislative act.

   The objectives, content, scope and duration of the delegation of power shall be explicitly defined in the legislative acts. The essential elements of an area shall be reserved for the legislative act and accordingly shall not be the subject of a delegation of power.

2. Legislative acts shall explicitly lay down the conditions to which the delegation is subject; these conditions may be as follows:
   (a) the European Parliament or the Council may decide to revoke the delegation;
   (b) the delegated act may enter into force only if no objection has been expressed by the European Parliament or the Council within a period set by the legislative act.
   For the purposes of (a) and (b), the European Parliament shall act by a majority of its component members, and the Council by a qualified majority.

3. The adjective 'delegated' shall be inserted in the title of delegated acts.

Article 291
1.   Member States shall adopt all measures of national law necessary to implement legally binding Union acts.

2.   Where uniform conditions for implementing legally binding Union acts are needed, those acts shall confer implementing powers on the Commission, or, in duly justified specific cases and in the cases provided for in Articles 24 and 26 of the Treaty on European Union, on the Council.

3.   For the purposes of paragraph 2, the European Parliament and the Council, acting by means of regulations in accordance with the ordinary legislative procedure, shall lay down in advance the rules and general principles concerning mechanisms for control by Member States of the Commission's exercise of implementing powers.

4.   The word 'implementing' shall be inserted in the title of implementing acts.

Article 292
The Council shall adopt recommendations. It shall act on a proposal from the Commission in all cases where the Treaties provide that it shall adopt acts on a proposal from the Commission. It shall act unanimously in those areas in which unanimity is required for the adoption of a Union act. The Commission, and the European Central Bank in the specific cases provided for in the Treaties, shall adopt recommendations.

SECTION 2 PROCEDURES FOR THE ADOPTION OF ACTS AND OTHER PROVISIONS

Article 293 (ex Article 250 TEC)
1.   Where, pursuant to the Treaties, the Council acts on a proposal from the Commission, it may amend that proposal only by acting unanimously, except in the cases referred to in paragraphs 10 and 13 of Article 294, in Articles 310, 312 and 314 and in the second paragraph of Article 315.

2.   As long as the Council has not acted, the Commission may alter its proposal at any time during the procedures leading to the adoption of a Union act.

Article 294 (ex Article 251 TEC)
1.   Where reference is made in the Treaties to the ordinary legislative procedure for the adoption of an act, the following procedure shall apply.

2.   The Commission shall submit a proposal to the European Parliament and the Council.

First reading
3.   The European Parliament shall adopt its position at first reading and communicate it to the Council.

4.   If the Council approves the European Parliament's position, the act concerned shall be adopted in the wording which corresponds to the position of the European Parliament.

5.   If the Council does not approve the European Parliament's position, it shall adopt its position at first reading and communicate it to the European Parliament.

6.   The Council shall inform the European Parliament fully of the reasons which led it to adopt its position at first reading. The Commission shall inform the European Parliament fully of its position.

Second reading

7.   If, within three months of such communication, the European Parliament:

(a)   approves the Council's position at first reading or has not taken a decision, the act concerned shall be deemed to have been adopted in the wording which corresponds to the position of the Council;

(b)   rejects, by a majority of its component members, the Council's position at first reading, the proposed act shall be deemed not to have been adopted;

(c)   proposes, by a majority of its component members, amendments to the Council's position at first reading, the text thus amended shall be forwarded to the Council and to the Commission, which shall deliver an opinion on those amendments.

8.   If, within three months of receiving the European Parliament's amendments, the Council, acting by a qualified majority:

(a)   approves all those amendments, the act in question shall be deemed to have been adopted;

(b)   does not approve all the amendments, the President of the Council, in agreement with the President of the European Parliament, shall within six weeks convene a meeting of the Conciliation Committee.

9.   The Council shall act unanimously on the amendments on which the Commission has delivered a negative opinion.

Conciliation

10.   The Conciliation Committee, which shall be composed of the members of the Council or their representatives and an equal number of members representing the European Parliament, shall have the task of reaching agreement on a joint text, by a qualified majority of the members of the Council or their representatives and by a majority of the members representing the European Parliament within six weeks of its being convened, on the basis of the positions of the European Parliament and the Council at second reading.

11.   The Commission shall take part in the Conciliation Committee's proceedings and shall take all necessary initiatives with a view to reconciling the positions of the European Parliament and the Council.

12.   If, within six weeks of its being convened, the Conciliation Committee does not approve the joint text, the proposed act shall be deemed not to have been adopted.

Third reading

13.   If, within that period, the Conciliation Committee approves a joint text, the European Parliament, acting by a majority of the votes cast, and the Council, acting by a qualified majority, shall each have a period of six weeks from that approval in which to adopt the act in question in accordance with the joint text. If they fail to do so, the proposed act shall be deemed not to have been adopted.

14.   The periods of three months and six weeks referred to in this Article shall be extended by a maximum of one month and two weeks respectively at the initiative of the European Parliament or the Council.

Special provisions

15.   Where, in the cases provided for in the Treaties, a legislative act is submitted to the ordinary legislative procedure on the initiative of a group of Member States, on a recommendation by the European Central Bank, or at the request of the Court of Justice, paragraph 2, the second sentence of paragraph 6, and paragraph 9 shall not apply.

In such cases, the European Parliament and the Council shall communicate the proposed act to the Commission with their positions at first and second readings. The European Parliament or the Council may request the opinion of the Commission throughout the procedure, which the Commission may also deliver on its own initiative. It may also, if it deems it necessary, take part in the Conciliation Committee in accordance with paragraph 11.

Article 295

The European Parliament, the Council and the Commission shall consult each other and by common agreement make arrangements for their cooperation. To that end, they may, in compliance with the Treaties, conclude interinstitutional agreements which may be of a binding nature.

Article 296 (ex Article 253 TEC)

Where the Treaties do not specify the type of act to be adopted, the institutions shall select it on a case-by-case basis, in compliance with the applicable procedures and with the principle of proportionality.

Legal acts shall state the reasons on which they are based and shall refer to any proposals, initiatives, recommendations, requests or opinions required by the Treaties.

When considering draft legislative acts, the European Parliament and the Council shall refrain from adopting acts not provided for by the relevant legislative procedure in the area in question.

Article 297 (ex Article 254 TEC)

1. Legislative acts adopted under the ordinary legislative procedure shall be signed by the President of the European Parliament and by the President of the Council.

    Legislative acts adopted under a special legislative procedure shall be signed by the President of the institution which adopted them.

    Legislative acts shall be published in the *Official Journal of the European Union*. They shall enter into force on the date specified in them or, in the absence thereof, on the twentieth day following that of their publication.

2. Non-legislative acts adopted in the form of regulations, directives or decisions, when the latter do not specify to whom they are addressed, shall be signed by the President of the institution which adopted them.

    Regulations and directives which are addressed to all Member States, as well as decisions which do not specify to whom they are addressed, shall be published in the *Official Journal of the European Union*. They shall enter into force on the date specified in them or, in the absence thereof, on the twentieth day following that of their publication.

    Other directives, and decisions which specify to whom they are addressed, shall be notified to those to whom they are addressed and shall take effect upon such notification.

Article 298

1. In carrying out their missions, the institutions, bodies, offices and agencies of the Union shall have the support of an open, efficient and independent European administration.

2. In compliance with the Staff Regulations and the Conditions of Employment adopted on the basis of Article 336, the European Parliament and the Council, acting by means of regulations in accordance with the ordinary legislative procedure, shall establish provisions to that end.

Article 299 (ex Article 256 TEC)
Acts of the Council, the Commission or the European Central Bank which impose a pecuniary obligation on persons other than States, shall be enforceable.

Enforcement shall be governed by the rules of civil procedure in force in the State in the territory of which it is carried out. The order for its enforcement shall be appended to the decision, without other formality than verification of the authenticity of the decision, by the national authority which the government of each Member State shall designate for this purpose and shall make known to the Commission and to the Court of Justice of the European Union.

When these formalities have been completed on application by the party concerned, the latter may proceed to enforcement in accordance with the national law, by bringing the matter directly before the competent authority.

Enforcement may be suspended only by a decision of the Court. However, the courts of the country concerned shall have jurisdiction over complaints that enforcement is being carried out in an irregular manner.

Chapter 3 THE UNION'S ADVISORY BODIES

Article 300
1.   The European Parliament, the Council and the Commission shall be assisted by an Economic and Social Committee and a Committee of the Regions, exercising advisory functions.

2.   The Economic and Social Committee shall consist of representatives of organisations of employers, of the employed, and of other parties representative of civil society, notably in socio-economic, civic, professional and cultural areas.

3.   The Committee of the Regions shall consist of representatives of regional and local bodies who either hold a regional or local authority electoral mandate or are politically accountable to an elected assembly.

4.   The members of the Economic and Social Committee and of the Committee of the Regions shall not be bound by any mandatory instructions. They shall be completely independent in the performance of their duties, in the Union's general interest.

5.   The rules referred to in paragraphs 2 and 3 governing the nature of the composition of the Committees shall be reviewed at regular intervals by the Council to take account of economic, social and demographic developments within the Union. The Council, on a proposal from the Commission, shall adopt decisions to that end.

SECTION 1 THE ECONOMIC AND SOCIAL COMMITTEE

Article 301 (ex Article 258 TEC)
The number of members of the Economic and Social Committee shall not exceed 350.

The Council, acting unanimously on a proposal from the Commission, shall adopt a decision determining the Committee's composition.

The Council shall determine the allowances of members of the Committee.

Article 302 (ex Article 259 TEC)
1.   The members of the Committee shall be appointed for five years The Council shall adopt the list of members drawn up in accordance with the proposals made by each Member State. The term of office of the members of the Committee shall be renewable.

2.   The Council shall act after consulting the Commission. It may obtain the opinion of European bodies which are representative of the various economic and social sectors and of civil society to which the Union's activities are of concern.

Article 303 (ex Article 260 TEC)
The Committee shall elect its chairman and officers from among its members for a term of two and a half years.

It shall adopt its Rules of Procedure.

The Committee shall be convened by its chairman at the request of the European Parliament, the Council or of the Commission. It may also meet on its own initiative.

Article 304 (ex Article 262 TEC)
The Committee shall be consulted by the European Parliament, by the Council or by the Commission where the Treaties so provide. The Committee may be consulted by these institutions in all cases in which they consider it appropriate. It may issue an opinion on its own initiative in cases in which it considers such action appropriate.

The European Parliament, the Council or the Commission shall, if it considers it necessary, set the Committee, for the submission of its opinion, a time limit which may not be less than one month from the date on which the chairman receives notification to this effect. Upon expiry of the time limit, the absence of an opinion shall not prevent further action.

The opinion of the Committee, together with a record of the proceedings, shall be forwarded to the European Parliament, to the Council and to the Commission.

SECTION 2 THE COMMITTEE OF THE REGIONS

Article 305 (ex Article 263, second, third and fourth paragraphs, TEC)
The number of members of the Committee of the Regions shall not exceed 350.

The Council, acting unanimously on a proposal from the Commission, shall adopt a decision determining the Committee's composition.

The members of the Committee and an equal number of alternate members shall be appointed for five years. Their term of office shall be renewable. The Council shall adopt the list of members and alternate members drawn up in accordance with the proposals made by each Member State. When the mandate referred to in Article 300(3) on the basis of which they were proposed comes to an end, the term of office of members of the Committee shall terminate automatically and they shall then be replaced for the remainder of the said term of office in accordance with the same procedure. No member of the Committee shall at the same time be a Member of the European Parliament.

Article 306 (ex Article 264 TEC)
The Committee of the Regions shall elect its chairman and officers from among its members for a term of two and a half years.

It shall adopt its Rules of Procedure.

The Committee shall be convened by its chairman at the request of the European Parliament, the Council or of the Commission. It may also meet on its own initiative.

Article 307 (ex Article 265 TEC)
The Committee of the Regions shall be consulted by the European Parliament, by the Council or by the Commission where the Treaties so provide and in all other cases, in particular those which concern cross-border cooperation, in which one of these institutions considers it appropriate.

The European Parliament, the Council or the Commission shall, if it considers it necessary, set the Committee, for the submission of its opinion, a time limit which may not be less than one month from the date on which the chairman receives notification to this effect. Upon expiry of the time limit, the absence of an opinion shall not prevent further action.

Where the Economic and Social Committee is consulted pursuant to Article 304, the Committee of the Regions shall be informed by the European Parliament, the Council or the Commission of the request for an opinion. Where it considers that specific regional interests are involved, the Committee of the Regions may issue an opinion on the matter.

It may issue an opinion on its own initiative in cases in which it considers such action appropriate.

The opinion of the Committee, together with a record of the proceedings, shall be forwarded to the European Parliament, to the Council and to the Commission.

Chapter 4 THE EUROPEAN INVESTMENT BANK

Article 308 (ex Article 266 TEC)
The European Investment Bank shall have legal personality.

The members of the European Investment Bank shall be the Member States.

The Statute of the European Investment Bank is laid down in a Protocol annexed to the Treaties. The Council acting unanimously in accordance with a special legislative procedure, at the request of the European Investment Bank and after consulting the European Parliament and the Commission, or on a proposal from the Commission and after consulting the European Parliament and the European Investment Bank, may amend the Statute of the Bank.

Article 309 (ex Article 267 TEC)
The task of the European Investment Bank shall be to contribute, by having recourse to the capital market and utilising its own resources, to the balanced and steady development of the internal market in the interest of the Union. For this purpose the Bank shall, operating on a non-profit-making basis, grant loans and give guarantees which facilitate the financing of the following projects in all sectors of the economy:
(a)   projects for developing less-developed regions;

(b)   projects for modernising or converting undertakings or for developing fresh activities called for by the establishment or functioning of the internal market, where these projects are of such a size or nature that they cannot be entirely financed by the various means available in the individual Member States;

(c)   projects of common interest to several Member States which are of such a size or nature that they cannot be entirely financed by the various means available in the individual Member States.

In carrying out its task, the Bank shall facilitate the financing of investment programmes in conjunction with assistance from the Structural Funds and other Union Financial Instruments.

TITLE II
FINANCIAL PROVISIONS

Article 310 (ex Article 268 TEC)
1.   All items of revenue and expenditure of the Union shall be included in estimates to be drawn up for each financial year and shall be shown in the budget.

The Union's annual budget shall be established by the European Parliament and the Council in accordance with Article 314.

The revenue and expenditure shown in the budget shall be in balance.

2. The expenditure shown in the budget shall be authorised for the annual budgetary period in accordance with the regulation referred to in Article 322.

3. The implementation of expenditure shown in the budget shall require the prior adoption of a legally binding Union act providing a legal basis for its action and for the implementation of the corresponding expenditure in accordance with the regulation referred to in Article 322, except in cases for which that law provides.

4. With a view to maintaining budgetary discipline, the Union shall not adopt any act which is likely to have appreciable implications for the budget without providing an assurance that the expenditure arising from such an act is capable of being financed within the limit of the Union's own resources and in compliance with the multiannual financial framework referred to in Article 312.

5. The budget shall be implemented in accordance with the principle of sound financial management. Member States shall cooperate with the Union to ensure that the appropriations entered in the budget are used in accordance with this principle.

6. The Union and the Member States, in accordance with Article 325, shall counter fraud and any other illegal activities affecting the financial interests of the Union.

CHAPTER 1 THE UNION'S OWN RESOURCES

Article 311 (ex Article 269 TEC)
The Union shall provide itself with the means necessary to attain its objectives and carry through its policies.

Without prejudice to other revenue, the budget shall be financed wholly from own resources.

The Council, acting in accordance with a special legislative procedure, shall unanimously and after consulting the European Parliament adopt a decision laying down the provisions relating to the system of own resources of the Union. In this context it may establish new categories of own resources or abolish an existing category. That decision shall not enter into force until it is approved by the Member States in accordance with their respective constitutional requirements.

The Council, acting by means of regulations in accordance with a special legislative procedure, shall lay down implementing measures for the Union's own resources system in so far as this is provided for in the decision adopted on the basis of the third paragraph. The Council shall act after obtaining the consent of the European Parliament.

Chapter 2 THE MULTIANNUAL FINANCIAL FRAMEWORK

Article 312
1. The multiannual financial framework shall ensure that Union expenditure develops in an orderly manner and within the limits of its own resources.

It shall be established for a period of at least five years.

The annual budget of the Union shall comply with the multiannual financial framework.

2. The Council, acting in accordance with a special legislative procedure, shall adopt a regulation laying down the multiannual financial framework. The Council shall act unanimously after obtaining the consent of the European Parliament, which shall be given by a majority of its component members.

The European Council may, unanimously, adopt a decision authorising the Council to act by a qualified majority when adopting the regulation referred to in the first subparagraph.

3.   The financial framework shall determine the amounts of the annual ceilings on commitment appropriations by category of expenditure and of the annual ceiling on payment appropriations. The categories of expenditure, limited in number, shall correspond to the Union's major sectors of activity.

The financial framework shall lay down any other provisions required for the annual budgetary procedure to run smoothly.

4.   Where no Council regulation determining a new financial framework has been adopted by the end of the previous financial framework, the ceilings and other provisions corresponding to the last year of that framework shall be extended until such time as that act is adopted.

5.   Throughout the procedure leading to the adoption of the financial framework, the European Parliament, the Council and the Commission shall take any measure necessary to facilitate its adoption.

Chapter 3 THE UNION'S ANNUAL BUDGET

Article 313 (ex Article 272(1), TEC)
The financial year shall run from 1 January to 31 December.

Article 314 (ex Article 272(2) to (10), TEC)
The European Parliament and the Council, acting in accordance with a special legislative procedure, shall establish the Union's annual budget in accordance with the following provisions.
1.   With the exception of the European Central Bank, each institution shall, before 1 July, draw up estimates of its expenditure for the following financial year. The Commission shall consolidate these estimates in a draft budget. which may contain different estimates.

The draft budget shall contain an estimate of revenue and an estimate of expenditure.

2.   The Commission shall submit a proposal containing the draft budget to the European Parliament and to the Council not later than 1 September of the year preceding that in which the budget is to be implemented.

The Commission may amend the draft budget during the procedure until such time as the Conciliation Committee, referred to in paragraph 5, is convened.

3.   The Council shall adopt its position on the draft budget and forward it to the European Parliament not later than 1 October of the year preceding that in which the budget is to be implemented. The Council shall inform the European Parliament in full of the reasons which led it to adopt its position.

4.   If, within forty-two days of such communication, the European Parliament:
(a) approves the position of the Council, the budget shall be adopted;
(b) has not taken a decision, the budget shall be deemed to have been adopted;
(c) adopts amendments by a majority of its component members, the amended draft shall be forwarded to the Council and to the Commission. The President of the European Parliament, in agreement with the President of the Council, shall immediately convene a meeting of the Conciliation Committee. However, if within ten days of the draft being forwarded the Council informs the European Parliament that it has approved all its amendments, the Conciliation Committee shall not meet.

5.   The Conciliation Committee, which shall be composed of the members of the Council or their representatives and an equal number of members representing the European Parliament, shall have the task of reaching agreement on a joint text, by a qualified majority of the members of the Council or their representatives and by a majority of the representatives of the European Parliament within twenty-one days of its being convened, on the basis of the positions of the European Parliament and the Council.

The Commission shall take part in the Conciliation Committee's proceedings and shall take all the necessary initiatives with a view to reconciling the positions of the European Parliament and the Council.

6.   If, within the twenty-one days referred to in paragraph 5, the Conciliation Committee agrees on a joint text, the European Parliament and the Council shall each have a period of fourteen days from the date of that agreement in which to approve the joint text.

7.   If, within the period of fourteen days referred to in paragraph 6:
   (a) the European Parliament and the Council both approve the joint text or fail to take a decision, or if one of these institutions approves the joint text while the other one fails to take a decision, the budget shall be deemed to be definitively adopted in accordance with the joint text; or
   (b) the European Parliament, acting by a majority of its component members, and the Council both reject the joint text, or if one of these institutions rejects the joint text while the other one fails to take a decision, a new draft budget shall be submitted by the Commission; or
   (c) the European Parliament, acting by a majority of its component members, rejects the joint text while the Council approves it, a new draft budget shall be submitted by the Commission; or
   (d) the European Parliament approves the joint text whilst the Council rejects it, the European Parliament may, within fourteen days from the date of the rejection by the Council and acting by a majority of its component members and three-fifths of the votes cast, decide to confirm all or some of the amendments referred to in paragraph 4(c). Where a European Parliament amendment is not confirmed, the position agreed in the Conciliation Committee on the budget heading which is the subject of the amendment shall be retained. The budget shall be deemed to be definitively adopted on this basis.

8.   If, within the twenty-one days referred to in paragraph 5, the Conciliation Committee does not agree on a joint text, a new draft budget shall be submitted by the Commission.

9.   When the procedure provided for in this Article has been completed, the President of the European Parliament shall declare that the budget has been definitively adopted.

10.   Each institution shall exercise the powers conferred upon it under this Article in compliance with the Treaties and the acts adopted thereunder, with particular regard to the Union's own resources and the balance between revenue and expenditure.

Article 315 (ex Article 273 TEC)

If, at the beginning of a financial year, the budget has not yet been definitively adopted, a sum equivalent to not more than one twelfth of the budget appropriations for the preceding financial year may be spent each month in respect of any chapter of the budget in accordance with the provisions of the Regulations made pursuant to Article 322; that sum shall not, however, exceed one twelfth of the appropriations provided for in the same chapter of the draft budget.

The Council on a proposal by the Commission, may, provided that the other conditions laid down in the first paragraph are observed, authorise expenditure in excess of one twelfth in accordance with the regulations made pursuant to Article 322. The Council shall forward the decision immediately to the European Parliament.

The decision referred to in the second paragraph shall lay down the necessary measures relating to resources to ensure application of this Article, in accordance with the acts referred to in Article 311.

It shall enter into force thirty days following its adoption if the European Parliament, acting by a majority of its component Members, has not decided to reduce this expenditure within that time-limit.

Article 316 (ex Article 271 TEC)
In accordance with conditions to be laid down pursuant to Article 322, any appropriations, other than those relating to staff expenditure, that are unexpended at the end of the financial year may be carried forward to the next financial year only.

Appropriations shall be classified under different chapters grouping items of expenditure according to their nature or purpose and subdivided in accordance with the regulations made pursuant to Article 322.

The expenditure of the European Parliament, the European Council and the Council, the Commission and the Court of Justice of the European Union shall be set out in separate parts of the budget, without prejudice to special arrangements for certain common items of expenditure.

Chapter 4 IMPLEMENTATION OF THE BUDGET AND DISCHARGE

Article 317 (ex Article 274 TEC)
The Commission shall implement the budget in cooperation with the Member States, in accordance with the provisions of the regulations made pursuant to Article 322, on its own responsibility and within the limits of the appropriations, having regard to the principles of sound financial management. Member States shall cooperate with the Commission to ensure that the appropriations are used in accordance with the principles of sound financial management.

The regulations shall lay down the control and audit obligations of the Member States in the implementation of the budget and the resulting responsibilities. They shall also lay down the responsibilities and detailed rules for each institution concerning its part in effecting its own expenditure.

Within the budget, the Commission may, subject to the limits and conditions laid down in the regulations made pursuant to Article 322, transfer appropriations from one chapter to another or from one subdivision to another.

Article 318 (ex Article 275 TEC)
The Commission shall submit annually to the European Parliament and to the Council the accounts of the preceding financial year relating to the implementation of the budget. The Commission shall also forward to them a financial statement of the assets and liabilities of the Union.

The Commission shall also submit to the European Parliament and to the Council an evaluation report on the Union's finances based on the results achieved, in particular in relation to the indications given by the European Parliament and the Council pursuant to Article 319.

Article 319 (ex Article 276 TEC)
1.   The European Parliament, acting on a recommendation from the Council, shall give a discharge to the Commission in respect of the implementation of the budget. To this end, the Council and the European Parliament in turn shall examine the accounts, the financial statement and the evaluation report referred to in Article 318, the annual report by the Court

of Auditors together with the replies of the institutions under audit to the observations of the Court of Auditors, the statement of assurance referred to in Article 287(1), second subparagraph and any relevant special reports by the Court of Auditors.

2.   Before giving a discharge to the Commission, or for any other purpose in connection with the exercise of its powers over the implementation of the budget, the European Parliament may ask to hear the Commission give evidence with regard to the execution of expenditure or the operation of financial control systems. The Commission shall submit any necessary information to the European Parliament at the latter's request.

3.   The Commission shall take all appropriate steps to act on the observations in the decisions giving discharge and on other observations by the European Parliament relating to the execution of expenditure, as well as on comments accompanying the recommendations on discharge adopted by the Council.

At the request of the European Parliament or the Council, the Commission shall report on the measures taken in the light of these observations and comments and in particular on the instructions given to the departments which are responsible for the implementation of the budget. These reports shall also be forwarded to the Court of Auditors.

Chapter 5 COMMON PROVISIONS

Article 320 (ex Article 277 TEC)
The multiannual financial framework and the annual budget shall be drawn up in euro.

Article 321 (ex Article 278 TEC)
The Commission may, provided it notifies the competent authorities of the Member States concerned, transfer into the currency of one of the Member States its holdings in the currency of another Member State, to the extent necessary to enable them to be used for purposes which come within the scope of the Treaties. The Commission shall as far as possible avoid making such transfers if it possesses cash or liquid assets in the currencies which it needs.

The Commission shall deal with each Member State through the authority designated by the State concerned. In carrying out financial operations the Commission shall employ the services of the bank of issue of the Member State concerned or of any other financial institution approved by that State.

Article 322 (ex Article 279 TEC)
1.   The European Parliament and the Council, acting in accordance with the ordinary legislative procedure, and after consulting the Court of Auditors, shall adopt by means of regulations:
   (a) the financial rules which determine in particular the procedure to be adopted for establishing and implementing the budget and for presenting and auditing accounts;
   (b) rules providing for checks on the responsibility of financial actors, in particular authorising officers and accounting officers.

2.   The Council, acting on a proposal from the Commission and after consulting the European Parliament and the Court of Auditors, shall determine the methods and procedure whereby the budget revenue provided under the arrangements relating to the Union's own resources shall be made available to the Commission, and determine the measures to be applied, if need be, to meet cash requirements.

Article 323
The European Parliament, the Council and the Commission shall ensure that the financial means are made available to allow the Union to fulfil its legal obligations in respect of third parties.

Article 324

Regular meetings between the Presidents of the European Parliament, the Council and the Commission shall be convened, on the initiative of the Commission, under the budgetary procedures referred to in this Title. The Presidents shall take all the necessary steps to promote consultation and the reconciliation of the positions of the institutions over which they preside in order to facilitate the implementation of this Title.

Chapter 6 COMBATTING FRAUD

Article 325 (ex Article 280 TEC)

1. The Union and the Member States shall counter fraud and any other illegal activities affecting the financial interests of the Union through measures to be taken in accordance with this Article, which shall act as a deterrent and be such as to afford effective protection in the Member States, and in all the Union's institutions, bodies, offices and agencies.

2. Member States shall take the same measures to counter fraud affecting the financial interests of the Union as they take to counter fraud affecting their own financial interests.

3. Without prejudice to other provisions of the Treaties, the Member States shall coordinate their action aimed at protecting the financial interests of the Union against fraud. To this end they shall organise, together with the Commission, close and regular cooperation between the competent authorities.

4. The European Parliament and the Council, acting in accordance with the ordinary legislative procedure, after consulting the Court of Auditors, shall adopt the necessary measures in the fields of the prevention of and fight against fraud affecting the financial interests of the Union with a view to affording effective and equivalent protection in the Member States and in all the Union's institutions, bodies, offices and agencies.

5. The Commission, in cooperation with Member States, shall each year submit to the European Parliament and to the Council a report on the measures taken for the implementation of this Article.

TITLE III
ENHANCED COOPERATION

Article 326 (ex Articles 27a to 27e, 40 to 40b and 43 to 45 TEU and ex Articles 11 and 11a TEC)

Any enhanced cooperation shall comply with the Treaties and Union law.

Such cooperation shall not undermine the internal market or economic, social and territorial cohesion. It shall not constitute a barrier to or discrimination in trade between Member States, nor shall it distort competition between them.

Article 327 (ex Articles 27a to 27e, 40 to 40b and 43 to 45 TEU and ex Articles 11 and 11a TEC)

Any enhanced cooperation shall respect the competences, rights and obligations of those Member States which do not participate in it. Those Member States shall not impede its implementation by the participating Member States.

Article 328 (ex Articles 27a to 27e, 40 to 40b and 43 to 45 TEU and ex Articles 11 and 11a TEC)

1. When enhanced cooperation is being established, it shall be open to all Member States, subject to compliance with any conditions of participation laid down by the authorising

decision. It shall also be open to them at any other time, subject to compliance with the acts already adopted within that framework, in addition to those conditions.

The Commission and the Member States participating in enhanced cooperation shall ensure that they promote participation by as many Member States as possible.

2.   The Commission and, where appropriate, the High Representative of the Union for Foreign Affairs and Security Policy shall keep the European Parliament and the Council regularly informed regarding developments in enhanced cooperation.

Article 329 (ex Articles 27a to 27e, 40 to 40b and 43 to 45 TEU and ex Articles 11 and 11a TEC)
1.   Member States which wish to establish enhanced cooperation between themselves in one of the areas covered by the Treaties, with the exception of fields of exclusive competence and the common foreign and security policy, shall address a request to the Commission, specifying the scope and objectives of the enhanced cooperation proposed. The Commission may submit a proposal to the Council to that effect. In the event of the Commission not submitting a proposal, it shall inform the Member States concerned of the reasons for not doing so.

Authorisation to proceed with the enhanced cooperation referred to in the first subparagraph shall be granted by the Council, on a proposal from the Commission and after obtaining the consent of the European Parliament.

2.   The request of the Member States which wish to establish enhanced cooperation between themselves within the framework of the common foreign and security policy shall be addressed to the Council. It shall be forwarded to the High Representative of the Union for Foreign Affairs and Security Policy, who shall give an opinion on whether the enhanced cooperation proposed is consistent with the Union's common foreign and security policy, and to the Commission, which shall give its opinion in particular on whether the enhanced cooperation proposed is consistent with other Union policies. It shall also be forwarded to the European Parliament for information.

Authorisation to proceed with enhanced cooperation shall be granted by a decision of the Council acting unanimously.

Article 330 (ex Articles 27a to 27e, 40 to 40b and 43 to 45 TEU and ex Articles 11 and 11a TEC)
All members of the Council may participate in its deliberations, but only members of the Council representing the Member States participating in enhanced cooperation shall take part in the vote.

Unanimity shall be constituted by the votes of the representatives of the participating Member States only.

A qualified majority shall be defined in accordance with Article 238(3).

Article 331 (ex Articles 27a to 27e, 40 to 40b and 43 to 45 TEU and ex Articles 11 and 11a TEC)
1.   Any Member State which wishes to participate in enhanced cooperation in progress in one of the areas referred to in Article 329(1) shall notify its intention to the Council and the Commission.

The Commission shall, within four months of the date of receipt of the notification, confirm the participation of the Member State concerned. It shall note where necessary that the conditions of participation have been fulfilled and shall adopt any transitional measures necessary with regard to the application of the acts already adopted within the framework of enhanced cooperation.

However, if the Commission considers that the conditions of participation have not been fulfilled, it shall indicate the arrangements to be adopted to fulfil those conditions and shall set a deadline for re-examining the request. On the expiry of that deadline, it shall re-examine the request, in accordance with the procedure set out in the second subparagraph. If the Commission considers that the conditions of participation have still not been met, the Member State concerned may refer the matter to the Council, which shall decide on the request. The Council shall act in accordance with Article 330. It may also adopt the transitional measures referred to in the second subparagraph on a proposal from the Commission.

2.   Any Member State which wishes to participate in enhanced cooperation in progress in the framework of the common foreign and security policy shall notify its intention to the Council, the High Representative of the Union for Foreign Affairs and Security Policy and the Commission.

The Council shall confirm the participation of the Member State concerned, after consulting the High Representative of the Union for Foreign Affairs and Security Policy and after noting, where necessary, that the conditions of participation have been fulfilled. The Council, on a proposal from the High Representative, may also adopt any transitional measures necessary with regard to the application of the acts already adopted within the framework of enhanced cooperation. However, if the Council considers that the conditions of participation have not been fulfilled, it shall indicate the arrangements to be adopted to fulfil those conditions and shall set a deadline for re-examining the request for participation.

For the purposes of this paragraph, the Council shall act unanimously and in accordance with Article 330.

Article 332 (ex Articles 27a to 27e, 40 to 40b and 43 to 45 TEU and ex Articles 11 and 11a TEC)

Expenditure resulting from implementation of enhanced cooperation, other than administrative costs entailed for the institutions, shall be borne by the participating Member States, unless all members of the Council, acting unanimously after consulting the European Parliament, decide otherwise.

Article 333 (ex Articles 27a to 27e, 40 to 40b and 43 to 45 TEU and ex Articles 11 and 11a TEC)

1.   Where a provision of the Treaties which may be applied in the context of enhanced cooperation stipulates that the Council shall act unanimously, the Council, acting unanimously in accordance with the arrangements laid down in Article 330, may adopt a decision stipulating that it will act by a qualified majority.

2.   Where a provision of the Treaties which may be applied in the context of enhanced cooperation stipulates that the Council shall adopt acts under a special legislative procedure, the Council, acting unanimously in accordance with the arrangements laid down in Article 330, may adopt a decision stipulating that it will act under the ordinary legislative procedure. The Council shall act after consulting the European Parliament.

3.   Paragraphs 1 and 2 shall not apply to decisions having military or defence implications.

Article 334 (ex Articles 27a to 27e, 40 to 40b and 43 to 45 TEU and ex Articles 11 and 11a TEC)

The Council and the Commission shall ensure the consistency of activities undertaken in the context of enhanced cooperation and the consistency of such activities with the policies of the Union, and shall cooperate to that end.

Part Seven GENERAL AND FINAL PROVISIONS

Article 335 (ex Article 282 TEC)

In each of the Member States, the Union shall enjoy the most extensive legal capacity accorded to legal persons under their laws; it may, in particular, acquire or dispose of movable and immovable property and may be a party to legal proceedings. To this end, the Union shall be represented by the Commission. However, the Union shall be represented by each of the institutions, by virtue of their administrative autonomy, in matters relating to their respective operation.

Article 336 (ex Article 283 TEC)

The European Parliament and the Council shall, acting by means of regulations in accordance with the ordinary legislative procedure and after consulting the other institutions concerned, lay down the Staff Regulations of Officials of the European Union and the Conditions of Employment of other servants of the Union.

Article 337 (ex Article 284 TEC)

The Commission may, within the limits and under conditions laid down by the Council acting by a simple majority in accordance with the provisions of the Treaties, collect any information and carry out any checks required for the performance of the tasks entrusted to it.

Article 338 (ex Article 285 TEC)

1. Without prejudice to Article 5 of the Protocol on the Statute of the European System of Central Banks and of the European Central Bank, the European Parliament and the Council, acting in accordance with the ordinary legislative procedure, shall adopt measures for the production of statistics where necessary for the performance of the activities of the Union.

2. The production of Union statistics shall conform to impartiality, reliability, objectivity, scientific independence, cost-effectiveness and statistical confidentiality; it shall not entail excessive burdens on economic operators.

Article 339 (ex Article 287 TEC)

The members of the institutions of the Union, the members of committees, and the officials and other servants of the Union shall be required, even after their duties have ceased, not to disclose information of the kind covered by the obligation of professional secrecy, in particular information about undertakings, their business relations or their cost components.

Article 340 (ex Article 288 TEC)

The contractual liability of the Union shall be governed by the law applicable to the contract in question.

In the case of non-contractual liability, the Union shall, in accordance with the general principles common to the laws of the Member States, make good any damage caused by its institutions or by its servants in the performance of their duties.

Notwithstanding the second paragraph, the European Central Bank shall, in accordance with the general principles common to the laws of the Member States, make good any damage caused by it or by its servants in the performance of their duties.

The personal liability of its servants towards the Union shall be governed by the provisions laid down in their Staff Regulations or in the Conditions of Employment applicable to them.

Article 341 (ex Article 289 TEC)

The seat of the institutions of the Union shall be determined by common accord of the governments of the Member States.

Article 342 (ex Article 290 TEC)
The rules governing the languages of the institutions of the Union shall, without prejudice to the provisions contained in the Statute of the Court of Justice of the European Union, be determined by the Council, acting unanimously by means of regulations.

Article 343 (ex Article 291 TEC)
The Union shall enjoy in the territories of the Member States such privileges and immunities as are necessary for the performance of its tasks, under the conditions laid down in the Protocol of 8 April 1965 on the privileges and immunities of the European Union. The same shall apply to the European Central Bank and the European Investment Bank.

Article 344 (ex Article 292 TEC)
Member States undertake not to submit a dispute concerning the interpretation or application of the Treaties to any method of settlement other than those provided for therein.

Article 345 (ex Article 295 TEC)
The Treaties shall in no way prejudice the rules in Member States governing the system of property ownership.

Article 346 (ex Article 296 TEC)
1. The provisions of the Treaties shall not preclude the application of the following rules:
    (a) no Member State shall be obliged to supply information the disclosure of which it considers contrary to the essential interests of its security;
    (b) any Member State may take such measures as it considers necessary for the protection of the essential interests of its security which are connected with the production of or trade in arms, munitions and war material; such measures shall not adversely affect the conditions of competition in the internal market regarding products which are not intended for specifically military purposes.

2. The Council may, acting unanimously on a proposal from the Commission, make changes to the list, which it drew up on 15 April 1958, of the products to which the provisions of paragraph 1(b) apply.

Article 347 (ex Article 297 TEC)
Member States shall consult each other with a view to taking together the steps needed to prevent the functioning of the internal market being affected by measures which a Member State may be called upon to take in the event of serious internal disturbances affecting the maintenance of law and order, in the event of war, serious international tension constituting a threat of war, or in order to carry out obligations it has accepted for the purpose of maintaining peace and international security.

Article 348 (ex Article 298 TEC)
If measures taken in the circumstances referred to in Articles 346 and 347 have the effect of distorting the conditions of competition in the internal market, the Commission shall, together with the State concerned, examine how these measures can be adjusted to the rules laid down in the Treaties.

By way of derogation from the procedure laid down in Articles 258 and 259, the Commission or any Member State may bring the matter directly before the Court of Justice if it considers that another Member State is making improper use of the powers provided for in Articles 346 and 347. The Court of Justice shall give its ruling in camera.

Article 349 (ex Article 299(2), second, third and fourth subparagraphs, TEC)
Taking account of the structural social and economic situation of Guadeloupe, French Guiana, Martinique, Réunion, Saint-Barthélemy, Saint-Martin, the Azores, Madeira and the Canary Islands, which is compounded by their remoteness, insularity, small size, difficult topography and climate, economic dependence on a few products, the permanence and combination of which severely restrain their development, the Council, on a proposal from the Commission and after consulting the European Parliament, shall adopt specific measures aimed, in particular, at laying down the conditions of application of the Treaties to those regions, including common policies. Where the specific measures in question are adopted by the Council in accordance with a special legislative procedure, it shall also act on a proposal from the Commission and after consulting the European Parliament.

The measures referred to in the first paragraph concern in particular areas such as customs and trade policies, fiscal policy, free zones, agriculture and fisheries policies, conditions for supply of raw materials and essential consumer goods, State aids and conditions of access to structural funds and to horizontal Union programmes.

The Council shall adopt the measures referred to in the first paragraph taking into account the special characteristics and constraints of the outermost regions without undermining the integrity and the coherence of the Union legal order, including the internal market and common policies.

Article 350 (ex Article 306 TEC)
The provisions of the Treaties shall not preclude the existence or completion of regional unions between Belgium and Luxembourg, or between Belgium, Luxembourg and the Netherlands, to the extent that the objectives of these regional unions are not attained by application of the Treaties.

Article 351 (ex Article 307 TEC)
The rights and obligations arising from agreements concluded before 1 January 1958 or, for acceding States, before the date of their accession, between one or more Member States on the one hand, and one or more third countries on the other, shall not be affected by the provisions of the Treaties.

To the extent that such agreements are not compatible with the Treaties, the Member State or States concerned shall take all appropriate steps to eliminate the incompatibilities established. Member States shall, where necessary, assist each other to this end and shall, where appropriate, adopt a common attitude.

In applying the agreements referred to in the first paragraph, Member States shall take into account the fact that the advantages accorded under the Treaties by each Member State form an integral part of the establishment of the Union and are thereby inseparably linked with the creation of common institutions, the conferring of powers upon them and the granting of the same advantages by all the other Member States.

Article 352 (ex Article 308 TEC)
1.   If action by the Union should prove necessary, within the framework of the policies defined in the Treaties, to attain one of the objectives set out in the Treaties, and the Treaties have not provided the necessary powers, the Council, acting unanimously on a proposal from the Commission and after obtaining the consent of the European Parliament, shall adopt the appropriate measures. Where the measures in question are adopted by the Council in accordance with a special legislative procedure, it shall also act unanimously on a proposal from the Commission and after obtaining the consent of the European Parliament.

2.   Using the procedure for monitoring the subsidiarity principle referred to in Article 5(3) of the Treaty on European Union, the Commission shall draw national Parliaments' attention to proposals based on this Article.

3.   Measures based on this Article shall not entail harmonisation of Member States' laws or regulations in cases where the Treaties exclude such harmonisation.

4.   This Article cannot serve as a basis for attaining objectives pertaining to the common foreign and security policy and any acts adopted pursuant to this Article shall respect the limits set out in Article 40, second paragraph, of the Treaty on European Union.

Article 353
Article 48(7) of the Treaty on European Union shall not apply to the following Articles:
—   Article 311, third and fourth paragraphs,

—   Article 312(2), first subparagraph,

—   Article 352, and

—   Article 354.

Article 354 (ex Article 309 TEC)
For the purposes of Article 7 of the Treaty on European Union on the suspension of certain rights resulting from Union membership, the member of the European Council or of the Council representing the Member State in question shall not take part in the vote and the Member State in question shall not be counted in the calculation of the one third or four fifths of Member States referred to in paragraphs 1 and 2 of that Article. Abstentions by members present in person or represented shall not prevent the adoption of decisions referred to in paragraph 2 of that Article.

For the adoption of the decisions referred to in paragraphs 3 and 4 of Article 7 of the Treaty on European Union, a qualified majority shall be defined in accordance with Article 238(3)(b) of this Treaty.

Where, following a decision to suspend voting rights adopted pursuant to paragraph 3 of Article 7 of the Treaty on European Union, the Council acts by a qualified majority on the basis of a provision of the Treaties, that qualified majority shall be defined in accordance with Article 238(3)(b) of this Treaty, or, where the Council acts on a proposal from the Commission or from the High Representative of the Union for Foreign Affairs and Security Policy, in accordance with Article 238(3)(a).

For the purposes of Article 7 of the Treaty on European Union, the European Parliament shall act by a two-thirds majority of the votes cast, representing the majority of its component Members.

Article 355 (ex Article 299(2), first subparagraph, and Article 299(3) to (6) TEC)
In addition to the provisions of Article 52 of the Treaty on European Union relating to the territorial scope of the Treaties, the following provisions shall apply:
1.   The provisions of the Treaties shall apply to Guadeloupe, French Guiana, Martinique, Réunion, Saint-Barthélemy, Saint-Martin, the Azores, Madeira and the Canary Islands in accordance with Article 349.

2.   The special arrangements for association set out in Part Four shall apply to the overseas countries and territories listed in Annex II.

The Treaties shall not apply to those overseas countries and territories having special relations with the United Kingdom of Great Britain and Northern Ireland which are not included in the aforementioned list.

3.   The provisions of the Treaties shall apply to the European territories for whose external relations a Member State is responsible.

4.   The provisions of the Treaties shall apply to the Åland Islands in accordance with the provisions set out in Protocol 2 to the Act concerning the conditions of accession of the Republic of Austria, the Republic of Finland and the Kingdom of Sweden.

5.   Notwithstanding Article 52 of the Treaty on European Union and paragraphs 1 to 4 of this Article:
      (a) the Treaties shall not apply to the Faeroe Islands;
      (b) the Treaties shall not apply to the United Kingdom Sovereign Base Areas of Akrotiri and Dhekelia in Cyprus except to the extent necessary to ensure the implementation of the arrangements set out in the Protocol on the Sovereign Base Areas of the United Kingdom of Great Britain and Northern Ireland in Cyprus annexed to the Act concerning the conditions of accession of the Czech Republic, the Republic of Estonia, the Republic of Cyprus, the Republic of Latvia, the Republic of Lithuania, the Republic of Hungary, the Republic of Malta, the Republic of Poland, the Republic of Slovenia and the Slovak Republic to the European Union and in accordance with the terms of that Protocol;
      (c) the Treaties shall apply to the Channel Islands and the Isle of Man only to the extent necessary to ensure the implementation of the arrangements for those islands set out in the Treaty concerning the accession of new Member States to the European Economic Community and to the European Atomic Energy Community signed on 22 January 1972.

6.   The European Council may, on the initiative of the Member State concerned, adopt a decision amending the status, with regard to the Union, of a Danish, French or Netherlands country or territory referred to in paragraphs 1 and 2. The European Council shall act unanimously after consulting the Commission.

Article 356 (ex Article 312 TEC)
This Treaty is concluded for an unlimited period.

Article 357 (ex Article 313 TEC)
This Treaty shall be ratified by the High Contracting Parties in accordance with their respective constitutional requirements. The Instruments of ratification shall be deposited with the Government of the Italian Republic.

This Treaty shall enter into force on the first day of the month following the deposit of the Instrument of ratification by the last signatory State to take this step. If, however, such deposit is made less than 15 days before the beginning of the following month, this Treaty shall not enter into force until the first day of the second month after the date of such deposit.

Article 358
The provisions of Article 55 of the Treaty on European Union shall apply to this Treaty.

IN WITNESS WHEREOF, the undersigned Plenipotentiaries have signed this Treaty.

Done at Rome this twenty-fifth day of March in the year one thousand nine hundred and fifty-seven.

(List of signatories not reproduced)

PROTOCOLS
OJ C 83, 30.3.2010, P. 201*

PROTOCOL (NO 1) ON THE ROLE OF NATIONAL PARLIAMENTS IN THE EUROPEAN UNION

THE HIGH CONTRACTING PARTIES,

RECALLING that the way in which national Parliaments scrutinise their governments in relation to the activities of the Union is a matter for the particular constitutional organisation and practice of each Member State,

*   EDITOR'S NOTE: The following Protocols have been omitted: Nos 4–7, 10–11, 16–18, 22–23, 28–29, 31–35 and 37.

DESIRING to encourage greater involvement of national Parliaments in the activities of the European Union and to enhance their ability to express their views on draft legislative acts of the Union as well as on other matters which may be of particular interest to them,

HAVE AGREED UPON the following provisions, which shall be annexed to the Treaty on European Union, to the Treaty on the Functioning of the European Union and to the Treaty establishing the European Atomic Energy Community:

TITLE I
INFORMATION FOR NATIONAL PARLIAMENTS

Article 1
Commission consultation documents (green and white papers and communications) shall be forwarded directly by the Commission to national Parliaments upon publication. The Commission shall also forward the annual legislative programme as well as any other instrument of legislative planning or policy to national Parliaments, at the same time as to the European Parliament and the Council.

Article 2
Draft legislative acts sent to the European Parliament and to the Council shall be forwarded to national Parliaments.

For the purposes of this Protocol, 'draft legislative acts' shall mean proposals from the Commission, initiatives from a group of Member States, initiatives from the European Parliament, requests from the Court of Justice, recommendations from the European Central Bank and requests from the European Investment Bank, for the adoption of a legislative act.

Draft legislative acts originating from the Commission shall be forwarded to national Parliaments directly by the Commission, at the same time as to the European Parliament and the Council.

Draft legislative acts originating from the European Parliament shall be forwarded to national Parliaments directly by the European Parliament.

Draft legislative acts originating from a group of Member States, the Court of Justice, the European Central Bank or the European Investment Bank shall be forwarded to national Parliaments by the Council.

Article 3
National Parliaments may send to the Presidents of the European Parliament, the Council and the Commission a reasoned opinion on whether a draft legislative act complies with the principle of subsidiarity, in accordance with the procedure laid down in the Protocol on the application of the principles of subsidiarity and proportionality.

If the draft legislative act originates from a group of Member States, the President of the Council shall forward the reasoned opinion or opinions to the governments of those Member States.

If the draft legislative act originates from the Court of Justice, the European Central Bank or the European Investment Bank, the President of the Council shall forward the reasoned opinion or opinions to the institution or body concerned.

Article 4
An eight-week period shall elapse between a draft legislative act being made available to national Parliaments in the official languages of the Union and the date when it is placed on a provisional agenda for the Council for its adoption or for adoption of a position under a legislative procedure. Exceptions shall be possible in cases of urgency, the reasons for which

shall be stated in the act or position of the Council. Save in urgent cases for which due reasons have been given, no agreement may be reached on a draft legislative act during those eight weeks. Save in urgent cases for which due reasons have been given, a ten-day period shall elapse between the placing of a draft legislative act on the provisional agenda for the Council and the adoption of a position.

Article 5
The agendas for and the outcome of meetings of the Council, including the minutes of meetings where the Council is deliberating on draft legislative acts, shall be forwarded directly to national Parliaments, at the same time as to Member States' governments.

Article 6
When the European Council intends to make use of the first or second subparagraphs of Article 48(7) of the Treaty on European Union, national Parliaments shall be informed of the initiative of the European Council at least six months before any decision is adopted.

Article 7
The Court of Auditors shall forward its annual report to national Parliaments, for information, at the same time as to the European Parliament and to the Council.

Article 8
Where the national Parliamentary system is not unicameral, Articles 1 to 7 shall apply to the component chambers.

TITLE II
INTERPARLIAMENTARY COOPERATION

Article 9
The European Parliament and national Parliaments shall together determine the organisation and promotion of effective and regular interparliamentary cooperation within the Union.

Article 10
A conference of Parliamentary Committees for Union Affairs may submit any contribution it deems appropriate for the attention of the European Parliament, the Council and the Commission. That conference shall in addition promote the exchange of information and best practice between national Parliaments and the European Parliament, including their special committees. It may also organise interparliamentary conferences on specific topics, in particular to debate matters of common foreign and security policy, including common security and defence policy. Contributions from the conference shall not bind national Parliaments and shall not prejudge their positions.

PROTOCOL (NO 2) ON THE APPLICATION OF THE PRINCIPLES OF SUBSIDIARITY AND PROPORTIONALITY

THE HIGH CONTRACTING PARTIES,

WISHING to ensure that decisions are taken as closely as possible to the citizens of the Union,

RESOLVED to establish the conditions for the application of the principles of subsidiarity and proportionality, as laid down in Article 5 of the Treaty on European Union, and to establish a system for monitoring the application of those principles,

HAVE AGREED UPON the following provisions, which shall be annexed to the Treaty on European Union and to the Treaty on the Functioning of the European Union:

Article 1
Each institution shall ensure constant respect for the principles of subsidiarity and proportionality, as laid down in Article 5 of the Treaty on European Union.

Article 2
Before proposing legislative acts, the Commission shall consult widely. Such consultations shall, where appropriate, take into account the regional and local dimension of the action envisaged. In cases of exceptional urgency, the Commission shall not conduct such consultations. It shall give reasons for its decision in its proposal.

Article 3
For the purposes of this Protocol, 'draft legislative acts' shall mean proposals from the Commission, initiatives from a group of Member States, initiatives from the European Parliament, requests from the Court of Justice, recommendations from the European Central Bank and requests from the European Investment Bank, for the adoption of a legislative act.

Article 4
The Commission shall forward its draft legislative acts and its amended drafts to national Parliaments at the same time as to the Union legislator.

The European Parliament shall forward its draft legislative acts and its amended drafts to national Parliaments.

The Council shall forward draft legislative acts originating from a group of Member States, the Court of Justice, the European Central Bank or the European Investment Bank and amended drafts to national Parliaments.

Upon adoption, legislative resolutions of the European Parliament and positions of the Council shall be forwarded by them to national Parliaments.

Article 5
Draft legislative acts shall be justified with regard to the principles of subsidiarity and proportionality. Any draft legislative act should contain a detailed statement making it possible to appraise compliance with the principles of subsidiarity and proportionality. This statement should contain some assessment of the proposal's financial impact and, in the case of a directive, of its implications for the rules to be put in place by Member States, including, where necessary, the regional legislation. The reasons for concluding that a Union objective can be better achieved at Union level shall be substantiated by qualitative and, wherever possible, quantitative indicators. Draft legislative acts shall take account of the need for any burden, whether financial or administrative, falling upon the Union, national governments, regional or local authorities, economic operators and citizens, to be minimised and commensurate with the objective to be achieved.

Article 6
Any national Parliament or any chamber of a national Parliament may, within eight weeks from the date of transmission of a draft legislative act, in the official languages of the Union, send to the Presidents of the European Parliament, the Council and the Commission a reasoned opinion stating why it considers that the draft in question does not comply with the principle of subsidiarity. It will be for each national Parliament or each chamber of a national Parliament to consult, where appropriate, regional parliaments with legislative powers.

If the draft legislative act originates from a group of Member States, the President of the Council shall forward the opinion to the governments of those Member States.

If the draft legislative act originates from the Court of Justice, the European Central Bank or the European Investment Bank, the President of the Council shall forward the opinion to the institution or body concerned.

Article 7

1. The European Parliament, the Council and the Commission, and, where appropriate, the group of Member States, the Court of Justice, the European Central Bank or the European Investment Bank, if the draft legislative act originates from them, shall take account of the reasoned opinions issued by national Parliaments or by a chamber of a national Parliament.

    Each national Parliament shall have two votes, shared out on the basis of the national Parliamentary system. In the case of a bicameral Parliamentary system, each of the two chambers shall have one vote.

2. Where reasoned opinions on a draft legislative act's non-compliance with the principle of subsidiarity represent at least one third of all the votes allocated to the national Parliaments in accordance with the second subparagraph of paragraph 1, the draft must be reviewed. This threshold shall be a quarter in the case of a draft legislative act submitted on the basis of Article 76 of the Treaty on the Functioning of the European Union on the area of freedom, security and justice.

    After such review, the Commission or, where appropriate, the group of Member States, the European Parliament, the Court of Justice, the European Central Bank or the European Investment Bank, if the draft legislative act originates from them, may decide to maintain, amend or withdraw the draft. Reasons must be given for this decision.

3. Furthermore, under the ordinary legislative procedure, where reasoned opinions on the non-compliance of a proposal for a legislative act with the principle of subsidiarity represent at least a simple majority of the votes allocated to the national Parliaments in accordance with the second subparagraph of paragraph 1, the proposal must be reviewed. After such review, the Commission may decide to maintain, amend or withdraw the proposal.

    If it chooses to maintain the proposal, the Commission will have, in a reasoned opinion, to justify why it considers that the proposal complies with the principle of subsidiarity. This reasoned opinion, as well as the reasoned opinions of the national Parliaments, will have to be submitted to the Union legislator, for consideration in the procedure:
    (a) before concluding the first reading, the legislator (the European Parliament and the Council) shall consider whether the legislative proposal is compatible with the principle of subsidiarity, taking particular account of the reasons expressed and shared by the majority of national Parliaments as well as the reasoned opinion of the Commission;
    (b) if, by a majority of 55 % of the members of the Council or a majority of the votes cast in the European Parliament, the legislator is of the opinion that the proposal is not compatible with the principle of subsidiarity, the legislative proposal shall not be given further consideration.

Article 8

The Court of Justice of the European Union shall have jurisdiction in actions on grounds of infringement of the principle of subsidiarity by a legislative act, brought in accordance with the rules laid down in Article 263 of the Treaty on the Functioning of the European Union by Member States, or notified by them in accordance with their legal order on behalf of their national Parliament or a chamber thereof.

In accordance with the rules laid down in the said Article, the Committee of the Regions may also bring such actions against legislative acts for the adoption of which the Treaty on the Functioning of the European Union provides that it be consulted.

Article 9
The Commission shall submit each year to the European Council, the European Parliament, the Council and national Parliaments a report on the application of Article 5 of the Treaty on European Union. This annual report shall also be forwarded to the Economic and Social Committee and the Committee of the Regions.

PROTOCOL (NO 3) ON THE STATUTE OF THE COURT OF JUSTICE OF THE EUROPEAN UNION

> Forthcoming amendments have been published on 28 March 2011 on the web pages of the Court of Justice of the EU: http://curia.europa.eu/jcms/jcms/Jo2_7031

THE HIGH CONTRACTING PARTIES,

DESIRING to lay down the Statute of the Court of Justice of the European Union provided for in Article 281 of the Treaty on the Functioning of the European Union,

HAVE AGREED UPON the following provisions, which shall be annexed to the Treaty on European Union, the Treaty on the Functioning of the European Union and the Treaty establishing the European Atomic Energy Community:

Article 1
The Court of Justice of the European Union shall be constituted and shall function in accordance with the provisions of the Treaties, of the Treaty establishing the European Atomic Energy Community (EAEC Treaty) and of this Statute.

TITLE I
JUDGES AND ADVOCATES-GENERAL

Article 2
Before taking up his duties each Judge shall, before the Court of Justice sitting in open court, take an oath to perform his duties impartially and conscientiously and to preserve the secrecy of the deliberations of the Court.

Article 3
The Judges shall be immune from legal proceedings. After they have ceased to hold office, they shall continue to enjoy immunity in respect of acts performed by them in their official capacity, including words spoken or written.

The Court of Justice, sitting as a full Court, may waive the immunity. If the decision concerns a member of the General Court or of a specialised court, the Court shall decide after consulting the court concerned.

Where immunity has been waived and criminal proceedings are instituted against a Judge, he shall be tried, in any of the Member States, only by the court competent to judge the members of the highest national judiciary.

Articles 11 to 14 and Article 17 of the Protocol on the privileges and immunities of the European Union shall apply to the Judges, Advocates-General, Registrar and Assistant Rapporteurs of the Court of Justice of the European Union, without prejudice to the provisions relating to immunity from legal proceedings of Judges which are set out in the preceding paragraphs.

Article 4
The Judges may not hold any political or administrative office.

They may not engage in any occupation, whether gainful or not, unless exemption is exceptionally granted by the Council, acting by a simple majority.

When taking up their duties, they shall give a solemn undertaking that, both during and after their term of office, they will respect the obligations arising therefrom, in particular the duty to behave with integrity and discretion as regards the acceptance, after they have ceased to hold office, of certain appointments or benefits.

Any doubt on this point shall be settled by decision of the Court of Justice. If the decision concerns a member of the General Court or of a specialised court, the Court shall decide after consulting the court concerned.

Article 5
Apart from normal replacement, or death, the duties of a Judge shall end when he resigns.

Where a Judge resigns, his letter of resignation shall be addressed to the President of the Court of Justice for transmission to the President of the Council. Upon this notification a vacancy shall arise on the bench.

Save where Article 6 applies, a Judge shall continue to hold office until his successor takes up his duties.

Article 6
A Judge may be deprived of his office or of his right to a pension or other benefits in its stead only if, in the unanimous opinion of the Judges and Advocates-General of the Court of Justice, he no longer fulfils the requisite conditions or meets the obligations arising from his office. The Judge concerned shall not take part in any such deliberations. If the person concerned is a member of the General Court or of a specialised court, the Court shall decide after consulting the court concerned.

The Registrar of the Court shall communicate the decision of the Court to the President of the European Parliament and to the President of the Commission and shall notify it to the President of the Council.

In the case of a decision depriving a Judge of his office, a vacancy shall arise on the bench upon this latter notification.

Article 7
A Judge who is to replace a member of the Court whose term of office has not expired shall be appointed for the remainder of his predecessor's term.

Article 8
The provisions of Articles 2 to 7 shall apply to the Advocates-General.

TITLE II
ORGANISATION OF THE COURT OF JUSTICE

Article 9
When, every three years, the Judges are partially replaced, 14 and 13 Judges shall be replaced alternately.

When, every three years, the Advocates-General are partially replaced, four Advocates-General shall be replaced on each occasion.

Article 10
The Registrar shall take an oath before the Court of Justice to perform his duties impartially and conscientiously and to preserve the secrecy of the deliberations of the Court of Justice.

Article 11
The Court of Justice shall arrange for replacement of the Registrar on occasions when he is prevented from attending the Court of Justice.

Article 12
Officials and other servants shall be attached to the Court of Justice to enable it to function. They shall be responsible to the Registrar under the authority of the President.

Article 13
At the request of the Court of Justice, the European Parliament and the Council may, acting in accordance with the ordinary legislative procedure, provide for the appointment of Assistant Rapporteurs and lay down the rules governing their service. The Assistant Rapporteurs may be required, under conditions laid down in the Rules of Procedure, to participate in preparatory inquiries in cases pending before the Court and to cooperate with the Judge who acts as Rapporteur.

The Assistant Rapporteurs shall be chosen from persons whose independence is beyond doubt and who possess the necessary legal qualifications; they shall be appointed by the Council, acting by a simple majority. They shall take an oath before the Court to perform their duties impartially and conscientiously and to preserve the secrecy of the deliberations of the Court.

Article 14
The Judges, the Advocates-General and the Registrar shall be required to reside at the place where the Court of Justice has its seat.

Article 15
The Court of Justice shall remain permanently in session. The duration of the judicial vacations shall be determined by the Court with due regard to the needs of its business.

Article 16
The Court of Justice shall form chambers consisting of three and five Judges. The Judges shall elect the Presidents of the chambers from among their number. The Presidents of the chambers of five Judges shall be elected for three years. They may be re-elected once.

The Grand Chamber shall consist of 13 Judges. It shall be presided over by the President of the Court. The Presidents of the chambers of five Judges and other Judges appointed in accordance with the conditions laid down in the Rules of Procedure shall also form part of the Grand Chamber.

The Court shall sit in a Grand Chamber when a Member State or an institution of the Union that is party to the proceedings so requests.

The Court shall sit as a full Court where cases are brought before it pursuant to Article 228(2), Article 245(2), Article 247 or Article 286(6) of the Treaty on the Functioning of the European Union.

Moreover, where it considers that a case before it is of exceptional importance, the Court may decide, after hearing the Advocate-General, to refer the case to the full Court.

Article 17
Decisions of the Court of Justice shall be valid only when an uneven number of its members is sitting in the deliberations.

Decisions of the chambers consisting of either three or five Judges shall be valid only if they are taken by three Judges.

Decisions of the Grand Chamber shall be valid only if nine Judges are sitting.

Decisions of the full Court shall be valid only if 15 Judges are sitting.

In the event of one of the Judges of a chamber being prevented from attending, a Judge of another chamber may be called upon to sit in accordance with conditions laid down in the Rules of Procedure.

Article 18
No Judge or Advocate-General may take part in the disposal of any case in which he has previously taken part as agent or adviser or has acted for one of the parties, or in which he has been called upon to pronounce as a member of a court or tribunal, of a commission of inquiry or in any other capacity.

If, for some special reason, any Judge or Advocate-General considers that he should not take part in the judgment or examination of a particular case, he shall so inform the President. If, for some special reason, the President considers that any Judge or Advocate-General should not sit or make submissions in a particular case, he shall notify him accordingly.

Any difficulty arising as to the application of this Article shall be settled by decision of the Court of Justice.

A party may not apply for a change in the composition of the Court or of one of its chambers on the grounds of either the nationality of a Judge or the absence from the Court or from the chamber of a Judge of the nationality of that party.

TITLE III
PROCEDURE BEFORE THE COURT OF JUSTICE

Article 19
The Member States and the institutions of the Union shall be represented before the Court of Justice by an agent appointed for each case; the agent may be assisted by an adviser or by a lawyer.

The States, other than the Member States, which are parties to the Agreement on the European Economic Area and also the EFTA Surveillance Authority referred to in that Agreement shall be represented in same manner.

Other parties must be represented by a lawyer.

Only a lawyer authorised to practise before a court of a Member State or of another State which is a party to the Agreement on the European Economic Area may represent or assist a party before the Court.

Such agents, advisers and lawyers shall, when they appear before the Court, enjoy the rights and immunities necessary to the independent exercise of their duties, under conditions laid down in the Rules of Procedure.

As regards such advisers and lawyers who appear before it, the Court shall have the powers normally accorded to courts of law, under conditions laid down in the Rules of Procedure.

University teachers being nationals of a Member State whose law accords them a right of audience shall have the same rights before the Court as are accorded by this Article to lawyers.

Article 20

The procedure before the Court of Justice shall consist of two parts: written and oral.

The written procedure shall consist of the communication to the parties and to the institutions of the Union whose decisions are in dispute, of applications, statements of case, defences and observations, and of replies, if any, as well as of all papers and documents in support or of certified copies of them.

Communications shall be made by the Registrar in the order and within the time laid down in the Rules of Procedure.

The oral procedure shall consist of the reading of the report presented by a Judge acting as Rapporteur, the hearing by the Court of agents, advisers and lawyers and of the submissions of the Advocate-General, as well as the hearing, if any, of witnesses and experts.

Where it considers that the case raises no new point of law, the Court may decide, after hearing the Advocate-General, that the case shall be determined without a submission from the Advocate-General.

Article 21

A case shall be brought before the Court of Justice by a written application addressed to the Registrar. The application shall contain the applicant's name and permanent address and the description of the signatory, the name of the party or names of the parties against whom the application is made, the subject-matter of the dispute, the form of order sought and a brief statement of the pleas in law on which the application is based.

The application shall be accompanied, where appropriate, by the measure the annulment of which is sought or, in the circumstances referred to in Article 265 of the Treaty on the Functioning of the European Union, by documentary evidence of the date on which an institution was, in accordance with those Articles, requested to act. If the documents are not submitted with the application, the Registrar shall ask the party concerned to produce them within a reasonable period, but in that event the rights of the party shall not lapse even if such documents are produced after the time limit for bringing proceedings.

Article 22

A case governed by Article 18 of the EAEC Treaty shall be brought before the Court of Justice by an appeal addressed to the Registrar. The appeal shall contain the name and permanent address of the applicant and the description of the signatory, a reference to the decision against which the appeal is brought, the names of the respondents, the subject-matter of the dispute, the submissions and a brief statement of the grounds on which the appeal is based.

The appeal shall be accompanied by a certified copy of the decision of the Arbitration Committee which is contested.

If the Court rejects the appeal, the decision of the Arbitration Committee shall become final.

If the Court annuls the decision of the Arbitration Committee, the matter may be re-opened, where appropriate, on the initiative of one of the parties in the case, before the Arbitration Committee. The latter shall conform to any decisions on points of law given by the Court.

Article 23

In the cases governed by Article 267 of the Treaty on the Functioning of the European Union, the decision of the court or tribunal of a Member State which suspends its proceedings and refers a case to the Court of Justice shall be notified to the Court by the court or tribunal concerned. The decision shall then be notified by the Registrar of the Court to the parties, to the Member States and to the Commission, and to the institution, body, office or agency of the Union which adopted the act the validity or interpretation of which is in dispute.

Within two months of this notification, the parties, the Member States, the Commission and, where appropriate, the institution, body, office or agency which adopted the act the validity or interpretation of which is in dispute, shall be entitled to submit statements of case or written observations to the Court.

In the cases governed by Article 267 of the Treaty on the Functioning of the European Union, the decision of the national court or tribunal shall, moreover, be notified by the Registrar of the Court to the States, other than the Member States, which are parties to the Agreement on the European Economic Area and also to the EFTA Surveillance Authority referred to in that Agreement which may, within two months of notification, where one of the fields of application of that Agreement is concerned, submit statements of case or written observations to the Court.

Where an agreement relating to a specific subject matter, concluded by the Council and one or more non-member States, provides that those States are to be entitled to submit statements of case or written observations where a court or tribunal of a Member State refers to the Court of Justice for a preliminary ruling a question falling within the scope of the agreement, the decision of the national court or tribunal containing that question shall also be notified to the non-member States concerned. Within two months from such notification, those States may lodge at the Court statements of case or written observations.

Article 23a (1)

The Rules of Procedure may provide for an expedited or accelerated procedure and, for references for a preliminary ruling relating to the area of freedom, security and justice, an urgent procedure.

Those procedures may provide, in respect of the submission of statements of case or written observations, for a shorter period than that provided for by Article 23, and, in derogation from the fourth paragraph of Article 20, for the case to be determined without a submission from the Advocate General.

In addition, the urgent procedure may provide for restriction of the parties and other interested persons mentioned in Article 23, authorised to submit statements of case or written observations and, in cases of extreme urgency, for the written stage of the procedure to be omitted.

Article 24

The Court of Justice may require the parties to produce all documents and to supply all information which the Court considers desirable. Formal note shall be taken of any refusal.

The Court may also require the Member States and institutions, bodies, offices and agencies not being parties to the case to supply all information which the Court considers necessary for the proceedings.

Article 25
The Court of Justice may at any time entrust any individual, body, authority, committee or other organisation it chooses with the task of giving an expert opinion.

Article 26
Witnesses may be heard under conditions laid down in the Rules of Procedure.

Article 27
With respect to defaulting witnesses the Court of Justice shall have the powers generally granted to courts and tribunals and may impose pecuniary penalties under conditions laid down in the Rules of Procedure.

Article 28
Witnesses and experts may be heard on oath taken in the form laid down in the Rules of Procedure or in the manner laid down by the law of the country of the witness or expert.

Article 29
The Court of Justice may order that a witness or expert be heard by the judicial authority of his place of permanent residence.

The order shall be sent for implementation to the competent judicial authority under conditions laid down in the Rules of Procedure. The documents drawn up in compliance with the letters rogatory shall be returned to the Court under the same conditions.

The Court shall defray the expenses, without prejudice to the right to charge them, where appropriate, to the parties.

Article 30
A Member State shall treat any violation of an oath by a witness or expert in the same manner as if the offence had been committed before one of its courts with jurisdiction in civil proceedings. At the instance of the Court of Justice, the Member State concerned shall prosecute the offender before its competent court.

Article 31
The hearing in court shall be public, unless the Court of Justice, of its own motion or on application by the parties, decides otherwise for serious reasons.

Article 32
During the hearings the Court of Justice may examine the experts, the witnesses and the parties themselves. The latter, however, may address the Court of Justice only through their representatives.

Article 33
Minutes shall be made of each hearing and signed by the President and the Registrar.

Article 34
The case list shall be established by the President.

Article 35
The deliberations of the Court of Justice shall be and shall remain secret.

Article 36
Judgments shall state the reasons on which they are based. They shall contain the names of the Judges who took part in the deliberations.

Article 37
Judgments shall be signed by the President and the Registrar. They shall be read in open court.

Article 38
The Court of Justice shall adjudicate upon costs.

Article 39
The President of the Court of Justice may, by way of summary procedure, which may, in so far as necessary, differ from some of the rules contained in this Statute and which shall be laid down in the Rules of Procedure, adjudicate upon applications to suspend execution, as provided for in Article 278 of the Treaty on the Functioning of the European Union and Article 157 of the EAEC Treaty, or to prescribe interim measures pursuant to Article 279 of the Treaty on the Functioning of the European Union, or to suspend enforcement in accordance with the fourth paragraph of Article 299 of the Treaty on the Functioning of the European Union or the third paragraph of Article 164 of the EAEC Treaty.

Should the President be prevented from attending, his place shall be taken by another Judge under conditions laid down in the Rules of Procedure.

The ruling of the President or of the Judge replacing him shall be provisional and shall in no way prejudice the decision of the Court on the substance of the case.

Article 40
Member States and institutions of the Union may intervene in cases before the Court of Justice.

The same right shall be open to the bodies, offices and agencies of the Union and to any other person which can establish an interest in the result of a case submitted to the Court. Natural or legal persons shall not intervene in cases between Member States, between institutions of the Union or between Member States and institutions of the Union.

Without prejudice to the second paragraph, the States, other than the Member States, which are parties to the Agreement on the European Economic Area, and also the EFTA Surveillance Authority referred to in that Agreement, may intervene in cases before the Court where one of the fields of application of that Agreement is concerned.

An application to intervene shall be limited to supporting the form of order sought by one of the parties.

Article 41
Where the defending party, after having been duly summoned, fails to file written submissions in defence, judgment shall be given against that party by default. An objection may be lodged against the judgment within one month of it being notified. The objection shall not have the effect of staying enforcement of the judgment by default unless the Court of Justice decides otherwise.

Article 42
Member States, institutions, bodies, offices and agencies of the Union and any other natural or legal persons may, in cases and under conditions to be determined by the Rules of Procedure, institute third-party proceedings to contest a judgment rendered without their being heard, where the judgment is prejudicial to their rights.

Article 43

If the meaning or scope of a judgment is in doubt, the Court of Justice shall construe it on application by any party or any institution of the Union establishing an interest therein.

Article 44

An application for revision of a judgment may be made to the Court of Justice only on discovery of a fact which is of such a nature as to be a decisive factor, and which, when the judgment was given, was unknown to the Court and to the party claiming the revision.

The revision shall be opened by a judgment of the Court expressly recording the existence of a new fact, recognising that it is of such a character as to lay the case open to revision and declaring the application admissible on this ground.

No application for revision may be made after the lapse of 10 years from the date of the judgment.

Article 45

Periods of grace based on considerations of distance shall be determined by the Rules of Procedure.

No right shall be prejudiced in consequence of the expiry of a time limit if the party concerned proves the existence of unforeseeable circumstances or of force majeure.

Article 46

Proceedings against the Union in matters arising from non-contractual liability shall be barred after a period of five years from the occurrence of the event giving rise thereto. The period of limitation shall be interrupted if proceedings are instituted before the Court of Justice or if prior to such proceedings an application is made by the aggrieved party to the relevant institution of the Union. In the latter event the proceedings must be instituted within the period of two months provided for in Article 263 of the Treaty on the Functioning of the European Union; the provisions of the second paragraph of Article 265 of the Treaty on the Functioning of the European Union shall apply where appropriate.

This Article shall also apply to proceedings against the European Central Bank regarding non-contractual liability.

TITLE IV
GENERAL COURT

Article 47

The first paragraph of Article 9, Articles 14 and 15, the first, second, fourth and fifth paragraphs of Article 17 and Article 18 shall apply to the General Court and its members.

The fourth paragraph of Article 3 and Articles 10, 11 and 14 shall apply to the Registrar of the General Court mutatis mutandis.

Article 48

The General Court shall consist of 27 Judges.

Article 49

The Members of the General Court may be called upon to perform the task of an Advocate-General.

It shall be the duty of the Advocate-General, acting with complete impartiality and independence, to make, in open court, reasoned submissions on certain cases brought before the General Court in order to assist the General Court in the performance of its task.

The criteria for selecting such cases, as well as the procedures for designating the Advocates-General, shall be laid down in the Rules of Procedure of the General Court.

A Member called upon to perform the task of Advocate-General in a case may not take part in the judgment of the case.

Article 50

The General Court shall sit in chambers of three or five Judges. The Judges shall elect the Presidents of the chambers from among their number. The Presidents of the chambers of five Judges shall be elected for three years. They may be re-elected once.

The composition of the chambers and the assignment of cases to them shall be governed by the Rules of Procedure. In certain cases governed by the Rules of Procedure, the General Court may sit as a full court or be constituted by a single Judge.

The Rules of Procedure may also provide that the General Court may sit in a Grand Chamber in cases and under the conditions specified therein.

Article 51

By way of derogation from the rule laid down in Article 256(1) of the Treaty on the Functioning of the European Union, jurisdiction shall be reserved to the Court of Justice in the actions referred to in Articles 263 and 265 of the Treaty on the Functioning of the European Union when they are brought by a Member State against:
(a)   an act of or failure to act by the European Parliament or the Council, or by those institutions acting jointly, except for:
    — decisions taken by the Council under the third subparagraph of Article 108(2) of the Treaty on the Functioning of the European Union;
    — acts of the Council adopted pursuant to a Council regulation concerning measures to protect trade within the meaning of Article 207 of the Treaty on the Functioning of the European Union;
    — acts of the Council by which the Council exercises implementing powers in accordance with the second paragraph of Article 291 of the Treaty on the Functioning of the European Union;
(b)   against an act of or failure to act by the Commission under the first paragraph of Article 331 of the Treaty on the Functioning of the European Union.

Jurisdiction shall also be reserved to the Court of Justice in the actions referred to in the same Articles when they are brought by an institution of the Union against an act of or failure to act by the European Parliament, the Council, both those institutions acting jointly, or the Commission, or brought by an institution of the Union against an act of or failure to act by the European Central Bank.

Article 52

The President of the Court of Justice and the President of the General Court shall determine, by common accord, the conditions under which officials and other servants attached to the Court of Justice shall render their services to the General Court to enable it to function. Certain officials or other servants shall be responsible to the Registrar of the General Court under the authority of the President of the General Court.

Article 53

The procedure before the General Court shall be governed by Title III.

Such further and more detailed provisions as may be necessary shall be laid down in its Rules of Procedure. The Rules of Procedure may derogate from the fourth paragraph of Article 40 and from Article 41 in order to take account of the specific features of litigation in the field of intellectual property.

Notwithstanding the fourth paragraph of Article 20, the Advocate-General may make his reasoned submissions in writing.

Article 54
Where an application or other procedural document addressed to the General Court is lodged by mistake with the Registrar of the Court of Justice, it shall be transmitted immediately by that Registrar to the Registrar of the General Court; likewise, where an application or other procedural document addressed to the Court of Justice is lodged by mistake with the Registrar of the General Court, it shall be transmitted immediately by that Registrar to the Registrar of the Court of Justice.

Where the General Court finds that it does not have jurisdiction to hear and determine an action in respect of which the Court of Justice has jurisdiction, it shall refer that action to the Court of Justice; likewise, where the Court of Justice finds that an action falls within the jurisdiction of the General Court, it shall refer that action to the General Court, whereupon that Court may not decline jurisdiction.

Where the Court of Justice and the General Court are seised of cases in which the same relief is sought, the same issue of interpretation is raised or the validity of the same act is called in question, the General Court may, after hearing the parties, stay the proceedings before it until such time as the Court of Justice has delivered judgment or, where the action is one brought pursuant to Article 263 of the Treaty on the Functioning of the European Union, may decline jurisdiction so as to allow the Court of Justice to rule on such actions. In the same circumstances, the Court of Justice may also decide to stay the proceedings before it; in that event, the proceedings before the General Court shall continue.

Where a Member State and an institution of the Union are challenging the same act, the General Court shall decline jurisdiction so that the Court of Justice may rule on those applications.

Article 55
Final decisions of the General Court, decisions disposing of the substantive issues in part only or disposing of a procedural issue concerning a plea of lack of competence or inadmissibility, shall be notified by the Registrar of the General Court to all parties as well as all Member States and the institutions of the Union even if they did not intervene in the case before the General Court.

Article 56
An appeal may be brought before the Court of Justice, within two months of the notification of the decision appealed against, against final decisions of the General Court and decisions of that Court disposing of the substantive issues in part only or disposing of a procedural issue concerning a plea of lack of competence or inadmissibility.

Such an appeal may be brought by any party which has been unsuccessful, in whole or in part, in its submissions. However, interveners other than the Member States and the institutions of the Union may bring such an appeal only where the decision of the General Court directly affects them.

With the exception of cases relating to disputes between the Union and its servants, an appeal may also be brought by Member States and institutions of the Union which did not intervene in the proceedings before the General Court. Such Member States and institutions shall be in the same position as Member States or institutions which intervened at first instance.

Article 57

Any person whose application to intervene has been dismissed by the General Court may appeal to the Court of Justice within two weeks from the notification of the decision dismissing the application.

The parties to the proceedings may appeal to the Court of Justice against any decision of the General Court made pursuant to Article 278 or Article 279 or the fourth paragraph of Article 299 of the Treaty on the Functioning of the European Union or Article 157 or the third paragraph of Article 164 of the EAEC Treaty within two months from their notification.

The appeal referred to in the first two paragraphs of this Article shall be heard and determined under the procedure referred to in Article 39.

Article 58

An appeal to the Court of Justice shall be limited to points of law. It shall lie on the grounds of lack of competence of the General Court, a breach of procedure before it which adversely affects the interests of the appellant as well as the infringement of Union law by the General Court.

No appeal shall lie regarding only the amount of the costs or the party ordered to pay them.

Article 59

Where an appeal is brought against a decision of the General Court, the procedure before the Court of Justice shall consist of a written part and an oral part. In accordance with conditions laid down in the Rules of Procedure, the Court of Justice, having heard the Advocate-General and the parties, may dispense with the oral procedure.

Article 60

Without prejudice to Articles 278 and 279 of the Treaty on the Functioning of the European Union or Article 157 of the EAEC Treaty, an appeal shall not have suspensory effect.

By way of derogation from Article 280 of the Treaty on the Functioning of the European Union, decisions of the General Court declaring a regulation to be void shall take effect only as from the date of expiry of the period referred to in the first paragraph of Article 56 of this Statute or, if an appeal shall have been brought within that period, as from the date of dismissal of the appeal, without prejudice, however, to the right of a party to apply to the Court of Justice, pursuant to Articles 278 and 279 of the Treaty on the Functioning of the European Union or Article 157 of the EAEC Treaty, for the suspension of the effects of the regulation which has been declared void or for the prescription of any other interim measure.

Article 61

If the appeal is well founded, the Court of Justice shall quash the decision of the General Court. It may itself give final judgment in the matter, where the state of the proceedings so permits, or refer the case back to the General Court for judgment.

Where a case is referred back to the General Court, that Court shall be bound by the decision of the Court of Justice on points of law.

When an appeal brought by a Member State or an institution of the Union, which did not intervene in the proceedings before the General Court, is well founded, the Court of Justice may, if it considers this necessary, state which of the effects of the decision of the General Court which has been quashed shall be considered as definitive in respect of the parties to the litigation.

Article 62

In the cases provided for in Article 256(2) and (3) of the Treaty on the Functioning of the European Union, where the First Advocate-General considers that there is a serious risk of the unity or consistency of Union law being affected, he may propose that the Court of Justice review the decision of the General Court.

The proposal must be made within one month of delivery of the decision by the General Court. Within one month of receiving the proposal made by the First Advocate-General, the Court of Justice shall decide whether or not the decision should be reviewed.

Article 62a

The Court of Justice shall give a ruling on the questions which are subject to review by means of an urgent procedure on the basis of the file forwarded to it by the General Court.

Those referred to in Article 23 of this Statute and, in the cases provided for in Article 256(2) of the EC Treaty, the parties to the proceedings before the General Court shall be entitled to lodge statements or written observations with the Court of Justice relating to questions which are subject to review within a period prescribed for that purpose.

The Court of Justice may decide to open the oral procedure before giving a ruling.

Article 62b

In the cases provided for in Article 256(2) of the Treaty on the Functioning of the European Union, without prejudice to Articles 278 and 279 of the Treaty on the Functioning of the European Union, proposals for review and decisions to open the review procedure shall not have suspensory effect. If the Court of Justice finds that the decision of the General Court affects the unity or consistency of Union law, it shall refer the case back to the General Court which shall be bound by the points of law decided by the Court of Justice; the Court of Justice may state which of the effects of the decision of the General Court are to be considered as definitive in respect of the parties to the litigation. If, however, having regard to the result of the review, the outcome of the proceedings flows from the findings of fact on which the decision of the General Court was based, the Court of Justice shall give final judgment.

In the cases provided for in Article 256(3) of the Treaty on the Functioning of the European Union, in the absence of proposals for review or decisions to open the review procedure, the answer(s) given by the General Court to the questions submitted to it shall take effect upon expiry of the periods prescribed for that purpose in the second paragraph of Article 62. Should a review procedure be opened, the answer(s) subject to review shall take effect following that procedure, unless the Court of Justice decides otherwise. If the Court of Justice finds that the decision of the General Court affects the unity or consistency of Union law, the answer given by the Court of Justice to the questions subject to review shall be substituted for that given by the General Court.

TITLE IVA
SPECIALISED COURTS

Article 62c

The provisions relating to the jurisdiction, composition, organisation and procedure of the specialised courts established under Article 257 of the Treaty on the Functioning of the European Union are set out in an Annex to this Statute.

TITLE V
FINAL PROVISIONS

Article 63
The Rules of Procedure of the Court of Justice and of the General Court shall contain any provisions necessary for applying and, where required, supplementing this Statute.

Article 64
The rules governing the language arrangements applicable at the Court of Justice of the European Union shall be laid down by a regulation of the Council acting unanimously. This regulation shall be adopted either at the request of the Court of Justice and after consultation of the Commission and the European Parliament, or on a proposal from the Commission and after consultation of the Court of Justice and of the European Parliament.

Until those rules have been adopted, the provisions of the Rules of Procedure of the Court of Justice and of the Rules of Procedure of the General Court governing language arrangements shall continue to apply. By way of derogation from Articles 253 and 254 of the Treaty on the Functioning of the European Union, those provisions may only be amended or repealed with the unanimous consent of the Council.

ANNEX I (omitted).
(1)   Article inserted by Decision 2008/79/EC, Euratom (OJ L 24, 29.1.2008, p. 42).

PROTOCOL (NO 8) RELATING TO ARTICLE 6(2) OF THE TREATY ON EUROPEAN UNION ON THE ACCESSION OF THE UNION TO THE EUROPEAN CONVENTION ON THE PROTECTION OF HUMAN RIGHTS AND FUNDAMENTAL FREEDOMS

THE HIGH CONTRACTING PARTIES,

HAVE AGREED UPON the following provisions, which shall be annexed to the Treaty on European Union and to the Treaty on the Functioning of the European Union:

Article 1
The agreement relating to the accession of the Union to the European Convention on the Protection of Human Rights and Fundamental Freedoms (hereinafter referred to as the 'European Convention') provided for in Article 6(2) of the Treaty on European Union shall make provision for preserving the specific characteristics of the Union and Union law, in particular with regard to:
(a)   the specific arrangements for the Union's possible participation in the control bodies of the European Convention;

(b)   the mechanisms necessary to ensure that proceedings by non-Member States and individual applications are correctly addressed to Member States and/or the Union as appropriate.

Article 2
The agreement referred to in Article 1 shall ensure that accession of the Union shall not affect the competences of the Union or the powers of its institutions. It shall ensure that nothing therein affects the situation of Member States in relation to the European Convention, in particular in relation to the Protocols thereto, measures taken by Member States derogating from the European Convention in accordance with Article 15 thereof and reservations to the European Convention made by Member States in accordance with Article 57 thereof.

Article 3
Nothing in the agreement referred to in Article 1 shall affect Article 344 of the Treaty on the Functioning of the European Union.

PROTOCOL (NO 9) ON THE DECISION OF THE COUNCIL RELATING TO THE IMPLEMENTATION OF ARTICLE 16(4) OF THE TREATY ON EUROPEAN UNION AND ARTICLE 238(2) OF THE TREATY ON THE FUNCTIONING OF THE EUROPEAN UNION BETWEEN 1 NOVEMBER 2014 AND 31 MARCH 2017 ON THE ONE HAND, AND AS FROM 1 APRIL 2017 ON THE OTHER

THE HIGH CONTRACTING PARTIES,

TAKING INTO ACCOUNT the fundamental importance that agreeing on the Decision of the Council relating to the implementation of Article 16(4) of the Treaty on European Union and Article 238(2) of the Treaty on the Functioning of the European Union between 1 November 2014 and 31 March 2017 on the one hand, and as from 1 April 2017 on the other (hereinafter 'the Decision'), had when approving the Treaty of Lisbon,

HAVE AGREED UPON the following provisions, which shall be annexed to the Treaty on European Union and to the Treaty on the Functioning of the European Union:

Sole Article
Before the examination by the Council of any draft which would aim either at amending or abrogating the Decision or any of its provisions, or at modifying indirectly its scope or its meaning through the modification of another legal act of the Union, the European Council shall hold a preliminary deliberation on the said draft, acting by consensus in accordance with Article 15(4) of the Treaty on European Union.

PROTOCOL (NO 12) ON THE EXCESSIVE DEFICIT PROCEDURE

THE HIGH CONTRACTING PARTIES,

DESIRING TO lay down the details of the excessive deficit procedure referred to in Article 126 of the Treaty on the Functioning of the European Union,

HAVE AGREED upon the following provisions, which shall be annexed to the Treaty on European Union and to the Treaty on the Functioning of the European Union:

Article 1
The reference values referred to in Article 126(2) of the Treaty on the Functioning of the European Union are:
—   3 % for the ratio of the planned or actual government deficit to gross domestic product at market prices;

—   60 % for the ratio of government debt to gross domestic product at market prices.

Article 2
In Article 126 of the said Treaty and in this Protocol:
—   'government' means general government, that is central government, regional or local government and social security funds, to the exclusion of commercial operations, as defined in the European System of Integrated Economic Accounts;

—   'deficit' means net borrowing as defined in the European System of Integrated Economic Accounts;

—   'investment' means gross fixed capital formation as defined in the European System of Integrated Economic Accounts;

—   'debt' means total gross debt at nominal value outstanding at the end of the year and consolidated between and within the sectors of general government as defined in the first indent.

Article 3
In order to ensure the effectiveness of the excessive deficit procedure, the governments of the Member States shall be responsible under this procedure for the deficits of general government as defined in the first indent of Article 2. The Member States shall ensure that national procedures in the budgetary area enable them to meet their obligations in this area deriving from these Treaties. The Member States shall report their planned and actual deficits and the levels of their debt promptly and regularly to the Commission.

Article 4
The statistical data to be used for the application of this Protocol shall be provided by the Commission.

PROTOCOL (NO 13) ON THE CONVERGENCE CRITERIA

THE HIGH CONTRACTING PARTIES,

DESIRING to lay down the details of the convergence criteria which shall guide the Union in taking decisions to end the derogations of those Member States with a derogation, referred to in Article 140 of the Treaty on the Functioning of the European Union,

HAVE AGREED upon the following provisions, which shall be annexed to the Treaty on European Union and to the Treaty on the Functioning of the European Union:

Article 1
The criterion on price stability referred to in the first indent of Article 140(1) of the Treaty on the Functioning of the European Union shall mean that a Member State has a price performance that is sustainable and an average rate of inflation, observed over a period of one year before the examination, that does not exceed by more than 1½ percentage points that of, at most, the three best performing Member States in terms of price stability. Inflation shall be measured by means of the consumer price index on a comparable basis taking into account differences in national definitions.

Article 2
The criterion on the government budgetary position referred to in the second indent of Article 140(1) of the said Treaty shall mean that at the time of the examination the Member State is not the subject of a Council decision under Article 126(6) of the said Treaty that an excessive deficit exists.

Article 3
The criterion on participation in the Exchange Rate mechanism of the European Monetary System referred to in the third indent of Article 140(1) of the said Treaty shall mean that a Member State has respected the normal fluctuation margins provided for by the exchange-rate mechanism on the European Monetary System without severe tensions for at least the last two years before the examination. In particular, the Member State shall not have devalued its currency's bilateral central rate against the euro on its own initiative for the same period.

Article 4

The criterion on the convergence of interest rates referred to in the fourth indent of Article 140(1) of the said Treaty shall mean that, observed over a period of one year before the examination, a Member State has had an average nominal long-term interest rate that does not exceed by more than two percentage points that of, at most, the three best performing Member States in terms of price stability. Interest rates shall be measured on the basis of long-term government bonds or comparable securities, taking into account differences in national definitions.

Article 5

The statistical data to be used for the application of this Protocol shall be provided by the Commission.

Article 6

The Council shall, acting unanimously on a proposal from the Commission and after consulting the European Parliament, the ECB and the Economic and Financial Committee, adopt appropriate provisions to lay down the details of the convergence criteria referred to in Article 140(1) of the said Treaty, which shall then replace this Protocol.

PROTOCOL (NO 14) ON THE EURO GROUP

THE HIGH CONTRACTING PARTIES,

DESIRING to promote conditions for stronger economic growth in the European Union and, to that end, to develop ever-closer coordination of economic policies within the euro area,

CONSCIOUS of the need to lay down special provisions for enhanced dialogue between the Member States whose currency is the euro, pending the euro becoming the currency of all Member States of the Union,

HAVE AGREED UPON the following provisions, which shall be annexed to the Treaty on European Union and to the Treaty on the Functioning of the European Union:

Article 1

The Ministers of the Member States whose currency is the euro shall meet informally. Such meetings shall take place, when necessary, to discuss questions related to the specific responsibilities they share with regard to the single currency. The Commission shall take part in the meetings. The European Central Bank shall be invited to take part in such meetings, which shall be prepared by the representatives of the Ministers with responsibility for finance of the Member States whose currency is the euro and of the Commission.

Article 2

The Ministers of the Member States whose currency is the euro shall elect a president for two and a half years, by a majority of those Member States.

PROTOCOL (NO 15) ON CERTAIN PROVISIONS RELATING TO THE UNITED KINGDOM OF GREAT BRITAIN AND NORTHERN IRELAND

THE HIGH CONTRACTING PARTIES,

RECOGNISING that the United Kingdom shall not be obliged or committed to adopt the euro without a separate decision to do so by its government and parliament,

GIVEN that on 16 October 1996 and 30 October 1997 the United Kingdom government notified the Council of its intention not to participate in the third stage of economic and monetary union,

NOTING the practice of the government of the United Kingdom to fund its borrowing requirement by the sale of debt to the private sector,

HAVE AGREED upon the following provisions, which shall be annexed to the Treaty on European Union and to the Treaty on the Functioning of the European Union:

1.   Unless the United Kingdom notifies the Council that it intends to adopt the euro, it shall be under no obligation to do so.

2.   In view of the notice given to the Council by the United Kingdom government on 16 October 1996 and 30 October 1997, paragraphs 3 to 8 and 10 shall apply to the United Kingdom.

3.   The United Kingdom shall retain its powers in the field of monetary policy according to national law.

4.   Articles 119, second paragraph, 126(1), (9) and (11), 127(1) to (5), 128, 130, 131, 132, 133, 138, 140(3), 219, 282(2), with the exception of the first and last sentences thereof, 282(5), and 283 of the Treaty on the Functioning of the European Union shall not apply to the United Kingdom. The same applies to Article 121(2) of this Treaty as regards the adoption of the parts of the broad economic policy guidelines which concern the euro area generally. In these provisions references to the Union or the Member States shall not include the United Kingdom and references to national central banks shall not include the Bank of England.

5.   The United Kingdom shall endeavour to avoid an excessive government deficit.

Articles 143 and 144 of the Treaty on the Functioning of the European Union shall continue to apply to the United Kingdom. Articles 134(4) and 142 shall apply to the United Kingdom as if it had a derogation.

6.   The voting rights of the United Kingdom shall be suspended in respect of acts of the Council referred to in the Articles listed in paragraph 4 and in the instances referred to in the first subparagraph of Article 139(4) of the Treaty on the Functioning of the European Union. For this purpose the second subparagraph of Article 139(4) of the Treaty shall apply.

The United Kingdom shall also have no right to participate in the appointment of the President, the Vice-President and the other members of the Executive Board of the ECB under the second subparagraph of Article 283(2) of the said Treaty.

7.   Articles 3, 4, 6, 7, 9.2, 10.1, 10.3, 11.2, 12.1, 14, 16, 18 to 20, 22, 23, 26, 27, 30 to 34 and 49 of the Protocol on the Statute of the European System of Central Banks and of the European Central Bank ('the Statute') shall not apply to the United Kingdom.

In those Articles, references to the Union or the Member States shall not include the United Kingdom and references to national central banks or shareholders shall not include the Bank of England.

References in Articles 10.3 and 30.2 of the Statute to 'subscribed capital of the ECB' shall not include capital subscribed by the Bank of England.

8.   Article 141(1) of the Treaty on the Functioning of the European Union and Articles 43 to 47 of the Statute shall have effect, whether or not there is any Member State with a derogation, subject to the following amendments:

(a) References in Article 43 to the tasks of the ECB and the EMI shall include those tasks that still need to be performed in the third stage owing to any decision of the United Kingdom not to adopt the euro.

(b) In addition to the tasks referred to in Article 46, the ECB shall also give advice in relation to and contribute to the preparation of any decision of the Council with regard to the United Kingdom taken in accordance with paragraphs 9(a) and 9(c).

(c) The Bank of England shall pay up its subscription to the capital of the ECB as a contribution to its operational costs on the same basis as national central banks of Member States with a derogation.

9. The United Kingdom may notify the Council at any time of its intention to adopt the euro. In that event:

(a) The United Kingdom shall have the right to adopt the euro provided only that it satisfies the necessary conditions. The Council, acting at the request of the United Kingdom and under the conditions and in accordance with the procedure laid down in Article 140(1) and (2) of the Treaty on the Functioning of the European Union, shall decide whether it fulfils the necessary conditions.

(b) The Bank of England shall pay up its subscribed capital, transfer to the ECB foreign reserve assets and contribute to its reserves on the same basis as the national central bank of a Member State whose derogation has been abrogated.

(c) The Council, acting under the conditions and in accordance with the procedure laid down in Article 140(3) of the said Treaty, shall take all other necessary decisions to enable the United Kingdom to adopt the euro.

If the United Kingdom adopts the euro pursuant to the provisions of this Protocol, paragraphs 3 to 8 shall cease to have effect.

10. Notwithstanding Article 123 of the Treaty on the Functioning of the European Union and Article 21.1 of the Statute, the Government of the United Kingdom may maintain its 'ways and means' facility with the Bank of England if and so long as the United Kingdom does not adopt the euro.

PROTOCOL (NO 19) ON THE SCHENGEN *ACQUIS* INTEGRATED INTO THE FRAMEWORK OF THE EUROPEAN UNION

THE HIGH CONTRACTING PARTIES,

NOTING that the Agreements on the gradual abolition of checks at common borders signed by some Member States of the European Union in Schengen on 14 June 1985 and on 19 June 1990, as well as related agreements and the rules adopted on the basis of these agreements, have been integrated into the framework of the European Union by the Treaty of Amsterdam of 2 October 1997,

DESIRING to preserve the Schengen *acquis*, as developed since the entry into force of the Treaty of Amsterdam, and to develop this *acquis* in order to contribute towards achieving the objective of offering citizens of the Union an area of freedom, security and justice without internal borders,

TAKING INTO ACCOUNT the special position of Denmark,

TAKING INTO ACCOUNT the fact that Ireland and the United Kingdom of Great Britain and Northern Ireland do not participate in all the provisions of the Schengen *acquis*; that provision should, however, be made to allow those Member States to accept other provisions of this *acquis* in full or in part,

RECOGNISING that, as a consequence, it is necessary to make use of the provisions of the Treaties concerning closer cooperation between some Member States,

TAKING INTO ACCOUNT the need to maintain a special relationship with the Republic of Iceland and the Kingdom of Norway, both States being bound by the provisions of the Nordic passport union, together with the Nordic States which are members of the European Union,

HAVE AGREED UPON the following provisions, which shall be annexed to the Treaty on European Union and to the Treaty on the Functioning of the European Union:

Article 1

The Kingdom of Belgium, the Republic of Bulgaria, the Czech Republic, the Kingdom of Denmark, the Federal Republic of Germany, the Republic of Estonia, the Hellenic Republic, the Kingdom of Spain, the French Republic, the Italian Republic, the Republic of Cyprus, the Republic of Latvia, the Republic of Lithuania, the Grand Duchy of Luxembourg, the Republic of Hungary, Malta, the Kingdom of the Netherlands, the Republic of Austria, the Republic of Poland, the Portuguese Republic, Romania, the Republic of Slovenia, the Slovak Republic, the Republic of Finland and the Kingdom of Sweden shall be authorised to establish closer cooperation among themselves in areas covered by provisions defined by the Council which constitute the Schengen *acquis*. This cooperation shall be conducted within the institutional and legal framework of the European Union and with respect for the relevant provisions of the Treaties.

Article 2

The Schengen *acquis* shall apply to the Member States referred to in Article 1, without prejudice to Article 3 of the Act of Accession of 16 April 2003 or to Article 4 of the Act of Accession of 25 April 2005. The Council will substitute itself for the Executive Committee established by the Schengen agreements.

Article 3

The participation of Denmark in the adoption of measures constituting a development of the Schengen *acquis*, as well as the implementation of these measures and their application to Denmark, shall be governed by the relevant provisions of the Protocol on the position of Denmark.

Article 4

Ireland and the United Kingdom of Great Britain and Northern Ireland may at any time request to take part in some or all of the provisions of the Schengen *acquis*.

The Council shall decide on the request with the unanimity of its members referred to in Article 1 and of the representative of the Government of the State concerned.

Article 5

1. Proposals and initiatives to build upon the Schengen *acquis* shall be subject to the relevant provisions of the Treaties.

   In this context, where either Ireland or the United Kingdom has not notified the Council in writing within a reasonable period that it wishes to take part, the authorisation referred to in Article 329 of the Treaty on the Functioning of the European Union shall be deemed to have been granted to the Member States referred to in Article 1 and to Ireland or the United Kingdom where either of them wishes to take part in the areas of cooperation in question.

2. Where either Ireland or the United Kingdom is deemed to have given notification pursuant to a decision under Article 4, it may nevertheless notify the Council in writing, within three months, that it does not wish to take part in such a proposal or initiative. In that case, Ireland or the United Kingdom shall not take part in its adoption.

As from the latter notification, the procedure for adopting the measure building upon the Schengen *acquis* shall be suspended until the end of the procedure set out in paragraphs 3 or 4 or until the notification is withdrawn at any moment during that procedure.

3. For the Member State having made the notification referred to in paragraph 2, any decision taken by the Council pursuant to Article 4 shall, as from the date of entry into force of the proposed measure, cease to apply to the extent considered necessary by the Council and under the conditions to be determined in a decision of the Council acting by a qualified majority on a proposal from the Commission. That decision shall be taken in accordance with the following criteria: the Council shall seek to retain the widest possible measure of participation of the Member State concerned without seriously affecting the practical operability of the various parts of the Schengen *acquis*, while respecting their coherence. The Commission shall submit its proposal as soon as possible after the notification referred to in paragraph 2. The Council shall, if needed after convening two successive meetings, act within four months of the Commission proposal.

4. If, by the end of the period of four months, the Council has not adopted a decision, a Member State may, without delay, request that the matter be referred to the European Council. In that case, the European Council shall, at its next meeting, acting by a qualified majority on a proposal from the Commission, take a decision in accordance with the criteria referred to in paragraph 3.

5. If, by the end of the procedure set out in paragraphs 3 or 4, the Council or, as the case may be, the European Council has not adopted its decision, the suspension of the procedure for adopting the measure building upon the Schengen *acquis* shall be terminated. If the said measure is subsequently adopted any decision taken by the Council pursuant to Article 4 shall, as from the date of entry into force of that measure, cease to apply for the Member State concerned to the extent and under the conditions decided by the Commission, unless the said Member State has withdrawn its notification referred to in paragraph 2 before the adoption of the measure. The Commission shall act by the date of this adoption. When taking its decision, the Commission shall respect the criteria referred to in paragraph 3.

Article 6
The Republic of Iceland and the Kingdom of Norway shall be associated with the implementation of the Schengen *acquis* and its further development. Appropriate procedures shall be agreed to that effect in an Agreement to be concluded with those States by the Council, acting by the unanimity of its Members mentioned in Article 1. Such Agreement shall include provisions on the contribution of Iceland and Norway to any financial consequences resulting from the implementation of this Protocol.

A separate Agreement shall be concluded with Iceland and Norway by the Council, acting unanimously, for the establishment of rights and obligations between Ireland and the United Kingdom of Great Britain and Northern Ireland on the one hand, and Iceland and Norway on the other, in domains of the Schengen *acquis* which apply to these States.

Article 7
For the purposes of the negotiations for the admission of new Member States into the European Union, the Schengen *acquis* and further measures taken by the institutions within its scope shall be regarded as an *acquis* which must be accepted in full by all States candidates for admission.

PROTOCOL (NO 20) ON THE APPLICATION OF CERTAIN ASPECTS OF
ARTICLE 26 OF THE TREATY ON THE FUNCTIONING OF THE EUROPEAN UNION
TO THE UNITED KINGDOM AND TO IRELAND

THE HIGH CONTRACTING PARTIES,

DESIRING to settle certain questions relating to the United Kingdom and Ireland,

HAVING REGARD to the existence for many years of special travel arrangements between the
United Kingdom and Ireland,

HAVE AGREED UPON the following provisions, which shall be annexed to the Treaty on
European Union and the Treaty on the Functioning of the European Union:

Article 1
The United Kingdom shall be entitled, notwithstanding Articles 26 and 77 of the Treaty on the
Functioning of the European Union, any other provision of that Treaty or of the Treaty on
European Union, any measure adopted under those Treaties, or any international agreement
concluded by the Union or by the Union and its Member States with one or more third States,
to exercise at its frontiers with other Member States such controls on persons seeking to enter
the United Kingdom as it may consider necessary for the purpose:
(a)   of verifying the right to enter the United Kingdom of citizens of Member States and of
       their dependants exercising rights conferred by Union law, as well as citizens of other
       States on whom such rights have been conferred by an agreement by which the United
       Kingdom is bound; and

(b)   of determining whether or not to grant other persons permission to enter the United
       Kingdom.

Nothing in Articles 26 and 77 of the Treaty on the Functioning of the European Union or in any
other provision of that Treaty or of the Treaty on European Union or in any measure adopted
under them shall prejudice the right of the United Kingdom to adopt or exercise any such
controls. References to the United Kingdom in this Article shall include territories for whose
external relations the United Kingdom is responsible.

Article 2
The United Kingdom and Ireland may continue to make arrangements between themselves
relating to the movement of persons between their territories ('the Common Travel Area'), while
fully respecting the rights of persons referred to in Article 1, first paragraph, point (a) of this
Protocol.

Accordingly, as long as they maintain such arrangements, the provisions of Article 1 of this
Protocol shall apply to Ireland under the same terms and conditions as for the United Kingdom.
Nothing in Articles 26 and 77 of the Treaty on the Functioning of the European Union, in any
other provision of that Treaty or of the Treaty on European Union or in any measure adopted
under them, shall affect any such arrangements.

Article 3
The other Member States shall be entitled to exercise at their frontiers or at any point of entry
into their territory such controls on persons seeking to enter their territory from the United
Kingdom or any territories whose external relations are under its responsibility for the same
purposes stated in Article 1 of this Protocol, or from Ireland as long as the provisions of
Article 1 of this Protocol apply to Ireland.

Nothing in Articles 26 and 77 of the Treaty on the Functioning of the European Union or in any other provision of that Treaty or of the Treaty on European Union or in any measure adopted under them shall prejudice the right of the other Member States to adopt or exercise any such controls.

PROTOCOL (NO 21) ON THE POSITION OF THE UNITED KINGDOM AND IRELAND IN RESPECT OF THE AREA OF FREEDOM, SECURITY AND JUSTICE

THE HIGH CONTRACTING PARTIES,

DESIRING to settle certain questions relating to the United Kingdom and Ireland,

HAVING REGARD to the Protocol on the application of certain aspects of Article 26 of the Treaty on the Functioning of the European Union to the United Kingdom and to Ireland,

HAVE AGREED UPON the following provisions, which shall be annexed to the Treaty on European Union and the Treaty on the Functioning of the European Union:

Article 1
Subject to Article 3, the United Kingdom and Ireland shall not take part in the adoption by the Council of proposed measures pursuant to Title V of Part Three of the Treaty on the Functioning of the European Union. The unanimity of the members of the Council, with the exception of the representatives of the governments of the United Kingdom and Ireland, shall be necessary for decisions of the Council which must be adopted unanimously.

For the purposes of this Article, a qualified majority shall be defined in accordance with Article 238(3) of the Treaty on the Functioning of the European Union.

Article 2
In consequence of Article 1 and subject to Articles 3, 4 and 6, none of the provisions of Title V of Part Three of the Treaty on the Functioning of the European Union, no measure adopted pursuant to that Title, no provision of any international agreement concluded by the Union pursuant to that Title, and no decision of the Court of Justice interpreting any such provision or measure shall be binding upon or applicable in the United Kingdom or Ireland; and no such provision, measure or decision shall in any way affect the competences, rights and obligations of those States; and no such provision, measure or decision shall in any way affect the Community or Union *acquis* nor form part of Union law as they apply to the United Kingdom or Ireland.

Article 3
1. The United Kingdom or Ireland may notify the President of the Council in writing, within three months after a proposal or initiative has been presented to the Council pursuant to Title V of Part Three of the Treaty on the Functioning of the European Union, that it wishes to take part in the adoption and application of any such proposed measure, whereupon that State shall be entitled to do so.

    The unanimity of the members of the Council, with the exception of a member which has not made such a notification, shall be necessary for decisions of the Council which must be adopted unanimously. A measure adopted under this paragraph shall be binding upon all Member States which took part in its adoption.

    Measures adopted pursuant to Article 70 of the Treaty on the Functioning of the European Union shall lay down the conditions for the participation of the United Kingdom and Ireland in the evaluations concerning the areas covered by Title V of Part Three of that Treaty.

For the purposes of this Article, a qualified majority shall be defined in accordance with Article 238(3) of the Treaty on the Functioning of the European Union.

2. If after a reasonable period of time a measure referred to in paragraph 1 cannot be adopted with the United Kingdom or Ireland taking part, the Council may adopt such measure in accordance with Article 1 without the participation of the United Kingdom or Ireland. In that case Article 2 applies.

Article 4

The United Kingdom or Ireland may at any time after the adoption of a measure by the Council pursuant to Title V of Part Three of the Treaty on the Functioning of the European Union notify its intention to the Council and to the Commission that it wishes to accept that measure. In that case, the procedure provided for in Article 331(1) of the Treaty on the Functioning of the European Union shall apply mutatis mutandis.

Article 4a

1. The provisions of this Protocol apply for the United Kingdom and Ireland also to measures proposed or adopted pursuant to Title V of Part Three of the Treaty on the Functioning of the European Union amending an existing measure by which they are bound.

2. However, in cases where the Council, acting on a proposal from the Commission, determines that the non-participation of the United Kingdom or Ireland in the amended version of an existing measure makes the application of that measure inoperable for other Member States or the Union, it may urge them to make a notification under Article 3 or 4. For the purposes of Article 3, a further period of two months starts to run as from the date of such determination by the Council.

    If at the expiry of that period of two months from the Council's determination the United Kingdom or Ireland has not made a notification under Article 3 or Article 4, the existing measure shall no longer be binding upon or applicable to it, unless the Member State concerned has made a notification under Article 4 before the entry into force of the amending measure. This shall take effect from the date of entry into force of the amending measure or of expiry of the period of two months, whichever is the later.

    For the purpose of this paragraph, the Council shall, after a full discussion of the matter, act by a qualified majority of its members representing the Member States participating or having participated in the adoption of the amending measure. A qualified majority of the Council shall be defined in accordance with Article 238(3)(a) of the Treaty on the Functioning of the European Union.

3. The Council, acting by a qualified majority on a proposal from the Commission, may determine that the United Kingdom or Ireland shall bear the direct financial consequences, if any, necessarily and unavoidably incurred as a result of the cessation of its participation in the existing measure.

4. This Article shall be without prejudice to Article 4.

Article 5

A Member State which is not bound by a measure adopted pursuant to Title V of Part Three of the Treaty on the Functioning of the European Union shall bear no financial consequences of that measure other than administrative costs entailed for the institutions, unless all members of the Council, acting unanimously after consulting the European Parliament, decide otherwise.

Article 6

Where, in cases referred to in this Protocol, the United Kingdom or Ireland is bound by a measure adopted by the Council pursuant to Title V of Part Three of the Treaty on the Functioning of the European Union, the relevant provisions of the Treaties shall apply to that State in relation to that measure.

Article 6a

The United Kingdom and Ireland shall not be bound by the rules laid down on the basis of Article 16 of the Treaty on the Functioning of the European Union which relate to the processing of personal data by the Member States when carrying out activities which fall within the scope of Chapter 4 or Chapter 5 of Title V of Part Three of that Treaty where the United Kingdom and Ireland are not bound by the rules governing the forms of judicial cooperation in criminal matters or police cooperation which require compliance with the provisions laid down on the basis of Article 16.

Article 7

Articles 3, 4 and 4a shall be without prejudice to the Protocol on the Schengen *acquis* integrated into the framework of the European Union.

Article 8

Ireland may notify the Council in writing that it no longer wishes to be covered by the terms of this Protocol. In that case, the normal treaty provisions will apply to Ireland.

Article 9

With regard to Ireland, this Protocol shall not apply to Article 75 of the Treaty on the Functioning of the European Union.

PROTOCOL (NO 23) ON EXTERNAL RELATIONS OF THE MEMBER STATES WITH REGARD TO THE CROSSING OF EXTERNAL BORDERS

THE HIGH CONTRACTING PARTIES,

TAKING INTO ACCOUNT the need of the Member States to ensure effective controls at their external borders, in cooperation with third countries where appropriate,

HAVE AGREED UPON the following provisions, which shall be annexed to the Treaty on European Union and to the Treaty on the Functioning of the European Union:

The provisions on the measures on the crossing of external borders included in Article 77(2)(b) of the Treaty on the Functioning of the European Union shall be without prejudice to the competence of Member States to negotiate or conclude agreements with third countries as long as they respect Union law and other relevant international agreements.

PROTOCOL (NO 24) ON ASYLUM FOR NATIONALS OF MEMBER STATES OF THE EUROPEAN UNION

THE HIGH CONTRACTING PARTIES,

WHEREAS, in accordance with Article 6(1) of the Treaty on European Union, the Union recognises the rights, freedoms and principles set out in the Charter of Fundamental Rights,

WHEREAS pursuant to Article 6(3) of the Treaty on European Union, fundamental rights, as guaranteed by the European Convention for the Protection of Human Rights and Fundamental Freedoms, constitute part of the Union's law as general principles,

WHEREAS the Court of Justice of the European Union has jurisdiction to ensure that in the interpretation and application of Article 6, paragraphs (1) and (3) of the Treaty on European Union the law is observed by the European Union,

WHEREAS pursuant to Article 49 of the Treaty on European Union any European State, when applying to become a Member of the Union, must respect the values set out in Article 2 of the Treaty on European Union,

BEARING IN MIND that Article 7 of the Treaty on European Union establishes a mechanism for the suspension of certain rights in the event of a serious and persistent breach by a Member State of those values,

RECALLING that each national of a Member State, as a citizen of the Union, enjoys a special status and protection which shall be guaranteed by the Member States in accordance with the provisions of Part Two of the Treaty on the Functioning of the European Union,

BEARING IN MIND that the Treaties establish an area without internal frontiers and grant every citizen of the Union the right to move and reside freely within the territory of the Member States,

WISHING to prevent the institution of asylum being resorted to for purposes alien to those for which it is intended,

WHEREAS this Protocol respects the finality and the objectives of the Geneva Convention of 28 July 1951 relating to the status of refugees,

HAVE AGREED UPON the following provisions, which shall be annexed to the Treaty on European Union and to the Treaty on the Functioning of the European Union:

Sole Article
Given the level of protection of fundamental rights and freedoms by the Member States of the European Union, Member States shall be regarded as constituting safe countries of origin in respect of each other for all legal and practical purposes in relation to asylum matters. Accordingly, any application for asylum made by a national of a Member State may be taken into consideration or declared admissible for processing by another Member State only in the following cases:

(a)   if the Member State of which the applicant is a national proceeds after the entry into force of the Treaty of Amsterdam, availing itself of the provisions of Article 15 of the European Convention for the Protection of Human Rights and Fundamental Freedoms, to take measures derogating in its territory from its obligations under that Convention;

(b)   if the procedure referred to Article 7(1) of the Treaty on European Union has been initiated and until the Council, or, where appropriate, the European Council, takes a decision in respect thereof with regard to the Member State of which the applicant is a national;

(c)   if the Council has adopted a decision in accordance with Article 7(1) of the Treaty on European Union in respect of the Member State of which the applicant is a national or if the European Council has adopted a decision in accordance with Article 7(2) of that Treaty in respect of the Member State of which the applicant is a national;

(d)   if a Member State should so decide unilaterally in respect of the application of a national of another Member State; in that case the Council shall be immediately informed; the application shall be dealt with on the basis of the presumption that it is manifestly unfounded without affecting in any way, whatever the cases may be, the decision-making power of the Member State.

PROTOCOL (No 25) ON THE EXERCISE OF SHARED COMPETENCE

THE HIGH CONTRACTING PARTIES,

HAVE AGREED UPON the following provisions, which shall be annexed to the Treaty on European Union and to the Treaty on the Functioning of the European Union:

Sole Article
With reference to Article 2(2) of the Treaty on the Functioning of the European Union on shared competence, when the Union has taken action in a certain area, the scope of this exercise of competence only covers those elements governed by the Union act in question and therefore does not cover the whole area.

PROTOCOL (NO 26) ON SERVICES OF GENERAL INTEREST

THE HIGH CONTRACTING PARTIES,

WISHING to emphasise the importance of services of general interest,

HAVE AGREED UPON the following interpretative provisions, which shall be annexed to the Treaty on European Union and to the Treaty on the Functioning of the European Union:

Article 1
The shared values of the Union in respect of services of general economic interest within the meaning of Article 14 of the Treaty on the Functioning of the European Union include in particular:
— 	the essential role and the wide discretion of national, regional and local authorities in providing, commissioning and organising services of general economic interest as closely as possible to the needs of the users;

— 	the diversity between various services of general economic interest and the differences in the needs and preferences of users that may result from different geographical, social or cultural situations;

— 	a high level of quality, safety and affordability, equal treatment and the promotion of universal access and of user rights.

Article 2
The provisions of the Treaties do not affect in any way the competence of Member States to provide, commission and organise non-economic services of general interest.

PROTOCOL (No 27) ON THE INTERNAL MARKET AND COMPETITION

THE HIGH CONTRACTING PARTIES,

CONSIDERING that the internal market as set out in Article 3 of the Treaty on European Union includes a system ensuring that competition is not distorted,

HAVE AGREED that:

To this end, the Union shall, if necessary, take action under the provisions of the Treaties, including under Article 352 of the Treaty on the Functioning of the European Union.

This protocol shall be annexed to the Treaty on European Union and to the Treaty on the Functioning of the European Union.

PROTOCOL (NO 30) ON THE APPLICATION OF THE CHARTER OF FUNDAMENTAL
RIGHTS OF THE EUROPEAN UNION TO POLAND AND TO THE UNITED KINGDOM

THE HIGH CONTRACTING PARTIES,

WHEREAS in Article 6 of the Treaty on European Union, the Union recognises the rights,
freedoms and principles set out in the Charter of Fundamental Rights of the European Union,

WHEREAS the Charter is to be applied in strict accordance with the provisions of the
aforementioned Article 6 and Title VII of the Charter itself,

WHEREAS the aforementioned Article 6 requires the Charter to be applied and interpreted by
the courts of Poland and of the United Kingdom strictly in accordance with the explanations
referred to in that Article,

WHEREAS the Charter contains both rights and principles,

WHEREAS the Charter contains both provisions which are civil and political in character and
those which are economic and social in character,

WHEREAS the Charter reaffirms the rights, freedoms and principles recognised in the Union
and makes those rights more visible, but does not create new rights or principles,

RECALLING the obligations devolving upon Poland and the United Kingdom under the Treaty
on European Union, the Treaty on the Functioning of the European Union, and Union law
generally,

NOTING the wish of Poland and the United Kingdom to clarify certain aspects of the
application of the Charter,

DESIROUS therefore of clarifying the application of the Charter in relation to the laws and
administrative action of Poland and of the United Kingdom and of its justiciability within
Poland and within the United Kingdom,

REAFFIRMING that references in this Protocol to the operation of specific provisions of the
Charter are strictly without prejudice to the operation of other provisions of the Charter,

REAFFIRMING that this Protocol is without prejudice to the application of the Charter to
other Member States,

REAFFIRMING that this Protocol is without prejudice to other obligations devolving upon
Poland and the United Kingdom under the Treaty on European Union, the Treaty on the
Functioning of the European Union, and Union law generally,

HAVE AGREED UPON the following provisions, which shall be annexed to the Treaty on
European Union and to the Treaty on the Functioning of the European Union:

Article 1

1. The Charter does not extend the ability of the Court of Justice of the European Union, or
    any court or tribunal of Poland or of the United Kingdom, to find that the laws, regulations
    or administrative provisions, practices or action of Poland or of the United Kingdom are
    inconsistent with the fundamental rights, freedoms and principles that it reaffirms.

2. In particular, and for the avoidance of doubt, nothing in Title IV of the Charter creates
    justiciable rights applicable to Poland or the United Kingdom except in so far as Poland or
    the United Kingdom has provided for such rights in its national law.

Article 2

To the extent that a provision of the Charter refers to national laws and practices, it shall only
apply to Poland or the United Kingdom to the extent that the rights or principles that it
contains are recognised in the law or practices of Poland or of the United Kingdom.

PROTOCOL (NO 36) ON TRANSITIONAL PROVISIONS

THE HIGH CONTRACTING PARTIES,

WHEREAS, in order to organise the transition from the institutional provisions of the Treaties applicable prior to the entry into force of the Treaty of Lisbon to the provisions contained in that Treaty, it is necessary to lay down transitional provisions,

HAVE AGREED UPON the following provisions, which shall be annexed to the Treaty on European Union, to the Treaty on the Functioning of the European Union and to the Treaty establishing the European Atomic Energy Community:

Article 1
In this Protocol, the words 'the Treaties' shall mean the Treaty on European Union, the Treaty on the Functioning of the European Union and the Treaty establishing the European Atomic Energy Community.

TITLE I
PROVISIONS CONCERNING THE EUROPEAN PARLIAMENT

Article 2
In accordance with the second subparagraph of Article 14(2) of the Treaty on European Union, the European Council shall adopt a decision determining the composition of the European Parliament in good time before the 2009 European Parliament elections.

Until the end of the 2004–2009 parliamentary term, the composition and the number of representatives elected to the European Parliament shall remain the same as on the date of the entry into force of the Treaty of Lisbon.

TITLE II
PROVISIONS CONCERNING THE QUALIFIED MAJORITY

Article 3
1. In accordance with Article 16(4) of the Treaty on European Union, the provisions of that paragraph and of Article 238(2) of the Treaty on the Functioning of the European Union relating to the definition of the qualified majority in the European Council and the Council shall take effect on 1 November 2014.

2. Between 1 November 2014 and 31 March 2017, when an act is to be adopted by qualified majority, a member of the Council may request that it be adopted in accordance with the qualified majority as defined in paragraph 3. In that case, paragraphs 3 and 4 shall apply.

3. Until 31 October 2014, the following provisions shall remain in force, without prejudice to the second subparagraph of Article 235(1) of the Treaty on the Functioning of the European Union.

   For acts of the European Council and of the Council requiring a qualified majority, members' votes shall be weighted as follows:

Belgium 12	Luxembourg 4
Bulgaria 10	Hungary 12
Czech Republic 12	Malta 3
Denmark 7	Netherlands 13
Germany 29	Austria 10

Estonia 4	Poland 27
Ireland 7	Portugal 12
Greece 12	Romania 14
Spain 27	Slovenia 4
France 29	Slovakia 7
Italy 29	Finland 7
Cyprus 4	Sweden 10
Latvia 4	United Kingdom 29
Lithuania 7	

Acts shall be adopted if there are at least 255 votes in favour representing a majority of the members where, under the Treaties, they must be adopted on a proposal from the Commission. In other cases decisions shall be adopted if there are at least 255 votes in favour representing at least two thirds of the members.

A member of the European Council or the Council may request that, where an act is adopted by the European Council or the Council by a qualified majority, a check is made to ensure that the Member States comprising the qualified majority represent at least 62 % of the total population of the Union. If that proves not to be the case, the act shall not be adopted.

4. Until 31 October 2014, the qualified majority shall, in cases where, under the Treaties, not all the members of the Council participate in voting, namely in the cases where reference is made to the qualified majority as defined in Article 238(3) of the Treaty on the Functioning of the European Union, be defined as the same proportion of the weighted votes and the same proportion of the number of the Council members and, if appropriate, the same percentage of the population of the Member States concerned as laid down in paragraph 3 of this Article.

TITLE III
PROVISIONS CONCERNING THE CONFIGURATIONS OF THE COUNCIL

Article 4
Until the entry into force of the decision referred to in the first subparagraph of Article 16(6) of the Treaty on European Union, the Council may meet in the configurations laid down in the second and third subparagraphs of that paragraph and in the other configurations on the list established by a decision of the General Affairs Council, acting by a simple majority.

TITLE IV
PROVISIONS CONCERNING THE COMMISSION, INCLUDING
THE HIGH REPRESENTATIVE OF THE UNION FOR FOREIGN
AFFAIRS AND SECURITY POLICY

Article 5
The members of the Commission in office on the date of entry into force of the Treaty of Lisbon shall remain in office until the end of their term of office. However, on the day of the appointment of the High Representative of the Union for Foreign Affairs and Security Policy, the term of office of the member having the same nationality as the High Representative shall end.

TITLE V
PROVISIONS CONCERNING THE SECRETARY-GENERAL OF THE COUNCIL,
HIGH REPRESENTATIVE FOR THE COMMON FOREIGN AND SECURITY
POLICY, AND THE DEPUTY SECRETARY-GENERAL OF THE COUNCIL

Article 6
The terms of office of the Secretary-General of the Council, High Representative for the common foreign and security policy, and the Deputy Secretary-General of the Council shall end on the date

of entry into force of the Treaty of Lisbon. The Council shall appoint a Secretary-General in conformity with Article 240(2) of the Treaty on the Functioning of the European Union.

TITLE VI
PROVISIONS CONCERNING ADVISORY BODIES

Article 7
Until the entry into force of the decision referred to in Article 301 of the Treaty on the Functioning of the European Union, the allocation of members of the Economic and Social Committee shall be as follows:

Belgium 12	Spain 21
Bulgaria 12	France 24
Czech Republic 12	Italy 24
Denmark 9	Cyprus 6
Germany 24	Latvia 7
Estonia 7	Lithuania 9
Ireland 9	Luxembourg 6
Greece 12	Hungary 12
Malta 5	Slovenia 7
Netherlands 12	Slovakia 9
Austria 12	Finland 9
Poland 21	Sweden 12
Portugal 12	United Kingdom 24
Romania 15	

Article 8
Until the entry into force of the decision referred to in Article 305 of the Treaty on the Functioning of the European Union, the allocation of members of the Committee of the Regions shall be as follows:

Belgium 12	Luxembourg 6
Bulgaria 12	Hungary 12
Czech Republic 12	Malta 5
Denmark 9	Netherlands 12
Germany 24	Austria 12
Estonia 7	Poland 21
Ireland 9	Portugal 12
Greece 12	Romania 15
Spain 21	Slovenia 7
France 24	Slovakia 9
Italy 24	Finland 9
Cyprus 6	Sweden 12
Latvia 7	United Kingdom 24
Lithuania 9	

TITLE VII
TRANSITIONAL PROVISIONS CONCERNING ACTS ADOPTED ON THE BASIS OF TITLES V AND VI OF THE TREATY ON EUROPEAN UNION PRIOR TO THE ENTRY INTO FORCE OF THE TREATY OF LISBON

Article 9
The legal effects of the acts of the institutions, bodies, offices and agencies of the Union adopted on the basis of the Treaty on European Union prior to the entry into force of the Treaty of

Lisbon shall be preserved until those acts are repealed, annulled or amended in implementation of the Treaties. The same shall apply to agreements concluded between Member States on the basis of the Treaty on European Union.

Article 10

1.   As a transitional measure, and with respect to acts of the Union in the field of police cooperation and judicial cooperation in criminal matters which have been adopted before the entry into force of the Treaty of Lisbon, the powers of the institutions shall be the following at the date of entry into force of that Treaty: the powers of the Commission under Article 258 of the Treaty on the Functioning of the European Union shall not be applicable and the powers of the Court of Justice of the European Union under Title VI of the Treaty on European Union, in the version in force before the entry into force of the Treaty of Lisbon, shall remain the same, including where they have been accepted under Article 35(2) of the said Treaty on European Union.

2.   The amendment of an act referred to in paragraph 1 shall entail the applicability of the powers of the institutions referred to in that paragraph as set out in the Treaties with respect to the amended act for those Member States to which that amended act shall apply.

3.   In any case, the transitional measure mentioned in paragraph 1 shall cease to have effect five years after the date of entry into force of the Treaty of Lisbon.

4.   At the latest six months before the expiry of the transitional period referred to in paragraph 3, the United Kingdom may notify to the Council that it does not accept, with respect to the acts referred to in paragraph 1, the powers of the institutions referred to in paragraph 1 as set out in the Treaties. In case the United Kingdom has made that notification, all acts referred to in paragraph 1 shall cease to apply to it as from the date of expiry of the transitional period referred to in paragraph 3. This subparagraph shall not apply with respect to the amended acts which are applicable to the United Kingdom as referred to in paragraph 2.

The Council, acting by a qualified majority on a proposal from the Commission, shall determine the necessary consequential and transitional arrangements. The United Kingdom shall not participate in the adoption of this decision. A qualified majority of the Council shall be defined in accordance with Article 238(3)(a) of the Treaty on the Functioning of the European Union.

The Council, acting by a qualified majority on a proposal from the Commission, may also adopt a decision determining that the United Kingdom shall bear the direct financial consequences, if any, necessarily and unavoidably incurred as a result of the cessation of its participation in those acts.

5.   The United Kingdom may, at any time afterwards, notify the Council of its wish to participate in acts which have ceased to apply to it pursuant to paragraph 4, first subparagraph. In that case, the relevant provisions of the Protocol on the Schengen *acquis* integrated into the framework of the European Union or of the Protocol on the position of the United Kingdom and Ireland in respect of the area of freedom, security and justice, as the case may be, shall apply. The powers of the institutions with regard to those acts shall be those set out in the Treaties. When acting under the relevant Protocols, the Union institutions and the United Kingdom shall seek to re-establish the widest possible measure of participation of the United Kingdom in the *acquis* of the Union in the area of freedom, security and justice without seriously affecting the practical operability of the various parts thereof, while respecting their coherence.

DECLARATIONS ANNEXED TO THE FINAL ACT OF THE INTERGOVERNMENTAL CONFERENCE WHICH ADOPTED THE TREATY OF LISBON, SIGNED ON 13 DECEMBER 2007
OJ C83, 30.3.2010, P. 335

A. DECLARATIONS CONCERNING PROVISIONS OF THE TREATIES*

DECLARATION (NO 1) CONCERNING THE CHARTER OF FUNDAMENTAL RIGHTS OF THE EUROPEAN UNION
The Charter of Fundamental Rights of the European Union, which has legally binding force, confirms the fundamental rights guaranteed by the European Convention for the Protection of Human Rights and Fundamental Freedoms and as they result from the constitutional traditions common to the Member States.

The Charter does not extend the field of application of Union law beyond the powers of the Union or establish any new power or task for the Union, or modify powers and tasks as defined by the Treaties.

DECLARATION (NO 2) ON ARTICLE 6(2) OF THE TREATY ON EUROPEAN UNION
The Conference agrees that the Union's accession to the European Convention for the Protection of Human Rights and Fundamental Freedoms should be arranged in such a way as to preserve the specific features of Union law. In this connection, the Conference notes the

---

*   EDITOR'S NOTE: The following Declarations have been omitted: Nos 3–9, 11–12, 15–16, 19–23, 25–37, 39–40 and 43. Annexed Declarations on the Protocols (Part B) and by the Member States (Part C) have also been omitted.

existence of a regular dialogue between the Court of Justice of the European Union and the European Court of Human Rights; such dialogue could be reinforced when the Union accedes to that Convention.

DECLARATION (NO 10) ON ARTICLE 17 OF THE TREATY ON EUROPEAN UNION
The Conference considers that when the Commission no longer includes nationals of all Member States, the Commission should pay particular attention to the need to ensure full transparency in relations with all Member States. Accordingly, the Commission should liaise closely with all Member States, whether or not they have a national serving as member of the Commission, and in this context pay special attention to the need to share information and consult with all Member States.

The Conference also considers that the Commission should take all the necessary measures to ensure that political, social and economic realities in all Member States, including those which have no national serving as member of the Commission, are fully taken into account.

These measures should include ensuring that the position of those Member States is addressed by appropriate organisational arrangements.

DECLARATION (NO 13) CONCERNING THE COMMON FOREIGN AND SECURITY POLICY
The Conference underlines that the provisions in the Treaty on European Union covering the Common Foreign and Security Policy, including the creation of the office of High Representative of the Union for Foreign Affairs and Security Policy and the establishment of an External Action Service, do not affect the responsibilities of the Member States, as they currently exist, for the formulation and conduct of their foreign policy nor of their national representation in third countries and international organisations.

The Conference also recalls that the provisions governing the Common Security and Defence Policy do not prejudice the specific character of the security and defence policy of the Member States.

It stresses that the European Union and its Member States will remain bound by the provisions of the Charter of the United Nations and, in particular, by the primary responsibility of the Security Council and of its Members for the maintenance of international peace and security.

DECLARATION (NO 14) CONCERNING THE COMMON FOREIGN AND SECURITY POLICY
In addition to the specific rules and procedures referred to in paragraph 1 of Article 24 of the Treaty on European Union, the Conference underlines that the provisions covering the Common Foreign and Security Policy including in relation to the High Representative of the Union for Foreign Affairs and Security Policy and the External Action Service will not affect the existing legal basis, responsibilities, and powers of each Member State in relation to the formulation and conduct of its foreign policy, its national diplomatic service, relations with third countries and participation in international organisations, including a Member State's membership of the Security Council of the United Nations.

The Conference also notes that the provisions covering the Common Foreign and Security Policy do not give new powers to the Commission to initiate decisions nor do they increase the role of the European Parliament.

The Conference also recalls that the provisions governing the Common Security and Defence Policy do not prejudice the specific character of the security and defence policy of the Member States.

DECLARATION (NO 17) CONCERNING PRIMACY

The Conference recalls that, in accordance with well settled case law of the Court of Justice of the European Union, the Treaties and the law adopted by the Union on the basis of the Treaties have primacy over the law of Member States, under the conditions laid down by the said case law.

The Conference has also decided to attach as an Annex to this Final Act the Opinion of the Council Legal Service on the primacy of EC law as set out in 11197/07 (JUR 260):

'Opinion of the Council Legal Service of 22 June 2007

It results from the case-law of the Court of Justice that primacy of EC law is a cornerstone principle of Community law. According to the Court, this principle is inherent to the specific nature of the European Community. At the time of the first judgment of this established case law (*Costa/ENEL*, 15 July 1964, Case 6/641* there was no mention of primacy in the treaty. It is still the case today. The fact that the principle of primacy will not be included in the future treaty shall not in any way change the existence of the principle and the existing case-law of the Court of Justice.

*   "It follows (. . .) that the law stemming from the treaty, an independent source of law, could not, because of its special and original nature, be overridden by domestic legal provisions, however framed, without being deprived of its character as Community law and without the legal basis of the Community itself being called into question." '

DECLARATION (NO 18) IN RELATION TO THE DELIMITATION OF COMPETENCES

The Conference underlines that, in accordance with the system of division of competences between the Union and the Member States as provided for in the Treaty on European Union and the Treaty on the Functioning of the European Union, competences not conferred upon the Union in the Treaties remain with the Member States.

When the Treaties confer on the Union a competence shared with the Member States in a specific area, the Member States shall exercise their competence to the extent that the Union has not exercised, or has decided to cease exercising, its competence. The latter situation arises when the relevant EU institutions decide to repeal a legislative act, in particular better to ensure constant respect for the principles of subsidiarity and proportionality. The Council may, at the initiative of one or several of its members (representatives of Member States) and in accordance with Article 241 of the Treaty on the Functioning of the European Union, request the Commission to submit proposals for repealing a legislative act. The Conference welcomes the Commission's declaration that it will devote particular attention to these requests.

Equally, the representatives of the governments of the Member States, meeting in an Intergovernmental Conference, in accordance with the ordinary revision procedure provided for in Article 48(2) to (5) of the Treaty on European Union, may decide to amend the Treaties upon which the Union is founded, including either to increase or to reduce the competences conferred on the Union in the said Treaties.

DECLARATION (NO 24) CONCERNING THE LEGAL PERSONALITY OF THE EUROPEAN UNION

The Conference confirms that the fact that the European Union has a legal personality will not in any way authorise the Union to legislate or to act beyond the competences conferred upon it by the Member States in the Treaties.

DECLARATION (NO 38) ON ARTICLE 252 OF THE TREATY ON THE FUNCTIONING OF THE EUROPEAN UNION REGARDING THE NUMBER OF ADVOCATES-GENERAL IN THE COURT OF JUSTICE

The Conference declares that if, in accordance with Article 252, first paragraph, of the Treaty on the Functioning of the European Union, the Court of Justice requests that the number of

Advocates-General be increased by three (eleven instead of eight), the Council will, acting unanimously, agree on such an increase.

In that case, the Conference agrees that Poland will, as is already the case for Germany, France, Italy, Spain and the United Kingdom, have a permanent Advocate-General and no longer take part in the rotation system, while the existing rotation system will involve the rotation of five Advocates-General instead of three.

DECLARATION (NO 41) ON ARTICLE 352 OF THE TREATY ON THE FUNCTIONING OF THE EUROPEAN UNION

The Conference declares that the reference in Article 352(1) of the Treaty on the Functioning of the European Union to objectives of the Union refers to the objectives as set out in Article 3(2) and (3) of the Treaty on European Union and to the objectives of Article 3(5) of the said Treaty with respect to external action under Part Five of the Treaty on the Functioning of the European Union. It is therefore excluded that an action based on Article 352 of the Treaty on the Functioning of the European Union would only pursue objectives set out in Article 3(1) of the Treaty on European Union. In this connection, the Conference notes that in accordance with Article 31(1) of the Treaty on European Union, legislative acts may not be adopted in the area of the Common Foreign and Security Policy.

DECLARATION (NO 42) ON ARTICLE 352 OF THE TREATY ON THE FUNCTIONING OF THE EUROPEAN UNION

The Conference underlines that, in accordance with the settled case law of the Court of Justice of the European Union, Article 352 of the Treaty on the Functioning of the European Union, being an integral part of an institutional system based on the principle of conferred powers, cannot serve as a basis for widening the scope of Union powers beyond the general framework created by the provisions of the Treaties as a whole and, in particular, by those that define the tasks and the activities of the Union. In any event, this Article cannot be used as a basis for the adoption of provisions whose effect would, in substance, be to amend the Treaties without following the procedure which they provide for that purpose.

II Tables of Equivalences for Converting Treaty Numbers

CONSOLIDATED VERSION OF THE TREATY ON EUROPEAN UNION – TABLES OF EQUIVALENCES*
OJ C 83, 30.3.2010, P. 361

TREATY ON EUROPEAN UNION[1]

Old numbering of the TEU	New numbering of the TEU
TITLE I — COMMON PROVISIONS	TITLE I — COMMON PROVISIONS
Article 1	Article 1
	Article 2
Article 2	Article 3
Article 3 (repealed) (1)	
	Article 4
	Article 5 (2)
Article 4 (repealed) (3)	
Article 5 (repealed) (4)	
Article 6	Article 6
Article 7	Article 7
	Article 8
TITLE II — PROVISIONS AMENDING THE TEC WITH A VIEW TO ESTABLISHING THE EC	TITLE II — PROVISIONS ON DEMOCRATIC PRINCIPLES
Article 8 (repealed) (5)	Article 9
	Article 10 (6)
	Article 11
	Article 12
TITLE III — PROVISIONS AMENDING THE TREATY ESTABLISHING THE EUROPEAN COAL AND STEEL COMMUNITY	TITLE III — PROVISIONS ON THE INSTITUTIONS
Article 9 (repealed) (7)	Article 13

* Tables of equivalences as referred to in Article 5 of the Treaty of Lisbon. The original centre column, which set out the intermediate numbering as used in that Treaty, has been omitted.

Old numbering of the TEU	New numbering of the TEU
	Article 14 (8)
	Article 15 (9)
	Article 16 (10)
	Article 17 (11)
	Article 18
	Article 19 (12)
TITLE IV — PROVISIONS AMENDING THE TREATY ESTABLISHING THE EUROPEAN ATOMIC ENERGY COMMUNITY	TITLE IV — PROVISIONS ON ENHANCED COOPERATION
Article 10 (repealed) (13)	
Articles 27a to 27e (replaced)	
Articles 40 to 40b (replaced)	
Articles 43 to 45 (replaced)	
	Article 20 (14)
TITLE V — PROVISIONS ON A COMMON FOREIGN AND SECURITY POLICY	TITLE V — GENERAL PROVISIONS ON THE UNION'S EXTERNAL ACTION AND SPECIFIC PROVISIONS ON THE COMMON FOREIGN AND SECURITY POLICY
	Chapter 1 — General provisions on the Union's external action
	Article 21
	Article 22
	Chapter 2 — Specific provisions on the common foreign and security policy
	Section 1 — Common provisions
	Article 23
Article 11	Article 24
Article 12	Article 25
Article 13	Article 26
	Article 27
Article 14	Article 28
Article 15	Article 29
Article 22 (moved)	Article 30
Article 23 (moved)	Article 31
Article 16	Article 32
Article 17 (moved)	*Article 42*
Article 18	Article 33
Article 19	Article 34
Article 20	Article 35
Article 21	Article 36
Article 22 (moved)	*Article 30*
Article 23 (moved)	*Article 31*
Article 24	Article 37
Article 25	Article 38
	Article 39

Old numbering of the TEU	New numbering of the TEU
Article 47 (moved)	Article 40
Article 26 (repealed)	
Article 27 (repealed)	
Article 27*a* (replaced) (15)	*Article 20*
Article 27*b* (replaced) (15)	*Article 20*
Article 27*c* (replaced) (15)	*Article 20*
Article 27*d* (replaced) (15)	*Article 20*
Article 27*e* (replaced) (15)	*Article 20*
Article 28	Article 41
	Section 2 — Provisions on the common security and defence policy
Article 17 (moved)	Article 42
	Article 43
	Article 44
	Article 45
	Article 46
TITLE VI — PROVISIONS ON POLICE AND JUDICIAL COOPERATION IN CRIMINAL MATTERS (repealed) (16)	
Article 29 (replaced) (17)	
Article 30 (replaced) (18)	
Article 31 (replaced) (19)	
Article 32 (replaced) (20)	
Article 33 (replaced) (21)	
Article 34 (repealed)	
Article 35 (repealed)	
Article 36 (replaced) (22)	
Article 37 (repealed)	
Article 38 (repealed)	
Article 39 (repealed)	
Article 40 (replaced) (23)	*Article 20*
Article 40 A (replaced) (23)	*Article 20*
Article 40 B (replaced) (23)	*Article 20*
Article 41 (repealed)	
Article 42 (repealed)	
TITLE VII — PROVISIONS ON ENHANCED COOPERATION (replaced) (24)	
TITLE IV — PROVISIONS ON ENHANCED COOPERATION	
Article 43 (replaced) (24)	*Article 20*
Article 43 A (replaced) (24)	*Article 20*
Article 43 B (replaced) (24)	*Article 20*
Article 44 (replaced) (24)	*Article 20*
Article 44 A (replaced) (24)	*Article 20*
Article 45 (replaced) (24)	*Article 20*

Old numbering of the TEU	New numbering of the TEU
TITLE VIII — FINAL PROVISIONS	TITLE VI — FINAL PROVISIONS
Article 46 (repealed)	
	Article 47
Article 47 (replaced)	*Article 40*
Article 48	Article 48
Article 49	Article 49
	Article 50
	Article 51
	Article 52
Article 50 (repealed)	
Article 51	Article 53
Article 52	Article 54
Article 53	Article 55

(1) Replaced, in substance, by Article 7 of the Treaty on the Functioning of the European Union ('TFEU') and by Articles 13(1) and 21, paragraph 3, second subparagraph of the Treaty on European Union ('TEU').

(2) Replaces Article 5 of the Treaty establishing the European Community ('TEC').

(3) Replaced, in substance, by Article 15.

(4) Replaced, in substance, by Article 13, paragraph 2.

(5) Article 8 TEU, which was in force until the entry into force of the Treaty of Lisbon (hereinafter 'current'), amended the TEC. Those amendments are incorporated into the latter Treaty and Article 8 is repealed. Its number is used to insert a new provision.

(6) Paragraph 4 replaces, in substance, the first subparagraph of Article 191 TEC.

(7) The current Article 9 TEU amended the Treaty establishing the European Coal and Steel Community. This latter expired on 23 July 2002. Article 9 is repealed and the number thereof is used to insert another provision.

(8) — Paragraphs 1 and 2 replace, in substance, Article 189 TEC;
— paragraphs 1 to 3 replace, in substance, paragraphs 1 to 3 of Article 190 TEC;
— paragraph 1 replaces, in substance, the first subparagraph of Article 192 TEC;
— paragraph 4 replaces, in substance, the first subparagraph of Article 197 TEC.

(9) Replaces, in substance, Article 4.

(10) — Paragraph 1 replaces, in substance, the first and second indents of Article 202 TEC;
— paragraphs 2 and 9 replace, in substance, Article 203 TEC;
— paragraphs 4 and 5 replace, in substance, paragraphs 2 and 4 of Article 205 TEC.

(11) Paragraph 1 replaces, in substance, Article 211 TEC;
— paragraphs 3 and 7 replace, in substance, Article 214 TEC.

(12) — paragraph 6 replaces, in substance, paragraphs 1, 3 and 4 of Article 217 TEC.
— Replaces, in substance, Article 220 TEC.
— the second subparagraph of paragraph 2 replaces, in substance, the first subparagraph of Article 221 TEC.

(13) Thecurrent Article 10 TEU amended the Treaty establishing the European Atomic Energy Community. Those amendments are incorporated into the Treaty of Lisbon. Article 10 is repealed and the number thereof is used to insert another provision.

(14) Also replaces Articles 11 and 11a TEC.

(15) The current Articles 27a to 27e, on enhanced cooperation, are also replaced by Articles 326 to 334 TFEU.

(16) The current provisions of Title VI of the TEU, on police and judicial cooperation in criminal matters, are replaced by the provisions of Chapters 1, 5 and 5 of Title IV of Part Three of the TFEU.

(17) Replaced by Article 67 TFEU.

(18) Replaced by Articles 87 and 88 TFEU.

(19) Replaced by Articles 82, 83 and 85 TFEU.

(20) Replaced by Article 89 TFEU.

(21) Replaced by Article 72 TFEU.

(22) Replaced by Article 71 TFEU.

(23) The current Articles 40 to 40 B TEU, on enhanced cooperation, are also replaced by Articles 326 to 334 TFEU.

(24) The current Articles 43 to 45 and Title VII of the TEU, on enhanced cooperation, are also replaced by Articles 326 to 334 TFEU.

CONSOLIDATED VERSION OF THE TREATY ON THE FUNCTIONING OF THE EUROPEAN UNION – TABLES OF EQUIVALENCES*
OJ C 83, 30.3.2010, P. 361

TREATY ON THE FUNCTIONING OF THE EUROPEAN UNION

Old numbering of the TEC (Treaty establishing the European Community)	New numbering of the TFEU
PART ONE — PRINCIPLES	PART ONE — PRINCIPLES
Article 1 (repealed)	
	Article 1
Article 2 (repealed) (25)	
	Title I — Categories and areas of Union competence
	Article 2
	Article 3
	Article 4
	Article 5
	Article 6
	Title II — Provisions having general Application
	Article 7
Article 3, paragraph 1 (repealed) (26)	
Article 3, paragraph 2	Article 8
Article 4 (moved)	*Article 119*
Article 5 (replaced) (27)	
	Article 9
	Article 10
Article 6	Article 11
Article 153, paragraph 2 (moved)	Article 12
	Article 13 (28)

---

*   Tables of equivalences as referred to in Article 5 of the Treaty of Lisbon. The original centre column, which set out the intermediate numbering as used in that Treaty, has been omitted.

Old numbering of the TEC (Treaty establishing the European Community)	New numbering of the TFEU
Article 7 (repealed) (29)	
Article 8 (repealed) (30)	
Article 9 (repealed)	
Article 10 (repealed) (31)	
Article 11 (replaced) (32)	*Articles 326 to 334*
Article 11a (replaced) (32)	*Articles 326 to 334*
Article 12 (repealed)	*Article 18*
Article 13 (moved)	*Article 19*
Article 14 (moved)	*Article 26*
Article 15 (moved)	*Article 27*
Article 16	Article 14
Article 255 (moved)	Article 15
Article 286 (moved)	Article 16
	Article 17
PART TWO — CITIZENSHIP OF THE UNION	PART TWO — NON-DISCRIMINATION AND CITIZENSHIP OF THE UNION
Article 12 (moved)	Article 18
Article 13 (moved)	Article 19
Article 17	Article 20
Article 18	Article 21
Article 19	Article 22
Article 20	Article 23
Article 21	Article 24
Article 22	Article 25
PART THREE — COMMUNITY POLICIES	PART THREE — POLICIES AND INTERNAL ACTIONS OF THE UNION
	Title I — The internal market
Article 14 (moved)	Article 26
Article 15 (moved)	Article 27
Title I — Free movement of goods	Title II — Free movement of goods
Article 23	Article 28
Article 24	Article 29
Chapter 1 — The customs union	Chapter 1 — The customs union
Article 25	Article 30

Old numbering of the TEC (Treaty establishing the European Community)	New numbering of the TFEU
Article 26	Article 31
Article 27	Article 32
Part Three, Title X, Customs cooperation (moved)	Chapter 2 — Customs cooperation
Article 135 (moved)	Article 33
Chapter 2 — Prohibition of quantitative restrictions between Member States	Chapter 3 — Prohibition of quantitative restrictions between Member States
Article 28	Article 34
Article 29	Article 35
Article 30	Article 36
Article 31	Article 37
Title II — Agriculture	Title III — Agriculture and fisheries
Article 32	Article 38
Article 33	Article 39
Article 34	Article 40
Article 35	Article 41
Article 36	Article 42
Article 37	Article 43
Article 38	Article 44
Title III — Free movement of persons, services and capital	Title IV — Free movement of persons, services and capital
Chapter 1 — Workers	Chapter 1 — Workers
Article 39	Article 45
Article 40	Article 46
Article 41	Article 47
Article 42	Article 48
Chapter 2 — Right of establishment	Chapter 2 — Right of establishment
Article 43	Article 49
Article 44	Article 50
Article 45	Article 51
Article 46	Article 52
Article 47	Article 53
Article 48	Article 54
Article 294 (moved)	Article 55

Old numbering of the TEC (Treaty establishing the European Community)	New numbering of the TFEU
Chapter 3 — Services	Chapter 3 — Services
Article 49	Article 56
Article 50	Article 57
Article 51	Article 58
Article 52	Article 59
Article 53	Article 60
Article 54	Article 61
Article 55	Article 62
Chapter 4 — Capital and payments	Chapter 4 — Capital and payments
Article 56	Article 63
Article 57	Article 64
Article 58	Article 65
Article 59	Article 66
Article 60 (moved)	*Article 75*
Title IV — Visas, asylum, immigration and other policies related to free movement of persons	Title V — Area of freedom, security and justice
	Chapter 1 — General provisions
Article 61	Article 67 (33)
	Article 68
	Article 69
	Article 70
	Article 71 (34)
Article 64, paragraph 1 (replaced)	Article 72 (35)
	Article 73
Article 66 (replaced)	Article 74
Article 60 (moved)	Article 75
	Article 76
	Chapter 2 — Policies on border checks, -asylum and immigration
Article 62	Article 77
Article 63, points 1 et 2, and Article 64, paragraph 2 (36)	Article 78
Article 63, points 3 and 4	Article 79
	Article 80
Article 64, paragraph 1 (replaced)	*Article 72*

Old numbering of the TEC (Treaty establishing the European Community)	New numbering of the TFEU
	Chapter 3 — Judicial cooperation in civil matters
Article 65	Article 81
Article 66 (replaced)	*Article 74*
Article 67 (repealed)	
Article 68 (repealed)	
Article 69 (repealed)	
	Chapter 4 — Judicial cooperation in criminal matters
	Article 82 (37)
	Article 83 (37)
	Article 84
	Article 85 (37)
	Article 86
	Chapter 5 — Police cooperation
	Article 87 (38)
	Article 88 (38)
	Article 89 (39)
Title V — Transport	Title VI — Transport
Article 70	Article 90
Article 71	Article 91
Article 72	Article 92
Article 73	Article 93
Article 74	Article 94
Article 75	Article 95
Article 76	Article 96
Article 77	Article 97
Article 78	Article 98
Article 79	Article 99
Article 80	Article 100
Title VI — Common rules on competition, competition, taxation and approximation	Title VII — Common rules on competition, taxation and approximation of laws
Chapter 1 — Rules on competition	Chapter 1 — Rules on competition
Section 1 — Rules applying to undertakings	Section 1 — Rules applying to undertakings
Article 81	Article 101
Article 82	Article 102

Old numbering of the TEC (Treaty establishing the European Community)	New numbering of the TFEU
Article 83	Article 103
Article 84	Article 104
Article 85	Article 105
Article 86	Article 106
Section 2 — Aids granted by States	Section 2 — Aids granted by States
Article 87	Article 107
Article 88	Article 108
Article 89	Article 109
Chapter 2 — Tax provisions	Chapter 2 — Tax provisions
Article 90	Article 110
Article 91	Article 111
Article 92	Article 112
Article 93	Article 113
Chapter 3 — Approximation of laws	Chapter 3 — Approximation of laws
Article 95 (moved)	Article 114
Article 94 (moved)	Article 115
Article 96	Article 116
Article 97	Article 117
	Article 118
Title VII — Economic and monetary policy	Title VIII — Economic and monetary policy
Article 4 (moved)	Article 119
Chapter 1 — Economic policy	Chapter 1 — Economic policy
Article 98	Article 120
Article 99	Article 121
Article 100	Article 122
Article 101	Article 123
Article 102	Article 124
Article 103	Article 125
Article 104	Article 126
Chapter 2 — Monetary policy	Chapter 2 — Monetary policy
Article 105	Article 127
Article 106	Article 128
Article 107	Article 129
Article 108	Article 130
Article 109	Article 131

Old numbering of the TEC (Treaty establishing the European Community)	New numbering of the TFEU
Article 110	Article 132
Article 111, paras. 1 to 3 & 5 (moved)	*Article 219*
Article 111, para. 4 (moved)	*Article 138*
	Article 133
Chapter 3 — Institutional provisions	Chapter 3 — Institutional provisions
Article 112 (moved)	Article 283
Article 113 (moved)	Article 284
Article 114	Article 134
Article 115	Article 135
	Chapter 4 — Provisions specific to Member States whose currency is the euro
	Article 136
	Article 137
Article 111, paragraph 4 (moved)	Article 138
Chapter 4 — Transitional provisions	Chapter 5 — Transitional provisions
Article 116 (repealed)	
	Article 139
Article 117, paras. 1, 2, sixth indent, and 3 to 9 (repealed)	
Article 117, para. 2, first five indents (moved)	*Article 141, para. 2*
Article 121, para. 1 (moved)	Article 140 (40)
Article 122, para. 2, second sentence (moved)	
Article 123, para. 5 (moved)	
Article 118 (repealed)	
Article 123, para. 3 (moved)	Article 141 (41)
Article 117, para. 2, first five indents (moved)	
Article 124, para. 1 (moved)	Article 142
Article 119	Article 143
Article 120	Article 144
Article 121, para. 1 (moved)	*Article 140, para. 1*
Article 121, paras. 2 to 4 (repealed)	
Article 122, paras. 1, 2, first sentence, 3, 4, 5 and 6 (repealed)	
Article 122, para. 2, second sentence (moved)	*Article 140, para. 2, first subpara.*
Article 123, paragraphs 1, 2 and 4 (repealed)	
Article 123, para. 3 (moved)	*Article 141, para. 1*

Old numbering of the TEC (Treaty establishing the European Community)	New numbering of the TFEU
Article 123, para. 5 (moved)	*Article 140, para. 3*
Article 124, para. 1 (moved)	Article 142
Article 124, para. 2 (repealed)	
Title VIII — Employment	Title IX — Employment
Article 125	Article 145
Article 126	Article 146
Article 127	Article 147
Article 128	Article 148
Article 129	Article 149
Article 130	Article 150
Title IX — Common commercial policy (moved)	*Part Five, Title II, common commercial policy*
Article 131 (moved)	*Article 206*
Article 132 (repealed)	
Article 133 (moved)	*Article 207*
Article 134 (repealed)	
Title X — Customs cooperation (moved)	*Part Three, Title II, Chapter 2, Customs cooperation*
Article 135 (moved)	*Article 33*
Title XI — Social policy, education, vocational training and youth	Title X — Social policy
Chapter 1 — social provisions (repealed)	
Article 136	Article 151
	Article 152
Article 137	Article 153
Article 138	Article 154
Article 139	Article 155
Article 140	Article 156
Article 141	Article 157
Article 142	Article 158
Article 143	Article 159
Article 144	Article 160
Article 145	Article 161
Chapter 2 — The European Social Fund	Title XI — The European Social Fund
Article 146	Article 162
Article 147	Article 163

Old numbering of the TEC (Treaty establishing the European Community)	New numbering of the TFEU
Article 148	Article 164
Chapter 3 — Education, vocational training and youth	Title XII — Education, vocational training, youth and sport
Article 149	Article 165
Article 150	Article 166
Title XII — Culture	Title XIII — Culture
Article 151	Article 167
Title XIII — Public health	Title XIV — Public health
Article 152	Article 168
Title XIV — Consumer protection	Title XV — Consumer protection
Article 153, paras. 1, 3, 4 and 5	Article 169
Article 153, para. 2 (moved)	Article 12
Title XV — Trans–European networks	Title XVI — Trans–European networks
Article 154	Article 170
Article 155	Article 171
Article 156	Article 172
Title XVI — Industry	Title XVII — Industry
Article 157	Article 173
Title XVII — Economic and social cohesion	Title XVIII — Economic, social and territorial cohesion
Article 158	Article 174
Article 159	Article 175
Article 160	Article 176
Article 161	Article 177
Article 162	Article 178
Title XVIII — Research and technological development	Title XIX — Research and technological development and space
Article 163	Article 179
Article 164	Article 180
Article 165	Article 181
Article 166	Article 182
Article 167	Article 183
Article 168	Article 184
Article 169	Article 185
Article 170	Article 186
Article 171	Article 187

Old numbering of the TEC (Treaty establishing the European Community)	New numbering of the TFEU
Article 172	Article 188
	Article 189
Article 173	Article 190
Title XIX — Environment	Title XX — Environment
Article 174	Article 191
Article 175	Article 192
Article 176	Article 193
	Title XXI — Energy
	Article 194
	Title XXII — Tourism
	Article 195
	Title XXIII — Civil protection
	Article 196
	Title XXIV — Administrative cooperation
	Article 197
Title XX — Development cooperation (moved)	*Part Five, Title III, Chapter 1, Development cooperation*
Article 177 (moved)	*Article 208*
Article 178 (repealed) (42)	
Article 179 (moved)	*Article 209*
Article 180 (moved)	*Article 210*
Article 181 (moved)	*Article 211*
Title XXI — Economic, financial and technical cooperation with third countries (moved)	*Part Five, Title III, Chapter 2, Economic, financial and technical cooperation with third countries*
Article 181*a* (moved)	*Article 212*
PART FOUR — ASSOCIATION OF THE OVERSEAS COUNTRIES AND TERRITORIES	PART FOUR — ASSOCIATION OF THE OVERSEAS COUNTRIES AND TERRITORIES
Article 182	Article 198
Article 183	Article 199
Article 184	Article 200
Article 185	Article 201
Article 186	Article 202
Article 187	Article 203
Article 188	Article 204

Old numbering of the TEC (Treaty establishing the European Community)	New numbering of the TFEU
	PART FIVE — EXTERNAL ACTION BY THE UNION
	Title I — General provisions on the Union's external action
	Article 205
Part Three, Title IX, Common commercial policy (moved)	Title II — Common commercial policy
Article 131 (moved)	Article 206
Article 133 (moved)	Article 207
	Title III — Cooperation with third countries and humanitarian aid
Part Three, Title XX, Development cooperation (moved)	Chapter 1 — Development cooperation
Article 177 (moved)	Article 208 (43)
Article 179 (moved)	Article 209
Article 180 (moved)	Article 210
Article 181 (moved)	Article 211
Part Three, Title XXI, Economic, financial and technical cooperation with third countries (moved)	Chapter 2 — Economic, financial and technical cooperation with third countries
Article 181a (moved)	Article 212
	Article 213
	Chapter 3 — Humanitarian aid
	Article 214
	Title IV — Restrictive measures
Article 301 (replaced)	Article 215
	Title V — International agreements
	Article 216
Article 310 (moved)	Article 217
Article 300 (replaced)	Article 218
Article 111, paras. 1 to 3 and 5 (moved)	Article 219
	Title VI — The Union's relations with international organisations and third countries and the Union delegations
Articles 302 to 304 (replaced)	Article 220
	Article 221

Old numbering of the TEC (Treaty establishing the European Community)	New numbering of the TFEU
	Title VII — Solidarity clause
	Article 222
PART FIVE — INSTITUTIONS OF THE COMMUNITY	**PART SIX — INSTITUTIONAL AND FINANCIAL PROVISIONS**
Title I — Institutional provisions	Title I — Institutional provisions
Chapter 1 — The institutions	Chapter 1 — The institutions
Section 1 — The European Parliament	Section 1 — The European Parliament
Article 189 (repealed) (44)	
Article 190, paras. 1 to 3 (repealed) (45)	
Article 190, paras. 4 and 5	Article 223
Article 191, first para. (repealed) (46)	
Article 191, second para.	Article 224
Article 192, first para. (repealed) (47)	
Article 192, second para.	Article 225
Article 193	Article 226
Article 194	Article 227
Article 195	Article 228
Article 196	Article 229
Article 197, first para. (repealed) (48)	
Article 197, second, third & fourth paras.	
	Article 230
Article 198	Article 231
Article 199	Article 232
Article 200	Article 233
Article 201	Article 234
	Section 2 — The European Council
	Article 235
	Article 236
Section 2 — The Council	Section 3 — The Council
Article 202 (repealed) (49)	
Article 203 (repealed) (50)	
Article 204	Article 237
Article 205, paras. 2 and 4 (repealed) (51)	
Article 205, paras. 1 and 3	Article 238
Article 206	Article 239

Old numbering of the TEC (Treaty establishing the European Community)	New numbering of the TFEU
Article 207	Article 240
Article 208	Article 241
Article 209	Article 242
Article 210	Article 243
Section 3 — The Commission	Section 4 — The Commission
Article 211 (repealed) (52)	
	Article 244
Article 212 (moved)	*Article 249, para. 2*
Article 213	Article 245
Article 214 (repealed) (53)	
Article 215	Article 246
Article 216	Article 247
Article 217, paras. 1, 3 and 4 (repealed) (54)	
Article 217, para. 2	Article 248
Article 218, para. 1 (repealed) (55)	
Article 218, para. 2	Article 249
Article 219	Article 250
Section 4 — The Court of Justice	Section 5 — The Court of Justice of the European Union
Article 220 (repealed) (56)	
Article 221, first para. (repealed) (57)	
Article 221, second and third paras.	Article 251
Article 222	Article 252
Article 223	Article 253
Article 224 (58)	Article 254
	Article 255
Article 225	Article 256
Article 225a	Article 257
Article 226	Article 258
Article 227	Article 259
Article 228	Article 260
Article 229	Article 261
Article 229a	Article 262
Article 230	Article 263
Article 231	Article 264

Old numbering of the TEC (Treaty establishing the European Community)	New numbering of the TFEU
Article 232	Article 265
Article 233	Article 266
Article 234	Article 267
Article 235	Article 268
	Article 269
Article 236	Article 270
Article 237	Article 271
Article 238	Article 272
Article 239	Article 273
Article 240	Article 274
	Article 275
	Article 276
Article 241	Article 277
Article 242	Article 278
Article 243	Article 279
Article 244	Article 280
Article 245	Article 281
	Section 6 — The European Central Bank
	Article 282
Article 112 (moved)	Article 283
Article 113 (moved)	Article 284
Section 5 — The Court of Auditors	Section 7 — The Court of Auditors
Article 246	Article 285
Article 247	Article 286
Article 248	Article 287
Chapter 2 — Provisions common to several institutions	Chapter 2 — Legal acts of the Union, adoption procedures and other provisions
	Section 1 — The legal acts of the Union
Article 249	Article 288
	Article 289
	Article 290 (59)
	Article 291 (59)
	Article 292
	Section 2 — Procedures for the adoption of acts and other provisions

Old numbering of the TEC (Treaty establishing the European Community)	New numbering of the TFEU
Article 250	Article 293
Article 251	Article 294
Article 252 (repealed)	
	Article 295
Article 253	Article 296
Article 254	Article 297
	Article 298
Article 255 (moved)	Article 15
Article 256	Article 299
	Chapter 3 — The Union's advisory bodies
	Article 300
Chapter 3 — The Economic and Social Committee	Section 1 — The Economic and Social Committee
Article 257 (repealed) (60)	
Article 258, first, second and fourth paras.	Article 301
Article 258, third para. (repealed) (61)	
Article 259	Article 302
Article 260	Article 303
Article 261 (repealed)	
Article 262	Article 304
Chapter 4 — The Committee of the Regions	Section 2 — The Committee of the Regions
Article 263, first and fifth paras. (repealed) (62)	
Article 263, second to fourth paras.	Article 305
Article 264	Article 306
Article 265	Article 307
Chapter 5 — The European Investment Bank	Chapter 4 — The European Investment
Article 266	Article 308
Article 267	Article 309
Title II — Financial provisions	Title II — Financial provisions
Article 268	Article 310
	Chapter 1 — The Union's own resources
Article 269	Article 311
Article 270 (repealed) (63)	

Old numbering of the TEC (Treaty establishing the European Community)	New numbering of the TFEU
	Chapter 2 — The multiannual financial framework
	Article 312
	Chapter 3 — The Union's annual budget
Article 272, para. 1 (moved)	Article 313
Article 271 (moved)	*Article 316*
Article 272, para. 1 (moved)	Article 313
Article 272, paras. 2 to 10	Article 314
Article 273	Article 315
Article 271 (moved)	Article 316
	Chapter 4 — Implementation of the budget and discharge
Article 274	Article 317
Article 275	Article 318
Article 276	Article 319
	Chapter 5 — Common provisions
Article 277	Article 320
Article 278	Article 321
Article 279	Article 322
	Article 323
	Article 324
	Chapter 6 — Combating fraud
Article 280	Article 325
	Title III — Enhanced cooperation
Articles 11 and 11a (replaced)	Article 326 (64)
Articles 11 and 11a (replaced)	Article 327 (64)
Articles 11 and 11a (replaced)	Article 328 (64)
Articles 11 and 11a (replaced)	Article 329 (64)
Articles 11 and 11a (replaced)	Article 330 (64)
Articles 11 and 11a (replaced)	Article 331 (64)
Articles 11 and 11a (replaced)	Article 332 (64)
Articles 11 and 11a (replaced)	Article 333 (64)
Articles 11 and 11a (replaced)	Article 334 (64)
PART SIX — GENERAL AND FINAL PROVISIONS	PART SEVEN — GENERAL AND FINAL PROVISIONS
Article 281 (repealed) (65)	

Old numbering of the TEC (Treaty establishing the European Community)	New numbering of the TFEU
Article 282	Article 335
Article 283	Article 336
Article 284	Article 337
Article 285	Article 338
Article 286 (replaced)	*Article 16*
Article 287	Article 339
Article 288	Article 340
Article 289	Article 341
Article 290	Article 342
Article 291	Article 343
Article 292	Article 344
Article 293 (repealed)	
Article 294 (moved)	*Article 55*
Article 295	Article 345
Article 296	Article 346
Article 297	Article 347
Article 298	Article 348
Article 299, para. 1 (repealed) (66)	
Article 299, para. 2, second, third & fourth subparas.	Article 349
Article 299, para. 2, first subpara. and paras. 3 to 6 (moved)	*Article 355*
Article 300 (replaced)	*Article 218*
Article 301 (replaced)	*Article 215*
Article 302 (replaced)	*Article 220*
Article 303 (replaced)	*Article 220*
Article 304 (replaced)	*Article 220*
Article 305 (repealed)	
Article 306	Article 350
Article 307	Article 351
Article 308	Article 352
	Article 353
Article 309	Article 354
Article 310 (moved)	*Article 217*
Article 311 (repealed) (67)	

Old numbering of the TEC (Treaty establishing the European Community)	New numbering of the TFEU
Article 299, para. 2, first subpara., and paras. 3 to 6 (moved)	Article 355
Article 312	Article 356
	Final Provisions
Article 313	Article 357
	Article 358
Article 314 (repealed) (68)	

(25) Replaced, in substance, by Article 3 TEU.
(26) Replaced, in substance, by Articles 3 to 6 TFEU.
(27) Replaced, in substance, by Article 5 TEU.
(28) Insertion of the operative part of the protocol on protection and welfare of animals.
(29) Replaced, in substance, by Article 13 TEU.
(30) Replaced, in substance, by Article 13 TEU and Article 282, para. 1, TFEU.
(31) Replaced, in substance, by Article 4, para. 3, TEU.
(32) Also replaced by Article 20 TEU.
(33) Also replaces the current Article 29 TEU.
(34) Also replaces the current Article 36 TEU.
(35) Also replaces the current Article 33 TEU.
(36) Points 1 and 2 of Article 63 EC are replaced by paragraphs 1 and 2 of Article 78 TFEU, and paragraph 2 of Article 64 is replaced by paragraph 3 of Article 78 TFEU.
(37) Replaces the current Article 31 TEU.
(38) Replaces the current Article 30 TEU.
(39) Replaces the current Article 32 TEU.
(40) — Article 140, para. 1 takes over the wording of para. 1 of Article 121.
       — Article 140, para. 2 takes over the second sentence of para. 2 of Article 122.
       — Article 140, para. 3 takes over para. 5 of Article 123.
(41) — Article 141, para. 1 takes over para. 3 of Article 123.
       — Article 141, para. 2 takes over the first five indents of para. 2 of Article 117.
(42) Replaced, in substance, by the second sentence of the second subpara. of para. 1 of Article 208 TFUE.
(43) The second sentence of the second subpara. of para. 1 replaces, in substance, Article 178 TEC.
(44) Replaced, in substance, by Article 14, paras. 1 and 2, TEU.
(45) Replaced, in substance, by Article 14, paras. 1 to 3, TEU.
(46) Replaced, in substance, by Article 11, para. 4, TEU.
(47) Replaced, in substance, by Article 14, para. 1, TEU.
(48) Replaced, in substance, by Article 14, para. 4, TEU.
(49) Replaced, in substance, by Article 16, para. 1, TEU and by Articles 290 and 291 TFEU.
(50) Replaced, in substance, by Article 16, paras. 2 and 9 TEU.
(51) Replaced, in substance, by Article 16, paras. 4 and 5 TEU.
(52) Replaced, in substance, by Article 17, para. 1 TEU.
(53) Replaced, in substance, by Article 17, paras. 3 and 7 TEU.
(54) Replaced, in substance, by Article 17, para. 6, TEU.
(55) Replaced, in substance, by Article 295 TFEU.
(56) Replaced, in substance, by Article 19 TEU.
(57) Replaced, in substance, by Article 19, para. 2, first subpara., of the TEU.
(58) The first sentence of the first subpara. is replaced, in substance, by Article 19, para. 2, second subpara. of the TEU.
(59) Replaces, in substance, the third indent of Article 202 TEC.
(60) Replaced, in substance, by Article 300, para. 2 of the TFEU.
(61) Replaced, in substance, by Article 300, para. 4 of the TFEU.
(62) Replaced, in substance, by Article 300, paras. 3 and 4, TFEU.
(63) Replaced, in substance, by Article 310, para. 4, TFEU.
(64) Also replaces the current Articles 27a to 27e, 40 to 40b, and 43 to 45 TEU.

(65) Replaced, in substance, by Article 47 TEU.
(66) Replaced, in substance by Article 52 TEU.
(67) Replaced, in substance by Article 51 TEU.
(68) Replaced, in substance by Article 55 TEU.

III Fundamental Rights

CHARTER OF FUNDAMENTAL RIGHTS OF THE EUROPEAN UNION
OJ C83, 30.3.2010, P. 389*

SOLEMN PROCLAMATION

The European Parliament, the Council and the Commission solemnly proclaim the following text as the Charter of Fundamental Rights of the European Union.

CHARTER OF FUNDAMENTAL RIGHTS OF THE EUROPEAN UNION

PREAMBLE

The peoples of Europe, in creating an ever closer union among them, are resolved to share a peaceful future based on common values.

....

* EDITOR'S NOTE: The text reproduced below adapts the wording of the Charter proclaimed on 7 December 2000 (OJ C 364, 18.12.2000, p. 1), and has replaced it from the date of entry into force of the Treaty of Lisbon, 1 December 2009. The adapted text was first published in 2007. The 'rights, freedoms and principles' set out in the Charter have the 'same legal value' as the Treaties according to Article 6(1) of the Treaty on European Union. The Charter is also subject to the provisions of Protocol (No 30), annexed to the Treaties, which concerns its application to Poland and the United Kingdom (see Part I of this edition). Under Article 6(1) TEU 'the Charter shall be interpreted in accordance with the general provisions in Title VII of the Charter governing its interpretation and application and with due regard to the explanations referred to in the Charter, that set out the sources of those provisions'. For the text of the 'explanations' see the next document in this Part of the edition.

Conscious of its spiritual and moral heritage, the Union is founded on the indivisible, universal values of human dignity, freedom, equality and solidarity; it is based on the principles of democracy and the rule of law. It places the individual at the heart of its activities, by establishing the citizenship of the Union and by creating an area of freedom, security and justice.

The Union contributes to the preservation and to the development of these common values while respecting the diversity of the cultures and traditions of the peoples of Europe as well as the national identities of the Member States and the organisation of their public authorities at national, regional and local levels; it seeks to promote balanced and sustainable development and ensures free movement of persons, services, goods and capital, and the freedom of establishment.

To this end, it is necessary to strengthen the protection of fundamental rights in the light of changes in society, social progress and scientific and technological developments by making those rights more visible in a Charter.

This Charter reaffirms, with due regard for the powers and tasks of the Union and for the principle of subsidiarity, the rights as they result, in particular, from the constitutional traditions and international obligations common to the Member States, the European Convention for the Protection of Human Rights and Fundamental Freedoms, the Social Charters adopted by the Union and by the Council of Europe and the case-law of the Court of Justice of the European Union and of the European Court of Human Rights. In this context the Charter will be interpreted by the courts of the Union and the Member States with due regard to the explanations prepared under the authority of the Praesidium of the Convention which drafted the Charter and updated under the responsibility of the Praesidium of the European Convention.

Enjoyment of these rights entails responsibilities and duties with regard to other persons, to the human community and to future generations.

The Union therefore recognises the rights, freedoms and principles set out hereafter.

TITLE I
DIGNITY

Article 1 Human dignity
Human dignity is inviolable. It must be respected and protected.

Article 2 Right to life
1.   Everyone has the right to life.

2.   No one shall be condemned to the death penalty, or executed.

Article 3 Right to the integrity of the person
1.   Everyone has the right to respect for his or her physical and mental integrity.

2.   In the fields of medicine and biology, the following must be respected in particular:
    (a) the free and informed consent of the person concerned, according to the procedures laid down by law;
    (b) the prohibition of eugenic practices, in particular those aiming at the selection of persons;
    (c) the prohibition on making the human body and its parts as such a source of financial gain;
    (d) the prohibition of the reproductive cloning of human beings.

Article 4 Prohibition of torture and inhuman or degrading treatment or punishment
No one shall be subjected to torture or to inhuman or degrading treatment or punishment.

Article 5 Prohibition of slavery and forced labour
1.   No one shall be held in slavery or servitude.

2.   No one shall be required to perform forced or compulsory labour.

3.   Trafficking in human beings is prohibited.

TITLE II
FREEDOMS

Article 6 Right to liberty and security
Everyone has the right to liberty and security of person.

Article 7 Respect for private and family life
Everyone has the right to respect for his or her private and family life, home and communications.

Article 8 Protection of personal data
1.   Everyone has the right to the protection of personal data concerning him or her.

2.   Such data must be processed fairly for specified purposes and on the basis of the consent of the person concerned or some other legitimate basis laid down by law. Everyone has the right of access to data which has been collected concerning him or her, and the right to have it rectified.

3.   Compliance with these rules shall be subject to control by an independent authority.

Article 9 Right to marry and right to found a family
The right to marry and the right to found a family shall be guaranteed in accordance with the national laws governing the exercise of these rights.

Article 10 Freedom of thought, conscience and religion
1.   Everyone has the right to freedom of thought, conscience and religion. This right includes freedom to change religion or belief and freedom, either alone or in community with others and in public or in private, to manifest religion or belief, in worship, teaching, practice and observance.

2.   The right to conscientious objection is recognised, in accordance with the national laws governing the exercise of this right.

Article 11 Freedom of expression and information
1.   Everyone has the right to freedom of expression. This right shall include freedom to hold opinions and to receive and impart information and ideas without interference by public authority and regardless of frontiers.

2.   The freedom and pluralism of the media shall be respected.

Article 12 Freedom of assembly and of association
1.   Everyone has the right to freedom of peaceful assembly and to freedom of association at all levels, in particular in political, trade union and civic matters, which implies the

right of everyone to form and to join trade unions for the protection of his or her interests.

2.   Political parties at Union level contribute to expressing the political will of the citizens of the Union.

Article 13 Freedom of the arts and sciences
The arts and scientific research shall be free of constraint. Academic freedom shall be respected.

Article 14 Right to education
1.   Everyone has the right to education and to have access to vocational and continuing training.

2.   This right includes the possibility to receive free compulsory education.

3.   The freedom to found educational establishments with due respect for democratic principles and the right of parents to ensure the education and teaching of their children in conformity with their religious, philosophical and pedagogical convictions shall be respected, in accordance with the national laws governing the exercise of such freedom and right.

Article 15 Freedom to choose an occupation and right to engage in work
1.   Everyone has the right to engage in work and to pursue a freely chosen or accepted occupation.

2.   Every citizen of the Union has the freedom to seek employment, to work, to exercise the right of establishment and to provide services in any Member State.

3.   Nationals of third countries who are authorised to work in the territories of the Member States are entitled to working conditions equivalent to those of citizens of the Union.

Article 16 Freedom to conduct a business
The freedom to conduct a business in accordance with Union law and national laws and practices is recognised.

Article 17 Right to property
1.   Everyone has the right to own, use, dispose of and bequeath his or her lawfully acquired possessions. No one may be deprived of his or her possessions, except in the public interest and in the cases and under the conditions provided for by law, subject to fair compensation being paid in good time for their loss. The use of property may be regulated by law in so far as is necessary for the general interest.

2.   Intellectual property shall be protected.

Article 18 Right to asylum
The right to asylum shall be guaranteed with due respect for the rules of the Geneva Convention of 28 July 1951 and the Protocol of 31 January 1967 relating to the status of refugees and in accordance with the Treaty on European Union and the Treaty on the Functioning of the European Union (hereinafter referred to as 'the Treaties').

Article 19 Protection in the event of removal, expulsion or extradition
1.   Collective expulsions are prohibited.

2.   No one may be removed, expelled or extradited to a State where there is a serious risk that he or she would be subjected to the death penalty, torture or other inhuman or degrading treatment or punishment.

TITLE III
EQUALITY

Article 20 Equality before the law
Everyone is equal before the law.

Article 21 Non-discrimination
1.   Any discrimination based on any ground such as sex, race, colour, ethnic or social origin, genetic features, language, religion or belief, political or any other opinion, membership of a national minority, property, birth, disability, age or sexual orientation shall be prohibited.

2.   Within the scope of application of the Treaties and without prejudice to any of their specific provisions, any discrimination on grounds of nationality shall be prohibited.

Article 22 Cultural, religious and linguistic diversity
The Union shall respect cultural, religious and linguistic diversity.

Article 23 Equality between women and men
Equality between women and men must be ensured in all areas, including employment, work and pay.

The principle of equality shall not prevent the maintenance or adoption of measures providing for specific advantages in favour of the under-represented sex.

Article 24 The rights of the child
1.   Children shall have the right to such protection and care as is necessary for their well-being. They may express their views freely. Such views shall be taken into consideration on matters which concern them in accordance with their age and maturity.

2.   In all actions relating to children, whether taken by public authorities or private institutions, the child's best interests must be a primary consideration.

3.   Every child shall have the right to maintain on a regular basis a personal relationship and direct contact with both his or her parents, unless that is contrary to his or her interests.

Article 25 The rights of the elderly
The Union recognises and respects the rights of the elderly to lead a life of dignity and independence and to participate in social and cultural life.

Article 26 Integration of persons with disabilities
The Union recognises and respects the right of persons with disabilities to benefit from measures designed to ensure their independence, social and occupational integration and participation in the life of the community.

TITLE IV
SOLIDARITY

Article 27 Workers' right to information and consultation within the undertaking
Workers or their representatives must, at the appropriate levels, be guaranteed information and consultation in good time in the cases and under the conditions provided for by Union law and national laws and practices.

Article 28 Right of collective bargaining and action
Workers and employers, or their respective organisations, have, in accordance with Union law and national laws and practices, the right to negotiate and conclude collective agreements at the appropriate levels and, in cases of conflicts of interest, to take collective action to defend their interests, including strike action.

Article 29 Right of access to placement services
Everyone has the right of access to a free placement service.

Article 30 Protection in the event of unjustified dismissal
Every worker has the right to protection against unjustified dismissal, in accordance with Union law and national laws and practices.

Article 31 Fair and just working conditions
1.   Every worker has the right to working conditions which respect his or her health, safety and dignity.

2.   Every worker has the right to limitation of maximum working hours, to daily and weekly rest periods and to an annual period of paid leave.

Article 32 Prohibition of child labour and protection of young people at work
The employment of children is prohibited. The minimum age of admission to employment may not be lower than the minimum school-leaving age, without prejudice to such rules as may be more favourable to young people and except for limited derogations.

Young people admitted to work must have working conditions appropriate to their age and be protected against economic exploitation and any work likely to harm their safety, health or physical, mental, moral or social development or to interfere with their education.

Article 33 Family and professional life
1.   The family shall enjoy legal, economic and social protection.

2.   To reconcile family and professional life, everyone shall have the right to protection from dismissal for a reason connected with maternity and the right to paid maternity leave and to parental leave following the birth or adoption of a child.

Article 34 Social security and social assistance
1.   The Union recognises and respects the entitlement to social security benefits and social services providing protection in cases such as maternity, illness, industrial accidents, dependency or old age, and in the case of loss of employment, in accordance with the rules laid down by Union law and national laws and practices.

2.   Everyone residing and moving legally within the European Union is entitled to social security benefits and social advantages in accordance with Union law and national laws and practices.

3.   In order to combat social exclusion and poverty, the Union recognises and respects the
      right to social and housing assistance so as to ensure a decent existence for all those who
      lack sufficient resources, in accordance with the rules laid down by Union law and
      national laws and practices.

Article 35 Health care

Everyone has the right of access to preventive health care and the right to benefit from medical
treatment under the conditions established by national laws and practices. A high level of
human health protection shall be ensured in the definition and implementation of all the Union's
policies and activities.

Article 36 Access to services of general economic interest

The Union recognises and respects access to services of general economic interest as provided
for in national laws and practices, in accordance with the Treaties, in order to promote the
social and territorial cohesion of the Union.

Article 37 Environmental protection

A high level of environmental protection and the improvement of the quality of the environment
must be integrated into the policies of the Union and ensured in accordance with the principle
of sustainable development.

Article 38 Consumer protection

Union policies shall ensure a high level of consumer protection.

TITLE V
CITIZENS' RIGHTS

Article 39 Right to vote and to stand as a candidate at elections to the European Parliament

1.   Every citizen of the Union has the right to vote and to stand as a candidate at elections to
      the European Parliament in the Member State in which he or she resides, under the same
      conditions as nationals of that State.

2.   Members of the European Parliament shall be elected by direct universal suffrage in a free
      and secret ballot.

Article 40 Right to vote and to stand as a candidate at municipal elections

Every citizen of the Union has the right to vote and to stand as a candidate at municipal
elections in the Member State in which he or she resides under the same conditions as nationals
of that State.

Article 41 Right to good administration

1.   Every person has the right to have his or her affairs handled impartially, fairly and within
      a reasonable time by the institutions, bodies, offices and agencies of the Union.

2.   This right includes:
      (a) the right of every person to be heard, before any individual measure which would
           affect him or her adversely is taken;
      (b) the right of every person to have access to his or her file, while respecting the
           legitimate interests of confidentiality and of professional and business secrecy;
      (c) the obligation of the administration to give reasons for its decisions.

3.   Every person has the right to have the Union make good any damage caused by its institutions or by its servants in the performance of their duties, in accordance with the general principles common to the laws of the Member States.

4.   Every person may write to the institutions of the Union in one of the languages of the Treaties and must have an answer in the same language.

Article 42 Right of access to documents
Any citizen of the Union, and any natural or legal person residing or having its registered office in a Member State, has a right of access to documents of the institutions, bodies, offices and agencies of the Union, whatever their medium.

Article 43 European Ombudsman
Any citizen of the Union and any natural or legal person residing or having its registered office in a Member State has the right to refer to the European Ombudsman cases of maladministration in the activities of the institutions, bodies, offices or agencies of the Union, with the exception of the Court of Justice of the European Union acting in its judicial role.

Article 44 Right to petition
Any citizen of the Union and any natural or legal person residing or having its registered office in a Member State has the right to petition the European Parliament.

Article 45 Freedom of movement and of residence
1.   Every citizen of the Union has the right to move and reside freely within the territory of the Member States.

2.   Freedom of movement and residence may be granted, in accordance with the Treaties, to nationals of third countries legally resident in the territory of a Member State.

Article 46 Diplomatic and consular protection
Every citizen of the Union shall, in the territory of a third country in which the Member State of which he or she is a national is not represented, be entitled to protection by the diplomatic or consular authorities of any Member State, on the same conditions as the nationals of that Member State.

TITLE VI
JUSTICE

Article 47 Right to an effective remedy and to a fair trial
Everyone whose rights and freedoms guaranteed by the law of the Union are violated has the right to an effective remedy before a tribunal in compliance with the conditions laid down in this Article.

Everyone is entitled to a fair and public hearing within a reasonable time by an independent and impartial tribunal previously established by law. Everyone shall have the possibility of being advised, defended and represented.

Legal aid shall be made available to those who lack sufficient resources in so far as such aid is necessary to ensure effective access to justice.

Article 48 Presumption of innocence and right of defence
1.   Everyone who has been charged shall be presumed innocent until proved guilty according to law.

2.   Respect for the rights of the defence of anyone who has been charged shall be guaranteed.

Article 49 Principles of legality and proportionality of criminal offences and penalties

1. No one shall be held guilty of any criminal offence on account of any act or omission which did not constitute a criminal offence under national law or international law at the time when it was committed. Nor shall a heavier penalty be imposed than the one that was applicable at the time the criminal offence was committed. If, subsequent to the commission of a criminal offence, the law provides for a lighter penalty, that penalty shall be applicable.

2. This Article shall not prejudice the trial and punishment of any person for any act or omission which, at the time when it was committed, was criminal according to the general principles recognised by the community of nations.

3. The severity of penalties must not be disproportionate to the criminal offence.

Article 50 Right not to be tried or punished twice in criminal proceedings for the same criminal offence

No one shall be liable to be tried or punished again in criminal proceedings for an offence for which he or she has already been finally acquitted or convicted within the Union in accordance with the law.

TITLE VII
GENERAL PROVISIONS GOVERNING THE INTERPRETATION AND APPLICATION OF THE CHARTER

Article 51 Field of application

1. The provisions of this Charter are addressed to the institutions, bodies, offices and agencies of the Union with due regard for the principle of subsidiarity and to the Member States only when they are implementing Union law. They shall therefore respect the rights, observe the principles and promote the application thereof in accordance with their respective powers and respecting the limits of the powers of the Union as conferred on it in the Treaties.

2. The Charter does not extend the field of application of Union law beyond the powers of the Union or establish any new power or task for the Union, or modify powers and tasks as defined in the Treaties.

Article 52 Scope and interpretation of rights and principles

1. Any limitation on the exercise of the rights and freedoms recognised by this Charter must be provided for by law and respect the essence of those rights and freedoms. Subject to the principle of proportionality, limitations may be made only if they are necessary and genuinely meet objectives of general interest recognised by the Union or the need to protect the rights and freedoms of others.

2. Rights recognised by this Charter for which provision is made in the Treaties shall be exercised under the conditions and within the limits defined by those Treaties.

3. In so far as this Charter contains rights which correspond to rights guaranteed by the Convention for the Protection of Human Rights and Fundamental Freedoms, the meaning and scope of those rights shall be the same as those laid down by the said Convention. This provision shall not prevent Union law providing more extensive protection.

4. In so far as this Charter recognises fundamental rights as they result from the constitutional traditions common to the Member States, those rights shall be interpreted in harmony with those traditions.

5.   The provisions of this Charter which contain principles may be implemented by legislative and executive acts taken by institutions, bodies, offices and agencies of the Union, and by acts of Member States when they are implementing Union law, in the exercise of their respective powers. They shall be judicially cognisable only in the interpretation of such acts and in the ruling on their legality.

6.   Full account shall be taken of national laws and practices as specified in this Charter.

7.   The explanations drawn up as a way of providing guidance in the interpretation of this Charter shall be given due regard by the courts of the Union and of the Member States.

Article 53 Level of protection
Nothing in this Charter shall be interpreted as restricting or adversely affecting human rights and fundamental freedoms as recognised, in their respective fields of application, by Union law and international law and by international agreements to which the Union or all the Member States are party, including the European Convention for the Protection of Human Rights and Fundamental Freedoms, and by the Member States' constitutions.

Article 54 Prohibition of abuse of rights
Nothing in this Charter shall be interpreted as implying any right to engage in any activity or to perform any act aimed at the destruction of any of the rights and freedoms recognised in this charter or at their limitation to a greater extent than is provided for herein.

EXPLANATIONS RELATING TO THE CHARTER OF FUNDAMENTAL RIGHTS
OJ C303, 14.12.2007, P. 17*

These explanations were originally prepared under the authority of the Praesidium of the Convention which drafted the Charter of Fundamental Rights of the European Union. They have been updated under the responsibility of the Praesidium of the European Convention, in the light of the drafting adjustments made to the text of the Charter by that Convention (notably to Articles 51 and 52) and of further developments of Union law. Although they do not as such have the status of law, they are a valuable tool of interpretation intended to clarify the provisions of the Charter.

TITLE I — DIGNITY

Explanation on Article 1 — Human dignity
The dignity of the human person is not only a fundamental right in itself but constitutes the real basis of fundamental rights. The 1948 Universal Declaration of Human Rights enshrined human dignity in its preamble: 'Whereas recognition of the inherent dignity and of the equal and inalienable rights of all members of the human family is the foundation of freedom, justice and peace in the world.' In its judgment of 9 October 2001 in Case C-377/98 *Netherlands v*

----

*   EDITOR'S NOTE: The text of the explanations was corrected and updated in 2007 following the publication of the adapted text of the Charter. Under Article 6(1) of the Treaty on European Union 'the Charter shall be interpreted in accordance with the general provisions in Title VII of the Charter governing its interpretation and application and with due regard to the explanations referred to in the Charter, that set out the sources of those provisions.'

European Parliament and Council [2001] ECR I-7079, at grounds 70–77, the Court of Justice confirmed that a fundamental right to human dignity is part of Union law.

It results that none of the rights laid down in this Charter may be used to harm the dignity of another person, and that the dignity of the human person is part of the substance of the rights laid down in this Charter. It must therefore be respected, even where a right is restricted.

Explanation on Article 2 — Right to life

1.   Paragraph 1 of this Article is based on the first sentence of Article 2(1) of the ECHR, which reads as follows:

'1.   Everyone's right to life shall be protected by law . . .'.

2.   The second sentence of the provision, which referred to the death penalty, was superseded by the entry into force of Article 1 of Protocol No 6 to the ECHR, which reads as follows:

'The death penalty shall be abolished. No-one shall be condemned to such penalty or executed.'

Article 2(2) of the Charter is based on that provision.

3.   The provisions of Article 2 of the Charter correspond to those of the above Articles of the ECHR and its Protocol.

They have the same meaning and the same scope, in accordance with Article 52(3) of the Charter. Therefore, the 'negative' definitions appearing in the ECHR must be regarded as also forming part of the Charter:

(a) Article 2(2) of the ECHR:

'Deprivation of life shall not be regarded as inflicted in contravention of this article when it results from the use of force which is no more than absolutely necessary:
(a) in defence of any person from unlawful violence;
(b) in order to effect a lawful arrest or to prevent the escape of a person lawfully detained;
(c) in action lawfully taken for the purpose of quelling a riot or insurrection.'

(b) Article 2 of Protocol No 6 to the ECHR:

'A State may make provision in its law for the death penalty in respect of acts committed in time of war or of imminent threat of war; such penalty shall be applied only in the instances laid down in the law and in accordance with its provisions. . .'.

Explanation on Article 3 — Right to the integrity of the person

1.   In its judgment of 9 October 2001 in Case C-377/98 *Netherlands v European Parliament and Council* [2001] ECR-I-7079, at grounds 70, 78 to 80, the Court of Justice confirmed that a fundamental right to human integrity is part of Union law and encompasses, in the context of medicine and biology, the free and informed consent of the donor and recipient.

2.   The principles of Article 3 of the Charter are already included in the Convention on Human Rights and Biomedicine, adopted by the Council of Europe (ETS 164 and additional protocol ETS 168). The Charter does not set out to depart from those principles, and therefore prohibits only reproductive cloning. It neither authorises nor prohibits other forms of cloning. Thus it does not in any way prevent the legislature from prohibiting other forms of cloning.

3.   The reference to eugenic practices, in particular those aiming at the selection of persons, relates to possible situations in which selection programmes are organised and implemented, involving campaigns for sterilisation, forced pregnancy, compulsory ethnic marriage among others, all acts deemed to be international crimes in the Statute of the International Criminal Court adopted in Rome on 17 July 1998 (see its Article 7(1)(g)).

Explanation on Article 4 — Prohibition of torture and inhuman or degrading treatment or punishment
The right in Article 4 is the right guaranteed by Article 3 of the ECHR, which has the same wording: 'No one shall be subjected to torture or to inhuman or degrading treatment or punishment'. By virtue of Article 52(3) of the Charter, it therefore has the same meaning and the same scope as the ECHR Article.

Explanation on Article 5 — Prohibition of slavery and forced labour
1.   The right in Article 5(1) and (2) corresponds to Article 4(1) and (2) of the ECHR, which has the same wording. It therefore has the same meaning and scope as the ECHR Article, by virtue of Article 52(3) of the Charter. Consequently:
    — no limitation may legitimately affect the right provided for in paragraph 1,
    — in paragraph 2, 'forced or compulsory labour' must be understood in the light of the 'negative' definitions contained in Article 4(3) of the ECHR:

'For the purpose of this article the term "forced or compulsory labour" shall not include:
(a)   any work required to be done in the ordinary course of detention imposed according to the provisions of Article 5 of this Convention or during conditional release from such detention;
(b)   any service of a military character or, in case of conscientious objectors in countries where they are recognised, service exacted instead of compulsory military service;
(c)   any service exacted in case of an emergency or calamity threatening the life or well-being of the community;
(d)   any work or service which forms part of normal civic obligations.'

2.   Paragraph 3 stems directly from human dignity and takes account of recent developments in organised crime, such as the organisation of lucrative illegal immigration or sexual exploitation networks. The Annex to the Europol Convention contains the following definition which refers to trafficking for the purpose of sexual exploitation:

'traffic in human beings: means subjection of a person to the real and illegal sway of other persons by using violence or menaces or by abuse of authority or intrigue with a view to the exploitation of prostitution, forms of sexual exploitation and assault of minors or trade in abandoned children'. Chapter VI of the Convention implementing the Schengen Agreement, which has been integrated into the Union's *acquis*, in which the United Kingdom and Ireland participate, contains the following wording in Article 27(1) which refers to illegal immigration networks: 'The Contracting Parties undertake to impose appropriate penalties on any person who, for financial gain, assists or tries to assist an alien to enter or reside within the territory of one of the Contracting Parties in breach of that Contracting Party's laws on the entry and residence of aliens.' On 19 July 2002, the Council adopted a framework decision on combating trafficking in human beings (OJ L 203, 1.8.2002, p. 1) whose Article 1 defines in detail the offences concerning trafficking in human beings for the purposes of labour exploitation or sexual exploitation, which the Member States must make punishable by virtue of that framework decision.

TITLE II — FREEDOMS

Explanation on Article 6 — Right to liberty and security
The rights in Article 6 are the rights guaranteed by Article 5 of the ECHR, and in accordance with Article 52(3) of the Charter, they have the same meaning and scope. Consequently, the limitations which may legitimately be imposed on them may not exceed those permitted by the ECHR, in the wording of Article 5:

'1.   Everyone has the right to liberty and security of person. No one shall be deprived of his liberty save in the following cases and in accordance with a procedure prescribed by law:

(a)   the lawful detention of a person after conviction by a competent court;

(b)   the lawful arrest or detention of a person for non-compliance with the lawful order of a court or in order to secure the fulfilment of any obligation prescribed by law;

(c)   the lawful arrest or detention of a person effected for the purpose of bringing him before the competent legal authority on reasonable suspicion of having committed an offence or when it is reasonably considered necessary to prevent his committing an offence or fleeing after having done so;

(d)   the detention of a minor by lawful order for the purpose of educational supervision or his lawful detention for the purpose of bringing him before the competent legal authority;

(e)   the lawful detention of persons for the prevention of the spreading of infectious diseases, of persons of unsound mind, alcoholics or drug addicts or vagrants;

(f)   the lawful arrest or detention of a person to prevent his effecting an unauthorised entry into the country or of a person against whom action is being taken with a view to deportation or extradition.

2.   Everyone who is arrested shall be informed promptly, in a language which he understands, of the reasons for his arrest and of any charge against him.

3.   Everyone arrested or detained in accordance with the provisions of paragraph 1.c of this Article shall be brought promptly before a judge or other officer authorised by law to exercise judicial power and shall be entitled to trial within a reasonable time or to release pending trial. Release may be conditioned by guarantees to appear for trial.

4.   Everyone who is deprived of his liberty by arrest or detention shall be entitled to take proceedings by which the lawfulness of his detention shall be decided speedily by a court and his release ordered if the detention is not lawful.

5.   Everyone who has been the victim of arrest or detention in contravention of the provisions of this Article shall have an enforceable right to compensation.'

The rights enshrined in Article 6 must be respected particularly when the European Parliament and the Council adopt legislative acts in the area of judicial cooperation in criminal matters, on the basis of Articles 82, 83 and 85 of the Treaty on the Functioning of the European Union, notably to define common minimum provisions as regards the categorisation of offences and punishments and certain aspects of procedural law.

Explanation on Article 7 — Respect for private and family life
The rights guaranteed in Article 7 correspond to those guaranteed by Article 8 of the ECHR. To take account of developments in technology the word 'correspondence' has been replaced by 'communications'.

In accordance with Article 52(3), the meaning and scope of this right are the same as those of the corresponding article of the ECHR. Consequently, the limitations which may legitimately be imposed on this right are the same as those allowed by Article 8 of the ECHR:

'1.   Everyone has the right to respect for his private and family life, his home and his correspondence.

2.   There shall be no interference by a public authority with the exercise of this right except such as is in accordance with the law and is necessary in a democratic society in the interests of national security, public safety or the economic wellbeing of the country, for the prevention of disorder or crime, for the protection of health or morals, or for the protection of the rights and freedoms of others.'

Explanation on Article 8 — Protection of personal data
This Article has been based on Article 286 of the Treaty establishing the European Community and Directive 95/46/EC of the European Parliament and of the Council on the protection of individuals with regard to the processing of personal data and on the free movement of such data (OJ L 281, 23.11.1995, p. 31) as well as on Article 8 of the ECHR and on the Council of Europe Convention of 28 January 1981 for the Protection of Individuals with regard to Automatic Processing of Personal Data, which has been ratified by all the Member States. Article 286 of the EC Treaty is now replaced by Article 16 of the Treaty on the Functioning of the European Union and Article 39 of the Treaty on European Union. Reference is also made to Regulation (EC) No 45/2001 of the European Parliament and of the Council on the protection of individuals with regard to the processing of personal data by the Community institutions and bodies and on the free movement of such data (OJ L 8, 12.1.2001, p. 1). The above-mentioned Directive and Regulation contain conditions and limitations for the exercise of the right to the protection of personal data.

Explanation on Article 9 — Right to marry and right to found a family
This Article is based on Article 12 of the ECHR, which reads as follows: 'Men and women of marriageable age have the right to marry and to found a family according to the national laws governing the exercising of this right.' The wording of the Article has been modernised to cover cases in which national legislation recognises arrangements other than marriage for founding a family. This Article neither prohibits nor imposes the granting of the status of marriage to unions between people of the same sex. This right is thus similar to that afforded by the ECHR, but its scope may be wider when national legislation so provides.

Explanation on Article 10 — Freedom of thought, conscience and religion
The right guaranteed in paragraph 1 corresponds to the right guaranteed in Article 9 of the ECHR and, in accordance with Article 52(3) of the Charter, has the same meaning and scope. Limitations must therefore respect Article 9(2) of the Convention, which reads as follows: 'Freedom to manifest one's religion or beliefs shall be subject only to such limitations as are prescribed by law and are necessary in a democratic society in the interests of public safety, for the protection of public order, health or morals, or for the protection of the rights and freedoms of others.'

The right guaranteed in paragraph 2 corresponds to national constitutional traditions and to the development of national legislation on this issue.

Explanation on Article 11 — Freedom of expression and information
1.   Article 11 corresponds to Article 10 of the European Convention on Human Rights, which reads as follows:

'1.   Everyone has the right to freedom of expression. This right shall include freedom to hold opinions and to receive and impart information and ideas without interference by public authority and regardless of frontiers.

This Article shall not prevent States from requiring the licensing of broadcasting, television or cinema enterprises.

2. The exercise of these freedoms, since it carries with it duties and responsibilities, may be subject to such formalities, conditions, restrictions or penalties as are prescribed by law and are necessary in a democratic society, in the interests of national security, territorial integrity or public safety, for the prevention of disorder or crime, for the protection of health or morals, for the protection of the reputation or rights of others, for preventing the disclosure of information received in confidence, or for maintaining the authority and impartiality of the judiciary.'

Pursuant to Article 52(3) of the Charter, the meaning and scope of this right are the same as those guaranteed by the ECHR. The limitations which may be imposed on it may therefore not exceed those provided for in Article 10(2) of the Convention, without prejudice to any restrictions which the competition law of the Union may impose on Member States' right to introduce the licensing arrangements referred to in the third sentence of Article 10(1) of the ECHR.

2. Paragraph 2 of this Article spells out the consequences of paragraph 1 regarding freedom of the media. It is based in particular on Court of Justice case-law regarding television, particularly in Case C-288/89 (judgment of 25 July 1991, *Stichting Collectieve Antennevoorziening Gouda and others* [1991] ECR I-4007), and on the Protocol on the system of public broadcasting in the Member States annexed to the EC Treaty and now to the Treaties, and on Council Directive 89/552/EC (particularly its seventeenth recital).

Explanation on Article 12 — Freedom of assembly and of association
1. Paragraph 1 of this Article corresponds to Article 11 of the ECHR, which reads as follows:

'1. Everyone has the right to freedom of peaceful assembly and to freedom of association with others, including the right to form and to join trade unions for the protection of his interests.

2. No restrictions shall be placed on the exercise of these rights other than such as are prescribed by law and are necessary in a democratic society in the interests of national security or public safety, for the prevention of disorder or crime, for the protection of health or morals or for the protection of the rights and freedoms of others. This article shall not prevent the imposition of lawful restrictions on the exercise of these rights by members of the armed forces, of the police or of the administration of the State.'

The meaning of the provisions of paragraph 1 of this Article 12 is the same as that of the ECHR, but their scope is wider since they apply at all levels including European level. In accordance with Article 52(3) of the Charter, limitations on that right may not exceed those considered legitimate by virtue of Article 11(2) of the ECHR.

2. This right is also based on Article 11 of the Community Charter of the Fundamental Social Rights of Workers.

3. Paragraph 2 of this Article corresponds to Article 10(4) of the Treaty on European Union.

Explanation on Article 13 — Freedom of the arts and sciences
This right is deduced primarily from the right to freedom of thought and expression. It is to be exercised having regard to Article 1 and may be subject to the limitations authorised by Article 10 of the ECHR.

Explanation on Article 14 — Right to education
1.   This Article is based on the common constitutional traditions of Member States and on
      Article 2 of the Protocol to the ECHR, which reads as follows:

      'No person shall be denied the right to education. In the exercise of any functions which it
      assumes in relation to education and to teaching, the State shall respect the right of
      parents to ensure such education and teaching in conformity with their own religious and
      philosophical convictions.'

      It was considered useful to extend this Article to access to vocational and continuing
      training (see point 15 of the Community Charter of the Fundamental Social Rights of
      Workers and Article 10 of the Social Charter) and to add the principle of free compulsory
      education. As it is worded, the latter principle merely implies that as regards compulsory
      education, each child has the possibility of attending an establishment which offers
      free education. It does not require all establishments which provide education or
      vocational and continuing training, in particular private ones, to be free of charge. Nor
      does it exclude certain specific forms of education having to be paid for, if the State
      takes measures to grant financial compensation. In so far as the Charter applies to the
      Union, this means that in its training policies the Union must respect free compulsory
      education, but this does not, of course, create new powers. Regarding the right of parents,
      it must be interpreted in conjunction with the provisions of Article 24.

2.   Freedom to found public or private educational establishments is guaranteed as one of the
      aspects of freedom to conduct a business but it is limited by respect for democratic principles
      and is exercised in accordance with the arrangements defined by national legislation.

Explanation on Article 15 — Freedom to choose an occupation and right to engage in work
Freedom to choose an occupation, as enshrined in Article 15(1), is recognised in Court of
Justice case-law (see *inter alia* judgment of 14 May 1974, Case 4/73 *Nold* [1974] ECR 491,
paragraphs 12 to 14 of the grounds; judgment of 13 December 1979, Case 44/79 *Hauer* [1979]
ECR 3727; judgment of 8 October 1986, Case 234/85 *Keller* [1986] ECR 2897, paragraph 8 of
the grounds).

This paragraph also draws upon Article 1(2) of the European Social Charter, which was signed
on 18 October 1961 and has been ratified by all the Member States, and on point 4 of the
Community Charter of the Fundamental Social Rights of Workers of 9 December 1989. The
expression 'working conditions' is to be understood in the sense of Article 156 of the Treaty on
the Functioning of the European Union.

Paragraph 2 deals with the three freedoms guaranteed by Articles 26, 45, 49 and 56 of the
Treaty on the Functioning of the European Union, namely freedom of movement for workers,
freedom of establishment and freedom to provide services.

Paragraph 3 has been based on Article 153(1)(g) of the Treaty on the Functioning of the
European Union, and on Article 19(4) of the European Social Charter signed on 18 October
1961 and ratified by all the Member States. Article 52(2) of the Charter is therefore applicable.
The question of recruitment of seamen having the nationality of third States for the crews of
vessels flying the flag of a Member State of the Union is governed by Union law and national
legislation and practice.

Explanation on Article 16 — Freedom to conduct a business
This Article is based on Court of Justice case-law which has recognised freedom to exercise an
economic or commercial activity (see judgments of 14 May 1974, Case 4/73 *Nold* [1974] ECR
491, paragraph 14 of the grounds, and of 27 September 1979, Case 230–78 *SpA Eridiana and*

others [1979] ECR 2749, paragraphs 20 and 31 of the grounds) and freedom of contract (see *inter alia Sukkerfabriken Nykøbing* judgment, Case 151/78 [1979] ECR 1, paragraph 19 of the grounds, and judgment of 5 October 1999, C-240/97 *Spain v Commission* [1999] ECR I-6571, paragraph 99 of the grounds) and Article 119(1) and (3) of the Treaty on the Functioning of the European Union, which recognises free competition. Of course, this right is to be exercised with respect for Union law and national legislation. It may be subject to the limitations provided for in Article 52(1) of the Charter.

Explanation on Article 17 — Right to property
This Article is based on Article 1 of the Protocol to the ECHR:

'Every natural or legal person is entitled to the peaceful enjoyment of his possessions. No one shall be deprived of his possessions except in the public interest and subject to the conditions provided for by law and by the general principles of international law.

The preceding provisions shall not, however, in any way impair the right of a State to enforce such laws as it deems necessary to control the use of property in accordance with the general interest or to secure the payment of taxes or other contributions or penalties.'

This is a fundamental right common to all national constitutions. It has been recognised on numerous occasions by the case-law of the Court of Justice, initially in the *Hauer* judgment (13 December 1979, [1979] ECR 3727). The wording has been updated but, in accordance with Article 52(3), the meaning and scope of the right are the same as those of the right guaranteed by the ECHR and the limitations may not exceed those provided for there.

Protection of intellectual property, one aspect of the right of property, is explicitly mentioned in paragraph 2 because of its growing importance and Community secondary legislation. Intellectual property covers not only literary and artistic property but also *inter alia* patent and trademark rights and associated rights. The guarantees laid down in paragraph 1 shall apply as appropriate to intellectual property.

Explanation on Article 18 — Right to asylum
The text of the Article has been based on TEC Article 63, now replaced by Article 78 of the Treaty on the Functioning of the European Union, which requires the Union to respect the Geneva Convention on refugees. Reference should be made to the Protocols relating to the United Kingdom and Ireland, annexed to the Treaties, and to Denmark, to determine the extent to which those Member States implement Union law in this area and the extent to which this Article is applicable to them. This Article is in line with the Protocol on Asylum annexed to the Treaties.

Explanation on Article 19 — Protection in the event of removal, expulsion or extradition
Paragraph 1 of this Article has the same meaning and scope as Article 4 of Protocol No 4 to the ECHR concerning collective expulsion. Its purpose is to guarantee that every decision is based on a specific examination and that no single measure can be taken to expel all persons having the nationality of a particular State (see also Article 13 of the Covenant on Civil and Political Rights).

Paragraph 2 incorporates the relevant case-law from the European Court of Human Rights regarding Article 3 of the ECHR (see Ahmed v. Austria, judgment of 17 December 1996, 1996-VI, p. 2206, and Soering, judgment of 7 July 1989).

TITLE III — EQUALITY

Explanation on Article 20 — Equality before the law
This Article corresponds to a general principle of law which is included in all European constitutions and has also been recognised by the Court of Justice as a basic principle of

Community law (judgment of 13 November 1984, Case 283/83 *Racke* [1984] ECR 3791, judgment of 17 April 1997, Case C-15/95 *EARL* [1997] ECR I-1961, and judgment of 13 April 2000, Case C-292/97 *Karlsson* [2000] ECR 2737).

Explanation on Article 21 — Non-discrimination

Paragraph 1 draws on Article 13 of the EC Treaty, now replaced by Article 19 of the Treaty on the Functioning of the European Union, Article 14 of the ECHR and Article 11 of the Convention on Human Rights and Biomedicine as regards genetic heritage. In so far as this corresponds to Article 14 of the ECHR, it applies in compliance with it.

There is no contradiction or incompatibility between paragraph 1 and Article 19 of the Treaty on the Functioning of the European Union which has a different scope and purpose: Article 19 confers power on the Union to adopt legislative acts, including harmonisation of the Member States' laws and regulations, to combat certain forms of discrimination, listed exhaustively in that Article. Such legislation may cover action of Member State authorities (as well as relations between private individuals) in any area within the limits of the Union's powers. In contrast, the provision in Article 21(1) does not create any power to enact anti-discrimination laws in these areas of Member State or private action, nor does it lay down a sweeping ban of discrimination in such wide-ranging areas. Instead, it only addresses discriminations by the institutions and bodies of the Union themselves, when exercising powers conferred under the Treaties, and by Member States only when they are implementing Union law. Paragraph 1 therefore does not alter the extent of powers granted under Article 19 nor the interpretation given to that Article.

Paragraph 2 corresponds to the first paragraph of Article 18 of the Treaty on the Functioning of the European Union and must be applied in compliance with that Article.

Explanation on Article 22 — Cultural, religious and linguistic diversity

This Article has been based on Article 6 of the Treaty on European Union and on Article 151(1) and (4) of the EC Treaty, now replaced by Article 167(1) and (4) of the Treaty on the Functioning of the European Union, concerning culture. Respect for cultural and linguistic diversity is now also laid down in Article 3(3) of the Treaty on European Union. The Article is also inspired by Declaration No 11 to the Final Act of the Amsterdam Treaty on the status of churches and nonconfessional organisations, now taken over in Article 17 of the Treaty on the Functioning of the European Union.

Explanation on Article 23 — Equality between women and men

The first paragraph has been based on Articles 2 and 3(2) of the EC Treaty, now replaced by Article 3 of the Treaty on European Union and Article 8 of the Treaty on the Functioning of the European Union which impose the objective of promoting equality between men and women on the Union, and on Article 157(1) of the Treaty on the Functioning of the European Union. It draws on Article 20 of the revised European Social Charter of 3 May 1996 and on point 16 of the Community Charter on the rights of workers.

It is also based on Article 157(3) of the Treaty on the Functioning of the European Union and Article 2(4) of Council Directive 76/207/EEC on the implementation of the principle of equal treatment for men and women as regards access to employment, vocational training and promotion, and working conditions.

The second paragraph takes over in shorter form Article 157(4) of the Treaty on the Functioning of the European Union which provides that the principle of equal treatment does not prevent the maintenance or adoption of measures providing for specific advantages in order to make it easier for the under-represented sex to pursue a vocational activity or to prevent or compensate for disadvantages in professional careers. In accordance with Article 52(2), the present paragraph does not amend Article 157(4).

Explanation on Article 24 — The rights of the child
This Article is based on the New York Convention on the Rights of the Child signed on
20 November 1989 and ratified by all the Member States, particularly Articles 3, 9, 12 and 13
thereof.

Paragraph 3 takes account of the fact that, as part of the establishment of an area of freedom,
security and justice, the legislation of the Union on civil matters having cross-border
implications, for which Article 81 of the Treaty on the Functioning of the European Union
confers power, may include notably visiting rights ensuring that children can maintain on a
regular basis a personal and direct contact with both of their parents.

Explanation on Article 25 — The rights of the elderly
This Article draws on Article 23 of the revised European Social Charter and Articles 24 and 25
of the Community Charter of the Fundamental Social Rights of Workers. Of course,
participation in social and cultural life also covers participation in political life.

Explanation on Article 26 — Integration of persons with disabilities
The principle set out in this Article is based on Article 15 of the European Social Charter and
also draws on point 26 of the Community Charter of the Fundamental Social Rights of
Workers.

TITLE IV — SOLIDARITY

*Explanation on Article 27 — Workers' right to information and consultation within
the undertaking*
This Article appears in the revised European Social Charter (Article 21) and in the Community
Charter on the rights of workers (points 17 and 18). It applies under the conditions laid down
by Union law and by national laws. The reference to appropriate levels refers to the levels laid
down by Union law or by national laws and practices, which might include the European level
when Union legislation so provides. There is a considerable Union *acquis* in this field: Articles
154 and 155 of the Treaty on the Functioning of the European Union, and Directives 2002/14/
EC (general framework for informing and consulting employees in the European Community),
98/59/EC (collective redundancies), 2001/23/EC (transfers of undertakings) and 94/45/EC
(European works councils).

Explanation on Article 28 — Right of collective bargaining and action
This Article is based on Article 6 of the European Social Charter and on the Community
Charter of the Fundamental Social Rights of Workers (points 12 to 14). The right of collective
action was recognised by the European Court of Human Rights as one of the elements of trade
union rights laid down by Article 11 of the ECHR. As regards the appropriate levels at which
collective negotiation might take place, see the explanation given for the above Article. The
modalities and limits for the exercise of collective action, including strike action, come under
national laws and practices, including the question of whether it may be carried out in parallel
in several Member States.

Explanation on Article 29 — Right of access to placement services
This Article is based on Article 1(3) of the European Social Charter and point 13 of the
Community Charter of the Fundamental Social Rights of Workers.

Explanation on Article 30 — Protection in the event of unjustified dismissal
This Article draws on Article 24 of the revised Social Charter. See also Directive 2001/23/EC on
the safeguarding of employees' rights in the event of transfers of undertakings, and Directive

80/987/EEC on the protection of employees in the event of the insolvency of their employer, as amended by Directive 2002/74/EC.

Explanation on Article 31 — Fair and just working conditions
1.   Paragraph 1 of this Article is based on Directive 89/391/EEC on the introduction of measures to encourage improvements in the safety and health of workers at work. It also draws on Article 3 of the Social Charter and point 19 of the Community Charter on the rights of workers, and, as regards dignity at work, on Article 26 of the revised Social Charter. The expression 'working conditions' is to be understood in the sense of Article 156 of the Treaty on the Functioning of the European Union.

2.   Paragraph 2 is based on Directive 93/104/EC concerning certain aspects of the organisation of working time, Article 2 of the European Social Charter and point 8 of the Community Charter on the rights of workers.

Explanation on Article 32 — Prohibition of child labour and protection of young people at work
This Article is based on Directive 94/33/EC on the protection of young people at work, Article 7 of the European Social Charter and points 20 to 23 of the Community Charter of the Fundamental Social Rights of Workers.

Explanation on Article 33 — Family and professional life
Article 33(1) is based on Article 16 of the European Social Charter.

Paragraph 2 draws on Council Directive 92/85/EEC on the introduction of measures to encourage improvements in the safety and health at work of pregnant workers and workers who have recently given birth or are breastfeeding and Directive 96/34/EC on the framework agreement on parental leave concluded by UNICE, CEEP and the ETUC. It is also based on Article 8 (protection of maternity) of the European Social Charter and draws on Article 27 (right of workers with family responsibilities to equal opportunities and equal treatment) of the revised Social Charter. 'Maternity' covers the period from conception to weaning.

Explanation on Article 34 — Social security and social assistance
The principle set out in Article 34(1) is based on Articles 153 and 156 of the Treaty on the Functioning of the European Union, Article 12 of the European Social Charter and point 10 of the Community Charter on the rights of workers. The Union must respect it when exercising the powers conferred on it by Articles 153 and 156 of the Treaty on the Functioning of the European Union. The reference to social services relates to cases in which such services have been introduced to provide certain advantages but does not imply that such services must be created where they do not exist. 'Maternity' must be understood in the same sense as in the preceding Article.

Paragraph 2 is based on Articles 12(4) and 13(4) of the European Social Charter and point 2 of the Community Charter of the Fundamental Social Rights of Workers and reflects the rules arising from Regulation (EEC) No 1408/71 and Regulation (EEC) No 1612/68.

Paragraph 3 draws on Article 13 of the European Social Charter and Articles 30 and 31 of the revised Social Charter and point 10 of the Community Charter. The Union must respect it in the context of policies based on Article 153 of the Treaty on the Functioning of the European Union.

Explanation on Article 35 — Health care
The principles set out in this Article are based on Article 152 of the EC Treaty, now replaced by Article 168 of the Treaty on the Functioning of the European Union, and on Articles 11 and 13 of the European Social Charter. The second sentence of the Article takes over Article 168(1).

Explanation on Article 36 — Access to services of general economic interest
This Article is fully in line with Article 14 of the Treaty on the Functioning of the European Union and does not create any new right. It merely sets out the principle of respect by the Union for the access to services of general economic interest as provided for by national provisions, when those provisions are compatible with Union law.

Explanation on Article 37 — Environmental protection
The principles set out in this Article have been based on Articles 2, 6 and 174 of the EC Treaty, which have now been replaced by Article 3(3) of the Treaty on European Union and Articles 11 and 191 of the Treaty on the Functioning of the European Union.

It also draws on the provisions of some national constitutions.

Explanation on Article 38 — Consumer protection
The principles set out in this Article have been based on Article 169 of the Treaty on the Functioning of the European Union.

TITLE V — CITIZENS' RIGHTS

Explanation on Article 39 — Right to vote and to stand as a candidate at elections to the European Parliament
Article 39 applies under the conditions laid down in the Treaties, in accordance with Article 52(2) of the Charter. Article 39(1) corresponds to the right guaranteed in Article 20(2) of the Treaty on the Functioning of the European Union (cf. also the legal base in Article 22 of the Treaty on the Functioning of the European Union for the adoption of detailed arrangements for the exercise of that right) and Article 39(2) corresponds to Article 14(3) of the Treaty on European Union. Article 39(2) takes over the basic principles of the electoral system in a democratic State.

Explanation on Article 40 — Right to vote and to stand as a candidate at municipal elections
This Article corresponds to the right guaranteed by Article 20(2) of the Treaty on the Functioning of the European Union (cf. also the legal base in Article 22 of the Treaty on the Functioning of the European Union for the adoption of detailed arrangements for the exercise of that right). In accordance with Article 52(2) of the Charter, it applies under the conditions defined in these Articles in the Treaties.

Explanation on Article 41 — Right to good administration
Article 41 is based on the existence of the Union as subject to the rule of law whose characteristics were developed in the case-law which enshrined *inter alia* good administration as a general principle of law (see *inter alia* Court of Justice judgment of 31 March 1992 in Case C-255/90 P *Burban* [1992] ECR I-2253, and Court of First Instance judgments of 18 September 1995 in Case T-167/94 *Nölle* [1995] ECR II-2589, and 9 July 1999 in Case T-231/97 *New Europe Consulting and others* [1999] ECR II-2403). The wording for that right in the first two paragraphs results from the case-law (Court of Justice judgment of 15 October 1987 in Case 222/86 *Heylens* [1987] ECR 4097, paragraph 15 of the grounds, judgment of 18 October 1989 in Case 374/87 *Orkem* [1989] ECR 3283, judgment of 21 November 1991 in Case C-269/90 *TU München* [1991] ECR I-5469, and Court of First Instance judgments of 6 December 1994 in Case T-450/93 *Lisrestal* [1994] ECR II-1177, 18 September 1995 in Case T-167/94 *Nölle* [1995] ECR II-2589) and the wording regarding the obligation to give reasons comes from Article 296 of the Treaty on the Functioning of the European Union (cf. also the legal base in Article 298 of the Treaty on the Functioning of the European Union for the adoption of legislation in the interest of an open, efficient and independent European administration).

Paragraph 3 reproduces the right now guaranteed by Article 340 of the Treaty on the Functioning of the European Union.

Paragraph 4 reproduces the right now guaranteed by Article 20(2)(d) and Article 25 of the Treaty on the Functioning of the European Union. In accordance with Article 52(2) of the Charter, those rights are to be applied under the conditions and within the limits defined by the Treaties.

The right to an effective remedy, which is an important aspect of this question, is guaranteed in Article 47 of this Charter.

Explanation on Article 42 — Right of access to documents
The right guaranteed in this Article has been taken over from Article 255 of the EC Treaty, on the basis of which Regulation (EC) No 1049/2001 has subsequently been adopted. The European Convention has extended this right to documents of institutions, bodies and agencies generally, regardless of their form (see Article 15(3) of the Treaty on the Functioning of the European Union). In accordance with Article 52(2) of the Charter, the right of access to documents is exercised under the conditions and within the limits for which provision is made in Article 15(3) of the Treaty on the Functioning of the European Union.

Explanation on Article 43 — European Ombudsman
The right guaranteed in this Article is the right guaranteed by Articles 20 and 228 of the Treaty on the Functioning of the European Union. In accordance with Article 52(2) of the Charter, it applies under the conditions defined in these two Articles.

Explanation on Article 44 — Right to petition
The right guaranteed in this Article is the right guaranteed by Articles 20 and 227 of the Treaty on the Functioning of the European Union. In accordance with Article 52(2) of the Charter, it applies under the conditions defined in these two Articles.

Explanation on Article 45 — Freedom of movement and of residence
The right guaranteed by paragraph 1 is the right guaranteed by Article 20(2)(a) of the Treaty on the Functioning of the European Union (cf. also the legal base in Article 21; and the judgment of the Court of Justice of 17 September 2002, Case C-413/99 *Baumbast* [2002] ECR I-7091). In accordance with Article 52(2) of the Charter, those rights are to be applied under the conditions and within the limits defined by the Treaties.

Paragraph 2 refers to the power granted to the Union by Articles 77, 78 and 79 of the Treaty on the Functioning of the European Union. Consequently, the granting of this right depends on the institutions exercising that power.

Explanation on Article 46 — Diplomatic and consular protection
The right guaranteed in this Article is the right guaranteed by Article 20 of the Treaty on the Functioning of the European Union (cf. also the legal base in Article 23). In accordance with Article 52(2) of the Charter, it applies under the conditions defined in these two Articles.

TITLE VI — JUSTICE

Explanation on Article 47 — Right to an effective remedy and to a fair trial
The first paragraph is based on Article 13 of the ECHR:

'Everyone whose rights and freedoms as set forth in this Convention are violated shall have an effective remedy before a national authority notwithstanding that the violation has been committed by persons acting in an official capacity.'

However, in Union law the protection is more extensive since it guarantees the right to an effective remedy before a court. The Court of Justice enshrined that right in its judgment of 15 May 1986 as a general principle of Union law (Case 222/84 *Johnston* [1986] ECR 1651; see also judgment of 15 October 1987, Case 222/86 *Heylens* [1987] ECR 4097 and judgment of 3 December 1992, Case C-97/91 *Borelli* [1992] ECR I-6313). According to the Court, that general principle of Union law also applies to the Member States when they are implementing Union law. The inclusion of this precedent in the Charter has not been intended to change the system of judicial review laid down by the Treaties, and particularly the rules relating to admissibility for direct actions before the Court of Justice of the European Union. The European Convention has considered the Union's system of judicial review including the rules on admissibility, and confirmed them while amending them as to certain aspects, as reflected in Articles 251 to 281 of the Treaty on the Functioning of the European Union, and in particular in the fourth paragraph of Article 263. Article 47 applies to the institutions of the Union and of Member States when they are implementing Union law and does so for all rights guaranteed by Union law.

The second paragraph corresponds to Article 6(1) of the ECHR which reads as follows:

'In the determination of his civil rights and obligations or of any criminal charge against him, everyone is entitled to a fair and public hearing within a reasonable time by an independent and impartial tribunal established by law. Judgment shall be pronounced publicly but the press and public may be excluded from all or part of the trial in the interests of morals, public order or national security in a democratic society, where the interests of juveniles or the protection of the private life of the parties so require, or to the extent strictly necessary in the opinion of the court in special circumstances where publicity would prejudice the interests of justice.'

In Union law, the right to a fair hearing is not confined to disputes relating to civil law rights and obligations. That is one of the consequences of the fact that the Union is a community based on the rule of law as stated by the Court in Case 294/83, *'Les Verts' v European Parliament* (judgment of 23 April 1986, [1986] ECR 1339). Nevertheless, in all respects other than their scope, the guarantees afforded by the ECHR apply in a similar way to the Union.

With regard to the third paragraph, it should be noted that in accordance with the case-law of the European Court of Human Rights, provision should be made for legal aid where the absence of such aid would make it impossible to ensure an effective remedy (ECHR judgment of 9 October 1979, Airey, Series A, Volume 32, p. 11). There is also a system of legal assistance for cases before the Court of Justice of the European Union.

Explanation on Article 48 — *Presumption of innocence and right of defence*
Article 48 is the same as Article 6(2) and (3) of the ECHR, which reads as follows:

'2.	Everyone charged with a criminal offence shall be presumed innocent until proved guilty according to law.

3.	Everyone charged with a criminal offence has the following minimum rights:
	(a)	to be informed promptly, in a language which he understands and in detail, of the nature and cause of the accusation against him;
	(b)	to have adequate time and facilities for the preparation of his defence;
	(c)	to defend himself in person or through legal assistance of his own choosing or, if he has not sufficient means to pay for legal assistance, to be given it free when the interests of justice so require;
	(d)	to examine or have examined witnesses against him and to obtain the attendance and examination of witnesses on his behalf under the same conditions as witnesses against him;

(e) to have the free assistance of an interpreter if he cannot understand or speak the language used in court.'

In accordance with Article 52(3), this right has the same meaning and scope as the right guaranteed by the ECHR.

Explanation on Article 49 — Principles of legality and proportionality of criminal offences and penalties
This Article follows the traditional rule of the non-retroactivity of laws and criminal sanctions. There has been added the rule of the retroactivity of a more lenient penal law, which exists in a number of Member States and which features in Article 15 of the Covenant on Civil and Political Rights.

Article 7 of the ECHR is worded as follows:

'1.   No one shall be held guilty of any criminal offence on account of any act or omission which did not constitute a criminal offence under national or international law at the time when it was committed. Nor shall a heavier penalty be imposed than the one that was applicable at the time the criminal offence was committed.

2.   This Article shall not prejudice the trial and punishment of any person for any act or omission which, at the time when it was committed, was criminal according to the general principles of law recognised by civilised nations.'

In paragraph 2, the reference to 'civilised' nations has been deleted; this does not change the meaning of this paragraph, which refers to crimes against humanity in particular. In accordance with Article 52(3), the right guaranteed here therefore has the same meaning and scope as the right guaranteed by the ECHR.

Paragraph 3 states the general principle of proportionality between penalties and criminal offences which is enshrined in the common constitutional traditions of the Member States and in the case-law of the Court of Justice of the Communities.

Explanation on Article 50 — Right not to be tried or punished twice in criminal proceedings for the same criminal offence
Article 4 of Protocol No 7 to the ECHR reads as follows:

'1.   No one shall be liable to be tried or punished again in criminal proceedings under the jurisdiction of the same State for an offence for which he has already been finally acquitted or convicted in accordance with the law and penal procedure of that State.

2.   The provisions of the preceding paragraph shall not prevent the reopening of the case in accordance with the law and the penal procedure of the State concerned, if there is evidence of new or newly discovered facts, or if there has been a fundamental defect in the previous proceedings, which could affect the outcome of the case.

3.   No derogation from this Article shall be made under Article 15 of the Convention.'

The '*non bis in idem*' rule applies in Union law (see, among the many precedents, the judgment of 5 May 1966, Joined Cases 18/65 and 35/65 *Gutmann v Commission* [1966] ECR 149 and a recent case, the decision of the Court of First Instance of 20 April 1999, Joined Cases T-305/94 and others *Limburgse Vinyl Maatschappij NV v Commission* [1999] ECR II 931). The rule prohibiting cumulation refers to cumulation of two penalties of the same kind, that is to say criminal-law penalties.

In accordance with Article 50, the '*non bis in idem*' rule applies not only within the jurisdiction of one State but also between the jurisdictions of several Member States. That corresponds to the *acquis* in Union law; see Articles 54 to 58 of the Schengen Convention and the judgment of the Court of Justice of 11 February 2003, C-187/01 *Gözütok* [2003] ECR I-1345, Article 7 of the Convention on the Protection of the European Communities' Financial Interests and Article 10 of the Convention on the fight against corruption. The very limited exceptions in those Conventions permitting the Member States to derogate from the '*non bis in idem*' rule are covered by the horizontal clause in Article 52(1) of the Charter concerning limitations. As regards the situations referred to by Article 4 of Protocol No 7, namely the application of the principle within the same Member State, the guaranteed right has the same meaning and the same scope as the corresponding right in the ECHR.

TITLE VII — GENERAL PROVISIONS GOVERNING THE INTERPRETATION AND APPLICATION OF THE CHARTER

Explanation on Article 51 — Field of application
The aim of Article 51 is to determine the scope of the Charter. It seeks to establish clearly that the Charter applies primarily to the institutions and bodies of the Union, in compliance with the principle of subsidiarity. This provision was drafted in keeping with Article 6(2) of the Treaty on European Union, which required the Union to respect fundamental rights, and with the mandate issued by the Cologne European Council. The term 'institutions' is enshrined in the Treaties. The expression 'bodies, offices and agencies' is commonly used in the Treaties to refer to all the authorities set up by the Treaties or by secondary legislation (see, e.g., Articles 15 or 16 of the Treaty on the Functioning of the European Union).

As regards the Member States, it follows unambiguously from the case-law of the Court of Justice that the requirement to respect fundamental rights defined in the context of the Union is only binding on the Member States when they act in the scope of Union law (judgment of 13 July 1989, Case 5/88 *Wachauf* [1989] ECR 2609; judgment of 18 June 1991, Case C-260/89 *ERT* [1991] ECR I-2925; judgment of 18 December 1997, Case C-309/96 *Annibaldi* [1997] ECR I-7493). The Court of Justice confirmed this case-law in the following terms: 'In addition, it should be remembered that the requirements flowing from the protection of fundamental rights in the Community legal order are also binding on Member States when they implement Community rules . . .' (judgment of 13 April 2000, Case C-292/97 [2000] ECR I-2737, paragraph 37 of the grounds). Of course this rule, as enshrined in this Charter, applies to the central authorities as well as to regional or local bodies, and to public organisations, when they are implementing Union law.

Paragraph 2, together with the second sentence of paragraph 1, confirms that the Charter may not have the effect of extending the competences and tasks which the Treaties confer on the Union. Explicit mention is made here of the logical consequences of the principle of subsidiarity and of the fact that the Union only has those powers which have been conferred upon it. The fundamental rights as guaranteed in the Union do not have any effect other than in the context of the powers determined by the Treaties. Consequently, an obligation, pursuant to the second sentence of paragraph 1, for the Union's institutions to promote principles laid down in the Charter may arise only within the limits of these same powers.

Paragraph 2 also confirms that the Charter may not have the effect of extending the field of application of Union law beyond the powers of the Union as established in the Treaties. The Court of Justice has already established this rule with respect to the fundamental rights recognised as part of Union law (judgment of 17 February 1998, C-249/96 *Grant* [1998] ECR I-621, paragraph 45 of the grounds). In accordance with this rule, it goes without saying that the reference to the Charter in Article 6 of the Treaty on European Union cannot be understood as extending by itself the range of Member State action considered to be 'implementation of Union law' (within the meaning of paragraph 1 and the above-mentioned case-law).

Explanation on Article 52 — Scope and interpretation of rights and principles
The purpose of Article 52 is to set the scope of the rights and principles of the Charter, and to lay down rules for their interpretation. Paragraph 1 deals with the arrangements for the limitation of rights. The wording is based on the case-law of the Court of Justice: '. . . it is well established in the case-law of the Court that restrictions may be imposed on the exercise of fundamental rights, in particular in the context of a common organisation of the market, provided that those restrictions in fact correspond to objectives of general interest pursued by the Community and do not constitute, with regard to the aim pursued, disproportionate and unreasonable interference undermining the very substance of those rights' (judgment of 13 April 2000, Case C-292/97, paragraph 45 of the grounds). The reference to general interests recognised by the Union covers both the objectives mentioned in Article 3 of the Treaty on European Union and other interests protected by specific provisions of the Treaties such as Article 4(1) of the Treaty on European Union and Articles 35(3), 36 and 346 of the Treaty on the Functioning of the European Union.

Paragraph 2 refers to rights which were already expressly guaranteed in the Treaty establishing the European Community and have been recognised in the Charter, and which are now found in the Treaties (notably the rights derived from Union citizenship). It clarifies that such rights remain subject to the conditions and limits applicable to the Union law on which they are based, and for which provision is made in the Treaties. The Charter does not alter the system of rights conferred by the EC Treaty and taken over by the Treaties.

Paragraph 3 is intended to ensure the necessary consistency between the Charter and the ECHR by establishing the rule that, in so far as the rights in the present Charter also correspond to rights guaranteed by the ECHR, the meaning and scope of those rights, including authorised limitations, are the same as those laid down by the ECHR. This means in particular that the legislator, in laying down limitations to those rights, must comply with the same standards as are fixed by the detailed limitation arrangements laid down in the ECHR, which are thus made applicable for the rights covered by this paragraph, without thereby adversely affecting the autonomy of Union law and of that of the Court of Justice of the European Union.

The reference to the ECHR covers both the Convention and the Protocols to it. The meaning and the scope of the guaranteed rights are determined not only by the text of those instruments, but also by the case-law of the European Court of Human Rights and by the Court of Justice of the European Union. The last sentence of the paragraph is designed to allow the Union to guarantee more extensive protection. In any event, the level of protection afforded by the Charter may never be lower than that guaranteed by the ECHR.

The Charter does not affect the possibilities of Member States to avail themselves of Article 15 ECHR, allowing derogations from ECHR rights in the event of war or of other public dangers threatening the life of the nation, when they take action in the areas of national defence in the event of war and of the maintenance of law and order, in accordance with their responsibilities recognised in Article 4(1) of the Treaty on European Union and in Articles 72 and 347 of the Treaty on the Functioning of the European Union.

The list of rights which may at the present stage, without precluding developments in the law, legislation and the Treaties, be regarded as corresponding to rights in the ECHR within the meaning of the present paragraph is given hereafter. It does not include rights additional to those in the ECHR.

1.   Articles of the Charter where both the meaning and the scope are the same as the corresponding Articles of the ECHR:
       — Article 2 corresponds to Article 2 of the ECHR,
       — Article 4 corresponds to Article 3 of the ECHR,
       — Article 5(1) and (2) corresponds to Article 4 of the ECHR,

— Article 6 corresponds to Article 5 of the ECHR,
— Article 7 corresponds to Article 8 of the ECHR,
— Article 10(1) corresponds to Article 9 of the ECHR,
— Article 11 corresponds to Article 10 of the ECHR without prejudice to any
restrictions which Union law may impose on Member States' right to introduce the
licensing arrangements referred to in the third sentence of Article 10(1) of the ECHR,
— Article 17 corresponds to Article 1 of the Protocol to the ECHR,
— Article 19(1) corresponds to Article 4 of Protocol No 4,
— Article 19(2) corresponds to Article 3 of the ECHR as interpreted by the European
Court of Human Rights,
— Article 48 corresponds to Article 6(2) and(3) of the ECHR,
— Article 49(1) (with the exception of the last sentence) and (2) correspond to Article 7
of the ECHR.

2.   Articles where the meaning is the same as the corresponding Articles of the ECHR, but
where the scope is wider:
— Article 9 covers the same field as Article 12 of the ECHR, but its scope may be
extended to other forms of marriage if these are established by national legislation,
— Article 12(1) corresponds to Article 11 of the ECHR, but its scope is extended to
European Union level,
— Article 14(1) corresponds to Article 2 of the Protocol to the ECHR, but its scope is
extended to cover access to vocational and continuing training,
— Article 14(3) corresponds to Article 2 of the Protocol to the ECHR as regards the
rights of parents,
— Article 47(2) and (3) corresponds to Article 6(1) of the ECHR, but the limitation to
the determination of civil rights and obligations or criminal charges does not apply as
regards Union law and its implementation,
— Article 50 corresponds to Article 4 of Protocol No 7 to the ECHR, but its scope is
extended to European Union level between the Courts of the Member States,
— Finally, citizens of the European Union may not be considered as aliens in the scope
of the application of Union law, because of the prohibition of any discrimination on
grounds of nationality. The limitations provided for by Article 16 of the ECHR as
regards the rights of aliens therefore do not apply to them in this context.

The rule of interpretation contained in paragraph 4 has been based on the wording of
Article 6(3) of the Treaty on European Union and takes due account of the approach to
common constitutional traditions followed by the Court of Justice (e.g., judgment of 13
December 1979, Case 44/79 *Hauer* [1979] ECR 3727; judgment of 18 May 1982, Case 155/79
AM&S [1982] ECR 1575). Under that rule, rather than following a rigid approach of 'a lowest
common denominator', the Charter rights concerned should be interpreted in a way offering a
high standard of protection which is adequate for the law of the Union and in harmony with the
common constitutional traditions.

Paragraph 5 clarifies the distinction between 'rights' and 'principles' set out in the Charter.
According to that distinction, subjective rights shall be respected, whereas principles shall be
observed (Article 51(1)). Principles may be implemented through legislative or executive acts
(adopted by the Union in accordance with its powers, and by the Member States only when they
implement Union law); accordingly, they become significant for the Courts only when such acts
are interpreted or reviewed. They do not however give rise to direct claims for positive action
by the Union's institutions or Member States authorities. This is consistent both with case-law
of the Court of Justice (cf. notably case-law on the 'precautionary principle' in Article 191(2) of
the Treaty on the Functioning of the European Union: judgment of the CFI of 11 September
2002, Case T-13/99 *Pfizer v Council*, with numerous references to earlier case-law; and a series

of judgments on Article 33 (ex-39) on the principles of agricultural law, e.g. judgment of the Court of Justice in Case 265/85 *Van den Berg* [1987] ECR 1155: scrutiny of the principle of market stabilisation and of reasonable expectations) and with the approach of the Member States' constitutional systems to 'principles', particularly in the field of social law. For illustration, examples for principles, recognised in the Charter include e.g. Articles 25, 26 and 37. In some cases, an Article of the Charter may contain both elements of a right and of a principle, e.g. Articles 23, 33 and 34.

Paragraph 6 refers to the various Articles in the Charter which, in the spirit of subsidiarity, make reference to national laws and practices.

Explanation on Article 53 — Level of protection
This provision is intended to maintain the level of protection currently afforded within their respective scope by Union law, national law and international law. Owing to its importance, mention is made of the ECHR.

Explanation on Article 54 — Prohibition of abuse of rights
This Article corresponds to Article 17 of the ECHR: 'Nothing in this Convention may be interpreted as implying for any State, group or person any right to engage in any activity or perform any act aimed at the destruction of any of the rights and freedoms set forth herein or at their limitation to a greater extent than is provided for in the Convention.'

REGULATION (EC) NO 168/2007 OF 15 FEBRUARY 2007 ESTABLISHING A EUROPEAN UNION AGENCY FOR FUNDAMENTAL RIGHTS
OJ L 53, 22.2.2007, P. 1[1]

(footnotes omitted)

THE COUNCIL OF THE EUROPEAN UNION,

Having regard to the Treaty establishing the European Community, and in particular Article 308 thereof,

Having regard to the proposal from the Commission,

Having regard to the opinion of the European Parliament,

Having regard to the opinion of the European Economic and Social Committee,

Having regard to the opinion of the Committee of the Regions,

Whereas:

(1)   The European Union is founded on the principles of liberty, democracy, respect for human rights and fundamental freedoms, and the rule of law, which are common values to the Member States.

---

[1]   EDITOR'S NOTE: Chapters 3–7 of the regulation have been omitted. As of 1 May 2012 this Regulation has not been amended following the entry into force of the Treaty of Lisbon. It may include references to the old version of the Treaty of European Union (TEU) and/or the now replaced Treaty establishing the European Community (TEC). Reference should be made to the Tables of Equivalences in Part II of this edition for the conversion of old Treaty numbers to new ones.

(2)   The Charter of Fundamental Rights of the European Union, bearing in mind its status and scope, and the accompanying explanations, reflects the rights as they result, in particular, from the constitutional traditions and international obligations common to the Member States, the Treaty on European Union, the Community Treaties, the European Convention for the Protection of Human Rights and Fundamental Freedoms, the social charters adopted by the Community and by the Council of Europe and the case law of the Court of Justice of the European Communities and of the European Court of Human Rights.

(3)   The Community and its Member States must respect fundamental rights when implementing Community law.

(4)   Greater knowledge of, and broader awareness of, fundamental rights issues in the Union are conducive to ensuring full respect of fundamental rights. It would contribute to the attainment of this objective to establish a Community agency whose tasks would be to provide information and data on fundamental rights matters. Moreover, developing effective institutions for the protection and promotion of human rights is a common value of the international and European societies, as expressed by Recommendation No R (97) 14 of the Committee of Ministers of the Council of Europe of 30 September 1997.

(5)   The Representatives of the Member States, meeting within the European Council on 13 December 2003, agreed to build upon the existing European Monitoring Centre on Racism and Xenophobia established by Regulation (EC) No 1035/97 and to extend its mandate to make it a Human Rights Agency. They also decided on that occasion that the seat of the Agency should remain in Vienna.

(6)   The Commission agreed and indicated its intention of presenting a proposal to amend Regulation (EC) No 1035/97 in that respect. The Commission subsequently issued its Communication of 25 October 2004 on the Fundamental Rights Agency, on the basis of which a large public consultation was carried out.

(7)   A European Union Agency for Fundamental Rights should accordingly be established, building upon the existing European Monitoring Centre on Racism and Xenophobia, to provide the relevant institutions and authorities of the Community and its Member States when implementing Community law with information, assistance and expertise on fundamental rights in order to support them when they take measures or formulate courses of action within their respective spheres of competence to fully respect fundamental rights.

(8)   It is recognised that the Agency should act only within the scope of application of Community law.

(9)   The Agency should refer in its work to fundamental rights within the meaning of Article 6(2) of the Treaty on European Union, including the European Convention on Human Rights and Fundamental Freedoms, and as reflected in particular in the Charter of Fundamental Rights, bearing in mind its status and the accompanying explanations. The close connection to the Charter should be reflected in the name of the Agency.

(10)   As the Agency is to be built upon the existing European Monitoring Centre on Racism and Xenophobia, the work of the Agency should continue to cover the phenomena of racism, xenophobia and anti-Semitism, the protection of rights of persons belonging to minorities, as well as gender equality, as essential elements for the protection of fundamental rights.

(11)   The thematic areas of activity of the Agency should be laid down in the Multiannual Framework, thus defining the limits of the work of the Agency. Due to the political significance of the Multiannual Framework, it is important that the Council itself should

adopt it, after consulting the European Parliament on the basis of a Commission proposal.

(12) The Agency should collect objective, reliable and comparable information on the development of the situation of fundamental rights, analyse this information in terms of causes of disrespect, consequences and effects and examine examples of good practice in dealing with these matters.

(13) The Agency should have the right to formulate opinions to the Union institutions and to the Member States when implementing Community law, either on its own initiative or at the request of the European Parliament, the Council or the Commission, without interference with the legislative and judicial procedures established in the Treaty. Nevertheless, the institutions should be able to request opinions on their legislative proposals or positions taken in the course of legislative procedures as far as their compatibility with fundamental rights are concerned.

(14) The Agency should present an annual report on fundamental rights issues covered by the areas of the Agency's activity, also highlighting examples of good practice. Furthermore, the Agency should produce thematic reports on topics of particular importance to the Union's policies.

(15) The Agency should take measures to raise the awareness of the general public about their fundamental rights, and about possibilities and different mechanisms for enforcing them in general, without, however, dealing itself with individual complaints.

(16) The Agency should work as closely as possible with all relevant Union institutions as well as the bodies, offices and agencies of the Community and the Union in order to avoid duplication, in particular as regards the future European Institute for Gender Equality.

(17) Since cooperation with the Member States is an essential element for the successful performance of the tasks of the Agency, it should cooperate closely with the Member States through its different bodies, for the purpose of which the Member States should nominate National Liaison Officers, as primary contact points for the Agency in the Member States. The Agency should, in particular, communicate with the National Liaison Officers as regards reports and other documents drawn up by the Agency.

(18) The Agency should collaborate closely with the Council of Europe. Such cooperation should guarantee that any overlap between the activities of the Agency and those of the Council of Europe is avoided, in particular by elaborating mechanisms to ensure complementarity and added value, such as the conclusion of a bilateral cooperation agreement and the participation of an independent person appointed by the Council of Europe in the management structures of the Agency with appropriately defined voting rights.

(19) Recognising the important role of civil society in the protection of fundamental rights, the Agency should promote dialogue with civil society and work closely with non-governmental organisations and with institutions of civil society active in the field of fundamental rights. It should set up a cooperation network called the "Fundamental Rights Platform" with a view to creating a structured and fruitful dialogue and close cooperation with all relevant stakeholders.

(20) Given the particular functions of the Agency, each Member State should appoint one independent expert to the Management Board. Having regard to the principles relating to the status and functioning of national institutions for the protection and promotion of human rights (the Paris Principles), the composition of that Board should ensure the Agency's independence from both Community institutions and Member State governments and assemble the broadest possible expertise in the field of fundamental rights.

(21) In order to ensure the high scientific quality of the work of the Agency, the Agency should avail itself of a Scientific Committee in order to guide its work by means of scientific objectivity.

(22) The authorities appointing members of the Management Board, the Executive Board and the Scientific Committee should aim to achieve a balanced participation between women and men on these bodies. Particular attention should also be given to the balanced representation of women and men on the staff of the Agency.

(23) Considering the significant role played by the European Parliament in the defence, mainstreaming and promotion of fundamental rights, it should be involved in the activities of the Agency, including the adoption of the Multiannual Framework for the Agency, and, given the exceptional nature and task of the Agency, the selection of the candidates proposed for the post of the Director of the Agency without setting a precedent for other Agencies.

(24) The Agency should apply the relevant Community legislation concerning public access to documents as set out in Regulation (EC) No 1049/2001 of the European Parliament and of the Council of 30 May 2001 regarding public access to European Parliament, Council and Commission documents, the protection of individuals with regard to the processing of personal data as set out in Regulation (EC) No 45/2001 of the European Parliament and of the Council of 18 December 2000 on the protection of individuals with regard to the processing of personal data by the Community institutions and bodies and on the free movement of such data, and concerning languages as set out in Regulation No 1 of 15 April 1958 determining the languages to be used by the European Economic Community and Regulation (EC) No 2965/94 of 28 November 1994 setting up a Translation Centre for bodies of the European Union.

(25) Commission Regulation (EC, Euratom) No 2343/2002 of 23 December 2002 on the framework Financial Regulation for the bodies referred to in Article 185 of Council Regulation (EC, Euratom) No 1605/2002 on the Financial Regulation applicable to the general budget of the European Communities should apply to the Agency, as well as Regulation (EC) No 1073/1999 of the European Parliament and of the Council of 25 May 1999 concerning investigations conducted by the European Antifraud Office (OLAF).

(26) The Staff Regulations of officials of the European Communities, the Conditions of Employment of other servants of the European Communities and the rules adopted jointly by the European Community institutions for the purpose of applying these Staff Regulations and Conditions of Employment should apply to the staff and to the Director of the Agency, including their rules relating to the dismissal of the Director.

(27) The Agency should have legal personality and succeed the European Monitoring Centre on Racism and Xenophobia as regards all legal obligations, financial commitments or liabilities carried out by the Centre or agreements made by the Centre as well as the employment contracts with the staff of the Centre.

(28) The Agency should be open to the participation of candidate countries. Furthermore, the countries with which a Stabilisation and Association agreement has been concluded should be allowed to participate in the Agency, since this will enable the Union to support their efforts towards European integration by facilitating a gradual alignment of their legislation with Community law as well as the transfer of know-how and good practice, particularly in those areas of the acquis that will serve as a central reference point for the reform process in the Western Balkans.

(29) The Agency should initiate the necessary evaluations of its activities in due time, on the basis of which the Agency's scope, tasks and working methods could be reviewed.

(30) Since the objectives of this Regulation, namely the provision of comparable and reliable information and data at European level in order to assist the Union institutions and the Member States in respecting fundamental rights, cannot be sufficiently achieved by the Member States and can therefore, by reason of the scale and impact of the proposed action, be better achieved at Community level, the Community may adopt measures, in accordance with the principle of subsidiarity set out in Article 5 of the Treaty. In accordance with the principle of proportionality as set out in that Article, this Regulation does not go beyond what is necessary in order to achieve those objectives.

(31) The contribution made by the Agency to ensuring full respect of fundamental rights in the framework of Community law is likely to help achieve the Community's objectives. With regard to the adoption of this Regulation, the Treaty does not provide for powers other than those set out in Article 308.

(32) Nothing in this Regulation should be interpreted in such a way as to prejudice the question of whether the remit of the Agency may be extended to cover the areas of police cooperation and judicial cooperation in criminal matters.

(33) As Regulation (EC) No 1035/97 would have to be substantially amended for the establishment of the Agency, it should be repealed in the interests of clarity,

HAS ADOPTED THIS REGULATION:

Chapter 1 SUBJECT MATTER, OBJECTIVE, SCOPE, TASKS AND AREAS OF ACTIVITY

Article 1 Subject matter
The European Union Agency for Fundamental Rights (the Agency) is hereby established.

Article 2 Objective
The objective of the Agency shall be to provide the relevant institutions, bodies, offices and agencies of the Community and its Member States when implementing Community law with assistance and expertise relating to fundamental rights in order to support them when they take measures or formulate courses of action within their respective spheres of competence to fully respect fundamental rights.

Article 3 Scope
1. The Agency shall carry out its tasks for the purpose of meeting the objective set in Article 2 within the competencies of the Community as laid down in the Treaty establishing the European Community.

2. The Agency shall refer in carrying out its tasks to fundamental rights as defined in Article 6(2) of the Treaty on European Union.

3. The Agency shall deal with fundamental-rights issues in the European Union and in its Member States when implementing Community law.

Article 4 Tasks
1. To meet the objective set in Article 2 and within its competences laid down in Article 3, the Agency shall:
   (a) collect, record, analyse and disseminate relevant, objective, reliable and comparable information and data, including results from research and monitoring communicated to it by Member States, Union institutions as well as bodies, offices and agencies of the Community and the Union, research centres, national bodies, non-governmental organisations, third countries and international organisations and in particular by the competent bodies of the Council of Europe;

(b) develop methods and standards to improve the comparability, objectivity and reliability of data at European level, in cooperation with the Commission and the Member States;

(c) carry out, cooperate with or encourage scientific research and surveys, preparatory studies and feasibility studies, including, where appropriate and compatible with its priorities and its annual work programme, at the request of the European Parliament, the Council or the Commission;

(d) formulate and publish conclusions and opinions on specific thematic topics, for the Union institutions and the Member States when implementing Community law, either on its own initiative or at the request of the European Parliament, the Council or the Commission;

(e) publish an annual report on fundamental-rights issues covered by the areas of the Agency's activity, also highlighting examples of good practice;

(f) publish thematic reports based on its analysis, research and surveys;

(g) publish an annual report on its activities; and

(h) develop a communication strategy and promote dialogue with civil society, in order to raise public awareness of fundamental rights and actively disseminate information about its work.

2. The conclusions, opinions and reports referred to in paragraph 1 may concern proposals from the Commission under Article 250 of the Treaty or positions taken by the institutions in the course of legislative procedures only where a request by the respective institution has been made in accordance with paragraph 1(d). They shall not deal with the legality of acts within the meaning of Article 230 of the Treaty or with the question of whether a Member State has failed to fulfil an obligation under the Treaty within the meaning of Article 226 of the Treaty.

Article 5 Areas of activity

1. The Council shall, acting on a proposal from the Commission and after consulting the European Parliament, adopt a Multiannual Framework for the Agency. When preparing its proposal, the Commission shall consult the Management Board.

2. The Framework shall:

(a) cover five years;

(b) determine the thematic areas of the Agency's activity, which must include the fight against racism, xenophobia and related intolerance;

(c) be in line with the Union's priorities, taking due account of the orientations resulting from European Parliament resolutions and Council conclusions in the field of fundamental rights;

(d) have due regard to the Agency's financial and human resources; and

(e) include provisions with a view to ensuring complementarity with the remit of other Community and Union bodies, offices and agencies, as well as with the Council of Europe and other international organisations active in the field of fundamental rights.

3. The Agency shall carry out its tasks within the thematic areas determined by the Multiannual Framework. This shall be without prejudice to the responses of the Agency to requests from the European Parliament, the Council or the Commission under Article 4(1)(c) and (d) outside these thematic areas, provided its financial and human resources so permit.

4. The Agency shall carry out its tasks in the light of its Annual Work Programme and with due regard to the available financial and human resources.

Chapter 2 WORKING METHODS AND COOPERATION

Article 6 Working methods

1. In order to ensure the provision of objective, reliable and comparable information, the Agency shall, drawing on the expertise of a variety of organisations and bodies in each Member State and taking account of the need to involve national authorities in the collection of data:
   (a) set up and coordinate information networks and use existing networks;
   (b) organise meetings of external experts; and
   (c) whenever necessary, set up ad hoc working parties.

2. In pursuing its activities, the Agency shall, in order to achieve complementarity and guarantee the best possible use of resources, take account, where appropriate, of information collected and of activities undertaken, in particular by:
   (a) Union institutions and bodies, offices and agencies of the Community and the Union, and bodies, offices and agencies of the Member States;
   (b) the Council of Europe, by referring to the findings and activities of the Council of Europe's monitoring and control mechanisms and of the Council of Europe Commissioner for Human Rights; and
   (c) the Organisation for Security and Cooperation in Europe (OSCE), the United Nations and other international organisations.

3. The Agency may enter into contractual relations, in particular subcontracting arrangements, with other organisations, in order to accomplish any tasks which it may entrust to them. The Agency may also award grants to promote appropriate cooperation and joint ventures, in particular to national and international organisations as referred to in Articles 8 and 9.

Article 7 Relations with relevant Community bodies, offices and agencies

The Agency shall ensure appropriate coordination with relevant Community bodies, offices and agencies. The terms of cooperation shall be laid down in memoranda of understanding where appropriate.

Article 8 Cooperation with organisations at Member State and international level

1. In order to ensure close cooperation with Member States, each Member State shall nominate a government official as a National Liaison Officer, who shall be the main contact point for the Agency in the Member State. The National Liaison Officers may, inter alia, submit opinions on the draft Annual Work Programme to the Director prior to its submission to the Management Board. The Agency shall communicate to the National Liaison Officers all documents drawn up in accordance with Article 4(1)(a), (b), (c), (d), (e), (f), (g) and (h).

2. To help it carry out its tasks, the Agency shall cooperate with:
   (a) governmental organisations and public bodies competent in the field of fundamental rights in the Member States, including national human rights institutions; and
   (b) the Organisation for Security and Cooperation in Europe (OSCE), especially the Office for Democratic Institutions and Human Rights (ODIHR), the United Nations and other international organisations.

3. The administrative arrangements for cooperation pursuant to paragraph 2 shall comply with Community law and shall be adopted by the Management Board on the basis of the draft submitted by the Director after the Commission has delivered an opinion. Where the Commission expresses its disagreement with these arrangements the Management Board shall re-examine and adopt them, with amendments where necessary, by a two-thirds majority of all members.

Article 9 Cooperation with the Council of Europe

In order to avoid duplication and in order to ensure complementarity and added value, the Agency shall coordinate its activities with those of the Council of Europe, particularly with regard to its Annual Work Programme pursuant to Article 12(6)(a) and cooperation with civil society in accordance with Article 10. To that end, the Community shall, in accordance with the procedure provided for in Article 300 of the Treaty, enter into an agreement with the Council of Europe for the purpose of establishing close cooperation between the latter and the Agency. This agreement shall include the appointment of an independent person by the Council of Europe, to sit on the Agency's Management Board and on its Executive Board, in accordance with Articles 12 and 13.

Article 10 Cooperation with civil society; Fundamental Rights Platform

1. The Agency shall closely cooperate with non-governmental organisations and with institutions of civil society, active in the field of fundamental rights including the combating of racism and xenophobia at national, European or international level. To that end, the Agency shall establish a cooperation network (Fundamental Rights Platform), composed of non-governmental organisations dealing with human rights, trade unions and employer's organisations, relevant social and professional organisations, churches, religious, philosophical and non-confessional organisations, universities and other qualified experts of European and international bodies and organisations.

2. The Fundamental Rights Platform shall constitute a mechanism for the exchange of information and pooling of knowledge. It shall ensure close cooperation between the Agency and relevant stakeholders.

3. The Fundamental Rights Platform shall be open to all interested and qualified stakeholders in accordance with paragraph 1. The Agency may address the members of the Fundamental Rights Platform in accordance with specific needs related to areas identified as a priority for the Agency's work.

4. The Agency shall call upon the Fundamental Rights Platform in particular, to:
    (a) make suggestions to the Management Board on the Annual Work Programme to be adopted pursuant to Article 12(6)(a);
    (b) give feedback and suggest follow-up to the Management Board on the annual report provided for in Article 4(1)(e); and
    (c) communicate outcomes and recommendations of conferences, seminars and meetings relevant to the work of the Agency to the Director and the Scientific Committee.

5. The Fundamental Rights Platform shall be coordinated under the authority of the Director.

IV Provisions Governing the Institutions

A) THE COURT OF JUSTICE – PROCEDURAL TEXTS

EXTRACTS FROM THE RULES OF PROCEDURE OF THE COURT OF JUSTICE

OJ L 176, 4.7.1991, P. 7 as amended and consolidated.[1]

....

[1] EDITOR'S NOTE: These Rules of Procedure were issued by the Court of Justice in accordance with its powers under Article 253 TFEU (ex 223 TEC). The Rules of Procedure are also subject to the institutional provisions contained in Articles 251–281 TFEU and Protocol (No. 3) on the Statute of the Court of Justice of the European Union. For the text of the Statute of the Court of Justice see the Protocols in Part I of this edition. Complete versions of the consolidated texts of the Rules of Procedure of the Court of Justice and the General Court (previously the Court of First Instance)can be found on the Court of Justice's web pages at: http://curia.europa.eu/jcms/jcms/Jo2_7031 (Court of Justice) and http://curia.europa.eu/jcms/jcms/Jo2_7040 (General Court). The most recent amendment took effect on 22 June 2011, OJ L162, 22.6.2011, p. 17, and was published as a consolidated text on 1 July 2011.

TITLE 1
ORGANISATION OF THE COURT

Chapter 1 JUDGES AND ADVOCATES GENERAL

Article 2
The term of office of a Judge shall begin on the date laid down in his instrument of appointment. In the absence of any provisions regarding the date, the term shall begin on the date of the instrument.

Article 3
1.   Before taking up his duties, a Judge shall at the first public sitting of the Court which he attends after his appointment take the following oath:

'I swear that I will perform my duties impartially and conscientiously; I swear that I will preserve the secrecy of the deliberations of the Court'.

2.   Immediately after taking the oath, a Judge shall sign a declaration by which he solemnly undertakes that, both during and after his term of office, he will respect the obligations arising therefrom, and in particular the duty to behave with integrity and discretion as regards the acceptance, after he has ceased to hold office, of certain appointments and benefits.

Article 4
When the Court is called upon to decide whether a Judge no longer fulfils the requisite conditions or no longer meets the obligations arising from his office, the President shall invite the Judge concerned to make representations to the Court, in closed session and in the absence of the Registrar.

Article 5
Articles 2, 3 and 4 of these Rules shall apply to Advocates General.

Article 6
Judges and Advocates General shall rank equally in precedence according to their seniority in office. Where there is equal seniority in office, precedence shall be determined by age.

Retiring Judges and Advocates General who are reappointed shall retain their former precedence.

Chapter 2   PRESIDENCY OF THE COURT AND CONSTITUTION OF THE CHAMBERS

Article 7

1.   The Judges shall, immediately after the partial replacement provided for in Article 253 TFEU, elect one of their number as President of the Court for a term of three years.

2.   If the office of the President of the Court falls vacant before the normal date of expiry thereof, the Court shall elect a successor for the remainder of the term.

3.   The elections provided for in this Article shall be by secret ballot. The Judge obtaining the votes of more than half the Judges composing the Court shall be elected. If no Judge obtains that majority, further ballots shall be held until that majority is attained.

Article 8

The President shall direct the judicial business and the administration of the Court; he shall preside at hearings and deliberations.

Article 9

1.   The Court shall set up Chambers of five and three Judges in accordance with Article 16 of the Statute and shall decide which Judges shall be attached to them.

The Court shall designate the Chamber or Chambers of five Judges which, for a period of one year, shall be responsible for cases of the kind referred to in Article 104b.

The composition of the Chambers and the designation of the Chamber or Chambers responsible for cases of the kind referred to in Article 104b shall be published in the *Official Journal of the European Union*.

2.   As soon as an application initiating proceedings has been lodged, the President shall designate a Judge to act as Rapporteur.

For cases of the kind referred to in Article 104b, the Judge-Rapporteur shall be selected from among the Judges of the Chamber designated in accordance with paragraph 1 of this Article, on a proposal from the President of that Chamber. If the Chamber decides that the case is not to be dealt with under the urgent procedure, the President of the Court may reassign the case to a Judge-Rapporteur attached to another Chamber.

The President of the Court shall take the necessary steps if a Judge-Rapporteur is absent or prevented from acting.

3.   For cases assigned to a formation of the Court in accordance with Article 44(3), the word 'Court' in these Rules shall mean that formation.

4.   In cases assigned to a Chamber of five or three Judges, the powers of the President of the Court shall be exercised by the President of the Chamber.

Article 10

1.   The Judges shall, immediately after the election of the President of the Court, elect the Presidents of the Chambers of five Judges for a term of three years.

The Judges shall elect the Presidents of the Chambers of three Judges for a term of one year.

The Court shall appoint for a period of one year the First Advocate General.

The provisions of Article 7(2) and (3) shall apply.

The elections and appointment made in pursuance of this paragraph shall be published in the *Official Journal of the European Union*.

2.   The First Advocate General shall assign each case to an Advocate General as soon as the Judge-Rapporteur has been designated by the President. He shall take the necessary steps if an Advocate General is absent or prevented from acting.

Article 11

When the President of the Court is absent or is prevented from attending or when the office of President is vacant, the functions of President shall be exercised by a President of a Chamber of five Judges according to the order of precedence laid down in Article 6 of these Rules.

When the President of the Court and the Presidents of the Chambers of five Judges are all absent or prevented from attending at the same time, or their posts are vacant at the same time, the functions of President shall be exercised by one of the Presidents of the Chambers of three Judges according to the order of precedence laid down in Article 6 of these Rules.

If the President of the Court and all the Presidents of Chambers are all absent or prevented from attending at the same time, or their posts are vacant at the same time, the functions of President shall be exercised by one of the other Judges according to the order of precedence laid down in Article 6 of these Rules.

Chapter 2A FORMATIONS OF THE COURT

Article 11a

The Court shall sit in the following formations:
—   the full Court, composed of all the Judges;

—   the Grand Chamber, composed of 13 Judges in accordance with Article 11b,

—   Chambers composed of five or three Judges in accordance with Article 11c.

Article 11b

1.   For each case the Grand Chamber shall be composed of the President of the Court, the Presidents of the Chambers of five Judges, the Judge-Rapporteur and the number of Judges necessary to reach 13. The last-mentioned Judges shall be designated from the list referred to in paragraph 2, following the order laid down therein. The starting-point on that list, in every case assigned to the Grand Chamber, shall be the name of the Judge immediately following the last Judge designated from the list for the preceding case assigned to that formation of the Court.

2.   After the election of the President of the Court and of the Presidents of the Chambers of five Judges, a list of the other Judges shall be drawn up for the purposes of determining the composition of the Grand Chamber. That list shall follow the order laid down in Article 6 of these Rules, alternating with the reverse order: the first Judge on that list shall be the first according to the order laid down in that Article, the second Judge shall be the last according to that order, the third Judge shall be the second according to that order, the fourth Judge the penultimate according to that order, and so on.

The list shall be published in the *Official Journal of the European Union*.

3.   In cases which are assigned to the Grand Chamber between the beginning of a year in which there is a partial replacement of Judges and the moment when that replacement has taken place, two substitute Judges shall also sit. Those substitute Judges shall be the two Judges appearing in the list referred to in the previous paragraph immediately after the last Judge designated for the composition of the Grand Chamber in the case.

The substitute Judges shall replace, in the order of the list referred to in the previous paragraph, such Judges as are unable to take part in the decision on the case.

Article 11c

1. The Chambers of five Judges and three Judges shall, for each case, be composed of the President of the Chamber, the Judge-Rapporteur and the number of Judges required to attain the number of five and three Judges respectively. Those last-mentioned Judges shall be designated from the lists referred to in paragraph 2 and following the order laid down in them.

    The starting point in those lists, for every case assigned to a Chamber, shall be the name of the Judge immediately following the last Judge designated from the list for the preceding case assigned to the Chamber concerned.

2. For the composition of the Chambers of five Judges, after the election of the Presidents of those Chambers lists shall be drawn up including all the Judges attached to the Chamber concerned, with the exception of its President. The lists shall be drawn up in the same way as the list referred to in Article 11b(2).

    For the composition of the Chambers of three Judges, after the election of the Presidents of those Chambers lists shall be drawn up including all the Judges attached to the Chamber concerned, with the exception of its President. The lists shall be drawn up according to the order laid down in Article 6 of these Rules.

    The lists referred to in this paragraph shall be published in the *Official Journal of the European Union*.

Article 11d

1. Where the Court considers that several cases must be heard and determined together by one and the same formation of the Court, the composition of that formation shall be that fixed for the case in respect of which the preliminary report was first examined.

2. Where a Chamber to which a case has been assigned refers the case back to the Court under Article 44(4), in order that it may be reassigned to a formation composed of a greater number of Judges, that formation shall include the members of the Chamber which has referred the case back.

Article 11e

When a member of the formation determining a case is prevented from attending, he shall be replaced by a Judge according to the order of the lists referred to in Article 11b(2) or 11c(2).

When the President of the Court is prevented from attending, the functions of the President of the Grand Chamber shall be exercised in accordance with the provisions of Article 11.

When the President of a Chamber of five Judges is prevented from attending, the functions of President of the Chamber shall be exercised by a President of a Chamber of three Judges, where necessary according to the order laid down in Article 6 of these Rules or, if that Chamber does not include a President of a Chamber of three Judges, by one of the other Judges according to the order laid down in Article 6.

When the President of a Chamber of three Judges is prevented from attending, the functions of President of the Chamber shall be exercised by a Judge of that Chamber according to the order laid down in Article 6 of these Rules.

(The remaining chapters in Title I have been omitted)

TITLE II
PROCEDURE

Chapter 1 WRITTEN PROCEDURE

Article 37

1.   The original of every pleading must be signed by the party's agent or lawyer.

The original, accompanied by all annexes referred to therein, shall be lodged together with five copies for the Court and a copy for every other party to the proceedings. Copies shall be certified by the party lodging them.

2.   Institutions shall in addition produce, within time-limits laid down by the Court, translations of all pleadings into the other languages provided for by Article 1 of Council Regulation No 1. The second subparagraph of paragraph 1 of this Article shall apply.

3.   All pleadings shall bear a date. In the reckoning of time-limits for taking steps in proceedings, only the date of lodgment at the Registry shall be taken into account.

4.   To every pleading there shall be annexed a file containing the documents relied on in support of it, together with a schedule listing them.

5.   Where in view of the length of a document only extracts from it are annexed to the pleading, the whole document or a full copy of it shall be lodged at the Registry.

6.   Without prejudice to the provisions of paragraphs 1 to 5, the date on which a copy of the signed original of a pleading, including the schedule of documents referred to in paragraph 4, is received at the Registry by telefax or other technical means of communication available to the Court shall be deemed to be the date of lodgment for the purposes of compliance with the time-limits for taking steps in proceedings, provided that the signed original of the pleading, accompanied by the annexes and copies referred to in the second subparagraph of paragraph 1 above, is lodged at the Registry no later than days thereafter. Article 81(2) shall not be applicable to this period of 10 days.

7.   Without prejudice to the first subparagraph of paragraph 1 or to paragraphs 2 to 5, the Court may by decision determine the criteria for a procedural document sent to the Registry by electronic means to be deemed to be the original of that document. That decision shall be published in the *Official Journal of the European Union*.

Article 38

1.   An application of the kind referred to in Article 21 of the Statute shall state:
      (a) the name and address of the applicant;
      (b) the designation of the party against whom the application is made;
      (c) the subject-matter of the proceedings and a summary of the pleas in law on which the application is based;
      (d) the form of order sought by the applicant;
      (e) where appropriate, the nature of any evidence offered in support.

2.   For the purpose of the proceedings, the application shall state an address for service in the place where the Court has its seat and the name of the person who is authorised and has expressed willingness to accept service.

In addition to, or instead of, specifying an address for service as referred to in the first subparagraph, the application may state that the lawyer or agent agrees that service is to be effected on him by telefax or other technical means of communication.

If the application does not comply with the requirements referred to in the first and second subparagraphs, all service on the party concerned for the purpose of the proceedings shall be effected, for so long as the defect has not been cured, by registered letter addressed to the agent or lawyer of that party. By way of derogation from Article 79(1), service shall then be deemed to be duly effected by the lodging of the registered letter at the post office of the place where the Court has its seat.

3.   The lawyer acting for a party must lodge at the Registry a certificate that he is authorised to practise before a court of a Member State or of another State which is a party to the EEA Agreement.

4.   The application shall be accompanied, where appropriate, by the documents specified in the second paragraph of Article 21 of the Statute.

5.   An application made by a legal person governed by private law shall be accompanied by:
     (a)   the instrument or instruments constituting or regulating that legal person or a recent extract from the register of companies, firms or associations or any other proof of its existence in law;
     (b)   proof that the authority granted to the applicant's lawyer has been properly conferred on him by someone authorised for the purpose.

6.   An application submitted under Article 273 TFEU shall be accompanied by a copy of the special agreement concluded between the Member States concerned.

7.   If an application does not comply with the requirements set out in paragraphs 3 to 6 of this Article, the Registrar shall prescribe a reasonable period within which the applicant is to comply with them whether by putting the application itself in order or by producing any of the abovementioned documents. If the applicant fails to put the application in order or to produce the required documents within the time prescribed, the Court shall, after hearing the Advocate General, decide whether the non-compliance with these conditions renders the application formally inadmissible.

Article 39
The application shall be served on the defendant. In a case where Article 38(7) applies, service shall be effected as soon as the application has been put in order or the Court has declared it admissible notwithstanding the failure to observe the formal requirements set out in that Article.

Article 40
1.   Within one month after service on him of the application, the defendant shall lodge a defence, stating:
     (a)   the name and address of the defendant;
     (b)   the arguments of fact and law relied on;
     (c)   the form of order sought by the defendant;
     (d)   the nature of any evidence offered by him.
     The provisions of Article 38(2) to (5) of these Rules shall apply to the defence.

2.   The time-limit laid down in paragraph 1 of this Article may be extended by the President on a reasoned application by the defendant.

Article 41
1.   The application initiating the proceedings and the defence may be supplemented by a reply from the applicant and by a rejoinder from the defendant.

2.   The President shall fix the time-limits within which these pleadings are to be lodged.

Article 42
1.   In reply or rejoinder a party may offer further evidence. The party must, however, give reasons for the delay in offering it.

2.   No new plea in law may be introduced in the course of proceedings unless it is based on matters of law or of fact which come to light in the course of the procedure.

If in the course of the procedure one of the parties puts forward a new plea in law which is so based, the President may, even after the expiry of the normal procedural time-limits, acting on a report of the Judge-Rapporteur and after hearing the Advocate General, allow the other party time to answer on that plea.

The decision on the admissibility of the plea shall be reserved for the final judgment.

Article 43
The Court may, at any time, after hearing the parties and the Advocate General, if the assignment referred to in Article 10(2) has taken place, order that two or more cases concerning the same subject-matter shall, on account of the connection between them, be joined for the purposes of the written or oral procedure or of the final judgment. The cases may subsequently be disjoined. The President may refer these matters to the Court.

Chapter 1A THE PRELIMINARY REPORT AND ASSIGNMENT OF CASES TO FORMATIONS

Article 44
1.   The President shall fix a date on which the Judge-Rapporteur is to present his preliminary report to the general meeting of the Court, either:
    (a) after the rejoinder has been lodged; or
    (b) where no reply or no rejoinder has been lodged within the time-limit fixed in accordance with Article 41(2); or
    (c) where the party concerned has waived his right to lodge a reply or rejoinder; or
    (d) where the expedited procedure referred to in Article 62a is to be applied,
    when the President fixes a date for the hearing.

2.   The preliminary report shall contain recommendations as to whether a preparatory inquiry or any other preparatory step should be undertaken and as to the formation to which the case should be assigned. It shall also contain the Judge-Rapporteur's recommendation, if any, as to whether to dispense with a hearing as provided for in Article 44a and as to whether to dispense with an Opinion of the Advocate General pursuant to the fifth subparagraph of Article 20 of the Statute.

The Court shall decide, after hearing the Advocate General, what action to take upon the recommendations of the Judge-Rapporteur.

3.   The Court shall assign to the Chambers of five and three Judges any case brought before it in so far as the difficulty or importance of the case or particular circumstances are not such as to require that it should be assigned to the Grand Chamber.

However, a case may not be assigned to a Chamber of five or three Judges if a Member State or an institution of the Union, being a party to the proceedings, has requested that the case be decided by the Grand Chamber. For the purposes of this provision, 'party to the proceedings' means any Member State or any institution which is a party to or an intervener in the proceedings or which has submitted written observations in any reference of a kind mentioned in Article 103. A request such as that referred to in this subparagraph may not be made in proceedings between the Union and its servants.

The Court shall sit as a full Court where cases are brought before it pursuant to the provisions referred to in the fourth paragraph of Article 16 of the Statute. It may assign a case to the full Court where, in accordance with the fifth paragraph of Article 16 of the Statute, it considers that the case is of exceptional importance.

4. The formation to which a case has been assigned may, at any stage of the proceedings, refer the case back to the Court in order that it may be reassigned to a formation composed of a greater number of Judges.

5. Where a preparatory inquiry has been opened, the formation determining the case may, if it does not undertake it itself, assign the inquiry to the Judge-Rapporteur. Where the oral procedure is opened without an inquiry, the President of the formation determining the case shall fix the opening date.

Article 44a

Without prejudice to any special provisions laid down in these Rules, the procedure before the Court shall also include an oral part. However, after the pleadings referred to in Article 40(1) and, as the case may be, in Article 41(1) have been lodged, the Court, acting on a report from the Judge-Rapporteur and after hearing the Advocate General, and if none of the parties has submitted an application setting out the reasons for which he wishes to be heard, may decide otherwise. The application shall be submitted within a period of three weeks from notification to the party of the close of the written procedure. That period may be extended by the President.

Chapter 2 PREPARATORY INQUIRIES AND OTHER PREPARATORY MEASURES

SECTION 1 – MEASURES OF INQUIRY

Article 45

1. The Court, after hearing the Advocate General, shall prescribe the measures of inquiry that it considers appropriate by means of an order setting out the facts to be proved. Before the Court decides on the measures of inquiry referred to in paragraph 2(c), (d) and (e) the parties shall be heard.

   The order shall be served on the parties.

2. Without prejudice to Articles 24 and 25 of the Statute, the following measures of inquiry may be adopted:
   (a) the personal appearance of the parties;
   (b) a request for information and production of documents;
   (c) oral testimony;
   (d) the commissioning of an expert's report;
   (e) an inspection of the place or thing in question.

3. The Advocate General shall take part in the measures of inquiry.

4. Evidence may be submitted in rebuttal and previous evidence may be amplified.

Article 46

The parties shall be entitled to attend the measures of inquiry.

SECTION 2 – THE SUMMONING AND EXAMINATION OF WITNESSES AND EXPERTS

Article 47

1. The Court may, either of its own motion or on application by a party, and after hearing the Advocate General, order that certain facts be proved by witnesses. The order of the Court shall set out the facts to be established.

    The Court may summon a witness of its own motion or on application by a party or at the instance of the Advocate General.

    An application by a party for the examination of a witness shall state precisely about what facts and for what reasons the witness should be examined.

2. The witness shall be summoned by an order of the Court containing the following information:
    (a) the surname, forenames, description and address of the witness;
    (b) an indication of the facts about which the witness is to be examined;
    (c) where appropriate, particulars of the arrangements made by the Court for reimbursement of expenses incurred by the witness, and of the penalties which may be imposed on defaulting witnesses.
    The order shall be served on the parties and the witnesses.

3. The Court may make the summoning of a witness for whose examination a party has applied conditional upon the deposit with the cashier of the Court of a sum sufficient to cover the taxed costs thereof; the Court shall fix the amount of the payment.

    The cashier shall advance the funds necessary in connection with the examination of any witness summoned by the Court of its own motion.

4. After the identity of the witness has been established, the President shall inform him that he will be required to vouch the truth of his evidence in the manner laid down in these Rules.

    The witness shall give his evidence to the Court, the parties having been given notice to attend. After the witness has given his main evidence the President may, at the request of a party or of his own motion, put questions to him.

    The other Judges and the Advocate General may do likewise.

    Subject to the control of the President, questions may be put to witnesses by the representatives of the parties.

5. After giving his evidence, the witness shall take the following oath:

    'I swear that I have spoken the truth, the whole truth and nothing but the truth.'

    The Court may, after hearing the parties, exempt a witness from taking the oath.

6. The Registrar shall draw up minutes in which the evidence of each witness is reproduced.

    The minutes shall be signed by the President or by the Judge-Rapporteur responsible for conducting the examination of the witness, and by the Registrar. Before the minutes are thus signed, witnesses must be given an opportunity to check the content of the minutes and to sign them.

    The minutes shall constitute an official record.

Article 48

1. Witnesses who have been duly summoned shall obey the summons and attend for examination.

2. If a witness who has been duly summoned fails to appear before the Court, the Court may impose upon him a pecuniary penalty not exceeding EUR 5 000* and may order that a further summons be served on the witness at his own expense. [*See Article 2 of Council Regulation (EC) No 1103/97 of 17 June 1997 on certain provisions relating to the introduction of the euro (OJ L 162 of 19.6.1997, p. 1].

    The same penalty may be imposed upon a witness who, without good reason, refuses to give evidence or to take the oath or where appropriate to make a solemn affirmation equivalent thereto.

3. If the witness proffers a valid excuse to the Court, the pecuniary penalty imposed on him may be cancelled. The pecuniary penalty imposed may be reduced at the request of the witness where he establishes that it is disproportionate to his income.

4. Penalties imposed and other measures ordered under this Article shall be enforced in accordance with Articles 280 TFEU and 299 TFEU and Article 164 TEAEC.

Article 49

1. The Court may order that an expert's report be obtained. The order appointing the expert shall define his task and set a time-limit within which he is to make his report.

2. The expert shall receive a copy of the order, together with all the documents necessary for carrying out his task. He shall be under the supervision of the Judge-Rapporteur, who may be present during his investigation and who shall be kept informed of his progress in carrying out his task.

    The Court may request the parties or one of them to lodge security for the costs of the expert's report.

3. At the request of the expert, the Court may order the examination of witnesses. Their examination shall be carried out in accordance with Article 47 of these Rules.

4. The expert may give his opinion only on points which have been expressly referred to him.

5. After the expert has made his report, the Court may order that he be examined, the parties having been given notice to attend.

    Subject to the control of the President, questions may be put to the expert by the representatives of the parties.

6. After making his report, the expert shall take the following oath before the Court:

    'I swear that I have conscientiously and impartially carried out my task.'

    The Court may, after hearing the parties, exempt the expert from taking the oath.

Article 50

1. If one of the parties objects to a witness or to an expert on the ground that he is not a competent or proper person to act as witness or expert or for any other reason, or if a witness or expert refuses to give evidence, to take the oath or to make a solemn affirmation equivalent thereto, the matter shall be resolved by the Court.

2. An objection to a witness or to an expert shall be raised within two weeks after service of the order summoning the witness or appointing the expert; the statement of

objection must set out the grounds of objection and indicate the nature of any evidence offered.

Article 51

1.   Witnesses and experts shall be entitled to reimbursement of their travel and subsistence expenses. The cashier of the Court may make a payment to them towards these expenses in advance.

2.   Witnesses shall be entitled to compensation for loss of earnings, and experts to fees for their services. The cashier of the Court shall pay witnesses and experts their compensation or fees after they have carried out their respective duties or tasks.

Article 52

The Court may, on application by a party or of its own motion, issue letters rogatory for the examination of witnesses or experts, as provided for in the supplementary rules mentioned in Article 125 of these Rules.

Article 53

1.   The Registrar shall draw up minutes of every hearing. The minutes shall be signed by the President and by the Registrar and shall constitute an official record.

2.   The parties may inspect the minutes and any expert's report at the Registry and obtain copies at their own expense.

SECTION 3 – CLOSURE OF THE PREPARATORY INQUIRY

Article 54

Unless the Court prescribes a period within which the parties may lodge written observations, the President shall fix the date for the opening of the oral procedure after the preparatory inquiry has been completed.

Where a period had been prescribed for the lodging of written observations, the President shall fix the date for the opening of the oral procedure after that period has expired.

SECTION 4 – PREPARATORY MEASURES

Article 54a

The Judge-Rapporteur and the Advocate General may request the parties to submit within a specified period all such information relating to the facts, and all such documents or other particulars, as they may consider relevant. The information and/or documents provided shall be communicated to the other parties.

Chapter Three ORAL PROCEDURE

Article 55

1.   Subject to the priority of decisions provided for in Article 85 of these Rules, the Court shall deal with the cases before it in the order in which the preparatory inquiries in them have been completed. Where the preparatory inquiries in several cases are completed simultaneously, the order in which they are to be dealt with shall be determined by the dates of entry in the register of the applications initiating them respectively.

2.   The President may in special circumstances order that a case be given priority over others.

The President may in special circumstances, after hearing the parties and the Advocate General, either on his own initiative or at the request of one of the parties, defer a case to be dealt with at a later date. On a joint application by the parties the President may order that a case be deferred.

Article 56

1. The proceedings shall be opened and directed by the President, who shall be responsible for the proper conduct of the hearing.

2. The oral proceedings in cases heard *in camera* shall not be published.

Article 57

The President may in the course of the hearing put questions to the agents, advisers or lawyers of the parties.

The other Judges and the Advocate General may do likewise.

Article 58

A party may address the Court only through his agent, adviser or lawyer.

Article 59

1. The Advocate General shall deliver his opinion orally at the end of the oral procedure.

2. After the Advocate General has delivered his opinion, the President shall declare the oral procedure closed.

Article 60

The Court may at any time, in accordance with Article 45(1), after hearing the Advocate General, order any measure of inquiry to be taken or that a previous inquiry be repeated or expanded. The Court may direct the Judge-Rapporteur to carry out the measures so ordered.

Article 61

The Court may after hearing the Advocate General order the reopening of the oral procedure.

Article 62

1. The Registrar shall draw up minutes of every hearing. The minutes shall be signed by the President and by the Registrar and shall constitute an official record.

2. The parties may inspect the minutes at the Registry and obtain copies at their own expense.

Chapter 3A EXPEDITED PROCEDURES

Article 62a

1. On application by the applicant or the defendant, the President may exceptionally decide, on the basis of a recommendation by the Judge-Rapporteur and after hearing the other party and the Advocate General, that a case is to be determined pursuant to an expedited procedure derogating from the provisions of these Rules, where the particular urgency of the case requires the Court to give its ruling with the minimum of delay.

   An application for a case to be decided under an expedited procedure shall be made by a separate document lodged at the same time as the application initiating the proceedings or the defence, as the case may be.

2. Under the expedited procedure, the originating application and the defence may be supplemented by a reply and a rejoinder only if the President considers this to be necessary.

An intervener may lodge a statement in intervention only if the President considers this to be necessary.

3.   Once the defence has been lodged or, if the decision to adjudicate under an expedited procedure is not made until after that pleading has been lodged, once that decision has been taken, the President shall fix a date for the hearing, which shall be communicated forthwith to the parties. He may postpone the date of the hearing where the organisation of measures of inquiry or of other preparatory measures so requires.

Without prejudice to Article 42, the parties may supplement their arguments and offer further evidence in the course of the oral procedure. They must, however, give reasons for the delay in offering such further evidence.

4.   The Court shall give its ruling after hearing the Advocate General.

Chapter 4 JUDGMENTS

Article 63
The judgment shall contain:
—   a statement that it is the judgment of the Court,

—   the date of its delivery,

—   the names of the President and of the Judges taking part in it,

—   the name of the Advocate General,

—   the name of the Registrar,

—   the description of the parties,

—   the names of the agents, advisers and lawyers of the parties,

—   a statement of the forms of order sought by the parties,

—   a statement that the Advocate General has been heard,

—   a summary of the facts,

—   the grounds for the decision,

—   the operative part of the judgment, including the decision as to costs.

Article 64
1.   The judgment shall be delivered in open court; the parties shall be given notice to attend to hear it.

2.   The original of the judgment, signed by the President, by the Judges who took part in the deliberations and by the Registrar, shall be sealed and deposited at the Registry; the parties shall be served with certified copies of the judgment.

3.   The Registrar shall record on the original of the judgment the date on which it was delivered.

Article 65
The judgment shall be binding from the date of its delivery.

Article 66
1.   Without prejudice to the provisions relating to the interpretation of judgments the Court may, of its own motion or on application by a party made within two weeks after the

delivery of a judgment, rectify clerical mistakes, errors in calculation and obvious slips in it.

2. The parties, whom the Registrar shall duly notify, may lodge written observations within a period prescribed by the President.

3. The Court shall take its decision in closed session after hearing the Advocate General.

4. The original of the rectification order shall be annexed to the original of the rectified judgment. A note of this order shall be made in the margin of the original of the rectified judgment.

Article 67
If the Court should omit to give a decision on a specific head of claim or on costs, any party may within a month after service of the judgment apply to the Court to supplement its judgment.

The application shall be served on the opposite party and the President shall prescribe a period within which that party may lodge written observations.

After these observations have been lodged, the Court shall, after hearing the Advocate General, decide both on the admissibility and on the substance of the application.

Article 68
The Registrar shall arrange for the publication of reports of cases before the Court.

(The remaining chapters in Title II have been omitted)

TITLE III
SPECIAL FORMS OF PROCEDURE
(Chapters 1–8 omitted)

Chapter 9 PRELIMINARY RULINGS AND OTHER REFERENCES FOR INTERPRETATION

Article 103
1. In cases governed by Article 23 of the Statute, the procedure shall be governed by the provisions of these Rules, subject to adaptations necessitated by the nature of the reference for a preliminary ruling.

2. The provisions of paragraph 1 shall apply to the references for a preliminary ruling provided for in the Protocol concerning the interpretation by the Court of Justice of the Convention of 29 February 1968 on the mutual recognition of companies and legal persons and the Protocol concerning the interpretation by the Court of Justice of the Convention of 27 September 1968 on jurisdiction and the enforcement of judgments in civil and commercial matters, signed at Luxembourg on 3 June 1971, and to the references provided for by Article 4 of the latter Protocol.

   The provisions of paragraph 1 shall apply also to references for interpretation provided for by other existing or future agreements.

Article 104
1. The decisions of national courts or tribunals referred to in Article 103 shall be communicated to the Member States in the original version, accompanied by a translation into the official language of the State to which they are addressed. Where appropriate on account of the length of the national court's decision, such translation shall be replaced by

the translation into the official language of the State to which it is addressed of a summary of the decision, which will serve as a basis for the position to be adopted by that State. The summary shall include the full text of the question or questions referred for a preliminary ruling. That summary shall contain, in particular, in so far as that information appears in the national court's decision, the subject-matter of the main proceedings, the essential arguments of the parties in the main proceedings, a succinct presentation of the reasoning in the reference for a preliminary ruling and the case-law and the provisions of European Union and domestic law relied on.

In the cases governed by the third paragraph of Article 23 of the Statute, the decisions of national courts or tribunals shall be notified to the States, other than the Member States, which are parties to the EEA Agreement and also to the EFTA Surveillance Authority in the original version, accompanied by a translation of the decision, or where appropriate of a summary, into one of the languages mentioned in Article 29(1), to be chosen by the addressee of the notification.

Where a non-Member State has the right to take part in proceedings for a preliminary ruling pursuant to the fourth paragraph of Article 23 of the Statute, the original version of the decision of the national court or tribunal shall be communicated to it together with a translation of the decision, or where appropriate of a summary, into one of the languages mentioned in Article 29(1), to be chosen by the non-Member State concerned.

2.   As regards the representation and attendance of the parties to the main proceedings in the preliminary ruling procedure the Court shall take account of the rules of procedure of the national court or tribunal which made the reference.

3.   Where a question referred to the Court for a preliminary ruling is identical to a question on which the Court has already ruled, or where the answer to such a question may be clearly deduced from existing case-law, the Court may, after hearing the Advocate General, at any time give its decision by reasoned order in which reference is made to its previous judgment or to the relevant case-law.

The Court may also give its decision by reasoned order, after informing the court or tribunal which referred the question to it, hearing any observations submitted by the persons referred to in Article 23 of the Statute and after hearing the Advocate General, where the answer to the question referred to the Court for a preliminary ruling admits of no reasonable doubt.

4.   Without prejudice to paragraph (3) of this Article, the procedure before the Court in the case of a reference for a preliminary ruling shall also include an oral part.

However, after the statements of case or written observations referred to Article 23 of the Statute have been submitted, the Court, acting on a report from the Judge Rapporteur, after informing the persons who under the aforementioned provisions are entitled to submit such statements or observations, may, after hearing the Advocate General, decide otherwise, provided that none of those persons has submitted an application setting out the reasons for which he wishes to be heard. The application shall be submitted within a period of three weeks from service on the party or person of the written statements of case or written observations which have been lodged. That period may be extended by the President.

5.   The Court may, after hearing the Advocate General, request clarification from the national court.

6.   It shall be for the national court or tribunal to decide as to the costs of the reference.

In special circumstances the Court may grant, by way of legal aid, assistance for the purpose of facilitating the representation or attendance of a party.

Article 104a

At the request of the national court, the President may exceptionally decide, on a proposal from the Judge-Rapporteur and after hearing the Advocate General, to apply an accelerated procedure derogating from the provisions of these Rules to a reference for a preliminary ruling, where the circumstances referred to establish that a ruling on the question put to the Court is a matter of exceptional urgency.

In that event, the President may immediately fix the date for the hearing, which shall be notified to the parties in the main proceedings and to the other persons referred to in Article 23 of the Statute when the decision making the reference is served.

The parties and other interested persons referred to in the preceding paragraph may lodge statements of case or written observations within a period prescribed by the President, which shall not be less than 15 days. The President may request the parties and other interested persons to restrict the matters addressed in their statement of case or written observations to the essential points of law raised by the question referred.

The statements of case or written observations, if any, shall be notified to the parties and to the other persons referred to above prior to the hearing.

The Court shall rule after hearing the Advocate General.

Article 104b

1.   A reference for a preliminary ruling which raises one or more questions in the areas covered by Title V of Part Three of the Treaty on the Functioning of the European Union may, at the request of the national court or tribunal or, exceptionally, of the Court's own motion, be dealt with under an urgent procedure which derogates from the provisions of these Rules.

The national court or tribunal shall set out, in its request, the matters of fact and law which establish the urgency and justify the application of that exceptional procedure and shall, in so far as possible, indicate the answer it proposes to the questions referred.

If the national court or tribunal has not submitted a request for the urgent procedure to be applied, the President of the Court may, if the application of that procedure appears, prima facie, to be required, ask the Chamber referred to below to consider whether it is necessary to deal with the reference under that procedure.

The decision to deal with a reference for a preliminary ruling under the urgent procedure shall be taken by the designated Chamber, acting on a report of the Judge-Rapporteur and after hearing the Advocate General. The composition of that Chamber shall be determined in accordance with Article 11c on the day on which the case is assigned to the Judge-Rapporteur if the application of the urgent procedure is requested by the national court or tribunal, or, if the application of that procedure is considered at the request of the President of the Court, on the day on which that request is made.

2.   A reference for a preliminary ruling of the kind referred to in the preceding paragraph shall, where the national court or tribunal has requested the application of the urgent procedure or where the President has requested the designated Chamber to consider whether it is necessary to deal with the reference under that procedure, be notified forthwith by the Registrar to the parties to the action before the national court or tribunal, to the Member State from which the reference is made and to the institutions referred to in the first paragraph of Article 23 of the Statute, in accordance with that provision.

The decision as to whether or not to deal with the reference for a preliminary ruling under the urgent procedure shall be notified forthwith to the national court or tribunal and to the parties, Member State and institutions referred to in the preceding subparagraph. The decision to deal with the reference under the urgent procedure shall prescribe the period within which those parties or entities may lodge statements of case or written observations. The decision may specify the matters of law to which such statements of case or written observations must relate and may specify the maximum length of those documents.

As soon as the notification referred to in the first subparagraph above has been made, the reference for a preliminary ruling shall also be communicated to the interested persons referred to in Article 23 of the Statute, other than the persons notified, and the decision whether or not to deal with the reference for a preliminary ruling under the urgent procedure shall be communicated to those interested persons as soon as the notification referred to in the second subparagraph has been made.

The parties and other interested persons referred to in Article 23 of the Statute shall be informed as soon as may be possible of the foreseeable date of the hearing.

Where the reference is not to be dealt with under the urgent procedure, the proceedings shall continue in accordance with the provisions of Article 23 of the Statute and the applicable provisions of these Rules.

3. A reference for a preliminary ruling which is to be dealt with under an urgent procedure, together with the statements of case or written observations which have been lodged, shall be served on the persons referred to in Article 23 of the Statute other than the parties and the entities referred to in the first subparagraph of the preceding paragraph of this Article. The reference for a preliminary ruling shall be accompanied by a translation, where appropriate in summary form, in accordance with Article 104(1).

    The statements of case or written observations which have been lodged shall also be served on the parties and the other persons referred to in the first subparagraph of Article 104b(2).

    The date of the hearing shall be notified to the parties and those other persons at the same time as the documents referred to in the preceding paragraphs are served.

4. The Chamber may, in cases of extreme urgency, decide to omit the written part of the procedure referred to in the second subparagraph of paragraph 2 of this Article.

5. The designated Chamber shall rule after hearing the Advocate General.

    It may decide to sit in a formation of three Judges. In that event, it shall be composed of the President of the designated Chamber, the Judge-Rapporteur and the first Judge or, as the case may be, the first two Judges designated from the list referred to in Article 11c(2) on the date on which the composition of the designated Chamber is determined in accordance with the fourth subparagraph of paragraph 1 of this Article.

    It may also decide to refer the case back to the Court in order for it to be assigned to a formation composed of a greater number of Judges. The urgent procedure shall continue before the new formation, where necessary after the reopening of the oral procedure.

6. The procedural documents referred to in this Article shall be deemed to have been lodged on the transmission to the Registry, by telefax or other technical means of communication available to the Court, of a copy of the signed original and the documents relied on in support of it, together with the schedule referred to in Article 37(4). The original of the document and the annexes referred to above shall be sent to the Registry.

    Where this Article requires that a document be notified to or served on a person, such notification or service may be effected by the transmission of a copy of the document by telefax or other technical means of communication available to the Court and the addressee.'

(Chapter 10 omitted)

Chapter 11 OPINIONS

Article 107
1.   A request by the European Parliament for an opinion pursuant to Article 218 TFEU shall be served on the Council, on the European Commission and on the Member States. Such a request by the Council shall be served on the European Commission and on the European Parliament. Such a request by the European Commission shall be served on the Council, on the European Parliament and on the Member States. Such a request by a Member State shall be served on the Council, on the European Commission, on the European Parliament and on the other Member States.

The President shall prescribe a period within which the institutions and Member States which have been served with a request may submit their written observations.

2.   The Opinion may deal not only with the question whether the envisaged agreement is compatible which the provisions of the Treaties but also with the question whether the Union or any Union institution has the power to enter into that agreement.

Article 108
1.   As soon as the request for an Opinion has been lodged, the President shall designate a Judge to act as Rapporteur.

2.   The Court sitting in closed session shall, after hearing the Advocates General, deliver a reasoned Opinion.

3.   The Opinion, signed by the President, by the Judges who took part in the deliberations and by the Registrar, shall be served on the Council, the European Commission, the European Parliament and the Member States.

Article 109
(repealed)

(The remaining chapters in Title III are omitted)

TITLE IV
APPEALS AGAINST DECISIONS OF THE GENERAL COURT

Article 110
Without prejudice to the arrangements laid down in Article 29(2)(b) and (c) and the fourth subparagraph of Article 29(3) of these Rules, in appeals against decisions of the General Court as referred to in Articles 56 and 57 of the Statute, the language of the case shall be the language of the decision of the General Court against which the appeal is brought.

Article 111
1.   An appeal shall be brought by lodging an application at the Registry of the Court of Justice or of the General Court.

2.   The Registry of the General Court shall immediately transmit to the Registry of the Court of Justice the papers in the case at first instance and, where necessary, the appeal.

Article 112
1.   An appeal shall contain:
      (a) the name and address of the appellant;
      (b) the names of the other parties to the proceedings before the General Court;
      (c) the pleas in law and legal arguments relied on;
      (d) the form or order sought by the appellant.
      Article 37 and Article 38(2) and (3) of these Rules shall apply to appeals.

2.   The decision of the General Court appealed against shall be attached to the appeal. The appeal shall state the date on which the decision appealed against was notified to the appellant.

3.   If an appeal does not comply with Article 38(3) or with paragraph 2 of this Article, Article 38(7) of these Rules shall apply.

Article 113
1.   An appeal may seek:
      — to set aside, in whole or in part, the decision of the General Court;
      — the same form of order, in whole or in part, as that sought at first instance and shall not seek a different form of order.

2.   The subject-matter of the proceedings before the General Court may not be changed in the appeal.

Article 114
Notice of the appeal shall be served on all the parties to the proceedings before the General Court. Article 39 of these Rules shall apply.

Article 115
1.   Any party to the proceedings before the General Court may lodge a response within two months after service on him of notice of the appeal. The time-limit for lodging a response shall not be extended.

2.   A response shall contain:
      (a) the name and address of the party lodging it;
      (b) the date on which notice of the appeal was served on him;
      (c) the pleas in law and legal arguments relied on;
      (d) the form of order sought by the respondent.
      Article 37 and Article 38(2) and (3) of these Rules shall apply.

Article 116
1.   A response may seek:
      — to dismiss, in whole or in part, the appeal or to set aside, in whole or in part, the decision of the General Court;
      — the same form of order, in whole or in part, as that sought at first instance and shall not seek a different form of order.

2.   The subject-matter of the proceedings before the General Court may not be changed in the response.

Article 117
1.   The appeal and the response may be supplemented by a reply and a rejoinder where the President, on application made by the appellant within seven days of service of the response, considers such further pleading necessary and expressly allows the submission of

a reply in order to enable the appellant to put forward his point of view or in order to provide a basis for the decision on the appeal. The President shall prescribe the date by which the reply is to be submitted and, upon service of that pleading, the date by which the rejoinder is to be submitted.

2.   Where the response seeks to set aside, in whole or in part, the decision of the General Court on a plea in law which was not raised in the appeal, the appellant or any other party may submit a reply on that plea alone within two months of the service of the response in question. Paragraph 1 shall apply to any further pleading following such a reply.

Article 118
Subject to the following provisions, Articles 42(2), 43, 44, 55 to 90, 93, 95 to 100 and 102 of these Rules shall apply to the procedure before the Court of Justice on appeal from a decision of the General Court.

Article 119
Where the appeal is, in whole or in part, clearly inadmissible or clearly unfounded, the Court may at any time, acting on a report from the Judge-Rapporteur and after hearing the Advocate General, by reasoned order dismiss the appeal in whole or in part.

Article 120
After the submission of pleadings as provided for in Article 115(1) and, if any, Article 117(1) and (2) of these Rules, the Court, acting on a report from the Judge-Rapporteur and after hearing the Advocate General and the parties, may decide to dispense with the oral part of the procedure unless one of the parties submits an application setting out the reasons for which he wishes to be heard. The application shall be submitted within a period of three weeks from notification to the party of the close of the written procedure.

That period may be extended by the President.

Article 121
The report referred to in Article 44(2) shall be presented to the Court after the pleadings provided for in Article 115(1) and where appropriate Article 117(1) and (2) of these Rules have been lodged. Where no such pleadings are lodged, the same procedure shall apply after the expiry of the period prescribed for lodging them.

Article 122
Where the appeal is unfounded or where the appeal is well founded and the Court itself gives final judgment in the case, the Court shall make a decision as to costs.

In proceedings between the Union and its servants:
—   Article 70 of these Rules shall apply only to appeals brought by institutions;

—   by way of derogation from Article 69(2) of these Rules, the Court may, in appeals brought by officials or other servants of an institution, order the parties to share the costs where equity so requires.

If the appeal is withdrawn Article 69(5) shall apply.

When an appeal brought by a Member State or an institution which did not intervene in the proceedings before the General Court is well founded, the Court of Justice may order that the parties share the costs or that the successful appellant pay the costs which the appeal has caused an unsuccessful party to incur.

Article 123
An application to intervene made to the Court in appeal proceedings shall be lodged before the expiry of a period of one month running from the publication referred to in Article 16(6).

TITLE IVA
REVIEW OF DECISIONS OF THE GENERAL COURT

Article 123a
Without prejudice to the arrangements laid down in Article 29(2)(b) and (c) and the fourth and fifth subparagraphs of Article 29(3) of these Rules, where, in accordance with the second paragraph of Article 62 of the Statute, the Court decides to review a decision of the General Court, the language of the case shall be the language of the decision of the General Court which is subject to review.

Article 123b
A special Chamber shall be set up for the purpose of deciding, in accordance with Article 123d, whether a decision of the General Court is to be reviewed in accordance with Article 62 of the Statute.

That Chamber shall be composed of the President of the Court and of four of the Presidents of the Chambers of five Judges designated according to the order of precedence laid down in Article 6 of these Rules.

Article 123c
As soon as the date for the delivery of a decision to be given under Article 256(2) or (3) TFEU is fixed, the Registry of the General Court shall inform the Registry of the Court of Justice. The decision shall be communicated immediately upon its delivery.

Article 123d
The proposal of the First Advocate General to review a decision of the General Court shall be forwarded to the President of the Court of Justice and notice of that transmission shall be given to the Registrar at the same time. Where the decision of the General Court has been given under Article 256(3) TFEU, the Registrar shall forthwith inform the General Court, the national court and the parties to the proceedings before the national court of the proposal to review.

As soon as the proposal to review has been received, the President shall designate the Judge-Rapporteur from among the Judges of the Chamber referred to in Article 123b.

That Chamber, acting on a report from the Judge-Rapporteur, shall decide whether the decision of the General Court is to be reviewed. The decision to review the decision of the General Court shall indicate the questions which are to be reviewed.

Where the decision of the General Court has been given under Article 256(2) TFEU, the General Court, the parties to the proceedings before it and the other interested parties referred to in the second paragraph of Article 62a of the Statute shall forthwith be informed by the Registrar of the decision of the Court of Justice to review the decision of the General Court.

Where the decision of the General Court has been given under Article 256(3) TFEU, the General Court, the national court, the parties to the proceedings before the national court and the other interested parties referred to in the second paragraph of Article 62a of the Statute shall forthwith be informed by the Registrar of the decision of the Court of Justice as to whether or not the decision of the General Court is to be reviewed. Notice of a decision to review the decision of the General Court shall be given in the *Official Journal of the European Union*.

Article 123e
The decision to review a decision of the General Court shall be notified to the parties and other interested parties referred to in the second paragraph of Article 62a of the Statute.

The notification to the Member States, and the States, other than the Member States, which are parties to the EEA Agreement, as well as the EFTA Surveillance Authority, shall be accompanied by a translation of the decision of the Court of Justice in accordance with the provisions of the first and second subparagraphs of Article 104(1) of these Rules. The decision of the Court of Justice shall also be communicated to the General Court and, in cases involving a decision given by that Court under Article 256(3) TFEU, to the national court concerned.

Within one month of the notification referred to in the preceding paragraph, the parties and other persons to whom the decision of the Court of Justice has been notified may lodge statements or written observations on the questions which are subject to review.

As soon as a decision to review a decision of the General Court has been taken, the First Advocate General shall assign the review to an Advocate General.

After designating the Judge-Rapporteur, the President shall fix the date on which the latter is to present a preliminary report to the general meeting of the Court. That report shall contain the recommendations of the Judge-Rapporteur as to whether any preparatory steps should be taken, as to the formation of the Court to which the review should be assigned and as to whether a hearing should take place, and also as to the manner in which the Advocate General should present his views. The Court shall decide, after hearing the Advocate General, what action to take upon the recommendations of the Judge-Rapporteur.

Where the decision of the General Court which is subject to review was given under Article 256(2) TFEU, the Court of Justice shall make a decision as to costs.

(Remaining provisions omitted)

COURT OF JUSTICE INFORMATION NOTE
on references from national courts for a preliminary ruling
OJ C 160, 28.5.2011, P. 1*

I. GENERAL

1. The preliminary ruling system is a fundamental mechanism of European Union law aimed at enabling national courts to ensure uniform interpretation and application of that law in all the Member States.

2. The Court of Justice of the European Union has jurisdiction to give preliminary rulings on the interpretation of European Union law and on the validity of acts of the institutions, bodies, offices or agencies of the Union. That general jurisdiction is conferred on it by Article 19(3)(b) of the Treaty on European Union (OJEU 2008 C 115, p. 13) ('the TEU') and Article 267 of the Treaty on the Functioning of the European Union (OJEU 2008 C 115, p. 47) ('the TFEU').

3. Article 256(3) TFEU provides that the General Court is to have jurisdiction to hear and determine questions referred for a preliminary ruling under Article 267, in specific areas laid down by the Statute. Since no provisions have been introduced into the Statute in that regard, the Court of Justice alone has jurisdiction to give preliminary rulings.

....

(* This note replaces the information note published in OJ 2009 C 297, p. 1.)

4.   While Article 267 TFEU confers on the Court of Justice a general jurisdiction, a number of provisions exist which lay down exceptions to or restrictions on that jurisdiction. This is true in particular of Articles 275 and 276 TFEU and Article 10 of Protocol (No 36) on Transitional Provisions of the Treaty of Lisbon (OJEU 2008 C 115, p. 322).

5.   The preliminary ruling procedure being based on cooperation between the Court of Justice and national courts, it may be helpful, in order to ensure that that cooperation is effective, to provide the national courts with the following information.

6.   This practical information, which is in no way binding, is intended to provide guidance to national courts as to whether it is appropriate to make a reference for a preliminary ruling and, should they proceed, to help them formulate and submit questions to the Court.

THE ROLE OF THE COURT OF JUSTICE IN THE PRELIMINARY RULING PROCEDURE

7.   Under the preliminary ruling procedure, the Court's role is to give an interpretation of European Union law or to rule on its validity, not to apply that law to the factual situation underlying the main proceedings, which is the task of the national court. It is not for the Court either to decide issues of fact raised in the main proceedings or to resolve differences of opinion on the interpretation or application of rules of national law.

8.   In ruling on the interpretation or validity of European Union law, the Court makes every effort to give a reply which will be of assistance in resolving the dispute, but it is for the referring court to draw the appropriate conclusions from that reply, if necessary by disapplying the rule of national law in question.

THE DECISION TO SUBMIT A QUESTION TO THE COURT

The originator of the question
9.   Under Article 267 TFEU, any court or tribunal of a Member State, in so far as it is called upon to give a ruling in proceedings intended to arrive at a decision of a judicial nature, may as a rule refer a question to the Court of Justice for a preliminary ruling (1). Status as a court or tribunal is interpreted by the Court of Justice as a self-standing concept of European Union law.

10.   It is for the national court alone to decide whether to refer a question to the Court of Justice for a preliminary ruling, whether or not the parties to the main proceedings have requested it to do so.

References on interpretation
11.   Any court or tribunal may refer a question to the Court of Justice on the interpretation of a rule of European Union law if it considers it necessary to do so in order to resolve a dispute brought before it.

12.   However, courts or tribunals against whose decisions there is no judicial remedy under national law must, as a rule, refer such a question to the Court, unless the Court has already ruled on the point (and there is no new context that raises any serious doubt as to whether that case-law may be applied), or unless the correct interpretation of the rule of law in question is obvious.

13.   Thus, a court or tribunal against whose decisions there is a judicial remedy may, in particular when it considers that sufficient guidance is given by the case-law of the Court

of Justice, itself decide on the correct interpretation of European Union law and its application to the factual situation before it. However, a reference for a preliminary ruling may prove particularly useful, at an appropriate stage of the proceedings, when there is a new question of interpretation of general interest for the uniform application of European Union law in all the Member States, or where the existing case-law does not appear to be applicable to a new set of facts.

14.   It is for the national court to explain why the interpretation sought is necessary to enable it to give judgment.

References on determination of validity

15.   Although national courts may reject pleas raised before them challenging the validity of acts of an institution, body, office or agency of the Union, the Court of Justice has exclusive jurisdiction to declare such an act invalid.

16.   All national courts must therefore refer a question to the Court when they have doubts about the validity of such an act, stating the reasons for which they consider that that act may be invalid.

17.   However, if a national court has serious doubts about the validity of an act of an institution, body, office or agency of the Union on which a national measure is based, it may exceptionally suspend application of that measure temporarily or grant other interim relief with respect to it. It must then refer the question of validity to the Court of Justice, stating the reasons for which it considers the act to be invalid.

THE STAGE AT WHICH TO SUBMIT A QUESTION FOR A PRELIMINARY RULING

18.   A national court or tribunal may refer a question to the Court for a preliminary ruling as soon as it finds that a ruling on the point or points of interpretation or validity is necessary to enable it to give judgment; it is the national court which is in the best position to decide at what stage of the proceedings such a question should be referred.

19.   It is, however, desirable that a decision to seek a preliminary ruling should be taken when the national proceedings have reached a stage at which the national court is able to define the factual and legal context of the question, so that the Court of Justice has available to it all the information necessary to check, where appropriate, that European Union law applies to the main proceedings. It may also be in the interests of justice to refer a question for a preliminary ruling only after both sides have been heard.

THE FORM OF THE REFERENCE FOR A PRELIMINARY RULING

20.   The decision by which a national court or tribunal refers a question to the Court of Justice for a preliminary ruling may be in any form allowed by national law as regards procedural steps. It must however be borne in mind that it is that document which serves as the basis of the proceedings before the Court and that it must therefore contain such information as will enable the latter to give a reply which is of assistance to the national court. Moreover, it is only the actual reference for a preliminary ruling which is notified to the interested persons entitled to submit observations to the Court, in particular the Member States and the institutions, and which is translated.

21.   Owing to the need to translate the reference, it should be drafted simply, clearly and precisely, avoiding superfluous detail.

22.   A maximum of about 10 pages is often sufficient to set out in a proper manner the context of a reference for a preliminary ruling. The order for reference must be succinct but

sufficiently complete and must contain all the relevant information to give the Court and the interested persons entitled to submit observations a clear understanding of the factual and legal context of the main proceedings. In particular, the order for reference must:

— include a brief account of the subject-matter of the dispute and the relevant findings of fact, or, at least, set out the factual situation on which the question referred is based;

— set out the tenor of any applicable national provisions and identify, where necessary, the relevant national case-law, giving in each case precise references (for example, a page of an official journal or specific law report, with any internet reference);

— identify the European Union law provisions relevant to the case as accurately as possible;

— explain the reasons which prompted the national court to raise the question of the interpretation or validity of the European Union law provisions, and the relationship between those provisions and the national provisions applicable to the main proceedings;

— include, if need be, a summary of the main relevant arguments of the parties to the main proceedings.

In order to make it easier to read and refer to the document, it is helpful if the different points or paragraphs of the order for reference are numbered.

23. Finally, the referring court may, if it considers itself able, briefly state its view on the answer to be given to the questions referred for a preliminary ruling.

24. The question or questions themselves should appear in a separate and clearly identified section of the order for reference, generally at the beginning or the end. It must be possible to understand them without referring to the statement of the grounds for the reference, which will however provide the necessary background for a proper assessment.

25. Under the preliminary ruling procedure, the Court will, as a rule, use the information contained in the order for reference, including nominative or personal data. It is therefore for the referring court itself, if it considers it necessary, to render anonymous, in the order for reference, one or more persons concerned by the dispute in the main proceedings.

THE EFFECTS OF THE REFERENCE FOR A PRELIMINARY RULING ON THE NATIONAL PROCEEDINGS

26. A reference for a preliminary ruling calls for the national proceedings to be stayed until the Court of Justice has given its ruling.

27. However, the national court may still order protective measures, particularly in connection with a reference on determination of validity (see point 17 above).

COSTS AND LEGAL AID

28. Preliminary ruling proceedings before the Court of Justice are free of charge and the Court does not rule on the costs of the parties to the main proceedings; it is for the national court to rule on those costs.

29. If a party has insufficient means and where it is possible under national rules, the national court may grant that party legal aid to cover the costs, including those of lawyers' fees, which it incurs before the Court. The Court itself may also grant legal aid where the

party in question is not already in receipt of legal aid under national rules or to the extent to which that aid does not cover, or covers only partly, costs incurred before the Court.

COMMUNICATION BETWEEN THE NATIONAL COURT AND THE COURT OF JUSTICE

30.   The order for reference and the relevant documents (including, where applicable, the case file or a copy of the case file) are to be sent by the national court directly to the Court of Justice, by registered post (addressed to the Registry of the Court of Justice, L-2925 Luxembourg, telephone +352 4303-1).

31.   The Court Registry will stay in contact with the national court until a ruling is given, and will send it copies of the procedural documents.

32.   The Court of Justice will send its ruling to the national court. It would welcome information from the national court on the action taken upon its ruling in the national proceedings and, where appropriate, a copy of the national court's final decision.

II. THE URGENT PRELIMINARY RULING PROCEDURE (PPU)

33.   This part of the note provides practical information on the urgent preliminary ruling procedure applicable to references relating to the area of freedom, security and justice. The procedure is governed by Article 23a of Protocol (No 3) on the Statute of the Court of Justice of the European Union (OJEU 2008 C 115, p. 210) and Article 104b of the Rules of Procedure of the Court of Justice. National courts may request that this procedure be applied or request the application of the accelerated procedure under the conditions laid down in Article 23a of the Protocol and Article 104a of the Rules of Procedure.

CONDITIONS FOR THE APPLICATION OF THE URGENT PRELIMINARY RULING PROCEDURE

34.   The urgent preliminary ruling procedure is applicable only in the areas covered by Title V of Part Three of the TFEU, which relates to the area of freedom, security and justice.

35.   The Court of Justice decides whether this procedure is to be applied. Such a decision is generally taken only on a reasoned request from the referring court. Exceptionally, the Court may decide of its own motion to deal with a reference under the urgent preliminary ruling procedure, where that appears to be required.

36.   The urgent preliminary ruling procedure simplifies the various stages of the proceedings before the Court, but its application entails significant constraints for the Court and for the parties and other interested persons participating in the procedure, particularly the Member States.

37.   It should therefore be requested only where it is absolutely necessary for the Court to give its ruling on the reference as quickly as possible. Although it is not possible to provide an exhaustive list of such situations, particularly because of the varied and evolving nature of the rules of European Union law governing the area of freedom, security and justice, a national court or tribunal might, for example, consider submitting a request for the urgent preliminary ruling procedure to be applied in the following situations: in the case, referred to in the fourth paragraph of Article 267 TFEU, of a person in custody or deprived of his liberty, where the answer to the question raised is decisive as to the assessment of that

person's legal situation or, in proceedings concerning parental authority or custody of children, where the identity of the court having jurisdiction under European Union law depends on the answer to the question referred for a preliminary ruling.

THE REQUEST FOR APPLICATION OF THE URGENT PRELIMINARY RULING PROCEDURE

38. To enable the Court to decide quickly whether the urgent preliminary ruling procedure should be applied, the request must set out the matters of fact and law which establish the urgency and, in particular, the risks involved in following the normal preliminary ruling procedure.

39. In so far as it is able to do so, the referring court should briefly state its view on the answer to be given to the question(s) referred. Such a statement makes it easier for the parties and other interested persons participating in the procedure to define their positions and facilitates the Court's decision, thereby contributing to the rapidity of the procedure.

40. The request for the urgent preliminary ruling procedure must be submitted in an unambiguous form that enables the Court Registry to establish immediately that the file must be dealt with in a particular way. Accordingly, the referring court is asked to couple its request with a mention of Article 104b of the Rules of Procedure and to include that mention in a clearly identifiable place in its reference (for example at the head of the page or in a separate judicial document). Where appropriate, a covering letter from the referring court can usefully refer to that request.

41. As regards the order for reference itself, it is particularly important that it should be succinct where the matter is urgent, as this will help to ensure the rapidity of the procedure.

COMMUNICATION BETWEEN THE COURT OF JUSTICE, THE NATIONAL COURT AND THE PARTIES

42. As regards communication with the national court or tribunal and the parties before it, national courts or tribunals which submit a request for an urgent preliminary ruling procedure are requested to state the e-mail address or any fax number which may be used by the Court of Justice, together with the e-mail addresses or any fax numbers of the representatives of the parties to the proceedings.

43. A copy of the signed order for reference together with a request for the urgent preliminary ruling procedure can initially be sent to the Court by e-mail (ECJ-Registry@curia.europa. eu) or by fax (+352 43 37 66). Processing of the reference and of the request can then begin upon receipt of the e-mailed or faxed copy. The originals of those documents must, however, be sent to the Court Registry as soon as possible.

(1) Article 10(1) to (3) of Protocol No 36 provides that the powers of the Court of Justice in relation to acts adopted before the entry into force of the Treaty of Lisbon (OJ 2007 C 306, p. 1) under Title VI of the TEU, in the field of police cooperation and judicial cooperation in criminal matters, and which have not since been amended, are, however, to remain the same for a maximum period of five years from the date of entry into force of the Treaty of Lisbon (1 December 2009). During that period, such acts may, therefore, form the subject-matter of a reference for a preliminary ruling only where the order for reference is made by a court of a Member State which has accepted the jurisdiction of the Court of Justice, it being a matter for each State to determine whether the right to refer a question to the Court is to be available to all of its national courts or is to be reserved to the courts of last instance.

B) PRESIDENCY OF THE COUNCIL

EUROPEAN COUNCIL DECISION OF 1 DECEMBER 2009
on the exercise of the Presidency of the Council OJ L 315, 2.12.2009, p. 50

THE EUROPEAN COUNCIL,

Having regard to the Treaty on the European Union, and in particular Article 16(9) thereof,

Having regard to the Treaty on the Functioning of the European Union, and in particular Article 236(b) thereof,

Whereas:
(1) Declaration (no 9) annexed to the Final Act of the Intergovernmental Conference which has adopted the Treaty of Lisbon foresees that the European Council adopts, on the date of entry into force of the Treaty, the Decision the text of which is contained in the said Declaration.

(2) It is therefore appropriate to adopt that Decision,

HAS ADOPTED THIS DECISION:

Article 1
1. The Presidency of the Council, with the exception of the Foreign Affairs configuration, shall be held by pre-established groups of three Member States for a period of 18 months. The groups shall be made up on a basis of equal rotation among the Member States, taking into account their diversity and geographical balance within the Union.

2. Each member of the group shall in turn chair for a six-month period all configurations of the Council, with the exception of the Foreign Affairs configuration. The other members of the group shall assist the Chair in all its responsibilities on the basis of a common programme. Members of the team may decide alternative arrangements among themselves.

Article 2
The Committee of Permanent Representatives of the Governments of the Member States shall be chaired by a representative of the Member State chairing the General Affairs Council. The Chair of the Political and Security Committee shall be held by a representative of the High Representative of the Union for Foreign Affairs and Security Policy. The chair of the preparatory bodies of the various Council configurations, with the exception of the Foreign Affairs configuration, shall fall to the member of the group chairing the relevant configuration, unless decided otherwise in accordance with Article 4.

Article 3
The General Affairs Council shall ensure consistency and continuity in the work of the different Council configurations in the framework of multiannual programmes in cooperation with the Commission. The Member States holding the Presidency shall take all necessary measures for the organisation and smooth operation of the Council's work, with the assistance of the General Secretariat of the Council.

Article 4
The Council shall adopt a decision establishing the measures for the implementation of this decision.

Article 5
This Decision shall enter into force on the day of its adoption. It shall be published in the *Official Journal of the European Union.*

C) THE EUROPEAN PARLIAMENT AND THE EUROPEAN COMMISSION

FRAMEWORK AGREEMENT

on relations between the Parliament and the European Commission OJ L 304, 20.11.2010, p. 47

(footnotes and annexes omitted)

THE EUROPEAN PARLIAMENT AND THE EUROPEAN COMMISSION (hereinafter referred to as "the two Institutions"),

having regard to the Treaty on European Union (TEU), the Treaty on the Functioning of the European Union (TFEU), in particular Article 295 thereof, and the Treaty establishing the European Atomic Energy Community (hereinafter referred to as "the Treaties"),

having regard to the Interinstitutional Agreements and texts governing relations between the two Institutions,

having regard to Parliament's Rules of Procedure, and in particular Rules 105, 106 and 127 thereof and Annexes VIII and XIV thereto,

having regard to the political guidelines issued, and the relevant statements made, by the President-elect of the Commission on 15 September 2009 and 9 February 2010 and the statements made by each of the candidate Members of the Commission in the course of their hearings by parliamentary committees,

A.   whereas the Lisbon Treaty strengthens the democratic legitimacy of the Union's decision-making process,

B.   whereas the two Institutions attach the utmost importance to the effective transposition and implementation of Union law,

C.   whereas this Framework Agreement does not affect the powers and prerogatives of Parliament, the Commission or any other institution or organ of the Union but seeks to ensure that those powers and prerogatives are exercised as effectively and transparently as possible,

D.   whereas this Framework Agreement should be interpreted in conformity with the institutional framework as organised by the Treaties,

E.   whereas the Commission will take due account of the respective roles conferred by the Treaties on Parliament and the Council, in particular with reference to the basic principle of equal treatment laid down under point 9,

F.   whereas it is appropriate to update the Framework Agreement concluded in May 2005
      and to replace it by the following text,

AGREE AS FOLLOWS:

I. SCOPE

1.   To better reflect the new "special partnership" between Parliament and the Commission,
      the two Institutions agree on the following measures to strengthen the political
      responsibility and legitimacy of the Commission, extend constructive dialogue, improve
      the flow of information between the two Institutions and improve cooperation on
      procedures and planning.

      They also agree on specific provisions:
      — on Commission meetings with national experts, as set out in Annex I,
      — on the forwarding of confidential information to Parliament, as set out in Annex II,
      — on the negotiation and conclusion of international agreements, as set out in Annex III,
        and
      — on the timetable for the Commission Work Programme, as set out in Annex IV.

II. POLITICAL RESPONSIBILITY

2.   After being nominated by the European Council, the President-designate of the
      Commission will submit to Parliament political guidelines for his/her term of office in
      order to enable an informed exchange of views to take place with Parliament before its
      election vote.

3.   In conformity with Rule 106 of its Rules of Procedure, Parliament shall communicate with
      the President-elect of the Commission in good time before the opening of the procedures
      relating to giving its consent to the new Commission. Parliament shall take into account
      the remarks expressed by the President-elect.

      The designated Members of the Commission shall ensure full disclosure of all relevant
      information, in conformity with the obligation of independence laid down in Article 245
      TFEU.

      The procedures shall be designed in such a way as to ensure that the entire Commission-
      designate is assessed in an open, fair and consistent manner.

4.   Each Member of the Commission shall take political responsibility for action in the
      field of which he/she is in charge, without prejudice to the principle of Commission
      collegiality.

      The President of the Commission shall be fully responsible for identifying any conflict of
      interest which renders a Member of the Commission unable to perform his/her duties.

      The President of the Commission shall likewise be responsible for any subsequent action
      taken in such circumstances and shall inform the President of Parliament thereof
      immediately and in writing.

      The participation of Members of the Commission in electoral campaigns is governed by
      the Code of Conduct for Commissioners.

      Members of the Commission participating actively in electoral campaigns as candidates in
      elections to the Parliament should take unpaid electoral leave with effect from the end of
      the last part-session before the elections.

The President of the Commission shall inform Parliament in due time of his/her decision to grant such leave, indicating which Member of the Commission will take over the relevant responsibilities for that period of leave.

5.   If Parliament asks the President of the Commission to withdraw confidence in an individual Member of the Commission, he/she will seriously consider whether to request that Member to resign, in accordance with Article 17(6) TEU. The President shall either require the resignation of that Member or explain his/her refusal to do so before Parliament in the following part-session.

6.   Where it becomes necessary to arrange for the replacement of a Member of the Commission during his/her term of office pursuant to the second paragraph of Article 246 TFEU, the President of the Commission will seriously consider the result of Parliament's consultation before giving accord to the decision of the Council.

Parliament shall ensure that its procedures are conducted with the utmost dispatch, in order to enable the President of the Commission to seriously consider Parliament's opinion before the new Member is appointed.

Similarly, pursuant to the third paragraph of Article 246 TFEU, when the remainder of the Commission's term of office is short, the President of the Commission will seriously consider Parliament's position.

7.   If the President of the Commission intends to reshuffle the allocation of responsibilities amongst the Members of the Commission during its term of office, pursuant to Article 248 TFEU, he/she shall inform Parliament in due time for the relevant parliamentary consultation with regard to those changes. The President's decision to reshuffle the portfolios can take effect immediately.

8.   When the Commission comes forward with a revision of the Code of Conduct for Commissioners relating to conflict of interest or ethical behaviour, it will seek Parliament's opinion.

III. CONSTRUCTIVE DIALOGUE AND FLOW OF INFORMATION

(i) **General provisions**

9.   The Commission guarantees that it will apply the basic principle of equal treatment for Parliament and the Council, especially as regards access to meetings and the provision of contributions or other information, in particular on legislative and budgetary matters.

10. Within its competences, the Commission shall take measures to better involve Parliament in such a way as to take Parliament's views into account as far as possible in the area of the Common Foreign and Security Policy.

11. A number of arrangements are made to implement the "special partnership" between Parliament and the Commission, as follows:
— the President of the Commission will at Parliament's request meet the Conference of Presidents at least twice a year to discuss issues of common interest,
— the President of the Commission will have a regular dialogue with the President of Parliament on key horizontal issues and major legislative proposals. This dialogue should also include invitations to the President of Parliament to attend meetings of the College of Commissioners,
— the President of the Commission or the Vice-President responsible for interinstitutional relations is to be invited to attend meetings of the Conference of Presidents and the Conference of Committee Chairs when specific issues relating to

plenary agenda-setting, interinstitutional relations between Parliament and the Commission and legislative and budgetary matters are to be discussed,

— meetings shall take place annually between the Conference of Presidents and the Conference of Committee Chairs and the College of Commissioners, to discuss relevant issues including the preparation and implementation of the Commission Work Programme,

— the Conference of Presidents and the Conference of Committee Chairs shall inform the Commission in due time of the results of their discussions having an interinstitutional dimension. Parliament shall also keep the Commission fully and regularly informed of the outcome of its meetings dealing with the preparation of the part-sessions, taking into account the Commission's views. This is without prejudice to point 45,

— to ensure a regular flow of relevant information between the two Institutions, the Secretaries-General of Parliament and of the Commission shall meet on a regular basis.

12. Each Member of the Commission shall make sure that there is a regular and direct flow of information between the Member of the Commission and the chair of the relevant parliamentary committee.

13. The Commission shall not make public any legislative proposal or any significant initiative or decision before notifying Parliament thereof in writing.

On the basis of the Commission Work Programme, the two Institutions shall identify in advance, by common agreement, key initiatives to be presented in plenary. In principle, the Commission will present these initiatives first in plenary and only afterwards to the public.

Similarly, they shall identify those proposals and initiatives for which information is to be provided before the Conference of Presidents or conveyed, in an appropriate manner, to the relevant parliamentary committee or its chair.

These decisions shall be taken within the framework of the regular dialogue between the two Institutions, as provided for in point 11, and shall be updated on a regular basis, taking due account of any political developments.

14. If an internal Commission document – of which Parliament has not been informed pursuant to this Framework Agreement – is circulated outside the Institutions, the President of Parliament may request that the document concerned be forwarded to Parliament without delay, in order to communicate it to any Member of Parliament who may request it.

15. The Commission will provide full information and documentation on its meetings with national experts within the framework of its work on the preparation and implementation of Union legislation, including soft law and delegated acts. If so requested by Parliament, the Commission may also invite Parliament's experts to attend those meetings.

The relevant provisions are laid down in Annex I.

16. Within 3 months after the adoption of a parliamentary resolution, the Commission shall provide information to Parliament in writing on action taken in response to specific requests addressed to it in Parliament's resolutions, including in cases where it has not been able to follow Parliament's views. That period may be shortened where a request is urgent. It may be extended by 1 month where a request calls for more exhaustive work and this is duly substantiated. Parliament will make sure that this information is widely distributed within the institution.

Parliament will endeavour to avoid asking oral or written questions concerning issues in respect of which the Commission has already informed Parliament of its position through a written follow-up communication.

The Commission shall commit itself to report on the concrete follow-up of any request to submit a proposal pursuant to Article 225 TFEU (legislative initiative report) within 3 months following adoption of the corresponding resolution in plenary. The Commission shall come forward with a legislative proposal at the latest after 1 year or shall include the proposal in its next year's Work Programme. If the Commission does not submit a proposal, it shall give Parliament detailed explanations of the reasons.

The Commission shall also commit itself to a close and early cooperation with Parliament on any legislative initiative requests emanating from citizens' initiatives.

As regards the discharge procedure, the specific provisions laid down in point 31 shall apply.

17. Where initiatives, recommendations or requests for legislative acts are made pursuant to Article 289(4) TFEU, the Commission shall inform Parliament, if so requested, of its position on those proposals before the relevant parliamentary committee.

18. The two Institutions agree to cooperate in the area of relations with national Parliaments.

Parliament and the Commission shall cooperate on the implementation of TFEU Protocol No 2 on the application of the principles of subsidiarity and proportionality. Such cooperation shall include arrangements related to any necessary translation of reasoned opinions presented by national Parliaments.

When the thresholds mentioned in Article 7 of TFEU Protocol No 2 are met, the Commission shall provide the translations of all the reasoned opinions presented by national Parliaments together with its position thereon.

19. The Commission shall inform Parliament of the list of its expert groups set up in order to assist the Commission in the exercise of its right of initiative. That list shall be updated on a regular basis and made public.

Within this framework, the Commission shall, in an appropriate manner, inform the competent parliamentary committee, at the specific and reasoned request of its chair, on the activities and composition of such groups.

20. The two Institutions shall hold, through the appropriate mechanisms, a constructive dialogue on questions concerning important administrative matters, notably on issues having direct implications for Parliament's own administration.

21. Parliament will seek the opinion of the Commission when it comes forward with a revision of its Rules of Procedures concerning relations with the Commission.

22. Where confidentiality is invoked as regards any of the information forwarded pursuant to this Framework Agreement, the provisions laid down in Annex II shall be applied.

(ii) International agreements and enlargement

23. Parliament shall be immediately and fully informed at all stages of the negotiation and conclusion of international agreements, including the definition of negotiating directives. The Commission shall act in a manner to give full effect to its obligations pursuant to Article 218 TFEU, while respecting each Institution's role in accordance with Article 13(2) TEU.

The Commission shall apply the arrangements set out in Annex III.

24. The information referred to in point 23 shall be provided to Parliament in sufficient time for it to be able to express its point of view if appropriate, and for the Commission to be able to take Parliament's views as far as possible into account. This information shall, as a general rule, be provided to Parliament through the responsible parliamentary committee and, where appropriate, at a plenary sitting. In duly justified cases, it shall be provided to more than one parliamentary committee.

    Parliament and the Commission undertake to establish appropriate procedures and safeguards for the forwarding of confidential information from the Commission to Parliament, in accordance with the provisions of Annex II.

25. The two Institutions acknowledge that, due to their different institutional roles, the Commission is to represent the European Union in international negotiations, with the exception of those concerning the Common Foreign and Security Policy and other cases as provided for in the Treaties.

    Where the Commission represents the Union in international conferences, it shall, at Parliament's request, facilitate the inclusion of a delegation of Members of the European Parliament as observers in Union delegations, so that it may be immediately and fully informed about the conference proceedings. The Commission undertakes, where applicable, to systematically inform the Parliament delegation about the outcome of negotiations.

    Members of the European Parliament may not participate directly in these negotiations. Subject to the legal, technical and diplomatic possibilities, they may be granted observer status by the Commission. In the event of refusal, the Commission will inform Parliament of the reasons therefor.

    In addition, the Commission shall facilitate the participation of Members of the European Parliament as observers in all relevant meetings under its responsibility before and after negotiation sessions.

26. Under the same conditions, the Commission shall keep Parliament systematically informed about, and facilitate access as observers for Members of the European Parliament forming part of Union delegations to, meetings of bodies set up by multilateral international agreements involving the Union, whenever such bodies are called upon to take decisions which require the consent of Parliament or the implementation of which may require the adoption of legal acts in accordance with the ordinary legislative procedure.

27. The Commission shall also give Parliament's delegation included in Union delegations to international conferences access to use all Union delegation facilities on these occasions, in line with the general principle of good cooperation between the institutions and taking into account the available logistics.

    The President of Parliament shall send to the President of the Commission a proposal for the inclusion of a Parliament delegation in the Union delegation no later than 4 weeks before the start of the conference, specifying the head of the Parliament delegation and the number of Members of the European Parliament to be included. In duly justified cases, this deadline can exceptionally be shortened.

    The number of Members of the European Parliament included in the Parliament delegation and of supporting staff shall be proportionate to the overall size of the Union delegation.

28. The Commission shall keep Parliament fully informed of the progress of accession negotiations and in particular on major aspects and developments, so as to enable it to express its views in good time through the appropriate parliamentary procedures.

29. When Parliament adopts a recommendation on matters referred to in point 28, pursuant to Rule 90(4) of its Rules of Procedure, and when, for important reasons, the Commission

decides that it cannot support such a recommendation, it shall explain the reasons before Parliament, at a plenary sitting or at the next meeting of the relevant parliamentary committee.

(iii) Budgetary implementation

30. Before making, at donors' conferences, financial pledges which involve new financial undertakings and require the agreement of the budgetary authority, the Commission shall inform the budgetary authority and examine its remarks.

31. In connection with the annual discharge governed by Article 319 TFEU, the Commission shall forward all information necessary for supervising the implementation of the budget for the year in question, which the chair of the parliamentary committee responsible for the discharge procedure pursuant to Annex VII to Parliament's Rules of Procedure requests from it for that purpose.

    If new aspects come to light concerning previous years for which discharge has already been given, the Commission shall forward all the necessary information on the matter with a view to arriving at a solution acceptable to both sides.

(iv) Relationship with regulatory agencies

32. Nominees for the post of Executive Director of regulatory agencies should come to parliamentary committee hearings.

    In addition, in the context of the discussions of the interinstitutional Working Group on Agencies set up in March 2009, the Commission and Parliament will aim at a common approach on the role and position of decentralised agencies in the Union's institutional landscape, accompanied by common guidelines for the creation, structure and operation of those agencies, together with funding, budgetary, supervision and management issues.

IV. COOPERATION AS REGARDS LEGISLATIVE PROCEDURES AND PLANNING

(i) Commission Work Programme and the European Union's programming

33. The Commission shall initiate the Union's annual and multiannual programming, with a view to achieving interinstitutional agreements.

34. Every year the Commission shall present its Work Programme.

35. The two Institutions shall cooperate in accordance with the timetable set out in Annex IV.

    The Commission shall take into account the priorities expressed by Parliament.

    The Commission shall provide sufficient detail as to what is envisaged under each point in its Work Programme.

36. The Commission shall explain when it cannot deliver individual proposals in its Work Programme for the year in question or when it departs from it. The Vice-President of the Commission responsible for interinstitutional relations undertakes to report to the Conference of Committee Chairs regularly, outlining the political implementation of the Commission Work Programme for the year in question.

(ii) Procedures for the adoption of acts

37. The Commission undertakes to carefully examine amendments to its legislative proposals adopted by Parliament, with a view to taking them into account in any amended proposal.

When delivering its opinion on Parliament's amendments pursuant to Article 294 TFEU, the Commission undertakes to take the utmost account of amendments adopted at second reading; should it decide, for important reasons and after consideration by the College, not to adopt or support such amendments, it shall explain its decision before Parliament, and in any event in its opinion on Parliament's amendments by virtue of point (c) of Article 294(7) TFEU.

38. Parliament undertakes, when dealing with an initiative submitted by at least a quarter of Member States, in conformity with Article 76 TFEU, not to adopt any report in the relevant committee before receiving the Commission's opinion on the initiative.

The Commission undertakes to issue its opinion on such an initiative no later than 10 weeks after it has been submitted.

39. The Commission shall provide a detailed explanation in due time before withdrawing any proposals on which Parliament has already expressed a position at first reading.

The Commission shall proceed with a review of all pending proposals at the beginning of the new Commission's term of office, in order to politically confirm or withdraw them, taking due account of the views expressed by Parliament.

40. For special legislative procedures on which Parliament is to be consulted, including other procedures such as that laid down in Article 148 TFEU, the Commission:
   (i)   shall take measures to better involve Parliament in such a way as to take Parliament's views into account as far as possible, in particular to ensure that Parliament has the necessary time to consider the Commission's proposal;
   (ii) shall ensure that Council bodies are reminded in good time not to reach a political agreement on its proposals before Parliament has adopted its opinion. It shall ask for discussion to be concluded at ministerial level after a reasonable period has been given to the members of the Council to examine Parliament's opinion;
   (iii) shall ensure that the Council adheres to the rules developed by the Court of Justice of the European Union requiring Parliament to be reconsulted if the Council substantially amends a Commission proposal. The Commission shall inform Parliament of any reminder to the Council of the need for reconsultation;
   (iv) undertakes, if appropriate, to withdraw a legislative proposal that Parliament has rejected. If, for important reasons and after consideration by the College, the Commission decides to maintain its proposal, it shall explain the reasons for that decision in a statement before Parliament.

41. For its part, in order to improve legislative planning, Parliament undertakes:
   (i)   to plan the legislative sections of its agendas, bringing them into line with the current Commission Work Programme and with the resolutions it has adopted on that programme, in particular with a view to the improved planning of the priority debates;
   (ii) to meet reasonable deadlines, in so far as is useful for the procedure, when adopting its position at first reading under the ordinary legislative procedure or its opinion under the consultation procedure;
   (iii) as far as possible to appoint rapporteurs on future proposals as soon as the Commission Work Programme is adopted;
   (iv) to consider requests for reconsultation as a matter of absolute priority provided that all the necessary information has been forwarded to it.

(iii) Issues linked to better lawmaking
42. The Commission shall ensure that its impact assessments are conducted under its responsibility by means of a transparent procedure which guarantees an independent

assessment. Impact assessments shall be published in due time, taking into consideration a number of different scenarios, including a "do nothing" option, and shall in principle be presented to the relevant parliamentary committee during the phase of the provision of information to national Parliaments under TFEU Protocols Nos 1 and 2.

43.   In areas where Parliament is usually involved in the legislative process, the Commission shall use soft law, where appropriate and on a duly justified basis after having given Parliament the opportunity to express its views. The Commission shall provide a detailed explanation to Parliament on how its views have been taken into account when it adopts its proposal.

44.   In order to ensure better monitoring of the transposition and application of Union law, the Commission and Parliament shall endeavour to include compulsory correlation tables and a binding time limit for transposition, which in directives should not normally exceed a period of 2 years.

In addition to specific reports and the annual report on the application of Union law, the Commission shall make available to Parliament summary information concerning all infringement procedures from the letter of formal notice, including, if so requested by Parliament, on a case-by-case basis and respecting the confidentiality rules, in particular those acknowledged by the Court of Justice of the European Union, on the issues to which the infringement procedure relates.

V. THE COMMISSION'S PARTICIPATION IN PARLIAMENTARY PROCEEDINGS

45.   The Commission shall give priority to its presence, if requested, at the plenary sittings or meetings of other bodies of Parliament, as compared to other competing events or invitations.

In particular, the Commission shall ensure that, as a general rule, Members of the Commission are present at plenary sittings for agenda items falling under their responsibility, whenever Parliament so requests. This is applicable to the preliminary draft agendas approved by the Conference of Presidents during the previous part-session.

Parliament shall seek to ensure that, as a general rule, agenda items of the part-sessions falling under the responsibility of a Member of the Commission are grouped together.

46.   At the request of Parliament, provision will be made for a regular Question Hour with the President of the Commission. This Question Hour will comprise two parts: the first with leaders of political groups or their representatives, conducted on an entirely spontaneous basis; the second devoted to a policy theme agreed upon in advance, at the latest on the Thursday before the relevant part-session, but without prepared questions.

Furthermore, a Question Hour with Members of the Commission, including the Vice-President for External Relations/High Representative of the Union for Foreign Affairs and Security Policy shall be introduced, following the model of the Question Hour with the President of the Commission, with the aim of reforming the existing Question Time. This Question Hour shall relate to the portfolio of the respective Members of the Commission.

47.   Members of the Commission shall be heard at their request.

Without prejudice to Article 230 TFEU, the two Institutions shall agree on general rules relating to the allocation of speaking time between the Institutions.

The two Institutions agree that their indicative allocation of speaking time should be respected.

48.   With a view to ensuring the presence of Members of the Commission, Parliament undertakes to do its best to maintain its final draft agendas.

Where Parliament amends its final draft agenda, or where it moves items within the agenda within a part-session, Parliament shall immediately inform the Commission. The Commission shall use its best endeavours to ensure the presence of the Member of the Commission responsible.

49.   The Commission may propose the inclusion of items on the agenda not later than the meeting of the Conference of Presidents that decides on the final draft agenda of a part-session. Parliament shall take the fullest account of such proposals.

50.   Parliamentary committees shall seek to maintain their draft agendas and agendas.

Whenever a parliamentary committee amends its draft agenda or its agenda, the Commission shall be immediately informed thereof. In particular, parliamentary committees shall endeavour to respect a reasonable deadline so as to allow for the presence of Members of the Commission at their meetings.

Where the presence of a Member of the Commission is not explicitly required at a parliamentary committee meeting, the Commission shall ensure that it is represented by a competent official at an appropriate level.

Parliamentary committees will endeavour to coordinate their work, including avoiding parallel meetings on the same issue, and will endeavour not to deviate from the draft agenda, so that the Commission can ensure an appropriate level of representation.

If the presence of a high-level official (Director-General or Director) has been requested at a committee meeting dealing with a Commission proposal, the representative of the Commission shall be allowed to intervene.

VI. FINAL PROVISIONS

51.   The Commission confirms its commitment to examine as soon as possible the legislative acts which were not adapted to the regulatory procedure with scrutiny before the entry into force of the Lisbon Treaty, in order to assess whether those instruments need to be adapted to the regime of delegated acts introduced by Article 290 TFEU.

As a final goal, a coherent system of delegated and implementing acts, fully consistent with the Treaty, should be achieved through a progressive assessment of the nature and contents of measures currently subject to the regulatory procedure with scrutiny, in order to adapt them in due course to the regime laid down by Article 290 TFEU.

52.   The provisions of this Framework Agreement complement the Interinstitutional Agreement on better lawmaking without affecting it and do not prejudice any further revision thereof. Without prejudice to forthcoming negotiations between Parliament, the Commission and the Council, the two Institutions commit to agree on key changes in preparation of future negotiations on adaptation of the Interinstitutional Agreement on better lawmaking to the new provisions introduced by the Lisbon Treaty, taking into account current practices and this Framework Agreement.

They also agree on the need to reinforce the existing interinstitutional contact mechanism, at political and at technical level, in relation to better lawmaking, so as to ensure effective interinstitutional cooperation between Parliament, the Commission and the Council.

53.   The Commission commits to initiate rapidly the Union's annual and multiannual programming with a view to achieving interinstitutional agreements, in accordance with Article 17 TEU.

The Commission Work Programme is the Commission's contribution to the Union's annual and multiannual programming. Following its adoption by the Commission, a trialogue between Parliament, the Council and the Commission should take place with a view to reaching an agreement on the Union's programming.

In this context and as soon as Parliament, the Council and the Commission have reached a common understanding on the Union's programming, the two Institutions shall review the provisions of this Framework Agreement related to programming.

Parliament and the Commission call on the Council to engage as soon as possible in discussions on the Union's programming as provided for in Article 17 TEU.

54.   The practical implementation of this Framework Agreement and its Annexes shall be assessed periodically by the two Institutions. A review shall be carried out by the end of 2011, in the light of practical experience.

(Date, place of signing and signatories omitted)

D) IMPLEMENTING POWERS AND LAW MAKING

INTERINSTITUTIONAL AGREEMENT OF 16 DECEMBER 2003
on better law-making OJ C 321, 31.12.2003, p. 1[1]

THE EUROPEAN PARLIAMENT, THE COUNCIL OF THE EUROPEAN UNION AND THE COMMISSION OF THE EUROPEAN COMMUNITIES,

Having regard to the Treaty establishing the European Community and, in particular, to Article 5 thereof and the Protocol on the application of the principles of subsidiarity and proportionality annexed thereto,

Having regard to the Treaty on European Union,

Drawing attention to Declaration No 18 on the estimated costs under Commission proposals and to Declaration No 19 on the implementation of Community law, both of which are annexed to the Maastricht Final Act,

Drawing attention to the Interinstitutional Agreements of 25 October 1993 on the procedures for implementing the principle of subsidiarity(1), of 20 December 1994 on accelerated working method for the official codification of legislative texts(2), of 22 December 1998 on common

----

[1]   EDITOR'S NOTE: As of 1 May 2012 this Agreement has not been amended following the entry into force of the Treaty of Lisbon. It may include references to the old version of the Treaty on European Union (TEU) and/or the now replaced Treaty establishing the European Community (TEC). Reference should be made to the Tables of Equivalences accompanying the consolidated Treaties in Part II of this edition for the conversion of old Treaty article numbers to new ones.

guidelines for the quality of drafting of Community legislation(3), and of 28 November 2001 on a more structured use of the recasting technique for legal acts(4),

Noting the Presidency Conclusions of the meetings of the European Council held on 21 and 22 June 2002 in Seville and on 20 and 21 March 2003 in Brussels,

Emphasising that this Agreement is concluded without prejudice to the outcome of the Intergovernmental Conference which will be held following the Convention on the Future of Europe,

HAVE AGREED AS FOLLOWS:

COMMON COMMITMENTS AND OBJECTIVES

1. The European Parliament, the Council of the European Union and the Commission of the European Communities hereby agree to improve the quality of law-making by means of a series of initiatives and procedures set out in this interinstitutional agreement.

2. In exercising the powers and in compliance with the procedures laid down in the Treaty, and recalling the importance which they attach to the Community method, the three Institutions agree to observe general principles such as democratic legitimacy, subsidiarity and proportionality, and legal certainty. They further agree to promote simplicity, clarity and consistency in the drafting of laws and the utmost transparency of the legislative process.

    They call on the Member States to ensure a proper and prompt transposition of Community law into national law within the prescribed time limits, pursuant to the Presidency Conclusions of the European Council at its Stockholm, Barcelona and Seville meetings.

BETTER COORDINATION OF THE LEGISLATIVE PROCESS

3. The three Institutions agree to ensure that general coordination of their legislative activity is improved, thereby providing an essential foundation for better law-making within the European Union.

4. The three Institutions agree to improve the coordination of their preparatory and legislative work in the context of the codecision procedure and to publicise it in appropriate fashion.

    The Council will inform the European Parliament in good time of the draft multiannual strategic programme which it recommends for adoption by the European Council. The three Institutions will forward to each other their respective annual legislative timetables with a view to reaching agreement on joint annual programming.

    In particular, the European Parliament and the Council will seek to establish, for each legislative proposal, an indicative timetable for the various stages leading to the final adoption of that proposal.

    Wherever multiannual programming has an interinstitutional impact, the three Institutions will initiate cooperation through the appropriate channels.

    As far as possible, the Commission's annual law-making and work programme will include indications as to the choice of legislative instrument and the legal basis envisaged for each measure to be put forward.

5. The three Institutions will, in the interests of efficiency, ensure as far as possible a better synchronisation of the treatment of common dossiers by the preparatory bodies(5) of each branch of the legislative authority(6).

6. The three Institutions will keep each other permanently informed about their work throughout the legislative process. This information will be based on appropriate procedures, including dialogue between the European Parliament, in committee and plenary, and the Council Presidency and the Commission.

7. The Commission will submit an annual progress report on its legislative proposals.

8. The Commission will ensure that, as a general rule, Commissioners are present for discussions at European Parliament committee meetings and plenary sittings on draft legislation for which they are responsible.

   The Council will continue the practice of maintaining intensive contact with the European Parliament by means of regular participation in plenary debates, as far as possible by the Ministers concerned. The Council will also endeavour to participate regularly in the work of the parliamentary committees and in other meetings, preferably at ministerial level or at some other appropriate level.

9. The Commission will take account of requests made by the European Parliament or the Council, on the basis respectively of Article 192 or Article 208 of the EC Treaty, for the submission of legislative proposals. It will reply rapidly and appropriately to the parliamentary committees concerned and to the Council's preparatory bodies.

GREATER TRANSPARENCY AND ACCESSIBILITY

10. The three Institutions confirm the importance which they attach to greater transparency and to the increased provision of information to the public at every stage of their legislative work, whilst taking into account their respective rules of procedure. They will ensure in particular that public debates at political level are broadcast as widely as possible through the systematic use of new communication technologies such as, inter alia, satellite broadcasting and Internet video-streaming. They will also ensure that the public has greater access to EUR-Lex.

11. The three Institutions will hold a joint press conference to announce the successful outcome of the legislative process in the codecision procedure, once they have reached agreement, whether after first reading, second reading or conciliation.

CHOICE OF LEGISLATIVE INSTRUMENT AND LEGAL BASIS

12. The Commission will explain and justify to the European Parliament and to the Council its choice of legislative instrument, where possible as part of its annual work programme or of the normal dialogue procedures and, at all events, in the explanatory memoranda attached to its initiatives. It will consider any request in this connection from the legislative authority, and it will take account of the results of any consultations which it has undertaken before tabling its proposals.

   It will ensure that the action it proposes is as simple as is compatible with the proper attainment of the objective of the measure and the need for effective implementation.

13. The three Institutions recall the definition of the term "directive" (Article 249 of the EC Treaty) and the relevant provisions of the Protocol on the application of the principles of subsidiarity and proportionality. In its proposals for directives, the Commission will

ensure that a proper balance is struck between general principles and detailed provisions, in a manner that avoids excessive use of Community implementing measures.

14. The Commission will provide a clear and comprehensive justification for the legal basis used for each proposal. In the event of a change being made to the legal basis after any Commission proposal has been presented, the European Parliament will be duly re-consulted by the Institution concerned, in full compliance with the case-law of the Court of Justice of the European Communities.

15. In the explanatory memoranda to its proposals, the Commission will, in every instance, set out the legal arrangements which currently exist at Community level in the area affected by the proposal. The Commission will also explain in its explanatory memoranda how the measures proposed are justified in the light of the principles of subsidiarity and proportionality. The Commission will also give an account of the scope and the results of the prior consultation and the impact analyses that it has undertaken.

USE OF ALTERNATIVE METHODS OF REGULATION

16. The three Institutions recall the Community's obligation to legislate only where it is necessary, in accordance with the Protocol on the application of the principles of subsidiarity and proportionality. They recognise the need to use, in suitable cases or where the Treaty does not specifically require the use of a legal instrument, alternative regulation mechanisms.

17. The Commission will ensure that any use of co-regulation or self-regulation is always consistent with Community law and that it meets the criteria of transparency (in particular the publicising of agreements) and representativeness of the parties involved. It must also represent added value for the general interest. These mechanisms will not be applicable where fundamental rights or important political options are at stake or in situations where the rules must be applied in a uniform fashion in all Member States. They must ensure swift and flexible regulation which does not affect the principles of competition or the unity of the internal market.

CO-REGULATION

18. Co-regulation means the mechanism whereby a Community legislative act entrusts the attainment of the objectives defined by the legislative authority to parties which are recognised in the field (such as economic operators, the social partners, non-governmental organisations, or associations).

    This mechanism may be used on the basis of criteria defined in the legislative act so as to enable the legislation to be adapted to the problems and sectors concerned, to reduce the legislative burden by concentrating on essential aspects and to draw on the experience of the parties concerned.

19. The legislative act must abide by the principle of proportionality defined in the EC Treaty. Agreements between social partners must comply with the provisions laid down in Articles 138 and 139 of the EC Treaty. In the explanatory memoranda to its proposals, the Commission will explain to the competent legislative authority its reasons for proposing the use of this mechanism.

20. In the context defined by the basic legislative act, the parties affected by that act may conclude voluntary agreements for the purpose of determining practical arrangements.

The draft agreements will be forwarded by the Commission to the legislative authority. In accordance with its responsibilities, the Commission will verify whether or not those draft agreements comply with Community law (and, in particular, with the basic legislative act).

At the request of inter alia the European Parliament or of the Council, on a case-by-case basis and depending on the subject, the basic legislative act may include a provision for a two-month period of grace following notification of a draft agreement to the European Parliament and the Council. During that period, each Institution may either suggest amendments, if it is considered that the draft agreement does not meet the objectives laid down by the legislative authority, or object to the entry into force of that agreement and, possibly, ask the Commission to submit a proposal for a legislative act.

21. A legislative act which serves as the basis for a co-regulation mechanism will indicate the possible extent of co-regulation in the area concerned. The competent legislative authority will define in the act the relevant measures to be taken in order to follow up its application, in the event of non-compliance by one or more parties or if the agreement fails. These measures may provide, for example, for the regular supply of information by the Commission to the legislative authority on follow-up to application or for a revision clause under which the Commission will report at the end of a specific period and, where necessary, propose an amendment to the legislative act or any other appropriate legislative measure.

SELF-REGULATION

22. Self-regulation is defined as the possibility for economic operators, the social partners, non-governmental organisations or associations to adopt amongst themselves and for themselves common guidelines at European level (particularly codes of practice or sectoral agreements).

As a general rule, this type of voluntary initiative does not imply that the Institutions have adopted any particular stance, in particular where such initiatives are undertaken in areas which are not covered by the Treaties or in which the Union has not hitherto legislated. As one of its responsibilities, the Commission will scrutinise self-regulation practices in order to verify that they comply with the provisions of the EC Treaty.

23. The Commission will notify the European Parliament and the Council of the self-regulation practices which it regards, on the one hand, as contributing to the attainment of the EC Treaty objectives and as being compatible with its provisions and, on the other, as being satisfactory in terms of the representativeness of the parties concerned, sectoral and geographical cover and the added value of the commitments given. It will, nonetheless, consider the possibility of putting forward a proposal for a legislative act, in particular at the request of the competent legislative authority or in the event of a failure to observe the above practices.

IMPLEMENTING MEASURES (COMMITTEE PROCEDURE)

24. The three Institutions emphasise the important role played by implementing measures in legislation. They note the outcome of the Convention on the Future of Europe relating to the establishment of rules governing the exercise by the Commission of the implementing powers conferred on it.

The European Parliament and the Council emphasise that, in accordance with their respective powers, they have begun consideration of the proposal which the Commission adopted on 11 December 2002 with a view to amending Council Decision 1999/468/EC(7).

IMPROVING THE QUALITY OF LEGISLATION

25.   The three Institutions, exercising their respective powers, will ensure that legislation is of good quality, namely that it is clear, simple and effective. The Institutions consider that improvement of the pre-legislative consultation process and more frequent use of impact assessments (both ex ante and ex post) will help towards this objective. They are committed to the full application of the Interinstitutional Agreement of 22 December 1998 on common guidelines for the quality of drafting of Community legislation.

(a) Pre-legislative consultation

26.   During the period preceding the submission of legislative proposals, the Commission will, having informed the European Parliament and the Council, conduct the widest possible consultations, the results of which will be made public. In certain cases, where the Commission deems it appropriate, the Commission may submit a pre-legislative consultation document on which the European Parliament and the Council may choose to deliver an opinion.

(b) Impact analyses

27.   Pursuant to the Protocol on the application of the principles of subsidiarity and proportionality, the Commission will take due account in its legislative proposals of their financial or administrative implications, for the Union and the Member States in particular. Furthermore, each of the three Institutions will take into account the objective of ensuring that application in the Member States is appropriate and effective.

28.   The three Institutions agree on the positive contribution of impact assessments in improving the quality of Community legislation, with particular regard to the scope and substance thereof.

29.   The Commission will continue to implement the integrated advance impact-assessment process for major items of draft legislation, combining in one single evaluation the impact assessments relating inter alia to social, economic and environmental aspects. The results of the assessments will be made fully and freely available to the European Parliament, the Council and the general public. In the explanatory memorandum to its proposals, the Commission will indicate the manner in which the impact assessments have influenced them.

30.   Where the codecision procedure applies, the European Parliament and Council may, on the basis of jointly defined criteria and procedures, have impact assessments carried out prior to the adoption of any substantive amendment, either at first reading or at the conciliation stage. As soon as possible after this Agreement is adopted, the three Institutions will carry out an assessment of their respective experiences and will consider the possibility of establishing a common methodology.

(c) Consistency of texts

31.   The European Parliament and the Council will make all appropriate arrangements for improving the scrutiny carried out by their respective departments of the wording of texts adopted under the codecision procedure, with a view to avoiding any inaccuracies or inconsistencies. To this end, the Institutions may agree on a short period of grace in order to allow such legal verification to be performed before the act is finally adopted.

BETTER TRANSPOSITION AND APPLICATION

32.   The three Institutions emphasise the need for Member States to comply with Article 10 of the EC Treaty, they call upon the Member States to ensure that Community law is

properly and promptly transposed into national law within the prescribed deadlines; and they deem such transposition to be essential to the consistent and effective application of that legislation by the courts, the administrations, members of the public and economic and social operators.

33.   The three Institutions will ensure that all directives include a binding time limit for the transposition of their provisions into national law. They will insert into directives a time limit for transposition that is as short as possible and that generally does not exceed two years. The three Institutions hope that the Member States will make a renewed effort as regards the transposition of directives within the time limits which they specify. In this connection, the European Parliament and the Council note that the Commission is proposing to step up cooperation with the Member States.

The three Institutions point out that, under the EC Treaty, the Commission has the power to initiate an infringement procedure in instances where a Member State fails to transpose legislation within the stipulated time limit; and the European Parliament and Council note the commitments given by the Commission on this subject(8).

34.   The Commission will draw up annual reports on the transposition of directives in the various Member States, with tables showing transposition rates. Those reports will be communicated to the European Parliament and to the Council, and will be made public.

The Council will encourage the Member States to draw up, for themselves and in the interests of the Community, their own tables which will, as far as possible, illustrate the correlation between the directives and the transposition measures and to make them public. It calls on those Member States which have not yet done so to appoint a transposition coordinator as soon as possible.

SIMPLIFYING AND REDUCING THE VOLUME OF LEGISLATION

35.   In order to make Community law easier to read and to apply, the three Institutions agree, firstly, to update and condense existing legislation and, secondly, significantly to simplify it. They will take the Commission's multiannual programme as a basis for this task.

Legislation will be updated and condensed inter alia through the repeal of acts which are no longer applied and through the codification or recasting of other acts.

The purpose of legislative simplification is to improve and adapt legislation by amending or replacing acts and provisions which are too unwieldy and too complex to be applied. Such simplification will be carried out through the recasting of existing acts or by means of new legislative proposals, whilst maintaining the substance of Community policies. In this connection, the Commission will select the areas of current law which are suitable for simplification, on the basis of criteria laid down once the legislative authority has been consulted.

36.   Within six months of the date upon which this Agreement comes into force, the European Parliament and the Council, whose task it would be as legislative authority to adopt at the final stage the proposals for simplified acts, need to modify their working methods by introducing, for example, ad hoc structures with the specific task of simplifying legislation.

IMPLEMENTATION AND MONITORING OF THE AGREEMENT

37.   The implementation of this Agreement will be monitored by the High-Level Technical Group for Interinstitutional Cooperation.

38.   The three Institutions will take the necessary steps to ensure that their staff have the means and resources required for the proper implementation of the provisions of this Agreement.

(Signatories omitted)

(1)   OJ 1993, C329/135.

(2)   OJ 1996, C102/2.

(3)   OJ 1999, C73/1.

(4)   OJ 2002, C77/1.

(5)   Committee at the European Parliament; the working party and Permanent Representatives' Committee at the Council.

(6)   For the purposes of this Agreement, "legislative authority" means only the European Parliament and the Council.

(7)   OJ 1999, L184/23.

(8)   Commission communication of 12 December 2002 on better monitoring of the application of Community law, COM(2002) 725 final, p. 20 and 21.

JOINT DECLARATION OF THE EUROPEAN PARLIAMENT, COUNCIL AND COMMISSION OF 13 JUNE 2007

on practical arrangements for the codecision procedure [Article 294 TFEU][1]
OJ C 145, 30.6.2007, P. 5

(footnotes omitted)

GENERAL PRINCIPLES

1.   The European Parliament, the Council and the Commission, hereinafter referred to collectively as "the institutions", note that current practice involving talks between the Council Presidency, the Commission and the chairs of the relevant committees and/or rapporteurs of the European Parliament and between the co-chairs of the Conciliation Committee has proved its worth.

2.   The institutions confirm that this practice, which has developed at all stages of the codecision procedure, must continue to be encouraged. The institutions undertake to examine their working methods with a view to making even more effective use of the full scope of the codecision procedure as established by the EC Treaty.

3.   This Joint Declaration clarifies these working methods, and the practical arrangements for pursuing them. It complements the Interinstitutional Agreement on Better Lawmaking and notably its provisions relating to the co-decision procedure. The institutions undertake

----

[1]   EDITOR'S NOTE: This Declaration refers to the article numbers from the Treaty establishing the European Community (TEC) in force at the time of its adoption. The replacement article numbers contained in the Treaty on the Functioning of the European Union (TFEU) have been inserted in closed brackets for ease of conversion. The co-decision procedure in Article 251 TEC has been renamed the 'ordinary legislative procedure' by the replacement provision, Article 294 TFEU.

fully to respect such commitments in line with the principles of transparency, accountability and efficiency. In this respect, the institutions should pay particular attention to making progress on simplification proposals while respecting the acquis communautaire.

4.   The institutions shall cooperate in good faith throughout the procedure with a view to reconciling their positions as far as possible and thereby clearing the way, where appropriate, for the adoption of the act concerned at an early stage of the procedure.

5.   With that aim in view, they shall cooperate through appropriate interinstitutional contacts to monitor the progress of the work and analyse the degree of convergence at all stages of the codecision procedure.

6.   The institutions, in accordance with their internal rules of procedure, undertake to exchange information regularly on the progress of codecision files. They shall ensure that their respective calendars of work are coordinated as far as possible in order to enable proceedings to be conducted in a coherent and convergent fashion. They will therefore seek to establish an indicative timetable for the various stages leading to the final adoption of different legislative proposals, while fully respecting the political nature of the decision-making process.

7.   Cooperation between the institutions in the context of codecision often takes the form of tripartite meetings ("trilogues"). This trilogue system has demonstrated its vitality and flexibility in increasing significantly the possibilities for agreement at first and second reading stages, as well as contributing to the preparation of the work of the Conciliation Committee.

8.   Such trilogues are usually conducted in an informal framework. They may be held at all stages of the procedure and at different levels of representation, depending on the nature of the expected discussion. Each institution, in accordance with its own rules of procedure, will designate its participants for each meeting, define its mandate for the negotiations and inform the other institutions of arrangements for the meetings in good time.

9.   As far as possible, any draft compromise texts submitted for discussion at a forthcoming meeting shall be circulated in advance to all participants. In order to enhance transparency, trilogues taking place within the European Parliament and Council shall be announced, where practicable.

10.   The Council Presidency will endeavour to attend the meetings of the parliamentary committees. It will carefully consider any request it receives to provide information related to the Council position, as appropriate.

FIRST READING

11.   The institutions shall cooperate in good faith with a view to reconciling their positions as far as possible so that, wherever possible, acts can be adopted at first reading.

Agreement at the stage of first reading in the European Parliament

12.   Appropriate contacts shall be established to facilitate the conduct of proceedings at first reading.

13.   The Commission shall facilitate such contacts and shall exercise its right of initiative in a constructive manner with a view to reconciling the positions of the European Parliament and the Council, with due regard for the balance between the institutions and the role conferred on it by the Treaty.

14. Where an agreement is reached through informal negotiations in trilogues, the chair of Coreper shall forward, in a letter to the chair of the relevant parliamentary committee, details of the substance of the agreement, in the form of amendments to the Commission proposal. That letter shall indicate the Council's willingness to accept that outcome, subject to legal-linguistic verification, should it be confirmed by the vote in plenary. A copy of that letter shall be forwarded to the Commission.

15. In this context, where conclusion of a dossier at first reading is imminent, information on the intention to conclude an agreement should be made readily available as early as possible.

Agreement at the stage of Council common position

16. Where no agreement is reached at the European Parliament's first reading, contacts may be continued with a view to concluding an agreement at the common position stage.

17. The Commission shall facilitate such contacts and shall exercise its right of initiative in a constructive manner with a view to reconciling the positions of the European Parliament and the Council, with due regard for the balance between the institutions and the role conferred on it by the Treaty.

18. Where an agreement is reached at this stage, the chair of the relevant parliamentary committee shall indicate, in a letter to the chair of Coreper, his recommendation to the plenary to accept the Council common position without amendment, subject to confirmation of the common position by the Council and to legal-linguistic verification. A copy of the letter shall be forwarded to the Commission.

SECOND READING

19. In its statement of reasons, the Council shall explain as clearly as possible the reasons that led it to adopt its common position. During its second reading, the European Parliament shall take the greatest possible account of those reasons and of the Commission's position.

20. Before transmitting the common position, the Council shall endeavour to consider in consultation with the European Parliament and the Commission the date for its transmission in order to ensure the maximum efficiency of the legislative procedure at second reading.

Agreement at the stage of second reading in the European Parliament

21. Appropriate contacts will continue as soon as the Council common position is forwarded to the European Parliament, with a view to achieving a better understanding of the respective positions and thus to bringing the legislative procedure to a conclusion as quickly as possible.

22. The Commission shall facilitate such contacts and give its opinion with a view to reconciling the positions of the European Parliament and the Council, with due regard for the balance between the institutions and the role conferred on it by the Treaty.

23. Where an agreement is reached through informal negotiations in trilogues, the chair of Coreper shall forward, in a letter to the chair of the relevant parliamentary committee, details of the substance of the agreement, in the form of amendments to the Council common position. That letter shall indicate the Council's willingness to accept that outcome, subject to legal-linguistic verification, should it be confirmed by the vote in plenary. A copy of that letter shall be forwarded to the Commission.

CONCILIATION

24. If it becomes clear that the Council will not be in a position to accept all the amendments of the European Parliament at second reading and when the Council is ready to present its position, a first trilogue will be organised. Each institution, in accordance with its own rules of procedure, will designate its participants for each meeting and define its mandate for the negotiations. The Commission will indicate to both delegations at the earliest possible stage its intentions with regard to its opinion on the European Parliament's second reading amendments.

25. Trilogues shall take place throughout the conciliation procedure with the aim of resolving outstanding issues and preparing the ground for an agreement to be reached in the Conciliation Committee. The results of the trilogues shall be discussed and possibly approved at the meetings of the respective institutions.

26. The Conciliation Committee shall be convened by the President of the Council, with the agreement of the President of the European Parliament and with due regard to the provisions of the Treaty.

27. The Commission shall take part in the conciliation proceedings and shall take all the necessary initiatives with a view to reconciling the positions of the European Parliament and the Council. Such initiatives may include, draft compromise texts having regard to the positions of the European Parliament and of the Council and with due regard for the role conferred upon the Commission by the Treaty.

28. The Conciliation Committee shall be chaired jointly by the President of the European Parliament and the President of the Council. Committee meetings shall be chaired alternately by each co-chair.

29. The dates and the agendas for the Conciliation Committee's meetings shall be set jointly by the co-chairs with a view to the effective functioning of the Conciliation Committee throughout the conciliation procedure. The Commission shall be consulted on the dates envisaged. The European Parliament and the Council shall set aside, for guidance, appropriate dates for conciliation proceedings and shall notify the Commission thereof.

30. The co-chairs may put several dossiers on the agenda of any one meeting of the Conciliation Committee. As well as the principal topic ("B-item"), where agreement has not yet been reached, conciliation procedures on other topics may be opened and/or closed without discussion on these items ("A-item").

31. While respecting the Treaty provisions regarding time-limits, the European Parliament and the Council shall, as far as possible, take account of scheduling requirements, in particular those resulting from breaks in the institutions' activities and from the European Parliament's elections. At all events, the break in activities shall be as short as possible.

32. The Conciliation Committee shall meet alternately at the premises of the European Parliament and the Council, with a view to an equal sharing of facilities, including interpretation facilities.

33. The Conciliation Committee shall have available to it the Commission proposal, the Council common position and the Commission's opinion thereon, the amendments proposed by the European Parliament and the Commission's opinion thereon, and a joint working document by the European Parliament and Council delegations. This working document should enable users to identify the issues at stake easily and to refer to them efficiently. The Commission shall, as a general rule, submit its opinion within three weeks of official receipt of the outcome of the European Parliament's vote and at the latest by the commencement of conciliation proceedings.

34.   The co-chairs may submit texts for the Conciliation Committee's approval.

35.   Agreement on a joint text shall be established at a meeting of the Conciliation Committee or, subsequently, by an exchange of letters between the co-chairs. Copies of such letters shall be forwarded to the Commission.

36.   If the Conciliation Committee reaches agreement on a joint text, the text shall, after legal-linguistic finalisation, be submitted to the co-chairs for formal approval. However, in exceptional cases in order to respect the deadlines, a draft joint text may be submitted to the co-chairs for approval.

37.   The co-chairs shall forward the approved joint text to the Presidents of the European Parliament and of the Council by means of a jointly signed letter. Where the Conciliation Committee is unable to agree on a joint text, the co-chairs shall notify the Presidents of the European Parliament and of the Council thereof in a jointly signed letter. Such letters shall serve as an official record. Copies of such letters shall be forwarded to the Commission for information. The working documents used during the conciliation procedure will be accessible in the Register of each institution once the procedure has been concluded.

38.   The Secretariat of the European Parliament and the General- Secretariat of the Council shall act jointly as the Conciliation Committee's secretariat, in association with the Secretariat-General of the Commission.

GENERAL PROVISIONS

39.   Should the European Parliament or the Council deem it essential to extend the time-limits referred to in [Article 294 TFEU], they shall notify the President of the other institution and the Commission accordingly.

40.   Where an agreement is reached at first or second reading, or during conciliation, the agreed text shall be finalised by the legal-linguistic services of the European Parliament and of the Council acting in close cooperation and by mutual agreement.

41.   No changes shall be made to any agreed texts without the explicit agreement, at the appropriate level, of both the European Parliament and the Council.

42.   Finalisation shall be carried out with due regard to the different procedures of the European Parliament and the Council, in particular with respect to deadlines for conclusion of internal procedures. The institutions undertake not to use the time-limits laid down for the legal-linguistic finalisation of acts to reopen discussions on substantive issues.

43.   The European Parliament and the Council shall agree on a common presentation of the texts prepared jointly by those institutions.

44.   As far as possible, the institutions undertake to use mutually acceptable standard clauses to be incorporated in the acts adopted under codecision in particular as regards provisions concerning the exercise of implementing powers (in accordance with the "comitology" decision, entry into force, transposition and the application of acts and respect for the Commission's right of initiative.

45.   The institutions will endeavour to hold a joint press conference to announce the successful outcome of the legislative process at first or second reading or during conciliation. They will also endeavour to issue joint press releases.

46.   Following adoption of a legislative act under the codecision procedure by the European Parliament and the Council, the text shall be submitted, for signature, to the President of the European Parliament and the President of the Council and to the Secretaries-General of those institutions.

47.   The Presidents of the European Parliament and the Council shall receive the text for signature in their respective languages and shall, as far as possible, sign the text together at a joint ceremony to be organised on a monthly basis with a view to signing important acts in the presence of the media.

48.   The jointly signed text shall be forwarded for publication in the Official Journal of the European Union. Publication shall normally follow within two months of the adoption of the legislative act by the European Parliament and the Council.

49.   If one of the institutions identifies a clerical or obvious error in a text (or in one of the language versions thereof), it shall immediately notify the other institutions. If the error concerns an act that has not yet been adopted by either the European Parliament or the Council, the legal-linguistic services of the European Parliament and the Council shall prepare the necessary corrigendum in close cooperation. Where this error concerns an act that has already been adopted by one or both of those institutions, whether published or not, the European Parliament and the Council shall adopt, by common agreement, a corrigendum drawn up under their respective procedures.

(Date and signatories omitted)

REGULATION (EU) NO 182/2011 OF THE EUROPEAN PARLIAMENT AND OF THE COUNCIL OF 16 FEBRUARY 2011

laying down the rules and general principles concerning mechanisms for control by Member States of the Commission's exercise of implementing powers OJ L55, 28.02.2011, p. 13*

(footnotes omitted)

THE EUROPEAN PARLIAMENT AND THE COUNCIL OF THE EUROPEAN UNION,

Having regard to the Treaty on the Functioning of the European Union, and in particular Article 291(3) thereof,

Having regard to the proposal from the Commission,

After transmission of the draft legislative act to the national parliaments,

Acting in accordance with the ordinary legislative procedure,

....

*   EDITOR'S NOTE: This Regulation repeals Council Decision 1999/468/EC of 28 June 1999 laying down the procedures for the exercise of implementing powers conferred on the Commission, OJ L 184, 17.7.1999, p. 23, reproduced in the 2010 edition.

Whereas:
(1)   Where uniform conditions for the implementation of legally binding Union acts are
       needed, those acts (hereinafter "basic acts") are to confer implementing powers on the
       Commission, or, in duly justified specific cases and in the cases provided for in Articles 24
       and 26 of the Treaty on European Union, on the Council.

(2)   It is for the legislator, fully respecting the criteria laid down in the Treaty on the Functioning
       of the European Union ("TFEU"), to decide in respect of each basic act whether to confer
       implementing powers on the Commission in accordance with Article 291(2) of that Treaty.

(3)   Hitherto, the exercise of implementing powers by the Commission has been governed by
       Council Decision 1999/468/EC.

(4)   The TFEU now requires the European Parliament and the Council to lay down the rules
       and general principles concerning mechanisms for control by Member States of the
       Commission's exercise of implementing powers.

(5)   It is necessary to ensure that the procedures for such control are clear, effective and
       proportionate to the nature of the implementing acts and that they reflect the institutional
       requirements of the TFEU as well as the experience gained and the common practice
       followed in the implementation of Decision 1999/468/EC.

(6)   In those basic acts which require the control of the Member States for the adoption by the
       Commission of implementing acts, it is appropriate, for the purposes of such control, that
       committees composed of the representatives of the Member States and chaired by the
       Commission be set up.

(7)   Where appropriate, the control mechanism should include referral to an appeal committee
       which should meet at the appropriate level.

(8)   In the interests of simplification, the Commission should exercise implementing powers in
       accordance with one of only two procedures, namely the advisory procedure or the
       examination procedure.

(9)   In order to simplify further, common procedural rules should apply to the committees,
       including the key provisions relating to their functioning and the possibility of delivering
       an opinion by written procedure.

(10)   Criteria should be laid down to determine the procedure to be used for the adoption of
       implementing acts by the Commission. In order to achieve greater consistency, the
       procedural requirements should be proportionate to the nature and impact of the
       implementing acts to be adopted.

(11)   The examination procedure should in particular apply for the adoption of acts of general
       scope designed to implement basic acts and specific implementing acts with a potentially
       important impact. That procedure should ensure that implementing acts cannot be
       adopted by the Commission if they are not in accordance with the opinion of the
       committee, except in very exceptional circumstances, where they may apply for a limited
       period of time. The procedure should also ensure that the Commission is able to review
       the draft implementing acts where no opinion is delivered by the committee, taking into
       account the views expressed within the committee.

(12)   Provided that the basic act confers implementing powers on the Commission relating to
       programmes with substantial budgetary implications or directed to third countries, the
       examination procedure should apply.

(13)   The chair of a committee should endeavour to find solutions which command the widest
       possible support within the committee or the appeal committee and should explain the

manner in which the discussions and suggestions for amendments have been taken into account. For that purpose, the Commission should pay particular attention to the views expressed within the committee or the appeal committee as regards draft definitive anti-dumping or countervailing measures.

(14) When considering the adoption of other draft implementing acts concerning particularly sensitive sectors, notably taxation, consumer health, food safety and protection of the environment, the Commission, in order to find a balanced solution, will, as far as possible, act in such a way as to avoid going against any predominant position which might emerge within the appeal committee against the appropriateness of an implementing act.

(15) The advisory procedure should, as a general rule, apply in all other cases or where it is considered more appropriate.

(16) It should be possible, where this is provided for in a basic act, to adopt implementing acts which are to apply immediately on imperative grounds of urgency.

(17) The European Parliament and the Council should be promptly informed of committee proceedings on a regular basis.

(18) Either the European Parliament or the Council should be able at any time to indicate to the Commission that, in its view, a draft implementing act exceeds the implementing powers provided for in the basic act, taking into account their rights relating to the review of the legality of Union acts.

(19) Public access to information on committee proceedings should be ensured in accordance with Regulation (EC) No 1049/2001 of the European Parliament and of the Council of 30 May 2001 regarding public access to European Parliament, Council and Commission documents.

(20) A register containing information on committee proceedings should be kept by the Commission. Consequently, rules relating to the protection of classified documents applicable to the Commission should also apply to the use of the register.

(21) Decision 1999/468/EC should be repealed. In order to ensure the transition between the regime provided for in Decision 1999/468/EC and this Regulation, any reference in existing legislation to the procedures provided for in that Decision should, with the exception of the regulatory procedure with scrutiny provided for in Article 5a thereof, be understood as a reference to the corresponding procedures provided for in this Regulation. The effects of Article 5a of Decision 1999/468/EC should be provisionally maintained for the purposes of existing basic acts which refer to that Article.

(22) The Commission's powers, as laid down by the TFEU, concerning the implementation of the competition rules are not affected by this Regulation,

HAVE ADOPTED THIS REGULATION:

Article 1 Subject-matter
This Regulation lays down the rules and general principles governing the mechanisms which apply where a legally binding Union act (hereinafter a "basic act") identifies the need for uniform conditions of implementation and requires that the adoption of implementing acts by the Commission be subject to the control of Member States.

Article 2 Selection of procedures
1.   A basic act may provide for the application of the advisory procedure or the examination procedure, taking into account the nature or the impact of the implementing act required.

2. The examination procedure applies, in particular, for the adoption of:
    (a) implementing acts of general scope;
    (b) other implementing acts relating to:
        (i)   programmes with substantial implications;
        (ii) the common agricultural and common fisheries policies;
        (iii) the environment, security and safety, or protection of the health or safety, of humans, animals or plants;
        (iv) the common commercial policy;
        (v)   taxation.

3. The advisory procedure applies, as a general rule, for the adoption of implementing acts not falling within the ambit of paragraph 2. However, the advisory procedure may apply for the adoption of the implementing acts referred to in paragraph 2 in duly justified cases.

Article 3 Common provisions

1. The common provisions set out in this Article shall apply to all the procedures referred to in Articles 4 to 8.

2. The Commission shall be assisted by a committee composed of representatives of the Member States. The committee shall be chaired by a representative of the Commission. The chair shall not take part in the committee vote.

3. The chair shall submit to the committee the draft implementing act to be adopted by the Commission.

    Except in duly justified cases, the chair shall convene a meeting not less than 14 days from submission of the draft implementing act and of the draft agenda to the committee. The committee shall deliver its opinion on the draft implementing act within a time limit which the chair may lay down according to the urgency of the matter. Time limits shall be proportionate and shall afford committee members early and effective opportunities to examine the draft implementing act and express their views.

4. Until the committee delivers an opinion, any committee member may suggest amendments and the chair may present amended versions of the draft implementing act.

    The chair shall endeavour to find solutions which command the widest possible support within the committee. The chair shall inform the committee of the manner in which the discussions and suggestions for amendments have been taken into account, in particular as regards those suggestions which have been largely supported within the committee.

5. In duly justified cases, the chair may obtain the committee's opinion by written procedure. The chair shall send the committee members the draft implementing act and shall lay down a time limit for delivery of an opinion according to the urgency of the matter. Any committee member who does not oppose the draft implementing act or who does not explicitly abstain from voting thereon before the expiry of that time limit shall be regarded as having tacitly agreed to the draft implementing act.

    Unless otherwise provided in the basic act, the written procedure shall be terminated without result where, within the time limit referred to in the first subparagraph, the chair so decides or a committee member so requests. In such a case, the chair shall convene a committee meeting within a reasonable time.

6. The committee's opinion shall be recorded in the minutes. Committee members shall have the right to ask for their position to be recorded in the minutes. The chair shall send the minutes to the committee members without delay.

7.   Where applicable, the control mechanism shall include referral to an appeal committee.

The appeal committee shall adopt its own rules of procedure by a simple majority of its component members, on a proposal from the Commission.

Where the appeal committee is seised, it shall meet at the earliest 14 days, except in duly justified cases, and at the latest 6 weeks, after the date of referral. Without prejudice to paragraph 3, the appeal committee shall deliver its opinion within 2 months of the date of referral.

A representative of the Commission shall chair the appeal committee.

The chair shall set the date of the appeal committee meeting in close cooperation with the members of the committee, in order to enable Member States and the Commission to ensure an appropriate level of representation. By 1 April 2011, the Commission shall convene the first meeting of the appeal committee in order to adopt its rules of procedure.

Article 4 Advisory procedure

1.   Where the advisory procedure applies, the committee shall deliver its opinion, if necessary by taking a vote. If the committee takes a vote, the opinion shall be delivered by a simple majority of its component members.

2.   The Commission shall decide on the draft implementing act to be adopted, taking the utmost account of the conclusions drawn from the discussions within the committee and of the opinion delivered.

Article 5 Examination procedure

1.   Where the examination procedure applies, the committee shall deliver its opinion by the majority laid down in Article 16(4) and (5) of the Treaty on European Union and, where applicable, Article 238(3) TFEU, for acts to be adopted on a proposal from the Commission. The votes of the representatives of the Member States within the committee shall be weighted in the manner set out in those Articles.

2.   Where the committee delivers a positive opinion, the Commission shall adopt the draft implementing act.

3.   Without prejudice to Article 7, if the committee delivers a negative opinion, the Commission shall not adopt the draft implementing act. Where an implementing act is deemed to be necessary, the chair may either submit an amended version of the draft implementing act to the same committee within 2 months of delivery of the negative opinion, or submit the draft implementing act within 1 month of such delivery to the appeal committee for further deliberation.

4.   Where no opinion is delivered, the Commission may adopt the draft implementing act, except in the cases provided for in the second subparagraph. Where the Commission does not adopt the draft implementing act, the chair may submit to the committee an amended version thereof.

Without prejudice to Article 7, the Commission shall not adopt the draft implementing act where:
(a) that act concerns taxation, financial services, the protection of the health or safety of humans, animals or plants, or definitive multilateral safeguard measures;
(b) the basic act provides that the draft implementing act may not be adopted where no opinion is delivered; or
(c) a simple majority of the component members of the committee opposes it.

In any of the cases referred to in the second subparagraph, where an implementing act is deemed to be necessary, the chair may either submit an amended version of that act to the same committee within 2 months of the vote, or submit the draft implementing act within 1 month of the vote to the appeal committee for further deliberation.

5.   By way of derogation from paragraph 4, the following procedure shall apply for the adoption of draft definitive anti-dumping or countervailing measures, where no opinion is delivered by the committee and a simple majority of its component members opposes the draft implementing act.

The Commission shall conduct consultations with the Member States. 14 days at the earliest and 1 month at the latest after the committee meeting, the Commission shall inform the committee members of the results of those consultations and submit a draft implementing act to the appeal committee. By way of derogation from Article 3(7), the appeal committee shall meet 14 days at the earliest and 1 month at the latest after the submission of the draft implementing act. The appeal committee shall deliver its opinion in accordance with Article 6. The time limits laid down in this paragraph shall be without prejudice to the need to respect the deadlines laid down in the relevant basic acts.

Article 6 Referral to the appeal committee

1.   The appeal committee shall deliver its opinion by the majority provided for in Article 5(1).

2.   Until an opinion is delivered, any member of the appeal committee may suggest amendments to the draft implementing act and the chair may decide whether or not to modify it.

The chair shall endeavour to find solutions which command the widest possible support within the appeal committee.

The chair shall inform the appeal committee of the manner in which the discussions and suggestions for amendments have been taken into account, in particular as regards suggestions for amendments which have been largely supported within the appeal committee.

3.   Where the appeal committee delivers a positive opinion, the Commission shall adopt the draft implementing act.

Where no opinion is delivered, the Commission may adopt the draft implementing act.

Where the appeal committee delivers a negative opinion, the Commission shall not adopt the draft implementing act.

4.   By way of derogation from paragraph 3, for the adoption of definitive multilateral safeguard measures, in the absence of a positive opinion voted by the majority provided for in Article 5(1), the Commission shall not adopt the draft measures.

5.   By way of derogation from paragraph 1, until 1 September 2012, the appeal committee shall deliver its opinion on draft definitive anti-dumping or countervailing measures by a simple majority of its component members.

Article 7 Adoption of implementing acts in exceptional cases

By way of derogation from Article 5(3) and the second subparagraph of Article 5(4), the Commission may adopt a draft implementing act where it needs to be adopted without delay in order to avoid creating a significant disruption of the markets in the area of agriculture or a risk for the financial interests of the Union within the meaning of Article 325 TFEU.

In such a case, the Commission shall immediately submit the adopted implementing act to the appeal committee. Where the appeal committee delivers a negative opinion on the adopted implementing act, the Commission shall repeal that act immediately. Where the appeal committee delivers a positive opinion or no opinion is delivered, the implementing act shall remain in force.

Article 8 Immediately applicable implementing acts

1. By way of derogation from Articles 4 and 5, a basic act may provide that, on duly justified imperative grounds of urgency, this Article is to apply.

2. The Commission shall adopt an implementing act which shall apply immediately, without its prior submission to a committee, and shall remain in force for a period not exceeding 6 months unless the basic act provides otherwise.

3. At the latest 14 days after its adoption, the chair shall submit the act referred to in paragraph 2 to the relevant committee in order to obtain its opinion.

4. Where the examination procedure applies, in the event of the committee delivering a negative opinion, the Commission shall immediately repeal the implementing act adopted in accordance with paragraph 2.

5. Where the Commission adopts provisional anti-dumping or countervailing measures, the procedure provided for in this Article shall apply. The Commission shall adopt such measures after consulting or, in cases of extreme urgency, after informing the Member States. In the latter case, consultations shall take place 10 days at the latest after notification to the Member States of the measures adopted by the Commission.

Article 9 Rules of procedure

1. Each committee shall adopt by a simple majority of its component members its own rules of procedure on the proposal of its chair, on the basis of standard rules to be drawn up by the Commission following consultation with Member States. Such standard rules shall be published by the Commission in the Official Journal of the European Union.

    In so far as may be necessary, existing committees shall adapt their rules of procedure to the standard rules.

2. The principles and conditions on public access to documents and the rules on data protection applicable to the Commission shall apply to the committees.

Article 10 Information on committee proceedings

1. The Commission shall keep a register of committee proceedings which shall contain:
    (a) a list of committees;
    (b) the agendas of committee meetings;
    (c) the summary records, together with the lists of the authorities and organisations to which the persons designated by the Member States to represent them belong;
    (d) the draft implementing acts on which the committees are asked to deliver an opinion;
    (e) the voting results;
    (f) the final draft implementing acts following delivery of the opinion of the committees;
    (g) information concerning the adoption of the final draft implementing acts by the Commission; and
    (h) statistical data on the work of the committees.

2. The Commission shall also publish an annual report on the work of the committees.

    The European Parliament and the Council shall have access to the information referred to in paragraph 1 in accordance with the applicable rules.

3.   At the same time as they are sent to the committee members, the Commission shall make available to the European Parliament and the Council the documents referred to in points (b), (d) and (f) of paragraph 1 whilst also informing them of the availability of such documents.

4.   The references of all documents referred to in points (a) to (g) of paragraph 1 as well as the information referred to in paragraph 1(h) shall be made public in the register.

Article 11 Right of scrutiny for the European Parliament and the Council
Where a basic act is adopted under the ordinary legislative procedure, either the European Parliament or the Council may at any time indicate to the Commission that, in its view, a draft implementing act exceeds the implementing powers provided for in the basic act. In such a case, the Commission shall review the draft implementing act, taking account of the positions expressed, and shall inform the European Parliament and the Council whether it intends to maintain, amend or withdraw the draft implementing act.

Article 12 Repeal of Decision 1999/468/EC
Decision 1999/468/EC is hereby repealed.

The effects of Article 5a of Decision 1999/468/EC shall be maintained for the purposes of existing basic acts making reference thereto.

Article 13 Transitional provisions: adaptation of existing basic acts
1.   Where basic acts adopted before the entry into force of this Regulation provide for the exercise of implementing powers by the Commission in accordance with Decision 1999/468/EC, the following rules shall apply:
      (a) where the basic act makes reference to Article 3 of Decision 1999/468/EC, the advisory procedure referred to in Article 4 of this Regulation shall apply;
      (b) where the basic act makes reference to Article 4 of Decision 1999/468/EC, the examination procedure referred to in Article 5 of this Regulation shall apply, with the exception of the second and third subparagraphs of Article 5(4);
      (c) where the basic act makes reference to Article 5 of Decision 1999/468/EC, the examination procedure referred to in Article 5 of this Regulation shall apply and the basic act shall be deemed to provide that, in the absence of an opinion, the Commission may not adopt the draft implementing act, as envisaged in point (b) of the second subparagraph of Article 5(4);
      (d) where the basic act makes reference to Article 6 of Decision 1999/468/EC, Article 8 of this Regulation shall apply;
      (e) where the basic act makes reference to Articles 7 and 8 of Decision 1999/468/EC, Articles 10 and 11 of this Regulation shall apply.

2.   Articles 3 and 9 of this Regulation shall apply to all existing committees for the purposes of paragraph 1.

3.   Article 7 of this Regulation shall apply only to existing procedures which make reference to Article 4 of Decision 1999/468/EC.

4.   The transitional provisions laid down in this Article shall not prejudice the nature of the acts concerned.

Article 14 Transitional arrangement
This Regulation shall not affect pending procedures in which a committee has already delivered its opinion in accordance with Decision 1999/468/EC.

Article 15 Review
By 1 March 2016, the Commission shall present a report to the European Parliament and the Council on the implementation of this Regulation, accompanied, if necessary, by appropriate legislative proposals.

Article 16 Entry into force
This Regulation shall enter into force on 1 March 2011.

This Regulation is binding in its entirety and directly applicable in all Member States.

(Date of signing and signatories omitted)

E) ACCESS TO DOCUMENTS

REGULATION (EC) NO 1049/2001 OF THE EUROPEAN PARLIAMENT AND OF THE COUNCIL
of 30 May 2001

regarding public access to European Parliament, Council and Commission documents
OJ L 145, 31.5.2001, p. 43[1]

FORTHCOMING AMENDMENTS: The European Commission has proposed amendments to this regulation in a Communication published on 21 March 2011, COM(2011) 137, available on EUR-Lex: http://eur-lex.europa.eu/en/index.htm

(footnotes omitted)

THE EUROPEAN PARLIAMENT AND THE COUNCIL OF THE EUROPEAN UNION,

Having regard to the Treaty establishing the European Community, and in particular Article 255(2) thereof,

Having regard to the proposal from the Commission,

Acting in accordance with the procedure referred to in Article 251 of the Treaty,

Whereas:

(1) The second subparagraph of Article 1 of the Treaty on European Union enshrines the concept of openness, stating that the Treaty marks a new stage in the process of creating an ever closer union among the peoples of Europe, in which decisions are taken as openly as possible and as closely as possible to the citizen.

----

[1] EDITOR'S NOTE: As of 1 May 2012 this Regulation has not been amended following the entry into force of the Treaty of Lisbon. It may include references to the old version of the Treaty on European Union (TEU) and/or the now replaced Treaty establishing the European Community (TEC). Reference should be made to the Tables of Equivalences accompanying the consolidated Treaties in Part II of this edition for the conversion of old Treaty article numbers to new ones.

(2)　Openness enables citizens to participate more closely in the decision-making process and guarantees that the administration enjoys greater legitimacy and is more effective and more accountable to the citizen in a democratic system. Openness contributes to strengthening the principles of democracy and respect for fundamental rights as laid down in Article 6 of the EU Treaty and in the Charter of Fundamental Rights of the European Union.

(3)　The conclusions of the European Council meetings held at Birmingham, Edinburgh and Copenhagen stressed the need to introduce greater transparency into the work of the Union institutions. This Regulation consolidates the initiatives that the institutions have already taken with a view to improving the transparency of the decision-making process.

(4)　The purpose of this Regulation is to give the fullest possible effect to the right of public access to documents and to lay down the general principles and limits on such access in accordance with Article 255(2) of the EC Treaty.

(5)　Since the question of access to documents is not covered by provisions of the Treaty establishing the European Coal and Steel Community and the Treaty establishing the European Atomic Energy Community, the European Parliament, the Council and the Commission should, in accordance with Declaration No 41 attached to the Final Act of the Treaty of Amsterdam, draw guidance from this Regulation as regards documents concerning the activities covered by those two Treaties.

(6)　Wider access should be granted to documents in cases where the institutions are acting in their legislative capacity, including under delegated powers, while at the same time preserving the effectiveness of the institutions' decision-making process. Such documents should be made directly accessible to the greatest possible extent.

(7)　In accordance with Articles 28(1) and 41(1) of the EU Treaty, the right of access also applies to documents relating to the common foreign and security policy and to police and judicial cooperation in criminal matters. Each institution should respect its security rules.

(8)　In order to ensure the full application of this Regulation to all activities of the Union, all agencies established by the institutions should apply the principles laid down in this Regulation.

(9)　On account of their highly sensitive content, certain documents should be given special treatment. Arrangements for informing the European Parliament of the content of such documents should be made through interinstitutional agreement.

(10)　In order to bring about greater openness in the work of the institutions, access to documents should be granted by the European Parliament, the Council and the Commission not only to documents drawn up by the institutions, but also to documents received by them. In this context, it is recalled that Declaration No 35 attached to the Final Act of the Treaty of Amsterdam provides that a Member State may request the Commission or the Council not to communicate to third parties a document originating from that State without its prior agreement.

(11)　In principle, all documents of the institutions should be accessible to the public. However, certain public and private interests should be protected by way of exceptions. The institutions should be entitled to protect their internal consultations and deliberations where necessary to safeguard their ability to carry out their tasks. In assessing the exceptions, the institutions should take account of the principles in Community legislation concerning the protection of personal data, in all areas of Union activities.

(12)　All rules concerning access to documents of the institutions should be in conformity with this Regulation.

(13) In order to ensure that the right of access is fully respected, a two-stage administrative procedure should apply, with the additional possibility of court proceedings or complaints to the Ombudsman.

(14) Each institution should take the measures necessary to inform the public of the new provisions in force and to train its staff to assist citizens exercising their rights under this Regulation. In order to make it easier for citizens to exercise their rights, each institution should provide access to a register of documents.

(15) Even though it is neither the object nor the effect of this Regulation to amend national legislation on access to documents, it is nevertheless clear that, by virtue of the principle of loyal cooperation which governs relations between the institutions and the Member States, Member States should take care not to hamper the proper application of this Regulation and should respect the security rules of the institutions.

(16) This Regulation is without prejudice to existing rights of access to documents for Member States, judicial authorities or investigative bodies.

(17) In accordance with Article 255(3) of the EC Treaty, each institution lays down specific provisions regarding access to its documents in its rules of procedure. Council Decision 93/731/EC of 20 December 1993 on public access to Council documents, Commission Decision 94/90/ECSC, EC, Euratom of 8 February 1994 on public access to Commission documents, European Parliament Decision 97/632/EC, ECSC, Euratom of 10 July 1997 on public access to European Parliament documents, and the rules on confidentiality of Schengen documents should therefore, if necessary, be modified or be repealed,

HAVE ADOPTED THIS REGULATION:

Article 1 Purpose
The purpose of this Regulation is:
(a) to define the principles, conditions and limits on grounds of public or private interest governing the right of access to European Parliament, Council and Commission (hereinafter referred to as "the institutions") documents provided for in Article 255 of the EC Treaty in such a way as to ensure the widest possible access to documents,

(b) to establish rules ensuring the easiest possible exercise of this right, and

(c) to promote good administrative practice on access to documents.

Article 2 Beneficiaries and scope
1. Any citizen of the Union, and any natural or legal person residing or having its registered office in a Member State, has a right of access to documents of the institutions, subject to the principles, conditions and limits defined in this Regulation.

2. The institutions may, subject to the same principles, conditions and limits, grant access to documents to any natural or legal person not residing or not having its registered office in a Member State.

3. This Regulation shall apply to all documents held by an institution, that is to say, documents drawn up or received by it and in its possession, in all areas of activity of the European Union.

4. Without prejudice to Articles 4 and 9, documents shall be made accessible to the public either following a written application or directly in electronic form or through a register.

In particular, documents drawn up or received in the course of a legislative procedure shall be made directly accessible in accordance with Article 12.

5.   Sensitive documents as defined in Article 9(1) shall be subject to special treatment in accordance with that Article.

6.   This Regulation shall be without prejudice to rights of public access to documents held by the institutions which might follow from instruments of international law or acts of the institutions implementing them.

Article 3 Definitions
For the purpose of this Regulation:
(a)   "document" shall mean any content whatever its medium (written on paper or stored in electronic form or as a sound, visual or audiovisual recording) concerning a matter relating to the policies, activities and decisions falling within the institution's sphere of responsibility;

(b)   "third party" shall mean any natural or legal person, or any entity outside the institution concerned, including the Member States, other Community or non-Community institutions and bodies and third countries.

Article 4 Exceptions
1.   The institutions shall refuse access to a document where disclosure would undermine the protection of:
    (a) the public interest as regards:
        — public security,
        — defence and military matters,
        — international relations,
        — the financial, monetary or economic policy of the Community or a Member State;
    (b) privacy and the integrity of the individual, in particular in accordance with Community legislation regarding the protection of personal data.

2.   The institutions shall refuse access to a document where disclosure would undermine the protection of:
    — commercial interests of a natural or legal person, including intellectual property,
    — court proceedings and legal advice,
    — the purpose of inspections, investigations and audits,
unless there is an overriding public interest in disclosure.

3.   Access to a document, drawn up by an institution for internal use or received by an institution, which relates to a matter where the decision has not been taken by the institution, shall be refused if disclosure of the document would seriously undermine the institution's decision-making process, unless there is an overriding public interest in disclosure.

Access to a document containing opinions for internal use as part of deliberations and preliminary consultations within the institution concerned shall be refused even after the decision has been taken if disclosure of the document would seriously undermine the institution's decision-making process, unless there is an overriding public interest in disclosure.

4.   As regards third-party documents, the institution shall consult the third party with a view to assessing whether an exception in paragraph 1 or 2 is applicable, unless it is clear that the document shall or shall not be disclosed.

5.   A Member State may request the institution not to disclose a document originating from that Member State without its prior agreement.

6.   If only parts of the requested document are covered by any of the exceptions, the remaining parts of the document shall be released.

7.   The exceptions as laid down in paragraphs 1 to 3 shall only apply for the period during which protection is justified on the basis of the content of the document. The exceptions may apply for a maximum period of 30 years. In the case of documents covered by the exceptions relating to privacy or commercial interests and in the case of sensitive documents, the exceptions may, if necessary, continue to apply after this period.

Article 5 Documents in the Member States

Where a Member State receives a request for a document in its possession, originating from an institution, unless it is clear that the document shall or shall not be disclosed, the Member State shall consult with the institution concerned in order to take a decision that does not jeopardise the attainment of the objectives of this Regulation.

The Member State may instead refer the request to the institution.

Article 6 Applications

1.   Applications for access to a document shall be made in any written form, including electronic form, in one of the languages referred to in Article 314 of the EC Treaty and in a sufficiently precise manner to enable the institution to identify the document. The applicant is not obliged to state reasons for the application.

2.   If an application is not sufficiently precise, the institution shall ask the applicant to clarify the application and shall assist the applicant in doing so, for example, by providing information on the use of the public registers of documents.

3.   In the event of an application relating to a very long document or to a very large number of documents, the institution concerned may confer with the applicant informally, with a view to finding a fair solution.

4.   The institutions shall provide information and assistance to citizens on how and where applications for access to documents can be made.

Article 7 Processing of initial applications

1.   An application for access to a document shall be handled promptly. An acknowledgement of receipt shall be sent to the applicant. Within 15 working days from registration of the application, the institution shall either grant access to the document requested and provide access in accordance with Article 10 within that period or, in a written reply, state the reasons for the total or partial refusal and inform the applicant of his or her right to make a confirmatory application in accordance with paragraph 2 of this Article.

2.   In the event of a total or partial refusal, the applicant may, within 15 working days of receiving the institution's reply, make a confirmatory application asking the institution to reconsider its position.

3.   In exceptional cases, for example in the event of an application relating to a very long document or to a very large number of documents, the time-limit provided for in paragraph 1 may be extended by 15 working days, provided that the applicant is notified in advance and that detailed reasons are given.

4.   Failure by the institution to reply within the prescribed time-limit shall entitle the applicant to make a confirmatory application.

Article 8 Processing of confirmatory applications

1. A confirmatory application shall be handled promptly. Within 15 working days from registration of such an application, the institution shall either grant access to the document requested and provide access in accordance with Article 10 within that period or, in a written reply, state the reasons for the total or partial refusal. In the event of a total or partial refusal, the institution shall inform the applicant of the remedies open to him or her, namely instituting court proceedings against the institution and/or making a complaint to the Ombudsman, under the conditions laid down in Articles 230 and 195 of the EC Treaty, respectively.

2. In exceptional cases, for example in the event of an application relating to a very long document or to a very large number of documents, the time limit provided for in paragraph 1 may be extended by 15 working days, provided that the applicant is notified in advance and that detailed reasons are given.

3. Failure by the institution to reply within the prescribed time limit shall be considered as a negative reply and entitle the applicant to institute court proceedings against the institution and/or make a complaint to the Ombudsman, under the relevant provisions of the EC Treaty.

Article 9 Treatment of sensitive documents

1. Sensitive documents are documents originating from the institutions or the agencies established by them, from Member States, third countries or International Organisations, classified as "TRÈS SECRET/TOP SECRET", "SECRET" or "CONFIDENTIEL" in accordance with the rules of the institution concerned, which protect essential interests of the European Union or of one or more of its Member States in the areas covered by Article 4(1)(a), notably public security, defence and military matters.

2. Applications for access to sensitive documents under the procedures laid down in Articles 7 and 8 shall be handled only by those persons who have a right to acquaint themselves with those documents. These persons shall also, without prejudice to Article 11(2), assess which references to sensitive documents could be made in the public register.

3. Sensitive documents shall be recorded in the register or released only with the consent of the originator.

4. An institution which decides to refuse access to a sensitive document shall give the reasons for its decision in a manner which does not harm the interests protected in Article 4.

5. Member States shall take appropriate measures to ensure that when handling applications for sensitive documents the principles in this Article and Article 4 are respected.

6. The rules of the institutions concerning sensitive documents shall be made public.

7. The Commission and the Council shall inform the European Parliament regarding sensitive documents in accordance with arrangements agreed between the institutions.

Article 10 Access following an application

1. The applicant shall have access to documents either by consulting them on the spot or by receiving a copy, including, where available, an electronic copy, according to the applicant's preference. The cost of producing and sending copies may be charged to the applicant. This charge shall not exceed the real cost of producing and sending the copies. Consultation on the spot, copies of less than 20 A4 pages and direct access in electronic form or through the register shall be free of charge.

2.   If a document has already been released by the institution concerned and is easily accessible to the applicant, the institution may fulfil its obligation of granting access to documents by informing the applicant how to obtain the requested document.

3.   Documents shall be supplied in an existing version and format (including electronically or in an alternative format such as Braille, large print or tape) with full regard to the applicant's preference.

Article 11 Registers

1.   To make citizens' rights under this Regulation effective, each institution shall provide public access to a register of documents. Access to the register should be provided in electronic form. References to documents shall be recorded in the register without delay.

2.   For each document the register shall contain a reference number (including, where applicable, the interinstitutional reference), the subject matter and/or a short description of the content of the document and the date on which it was received or drawn up and recorded in the register. References shall be made in a manner which does not undermine protection of the interests in Article 4.

3.   The institutions shall immediately take the measures necessary to establish a register which shall be operational by 3 June 2002.

Article 12 Direct access in electronic form or through a register

1.   The institutions shall as far as possible make documents directly accessible to the public in electronic form or through a register in accordance with the rules of the institution concerned.

2.   In particular, legislative documents, that is to say, documents drawn up or received in the course of procedures for the adoption of acts which are legally binding in or for the Member States, should, subject to Articles 4 and 9, be made directly accessible.

3.   Where possible, other documents, notably documents relating to the development of policy or strategy, should be made directly accessible.

4.   Where direct access is not given through the register, the register shall as far as possible indicate where the document is located.

Article 13 Publication in the *Official Journal*

1.   In addition to the acts referred to in Article 254(1) and (2) of the EC Treaty and the first paragraph of Article 163 of the Euratom Treaty, the following documents shall, subject to Articles 4 and 9 of this Regulation, be published in the *Official Journal*:
    (a) Commission proposals;
    (b) common positions adopted by the Council in accordance with the procedures referred to in Articles 251 and 252 of the EC Treaty and the reasons underlying those common positions, as well as the European Parliament's positions in these procedures;
    (c) framework decisions and decisions referred to in Article 34(2) of the EU Treaty;
    (d) conventions established by the Council in accordance with Article 34(2) of the EU Treaty;
    (e) conventions signed between Member States on the basis of Article 293 of the EC Treaty;
    (f) international agreements concluded by the Community or in accordance with Article 24 of the EU Treaty.

2.   As far as possible, the following documents shall be published in the *Official Journal*:
    (a) initiatives presented to the Council by a Member State pursuant to Article 67(1) of the EC Treaty or pursuant to Article 34(2) of the EU Treaty;
    (b) common positions referred to in Article 34(2) of the EU Treaty;

(c)   directives other than those referred to in Article 254(1) and (2) of the EC Treaty, decisions other than those referred to in Article 254(1) of the EC Treaty, recommendations and opinions.

3.   Each institution may in its rules of procedure establish which further documents shall be published in the *Official Journal*.

Article 14 Information
1.   Each institution shall take the requisite measures to inform the public of the rights they enjoy under this Regulation.

2.   The Member States shall cooperate with the institutions in providing information to the citizens.

Article 15 Administrative practice in the institutions
1.   The institutions shall develop good administrative practices in order to facilitate the exercise of the right of access guaranteed by this Regulation.

2.   The institutions shall establish an interinstitutional committee to examine best practice, address possible conflicts and discuss future developments on public access to documents.

Article 16 Reproduction of documents
This Regulation shall be without prejudice to any existing rules on copyright which may limit a third party's right to reproduce or exploit released documents.

Article 17 Reports
1.   Each institution shall publish annually a report for the preceding year including the number of cases in which the institution refused to grant access to documents, the reasons for such refusals and the number of sensitive documents not recorded in the register.

2.   At the latest by 31 January 2004, the Commission shall publish a report on the implementation of the principles of this Regulation and shall make recommendations, including, if appropriate, proposals for the revision of this Regulation and an action programme of measures to be taken by the institutions.

Article 18 Application measures
1.   Each institution shall adapt its rules of procedure to the provisions of this Regulation. The adaptations shall take effect from 3 December 2001.

2.   Within six months of the entry into force of this Regulation, the Commission shall examine the conformity of Council Regulation (EEC, Euratom) No 354/83 of 1 February 1983 concerning the opening to the public of the historical archives of the European Economic Community and the European Atomic Energy Community with this Regulation in order to ensure the preservation and archiving of documents to the fullest extent possible.

3.   Within six months of the entry into force of this Regulation, the Commission shall examine the conformity of the existing rules on access to documents with this Regulation.

Article 19 Entry into force
This Regulation shall enter into force on the third day following that of its publication in the *Official Journal* of the European Communities.

It shall be applicable from 3 December 2001.

This Regulation shall be binding in its entirety and directly applicable in all Member States.

(Date of signing and signatories omitted)

INTERINSTITUTIONAL AGREEMENT OF 20 NOVEMBER 2002

between the European Parliament and the Council concerning access by the European Parliament to sensitive information of the Council in the field of security and defence policy

OJ C298, 30.11.2002, P. 1[1]

(footnotes omitted)

THE EUROPEAN PARLIAMENT AND THE COUNCIL,

Whereas:

(1)   Article 21 of the Treaty on European Union states that the Council Presidency shall consult the European Parliament on the main aspects and the basic choices of the common foreign and security policy and shall ensure that the views of the European Parliament are duly taken into consideration. That Article also stipulates that the European Parliament shall be kept regularly informed by the Council Presidency and the Commission of the development of the common foreign and security policy. A mechanism should be introduced to ensure that these principles are implemented in this field.

(2)   In view of the specific nature and the especially sensitive content of certain highly classified information in the field of security and defence policy, special arrangements should be introduced for the handling of documents containing such information.

(3)   In conformity with Article 9(7) of Regulation (EC) No 1049/2001 of the European Parliament and of the Council of 30 May 2001 regarding public access to European Parliament, Council and Commission documents(1), the Council is to inform the European Parliament regarding sensitive documents as defined in Article 9(1) of that Regulation in accordance with arrangements agreed between the institutions.

(4)   In most Member States there are specific mechanisms for the transmission and handling of classified information between governments and national parliaments. This Interinstitutional Agreement should provide the European Parliament with treatment inspired by best practices in Member States,

HAVE CONCLUDED THIS INTERINSTITUTIONAL AGREEMENT:

1 SCOPE

1.1   This Interinstitutional Agreement deals with access by the European Parliament to sensitive information, i.e. information classified as TRÈS SECRET/TOP SECRET,

---

[1]   EDITOR'S NOTE: As of 1 May 2012 this Agreement has not been amended following the entry into force of the Treaty of Lisbon. It may include references to the old version of the Treaty on European Union (TEU) and/or the now replaced Treaty establishing the European Community (TEC). Reference should be made to the Tables of Equivalences accompanying the consolidated Treaties in Part II of this edition for the conversion of old Treaty article numbers to new ones.

SECRET or CONFIDENTIEL, whatever its origin, medium or state of completion, held by the Council in the field of security and defence policy and the handling of documents so classified.

1.2   Information originating from a third State or international organisation shall be transmitted with the agreement of that State or organisation.

Where information originating from a Member State is transmitted to the Council without explicit restriction on its dissemination to other institutions other than its classification, the rules in sections 2 and 3 of this Interinstitutional Agreement shall apply. Otherwise, such information shall be transmitted with the agreement of the Member State in question.

In the case of a refusal of the transmission of information originating from a third State, an international organisation or a Member State, the Council shall give the reasons.

1.3   The provisions of this Interinstitutional Agreement shall apply in accordance with applicable law and without prejudice to Decision 95/167/EC, Euratom, ECSC of the European Parliament, the Council and the Commission of 19 April 1995 on the detailed provisions governing the exercise of the European Parliament's right of inquiry(2) and without prejudice to existing arrangements, especially the Interinstitutional Agreement of 6 May 1999 between the European Parliament, the Council and the Commission on budgetary discipline and improvement of the budgetary procedure(3).

2 GENERAL RULES

2.1   The two institutions shall act in accordance with their mutual duties of sincere cooperation and in a spirit of mutual trust as well as in conformity with the relevant Treaty provisions. Communication and handling of the information covered by this Interinstitutional Agreement must have due regard for the interests which classification is designed to protect, and in particular the public interest as regards the security and defence of the European Union or of one or more of its Member States or military and non-military crisis management.

2.2   At the request of one of the persons referred to in point 3.1 below, the Presidency of the Council or the Secretary-General/High Representative shall inform them with all due despatch of the content of any sensitive information required for the exercise of the powers conferred on the European Parliament by the Treaty on European Union in the field covered by the present Interinstitutional Agreement, taking into account the public interest in matters relating to the security and defence of the European Union or of one or more of its Member States or military and non-military crisis management, in accordance with the arrangements laid down in section 3 below.

3 ARRANGEMENTS FOR ACCESS TO AND HANDLING OF SENSITIVE INFORMATION

3.1   In the context of this Interinstitutional Agreement, the President of the European Parliament or the Chairman of the European Parliament's Committee on Foreign Affairs, Human Rights, Common Security and Defence Policy may request that the Presidency of the Council or the Secretary-General/High Representative convey information to this committee on developments in European security and defence policy, including sensitive information to which point 3.3 applies.

3.2   In the event of a crisis or at the request of the President of the European Parliament or of the Chairman of the Committee on Foreign Affairs, Human Rights, Common Security and Defence Policy, such information shall be provided at the earliest opportunity.

3.3   In this framework, the President of the European Parliament and a special committee chaired by the Chairman of the Committee on Foreign Affairs, Human Rights, Common Security and Defence Policy and composed of four members designated by the Conference of Presidents shall be informed by the Presidency of the Council or the Secretary-General/High Representative of the content of the sensitive information where it is required for the exercise of the powers conferred on the European Parliament by the Treaty on European Union in the field covered by the present Interinstitutional Agreement. The President of the European Parliament and the special committee may ask to consult the documents in question on the premises of the Council.

Where this is appropriate and possible in the light of the nature and content of the information or documents concerned, these shall be made available to the President of the European Parliament, who shall select one of the following options:

(a)   information intended for the chairman of the Committee on Foreign Affairs, Human Rights, Common Security and Defence Policy;

(b)   access to information restricted to the members of the Committee on Foreign Affairs, Human Rights, Common Security and Defence Policy only;

(c)   discussion in the Committee on Foreign Affairs, Human Rights, Common Security and Defence Policy, meeting in camera, in accordance with arrangements which may vary by virtue of the degree of confidentiality involved;

(d)   communication of documents from which information has been expunged in the light of the degree of secrecy required.

These options are not applicable if sensitive information is classified as TRÈS SECRET//TOP SECRET.

As to information or documents classified as SECRET or CONFIDENTIEL, the selection by the President of the European Parliament of one of these options shall be previously agreed with the Council.

The information or documents in question shall not be published or forwarded to any other addressee.

4   FINAL PROVISIONS

4.1   The European Parliament and the Council, each for its own part, shall take all necessary measures to ensure the implementation of this Interinstitutional Agreement, including the steps required for the security clearance of the persons involved.

4.2   The two institutions are willing to discuss comparable Interinstitutional Agreements covering classified information in other areas of the Council's activities, on the understanding that the provisions of this Interinstitutional Agreement do not constitute a precedent for the Union's or the Community's other areas of activity and shall not affect the substance of any other Interinstitutional Agreements.

4.3   This Interinstitutional Agreement shall be reviewed after two years at the request of either of the two institutions in the light of experience gained in implementing it.

(*Date of signing and signatories omitted*)

ANNEX

This Interinstitutional Agreement shall be implemented in conformity with the relevant applicable regulations and in particular with the principle according to which the consent of the originator is a necessary condition for the transmission of classified information as laid down in point 1.2.

Consultation of sensitive documents by the members of the Special Committee of the European Parliament shall take place in a secured room at the Council premises.

This Interinstitutional Agreement shall enter into force after the European Parliament has adopted internal security measures which are in accordance with the principles laid down in point 2.1 and comparable to those of the other institutions in order to guarantee an equivalent level of protection of the sensitive information concerned.

F) CITIZENS' INITIATIVE

REGULATION (EU) NO 211/2011 OF THE EUROPEAN PARLIAMENT AND OF THE COUNCIL OF 16 FEBRUARY 2011

on the citizens' initiative OJ L 65, 11.03.2011, p. 1

(footnotes omitted)

THE EUROPEAN PARLIAMENT AND THE COUNCIL OF THE EUROPEAN UNION,

Having regard to the Treaty on the Functioning of the European Union, and in particular the first paragraph of Article 24 thereof,

Having regard to the proposal from the European Commission,

After transmission of the draft legislative act to the national parliaments,

Having regard to the opinion of the European Economic and Social Committee,

Having regard to the opinion of the Committee of the Regions,

Acting in accordance with the ordinary legislative procedure,

Whereas:

(1)   The Treaty on European Union (TEU) reinforces citizenship of the Union and enhances further the democratic functioning of the Union by providing, inter alia, that every citizen is to have the right to participate in the democratic life of the Union by way of a European citizens' initiative. That procedure affords citizens the possibility of directly approaching the Commission with a request inviting it to submit a proposal for a legal act of the Union for the purpose of implementing the Treaties similar to the right conferred on the European Parliament under Article 225 of the Treaty on the Functioning of the European Union (TFEU) and on the Council under Article 241 TFEU.

(2)   The procedures and conditions required for the citizens' initiative should be clear, simple, user-friendly and proportionate to the nature of the citizens' initiative so as to encourage participation by citizens and to make the Union more accessible. They should strike a judicious balance between rights and obligations.

(3)   They should also ensure that citizens of the Union are subject to similar conditions for supporting a citizens' initiative regardless of the Member State from which they come.

(4)   The Commission should, upon request, provide citizens with information and informal advice about citizens' initiatives, notably as regards the registration criteria.

(5)   It is necessary to establish the minimum number of Member States from which citizens must come. In order to ensure that a citizens' initiative is representative of a Union interest, while ensuring that the instrument remains easy to use, that number should be set at one quarter of Member States.

(6)   For that purpose, it is also appropriate to establish the minimum number of signatories coming from each of those Member States. In order to ensure similar conditions for citizens to support a citizens' initiative, those minimum numbers should be degressively proportional. For the purpose of clarity, those minimum numbers should be set out for each Member State in an annex to this Regulation. The minimum number of signatories required in each Member State should correspond to the number of Members of the European Parliament elected in each Member State, multiplied by 750. The Commission should be empowered to amend that annex in order to reflect any modification in the composition of the European Parliament.

(7)   It is appropriate to fix a minimum age for supporting a citizens' initiative. That should be set as the age at which citizens are entitled to vote in elections to the European Parliament.

(8)   A minimum organised structure is needed in order to successfully carry through a citizens' initiative. That should take the form of a citizens' committee, composed of natural persons (organisers) coming from at least seven different Member States, in order to encourage the emergence of European-wide issues and to foster reflection on those issues. For the sake of transparency and smooth and efficient communication, the citizens' committee should designate representatives to liaise between the citizens' committee and the institutions of the Union throughout the procedure.

(9)   Entities, notably organisations which under the Treaties contribute to forming European political awareness and to expressing the will of citizens of the Union, should be able to promote a citizens' initiative, provided that they do so with full transparency.

(10)   In order to ensure coherence and transparency in relation to proposed citizens' initiatives and to avoid a situation where signatures are being collected for a proposed citizens' initiative which does not comply with the conditions laid down in this Regulation, it should be mandatory to register such initiatives on a website made available by the Commission prior to collecting the necessary statements of support from citizens. All proposed citizens' initiatives that comply with the conditions laid down in this Regulation should be registered by the Commission. The Commission should deal with registration in accordance with the general principles of good administration.

(11)   Once a proposed citizens' initiative is registered, statements of support from citizens may be collected by the organisers.

(12)   It is appropriate to set out the form for the statement of support in an annex to this Regulation, specifying the data required for the purposes of verification by the Member States. The Commission should be empowered to amend that annex in accordance with Article 290 TFEU, taking into account information forwarded to it by Member States.

(13)   With due respect for the principle that personal data must be adequate, relevant and not excessive in relation to the purposes for which they are collected, the provision of personal data, including, where applicable, a personal identification number or a personal identification document number by signatories of a proposed citizens' initiative is required as far as may be necessary in order to allow for the verification of statements of support by Member States, in accordance with national law and practice.

(14) In order to put modern technology to good use as a tool of participatory democracy, it is appropriate to provide for statements of support to be collected online as well as in paper form. Online collection systems should have adequate security features in place in order to ensure, inter alia, that the data are securely collected and stored. For that purpose, the Commission should set out detailed technical specifications for online collection systems.

(15) It is appropriate for Member States to verify the conformity of online collection systems with the requirements of this Regulation before statements of support are collected.

(16) The Commission should make available an open-source software incorporating the relevant technical and security features necessary in order to comply with the provisions of this Regulation as regards online collection systems.

(17) It is appropriate to ensure that statements of support for a citizens' initiative are collected within a specific time limit. In order to ensure that proposed citizens' initiatives remain relevant, whilst taking account of the complexity of collecting statements of support across the Union, that time limit should not be longer than 12 months from the date of registration of the proposed citizens' initiative.

(18) It is appropriate to provide that, where a citizens' initiative has received the necessary statements of support from signatories, each Member State should be responsible for the verification and certification of statements of support collected from signatories coming from that Member State. Taking account of the need to limit the administrative burden for Member States, they should, within a period of three months from receipt of a request for certification, carry out such verifications on the basis of appropriate checks, which may be based on random sampling, and should issue a document certifying the number of valid statements of support received.

(19) Organisers should ensure that all the relevant conditions set out in this Regulation are met prior to submitting a citizens' initiative to the Commission.

(20) The Commission should examine a citizens' initiative and set out its legal and political conclusions separately. It should also set out the action it intends to take in response to it, within a period of three months. In order to demonstrate that a citizens' initiative supported by at least one million Union citizens and its possible follow-up are carefully examined, the Commission should explain in a clear, comprehensible and detailed manner the reasons for its intended action, and should likewise give its reasons if it does not intend to take any action. When the Commission has received a citizens' initiative supported by the requisite number of signatories which fulfils the other requirements of this Regulation, the organisers should be entitled to present that initiative at a public hearing at Union level.

(21) Directive 95/46/EC of the European Parliament and of the Council of 24 October 1995 on the protection of individuals with regard to the processing of personal data and on the free movement of such data is fully applicable to the processing of personal data carried out in application of this Regulation. In this respect, for the sake of legal certainty, it is appropriate to clarify that the organisers of a citizens' initiative and the competent authorities of the Member States are the data controllers within the meaning of Directive 95/46/EC and to specify the maximum period within which the personal data collected for the purposes of a citizens' initiative may be retained. In their capacity as data controllers, organisers need to take all the appropriate measures to comply with the obligations imposed by Directive 95/46/EC, in particular those relating to the lawfulness of the processing, the security of the processing activities, the provision of information and the rights of data subjects to have access to their personal data, as well as to procure the correction and erasure of their personal data.

(22) The provisions of Chapter III of Directive 95/46/EC on judicial remedies, liability and sanctions are fully applicable as regards the data processing carried out in application of this Regulation. Organisers of a citizens' initiative should be liable in accordance with applicable national law for any damage that they cause. In addition, Member States should ensure that organisers are subject to appropriate penalties for infringements of this Regulation.

(23) Regulation (EC) No 45/2001 of the European Parliament and of the Council of 18 December 2000 on the protection of individuals with regard to the processing of personal data by the Community institutions and bodies and on the free movement of such data is fully applicable to the processing of personal data carried out by the Commission in application of this Regulation.

(24) In order to address future adaptation needs, the Commission should be empowered to adopt delegated acts in accordance with Article 290 TFEU for the purpose of amending the Annexes to this Regulation. It is of particular importance that the Commission carry out appropriate consultations during its preparatory work, including at expert level.

(25) The measures necessary for the implementation of this Regulation should be adopted in accordance with Council Decision 1999/468/EC of 28 June 1999 laying down the procedures for the exercise of implementing powers conferred on the Commission.

(26) This Regulation respects fundamental rights and observes the principles enshrined in the Charter of Fundamental Rights of the European Union, in particular Article 8 thereof, which states that everyone has the right to the protection of personal data concerning him or her.

(27) The European Data Protection Supervisor was consulted and adopted an opinion,

HAVE ADOPTED THIS REGULATION:

Article 1 Subject matter
This Regulation establishes the procedures and conditions required for a citizens' initiative as provided for in Article 11 TEU and Article 24 TFEU.

Article 2 Definitions
For the purpose of this Regulation the following definitions shall apply:
1. "citizens' initiative" means an initiative submitted to the Commission in accordance with this Regulation, inviting the Commission, within the framework of its powers, to submit any appropriate proposal on matters where citizens consider that a legal act of the Union is required for the purpose of implementing the Treaties, which has received the support of at least one million eligible signatories coming from at least one quarter of all Member States;

2. "signatories" means citizens of the Union who have supported a given citizens' initiative by completing a statement of support form for that initiative;

3. "organisers" means natural persons forming a citizens' committee responsible for the preparation of a citizens' initiative and its submission to the Commission.

Article 3 Requirements for organisers and for signatories
1. The organisers shall be citizens of the Union and be of the age to be entitled to vote in elections to the European Parliament.

2. The organisers shall form a citizens' committee of at least seven persons who are residents of at least seven different Member States.

The organisers shall designate one representative and one substitute ("the contact persons"), who shall liaise between the citizens' committee and the institutions of the Union throughout the procedure and who shall be mandated to speak and act on behalf of the citizens' committee.

Organisers who are Members of the European Parliament shall not be counted for the purposes of reaching the minimum number required to form a citizens' committee.

For the purpose of registering a proposed citizens' initiative in accordance with Article 4, only the information concerning the seven members of the citizens' committee who are needed in order to comply with the requirements laid down in paragraph 1 of this Article and in this paragraph shall be considered by the Commission.

3. The Commission may request the organisers to provide appropriate proof that the requirements laid down in paragraphs 1 and 2 are fulfilled.

4. In order to be eligible to support a proposed citizens' initiative, signatories shall be citizens of the Union and shall be of the age to be entitled to vote in elections to the European Parliament.

Article 4 Registration of a proposed citizens' initiative

1. Prior to initiating the collection of statements of support from signatories for a proposed citizens' initiative, the organisers shall be required to register it with the Commission, providing the information set out in Annex II, in particular on the subject matter and objectives of the proposed citizens' initiative.

    That information shall be provided in one of the official languages of the Union, in an online register made available for that purpose by the Commission ("the register").

    The organisers shall provide, for the register and where appropriate on their website, regularly updated information on the sources of support and funding for the proposed citizens' initiative.

    After the registration is confirmed in accordance with paragraph 2, the organisers may provide the proposed citizens' initiative in other official languages of the Union for inclusion in the register. The translation of the proposed citizens' initiative into other official languages of the Union shall be the responsibility of the organisers.

    The Commission shall establish a point of contact which provides information and assistance.

2. Within two months from the receipt of the information set out in Annex II, the Commission shall register a proposed citizens' initiative under a unique registration number and send a confirmation to the organisers, provided that the following conditions are fulfilled:
    (a) the citizens' committee has been formed and the contact persons have been designated in accordance with Article 3(2);
    (b) the proposed citizens' initiative does not manifestly fall outside the framework of the Commission's powers to submit a proposal for a legal act of the Union for the purpose of implementing the Treaties;
    (c) the proposed citizens' initiative is not manifestly abusive, frivolous or vexatious; and
    (d) the proposed citizens' initiative is not manifestly contrary to the values of the Union as set out in Article 2 TEU.

3. The Commission shall refuse the registration if the conditions laid down in paragraph 2 are not met.

Where it refuses to register a proposed citizens' initiative, the Commission shall inform the organisers of the reasons for such refusal and of all possible judicial and extrajudicial remedies available to them.

4.   A proposed citizens' initiative that has been registered shall be made public in the register. Without prejudice to their rights under Regulation (EC) No 45/2001, data subjects shall be entitled to request the removal of their personal data from the register after the expiry of a period of two years from the date of registration of a proposed citizens' initiative.

5.   At any time before the submission of statements of support in accordance with Article 8, the organisers may withdraw a proposed citizens' initiative that has been registered. In that case, an indication to that effect shall be entered in the register.

Article 5 Procedures and conditions for the collection of statements of support

1.   The organisers shall be responsible for the collection of the statements of support from signatories for a proposed citizens' initiative which has been registered in accordance with Article 4.

Only forms which comply with the models set out in Annex III and which are in one of the language versions included in the register for that proposed citizens' initiative may be used for the collection of statements of support. The organisers shall complete the forms as indicated in Annex III prior to initiating the collection of statements of support from signatories. The information given in the forms shall correspond to the information contained in the register.

2.   The organisers may collect statements of support in paper form or electronically. Where statements of support are collected online, Article 6 shall apply.

For the purpose of this Regulation, statements of support which are electronically signed using an advanced electronic signature, within the meaning of Directive 1999/93/EC of the European Parliament and of the Council of 13 December 1999 on a Community framework for electronic signatures, shall be treated in the same way as statements of support in paper form.

3.   Signatories shall be required to complete statement of support forms made available by the organisers. They shall indicate only the personal data that are required for the purposes of verification by the Member States, as set out in Annex III.

Signatories may only support a given proposed citizens' initiative once.

4.   Member States shall forward to the Commission any changes to the information set out in Annex III. Taking into account those changes, the Commission may adopt, by means of delegated acts, in accordance with Article 17 and subject to the conditions of Articles 18 and 19, amendments to Annex III.

5.   All statements of support shall be collected after the date of registration of the proposed citizens' initiative and within a period not exceeding 12 months.

At the end of that period, the register shall indicate that the period has expired and, where appropriate, that the required number of statements of support was not collected.

Article 6 Online collection systems

1.   Where statements of support are collected online, the data obtained through the online collection system shall be stored in the territory of a Member State.

The online collection system shall be certified in accordance with paragraph 3 in the Member State in which the data collected through the online collection system will be stored. The organisers may use one online collection system for the purpose of collecting statements of support in several or all Member States.

The models for the statement of support forms may be adapted for the purpose of the online collection.

2.   The organisers shall ensure that the online collection system used for the collection of statements of support complies with paragraph 4.

Prior to initiating the collection of statements of support, the organisers shall request the competent authority of the relevant Member State to certify that the online collection system used for that purpose complies with paragraph 4.

The organisers may only start collecting statements of support through the online collection system once they have obtained the certificate referred to in paragraph 3. The organisers shall make a copy of that certificate publicly available on the website used for the online collection system.

By 1 January 2012, the Commission shall set up and thereafter shall maintain open-source software incorporating the relevant technical and security features necessary for compliance with the provisions of this Regulation regarding the online collection systems. The software shall be made available free of charge.

3.   Where the online collection system complies with paragraph 4, the relevant competent authority shall within one month issue a certificate to that effect in accordance with the model set out in Annex IV.

Member States shall recognise the certificates issued by the competent authorities of other Member States.

4.   Online collection systems shall have adequate security and technical features in place in order to ensure that:
(a)   only natural persons may submit a statement of support form online;
(b)   the data provided online are securely collected and stored, in order to ensure, inter alia, that they may not be modified or used for any purpose other than their indicated support of the given citizens' initiative and to protect personal data against accidental or unlawful destruction or accidental loss, alteration or unauthorised disclosure or access;
(c)   the system can generate statements of support in a form complying with the models set out in Annex III, in order to allow for the verification by the Member States in accordance with Article 8(2).

5.   By 1 January 2012, the Commission shall adopt technical specifications for the implementation of paragraph 4, in accordance with the regulatory procedure referred to in Article 20(2).

Article 7 Minimum number of signatories per Member State

1.   The signatories of a citizens' initiative shall come from at least one quarter of Member States.

2.   In at least one quarter of Member States, signatories shall comprise at least the minimum number of citizens set out, at the time of registration of the proposed citizens' initiative, in Annex I. Those minimum numbers shall correspond to the number of the Members of the European Parliament elected in each Member State, multiplied by 750.

3.   The Commission shall adopt, by means of delegated acts, in accordance with Article 17 and subject to the conditions of Articles 18 and 19, appropriate adjustments to Annex I in order to reflect any modification in the composition of the European Parliament.

4.   Signatories shall be considered as coming from the Member State which is responsible for the verification of their statement of support in accordance with the second subparagraph of Article 8(1).

Article 8 Verification and certification by Member States of statements of support

1.   After collecting the necessary statements of support from signatories in accordance with Articles 5 and 7, the organisers shall submit the statements of support, in paper or electronic form, to the relevant competent authorities referred to in Article 15 for verification and certification. For that purpose the organisers shall use the form set out in Annex V and shall separate those statements of support collected in paper form, those which were electronically signed using an advanced electronic signature and those collected through an online collection system.

The organisers shall submit statements of support to the relevant Member State as follows:
(a) to the Member State of residence or of nationality of the signatory, as specified in point 1 of Part C of Annex III, or
(b) to the Member State that issued the personal identification number or the personal identification document indicated in the statement of support, as specified in point 2 of Part C of Annex III.

2.   The competent authorities shall, within a period not exceeding three months from receipt of the request, verify the statements of support submitted on the basis of appropriate checks, in accordance with national law and practice, as appropriate. On that basis they shall deliver to the organisers a certificate in accordance with the model set out in Annex VI, certifying the number of valid statements of support for the Member State concerned.

For the purpose of the verification of statements of support, the authentication of signatures shall not be required.

3.   The certificate provided for in paragraph 2 shall be issued free of charge.

Article 9 Submission of a citizens' initiative to the Commission

After obtaining the certificates provided for in Article 8(2), and provided that all relevant procedures and conditions set out in this Regulation have been complied with, the organisers may submit the citizens' initiative to the Commission, accompanied by information regarding any support and funding received for that initiative. That information shall be published in the register.

The amount of support and funding received from any source in excess of which information is to be provided shall be identical to that set out in Regulation (EC) No 2004/2003 of the European Parliament and of the Council of 4 November 2003 on the regulations governing political parties at European level and the rules regarding their funding.

For the purpose of this Article, the organisers shall make use of the form set out in Annex VII and shall submit the completed form together with copies, in paper or electronic form, of the certificates provided for in Article 8(2).

Article 10 Procedure for the examination of a citizens' initiative by the Commission

1.   Where the Commission receives a citizens' initiative in accordance with Article 9 it shall:
(a) publish the citizens' initiative without delay in the register;
(b) receive the organisers at an appropriate level to allow them to explain in detail the matters raised by the citizens' initiative;
(c) within three months, set out in a communication its legal and political conclusions on the citizens' initiative, the action it intends to take, if any, and its reasons for taking or not taking that action.

2.   The communication referred to in paragraph 1(c) shall be notified to the organisers as well as to the European Parliament and the Council and shall be made public.

Article 11 Public hearing

Where the conditions of Article 10(1)(a) and (b) are fulfilled, and within the deadline laid down in Article 10(1)(c), the organisers shall be given the opportunity to present the citizens' initiative at a public hearing. The Commission and the European Parliament shall ensure that this hearing is organised at the European Parliament, if appropriate together with such other institutions and bodies of the Union as may wish to participate, and that the Commission is represented at an appropriate level.

Article 12 Protection of personal data

1.   In processing personal data pursuant to this Regulation, the organisers of a citizens' initiative and the competent authorities of the Member State shall comply with Directive 95/46/EC and the national provisions adopted pursuant thereto.

2.   For the purposes of their respective processing of personal data, the organisers of a citizens' initiative and the competent authorities designated in accordance with Article 15(2) shall be considered as data controllers in accordance with Article 2(d) of Directive 95/46/EC.

3.   The organisers shall ensure that personal data collected for a given citizen's initiative are not used for any purpose other than their indicated support for that initiative, and shall destroy all statements of support received for that initiative and any copies thereof at the latest one month after submitting that initiative to the Commission in accordance with Article 9 or 18 months after the date of registration of the proposed citizens' initiative, whichever is the earlier.

4.   The competent authority shall use the personal data it receives for a given citizens' initiative only for the purpose of verifying the statements of support in accordance with Article 8(2), and shall destroy all statements of support and copies thereof at the latest one month after issuing the certificate referred to in that Article.

5.   Statements of support for a given citizens' initiative and copies thereof may be retained beyond the time limits laid down in paragraphs 3 and 4 if necessary for the purpose of legal or administrative proceedings relating to a proposed citizen's initiative. The organisers and the competent authority shall destroy all statements of support and copies thereof at the latest one week after the date of conclusion of the said proceedings by a final decision.

6.   The organisers shall implement appropriate technical and organisational measures to protect personal data against accidental or unlawful destruction or accidental loss, alteration, unauthorised disclosure or access, in particular where the processing involves the transmission of data over a network, and against all other unlawful forms of processing.

Article 13 Liability

Organisers shall be liable for any damage they cause in the organisation of a citizens' initiative in accordance with applicable national law.

Article 14 Penalties

1.   Member States shall ensure that organisers are subject to appropriate penalties for infringements of this Regulation and in particular for:
    (a) false declarations made by organisers;
    (b) the fraudulent use of data.

2.   The penalties referred to in paragraph 1 shall be effective, proportionate and dissuasive.

Article 15 Competent authorities within the Member States

1.   For the purpose of the implementation of Article 6(3), Member States shall designate competent authorities responsible for issuing the certificate provided for therein.

2.   For the purpose of the implementation of Article 8(2), each Member State shall designate one competent authority responsible for coordinating the process of verification of statements of support and for delivering the certificates provided for therein.

3.   Not later than 1 March 2012, Member States shall forward the names and addresses of the competent authorities to the Commission.

4.   The Commission shall make the list of competent authorities publicly available.

Article 16 Amendment of the Annexes

The Commission may adopt, by means of delegated acts in accordance with Article 17 and subject to the conditions of Articles 18 and 19, amendments to the Annexes to this Regulation within the scope of the relevant provisions of this Regulation.

Article 17 Exercise of the delegation

1.   The power to adopt the delegated acts referred to in Article 16 shall be conferred on the Commission for an indeterminate period of time.

2.   As soon as it adopts a delegated act, the Commission shall notify it simultaneously to the European Parliament and to the Council.

3.   The power to adopt delegated acts is conferred on the Commission subject to the conditions laid down in Articles 18 and 19.

Article 18 Revocation of the delegation

1.   The delegation of power referred to in Article 16 may be revoked at any time by the European Parliament or by the Council.

2.   The institution which has commenced an internal procedure for deciding whether to revoke the delegation of power shall endeavour to inform the other institution and the Commission within a reasonable time before the final decision is taken, indicating the delegated powers which could be subject to revocation and possible reasons for a revocation.

3.   The decision of revocation shall put an end to the delegation of the powers specified in that decision. It shall take effect immediately or at a later date specified therein. It shall not affect the validity of the delegated acts already in force. It shall be published in the Official Journal of the European Union.

Article 19 Objections to delegated acts

1.   The European Parliament or the Council may object to the delegated act within a period of two months from the date of notification. At the initiative of the European Parliament or the Council this period shall be extended by two months.

2.   If, on expiry of the period referred to in paragraph 1, neither the European Parliament nor the Council has objected to the delegated act it shall be published in the Official Journal of the European Union and shall enter into force on the date stated therein.

The delegated act may be published in the Official Journal of the European Union and enter into force before the expiry of that period if the European Parliament and the Council have both informed the Commission of their intention not to raise objections.

3.   If either the European Parliament or the Council objects to a delegated act within the period referred to in paragraph 1, it shall not enter into force. The institution which objects shall state the reasons for objecting to the delegated act.

Article 20 Committee

1.   For the purpose of the implementation of Article 6(5), the Commission shall be assisted by a committee.

2.   Where reference is made to this paragraph, Articles 5 and 7 of Decision 1999/468/EC shall apply, having regard to the provisions of Article 8 thereof.

The period laid down in Article 5(6) of Decision 1999/468/EC shall be set at three months.

Article 21 Notification of national provisions

Each Member State shall notify to the Commission the specific provisions it adopts in order to implement this Regulation.

The Commission shall inform the other Member States thereof.

Article 22 Review

By 1 April 2015, and every three years thereafter, the Commission shall present a report to the European Parliament and the Council on the application of this Regulation.

Article 23 Entry into force and application

This Regulation shall enter into force on the 20th day following its publication in the Official Journal of the European Union.

It shall apply from 1 April 2012.

This Regulation shall be binding in its entirety and directly applicable in all Member States.

(Date and place of signing and signatories omitted)

ANNEX I
MINIMUM NUMBER OF SIGNATORIES PER MEMBER STATE

Belgium 16500

Bulgaria 12750

Czech Republic 16500

Denmark 9750

Germany 74250

Estonia 4500

Ireland 9000

Greece 16500

Spain 37500

France 54000

Italy 54000

Cyprus 4500

Latvia 6000

Lithuania 9000

Luxembourg 4500

Hungary 16500

Malta 3750

Netherlands 18750

Austria 12750

Poland 37500

Portugal 16500

Romania 24750

Slovenia 5250

Slovakia 9750

Finland 9750

Sweden 13500

United Kingdom 54000

(Annexes II–VII omitted)

V Internal Market

A) FREE MOVEMENT OF GOODS

COMMUNICATION FROM THE COMMISSION
concerning the consequences of the judgment given by the Court of Justice on 20 February 1979 in Case 120/78 ('Cassis de Dijon')

OJ C 256, 3.10.1980, P. 2[1]

The following is the text of a letter which has been sent to the Member States; the European Parliament and the Council have also been notified of it.

In the Commission's Communication of 6 November 1978 on "Safeguarding free trade within the Community", it was emphasized that the free movement of goods is being affected by a growing number of restrictive measures.

The judgment delivered by the Court of Justice on 20 February 1979 in Case 120/78 (the "Cassis de Dijon" case), and recently reaffirmed in the judgment of 26 June 1980 in Case 788/79, has given the Commission some interpretative guidance enabling it to monitor more strictly the application of the Treaty rules on the free movement of goods, particularly Articles 30 to 36 of the EEC Treaty [Articles 34–36 TFEU].

The Court gives a very general definition of the barriers to free trade which are prohibited by the provisions of Article 30 et seq. of the EEC Treaty [Article 34 et.seq TFEU]. These are taken to include "any national measure capable of hindering, directly or indirectly, actually or potentially, intra-Community trade".

In its judgment of 20 February 1979 the Court indicates the scope of this definition as it applies to technical and commercial rules.

Any product lawfully produced and marketed in one Member State must, in principle, be admitted to the market of any other Member State.

Technical and commercial rules, even those equally applicable to national and imported products, may create barriers to trade only where those rules are necessary to satisfy mandatory requirements and to serve a purpose which is in the general interest and for which they are an essential guarantee. This purpose must be such as to take precedence over the

[1]   EDITOR'S NOTE: This Communication refers to the original European Economic Community (EEC) Treaty article numbers in force at the time of its publication. The replacement article numbers contained in the Treaty on the Functioning of the European Union (TFEU) have been inserted in closed brackets after each Treaty reference for ease of conversion.

requirements of the free movement of goods, which constitutes one of the fundamental rules of the Community.

The conclusions in terms of policy which the Commission draws from this new guidance are set out below. – Whereas Member States may, with respect to domestic products and in the absence of relevant Community provisions, regulate the terms on which such products are marketed, the case is different for products imported from other Member States.

Any product imported from another Member State must in principle be admitted to the territory of the importing Member State if it has been lawfully produced, that is, conforms to rules and processes of manufacture that are customarily and traditionally accepted in the exporting country, and is marketed in the territory of the latter.

This principle implies that Member States, when drawing up commercial or technical rules liable to affect the free movement of goods, may not take an exclusively national viewpoint and take account only of requirements confined to domestic products. The proper functioning of the common market demands that each Member State also give consideration to the legitimate requirements of the other Member States.

— Only under very strict conditions does the Court accept exceptions to this principle; barriers to trade resulting from differences between commercial and technical rules are only admissible: – if the rules are necessary, that is appropriate and not excessive, in order to satisfy mandatory requirements (public health, protection of consumers or the environment, the fairness of commercial transactions, etc.);
— if the rules serve a purpose in the general interest which is compelling enough to justify an exception to a fundamental rule of the Treaty such as the free movement of goods;
— if the rules are essential for such a purpose to be attained, i.e. are the means which are the most appropriate and at the same time least hinder trade.

The Court's interpretation has induced the Commission to set out a number of guidelines.
— The principles deduced by the Court imply that a Member State may not in principle prohibit the sale in its territory of a product lawfully produced and marketed in another Member State even if the product is produced according to technical or quality requirements which differ from those imposed on its domestic products. Where a product "suitably and satisfactorily" fulfils the legitimate objective of a Member State's own rules (public safety, protection of the consumer or the environment, etc.), the importing country cannot justify prohibiting its sale in its territory by claiming that the way it fulfils the objective is different from that imposed on domestic products.

In such a case, an absolute prohibition of sale could not be considered "necessary" to satisfy a "mandatory requirement" because it would not be an "essential guarantee" in the sense defined in the Court's judgment.

The Commission will therefore have to tackle a whole body of commercial rules which lay down that products manufactured and marketed in one Member State must fulfil technical or qualitative conditions in order to be admitted to the market of another and specifically in all cases where the trade barriers occasioned by such rules are inadmissible according to the very strict criteria set out by the Court.

The Commission is referring in particular to rules covering the composition, designation, presentation and packaging of products as well as rules requiring compliance with certain technical standards.

— The Commission's work of harmonization will henceforth have to be directed mainly at national laws having an impact on the functioning of the common market where barriers to trade to be removed arise from national provisions which are admissible under the criteria set by the Court.

The Commission will be concentrating on sectors deserving priority because of their economic relevance to the creation of a single internal market.

To forestall later difficulties, the Commission will be informing Member States of potential objections, under the terms of Community law, to provisions they may be considering introducing which come to the attention of the Commission.

It will be producing suggestions soon on the procedures to be followed in such cases.

The Commission is confident that this approach will secure greater freedom of trade for the Community's manufacturers, so strengthening the industrial base of the Community, while meeting the expectations of consumers.

COUNCIL REGULATION (EC) NO 2679/98 OF 7 DECEMBER 1998

on the functioning of the internal market in relation to the free movement of goods among the Member States,[1]

OJ L 337, 12.12.1998, P. 8

(*footnotes omitted*)

THE COUNCIL OF THE EUROPEAN UNION,

Having regard to the Treaty establishing the European Community, and in particular Article 235 [Article 352 TFEU] thereof,

Having regard to the proposal from the Commission,

Having regard to the opinion of the European Parliament,

Having regard to the opinion of the Economic and Social Committee,

(1) Whereas, as provided for in Article 7a of the Treaty [Article 26 TFEU], the internal market comprises an area without internal frontiers in which, in particular, the free movement of goods is ensured in accordance with Articles 30 to 36 of the Treaty [Articles 34–36 TFEU];

(2) Whereas breaches of this principle, such as occur when in a given Member State the free movement of goods is obstructed by actions of private individuals, may cause grave disruption to the proper functioning of the internal market and inflict serious losses on the individuals affected;

(3) Whereas, in order to ensure fulfilment of the obligations arising from the Treaty, and, in particular, to ensure the proper functioning of the internal market, Member States should, on the one hand, abstain from adopting measures or engaging in conduct liable to

....

[1]   EDITOR'S NOTE: This Regulation refers to the old EC Treaty article numbers effective prior to the Treaty of Amsterdam, 1999. The replacement article numbers contained in the Treaty on the Functioning of the European Union (TFEU) have been inserted in closed brackets after each Treaty reference for ease of conversion.

constitute an obstacle to trade and, on the other hand, take all necessary and proportionate measures with a view to facilitating the free movement of goods in their territory;

(4)   Whereas such measures must not affect the exercise of fundamental rights, including the right or freedom to strike;

(5)   Whereas this Regulation does not prevent any actions which may be necessary in certain cases at Community level to respond to problems in the functioning of the internal market, taking into account, where appropriate, the application of this Regulation;

(6)   Whereas Member States have exclusive competence as regards the maintenance of public order and the safeguarding of internal security as well as in determining whether, when and which measures are necessary and proportionate in order to facilitate the free movement of goods in their territory in a given situation;

(7)   Whereas there should be adequate and rapid exchange of information between the Member States and the Commission on obstacles to the free movement of goods;

(8)   Whereas a Member State on the territory of which obstacles to the free movement of goods occur should take all necessary and proportionate measures to restore as soon as possible the free movement of goods in their territory in order to avoid the risk that the disruption or loss in question will continue, increase or intensify and that there may be a breakdown in trade and in the contractual relations which underlie it; whereas such Member State should inform the Commission and, if requested, other Member States of the measures it has taken or intends to take in order to fulfil this objective;

(9)   Whereas the Commission, in fulfilment of its duty under the Treaty, should notify the Member State concerned of its view that a breach has occurred and the Member State should respond to that notification;

(10)   Whereas the Treaty provides for no powers, other than those in Article 235 [Article 352 TFEU] thereof, for the adoption of this Regulation,

HAS ADOPTED THIS REGULATION:

Article 1
For the purpose of this Regulation:

1.   the term 'obstacle' shall mean an obstacle to the free movement of goods among Member States which is attributable to a Member State, whether it involves action or inaction on its part, which may constitute a breach of Articles 30 to 36 of the Treaty [Articles 34–36 TFEU] and which:
      (a) leads to serious disruption of the free movement of goods by physically or otherwise preventing, delaying or diverting their import into, export from or transport across a Member State,
      (b) causes serious loss to the individuals affected, and
      (c) requires immediate action in order to prevent any continuation, increase or intensification of the disruption or loss in question;

2.   the term 'inaction' shall cover the case when the competent authorities of a Member State, in the presence of an obstacle caused by actions taken by private individuals, fail to take all necessary and proportionate measures within their powers with a view to removing the obstacle and ensuring the free movement of goods in their territory.

Article 2

This Regulation may not be interpreted as affecting in any way the exercise of fundamental rights as recognised in Member States, including the right or freedom to strike. These rights may also include the right or freedom to take other actions covered by the specific industrial relations systems in Member States.

Article 3

1. When an obstacle occurs or when there is a threat thereof
    (a) any Member State (whether or not it is the Member State concerned) which has relevant information shall immediately transmit it to the Commission, and
    (b) the Commission shall immediately transmit to the Member States that information and any information from any other source which it may consider relevant.

2. The Member State concerned shall respond as soon as possible to requests for information from the Commission and from other Member States concerning the nature of the obstacle or threat and the action which it has taken or proposes to take. Information exchange between Member States shall also be transmitted to the Commission.

Article 4

1. When an obstacle occurs, and subject to Article 2, the Member State concerned shall
    (a) take all necessary and proportionate measures so that the free movement of goods is assured in the territory of the Member State in accordance with the Treaty, and
    (b) inform the Commission of the actions which its authorities have taken or intend to take.

2. The Commission shall immediately transmit the information received under paragraph 1(b) to the other Member States.

Article 5

1. Where the Commission considers that an obstacle is occurring in a Member State, it shall notify the Member State concerned of the reasons that have led the Commission to such a conclusion and shall request the Member State to take all necessary and proportionate measures to remove the said obstacle within a period which it shall determine with reference to the urgency of the case.

2. In reaching its conclusion, the Commission shall have regard to Article 2.

3. The Commission may publish in the *Official Journal of the European Communities* the text of the notification which it has sent to the Member State concerned and shall immediately transmit the text to any party which requests it.

4. The Member State shall, within five working days of receipt of the text, either:
    — inform the Commission of the steps which it has taken or intends to take to implement paragraph 1, or
    — communicate a reasoned submission as to why there is no obstacle constituting a breach of Articles 30 to 36 of the Treaty [Articles 34–36 TFEU].

5. In exceptional cases, the Commission may allow an extension of the deadline mentioned in paragraph 4 if the Member State submits a duly substantiated request and the grounds cited are deemed acceptable.

    This Regulation shall be binding in its entirety and directly applicable in all Member States.

(Date of signing and signatory omitted)

RESOLUTION OF THE COUNCIL AND OF THE REPRESENTATIVES OF THE GOVERNMENTS OF THE MEMBER STATES, MEETING WITHIN THE COUNCIL OF 7 DECEMBER 1998

on the free movement of goods,
OJ L 337, 12.12.98, P. 10[1]

(preamble and footnote omitted)

1. MEMBER STATES undertake to do all within their powers, taking into account the protection of fundamental rights, including the right or freedom to strike, to maintain the free movement of goods and to deal rapidly with actions which seriously disrupt the free movement of goods, as defined in Regulation (EC) No 2679/98.

2. MEMBER STATES undertake to inform their economic operators of such disruptions and of efforts to overcome them.

3. MEMBER STATES agree to ensure that rapid and effective review procedures are available for any person who has been harmed as a result of a breach of the Treaty caused by an obstacle within the meaning of Article 1 of Regulation (EC) No 2679/98. They undertake to take all reasonable and proportionate steps to inform persons affected by a breach of the Treaty of this kind, of the existence of such remedies and of the procedure to be followed in pursuing them.

4. MEMBER STATES also agree to take the necessary steps, in accordance with the provisions of the Treaty, to make sure that requests for debate on the free movement of goods can be dealt with swiftly at the appropriate level within the Council, should a given situation warrant such attention.

5. THE COUNCIL notes the Commission's intention to impose tight deadlines for procedures under Article 169 of the Treaty [Article 258 TFEU] regarding cases falling within the scope of Regulation (EC) No 2679/98 and requests the Commission to inform the Council of specific initiatives to be taken in this respect.

6. MEMBER STATES take note that in cases referred to in paragraph 5 the time set by the Commission for submission of observations may be as short as five working days, as may also the time for response to a reasoned opinion.

7. THE COUNCIL invites the Court of Justice of the European Communities to consider whether cases within the scope of Regulation (EC) No 2679/98 can be expedited and promises to examine any proposals to amend the Rules of Procedure of the Court of Justice urgently and with an open mind.

8. THE COUNCIL invites the Commission to submit a report on the application of Regulation (EC) No 2679/98 two years after the entry into force thereof.

---

[1]   EDITOR'S NOTE: This Resolution refers to the old EC Treaty article numbers effective prior to the Treaty of Amsterdam, 1999. The replacement article numbers contained in the Treaty on the Functioning of the European Union (TFEU) have been inserted in closed brackets after each Treaty reference for ease of conversion.

B) FREE MOVEMENT OF PERSONS

DIRECTIVE 2004/38/EC OF THE EUROPEAN PARLIAMENT AND OF THE COUNCIL OF 29 APRIL 2004

on the right of citizens of the Union and their family members to move and reside freely within the territory of the Member States amending Regulation (EEC) No 1612/68 and repealing Directives 64/221/EEC, 68/360/EEC, 72/194/EEC, 73/148/EEC, 75/34/EEC, 75/35/EEC, 90/364/EEC, 90/365/EEC and 93//96/EEC

OJ L 229, 29.6.2004, P. 35*[1]

(footnotes omitted)

THE EUROPEAN PARLIAMENT AND THE COUNCIL OF THE EUROPEAN UNION,

Having regard to the Treaty establishing the European Community, and in particular Articles 12, 18, 40, 44 and 52 thereof,

Having regard to the proposal from the Commission,

Having regard to the opinion of the European Economic and Social Committee,

Having regard to the opinion of the Committee of the Regions,

Acting in accordance with the procedure laid down in Article 251 of the Treaty,

Whereas:

(1) Citizenship of the Union confers on every citizen of the Union a primary and individual right to move and reside freely within the territory of the Member States, subject to the limitations and conditions laid down in the Treaty and to the measures adopted to give it effect.

(2) The free movement of persons constitutes one of the fundamental freedoms of the internal market, which comprises an area without internal frontiers, in which freedom is ensured in accordance with the provisions of the Treaty.

(3) Union citizenship should be the fundamental status of nationals of the Member States when they exercise their right of free movement and residence. It is therefore necessary to codify and review the existing Community instruments dealing separately with workers, self-employed persons, as well as students and other inactive persons in order to simplify and strengthen the right of free movement and residence of all Union citizens.

....

(*as corrected at: OJ L 30, 3.2.2005, p. 27, and OJ L 197, 28.7.2005)

[1] EDITOR'S NOTE: As of 1 May 2012 this Directive has not been amended following the entry into force of the Treaty of Lisbon. It includes references to the old Treaty article numbers. Reference should be made to the Tables of Equivalences accompanying the consolidated Treaties in Part II of this edition for the conversion of old Treaty article numbers to new ones.

(4)   With a view to remedying this sector-by-sector, piecemeal approach to the right of free movement and residence and facilitating the exercise of this right, there needs to be a single legislative act to amend Council Regulation (EEC) No 1612/68 of 15 October 1968 on freedom of movement for workers within the Community, and to repeal the following acts: Council Directive 68/360/EEC of 15 October 1968 on the abolition of restrictions on movement and residence within the Community for workers of Member States and their families, Council Directive 73/148/EEC of 21 May 1973 on the abolition of restrictions on movement and residence within the Community for nationals of Member States with regard to establishment and the provision of services, Council Directive 90/364/EEC of 28 June 1990 on the right of residence, Council Directive 90/365/EEC of 28 June 1990 on the right of residence for employees and self-employed persons who have ceased their occupational activity and Council Directive 93/96/EEC of 29 October 1993 on the right of residence for students.

(5)   The right of all Union citizens to move and reside freely within the territory of the Member States should, if it is to be exercised under objective conditions of freedom and dignity, be also granted to their family members, irrespective of nationality. For the purposes of this Directive, the definition of «family member» should also include the registered partner if the legislation of the host Member State treats registered partnership as equivalent to marriage.

(6)   In order to maintain the unity of the family in a broader sense and without prejudice to the prohibition of discrimination on grounds of nationality, the situation of those persons who are not included in the definition of family members under this Directive, and who therefore do not enjoy an automatic right of entry and residence in the host Member State, should be examined by the host Member State on the basis of its own national legislation, in order to decide whether entry and residence could be granted to such persons, taking into consideration their relationship with the Union citizen or any other circumstances, such as their financial or physical dependence on the Union citizen.

(7)   The formalities connected with the free movement of Union citizens within the territory of Member States should be clearly defined, without prejudice to the provisions applicable to national border controls.

(8)   With a view to facilitating the free movement of family members who are not nationals of a Member State, those who have already obtained a residence card should be exempted from the requirement to obtain an entry visa within the meaning of Council Regulation (EC) No 539/2001 of 15 March 2001 listing the third countries whose nationals must be in possession of visas when crossing the external borders and those whose nationals are exempt from that requirement or, where appropriate, of the applicable national legislation.

(9)   Union citizens should have the right of residence in the host Member State for a period not exceeding three months without being subject to any conditions or any formalities other than the requirement to hold a valid identity card or passport, without prejudice to a more favourable treatment applicable to job-seekers as recognised by the case-law of the Court of Justice.

(10)   Persons exercising their right of residence should not, however, become an unreasonable burden on the social assistance system of the host Member State during an initial period of residence. Therefore, the right of residence for Union citizens and their family members for periods in excess of three months should be subject to conditions.

(11) The fundamental and personal right of residence in another Member State is conferred directly on Union citizens by the Treaty and is not dependent upon their having fulfilled administrative procedures.

(12) For periods of residence of longer than three months, Member States should have the possibility to require Union citizens to register with the competent authorities in the place of residence, attested by a registration certificate issued to that effect.

(13) The residence card requirement should be restricted to family members of Union citizens who are not nationals of a Member State for periods of residence of longer than three months.

(14) The supporting documents required by the competent authorities for the issuing of a registration certificate or of a residence card should be comprehensively specified in order to avoid divergent administrative practices or interpretations constituting an undue obstacle to the exercise of the right of residence by Union citizens and their family members.

(15) Family members should be legally safeguarded in the event of the death of the Union citizen, divorce, annulment of marriage or termination of a registered partnership. With due regard for family life and human dignity, and in certain conditions to guard against abuse, measures should therefore be taken to ensure that in such circumstances family members already residing within the territory of the host Member State retain their right of residence exclusively on a personal basis.

(16) As long as the beneficiaries of the right of residence do not become an unreasonable burden on the social assistance system of the host Member State they should not be expelled. Therefore, an expulsion measure should not be the automatic consequence of recourse to the social assistance system. The host Member State should examine whether it is a case of temporary difficulties and take into account the duration of residence, the personal circumstances and the amount of aid granted in order to consider whether the beneficiary has become an unreasonable burden on its social assistance system and to proceed to his expulsion. In no case should an expulsion measure be adopted against workers, self-employed persons or job-seekers as defined by the Court of Justice save on grounds of public policy or public security.

(17) Enjoyment of permanent residence by Union citizens who have chosen to settle long term in the host Member State would strengthen the feeling of Union citizenship and is a key element in promoting social cohesion, which is one of the fundamental objectives of the Union. A right of permanent residence should therefore be laid down for all Union citizens and their family members who have resided in the host Member State in compliance with the conditions laid down in this Directive during a continuous period of five years without becoming subject to an expulsion measure.

(18) In order to be a genuine vehicle for integration into the society of the host Member State in which the Union citizen resides, the right of permanent residence, once obtained, should not be subject to any conditions.

(19) Certain advantages specific to Union citizens who are workers or self-employed persons and to their family members, which may allow these persons to acquire a right of permanent residence before they have resided five years in the host Member State, should be maintained, as these constitute acquired rights, conferred by Commission Regulation (EEC) No 1251/70 of 29 June 1970 on the right of workers to remain in the territory of a Member State after having been employed in that State and Council Directive 75/34/EEC

of 17 December 1974 concerning the right of nationals of a Member State to remain in the territory of another Member State after having pursued therein an activity in a self-employed capacity.

(20) In accordance with the prohibition of discrimination on grounds of nationality, all Union citizens and their family members residing in a Member State on the basis of this Directive should enjoy, in that Member State, equal treatment with nationals in areas covered by the Treaty, subject to such specific provisions as are expressly provided for in the Treaty and secondary law.

(21) However, it should be left to the host Member State to decide whether it will grant social assistance during the first three months of residence, or for a longer period in the case of job-seekers, to Union citizens other than those who are workers or self-employed persons or who retain that status or their family members, or maintenance assistance for studies, including vocational training, prior to acquisition of the right of permanent residence, to these same persons.

(22) The Treaty allows restrictions to be placed on the right of free movement and residence on grounds of public policy, public security or public health. In order to ensure a tighter definition of the circumstances and procedural safeguards subject to which Union citizens and their family members may be denied leave to enter or may be expelled, this Directive should replace Council Directive 64/221/EEC of 25 February 1964 on the coordination of special measures concerning the movement and residence of foreign nationals, which are justified on grounds of public policy, public security or public health.

(23) Expulsion of Union citizens and their family members on grounds of public policy or public security is a measure that can seriously harm persons who, having availed themselves of the rights and freedoms conferred on them by the Treaty, have become genuinely integrated into the host Member State. The scope for such measures should therefore be limited in accordance with the principle of proportionality to take account of the degree of integration of the persons concerned, the length of their residence in the host Member State, their age, state of health, family and economic situation and the links with their country of origin.

(24) Accordingly, the greater the degree of integration of Union citizens and their family members in the host Member State, the greater the degree of protection against expulsion should be. Only in exceptional circumstances, where there are imperative grounds of public security, should an expulsion measure be taken against Union citizens who have resided for many years in the territory of the host Member State, in particular when they were born and have resided there throughout their life. In addition, such exceptional circumstances should also apply to an expulsion measure taken against minors, in order to protect their links with their family, in accordance with the United Nations Convention on the Rights of the Child, of 20 November 1989.

(25) Procedural safeguards should also be specified in detail in order to ensure a high level of protection of the rights of Union citizens and their family members in the event of their being denied leave to enter or reside in another Member State, as well as to uphold the principle that any action taken by the authorities must be properly justified.

(26) In all events, judicial redress procedures should be available to Union citizens and their family members who have been refused leave to enter or reside in another Member State.

(27) In line with the case-law of the Court of Justice prohibiting Member States from issuing orders excluding for life persons covered by this Directive from their territory, the right of Union citizens and their family members who have been excluded from the territory of a Member State to submit a fresh application after a reasonable period, and in any event after a three year period from enforcement of the final exclusion order, should be confirmed.

(28) To guard against abuse of rights or fraud, notably marriages of convenience or any other form of relationships contracted for the sole purpose of enjoying the right of free movement and residence, Member States should have the possibility to adopt the necessary measures.

(29) This Directive should not affect more favourable national provisions.

(30) With a view to examining how further to facilitate the exercise of the right of free movement and residence, a report should be prepared by the Commission in order to evaluate the opportunity to present any necessary proposals to this effect, notably on the extension of the period of residence with no conditions.

(31) This Directive respects the fundamental rights and freedoms and observes the principles recognised in particular by the Charter of Fundamental Rights of the European Union. In accordance with the prohibition of discrimination contained in the Charter, Member States should implement this Directive without discrimination between the beneficiaries of this Directive on grounds such as sex, race, colour, ethnic or social origin, genetic characteristics, language, religion or beliefs, political or other opinion, membership of an ethnic minority, property, birth, disability, age or sexual orientation,

HAVE ADOPTED THIS DIRECTIVE:

Chapter I GENERAL PROVISIONS

Article 1 Subject
This Directive lays down:
(a)   the conditions governing the exercise of the right of free movement and residence within the territory of the Member States by Union citizens and their family members;

(b)   the right of permanent residence in the territory of the Member States for Union citizens and their family members;

(c)   the limits placed on the rights set out in (a) and (b) on grounds of public policy, public security or public health.

Article 2 Definitions
For the purposes of this Directive:
1.   'Union citizen' means any person having the nationality of a Member State;

2.   'family member' means:
(a) the spouse;
(b) the partner with whom the Union citizen has contracted a registered partnership, on the basis of the legislation of a Member State, if the legislation of the host Member State treats registered partnerships as equivalent to marriage and in accordance with the conditions laid down in the relevant legislation of the host Member State;
(c) the direct descendants who are under the age of 21 or are dependants and those of the spouse or partner as defined in point (b);

(d) the dependent direct relatives in the ascending line and those of the spouse or partner as defined in point (b);

3. 'host Member State' means the Member State to which a Union citizen moves in order to exercise his/her right of free movement and residence.

Article 3 Beneficiaries

1. This Directive shall apply to all Union citizens who move to or reside in a Member State other than that of which they are a national, and to their family members as defined in point 2 of Article 2 who accompany or join them.

2. Without prejudice to any right to free movement and residence the persons concerned may have in their own right, the host Member State shall, in accordance with its national legislation, facilitate entry and residence for the following persons:
   (a) any other family members, irrespective of their nationality, not falling under the definition in point 2 of Article 2 who, in the country from which they have come, are dependants or members of the household of the Union citizen having the primary right of residence, or where serious health grounds strictly require the personal care of the family member by the Union citizen;
   (b) the partner with whom the Union citizen has a durable relationship, duly attested.
   The host Member State shall undertake an extensive examination of the personal circumstances and shall justify any denial of entry or residence to these people.

Chapter II RIGHT OF EXIT AND ENTRY

Article 4 Right of exit

1. Without prejudice to the provisions on travel documents applicable to national border controls, all Union citizens with a valid identity card or passport and their family members who are not nationals of a Member State and who hold a valid passport shall have the right to leave the territory of a Member State to travel to another Member State.

2. No exit visa or equivalent formality may be imposed on the persons to whom paragraph 1 applies.

3. Member States shall, acting in accordance with their laws, issue to their own nationals, and renew, an identity card or passport stating their nationality.

4. The passport shall be valid at least for all Member States and for countries through which the holder must pass when travelling between Member States. Where the law of a Member State does not provide for identity cards to be issued, the period of validity of any passport on being issued or renewed shall be not less than five years.

Article 5 Right of entry

1. Without prejudice to the provisions on travel documents applicable to national border controls, Member States shall grant Union citizens leave to enter their territory with a valid identity card or passport and shall grant family members who are not nationals of a Member State leave to enter their territory with a valid passport.

   No entry visa or equivalent formality may be imposed on Union citizens.

2. Family members who are not nationals of a Member State shall only be required to have an entry visa in accordance with Regulation (EC) No 539/2001 or, where appropriate, with national law. For the purposes of this Directive, possession of the valid residence card referred to in Article 10 shall exempt such family members from the visa requirement.

Member States shall grant such persons every facility to obtain the necessary visas. Such visas shall be issued free of charge as soon as possible and on the basis of an accelerated procedure.

3.   The host Member State shall not place an entry or exit stamp in the passport of family members who are not nationals of a Member State provided that they present the residence card provided for in Article 10.

4.   Where a Union citizen, or a family member who is not a national of a Member State, does not have the necessary travel documents or, if required, the necessary visas, the Member State concerned shall, before turning them back, give such persons every reasonable opportunity to obtain the necessary documents or have them brought to them within a reasonable period of time or to corroborate or prove by other means that they are covered by the right of free movement and residence.

5.   The Member State may require the person concerned to report his/her presence within its territory within a reasonable and non-discriminatory period of time. Failure to comply with this requirement may make the person concerned liable to proportionate and non-discriminatory sanctions.

Chapter III RIGHT OF RESIDENCE

Article 6 Right of residence for up to three months

1.   Union citizens shall have the right of residence on the territory of another Member State for a period of up to three months without any conditions or any formalities other than the requirement to hold a valid identity card or passport.

2.   The provisions of paragraph 1 shall also apply to family members in possession of a valid passport who are not nationals of a Member State, accompanying or joining the Union citizen.

Article 7 Right of residence for more than three months

1.   All Union citizens shall have the right of residence on the territory of another Member State for a period of longer than three months if they:
   (a)   are workers or self-employed persons in the host Member State; or
   (b)   have sufficient resources for themselves and their family members not to become a burden on the social assistance system of the host Member State during their period of residence and have comprehensive sickness insurance cover in the host Member State; or
   (c)   are enrolled at a private or public establishment, accredited or financed by the host Member State on the basis of its legislation or administrative practice, for the principal purpose of following a course of study, including vocational training; and have comprehensive sickness insurance cover in the host Member State and assure the relevant national authority, by means of a declaration or by such equivalent means as they may choose, that they have sufficient resources for themselves and their family members not to become a burden on the social assistance system of the host Member State during their period of residence; or

   (d)   are family members accompanying or joining a Union citizen who satisfies the conditions referred to in points (a), (b) or (c).

2.   The right of residence provided for in paragraph 1 shall extend to family members who are not nationals of a Member State, accompanying or joining the Union citizen in the host Member State, provided that such Union citizen satisfies the conditions referred to in paragraph 1(a), (b) or (c).

3. For the purposes of paragraph 1(a), a Union citizen who is no longer a worker or self-employed person shall retain the status of worker or self-employed person in the following circumstances:

    (a) he/she is temporarily unable to work as the result of an illness or accident;

    (b) he/she is in duly recorded involuntary unemployment after having been employed for more than one year and has registered as a job-seeker with the relevant employment office;

    (c) he/she is in duly recorded involuntary unemployment after completing a fixed-term employment contract of less than a year or after having become involuntarily unemployed during the first twelve months and has registered as a job-seeker with the relevant employment office. In this case, the status of worker shall be retained for no less than six months;

    (d) he/she embarks on vocational training. Unless he/she is involuntarily unemployed, the retention of the status of worker shall require the training to be related to the previous employment.

4. By way of derogation from paragraphs 1(d) and 2 above, only the spouse, the registered partner provided for in Article 2(2)(b) and dependent children shall have the right of residence as family members of a Union citizen meeting the conditions under 1(c) above. Article 3(2) shall apply to his/her dependent direct relatives in the ascending lines and those of his/her spouse or registered partner.

Article 8 Administrative formalities for Union citizens

1. Without prejudice to Article 5(5), for periods of residence longer than three months, the host Member State may require Union citizens to register with the relevant authorities.

2. The deadline for registration may not be less than three months from the date of arrival. A registration certificate shall be issued immediately, stating the name and address of the person registering and the date of the registration. Failure to comply with the registration requirement may render the person concerned liable to proportionate and non-discriminatory sanctions.

3. For the registration certificate to be issued, Member States may only require that

    Union citizens to whom point (a) of Article 7(1) applies present a valid identity card or passport, a confirmation of engagement from the employer or a certificate of employment, or proof that they are self-employed persons,

    Union citizens to whom point (b) of Article 7(1) applies present a valid identity card or passport and provide proof that they satisfy the conditions laid down therein,

    Union citizens to whom point (c) of Article 7(1) applies present a valid identity card or passport, provide proof of enrolment at an accredited establishment and of comprehensive sickness insurance cover and the declaration or equivalent means referred to in point (c) of Article 7(1). Member States may not require this declaration to refer to any specific amount of resources.

4. Member States may not lay down a fixed amount which they regard as 'sufficient resources', but they must take into account the personal situation of the person concerned. In all cases this amount shall not be higher than the threshold below which nationals of the host Member State become eligible for social assistance, or, where this criterion is not applicable, higher than the minimum social security pension paid by the host Member State.

5. For the registration certificate to be issued to family members of Union citizens, who are themselves Union citizens, Member States may require the following documents to be presented:

(a) a valid identity card or passport;
(b) a document attesting to the existence of a family relationship or of a registered partnership;
(c) where appropriate, the registration certificate of the Union citizen whom they are accompanying or joining;
(d) in cases falling under points (c) and (d) of Article 2(2), documentary evidence that the conditions laid down therein are met;
(e) in cases falling under Article 3(2)(a), a document issued by the relevant authority in the country of origin or country from which they are arriving certifying that they are dependants or members of the household of the Union citizen, or proof of the existence of serious health grounds which strictly require the personal care of the family member by the Union citizen;
(f) in cases falling under Article 3(2)(b), proof of the existence of a durable relationship with the Union citizen.

Article 9 Administrative formalities for family members who are not nationals of a Member State

1.   Member States shall issue a residence card to family members of a Union citizen who are not nationals of a Member State, where the planned period of residence is for more than three months.

2.   The deadline for submitting the residence card application may not be less than three months from the date of arrival.

3.   Failure to comply with the requirement to apply for a residence card may make the person concerned liable to proportionate and non-discriminatory sanctions.

Article 10 Issue of residence cards

1.   The right of residence of family members of a Union citizen who are not nationals of a Member State shall be evidenced by the issuing of a document called 'Residence card of a family member of a Union citizen' no later than six months from the date on which they submit the application. A certificate of application for the residence card shall be issued immediately.

2.   For the residence card to be issued, Member States shall require presentation of the following documents:
(a) a valid passport;
(b) a document attesting to the existence of a family relationship or of a registered partnership;
(c) the registration certificate or, in the absence of a registration system, any other proof of residence in the host Member State of the Union citizen whom they are accompanying or joining;
(d) in cases falling under points (c) and (d) of Article 2(2), documentary evidence that the conditions laid down therein are met;
(e) in cases falling under Article 3(2)(a), a document issued by the relevant authority in the country of origin or country from which they are arriving certifying that they are dependants or members of the household of the Union citizen, or proof of the existence of serious health grounds which strictly require the personal care of the family member by the Union citizen;
(f) in cases falling under Article 3(2)(b), proof of the existence of a durable relationship with the Union citizen.

Article 11 Validity of the residence card

1. The residence card provided for by Article 10(1) shall be valid for five years from the date of issue or for the envisaged period of residence of the Union citizen, if this period is less than five years.

2. The validity of the residence card shall not be affected by temporary absences not exceeding six months a year, or by absences of a longer duration for compulsory military service or by one absence of a maximum of 12 consecutive months for important reasons such as pregnancy and childbirth, serious illness, study or vocational training, or a posting in another Member State or a third country.

Article 12 Retention of the right of residence by family members in the event of death or departure of the Union citizen

1. Without prejudice to the second subparagraph, the Union citizen's death or departure from the host Member State shall not affect the right of residence of his/her family members who are nationals of a Member State.

   Before acquiring the right of permanent residence, the persons concerned must meet the conditions laid down in points (a), (b), (c) or (d) of Article 7(1).

2. Without prejudice to the second subparagraph, the Union citizen's death shall not entail loss of the right of residence of his/her family members who are not nationals of a Member State and who have been residing in the host Member State as family members for at least one year before the Union citizen's death.

   Before acquiring the right of permanent residence, the right of residence of the persons concerned shall remain subject to the requirement that they are able to show that they are workers or self-employed persons or that they have sufficient resources for themselves and their family members not to become a burden on the social assistance system of the host Member State during their period of residence and have comprehensive sickness insurance cover in the host Member State, or that they are members of the family, already constituted in the host Member State, of a person satisfying these requirements.

   'Sufficient resources' shall be as defined in Article 8(4).

   Such family members shall retain their right of residence exclusively on a personal basis.

3. The Union citizen's departure from the host Member State or his/her death shall not entail loss of the right of residence of his/her children or of the parent who has actual custody of the children, irrespective of nationality, if the children reside in the host Member State and are enrolled at an educational establishment, for the purpose of studying there, until the completion of their studies.

Article 13 Retention of the right of residence by family members in the event of divorce, annulment of marriage or termination of registered partnership

1. Without prejudice to the second subparagraph, divorce, annulment of the Union citizen's marriage or termination of his/her registered partnership, as referred to in point 2(b) of Article 2 shall not affect the right of residence of his/her family members who are nationals of a Member State.

   Before acquiring the right of permanent residence, the persons concerned must meet the conditions laid down in points (a), (b), (c) or (d) of Article 7(1).

2. Without prejudice to the second subparagraph, divorce, annulment of marriage or termination of the registered partnership referred to in point 2(b) of Article 2 shall not entail loss of the right of residence of a Union citizen's family members who are not nationals of a Member State where:

(a) prior to initiation of the divorce or annulment proceedings or termination of the registered partnership referred to in point 2(b) of Article 2, the marriage or registered partnership has lasted at least three years, including one year in the host Member State; or

(b) by agreement between the spouses or the partners referred to in point 2(b) of Article 2 or by court order, the spouse or partner who is not a national of a Member State has custody of the Union citizen's children; or

(c) this is warranted by particularly difficult circumstances, such as having been a victim of domestic violence while the marriage or registered partnership was subsisting; or

(d) by agreement between the spouses or partners referred to in point 2(b) of Article 2 or by court order, the spouse or partner who is not a national of a Member State has the right of access to a minor child, provided that the court has ruled that such access must be in the host Member State, and for as long as is required.

Before acquiring the right of permanent residence, the right of residence of the persons concerned shall remain subject to the requirement that they are able to show that they are workers or self-employed persons or that they have sufficient resources for themselves and their family members not to become a burden on the social assistance system of the host Member State during their period of residence and have comprehensive sickness insurance cover in the host Member State, or that they are members of the family, already constituted in the host Member State, of a person satisfying these requirements. 'Sufficient resources' shall be as defined in Article 8(4).

Such family members shall retain their right of residence exclusively on personal basis.

Article 14 Retention of the right of residence

1. Union citizens and their family members shall have the right of residence provided for in Article 6, as long as they do not become an unreasonable burden on the social assistance system of the host Member State.

2. Union citizens and their family members shall have the right of residence provided for in Articles 7, 12 and 13 as long as they meet the conditions set out therein.

   In specific cases where there is a reasonable doubt as to whether a Union citizen or his/her family members satisfies the conditions set out in Articles 7, 12 and 13, Member States may verify if these conditions are fulfilled. This verification shall not be carried out systematically.

3. An expulsion measure shall not be the automatic consequence of a Union citizen's or his or her family member's recourse to the social assistance system of the host Member State.

4. By way of derogation from paragraphs 1 and 2 and without prejudice to the provisions of Chapter VI, an expulsion measure may in no case be adopted against Union citizens or their family members if:
   (a) the Union citizens are workers or self-employed persons, or
   (b) the Union citizens entered the territory of the host Member State in order to seek employment. In this case, the Union citizens and their family members may not be expelled for as long as the Union citizens can provide evidence that they are continuing to seek employment and that they have a genuine chance of being engaged.

Article 15 Procedural safeguards

1. The procedures provided for by Articles 30 and 31 shall apply by analogy to all decisions restricting free movement of Union citizens and their family members on grounds other than public policy, public security or public health.

2.   Expiry of the identity card or passport on the basis of which the person concerned entered the host Member State and was issued with a registration certificate or residence card shall not constitute a ground for expulsion from the host Member State.

3.   The host Member State may not impose a ban on entry in the context of an expulsion decision to which paragraph 1 applies.

Chapter IV RIGHT OF PERMANENT RESIDENCE

SECTION I ELIGIBILITY

Article 16 General rule for Union citizens and their family members

1.   Union citizens who have resided legally for a continuous period of five years in the host Member State shall have the right of permanent residence there. This right shall not be subject to the conditions provided for in Chapter III.

2.   Paragraph 1 shall apply also to family members who are not nationals of a Member State and have legally resided with the Union citizen in the host Member State for a continuous period of five years.

3.   Continuity of residence shall not be affected by temporary absences not exceeding a total of six months a year, or by absences of a longer duration for compulsory military service, or by one absence of a maximum of 12 consecutive months for important reasons such as pregnancy and childbirth, serious illness, study or vocational training, or a posting in another Member State or a third country.

4.   Once acquired, the right of permanent residence shall be lost only through absence from the host Member State for a period exceeding two consecutive years.

Article 17 Exemptions for persons no longer working in the host Member State and their family members

1.   By way of derogation from Article 16, the right of permanent residence in the host Member State shall be enjoyed before completion of a continuous period of five years of residence by:
    (a) workers or self-employed persons who, at the time they stop working, have reached the age laid down by the law of that Member State for entitlement to an old age pension or workers who cease paid employment to take early retirement, provided that they have been working in that Member State for at least the preceding twelve months and have resided there continuously for more than three years.
    If the law of the host Member State does not grant the right to an old age pension to certain categories of self-employed persons, the age condition shall be deemed to have been met once the person concerned has reached the age of 60;
    (b) workers or self-employed persons who have resided continuously in the host Member State for more than two years and stop working there as a result of permanent incapacity to work.
    If such incapacity is the result of an accident at work or an occupational disease entitling the person concerned to a benefit payable in full or in part by an institution in the host Member State, no condition shall be imposed as to length of residence;
    (c) workers or self-employed persons who, after three years of continuous employment and residence in the host Member State, work in an employed or self-employed capacity in another Member State, while retaining their place of residence in the host Member State, to which they return, as a rule, each day or at least once a week.
    For the purposes of entitlement to the rights referred to in points (a) and (b), periods of employment spent in the Member State in which the person concerned is working shall be regarded as having been spent in the host Member State.

Periods of involuntary unemployment duly recorded by the relevant employment office, periods not worked for reasons not of the person's own making and absences from work or cessation of work due to illness or accident shall be regarded as periods of employment.

2.   The conditions as to length of residence and employment laid down in point (a) of paragraph 1 and the condition as to length of residence laid down in point (b) of paragraph 1 shall not apply if the worker's or the self-employed person's spouse or partner as referred to in point 2(b) of Article 2 is a national of the host Member State or has lost the nationality of that Member State by marriage to that worker or self-employed person.

3.   Irrespective of nationality, the family members of a worker or a self-employed person who are residing with him in the territory of the host Member State shall have the right of permanent residence in that Member State, if the worker or self-employed person has acquired himself the right of permanent residence in that Member State on the basis of paragraph 1.

4.   If, however, the worker or self-employed person dies while still working but before acquiring permanent residence status in the host Member State on the basis of paragraph 1, his family members who are residing with him in the host Member State shall acquire the right of permanent residence there, on condition that:
(a) the worker or self-employed person had, at the time of death, resided continuously on the territory of that Member State for two years; or
(b) the death resulted from an accident at work or an occupational disease; or
(c) the surviving spouse lost the nationality of that Member State following marriage to the worker or self-employed person.

Article 18 Acquisition of the right of permanent residence by certain family members who are not nationals of a Member State

Without prejudice to Article 17, the family members of a Union citizen to whom Articles 12(2) and 13(2) apply, who satisfy the conditions laid down therein, shall acquire the right of permanent residence after residing legally for a period of five consecutive years in the host Member State.

SECTION II ADMINISTRATIVE FORMALITIES

Article 19 Document certifying permanent residence for Union citizens

1.   Upon application Member States shall issue Union citizens entitled to permanent residence, after having verified duration of residence, with a document certifying permanent residence.

2.   The document certifying permanent residence shall be issued as soon as possible.

Article 20 Permanent residence card for family members who are not nationals of a Member State

1.   Member States shall issue family members who are not nationals of a Member State entitled to permanent residence with a permanent residence card within six months of the submission of the application. The permanent residence card shall be renewable automatically every 10 years.

2.   The application for a permanent residence card shall be submitted before the residence card expires. Failure to comply with the requirement to apply for a permanent residence card may render the person concerned liable to proportionate and non-discriminatory sanctions.

3.   Interruption in residence not exceeding two consecutive years shall not affect the validity of the permanent residence card.

Article 21 Continuity of residence

For the purposes of this Directive, continuity of residence may be attested by any means of proof in use in the host Member State. Continuity of residence is broken by any expulsion decision duly enforced against the person concerned.

Chapter V PROVISIONS COMMON TO THE RIGHT OF RESIDENCE AND THE RIGHT OF PERMANENT RESIDENCE

Article 22 Territorial scope

The right of residence and the right of permanent residence shall cover the whole territory of the host Member State. Member States may impose territorial restrictions on the right of residence and the right of permanent residence only where the same restrictions apply to their own nationals.

Article 23 Related rights

Irrespective of nationality, the family members of a Union citizen who have the right of residence or the right of permanent residence in a Member State shall be entitled to take up employment or self-employment there.

Article 24 Equal treatment

1.   Subject to such specific provisions as are expressly provided for in the Treaty and secondary law, all Union citizens residing on the basis of this Directive in the territory of the host Member State shall enjoy equal treatment with the nationals of that Member State within the scope of the Treaty. The benefit of this right shall be extended to family members who are not nationals of a Member State and who have the right of residence or permanent residence.

2.   By way of derogation from paragraph 1, the host Member State shall not be obliged to confer entitlement to social assistance during the first three months of residence or, where appropriate, the longer period provided for in Article 14(4)(b), nor shall it be obliged, prior to acquisition of the right of permanent residence, to grant maintenance aid for studies, including vocational training, consisting in student grants or student loans to persons other than workers, self-employed persons, persons who retain such status and members of their families.

Article 25 General provisions concerning residence documents

1.   Possession of a registration certificate as referred to in Article 8, of a document certifying permanent residence, of a certificate attesting submission of an application for a family member residence card, of a residence card or of a permanent residence card, may under no circumstances be made a precondition for the exercise of a right or the completion of an administrative formality, as entitlement to rights may be attested by any other means of proof.

2.   All documents mentioned in paragraph 1 shall be issued free of charge or for a charge not exceeding that imposed on nationals for the issuing of similar documents.

Article 26 Checks

Member States may carry out checks on compliance with any requirement deriving from their national legislation for non-nationals always to carry their registration certificate or residence card, provided that the same requirement applies to their own nationals as regards their identity card. In the event of failure to comply with this requirement, Member States may impose the same sanctions as those imposed on their own nationals for failure to carry their identity card.

Chapter VI RESTRICTIONS ON THE RIGHT OF ENTRY AND THE RIGHT OF RESIDENCE ON GROUNDS OF PUBLIC POLICY, PUBLIC SECURITY OR PUBLIC HEALTH

Article 27 General principles

1. Subject to the provisions of this Chapter, Member States may restrict the freedom of movement and residence of Union citizens and their family members, irrespective of nationality, on grounds of public policy, public security or public health. These grounds shall not be invoked to serve economic ends.

2. Measures taken on grounds of public policy or public security shall comply with the principle of proportionality and shall be based exclusively on the personal conduct of the individual concerned. Previous criminal convictions shall not in themselves constitute grounds for taking such measures.

   The personal conduct of the individual concerned must represent a genuine, present and sufficiently serious threat affecting one of the fundamental interests of society. Justifications that are isolated from the particulars of the case or that rely on considerations of general prevention shall not be accepted.

3. In order to ascertain whether the person concerned represents a danger for public policy or public security, when issuing the registration certificate or, in the absence of a registration system, not later than three months from the date of arrival of the person concerned on its territory or from the date of reporting his/her presence within the territory, as provided for in Article 5(5), or when issuing the residence card, the host Member State may, should it consider this essential, request the Member State of origin and, if need be, other Member States to provide information concerning any previous police record the person concerned may have. Such enquiries shall not be made as a matter of routine. The Member State consulted shall give its reply within two months.

4. The Member State which issued the passport or identity card shall allow the holder of the document who has been expelled on grounds of public policy, public security, or public health from another Member State to re-enter its territory without any formality even if the document is no longer valid or the nationality of the holder is in dispute.

Article 28 Protection against expulsion

1. Before taking an expulsion decision on grounds of public policy or public security, the host Member State shall take account of considerations such as how long the individual concerned has resided on its territory, his/her age, state of health, family and economic situation, social and cultural integration into the host Member State and the extent of his/her links with the country of origin.

2. The host Member State may not take an expulsion decision against Union citizens or their family members, irrespective of nationality, who have the right of permanent residence on its territory, except on serious grounds of public policy or public security.

3. An expulsion decision may not be taken against Union citizens, except if the decision is based on imperative grounds of public security, as defined by Member States, if they:
   (a) have resided in the host Member State for the previous 10 years; or
   (b) are a minor, except if the expulsion is necessary for the best interests of the child, as provided for in the United Nations Convention on the Rights of the Child of 20 November 1989.

Article 29 Public health

1.   The only diseases justifying measures restricting freedom of movement shall be the diseases with epidemic potential as defined by the relevant instruments of the World Health Organisation and other infectious diseases or contagious parasitic diseases if they are the subject of protection provisions applying to nationals of the host Member State.

2.   Diseases occurring after a three-month period from the date of arrival shall not constitute grounds for expulsion from the territory.

3.   Where there are serious indications that it is necessary, Member States may, within three months of the date of arrival, require persons entitled to the right of residence to undergo, free of charge, a medical examination to certify that they are not suffering from any of the conditions referred to in paragraph 1. Such medical examinations may not be required as a matter of routine.

Article 30 Notification of decisions

1.   The persons concerned shall be notified in writing of any decision taken under Article 27(1), in such a way that they are able to comprehend its content and the implications for them.

2.   The persons concerned shall be informed, precisely and in full, of the public policy, public security or public health grounds on which the decision taken in their case is based, unless this is contrary to the interests of State security.

3.   The notification shall specify the court or administrative authority with which the person concerned may lodge an appeal, the time limit for the appeal and, where applicable, the time allowed for the person to leave the territory of the Member State. Save in duly substantiated cases of urgency, the time allowed to leave the territory shall be not less than one month from the date of notification.

Article 31 Procedural safeguards

1.   The persons concerned shall have access to judicial and, where appropriate, administrative redress procedures in the host Member State to appeal against or seek review of any decision taken against them on the grounds of public policy, public security or public health.

2.   Where the application for appeal against or judicial review of the expulsion decision is accompanied by an application for an interim order to suspend enforcement of that decision, actual removal from the territory may not take place until such time as the decision on the interim order has been taken, except:

where the expulsion decision is based on a previous judicial decision; or

where the persons concerned have had previous access to judicial review; or

where the expulsion decision is based on imperative grounds of public security under Article 28(3).

3.   The redress procedures shall allow for an examination of the legality of the decision, as well as of the facts and circumstances on which the proposed measure is based. They shall ensure that the decision is not disproportionate, particularly in view of the requirements laid down in Article 28.

4.   Member States may exclude the individual concerned from their territory pending the redress procedure, but they may not prevent the individual from submitting his/her defence in person, except when his/her appearance may cause serious troubles to public policy or public security or when the appeal or judicial review concerns a denial of entry to the territory.

Article 32 Duration of exclusion orders

1. Persons excluded on grounds of public policy or public security may submit an application for lifting of the exclusion order after a reasonable period, depending on the circumstances, and in any event after three years from enforcement of the final exclusion order which has been validly adopted in accordance with Community law, by putting forward arguments to establish that there has been a material change in the circumstances which justified the decision ordering their exclusion.

    The Member State concerned shall reach a decision on this application within six months of its submission.

2. The persons referred to in paragraph 1 shall have no right of entry to the territory of the Member State concerned while their application is being considered.

Article 33 Expulsion as a penalty or legal consequence

1. Expulsion orders may not be issued by the host Member State as a penalty or legal consequence of a custodial penalty, unless they conform to the requirements of Articles 27, 28 and 29.

2. If an expulsion order, as provided for in paragraph 1, is enforced more than two years after it was issued, the Member State shall check that the individual concerned is currently and genuinely a threat to public policy or public security and shall assess whether there has been any material change in the circumstances since the expulsion order was issued.

Chapter VII FINAL PROVISIONS

Article 34 Publicity

Member States shall disseminate information concerning the rights and obligations of Union citizens and their family members on the subjects covered by this Directive, particularly by means of awareness-raising campaigns conducted through national and local media and other means of communication.

Article 35 Abuse of rights

Member States may adopt the necessary measures to refuse, terminate or withdraw any right conferred by this Directive in the case of abuse of rights or fraud, such as marriages of convenience. Any such measure shall be proportionate and subject to the procedural safeguards provided for in Articles 30 and 31.

Article 36 Sanctions

Member States shall lay down provisions on the sanctions applicable to breaches of national rules adopted for the implementation of this Directive and shall take the measures required for their application. The sanctions laid down shall be effective and proportionate. Member States shall notify the Commission of these provisions not later than 30 April 2006 and as promptly as possible in the case of any subsequent changes.

Article 37 More favourable national provisions

The provisions of this Directive shall not affect any laws, regulations or administrative provisions laid down by a Member State which would be more favourable to the persons covered by this Directive.

Article 38 Repeals

1. Articles 10 and 11 of Regulation (EEC) No 1612/68 shall be repealed with effect from 30 April 2006.

2. Directives 64/221/EEC, 68/360/EEC, 72/194/EEC, 73/148/EEC, 75/34/EEC, 75/35/EEC, 90/364/EEC, 90/365/EEC and 93/96/EEC shall be repealed with effect from 30 April 2006.

3.   References made to the repealed provisions and Directives shall be construed as being made to this Directive.

Article 39 Report

No later than 30 April 2008 the Commission shall submit a report on the application of this Directive to the European Parliament and the Council, together with any necessary proposals, notably on the opportunity to extend the period of time during which Union citizens and their family members may reside in the territory of the host Member State without any conditions. The Member States shall provide the Commission with the information needed to produce the report.

Article 40 Transposition

1.   Member States shall bring into force the laws, regulations and administrative provisions necessary to comply with this Directive by 30 April 2006.
      When Member States adopt those measures, they shall contain a reference to this Directive or shall be accompanied by such a reference on the occasion of their official publication. The methods of making such reference shall be laid down by the Member States.

2.   Member States shall communicate to the Commission the text of the provisions of national law which they adopt in the field covered by this Directive together with a table showing how the provisions of this Directive correspond to the national provisions adopted.

Article 41 Entry into force

This Directive shall enter into force on the day of its publication in the *Official Journal of the European Union*.

Article 42 Addressees

This Directive is addressed to the Member States.

(*Date of signing and signatories omitted*)

DIRECTIVE 2005/36/EC OF THE EUROPEAN PARLIAMENT AND OF THE COUNCIL OF 7 SEPTEMBER 2005

on the recognition of professional qualifications

OJ L 255, 30.9.2005, P. 22, AS AMENDED AND CORRECTED*

(*As amended by: Council Directive 2006/100/EC of 20 November 2006 L 363/141, 20.12.2006; Commission Regulation (EC) No 1430/2007 of 5 December 2007 L 320/3, 6.12.2007; Commission Regulation (EC) No 755/2008 of 31 July 2008 L205/10, 1.8.2008; and Regulation (EC) No 1137/2008 of the European Parliament and of the Council of 22 October 2008 L 311/1, 21.11.2008). Corrected at: OJ L 271/18, 16.10.2007, (2005/36/EC); and OJ L 93/28, 4.4.2008, (2005/36/EC).[1]

(*Annexes II–VII are omitted due to their length*)

....

[1]   EDITOR'S NOTE: As of 1 May 2012 this Directive has not been amended following the entry into force of the Treaty of Lisbon. It includes references to the old Treaty article numbers. Reference should be made to the Tables of Equivalences accompanying the consolidated Treaties in Part II of this edition for the conversion of old Treaty article numbers to new ones.

THE EUROPEAN PARLIAMENT AND THE COUNCIL OF THE EUROPEAN UNION,

Having regard to the Treaty establishing the European Community, and in particular Article 40, Article 47(1), the first and third sentences of Article 47(2), and Article 55 thereof,

Having regard to the proposal from the Commission,

Having regard to the opinion of the European Economic and Social Committee,

Acting in accordance with the procedure laid down in Article 251 of the Treaty,

Whereas:

(1) Pursuant to Article 3(1)(c) of the Treaty, the abolition, as between Member States, of obstacles to the free movement of persons and services is one of the objectives of the Community. For nationals of the Member States, this includes, in particular, the right to pursue a profession, in a self-employed or employed capacity, in a Member State other than the one in which they have obtained their professional qualifications. In addition, Article 47(1) of the Treaty lays down that directives shall be issued for the mutual recognition of diplomas, certificates and other evidence of formal qualifications.

(Recital 2 omitted)

(3) The guarantee conferred by this Directive on persons having acquired their professional qualifications in a Member State to have access to the same profession and pursue it in another Member State with the same rights as nationals is without prejudice to compliance by the migrant professional with any non-discriminatory conditions of pursuit which might be laid down by the latter Member State, provided that these are objectively justified and proportionate.

(Remainder of the preamble and all footnotes omitted)

TITLE I
GENERAL PROVISIONS

Article 1 Purpose
This Directive establishes rules according to which a Member State which makes access to or pursuit of a regulated profession in its territory contingent upon possession of specific professional qualifications (referred to hereinafter as the host Member State) shall recognise professional qualifications obtained in one or more other Member States (referred to hereinafter as the home Member State) and which allow the holder of the said qualifications to pursue the same profession there, for access to and pursuit of that profession.

Article 2 Scope
1. This Directive shall apply to all nationals of a Member State wishing to pursue a regulated profession in a Member State, including those belonging to the liberal professions, other than that in which they obtained their professional qualifications, on either a self-employed or employed basis.

2. Each Member State may permit Member State nationals in possession of evidence of professional qualifications not obtained in a Member State to pursue a regulated profession within the meaning of Article 3(1)(a) on its territory in accordance with its rules. In the case of professions covered by Title III, Chapter III, this initial recognition shall respect the minimum training conditions laid down in that Chapter.

3. Where, for a given regulated profession, other specific arrangements directly related to the recognition of professional qualifications are established in a separate instrument of Community law, the corresponding provisions of this Directive shall not apply.

Article 3 Definitions

1.   For the purposes of this Directive, the following definitions apply:

(a) "regulated profession": a professional activity or group of professional activities, access to which, the pursuit of which, or one of the modes of pursuit of which is subject, directly or indirectly, by virtue of legislative, regulatory or administrative provisions to the possession of specific professional qualifications; in particular, the use of a professional title limited by legislative, regulatory or administrative provisions to holders of a given professional qualification shall constitute a mode of pursuit. Where the first sentence of this definition does not apply, a profession referred to in paragraph 2 shall be treated as a regulated profession;

(b) "professional qualifications": qualifications attested by evidence of formal qualifications, an attestation of competence referred to in Article 11, point (a) (i) and/or professional experience;

(c) "evidence of formal qualifications": diplomas, certificates and other evidence issued by an authority in a Member State designated pursuant to legislative, regulatory or administrative provisions of that Member State and certifying successful completion of professional training obtained mainly in the Community. Where the first sentence of this definition does not apply, evidence of formal qualifications referred to in paragraph 3 shall be treated as evidence of formal qualifications;

(d) "competent authority": any authority or body empowered by a Member State specifically to issue or receive training diplomas and other documents or information and to receive the applications, and take the decisions, referred to in this Directive;

(e) "regulated education and training": any training which is specifically geared to the pursuit of a given profession and which comprises a course or courses complemented, where appropriate, by professional training, or probationary or professional practice. The structure and level of the professional training, probationary or professional practice shall be determined by the laws, regulations or administrative provisions of the Member State concerned or monitored or approved by the authority designated for that purpose;

(f) "professional experience": the actual and lawful pursuit of the profession concerned in a Member State;

(g) "adaptation period": the pursuit of a regulated profession in the host Member State under the responsibility of a qualified member of that profession, such period of supervised practice possibly being accompanied by further training. This period of supervised practice shall be the subject of an assessment. The detailed rules governing the adaptation period and its assessment as well as the status of a migrant under supervision shall be laid down by the competent authority in the host Member State. The status enjoyed in the host Member State by the person undergoing the period of supervised practice, in particular in the matter of right of residence as well as obligations, social rights and benefits, allowances and remuneration, shall be established by the competent authorities in that Member State in accordance with applicable Community law;

(h) "aptitude test": a test limited to the professional knowledge of the applicant, made by the competent authorities of the host Member State with the aim of assessing the ability of the applicant to pursue a regulated profession in that Member State. In order to permit this test to be carried out, the competent authorities shall draw up a list of subjects which, on the basis of a comparison of the education and training required in the Member State and that received by the applicant, are not covered by the diploma or other evidence of formal qualifications possessed by the applicant. The aptitude test must take account of the fact that the applicant is a qualified professional in the home Member State or the Member State from which he comes. It shall cover subjects to be selected from those on the list, knowledge of which is essential in order to be able to pursue the profession in the host Member State. The test may also include knowledge of the professional rules applicable to the activities in question in the host Member State.

The detailed application of the aptitude test and the status, in the host Member State, of the applicant who wishes to prepare himself for the aptitude test in that State shall be determined by the competent authorities in that Member State;

(i) "manager of an undertaking": any person who in an undertaking in the occupational field in question has pursued an activity:

  (i) as a manager of an undertaking or a manager of a branch of an undertaking; or

  (ii) as a deputy to the proprietor or the manager of an undertaking where that post involves responsibility equivalent to that of the proprietor or manager represented; or

  (iii) in a managerial post with duties of a commercial and/or technical nature and with responsibility for one or more departments of the undertaking.

2. A profession practised by the members of an association or organisation listed in Annex I shall be treated as a regulated profession.

The purpose of the associations or organisations referred to in the first subparagraph is, in particular, to promote and maintain a high standard in the professional field concerned. To that end they are recognised in a special form by a Member State and award evidence of formal qualifications to their members, ensure that their members respect the rules of professional conduct which they prescribe, and confer on them the right to use a title or designatory letters or to benefit from a status corresponding to those formal qualifications.

On each occasion that a Member State grants recognition to an association or organisation referred to in the first subparagraph, it shall inform the Commission, which shall publish an appropriate notification in the *Official Journal of the European Union.*

3. Evidence of formal qualifications issued by a third country shall be regarded as evidence of formal qualifications if the holder has three years' professional experience in the profession concerned on the territory of the Member State which recognised that evidence of formal qualifications in accordance with Article 2(2), certified by that Member State.

Article 4 Effects of recognition

1. The recognition of professional qualifications by the host Member State allows the beneficiary to gain access in that Member State to the same profession as that for which he is qualified in the home Member State and to pursue it in the host Member State under the same conditions as its nationals.

2. For the purposes of this Directive, the profession which the applicant wishes to pursue in the host Member State is the same as that for which he is qualified in his home Member State if the activities covered are comparable.

TITLE II
FREE PROVISION OF SERVICES

Article 5 Principle of the free provision of services

1. Without prejudice to specific provisions of Community law, as well as to Articles 6 and 7 of this Directive, Member States shall not restrict, for any reason relating to professional qualifications, the free provision of services in another Member State:

  (a) if the service provider is legally established in a Member State for the purpose of pursuing the same profession there (hereinafter referred to as the Member State of establishment), and

(b) where the service provider moves, if he has pursued that profession in the Member State of establishment for at least two years during the 10 years preceding the provision of services when the profession is not regulated in that Member State. The condition requiring two years' pursuit shall not apply when either the profession or the education and training leading to the profession is regulated.

2.   The provisions of this title shall only apply where the service provider moves to the territory of the host Member State to pursue, on a temporary and occasional basis, the profession referred to in paragraph 1.

The temporary and occasional nature of the provision of services shall be assessed case by case, in particular in relation to its duration, its frequency, its regularity and its continuity.

3.   Where a service provider moves, he shall be subject to professional rules of a professional, statutory or administrative nature which are directly linked to professional qualifications, such as the definition of the profession, the use of titles and serious professional malpractice which is directly and specifically linked to consumer protection and safety, as well as disciplinary provisions which are applicable in the host Member State to professionals who pursue the same profession in that Member State.

Article 6 Exemptions
Pursuant to Article 5(1), the host Member State shall exempt service providers established in another Member State from the requirements which it places on professionals established in its territory relating to:

(a)   authorisation by, registration with or membership of a professional organisation or body. In order to facilitate the application of disciplinary provisions in force on their territory according to Article 5(3), Member States may provide either for automatic temporary registration with or for pro forma membership of such a professional organisation or body, provided that such registration or membership does not delay or complicate in any way the provision of services and does not entail any additional costs for the service provider. A copy of the declaration and, where applicable, of the renewal referred to in Article 7(1), accompanied, for professions which have implications for public health and safety referred to in Article 7(4) or which benefit from automatic recognition under Title III Chapter III, by a copy of the documents referred to in Article 7(2) shall be sent by the competent authority to the relevant professional organisation or body, and this shall constitute automatic temporary registration or pro forma membership for this purpose;

(b)   registration with a public social security body for the purpose of settling accounts with an insurer relating to activities pursued for the benefit of insured persons.

The service provider shall, however, inform in advance or, in an urgent case, afterwards, the body referred to in point (b) of the services which he has provided.

Article 7 Declaration to be made in advance, if the service provider moves
1.   Member States may require that, where the service provider first moves from one Member State to another in order to provide services, he shall inform the competent authority in the host Member State in a written declaration to be made in advance including the details of any insurance cover or other means of personal or collective protection with regard to professional liability. Such declaration shall be renewed once a year if the service provider intends to provide temporary or occasional services in that Member State during that year. The service provider may supply the declaration by any means.

2.   Moreover, for the first provision of services or if there is a material change in the situation substantiated by the documents, Member States may require that the declaration be accompanied by the following documents:

(a) proof of the nationality of the service provider;

(b) an attestation certifying that the holder is legally established in a Member State for the purpose of pursuing the activities concerned and that he is not prohibited from practising, even temporarily, at the moment of delivering the attestation;

(c) evidence of professional qualifications;

(d) for cases referred to in Article 5(1)(b), any means of proof that the service provider has pursued the activity concerned for at least two years during the previous ten years;

(e) for professions in the security sector, where the Member State so requires for its own nationals, evidence of no criminal convictions.

3.   The service shall be provided under the professional title of the Member State of establishment, in so far as such a title exists in that Member State for the professional activity in question. That title shall be indicated in the official language or one of the official languages of the Member State of establishment in such a way as to avoid any confusion with the professional title of the host Member State. Where no such professional title exists in the Member State of establishment, the service provider shall indicate his formal qualification in the official language or one of the official languages of that Member State. By way of exception, the service shall be provided under the professional title of the host Member State for cases referred to in Title III Chapter III.

4.   For the first provision of services, in the case of regulated professions having public health or safety implications, which do not benefit from automatic recognition under Title III Chapter III, the competent authority of the host Member State may check the professional qualifications of the service provider prior to the first provision of services. Such a prior check shall be possible only where the purpose of the check is to avoid serious damage to the health or safety of the service recipient due to a lack of professional qualification of the service provider and where this does not go beyond what is necessary for that purpose.

Within a maximum of one month of receipt of the declaration and accompanying documents, the competent authority shall endeavour to inform the service provider either of its decision not to check his qualifications or of the outcome of such check. Where there is a difficulty which would result in delay, the competent authority shall notify the service provider within the first month of the reason for the delay and the timescale for a decision, which must be finalised within the second month of receipt of completed documentation.

Where there is a substantial difference between the professional qualifications of the service provider and the training required in the host Member State, to the extent that that difference is such as to be harmful to public health or safety, the host Member State shall give the service provider the opportunity to show, in particular by means of an aptitude test, that he has acquired the knowledge or competence lacking. In any case, it must be possible to provide the service within one month of a decision being taken in accordance with the previous subparagraph.

In the absence of a reaction of the competent authority within the deadlines set in the previous subparagraphs, the service may be provided.

In cases where qualifications have been verified under this paragraph, the service shall be provided under the professional title of the host Member State.

Article 8 Administrative cooperation

1.   The competent authorities of the host Member State may ask the competent authorities of the Member State of establishment, for each provision of services, to provide any information relevant to the legality of the service provider's establishment and his good

conduct, as well as the absence of any disciplinary or criminal sanctions of a professional nature. The competent authorities of the Member State of establishment shall provide this information in accordance with the provisions of Article 56.

2.   The competent authorities shall ensure the exchange of all information necessary for complaints by a recipient of a service against a service provider to be correctly pursued. Recipients shall be informed of the outcome of the complaint.

Article 9 Information to be given to the recipients of the service
In cases where the service is provided under the professional title of the Member State of establishment or under the formal qualification of the service provider, in addition to the other requirements relating to information contained in Community law, the competent authorities of the host Member State may require the service provider to furnish the recipient of the service with any or all of the following information:

(a)   if the service provider is registered in a commercial register or similar public register, the register in which he is registered, his registration number, or equivalent means of identification contained in that register;

(b)   if the activity is subject to authorisation in the Member State of establishment, the name and address of the competent supervisory authority;

(c)   any professional association or similar body with which the service provider is registered;

(d)   the professional title or, where no such title exists, the formal qualification of the service provider and the Member State in which it was awarded;

(e)   if the service provider performs an activity which is subject to VAT, the VAT identification number referred to in Article 22(1) of the sixth Council Directive 77/388/EEC of 17 May 1977 on the harmonisation of the laws of the Member States relating to turnover taxes – Common system of value added tax: uniform basis of assessment [23];

(f)   details of any insurance cover or other means of personal or collective protection with regard to professional liability.

TITLE III
FREEDOM OF ESTABLISHMENT

Chapter I GENERAL SYSTEM FOR THE RECOGNITION OF EVIDENCE OF TRAINING

Article 10 Scope
This Chapter applies to all professions which are not covered by Chapters II and III of this Title and in the following cases in which the applicant, for specific and exceptional reasons, does not satisfy the conditions laid down in those Chapters:

(a)   for activities listed in Annex IV, when the migrant does not meet the requirements set out in Articles 17, 18 and 19;

(b)   for doctors with basic training, specialised doctors, nurses responsible for general care, dental practitioners, specialised dental practitioners, veterinary surgeons, midwives, pharmacists and architects, when the migrant does not meet the requirements of effective and lawful professional practice referred to in Articles 23, 27, 33, 37, 39, 43 and 49;

(c)   for architects, when the migrant holds evidence of formal qualification not listed in Annex V, point 5.7;

(d)   without prejudice to Article 21(1), 23 and 27, for doctors, nurses, dental practitioners, veterinary surgeons, midwives, pharmacists and architects holding evidence of formal qualifications as a specialist who must have taken part in the training leading to the possession of a title listed in Annex V, points 5.1.1, 5.2.2, 5.3.2, 5.4.2, 5.5.2, 5.6.2 and 5.7.1, and solely for the purpose of the recognition of the relevant specialty;

(e) for nurses responsible for general care and specialized nurses holding evidence of formal qualifications as a specialist who have taken part in the training leading to the possession of a title listed in Annex V, point 5.2.2, when the migrant seeks recognition in another Member State where the relevant professional activities are pursued by specialised nurses without training as general care nurse;

(f) for specialised nurses without training as general care nurse, when the migrant seeks recognition in another Member State where the relevant professional activities are pursued by nurses responsible for general care, specialised nurses without training as general care nurse or specialised nurses holding evidence of formal qualifications as a specialist who have taken part in the training leading to the possession of the titles listed in Annex V, point 5.22;

(g) for migrants meeting the requirements set out in Article 3(3).

Article 11 Levels of qualification

For the purpose of applying Article 13, the professional qualifications are grouped under the following levels as described below:

(a) an attestation of competence issued by a competent authority in the home Member State designated pursuant to legislative, regulatory or administrative provisions of that Member State, on the basis of:
  (i) either a training course not forming part of a certificate or diploma within the meaning of points (b), (c), (d) or (e), or a specific examination without prior training, or full-time pursuit of the profession in a Member State for three consecutive years or for an equivalent duration on a part-time basis during the previous 10 years,
  (ii) or general primary or secondary education, attesting that the holder has acquired general knowledge;

(b) a certificate attesting to a successful completion of a secondary course,
  (i) either general in character, supplemented by a course of study or professional training other than those referred to in point (c) and/or by the probationary or professional practice required in addition to that course,
  (ii) or technical or professional in character, supplemented where appropriate by a course of study or professional training as referred to in point (i), and/or by the probationary or professional practice required in addition to that course;

(c) a diploma certifying successful completion of
  (i) either training at post-secondary level other than that referred to in points (d) and (e) of a duration of at least one year or of an equivalent duration on a part-time basis, one of the conditions of entry of which is, as a general rule, the successful completion of the secondary course required to obtain entry to university or higher education or the completion of equivalent school education of the second secondary level, as well as the professional training which may be required in addition to that post-secondary course; or
  (ii) in the case of a regulated profession, training with a special structure, included in Annex II, equivalent to the level of training provided for under (i), which provides a comparable professional standard and which prepares the trainee for a comparable level of responsibilities and functions;

(d) a diploma certifying successful completion of training at post-secondary level of at least three and not more than four years' duration, or of an equivalent duration on a part-time basis, at a university or establishment of higher education or another establishment providing the same level of training, as well as the professional training which may be required in addition to that post-secondary course;

(e)   a diploma certifying that the holder has successfully completed a post-secondary course of at least four years' duration, or of an equivalent duration on a part-time basis, at a university or establishment of higher education or another establishment of equivalent level and, where appropriate, that he has successfully completed the professional training required in addition to the post-secondary course.

The Commission may adapt the list in Annex II to take account of training which meets the requirements provided for in point (c)(ii) of the first paragraph. Those measures, designed to amend non-essential elements of this Directive, shall be adopted in accordance with the regulatory procedure with scrutiny referred to in Article 58(3).

Article 12 Equal treatment of qualifications

Any evidence of formal qualifications or set of evidence of formal qualifications issued by a competent authority in a Member State, certifying successful completion of training in the Community which is recognised by that Member State as being of an equivalent level and which confers on the holder the same rights of access to or pursuit of a profession or prepares for the pursuit of that profession, shall be treated as evidence of formal qualifications of the type covered by Article 11, including the level in question.

Any professional qualification which, although not satisfying the requirements contained in the legislative, regulatory or administrative provisions in force in the home Member State for access to or the pursuit of a profession, confers on the holder acquired rights by virtue of these provisions, shall also be treated as such evidence of formal qualifications under the same conditions as set out in the first subparagraph. This applies in particular if the home Member State raises the level of training required for admission to a profession and for its exercise, and if an individual who has undergone former training, which does not meet the requirements of the new qualification, benefits from acquired rights by virtue of national legislative, regulatory or administrative provisions; in such case this former training is considered by the host Member State, for the purposes of the application of Article 13, as corresponding to the level of the new training.

Article 13 Conditions for recognition

1.   If access to or pursuit of a regulated profession in a host Member State is contingent upon possession of specific professional qualifications, the competent authority of that Member State shall permit access to and pursuit of that profession, under the same conditions as apply to its nationals, to applicants possessing the attestation of competence or evidence of formal qualifications required by another Member State in order to gain access to and pursue that profession on its territory.

Attestations of competence or evidence of formal qualifications shall satisfy the following conditions:
(a)   they shall have been issued by a competent authority in a Member State, designated in accordance with the legislative, regulatory or administrative provisions of that Member State;
(b)   they shall attest a level of professional qualification at least equivalent to the level immediately prior to that which is required in the host Member State, as described in Article 11.

2.   Access to and pursuit of the profession, as described in paragraph 1, shall also be granted to applicants who have pursued the profession referred to in that paragraph on a full-time basis for two years during the previous 10 years in another Member State which does not regulate that profession, providing they possess one or more attestations of competence or documents providing evidence of formal qualifications.

Attestations of competence and evidence of formal qualifications shall satisfy the following conditions:

(a) they shall have been issued by a competent authority in a Member State, designated in accordance with the legislative, regulatory or administrative provisions of that Member State;

(b) they shall attest a level of professional qualification at least equivalent to the level immediately prior to that required in the host Member State, as described in Article 11;

(c) they shall attest that the holder has been prepared for the pursuit of the profession in question.

The two years' professional experience referred to in the first subparagraph may not, however, be required if the evidence of formal qualifications which the applicant possesses certifies regulated education and training within the meaning of Article 3(1)(e) at the levels of qualifications described in Article 11, points (b), (c), (d) or (e). The regulated education and training listed in Annex III shall be considered as such regulated education and training at the level described in Article 11, point (c).

The Commission may adapt the list in Annex III to take account of regulated education and training which provides a comparable professional standard and which prepares the trainee for a comparable level of responsibilities and functions. Those measures, designed to amend non-essential elements of this Directive, shall be adopted in accordance with the regulatory procedure with scrutiny referred to in Article 58(3).

3.   By way of derogation from paragraph 1, point (b) and to paragraph 2, point (b), the host Member State shall permit access and pursuit of a regulated profession where access to this profession is contingent in its territory upon possession of a qualification certifying successful completion of higher or university education of four years' duration, and where the applicant possesses a qualification referred to in Article 11, point (c).

Article 14 Compensation measures

1.   Article 13 does not preclude the host Member State from requiring the applicant to complete an adaptation period of up to three years or to take an aptitude test if:

(a) the duration of the training of which he provides evidence under the terms of Article 13, paragraph 1 or 2, is at least one year shorter than that required by the host Member State;

(b) the training he has received covers substantially different matters than those covered by the evidence of formal qualifications required in the host Member State;

(c) the regulated profession in the host Member State comprises one or more regulated professional activities which do not exist in the corresponding profession in the applicant's home Member State within the meaning of Article 4(2), and that difference consists in specific training which is required in the host Member State and which covers substantially different matters from those covered by the applicant's attestation of competence or evidence of formal qualifications.

2.   If the host Member State makes use of the option provided for in paragraph 1, it must offer the applicant the choice between an adaptation period and an aptitude test.

Where a Member State considers, with respect to a given profession, that it is necessary to derogate from the requirement, set out in the previous subparagraph, that it give the applicant a choice between an adaptation period and an aptitude test, it shall inform the other Member States and the Commission in advance and provide sufficient justification for the derogation.

If, after receiving all necessary information, the Commission considers that the derogation referred to in the second subparagraph is inappropriate or that it is not in accordance with

Community law, it shall, within three months, ask the Member State in question to refrain from taking the envisaged measure. In the absence of a response from the Commission within the abovementioned deadline, the derogation may be applied.

3.   By way of derogation from the principle of the right of the applicant to choose, as laid down in paragraph 2, for professions whose pursuit requires precise knowledge of national law and in respect of which the provision of advice and/or assistance concerning national law is an essential and constant aspect of the professional activity, the host Member State may stipulate either an adaptation period or an aptitude test.

This applies also to the cases provided for in Article 10 points (b) and (c), in Article 10 point (d) concerning doctors and dental practitioners in Article 10 point (f) when the migrant seeks recognition in another Member State where the relevant professional activities are pursued by nurses responsible for general care or specialised nurses holding evidence of formal qualifications as a specialist who have taken part in the training leading to the possession of the titles listed in Annex V, point 5.2.2 and in Article 10 point (g).

In the cases covered by Article 10 point (a), the host Member State may require an adaptation period or an aptitude test if the migrant envisages pursuing professional activities in a self-employed capacity or as a manager of an undertaking which require the knowledge and the application of the specific national rules in force, provided that knowledge and application of those rules are required by the competent authorities of the host Member State for access to such activities by its own nationals.

4.   For the purpose of applying paragraph 1 points (b) and (c), "substantially different matters" means matters of which knowledge is essential for pursuing the profession and with regard to which the training received by the migrant shows important differences in terms of duration or content from the training required by the host Member State.

5.   Paragraph 1 shall be applied with due regard to the principle of proportionality. In particular, if the host Member State intends to require the applicant to complete an adaptation period or take an aptitude test, it must first ascertain whether the knowledge acquired by the applicant in the course of his professional experience in a Member State or in a third country, is of a nature to cover, in full or in part, the substantial difference referred to in paragraph 4.

Article 15 Waiving of compensation measures on the basis of common platforms
1.   For the purpose of this Article, "common platforms" is defined as a set of criteria of professional qualifications which are suitable for compensating for substantial differences which have been identified between the training requirements existing in the various Member States for a given profession. These substantial differences shall be identified by comparison between the duration and contents of the training in at least two thirds of the Member States, including all Member States which regulate this profession. The differences in the contents of the training may result from substantial differences in the scope of the professional activities.

2.   Common platforms as defined in paragraph 1 may be submitted to the Commission by Member States or by professional associations or organisations which are representative at national and European level. If the Commission, after consulting the Member States, is of the opinion that a draft common platform facilitates the mutual recognition of professional qualifications, it may present draft measures with a view to their adoption. Those measures, designed to amend non-essential elements of this Directive by supplementing it, shall be adopted in accordance with the regulatory procedure with scrutiny referred to in Article 58(3).

3.   Where the applicant's professional qualifications satisfy the criteria established in the measure adopted in accordance with paragraph 2, the host Member State shall waive the application of compensation measures under Article 14.

4.   Paragraphs 1 to 3 shall not affect the competence of Member States to decide the professional qualifications required for the pursuit of professions in their territory as well as the contents and the organisation of their systems of education and professional training.

5.   If a Member State considers that the criteria established in a measure adopted in accordance with paragraph 2 no longer offer adequate guarantees with regard to professional qualifications, it shall inform the Commission accordingly. The Commission shall, if appropriate, present a draft measure for adoption. That measure, designed to amend non-essential elements of this Directive by supplementing it, shall be adopted in accordance with the regulatory procedure with scrutiny referred to in Article 58(3).

6.   The Commission shall, by 20 October 2010, submit to the European Parliament and the Council a report on the operation of this Article and, if necessary, appropriate proposals for amending this Article.

Chapter II RECOGNITION OF PROFESSIONAL EXPERIENCE

Article 16 Requirements regarding professional experience
If, in a Member State, access to or pursuit of one of the activities listed in Annex IV is contingent upon possession of general, commercial or professional knowledge and aptitudes, that Member State shall recognise previous pursuit of the activity in another Member State as sufficient proof of such knowledge and aptitudes. The activity must have been pursued in accordance with Articles 17, 18 and 19.

Article 17 Activities referred to in list I of Annex IV
1.   For the activities in list I of Annex IV, the activity in question must have been previously pursued:
   (a) for six consecutive years on a self-employed basis or as a manager of an undertaking; or
   (b) for three consecutive years on a self-employed basis or as a manager of an undertaking, where the beneficiary proves that he has received previous training of at least three years for the activity in question, evidenced by a certificate recognised by the Member State or judged by a competent professional body to be fully valid; or
   (c) for four consecutive years on a self-employed basis or as a manager of an undertaking, where the beneficiary can prove that he has received, for the activity in question, previous training of at least two years' duration, attested by a certificate recognised by the Member State or judged by a competent professional body to be fully valid; or
   (d) for three consecutive years on a self-employed basis, if the beneficiary can prove that he has pursued the activity in question on an employed basis for at least five years; or
   (e) for five consecutive years in an executive position, of which at least three years involved technical duties and responsibility for at least one department of the company, if the beneficiary can prove that he has received, for the activity in question, previous training of at least three years' duration, as attested by a certificate recognised by the Member State or judged by a competent professional body to be fully valid.

2.   In cases (a) and (d), the activity must not have finished more than 10 years before the date on which the complete application was submitted by the person concerned to the competent authority referred to in Article 56.

3.   Paragraph 1(e) shall not apply to activities in Group ex 855, hairdressing establishments, of the ISIC Nomenclature.

Article 18 Activities referred to in list II of Annex IV

1.   For the activities in list II of Annex IV, the activity in question must have been previously pursued:

(a) for five consecutive years on a self-employed basis or as a manager of an undertaking, or

(b) for three consecutive years on a self-employed basis or as a manager of an undertaking, where the beneficiary proves that he has received previous training of at least three years for the activity in question, evidenced by a certificate recognised by the Member State or judged by a competent professional body to be fully valid, or

(c) for four consecutive years on a self-employed basis or as a manager of an undertaking, where the beneficiary can prove that he has received, for the activity in question, previous training of at least two years' duration, attested by a certificate recognised by the Member State or judged by a competent professional body to be fully valid, or

(d) for three consecutive years on a self-employed basis or as a manager of an undertaking, if the beneficiary can prove that he has pursued the activity in question on an employed basis for at least five years, or

(e) for five consecutive years on an employed basis, if the beneficiary can prove that he has received, for the activity in question, previous training of at least three years' duration, as attested by a certificate recognised by the Member State or judged by a competent professional body to be fully valid, or

(f) for six consecutive years on an employed basis, if the beneficiary can prove that he has received previous training in the activity in question of at least two years' duration, as attested by a certificate recognised by the Member State or judged by a competent professional body to be fully valid.

2.   In cases (a) and (d), the activity must not have finished more than 10 years before the date on which the complete application was submitted by the person concerned to the competent authority referred to in Article 56.

Article 19 Activities referred to in list III of Annex IV

1.   For the activities in list III of Annex IV, the activity in question must have been previously pursued:

(a) for three consecutive years, either on a self-employed basis or as a manager of an undertaking, or

(b) for two consecutive years, either on a self-employed basis or as a manager of an undertaking, if the beneficiary can prove that he has received previous training for the activity in question, as attested by a certificate recognised by the Member State or judged by a competent professional body to be fully valid, or

(c) for two consecutive years, either on a self-employed basis or as a manager of an undertaking, if the beneficiary can prove that he has pursued the activity in question on an employed basis for at least three years, or

(d) for three consecutive years, on an employed basis, if the beneficiary can prove that he has received previous training for the activity in question, as attested by a certificate recognised by the Member State or judged by a competent professional body to be fully valid.

2.   In cases (a) and (c), the activity must not have finished more than 10 years before the date on which the complete application was submitted by the person concerned to the competent authority referred to in Article 56.

Article 20 Adaptation of the lists of activities in Annex IV
The Commission may adapt the lists of activities in Annex IV which are the subject of recognition of professional experience pursuant to Article 16 with a view to updating or clarifying the nomenclature, provided that this does not involve any change in the activities related to the individual categories. Those measures, designed to amend non-essential elements of this Directive, shall be adopted in accordance with the regulatory procedure with scrutiny referred to in Article 58(3).

Chapter III RECOGNITION ON THE BASIS OF COORDINATION OF MINIMUM TRAINING CONDITIONS

SECTION 1 GENERAL PROVISIONS

Article 21 Principle of automatic recognition
1.   Each Member State shall recognise evidence of formal qualifications as doctor giving access to the professional activities of doctor with basic training and specialised doctor, as nurse responsible for general care, as dental practitioner, as specialised dental practitioner, as veterinary surgeon, as pharmacist and as architect, listed in Annex V, points 5.1.1, 5.1.2, 5.2.2, 5.3.2, 5.3.3, 5.4.2, 5.6.2 and 5.7.1 respectively, which satisfy the minimum training conditions referred to in Articles 24, 25, 31, 34, 35, 38, 44 and 46 respectively, and shall, for the purposes of access to and pursuit of the professional activities, give such evidence the same effect on its territory as the evidence of formal qualifications which it itself issues.

Such evidence of formal qualifications must be issued by the competent bodies in the Member States and accompanied, where appropriate, by the certificates listed in Annex V, points 5.1.1, 5.1.2, 5.2.2, 5.3.2, 5.3.3, 5.4.2, 5.6.2 and 5.7.1 respectively.

The provisions of the first and second subparagraphs do not affect the acquired rights referred to in Articles 23, 27, 33, 37, 39 and 49.

2.   Each Member State shall recognise, for the purpose of pursuing general medical practice in the framework of its national social security system, evidence of formal qualifications listed in Annex V, point 5.1.4 and issued to nationals of the Member States by the other Member States in accordance with the minimum training conditions laid down in Article 28.

The provisions of the previous subparagraph do not affect the acquired rights referred to in Article 30.

3.   Each Member State shall recognise evidence of formal qualifications as a midwife, awarded to nationals of Member States by the other Member States, listed in Annex V, point 5.5.2, which complies with the minimum training conditions referred to in Article 40 and satisfies the criteria set out in Article 41, and shall, for the purposes of access to and pursuit of the professional activities, give such evidence the same effect on its territory as the evidence of formal qualifications which it itself issues. This provision does not affect the acquired rights referred to in Articles 23 and 43.

4.   Member States shall not be obliged to give effect to evidence of formal qualifications referred to in Annex V, point 5.6.2, for the setting up of new pharmacies open to the public. For the purposes of this paragraph, pharmacies which have been open for less than three years shall also be considered as new pharmacies.

5.   Evidence of formal qualifications as an architect referred to in Annex V, point 5.7.1, which is subject to automatic recognition pursuant to paragraph 1, proves completion of a course of training which began not earlier than during the academic reference year referred to in that Annex.

6. Each Member State shall make access to and pursuit of the professional activities of doctors, nurses responsible for general care, dental practitioners, veterinary surgeons, midwives and pharmacists subject to possession of evidence of formal qualifications referred to in Annex V, points 5.1.1, 5.1.2, 5.1.4, 5.2.2, 5.3.2, 5.3.3, 5.4.2, 5.5.2 and 5.6.2 respectively, attesting that the person concerned has acquired, over the duration of his training, and where appropriate, the knowledge and skills referred to in Articles 24(3), 31(6), 34(3), 38(3), 40(3) and 44(3).

The Commission may adapt the knowledge and skills referred to in Articles 24(3), 31(6), 34(3), 38(3), 40(3) and 44(3) to scientific and technical progress. Those measures, designed to amend non-essential elements of this Directive, shall be adopted in accordance with the regulatory procedure with scrutiny referred to in Article 58(3).

Such updates shall not entail, for any Member State, an amendment of its existing legislative principles regarding the structure of professions as regards training and conditions of access by natural persons.

7. Each Member State shall notify the Commission of the legislative, regulatory and administrative provisions which it adopts with regard to the issuing of evidence of formal qualifications in the area covered by this Chapter. In addition, for evidence of formal qualifications in the area referred to in Section 8, this notification shall be addressed to the other Member States.

The Commission shall publish an appropriate communication in the *Official Journal of the European Union,* indicating the titles adopted by the Member States for evidence of formal qualifications and, where appropriate, the body which issues the evidence of formal qualifications, the certificate which accompanies it and the corresponding professional title referred to in Annex V, points 5.1.1, 5.1.2, 5.1.3, 5.1.4, 5.2.2, 5.3.2, 5.3.3, 5.4.2, 5.5.2, 5.6.2 and 5.7.1 respectively.

Article 22 Common provisions on training
With regard to the training referred to in Articles 24, 25, 28, 31, 34, 35, 38, 40, 44 and 46:
(a) Member States may authorise part-time training under conditions laid down by the competent authorities; those authorities shall ensure that the overall duration, level and quality of such training is not lower than that of continuous full-time training;

(b) in accordance with the procedures specific to each Member State, continuing education and training shall ensure that persons who have completed their studies are able to keep abreast of professional developments to the extent necessary to maintain safe and effective practice.

Article 23 Acquired rights
1. Without prejudice to the acquired rights specific to the professions concerned, in cases where the evidence of formal qualifications as doctor giving access to the professional activities of doctor with basic training and specialised doctor, as nurse responsible for general care, as dental practitioner, as specialised dental practitioner, as veterinary surgeon, as midwife and as pharmacist held by Member States nationals does not satisfy all the training requirements referred to in Articles 24, 25, 31, 34, 35, 38, 40 and 44, each Member State shall recognise as sufficient proof evidence of formal qualifications issued by those Member States insofar as such evidence attests successful completion of training which began before the reference dates laid down in Annex V, points 5.1.1, 5.1.2, 5.2.2, 5.3.2, 5.3.3, 5.4.2, 5.5.2 and 5.6.2 and is accompanied by a certificate stating that the holders have been effectively and lawfully engaged in the activities in question for at least three consecutive years during the five years preceding the award of the certificate.

2.   The same provisions shall apply to evidence of formal qualifications as doctor giving access to the professional activities of doctor with basic training and specialised doctor, as nurse responsible for general care, as dental practitioner, as specialised dental practitioner, as veterinary surgeon, as midwife and as pharmacist, obtained in the territory of the former German Democratic Republic, which does not satisfy all the minimum training requirements laid down in Articles 24, 25, 31, 34, 35, 38, 40 and 44 if such evidence certifies successful completion of training which began before:

(a) 3 October 1990 for doctors with basic training, nurses responsible for general care, dental practitioners with basic training, specialised dental practitioners, veterinary surgeons, midwives and pharmacists, and

(b) 3 April 1992 for specialised doctors.

The evidence of formal qualifications referred to in the first subparagraph confers on the holder the right to pursue professional activities throughout German territory under the same conditions as evidence of formal qualifications issued by the competent German authorities referred to in Annex V, points 5.1.1, 5.1.2, 5.2.2, 5.3.2, 5.3.3, 5.4.2, 5.5.2 and 5.6.2.

3.   Without prejudice to the provisions of Article 37(1), each Member State shall recognise evidence of formal qualifications as doctor giving access to the professional activities of doctor with basic training and specialised doctor, as nurse responsible for general care, as veterinary surgeon, as midwife, as pharmacist and as architect held by Member States nationals and issued by the former Czechoslovakia, or whose training commenced, for the Czech Republic and Slovakia, before 1 January 1993, where the authorities of either of the two aforementioned Member States attest that such evidence of formal qualifications has the same legal validity within their territory as the evidence of formal qualifications which they issue and, with respect to architects, as the evidence of formal qualifications specified for those Member States in Annex VI, point 6, as regards access to the professional activities of doctor with basic training, specialised doctor, nurse responsible for general care, veterinary surgeon, midwife, pharmacist with respect to the activities referred to in Article 45(2), and architect with respect to the activities referred to in Article 48, and the pursuit of such activities.

Such an attestation must be accompanied by a certificate issued by those same authorities stating that such persons have effectively and lawfully been engaged in the activities in question within their territory for at least three consecutive years during the five years prior to the date of issue of the certificate.

4.   Each Member State shall recognise evidence of formal qualifications as doctor giving access to the professional activities of doctor with basic training and specialised doctor, as nurse responsible for general care, as dental practitioner, as specialised dental practitioner, as veterinary surgeon, as midwife, as pharmacist and as architect held by nationals of the Member States and issued by the former Soviet Union, or whose training commenced

(a) for Estonia, before 20 August 1991,

(b) for Latvia, before 21 August 1991,

(c) for Lithuania, before 11 March 1990,

where the authorities of any of the three aforementioned Member States attest that such evidence has the same legal validity within their territory as the evidence which they issue and, with respect to architects, as the evidence of formal qualifications specified for those Member States in Annex VI, point 6, as regards access to the professional activities of doctor with basic training, specialised doctor, nurse responsible for general care, dental practitioner, specialised dental practitioner, veterinary surgeon, midwife, pharmacist with respect to the activities referred to in Article 45(2), and architect with respect to the activities referred to in Article 48, and the pursuit of such activities.

Such an attestation must be accompanied by a certificate issued by those same authorities stating that such persons have effectively and lawfully been engaged in the activities in question within their territory for at least three consecutive years during the five years prior to the date of issue of the certificate.

With regard to evidence of formal qualifications as veterinary surgeons issued by the former Soviet Union or in respect of which training commenced, for Estonia, before 20 August 1991, the attestation referred to in the preceding subparagraph must be accompanied by a certificate issued by the Estonian authorities stating that such persons have effectively and lawfully been engaged in the activities in question within their territory for at least five consecutive years during the seven years prior to the date of issue of the certificate.

5.   Each Member State shall recognise evidence of formal qualifications as doctor giving access to the professional activities of doctor with basic training and specialised doctor, as nurse responsible for general care, as dental practitioner, as specialised dental practitioner, as veterinary surgeon, as midwife, as pharmacist and as architect held by nationals of the Member States and issued by the former Yugoslavia, or whose training commenced, for Slovenia, before 25 June 1991, where the authorities of the aforementioned Member State attest that such evidence has the same legal validity within their territory as the evidence which they issue and, with respect to architects, as the evidence of formal qualifications specified for those Member States in Annex VI, point 6, as regards access to the professional activities of doctor with basic training, specialised doctor, nurse responsible for general care, dental practitioner, specialised dental practitioner, veterinary surgeon, midwife, pharmacist with respect to the activities referred to in Article 45(2), and architect with respect to the activities referred to in Article 48, and the pursuit of such activities.

Such an attestation must be accompanied by a certificate issued by those same authorities stating that such persons have effectively and lawfully been engaged in the activities in question within their territory for at least three consecutive years during the five years prior to the date of issue of the certificate.

6.   Each Member State shall recognise as sufficient proof for Member State nationals whose evidence of formal qualifications as a doctor, nurse responsible for general care, dental practitioner, veterinary surgeon, midwife and pharmacist does not correspond to the titles given for that Member State in Annex V, points 5.1.1, 5.1.2, 5.1.3, 5.1.4, 5.2.2, 5.3.2, 5.3.3, 5.4.2, 5.5.2 and 5.6.2, evidence of formal qualifications issued by those Member States accompanied by a certificate issued by the competent authorities or bodies.

The certificate referred to in the first subparagraph shall state that the evidence of formal qualifications certifies successful completion of training in accordance with Articles 24, 25, 28, 31, 34, 35, 38, 40 and 44 respectively and is treated by the Member State which issued it in the same way as the qualifications whose titles are listed in Annex V, points 5.1.1, 5.1.2, 5.1.3, 5.1.4, 5.2.2, 5.3.2, 5.3.3, 5.4.2, 5.5.2 and 5.6.2.

Article 23a Specific circumstances

1.   By way of derogation from the present Directive, Bulgaria may authorise the holders of the qualification of фелдшер' (feldsher) awarded in Bulgaria before 31 December 1999 and exercising this profession under the Bulgarian national social security scheme on 1 January 2000 to continue to exercise the said profession, even if parts of their activity fall under the provisions of the present Directive concerning doctors of medicine and nurses responsible for general care respectively.

2.   The holders of the Bulgarian qualification of 'фелдшер' (feldsher) referred to in paragraph 1 are not entitled to obtain professional recognition in other Member States as doctors of medicine nor as nurses responsible for general care under this Directive.

SECTION 2 DOCTORS OF MEDICINE

Article 24 Basic medical training
1.   Admission to basic medical training shall be contingent upon possession of a diploma or certificate providing access, for the studies in question, to universities.

2.   Basic medical training shall comprise a total of at least six years of study or 5500 hours of theoretical and practical training provided by, or under the supervision of, a university.

   For persons who began their studies before 1 January 1972, the course of training referred to in the first subparagraph may comprise six months of full-time practical training at university level under the supervision of the competent authorities.

3.   Basic medical training shall provide an assurance that the person in question has acquired the following knowledge and skills:
   (a) adequate knowledge of the sciences on which medicine is based and a good understanding of the scientific methods including the principles of measuring biological functions, the evaluation of scientifically established facts and the analysis of data;
   (b) sufficient understanding of the structure, functions and behaviour of healthy and sick persons, as well as relations between the state of health and physical and social surroundings of the human being;
   (c) adequate knowledge of clinical disciplines and practices, providing him with a coherent picture of mental and physical diseases, of medicine from the points of view of prophylaxis, diagnosis and therapy and of human reproduction;
   (d) suitable clinical experience in hospitals under appropriate supervision.

Article 25 Specialist medical training
1.   Admission to specialist medical training shall be contingent upon completion and validation of six years of study as part of a training programme referred to in Article 24 in the course of which the trainee has acquired the relevant knowledge of basic medicine.

2.   Specialist medical training shall comprise theoretical and practical training at a university or medical teaching hospital or, where appropriate, a medical care establishment approved for that purpose by the competent authorities or bodies.

   The Member States shall ensure that the minimum duration of specialist medical training courses referred to in Annex V, point 5.1.3 is not less than the duration provided for in that point. Training shall be given under the supervision of the competent authorities or bodies. It shall include personal participation of the trainee specialised doctor in the activity and responsibilities entailed by the services in question.

3.   Training shall be given on a full-time basis at specific establishments which are recognised by the competent authorities. It shall entail participation in the full range of medical activities of the department where the training is given, including duty on call, in such a way that the trainee specialist devotes all his professional activity to his practical and theoretical training throughout the entire working week and throughout the year, in accordance with the procedures laid down by the competent authorities. Accordingly, these posts shall be the subject of appropriate remuneration.

4.   The Member States shall make the issuance of evidence of specialist medical training contingent upon possession of evidence of basic medical training referred to in Annex V, point 5.1.1.

5.   The Commission may adapt the minimum periods of training referred to in Annex V, point 5.1.3, to scientific and technical progress. Those measures, designed to amend

non-essential elements of this Directive, shall be adopted in accordance with the regulatory procedure with scrutiny referred to in Article 58(3).

Article 26 Types of specialist medical training

Evidence of formal qualifications as a specialised doctor referred to in Article 21 is such evidence awarded by the competent authorities or bodies referred to in Annex V, point 5.1.2 as corresponds, for the specialised training in question, to the titles in use in the various Member States and referred to in Annex V, point 5.1.3.

The Commission may include in Annex V, point 5.1.3, new medical specialties common to at least two-fifths of the Member States with a view to updating this Directive in the light of changes in national legislation. That measure, designed to amend non-essential elements of this Directive, shall be adopted in accordance with the regulatory procedure with scrutiny referred to in Article 58(3).

Article 27 Acquired rights specific to specialised doctors

1. A host Member State may require of specialised doctors whose part-time specialist medical training was governed by legislative, regulatory and administrative provisions in force as of 20 June 1975 and who began their specialist training no later than 31 December 1983 that their evidence of formal qualifications be accompanied by a certificate stating that they have been effectively and lawfully engaged in the relevant activities for at least three consecutive years during the five years preceding the award of that certificate.

2. Every Member State shall recognise the qualification of specialised doctors awarded in Spain to doctors who completed their specialist training before 1 January 1995, even if that training does not satisfy the minimum training requirements provided for in Article 25, in so far as that qualification is accompanied by a certificate issued by the competent Spanish authorities and attesting that the person concerned has passed the examination in specific professional competence held in the context of exceptional measures concerning recognition laid down in Royal Decree 1497/99, with a view to ascertaining that the person concerned possesses a level of knowledge and skill comparable to that of doctors who possess a qualification as a specialised doctor defined for Spain in Annex V, points 5.1.2 and 5.1.3.

3. Every Member State which has repealed its legislative, regulatory or administrative provisions relating to the award of evidence of formal qualifications as a specialised doctor referred to in Annex V, points 5.1.2 and 5.1.3 and which has adopted measures relating to acquired rights benefiting its nationals, shall grant nationals of other Member States the right to benefit from those measures, in so far as such evidence of formal qualifications was issued before the date on which the host Member State ceased to issue such evidence for the specialty in question.

   The dates on which these provisions were repealed are set out in Annex V, point 5.1.3.

Article 28 Specific training in general medical practice

1. Admission to specific training in general medical practice shall be contingent on the completion and validation of six years of study as part of a training programme referred to in Article 24.

2. The specific training in general medical practice leading to the award of evidence of formal qualifications issued before 1 January 2006 shall be of a duration of at least two years on a full-time basis. In the case of evidence of formal qualifications issued after that date, the training shall be of a duration of at least three years on a full-time basis.

Where the training programme referred to in Article 24 comprises practical training given by an approved hospital possessing appropriate general medical equipment and services or as part of an approved general medical practice or an approved centre in which doctors provide primary medical care, the duration of that practical training may, up to a maximum of one year, be included in the duration provided for in the first subparagraph for certificates of training issued on or after 1 January 2006.

The option provided for in the second subparagraph shall be available only for Member States in which the specific training in general medical practice lasted two years as of 1 January 2001.

3.   The specific training in general medical practice shall be carried out on a full-time basis, under the supervision of the competent authorities or bodies. It shall be more practical than theoretical.

The practical training shall be given, on the one hand, for at least six months in an approved hospital possessing appropriate equipment and services and, on the other hand, for at least six months as part of an approved general medical practice or an approved centre at which doctors provide primary health care.

The practical training shall take place in conjunction with other health establishments or structures concerned with general medicine. Without prejudice to the minimum periods laid down in the second subparagraph, however, the practical training may be given during a period of not more than six months in other approved establishments or health structures concerned with general medicine.

The training shall require the personal participation of the trainee in the professional activity and responsibilities of the persons with whom he is working.

4.   Member States shall make the issuance of evidence of formal qualifications in general medical practice subject to possession of evidence of formal qualifications in basic medical training referred to in Annex V, point 5.1.1.

5.   Member States may issue evidence of formal qualifications referred to in Annex V, point 5.1.4 to a doctor who has not completed the training provided for in this Article but who has completed a different, supplementary training, as attested by evidence of formal qualifications issued by the competent authorities in a Member State. They may not, however, award evidence of formal qualifications unless it attests knowledge of a level qualitatively equivalent to the knowledge acquired from the training provided for in this Article.

Member States shall determine, inter alia, the extent to which the complementary training and professional experience already acquired by the applicant may replace the training provided for in this Article.

The Member States may only issue the evidence of formal qualifications referred to in Annex V, point 5.1.4 if the applicant has acquired at least six months' experience of general medicine in a general medical practice or a centre in which doctors provide primary health care of the types referred to in paragraph 3.

Article 29 Pursuit of the professional activities of general practitioners
Each Member State shall, subject to the provisions relating to acquired rights, make the pursuit of the activities of a general practitioner in the framework of its national social security system contingent upon possession of evidence of formal qualifications referred to in Annex V, point 5.1.4.

Member States may exempt persons who are currently undergoing specific training in general medicine from this condition.

Article 30 Acquired rights specific to general practitioners

1. Each Member State shall determine the acquired rights. It shall, however, confer as an acquired right the right to pursue the activities of a general practitioner in the framework of its national social security system, without the evidence of formal qualifications referred to in Annex V, point 5.1.4, on all doctors who enjoy this right as of the reference date stated in that point by virtue of provisions applicable to the medical profession giving access to the professional activities of doctor with basic training and who are established as of that date on its territory, having benefited from the provisions of Articles 21 or 23.

    The competent authorities of each Member State shall, on demand, issue a certificate stating the holder's right to pursue the activities of general practitioner in the framework of their national social security systems, without the evidence of formal qualifications referred to in Annex V, point 5.1.4, to doctors who enjoy acquired rights pursuant to the first subparagraph.

2. Every Member State shall recognise the certificates referred to in paragraph 1, second subparagraph, awarded to nationals of Member States by the other Member States, and shall give such certificates the same effect on its territory as evidence of formal qualifications which it awards and which permit the pursuit of the activities of a general practitioner in the framework of its national social security system.

SECTION 3 NURSES RESPONSIBLE FOR GENERAL CARE

Article 31 Training of nurses responsible for general care

1. Admission to training for nurses responsible for general care shall be contingent upon completion of general education of 10 years, as attested by a diploma, certificate or other evidence issued by the competent authorities or bodies in a Member State or by a certificate attesting success in an examination, of an equivalent level, for admission to a school of nursing.

2. Training of nurses responsible for general care shall be given on a full-time basis and shall include at least the programme described in Annex V, point 5.2.1.

    The Commission may adapt the content listed in Annex V, point 5.2.1, to scientific and technical progress. That measure, designed to amend non-essential elements of this Directive, shall be adopted in accordance with the regulatory procedure with scrutiny referred to in Article 58(3).

    Such updates may not entail, for any Member State, any amendment of its existing legislative principles relating to the structure of professions as regards training and the conditions of access by natural persons.

3. The training of nurses responsible for general care shall comprise at least three years of study or 4600 hours of theoretical and clinical training, the duration of the theoretical training representing at least one-third and the duration of the clinical training at least one half of the minimum duration of the training. Member States may grant partial exemptions to persons who have received part of their training on courses which are of at least an equivalent level.

    The Member States shall ensure that institutions providing nursing training are responsible for the coordination of theoretical and clinical training throughout the entire study programme.

4. Theoretical training is that part of nurse training from which trainee nurses acquire the professional knowledge, insights and skills necessary for organising, dispensing and

evaluating overall health care. The training shall be given by teachers of nursing care and by other competent persons, in nursing schools and other training establishments selected by the training institution.

5. Clinical training is that part of nurse training in which trainee nurses learn, as part of a team and in direct contact with a healthy or sick individual and/or community, to organise, dispense and evaluate the required comprehensive nursing care, on the basis of the knowledge and skills which they have acquired. The trainee nurse shall learn not only how to work in a team, but also how to lead a team and organise overall nursing care, including health education for individuals and small groups, within the health institute or in the community.

This training shall take place in hospitals and other health institutions and in the community, under the responsibility of nursing teachers, in cooperation with and assisted by other qualified nurses. Other qualified personnel may also take part in the teaching process.

Trainee nurses shall participate in the activities of the department in question insofar as those activities are appropriate to their training, enabling them to learn to assume the responsibilities involved in nursing care.

6. Training for nurses responsible for general care shall provide an assurance that the person in question has acquired the following knowledge and skills:
(a) adequate knowledge of the sciences on which general nursing is based, including sufficient understanding of the structure, physiological functions and behaviour of healthy and sick persons, and of the relationship between the state of health and the physical and social environment of the human being;
(b) sufficient knowledge of the nature and ethics of the profession and of the general principles of health and nursing;
(c) adequate clinical experience; such experience, which should be selected for its training value, should be gained under the supervision of qualified nursing staff and in places where the number of qualified staff and equipment are appropriate for the nursing care of the patient;
(d) the ability to participate in the practical training of health personnel and experience of working with such personnel;
(e) experience of working with members of other professions in the health sector.

Article 32 Pursuit of the professional activities of nurses responsible for general care
For the purposes of this Directive, the professional activities of nurses responsible for general care are the activities pursued on a professional basis and referred to in Annex V, point 5.2.2.

Article 33 Acquired rights specific to nurses responsible for general care
1. Where the general rules of acquired rights apply to nurses responsible for general care, the activities referred to in Article 23 must have included full responsibility for the planning, organisation and administration of nursing care delivered to the patient.

2. As regards the Polish qualification of nurse responsible for general care, only the following acquired rights provisions shall apply. In the case of nationals of the Member States whose evidence of formal qualifications as nurse responsible for general care was awarded by, or whose training started in, Poland before 1 May 2004 and who do not satisfy the minimum training requirements laid down in Article 31, Member States shall recognise the following evidence of formal qualifications as nurse responsible for general care as being sufficient proof if accompanied by a certificate stating that those Member State nationals have effectively and lawfully been engaged in the activities of a nurse responsible for general care in Poland for the period specified below:

(a) evidence of formal qualifications as a nurse at degree level (dyplom licencjata
     pielealegniarstwa) — at least three consecutive years during the five years prior to
     the date of issue of the certificate,

(b) evidence of formal qualifications as a nurse certifying completion of post-secondary
     education obtained from a medical vocational school (dyplom pielealegniarki albo
     pielealegniarki dyplomowanej) — at least five consecutive years during the seven
     years prior to the date of issue of the certificate.

The said activities must have included taking full responsibility for the planning,
organisation and administration of nursing care delivered to the patient.

3.   Member States shall recognise evidence of formal qualifications in nursing awarded in
      Poland, to nurses who completed training before 1 May 2004, which did not comply with
      the minimum training requirements laid down in Article 31, attested by the diploma
      "bachelor" which has been obtained on the basis of a special upgrading programme
      contained in Article 11 of the Act of 20 April 2004 on the amendment of the Act on
      professions of nurse and midwife and on some other legal acts (Official Journal of the
      Republic of Poland of 30 April 2004 No 92, pos. 885), and the Regulation of the Minister
      of Health of 11 May 2004 on the detailed conditions of delivering studies for nurses and
      midwives, who hold a certificate of secondary school (final examination — matura) and
      are graduates of medical lyceum and medical vocational schools teaching in a profession
      of a nurse and a midwife (Official Journal of the Republic of Poland of 13 May 2004 No
      110, pos. 1170), with the aim of verifying that the person concerned has a level of
      knowledge and competence comparable to that of nurses holding the qualifications which,
      in the case of Poland, are defined in Annex V, point 5.2.2.

Article 33(a)

As regards the Romanian qualification of nurse responsible for general care, only the following
acquired rights provisions will apply:

In the case of nationals of the Member States whose evidence of formal qualifications as nurse
responsible for general care were awarded by, or whose training started in, Romania before the
date of accession and which does not satisfy the minimum training requirements laid down in
Article 31, Member States shall recognise the evidence of formal qualification as nurse
responsible for general care (*Certificat de competence profesionale de asistent medical
generalist*) with postsecondary education obtained from a *scoală postliceală*, as being sufficient
proof if accompanied by a certificate stating that those Member State nationals have effectively
and lawfully been engaged in the activities of a nurse responsible for general care in Romania
for a period of at least five consecutive years during the seven years prior to the date of issue of
the certificate.

The said activities must have included taking full responsibility for the planning, organisation
and carrying out of the nursing care of the patient.

SECTION 4 DENTAL PRACTITIONERS

Article 34 Basic dental training

1.   Admission to basic dental training presupposes possession of a diploma or certificate
      giving access, for the studies in question, to universities or higher institutes of a level
      recognised as equivalent, in a Member State.

2.   Basic dental training shall comprise a total of at least five years of full-time theoretical and
      practical study, comprising at least the programme described in Annex V, point 5.3.1 and
      given in a university, in a higher institute providing training recognised as being of an
      equivalent level or under the supervision of a university.

The Commission may adapt the content listed in Annex V, point 5.3.1, to scientific and technical progress. That measure, designed to amend non-essential elements of this Directive, shall be adopted in accordance with the regulatory procedure with scrutiny referred to in Article 58(3).

Such updates may not entail, for any Member State, any amendment of its existing legislative principles relating to the system of professions as regards training and the conditions of access by natural persons.

3. Basic dental training shall provide an assurance that the person in question has acquired the following knowledge and skills:
    (a) adequate knowledge of the sciences on which dentistry is based and a good understanding of scientific methods, including the principles of measuring biological functions, the evaluation of scientifically established facts and the analysis of data;
    (b) adequate knowledge of the constitution, physiology and behaviour of healthy and sick persons as well as the influence of the natural and social environment on the state of health of the human being, in so far as these factors affect dentistry;
    (c) adequate knowledge of the structure and function of the teeth, mouth, jaws and associated tissues, both healthy and diseased, and their relationship to the general state of health and to the physical and social well-being of the patient;
    (d) adequate knowledge of clinical disciplines and methods, providing the dentist with a coherent picture of anomalies, lesions and diseases of the teeth, mouth, jaws and associated tissues and of preventive, diagnostic and therapeutic dentistry;
    (e) suitable clinical experience under appropriate supervision.
    This training shall provide him with the skills necessary for carrying out all activities involving the prevention, diagnosis and treatment of anomalies and diseases of the teeth, mouth, jaws and associated tissues.

Article 35 Specialist dental training

1. Admission to specialist dental training shall entail the completion and validation of five years of theoretical and practical instruction within the framework of the training referred to in Article 34, or possession of the documents referred to in Articles 23 and 37.

2. Specialist dental training shall comprise theoretical and practical instruction in a university centre, in a treatment teaching and research centre or, where appropriate, in a health establishment approved for that purpose by the competent authorities or bodies.

    Full-time specialist dental courses shall be of a minimum of three years' duration supervised by the competent authorities or bodies. It shall involve the personal participation of the dental practitioner training to be a specialist in the activity and in the responsibilities of the establishment concerned.

    The Commission may adapt the minimum period of training referred to in the second subparagraph to scientific and technical progress. That measure, designed to amend non-essential elements of this Directive, shall be adopted in accordance with the regulatory procedure with scrutiny referred to in Article 58(3).

3. The Member States shall make the issuance of evidence of specialist dental training contingent upon possession of evidence of basic dental training referred to in Annex V, point 5.3.2.

Article 36 Pursuit of the professional activities of dental practitioners

1. For the purposes of this Directive, the professional activities of dental practitioners are the activities defined in paragraph 3 and pursued under the professional qualifications listed in Annex V, point 5.3.2.

2. The profession of dental practitioner shall be based on dental training referred to in Article 34 and shall constitute a specific profession which is distinct from other general or specialised medical professions. Pursuit of the activities of a dental practitioner requires the possession of evidence of formal qualifications referred to in Annex V, point 5.3.2. Holders of such evidence of formal qualifications shall be treated in the same way as those to whom Articles 23 or 37 apply.

3. The Member States shall ensure that dental practitioners are generally able to gain access to and pursue the activities of prevention, diagnosis and treatment of anomalies and diseases affecting the teeth, mouth, jaws and adjoining tissue, having due regard to the regulatory provisions and rules of professional ethics on the reference dates referred to in Annex V, point 5.3.2.

Article 37 Acquired rights specific to dental practitioners

1. Every Member State shall, for the purposes of the pursuit of the professional activities of dental practitioners under the qualifications listed in Annex V, point 5.3.2, recognise evidence of formal qualifications as a doctor issued in Italy, Spain, Austria, the Czech Republic, Slovakia and Romania to persons who began their medical training on or before the reference date stated in that Annex for the Member State concerned, accompanied by a certificate issued by the competent authorities of that Member State.

   The certificate must show that the two following conditions are met:
   (a) that the persons in question have been effectively, lawfully and principally engaged in that Member State in the activities referred to in Article 36 for at least three consecutive years during the five years preceding the award of the certificate;
   (b) that those persons are authorised to pursue the said activities under the same conditions as holders of evidence of formal qualifications listed for that Member State in Annex V, point 5.3.2.
   Persons who have successfully completed at least three years of study, certified by the competent authorities in the Member State concerned as being equivalent to the training referred to in Article 34, shall be exempt from the three-year practical work experience referred to in the second subparagraph, point (a).

   With regard to the Czech Republic and Slovakia, evidence of formal qualifications obtained in the former Czechoslovakia shall be accorded the same level of recognition as Czech and Slovak evidence of formal qualifications and under the same conditions as set out in the preceding subparagraphs.

2. Each Member State shall recognise evidence of formal qualifications as a doctor issued in Italy to persons who began their university medical training after 28 January 1980 and no later than 31 December 1984, accompanied by a certificate issued by the competent Italian authorities.

   The certificate must show that the three following conditions are met:
   (a) that the persons in question passed the relevant aptitude test held by the competent Italian authorities with a view to establishing that those persons possess a level of knowledge and skills comparable to that of persons possessing evidence of formal qualifications listed for Italy in Annex V, point 5.3.2;
   (b) that they have been effectively, lawfully and principally engaged in the activities referred to in Article 36 in Italy for at least three consecutive years during the five years preceding the award of the certificate;
   (c) that they are authorised to engage in or are effectively, lawfully and principally engaged in the activities referred to in Article 36, under the same conditions as the holders of evidence of formal qualifications listed for Italy in Annex V, point 5.3.2.

Persons who have successfully completed at least three years of study certified by the competent authorities as being equivalent to the training referred to in Article 34 shall be exempt from the aptitude test referred to in the second subparagraph, point (a).

Persons who began their university medical training after 31 December 1984 shall be treated in the same way as those referred to above, provided that the abovementioned three years of study began before 31 December 1994.

SECTION 5 VETERINARY SURGEONS

Article 38 The training of veterinary surgeons
1. The training of veterinary surgeons shall comprise a total of at least five years of full-time theoretical and practical study at a university or at a higher institute providing training recognised as being of an equivalent level, or under the supervision of a university, covering at least the study programme referred to in Annex V, point 5.4.1.

   The Commission may adapt the content listed in Annex V, point 5.4.1, to scientific and technical progress. That measure, designed to amend non-essential elements of this Directive, shall be adopted in accordance with the regulatory procedure with scrutiny referred to in Article 58(3).

   Such updates may not entail, for any Member State, any amendment of its existing legislative principles relating to the structure of professions as regards training and conditions of access by natural persons.

2. Admission to veterinary training shall be contingent upon possession of a diploma or certificate entitling the holder to enter, for the studies in question, university establishments or institutes of higher education recognised by a Member State to be of an equivalent level for the purpose of the relevant study.

3. Training as a veterinary surgeon shall provide an assurance that the person in question has acquired the following knowledge and skills:
   (a) adequate knowledge of the sciences on which the activities of the veterinary surgeon are based;
   (b) adequate knowledge of the structure and functions of healthy animals, of their husbandry, reproduction and hygiene in general, as well as their feeding, including the technology involved in the manufacture and preservation of foods corresponding to their needs;
   (c) adequate knowledge of the behaviour and protection of animals;
   (d) adequate knowledge of the causes, nature, course, effects, diagnosis and treatment of the diseases of animals, whether considered individually or in groups, including a special knowledge of the diseases which may be transmitted to humans;
   (e) adequate knowledge of preventive medicine;
   (f) adequate knowledge of the hygiene and technology involved in the production, manufacture and putting into circulation of animal foodstuffs or foodstuffs of animal origin intended for human consumption;
   (g) adequate knowledge of the laws, regulations and administrative provisions relating to the subjects listed above;
   (h) adequate clinical and other practical experience under appropriate supervision.

Article 39 Acquired rights specific to veterinary surgeons
Without prejudice to Article 23(4), with regard to nationals of Member States whose evidence of formal qualifications as a veterinary surgeon was issued by, or whose training commenced in, Estonia before 1 May 2004, Member States shall recognise such evidence of formal

qualifications as a veterinary surgeon if it is accompanied by a certificate stating that such persons have effectively and lawfully been engaged in the activities in question in Estonia for at least five consecutive years during the seven years prior to the date of issue of the certificate.

SECTION 6 MIDWIVES

Article 40 The training of midwives

1.   The training of midwives shall comprise a total of at least:
   (a) specific full-time training as a midwife comprising at least three years of theoretical and practical study (route I) comprising at least the programme described in Annex V, point 5.5.1, or
   (b) specific full-time training as a midwife of 18 months' duration (route II), comprising at least the study programme described in Annex V, point 5.5.1, which was not the subject of equivalent training of nurses responsible for general care.
   The Member States shall ensure that institutions providing midwife training are responsible for coordinating theory and practice throughout the programme of study.

   The Commission may adapt the content listed in Annex V, point 5.5.1, to scientific and technical progress. That measure, designed to amend non-essential elements of this Directive, shall be adopted in accordance with the regulatory procedure with scrutiny referred to in Article 58(3).

   Such updates must not entail, for any Member State, any amendment of existing legislative principles relating to the structure of professions as regards training and the conditions of access by natural persons.

2.   Access to training as a midwife shall be contingent upon one of the following conditions:
   (a) completion of at least the first 10 years of general school education for route I, or
   (b) possession of evidence of formal qualifications as a nurse responsible for general care referred to in Annex V, point 5.2.2 for route II.

3.   Training as a midwife shall provide an assurance that the person in question has acquired the following knowledge and skills:
   (a) adequate knowledge of the sciences on which the activities of midwives are based, particularly obstetrics and gynaecology;
   (b) adequate knowledge of the ethics of the profession and the professional legislation;
   (c) detailed knowledge of biological functions, anatomy and physiology in the field of obstetrics and of the newly born, and also a knowledge of the relationship between the state of health and the physical and social environment of the human being, and of his behaviour;
   (d) adequate clinical experience gained in approved institutions under the supervision of staff qualified in midwifery and obstetrics;
   (e) adequate understanding of the training of health personnel and experience of working with such.

Article 41 Procedures for the recognition of evidence of formal qualifications as a midwife

1.   The evidence of formal qualifications as a midwife referred to in Annex V, point 5.5.2 shall be subject to automatic recognition pursuant to Article 21 in so far as they satisfy one of the following criteria:
   (a) full-time training of at least three years as a midwife:
      (i) either made contingent upon possession of a diploma, certificate or other evidence of qualification giving access to universities or higher education institutes, or otherwise guaranteeing an equivalent level of knowledge; or

(ii) followed by two years of professional practice for which a certificate has been issued in accordance with paragraph 2;

(b) full-time training as a midwife of at least two years or 3600 hours, contingent upon possession of evidence of formal qualifications as a nurse responsible for general care referred to in Annex V, point 5.2.2;

(c) full-time training as a midwife of at least 18 months or 3000 hours, contingent upon possession of evidence of formal qualifications as a nurse responsible for general care referred to in Annex V, point 5.2.2 and followed by one year's professional practice for which a certificate has been issued in accordance with paragraph 2.

2. The certificate referred to in paragraph 1 shall be issued by the competent authorities in the home Member State. It shall certify that the holder, after obtaining evidence of formal qualifications as a midwife, has satisfactorily pursued all the activities of a midwife for a corresponding period in a hospital or a health care establishment approved for that purpose.

Article 42 Pursuit of the professional activities of a midwife

1. The provisions of this section shall apply to the activities of midwives as defined by each Member State, without prejudice to paragraph 2, and pursued under the professional titles set out in Annex V, point 5.5.2.

2. The Member States shall ensure that midwives are able to gain access to and pursue at least the following activities:

(a) provision of sound family planning information and advice;

(b) diagnosis of pregnancies and monitoring normal pregnancies; carrying out the examinations necessary for the monitoring of the development of normal pregnancies;

(c) prescribing or advising on the examinations necessary for the earliest possible diagnosis of pregnancies at risk;

(d) provision of programmes of parenthood preparation and complete preparation for childbirth including advice on hygiene and nutrition;

(e) caring for and assisting the mother during labour and monitoring the condition of the foetus in utero by the appropriate clinical and technical means;

(f) conducting spontaneous deliveries including where required episiotomies and in urgent cases breech deliveries;

(g) recognising the warning signs of abnormality in the mother or infant which necessitate referral to a doctor and assisting the latter where appropriate; taking the necessary emergency measures in the doctor's absence, in particular the manual removal of the placenta, possibly followed by manual examination of the uterus;

(h) examining and caring for the new-born infant; taking all initiatives which are necessary in case of need and carrying out where necessary immediate resuscitation;

(i) caring for and monitoring the progress of the mother in the post-natal period and giving all necessary advice to the mother on infant care to enable her to ensure the optimum progress of the new-born infant;

(j) carrying out treatment prescribed by doctors;

(k) drawing up the necessary written reports.

Article 43 Acquired rights specific to midwives

1. Every Member State shall, in the case of Member State nationals whose evidence of formal qualifications as a midwife satisfies all the minimum training requirements laid down in Article 40 but, by virtue of Article 41, is not recognised unless it is accompanied by a certificate of professional practice referred to in Article 41(2), recognise as sufficient proof evidence of formal qualifications issued by those Member States before the reference date referred to in Annex V, point 5.5.2, accompanied by a certificate stating that those

nationals have been effectively and lawfully engaged in the activities in question for at least two consecutive years during the five years preceding the award of the certificate.

2.   The conditions laid down in paragraph 1 shall apply to the nationals of Member States whose evidence of formal qualifications as a midwife certifies completion of training received in the territory of the former German Democratic Republic and satisfying all the minimum training requirements laid down in Article 40 but where the evidence of formal qualifications, by virtue of Article 41, is not recognised unless it is accompanied by the certificate of professional experience referred to in Article 41(2), where it attests a course of training which began before 3 October 1990.

3.   As regards the Polish evidence of formal qualifications as a midwife, only the following acquired rights provisions shall apply.

In the case of Member States nationals whose evidence of formal qualifications as a midwife was awarded by, or whose training commenced in, Poland before 1 May 2004, and who do not satisfy the minimum training requirements as set out in Article 40, Member States shall recognise the following evidence of formal qualifications as a midwife if accompanied by a certificate stating that such persons have effectively and lawfully been engaged in the activities of a midwife for the period specified below:
(a) evidence of formal qualifications as a midwife at degree level (dyplom licencjata położ.nictwa): at least three consecutive years during the five years prior to the date of issue of the certificate,
(b) evidence of formal qualifications as a midwife certifying completion of post-secondary education obtained from a medical vocational school (dyplom położ.nej): at least five consecutive years during the seven years prior to the date of issue of the certificate.

4.   Member States shall recognise evidence of formal qualifications in midwifery awarded in Poland, to midwives who completed training before 1 May 2004, which did not comply with the minimum training requirements laid down in Article 40, attested by the diploma "bachelor" which has been obtained on the basis of a special upgrading programme contained in Article 11 of the Act of 20 April 2004 on the amendment of the Act on professions of nurse and midwife and on some other legal acts (Official Journal of the Republic of Poland of 30 April 2004 No 92, pos. 885), and the Regulation of the Minister of Health of 11 May 2004 on the detailed conditions of delivering studies for nurses and midwives, who hold a certificate of secondary school (final examination — matura) and are graduates of medical lyceum and medical vocational schools teaching in a profession of a nurse and a midwife (Official Journal of the Republic of Poland of 13 May 2004 No 110, pos 1170), with the aim of verifying that the person concerned has a level of knowledge and competence comparable to that of midwives holding the qualifications which, in the case of Poland, are defined in Annex V, point 5.5.2.

Article 43(a)
As regards the Romanian qualifications in midwifery, only the following acquired rights provisions will apply:

In the case of nationals of the Member States whose evidence of formal qualifications as a midwife (asistent medical obstetrica?-ginecologie/obstetrics-gynecology nurse) were awarded by Romania before the date of accession and which do not satisfy the minimum training requirements laid down in Article 40, Member States shall recognise the said evidence of formal qualifications as being sufficient proof for the purposes of carrying out the activities of midwife, if they are accompanied by a certificate stating that those Member State nationals have effectively and lawfully been engaged in the activities of midwife in Romania, for at least five consecutive years during the seven years prior to the issue of the certificate.

SECTION 7 PHARMACIST

Article 44 Training as a pharmacist

1. Admission to a course of training as a pharmacist shall be contingent upon possession of a diploma or certificate giving access, in a Member State, to the studies in question, at universities or higher institutes of a level recognised as equivalent.

2. Evidence of formal qualifications as a pharmacist shall attest to training of at least five years' duration, including at least:
    (a) four years of full-time theoretical and practical training at a university or at a higher institute of a level recognised as equivalent, or under the supervision of a university;
    (b) six-month traineeship in a pharmacy which is open to the public or in a hospital, under the supervision of that hospital's pharmaceutical department.
    That training cycle shall include at least the programme described in Annex V, point 5.6.1. The Commission may adapt the content listed in Annex V, point 5.6.1, to scientific and technical progress. That measure, designed to amend non-essential elements of this Directive, shall be adopted in accordance with the regulatory procedure with scrutiny referred to in Article 58(3).

    Such updates must not entail, for any Member State, any amendment of existing legislative principles relating to the structure of professions as regards training and the conditions of access by natural persons.

3. Training for pharmacists shall provide an assurance that the person concerned has acquired the following knowledge and skills:
    (a) adequate knowledge of medicines and the substances used in the manufacture of medicines;
    (b) adequate knowledge of pharmaceutical technology and the physical, chemical, biological and microbiological testing of medicinal products;
    (c) adequate knowledge of the metabolism and the effects of medicinal products and of the action of toxic substances, and of the use of medicinal products;
    (d) adequate knowledge to evaluate scientific data concerning medicines in order to be able to supply appropriate information on the basis of this knowledge;
    (e) adequate knowledge of the legal and other requirements associated with the pursuit of pharmacy.

Article 45 Pursuit of the professional activities of a pharmacist

1. For the purposes of this Directive, the activities of a pharmacist are those, access to which and pursuit of which are contingent, in one or more Member States, upon professional qualifications and which are open to holders of evidence of formal qualifications of the types listed in Annex V, point 5.6.2.

2. The Member States shall ensure that the holders of evidence of formal qualifications in pharmacy at university level or a level deemed to be equivalent, which satisfies the provisions of Article 44, are able to gain access to and pursue at least the following activities, subject to the requirement, where appropriate, of supplementary professional experience:
    (a) preparation of the pharmaceutical form of medicinal products;
    (b) manufacture and testing of medicinal products;
    (c) testing of medicinal products in a laboratory for the testing of medicinal products;
    (d) storage, preservation and distribution of medicinal products at the wholesale stage;
    (e) preparation, testing, storage and supply of medicinal products in pharmacies open to the public;
    (f) preparation, testing, storage and dispensing of medicinal products in hospitals;
    (g) provision of information and advice on medicinal products.

3.   If a Member State makes access to or pursuit of one of the activities of a pharmacist contingent upon supplementary professional experience, in addition to possession of evidence of formal qualifications referred to in Annex V, point 5.6.2, that Member State shall recognise as sufficient proof in this regard a certificate issued by the competent authorities in the home Member State stating that the person concerned has been engaged in those activities in the home Member State for a similar period.

4.   The recognition referred to in paragraph 3 shall not apply with regard to the two-year period of professional experience required by the Grand Duchy of Luxembourg for the grant of a State public pharmacy concession.

5.   If, on 16 September 1985, a Member State had a competitive examination in place designed to select from among the holders referred to in paragraph 2, those who are to be authorised to become owners of new pharmacies whose creation has been decided on as part of a national system of geographical division, that Member State may, by way of derogation from paragraph 1, proceed with that examination and require nationals of Member States who possess evidence of formal qualifications as a pharmacist referred to in Annex V, point 5.6.2 or who benefit from the provisions of Article 23 to take part in it.

SECTION 8 ARCHITECT

Article 46 Training of architects

1.   Training as an architect shall comprise a total of at least four years of full-time study or six years of study, at least three years of which on a full-time basis, at a university or comparable teaching institution. The training must lead to successful completion of a university-level examination.

That training, which must be of university level, and of which architecture is the principal component, must maintain a balance between theoretical and practical aspects of architectural training and guarantee the acquisition of the following knowledge and skills:
  (a) ability to create architectural designs that satisfy both aesthetic and technical requirements;
  (b) adequate knowledge of the history and theories of architecture and the related arts, technologies and human sciences;
  (c) knowledge of the fine arts as an influence on the quality of architectural design;
  (d) adequate knowledge of urban design, planning and the skills involved in the planning process;
  (e) understanding of the relationship between people and buildings, and between buildings and their environment, and of the need to relate buildings and the spaces between them to human needs and scale;
  (f) understanding of the profession of architecture and the role of the architect in society, in particular in preparing briefs that take account of social factors;
  (g) understanding of the methods of investigation and preparation of the brief for a design project;
  (h) understanding of the structural design, constructional and engineering problems associated with building design;
  (i) adequate knowledge of physical problems and technologies and of the function of buildings so as to provide them with internal conditions of comfort and protection against the climate;
  (j) the necessary design skills to meet building users' requirements within the constraints imposed by cost factors and building regulations;
  (k) adequate knowledge of the industries, organisations, regulations and procedures involved in translating design concepts into buildings and integrating plans into overall planning.

2.   The Commission may adapt the knowledge and skills listed in paragraph 1 to scientific and technical progress. That measure, designed to amend non-essential elements of this Directive, shall be adopted in accordance with the regulatory procedure with scrutiny referred to in Article 58(3).

Such updates must not entail, for any Member State, any amendment of existing legislative principles relating to the structure of professions as regards training and the conditions of access by natural persons.

Article 47 Derogations from the conditions for the training of architects

1.   By way of derogation from Article 46, the following shall also be recognised as satisfying Article 21: training existing as of 5 August 1985, provided by "Fachhochschulen" in the Federal Republic of Germany over a period of three years, satisfying the requirements referred to in Article 46 and giving access to the activities referred to in Article 48 in that Member State under the professional title of "architect", in so far as the training was followed by a four-year period of professional experience in the Federal Republic of Germany, as attested by a certificate issued by the professional association in whose roll the name of the architect wishing to benefit from the provisions of this Directive appears.

The professional association must first ascertain that the work performed by the architect concerned in the field of architecture represents convincing application of the full range of knowledge and skills listed in Article 46(1). That certificate shall be awarded in line with the same procedure as that applying to registration in the professional association's roll.

2.   By way of derogation from Article 46, the following shall also be recognised as satisfying Article 21: training as part of social betterment schemes or part-time university studies which satisfies the requirements referred to in Article 46, as attested by an examination in architecture passed by a person who has been working for seven years or more in the field of architecture under the supervision of an architect or architectural bureau. The examination must be of university level and be equivalent to the final examination referred to in Article 46(1), first subparagraph.

Article 48 Pursuit of the professional activities of architects

1.   For the purposes of this Directive, the professional activities of an architect are the activities regularly carried out under the professional title of "architect".

2.   Nationals of a Member State who are authorised to use that title pursuant to a law which gives the competent authority of a Member State the power to award that title to Member States nationals who are especially distinguished by the quality of their work in the field of architecture shall be deemed to satisfy the conditions required for the pursuit of the activities of an architect, under the professional title of "architect". The architectural nature of the activities of the persons concerned shall be attested by a certificate awarded by their home Member State.

Article 49 Acquired rights specific to architects

1.   Each Member State shall accept evidence of formal qualifications as an architect listed in Annex VI, awarded by the other Member States, and attesting a course of training which began no later than the reference academic year referred to in that Annex, even if they do not satisfy the minimum requirements laid down in Article 46, and shall, for the purposes of access to and pursuit of the professional activities of an architect, give such evidence the same effect on its territory as evidence of formal qualifications as an architect which it itself issues.

Under these circumstances, certificates issued by the competent authorities of the Federal Republic of Germany attesting that evidence of formal qualifications issued on or after

8 May 1945 by the competent authorities of the German Democratic Republic is equivalent to such evidence listed in that Annex, shall be recognised.

2.   Without prejudice to paragraph 1, every Member State shall recognise the following evidence of formal qualifications and shall, for the purposes of access to and pursuit of the professional activities of an architect performed, give them the same effect on its territory as evidence of formal qualifications which it itself issues: certificates issued to nationals of Member States by the Member States which have enacted rules governing the access to and pursuit of the activities of an architect as of the following dates:
(a) 1 January 1995 for Austria, Finland and Sweden;
(b) 1 May 2004 for the Czech Republic, Estonia, Cyprus, Latvia, Lithuania, Hungary, Malta, Poland, Slovenia and Slovakia;
(c) 5 August 1987 for the other Member States.
The certificates referred to in the first subparagraph shall certify that the holder was authorized, no later than the respective date, to use the professional title of architect, and that he has been effectively engaged, in the context of those rules, in the activities in question for at least three consecutive years during the five years preceding the award of the certificate.

Chapter IV COMMON PROVISIONS ON ESTABLISHMENT

Article 50 Documentation and formalities
1.   Where the competent authorities of the host Member State decide on an application for authorisation to pursue the regulated profession in question by virtue of this Title, those authorities may demand the documents and certificates listed in Annex VII.

The documents referred to in Annex VII, point 1(d), (e) and (f), shall not be more than three months old by the date on which they are submitted.

The Member States, bodies and other legal persons shall guarantee the confidentiality of the information which they receive.

2.   In the event of justified doubts, the host Member State may require from the competent authorities of a Member State confirmation of the authenticity of the attestations and evidence of formal qualifications awarded in that other Member State, as well as, where applicable, confirmation of the fact that the beneficiary fulfils, for the professions referred to in Chapter III of this Title, the minimum training conditions set out respectively in Articles 24, 25, 28, 31, 34, 35, 38, 40, 44 and 46.

3.   In cases of justified doubt, where evidence of formal qualifications, as defined in Article 3(1)(c), has been issued by a competent authority in a Member State and includes training received in whole or in part in an establishment legally established in the territory of another Member State, the host Member State shall be entitled to verify with the competent body in the Member State of origin of the award:
(a) whether the training course at the establishment which gave the training has been formally certified by the educational establishment based in the Member State of origin of the award;
(b) whether the evidence of formal qualifications issued is the same as that which would have been awarded if the course had been followed entirely in the Member State of origin of the award; and
(c) whether the evidence of formal qualifications confers the same professional rights in the territory of the Member State of origin of the award.

4.   Where a host Member State requires its nationals to swear a solemn oath or make a sworn statement in order to gain access to a regulated profession, and where the wording

of that oath or statement cannot be used by nationals of the other Member States, the host Member State shall ensure that the persons concerned can use an appropriate equivalent wording.

Article 51 Procedure for the mutual recognition of professional qualifications

1.   The competent authority of the host Member State shall acknowledge receipt of the application within one month of receipt and inform the applicant of any missing document.

2.   The procedure for examining an application for authorisation to practise a regulated profession must be completed as quickly as possible and lead to a duly substantiated decision by the competent authority in the host Member State in any case within three months after the date on which the applicant's complete file was submitted. However, this deadline may be extended by one month in cases falling under Chapters I and II of this Title.

3.   The decision, or failure to reach a decision within the deadline, shall be subject to appeal under national law.

Article 52 Use of professional titles

1.   If, in a host Member State, the use of a professional title relating to one of the activities of the profession in question is regulated, nationals of the other Member States who are authorised to practise a regulated profession on the basis of Title III shall use the professional title of the host Member State, which corresponds to that profession in that Member State, and make use of any associated initials.

2.   Where a profession is regulated in the host Member State by an association or organisation within the meaning of Article 3(2), nationals of Member States shall not be authorised to use the professional title issued by that organisation or association, or its abbreviated form, unless they furnish proof that they are members of that association or organisation.

If the association or organisation makes membership contingent upon certain qualifications, it may do so, only under the conditions laid down in this Directive, in respect of nationals of other Member States who possess professional qualifications.

TITLE IV
DETAILED RULES FOR PURSUING THE PROFESSION

Article 53 Knowledge of languages
Persons benefiting from the recognition of professional qualifications shall have a knowledge of languages necessary for practising the profession in the host Member State.

Article 54 Use of academic titles
Without prejudice to Articles 7 and 52, the host Member State shall ensure that the right shall be conferred on the persons concerned to use academic titles conferred on them in the home Member State, and possibly an abbreviated form thereof, in the language of the home Member State. The host Member State may require that title to be followed by the name and address of the establishment or examining board which awarded it. Where an academic title of the home Member State is liable to be confused in the host Member State with a title which, in the latter Member State, requires supplementary training not acquired by the beneficiary, the host Member State may require the beneficiary to use the academic title of the home Member State in an appropriate form, to be laid down by the host Member State.

Article 55 Approval by health insurance funds
Without prejudice to Article 5(1) and Article 6, first subparagraph, point (b), Member States which require persons who acquired their professional qualifications in their territory to complete a preparatory period of in-service training and/or a period of professional experience

in order to be approved by a health insurance fund, shall waive this obligation for the holders of evidence of professional qualifications of doctor and dental practitioner acquired in other Member States.

TITLE V
ADMINISTRATIVE COOPERATION AND RESPONSIBILITY FOR IMPLEMENTATION

Article 56 Competent authorities

1.   The competent authorities of the host Member State and of the home Member State shall work in close collaboration and shall provide mutual assistance in order to facilitate application of this Directive. They shall ensure the confidentiality of the information which they exchange.

2.   The competent authorities of the host and home Member States shall exchange information regarding disciplinary action or criminal sanctions taken or any other serious, specific circumstances which are likely to have consequences for the pursuit of activities under this Directive, respecting personal data protection legislation provided for in Directives 95/46/EC of the European Parliament and of the Council of 24 October 1995 on the protection of individuals with regard to the processing of personal data and on the free movement of such data [24] and 2002/58/EC of the European Parliament and of the Council of 12 July 2002 concerning the processing of personal data and the protection of privacy in the electronic communications sector (Directive on privacy and electronic communications) [25].

The home Member State shall examine the veracity of the circumstances and its authorities shall decide on the nature and scope of the investigations which need to be carried out and shall inform the host Member State of the conclusions which it draws from the information available to it.

3.   Each Member State shall, no later than 20 October 2007, designate the authorities and bodies competent to award or receive evidence of formal qualifications and other documents or information, and those competent to receive applications and take the decisions referred to in this Directive, and shall forthwith inform the other Member States and the Commission thereof.

4.   Each Member State shall designate a coordinator for the activities of the authorities referred to in paragraph 1 and shall inform the other Member States and the Commission thereof.

The coordinators' remit shall be:
(a) to promote uniform application of this Directive;
(b) to collect all the information which is relevant for application of this Directive, such as on the conditions for access to regulated professions in the Member States.
For the purpose of fulfilling the remit described in point (b), the coordinators may solicit the help of the contact points referred to in Article 57.

Article 57 Contact points
Each Member State shall designate, no later than 20 October 2007, a contact point whose remit shall be:
(a) to provide the citizens and contact points of the other Member States with such information as is necessary concerning the recognition of professional qualifications provided for in this Directive, such as information on the national legislation governing the professions and the pursuit of those professions, including social legislation, and, where appropriate, the rules of ethics;

(b)   to assist citizens in realising the rights conferred on them by this Directive, in cooperation, where appropriate, with the other contact points and the competent authorities in the host Member State.

At the Commission's request, the contact points shall inform the Commission of the result of enquiries with which they are dealing pursuant to the provisions of point (b) within two months of receiving them.

Article 58 Committee procedure

1.   The Commission shall be assisted by a Committee on the recognition of professional qualifications.

2.   Where reference is made to this paragraph, Articles 5 and 7 of Decision 1999/468/EC shall apply, having regard to the provisions of Article 8 thereof. The period provided for in Article 5(6) of Decision 1999/468/EC shall be set at two months.

3.   Where reference is made to this paragraph, Article 5a(1) to (4) and Article 7 of Decision 1999/468/EC shall apply, having regard to the provisions of Article 8 thereof.

Article 59 Consultation

The Commission shall ensure the consultation of experts from the professional groups concerned in an appropriate manner in particular in the context of the work of the committee referred to in Article 58 and shall provide a reasoned report on these consultations to that committee.

TITLE VI
OTHER PROVISIONS

Article 60 Reports

1.   As from 20 October 2007, Member States shall, every two years, send a report to the Commission on the application of the system. In addition to general observations, the report shall contain a statistical summary of decisions taken and a description of the main problems arising from the application of this Directive.

2.   As from 20 October 2007, the Commission shall draw up every five years a report on the implementation of this Directive.

Article 61 Derogation clause

If, for the application of one of the provisions of this Directive, a Member State encounters major difficulties in a particular area, the Commission shall examine those difficulties in collaboration with the Member State concerned.

Where appropriate, the Commission shall decide, in accordance with the procedure referred to in Article 58(2), to permit the Member State in question to derogate from the provision in question for a limited period.

Article 62 Repeal

Directives 77/452/EEC, 77/453/EEC, 78/686/EEC, 78/687/EEC, 78/1026/EEC, 78/1027/EEC, 80/154/EEC, 80/155/EEC, 85/384/EEC, 85/432/EEC, 85/433/EEC, 89/48/EEC, 92/51/EEC, 93/16/EEC and 1999/42/EC are repealed with effect from 20 October 2007. References to the repealed Directives shall be understood as references to this Directive and the acts adopted on the basis of those Directives shall not be affected by the repeal.

Article 63 Transposition

Member States shall bring into force the laws, regulations and administrative provisions necessary to comply with this Directive by 20 October 2007 at the latest. They shall forthwith inform the Commission thereof.

When Member States adopt these measures, they shall contain a reference to this Directive or be accompanied by such a reference on the occasion of their official publication. Member States shall determine how such reference is to be made.

Article 64 Entry into force
This Directive shall enter into force on the 20th day following its publication in the *Official Journal of the European Union.*

Article 65 Addressees
This Directive is addressed to the Member States.

(*Date of signing and signatories omitted*)

ANNEX I

List of professional associations or organisations fulfilling the conditions of Article 3(2)

IRELAND [1]
1.   The Institute of Chartered Accountants in Ireland [2]

2.   The Institute of Certified Public Accountants in Ireland [2]

3.   The Association of Certified Accountants [2]

4.   Institution of Engineers of Ireland

5.   Irish Planning Institute

UNITED KINGDOM
1.   Institute of Chartered Accountants in England and Wales

2.   Institute of Chartered Accountants of Scotland

3.   Institute of Chartered Accountants in Ireland

4.   Chartered Association of Certified Accountants

5.   Chartered Institute of Loss Adjusters

6.   Chartered Institute of Management Accountants

7.   Institute of Chartered Secretaries and Administrators

8.   Chartered Insurance Institute

9.   Institute of Actuaries

10. Faculty of Actuaries

11. Chartered Institute of Bankers

12. Institute of Bankers in Scotland

13. Royal Institution of Chartered Surveyors

14. Royal Town Planning Institute

15. Chartered Society of Physiotherapy

16. Royal Society of Chemistry

17. British Psychological Society

18. Library Association

19. Institute of Chartered Foresters

20. Chartered Institute of Building

21. Engineering Council

22. Institute of Energy

23. Institution of Structural Engineers

24. Institution of Civil Engineers

25. Institution of Mining Engineers

26. Institution of Mining and Metallurgy

27. Institution of Electrical Engineers

28. Institution of Gas Engineers

29. Institution of Mechanical Engineers

30. Institution of Chemical Engineers

31. Institution of Production Engineers

32. Institution of Marine Engineers

33. Royal Institution of Naval Architects

34. Royal Aeronautical Society

35. Institute of Metals

36. Chartered Institution of Building Services Engineers

37. Institute of Measurement and Control

38. British Computer Society

[1] Irish nationals are also members of the following associations or organisations in the United Kingdom:
— Institute of Chartered Accountants in England and Wales
— Institute of Chartered Accountants of Scotland
— Institute of Actuaries
— Faculty of Actuaries
— The Chartered Institute of Management Accountants
— Institute of Chartered Secretaries and Administrators
— Royal Town Planning Institute
— Royal Institution of Chartered Surveyors
— Chartered Institute of Building.
[2] Only for the activity of auditing accounts.

(*Annexes II–VII omitted*)

DIRECTIVE 2011/24/EU OF THE EUROPEAN PARLIAMENT AND OF THE COUNCIL OF 9 MARCH 2011
on the application of patients' rights in cross-border healthcare
OJ L 88, 4.4.2011, P. 45

(preamble and footnotes omitted)

Chapter I GENERAL PROVISIONS

Article 1 Subject matter and scope
1.   This Directive provides rules for facilitating the access to safe and high-quality cross-border healthcare and promotes cooperation on healthcare between Member States, in full respect of national competencies in organising and delivering healthcare. This Directive also aims at clarifying its relationship with the existing framework on the coordination of social security systems, Regulation (EC) No 883/2004, with a view to application of patients' rights.

2.   This Directive shall apply to the provision of healthcare to patients, regardless of how it is organised, delivered and financed.

3.   This Directive shall not apply to:
   (a) services in the field of long-term care the purpose of which is to support people in need of assistance in carrying out routine, everyday tasks;
   (b) allocation of and access to organs for the purpose of organ transplants;
   (c) with the exception of Chapter IV, public vaccination programmes against infectious diseases which are exclusively aimed at protecting the health of the population on the territory of a Member State and which are subject to specific planning and implementation measures.

4.   This Directive shall not affect laws and regulations in Member States relating to the organisation and financing of healthcare in situations not related to cross-border healthcare. In particular, nothing in this Directive obliges a Member State to reimburse costs of healthcare provided by healthcare providers established on its own territory if those providers are not part of the social security system or public health system of that Member State.

Article 2 Relationship with other Union provisions
This Directive shall apply without prejudice to:
(a) Council Directive 89/105/EEC of 21 December 1988 relating to the transparency of measures regulating the prices of medicinal products for human use and their inclusion in the scope of national health insurance systems;

(b) Council Directive 90/385/EEC of 20 June 1990 on the approximation of the laws of the Member States relating to active implantable medical devices, Council Directive 93/42/EEC of 14 June 1993 concerning medical devices and Directive 98/79/EC of the European Parliament and of the Council of 27 October 1998 on in vitro diagnostic medical devices;

(c) Directive 95/46/EC and Directive 2002/58/EC of the European Parliament and of the Council of 12 July 2002 concerning the processing of personal data and the protection of privacy in the electronic communications sector;

(d) Directive 96/71/EC of the European Parliament and of the Council of 16 December 1996 concerning the posting of workers in the framework of the provision of services;

(e) Directive 2000/31/EC;

(f)   Council Directive 2000/43/EC of 29 June 2000 implementing the principle of equal treatment between persons irrespective of racial or ethnic origin;

(g)   Directive 2001/20/EC of the European Parliament and of the Council of 4 April 2001 on the approximation of the laws, regulations and administrative provisions of the Member States relating to the implementation of good clinical practice in the conduct of clinical trials on medicinal products for human use;

(h)   Directive 2001/83/EC of the European Parliament and of the Council of 6 November 2001 on the Community code relating to medicinal products for human use;

(i)   Directive 2002/98/EC of the European Parliament and of the Council of 27 January 2003 setting standards of quality and safety for the collection, testing, processing, storage and distribution of human blood and blood components;

(j)   Regulation (EC) No 859/2003;

(k)   Directive 2004/23/EC of the European Parliament and of the Council of 31 March 2004 on setting standards of quality and safety for the donation, procurement, testing, processing, preservation, storage and distribution of human tissues and cells;

(l)   Regulation (EC) No 726/2004 of the European Parliament and of the Council of 31 March 2004 laying down Community procedures for the authorisation and supervision of medicinal products for human and veterinary use and establishing a European Medicines Agency;

(m)   Regulation (EC) No 883/2004 and Regulation (EC) No 987/2009 of the European Parliament and of the Council of 16 September 2009 laying down the procedure for implementing Regulation (EC) No 883/2004 on the coordination of social security systems;

(n)   Directive 2005/36/EC;

(o)   Regulation (EC) No 1082/2006 of the European Parliament and of the Council of 5 July 2006 on a European grouping of territorial cooperation (EGTC);

(p)   Regulation (EC) No 1338/2008 of the European Parliament and of the Council of 16 December 2008 on Community statistics on public health and health and safety at work;

(q)   Regulation (EC) No 593/2008 of the European Parliament and of the Council of 17 June 2008 on the law applicable to contractual obligations (Rome I), Regulation (EC) No 864/2007 of the European Parliament and of the Council of 11 July 2007 on the law applicable to non-contractual obligations (Rome II) and other Union rules on private international law, in particular rules related to court jurisdiction and the applicable law;

(r)   Directive 2010/53/EU of the European Parliament and of the Council of 7 July 2010 on standards of quality and safety of human organs intended for transplantation;

(s)   Regulation (EU) No 1231/2010.

Article 3 Definitions
For the purposes of this Directive, the following definitions shall apply:
(a)   "healthcare" means health services provided by health professionals to patients to assess, maintain or restore their state of health, including the prescription, dispensation and provision of medicinal products and medical devices;

(b)   "insured person" means:
   (i)   persons, including members of their families and their survivors, who are covered by Article 2 of Regulation (EC) No 883/2004 and who are insured persons within the meaning of Article 1(c) of that Regulation; and

      (ii) nationals of a third country who are covered by Regulation (EC) No 859/2003 or Regulation (EU) No 1231/2010, or who satisfy the conditions of the legislation of the Member State of affiliation for entitlement to benefits;

(c) "Member State of affiliation" means:
      (i) for persons referred to in point (b)(i), the Member State that is competent to grant to the insured person a prior authorisation to receive appropriate treatment outside the Member State of residence according to Regulations (EC) No 883/2004 and (EC) No 987/2009;
      (ii) for persons referred to in point (b)(ii), the Member State that is competent to grant to the insured person a prior authorisation to receive appropriate treatment in another Member State according to Regulation (EC) No 859/2003 or Regulation (EU) No 1231/2010. If no Member State is competent according to those Regulations, the Member State of affiliation shall be the Member State where the person is insured or has the rights to sickness benefits according to the legislation of that Member State;

(d) "Member State of treatment" means the Member State on whose territory healthcare is actually provided to the patient. In the case of telemedicine, healthcare is considered to be provided in the Member State where the healthcare provider is established;

(e) "cross-border healthcare" means healthcare provided or prescribed in a Member State other than the Member State of affiliation;

(f) "health professional" means a doctor of medicine, a nurse responsible for general care, a dental practitioner, a midwife or a pharmacist within the meaning of Directive 2005/36/EC, or another professional exercising activities in the healthcare sector which are restricted to a regulated profession as defined in Article 3(1)(a) of Directive 2005/36/EC, or a person considered to be a health professional according to the legislation of the Member State of treatment;

(g) "healthcare provider" means any natural or legal person or any other entity legally providing healthcare on the territory of a Member State;

(h) "patient" means any natural person who seeks to receive or receives healthcare in a Member State;

(i) "medicinal product" means a medicinal product as defined by Directive 2001/83/EC;

(j) "medical device" means a medical device as defined by Directive 90/385/EEC, Directive 93/42/EEC or Directive 98/79/EC;

(k) "prescription" means a prescription for a medicinal product or for a medical device issued by a member of a regulated health profession within the meaning of Article 3(1)(a) of Directive 2005/36/EC who is legally entitled to do so in the Member State in which the prescription is issued;

(l) "health technology" means a medicinal product, a medical device or medical and surgical procedures as well as measures for disease prevention, diagnosis or treatment used in healthcare;

(m) "medical records" means all the documents containing data, assessments and information of any kind on a patient's situation and clinical development throughout the care process.

Chapter II RESPONSIBILITIES OF MEMBER STATES WITH REGARD TO CROSS-BORDER HEALTH CARE

Article 4 Responsibilities of the Member State of treatment

1. Taking into account the principles of universality, access to good quality care, equity and solidarity, cross-border healthcare shall be provided in accordance with:

(a) the legislation of the Member State of treatment;

(b) standards and guidelines on quality and safety laid down by the Member State of treatment; and

(c) Union legislation on safety standards.

2. The Member State of treatment shall ensure that:

(a) patients receive from the national contact point referred to in Article 6, upon request, relevant information on the standards and guidelines referred to in paragraph 1(b) of this Article, including provisions on supervision and assessment of healthcare providers, information on which healthcare providers are subject to these standards and guidelines and information on the accessibility of hospitals for persons with disabilities;

(b) healthcare providers provide relevant information to help individual patients to make an informed choice, including on treatment options, on the availability, quality and safety of the healthcare they provide in the Member State of treatment and that they also provide clear invoices and clear information on prices, as well as on their authorisation or registration status, their insurance cover or other means of personal or collective protection with regard to professional liability. To the extent that healthcare providers already provide patients resident in the Member State of treatment with relevant information on these subjects, this Directive does not oblige healthcare providers to provide more extensive information to patients from other Member States;

(c) there are transparent complaints procedures and mechanisms in place for patients, in order for them to seek remedies in accordance with the legislation of the Member State of treatment if they suffer harm arising from the healthcare they receive;

(d) systems of professional liability insurance, or a guarantee or similar arrangement that is equivalent or essentially comparable as regards its purpose and which is appropriate to the nature and the extent of the risk, are in place for treatment provided on its territory;

(e) the fundamental right to privacy with respect to the processing of personal data is protected in conformity with national measures implementing Union provisions on the protection of personal data, in particular Directives 95/46/EC and 2002/58/EC;

(f) in order to ensure continuity of care, patients who have received treatment are entitled to a written or electronic medical record of such treatment, and access to at least a copy of this record in conformity with and subject to national measures implementing Union provisions on the protection of personal data, in particular Directives 95/46/EC and 2002/58/EC.

3. The principle of non-discrimination with regard to nationality shall be applied to patients from other Member States.

This shall be without prejudice to the possibility for the Member State of treatment, where it is justified by overriding reasons of general interest, such as planning requirements relating to the aim of ensuring sufficient and permanent access to a balanced range of high-quality treatment in the Member State concerned or to the wish to control costs and avoid, as far as possible, any waste of financial, technical and human resources, to adopt measures regarding access to treatment aimed at fulfilling its fundamental responsibility to ensure sufficient and permanent access to healthcare within its territory. Such measures shall be limited to what is necessary and proportionate and may not constitute a means of arbitrary discrimination and shall be made publicly available in advance.

4. Member States shall ensure that the healthcare providers on their territory apply the same scale of fees for healthcare for patients from other Member States, as for domestic patients in a comparable medical situation, or that they charge a price calculated

according to objective, non-discriminatory criteria if there is no comparable price for domestic patients.

This paragraph shall be without prejudice to national legislation which allows healthcare providers to set their own prices, provided that they do not discriminate against patients from other Member States.

5.   This Directive shall not affect laws and regulations in Member States on the use of languages. Member States may choose to deliver information in other languages than those which are official languages in the Member State concerned.

Article 5 Responsibilities of the Member State of affiliation
The Member State of affiliation shall ensure that:

(a)   the cost of cross-border healthcare is reimbursed in accordance with Chapter III;

(b)   there are mechanisms in place to provide patients on request with information on their rights and entitlements in that Member State relating to receiving cross-border healthcare, in particular as regards the terms and conditions for reimbursement of costs in accordance with Article 7(6) and procedures for accessing and determining those entitlements and for appeal and redress if patients consider that their rights have not been respected, in accordance with Article 9. In information about cross-border healthcare, a clear distinction shall be made between the rights which patients have by virtue of this Directive and rights arising from Regulation (EC) No 883/2004;

(c)   where a patient has received cross-border healthcare and where medical follow-up proves necessary, the same medical follow-up is available as would have been if that healthcare had been provided on its territory;

(d)   patients who seek to receive or do receive cross-border healthcare have remote access to or have at least a copy of their medical records, in conformity with, and subject to, national measures implementing Union provisions on the protection of personal data, in particular Directives 95/46/EC and 2002/58/EC.

Article 6 National contact points for cross-border healthcare
1.   Each Member State shall designate one or more national contact points for cross-border healthcare and communicate their names and contact details to the Commission. The Commission and the Member States shall make this information publicly available. Member States shall ensure that the national contact points consult with patient organisations, healthcare providers and healthcare insurers.

2.   National contact points shall facilitate the exchange of information referred to in paragraph 3 and shall cooperate closely with each other and with the Commission. National contact points shall provide patients on request with contact details of national contact points in other Member States.

3.   In order to enable patients to make use of their rights in relation to cross-border healthcare, national contact points in the Member State of treatment shall provide them with information concerning healthcare providers, including, on request, information on a specific provider's right to provide services or any restrictions on its practice, information referred to in Article 4(2)(a), as well as information on patients' rights, complaints procedures and mechanisms for seeking remedies, according to the legislation of that Member State, as well as the legal and administrative options available to settle disputes, including in the event of harm arising from cross-border healthcare.

4.   National contact points in the Member State of affiliation shall provide patients and health professionals with the information referred to in Article 5(b).

5.   The information referred to in this Article shall be easily accessible and shall be made available by electronic means and in formats accessible to people with disabilities, as appropriate.

Chapter III REIMBURSEMENT OF COSTS OF CROSS-BORDER HEALTHCARE

Article 7 General principles for reimbursement of costs

1.   Without prejudice to Regulation (EC) No 883/2004 and subject to the provisions of Articles 8 and 9, the Member State of affiliation shall ensure the costs incurred by an insured person who receives cross-border healthcare are reimbursed, if the healthcare in question is among the benefits to which the insured person is entitled in the Member State of affiliation.

2.   By way of derogation from paragraph 1:
(a)   if a Member State is listed in Annex IV to Regulation (EC) No 883/2004 and in compliance with that Regulation has recognised the rights to sickness benefits for pensioners and the members of their families, being resident in a different Member State, it shall provide them healthcare under this Directive at its own expense when they stay on its territory, in accordance with its legislation, as though the persons concerned were residents in the Member State listed in that Annex;
(b)   if the healthcare provided in accordance with this Directive is not subject to prior authorisation, is not provided in accordance with Chapter 1 of Title III of the Regulation (EC) No 883/2004, and is provided in the territory of the Member State that according to that Regulation and Regulation (EC) No 987/2009 is, in the end, responsible for reimbursement of the costs, the costs shall be assumed by that Member State. That Member State may assume the costs of the healthcare in accordance with the terms, conditions, criteria for eligibility and regulatory and administrative formalities that it has established, provided that these are compatible with the TFEU.

3.   It is for the Member State of affiliation to determine, whether at a local, regional or national level, the healthcare for which an insured person is entitled to assumption of costs and the level of assumption of those costs, regardless of where the healthcare is provided.

4.   The costs of cross-border healthcare shall be reimbursed or paid directly by the Member State of affiliation up to the level of costs that would have been assumed by the Member State of affiliation, had this healthcare been provided in its territory without exceeding the actual costs of healthcare received.

Where the full cost of cross-border healthcare exceeds the level of costs that would have been assumed had the healthcare been provided in its territory the Member State of affiliation may nevertheless decide to reimburse the full cost.

The Member State of affiliation may decide to reimburse other related costs, such as accommodation and travel costs, or extra costs which persons with disabilities might incur due to one or more disabilities when receiving cross-border healthcare, in accordance with national legislation and on the condition that there be sufficient documentation setting out these costs.

5.   Member States may adopt provisions in accordance with the TFEU aimed at ensuring that patients enjoy the same rights when receiving cross-border healthcare as they would have enjoyed if they had received healthcare in a comparable situation in the Member State of affiliation.

6.   For the purposes of paragraph 4, Member States shall have a transparent mechanism for calculation of costs of cross-border healthcare that are to be reimbursed to the insured

person by the Member State of affiliation. This mechanism shall be based on objective, non-discriminatory criteria known in advance and applied at the relevant (local, regional or national) administrative level.

7.   The Member State of affiliation may impose on an insured person seeking reimbursement of the costs of cross-border healthcare, including healthcare received through means of telemedicine, the same conditions, criteria of eligibility and regulatory and administrative formalities, whether set at a local, regional or national level, as it would impose if this healthcare were provided in its territory. This may include an assessment by a health professional or healthcare administrator providing services for the statutory social security system or national health system of the Member State of affiliation, such as the general practitioner or primary care practitioner with whom the patient is registered, if this is necessary for determining the individual patient's entitlement to healthcare. However, no conditions, criteria of eligibility and regulatory and administrative formalities imposed according to this paragraph may be discriminatory or constitute an obstacle to the free movement of patients, services or goods, unless it is objectively justified by planning requirements relating to the object of ensuring sufficient and permanent access to a balanced range of high-quality treatment in the Member State concerned or to the wish to control costs and avoid, as far as possible, any waste of financial, technical and human resources.

8.   The Member State of affiliation shall not make the reimbursement of costs of cross-border healthcare subject to prior authorisation except in the cases set out in Article 8.

9.   The Member State of affiliation may limit the application of the rules on reimbursement for cross-border healthcare based on overriding reasons of general interest, such as planning requirements relating to the aim of ensuring sufficient and permanent access to a balanced range of high-quality treatment in the Member State concerned or to the wish to control costs and avoid, as far as possible, any waste of financial, technical and human resources.

10.   Notwithstanding paragraph 9, Member States shall ensure that the cross-border healthcare for which a prior authorisation has been granted is reimbursed in accordance with the authorisation.

11.   The decision to limit the application of this Article pursuant to paragraph 9 shall be restricted to what is necessary and proportionate, and may not constitute a means of arbitrary discrimination or an unjustified obstacle to the free movement of goods, persons or services. Member States shall notify the Commission of any decisions to limit reimbursement on the grounds stated in paragraph 9.

Article 8 Healthcare that may be subject to prior authorisation

1.   The Member State of affiliation may provide for a system of prior authorisation for reimbursement of costs of cross-border healthcare, in accordance with this Article and Article 9. The system of prior authorisation, including the criteria and the application of those criteria, and individual decisions of refusal to grant prior authorisation, shall be restricted to what is necessary and proportionate to the objective to be achieved, and may not constitute a means of arbitrary discrimination or an unjustified obstacle to the free movement of patients.

2.   Healthcare that may be subject to prior authorisation shall be limited to healthcare which:
      (a) is made subject to planning requirements relating to the object of ensuring sufficient and permanent access to a balanced range of high-quality treatment in the Member State concerned or to the wish to control costs and avoid, as far as possible, any waste of financial, technical and human resources and:

(i)   involves overnight hospital accommodation of the patient in question for at least one night; or

(ii)   requires use of highly specialised and cost-intensive medical infrastructure or medical equipment;

(b)   involves treatments presenting a particular risk for the patient or the population; or

(c)   is provided by a healthcare provider that, on a case-by-case basis, could give rise to serious and specific concerns relating to the quality or safety of the care, with the exception of healthcare which is subject to Union legislation ensuring a minimum level of safety and quality throughout the Union.

Member States shall notify the categories of healthcare referred to in point (a) to the Commission.

3.   With regard to requests for prior authorisation made by an insured person with a view to receiving cross-border healthcare, the Member State of affiliation shall ascertain whether the conditions laid down in Regulation (EC) No 883/2004 have been met. Where those conditions are met, the prior authorisation shall be granted pursuant to that Regulation unless the patient requests otherwise.

4.   When a patient affected, or suspected of being affected, by a rare disease applies for prior authorisation, a clinical evaluation may be carried out by experts in that field. If no experts can be found within the Member State of affiliation or if the expert's opinion is inconclusive, the Member State of affiliation may request scientific advice.

5.   Without prejudice to points (a) to (c) of paragraph 6, the Member State of affiliation may not refuse to grant prior authorisation when the patient is entitled to the healthcare in question in accordance with Article 7, and when this healthcare cannot be provided on its territory within a time limit which is medically justifiable, based on an objective medical assessment of the patient's medical condition, the history and probable course of the patient's illness, the degree of the patient's pain and/or the nature of the patient's disability at the time when the request for authorisation was made or renewed.

6.   The Member State of affiliation may refuse to grant prior authorisation for the following reasons:

(a)   the patient will, according to a clinical evaluation, be exposed with reasonable certainty to a patient-safety risk that cannot be regarded as acceptable, taking into account the potential benefit for the patient of the sought cross-border healthcare;

(b)   the general public will be exposed with reasonable certainty to a substantial safety hazard as a result of the cross-border healthcare in question;

(c)   this healthcare is to be provided by a healthcare provider that raises serious and specific concerns relating to the respect of standards and guidelines on quality of care and patient safety, including provisions on supervision, whether these standards and guidelines are laid down by laws and regulations or through accreditation systems established by the Member State of treatment;

(d)   this healthcare can be provided on its territory within a time limit which is medically justifiable, taking into account the current state of health and the probable course of the illness of each patient concerned.

7.   The Member State of affiliation shall make publicly available which healthcare is subject to prior authorisation for the purposes of this Directive, as well as all relevant information on the system of prior authorisation.

Article 9 Administrative procedures regarding cross-border healthcare

1.   The Member State of affiliation shall ensure that administrative procedures regarding the use of cross-border healthcare and reimbursement of costs of healthcare incurred in

another Member State are based on objective, non-discriminatory criteria which are necessary and proportionate to the objective to be achieved.

2.   Any administrative procedure of the kind referred to in paragraph 1 shall be easily accessible and information relating to such a procedure shall be made publicly available at the appropriate level. Such a procedure shall be capable of ensuring that requests are dealt with objectively and impartially.

3.   Member States shall set out reasonable periods of time within which requests for cross-border healthcare must be dealt with and make them public in advance. When considering a request for cross-border healthcare, Member States shall take into account:
(a) the specific medical condition;
(b) the urgency and individual circumstances.

4.   Member States shall ensure that individual decisions regarding the use of cross-border healthcare and reimbursement of costs of healthcare incurred in another Member State are properly reasoned and subject, on a case-by-case basis, to review and are capable of being challenged in judicial proceedings, which include provision for interim measures.

5.   This Directive is without prejudice to Member States' right to offer patients a voluntary system of prior notification whereby, in return for such notification, the patient receives a written confirmation of the amount to be reimbursed on the basis of an estimate. This estimate shall take into account the patient's clinical case, specifying the medical procedures likely to apply.

Member States may choose to apply the mechanisms of financial compensation between the competent institutions as provided for by Regulation (EC) No 883/2004. Where a Member State of affiliation does not apply such mechanisms, it shall ensure that patients receive reimbursement without undue delay.

Chapter IV COOPERATION IN HEALTHCARE

Article 10 Mutual assistance and cooperation
1.   Member States shall render such mutual assistance as is necessary for the implementation of this Directive, including cooperation on standards and guidelines on quality and safety and the exchange of information, especially between their national contact points in accordance with Article 6, including on provisions on supervision and mutual assistance to clarify the content of invoices.

2.   Member States shall facilitate cooperation in cross-border healthcare provision at regional and local level as well as through ICT and other forms of cross-border cooperation.

3.   The Commission shall encourage Member States, particularly neighbouring countries, to conclude agreements among themselves. The Commission shall also encourage the Member States to cooperate in cross-border healthcare provision in border regions.

4.   Member States of treatment shall ensure that information on the right to practise of health professionals listed in national or local registers established on their territory is, upon request, made available to the authorities of other Member States, for the purpose of cross-border healthcare, in accordance with Chapters II and III and with national measures implementing Union provisions on the protection of personal data, in particular Directives 95/46/EC and 2002/58/EC, and the principle of presumption of innocence. The exchange of information shall take place via the Internal Market Information system established pursuant to Commission Decision 2008/49/EC of 12 December 2007 concerning the implementation of the Internal Market Information System (IMI) as regards the protection of personal data.

Article 11 Recognition of prescriptions issued in another Member State

1. If a medicinal product is authorised to be marketed on their territory, in accordance with Directive 2001/83/EC or Regulation (EC) No 726/2004, Member States shall ensure that prescriptions issued for such a product in another Member State for a named patient can be dispensed on their territory in compliance with their national legislation in force, and that any restrictions on recognition of individual prescriptions are prohibited unless such restrictions are:
   (a) limited to what is necessary and proportionate to safeguard human health, and non-discriminatory; or
   (b) based on legitimate and justified doubts about the authenticity, content or comprehensibility of an individual prescription.

   The recognition of such prescriptions shall not affect national rules governing prescribing and dispensing, if those rules are compatible with Union law, including generic or other substitution. The recognition of prescriptions shall not affect the rules on reimbursement of medicinal products. Reimbursement of costs of medicinal products is covered by Chapter III of this Directive.

   In particular, the recognition of prescriptions shall not affect a pharmacist's right, by virtue of national rules, to refuse, for ethical reasons, to dispense a product that was prescribed in another Member State, where the pharmacist would have the right to refuse to dispense, had the prescription been issued in the Member State of affiliation.

   The Member State of affiliation shall take all necessary measures, in addition to the recognition of the prescription, in order to ensure continuity of treatment in cases where a prescription is issued in the Member State of treatment for medicinal products or medical devices available in the Member State of affiliation and where dispensing is sought in the Member State of affiliation.

   This paragraph shall also apply to medical devices that are legally placed on the market in the respective Member State.

2. In order to facilitate implementation of paragraph 1, the Commission shall adopt:
   (a) measures enabling a health professional to verify the authenticity of the prescription and whether the prescription was issued in another Member State by a member of a regulated health profession who is legally entitled to do so through developing a non-exhaustive list of elements to be included in the prescriptions and which must be clearly identifiable in all prescription formats, including elements to facilitate, if needed, contact between the prescribing party and the dispensing party in order to contribute to a complete understanding of the treatment, in due respect of data protection;
   (b) guidelines supporting the Member States in developing the interoperability of ePrescriptions;
   (c) measures to facilitate the correct identification of medicinal products or medical devices prescribed in one Member State and dispensed in another, including measures to address patient safety concerns in relation to their substitution in cross border healthcare where the legislation of the dispensing Member State permits such substitution. The Commission shall consider, inter alia, using the International Non-proprietary Name and the dosage of medicinal products;
   (d) measures to facilitate the comprehensibility of the information to patients concerning the prescription and the instructions included on the use of the product, including an indication of active substance and dosage.

   Measures referred in point (a) shall be adopted by the Commission no later than 25 December 2012 and measures in points (c) and (d) shall be adopted by the Commission no later than 25 October 2012.

3.   The measures and guidelines referred to in points (a) to (d) of paragraph 2 shall be adopted in accordance with the regulatory procedure referred to in Article 16(2).

4.   In adopting measures or guidelines under paragraph 2, the Commission shall have regard to the proportionality of any costs of compliance with, as well as the likely benefits of, the measures or guidelines.

5.   For the purpose of paragraph 1, the Commission shall also adopt, by means of delegated acts in accordance with Article 17 and subject to the conditions of Articles 18 and 19 and no later than 25 October 2012 measures to exclude specific categories of medicinal products or medical devices from the recognition of prescriptions provided for under this Article, where necessary in order to safeguard public health.

6.   Paragraph 1 shall not apply to medicinal products subject to special medical prescription provided for in Article 71(2) of Directive 2001/83/EC.

Article 12 European reference networks
1.   The Commission shall support Member States in the development of European reference networks between healthcare providers and centres of expertise in the Member States, in particular in the area of rare diseases. The networks shall be based on voluntary participation by its members, which shall participate and contribute to the networks' activities in accordance with the legislation of the Member State where the members are established and shall at all times be open to new healthcare providers which might wish to join them, provided that such healthcare providers fulfil all the required conditions and criteria referred to in paragraph 4.

2.   European reference networks shall have at least three of the following objectives:
    (a) to help realise the potential of European cooperation regarding highly specialised healthcare for patients and for healthcare systems by exploiting innovations in medical science and health technologies;
    (b) to contribute to the pooling of knowledge regarding sickness prevention;
    (c) to facilitate improvements in diagnosis and the delivery of high-quality, accessible and cost-effective healthcare for all patients with a medical condition requiring a particular concentration of expertise in medical domains where expertise is rare;
    (d) to maximise the cost-effective use of resources by concentrating them where appropriate;
    (e) to reinforce research, epidemiological surveillance like registries and provide training for health professionals;
    (f) to facilitate mobility of expertise, virtually or physically, and to develop, share and spread information, knowledge and best practice and to foster developments of the diagnosis and treatment of rare diseases, within and outside the networks;
    (g) to encourage the development of quality and safety benchmarks and to help develop and spread best practice within and outside the network;
    (h) to help Member States with an insufficient number of patients with a particular medical condition or lacking technology or expertise to provide highly specialised services of high quality.

3.   Member States are encouraged to facilitate the development of the European reference networks:
    (a) by connecting appropriate healthcare providers and centres of expertise throughout their national territory and ensuring the dissemination of information towards appropriate healthcare providers and centres of expertise throughout their national territory;
    (b) by fostering the participation of healthcare providers and centres of expertise in the European reference networks.

4. For the purposes of paragraph 1, the Commission shall:
   (a) adopt a list of specific criteria and conditions that the European reference networks must fulfil and the conditions and criteria required from healthcare providers wishing to join the European reference network. These criteria and conditions shall ensure, inter alia, that European reference networks:
       (i) have knowledge and expertise to diagnose, follow-up and manage patients with evidence of good outcomes, as far as applicable;
       (ii) follow a multi-disciplinary approach;
       (iii) offer a high level of expertise and have the capacity to produce good practice guidelines and to implement outcome measures and quality control;
       (iv) make a contribution to research;
       (v) organise teaching and training activities; and
       (vi) collaborate closely with other centres of expertise and networks at national and international level;
   (b) develop and publish criteria for establishing and evaluating European reference networks;
   (c) facilitate the exchange of information and expertise in relation to the establishment of European reference networks and their evaluation.

5. The Commission shall adopt the measures referred to in paragraph 4(a) by means of delegated acts in accordance with Article 17 and subject to the conditions of Articles 18 and 19. The measures referred to in points (b) and (c) of paragraph 4 shall be adopted in accordance with the regulatory procedure referred to in Article 16(2).

6. Measures adopted pursuant to this Article shall not harmonise any laws or regulations of the Member States and shall fully respect the responsibilities of the Member States for the organisation and delivery of health services and medical care.

Article 13 Rare diseases

The Commission shall support Member States in cooperating in the development of diagnosis and treatment capacity in particular by aiming to:

(a) make health professionals aware of the tools available to them at Union level to assist them in the correct diagnosis of rare diseases, in particular the Orphanet database, and the European reference networks;

(b) make patients, health professionals and those bodies responsible for the funding of healthcare aware of the possibilities offered by Regulation (EC) No 883/2004 for referral of patients with rare diseases to other Member States even for diagnosis and treatments which are not available in the Member State of affiliation.

Article 14 eHealth

1. The Union shall support and facilitate cooperation and the exchange of information among Member States working within a voluntary network connecting national authorities responsible for eHealth designated by the Member States.

2. The objectives of the eHealth network shall be to:
   (a) work towards delivering sustainable economic and social benefits of European eHealth systems and services and interoperable applications, with a view to achieving a high level of trust and security, enhancing continuity of care and ensuring access to safe and high-quality healthcare;
   (b) draw up guidelines on:
       (i) a non-exhaustive list of data that are to be included in patients' summaries and that can be shared between health professionals to enable continuity of care and patient safety across borders; and

(ii) effective methods for enabling the use of medical information for public health and research;

(c) support Member States in developing common identification and authentication measures to facilitate transferability of data in cross-border healthcare.

The objectives referred to in points (b) and (c) shall be pursued in due observance of the principles of data protection as set out, in particular, in Directives 95/46/EC and 2002/58/EC.

3.   The Commission shall, in accordance with the regulatory procedure referred to in Article 16(2), adopt the necessary measures for the establishment, management and transparent functioning of this network.

Article 15 Cooperation on health technology assessment

1.   The Union shall support and facilitate cooperation and the exchange of scientific information among Member States within a voluntary network connecting national authorities or bodies responsible for health technology assessment designated by the Member States. The Member States shall communicate their names and contact details to the Commission. The members of such a health technology assessment network shall participate in, and contribute to, the network's activities in accordance with the legislation of the Member State where they are established. That network shall be based on the principle of good governance including transparency, objectivity, independence of expertise, fairness of procedure and appropriate stakeholder consultations.

2.   The objectives of the health technology assessment network shall be to:
(a) support cooperation between national authorities or bodies;
(b) support Member States in the provision of objective, reliable, timely, transparent, comparable and transferable information on the relative efficacy as well as on the short- and long-term effectiveness, when applicable, of health technologies and to enable an effective exchange of this information between the national authorities or bodies;
(c) support the analysis of the nature and type of information that can be exchanged;
(d) avoid duplication of assessments.

3.   In order to fulfil the objectives set out in paragraph 2, the network on health technology assessment may receive Union aid. Aid may be granted in order to:
(a) contribute to the financing of administrative and technical support;
(b) support collaboration between Member States in developing and sharing methodologies for health technology assessment including relative effectiveness assessment;
(c) contribute to the financing of the provision of transferable scientific information for use in national reporting and case studies commissioned by the network;
(d) facilitate cooperation between the network and other relevant institutions and bodies of the Union;
(e) facilitate the consultation of stakeholders on the work of the network.

4.   The Commission shall, in accordance with the regulatory procedure referred to in Article 16(2), adopt the necessary measures for the establishment, management and transparent functioning of this network.

5.   Arrangements for granting the aid, the conditions to which it may be subject and the amount of the aid, shall be adopted in accordance with the regulatory procedure referred to in Article 16(2). Only those authorities and bodies in the network designated as beneficiaries by the participating Member States shall be eligible for Union aid.

6.   The appropriations required for measures provided for in this Article shall be decided each year as part of the budgetary procedure.

7. Measures adopted pursuant to this Article shall not interfere with Member States' competences in deciding on the implementation of health technology assessment conclusions and shall not harmonise any laws or regulations of the Member States and shall fully respect the responsibilities of the Member States for the organisation and delivery of health services and medical care.

Chapter V IMPLEMENTING AND FINAL PROVISIONS

Article 16 Committee

1. The Commission shall be assisted by a Committee, consisting of representatives of the Member States and chaired by the Commission representative.

2. Where reference is made to this paragraph, Articles 5 and 7 of Decision 1999/468/EC shall apply, having regard to the provisions of Article 8 thereof.

    The period laid down in Article 5(6) of Decision 1999/468/EC shall be set at 3 months.

Article 17 Exercise of the delegation

1. The powers to adopt delegated acts referred to in Articles 11(5) and 12(5) shall be conferred on the Commission for a period of 5 years from 24 April 2011. The Commission shall make a report in respect of the delegated powers not later than 6 months before the end of the five-year period. The delegation of powers shall be automatically extended for periods of an identical duration, unless the European Parliament or the Council revokes it in accordance with Article 18.

2. As soon as it adopts a delegated act, the Commission shall notify it simultaneously to the European Parliament and to the Council.

3. The powers to adopt delegated acts are conferred on the Commission subject to the conditions laid down in Articles 18 and 19.

Article 18 Revocation of the delegation

1. The delegation of power referred to in Articles 11(5) and 12(5) may be revoked at any time by the European Parliament or by the Council.

2. The institution which has commenced an internal procedure for deciding whether to revoke the delegation of power shall endeavour to inform the other institution and the Commission within a reasonable time before the final decision is taken, indicating the delegated powers which could be subject to revocation and possible reasons for a revocation.

3. The decision of revocation shall put an end to the delegation of the powers specified in that decision. It shall take effect immediately or at a later date specified therein. It shall not affect the validity of the delegated acts already in force. It shall be published in the Official Journal of the European Union.

Article 19 Objections to delegated acts

1. The European Parliament or the Council may object to the delegated act within a period of 2 months from the date of notification.

    At the initiative of the European Parliament or the Council this period shall be extended by 2 months.

2. If, on expiry of the period referred to in paragraph 1, neither the European Parliament nor the Council has objected to the delegated act, it shall be published in the Official Journal of the European Union and shall enter into force on the date stated therein.

The delegated act may be published in the Official Journal of the European Union and enter into force before the expiry of that period if the European Parliament and the Council have both informed the Commission of their intention not to raise objections.

3. If the European Parliament or the Council objects to a delegated act within the period referred to in paragraph 1, it shall not enter into force. The institution which objects shall state the reasons for objecting to the delegated act.

Article 20 Reports

1. The Commission shall by 25 October 2015 and subsequently every 3 years thereafter, draw up a report on the operation of this Directive and submit it to the European Parliament and to the Council.

2. The report shall in particular include information on patient flows, financial dimensions of patient mobility, the implementation of Article 7(9) and Article 8, and on the functioning of the European reference networks and national contact points. To this end, the Commission shall conduct an assessment of the systems and practices put in place in the Member States, in the light of the requirements of this Directive and the other Union legislation relating to patient mobility.

    The Member States shall provide the Commission with assistance and all available information for carrying out the assessment and preparing the reports.

3. Member States and the Commission shall have recourse to the Administrative Commission established pursuant to Article 71 of Regulation (EC) No 883/2004, in order to address the financial consequences of the application of this Directive on the Member States which have opted for reimbursement on the basis of fixed amounts, in cases covered by Articles 20(4) and 27(5) of that Regulation.

    The Commission shall monitor and regularly report on the effect of Article 3(c)(i) and Article 8 of this Directive. A first report shall be presented by 25 October 2013. On the basis of these reports, the Commission shall, where appropriate, make proposals to alleviate any disproportionalities.

Article 21 Transposition

1. Member States shall bring into force the laws, regulations and administrative provisions necessary to comply with this Directive by 25 October 2013. They shall forthwith inform the Commission thereof.

    When Member States adopt those provisions, they shall contain a reference to this Directive or be accompanied by such a reference on the occasion of their official publication. The methods of making such reference shall be laid down by the Member States.

2. Member States shall communicate to the Commission the text of the main provisions of national law which they adopt in the field covered by this Directive.

Article 22 Entry into force

This Directive shall enter into force on the 20th day following its publication in the Official Journal of the European Union.

Article 23 Addressees

This Directive is addressed to the Member States.

(Date and names of signatories omitted)

REGULATION (EU) NO 492/2011

of the European Parliament and of the Council of 5 April 2011 on (freedom of movement for workers within the Union)

(codification)[1]

OJ L 141, 27.05.2011, P. 1

(footnotes omitted)

THE EUROPEAN PARLIAMENT AND THE COUNCIL OF THE EUROPEAN UNION,

Having regard to the Treaty on the Functioning of the European Union, and in particular Article 46 thereof,

Having regard to the proposal from the European Commission,

After transmission of the draft legislative act to the national parliaments,

Having regard to the opinion of the European Economic and Social Committee,

Acting in accordance with the ordinary legislative procedure,

Whereas:

(1)   Regulation (EEC) No 1612/68 of the Council of 15 October 1968 on freedom of movement for workers within the Community has been substantially amended several times. In the interests of clarity and rationality the said Regulation should be codified.

(2)   Freedom of movement for workers should be secured within the Union. The attainment of this objective entails the abolition of any discrimination based on nationality between workers of the Member States as regards employment, remuneration and other conditions of work and employment, as well as the right of such workers to move freely within the Union in order to pursue activities as employed persons subject to any limitations justified on grounds of public policy, public security or public health.

(3)   Provisions should be laid down to enable the objectives laid down in Articles 45 and 46 of the Treaty on the Functioning of the European Union in the field of freedom of movement to be achieved.

(4)   Freedom of movement constitutes a fundamental right of workers and their families. Mobility of labour within the Union must be one of the means by which workers are guaranteed the possibility of improving their living and working conditions and promoting their social advancement, while helping to satisfy the requirements of the economies of the Member States. The right of all workers in the Member States to pursue the activity of their choice within the Union should be affirmed.

(5)   Such right should be enjoyed without discrimination by permanent, seasonal and frontier workers and by those who pursue their activities for the purpose of providing services.

(6)   The right of freedom of movement, in order that it may be exercised, by objective standards, in freedom and dignity, requires that equality of treatment be ensured in fact and in law in respect of all matters relating to the actual pursuit of activities as employed persons and to eligibility for housing, and also that obstacles to the mobility of workers be

....

[1]   See Annex I for reference to the repealed Regulation, 1612/68/EEC and the list of its amendments.

eliminated, in particular as regards the conditions for the integration of the worker's family into the host country.

(7)   The principle of non-discrimination between workers in the Union means that all nationals of Member States have the same priority as regards employment as is enjoyed by national workers.

(8)   The machinery for vacancy clearance, in particular by means of direct cooperation between the central employment services and also between the regional services, as well as by coordination of the exchange of information, ensures in a general way a clearer picture of the labour market. Workers wishing to move should also be regularly informed of living and working conditions.

(9)   Close links exist between freedom of movement for workers, employment and vocational training, particularly where the latter aims at putting workers in a position to take up concrete offers of employment from other regions of the Union. Such links make it necessary that the problems arising in this connection should no longer be studied in isolation but viewed as interdependent, account also being taken of the problems of employment at the regional level. It is therefore necessary to direct the efforts of Member States toward coordinating their employment policies,

HAVE ADOPTED THIS REGULATION:

Chapter I EMPLOYMENT, EQUAL TREATMENT AND WORKERS' FAMILIES

SECTION 1 ELIGIBILITY FOR EMPLOYMENT

Article 1
1.   Any national of a Member State shall, irrespective of his place of residence, have the right to take up an activity as an employed person, and to pursue such activity, within the territory of another Member State in accordance with the provisions laid down by law, regulation or administrative action governing the employment of nationals of that State.

2.   He shall, in particular, have the right to take up available employment in the territory of another Member State with the same priority as nationals of that State.

Article 2
Any national of a Member State and any employer pursuing an activity in the territory of a Member State may exchange their applications for and offers of employment, and may conclude and perform contracts of employment in accordance with the provisions in force laid down by law, regulation or administrative action, without any discrimination resulting therefrom.

Article 3
1.   Under this Regulation, provisions laid down by law, regulation or administrative action or administrative practices of a Member State shall not apply:
    (a) where they limit application for and offers of employment, or the right of foreign nationals to take up and pursue employment or subject these to conditions not applicable in respect of their own nationals; or
    (b) where, though applicable irrespective of nationality, their exclusive or principal aim or effect is to keep nationals of other Member States away from the employment offered.
    The first subparagraph shall not apply to conditions relating to linguistic knowledge required by reason of the nature of the post to be filled.

2.   There shall be included in particular among the provisions or practices of a Member State referred to in the first subparagraph of paragraph 1 those which:
       (a) prescribe a special recruitment procedure for foreign nationals;
       (b) limit or restrict the advertising of vacancies in the press or through any other medium or subject it to conditions other than those applicable in respect of employers pursuing their activities in the territory of that Member State;
       (c) subject eligibility for employment to conditions of registration with employment offices or impede recruitment of individual workers, where persons who do not reside in the territory of that State are concerned.

Article 4
1.   Provisions laid down by law, regulation or administrative action of the Member States which restrict by number or percentage the employment of foreign nationals in any undertaking, branch of activity or region, or at a national level, shall not apply to nationals of the other Member States.

2.   When in a Member State the granting of any benefit to undertakings is subject to a minimum percentage of national workers being employed, nationals of the other Member States shall be counted as national workers, subject to Directive 2005/36/EC of the European Parliament and of the Council of 7 September 2005 on the recognition of professional qualifications.

Article 5
A national of a Member State who seeks employment in the territory of another Member State shall receive the same assistance there as that afforded by the employment offices in that State to their own nationals seeking employment.

Article 6
1.   The engagement and recruitment of a national of one Member State for a post in another Member State shall not depend on medical, vocational or other criteria which are discriminatory on grounds of nationality by comparison with those applied to nationals of the other Member State who wish to pursue the same activity.

2.   A national who holds an offer in his name from an employer in a Member State other than that of which he is a national may have to undergo a vocational test, if the employer expressly requests this when making his offer of employment.

SECTION 2 EMPLOYMENT AND EQUALITY OF TREATMENT

Article 7
1.   A worker who is a national of a Member State may not, in the territory of another Member State, be treated differently from national workers by reason of his nationality in respect of any conditions of employment and work, in particular as regards remuneration, dismissal, and, should he become unemployed, reinstatement or re-employment.

2.   He shall enjoy the same social and tax advantages as national workers.

3.   He shall also, by virtue of the same right and under the same conditions as national workers, have access to training in vocational schools and retraining centres.

4.   Any clause of a collective or individual agreement or of any other collective regulation concerning eligibility for employment, remuneration and other conditions of work or dismissal shall be null and void in so far as it lays down or authorises discriminatory conditions in respect of workers who are nationals of the other Member States.

Article 8

A worker who is a national of a Member State and who is employed in the territory of another Member State shall enjoy equality of treatment as regards membership of trade unions and the exercise of rights attaching thereto, including the right to vote and to be eligible for the administration or management posts of a trade union. He may be excluded from taking part in the management of bodies governed by public law and from holding an office governed by public law. Furthermore, he shall have the right of eligibility for workers' representative bodies in the undertaking.

The first paragraph of this Article shall not affect laws or regulations in certain Member States which grant more extensive rights to workers coming from the other Member States.

Article 9

1.   A worker who is a national of a Member State and who is employed in the territory of another Member State shall enjoy all the rights and benefits accorded to national workers in matters of housing, including ownership of the housing he needs.

2.   A worker referred to in paragraph 1 may, with the same right as nationals, put his name down on the housing lists in the region in which he is employed, where such lists exist, and shall enjoy the resultant benefits and priorities.

    If his family has remained in the country whence he came, they shall be considered for this purpose as residing in the said region, where national workers benefit from a similar presumption.

SECTION 3 WORKERS' FAMILIES

Article 10[2]

The children of a national of a Member State who is or has been employed in the territory of another Member State shall be admitted to that State's general educational, apprenticeship and vocational training courses under the same conditions as the nationals of that State, if such children are residing in its territory.

Member States shall encourage all efforts to enable such children to attend these courses under the best possible conditions.

ANNEX I

REPEALED REGULATION WITH LIST OF ITS SUCCESSIVE AMENDMENTS

Council Regulation (EEC) No 1612/68 (OJ L 257, 19.10.1968, p. 2)

Council Regulation (EEC) No 312/76 (OJ L 39, 14.2.1976, p. 2)

Council Regulation (EEC) No 2434/92 (OJ L 245, 26.8.1992, p. 1)

Directive 2004/38/EC of the European Parliament and of the Council (OJ L 158, 30.4.2004, p. 77) Only Article 38(1)

(Parts II–IV and Annex II omitted)

---

[2]   Previously Article 12 of Regulation 1612/68/EEC.

C) FREE MOVEMENT OF SERVICES

DIRECTIVE 2006/123/EC OF THE EUROPEAN PARLIAMENT AND OF THE COUNCIL OF 12 DECEMBER 2006

on services in the internal market

OJ L 376, 27.12.2006, P. 36[1]

(footnotes omitted)

THE EUROPEAN PARLIAMENT AND THE COUNCIL OF THE EUROPEAN UNION,

Having regard to the Treaty establishing the European Community, and in particular the first and third sentence of Article 47(2) and Article 55 thereof,

Having regard to the proposal from the Commission,

Having regard to the Opinion of the European Economic and Social Committee,

Having regard to the opinion of the Committee of the Regions,

Acting in accordance with the procedure laid down in Article 251 of the Treaty,

Whereas:

(1)   The European Community is seeking to forge ever closer links between the States and peoples of Europe and to ensure economic and social progress. In accordance with Article 14(2) of the Treaty, the internal market comprises an area without internal frontiers in which the free movement of services is ensured. In accordance with Article 43 of the Treaty the freedom of establishment is ensured. Article 49 of the Treaty establishes the right to provide services within the Community. The elimination of barriers to the development of service activities between Member States is essential in order to strengthen the integration of the peoples of Europe and to promote balanced and sustainable economic and social progress. In eliminating such barriers it is essential to ensure that the development of service activities contributes to the fulfilment of the task laid down in Article 2 of the Treaty of promoting throughout the Community a harmonious, balanced and sustainable development of economic activities, a high level of employment and of social protection, equality between men and women, sustainable and non-inflationary growth, a high degree of competitiveness and convergence of economic performance, a high level of protection and improvement of the quality of the environment, the raising of the standard of living and quality of life and economic and social cohesion and solidarity among Member States.

(2)   A competitive market in services is essential in order to promote economic growth and create jobs in the European Union. At present numerous barriers within the internal market prevent providers, particularly small and medium-sized enterprises (SMEs), from extending their operations beyond their national borders and from taking full advantage of the internal

---

[1]   EDITOR'S NOTE: As of 1 May 2012 this Directive has not been amended following the entry into force of the Treaty of Lisbon. It includes references to the old Treaty article numbers. Reference should be made to the Tables of Equivalences accompanying the consolidated Treaties in Part II of this edition for the conversion of old Treaty article numbers to new ones.

market. This weakens the worldwide competitiveness of European Union providers. A free market which compels the Member States to eliminate restrictions on cross-border provision of services while at the same time increasing transparency and information for consumers would give consumers wider choice and better services at lower prices.

(3)   The report from the Commission on "The State of the Internal Market for Services" drew up an inventory of a large number of barriers which are preventing or slowing down the development of services between Member States, in particular those provided by SMEs, which are predominant in the field of services. The report concludes that a decade after the envisaged completion of the internal market, there is still a huge gap between the vision of an integrated European Union economy and the reality as experienced by European citizens and providers. The barriers affect a wide variety of service activities across all stages of the provider's activity and have a number of common features, including the fact that they often arise from administrative burdens, the legal uncertainty associated with cross-border activity and the lack of mutual trust between Member States.

(4)   Since services constitute the engine of economic growth and account for 70 % of GDP and employment in most Member States, this fragmentation of the internal market has a negative impact on the entire European economy, in particular on the competitiveness of SMEs and the movement of workers, and prevents consumers from gaining access to a greater variety of competitively priced services. It is important to point out that the services sector is a key employment sector for women in particular, and that they therefore stand to benefit greatly from new opportunities offered by the completion of the internal market for services. The European Parliament and the Council have emphasised that the removal of legal barriers to the establishment of a genuine internal market is a matter of priority for achieving the goal set by the European Council in Lisbon of 23 and 24 March 2000 of improving employment and social cohesion and achieving sustainable economic growth so as to make the European Union the most competitive and dynamic knowledge-based economy in the world by 2010, with more and better jobs. Removing those barriers, while ensuring an advanced European social model, is thus a basic condition for overcoming the difficulties encountered in implementing the Lisbon Strategy and for reviving the European economy, particularly in terms of employment and investment. It is therefore important to achieve an internal market for services, with the right balance between market opening and preserving public services and social and consumer rights.

(5)   It is therefore necessary to remove barriers to the freedom of establishment for providers in Member States and barriers to the free movement of services as between Member States and to guarantee recipients and providers the legal certainty necessary for the exercise in practice of those two fundamental freedoms of the Treaty. Since the barriers in the internal market for services affect operators who wish to become established in other Member States as well as those who provide a service in another Member State without being established there, it is necessary to enable providers to develop their service activities within the internal market either by becoming established in a Member State or by making use of the free movement of services. Providers should be able to choose between those two freedoms, depending on their strategy for growth in each Member State.

(6)   Those barriers cannot be removed solely by relying on direct application of Articles 43 and 49 of the Treaty, since, on the one hand, addressing them on a case-by-case basis through infringement procedures against the Member States concerned would, especially following enlargement, be extremely complicated for national and Community institutions, and, on the other hand, the lifting of many barriers requires prior coordination of national legal schemes, including the setting up of administrative cooperation. As the European Parliament and the Council have recognised, a Community legislative instrument makes it possible to achieve a genuine internal market for services.

(7)   This Directive establishes a general legal framework which benefits a wide variety of services while taking into account the distinctive features of each type of activity or profession and its system of regulation. That framework is based on a dynamic and selective approach consisting in the removal, as a matter of priority, of barriers which may be dismantled quickly and, for the others, the launching of a process of evaluation, consultation and complementary harmonisation of specific issues, which will make possible the progressive and coordinated modernisation of national regulatory systems for service activities which is vital in order to achieve a genuine internal market for services by 2010. Provision should be made for a balanced mix of measures involving targeted harmonisation, administrative cooperation, the provision on the freedom to provide services and encouragement of the development of codes of conduct on certain issues. That coordination of national legislative regimes should ensure a high degree of Community legal integration and a high level of protection of general interest objectives, especially protection of consumers, which is vital in order to establish trust between Member States. This Directive also takes into account other general interest objectives, including the protection of the environment, public security and public health as well as the need to comply with labour law.

(8)   It is appropriate that the provisions of this Directive concerning the freedom of establishment and the free movement of services should apply only to the extent that the activities in question are open to competition, so that they do not oblige Member States either to liberalise services of general economic interest or to privatise public entities which provide such services or to abolish existing monopolies for other activities or certain distribution services.

(9)   This Directive applies only to requirements which affect the access to, or the exercise of, a service activity. Therefore, it does not apply to requirements, such as road traffic rules, rules concerning the development or use of land, town and country planning, building standards as well as administrative penalties imposed for non-compliance with such rules which do not specifically regulate or specifically affect the service activity but have to be respected by providers in the course of carrying out their economic activity in the same way as by individuals acting in their private capacity.

(10) This Directive does not concern requirements governing access to public funds for certain providers. Such requirements include notably those laying down conditions under which providers are entitled to receive public funding, including specific contractual conditions, and in particular quality standards which need to be observed as a condition for receiving public funds, for example for social services.

(11) This Directive does not interfere with measures taken by Member States, in accordance with Community law, in relation to the protection or promotion of cultural and linguistic diversity and media pluralism, including the funding thereof. This Directive does not prevent Member States from applying their fundamental rules and principles relating to the freedom of press and freedom of expression. This Directive does not affect Member State laws prohibiting discrimination on grounds of nationality or on grounds such as those set out in Article 13 of the Treaty.

(12) This Directive aims at creating a legal framework to ensure the freedom of establishment and the free movement of services between the Member States and does not harmonise or prejudice criminal law. However, Member States should not be able to restrict the freedom to provide services by applying criminal law provisions which specifically affect the access to or the exercise of a service activity in circumvention of the rules laid down in this Directive.

(13) It is equally important that this Directive fully respect Community initiatives based on Article 137 of the Treaty with a view to achieving the objectives of Article 136 thereof concerning the promotion of employment and improved living and working conditions.

(14) This Directive does not affect terms and conditions of employment, including maximum work periods and minimum rest periods, minimum paid annual holidays, minimum rates of pay as well as health, safety and hygiene at work, which Member States apply in compliance with Community law, nor does it affect relations between social partners, including the right to negotiate and conclude collective agreements, the right to strike and to take industrial action in accordance with national law and practices which respect Community law, nor does it apply to services provided by temporary work agencies. This Directive does not affect Member States' social security legislation.

(15) This Directive respects the exercise of fundamental rights applicable in the Member States and as recognised in the Charter of fundamental Rights of the European Union and the accompanying explanations, reconciling them with the fundamental freedoms laid down in Articles 43 and 49 of the Treaty. Those fundamental rights include the right to take industrial action in accordance with national law and practices which respect Community law.

(16) This Directive concerns only providers established in a Member State and does not cover external aspects. It does not concern negotiations within international organisations on trade in services, in particular in the framework of the General Agreement on Trade in Services (GATS).

(17) This Directive covers only services which are performed for an economic consideration. Services of general interest are not covered by the definition in Article 50 of the Treaty and therefore do not fall within the scope of this Directive. Services of general economic interest are services that are performed for an economic consideration and therefore do fall within the scope of this Directive. However, certain services of general economic interest, such as those that may exist in the field of transport, are excluded from the scope of this Directive and certain other services of general economic interest, for example, those that may exist in the area of postal services, are the subject of a derogation from the provision on the freedom to provide services set out in this Directive. This Directive does not deal with the funding of services of general economic interest and does not apply to systems of aids granted by Member States, in particular in the social field, in accordance with Community rules on competition. This Directive does not deal with the follow-up to the Commission White Paper on Services of General Interest.

(18) Financial services should be excluded from the scope of this Directive since these activities are the subject of specific Community legislation aimed, as is this Directive, at achieving a genuine internal market for services. Consequently, this exclusion should cover all financial services such as banking, credit, insurance, including reinsurance, occupational or personal pensions, securities, investment funds, payments and investment advice, including the services listed in Annex I to Directive 2006/48/EC of the European Parliament and of the Council of 14 June 2006 relating to the taking up and pursuit of the business of credit institutions.

(19) In view of the adoption in 2002 of a package of legislative instruments relating to electronic communications networks and services, as well as to associated resources and services, which has established a regulatory framework facilitating access to those activities within the internal market, notably through the elimination of most individual authorisation schemes, it is necessary to exclude issues dealt with by those instruments from the scope of this Directive.

(20) The exclusion from the scope of this Directive as regards matters of electronic communications services as covered by Directives 2002/19/EC of the European Parliament and of the Council of 7 March 2002 on access to, and interconnection of, electronic communications networks and associated facilities (Access Directive), 2002/20/EC of the European Parliament and of the Council of 7 March 2002 on the authorisation of electronic communications networks and services (Authorisation Directive), 2002/21/EC

of the European Parliament and of the Council of 7 March 2002 on a common regulatory framework for electronic communications networks and services (Framework Directive), 2002/22/EC of the European Parliament and of the Council of 7 March 2002 on universal service and users' rights relating to electronic communications networks and services (Universal Service Directive) and 2002/58/EC of the European Parliament and of the Council of 12 July 2002 concerning the processing of personal data and the protection of privacy in the electronic communications sector (Directive on privacy and electronic communications) should apply not only to questions specifically dealt with in these Directives but also to matters for which the Directives explicitly leave to Member States the possibility of adopting certain measures at national level.

(21) Transport services, including urban transport, taxis and ambulances as well as port services, should be excluded from the scope of this Directive.

(22) The exclusion of healthcare from the scope of this Directive should cover healthcare and pharmaceutical services provided by health professionals to patients to assess, maintain or restore their state of health where those activities are reserved to a regulated health profession in the Member State in which the services are provided.

(23) This Directive does not affect the reimbursement of healthcare provided in a Member State other than that in which the recipient of the care is resident. This issue has been addressed by the Court of Justice on numerous occasions, and the Court has recognised patients' rights. It is important to address this issue in another Community legal instrument in order to achieve greater legal certainty and clarity to the extent that this issue is not already addressed in Council Regulation (EEC) No 1408/71 of 14 June 1971 on the application of social security schemes to employed persons, to self-employed persons and to members of their families moving within the Community.

(24) Audiovisual services, whatever their mode of transmission, including within cinemas, should also be excluded from the scope of this Directive. Furthermore, this Directive should not apply to aids granted by Member States in the audiovisual sector which are covered by Community rules on competition.

(25) Gambling activities, including lottery and betting transactions, should be excluded from the scope of this Directive in view of the specific nature of these activities, which entail implementation by Member States of policies relating to public policy and consumer protection.

(26) This Directive is without prejudice to the application of Article 45 of the Treaty.

(27) This Directive should not cover those social services in the areas of housing, childcare and support to families and persons in need which are provided by the State at national, regional or local level by providers m andated by the State or by charities recognised as such by the State with the objective of ensuring support for those who are permanently or temporarily in a particular state of need because of their insufficient family income or total or partial lack of independence and for those who risk being marginalised. These services are essential in order to guarantee the fundamental right to human dignity and integrity and are a manifestation of the principles of social cohesion and solidarity and should not be affected by this Directive.

(28) This Directive does not deal with the funding of, or the system of aids linked to, social services. Nor does it affect the criteria or conditions set by Member States to ensure that social services effectively carry out a function to the benefit of the public interest and social cohesion. In addition, this Directive should not affect the principle of universal service in Member States' social services.

(29) Given that the Treaty provides specific legal bases for taxation matters and given the Community instruments already adopted in that field, it is necessary to exclude the field of taxation from the scope of this Directive.

(30) There is already a considerable body of Community law on service activities. This Directive builds on, and thus complements, the Community acquis. Conflicts between this Directive and other Community instruments have been identified and are addressed by this Directive, including by means of derogations. However, it is necessary to provide a rule for any residual and exceptional cases where there is a conflict between a provision of this Directive and a provision of another Community instrument. The existence of such a conflict should be determined in compliance with the rules of the Treaty on the right of establishment and the free movement of services.

(31) This Directive is consistent with and does not affect Directive 2005/36/EC of the European Parliament and of the Council of 7 September 2005 on the recognition of professional qualifications. It deals with questions other than those relating to professional qualifications, for example professional liability insurance, commercial communications, multidisciplinary activities and administrative simplification. With regard to temporary cross-border service provision, a derogation from the provision on the freedom to provide services in this Directive ensures that Title II on the free provision of services of Directive 2005/36/EC is not affected. Therefore, none of the measures applicable under that Directive in the Member State where the service is provided is affected by the provision on the freedom to provide services.

(32) This Directive is consistent with Community legislation on consumer protection, such as Directive 2005/29/EC of the European Parliament and of the Council of 11 May 2005 concerning unfair business-to-consumer commercial practices in the internal market (the Unfair Commercial Practices Directive) and Regulation (EC) No 2006/2004 of the European Parliament and of the Council of 27 October 2004 on cooperation between national authorities responsible for the enforcement of consumer protection laws (the Regulation on consumer protection cooperation).

(33) The services covered by this Directive concern a wide variety of ever-changing activities, including business services such as management consultancy, certification and testing; facilities management, including office maintenance; advertising; recruitment services; and the services of commercial agents. The services covered are also services provided both to businesses and to consumers, such as legal or fiscal advice; real estate services such as estate agencies; construction, including the services of architects; distributive trades; the organisation of trade fairs; car rental; and travel agencies. Consumer services are also covered, such as those in the field of tourism, including tour guides; leisure services, sports centres and amusement parks; and, to the extent that they are not excluded from the scope of application of the Directive, household support services, such as help for the elderly. Those activities may involve services requiring the proximity of provider and recipient, services requiring travel by the recipient or the provider and services which may be provided at a distance, including via the Internet.

(34) According to the case-law of the Court of Justice, the assessment of whether certain activities, in particular activities which are publicly funded or provided by public entities, constitute a "service" has to be carried out on a case by case basis in the light of all their characteristics, in particular the way they are provided, organised and financed in the Member State concerned. The Court of Justice has held that the essential characteristic of remuneration lies in the fact that it constitutes consideration for the services in question and has recognised that the characteristic of remuneration is absent in the case of activities performed, for no consideration, by the State or on behalf of the State in the context of its

duties in the social, cultural, educational and judicial fields, such as courses provided under the national education system, or the management of social security schemes which do not engage in economic activity. The payment of a fee by recipients, for example, a tuition or enrolment fee paid by students in order to make a certain contribution to the operating expenses of a system, does not in itself constitute remuneration because the service is still essentially financed by public funds. These activities are, therefore, not covered by the definition of service in Article 50 of the Treaty and do not therefore fall within the scope of this Directive.

(35) Non-profit making amateur sporting activities are of considerable social importance. They often pursue wholly social or recreational objectives. Thus, they might not constitute economic activities within the meaning of Community law and should fall outside the scope of this Directive.

(36) The concept of "provider" should cover any natural person who is a national of a Member State or any legal person engaged in a service activity in a Member State, in exercise either of the freedom of establishment or of the free movement of services. The concept of provider should thus not be limited solely to cross-border service provision within the framework of the free movement of services but should also cover cases in which an operator establishes itself in a Member State in order to develop its service activities there. On the other hand, the concept of a provider should not cover the case of branches in a Member State of companies from third countries because, under Article 48 of the Treaty, the freedom of establishment and free movement of services may benefit only companies constituted in accordance with the laws of a Member State and having their registered office, central administration or principal place of business within the Community. The concept of "recipient" should also cover third country nationals who already benefit from rights conferred upon them by Community acts such as Regulation (EEC) No 1408/71, Council Directive 2003/109/EC of 25 November 2003 concerning the status of third-country nationals who are long-term residents, Council Regulation (EC) No 859/2003 of 14 May 2003 extending the provisions of Regulation (EEC) No 1408/71 and Regulation (EEC) No 574/72 to nationals of third countries who are not already covered by those provisions solely on the ground of their nationality and Directive 2004/38/ECof the European Parliament and of the Council of 29 April 2004 on the right of citizens of the Union and their family members to move and reside freely within the territory of the Member States. Furthermore, Member States may extend the concept of recipient to other third country nationals that are present within their territory.

(37) The place at which a provider is established should be determined in accordance with the case law of the Court of Justice according to which the concept of establishment involves the actual pursuit of an economic activity through a fixed establishment for an indefinite period. This requirement may also be fulfilled where a company is constituted for a given period or where it rents the building or installation through which it pursues its activity. It may also be fulfilled where a Member State grants authorisations for a limited duration only in relation to particular services. An establishment does not need to take the form of a subsidiary, branch or agency, but may consist of an office managed by a provider's own staff or by a person who is independent but authorised to act on a permanent basis for the undertaking, as would be the case with an agency. According to this definition, which requires the actual pursuit of an economic activity at the place of establishment of the provider, a mere letter box does not constitute an establishment. Where a provider has several places of establishment, it is important to determine the place of establishment from which the actual service concerned is provided. Where it is difficult to determine from which of several places of establishment a given service is provided, the location of the provider's centre of activities relating to this particular service should be that place of establishment.

(38) The concept of "legal persons", according to the Treaty provisions on establishment, leaves operators free to choose the legal form which they deem suitable for carrying out their activity. Accordingly, "legal persons", within the meaning of the Treaty, means all entities constituted under, or governed by, the law of a Member State, irrespective of their legal form.

(39) The concept of "authorisation scheme" should cover, inter alia, the administrative procedures for granting authorisations, licences, approvals or concessions, and also the obligation, in order to be eligible to exercise the activity, to be registered as a member of a profession or entered in a register, roll or database, to be officially appointed to a body or to obtain a card attesting to membership of a particular profession. Authorisation may be granted not only by a formal decision but also by an implicit decision arising, for example, from the silence of the competent authority or from the fact that the interested party must await acknowledgement of receipt of a declaration in order to commence the activity in question or for the latter to become lawful.

(40) The concept of "overriding reasons relating to the public interest" to which reference is made in certain provisions of this Directive has been developed by the Court of Justice in its case law in relation to Articles 43 and 49 of the Treaty and may continue to evolve. The notion as recognised in the case law of the Court of Justice covers at least the following grounds: public policy, public security and public health, within the meaning of Articles 46 and 55 of the Treaty; the maintenance of order in society; social policy objectives; the protection of the recipients of services; consumer protection; the protection of workers, including the social protection of workers; animal welfare; the preservation of the financial balance of the social security system; the prevention of fraud; the prevention of unfair competition; the protection of the environment and the urban environment, including town and country planning; the protection of creditors; safeguarding the sound administration of justice; road safety; the protection of intellectual property; cultural policy objectives, including safeguarding the freedom of expression of various elements, in particular social, cultural, religious and philosophical values of society; the need to ensure a high level of education, the maintenance of press diversity and the promotion of the national language; the preservation of national historical and artistic heritage; and veterinary policy.

(41) The concept of "public policy", as interpreted by the Court of Justice, covers the protection against a genuine and sufficiently serious threat affecting one of the fundamental interests of society and may include, in particular, issues relating to human dignity, the protection of minors and vulnerable adults and animal welfare. Similarly, the concept of public security includes issues of public safety.

(42) The rules relating to administrative procedures should not aim at harmonising administrative procedures but at removing overly burdensome authorisation schemes, procedures and formalities that hinder the freedom of establishment and the creation of new service undertakings therefrom.

(43) One of the fundamental difficulties faced, in particular by SMEs, in accessing service activities and exercising them is the complexity, length and legal uncertainty of administrative procedures. For this reason, following the example of certain modernising and good administrative practice initiatives undertaken at Community and national level, it is necessary to establish principles of administrative simplification, inter alia through the limitation of the obligation of prior authorisation to cases in which it is essential and the introduction of the principle of tacit authorisation by the competent authorities after a certain period of time elapsed. Such modernising action, while maintaining the requirements on transparency and the updating of information relating to operators, is intended to eliminate the delays, costs and dissuasive effects which arise, for example, from unnecessary or excessively complex and

burdensome procedures, the duplication of procedures, the "red tape" involved in submitting documents, the arbitrary use of powers by the competent authorities, indeterminate or excessively long periods before a response is given, the limited duration of validity of authorisations granted and disproportionate fees and penalties. Such practices have particularly significant dissuasive effects on providers wishing to develop their activities in other Member States and require coordinated modernisation within an enlarged internal market of twenty-five Member States.

(44) Member States should introduce, where appropriate, forms harmonised at Community level, as established by the Commission, which will serve as an equivalent to certificates, attestations or any other document in relation to establishment.

(45) In order to examine the need for simplifying procedures and formalities, Member States should be able, in particular, to take into account their necessity, number, possible duplication, cost, clarity and accessibility, as well as the delay and practical difficulties to which they could give rise for the provider concerned.

(46) In order to facilitate access to service activities and the exercise thereof in the internal market, it is necessary to establish an objective, common to all Member States, of administrative simplification and to lay down provisions concerning, inter alia, the right to information, procedures by electronic means and the establishment of a framework for authorisation schemes. Other measures adopted at national level to meet that objective could involve reduction of the number of procedures and formalities applicable to service activities and the restriction of such procedures and formalities to those which are essential in order to achieve a general interest objective and which do not duplicate each other in terms of content or purpose.

(47) With the aim of administrative simplification, general formal requirements, such as presentation of original documents, certified copies or a certified translation, should not be imposed, except where objectively justified by an overriding reason relating to the public interest, such as the protection of workers, public health, the protection of the environment or the protection of consumers. It is also necessary to ensure that an authorisation as a general rule permits access to, or exercise of, a service activity throughout the national territory, unless a new authorisation for each establishment, for example for each new hypermarket, or an authorisation that is restricted to a specific part of the national territory is objectively justified by an overriding reason relating to the public interest.

(48) In order to further simplify administrative procedures, it is appropriate to ensure that each provider has a single point through which he can complete all procedures and formalities (hereinafter referred to as "points of single contact"). The number of points of single contact per Member State may vary according to regional or local competencies or according to the activities concerned. The creation of points of single contact should not interfere with the allocation of functions among competent authorities within each national system. Where several authorities at regional or local level are competent, one of them may assume the role of point of single contact and coordinator. Points of single contact may be set up not only by administrative authorities but also by chambers of commerce or crafts, or by the professional organisations or private bodies to which a Member State decides to entrust that function. Points of single contact have an important role to play in providing assistance to providers either as the authority directly competent to issue the documents necessary to access a service activity or as an intermediary between the provider and the authorities which are directly competent.

(49) The fee which may be charged by points of single contact should be proportionate to the cost of the procedures and formalities with which they deal. This should not prevent

Member States from entrusting the points of single contact with the collection of other administrative fees, such as the fee of supervisory bodies.

(50) It is necessary for providers and recipients of services to have easy access to certain types of information It should be for each Member State to determine, within the framework of this Directive, the way in which providers and recipients are provided with information. In particular, the obligation on Member States to ensure that relevant information is easily accessible to providers and recipients and that it can be accessed by the public without obstacle could be fulfilled by making this information accessible through a website. Any information given should be provided in a clear and unambiguous manner.

(51) The information provided to providers and recipients of services should include, in particular, information on procedures and formalities, contact details of the competent authorities, conditions for access to public registers and data bases and information concerning available remedies and the contact details of associations and organisations from which providers or recipients can obtain practical assistance. The obligation on competent authorities to assist providers and recipients should not include the provision of legal advice in individual cases. Nevertheless, general information on the way in which requirements are usually interpreted or applied should be given. Issues such as liability for providing incorrect or misleading information should be determined by Member States.

(52) The setting up, in the reasonably near future, of electronic means of completing procedures and formalities will be vital for administrative simplification in the field of service activities, for the benefit of providers, recipients and competent authorities. In order to meet that obligation as to results, national laws and other rules applicable to services may need to be adapted. This obligation should not prevent Member States from providing other means of completing such procedures and formalities, in addition to electronic means. The fact that it must be possible to complete those procedures and formalities at a distance means, in particular, that Member States must ensure that they may be completed across borders. The obligation as to results does not cover procedures or formalities which by their very nature are impossible to complete at a distance. Furthermore, this does not interfere with Member States' legislation on the use of languages.

(53) The granting of licences for certain service activities may require an interview with the applicant by the competent authority in order to assess the applicant's personal integrity and suitability for carrying out the service in question. In such cases, the completion of formalities by electronic means may not be appropriate.

(54) The possibility of gaining access to a service activity should be made subject to authorisation by the competent authorities only if that decision satisfies the criteria of non-discrimination, necessity and proportionality. That means, in particular, that authorisation schemes should be permissible only where an a posteriori inspection would not be effective because of the impossibility of ascertaining the defects of the services concerned a posteriori, due account being taken of the risks and dangers which could arise in the absence of a prior inspection. However, the provision to that effect made by this Directive cannot be relied upon in order to justify authorisation schemes which are prohibited by other Community instruments such as Directive 1999/93/EC of the European Parliament and the Council of 13 December 1999 on a Community framework for electronic signatures, or Directive 2000/31/EC of the European Parliament and of the Council of 8 June 2000 on certain legal aspects of information society services, in particular electronic commerce, in the internal market (Directive on electronic commerce). The results of the process of mutual evaluation will make it possible to determine, at Community level, the types of activity for which authorisation schemes should be eliminated.

(55) This Directive should be without prejudice to the possibility for Member States to withdraw authorisations after they have been issued, if the conditions for the granting of the authorisation are no longer fulfilled.

(56) According to the case law of the Court of Justice, public health, consumer protection, animal health and the protection of the urban environment constitute overriding reasons relating to the public interest. Such overriding reasons may justify the application of authorisation schemes and other restrictions. However, no such authorisation scheme or restriction should discriminate on grounds of nationality. Further, the principles of necessity and proportionality should always be respected.

(57) The provisions of this Directive relating to authorisation schemes should concern cases where the access to or exercise of a service activity by operators requires a decision by a competent authority. This concerns neither decisions by competent authorities to set up a public or private entity for the provision of a particular service nor the conclusion of contracts by competent authorities for the provision of a particular service which is governed by rules on public procurement, since this Directive does not deal with rules on public procurement.

(58) In order to facilitate access to and exercise of service activities, it is important to evaluate and report on authorisation schemes and their justification. This reporting obligation concerns only the existence of authorisation schemes and not the criteria and conditions for the granting of an authorisation.

(59) The authorisation should as a general rule enable the provider to have access to the service activity, or to exercise that activity, throughout the national territory, unless a territorial limit is justified by an overriding reason relating to the public interest. For example, environmental protection may justify the requirement to obtain an individual authorisation for each installation on the national territory. This provision should not affect regional or local competences for the granting of authorisations within the Member States.

(60) This Directive, and in particular the provisions concerning authorisation schemes and the territorial scope of an authorisation, should not interfere with the division of regional or local competences within the Member States, including regional and local self-government and the use of official languages.

(61) The provision relating to the non-duplication of conditions for the granting of an authorisation should not prevent Member States from applying their own conditions as specified in the authorisation scheme. It should only require that competent authorities, when considering whether these conditions are met by the applicant, take into account the equivalent conditions which have already been satisfied by the applicant in another Member State. This provision should not require the application of the conditions for the granting of an authorisation provided for in the authorisation scheme of another Member State.

(62) Where the number of authorisations available for an activity is limited because of scarcity of natural resources or technical capacity, a procedure for selection from among several potential candidates should be adopted with the aim of developing through open competition the quality and conditions for supply of services available to users. Such a procedure should provide guarantees of transparency and impartiality and the authorisation thus granted should not have an excessive duration, be subject to automatic renewal or confer any advantage on the provider whose authorisation has just expired. In particular, the duration of the authorisation granted should be fixed in such a way that it does not restrict or limit free competition beyond what is necessary in order to enable the provider to recoup the cost of investment and to make a fair return on the capital invested. This provision should not prevent Member States from limiting the number of authorisations for reasons other than scarcity of natural resources or technical capacity. These authorisations

should remain in any case subject to the other provisions of this Directive relating to authorisation schemes.

(63) In the absence of different arrangements, failing a response within a time period, an authorisation should be deemed to have been granted. However, different arrangements may be put in place in respect of certain activities, where objectively justified by overriding reasons relating to the public interest, including a legitimate interest of third parties. Such different arrangements could include national rules according to which, in the absence of a response of the competent authority, the application is deemed to have been rejected, this rejection being open to challenge before the courts.

(64) In order to establish a genuine internal market for services, it is necessary to abolish any restrictions on the freedom of establishment and the free movement of services which are still enshrined in the laws of certain Member States and which are incompatible with Articles 43 and 49 of the Treaty respectively. The restrictions to be prohibited particularly affect the internal market for services and should be systematically dismantled as soon as possible.

(65) Freedom of establishment is predicated, in particular, upon the principle of equal treatment, which entails the prohibition not only of any discrimination on grounds of nationality but also of any indirect discrimination based on other grounds but capable of producing the same result. Thus, access to a service activity or the exercise thereof in a Member State, either as a principal or secondary activity, should not be made subject to criteria such as place of establishment, residence, domicile or principal provision of the service activity. However, these criteria should not include requirements according to which a provider or one of his employees or a representative must be present during the exercise of the activity when this is justified by an overriding reason relating to the public interest. Furthermore, a Member State should not restrict the legal capacity or the right of companies, incorporated in accordance with the law of another Member State on whose territory they have their primary establishment, to bring legal proceedings. Moreover, a Member State should not be able to confer any advantages on providers having a particular national or local socio-economic link; nor should it be able to restrict, on grounds of place of establishment, the provider's freedom to acquire, exploit or dispose of rights and goods or to access different forms of credit or accommodation in so far as those choices are useful for access to his activity or for the effective exercise thereof.

(66) Access to or the exercise of a service activity in the territory of a Member State should not be subject to an economic test. The prohibition of economic tests as a prerequisite for the grant of authorisation should cover economic tests as such, but not requirements which are objectively justified by overriding reasons relating to the public interest, such as the protection of the urban environment, social policy or public health. The prohibition should not affect the exercise of the powers of the authorities responsible for applying competition law.

(67) With respect to financial guarantees or insurance, the prohibition of requirements should concern only the obligation that the requested financial guarantees or insurance must be obtained from a financial institution established in the Member State concerned.

(68) With respect to pre-registration, the prohibition of requirements should concern only the obligation that the provider, prior to the establishment, be pre-registered for a given period in a register held in the Member State concerned.

(69) In order to coordinate the modernisation of national rules and regulations in a manner consistent with the requirements of the internal market, it is necessary to evaluate certain non-discriminatory national requirements which, by their very nature, could severely restrict or even prevent access to an activity or the exercise thereof under the freedom of establishment. This evaluation process should be limited to the compatibility of these requirements with the criteria already established by the Court of Justice on the freedom

of establishment. It should not concern the application of Community competition law. Where such requirements are discriminatory or not objectively justified by an overriding reason relating to the public interest, or where they are disproportionate, they must be abolished or amended. The outcome of this assessment will be different according to the nature of the activity and the public interest concerned. In particular, such requirements could be fully justified when they pursue social policy objectives.

(70) For the purposes of this Directive, and without prejudice to Article 16 of the Treaty, services may be considered to be services of general economic interest only if they are provided in application of a special task in the public interest entrusted to the provider by the Member State concerned. This assignment should be made by way of one or more acts, the form of which is determined by the Member State concerned, and should specify the precise nature of the special task.

(71) The mutual evaluation process provided for in this Directive should not affect the freedom of Member States to set in their legislation a high level of protection of the public interest, in particular in relation to social policy objectives. Furthermore, it is necessary that the mutual evaluation process take fully into account the specificity of services of general economic interest and of the particular tasks assigned to them. This may justify certain restrictions on the freedom of establishment, in particular where such restrictions pursue the protection of public health and social policy objectives and where they satisfy the conditions set out in Article 15(3)(a), (b) and (c). For example, with regard to the obligation to take a specific legal form in order to exercise certain services in the social field, the Court of Justice has already recognised that it may be justified to subject the provider to a requirement to be non-profit making.

(72) Services of a general economic interest are entrusted with important tasks relating to social and territorial cohesion. The performance of these tasks should not be obstructed as a result of the evaluation process provided for in this Directive. Requirements which are necessary for the fulfilment of such tasks should not be affected by this process while, at the same time, unjustified restrictions on the freedom of establishment should be addressed.

(73) The requirements to be examined include national rules which, on grounds other than those relating to professional qualifications, reserve access to certain activities to particular providers. These requirements also include obligations on a provider to take a specific legal form, in particular to be a legal person, to be a company with individual ownership, to be a non-profit making organisation or a company owned exclusively by natural persons, and requirements which relate to the shareholding of a company, in particular obligations to hold a minimum amount of capital for certain service activities or to have a specific qualification in order to hold share capital in or to manage certain companies. The evaluation of the compatibility of fixed minimum and/or maximum tariffs with the freedom of establishment concerns only tariffs imposed by competent authorities specifically for the provision of certain services and not, for example, general rules on price determination, such as for the renting of houses.

(74) The mutual evaluation process means that during the transposition period Member States will first have to conduct a screening of their legislation in order to ascertain whether any of the above mentioned requirements exists in their legal systems. At the latest by the end of the transposition period, Member States should draw up a report on the results of this screening. Each report will be submitted to all other Member States and interested parties. Member States will then have six months in which to submit their observations on these reports. At the latest by one year after the date of transposition of this Directive, the Commission should draw up a summary report, accompanied where appropriate by proposals for further initiatives. If necessary the Commission, in cooperation with the Member States, could assist them to design a common method.

(75)   The fact that this Directive specifies a number of requirements to be abolished or evaluated by the Member States during the transposition period is without prejudice to any infringement proceedings against a Member State for failure to fulfil its obligations under Articles 43 or 49 of the Treaty.

(76)   This Directive does not concern the application of Articles 28 to 30 of the Treaty relating to the free movement of goods. The restrictions prohibited pursuant to the provision on the freedom to provide services cover the requirements applicable to access to service activities or to the exercise thereof and not those applicable to goods as such.

(77)   Where an operator travels to another Member State to exercise a service activity there, a distinction should be made between situations covered by the freedom of establishment and those covered, due to the temporary nature of the activities concerned, by the free movement of services. As regards the distinction between the freedom of establishment and the free movement of services, according to the case law of the Court of Justice the key element is whether or not the operator is established in the Member State where it provides the service concerned. If the operator is established in the Member State where it provides its services, it should come under the scope of application of the freedom of establishment. If, by contrast, the operator is not established in the Member State where the service is provided, its activities should be covered by the free movement of services. The Court of Justice has consistently held that the temporary nature of the activities in question should be determined in the light not only of the duration of the provision of the service, but also of its regularity, periodical nature or continuity. The fact that the activity is temporary should not mean that the provider may not equip itself with some forms of infrastructure in the Member State where the service is provided, such as an office, chambers or consulting rooms, in so far as such infrastructure is necessary for the purposes of providing the service in question.

(78)   In order to secure effective implementation of the free movement of services and to ensure that recipients and providers can benefit from and supply services throughout the Community regardless of borders, it is necessary to clarify the extent to which requirements of the Member State where the service is provided can be imposed. It is indispensable to provide that the provision on the freedom to provide services does not prevent the Member State where the service is provided from imposing, in compliance with the principles set out in Article 16(1)(a) to (c), its specific requirements for reasons of public policy or public security or for the protection of public health or the environment.

(79)   The Court of Justice has consistently held that Member States retain the right to take measures in order to prevent providers from abusively taking advantage of the internal market principles. Abuse by a provider should be established on a case by case basis.

(80)   It is necessary to ensure that providers are able to take equipment which is integral to the provision of their service with them when they travel to provide services in another Member State. In particular, it is important to avoid cases in which the service could not be provided without the equipment or situations in which providers incur additional costs, for example, by hiring or purchasing different equipment to that which they habitually use or by needing to deviate significantly from the way they habitually carry out their activity.

(81)   The concept of equipment does not refer to physical objects which are either supplied by the provider to the client or become part of a physical object as a result of the service activity, such as building materials or spare parts, or which are consumed or left in situ in the course of the service provision, such as combustible fuels, explosives, fireworks, pesticides, poisons or medicines.

(82)   The provisions of this Directive should not preclude the application by a Member State of rules on employment conditions. Rules laid down by law, regulation or administrative

provisions should, in accordance with the Treaty, be justified for reasons relating to the protection of workers and be non-discriminatory, necessary, and proportionate, as interpreted by the Court of Justice, and comply with other relevant Community law.

(83) It is necessary to ensure that the provision on the freedom to provide services may be departed from only in the areas covered by derogations. Those derogations are necessary in order to take into account the level of integration of the internal market or certain Community instruments relating to services pursuant to which a provider is subject to the application of a law other than that of the Member State of establishment. Moreover, by way of exception, measures against a given provider should also be adopted in certain individual cases and under certain strict procedural and substantive conditions. In addition, any restriction of the free movement of services should be permitted, by way of exception, only if it is consistent with fundamental rights which form an integral part of the general principles of law enshrined in the Community legal order.

(84) The derogation from the provision on the freedom to provide services concerning postal services should cover both activities reserved to the universal service provider and other postal services.

(85) The derogation from the provision on the freedom to provide services relating to the judicial recovery of debts and the reference to a possible future harmonisation instrument should concern only the access to and the exercise of activities which consist, notably, in bringing actions before a court relating to the recovery of debts.

(86) This Directive should not affect terms and conditions of employment which, pursuant to Directive 96/71/EC of the European Parliament and of the Council of 16 December 1996 concerning the posting of workers in the framework of the provision of services, apply to workers posted to provide a service in the territory of another Member State. In such cases, Directive 96/71/EC stipulates that providers have to comply with terms and conditions of employment in a listed number of areas applicable in the Member State where the service is provided. These are: maximum work periods and minimum rest periods, minimum paid annual holidays, minimum rates of pay, including overtime rates, the conditions of hiring out of workers, in particular the protection of workers hired out by temporary employment undertakings, health, safety and hygiene at work, protective measures with regard to the terms and conditions of employment of pregnant women or women who have recently given birth and of children and young people and equality of treatment between men and women and other provisions on non-discrimination. This not only concerns terms and conditions of employment which are laid down by law but also those laid down in collective agreements or arbitration awards that are officially declared or de facto universally applicable within the meaning of Directive 96/71/EC. Moreover, this Directive should not prevent Member States from applying terms and conditions of employment on matters other than those listed in Article 3(1) of Directive 96/71/EC on the grounds of public policy.

(87) Neither should this Directive affect terms and conditions of employment in cases where the worker employed for the provision of a cross-border service is recruited in the Member State where the service is provided. Furthermore, this Directive should not affect the right for the Member State where the service is provided to determine the existence of an employment relationship and the distinction between self-employed persons and employed persons, including "false self-employed persons". In that respect the essential characteristic of an employment relationship within the meaning of Article 39 of the Treaty should be the fact that for a certain period of time a person provides services for and under the direction of another person in return for which he receives remuneration. Any activity which a person performs outside a relationship of subordination must be

classified as an activity pursued in a self-employed capacity for the purposes of Articles 43 and 49 of the Treaty.

(88) The provision on the freedom to provide services should not apply in cases where, in conformity with Community law, an activity is reserved in a Member State to a particular profession, for example requirements which reserve the provision of legal advice to lawyers.

(89) The derogation from the provision on the freedom to provide services concerning matters relating to the registration of vehicles leased in a Member State other than that in which they are used follows from the case law of the Court of Justice, which has recognised that a Member State may impose such an obligation, in accordance with proportionate conditions, in the case of vehicles used on its territory. That exclusion does not cover occasional or temporary rental.

(90) Contractual relations between the provider and the client as well as between an employer and employee should not be subject to this Directive. The applicable law regarding the contractual or non contractual obligations of the provider should be determined by the rules of private international law.

(91) It is necessary to afford Member States the possibility, exceptionally and on a case-by-case basis, of taking measures which derogate from the provision on the freedom to provide services in respect of a provider established in another Member State on grounds of the safety of services. However, it should be possible to take such measures only in the absence of harmonisation at Community level.

(92) Restrictions on the free movement of services, contrary to this Directive, may arise not only from measures applied to providers, but also from the many barriers to the use of services by recipients, especially consumers. This Directive mentions, by way of illustration, certain types of restriction applied to a recipient wishing to use a service performed by a provider established in another Member State. This also includes cases where recipients of a service are under an obligation to obtain authorisation from or to make a declaration to their competent authorities in order to receive a service from a provider established in another Member State. This does not concern general authorisation schemes which also apply to the use of a service supplied by a provider established in the same Member State.

(93) The concept of financial assistance provided for the use of a particular service should not apply to systems of aids granted by Member States, in particular in the social field or in the cultural sector, which are covered by Community rules on competition, nor to general financial assistance not linked to the use of a particular service, for example grants or loans to students.

(94) In accordance with the Treaty rules on the free movement of services, discrimination on grounds of the nationality of the recipient or national or local residence is prohibited. Such discrimination could take the form of an obligation, imposed only on nationals of another Member State, to supply original documents, certified copies, a certificate of nationality or official translations of documents in order to benefit from a service or from more advantageous terms or prices. However, the prohibition of discriminatory requirements should not preclude the reservation of advantages, especially as regards tariffs, to certain recipients, if such reservation is based on legitimate and objective criteria.

(95) The principle of non-discrimination within the internal market means that access by a recipient, and especially by a consumer, to a service on offer to the public may not be

denied or restricted by application of a criterion, included in general conditions made available to the public, relating to the recipient's nationality or place of residence. It does not follow that it will be unlawful discrimination if provision were made in such general conditions for different tariffs and conditions to apply to the provision of a service, where those tariffs, prices and conditions are justified for objective reasons that can vary from country to country, such as additional costs incurred because of the distance involved or the technical characteristics of the provision of the service, or different market conditions, such as higher or lower demand influenced by seasonality, different vacation periods in the Member States and pricing by different competitors, or extra risks linked to rules differing from those of the Member State of establishment. Neither does it follow that the non-provision of a service to a consumer for lack of the required intellectual property rights in a particular territory would constitute unlawful discrimination.

(96) It is appropriate to provide that, as one of the means by which the provider may make the information which he is obliged to supply easily accessible to the recipient, he supply his electronic address, including that of his website. Furthermore, the obligation to make available certain information in the provider's information documents which present his services in detail should not cover commercial communications of a general nature, such as advertising, but rather documents giving a detailed description of the services proposed, including documents on a website.

(97) It is necessary to provide in this Directive for certain rules on high quality of services, ensuring in particular information and transparency requirements. These rules should apply both in cases of cross border provision of services between Member States and in cases of services provided in a Member State by a provider established there, without imposing unnecessary burdens on SMEs. They should not in any way prevent Member States from applying, in conformity with this Directive and other Community law, additional or different quality requirements.

(98) Any operator providing services involving a direct and particular health, safety or financial risk for the recipient or a third person should, in principle, be covered by appropriate professional liability insurance, or by another form of guarantee which is equivalent or comparable, which means, in particular, that such an operator should as a general rule have adequate insurance cover for services provided in one or more Member States other than the Member State of establishment.

(99) The insurance or guarantee should be appropriate to the nature and extent of the risk. Therefore it should be necessary for the provider to have cross-border cover only if that provider actually provides services in other Member States. Member States should not lay down more detailed rules concerning the insurance cover and fix for example minimum thresholds for the insured sum or limits on exclusions from the insurance cover. Providers and insurance companies should maintain the necessary flexibility to negotiate insurance policies precisely targeted to the nature and extent of the risk. Furthermore, it is not necessary for an obligation of appropriate insurance to be laid down by law. It should be sufficient if an insurance obligation is part of the ethical rules laid down by professional bodies. Finally, there should be no obligation for insurance companies to provide insurance cover.

(100) It is necessary to put an end to total prohibitions on commercial communications by the regulated professions, not by removing bans on the content of a commercial communication but rather by removing those bans which, in a general way and for a given profession, forbid one or more forms of commercial communication, such as a ban on all advertising in one or more given media. As regards the content and methods of commercial communication, it is necessary to encourage professionals to draw up, in accordance with Community law, codes of conduct at Community level.

(101) It is necessary and in the interest of recipients, in particular consumers, to ensure that it is possible for providers to offer multidisciplinary services and that restrictions in this regard be limited to what is necessary to ensure the impartiality, independence and integrity of the regulated professions. This does not affect restrictions or prohibitions on carrying out particular activities which aim at ensuring independence in cases in which a Member State entrusts a provider with a particular task, notably in the area of urban development, nor should it affect the application of competition rules.

(102) In order to increase transparency and promote assessments based on comparable criteria with regard to the quality of the services offered and supplied to recipients, it is important that information on the meaning of quality labels and other distinctive marks relating to these services be easily accessible. That obligation of transparency is particularly important in areas such as tourism, especially the hotel business, in which the use of a system of classification is widespread. Moreover, it is appropriate to examine the extent to which European standardisation could facilitate compatibility and quality of services. European standards are drawn up by the European standards-setting bodies, the European Committee for Standardisation (CEN), the European Committee for Electrotechnical Standardisation (CENELEC) and the European Telecommunications Standards Institute (ETSI). Where appropriate, the Commission may, in accordance with the procedures laid down in Directive 98/34/EC of the European Parliament and of the Council of 22 June 1998 laying down a procedure for the provision of information in the field of technical standards and regulations and of rules on Information Society services, issue a mandate for the drawing up of specific European standards.

(103) In order to solve potential problems with compliance with judicial decisions, it is appropriate to provide that Member States recognise equivalent guarantees lodged with institutions or bodies such as banks, insurance providers or other financial services providers established in another Member State.

(104) The development of a network of Member States' consumer protection authorities, which is the subject of Regulation (EC) No 2006/2004, complements the cooperation provided for in this Directive. The application of consumer protection legislation in cross-border cases, in particular with regard to new marketing and selling practices, as well as the need to remove certain specific obstacles to cooperation in this field, necessitates a greater degree of cooperation between Member States. In particular, it is necessary in this area to ensure that Member States require the cessation of illegal practices by operators in their territory who target consumers in another Member State.

(105) Administrative cooperation is essential to make the internal market in services function properly. Lack of cooperation between Member States results in proliferation of rules applicable to providers or duplication of controls for cross-border activities, and can also be used by rogue traders to avoid supervision or to circumvent applicable national rules on services. It is, therefore, essential to provide for clear, legally binding obligations for Member States to cooperate effectively.

(106) For the purposes of the Chapter on administrative cooperation, "supervision" should cover activities such as monitoring and fact finding, problem solving, enforcement and imposition of sanctions and subsequent follow-up activities.

(107) In normal circumstances mutual assistance should take place directly between competent authorities. The liaison points designated by Member States should be required to facilitate this process only in the event of difficulties being encountered, for instance if assistance is required to identify the relevant competent authority.

(108) Certain obligations of mutual assistance should apply to all matters covered by this Directive, including those relating to cases where a provider establishes in another Member State. Other obligations of mutual assistance should apply only in cases of cross-border provision of services, where the provision on the freedom to provide services applies. A further set of obligations should apply in all cases of cross-border provision of services, including areas not covered by the provision on the freedom to provide services. Cross-border provision of services should include cases where services are provided at a distance and where the recipient travels to the Member State of establishment of the provider in order to receive services.

(109) In cases where a provider moves temporarily to a Member State other than the Member State of establishment, it is necessary to provide for mutual assistance between those two Member States so that the former can carry out checks, inspections and enquiries at the request of the Member State of establishment or carry out such checks on its own initiative if these are merely factual checks.

(110) It should not be possible for Member States to circumvent the rules laid down in this Directive, including the provision on the freedom to provide services, by conducting checks, inspections or investigations which are discriminatory or disproportionate.

(111) The provisions of this Directive concerning exchange of information regarding the good repute of providers should not pre-empt initiatives in the area of police and judicial cooperation in criminal matters, in particular on the exchange of information between law enforcement authorities of the Member States and on criminal records.

(112) Cooperation between Member States requires a well-functioning electronic information system in order to allow competent authorities easily to identify their relevant interlocutors in other Member States and to communicate in an efficient way.

(113) It is necessary to provide that the Member States, in cooperation with the Commission, are to encourage interested parties to draw up codes of conduct at Community level, aimed, in particular, at promoting the quality of services and taking into account the specific nature of each profession. Those codes of conduct should comply with Community law, especially competition law. They should be compatible with legally binding rules governing professional ethics and conduct in the Member States.

(114) Member States should encourage the setting up of codes of conduct, in particular, by professional bodies, organisations and associations at Community level. These codes of conduct should include, as appropriate to the specific nature of each profession, rules for commercial communications relating to the regulated professions and rules of professional ethics and conduct of the regulated professions which aim, in particular, at ensuring independence, impartiality and professional secrecy. In addition, the conditions to which the activities of estate agents are subject should be included in such codes of conduct. Member States should take accompanying measures to encourage professional bodies, organisations and associations to implement at national level the codes of conduct adopted at Community level.

(115) Codes of conduct at Community level are intended to set minimum standards of conduct and are complementary to Member States' legal requirements. They do not preclude Member States, in accordance with Community law, from taking more stringent measures in law or national professional bodies from providing for greater protection in their national codes of conduct.

(116) Since the objectives of this Directive, namely the elimination of barriers to the freedom of establishment for providers in the Member States and to the free provision of services between Member States, cannot be sufficiently achieved by the Member States and can

therefore, by reason of the scale of the action, be better achieved at Community level, the Community may adopt measures, in accordance with the principle of subsidiarity as set out in Article 5 of the Treaty. In accordance with the principle of proportionality, as set out in that Article, this Directive does not go beyond what is necessary in order to achieve those objectives.

(117) The measures necessary for the implementation of this Directive should be adopted in accordance with Council Decision 1999/468/EC of 28 June 1999 laying down the procedures for the exercise of implementing powers conferred on the Commission.

(118) In accordance with paragraph 34 of the Interinstitutional Agreement on better law-making, Member States are encouraged to draw up, for themselves and in the interest of the Community, their own tables, which will, as far as possible, illustrate the correlation between the Directive and the transposition measures, and to make them public,

HAVE ADOPTED THIS DIRECTIVE:

Chapter I GENERAL PROVISIONS

Article 1 Subject matter

1. This Directive establishes general provisions facilitating the exercise of the freedom of establishment for service providers and the free movement of services, while maintaining a high quality of services.

2. This Directive does not deal with the liberalisation of services of general economic interest, reserved to public or private entities, nor with the privatisation of public entities providing services.

3. This Directive does not deal with the abolition of monopolies providing services nor with aids granted by Member States which are covered by Community rules on competition.

   This Directive does not affect the freedom of Member States to define, in conformity with Community law, what they consider to be services of general economic interest, how those services should be organised and financed, in compliance with the State aid rules, and what specific obligations they should be subject to.

4. This Directive does not affect measures taken at Community level or at national level, in conformity with Community law, to protect or promote cultural or linguistic diversity or media pluralism.

5. This Directive does not affect Member States' rules of criminal law. However, Member States may not restrict the freedom to provide services by applying criminal law provisions which specifically regulate or affect access to or exercise of a service activity in circumvention of the rules laid down in this Directive.

6. This Directive does not affect labour law, that is any legal or contractual provision concerning employment conditions, working conditions, including health and safety at work and the relationship between employers and workers, which Member States apply in accordance with national law which respects Community law. Equally, this Directive does not affect the social security legislation of the Member States.

7. This Directive does not affect the exercise of fundamental rights as recognised in the Member States and by Community law. Nor does it affect the right to negotiate, conclude and enforce collective agreements and to take industrial action in accordance with national law and practices which respect Community law.

Article 2 Scope

1.   This Directive shall apply to services supplied by providers established in a Member State.

2.   This Directive shall not apply to the following activities:
     (a) non-economic services of general interest;
     (b) financial services, such as banking, credit, insurance and re-insurance, occupational or personal pensions, securities, investment funds, payment and investment advice, including the services listed in Annex I to Directive 2006/48/EC;
     (c) electronic communications services and networks, and associated facilities and services, with respect to matters covered by Directives 2002/19/EC, 2002/20/EC, 2002/21/EC, 2002/22/EC and 2002/58/EC;
     (d) services in the field of transport, including port services, falling within the scope of Title V of the Treaty;
     (e) services of temporary work agencies;
     (f) healthcare services whether or not they are provided via healthcare facilities, and regardless of the ways in which they are organised and financed at national level or whether they are public or private;
     (g) audiovisual services, including cinematographic services, whatever their mode of production, distribution and transmission, and radio broadcasting;
     (h) gambling activities which involve wagering a stake with pecuniary value in games of chance, including lotteries, gambling in casinos and betting transactions;
     (i) activities which are connected with the exercise of official authority as set out in Article 45 of the Treaty;
     (j) social services relating to social housing, childcare and support of families and persons permanently or temporarily in need which are provided by the State, by providers mandated by the State or by charities recognised as such by the State;
     (k) private security services;
     (l) services provided by notaries and bailiffs, who are appointed by an official act of government.

3.   This Directive shall not apply to the field of taxation.

Article 3 Relationship with other provisions of Community law

1.   If the provisions of this Directive conflict with a provision of another Community act governing specific aspects of access to or exercise of a service activity in specific sectors or for specific professions, the provision of the other Community act shall prevail and shall apply to those specific sectors or professions. These include:
     (a) Directive 96/71/EC;
     (b) Regulation (EEC) No 1408/71;
     (c) Council Directive 89/552/EEC of 3 October 1989 on the coordination of certain provisions laid down by law, regulation or administrative action in Member States concerning the pursuit of television broadcasting activities;
     (d) Directive 2005/36/EC.

2.   This Directive does not concern rules of private international law, in particular rules governing the law applicable to contractual and non contractual obligations, including those which guarantee that consumers benefit from the protection granted to them by the consumer protection rules laid down in the consumer legislation in force in their Member State.

3.   Member States shall apply the provisions of this Directive in compliance with the rules of the Treaty on the right of establishment and the free movement of services.

Article 4 Definitions

For the purposes of this Directive, the following definitions shall apply:

1.   "service" means any self-employed economic activity, normally provided for remuneration, as referred to in Article 50 of the Treaty;

2.   "provider" means any natural person who is a national of a Member State, or any legal person as referred to in Article 48 of the Treaty and established in a Member State, who offers or provides a service;

3.   "recipient" means any natural person who is a national of a Member State or who benefits from rights conferred upon him by Community acts, or any legal person as referred to in Article 48 of the Treaty and established in a Member State, who, for professional or non-professional purposes, uses, or wishes to use, a service;

4.   "Member State of establishment" means the Member State in whose territory the provider of the service concerned is established;

5.   "establishment" means the actual pursuit of an economic activity, as referred to in Article 43 of the Treaty, by the provider for an indefinite period and through a stable infrastructure from where the business of providing services is actually carried out;

6.   "authorisation scheme" means any procedure under which a provider or recipient is in effect required to take steps in order to obtain from a competent authority a formal decision, or an implied decision, concerning access to a service activity or the exercise thereof;

7.   "requirement" means any obligation, prohibition, condition or limit provided for in the laws, regulations or administrative provisions of the Member States or in consequence of case-law, administrative practice, the rules of professional bodies, or the collective rules of professional associations or other professional organisations, adopted in the exercise of their legal autonomy; rules laid down in collective agreements negotiated by the social partners shall not as such be seen as requirements within the meaning of this Directive;

8.   "overriding reasons relating to the public interest" means reasons recognised as such in the case law of the Court of Justice, including the following grounds: public policy; public security; public safety; public health; preserving the financial equilibrium of the social security system; the protection of consumers, recipients of services and workers; fairness of trade transactions; combating fraud; the protection of the environment and the urban environment; the health of animals; intellectual property; the conservation of the national historic and artistic heritage; social policy objectives and cultural policy objectives;

9.   "competent authority" means any body or authority which has a supervisory or regulatory role in a Member State in relation to service activities, including, in particular, administrative authorities, including courts acting as such, professional bodies, and those professional associations or other professional organisations which, in the exercise of their legal autonomy, regulate in a collective manner access to service activities or the exercise thereof;

10.   "Member State where the service is provided" means the Member State where the service is supplied by a provider established in another Member State;

11.   "regulated profession" means a professional activity or a group of professional activities as referred to in Article 3(1)(a) of Directive 2005/36/EC;

12.   "commercial communication" means any form of communication designed to promote, directly or indirectly, the goods, services or image of an undertaking, organisation or person engaged in commercial, industrial or craft activity or practising a regulated profession. The following do not in themselves constitute commercial communications:
       (a) information enabling direct access to the activity of the undertaking, organisation or person, including in particular a domain name or an electronic-mailing address;

(b) communications relating to the goods, services or image of the undertaking, organisation or person, compiled in an independent manner, particularly when provided for no financial consideration.

Chapter II ADMINISTRATIVE SIMPLIFICATION

Article 5 Simplification of procedures

1. Member States shall examine the procedures and formalities applicable to access to a service activity and to the exercise thereof. Where procedures and formalities examined under this paragraph are not sufficiently simple, Member States shall simplify them.

2. The Commission may introduce harmonised forms at Community level, in accordance with the procedure referred to in Article 40(2). These forms shall be equivalent to certificates, attestations and any other documents required of a provider.

3. Where Member States require a provider or recipient to supply a certificate, attestation or any other document proving that a requirement has been satisfied, they shall accept any document from another Member State which serves an equivalent purpose or from which it is clear that the requirement in question has been satisfied. They may not require a document from another Member State to be produced in its original form, or as a certified copy or as a certified translation, save in the cases provided for in other Community instruments or where such a requirement is justified by an overriding reason relating to the public interest, including public order and security.

   The first subparagraph shall not affect the right of Member States to require non-certified translations of documents in one of their official languages.

4. Paragraph 3 shall not apply to the documents referred to in Article 7(2) and 50 of Directive 2005/36/EC, in Articles 45(3), 46, 49 and 50 of Directive 2004/18/EC of the European Parliament and of the Council of 31 March 2004 on the coordination of procedures for the award of public works contracts, public supply contracts and public service contracts, in Article 3(2) of Directive 98/5/EC of the European Parliament and of the Council of 16 February 1998 to facilitate practice of the profession of lawyer on a permanent basis in a Member State other than that in which the qualification was obtained, in the First Council Directive 68/151/EEC of 9 March 1968 on coordination of safeguards which, for the protection of the interests of members and others, are required by Member States of companies within the meaning of the second paragraph of Article 58 of the Treaty, with a view to making such safeguards equivalent throughout the Community and in the Eleventh Council Directive 89/666/EECof 21 December 1989 concerning disclosure requirements in respect of branches opened in a Member State by certain types of company governed by the law of another State.

Article 6 Points of single contact

1. Member States shall ensure that it is possible for providers to complete the following procedures and formalities through points of single contact:
   (a) all procedures and formalities needed for access to his service activities, in particular, all declarations, notifications or applications necessary for authorisation from the competent authorities, including applications for inclusion in a register, a roll or a database, or for registration with a professional body or association;
   (b) any applications for authorisation needed to exercise his service activities.

2. The establishment of points of single contact shall be without prejudice to the allocation of functions and powers among the authorities within national systems.

Article 7 Right to information

1. Member States shall ensure that the following information is easily accessible to providers and recipients through the points of single contact:

    (a) requirements applicable to providers established in their territory, in particular those requirements concerning the procedures and formalities to be completed in order to access and to exercise service activities;

    (b) the contact details of the competent authorities enabling the latter to be contacted directly, including the details of those authorities responsible for matters concerning the exercise of service activities;

    (c) the means of, and conditions for, accessing public registers and databases on providers and services;

    (d) the means of redress which are generally available in the event of dispute between the competent authorities and the provider or the recipient, or between a provider and a recipient or between providers;

    (e) the contact details of the associations or organisations, other than the competent authorities, from which providers or recipients may obtain practical assistance.

2. Member States shall ensure that it is possible for providers and recipients to receive, at their request, assistance from the competent authorities, consisting in information on the way in which the requirements referred to in point (a) of paragraph 1 are generally interpreted and applied. Where appropriate, such advice shall include a simple step-by-step guide. The information shall be provided in plain and intelligible language.

3. Member States shall ensure that the information and assistance referred to in paragraphs 1 and 2 are provided in a clear and unambiguous manner, that they are easily accessible at a distance and by electronic means and that they are kept up to date.

4. Member States shall ensure that the points of single contact and the competent authorities respond as quickly as possible to any request for information or assistance as referred to in paragraphs 1 and 2 and, in cases where the request is faulty or unfounded, inform the applicant accordingly without delay.

5. Member States and the Commission shall take accompanying measures in order to encourage points of single contact to make the information provided for in this Article available in other Community languages. This does not interfere with Member States' legislation on the use of languages.

6. The obligation for competent authorities to assist providers and recipients does not require those authorities to provide legal advice in individual cases but concerns only general information on the way in which requirements are usually interpreted or applied.

Article 8 Procedures by electronic means

1. Member States shall ensure that all procedures and formalities relating to access to a service activity and to the exercise thereof may be easily completed, at a distance and by electronic means, through the relevant point of single contact and with the relevant competent authorities.

2. Paragraph 1 shall not apply to the inspection of premises on which the service is provided or of equipment used by the provider or to physical examination of the capability or of the personal integrity of the provider or of his responsible staff.

3. The Commission shall, in accordance with the procedure referred to in Article 40(2), adopt detailed rules for the implementation of paragraph 1 of this Article with a view to facilitating the interoperability of information systems and use of procedures by electronic means between Member States, taking into account common standards developed at Community level.

Chapter III FREEDOM OF ESTABLISHMENT FOR PROVIDERS

SECTION 1 AUTHORISATIONS

Article 9 Authorisation schemes

1. Member States shall not make access to a service activity or the exercise thereof subject to an authorisation scheme unless the following conditions are satisfied:
   (a) the authorisation scheme does not discriminate against the provider in question;
   (b) the need for an authorisation scheme is justified by an overriding reason relating to the public interest;
   (c) the objective pursued cannot be attained by means of a less restrictive measure, in particular because an a posteriori inspection would take place too late to be genuinely effective.

2. In the report referred to in Article 39(1), Member States shall identify their authorisation schemes and give reasons showing their compatibility with paragraph 1 of this Article.

3. This section shall not apply to those aspects of authorisation schemes which are governed directly or indirectly by other Community instruments.

Article 10 Conditions for the granting of authorisation

1. Authorisation schemes shall be based on criteria which preclude the competent authorities from exercising their power of assessment in an arbitrary manner.

2. The criteria referred to in paragraph 1 shall be:
   (a) non-discriminatory;
   (b) justified by an overriding reason relating to the public interest;
   (c) proportionate to that public interest objective;
   (d) clear and unambiguous;
   (e) objective;
   (f) made public in advance;
   (g) transparent and accessible.

3. The conditions for granting authorisation for a new establishment shall not duplicate requirements and controls which are equivalent or essentially comparable as regards their purpose to which the provider is already subject in another Member State or in the same Member State. The liaison points referred to in Article 28(2) and the provider shall assist the competent authority by providing any necessary information regarding those requirements.

4. The authorisation shall enable the provider to have access to the service activity, or to exercise that activity, throughout the national territory, including by means of setting up agencies, subsidiaries, branches or offices, except where an authorisation for each individual establishment or a limitation of the authorisation to a certain part of the territory is justified by an overriding reason relating to the public interest.

5. The authorisation shall be granted as soon as it is established, in the light of an appropriate examination, that the conditions for authorisation have been met.

6. Except in the case of the granting of an authorisation, any decision from the competent authorities, including refusal or withdrawal of an authorisation, shall be fully reasoned and shall be open to challenge before the courts or other instances of appeal.

7. This Article shall not call into question the allocation of the competences, at local or regional level, of the Member States' authorities granting authorisations.

Article 11 Duration of authorisation

1.   An authorisation granted to a provider shall not be for a limited period, except where:
     (a) the authorisation is being automatically renewed or is subject only to the continued fulfilment of requirements;
     (b) the number of available authorisations is limited by an overriding reason relating to the public interest; or
     (c) a limited authorisation period can be justified by an overriding reason relating to the public interest.

2.   Paragraph 1 shall not concern the maximum period before the end of which the provider must actually commence his activity after receiving authorisation.

3.   Member States shall require a provider to inform the relevant point of single contact provided for in Article 6 of the following changes:
     (a) the creation of subsidiaries whose activities fall within the scope of the authorisation scheme;
     (b) changes in his situation which result in the conditions for authorisation no longer being met.

4.   This Article shall be without prejudice to the Member States' ability to revoke authorisations, when the conditions for authorisation are no longer met.

Article 12 Selection from among several candidates

1.   Where the number of authorisations available for a given activity is limited because of the scarcity of available natural resources or technical capacity, Member States shall apply a selection procedure to potential candidates which provides full guarantees of impartiality and transparency, including, in particular, adequate publicity about the launch, conduct and completion of the procedure.

2.   In the cases referred to in paragraph 1, authorisation shall be granted for an appropriate limited period and may not be open to automatic renewal nor confer any other advantage on the provider whose authorisation has just expired or on any person having any particular links with that provider.

3.   Subject to paragraph 1 and to Articles 9 and 10, Member States may take into account, in establishing the rules for the selection procedure, considerations of public health, social policy objectives, the health and safety of employees or self-employed persons, the protection of the environment, the preservation of cultural heritage and other overriding reasons relating to the public interest, in conformity with Community law.

Article 13 Authorisation procedures

1.   Authorisation procedures and formalities shall be clear, made public in advance and be such as to provide the applicants with a guarantee that their application will be dealt with objectively and impartially.

2.   Authorisation procedures and formalities shall not be dissuasive and shall not unduly complicate or delay the provision of the service. They shall be easily accessible and any charges which the applicants may incur from their application shall be reasonable and proportionate to the cost of the authorisation procedures in question and shall not exceed the cost of the procedures.

3.   Authorisation procedures and formalities shall provide applicants with a guarantee that their application will be processed as quickly as possible and, in any event, within a reasonable period which is fixed and made public in advance. The period shall run only from the time when all documentation has been submitted. When justified by the

complexity of the issue, the time period may be extended once, by the competent authority, for a limited time. The extension and its duration shall be duly motivated and shall be notified to the applicant before the original period has expired.

4. Failing a response within the time period set or extended in accordance with paragraph 3, authorisation shall be deemed to have been granted. Different arrangements may nevertheless be put in place, where justified by overriding reasons relating to the public interest, including a legitimate interest of third parties.

5. All applications for authorisation shall be acknowledged as quickly as possible. The acknowledgement must specify the following:
   (a) the period referred to in paragraph 3;
   (b) the available means of redress;
   (c) where applicable, a statement that in the absence of a response within the period specified, the authorisation shall be deemed to have been granted.

6. In the case of an incomplete application, the applicant shall be informed as quickly as possible of the need to supply any additional documentation, as well as of any possible effects on the period referred to in paragraph 3.

7. When a request is rejected because it fails to comply with the required procedures or formalities, the applicant shall be informed of the rejection as quickly as possible.

SECTION 2 REQUIREMENTS PROHIBITED OR SUBJECT TO EVALUATION

Article 14 Prohibited requirements
Member States shall not make access to, or the exercise of, a service activity in their territory subject to compliance with any of the following:

1. discriminatory requirements based directly or indirectly on nationality or, in the case of companies, the location of the registered office, including in particular:
   (a) nationality requirements for the provider, his staff, persons holding the share capital or members of the provider's management or supervisory bodies;
   (b) a requirement that the provider, his staff, persons holding the share capital or members of the provider's management or supervisory bodies be resident within the territory;

2. a prohibition on having an establishment in more than one Member State or on being entered in the registers or enrolled with professional bodies or associations of more than one Member State;

3. restrictions on the freedom of a provider to choose between a principal or a secondary establishment, in particular an obligation on the provider to have its principal establishment in their territory, or restrictions on the freedom to choose between establishment in the form of an agency, branch or subsidiary;

4. conditions of reciprocity with the Member State in which the provider already has an establishment, save in the case of conditions of reciprocity provided for in Community instruments concerning energy;

5. the case-by-case application of an economic test making the granting of authorisation subject to proof of the existence of an economic need or market demand, an assessment of the potential or current economic effects of the activity or an assessment of the appropriateness of the activity in relation to the economic planning objectives set by the competent authority; this prohibition shall not concern planning requirements which do not pursue economic aims but serve overriding reasons relating to the public interest;

6.   the direct or indirect involvement of competing operators, including within consultative bodies, in the granting of authorisations or in the adoption of other decisions of the competent authorities, with the exception of professional bodies and associations or other organisations acting as the competent authority; this prohibition shall not concern the consultation of organisations, such as chambers of commerce or social partners, on matters other than individual applications for authorisation, or a consultation of the public at large;

7.   an obligation to provide or participate in a financial guarantee or to take out insurance from a provider or body established in their territory. This shall not affect the possibility for Member States to require insurance or financial guarantees as such, nor shall it affect requirements relating to the participation in a collective compensation fund, for instance for members of professional bodies or organisations;

8.   an obligation to have been pre-registered, for a given period, in the registers held in their territory or to have previously exercised the activity for a given period in their territory.

Article 15 Requirements to be evaluated

1.   Member States shall examine whether, under their legal system, any of the requirements listed in paragraph 2 are imposed and shall ensure that any such requirements are compatible with the conditions laid down in paragraph 3. Member States shall adapt their laws, regulations or administrative provisions so as to make them compatible with those conditions.

2.   Member States shall examine whether their legal system makes access to a service activity or the exercise of it subject to compliance with any of the following non-discriminatory requirements:
   (a)   quantitative or territorial restrictions, in particular in the form of limits fixed according to population or of a minimum geographical distance between providers;
   (b)   an obligation on a provider to take a specific legal form;
   (c)   requirements which relate to the shareholding of a company;
   (d)   requirements, other than those concerning matters covered by Directive 2005/36/EC or provided for in other Community instruments, which reserve access to the service activity in question to particular providers by virtue of the specific nature of the activity;
   (e)   a ban on having more than one establishment in the territory of the same State;
   (f)   requirements fixing a minimum number of employees;
   (g)   fixed minimum and/or maximum tariffs with which the provider must comply;
   (h)   an obligation on the provider to supply other specific services jointly with his service.

3.   Member States shall verify that the requirements referred to in paragraph 2 satisfy the following conditions:
   (a)   non-discrimination: requirements must be neither directly nor indirectly discriminatory according to nationality nor, with regard to companies, according to the location of the registered office;
   (b)   necessity: requirements must be justified by an overriding reason relating to the public interest;
   (c)   proportionality: requirements must be suitable for securing the attainment of the objective pursued; they must not go beyond what is necessary to attain that objective and it must not be possible to replace those requirements with other, less restrictive measures which attain the same result.

4.   Paragraphs 1, 2 and 3 shall apply to legislation in the field of services of general economic interest only insofar as the application of these paragraphs does not obstruct the performance, in law or in fact, of the particular task assigned to them.

5.   In the mutual evaluation report provided for in Article 39(1), Member States shall specify the following:
     (a) the requirements that they intend to maintain and the reasons why they consider that those requirements comply with the conditions set out in paragraph 3;
     (b) the requirements which have been abolished or made less stringent.

6.   From 28 December 2006 Member States shall not introduce any new requirement of a kind listed in paragraph 2, unless that requirement satisfies the conditions laid down in paragraph 3.

7.   Member States shall notify the Commission of any new laws, regulations or administrative provisions which set requirements as referred to in paragraph 6, together with the reasons for those requirements. The Commission shall communicate the provisions concerned to the other Member States. Such notification shall not prevent Member States from adopting the provisions in question.

Within a period of 3 months from the date of receipt of the notification, the Commission shall examine the compatibility of any new requirements with Community law and, where appropriate, shall adopt a decision requesting the Member State in question to refrain from adopting them or to abolish them.

The notification of a draft national law in accordance with Directive 98/34/EC shall fulfil the obligation of notification provided for in this Directive.

Chapter IV FREE MOVEMENT OF SERVICES

SECTION 1 FREEDOM TO PROVIDE SERVICES AND RELATED DEROGATIONS

Article 16 Freedom to provide services
1.   Member States shall respect the right of providers to provide services in a Member State other than that in which they are established.

The Member State in which the service is provided shall ensure free access to and free exercise of a service activity within its territory.

Member States shall not make access to or exercise of a service activity in their territory subject to compliance with any requirements which do not respect the following principles:
     (a) non-discrimination: the requirement may be neither directly nor indirectly discriminatory with regard to nationality or, in the case of legal persons, with regard to the Member State in which they are established;
     (b) necessity: the requirement must be justified for reasons of public policy, public security, public health or the protection of the environment;
     (c) proportionality: the requirement must be suitable for attaining the objective pursued, and must not go beyond what is necessary to attain that objective.

2.   Member States may not restrict the freedom to provide services in the case of a provider established in another Member State by imposing any of the following requirements:
     (a) an obligation on the provider to have an establishment in their territory;
     (b) an obligation on the provider to obtain an authorisation from their competent authorities including entry in a register or registration with a professional body or association in their territory, except where provided for in this Directive or other instruments of Community law;

(c) a ban on the provider setting up a certain form or type of infrastructure in their territory, including an office or chambers, which the provider needs in order to supply the services in question;

(d) the application of specific contractual arrangements between the provider and the recipient which prevent or restrict service provision by the self-employed;

(e) an obligation on the provider to possess an identity document issued by its competent authorities specific to the exercise of a service activity;

(f) requirements, except for those necessary for health and safety at work, which affect the use of equipment and material which are an integral part of the service provided;

(g) restrictions on the freedom to provide the services referred to in Article 19.

3. The Member State to which the provider moves shall not be prevented from imposing requirements with regard to the provision of a service activity, where they are justified for reasons of public policy, public security, public health or the protection of the environment and in accordance with paragraph 1. Nor shall that Member State be prevented from applying, in accordance with Community law, its rules on employment conditions, including those laid down in collective agreements.

4. By 28 December 2011 the Commission shall, after consultation of the Member States and the social partners at Community level, submit to the European Parliament and the Council a report on the application of this Article, in which it shall consider the need to propose harmonisation measures regarding service activities covered by this Directive.

Article 17 Additional derogations from the freedom to provide services
Article 16 shall not apply to:

1. services of general economic interest which are provided in another Member State, inter alia:

(a) in the postal sector, services covered by Directive 97/67/EC of the European Parliament and of the Council of 15 December 1997 on common rules for the development of the internal market of Community postal services and the improvement of quality of service;

(b) in the electricity sector, services covered by Directive 2003/54/EC of the European Parliament and of the Council of 26 June 2003 concerning common rules for the internal market in electricity;

(c) in the gas sector, services covered by Directive 2003/55/EC of the European Parliament and of the Council of 26 June 2003 concerning common rules for the internal market in natural gas;

(d) water distribution and supply services and waste water services;

(e) treatment of waste;

2. matters covered by Directive 96/71/EC;

3. matters covered by Directive 95/46/EC of the European Parliament and of the Council of 24 October 1995 on the protection of individuals with regard to the processing of personal data and on the free movement of such data;

4. matters covered by Council Directive 77/249/EEC of 22 March 1977 to facilitate the effective exercise by lawyers of freedom to provide services;

5. the activity of judicial recovery of debts;

6. matters covered by Title II of Directive 2005/36/EC, as well as requirements in the Member State where the service is provided which reserve an activity to a particular profession;

7. matters covered by Regulation (EEC) No 1408/71;

8.   as regards administrative formalities concerning the free movement of persons and their residence, matters covered by the provisions of Directive 2004/38/EC that lay down administrative formalities of the competent authorities of the Member State where the service is provided with which beneficiaries must comply;

9.   as regards third country nationals who move to another Member State in the context of the provision of a service, the possibility for Member States to require visa or residence permits for third country nationals who are not covered by the mutual recognition regime provided for in Article 21 of the Convention implementing the Schengen Agreement of 14 June 1985 on the gradual abolition of checks at the common borders or the possibility to oblige third country nationals to report to the competent authorities of the Member State in which the service is provided on or after their entry;

10. as regards the shipment of waste, matters covered by Council Regulation (EEC) No 259/93 of 1 February 1993 on the supervision and control of shipments of waste within, into and out of the European Community;

11. copyright, neighbouring rights and rights covered by Council Directive 87/54/EEC of 16 December 1986 on the legal protection of topographies of semiconductor products and by Directive 96/9/EC of the European Parliament and of the Council of 11 March 1996 on the legal protection of databases, as well as industrial property rights;

12. acts requiring by law the involvement of a notary;

13. matters covered by Directive 2006/43/EC of the European Parliament and of the Council of 17 May 2006 on statutory audit of annual accounts and consolidated accounts;

14. the registration of vehicles leased in another Member State;

15. provisions regarding contractual and non-contractual obligations, including the form of contracts, determined pursuant to the rules of private international law.

Article 18 Case-by-case derogations

1.   By way of derogation from Article 16, and in exceptional circumstances only, a Member State may, in respect of a provider established in another Member State, take measures relating to the safety of services.

2.   The measures provided for in paragraph 1 may be taken only if the mutual assistance procedure laid down in Article 35 is complied with and the following conditions are fulfilled:
   (a) the national provisions in accordance with which the measure is taken have not been subject to Community harmonisation in the field of the safety of services;
   (b) the measures provide for a higher level of protection of the recipient than would be the case in a measure taken by the Member State of establishment in accordance with its national provisions;
   (c) the Member State of establishment has not taken any measures or has taken measures which are insufficient as compared with those referred to in Article 35(2);
   (d) the measures are proportionate.

3.   Paragraphs 1 and 2 shall be without prejudice to provisions, laid down in Community instruments, which guarantee the freedom to provide services or which allow derogations therefrom.

SECTION 2 RIGHTS OF RECIPIENTS OF SERVICES

Article 19 Prohibited restrictions

Member States may not impose on a recipient requirements which restrict the use of a service supplied by a provider established in another Member State, in particular the following requirements:

(a)   an obligation to obtain authorisation from or to make a declaration to their competent authorities;

(b)   discriminatory limits on the grant of financial assistance by reason of the fact that the provider is established in another Member State or by reason of the location of the place at which the service is provided.

Article 20 Non-discrimination

1.   Member States shall ensure that the recipient is not made subject to discriminatory requirements based on his nationality or place of residence.

2.   Member States shall ensure that the general conditions of access to a service, which are made available to the public at large by the provider, do not contain discriminatory provisions relating to the nationality or place of residence of the recipient, but without precluding the possibility of providing for differences in the conditions of access where those differences are directly justified by objective criteria.

Article 21 Assistance for recipients

1.   Member States shall ensure that recipients can obtain, in their Member State of residence, the following information:
      (a)   general information on the requirements applicable in other Member States relating to access to, and exercise of, service activities, in particular those relating to consumer protection;
      (b)   general information on the means of redress available in the case of a dispute between a provider and a recipient;
      (c)   the contact details of associations or organisations, including the centres of the European Consumer Centres Network, from which providers or recipients may obtain practical assistance.
      Where appropriate, advice from the competent authorities shall include a simple step-by-step guide. Information and assistance shall be provided in a clear and unambiguous manner, shall be easily accessible at a distance, including by electronic means, and shall be kept up to date.

2.   Member States may confer responsibility for the task referred to in paragraph 1 on points of single contact or on any other body, such as the centres of the European Consumer Centres Network, consumer associations or Euro Info Centres.

      Member States shall communicate to the Commission the names and contact details of the designated bodies. The Commission shall transmit them to all Member States.

3.   In fulfilment of the requirements set out in paragraphs 1 and 2, the body approached by the recipient shall, if necessary, contact the relevant body for the Member State concerned. The latter shall send the information requested as soon as possible to the requesting body which shall forward the information to the recipient. Member States shall ensure that those bodies give each other mutual assistance and shall put in place all possible measures for effective cooperation. Together with the Commission, Member States shall put in place practical arrangements necessary for the implementation of paragraph 1.

4.   The Commission shall, in accordance with the procedure referred to in Article 40(2), adopt measures for the implementation of paragraphs 1, 2 and 3 of this Article, specifying the technical mechanisms for the exchange of information between the bodies of the various Member States and, in particular, the interoperability of information systems, taking into account common standards.

Chapter V QUALITY OF SERVICES

Article 22 Information on providers and their services

1. Member States shall ensure that providers make the following information available to the recipient:

    (a) the name of the provider, his legal status and form, the geographic address at which he is established and details enabling him to be contacted rapidly and communicated with directly and, as the case may be, by electronic means;

    (b) where the provider is registered in a trade or other similar public register, the name of that register and the provider's registration number, or equivalent means of identification in that register;

    (c) where the activity is subject to an authorisation scheme, the particulars of the relevant competent authority or the single point of contact;

    (d) where the provider exercises an activity which is subject to VAT, the identification number referred to in Article 22(1) of Sixth Council Directive 77/388/EEC of 17 May 1977 on the harmonisation of the laws of the Member States relating to turnover taxes – Common system of value added tax: uniform basis of assessment;

    (e) in the case of the regulated professions, any professional body or similar institution with which the provider is registered, the professional title and the Member State in which that title has been granted;

    (f) the general conditions and clauses, if any, used by the provider;

    (g) the existence of contractual clauses, if any, used by the provider concerning the law applicable to the contract and/or the competent courts;

    (h) the existence of an after-sales guarantee, if any, not imposed by law;

    (i) the price of the service, where a price is pre-determined by the provider for a given type of service;

    (j) the main features of the service, if not already apparent from the context;

    (k) the insurance or guarantees referred to in Article 23(1), and in particular the contact details of the insurer or guarantor and the territorial coverage.

2. Member States shall ensure that the information referred to in paragraph 1, according to the provider's preference:

    (a) is supplied by the provider on his own initiative;

    (b) is easily accessible to the recipient at the place where the service is provided or the contract concluded;

    (c) can be easily accessed by the recipient electronically by means of an address supplied by the provider;

    (d) appears in any information documents supplied to the recipient by the provider which set out a detailed description of the service he provides.

3. Member States shall ensure that, at the recipient's request, providers supply the following additional information:

    (a) where the price is not pre-determined by the provider for a given type of service, the price of the service or, if an exact price cannot be given, the method for calculating the price so that it can be checked by the recipient, or a sufficiently detailed estimate;

    (b) as regards the regulated professions, a reference to the professional rules applicable in the Member State of establishment and how to access them;

    (c) information on their multidisciplinary activities and partnerships which are directly linked to the service in question and on the measures taken to avoid conflicts of interest. That information shall be included in any information document in which providers give a detailed description of their services;

    (d) any codes of conduct to which the provider is subject and the address at which these codes may be consulted by electronic means, specifying the language version available;

(e) where a provider is subject to a code of conduct, or member of a trade association or professional body which provides for recourse to a non-judicial means of dispute settlement, information in this respect. The provider shall specify how to access detailed information on the characteristics of, and conditions for, the use of non-judicial means of dispute settlement.

4.   Member States shall ensure that the information which a provider must supply in accordance with this Chapter is made available or communicated in a clear and unambiguous manner, and in good time before conclusion of the contract or, where there is no written contract, before the service is provided.

5.   The information requirements laid down in this Chapter are in addition to requirements already provided for in Community law and do not prevent Member States from imposing additional information requirements applicable to providers established in their territory.

6.   The Commission may, in accordance with the procedure referred to in Article 40(2), specify the content of the information provided for in paragraphs 1 and 3 of this Article according to the specific nature of certain activities and may specify the practical means of implementing paragraph 2 of this Article.

Article 23 Professional liability insurance and guarantees

1.   Member States may ensure that providers whose services present a direct and particular risk to the health or safety of the recipient or a third person, or to the financial security of the recipient, subscribe to professional liability insurance appropriate to the nature and extent of the risk, or provide a guarantee or similar arrangement which is equivalent or essentially comparable as regards its purpose.

2.   When a provider establishes himself in their territory, Member States may not require professional liability insurance or a guarantee from the provider where he is already covered by a guarantee which is equivalent, or essentially comparable as regards its purpose and the cover it provides in terms of the insured risk, the insured sum or a ceiling for the guarantee and possible exclusions from the cover, in another Member State in which the provider is already established. Where equivalence is only partial, Member States may require a supplementary guarantee to cover those aspects not already covered.

When a Member State requires a provider established in its territory to subscribe to professional liability insurance or to provide another guarantee, that Member State shall accept as sufficient evidence attestations of such insurance cover issued by credit institutions and insurers established in other Member States.

3.   Paragraphs 1 and 2 shall not affect professional insurance or guarantee arrangements provided for in other Community instruments.

4.   For the implementation of paragraph 1, the Commission may, in accordance with the regulatory procedure referred to in Article 40(2), establish a list of services which exhibit the characteristics referred to in paragraph 1 of this Article. The Commission may also, in accordance with the procedure referred to in Article 40(3), adopt measures designed to amend non-essential elements of this Directive by supplementing it by establishing common criteria for defining, for the purposes of the insurance or guarantees referred to in paragraph 1 of this Article, what is appropriate to the nature and extent of the risk.

5.   For the purpose of this Article
— "direct and particular risk" means a risk arising directly from the provision of the service,
— "health and safety" means, in relation to a recipient or a third person, the prevention of death or serious personal injury,

— "financial security" means, in relation to a recipient, the prevention of substantial losses of money or of value of property,

— "professional liability insurance" means insurance taken out by a provider in respect of potential liabilities to recipients and, where applicable, third parties arising out of the provision of the service.

Article 24 Commercial communications by the regulated professions

1. Member States shall remove all total prohibitions on commercial communications by the regulated professions.

2. Member States shall ensure that commercial communications by the regulated professions comply with professional rules, in conformity with Community law, which relate, in particular, to the independence, dignity and integrity of the profession, as well as to professional secrecy, in a manner consistent with the specific nature of each profession. Professional rules on commercial communications shall be non-discriminatory, justified by an overriding reason relating to the public interest and proportionate.

Article 25 Multidisciplinary activities

1. Member States shall ensure that providers are not made subject to requirements which oblige them to exercise a given specific activity exclusively or which restrict the exercise jointly or in partnership of different activities.

   However, the following providers may be made subject to such requirements:
   (a) the regulated professions, in so far as is justified in order to guarantee compliance with the rules governing professional ethics and conduct, which vary according to the specific nature of each profession, and is necessary in order to ensure their independence and impartiality;
   (b) providers of certification, accreditation, technical monitoring, test or trial services, in so far as is justified in order to ensure their independence and impartiality.

2. Where multidisciplinary activities between providers referred to in points (a) and (b) of paragraph 1 are authorised, Member States shall ensure the following:
   (a) that conflicts of interest and incompatibilities between certain activities are prevented;
   (b) that the independence and impartiality required for certain activities is secured;
   (c) that the rules governing professional ethics and conduct for different activities are compatible with one another, especially as regards matters of professional secrecy.

3. In the report referred to in Article 39(1), Member States shall indicate which providers are subject to the requirements laid down in paragraph 1 of this Article, the content of those requirements and the reasons for which they consider them to be justified.

Article 26 Policy on quality of services

1. Member States shall, in cooperation with the Commission, take accompanying measures to encourage providers to take action on a voluntary basis in order to ensure the quality of service provision, in particular through use of one of the following methods:
   (a) certification or assessment of their activities by independent or accredited bodies;
   (b) drawing up their own quality charter or participation in quality charters or labels drawn up by professional bodies at Community level.

2. Member States shall ensure that information on the significance of certain labels and the criteria for applying labels and other quality marks relating to services can be easily accessed by providers and recipients.

3. Member States shall, in cooperation with the Commission, take accompanying measures to encourage professional bodies, as well as chambers of commerce and craft associations

and consumer associations, in their territory to cooperate at Community level in order to promote the quality of service provision, especially by making it easier to assess the competence of a provider.

4.   Member States shall, in cooperation with the Commission, take accompanying measures to encourage the development of independent assessments, notably by consumer associations, in relation to the quality and defects of service provision, and, in particular, the development at Community level of comparative trials or testing and the communication of the results.

5.   Member States, in cooperation with the Commission, shall encourage the development of voluntary European standards with the aim of facilitating compatibility between services supplied by providers in different Member States, information to the recipient and the quality of service provision.

Article 27 Settlement of disputes

1.   Member States shall take the general measures necessary to ensure that providers supply contact details, in particular a postal address, fax number or e-mail address and telephone number to which all recipients, including those resident in another Member State, can send a complaint or a request for information about the service provided. Providers shall supply their legal address if this is not their usual address for correspondence.

Member States shall take the general measures necessary to ensure that providers respond to the complaints referred to in the first subparagraph in the shortest possible time and make their best efforts to find a satisfactory solution.

2.   Member States shall take the general measures necessary to ensure that providers are obliged to demonstrate compliance with the obligations laid down in this Directive as to the provision of information and to demonstrate that the information is accurate.

3.   Where a financial guarantee is required for compliance with a judicial decision, Member States shall recognise equivalent guarantees lodged with a credit institution or insurer established in another Member State. Such credit institutions must be authorised in a Member State in accordance with Directive 2006/48/EC and such insurers in accordance, as appropriate, with First Council Directive 73/239/EEC of 24 July 1973 on the coordination of laws, regulations and administrative provisions relating to the taking-up and pursuit of the business of direct insurance other than life assurance and Directive 2002/83/EC of the European Parliament and of the Council of 5 November 2002 concerning life assurance.

4.   Member States shall take the general measures necessary to ensure that providers who are subject to a code of conduct, or are members of a trade association or professional body, which provides for recourse to a non-judicial means of dispute settlement inform the recipient thereof and mention that fact in any document which presents their services in detail, specifying how to access detailed information on the characteristics of, and conditions for, the use of such a mechanism.

Chapter VI ADMINISTRATIVE COOPERATION

Article 28 Mutual assistance – general obligations

1.   Member States shall give each other mutual assistance, and shall put in place measures for effective cooperation with one another, in order to ensure the supervision of providers and the services they provide.

2.   For the purposes of this Chapter, Member States shall designate one or more liaison points, the contact details of which shall be communicated to the other Member States

and the Commission. The Commission shall publish and regularly update the list of liaison points.

3. Information requests and requests to carry out any checks, inspections and investigations under this Chapter shall be duly motivated, in particular by specifying the reason for the request. Information exchanged shall be used only in respect of the matter for which it was requested.

4. In the event of receiving a request for assistance from competent authorities in another Member State, Member States shall ensure that providers established in their territory supply their competent authorities with all the information necessary for supervising their activities in compliance with their national laws.

5. In the event of difficulty in meeting a request for information or in carrying out checks, inspections or investigations, the Member State in question shall rapidly inform the requesting Member State with a view to finding a solution.

6. Member States shall supply the information requested by other Member States or the Commission by electronic means and within the shortest possible period of time.

7. Member States shall ensure that registers in which providers have been entered, and which may be consulted by the competent authorities in their territory, may also be consulted, in accordance with the same conditions, by the equivalent competent authorities of the other Member States.

8. Member States shall communicate to the Commission information on cases where other Member States do not fulfil their obligation of mutual assistance. Where necessary, the Commission shall take appropriate steps, including proceedings provided for in Article 226 of the Treaty, in order to ensure that the Member States concerned comply with their obligation of mutual assistance. The Commission shall periodically inform Member States about the functioning of the mutual assistance provisions.

Article 29 Mutual assistance – general obligations for the Member State of establishment

1. With respect to providers providing services in another Member State, the Member State of establishment shall supply information on providers established in its territory when requested to do so by another Member State and, in particular, confirmation that a provider is established in its territory and, to its knowledge, is not exercising his activities in an unlawful manner.

2. The Member State of establishment shall undertake the checks, inspections and investigations requested by another Member State and shall inform the latter of the results and, as the case may be, of the measures taken. In so doing, the competent authorities shall act to the extent permitted by the powers vested in them in their Member State. The competent authorities can decide on the most appropriate measures to be taken in each individual case in order to meet the request by another Member State.

3. Upon gaining actual knowledge of any conduct or specific acts by a provider established in its territory which provides services in other Member States, that, to its knowledge, could cause serious damage to the health or safety of persons or to the environment, the Member State of establishment shall inform all other Member States and the Commission within the shortest possible period of time.

Article 30 Supervision by the Member State of establishment in the event of the temporary movement of a provider to another Member State

1. With respect to cases not covered by Article 31(1), the Member State of establishment shall ensure that compliance with its requirements is supervised in conformity with the

powers of supervision provided for in its national law, in particular through supervisory measures at the place of establishment of the provider.

2.   The Member State of establishment shall not refrain from taking supervisory or enforcement measures in its territory on the grounds that the service has been provided or caused damage in another Member State.

3.   The obligation laid down in paragraph 1 shall not entail a duty on the part of the Member State of establishment to carry out factual checks and controls in the territory of the Member State where the service is provided. Such checks and controls shall be carried out by the authorities of the Member State where the provider is temporarily operating at the request of the authorities of the Member State of establishment, in accordance with Article 31.

Article 31 Supervision by the Member State where the service is provided in the event of the temporary movement of the provider

1.   With respect to national requirements which may be imposed pursuant to Articles 16 or 17, the Member State where the service is provided is responsible for the supervision of the activity of the provider in its territory. In conformity with Community law, the Member State where the service is provided:
  (a) shall take all measures necessary to ensure the provider complies with those requirements as regards the access to and the exercise of the activity;
  (b) shall carry out the checks, inspections and investigations necessary to supervise the service provided.

2.   With respect to requirements other than those referred to in paragraph 1, where a provider moves temporarily to another Member State in order to provide a service without being established there, the competent authorities of that Member State shall participate in the supervision of the provider in accordance with paragraphs 3 and 4.

3.   At the request of the Member State of establishment, the competent authorities of the Member State where the service is provided shall carry out any checks, inspections and investigations necessary for ensuring the effective supervision by the Member State of establishment. In so doing, the competent authorities shall act to the extent permitted by the powers vested in them in their Member State. The competent authorities may decide on the most appropriate measures to be taken in each individual case in order to meet the request by the Member State of establishment.

4.   On their own initiative, the competent authorities of the Member State where the service is provided may conduct checks, inspections and investigations on the spot, provided that those checks, inspections or investigations are not discriminatory, are not motivated by the fact that the provider is established in another Member State and are proportionate.

Article 32 Alert mechanism

1.   Where a Member State becomes aware of serious specific acts or circumstances relating to a service activity that could cause serious damage to the health or safety of persons or to the environment in its territory or in the territory of other Member States, that Member State shall inform the Member State of establishment, the other Member States concerned and the Commission within the shortest possible period of time.

2.   The Commission shall promote and take part in the operation of a European network of Member States' authorities in order to implement paragraph 1.

3.   The Commission shall adopt and regularly update, in accordance with the procedure referred to in Article 40(2), detailed rules concerning the management of the network referred to in paragraph 2 of this Article.

Article 33 Information on the good repute of providers

1.   Member States shall, at the request of a competent authority in another Member State, supply information, in conformity with their national law, on disciplinary or administrative actions or criminal sanctions and decisions concerning insolvency or bankruptcy involving fraud taken by their competent authorities in respect of the provider which are directly relevant to the provider's competence or professional reliability. The Member State which supplies the information shall inform the provider thereof.

A request made pursuant to the first subparagraph must be duly substantiated, in particular as regards the reasons for the request for information.

2.   Sanctions and actions referred to in paragraph 1 shall only be communicated if a final decision has been taken. With regard to other enforceable decisions referred to in paragraph 1, the Member State which supplies the information shall specify whether a particular decision is final or whether an appeal has been lodged in respect of it, in which case the Member State in question should provide an indication of the date when the decision on appeal is expected.

Moreover, that Member State shall specify the provisions of national law pursuant to which the provider was found guilty or penalised.

3.   Implementation of paragraphs 1 and 2 must comply with rules on the provision of personal data and with rights guaranteed to persons found guilty or penalised in the Member States concerned, including by professional bodies. Any information in question which is public shall be accessible to consumers.

Article 34 Accompanying measures

1.   The Commission, in cooperation with Member States, shall establish an electronic system for the exchange of information between Member States, taking into account existing information systems.

2.   Member States shall, with the assistance of the Commission, take accompanying measures to facilitate the exchange of officials in charge of the implementation of mutual assistance and training of such officials, including language and computer training.

3.   The Commission shall assess the need to establish a multi-annual programme in order to organise relevant exchanges of officials and training.

Article 35 Mutual assistance in the event of case-by-case derogations

1.   Where a Member State intends to take a measure pursuant to Article 18, the procedure laid down in paragraphs 2 to 6 of this Article shall apply without prejudice to court proceedings, including preliminary proceedings and acts carried out in the framework of a criminal investigation.

2.   The Member State referred to in paragraph 1 shall ask the Member State of establishment to take measures with regard to the provider, supplying all relevant information on the service in question and the circumstances of the case.

The Member State of establishment shall check, within the shortest possible period of time, whether the provider is operating lawfully and verify the facts underlying the request. It shall inform the requesting Member State within the shortest possible period of time of the measures taken or envisaged or, as the case may be, the reasons why it has not taken any measures.

3.   Following communication by the Member State of establishment as provided for in the second subparagraph of paragraph 2, the requesting Member State shall notify the

Commission and the Member State of establishment of its intention to take measures, stating the following:

(a) the reasons why it believes the measures taken or envisaged by the Member State of establishment are inadequate;

(b) the reasons why it believes the measures it intends to take fulfil the conditions laid down in Article 18.

4. The measures may not be taken until fifteen working days after the date of notification provided for in paragraph 3.

5. Without prejudice to the possibility for the requesting Member State to take the measures in question upon expiry of the period specified in paragraph 4, the Commission shall, within the shortest possible period of time, examine the compatibility with Community law of the measures notified.

Where the Commission concludes that the measure is incompatible with Community law, it shall adopt a decision asking the Member State concerned to refrain from taking the proposed measures or to put an end to the measures in question as a matter of urgency.

6. In the case of urgency, a Member State which intends to take a measure may derogate from paragraphs 2, 3 and 4. In such cases, the measures shall be notified within the shortest possible period of time to the Commission and the Member State of establishment, stating the reasons for which the Member State considers that there is urgency.

Article 36 Implementing measures

In accordance with the procedure referred to in Article 40(3), the Commission shall adopt the implementing measures designed to amend non-essential elements of this Chapter by supplementing it by specifying the time-limits provided for in Articles 28 and 35. The Commission shall also adopt, in accordance with the procedure referred to in Article 40(2), the practical arrangements for the exchange of information by electronic means between Member States, and in particular the interoperability provisions for information systems.

Chapter VII CONVERGENCE PROGRAMME

Article 37 Codes of conduct at Community level

1. Member States shall, in cooperation with the Commission, take accompanying measures to encourage the drawing up at Community level, particularly by professional bodies, organisations and associations, of codes of conduct aimed at facilitating the provision of services or the establishment of a provider in another Member State, in conformity with Community law.

2. Member States shall ensure that the codes of conduct referred to in paragraph 1 are accessible at a distance, by electronic means.

Article 38 Additional harmonisation

The Commission shall assess, by 28 December 2010 the possibility of presenting proposals for harmonisation instruments on the following subjects:

(a) access to the activity of judicial recovery of debts;

(b) private security services and transport of cash and valuables.

Article 39 Mutual evaluation

1. By 28 December 2009 at the latest, Member States shall present a report to the Commission, containing the information specified in the following provisions:

(a) Article 9(2), on authorisation schemes;

(b) Article 15(5), on requirements to be evaluated;

(c) Article 25(3), on multidisciplinary activities.

2. The Commission shall forward the reports provided for in paragraph 1 to the Member States, which shall submit their observations on each of the reports within six months of receipt. Within the same period, the Commission shall consult interested parties on those reports.

3. The Commission shall present the reports and the Member States' observations to the Committee referred to in Article 40(1), which may make observations.

4. In the light of the observations provided for in paragraphs 2 and 3, the Commission shall, by 28 December 2010 at the latest, present a summary report to the European Parliament and to the Council, accompanied where appropriate by proposals for additional initiatives.

5. By 28 December 2009 at the latest, Member States shall present a report to the Commission on the national requirements whose application could fall under the third subparagraph of Article 16(1) and the first sentence of Article 16(3), providing reasons why they consider that the application of those requirements fulfil the criteria referred to in the third subparagraph of Article 16(1) and the first sentence of Article 16(3).

Thereafter, Member States shall transmit to the Commission any changes in their requirements, including new requirements, as referred to above, together with the reasons for them.

The Commission shall communicate the transmitted requirements to other Member States. Such transmission shall not prevent the adoption by Member States of the provisions in question. The Commission shall on an annual basis thereafter provide analyses and orientations on the application of these provisions in the context of this Directive.

Article 40 Committee procedure

1. The Commission shall be assisted by a Committee.

2. Where reference is made to this paragraph, Articles 5 and 7 of Decision 1999/468/EC shall apply, having regard to the provisions of Article 8 thereof. The period laid down in Article 5(6) of Decision 1999/468/EC shall be set at three months.

3. Where reference is made to this paragraph, Article 5a(1) to (4), and Article 7 of Decision 1999/468/EC shall apply, having regard to the provisions of Article 8 thereof.

Article 41 Review clause

The Commission, by 28 December 2011 and every three years thereafter, shall present to the European Parliament and to the Council a comprehensive report on the application of this Directive. This report shall, in accordance with Article 16(4), address in particular the application of Article 16. It shall also consider the need for additional measures for matters excluded from the scope of application of this Directive. It shall be accompanied, where appropriate, by proposals for amendment of this Directive with a view to completing the Internal Market for services.

Article 42 Amendment of Directive 98/27/EC

In the Annex to Directive 98/27/EC of the European Parliament and of the Council of 19 May 1998 on injunctions for the protection of consumers' interests, the following point shall be added:

"13. Directive 2006/123/EC of the European Parliament and of the Council of 12 December 2006 on services in the internal market (OJ L 376, 27.12.2006, p. 36)"

Article 43 Protection of personal data

The implementation and application of this Directive and, in particular, the provisions on supervision shall respect the rules on the protection of personal data as provided for in Directives 95/46/EC and 2002/58/EC.

Chapter VIII FINAL PROVISIONS

Article 44 Transposition

1.   Member States shall bring into force the laws, regulations and administrative provisions necessary to comply with this Directive before 28 December 2009.

They shall forthwith communicate to the Commission the text of those measures.

When Member States adopt these measures, they shall contain a reference to this Directive or shall be accompanied by such a reference on the occasion of their official publication. The methods of making such reference shall be laid down by Member States.

2.   Member States shall communicate to the Commission the text of the main provisions of national law which they adopt in the field covered by this Directive.

Article 45 Entry into force

This Directive shall enter into force on the day following that of its publication in the *Official Journal of the European Union*.

Article 46 Addressees

This Directive is addressed to the Member States.

(date of signing, signatories and footnotes omitted)

VI Competition Law

A) COMMISSION NOTICES AND GUIDANCE

COMMISSION NOTICE

on the definition of relevant market for the purposes of Community competition law
OJ C 372, 09.12.1997, P. 5[1]

I. INTRODUCTION

1.   The purpose of this notice is to provide guidance as to how the Commission applies the concept of relevant product and geographic market in its ongoing enforcement of Community competition law, in particular the application of Council Regulation No 17 and (EEC) No 4064/89, their equivalents in other sectoral applications such as transport, coal and steel, and agriculture, and the relevant provisions of the EEA Agreement (1). Throughout this notice, references to Articles 85 and 86 of the Treaty [Articles 101 and 102 TFEU] and to merger control are to be understood as referring to the equivalent provisions in the EEA Agreement and the ECSC Treaty.

2.   Market definition is a tool to identify and define the boundaries of competition between firms. It serves to establish the framework within which competition policy is applied by the Commission. The main purpose of market definition is to identify in a systematic way the competitive constraints that the undertakings involved (2) face. The objective of defining a market in both its product and geographic dimension is to identify those actual competitors of the undertakings involved that are capable of constraining those undertakings' behaviour and of preventing them from behaving independently of effective competitive pressure. It is from this perspective that the market definition makes it possible inter alia to calculate market shares that would convey meaningful information regarding market power for the purposes of assessing dominance or for the purposes of applying Article 85 [Article 101].

3.   It follows from point 2 that the concept of 'relevant market' is different from other definitions of market often used in other contexts. For instance, companies often use the term 'market' to refer to the area where it sells its products or to refer broadly to the industry or sector where it belongs.

---

[1]   EDITOR'S NOTE: This Commission Notice refers to the old EC Treaty article numbers effective prior to the Treaty of Amsterdam, 1999. In this edition the replacement article numbers contained in the Treaty on the Functioning of the European Union (TFEU) have been inserted in closed brackets after each Treaty reference for ease of conversion.

4.   The definition of the relevant market in both its product and its geographic dimensions often has a decisive influence on the assessment of a competition case. By rendering public the procedures which the Commission follows when considering market definition and by indicating the criteria and evidence on which it relies to reach a decision, the Commission expects to increase the transparency of its policy and decision-making in the area of competition policy.

5.   Increased transparency will also result in companies and their advisers being able to better anticipate the possibility that the Commission may raise competition concerns in an individual case. Companies could, therefore, take such a possibility into account in their own internal decision-making when contemplating, for instance, acquisitions, the creation of joint ventures, or the establishment of certain agreements. It is also intended that companies should be in a better position to understand what sort of information the Commission considers relevant for the purposes of market definition.

6.   The Commission's interpretation of 'relevant market' is without prejudice to the interpretation which may be given by the Court of Justice or the Court of First Instance of the European Communities.

II. DEFINITION OF RELEVANT MARKET

Definition of relevant product market and relevant geographic market
7.   The Regulations based on Article 85 and 86 of the Treaty [Articles 101 and 102 TFEU], in particular in section 6 of Form A/B with respect to Regulation No 17, as well as in section 6 of Form CO with respect to Regulation (EEC) No 4064/89 on the control of concentrations having a Community dimension have laid down the following definitions, 'Relevant product markets' are defined as follows:

'A relevant product market comprises all those products and/or services which are regarded as interchangeable or substitutable by the consumer, by reason of the products' characteristics, their prices and their intended use'.

8.   'Relevant geographic markets' are defined as follows:

'The relevant geographic market comprises the area in which the undertakings concerned are involved in the supply and demand of products or services, in which the conditions of competition are sufficiently homogeneous and which can be distinguished from neighbouring areas because the conditions of competition are appreciably different in those area'.

9.   The relevant market within which to assess a given competition issue is therefore established by the combination of the product and geographic markets. The Commission interprets the definitions in paragraphs 7 an 8 (which reflect the case-law of the Court of Justice and the Court of First Instance as well as its own decision-making practice) according to the orientations defined in this notice.

Concept of relevant market and objectives of Community competition policy
10.   The concept of relevant market is closely related to the objectives pursued under Community competition policy. For example, under the Community's merger control, the objective in controlling structural changes in the supply of a product/service is to prevent the creation or reinforcement of a dominant position as a result of which effective competition would be significantly impeded in a substantial part of the common market. Under the Community's competition rules, a dominant position is such that a firm

or group of firms would be in a position to behave to an appreciable extent independently of its competitors, customers and ultimately of its consumers (3). Such a position would usually arise when a firm or group of firms accounted for a large share of the supply in any given market, provided that other factors analysed in the assessment (such as entry barriers, customers' capacity to react, etc.) point in the same direction.

11.   The same approach is followed by the Commission in its application of Article 86 of the Treaty [Article 102 TFEU] to firms that enjoy a single or collective dominant position. Within the meaning of Regulation No 17, the Commission has the power to investigate and bring to an end abuses of such a dominant position, which must also be defined by reference to the relevant market. Markets may also need to be defined in the application of Article 85 of the Treaty [Article 101 TFEU], in particular, in determining whether an appreciable restriction of competition exists or in establishing if the condition pursuant to Article 85 (3) (b) [Article 101(3)(b) TFEU] for an exemption from the application of Article 85 (1) [Article 101(1) TFEU] is met.

12.   The criteria for defining the relevant market are applied generally for the analysis of certain types of behaviour in the market and for the analysis of structural changes in the supply of products. This methodology, though, might lead to different results depending on the nature of the competition issue being examined. For instance, the scope of the geographic market might be different when analysing a concentration, where the analysis is essentially prospective, from an analysis of past behaviour. The different time horizon considered in each case might lead to the result that different geographic markets are defined for the same products depending on whether the Commission is examining a change in the structure of supply, such as a concentration or a cooperative joint venture, or examining issues relating to certain past behaviour.

Basic principles for market definition

Competitive constraints

13.   Firms are subject to three main sources or competitive constraints: demand substitutability, supply substitutability and potential competition. From an economic point of view, for the definition of the relevant market, demand substitution constitutes the most immediate and effective disciplinary force on the suppliers of a given product, in particular in relation to their pricing decisions. A firm or a group of firms cannot have a significant impact on the prevailing conditions of sale, such as prices, if its customers are in a position to switch easily to available substitute products or to suppliers located elsewhere. Basically, the exercise of market definition consists in identifying the effective alternative sources of supply for the customers of the undertakings involved, in terms both of products/services and of geographic location of suppliers.

14.   The competitive constraints arising from supply side substitutability other then those described in paragraphs 20 to 23 and from potential competition are in general less immediate and in any case require an analysis of additional factors. As a result such constraints are taken into account at the assessment stage of competition analysis.

Demand substitution

15.   The assessment of demand substitution entails a determination of the range of products which are viewed as substitutes by the consumer. One way of making this determination can be viewed as a speculative experiment, postulating a hypothetical small, lasting change in relative prices and evaluating the likely reactions of customers to that increase.

The exercise of market definition focuses on prices for operational and practical purposes, and more precisely on demand substitution arising from small, permanent changes in relative prices. This concept can provide clear indications as to the evidence that is relevant in defining markets.

16. Conceptually, this approach means that, starting from the type of products that the undertakings involved sell and the area in which they sell them, additional products and areas will be included in, or excluded from, the market definition depending on whether competition from these other products and areas affect or restrain sufficiently the pricing of the parties' products in the short term.

17. The question to be answered is whether the parties' customers would switch to readily available substitutes or to suppliers located elsewhere in response to a hypothetical small (in the range 5 % to 10 %) but permanent relative price increase in the products and areas being considered. If substitution were enough to make the price increase unprofitable because of the resulting loss of sales, additional substitutes and areas are included in the relevant market. This would be done until the set of products and geographical areas is such that small, permanent increases in relative prices would be profitable. The equivalent analysis is applicable in cases concerning the concentration of buying power, where the starting point would then be the supplier and the price test serves to identify the alternative distribution channels or outlets for the supplier's products. In the application of these principles, careful account should be taken of certain particular situations as described within paragraphs 56 and 58.

18. A practical example of this test can be provided by its application to a merger of, for instance, soft-drink bottlers. An issue to examine in such a case would be to decide whether different flavours of soft drinks belong to the same market. In practice, the question to address would be whether consumers of flavour A would switch to other flavours when confronted with a permanent price increase of 5 % to 10 % for flavour A. If a sufficient number of consumers would switch to, say, flavour B, to such an extent that the price increase for flavour A would not be profitable owing to the resulting loss of sales, then the market would comprise at least flavours A and B. The process would have to be extended in addition to other available flavours until a set of products is identified for which a price rise would not induce a sufficient substitution in demand.

19. Generally, and in particular for the analysis of merger cases, the price to take into account will be the prevailing market price. This may not be the case where the prevailing price has been determined in the absence of sufficient competition. In particular for the investigation of abuses of dominant positions, the fact that the prevailing price might already have been substantially increased will be taken into account.

Supply substitution
20. Supply-side substitutability may also be taken into account when defining markets in those situations in which its effects are equivalent to those of demand substitution in terms of effectiveness and immediacy. This means that suppliers are able to switch production to the relevant products and market them in the short term (4) without incurring significant additional costs or risks in response to small and permanent changes in relative prices. When these conditions are met, the additional production that is put on the market will have a disciplinary effect on the competitive behaviour of the companies involved. Such an impact in terms of effectiveness and immediacy is equivalent to the demand substitution effect.

21. These situations typically arise when companies market a wide range of qualities or grades of one product; even if, for a given final customer or group of consumers, the different qualities are not substitutable, the different qualities will be grouped into one product market, provided that most of the suppliers are able to offer and sell the various qualities immediately and without the significant increases in costs described above. In such cases, the relevant product market will encompass all products that are substitutable in demand and supply, and the current sales of those products will be aggregated so as to give the total value or volume of the market. The same reasoning may lead to group different geographic areas.

22. A practical example of the approach to supply-side substitutability when defining product markets is to be found in the case of paper. Paper is usually supplied in a range of different qualities, from standard writing paper to high quality papers to be used, for instance, to publish art books. From a demand point of view, different qualities of paper cannot be used for any given use, i.e. an art book or a high quality publication cannot be based on lower quality papers. However, paper plants are prepared to manufacture the different qualities, and production can be adjusted with negligible costs and in a short time-frame. In the absence of particular difficulties in distribution, paper manufacturers are able therefore, to compete for orders of the various qualities, in particular if orders are placed with sufficient lead time to allow for modification of production plans. Under such circumstances, the Commission would not define a separate market for each quality of paper and its respective use. The various qualities of paper are included in the relevant market, and their sales added up to estimate total market value and volume.

23. When supply-side substitutability would entail the need to adjust significantly existing tangible and intangible assets, additional investments, strategic decisions or time delays, it will not be considered at the stage of market definition. Examples where supply-side substitution did not induce the Commission to enlarge the market are offered in the area of consumer products, in particular for branded beverages. Although bottling plants may in principle bottle different beverages, there are costs and lead times involved (in terms of advertising, product testing and distribution) before the products can actually be sold. In these cases, the effects of supply-side substitutability and other forms of potential competition would then be examined at a later stage.

Potential competition

24. The third source of competitive constraint, potential competition, is not taken into account when defining markets, since the conditions under which potential competition will actually represent an effective competitive constraint depend on the analysis of specific factors and circumstances related to the conditions of entry. If required, this analysis is only carried out at a subsequent stage, in general once the position of the companies involved in the relevant market has already been ascertained, and when such position gives rise to concerns from a competition point of view.

III. EVIDENCE RELIED ON TO DEFINE RELEVANT MARKETS

THE PROCESS OF DEFINING THE RELEVANT MARKET IN PRACTICE

Product dimension

25. There is a range of evidence permitting an assessment of the extent to which substitution would take place. In individual cases, certain types of evidence will be determinant, depending very much on the characteristics and specificity of the industry and products or

services that are being examined. The same type of evidence may be of no importance in other cases. In most cases, a decision will have to be based on the consideration of a number of criteria and different items of evidence. The Commission follows an open approach to empirical evidence, aimed at making an effective use of all available information which may be relevant in individual cases. The Commission does not follow a rigid hierarchy of different sources of information or types of evidence.

26. The process of defining relevant markets may be summarized as follows: on the basis of the preliminary information available or information submitted by the undertakings involved, the Commission will usually be in a position to broadly establish the possible relevant markets within which, for instance, a concentration or a restriction of competition has to be assessed. In general, and for all practical purposes when handling individual cases, the question will usually be to decide on a few alternative possible relevant markets. For instance, with respect to the product market, the issue will often be to establish whether product A and product B belong or do not belong to the same product market. it is often the case that the inclusion of product B would be enough to remove any competition concerns.

27. In such situations it is not necessary to consider whether the market includes additional products, or to reach a definitive conclusion on the precise product market. If under the conceivable alternative market definitions the operation in question does not raise competition concerns, the question of market definition will be left open, reducing thereby the burden on companies to supply information.

Geographic dimension
28. The Commission's approach to geographic market definition might be summarized as follows: it will take a preliminary view of the scope of the geographic market on the basis of broad indications as to the distribution of market shares between the parties and their competitors, as well as a preliminary analysis of pricing and price differences at national and Community or EEA level. This initial view is used basically as a working hypothesis to focus the Commission's enquiries for the purposes of arriving at a precise geographic market definition.

29. The reasons behind any particular configuration of prices and market shares need to be explored. Companies might enjoy high market shares in their domestic markets just because of the weight of the past, and conversely, a homogeneous presence of companies throughout the EEA might be consistent with national or regional geographic markets. The initial working hypothesis will therefore be checked against an analysis of demand characteristics (importance of national or local preferences, current patterns of purchases of customers, product differentiation/brands, other) in order to establish whether companies in different areas do indeed constitute a real alternative source of supply for consumers. The theoretical experiment is again based on substitution arising from changes in relative prices, and the question to answer is again whether the customers of the parties would switch their orders to companies located elsewhere in the short term and at a negligible cost.

30. If necessary, a further check on supply factors will be carried out to ensure that those companies located in differing areas do not face impediments in developing their sales on competitive terms throughout the whole geographic market. This analysis will include an examination of requirements for a local presence in order to sell in that area the conditions of access to distribution channels, costs associated with setting up a distribution network, and the presence or absence of regulatory barriers arising from public procurement, price regulations, quotas and tariffs limiting trade or production, technical standards, monopolies, freedom of establishment, requirements for

administrative authorizations, packaging regulations, etc. In short, the Commission will identify possible obstacles and barriers isolating companies located in a given area from the competitive pressure of companies located outside that area, so as to determine the precise degree of market interpenetration at national, European or global level.

31.   The actual pattern and evolution of trade flows offers useful supplementary indications as to the economic importance of each demand or supply factor mentioned above, and the extent to which they may or may not constitute actual barriers creating different geographic markets. The analysis of trade flows will generally address the question of transport costs and the extent to which these may hinder trade between different areas, having regard to plant location, costs of production and relative price levels.

Market integration in the Community

32.   Finally, the Commission also takes into account the continuing process of market integration, in particular in the Community, when defining geographic markets, especially in the area of concentrations and structural joint ventures. The measures adopted and implemented in the internal market programme to remove barriers to trade and further integrate the Community markets cannot be ignored when assessing the effects on competition of a concentration or a structural joint venture. A situation where national markets have been artificially isolated from each other because of the existence of legislative barriers that have now been removed will generally lead to a cautious assessment of past evidence regarding prices, market shares or trade patterns. A process of market integration that would, in the short term, lead to wider geographic markets may therefore be taken into consideration when defining the geographic market for the purposes of assessing concentrations and joint ventures.

The process of gathering evidence

33.   When a precise market definition is deemed necessary, the Commission will often contact the main customers and the main companies in the industry to enquire into their views about the boundaries of product and geographic markets and to obtain the necessary factual evidence to reach a conclusion. The Commission might also contact the relevant professional associations, and companies active in upstream markets, so as to be able to define, in so far as necessary, separate product and geographic markets, for different levels of production or distribution of the products/services in question. It might also request additional information to the undertakings involved.

34.   Where appropriate, the Commission will address written requests for information to the market players mentioned above. These requests will usually include questions relating to the perceptions of companies about reactions to hypothetical price increases and their views of the boundaries of the relevant market. They will also ask for provision of the factual information the Commission deems necessary to reach a conclusion on the extent of the relevant market. The Commission might also discuss with marketing directors or other officers of those companies to gain a better understanding on how negotiations between suppliers and customers take place and better understand issues relating to the definition of the relevant market. Where appropriate, they might also carry out visits or inspections to the premises of the parties, their customers and/or their competitors, in order to better understand how products are manufactured and sold.

35.   The type of evidence relevant to reach a conclusion as to the product market can be categorized as follows:

Evidence to define markets – product dimension

36.   An analysis of the product characteristics and its intended use allows the Commission, as a first step, to limit the field of investigation of possible substitutes. However, product characteristics and intended use are insufficient to show whether two products are demand substitutes. Functional interchangeability or similarity in characteristics may not, in themselves, provide sufficient criteria, because the responsiveness of customers to relative price changes may be determined by other considerations as well. For example, there may be different competitive constraints in the original equipment market for car components and in spare parts, thereby leading to a separate delineation of two relevant markets. Conversely, differences in product characteristics are not in themselves sufficient to exclude demand substitutability, since this will depend to a large extent on how customers value different characteristics.

37.   The type of evidence the Commission considers relevant to assess whether two products are demand substitutes can be categorized as follows:

38.   Evidence of substitution in the recent past. In certain cases, it is possible to analyse evidence relating to recent past events or shocks in the market that offer actual examples of substitution between two products. When available, this sort of information will normally be fundamental for market definition. If there have been changes in relative prices in the past (all else being equal), the reactions in terms of quantities demanded will be determinant in establishing substitutability. Launches of new products in the past can also offer useful information, when it is possible to precisely analyse which products have lost sales to the new product.

39.   There are a number of quantitative tests that have specifically been designed for the purpose of delineating markets. These tests consist of various econometric and statistical approaches estimates of elasticities and cross-price elasticities (5) for the demand of a product, tests based on similarity of price movements over time, the analysis of causality between price series and similarity of price levels and/or their convergence. The Commission takes into account the available quantitative evidence capable of withstanding rigorous scrutiny for the purposes of establishing patterns of substitution in the past.

40.   Views of customers and competitors. The Commission often contacts the main customers and competitors of the companies involved in its enquiries, to gather their views on the boundaries of the product market as well as most of the factual information it requires to reach a conclusion on the scope of the market. Reasoned answers of customers and competitors as to what would happen if relative prices for the candidate products were to increase in the candidate geographic area by a small amount (for instance of 5 % to 10 %) are taken into account when they are sufficiently backed by factual evidence.

41.   Consumer preferences. In the case of consumer goods, it may be difficult for the Commission to gather the direct views of end consumers about substitute products. Marketing studies that companies have commissioned in the past and that are used by companies in their own decision-making as to pricing of their products and/or marketing actions may provide useful information for the Commission's delineation of the relevant market. Consumer surveys on usage patterns and attitudes, data from consumer's purchasing patterns, the views expressed by retailers and more generally, market research studies submitted by the parties and their competitors are taken into account to establish whether an economically significant proportion of consumers consider two products as substitutable, also taking into account the importance of brands for the products in question. The methodology followed in consumer surveys carried out ad hoc by the

undertakings involved or their competitors for the purposes of a merger procedure or a procedure pursuant to Regulation No 17 will usually be scrutinized with utmost care. Unlike pre-existing studies, they have not been prepared in the normal course of business for the adoption of business decisions.

42.   Barriers and costs associated with switching demand to potential substitutes. There are a number of barriers and costs that might prevent the Commission from considering two prima facie demand substitutes as belonging to one single product market. It is not possible to provide an exhaustive list of all the possible barriers to substitution and of switching costs. These barriers or obstacles might have a wide range of origins, and in its decisions, the Commission has been confronted with regulatory barriers or other forms of State intervention, constraints arising in downstream markets, need to incur specific capital investment or loss in current output in order to switch to alternative inputs, the location of customers, specific investment in production process, learning and human capital investment, retooling costs or other investments, uncertainty about quality and reputation of unknown suppliers, and others.

43.   Different categories of customers and price discrimination. The extent of the product market might be narrowed in the presence of distinct groups of customers. A distinct group of customers for the relevant product may constitute a narrower, distinct market when such ha group could be subject to price discrimination. This will usually be the case when two conditions are met: (a) it is possible to identify clearly which group an individual customer belongs to at the moment of selling the relevant products to him, and (b) trade among customers or arbitrage by third parties should not be feasible.

Evidence for defining markets – geographic dimension

44.   The type of evidence the Commission considers relevant to reach a conclusion as to the geographic market can be categorized as follows:

45.   Past evidence of diversion of orders to other areas. In certain cases, evidence on changes in prices between different areas and consequent reactions by customers might be available. Generally, the same quantitative tests used for product market definition might as well be used in geographic market definition, bearing in mind that international comparisons of prices might be more complex due to a number of factors such as exchange rate movements, taxation and product differentiation.

46.   Basic demand characteristics. The nature of demand for the relevant product may in itself determine the scope of the geographical market. Factors such as national preferences or preferences for national brands, language, culture and life style, and the need for a local presence have a strong potential to limit the geographic scope of competition.

47.   Views of customers and competitors. Where appropriate, the Commission will contact the main customers and competitors of the parties in its enquiries, to gather their views on the boundaries of the geographic market as well as most of the factual information it requires to reach a conclusion on the scope of the market when they are sufficiently backed by factual evidence.

48.   Current geographic pattern of purchases. An examination of the customers' current geographic pattern of purchases provides useful evidence as to the possible scope of the geographic market. When customers purchase from companies located anywhere in the Community or the EEA on similar terms, or they procure their supplies through effective tendering procedures in which companies from anywhere in the Community or the EEA submit bids, usually the geographic market will be considered to be Community-wide.

49. Trade flows/pattern of shipments. When the number of customers is so large that it is not possible to obtain through them a clear picture of geographic purchasing patterns, information on trade flows might be used alternatively, provided that the trade statistics are available with a sufficient degree of detail for the relevant products. Trade flows, and above all, the rationale behind trade flows provide useful insights and information for the purpose of establishing the scope of the geographic market but are not in themselves conclusive.

50. Barriers and switching costs associated to divert orders to companies located in other areas. The absence of trans-border purchases or trade flows, for instance, does not necessarily mean that the market is at most national in scope. Still, barriers isolating the national market have to identified before it is concluded that the relevant geographic market in such a case is national. Perhaps the clearest obstacle for a customer to divert its orders to other areas is the impact of transport costs and transport restrictions arising from legislation or from the nature of the relevant products. The impact of transport costs will usually limit the scope of the geographic market for bulky, low-value products, bearing in mind that a transport disadvantage might also be compensated by a comparative advantage in other costs (labour costs or raw materials). Access to distribution in a given area, regulatory barriers still existing in certain sectors, quotas and custom tariffs might also constitute barriers isolating a geographic area from the competitive pressure of companies located outside that area. Significant switching costs in procuring supplies from companies located in other countries constitute additional sources of such barriers.

51. On the basis of the evidence gathered, the Commission will then define a geographic market that could range from a local dimension to a global one, and there are examples of both local and global markets in past decisions of the Commission.

52. The paragraphs above describe the different factors which might be relevant to define markets. This does not imply that in each individual case it will be necessary to obtain evidence and assess each of these factors. Often in practice the evidence provided by a subset of these factors will be sufficient to reach a conclusion, as shown in the past decisional practice of the Commission.

IV. CALCULATION OF MARKET SHARE

53. The definition of the relevant market in both its product and geographic dimensions allows the identification the suppliers and the customers/consumers active on that market. On that basis, a total market size and market shares for each supplier can be calculated on the basis of their sales of the relevant products in the relevant area. In practice, the total market size and market shares are often available from market sources, i.e. companies' estimates, studies commissioned from industry consultants and/or trade associations. When this is not the case, or when available estimates are not reliable, the Commission will usually ask each supplier in the relevant market to provide its own sales in order to calculate total market size and market shares.

54. If sales are usually the reference to calculate market shares, there are nevertheless other indications that, depending on the specific products or industry in question, can offer useful information such as, in particular, capacity, the number of players in bidding markets, units of fleet as in aerospace, or the reserves held in the case of sectors such as mining.

55. As a rule of thumb, both volume sales and value sales provide useful information. In cases of differentiated products, sales in value and their associated market share will usually be considered to better reflect the relative position and strength of each supplier.

V. ADDITIONAL CONSIDERATIONS

56.   There are certain areas where the application of the principles above has to be undertaken with care. This is the case when considering primary and secondary markets, in particular, when the behaviour of undertakings at a point in time has to be analysed pursuant to Article 86 [Article 102 TFEU]. The method of defining markets in these cases is the same, i.e. assessing the responses of customers based on their purchasing decisions to relative price changes, but taking into account as well, constraints on substitution imposed by conditions in the connected markets. A narrow definition of market for secondary products, for instance, spare parts, may result when compatibility with the primary product is important. Problems of finding compatible secondary products together with the existence of high prices and a long lifetime of the primary products may render relative price increases of secondary products profitable. A different market definition may result if significant substitution between secondary products is possible or if the characteristics of the primary products make quick and direct consumer responses to relative price increases of the secondary products feasible.

57.   In certain cases, the existence of chains of substitution might lead to the definition of a relevant market where products or areas at the extreme of the market are not directly substitutable. An example might be provided by the geographic dimension of a product with significant transport costs. In such cases, deliveries from a given plant are limited to a certain area around each plant by the impact of transport costs. In principle, such an area could constitute the relevant geographic market. However, if the distribution of plants is such that there are considerable overlaps between the areas around different plants, it is possible that the pricing of those products will be constrained by a chain substitution effect, and lead to the definition of a broader geographic market. The same reasoning may apply if product B is a demand substitute for products A and C. Even if products A and C are not direct demand substitutes, they might be found to be in the same relevant product market since their respective pricing might be constrained by substitution to B.

58.   From a practical perspective, the concept of chains of substitution has to be corroborated by actual evidence, for instance related to price interdependence at the extremes of the chains of substitution, in order to lead to an extension of the relevant market in an individual case. Price levels at the extremes of the chains would have to be of the same magnitude as well.

(1)   The focus of assessment in State aid cases is the aid recipient and the industry/sector concerned rather than identification of competitive constraints faced by the aid recipient. When consideration of market power and therefore of the relevant market are raised in any particular case, elements of the approach outlined here might serve as a basis for the assessment of State aid cases.

(2)   For the purposes of this notice, the undertakings involved will be, in the case of a concentration, the parties to the concentration; in investigations within the meaning of Article 86 of the Treaty, [Article 102 TFEU] the undertaking being investigated or the complainants; for investigations within the meaning of Article 85 [Article 101 TFEU], the parties to the Agreement.

(3)   Definition given by the Court of Justice in its judgment of 13 February 1979 in Case 85/76, Hoffmann-La Roche [1979] ECR 461, and confirmed in subsequent judgments.

(4)   That is such a period that does not entail a significant adjustment of existing tangible and intangible assets (see paragraph 23).

(5)   Own-price elasticity of demand for product X is a measure of the responsiveness of demand for X to percentage change in its own price. Cross-price elasticity between products X and Y is the responsiveness of demand for product X to percentage change in the price of product Y.

COMMISSION NOTICE

on agreements of minor importance which do not appreciably restrict competition under Article 81(1) of the Treaty establishing the European Community (*de minimis*)(1)

OJ C 368, 22.12.2001, P. 13[1]

I

1. Article 81(1) prohibits agreements between undertakings which may affect trade between Member States and which have as their object or effect the prevention, restriction or distortion of competition within the common market. The Court of Justice of the European Communities has clarified that this provision is not applicable where the impact of the agreement on intra-Community trade or on competition is not appreciable.

2. In this notice the Commission quantifies, with the help of market share thresholds, what is not an appreciable restriction of competition under Article 81 of the EC Treaty. This negative definition of appreciability does not imply that agreements between undertakings which exceed the thresholds set out in this notice appreciably restrict competition. Such agreements may still have only a negligible effect on competition and may therefore not be prohibited by Article 81(1)(2).

3. Agreements may in addition not fall under Article 81(1) because they are not capable of appreciably affecting trade between Member States. This notice does not deal with this issue. It does not quantify what does not constitute an appreciable effect on trade. It is however acknowledged that agreements between small and medium-sized undertakings, as defined in the Annex to Commission Recommendation 96/280/EC(3), are rarely capable of appreciably affecting trade between Member States. Small and medium-sized undertakings are currently defined in that recommendation as undertakings which have fewer than 250 employees and have either an annual turnover not exceeding EUR 40 million or an annual balance-sheet total not exceeding EUR 27 million.

4. In cases covered by this notice the Commission will not institute proceedings either upon application or on its own initiative. Where undertakings assume in good faith that an agreement is covered by this notice, the Commission will not impose fines. Although not binding on them, this notice also intends to give guidance to the courts and authorities of the Member States in their application of Article 81.

5. This notice also applies to decisions by associations of undertakings and to concerted practices.

6. This notice is without prejudice to any interpretation of Article 81 which may be given by the Court of Justice or the Court of First Instance of the European Communities.

II

7. The Commission holds the view that agreements between undertakings which affect trade between Member States do not appreciably restrict competition within the meaning of Article 81(1):

---

[1]   EDITOR'S NOTE: As of 1 May 2012 this Commission Notice has not been reissued following the entry into force of the Treaty of Lisbon. It includes references to the old Treaty article numbers. Reference should be made to the Tables of Equivalences accompanying the consolidated Treaties in Part II of this edition for the conversion of old Treaty article numbers to new ones.

(a) if the aggregate market share held by the parties to the agreement does not exceed 10 % on any of the relevant markets affected by the agreement, where the agreement is made between undertakings which are actual or potential competitors on any of these markets (agreements between competitors)(4); or

(b) if the market share held by each of the parties to the agreement does not exceed 15 % on any of the relevant markets affected by the agreement, where the agreement is made between undertakings which are not actual or potential competitors on any of these markets (agreements between non-competitors).

In cases where it is difficult to classify the agreement as either an agreement between competitors or an agreement between non-competitors the 10 % threshold is applicable.

8.   Where in a relevant market competition is restricted by the cumulative effect of agreements for the sale of goods or services entered into by different suppliers or distributors (cumulative foreclosure effect of parallel networks of agreements having similar effects on the market), the market share thresholds under point 7 are reduced to 5 %, both for agreements between competitors and for agreements between non-competitors. Individual suppliers or distributors with a market share not exceeding 5 % are in general not considered to contribute significantly to a cumulative foreclosure effect(5). A cumulative foreclosure effect is unlikely to exist if less than 30 % of the relevant market is covered by parallel (networks of) agreements having similar effects.

9.   The Commission also holds the view that agreements are not restrictive of competition if the market shares do not exceed the thresholds of respectively 10 %, 15 % and 5 % set out in point 7 and 8 during two successive calendar years by more than 2 percentage points.

10. In order to calculate the market share, it is necessary to determine the relevant market. This consists of the relevant product market and the relevant geographic market. When defining the relevant market, reference should be had to the notice on the definition of the relevant market for the purposes of Community competition law(6). The market shares are to be calculated on the basis of sales value data or, where appropriate, purchase value data. If value data are not available, estimates based on other reliable market information, including volume data, may be used.

11. Points 7, 8 and 9 do not apply to agreements containing any of the following hardcore restrictions:

(1) as regards agreements between competitors as defined in point 7, restrictions which, directly or indirectly, in isolation or in combination with other factors under the control of the parties, have as their object(7):

(a) the fixing of prices when selling the products to third parties;

(b) the limitation of output or sales;

(c) the allocation of markets or customers;

(2) as regards agreements between non-competitors as defined in point 7, restrictions which, directly or indirectly, in isolation or in combination with other factors under the control of the parties, have as their object:

(a) the restriction of the buyer's ability to determine its sale price, without prejudice to the possibility of the supplier imposing a maximum sale price or recommending a sale price, provided that they do not amount to a fixed or minimum sale price as a result of pressure from, or incentives offered by, any of the parties;

(b) the restriction of the territory into which, or of the customers to whom, the buyer may sell the contract goods or services, except the following restrictions which are not hardcore:

> — the restriction of active sales into the exclusive territory or to an exclusive customer group reserved to the supplier or allocated by the supplier to another buyer, where such a restriction does not limit sales by the customers of the buyer,
> — the restriction of sales to end users by a buyer operating at the wholesale level of trade,
> — the restriction of sales to unauthorised distributors by the members of a selective distribution system, and
> — the restriction of the buyer's ability to sell components, supplied for the purposes of incorporation, to customers who would use them to manufacture the same type of goods as those produced by the supplier;

(c) the restriction of active or passive sales to end users by members of a selective distribution system operating at the retail level of trade, without prejudice to the possibility of prohibiting a member of the system from operating out of an unauthorised place of establishment;

(d) the restriction of cross-supplies between distributors within a selective distribution system, including between distributors operating at different levels of trade;

(e) the restriction agreed between a supplier of components and a buyer who incorporates those components, which limits the supplier's ability to sell the components as spare parts to end users or to repairers or other service providers not entrusted by the buyer with the repair or servicing of its goods;

(3) as regards agreements between competitors as defined in point 7, where the competitors operate, for the purposes of the agreement, at a different level of the production or distribution chain, any of the hardcore restrictions listed in paragraph (1) and (2) above.

12. (1) For the purposes of this notice, the terms "undertaking", "party to the agreement", "distributor", "supplier" and "buyer" shall include their respective connected undertakings.

(2) "Connected undertakings" are:

(a) undertakings in which a party to the agreement, directly or indirectly:
> — has the power to exercise more than half the voting rights, or
> — has the power to appoint more than half the members of the supervisory board, board of management or bodies legally representing the undertaking, or
> — has the right to manage the undertaking's affairs;

(b) undertakings which directly or indirectly have, over a party to the agreement, the rights or powers listed in (a);

(c) undertakings in which an undertaking referred to in (b) has, directly or indirectly, the rights or powers listed in (a);

(d) undertakings in which a party to the agreement together with one or more of the undertakings referred to in (a), (b) or (c), or in which two or more of the latter undertakings, jointly have the rights or powers listed in (a);

(e) undertakings in which the rights or the powers listed in (a) are jointly held by:
> — parties to the agreement or their respective connected undertakings referred to in (a) to (d), or
> — one or more of the parties to the agreement or one or more of their connected undertakings referred to in (a) to (d) and one or more third parties.

(3) For the purposes of paragraph 2(e), the market share held by these jointly held undertakings shall be apportioned equally to each undertaking having the rights or the powers listed in paragraph 2(a).

(1)   This notice replaces the notice on agreements of minor importance published in OJ C 372, 9.12.1997.

(2)   See, for instance, the judgment of the Court of Justice in Joined Cases C-215/96 and C-216/96 Bagnasco (Carlos)
      v Banca Popolare di Novara and Casa di Risparmio di Genova e Imperia (1999) ECR I-135, points 34–35. This
      notice is also without prejudice to the principles for assessment under Article 81(1) as expressed in the Commission
      notice "Guidelines on the applicability of Article 81 of the EC Treaty to horizontal cooperation agreements", OJ C 3,
      6.1.2001, in particular points 17–31 inclusive, and in the Commission notice "Guidelines on vertical restraints", OJ C
      291, 13.10.2000, in particular points 5–20 inclusive.

(3)   OJ L 107, 30.4.1996, p. 4. This recommendation will be revised. It is envisaged to increase the annual turnover
      threshold from EUR 40 million to EUR 50 million and the annual balance-sheet total threshold from EUR 27 million
      to EUR 43 million.

(4)   On what are actual or potential competitors, see the Commission notice "Guidelines on the applicability of Article 81
      of the EC Treaty to horizontal cooperation agreements", OJ C 3, 6.1.2001, paragraph 9. A firm is treated as an actual
      competitor if it is either active on the same relevant market or if, in the absence of the agreement, it is able to switch
      production to the relevant products and market them in the short term without incurring significant additional costs
      or risks in response to a small and permanent increase in relative prices (immediate supply-side substitutability). A
      firm is treated as a potential competitor if there is evidence that, absent the agreement, this firm could and would be
      likely to undertake the necessary additional investments or other necessary switching costs so that it could enter the
      relevant market in response to a small and permanent increase in relative prices.

(5)   See also the Commission notice "Guidelines on vertical restraints", OJ C 291, 13.10.2000, in particular para-
      graphs 73, 142, 143 and 189. While in the guidelines on vertical restraints in relation to certain restrictions reference
      is made not only to the total but also to the tied market share of a particular supplier or buyer, in this notice all
      market share thresholds refer to total market shares.

(6)   OJ C 372, 9.12.1997, p. 5.

(7)   Without prejudice to situations of joint production with or without joint distribution as defined in Article 5, para-
      graph 2, of Commission Regulation (EC) No 2658/2000 and Article 5, paragraph 2, of Commission Regulation (EC)
      No 2659/2000, OJ L 304, 5.12.2000, pp. 3 and 7 respectively.

COMMISSION NOTICE
on the handling of complaints by the Commission under [Articles 101 and 102 TFEU][1]
OJ C 101, 27.4.2004, P. 65

I. INTRODUCTION AND SUBJECT-MATTER OF THE NOTICE

1.   Regulation 1/2003(1) establishes a system of parallel competence for the application of
      Articles 81 and 82 of the EC Treaty by the Commission and the Member States'
      competition authorities and courts. The Regulation recognises in particular the
      complementary functions of the Commission and Member States' competition authorities
      acting as public enforcers and the Member States' courts that rule on private lawsuits in
      order to safeguard the rights of individuals deriving from Articles 81 and 82(2).

2.   Under Regulation 1/2003, the public enforcers may focus their action on the investigation
      of serious infringements of Articles 81 and 82 which are often difficult to detect. For their
      enforcement activity, they benefit from information supplied by undertakings and by
      consumers in the market.

---

[1]   EDITOR'S NOTE: As of 1 May 2012 this Commission Notice has not been reissued following the entry into force
      of the Treaty of Lisbon. It includes references to the old Treaty article numbers in the text. The title of the Notice has
      been updated to reflect that fact that Articles 81 and 82 TEC have been replaced by Articles 101 and 102 TFEU.
      Reference should be made to the Tables of Equivalences accompanying the consolidated Treaties in Part II of this
      edition for the conversion of old Treaty article numbers to new ones.

3. The Commission therefore wishes to encourage citizens and undertakings to address themselves to the public enforcers to inform them about suspected infringements of the competition rules. At the level of the Commission, there are two ways to do this, one is by lodging a complaint pursuant to Article 7(2) of Regulation 1/2003. Under Articles 5 to 9 of Regulation 773/2004(3), such complaints must fulfil certain requirements.

4. The other way is the provision of market information that does not have to comply with the requirements for complaints pursuant to Article 7(2) of Regulation 1/2003. For this purpose, the Commission has created a special website to collect information from citizens and undertakings and their associations who wish to inform the Commission about suspected infringements of Articles 81 and 82. Such information can be the starting point for an investigation by the Commission(4). Information about suspected infringements can be supplied to the following address:

    http://europa.eu.int/dgcomp/ info-on-anti-competitive-practices

    or to: Commission européenne/Europese Commissie Competition DG B – 1049 Bruxelles/ Brussel

5. Without prejudice to the interpretation of Regulation 1/2003 and of Commission Regulation 773/2004 by the Community Courts, the present Notice intends to provide guidance to citizens and undertakings that are seeking relief from suspected infringements of the competition rules. The Notice contains two main parts:
    — Part II gives indications about the choice between complaining to the Commission or bringing a lawsuit before a national court. Moreover, it recalls the principles related to the work-sharing between the Commission and the national competition authorities in the enforcement system established by Regulation 1/2003 that are explained in the Notice on cooperation within the network of competition authorities(5).
    — Part III explains the procedure for the treatment of complaints pursuant to Article 7(2) of Regulation 1/2003 by the Commission.

6. This Notice does not address the following situations:
    — complaints lodged by Member States pursuant to Article 7(2) of Regulation 1/2003,
    — complaints that ask the Commission to take action against a Member State pursuant to Article 86(3) in conjunction with Articles 81 or 82 of the Treaty,
    — complaints relating to Article 87 of the Treaty on state aids,
    — complaints relating to infringements by Member States that the Commission may pursue in the framework of Article 226 of the Treaty(6).

II. DIFFERENT POSSIBILITIES FOR LODGING COMPLAINTS ABOUT SUSPECTED INFRINGEMENTS OF ARTICLES 81 OR 82

A. COMPLAINTS IN THE NEW ENFORCEMENT SYSTEM ESTABLISHED BY REGULATION 1/2003

7. Depending on the nature of the complaint, a complainant may bring his complaint either to a national court or to a competition authority that acts as public enforcer. The present chapter of this Notice intends to help potential complainants to make an informed choice about whether to address themselves to the Commission, to one of the Member States' competition authorities or to a national court.

8. While national courts are called upon to safeguard the rights of individuals and are thus bound to rule on cases brought before them, public enforcers cannot investigate all complaints, but must set priorities in their treatment of cases. The Court of Justice has

held that the Commission, entrusted by Article 85(1) of the EC Treaty with the task of ensuring application of the principles laid down in Articles 81 and 82 of the Treaty, is responsible for defining and implementing the orientation of Community competition policy and that, in order to perform that task effectively, it is entitled to give differing degrees of priority to the complaints brought before it(7).

9. Regulation 1/2003 empowers Member States' courts and Member States' competition authorities to apply Articles 81 and 82 in their entirety alongside the Commission. Regulation 1/2003 pursues as one principal objective that Member States' courts and competition authorities should participate effectively in the enforcement of Articles 81 and 82(8).

10. Moreover, Article 3 of Regulation 1/2003 provides that Member States' courts and competition authorities have to apply Articles 81 and 82 to all cases of agreements or conduct that are capable of affecting trade between Member States to which they apply their national competition laws. In addition, Articles 11 and 15 of the Regulation create a range of mechanisms by which Member States' courts and competition authorities cooperate with the Commission in the enforcement of Articles 81 and 82.

11. In this new legislative framework, the Commission intends to refocus its enforcement resources along the following lines:
    — enforce the EC competition rules in cases for which it is well placed to act(9), concentrating its resources on the most serious infringements(10);
    — handle cases in relation to which the Commission should act with a view to define Community competition policy and/or to ensure coherent application of Articles 81 or 82.

B. THE COMPLEMENTARY ROLES OF PRIVATE AND PUBLIC ENFORCEMENT

12. It has been consistently held by the Community Courts that national courts are called upon to safeguard the rights of individuals created by the direct effect of Articles 81(1) and 82(11).

13. National courts can decide upon the nullity or validity of contracts and only national courts can grant damages to an individual in case of an infringement of Articles 81 and 82. Under the case law of the Court of Justice, any individual can claim damages for loss caused to him by a contract or by conduct which restricts or distorts competition, in order to ensure the full effectiveness of the Community competition rules. Such actions for damages before the national courts can make a significant contribution to the maintenance of effective competition in the Community as they discourage undertakings from concluding or applying restrictive agreements or practices(12).

14. Regulation 1/2003 takes express account of the fact that national courts have an essential part to play in applying the EC competition rules(13). By extending the power to apply Article 81(3) to national courts it removes the possibility for undertakings to delay national court proceedings by a notification to the Commission and thus eliminates an obstacle for private litigation that existed under Regulation No 17(14).

15. Without prejudice to the right or obligation of national courts to address a preliminary question to the Court of Justice in accordance with Article 234 EC, Article 15(1) of Regulation 1/2003 provides expressly that national courts may ask for opinions or information from the Commission. This provision aims at facilitating the application of Articles 81 and 82 by national courts(15).

16. Action before national courts has the following advantages for complainants:
     — National courts may award damages for loss suffered as a result of an infringement of
        Article 81 or 82.
     — National courts may rule on claims for payment or contractual obligations based on
        an agreement that they examine under Article 81.
     — It is for the national courts to apply the civil sanction of nullity of Article 81(2) in
        contractual relationships between individuals(16). They can in particular assess, in the
        light of the applicable national law, the scope and consequences of the nullity of
        certain contractual provisions under Article 81(2), with particular regard to all the
        other matters covered by the agreement(17).
     — National courts are usually better placed than the Commission to adopt interim
        measures(18).
     — Before national courts, it is possible to combine a claim under Community
        competition law with other claims under national law.
     — Courts normally have the power to award legal costs to the successful applicant. This
        is never possible in an administrative procedure before the Commission.

17. The fact that a complainant can secure the protection of his rights by an action before a
     national court, is an important element that the Commission may take into account in its
     examination of the Community interest for investigating a complaint(19).

18. The Commission holds the view that the new enforcement system established by
     Regulation 1/2003 strengthens the possibilities for complainants to seek and obtain
     effective relief before national courts.

C. WORK-SHARING BETWEEN THE PUBLIC ENFORCERS IN THE EUROPEAN COMMUNITY

19. Regulation 1/2003 creates a system of parallel competence for the application of Articles 81
     and 82 by empowering Member States' competition authorities to apply Articles 81 and 82
     in their entirety (Article 5). Decentralised enforcement by Member States' competition
     authorities is further encouraged by the possibility to exchange information (Article 12) and
     to provide each other assistance with investigations (Article 22).

20. The Regulation does not regulate the work-sharing between the Commission and the
     Member States' competition authorities but leaves the division of case work to the
     cooperation of the Commission and the Member States' competition authorities inside the
     European Competition Network (ECN). The Regulation pursues the objective of ensuring
     effective enforcement of Articles 81 and 82 through a flexible division of case work
     between the public enforcers in the Community.

21. Orientations for the work sharing between the Commission and the Member States'
     competition authorities are laid down in a separate Notice(20). The guidance contained in
     that Notice, which concerns the relations between the public enforcers, will be of interest
     to complainants as it permits them to address a complaint to the authority most likely to
     be well placed to deal with their case.

22. The Notice on cooperation within the Network of Competition Authorities states in
     particular(21):

     "An authority can be considered to be well placed to deal with a case if the following
     three cumulative conditions are met:
     — the agreement or practice has substantial direct actual or foreseeable effects on
        competition within its territory, is implemented within or originates from its territory;

— the authority is able effectively to bring to an end the entire infringement, i.e. it can adopt a cease-and desist order, the effect of which will be sufficient to bring an end to the infringement and it can, where appropriate, sanction the infringement adequately;

— it can gather, possibly with the assistance of other authorities, the evidence required to prove the infringement.

The above criteria indicate that a material link between the infringement and the territory of a Member State must exist in order for that Member State's competition authority to be considered well placed. It can be expected that in most cases the authorities of those Member States where competition is substantially affected by an infringement will be well placed provided they are capable of effectively bringing the infringement to an end through either single or parallel action unless the Commission is better placed to act (see below [. . .]).

It follows that a single NCA is usually well placed to deal with agreements or practices that substantially affect competition mainly within its territory [. . .].

Furthermore single action of an NCA might also be appropriate where, although more than one NCA can be regarded as well placed, the action of a single NCA is sufficient to bring the entire infringement to an end [. . .].

Parallel action by two or three NCAs may be appropriate where an agreement or practice has substantial effects on competition mainly in their respective territories and the action of only one NCA would not be sufficient to bring the entire infringement to an end and/or to sanction it adequately [. . .].

The authorities dealing with a case in parallel action will endeavour to coordinate their action to the extent possible. To that effect, they may find it useful to designate one of them as a lead authority and to delegate tasks to the lead authority such as for example the coordination of investigative measures, while each authority remains responsible for conducting its own proceedings.

The Commission is particularly well placed if one or several agreement(s) or practice(s), including networks of similar agreements or practices, have effects on competition in more than three Member States (cross-border markets covering more than three Member States or several national markets) [. . .].

Moreover, the Commission is particularly well placed to deal with a case if it is closely linked to other Community provisions which may be exclusively or more effectively applied by the Commission, if the Community interest requires the adoption of a Commission decision to develop Community competition policy when a new competition issue arises or to ensure effective enforcement.".

23. Within the European Competition Network, information on cases that are being investigated following a complaint will be made available to the other members of the network before or without delay after commencing the first formal investigative measure(22). Where the same complaint has been lodged with several authorities or where a case has not been lodged with an authority that is well placed, the members of the network will endeavour to determine within an indicative time-limit of two months which authority or authorities should be in charge of the case.

24. Complainants themselves have an important role to play in further reducing the potential need for reallocation of a case originating from their complaint by referring to the orientations on work sharing in the network set out in the present chapter when deciding on where to lodge their complaint. If nonetheless a case is reallocated within the network, the undertakings concerned and the complainant(s) are informed as soon as possible by the competition authorities involved(23).

25. The Commission may reject a complaint in accordance with Article 13 of Regulation 1/2003, on the grounds that a Member State competition authority is dealing or has dealt with the case. When doing so, the Commission must, in accordance with Article 9 of Regulation 773/2004, inform the complainant without delay of the national competition authority which is dealing or has already dealt with the case.

III. THE COMMISSION'S HANDLING OF COMPLAINTS PURSUANT TO ARTICLE 7(2) OF REGULATION 1/2003

A. GENERAL

26. According to Article 7(2) of Regulation 1/2003 natural or legal persons that can show a legitimate interest(24) are entitled to lodge a complaint to ask the Commission to find an infringement of Articles 81 and 82 EC and to require that the infringement be brought to an end in accordance with Article 7(1) of Regulation 1/2003. The present part of this Notice explains the requirements applicable to complaints based on Article 7(2) of Regulation 1/2003, their assessment and the procedure followed by the Commission.

27. The Commission, unlike civil courts, whose task is to safeguard the individual rights of private persons, is an administrative authority that must act in the public interest. It is an inherent feature of the Commission's task as public enforcer that it has a margin of discretion to set priorities in its enforcement activity(25).

28. The Commission is entitled to give different degrees of priority to complaints made to it and may refer to the Community interest presented by a case as a criterion of priority(26). The Commission may reject a complaint when it considers that the case does not display a sufficient Community interest to justify further investigation. Where the Commission rejects a complaint, the complainant is entitled to a decision of the Commission(27) without prejudice to Article 7(3) of Regulation 773/2004.

B. MAKING A COMPLAINT PURSUANT TO ARTICLE 7(2) OF REGULATION 1/2003

(a) Complaint form

29. A complaint pursuant to Article 7(2) of Regulation 1/2003 can only be made about an alleged infringement of Articles 81 or 82 with a view to the Commission taking action under Article 7(1) of Regulation 1/2003. A complaint under Article 7(2) of Regulation 1/2003 has to comply with Form C mentioned in Article 5(1) of Regulation 773/2004 and annexed to that Regulation.

30. Form C is available at http://europa.eu.int/dgcomp/ complaints-form and is also annexed to this Notice. The complaint must be submitted in three paper copies as well as, if possible, an electronic copy. In addition, the complainant must provide a non-confidential version of the complaint (Article 5(2) of Regulation 773/2004). Electronic transmission to the Commission is possible via the website indicated, the paper copies should be sent to the following address: Commission européenne/Europese Commissie Competition DG B – 1049 Bruxelles/Brussel

31. Form C requires complainants to submit comprehensive information in relation to their complaint. They should also provide copies of relevant supporting documentation reasonably available to them and, to the extent possible, provide indications as to where relevant information and documents that are unavailable to them could be obtained by the Commission. In particular cases, the Commission may dispense with the obligation to provide information in relation to part of the information required by Form C

(Article 5(1) of Regulation 773/2004). The Commission holds the view that this possibility can in particular play a role to facilitate complaints by consumer associations where they, in the context of an otherwise substantiated complaint, do not have access to specific pieces of information from the sphere of the undertakings complained of.

32.   Correspondence to the Commission that does not comply with the requirements of Article 5 of Regulation 773/2004 and therefore does not constitute a complaint within the meaning of Article 7(2) of Regulation 1/2003 will be considered by the Commission as general information that, where it is useful, may lead to an own-initiative investigation (cf. point 4 above).

(b) Legitimate interest

33.   The status of formal complainant under Article 7(2) of Regulation 1/2003 is reserved to legal and natural persons who can show a legitimate interest(28). Member States are deemed to have a legitimate interest for all complaints they choose to lodge.

34.   In the past practice of the Commission, the condition of legitimate interest was not often a matter of doubt as most complainants were in a position of being directly and adversely affected by the alleged infringement. However, there are situations where the condition of a "legitimate interest" in Article 7(2) requires further analysis to conclude that it is fulfilled. Useful guidance can best be provided by a non-exhaustive set of examples.

35.   The Court of First Instance has held that an association of undertakings may claim a legitimate interest in lodging a complaint regarding conduct concerning its members, even if it is not directly concerned, as an undertaking operating in the relevant market, by the conduct complained of, provided that, first, it is entitled to represent the interests of its members and secondly, the conduct complained of is liable to adversely affect the interests of its members(29). Conversely, the Commission has been found to be entitled not to pursue the complaint of an association of undertakings whose members were not involved in the type of business transactions complained of(30).

36.   From this case law, it can be inferred that undertakings (themselves or through associations that are entitled to represent their interests) can claim a legitimate interest where they are operating in the relevant market or where the conduct complained of is liable to directly and adversely affect their interests. This confirms the established practice of the Commission which has accepted that a legitimate interest can, for instance, be claimed by the parties to the agreement or practice which is the subject of the complaint, by competitors whose interests have allegedly been damaged by the behaviour complained of or by undertakings excluded from a distribution system.

37.   Consumer associations can equally lodge complaints with the Commission(31). The Commission moreover holds the view that individual consumers whose economic interests are directly and adversely affected insofar as they are the buyers of goods or services that are the object of an infringement can be in a position to show a legitimate interest(32).

38.   However, the Commission does not consider as a legitimate interest within the meaning of Article 7(2) the interest of persons or organisations that wish to come forward on general interest considerations without showing that they or their members are liable to be directly and adversely affected by the infringement (pro bono publico).

39.   Local or regional public authorities may be able to show a legitimate interest in their capacity as buyers or users of goods or services affected by the conduct complained of. Conversely, they cannot be considered as showing a legitimate interest within the meaning of Article 7(2) of Regulation 1/2003 to the extent that they bring to the attention of the Commission alleged infringements pro bono publico.

40.   Complainants have to demonstrate their legitimate interest. Where a natural or legal person lodging a complaint is unable to demonstrate a legitimate interest, the Commission is entitled, without prejudice to its right to initiate proceedings of its own initiative, not to pursue the complaint. The Commission may ascertain whether this condition is met at any stage of the investigation(33).

C. ASSESSMENT OF COMPLAINTS

(a) Community interest

41.   Under the settled case law of the Community Courts, the Commission is not required to conduct an investigation in each case(34) or, a fortiori, to take a decision within the meaning of Article 249 EC on the existence or non-existence of an infringement of Articles 81 or 82(35), but is entitled to give differing degrees of priority to the complaints brought before it and refer to the Community interest in order to determine the degree of priority to be applied to the various complaints it receives(36). The position is different only if the complaint falls within the exclusive competence of the Commission(37).

42.   The Commission must however examine carefully the factual and legal elements brought to its attention by the complainant in order to assess the Community interest in further investigation of a case(38).

43.   The assessment of the Community interest raised by a complaint depends on the circumstances of each individual case. Accordingly, the number of criteria of assessment to which the Commission may refer is not limited, nor is the Commission required to have recourse exclusively to certain criteria. As the factual and legal circumstances may differ considerably from case to case, it is permissible to apply new criteria which had not before been considered(39). Where appropriate, the Commission may give priority to a single criterion for assessing the Community interest(40).

44.   Among the criteria which have been held relevant in the case law for the assessment of the Community interest in the (further) investigation of a case are the following:
    — The Commission can reject a complaint on the ground that the complainant can bring an action to assert its rights before national courts(41).
    — The Commission may not regard certain situations as excluded in principle from its purview under the task entrusted to it by the Treaty but is required to assess in each case how serious the alleged infringements are and how persistent their consequences are. This means in particular that it must take into account the duration and the extent of the infringements complained of and their effect on the competition situation in the Community(42).
    — The Commission may have to balance the significance of the alleged infringement as regards the functioning of the common market, the probability of establishing the existence of the infringement and the scope of the investigation required in order to fulfil its task of ensuring that Articles 81 and 82 of the Treaty are complied with(43).
    — While the Commission's discretion does not depend on how advanced the investigation of a case is, the stage of the investigation forms part of the circumstances of the case which the Commission may have to take into consideration(44).
    — The Commission may decide that it is not appropriate to investigate a complaint where the practices in question have ceased. However, for this purpose, the Commission will have to ascertain whether anti-competitive effects persist and if the

seriousness of the infringements or the persistence of their effects does not give the complaint a Community interest(45).

— The Commission may also decide that it is not appropriate to investigate a complaint where the undertakings concerned agree to change their conduct in such a way that it can consider that there is no longer a sufficient Community interest to intervene(46).

45.   Where it forms the view that a case does not display sufficient Community interest to justify (further) investigation, the Commission may reject the complaint on that ground. Such a decision can be taken either before commencing an investigation or after taking investigative measures(47). However, the Commission is not obliged to set aside a complaint for lack of Community interest(48).

(b) Assessment under Articles 81 and 82

46.   The examination of a complaint under Articles 81 and 82 involves two aspects, one relating to the facts to be established to prove an infringement of Articles 81 or 82 and the other relating to the legal assessment of the conduct complained of.

47.   Where the complaint, while complying with the requirements of Article 5 of Regulation 773/2004 and Form C, does not sufficiently substantiate the allegations put forward, it may be rejected on that ground(49). In order to reject a complaint on the ground that the conduct complained of does not infringe the EC competition rules or does not fall within their scope of application, the Commission is not obliged to take into account circumstances that have not been brought to its attention by the complainant and that it could only have uncovered by the investigation of the case(50).

48.   The criteria for the legal assessment of agreements or practices under Articles 81 and 82 cannot be dealt with exhaustively in the present Notice. However, potential complainants should refer to the extensive guidance available from the Commission(51), in addition to other sources and in particular the case law of the Community Courts and the case practice of the Commission. Four specific issues are mentioned in the following points with indications on where to find further guidance.

49.   Agreements and practices fall within the scope of application of Articles 81 and 82 where they are capable of affecting trade between Member States. Where an agreement or practice does not fulfil this condition, national competition law may apply, but not EC competition law. Extensive guidance on this subject can be found in the Notice on the effect on trade concept(52).

50.   Agreements falling within the scope of Article 81 may be agreements of minor importance which are deemed not to restrict competition appreciably. Guidance on this issue can be found in the Commission's de minimis Notice(53).

51.   Agreements that fulfil the conditions of a block exemption regulation are deemed to satisfy the conditions of Article 81(3)(54). For the Commission to withdraw the benefit of the block exemption pursuant to Article 29 of Regulation 1/2003, it must find that upon individual assessment an agreement to which the exemption regulation applies has certain effects which are incompatible with Article 81(3).

52.   Agreements that restrict competition within the meaning of Article 81(1) EC may fulfil the conditions of Article 81(3) EC. Pursuant to Article 1(2) of Regulation 1/2003 and without a prior administrative decision being required, such agreements are not prohibited. Guidance on the conditions to be fulfilled by an agreement pursuant to Article 81(3) can be found in the Notice on Article 81(3)(55).

D. THE COMMISSION'S PROCEDURES WHEN DEALING WITH COMPLAINTS

(a) Overview

53.   As recalled above, the Commission is not obliged to carry out an investigation on the basis of every complaint submitted with a view to establishing whether an infringement has been committed. However, the Commission is under a duty to consider carefully the factual and legal issues brought to its attention by the complainant, in order to assess whether those issues indicate conduct which is liable to infringe Articles 81 and 82(56).

54.   In the Commission's procedure for dealing with complaints, different stages can be distinguished(57).

55.   During the first stage, following the submission of the complaint, the Commission examines the complaint and may collect further information in order to decide what action it will take on the complaint. That stage may include an informal exchange of views between the Commission and the complainant with a view to clarifying the factual and legal issues with which the complaint is concerned. In this stage, the Commission may give an initial reaction to the complainant allowing the complainant an opportunity to expand on his allegations in the light of that initial reaction.

56.   In the second stage, the Commission may investigate the case further with a view to initiating proceedings pursuant to Article 7(1) of Regulation 1/2003 against the undertakings complained of. Where the Commission considers that there are insufficient grounds for acting on the complaint, it will inform the complainant of its reasons and offer the complainant the opportunity to submit any further comments within a time-limit which it fixes (Article 7(1) of Regulation 773/2004).

57.   If the complainant fails to make known its views within the time-limit set by the Commission, the complaint is deemed to have been withdrawn (Article 7(3) of Regulation 773/2004). In all other cases, in the third stage of the procedure, the Commission takes cognisance of the observations submitted by the complainant and either initiates a procedure against the subject of the complaint or adopts a decision rejecting the complaint(58).

58.   Where the Commission rejects a complaint pursuant to Article 13 of Regulation 1/2003 on the grounds that another authority is dealing or has dealt with the case, the Commission proceeds in accordance with Article 9 of Regulation 773/2004.

59.   Throughout the procedure, complainants benefit from a range of rights as provided in particular in Articles 6 to 8 of Regulation 773/2004. However, proceedings of the Commission in competition cases do not constitute adversarial proceedings between the complainant on the one hand and the companies which are the subject of the investigation on the other hand. Accordingly, the procedural rights of complainants are less far-reaching than the right to a fair hearing of the companies which are the subject of an infringement procedure(59).

(b) Indicative time limit for informing the complainant of the Commission's proposed action

60.   The Commission is under an obligation to decide on complaints within a reasonable time(60). What is a reasonable duration depends on the circumstances of each case and in particular, its context, the various procedural steps followed by the Commission, the conduct of the parties in the course of the procedure, the complexity of the case and its importance for the various parties involved(61).

61. The Commission will in principle endeavour to inform complainants of the action that it proposes to take on a complaint within an indicative time frame of four months from the reception of the complaint. Thus, subject to the circumstances of the individual case and in particular the possible need to request complementary information from the complainant or third parties, the Commission will in principle inform the complainant within four months whether or not it intends to investigate its case further. This time-limit does not constitute a binding statutory term.

62. Accordingly, within this four month period, the Commission may communicate its proposed course of action to the complainant as an initial reaction within the first phase of the procedure (see point 55 above). The Commission may also, where the examination of the complaint has progressed to the second stage (see point 56 above), directly proceed to informing the complainant about its provisional assessment by a letter pursuant to Article 7(1) of Regulation 773/2004.

63. To ensure the most expeditious treatment of their complaint, it is desirable that complainants cooperate diligently in the procedures(62), for example by informing the Commission of new developments.

(c) **Procedural rights of the complainant**
64. Where the Commission addresses a statement of objections to the companies complained of pursuant to Article 10(1) of Regulation 773/2004, the complainant is entitled to receive a copy of this document from which business secrets and other confidential information of the companies concerned have been removed (non-confidential version of the statement of objections; cf. Article 6(1) of Regulation 773/2004). The complainant is invited to comment in writing on the statement of objections. A time-limit will be set for such written comments.

65. Furthermore, the Commission may, where appropriate, afford complainants the opportunity of expressing their views at the oral hearing of the parties to which a statement of objections has been addressed, if the complainants so request in their written comments(63).

66. Complainants may submit, of their own initiative or following a request by the Commission, documents that contain business secrets or other confidential information. Confidential information will be protected by the Commission(64). Under Article 16 of Regulation 773/2004, complainants are obliged to identify confidential information, give reasons why the information is considered confidential and submit a separate non-confidential version when they make their views known pursuant to Article 6(1) and 7(1) of Regulation 773/2004, as well as when they subsequently submit further information in the course of the same procedure. Moreover, the Commission may, in all other cases, request complainants which produce documents or statements to identify the documents or parts of the documents or statements which they consider to be confidential. It may in particular set a deadline for the complainant to specify why it considers a piece of information to be confidential and to provide a non-confidential version, including a concise description or non-confidential version of each piece of information deleted.

67. The qualification of information as confidential does not prevent the Commission from disclosing and using information where that is necessary to prove an infringement of Articles 81 or 82(65). Where business secrets and confidential information are necessary to prove an infringement, the Commission must assess for each individual document whether the need to disclose is greater than the harm which might result from disclosure.

68. Where the Commission takes the view that a complaint should not be further examined, because there is no sufficient Community interest in pursuing the case further or on other

grounds, it will inform the complainant in the form of a letter which indicates its legal basis (Article 7(1) of Regulation 773/2004), sets out the reasons that have led the Commission to provisionally conclude in the sense indicated and provides the complainant with the opportunity to submit supplementary information or observations within a time-limit set by the Commission. The Commission will also indicate the consequences of not replying pursuant to Article 7(3) of Regulation 773/2004, as explained below.

69.   Pursuant to Article 8(1) of Regulation 773/2004, the complainant has the right to access the information on which the Commission bases its preliminary view. Such access is normally provided by annexing to the letter a copy of the relevant documents.

70.   The time-limit for observations by the complainant on the letter pursuant to Article 7(1) of Regulation 773/2004 will be set in accordance with the circumstances of the case. It will not be shorter than four weeks (Article 17(2) of Regulation 773/2004). If the complainant does not respond within the time-limit set, the complaint is deemed to have been withdrawn pursuant to Article 7(3) of Regulation 773/2004. Complainants are also entitled to withdraw their complaint at any time if they so wish.

71.   The complainant may request an extension of the time-limit for the provision of comments. Depending on the circumstances of the case, the Commission may grant such an extension.

72.   In that case, where the complainant submits supplementary observations, the Commission takes cognisance of those observations. Where they are of such a nature as to make the Commission change its previous course of action, it may initiate a procedure against the companies complained of. In this procedure, the complainant has the procedural rights explained above.

73.   Where the observations of the complainant do not alter the Commission's proposed course of action, it rejects the complaint by decision(66).

(d) The Commission decision rejecting a complaint
74.   Where the Commission rejects a complaint by decision pursuant to Article 7(2) of Regulation 773/2004, it must state the reasons in accordance with Article 253 EC, i.e. in a way that is appropriate to the act at issue and takes into account the circumstances of each case.

75.   The statement of reasons must disclose in a clear and unequivocal fashion the reasoning followed by the Commission in such a way as to enable the complainant to ascertain the reasons for the decision and to enable the competent Community Court to exercise its power of review. However, the Commission is not obliged to adopt a position on all the arguments relied on by the complainant in support of its complaint. It only needs to set out the facts and legal considerations which are of decisive importance in the context of the decision(67).

76.   Where the Commission rejects a complaint in a case that also gives rise to a decision pursuant to Article 10 of Regulation 1/2003 (Finding of inapplicability of Articles 81 or 82) or Article 9 of Regulation 1/2003 (Commitments), the decision rejecting a complaint may refer to that other decision adopted on the basis of the provisions mentioned.

77.   A decision to reject a complaint is subject to appeal before the Community Courts(68).

78.   A decision rejecting a complaint prevents complainants from requiring the reopening of the investigation unless they put forward significant new evidence. Accordingly, further

correspondence on the same alleged infringement by former complainants cannot be regarded as a new complaint unless significant new evidence is brought to the attention of the Commission. However, the Commission may re-open a file under appropriate circumstances.

79.   A decision to reject a complaint does not definitively rule on the question of whether or not there is an infringement of Articles 81 or 82, even where the Commission has assessed the facts on the basis of Articles 81 and 82. The assessments made by the Commission in a decision rejecting a complaint therefore do not prevent a Member State court or competition authority from applying Articles 81 and 82 to agreements and practices brought before it. The assessments made by the Commission in a decision rejecting a complaint constitute facts which Member States' courts or competition authorities may take into account in examining whether the agreements or conduct in question are in conformity with Articles 81 and 82(69).

(e) Specific situations
80.   According to Article 8 of Regulation 1/2003 the Commission may on its own initiative order interim measures where there is the risk of serious and irreparable damage to competition. Article 8 of Regulation 1/2003 makes it clear that interim measures cannot be applied for by complainants under Article 7(2) of Regulation 1/2003. Requests for interim measures by undertakings can be brought before Member States' courts which are well placed to decide on such measures(70).

81.   Some persons may wish to inform the Commission about suspected infringements of Articles 81 or 82 without having their identity revealed to the undertakings concerned by the allegations. These persons are welcome to contact the Commission. The Commission is bound to respect an informant's request for anonymity(71), unless the request to remain anonymous is manifestly unjustified.

....

(1) Council Regulation (EC) No 1/2003 of 16 December 2002 on the implementation of the rules on competition laid down in Articles 81 and 82 of the Treaty (OJ L 1, 4.1.2003, pages 1–25).
(2) Cf. in particular Recitals 3–7 and 35 of Regulation 1/2003.
(3) Commission Regulation (EC) No 773/2004 of 7 April 2004 relating to the conduct of proceedings by the Commission pursuant to Articles 81 and 82 of the EC Treaty (OJ 123, 27.4.2004).
(4) The Commission handles correspondence from informants in accordance with its principles of good administrative practice.
(5) Notice on cooperation within the Network of competition authorities (p. 43).
(6) For the handling of such complaints, cf. Commission communication of 10 October 2002, COM(2002) 141.
(7) Case C-344/98, Masterfoods v HB Ice Cream, [2000] ECR I-11369, para 46; Case C-119/97 P, Union française de l'express (Ufex) and Others v Commission of the European Communities, [1999] ECR I-1341, para 88; Case T-24/90, Automec v Commission of the European Communities, [1992] ECR II-2223, paras 73–77.
(8) Cf. in particular Articles 5, 6, 11, 12, 15, 22, 29, 35 and Recitals 2 to 4 and 6 to 8 of Regulation 1/2003.
(9) Cf. Notice on cooperation within the network of competition authorities . . ., points 5 ss.
(10) Cf. Recital 3 of Regulation 1/2003.
(11) Settled case law, cf. Case 127/73, Belgische Radio en Televisie (BRT) v SABAM and Fonior, [1974] ECR 51, para 16; Case C-282/95 P, Guérin automobiles v Commission of the European Communities, [1997] ECR I-1503, para 39; Case C-453/99, Courage v Bernhard Crehan, [2001] ECR I-6297, para 23.
(12) Case C-453/99, Courage v Bernhard Crehan, [2001] ECR I-6297, paras 26 and 27; the power of national courts to grant damages is also underlined in Recital 7 of Regulation 1/2003.
(13) Cf. Articles 1, 6 and 15 as well as Recital 7 of Regulation 1/2003.
(14) Regulation No 17: First Regulation implementing Articles 85 and 86 of the Treaty; OJ P 13 of 21 February 1962, p. 204–211; English special edition: Series I Chapter 1959–1962 p. 87. Regulation No 17 is repealed by Article 43 of Regulation 1/2003 with effect from 1 May 2004.
(15) For more detailed explanations of this mechanism, cf. Notice on the co-operation between the Commission and the courts of the EU Member States in the application of Articles 81 and 82 EC . . .
(16) Case T-24/90, Automec v Commission of the European Communities, [1992] ECR II-2223, para 93.

(17) Case C-230/96, Cabour and Nord Distribution Automobile v Arnor "SOCO", [1998] ECR I-2055, para 51; Joined Cases T-185/96, T-189/96 and T-190/96, Dalmasso and Others v Commission of the European Communities, [1999] ECR II-93, para 50.

(18) Cf. Article 8 of Regulation 1/2003 and para 80 below. Depending on the case, Member States' competition authorities may equally be well placed to adopt interim measures.

(19) Cf. points 41 ss. below.

(20) Notice on cooperation within the Network of competition authorities (p. 43).

(21) Notice on cooperation within the Network of competition authorities . . ., points 8–15.

(22) Article 11(2) and (3) of Regulation 1/2003; Notice on cooperation within the Network of Competition Authorities . . ., points 16/17.

(23) Notice on cooperation within the Network of Competition Authorities, . . ., point 34.

(24) For more extensive explanations on this notion in particular, cf. points 33 ss. below.

(25) Case C-119/97 P, Union française de l'express (Ufex) and Others v Commission of the European Communities, [1999] ECR I-1341, para 88; Case T-24/90, Automec v Commission of the European Communities, [1992] ECR II-2223, paras 73–77 and 85.

(26) Settled case law since Case T-24/90, Automec v Commission of the European Communities, [1992] ECR II-2223, para 85.

(27) Case C-282/95 P, Guérin automobiles v Commission of the European Communities, [1997] ECR I-1503, para 36.

(28) Cf. Article 5(1) of Regulation 773/2004.

(29) Case T-114/92, Bureau Européen des Médias et de l'Industrie Musicale (BEMIM) v Commission of the European Communities, [1995] ECR II-147, para 28. Associations of undertakings were also the complainants in the cases underlying the judgments in Case 298/83, Comité des industries cinématographiques des Communautés européennes (CICCE) v Commission of the European Communities, [1985] ECR 1105 and Case T-319/99, Federacion Nacional de Empresas (FENIN) v Commission of the European Communities, not yet published in [2003] ECR.

(30) Joined Cases T-133/95 and T-204/95, International Express Carriers Conference (IECC) v Commission of the European Communities, [1998] ECR II-3645, paras 79–83.

(31) Case T-37/92, Bureau Européen des Unions des Consommateurs (BEUC) v Commission of the European Communities, [1994] ECR II-285, para 36.

(32) This question is currently raised in a pending procedure before the Court of First Instance (Joined cases T-213 and 214/01). The Commission has also accepted as complainant an individual consumer in its Decision of 9 December 1998 in Case IV/D-2/34.466, Greek Ferries, OJ L 109/24 of 27 April 1999, para 1.

(33) Joined Cases T-133/95 and T-204/95, International Express Carriers Conference (IECC) v Commission of the European Communities, [1998] ECR II-3645, para 79.

(34) Case T-24/90, Automec v Commission of the European Communities, [1992] ECR II-2223, para 76; Case C-91/95 P, Roger Tremblay and Others v Commission of the European Communities, [1996] ECR I-5547, para 30.

(35) Case 125/78, GEMA v Commission of the European Communities, [1979] ECR 3173, para 17; Case C-119/97/P, Union française de l'express (Ufex) and Others v Commission of the European Communities, [1999] ECR I-1341, para 87.

(36) Settled case law since the Case T-24/90, Automec v Commission of the European Communities, [1992] ECR II-2223, paras 77 and 85; Recital 18 of Regulation 1/2003 expressly confirms this possibility.

(37) European Communities, [1992] ECR II-2223, para 75. Under Regulation 1/2003, this principle may only be relevant in the context of Article 29 of that Regulation.

(38) Case 210/81, Oswald Schmidt, trading as Demo-Studio Schmidt v Commission of the European Communities, [1983] ECR 3045, para 19; Case C-119/97 P, Union française de l'express (Ufex) and Others v Commission of the European Communities, [1999] ECR I-1341, para 86.

(39) Case C-119/97 P, Union française de l'express (Ufex) and Others v Commission of the European Communities, [1999] ECR I-1341, paras 79–80.

(40) Case C-450/98 P, International Express Carriers Conference (IECC) v Commission of the European Communities, [2001] ECR I-3947, paras 57–59.

(41) Case T-24/90, Automec v Commission of the European Communities, [1992] ECR II-2223, paras 88ss.; Case T-5/93, Roger Tremblay and Others v Commission of the European Communities, [1995] ECR II-185, paras 65ss.; Case T-575/93, Casper Koelman v Commission of the European Communities, [1996] ECR II-1, paras 75–80; see also part II above where more detailed explanations concerning this situation are given.

(42) Case C-119/97 P, Union française de l'express (Ufex) and Others v Commission of the European Communities, [1999] ECR I-1341, paras 92/93.

(43) Settled case law since Case T-24/90, Automec v Commission of the European Communities, [1992] ECR II-2223, para 86.

(44) Case C-449/98 P, International Express Carriers Conference (IECC) v Commission of the European Communities [2001] ECR I-3875, para 37.

(45) Case T-77/95, Syndicat français de l'Express International and Others v Commission of the European Communities [1997] ECR II-1, para 57; Case C-119/97 P, Union française de l'express (Ufex) and Others v Commission of the European Communities, [1999] ECR I-1341, para 95. Cf. also Case T-37/92, Bureau Européen des Unions des Consommateurs (BEUC) v Commission of the European Communities, [1994] ECR II-285, para 113, where an unwritten commitment between a Member State and a third county outside the common commercial policy was held not to suffice to establish that the conduct complained of had ceased.

(46) Case T-110/95, International Express Carriers (IECC) v Commission of the European Communities and Others, [1998] ECR II-3605, para 57, upheld by Case 449/98 P, International Express Carriers (IECC) v Commission of the European Communities and Others, [2001] ECR I-3875, paras 44–47.

(47) Case C-449/98 P, International Express Carriers (IECC) v Commission of the European Communities e.a. [2001] ECR I-3875, para 37.

(48) Cf. Case T-77/92, Parker Pen v Commission of the European Communities, [1994] ECR II-549, paras 64/65.

(49) Case 298/83, Comité des industries cinématographiques des Communautés européennes (CICCE) v Commission of the European Communities, [1985] ECR 1105, paras 21–24; Case T-198/98, Micro Leader Business v Commission of the European Communities, [1999] ECR II-3989, paras 32–39.

(50) Case T-319/99, Federación Nacional de Empresas (FENIN) v Commission of the European Communities, not yet published in [2003] ECR, para 43.

(51) Extensive guidance can be found on the Commission's website at http://europa.eu.int/comm/ competition/index_en.html

(52) Notice on the effect on trade concept contained in Articles 81 and 82 of the Treaty (p. 81).

(53) Commission Notice on agreements of minor importance which do not appreciably restrict competition under Article 81(1) of the Treaty establishing the European Community (de minimis), OJ C 368 of 22 December 2002, p. 13.

(54) The texts of all block exemption regulations are available on the Commission's website at http://europa.eu.int/comm/ competition/index_en.html

(55) Commission Notice – Guidelines on the application of Article 81(3) of the Treaty (p. 97).

(56) Case 210/81, Oswald Schmidt, trading as Demo-Studio Schmidt v Commission of the European Communities, [1983] ECR 3045, para 19; Case T-24/90, Automec v Commission of the European Communities, [1992] ECR II-2223, para 79.

(57) Cf. Case T-64/89, Automec v Commission of the European Communities, [1990] ECR II-367, paras 45–47; Case T-37/92, Bureau Européen des Unions des Consommateurs (BEUC) v Commission of the European Communities, [1994] ECR II-285, para 29.

(58) Case C-282/95 P, Guérin automobiles v Commission of the European Communities, [1997] ECR I-1503, para 36.

(59) Joined Cases 142 and 156/84, British American Tobacco Company and R. J. Reynolds Industries v Commission of the European Communities [1987] ECR 249, paras 19/20.

(60) Case C-282/95 P, Guérin automobiles v Commission of the European Communities, [1997] ECR I-1503, para 37.

(61) Joined Cases T-213/95 and T-18/96, Stichting Certificatie Kraanverhuurbedrijf (SCK) and Federatie van Nederlandse Kraanbedrijven (FNK) v Commission of the European Communities, [1997] ECR 1739, para 57.

(62) The notion of "diligence" on the part of the complainant is used by the Court of First Instance in Case T-77/94, Vereniging van Groothandelaren in Bloemkwekerijprodukten and Others v Commission of the European Communities, [1997] ECR II-759, para 75.

(63) Article 6(2) of Commission Regulation 773/2004.

(64) Article 287 EC, Article 28 of Regulation 1/2003 and Articles 15 and 16 of Regulation 773/2004.

(65) Article 27(2) of Regulation 1/2003.

(66) Article 7(2) of Regulation 773/2004; Case C-282/95 P, Guérin automobiles v Commission of the European Communities, [1997] ECR I-1503, para 36.

(67) Settled case law, cf. i.a. Case T-114/92, Bureau Européen des Médias et de l'Industrie Musicale (BEMIM) v Commission of the European Communities, [1995] ECR II-147, para 41.

(68) Settled case law since Case 210/81, Oswald Schmidt, trading as Demo-Studio Schmidt v Commission of the European Communities, [1983] ECR 3045.

(69) Case T-575/93, Casper Koelman v Commission of the European Communities, [1996] ECR II-1, paras 41–43.

(70) Depending on the case, Member States' competition authorities may equally be well placed to adopt interim measures.

(71) Case 145/83, Stanley George Adams v Commission of the European Communities, [1985] ECR 3539.

COMMISSION NOTICE
Guidelines on the effect on trade concept contained in [Articles 101 and 102 TFEU][1]
OJ C101, 27.4.2004, P. 81

1. INTRODUCTION

1. Articles 81 and 82 of the Treaty are applicable to horizontal and vertical agreements and practices on the part of undertakings which "may affect trade between Member States".

2. In their interpretation of Articles 81 and 82, the Community Courts have already substantially clarified the content and scope of the concept of effect on trade between Member States.

3. The present guidelines set out the principles developed by the Community Courts in relation to the interpretation of the effect on trade concept of Articles 81 and 82. They further spell out a rule indicating when agreements are in general unlikely to be capable of appreciably affecting trade between Member States (the non-appreciable affectation of trade rule or NAAT-rule). The guidelines are not intended to be exhaustive. The aim is to set out the methodology for the application of the effect on trade concept and to provide guidance on its application in frequently occurring situations. Although not binding on them, these guidelines also intend to give guidance to the courts and authorities of the Member States in their application of the effect on trade concept contained in Articles 81 and 82.

4. The present guidelines do not address the issue of what constitutes an appreciable restriction of competition under Article 81(1). This issue, which is distinct from the ability of agreements to appreciably affect trade between Member States, is dealt with in the Commission Notice on agreements of minor importance which do not appreciably restrict competition under Article 81(1) of the Treaty(1) (the de minimis rule). The guidelines are also not intended to provide guidance on the effect on trade concept contained in Article 87(1) of the Treaty on State aid.

5. These guidelines, including the NAAT-rule, are without prejudice to the interpretation of Articles 81 and 82 which may be given by the Court of Justice and the Court of First Instance.

2. THE EFFECT ON TRADE CRITERION

2.1. General principles

6. Article 81(1) provides that "the following shall be prohibited as incompatible with the common market: all agreements between undertakings, decisions of associations of undertakings and concerted practices which may affect trade between Member States and which have as their object or effect the prevention, restriction or distortion of competition

---

[1]   EDITOR'S NOTE: As of 1 May 2012 this Commission Notice has not been reissued following the entry into force of the Treaty of Lisbon. It includes references to the old Treaty article numbers in the text. The title of the Notice has been updated to reflect that fact that Articles 81 and 82 TEC have been replaced by Articles 101 and 102 TFEU. Reference should be made to the Tables of Equivalences accompanying the consolidated Treaties in Part II of this edition for the conversion of old Treaty article numbers to new ones.

within the common market". For the sake of simplicity the terms "agreements, decisions of associations of undertakings and concerted practices" are collectively referred to as "agreements'.

7.   Article 82 on its part stipulates that "any abuse by one or more undertakings of a dominant position within the common market or in a substantial part thereof shall be prohibited as incompatible with the common market insofar as it may affect trade between Member States." In what follows the term "practices" refers to the conduct of dominant undertakings.

8.   The effect on trade criterion also determines the scope of application of Article 3 of Regulation 1/2003 on the implementation of the rules on competition laid down in Articles 81 and 82 of the Treaty(2).

9.   According to Article 3(1) of that Regulation the competition authorities and courts of the Member States must apply Article 81 to agreements, decisions by associations of undertakings or concerted practices within the meaning of Article 81(1) of the Treaty which may affect trade between Member States within the meaning of that provision, when they apply national competition law to such agreements, decisions or concerted practices. Similarly, when the competition authorities and courts of the Member States apply national competition law to any abuse prohibited by Article 82 of the Treaty, they must also apply Article 82 of the Treaty. Article 3(1) thus obliges the competition authorities and courts of the Member States to also apply Articles 81 and 82 when they apply national competition law to agreements and abusive practices which may affect trade between Member States. On the other hand, Article 3(1) does not oblige national competition authorities and courts to apply national competition law when they apply Articles 81 and 82 to agreements, decisions and concerted practices and to abuses which may affect trade between Member States. They may in such cases apply the Community competition rules on a stand alone basis.

10.   It follows from Article 3(2) that the application of national competition law may not lead to the prohibition of agreements, decisions by associations of undertakings or concerted practices which may affect trade between Member States but which do not restrict competition within the meaning of Article 81(1) of the Treaty, or which fulfil the conditions of Article 81(3) of the Treaty or which are covered by a Regulation for the application of Article 81(3) of the Treaty. Member States, however, are not under Regulation 1/2003 precluded from adopting and applying on their territory stricter national laws which prohibit or sanction unilateral conduct engaged in by undertakings.

11.   Finally it should be mentioned that Article 3(3) stipulates that without prejudice to general principles and other provisions of Community law, Article 3(1) and (2) do not apply when the competition authorities and the courts of the Member States apply national merger control laws, nor do they preclude the application of provisions of national law that predominantly pursue an objective different from that pursued by Articles 81 and 82 of the Treaty.

12.   The effect on trade criterion is an autonomous Community law criterion, which must be assessed separately in each case. It is a jurisdictional criterion, which defines the scope of application of Community competition law(3). Community competition law is not applicable to agreements and practices that are not capable of appreciably affecting trade between Member States.

13.   The effect on trade criterion confines the scope of application of Articles 81 and 82 to agreements and practices that are capable of having a minimum level of cross-border effects within the Community. In the words of the Court of Justice, the ability of

the agreement or practice to affect trade between Member States must be "appreciable"(4).

14. In the case of Article 81 of the Treaty, it is the agreement that must be capable of affecting trade between Member States. It is not required that each individual part of the agreement, including any restriction of competition which may flow from the agreement, is capable of doing so(5). If the agreement as a whole is capable of affecting trade between Member States, there is Community law jurisdiction in respect of the entire agreement, including any parts of the agreement that individually do not affect trade between Member States. In cases where the contractual relations between the same parties cover several activities, these activities must, in order to form part of the same agreement, be directly linked and form an integral part of the same overall business arrangement(6). If not, each activity constitutes a separate agreement.

15. It is also immaterial whether or not the participation of a particular undertaking in the agreement has an appreciable effect on trade between Member States(7). An undertaking cannot escape Community law jurisdiction merely because of the fact that its own contribution to an agreement, which itself is capable of affecting trade between Member States, is insignificant.

16. It is not necessary, for the purposes of establishing Community law jurisdiction, to establish a link between the alleged restriction of competition and the capacity of the agreement to affect trade between Member States. Non-restrictive agreements may also affect trade between Member States. For example, selective distribution agreements based on purely qualitative selection criteria justified by the nature of the products, which are not restrictive of competition within the meaning of Article 81(1), may nevertheless affect trade between Member States. However, the alleged restrictions arising from an agreement may provide a clear indication as to the capacity of the agreement to affect trade between Member States. For instance, a distribution agreement prohibiting exports is by its very nature capable of affecting trade between Member States, although not necessarily to an appreciable extent(8).

17. In the case of Article 82 it is the abuse that must affect trade between Member States. This does not imply, however, that each element of the behaviour must be assessed in isolation. Conduct that forms part of an overall strategy pursued by the dominant undertaking must be assessed in terms of its overall impact. Where a dominant undertaking adopts various practices in pursuit of the same aim, for instance practices that aim at eliminating or foreclosing competitors, in order for Article 82 to be applicable to all the practices forming part of this overall strategy, it is sufficient that at least one of these practices is capable of affecting trade between Member States(9).

18. It follows from the wording of Articles 81 and 82 and the case law of the Community Courts that in the application of the effect on trade criterion three elements in particular must be addressed:
(a) The concept of "trade between Member States",
(b) The notion of "may affect", and
(c) The concept of "appreciability".

2.2. The concept of "trade between Member States"

19. The concept of "trade" is not limited to traditional exchanges of goods and services across borders(10). It is a wider concept, covering all cross-border economic activity including establishment(11). This interpretation is consistent with the fundamental objective of the Treaty to promote free movement of goods, services, persons and capital.

20. According to settled case law the concept of "trade" also encompasses cases where agreements or practices affect the competitive structure of the market. Agreements and

practices that affect the competitive structure inside the Community by eliminating or threatening to eliminate a competitor operating within the Community may be subject to the Community competition rules(12). When an undertaking is or risks being eliminated the competitive structure within the Community is affected and so are the economic activities in which the undertaking is engaged.

21.   The requirement that there must be an effect on trade "between Member States" implies that there must be an impact on cross-border economic activity involving at least two Member States. It is not required that the agreement or practice affect trade between the whole of one Member State and the whole of another Member State. Articles 81 and 82 may be applicable also in cases involving part of a Member State, provided that the effect on trade is appreciable(13).

22.   The application of the effect on trade criterion is independent of the definition of relevant geographic markets. Trade between Member States may be affected also in cases where the relevant market is national or sub-national(14).

2.3. The notion "may affect"
23.   The function of the notion "may affect" is to define the nature of the required impact on trade between Member States. According to the standard test developed by the Court of Justice, the notion "may affect" implies that it must be possible to foresee with a sufficient degree of probability on the basis of a set of objective factors of law or fact that the agreement or practice may have an influence, direct or indirect, actual or potential, on the pattern of trade between Member States(15)(16). As mentioned in paragraph 20 above the Court of Justice has in addition developed a test based on whether or not the agreement or practice affects the competitive structure. In cases where the agreement or practice is liable to affect the competitive structure inside the Community, Community law jurisdiction is established.

24.   The "pattern of trade" -test developed by the Court of Justice contains the following main elements, which are dealt with in the following sections:
   (a) "A sufficient degree of probability on the basis of a set of objective factors of law or fact",
   (b) An influence on the "pattern of trade between Member States",
   (c) "A direct or indirect, actual or potential influence" on the pattern of trade.

2.3.1. A sufficient degree of probability on the basis of a set of objective factors of law or fact
25.   The assessment of effect on trade is based on objective factors. Subjective intent on the part of the undertakings concerned is not required. If, however, there is evidence that undertakings have intended to affect trade between Member States, for example because they have sought to hinder exports to or imports from other Member States, this is a relevant factor to be taken into account.

26.   The words "may affect" and the reference by the Court of Justice to "a sufficient degree of probability" imply that, in order for Community law jurisdiction to be established, it is not required that the agreement or practice will actually have or has had an effect on trade between Member States. It is sufficient that the agreement or practice is "capable" of having such an effect(17).

27.   There is no obligation or need to calculate the actual volume of trade between Member States affected by the agreement or practice. For example, in the case of agreements prohibiting exports to other Member States there is no need to estimate what would have been the level of parallel trade between the Member States concerned, in the absence of the agreement. This interpretation is consistent with the jurisdictional nature of the effect

on trade criterion. Community law jurisdiction extends to categories of agreements and practices that are capable of having cross-border effects, irrespective of whether a particular agreement or practice actually has such effects.

28. The assessment under the effect on trade criterion depends on a number of factors that individually may not be decisive(18). The relevant factors include the nature of the agreement and practice, the nature of the products covered by the agreement or practice and the position and importance of the undertakings concerned(19).

29. The nature of the agreement and practice provides an indication from a qualitative point of view of the ability of the agreement or practice to affect trade between Member States. Some agreements and practices are by their very nature capable of affecting trade between Member States, whereas others require more detailed analysis in this respect. Cross-border cartels are an example of the former, whereas joint ventures confined to the territory of a single Member State are an example of the latter. This aspect is further examined in section 3 below, which deals with various categories of agreements and practices.

30. The nature of the products covered by the agreements or practices also provides an indication of whether trade between Member States is capable of being affected. When by their nature products are easily traded across borders or are important for undertakings that want to enter or expand their activities in other Member States, Community jurisdiction is more readily established than in cases where due to their nature there is limited demand for products offered by suppliers from other Member States or where the products are of limited interest from the point of view of cross-border establishment or the expansion of the economic activity carried out from such place of establishment(20). Establishment includes the setting-up by undertakings in one Member State of agencies, branches or subsidiaries in another Member State.

31. The market position of the undertakings concerned and their sales volumes are indicative from a quantitative point of view of the ability of the agreement or practice concerned to affect trade between Member States. This aspect, which forms an integral part of the assessment of appreciability, is addressed in section 2.4 below.

32. In addition to the factors already mentioned, it is necessary to take account of the legal and factual environment in which the agreement or practice operates. The relevant economic and legal context provides insight into the potential for an effect on trade between Member States. If there are absolute barriers to cross-border trade between Member States, which are external to the agreement or practice, trade is only capable of being affected if those barriers are likely to disappear in the foreseeable future. In cases where the barriers are not absolute but merely render cross-border activities more difficult, it is of the utmost importance to ensure that agreements and practices do not further hinder such activities. Agreements and practices that do so are capable of affecting trade between Member States.

2.3.2. An influence on the "pattern of trade between Member States"

33. For Articles 81 and 82 to be applicable there must be an influence on the "pattern of trade between Member States".

34. The term "pattern of trade" is neutral. It is not a condition that trade be restricted or reduced(21). Patterns of trade can also be affected when an agreement or practice causes an increase in trade. Indeed, Community law jurisdiction is established if trade between Member States is likely to develop differently with the agreement or practice compared to the way in which it would probably have developed in the absence of the agreement or practice(22).

35.   This interpretation reflects the fact that the effect on trade criterion is a jurisdictional one, which serves to distinguish those agreements and practices which are capable of having cross-border effects, so as to warrant an examination under the Community competition rules, from those agreements and practices which do not.

2.3.3. A "direct or indirect, actual or potential influence" on the pattern of trade
36.   The influence of agreements and practices on patterns of trade between Member States can be "direct or indirect, actual or potential".

37.   Direct effects on trade between Member States normally occur in relation to the products covered by an agreement or practice. When, for example, producers of a particular product in different Member States agree to share markets, direct effects are produced on trade between Member States on the market for the products in question. Another example of direct effects being produced is when a supplier limits distributor rebates to products sold within the Member State in which the distributors are established. Such practices increase the relative price of products destined for exports, rendering export sales less attractive and less competitive.

38.   Indirect effects often occur in relation to products that are related to those covered by an agreement or practice. Indirect effects may, for example, occur where an agreement or practice has an impact on cross-border economic activities of undertakings that use or otherwise rely on the products covered by the agreement or practice(23). Such effects can, for instance, arise where the agreement or practice relates to an intermediate product, which is not traded, but which is used in the supply of a final product, which is traded. The Court of Justice has held that trade between Member States was capable of being affected in the case of an agreement involving the fixing of prices of spirits used in the production of cognac(24). Whereas the raw material was not exported, the final product – cognac – was exported. In such cases Community competition law is thus applicable, if trade in the final product is capable of being appreciably affected.

39.   Indirect effects on trade between Member States may also occur in relation to the products covered by the agreement or practice. For instance, agreements whereby a manufacturer limits warranties to products sold by distributors within their Member State of establishment create disincentives for consumers from other Member States to buy the products because they would not be able to invoke the warranty(25). Export by official distributors and parallel traders is made more difficult because in the eyes of consumers the products are less attractive without the manufacturer's warranty(26).

40.   Actual effects on trade between Member States are those that are produced by the agreement or practice once it is implemented. An agreement between a supplier and a distributor within the same Member State, for instance one that prohibits exports to other Member States, is likely to produce actual effects on trade between Member States. Without the agreement the distributor would have been free to engage in export sales. It should be recalled, however, that it is not required that actual effects are demonstrated. It is sufficient that the agreement or practice be capable of having such effects.

41.   Potential effects are those that may occur in the future with a sufficient degree of probability. In other words, foreseeable market developments must be taken into account(27). Even if trade is not capable of being affected at the time the agreement is concluded or the practice is implemented, Articles 81 and 82 remain applicable if the factors which led to that conclusion are likely to change in the foreseeable future. In this respect it is relevant to consider the impact of liberalisation measures adopted by the Community or by the Member State in question and other foreseeable measures aiming at eliminating legal barriers to trade.

42. Moreover, even if at a given point in time market conditions are unfavourable to cross-border trade, for example because prices are similar in the Member States in question, trade may still be capable of being affected if the situation may change as a result of changing market conditions(28). What matters is the ability of the agreement or practice to affect trade between Member States and not whether at any given point in time it actually does so.

43. The inclusion of indirect or potential effects in the analysis of effects on trade between Member States does not mean that the analysis can be based on remote or hypothetical effects. The likelihood of a particular agreement to produce indirect or potential effects must be explained by the authority or party claiming that trade between Member States is capable of being appreciably affected. Hypothetical or speculative effects are not sufficient for establishing Community law jurisdiction. For instance, an agreement that raises the price of a product which is not tradable reduces the disposable income of consumers. As consumers have less money to spend they may purchase fewer products imported from other Member States. However, the link between such income effects and trade between Member States is generally in itself too remote to establish Community law jurisdiction.

2.4. The concept of appreciability

2.4.1. General principle
44. The effect on trade criterion incorporates a quantitative element, limiting Community law jurisdiction to agreements and practices that are capable of having effects of a certain magnitude. Agreements and practices fall outside the scope of application of Articles 81 and 82 when they affect the market only insignificantly having regard to the weak position of the undertakings concerned on the market for the products in question(29). Appreciability can be appraised in particular by reference to the position and the importance of the relevant undertakings on the market for the products concerned(30).

45. The assessment of appreciability depends on the circumstances of each individual case, in particular the nature of the agreement and practice, the nature of the products covered and the market position of the undertakings concerned. When by its very nature the agreement or practice is capable of affecting trade between Member States, the appreciability threshold is lower than in the case of agreements and practices that are not by their very nature capable of affecting trade between Member States. The stronger the market position of the undertakings concerned, the more likely it is that an agreement or practice capable of affecting trade between Member States can be held to do so appreciably(31).

46. In a number of cases concerning imports and exports the Court of Justice has considered that the appreciability requirement was fulfilled when the sales of the undertakings concerned accounted for about 5 % of the market(32). Market share alone, however, has not always been considered the decisive factor. In particular, it is necessary also to take account of the turnover of the undertakings in the products concerned(33).

47. Appreciability can thus be measured both in absolute terms (turnover) and in relative terms, comparing the position of the undertaking(s) concerned to that of other players on the market (market share). This focus on the position and importance of the undertakings concerned is consistent with the concept "may affect", which implies that the assessment is based on the ability of the agreement or practice to affect trade between Member States rather than on the impact on actual flows of goods and services across borders. The market position of the undertakings concerned and their turnover in the products concerned are indicative of the ability of an agreement or practice to affect trade between Member States. These two elements are reflected in the presumptions set out in paragraphs and 53 below.

48. The application of the appreciability test does not necessarily require that relevant markets be defined and market shares calculated(34). The sales of an undertaking in absolute terms may be sufficient to support a finding that the impact on trade is appreciable. This is particularly so in the case of agreements and practices that by their very nature are liable to affect trade between Member States, for example because they concern imports or exports or because they cover several Member States. The fact that in such circumstances turnover in the products covered by the agreement may be sufficient for a finding of an appreciable effect on trade between Member States is reflected in the positive presumption set out in paragraph below.

49. Agreements and practices must always be considered in the economic and legal context in which they occur. In the case of vertical agreements it may be necessary to have regard to any cumulative effects of parallel networks of similar agreements(35). Even if a single agreement or network of agreements is not capable of appreciably affecting trade between Member States, the effect of parallel networks of agreements, taken as a whole, may be capable of doing so. For that to be the case, however, it is necessary that the individual agreement or network of agreements makes a significant contribution to the overall effect on trade(36).

2.4.2. Quantification of appreciability

50. It is not possible to establish general quantitative rules covering all categories of agreements indicating when trade between Member States is capable of being appreciably affected. It is possible, however, to indicate when trade is normally not capable of being appreciably affected. Firstly, in its notice on agreements of minor importance which do not appreciably restrict competition in the meaning of Article 81(1) of the Treaty (the de minimis rule)(37) the Commission has stated that agreements between small and medium-sized undertakings (SMEs) as defined in the Annex to Commission Recommendation 96/280/EC(38) are normally not capable of affecting trade between Member States. The reason for this presumption is the fact that the activities of SMEs are normally local or at most regional in nature. However, SMEs may be subject to Community law jurisdiction in particular where they engage in cross-border economic activity. Secondly, the Commission considers it appropriate to set out general principles indicating when trade is normally not capable of being appreciably affected, i.e. a standard defining the absence of an appreciable effect on trade between Member States (the NAAT-rule). When applying Article 81, the Commission will consider this standard as a negative rebuttable presumption applying to all agreements within the meaning of Article 81(1) irrespective of the nature of the restrictions contained in the agreement, including restrictions that have been identified as hardcore restrictions in Commission block exemption regulations and guidelines. In cases where this presumption applies the Commission will normally not institute proceedings either upon application or on its own initiative. Where the undertakings assume in good faith that an agreement is covered by this negative presumption, the Commission will not impose fines.

51. Without prejudice to paragraph below, this negative definition of appreciability does not imply that agreements, which do not fall within the criteria set out below, are automatically capable of appreciably affecting trade between Member States. A case by case analysis is necessary.

52. The Commission holds the view that in principle agreements are not capable of appreciably affecting trade between Member States when the following cumulative conditions are met:
   (a) The aggregate market share of the parties on any relevant market within the Community affected by the agreement does not exceed 5 %, and

(b) In the case of horizontal agreements, the aggregate annual Community turnover of the undertakings concerned(39) in the products covered by the agreement does not exceed 40 million euro. In the case of agreements concerning the joint buying of products the relevant turnover shall be the parties' combined purchases of the products covered by the agreement.

In the case of vertical agreements, the aggregate annual Community turnover of the supplier in the products covered by the agreement does not exceed 40 million euro. In the case of licence agreements the relevant turnover shall be the aggregate turnover of the licensees in the products incorporating the licensed technology and the licensor's own turnover in such products. In cases involving agreements concluded between a buyer and several suppliers the relevant turnover shall be the buyer's combined purchases of the products covered by the agreements.

The Commission will apply the same presumption where during two successive calendar years the above turnover threshold is not exceeded by more than 10 % and the above market threshold is not exceeded by more than 2 percentage points. In cases where the agreement concerns an emerging not yet existing market and where as a consequence the parties neither generate relevant turnover nor accumulate any relevant market share, the Commission will not apply this presumption. In such cases appreciability may have to be assessed on the basis of the position of the parties on related product markets or their strength in technologies relating to the agreement.

53. The Commission will also hold the view that where an agreement by its very nature is capable of affecting trade between Member States, for example, because it concerns imports and exports or covers several Member States, there is a rebuttable positive presumption that such effects on trade are appreciable when the turnover of the parties in the products covered by the agreement calculated as indicated in paragraphs 52 and 54 exceeds 40 million euro. In the case of agreements that by their very nature are capable of affecting trade between Member States it can also often be presumed that such effects are appreciable when the market share of the parties exceeds the 5 % threshold set out in the previous paragraph. However, this presumption does not apply where the agreement covers only part of a Member State (see paragraph 90 below).

54. With regard to the threshold of 40 million euro (cf. paragraph 52 above), the turnover is calculated on the basis of total Community sales excluding tax during the previous financial year by the undertakings concerned, of the products covered by the agreement (the contract products). Sales between entities that form part of the same undertaking are excluded(40).

55. In order to apply the market share threshold, it is necessary to determine the relevant market(41). This consists of the relevant product market and the relevant geographic market. The market shares are to be calculated on the basis of sales value data or, where appropriate, purchase value data. If value data are not available, estimates based on other reliable market information, including volume data, may be used.

56. In the case of networks of agreements entered into by the same supplier with different distributors, sales made through the entire network are taken into account.

57. Contracts that form part of the same overall business arrangement constitute a single agreement for the purposes of the NAAT-rule(42). Undertakings cannot bring themselves inside these thresholds by dividing up an agreement that forms a whole from an economic perspective.

3. THE APPLICATION OF THE ABOVE PRINCIPLES TO COMMON TYPES OF AGREEMENTS AND ABUSES

58.   The Commission will apply the negative presumption set out in the preceding section to all agreements, including agreements that by their very nature are capable of affecting trade between Member States as well as agreements that involve trade with undertakings located in third countries (cf. section 3.3 below).

59.   Outside the scope of negative presumption, the Commission will take account of qualitative elements relating to the nature of the agreement or practice and the nature of the products that they concern (see paragraphs and above). The relevance of the nature of the agreement is also reflected in the positive presumption set out in paragraph 53 above relating to appreciability in the case of agreements that by their very nature are capable of affecting trade between Member States. With a view to providing additional guidance on the application of the effect on trade concept it is therefore useful to consider various common types of agreements and practices.

60.   In the following sections a primary distinction is drawn between agreements and practices that cover several Member States and agreements and practices that are confined to a single Member State or to part of a single Member State. These two main categories are broken down into further subcategories based on the nature of the agreement or practice involved. Agreements and practices involving third countries are also dealt with.

3.1. Agreements and abuse covering or implemented in several Member States

61.   Agreements and practices covering or implemented in several Member States are in almost all cases by their very nature capable of affecting trade between Member States. When the relevant turnover exceeds the threshold set out in paragraph above it will therefore in most cases not be necessary to conduct a detailed analysis of whether trade between Member States is capable of being affected. However, in order to provide guidance also in these cases and to illustrate the principles developed in section 2 above, it is useful to explain what are the factors that are normally used to support a finding of Community law jurisdiction.

3.1.1. Agreements concerning imports and exports

62.   Agreements between undertakings in two or more Member States that concern imports and exports are by their very nature capable of affecting trade between Member States. Such agreements, irrespective of whether they are restrictive of competition or not, have a direct impact on patterns of trade between Member States. In Kerpen & Kerpen, for example, which concerned an agreement between a French producer and a German distributor covering more than 10 % of exports of cement from France to Germany, amounting in total to 350000 tonnes per year, the Court of Justice held that it was impossible to take the view that such an agreement was not capable of (appreciably) affecting trade between Member States(43).

63.   This category includes agreements that impose restrictions on imports and exports, including restrictions on active and passive sales and resale by buyers to customers in other Member States(44). In these cases there is an inherent link between the alleged restriction of competition and the effect on trade, since the very purpose of the restriction is to prevent flows of goods and services between Member States, which would otherwise be possible. It is immaterial whether the parties to the agreement are located in the same Member State or in different Member States.

3.1.2. Cartels covering several Member States

64.   Cartel agreements such as those involving price fixing and market sharing covering several Member States are by their very nature capable of affecting trade between Member States.

Cross-border cartels harmonise the conditions of competition and affect the interpenetration of trade by cementing traditional patterns of trade(45). When undertakings agree to allocate geographic territories, sales from other areas into the allocated territories are capable of being eliminated or reduced. When undertakings agree to fix prices, they eliminate competition and any resulting price differentials that would entice both competitors and customers to engage in cross-border trade. When undertakings agree on sales quotas traditional patterns of trade are preserved. The undertakings concerned abstain from expanding output and thereby from serving potential customers in other Member States.

65.   The effect on trade produced by cross-border cartels is generally also by its very nature appreciable due to the market position of the parties to the cartel. Cartels are normally only formed when the participating undertakings together hold a large share of the market, as this allows them to raise price or reduce output.

3.1.3. Horizontal cooperation agreements covering several Member States

66.   This section covers various types of horizontal cooperation agreements. Horizontal cooperation agreements may for instance take the form of agreements whereby two or more undertakings cooperate in the performance of a particular economic activity such as production and distribution(46). Often such agreements are referred to as joint ventures. However, joint ventures that perform on a lasting basis all the functions of an autonomous economic entity are covered by the Merger Regulation(47). At the level of the Community such full function joint ventures are not dealt with under Articles 81 and 82 except in cases where Article 2(4) of the Merger Regulation is applicable(48). This section therefore does not deal with full-function joint ventures. In the case of non-full function joint ventures the joint entity does not operate as an autonomous supplier (or buyer) on any market. It merely serves the parents, who themselves operate on the market(49).

67.   Joint ventures which engage in activities in two or more Member States or which produce an output that is sold by the parents in two or more Member States affect the commercial activities of the parties in those areas of the Community. Such agreements are therefore normally by their very nature capable of affecting trade between Member States compared to the situation without the agreement(50). Patterns of trade are affected when undertakings switch their activities to the joint venture or use it for the purpose of establishing a new source of supply in the Community.

68.   Trade may also be capable of being affected where a joint venture produces an input for the parent companies, which is subsequently further processed or incorporated into a product by the parent undertakings. This is likely to be the case where the input in question was previously sourced from suppliers in other Member States, where the parents previously produced the input in other Member States or where the final product is traded in more than one Member State.

69.   In the assessment of appreciability it is important to take account of the parents' sales of products related to the agreement and not only those of the joint entity created by the agreement, given that the joint venture does not operate as an autonomous entity on any market.

3.1.4. Vertical agreements implemented in several Member States

70.   Vertical agreements and networks of similar vertical agreements implemented in several Member States are normally capable of affecting trade between Member States if they cause trade to be channelled in a particular way. Networks of selective distribution

agreements implemented in two or more Member States for example, channel trade in a particular way because they limit trade to members of the network, thereby affecting patterns of trade compared to the situation without the agreement(51).

71. Trade between Member States is also capable of being affected by vertical agreements that have foreclosure effects. This may for instance be the case of agreements whereby distributors in several Member States agree to buy only from a particular supplier or to sell only its products. Such agreements may limit trade between the Member States in which the agreements are implemented, or trade from Member States not covered by the agreements. Foreclosure may result from individual agreements or from networks of agreements. When an agreement or networks of agreements that cover several Member States have foreclosure effects, the ability of the agreement or agreements to affect trade between Member States is normally by its very nature appreciable.

72. Agreements between suppliers and distributors which provide for resale price maintenance (RPM) and which cover two or more Member States are normally also by their very nature capable of affecting trade between Member States(52). Such agreements alter the price levels that would have been likely to exist in the absence of the agreements and thereby affect patterns of trade.

3.1.5. Abuses of dominant positions covering several Member States

73. In the case of abuse of a dominant position it is useful to distinguish between abuses that raise barriers to entry or eliminate competitors (exclusionary abuses) and abuses whereby the dominant undertaking exploits its economic power for instance by charging excessive or discriminatory prices (exploitative abuses). Both kinds of abuse may be carried out either through agreements, which are equally subject to Article 81(1), or through unilateral conduct, which as far as Community competition law is concerned is subject only to Article 82.

74. In the case of exploitative abuses such as discriminatory rebates, the impact is on downstream trading partners, which either benefit or suffer, altering their competitive position and affecting patterns of trade between Member States.

75. When a dominant undertaking engages in exclusionary conduct in more than one Member State, such abuse is normally by its very nature capable of affecting trade between Member States. Such conduct has a negative impact on competition in an area extending beyond a single Member State, being likely to divert trade from the course it would have followed in the absence of the abuse. For example, patterns of trade are capable of being affected where the dominant undertaking grants loyalty rebates. Customers covered by the exclusionary rebate system are likely to purchase less from competitors of the dominant firm than they would otherwise have done. Exclusionary conduct that aims directly at eliminating a competitor such as predatory pricing is also capable of affecting trade between Member States because of its impact on the competitive market structure inside the Community(53). When a dominant firm engages in behaviour with a view to eliminating a competitor operating in more than one Member State, trade is capable of being affected in several ways. First, there is a risk that the affected competitor will cease to be a source of supply inside the Community. Even if the targeted undertaking is not eliminated, its future competitive conduct is likely to be affected, which may also have an impact on trade between Member States. Secondly, the abuse may have an impact on other competitors. Through its abusive behaviour the dominant undertaking can signal to its competitors that it will discipline attempts to engage in real competition. Thirdly, the very fact of eliminating a competitor may be sufficient for trade between Member States to be capable of being affected. This may be the case even where the undertaking that

risks being eliminated mainly engages in exports to third countries(54). Once the effective competitive market structure inside the Community risks being further impaired, there is Community law jurisdiction.

76. Where a dominant undertaking engages in exploitative or exclusionary abuse in more than one Member State, the capacity of the abuse to affect trade between Member States will normally also by its very nature be appreciable. Given the market position of the dominant undertaking concerned, and the fact that the abuse is implemented in several Member States, the scale of the abuse and its likely impact on patterns of trade is normally such that trade between Member States is capable of being appreciably affected. In the case of an exploitative abuse such as price discrimination, the abuse alters the competitive position of trading partners in several Member States. In the case of exclusionary abuses, including abuses that aim at eliminating a competitor, the economic activity engaged in by competitors in several Member States is affected. The very existence of a dominant position in several Member States implies that competition in a substantial part of the common market is already weakened(55). When a dominant undertaking further weakens competition through recourse to abusive conduct, for example by eliminating a competitor, the ability of the abuse to affect trade between Member States is normally appreciable.

3.2. Agreements and abuses covering a single, or only part of a, Member State

77. When agreements or abusive practices cover the territory of a single Member State, it may be necessary to proceed with a more detailed inquiry into the ability of the agreements or abusive practices to affect trade between Member States. It should be recalled that for there to be an effect on trade between Member States it is not required that trade is reduced. It is sufficient that an appreciable change is capable of being caused in the pattern of trade between Member States. Nevertheless, in many cases involving a single Member State the nature of the alleged infringement, and in particular, its propensity to foreclose the national market, provides a good indication of the capacity of the agreement or practice to affect trade between Member States. The examples mentioned hereafter are not exhaustive. They merely provide examples of cases where agreements confined to the territory of a single Member State can be considered capable of affecting trade between Member States.

3.2.1. Cartels covering a single Member State

78. Horizontal cartels covering the whole of a Member State are normally capable of affecting trade between Member States. The Community Courts have held in a number of cases that agreements extending over the whole territory of a Member State by their very nature have the effect of reinforcing the partitioning of markets on a national basis by hindering the economic penetration which the Treaty is designed to bring about(56).

79. The capacity of such agreements to partition the internal market follows from the fact that undertakings participating in cartels in only one Member State, normally need to take action to exclude competitors from other Member States(57). If they do not, and the product covered by the agreement is tradable(58), the cartel risks being undermined by competition from undertakings from other Member States. Such agreements are normally also by their very nature capable of having an appreciable effect on trade between Member States, given the market coverage required for such cartels to be effective.

80. Given the fact that the effect on trade concept encompasses potential effects, it is not decisive whether such action against competitors from other Member States is in fact adopted at any given point in time. If the cartel price is similar to the price prevailing in other Member States, there may be no immediate need for the members of the cartel to

take action against competitors from other Member States. What matters is whether or not they are likely to do so, if market conditions change. The likelihood of that depends on the existence or otherwise of natural barriers to trade in the market, including in particular whether or not the product in question is tradable. In a case involving certain retail banking services(59) the Court of Justice has, for example, held that trade was not capable of being appreciably affected because the potential for trade in the specific products concerned was very limited and because they were not an important factor in the choice made by undertakings from other Member States regarding whether or not to establish themselves in the Member State in question(60).

81. The extent to which the members of a cartel monitor prices and competitors from other Member States can provide an indication of the extent to which the products covered by the cartel are tradable. Monitoring suggests that competition and competitors from other Member States are perceived as a potential threat to the cartel. Moreover, if there is evidence that the members of the cartel have deliberately fixed the price level in the light of the price level prevailing in other Member States (limit pricing), it is an indication that the products in question are tradable and that trade between Member States is capable of being affected.

82. Trade is normally also capable of being affected when the members of a national cartel temper the competitive constraint imposed by competitors from other Member States by inducing them to join the restrictive agreement, or if their exclusion from the agreement places the competitors at a competitive disadvantage(61). In such cases the agreement either prevents these competitors from exploiting any competitive advantage that they have, or raises their costs, thereby having a negative impact on their competitiveness and their sales. In both cases the agreement hampers the operations of competitors from other Member States on the national market in question. The same is true when a cartel agreement confined to a single Member State is concluded between undertakings that resell products imported from other Member States(62).

3.2.2. Horizontal cooperation agreements covering a single Member State

83. Horizontal cooperation agreements and in particular non-full function joint ventures (cf. paragraph 66 above), which are confined to a single Member State and which do not directly relate to imports and exports, do not belong to the category of agreements that by their very nature are capable of affecting trade between Member States. A careful examination of the capacity of the individual agreement to affect trade between Member States may therefore be required.

84. Horizontal cooperation agreements may, in particular, be capable of affecting trade between Member States where they have foreclosure effects. This may be the case with agreements that establish sector-wide standardisation and certification regimes, which either exclude undertakings from other Member States or which are more easily fulfilled by undertakings from the Member State in question due to the fact that they are based on national rules and traditions. In such circumstances the agreements make it more difficult for undertakings from other Member States to penetrate the national market.

85. Trade may also be affected where a joint venture results in undertakings from other Member States being cut off from an important channel of distribution or source of demand. If, for example, two or more distributors established within the same Member State, and which account for a substantial share of imports of the products in question, establish a purchasing joint venture combining their purchases of that product, the resulting reduction in the number of distribution channels limits the possibility for suppliers from other Member States of gaining access to the national market in question.

Trade is therefore capable of being affected(63). Trade may also be affected where undertakings which previously imported a particular product form a joint venture which is entrusted with the production of that same product. In this case the agreement causes a change in the patterns of trade between Member States compared to the situation before the agreement.

3.2.3. Vertical agreements covering a single Member State

86.   Vertical agreements covering the whole of a Member State may, in particular, be capable of affecting patterns of trade between Member States when they make it more difficult for undertakings from other Member States to penetrate the national market in question, either by means of exports or by means of establishment (foreclosure effect). When vertical agreements give rise to such foreclosure effects, they contribute to the partitioning of markets on a national basis, thereby hindering the economic interpenetration which the Treaty is designed to bring about(64).

87.   Foreclosure may, for example, occur when suppliers impose exclusive purchasing obligations on buyers(65). In Delimitis(66), which concerned agreements between a brewer and owners of premises where beer was consumed whereby the latter undertook to buy beer exclusively from the brewer, the Court of Justice defined foreclosure as the absence, due to the agreements, of real and concrete possibilities of gaining access to the market. Agreements normally only create significant barriers to entry when they cover a significant proportion of the market. Market share and market coverage can be used as an indicator in this respect. In making the assessment account must be taken not only of the particular agreement or network of agreements in question, but also of other parallel networks of agreements having similar effects(67).

88.   Vertical agreements which cover the whole of a Member State and which relate to tradable products may also be capable of affecting trade between Member States, even if they do not create direct obstacles to trade. Agreements whereby undertakings engage in resale price maintenance (RPM) may have direct effects on trade between Member States by increasing imports from other Member States and by decreasing exports from the Member State in question(68). Agreements involving RPM may also affect patterns of trade in much the same way as horizontal cartels. To the extent that the price resulting from RPM is higher than that prevailing in other Member States this price level is only sustainable if imports from other Member States can be controlled.

3.2.4. Agreements covering only part of a Member State

89.   In qualitative terms the assessment of agreements covering only part of a Member State is approached in the same way as in the case of agreements covering the whole of a Member State. This means that the analysis in section 2 applies. In the assessment of appreciability, however, the two categories must be distinguished, as it must be taken into account that only part of a Member State is covered by the agreement. It must also be taken into account what proportion of the national territory is susceptible to trade. If, for example, transport costs or the operating radius of equipment render it economically unviable for undertakings from other Member States to serve the entire territory of another Member State, trade is capable of being affected if the agreement forecloses access to the part of the territory of a Member State that is susceptible to trade, provided that this part is not insignificant(69).

90.   Where an agreement forecloses access to a regional market, then for trade to be appreciably affected, the volume of sales affected must be significant in proportion to the overall volume of sales of the products concerned inside the Member State in question. This assessment cannot be based merely on geographic coverage. The market share of the

parties to the agreement must also be given fairly limited weight. Even if the parties have a high market share in a properly defined regional market, the size of that market in terms of volume may still be insignificant when compared to total sales of the products concerned within the Member State in question. In general, the best indicator of the capacity of the agreement to (appreciably) affect trade between Member States is therefore considered to be the share of the national market in terms of volume that is being foreclosed. Agreements covering areas with a high concentration of demand will thus weigh more heavily than those covering areas where demand is less concentrated. For Community jurisdiction to be established the share of the national market that is being foreclosed must be significant.

91. Agreements that are local in nature are in themselves not capable of appreciably affecting trade between Member States. This is the case even if the local market is located in a border region. Conversely, if the foreclosed share of the national market is significant, trade is capable of being affected even where the market in question is not located in a border region.

92. In cases in this category some guidance may be derived from the case law concerning the concept in Article 82 of a substantial part of the common market(70). Agreements that, for example, have the effect of hindering competitors from other Member States from gaining access to part of a Member State, which constitutes a substantial part of the common market, should be considered to have an appreciable effect on trade between Member States.

3.2.5. Abuses of dominant positions covering a single Member State

93. Where an undertaking, which holds a dominant position covering the whole of a Member State, engages in exclusionary abuses, trade between Member States is normally capable of being affected. Such abusive conduct will generally make it more difficult for competitors from other Member States to penetrate the market, in which case patterns of trade are capable of being affected(71). In Michelin(72), for example, the Court of Justice held that a system of loyalty rebates foreclosed competitors from other Member States and therefore affected trade within the meaning of Article 82. In Rennet(73) the Court similarly held that an abuse in the form of an exclusive purchasing obligation on customers foreclosed products from other Member States.

94. Exclusionary abuses that affect the competitive market structure inside a Member State, for instance by eliminating or threatening to eliminate a competitor, may also be capable of affecting trade between Member States. Where the undertaking that risks being eliminated only operates in a single Member State, the abuse will normally not affect trade between Member States. However, trade between Member States is capable of being affected where the targeted undertaking exports to or imports from other Member States(74) and where it also operates in other Member States(75). An effect on trade may arise from the dissuasive impact of the abuse on other competitors. If through repeated conduct the dominant undertaking has acquired a reputation for adopting exclusionary practices towards competitors that attempt to engage in direct competition, competitors from other Member States are likely to compete less aggressively, in which case trade may be affected, even if the victim in the case at hand is not from another Member State.

95. In the case of exploitative abuses such as price discrimination and excessive pricing, the situation may be more complex. Price discrimination between domestic customers will normally not affect trade between Member States. However, it may do so if the buyers are engaged in export activities and are disadvantaged by the discriminatory pricing or if this practice is used to prevent imports(76). Practices consisting of offering lower prices to customers that are the most likely to import products from other Member States may

make it more difficult for competitors from other Member States to enter the market. In such cases trade between Member States is capable of being affected.

96. As long as an undertaking has a dominant position which covers the whole of a Member State it is normally immaterial whether the specific abuse engaged in by the dominant undertaking only covers part of its territory or affects certain buyers within the national territory. A dominant firm can significantly impede trade by engaging in abusive conduct in the areas or vis-à-vis the customers that are the most likely to be targeted by competitors from other Member States. For example, it may be the case that a particular channel of distribution constitutes a particularly important means of gaining access to broad categories of consumers. Hindering access to such channels can have a substantial impact on trade between Member States. In the assessment of appreciability it must also be taken into account that the very presence of the dominant undertaking covering the whole of a Member State is likely to make market penetration more difficult. Any abuse which makes it more difficult to enter the national market should therefore be considered to appreciably affect trade. The combination of the market position of the dominant undertaking and the anti-competitive nature of its conduct implies that such abuses have normally by their very nature an appreciable effect on trade. However, if the abuse is purely local in nature or involves only an insignificant share of the sales of the dominant undertaking within the Member State in question, trade may not be capable of being appreciably affected.

3.2.6. Abuse of a dominant position covering only part of a Member State

97. Where a dominant position covers only part of a Member State some guidance may, as in the case of agreements, be derived from the condition in Article 82 that the dominant position must cover a substantial part of the common market. If the dominant position covers part of a Member State that constitutes a substantial part of the common market and the abuse makes it more difficult for competitors from other Member States to gain access to the market where the undertaking is dominant, trade between Member States must normally be considered capable of being appreciably affected.

98. In the application of this criterion regard must be had in particular to the size of the market in question in terms of volume. Regions and even a port or an airport situated in a Member State may, depending on their importance, constitute a substantial part of the common market(77). In the latter cases it must be taken into account whether the infrastructure in question is used to provide cross-border services and, if so, to what extent. When infrastructures such as airports and ports are important in providing cross-border services, trade between Member States is capable of being affected.

99. As in the case of dominant positions covering the whole of a Member State (cf. paragraph 95 above), trade may not be capable of being appreciably affected if the abuse is purely local in nature or involves only an insignificant share of the sales of the dominant undertaking.

3.3. Agreements and abuses involving imports and exports with undertakings located in third countries, and agreements and practices involving undertakings located in third countries

3.3.1. General remarks

100. Articles 81 and 82 apply to agreements and practices that are capable of affecting trade between Member States even if one or more of the parties are located outside the Community(78). Articles 81 and 82 apply irrespective of where the undertakings are located or where the agreement has been concluded, provided that the agreement or practice is either implemented inside the Community(79), or produce effects inside the

Community(80). Articles 81 and 82 may also apply to agreements and practices that cover third countries, provided that they are capable of affecting trade between Member States. The general principle set out in section 2 above according to which the agreement or practice must be capable of having an appreciable influence, direct or indirect, actual or potential, on the pattern of trade between Member States, also applies in the case of agreements and abuses which involve undertakings located in third countries or which relate to imports or exports with third countries.

101. For the purposes of establishing Community law jurisdiction it is sufficient that an agreement or practice involving third countries or undertakings located in third countries is capable of affecting cross-border economic activity inside the Community. Import into one Member State may be sufficient to trigger effects of this nature. Imports can affect the conditions of competition in the importing Member State, which in turn can have an impact on exports and imports of competing products to and from other Member States. In other words, imports from third countries resulting from the agreement or practice may cause a diversion of trade between Member States, thus affecting patterns of trade.

102. In the application of the effect on trade criterion to the above mentioned agreements and practices it is relevant to examine, inter alia, what is the object of the agreement or practice as indicated by its content or the underlying intent of the undertakings involved(81).

103. Where the object of the agreement is to restrict competition inside the Community the requisite effect on trade between Member States is more readily established than where the object is predominantly to regulate competition outside the Community. Indeed in the former case the agreement or practice has a direct impact on competition inside the Community and trade between Member States. Such agreements and practices, which may concern both imports and exports, are normally by their very nature capable of affecting trade between Member States.

3.3.2. Arrangements that have as their object the restriction of competition inside the Community

104. In the case of imports, this category includes agreements that bring about an isolation of the internal market(82). This is, for instance, the case of agreements whereby competitors in the Community and in third countries share markets, e.g. by agreeing not to sell in each other's home markets or by concluding reciprocal (exclusive) distribution agreements(83).

105. In the case of exports, this category includes cases where undertakings that compete in two or more Member States agree to export certain (surplus) quantities to third countries with a view to co-ordinating their market conduct inside the Community. Such export agreements serve to reduce price competition by limiting output inside the Community, thereby affecting trade between Member States. Without the export agreement these quantities might have been sold inside the Community(84).

3.3.3. Other arrangements

106. In the case of agreements and practices whose object is not to restrict competition inside the Community, it is normally necessary to proceed with a more detailed analysis of whether or not cross-border economic activity inside the Community, and thus patterns of trade between Member States, are capable of being affected.

107. In this regard it is relevant to examine the effects of the agreement or practice on customers and other operators inside the Community that rely on the products of the undertakings that are parties to the agreement or practice(85). In Compagnie maritime belge(86), which concerned agreements between shipping companies operating between

Community ports and West African ports, the agreements were held to be capable of indirectly affecting trade between Member States because they altered the catchment areas of the Community ports covered by the agreements and because they affected the activities of other undertakings inside those areas. More specifically, the agreements affected the activities of undertakings that relied on the parties for transportation services, either as a means of transporting goods purchased in third countries or sold there, or as an important input into the services that the ports themselves offered.

108. Trade may also be capable of being affected when the agreement prevents re-imports into the Community. This may, for example, be the case with vertical agreements between Community suppliers and third country distributors, imposing restrictions on resale outside an allocated territory, including the Community. If in the absence of the agreement resale to the Community would be possible and likely, such imports may be capable of affecting patterns of trade inside the Community(87).

109. However, for such effects to be likely, there must be an appreciable difference between the prices of the products charged in the Community and those charged outside the Community, and this price difference must not be eroded by customs duties and transport osts. In addition, the product volumes exported compared to the total market for those products in the territory of the common market must not be insignificant(88). If these product volumes are insignificant compared to those sold inside the Community, the impact of any re-importation on trade between Member States is considered not to be appreciable. In making this assessment, regard must be had not only to the individual agreement concluded between the parties, but also to any cumulative effect of similar agreements concluded by the same and competing suppliers. It may be, for example, that the product volumes covered by a single agreement are quite small, but that the product volumes covered by several such agreements are significant. In that case the agreements taken as a whole may be capable of appreciably affecting trade between Member States. It should be recalled, however (cf. paragraph 49 above), that the individual agreement or network of agreements must make a significant contribution to the overall effect on trade.

....

(1) OJ C 368, 22.12.2001, p. 13.
(2) OJ L 1, 4.1.2003, p. 1.
(3) See e.g. Joined Cases 56/64 and 58/64, Consten and Grundig, [1966] ECR p. 429, and Joined Cases 6/73 and 7/73, Commercial Solvents, [1974] ECR p. 223.
(4) See in this respect Case 22/71, Béguelin, [1971] ECR p. 949, paragraph 16.
(5) See Case 193/83, Windsurfing, [1986] ECR p. 611, paragraph 96, and Case T-77/94, Vereniging van Groothandelaren in Bloemkwekerijprodukten, [1997] ECR II-759, paragraph 126.
(6) See paragraphs 142 to 144 of the judgment in Vereniging van Groothandelaren in Bloemkwekerijprodukteten cited in the previous footnote.
(7) See e.g. Case T-2/89, Petrofina, [1991] ECR II-1087, paragraph 226.
(8) The concept of appreciability is dealt with in section 2.4 below.
(9) See in this respect Case 85/76, Hoffmann-La Roche, [1979] ECR p. 461, paragraph 126.
(10) Throughout these guidelines the term "products" covers both goods and services.
(11) See Case 172/80, Züchner, [1981] ECR p. 2021, paragraph 18. See also Case C-309/99, Wouters, [2002] ECR I-1577, paragraph 95, Case C-475/99, Ambulanz Glöckner, [2001] ECR I-8089, paragraph 49, Joined Cases C-215/96 and 216/96, Bagnasco, [1999] ECR I-135, paragraph 51, Case C-55/96, Job Centre, [1997] ECR I-7119, paragraph 37, and Case C-41/90, Höfner and Elser, [1991] ECR I-1979, paragraph 33.
(12) See e.g. Joined Cases T-24/93 and others, Compagnie maritime belge, [1996] ECR II-1201, paragraph 203, and paragraph 23 of the judgment in Commercial Solvents cited in footnote.
(13) See e.g. Joined Cases T-213/95 and T-18/96, SCK and FNK, [1997] ECR II-1739, and sections 3.2.4 and 3.2.6 below.
(14) See section 3.2 below.
(15) See e.g. the judgment in Züchner cited in footnote 11 and Case 319/82, Kerpen & Kerpen, [1983] ECR 4173, Joined Cases 240/82 and others, Stichting Sigarettenindustrie, [1985] ECR 3831, paragraph 48, and Joined Cases T-25/95 and others, Cimenteries CBR, [2000] ECR II-491, paragraph 3930.

(16) In some judgments mainly relating to vertical agreements the Court of Justice has added wording to the effect that the agreement was capable of hindering the attainment of the objectives of a single market between Member States, see e.g. Case T-62/98, Volkswagen, [2000] ECR II-2707, paragraph 179, and paragraph 47 of the Bagnasco judgment cited in footnote 11, and Case 56/65, Société Technique Minière, [1966] ECR 337. The impact of an agreement on the single market objective is thus a factor which can be taken into account.

(17) See e.g. Case T-228/97, Irish Sugar, [1999] ECR II-2969, paragraph 170, and Case 19/77, Miller, [1978] ECR 131, paragraph 15.

(18) See e.g. Case C-250/92, Gøttrup-Klim [1994] ECR II-5641, paragraph 54.

(19) See e.g. Case C-306/96, Javico, [1998] ECR I-1983, paragraph 17, and paragraph 18 of the judgment in Béguelin cited in footnote 4.

(20) Compare in this respect the judgments in Bagnasco and Wouters cited in footnote 11.

(21) See e.g. Case T-141/89, Tréfileurope, [1995] ECR II-791, Case T-29/92, Vereniging van Samenwerkende Prijsregelende Organisaties in de Bouwnijverheid (SPO), [1995] ECR II-289, as far as exports were concerned, and Commission Decision in Volkswagen (II) (OJ L 264, 2.10.2001, p. 14).

(22) See in this respect Case 71/74, Frubo, [1975] ECR 563, paragraph 38, Joined Cases 209/78 and others, Van Landewyck, [1980] ECR 3125, paragraph 172, Case T-61/89, Dansk Pelsdyravler Forening, [1992] ECR II-1931, paragraph 143, and Case T-65/89, BPB Industries and British Gypsum, [1993] ECR II-389, paragraph 135.

(23) See in this respect Case T-86/95, Compagnie Générale Maritime and others, [2002] ECR II-1011, paragraph 148, and paragraph 202 of the judgment in Compagnie maritime belge cited in footnote 12.

(24) See Case 123/83, BNIC v Clair, [1985] ECR 391, paragraph 29.

(25) See Commission Decision in Zanussi, OJ L 322, 16.11.1978, p. 36, paragraph 11.

(26) See in this respect Case 31/85, ETA Fabrique d'Ébauches, [1985] ECR 3933, paragraphs 12 and 13.

(27) See Joined Cases C-241/91 P and C-242/91 P, RTE (Magill), [1995] ECR I-743, paragraph 70, and Case 107/82, AEG, [1983] ECR 3151, paragraph 60.

(28) See paragraph 60 of the AEG judgment cited in the previous footnote.

(29) See Case 5/69, Völk, [1969] ECR 295, paragraph 7.

(30) See e.g. paragraph 17 of the judgment in Javico cited in footnote 19, and paragraph 138 of the judgment in BPB Industries and British Gypsum cited in footnote 22.

(31) See paragraph 138 of the judgment in BPB Industries and British Gypsum cited in footnote 22.

(32) See e.g. paragraphs 9 and 10 of the Miller judgment cited in footnote 17, and paragraph 58 of the AEG judgment cited in footnote 27.

(33) See Joined Cases 100/80 and others, Musique Diffusion Française, [1983] ECR 1825, paragraph 86. In that case the products in question accounted for just above 3 % of sales on the national markets concerned. The Court held that the agreements, which hindered parallel trade, were capable of appreciably affecting trade between Member States due to the high turnover of the parties and the relative market position of the products, compared to those of products produced by competing suppliers.

(34) See in this respect paragraphs 179 and 231 of the Volkswagen judgment cited in footnote 16, and Case T-213/00, CMA CGM and others, [2003] ECR I-, paragraphs 219 and 220.

(35) See e.g. Case T-7/93, Langnese-Iglo, [1995] ECR II-1533, paragraph 120.

(36) See paragraphs 140 and 141 of the judgment in Vereniging van Groothandelaren in Bloemkwekerijprodukten cited in footnote 5.

(37) See Commission Notice on agreements of minor importance which do not appreciably restrict competition under Article 81(1) of the Treaty (OJ C 368, 22.12.2001, p. 13, paragraph 3).

(38) OJ L 107, 30.4.1996, p. 4. With effect from 1.1.2005 this recommendation will be replaced by Commission Recommendation 2003/361/EC concerning the definition of micro, small and medium-sized enterprises (OJ L 124, 20.5.2003, p. 36).

(39) The term "undertakings concerned" shall include connected undertakings as defined in paragraph 12.2 of the Commission's Notice on agreements of minor importance which do not appreciably restrict competition under Article 81(1) of the Treaty establishing the European Community (OJ C 368, 22.12.2001, p. 13).

(40) See the previous footnote.

(41) When defining the relevant market, reference should be made to the notice on the definition of the relevant market for the purposes of Community competition law (OJ C 372, 9.12.1997, p. 5).

(42) See also paragraph 14 above.

(43) See paragraph 8 of the judgment in Kerpen & Kerpen cited in footnote 15. It should be noted that the Court does not refer to market share but to the share of French exports and to the product volumes involved.

(44) See e.g. the judgment in Volkswagen cited in footnote 16 and Case T-175/95, BASF Coatings, [1999] ECR II-1581. For a horizontal agreement to prevent parallel trade see Joined Cases 96/82 and others, IAZ International, [1983] ECR 3369, paragraph 27.

(45) See e.g. Case T-142/89, Usines Gustave Boël, [1995] ECR II-867, paragraph 102.

(46) Horizontal cooperation agreements are dealt with in the Commission Guidelines on the applicability of Article 81 of the EC Treaty to horizontal cooperation agreements (OJ C 3, 6.1.2001, p. 2). Those guidelines deal with the substantive competition assessment of various types of agreements but do not deal with the effect on trade issue.

(47) See Council Regulation (EC) No 139/2004 on the control of concentrations between undertakings (OJ L 24, 29.1.2004, p. 1).

(48) The Commission Notice on the concept of full-function joint ventures under the Merger Regulation (OJ C 66, 2.3.1998, p. 1) gives guidance on the scope of this concept.

(49) See e.g. the Commission Decision in Ford/Volkswagen (OJ L 20, 28.1.1993, p. 14).

(50) See in this respect paragraph 146 of the Compagnie Générale Maritime judgment cited in footnote 23 above.

(51) See in this respect Joined Cases 43/82 and 63/82, VBVB and VBBB, [1984] ECR 19, paragraph 9.

(52) See in this respect Case T-66/89, Publishers Association, [1992] ECR II-1995.

(53) See in this respect the judgment in Commercial Solvents cited in footnote 3, in the judgment in Hoffmann-La Roche, cited in footnote, paragraph 125, and in RTE and ITP cited in footnote, as well as Case 6/72, Continental Can, [1973] ECR 215, paragraph 16, and Case 27/76, United Brands, [1978] ECR 207, paragraphs 197 to 203.

(54) See paragraphs 32 and 33 of the judgment in Commercial Solvents cited in footnote 3.

(55) According to settled case law dominance is a position of economic strength enjoyed by an undertaking which enables it to prevent effective competition being maintained on the relevant market by affording it the power to act to an appreciable extent independently of its competitors, its customers and ultimately of the consumers, see e.g. paragraph 38 of the judgment in Hoffmann-La Roche cited in footnote 9.

(56) See for a recent example paragraph 95 of the Wouters judgment cited in footnote 11.

(57) See e.g. Case 246/86, Belasco, [1989] ECR 2117, paragraph 32–38.

(58) See paragraph 34 of the Belasco judgment cited in the previous footnote and more recently Joined Cases T-202/98 a.o., British Sugar, [2001] ECR II-2035, paragraph 79. On the other hand this is not so when the market is not susceptible to imports, see paragraph 51 of the Bagnasco judgment cited in footnote 11.

(59) Guarantees for current account credit facilities.

(60) See paragraph 51 of the Bagnasco judgment cited in footnote 11.

(61) See in this respect Case 45/85, Verband der Sachversicherer, [1987] ECR 405, paragraph 50, and Case C-7/95 P, John Deere, [1998] ECR I-3111. See also paragraph 172 of the judgment in Van Landewyck cited in footnote 22, where the Court stressed that the agreement in question reduced appreciably the incentive to sell imported products.

(62) See e.g. the judgment in Stichting Sigarettenindustrie, cited in footnote 15, paragraphs 49 and 50.

(63) See in this respect Case T-22/97, Kesko, [1999] ECR II-3775, paragraph 109.

(64) See e.g. Case T-65/98, Van den Bergh Foods, [2003] ECR II-. . ., and the judgment in Langnese-Iglo, cited in footnote 35 paragraph 120.

(65) See e.g. judgment of 7.12.2000, Case C-214/99, Neste, ECR I-11121.

(66) See judgment of 28.2.1991, Case C-234/89, Delimitis, ECR I-935.

(67) See paragraph 120 of the Langnese-Iglo judgment cited in footnote 35.

(68) See e.g. Commission Decision in Volkswagen (II), cited in footnote 21, paragraphs 81 et seq.

(69) See in this respect paragraphs 177 to 181 of the judgment in SCK and FNK cited in footnote 13.

(70) See as to this notion the judgment in Ambulanz Glöckner, cited in footnote 11, paragraph 38, and Case C-179/90, Merci convenzionali porto di Genova, [1991] ECR I-5889, and Case C-242/95, GT-Link, [1997] ECR I-4449.

(71) See e.g. paragraph 135 of the judgment in BPB Industries and British Gypsum cited in footnote.

(72) See Case 322/81, Nederlandse Banden Industrie Michelin, [1983] ECR 3461

(73) See Case 61/80, Coöperative Stremsel- en Kleurselfabriek, [1981] ECR 851, paragraph 15.

(74) See in this respect judgment in Irish Sugar cited in footnote 17 paragraph 169.

(75) See paragraph 70 of the judgment in RTE (Magill) cited in footnote 27.

(76) See the judgment in Irish Sugar cited in footnote 17.

(77) See e.g. the case law cited in footnote 70.

(78) See in this respect Case 28/77, Tepea, [1978] ECR 1391, paragraph 48, and paragraph 16 of the judgment in Continental Can cited in footnote 53.

(79) See Joined Cases C-89/85 and others, Ahlström Osakeyhtiö (Woodpulp), [1988] ECR 651, paragraph 16.

(80) See in this respect Case T-102/96, Gencor, [1999] ECR II-753, which applies the effects test in the field of mergers.

(81) See to that effect paragraph 19 of the judgment in Javico cited in footnote 19.

(82) See in this respect Case 51/75, EMI v CBS, [1976] ECR 811, paragraphs 28 and 29.

(83) See Commission Decision in Siemens/Fanuc (OJ L 376, 31.12.1985, p. 29).

(84) See in this respect Joined Cases 29/83 and 30/83, CRAM and Rheinzinc, [1984] ECR 1679, and Joined Cases 40/73 and others, Suiker Unie, [1975] ECR 1663, paragraphs 564 and 580.

(85) See paragraph 22 of the judgment in Javico cited in footnote 19.

(86) See paragraph 203 of the judgment in Compagnie maritime belge cited in footnote 12.

(87) See in this respect the judgment in Javico cited in footnote 19.

(88) See in this respect paragraphs 24 to 26 of the Javico judgment cited in footnote 19.

COMMISSION NOTICE
Guidelines on the application of [Article 101(3) TFEU][1]
OJ C 101, 27.4.2004, P. 97

1. INTRODUCTION

1. Article 81(3) of the Treaty sets out an exception rule, which provides a defence to undertakings against a finding of an infringement of Article 81(1) of the Treaty. Agreements, decisions of associations of undertakings and concerted practices(1) caught by Article 81(1) which satisfy the conditions of Article 81(3) are valid and enforceable, no prior decision to that effect being required.

2. Article 81(3) can be applied in individual cases or to categories of agreements and concerted practices by way of block exemption regulation. Regulation 1/2003 on the implementation of the competition rules laid down in Articles 81 and 82(2) does not affect the validity and legal nature of block exemption regulations. All existing block exemption regulations remain in force and agreements covered by block exemption regulations are legally valid and enforceable even if they are restrictive of competition within the meaning of Article 81(1)(3). Such agreements can only be prohibited for the future and only upon formal withdrawal of the block exemption by the Commission or a national competition authority(4). Block exempted agreements cannot be held invalid by national courts in the context of private litigation.

3. The existing guidelines on vertical restraints, horizontal cooperation agreements and technology transfer agreements(5) deal with the application of Article 81 to various types of agreements and concerted practices. The purpose of those guidelines is to set out the Commission's view of the substantive assessment criteria applied to the various types of agreements and practices.

4. The present guidelines set out the Commission's interpretation of the conditions for exception contained in Article 81(3). It thereby provides guidance on how it will apply Article 81 in individual cases. Although not binding on them, these guidelines also intend to give guidance to the courts and authorities of the Member States in their application of Article 81(1) and (3) of the Treaty.

5. The guidelines establish an analytical framework for the application of Article 81(3). The purpose is to develop a methodology for the application of this Treaty provision. This methodology is based on the economic approach already introduced and developed in the guidelines on vertical restraints, horizontal co-operation agreements and technology transfer agreements. The Commission will follow the present guidelines, which provide more detailed guidance on the application of the four conditions of Article 81(3) than the guidelines on vertical restraints, horizontal co-operation agreements and technology transfer agreements, also with regard to agreements covered by those guidelines.

6. The standards set forth in the present guidelines must be applied in light of the circumstances specific to each case. This excludes a mechanical application. Each case must be assessed on its own facts and the guidelines must be applied reasonably and flexibly.

....

[1] EDITOR'S NOTE: As of 1 May 2012 this Commission Notice has not been reissued following the entry into force of the Treaty of Lisbon. It includes references to the old Treaty article numbers in the text. The title of the Notice has been updated to reflect that fact that Articles 81 and 82 TEC have been replaced by Articles 101 and 102 TFEU. Reference should be made to the Tables of Equivalences accompanying the consolidated Treaties in Part II of this edition for the conversion of old Treaty article numbers to new ones.

7.   With regard to a number of issues, the present guidelines outline the current state of the case law of the Court of Justice. However, the Commission also intends to explain its policy with regard to issues that have not been dealt with in the case law, or that are subject to interpretation. The Commission's position, however, is without prejudice to the case law of the Court of Justice and the Court of First Instance concerning the interpretation of Article 81(1) and (3), and to the interpretation that the Community Courts may give to those provisions in the future.

2. THE GENERAL FRAMEWORK OF ARTICLE 81 EC

2.1. The Treaty provisions

8.   Article 81(1) prohibits all agreements between undertakings, decisions by associations of undertakings and concerted practices which may affect trade between Member States(6) and which have as their object or effect the prevention, restriction or distortion of competition(7).

9.   As an exception to this rule Article 81(3) provides that the prohibition contained in Article 81(1) may be declared inapplicable in case of agreements which contribute to improving the production or distribution of goods or to promoting technical or economic progress, while allowing consumers a fair share of the resulting benefits, and which do not impose restrictions which are not indispensable to the attainment of these objectives, and do not afford such undertakings the possibility of eliminating competition in respect of a substantial part of the products concerned.

10.   According to Article 1(1) of Regulation 1/2003 agreements which are caught by Article 81(1) and which do not satisfy the conditions of Article 81(3) are prohibited, no prior decision to that effect being required(8). According to Article 1(2) of the same Regulation agreements which are caught by Article 81(1) but which satisfy the conditions of Article 81(3) are not prohibited, no prior decision to that effect being required. Such agreements are valid and enforceable from the moment that the conditions of Article 81(3) are satisfied and for as long as that remains the case.

11.   The assessment under Article 81 thus consists of two parts. The first step is to assess whether an agreement between undertakings, which is capable of affecting trade between Member States, has an anti-competitive object or actual or potential(9) anti-competitive effects. The second step, which only becomes relevant when an agreement is found to be restrictive of competition, is to determine the pro-competitive benefits produced by that agreement and to assess whether these pro-competitive effects outweigh the anti-competitive effects. The balancing of anti-competitive and pro-competitive effects is conducted exclusively within the framework laid down by Article 81(3)(10).

12.   The assessment of any countervailing benefits under Article 81(3) necessarily requires prior determination of the restrictive nature and impact of the agreement. To place Article 81(3) in its proper context it is appropriate to briefly outline the objective and principal content of the prohibition rule of Article 81(1). The Commission guidelines on vertical restraints, horizontal co-operation agreements and technology transfer agreements(11) contain substantial guidance on the application of Article 81(1) to various types of agreements. The present guidelines are therefore limited to recalling the basic analytical framework for applying Article 81(1).

2.2. The prohibition rule of Article 81(1)

2.2.1. General remarks

13. The objective of Article 81 is to protect competition on the market as a means of enhancing consumer welfare and of ensuring an efficient allocation of resources. Competition and market integration serve these ends since the creation and preservation of an open single market promotes an efficient allocation of resources throughout the Community for the benefit of consumers.

14. The prohibition rule of Article 81(1) applies to restrictive agreements and concerted practices between undertakings and decisions by associations of undertakings in so far as they are capable of affecting trade between Member States. A general principle underlying Article 81(1) which is expressed in the case law of the Community Courts is that each economic operator must determine independently the policy, which he intends to adopt on the market(12). In view of this the Community Courts have defined "agreements", "decisions" and "concerted practices" as Community law concepts which allow a distinction to be made between the unilateral conduct of an undertaking and co-ordination of behaviour or collusion between undertakings(13). Unilateral conduct is subject only to Article 82 of the Treaty as far as Community competition law is concerned. Moreover, the convergence rule set out in Article 3(2) of Regulation 1/2003 does not apply to unilateral conduct. This provision applies only to agreements, decisions and concerted practices, which are capable of affecting trade between Member States. Article 3(2) provides that when such agreements, decisions and concerted practices are not prohibited by Article 81, they cannot be prohibited by national competition law. Article 3 is without prejudice to the fundamental principle of primacy of Community law, which entails in particular that agreements and abusive practices that are prohibited by Articles 81 and 82 cannot be upheld by national law(14).

15. The type of co-ordination of behaviour or collusion between undertakings falling within the scope of Article 81(1) is that where at least one undertaking vis-à-vis another undertaking undertakes to adopt a certain conduct on the market or that as a result of contacts between them uncertainty as to their conduct on the market is eliminated or at least substantially reduced(15). It follows that co-ordination can take the form of obligations that regulate the market conduct of at least one of the parties as well as of arrangements that influence the market conduct of at least one of the parties by causing a change in its incentives. It is not required that co-ordination is in the interest of all the undertakings concerned(16). Co-ordination must also not necessarily be express. It can also be tacit. For an agreement to be capable of being regarded as having been concluded by tacit acceptance there must be an invitation from an undertaking to another undertaking, whether express or implied, to fulfil a goal jointly(17). In certain circumstances an agreement may be inferred from and imputed to an ongoing commercial relationship between the parties(18). However, the mere fact that a measure adopted by an undertaking falls within the context of on-going business relations is not sufficient(19).

16. Agreements between undertakings are caught by the prohibition rule of Article 81(1) when they are likely to have an appreciable adverse impact on the parameters of competition on the market, such as price, output, product quality, product variety and innovation. Agreements can have this effect by appreciably reducing rivalry between the parties to the agreement or between them and third parties.

2.2.2. The basic principles for assessing agreements under Article 81(1)

17. The assessment of whether an agreement is restrictive of competition must be made within the actual context in which competition would occur in the absence of the agreement with its alleged restrictions(20). In making this assessment it is necessary to take account of the

likely impact of the agreement on inter-brand competition (i.e. competition between suppliers of competing brands) and on intra-brand competition (i.e. competition between distributors of the same brand). Article 81(1) prohibits restrictions of both inter-brand competition and intra-brand competition(21).

18.   For the purpose of assessing whether an agreement or its individual parts may restrict inter-brand competition and/or intra-brand competition it needs to be considered how and to what extent the agreement affects or is likely to affect competition on the market. The following two questions provide a useful framework for making this assessment. The first question relates to the impact of the agreement on inter-brand competition while the second question relates to the impact of the agreement on intra-brand competition. As restraints may be capable of affecting both inter-brand competition and intra-brand competition at the same time, it may be necessary to analyse a restraint in light of both questions before it can be concluded whether or not competition is restricted within the meaning of Article 81(1):

(1) Does the agreement restrict actual or potential competition that would have existed without the agreement? If so, the agreement may be caught by Article 81(1). In making this assessment it is necessary to take into account competition between the parties and competition from third parties. For instance, where two undertakings established in different Member States undertake not to sell products in each other's home markets, (potential) competition that existed prior to the agreement is restricted. Similarly, where a supplier imposes obligations on his distributors not to sell competing products and these obligations foreclose third party access to the market, actual or potential competition that would have existed in the absence of the agreement is restricted. In assessing whether the parties to an agreement are actual or potential competitors the economic and legal context must be taken into account. For instance, if due to the financial risks involved and the technical capabilities of the parties it is unlikely on the basis of objective factors that each party would be able to carry out on its own the activities covered by the agreement the parties are deemed to be non-competitors in respect of that activity(22). It is for the parties to bring forward evidence to that effect.

(2) Does the agreement restrict actual or potential competition that would have existed in the absence of the contractual restraint(s)? If so, the agreement may be caught by Article 81(1). For instance, where a supplier restricts its distributors from competing with each other, (potential) competition that could have existed between the distributors absent the restraints is restricted. Such restrictions include resale price maintenance and territorial or customer sales restrictions between distributors. However, certain restraints may in certain cases not be caught by Article 81(1) when the restraint is objectively necessary for the existence of an agreement of that type or that nature(23). Such exclusion of the application of Article 81(1) can only be made on the basis of objective factors external to the parties themselves and not the subjective views and characteristics of the parties. The question is not whether the parties in their particular situation would not have accepted to conclude a less restrictive agreement, but whether given the nature of the agreement and the characteristics of the market a less restrictive agreement would not have been concluded by undertakings in a similar setting. For instance, territorial restraints in an agreement between a supplier and a distributor may for a certain period of time fall outside Article 81(1), if the restraints are objectively necessary in order for the distributor to penetrate a new market(24). Similarly, a prohibition imposed on all distributors not to sell to certain categories of end users may not be restrictive of competition if such restraint is objectively necessary for reasons of safety or health related to the dangerous nature of the product in question. Claims that in the absence of a restraint the supplier would have resorted to

vertical integration are not sufficient. Decisions on whether or not to vertically integrate depend on a broad range of complex economic factors, a number of which are internal to the undertaking concerned.

19. In the application of the analytical framework set out in the previous paragraph it must be taken into account that Article 81(1) distinguishes between those agreements that have a restriction of competition as their object and those agreements that have a restriction of competition as their effect. An agreement or contractual restraint is only prohibited by Article 81(1) if its object or effect is to restrict inter-brand competition and/or intra-brand competition.

20. The distinction between restrictions by object and restrictions by effect is important. Once it has been established that an agreement has as its object the restriction of competition, there is no need to take account of its concrete effects(25). In other words, for the purpose of applying Article 81(1) no actual anti-competitive effects need to be demonstrated where the agreement has a restriction of competition as its object. Article 81(3), on the other hand, does not distinguish between agreements that restrict competition by object and agreements that restrict competition by effect. Article 81(3) applies to all agreements that fulfil the four conditions contained therein(26).

21. Restrictions of competition by object are those that by their very nature have the potential of restricting competition. These are restrictions which in light of the objectives pursued by the Community competition rules have such a high potential of negative effects on competition that it is unnecessary for the purposes of applying Article 81(1) to demonstrate any actual effects on the market. This presumption is based on the serious nature of the restriction and on experience showing that restrictions of competition by object are likely to produce negative effects on the market and to jeopardise the objectives pursued by the Community competition rules. Restrictions by object such as price fixing and market sharing reduce output and raise prices, leading to a misallocation of resources, because goods and services demanded by customers are not produced. They also lead to a reduction in consumer welfare, because consumers have to pay higher prices for the goods and services in question.

22. The assessment of whether or not an agreement has as its object the restriction of competition is based on a number of factors. These factors include, in particular, the content of the agreement and the objective aims pursued by it. It may also be necessary to consider the context in which it is (to be) applied and the actual conduct and behaviour of the parties on the market(27). In other words, an examination of the facts underlying the agreement and the specific circumstances in which it operates may be required before it can be concluded whether a particular restriction constitutes a restriction of competition by object. The way in which an agreement is actually implemented may reveal a restriction by object even where the formal agreement does not contain an express provision to that effect. Evidence of subjective intent on the part of the parties to restrict competition is a relevant factor but not a necessary condition.

23. Non-exhaustive guidance on what constitutes restrictions by object can be found in Commission block exemption regulations, guidelines and notices. Restrictions that are black-listed in block exemptions or identified as hardcore restrictions in guidelines and notices are generally considered by the Commission to constitute restrictions by object. In the case of horizontal agreements restrictions of competition by object include price fixing, output limitation and sharing of markets and customers(28). As regards vertical agreements the category of restrictions by object includes, in particular, fixed and minimum resale price maintenance and restrictions providing absolute territorial protection, including restrictions on passive sales(29).

24. If an agreement is not restrictive of competition by object it must be examined whether it has restrictive effects on competition. Account must be taken of both actual and potential effects(30). In other words the agreement must have likely anti-competitive effects. In the case of restrictions of competition by effect there is no presumption of anti-competitive effects. For an agreement to be restrictive by effect it must affect actual or potential competition to such an extent that on the relevant market negative effects on prices, output, innovation or the variety or quality of goods and services can be expected with a reasonable degree of probability(31). Such negative effects must be appreciable. The prohibition rule of Article 81(1) does not apply when the identified anti-competitive effects are insignificant(32). This test reflects the economic approach which the Commission is applying. The prohibition of Article 81(1) only applies where on the basis of proper market analysis it can be concluded that the agreement has likely anti-competitive effects on the market(33). It is insufficient for such a finding that the market shares of the parties exceed the thresholds set out in the Commission's de minimis notice(34). Agreements falling within safe harbours of block exemption regulations may be caught by Article 81(1) but this is not necessarily so. Moreover, the fact that due to the market shares of the parties, an agreement falls outside the safe harbour of a block exemption is in itself an insufficient basis for finding that the agreement is caught by Article 81(1) or that it does not fulfil the conditions of Article 81(3). Individual assessment of the likely effects produced by the agreement is required.

25. Negative effects on competition within the relevant market are likely to occur when the parties individually or jointly have or obtain some degree of market power and the agreement contributes to the creation, maintenance or strengthening of that market power or allows the parties to exploit such market power. Market power is the ability to maintain prices above competitive levels for a significant period of time or to maintain output in terms of product quantities, product quality and variety or innovation below competitive levels for a significant period of time. In markets with high fixed costs undertakings must price significantly above their marginal costs of production in order to ensure a competitive return on their investment. The fact that undertakings price above their marginal costs is therefore not in itself a sign that competition in the market is not functioning well and that undertakings have market power that allows them to price above the competitive level. It is when competitive constraints are insufficient to maintain prices and output at competitive levels that undertakings have market power within the meaning of Article 81(1).

26. The creation, maintenance or strengthening of market power can result from a restriction of competition between the parties to the agreement. It can also result from a restriction of competition between any one of the parties and third parties, e.g. because the agreement leads to foreclosure of competitors or because it raises competitors' costs, limiting their capacity to compete effectively with the contracting parties. Market power is a question of degree. The degree of market power normally required for the finding of an infringement under Article 81(1) in the case of agreements that are restrictive of competition by effect is less than the degree of market power required for a finding of dominance under Article 82.

27. For the purposes of analysing the restrictive effects of an agreement it is normally necessary to define the relevant market(35). It is normally also necessary to examine and assess, inter alia, the nature of the products, the market position of the parties, the market position of competitors, the market position of buyers, the existence of potential competitors and the level of entry barriers. In some cases, however, it may be possible to show anti-competitive effects directly by analysing the conduct of the parties to the agreement on the market. It may for example be possible to ascertain that an agreement has led to price increases. The guidelines on horizontal cooperation agreements and on

vertical restraints set out a detailed framework for analysing the competitive impact of various types of horizontal and vertical agreements under Article 81(1)(36).

2.2.3. Ancillary restraints

28. Paragraph 18 above sets out a framework for analysing the impact of an agreement and its individual restrictions on inter-brand competition and intra-brand competition. If on the basis of those principles it is concluded that the main transaction covered by the agreement is not restrictive of competition, it becomes relevant to examine whether individual restraints contained in the agreement are also compatible with Article 81(1) because they are ancillary to the main non-restrictive transaction.

29. In Community competition law the concept of ancillary restraints covers any alleged restriction of competition which is directly related and necessary to the implementation of a main non-restrictive transaction and proportionate to it(37). If an agreement in its main parts, for instance a distribution agreement or a joint venture, does not have as its object or effect the restriction of competition, then restrictions, which are directly related to and necessary for the implementation of that transaction, also fall outside Article 81(1)(38). These related restrictions are called ancillary restraints. A restriction is directly related to the main transaction if it is subordinate to the implementation of that transaction and is inseparably linked to it. The test of necessity implies that the restriction must be objectively necessary for the implementation of the main transaction and be proportionate to it. It follows that the ancillary restraints test is similar to the test set out in paragraph 18(2) above. However, the ancillary restraints test applies in all cases where the main transaction is not restrictive of competition(39). It is not limited to determining the impact of the agreement on intra-brand competition.

30. The application of the ancillary restraint concept must be distinguished from the application of the defence under Article 81(3) which relates to certain economic benefits produced by restrictive agreements and which are balanced against the restrictive effects of the agreements. The application of the ancillary restraint concept does not involve any weighing of pro-competitive and anti-competitive effects. Such balancing is reserved for Article 81(3)(40).

31. The assessment of ancillary restraints is limited to determining whether, in the specific context of the main non-restrictive transaction or activity, a particular restriction is necessary for the implementation of that transaction or activity and proportionate to it. If on the basis of objective factors it can be concluded that without the restriction the main non-restrictive transaction would be difficult or impossible to implement, the restriction may be regarded as objectively necessary for its implementation and proportionate to it(41). If, for example, the main object of a franchise agreement does not restrict competition, then restrictions, which are necessary for the proper functioning of the agreement, such as obligations aimed at protecting the uniformity and reputation of the franchise system, also fall outside Article 81(1)(42). Similarly, if a joint venture is not in itself restrictive of competition, then restrictions that are necessary for the functioning of the agreement are deemed to be ancillary to the main transaction and are therefore not caught by Article 81(1). For instance in TPS(43) the Commission concluded that an obligation on the parties not to be involved in companies engaged in distribution and marketing of television programmes by satellite was ancillary to the creation of the joint venture during the initial phase. The restriction was therefore deemed to fall outside Article 81(1) for a period of three years. In arriving at this conclusion the Commission took account of the heavy investments and commercial risks involved in entering the market for pay-television.

2.3. The exception rule of Article 81(3)

32.   The assessment of restrictions by object and effect under Article 81(1) is only one side of the analysis. The other side, which is reflected in Article 81(3), is the assessment of the positive economic effects of restrictive agreements.

33.   The aim of the Community competition rules is to protect competition on the market as a means of enhancing consumer welfare and of ensuring an efficient allocation of resources. Agreements that restrict competition may at the same time have pro-competitive effects by way of efficiency gains(44). Efficiencies may create additional value by lowering the cost of producing an output, improving the quality of the product or creating a new product. When the pro-competitive effects of an agreement outweigh its anti-competitive effects the agreement is on balance pro-competitive and compatible with the objectives of the Community competition rules. The net effect of such agreements is to promote the very essence of the competitive process, namely to win customers by offering better products or better prices than those offered by rivals. This analytical framework is reflected in Article 81(1) and Article 81(3). The latter provision expressly acknowledges that restrictive agreements may generate objective economic benefits so as to outweigh the negative effects of the restriction of competition(45).

34.   The application of the exception rule of Article 81(3) is subject to four cumulative conditions, two positive and two negative:
   (a) The agreement must contribute to improving the production or distribution of goods or contribute to promoting technical or economic progress,
   (b) Consumers must receive a fair share of the resulting benefits,
   (c) The restrictions must be indispensable to the attainment of these objectives, and finally
   (d) The agreement must not afford the parties the possibility of eliminating competition in respect of a substantial part of the products in question.
   When these four conditions are fulfilled the agreement enhances competition within the relevant market, because it leads the undertakings concerned to offer cheaper or better products to consumers, compensating the latter for the adverse effects of the restrictions of competition.

35.   Article 81(3) can be applied either to individual agreements or to categories of agreements by way of a block exemption regulation. When an agreement is covered by a block exemption the parties to the restrictive agreement are relieved of their burden under Article 2 of Regulation 1/2003 of showing that their individual agreement satisfies each of the conditions of Article 81(3). They only have to prove that the restrictive agreement benefits from a block exemption. The application of Article 81(3) to categories of agreements by way of block exemption regulation is based on the presumption that restrictive agreements that fall within their scope(46) fulfil each of the four conditions laid down in Article 81(3).

36.   If in an individual case the agreement is caught by Article 81(1) and the conditions of Article 81(3) are not fulfilled the block exemption may be withdrawn. According to Article 29(1) of Regulation 1/2003 the Commission is empowered to withdraw the benefit of a block exemption when it finds that in a particular case an agreement covered by a block exemption regulation has certain effects which are incompatible with Article 81(3) of the Treaty. Pursuant to Article 29(2) of Regulation 1/2003 a competition authority of a Member State may also withdraw the benefit of a Commission block exemption regulation in respect of its territory (or part of its territory), if this territory has all the characteristics of a distinct geographic market. In the case of withdrawal it is for the competition authorities concerned to demonstrate that the agreement infringes Article 81(1) and that it does not fulfil the conditions of Article 81(3).

37.   The courts of the Member States have no power to withdraw the benefit of block
      exemption regulations. Moreover, in their application of block exemption regulations
      Member State courts may not modify their scope by extending their sphere of application
      to agreements not covered by the block exemption regulation in question(47). Outside the
      scope of block exemption regulations Member State courts have the power to apply
      Article 81 in full (cf. Article 6 of Regulation 1/2003).

3. THE APPLICATION OF THE FOUR CONDITIONS OF ARTICLE 81(3)

38.   The remainder of these guidelines will consider each of the four conditions of
      Article 81(3)(48). Given that these four conditions are cumulative(49) it is unnecessary to
      examine any remaining conditions once it is found that one of the conditions of
      Article 81(3) is not fulfilled. In individual cases it may therefore be appropriate to consider
      the four conditions in a different order.

39.   For the purposes of these guidelines it is considered appropriate to invert the order of the
      second and the third condition and thus deal with the issue of indispensability before the
      issue of pass-on to consumers. The analysis of pass-on requires a balancing of the negative
      and positive effects of an agreement on consumers. This analysis should not include the
      effects of any restrictions, which already fail the indispensability test and which for that
      reason are prohibited by Article 81.

3.1. General principles

40.   Article 81(3) of the Treaty only becomes relevant when an agreement between undertakings
      restricts competition within the meaning of Article 81(1). In the case of non-restrictive
      agreements there is no need to examine any benefits generated by the agreement.

41.   Where in an individual case a restriction of competition within the meaning of
      Article 81(1) has been proven, Article 81(3) can be invoked as a defence. According to
      Article 2 of Regulation 1/2003 the burden of proof under Article 81(3) rests on the
      undertaking(s) invoking the benefit of the exception rule. Where the conditions of
      Article 81(3) are not satisfied the agreement is null and void, cf. Article 81(2). However,
      such automatic nullity only applies to those parts of the agreement that are incompatible
      with Article 81, provided that such parts are severable from the agreement as a whole(50).
      If only part of the agreement is null and void, it is for the applicable national law to
      determine the consequences thereof for the remaining part of the agreement(51).

42.   According to settled case law the four conditions of Article 81(3) are cumulative(52), i.e.
      they must all be fulfilled for the exception rule to be applicable. If they are not, the
      application of the exception rule of Article 81(3) must be refused(53). The four conditions
      of Article 81(3) are also exhaustive. When they are met the exception is applicable and
      may not be made dependant on any other condition. Goals pursued by other Treaty
      provisions can be taken into account to the extent that they can be subsumed under the
      four conditions of Article 81(3)(54).

43.   The assessment under Article 81(3) of benefits flowing from restrictive agreements is in
      principle made within the confines of each relevant market to which the agreement relates.
      The Community competition rules have as their objective the protection of competition on
      the market and cannot be detached from this objective. Moreover, the condition that
      consumers(55) must receive a fair share of the benefits implies in general that efficiencies
      generated by the restrictive agreement within a relevant market must be sufficient to
      outweigh the anti-competitive effects produced by the agreement within that same
      relevant market(56). Negative effects on consumers in one geographic market or product

market cannot normally be balanced against and compensated by positive effects for consumers in another unrelated geographic market or product market. However, where two markets are related, efficiencies achieved on separate markets can be taken into account provided that the group of consumers affected by the restriction and benefiting from the efficiency gains are substantially the same(57). Indeed, in some cases only consumers in a downstream market are affected by the agreement in which case the impact of the agreement on such consumers must be assessed. This is for instance so in the case of purchasing agreements(58).

44.   The assessment of restrictive agreements under Article 81(3) is made within the actual context in which they occur(59) and on the basis of the facts existing at any given point in time. The assessment is sensitive to material changes in the facts. The exception rule of Article 81(3) applies as long as the four conditions are fulfilled and ceases to apply when that is no longer the case(60). When applying Article 81(3) in accordance with these principles it is necessary to take into account the initial sunk investments made by any of the parties and the time needed and the restraints required to commit and recoup an efficiency enhancing investment. Article 81 cannot be applied without taking due account of such ex ante investment. The risk facing the parties and the sunk investment that must be committed to implement the agreement can thus lead to the agreement falling outside Article 81(1) or fulfilling the conditions of Article 81(3), as the case may be, for the period of time required to recoup the investment.

45.   In some cases the restrictive agreement is an irreversible event. Once the restrictive agreement has been implemented the ex ante situation cannot be re-established. In such cases the assessment must be made exclusively on the basis of the facts pertaining at the time of implementation. For instance, in the case of a research and development agreement whereby each party agrees to abandon its respective research project and pool its capabilities with those of another party, it may from an objective point of view be technically and economically impossible to revive a project once it has been abandoned. The assessment of the anti-competitive and pro-competitive effects of the agreement to abandon the individual research projects must therefore be made as of the time of the completion of its implementation. If at that point in time the agreement is compatible with Article 81, for instance because a sufficient number of third parties have competing research and development projects, the parties' agreement to abandon their individual projects remains compatible with Article 81, even if at a later point in time the third party projects fail. However, the prohibition of Article 81 may apply to other parts of the agreement in respect of which the issue of irreversibility does not arise. If for example in addition to joint research and development, the agreement provides for joint exploitation, Article 81 may apply to this part of the agreement if due to subsequent market developments the agreement becomes restrictive of competition and does not (any longer) satisfy the conditions of Article 81(3) taking due account of ex ante sunk investments, cf. the previous paragraph.

46.   Article 81(3) does not exclude a priori certain types of agreements from its scope. As a matter of principle all restrictive agreements that fulfil the four conditions of Article 81(3) are covered by the exception rule(61). However, severe restrictions of competition are unlikely to fulfil the conditions of Article 81(3). Such restrictions are usually black-listed in block exemption regulations or identified as hardcore restrictions in Commission guidelines and notices. Agreements of this nature generally fail (at least) the two first conditions of Article 81(3). They neither create objective economic benefits(62) nor do they benefit consumers(63). For example, a horizontal agreement to fix prices limits output leading to misallocation of resources. It also transfers value from consumers to producers, since it leads to higher prices without producing any countervailing value to

consumers within the relevant market. Moreover, these types of agreements generally also fail the indispensability test under the third condition(64).

47. Any claim that restrictive agreements are justified because they aim at ensuring fair conditions of competition on the market is by nature unfounded and must be discarded(65). The purpose of Article 81 is to protect effective competition by ensuring that markets remain open and competitive. The protection of fair conditions of competition is a task for the legislator in compliance with Community law obligations(66) and not for undertakings to regulate themselves.

3.2. First condition of Article 81(3): Efficiency gains

3.2.1. General remarks

48. According to the first condition of Article 81(3) the restrictive agreement must contribute to improving the production or distribution of goods or to promoting technical or economic progress. The provision refers expressly only to goods, but applies by analogy to services.

49. It follows from the case law of the Court of Justice that only objective benefits can be taken into account(67). This means that efficiencies are not assessed from the subjective point of view of the parties(68). Cost savings that arise from the mere exercise of market power by the parties cannot be taken into account. For instance, when companies agree to fix prices or share markets they reduce output and thereby production costs. Reduced competition may also lead to lower sales and marketing expenditures. Such cost reductions are a direct consequence of a reduction in output and value. The cost reductions in question do not produce any pro-competitive effects on the market. In particular, they do not lead to the creation of value through an integration of assets and activities. They merely allow the undertakings concerned to increase their profits and are therefore irrelevant from the point of view of Article 81(3).

50. The purpose of the first condition of Article 81(3) is to define the types of efficiency gains that can be taken into account and be subject to the further tests of the second and third conditions of Article 81(3). The aim of the analysis is to ascertain what are the objective benefits created by the agreement and what is the economic importance of such efficiencies. Given that for Article 81(3) to apply the pro-competitive effects flowing from the agreement must outweigh its anti-competitive effects, it is necessary to verify what is the link between the agreement and the claimed efficiencies and what is the value of these efficiencies.

51. All efficiency claims must therefore be substantiated so that the following can be verified:
  (a) The nature of the claimed efficiencies;
  (b) The link between the agreement and the efficiencies;
  (c) The likelihood and magnitude of each claimed efficiency; and
  (d) How and when each claimed efficiency would be achieved.

52. Letter (a) allows the decision-maker to verify whether the claimed efficiencies are objective in nature, cf. paragraph 49 above.

53. Letter (b) allows the decision-maker to verify whether there is a sufficient causal link between the restrictive agreement and the claimed efficiencies. This condition normally requires that the efficiencies result from the economic activity that forms the object of the agreement. Such activities may, for example, take the form of distribution, licensing of technology, joint production or joint research and development. To the extent, however, that an agreement has wider efficiency enhancing effects within the relevant market, for example because it leads to a reduction in industry wide costs, these additional benefits are also taken into account.

54.   The causal link between the agreement and the claimed efficiencies must normally also be direct(69). Claims based on indirect effects are as a general rule too uncertain and too remote to be taken into account. A direct causal link exists for instance where a technology transfer agreement allows the licensees to produce new or improved products or a distribution agreement allows products to be distributed at lower cost or valuable services to be produced. An example of indirect effect would be a case where it is claimed that a restrictive agreement allows the undertakings concerned to increase their profits, enabling them to invest more in research and development to the ultimate benefit of consumers. While there may be a link between profitability and research and development, this link is generally not sufficiently direct to be taken into account in the context of Article 81(3).

55.   Letters (c) and (d) allow the decision-maker to verify the value of the claimed efficiencies, which in the context of the third condition of Article 81(3) must be balanced against the anti-competitive effects of the agreement, see paragraph 101 below. Given that Article 81(1) only applies in cases where the agreement has likely negative effects on competition and consumers (in the case of hardcore restrictions such effects are presumed) efficiency claims must be substantiated so that they can be verified. Unsubstantiated claims are rejected.

56.   In the case of claimed cost efficiencies the undertakings invoking the benefit of Article 81(3) must as accurately as reasonably possible calculate or estimate the value of the efficiencies and describe in detail how the amount has been computed. They must also describe the method(s) by which the efficiencies have been or will be achieved. The data submitted must be verifiable so that there can be a sufficient degree of certainty that the efficiencies have materialised or are likely to materialise.

57.   In the case of claimed efficiencies in the form of new or improved products and other non-cost based efficiencies, the undertakings claiming the benefit of Article 81(3) must describe and explain in detail what is the nature of the efficiencies and how and why they constitute an objective economic benefit.

58.   In cases where the agreement has yet to be fully implemented the parties must substantiate any projections as to the date from which the efficiencies will become operational so as to have a significant positive impact in the market.

3.2.2. The different categories of efficiencies

59.   The types of efficiencies listed in Article 81(3) are broad categories which are intended to cover all objective economic efficiencies. There is considerable overlap between the various categories mentioned in Article 81(3) and the same agreement may give rise to several kinds of efficiencies. It is therefore not appropriate to draw clear and firm distinctions between the various categories. For the purpose of these guidelines, a distinction is made between cost efficiencies and efficiencies of a qualitative nature whereby value is created in the form of new or improved products, greater product variety etc.

60.   In general, efficiencies stem from an integration of economic activities whereby undertakings combine their assets to achieve what they could not achieve as efficiently on their own or whereby they entrust another undertaking with tasks that can be performed more efficiently by that other undertaking.

61.   The research and development, production and distribution process may be viewed as a value chain that can be divided into a number of stages. At each stage of this chain an undertaking must make a choice between performing the activity itself, performing it together with (an)other undertaking(s) or outsourcing the activity entirely to (an)other undertaking(s).

62.   In each case where the choice made involves cooperation on the market with another undertaking, an agreement within the meaning of Article 81(1) normally needs to be

concluded. These agreements can be vertical, as is the case where the parties operate at different levels of the value chain or horizontal, as is the case where the firms operate at the same level of the value chain. Both categories of agreements may create efficiencies by allowing the undertakings in question to perform a particular task at lower cost or with higher added value for consumers. Such agreements may also contain or lead to restrictions of competition in which case the prohibition rule of Article 81(1) and the exception rule of Article 81(3) may become relevant.

63. The types of efficiencies mentioned in the following are only examples and are not intended to be exhaustive.

3.2.2.1. Cost efficiencies

64. Cost efficiencies flowing from agreements between undertakings can originate from a number of different sources. One very important source of cost savings is the development of new production technologies and methods. In general, it is when technological leaps are made that the greatest potential for cost savings is achieved. For instance, the introduction of the assembly line led to a very substantial reduction in the cost of producing motor vehicles.

65. Another very important source of efficiency is synergies resulting from an integration of existing assets. When the parties to an agreement combine their respective assets they may be able to attain a cost/output configuration that would not otherwise be possible. The combination of two existing technologies that have complementary strengths may reduce production costs or lead to the production of a higher quality product. For instance, it may be that the production assets of firm A generate a high output per hour but require a relatively high input of raw materials per unit of output, whereas the production assets of firm B generate lower output per hour but require a relatively lower input of raw materials per unit of output. Synergies are created if by establishing a production joint venture combining the production assets of A and B the parties can attain a high(er) level of output per hour with a low(er) input of raw materials per unit of output. Similarly, if one undertaking has optimised one part of the value chain and another undertaking has optimised another part of the value chain, the combination of their operations may lead to lower costs. Firm A may for instance have a highly automated production facility resulting in low production costs per unit whereas B has developed an efficient order processing system. The system allows production to be tailored to customer demand, ensuring timely delivery and reducing warehousing and obsolescence costs. By combining their assets A and B may be able to obtain cost reductions.

66. Cost efficiencies may also result from economies of scale, i.e. declining cost per unit of output as output increases. To give an example: investment in equipment and other assets often has to be made in indivisible blocks. If an undertaking cannot fully utilise a block, its average costs will be higher than if it could do so. For instance, the cost of operating a truck is virtually the same regardless of whether it is almost empty, half-full or full. Agreements whereby undertakings combine their logistics operations may allow them to increase the load factors and reduce the number of vehicles employed. Larger scale may also allow for better division of labour leading to lower unit costs. Firms may achieve economies of scale in respect of all parts of the value chain, including research and development, production, distribution and marketing. Learning economies constitute a related type of efficiency. As experience is gained in using a particular production process or in performing particular tasks, productivity may increase because the process is made to run more efficiently or because the task is performed more quickly.

67. Economies of scope are another source of cost efficiency, which occur when firms achieve cost savings by producing different products on the basis of the same input. Such

efficiencies may arise from the fact that it is possible to use the same components and the same facilities and personnel to produce a variety of products. Similarly, economies of scope may arise in distribution when several types of goods are distributed in the same vehicles. For instance, a producer of frozen pizzas and a producer of frozen vegetables may obtain economies of scope by jointly distributing their products. Both groups of products must be distributed in refrigerated vehicles and it is likely that there are significant overlaps in terms of customers. By combining their operations the two producers may obtain lower distribution costs per distributed unit.

68. Efficiencies in the form of cost reductions can also follow from agreements that allow for better planning of production, reducing the need to hold expensive inventory and allowing for better capacity utilisation. Efficiencies of this nature may for example stem from the use of "just in time" purchasing, i.e. an obligation on a supplier of components to continuously supply the buyer according to its needs thereby avoiding the need for the buyer to maintain a significant stock of components which risks becoming obsolete. Cost savings may also result from agreements that allow the parties to rationalise production across their facilities.

3.2.2.2. Qualitative efficiencies

69. Agreements between undertakings may generate various efficiencies of a qualitative nature which are relevant to the application of Article 81(3). In a number of cases the main efficiency enhancing potential of the agreement is not cost reduction; it is quality improvements and other efficiencies of a qualitative nature. Depending on the individual case such efficiencies may therefore be of equal or greater importance than cost efficiencies.

70. Technical and technological advances form an essential and dynamic part of the economy, generating significant benefits in the form of new or improved goods and services. By cooperating undertakings may be able to create efficiencies that would not have been possible without the restrictive agreement or would have been possible only with substantial delay or at higher cost. Such efficiencies constitute an important source of economic benefits covered by the first condition of Article 81(3). Agreements capable of producing efficiencies of this nature include, in particular, research and development agreements. An example would be A and B creating a joint venture for the development and, if successful, joint production of a cell-based tyre. The puncture of one cell does not affect other cells, which means that there is no risk of collapse of the tyre in the event of a puncture. The tyre is thus safer than traditional tyres. It also means that there is no immediate need to change the tyre and thus to carry a spare. Both types of efficiencies constitute objective benefits within the meaning of the first condition of Article 81(3).

71. In the same way that the combination of complementary assets can give rise to cost savings, combinations of assets may also create synergies that create efficiencies of a qualitative nature. The combination of production assets may for instance lead to the production of higher quality products or products with novel features. This may for instance be the case for licence agreements, and agreements providing for joint production of new or improved goods or services. Licence agreements may, in particular, ensure more rapid dissemination of new technology in the Community and enable the licensee(s) to make available new products or to employ new production techniques that lead to quality improvements. Joint production agreements may, in particular, allow new or improved products or services to be introduced on the market more quickly or at lower cost(70). In the telecommunications sector, for example, cooperation agreements have been held to create efficiencies by making available more quickly new global services(71). In the banking sector cooperation agreements that made available improved facilities for making cross-border payments have also been held to create efficiencies falling within the scope of the first condition of Article 81(3)(72).

72. Distribution agreements may also give rise to qualitative efficiencies. Specialised distributors, for example, may be able to provide services that are better tailored to customer needs or to provide quicker delivery or better quality assurance throughout the distribution chain(73).

3.3. Third condition of Article 81(3): Indispensability of the restrictions

73. According to the third condition of Article 81(3) the restrictive agreement must not impose restrictions, which are not indispensable to the attainment of the efficiencies created by the agreement in question. This condition implies a two-fold test. First, the restrictive agreement as such must be reasonably necessary in order to achieve the efficiencies. Secondly, the individual restrictions of competition that flow from the agreement must also be reasonably necessary for the attainment of the efficiencies.

74. In the context of the third condition of Article 81(3) the decisive factor is whether or not the restrictive agreement and individual restrictions make it possible to perform the activity in question more efficiently than would likely have been the case in the absence of the agreement or the restriction concerned. The question is not whether in the absence of the restriction the agreement would not have been concluded, but whether more efficiencies are produced with the agreement or restriction than in the absence of the agreement or restriction(74).

75. The first test contained in the third condition of Article 81(3) requires that the efficiencies be specific to the agreement in question in the sense that there are no other economically practicable and less restrictive means of achieving the efficiencies. In making this latter assessment the market conditions and business realities facing the parties to the agreement must be taken into account. Undertakings invoking the benefit of Article 81(3) are not required to consider hypothetical or theoretical alternatives. The Commission will not second guess the business judgment of the parties. It will only intervene where it is reasonably clear that there are realistic and attainable alternatives. The parties must only explain and demonstrate why such seemingly realistic and significantly less restrictive alternatives to the agreement would be significantly less efficient.

76. It is particularly relevant to examine whether, having due regard to the circumstances of the individual case, the parties could have achieved the efficiencies by means of another less restrictive type of agreement and, if so, when they would likely be able to obtain the efficiencies. It may also be necessary to examine whether the parties could have achieved the efficiencies on their own. For instance, where the claimed efficiencies take the form of cost reductions resulting from economies of scale or scope the undertakings concerned must explain and substantiate why the same efficiencies would not be likely to be attained through internal growth and price competition. In making this assessment it is relevant to consider, inter alia, what is the minimum efficient scale on the market concerned. The minimum efficient scale is the level of output required to minimise average cost and exhaust economies of scale(75). The larger the minimum efficient scale compared to the current size of either of the parties to the agreement, the more likely it is that the efficiencies will be deemed to be specific to the agreement. In the case of agreements that produce substantial synergies through the combination of complementary assets and capabilities the very nature of the efficiencies give rise to a presumption that the agreement is necessary to attain them.

77. These principles can be illustrated by the following hypothetical example:

A and B combine within a joint venture their respective production technologies to achieve higher output and lower raw material consumption. The joint venture is granted an exclusive licence to their respective production technologies. The parties transfer their existing production facilities to the joint venture. They also transfer key staff in order to ensure that existing learning economies can be exploited and further developed. It is estimated that these economies will reduce production costs by a further 5 %. The output of the joint venture is sold independently by A and B. In this case the indispensability condition necessitates an assessment of whether or not the benefits could be substantially achieved by means of a licence agreement, which would be likely to be less restrictive because A and B would continue to produce independently. In the circumstances described this is unlikely to be the case since under a licence agreement the parties would not be able to benefit in the same seamless and continued way from their respective experience in operating the two technologies, resulting in significant learning economies.

78.   Once it is found that the agreement in question is necessary in order to produce the efficiencies, the indispensability of each restriction of competition flowing from the agreement must be assessed. In this context it must be assessed whether individual restrictions are reasonably necessary in order to produce the efficiencies. The parties to the agreement must substantiate their claim with regard to both the nature of the restriction and its intensity.

79.   A restriction is indispensable if its absence would eliminate or significantly reduce the efficiencies that follow from the agreement or make it significantly less likely that they will materialise. The assessment of alternative solutions must take into account the actual and potential improvement in the field of competition by the elimination of a particular restriction or the application of a less restrictive alternative. The more restrictive the restraint the stricter the test under the third condition(76). Restrictions that are black listed in block exemption regulations or identified as hardcore restrictions in Commission guidelines and notices are unlikely to be considered indispensable.

80.   The assessment of indispensability is made within the actual context in which the agreement operates and must in particular take account of the structure of the market, the economic risks related to the agreement, and the incentives facing the parties. The more uncertain the success of the product covered by the agreement, the more a restriction may be required to ensure that the efficiencies will materialise. Restrictions may also be indispensable in order to align the incentives of the parties and ensure that they concentrate their efforts on the implementation of the agreement. A restriction may for instance be necessary in order to avoid hold-up problems once a substantial sunk investment has been made by one of the parties. Once for instance a supplier has made a substantial relationship-specific investment with a view to supplying a customer with an input, the supplier is locked into the customer. In order to avoid that ex post the customer exploits this dependence to obtain more favourable terms, it may be necessary to impose an obligation not to purchase the component from third parties or to purchase minimum quantities of the component from the supplier(77).

81.   In some cases a restriction may be indispensable only for a certain period of time, in which case the exception of Article 81(3) only applies during that period. In making this assessment it is necessary to take due account of the period of time required for the parties to achieve the efficiencies justifying the application of the exception rule(78). In cases where the benefits cannot be achieved without considerable investment, account must, in particular, be taken of the period of time required to ensure an adequate return on such investment, see also paragraph 44 above.

82.   These principles can be illustrated by the following hypothetical examples:

P produces and distributes frozen pizzas, holding 15 % of the market in Member State X. Deliveries are made directly to retailers. Since most retailers have limited storage capacity, relatively frequent deliveries are required, leading to low capacity utilisation and use of relatively small vehicles. T is a wholesaler of frozen pizzas and other frozen products, delivering to most of the same customers as P. The pizza products distributed by T hold 30 % of the market. T has a fleet of larger vehicles and has excess capacity. P concludes an exclusive distribution agreement with T for Member State X and undertakes to ensure that distributors in other Member States will not sell into T's territory either actively or passively. T undertakes to advertise the products, survey consumer tastes and satisfaction rates and ensure delivery to retailers of all products within 24 hours. The agreement leads to a reduction in total distribution costs of 30 % as capacity is better utilised and duplication of routes is eliminated. The agreement also leads to the provision of additional services to consumers. Restrictions on passive sales are hardcore restrictions under the block exemption regulation on vertical restraints(79) and can only be considered indispensable in exceptional circumstances. The established market position of T and the nature of the obligations imposed on it indicate this is not an exceptional case. The ban on active selling, on the other hand, is likely to be indispensable. T is likely to have less incentive to sell and advertise the P brand, if distributors in other Member States could sell actively in Member State X and thus get a free ride on the efforts of T. This is particularly so, as T also distributes competing brands and thus has the possibility of pushing more of the brands that are the least exposed to free riding.

S is a producer of carbonated soft drinks, holding 40 % of the market. The nearest competitor holds 20 %. S concludes supply agreements with customers accounting for 25 % of demand, whereby they undertake to purchase exclusively from S for 5 years. S concludes agreements with other customers accounting for 15 % of demand whereby they are granted quarterly target rebates, if their purchases exceed certain individually fixed targets. S claims that the agreements allow it to predict demand more accurately and thus to better plan production, reducing raw material storage and warehousing costs and avoiding supply shortages. Given the market position of S and the combined coverage of the restrictions, the restrictions are very unlikely to be considered indispensable. The exclusive purchasing obligation exceeds what is required to plan production and the same is true of the target rebate scheme. Predictability of demand can be achieved by less restrictive means. S could, for example, provide incentives for customers to order large quantities at a time by offering quantity rebates or by offering a rebate to customers that place firm orders in advance for delivery on specified dates.

3.4. Second condition of Article 81(3): Fair share for consumers

3.4.1. General remarks

83.   According to the second condition of Article 81(3) consumers must receive a fair share of the efficiencies generated by the restrictive agreement.

84.   The concept of "consumers" encompasses all direct or indirect users of the products covered by the agreement, including producers that use the products as an input, wholesalers, retailers and final consumers, i.e. natural persons who are acting for purposes which can be regarded as outside their trade or profession. In other words, consumers within the meaning of Article 81(3) are the customers of the parties to the agreement and subsequent purchasers. These customers can be undertakings as in the case of buyers of industrial machinery or an input for further processing or final consumers as for instance in the case of buyers of impulse ice-cream or bicycles.

85.   The concept of "fair share" implies that the pass-on of benefits must at least compensate consumers for any actual or likely negative impact caused to them by the restriction of competition found under Article 81(1). In line with the overall objective of Article 81 to prevent anti-competitive agreements, the net effect of the agreement must at least be neutral from the point of view of those consumers directly or likely affected by the

agreement(80). If such consumers are worse off following the agreement, the second condition of Article 81(3) is not fulfilled. The positive effects of an agreement must be balanced against and compensate for its negative effects on consumers(81). When that is the case consumers are not harmed by the agreement. Moreover, society as a whole benefits where the efficiencies lead either to fewer resources being used to produce the output consumed or to the production of more valuable products and thus to a more efficient allocation of resources.

86.   It is not required that consumers receive a share of each and every efficiency gain identified under the first condition. It suffices that sufficient benefits are passed on to compensate for the negative effects of the restrictive agreement. In that case consumers obtain a fair share of the overall benefits(82). If a restrictive agreement is likely to lead to higher prices, consumers must be fully compensated through increased quality or other benefits. If not, the second condition of Article 81(3) is not fulfilled.

87.   The decisive factor is the overall impact on consumers of the products within the relevant market and not the impact on individual members of this group of consumers(83). In some cases a certain period of time may be required before the efficiencies materialise. Until such time the agreement may have only negative effects. The fact that pass-on to the consumer occurs with a certain time lag does not in itself exclude the application of Article 81(3). However, the greater the time lag, the greater must be the efficiencies to compensate also for the loss to consumers during the period preceding the pass-on.

88.   In making this assessment it must be taken into account that the value of a gain for consumers in the future is not the same as a present gain for consumers. The value of saving 100 euro today is greater than the value of saving the same amount a year later. A gain for consumers in the future therefore does not fully compensate for a present loss to consumers of equal nominal size. In order to allow for an appropriate comparison of a present loss to consumers with a future gain to consumers, the value of future gains must be discounted. The discount rate applied must reflect the rate of inflation, if any, and lost interest as an indication of the lower value of future gains.

89.   In other cases the agreement may enable the parties to obtain the efficiencies earlier than would otherwise be possible. In such circumstances it is necessary to take account of the likely negative impact on consumers within the relevant market once this lead-time has lapsed. If through the restrictive agreement the parties obtain a strong position on the market, they may be able to charge a significantly higher price than would otherwise have been the case. For the second condition of Article 81(3) to be satisfied the benefit to consumers of having earlier access to the products must be equally significant. This may for instance be the case where an agreement allows two tyre manufacturers to bring to market three years earlier a new substantially safer tyre but at the same time, by increasing their market power, allows them to raise prices by 5 %. In such a case it is likely that having early access to a substantially improved product outweighs the price increase.

90.   The second condition of Article 81(3) incorporates a sliding scale. The greater the restriction of competition found under Article 81(1) the greater must be the efficiencies and the pass-on to consumers. This sliding scale approach implies that if the restrictive effects of an agreement are relatively limited and the efficiencies are substantial it is likely that a fair share of the cost savings will be passed on to consumers. In such cases it is therefore normally not necessary to engage in a detailed analysis of the second condition of Article 81(3), provided that the three other conditions for the application of this provision are fulfilled.

91.   If, on the other hand, the restrictive effects of the agreement are substantial and the cost savings are relatively insignificant, it is very unlikely that the second condition of

Article 81(3) will be fulfilled. The impact of the restriction of competition depends on the intensity of the restriction and the degree of competition that remains following the agreement.

92. If the agreement has both substantial anti-competitive effects and substantial pro-competitive effects a careful analysis is required. In the application of the balancing test in such cases it must be taken into account that competition is an important long-term driver of efficiency and innovation. Undertakings that are not subject to effective competitive constraints – such as for instance dominant firms – have less incentive to maintain or build on the efficiencies. The more substantial the impact of the agreement on competition, the more likely it is that consumers will suffer in the long run.

93. The following two sections describe in more detail the analytical framework for assessing consumer pass-on of efficiency gains. The first section deals with cost efficiencies, whereas the section that follows covers other types of efficiencies such as new or improved products (qualitative efficiencies). The framework, which is developed in these two sections, is particularly important in cases where it is not immediately obvious that the competitive harms exceed the benefits to consumers or vice versa(84).

94. In the application of the principles set out below the Commission will have regard to the fact that in many cases it is difficult to accurately calculate the consumer pass-on rate and other types of consumer pass-on. Undertakings are only required to substantiate their claims by providing estimates and other data to the extent reasonably possible, taking account of the circumstances of the individual case.

3.4.2. Pass-on and balancing of cost efficiencies

95. When markets, as is normally the case, are not perfectly competitive, undertakings are able to influence the market price to a greater or lesser extent by altering their output(85). They may also be able to price discriminate amongst customers.

96. Cost efficiencies may in some circumstances lead to increased output and lower prices for the affected consumers. If due to cost efficiencies the undertakings in question can increase profits by expanding output, consumer pass-on may occur. In assessing the extent to which cost efficiencies are likely to be passed on to consumers and the outcome of the balancing test contained in Article 81(3) the following factors are in particular taken into account:
     (a) The characteristics and structure of the market,
     (b) The nature and magnitude of the efficiency gains,
     (c) The elasticity of demand, and
     (d) The magnitude of the restriction of competition.
All factors must normally be considered. Since Article 81(3) only applies in cases where competition on the market is being appreciably restricted, see paragraph 24 above, there can be no presumption that residual competition will ensure that consumers receive a fair share of the benefits. However, the degree of competition remaining on the market and the nature of this competition influences the likelihood of pass-on.

97. The greater the degree of residual competition the more likely it is that individual undertakings will try to increase their sales by passing on cost efficiencies. If undertakings compete mainly on price and are not subject to significant capacity constraints, pass-on may occur relatively quickly. If competition is mainly on capacity and capacity adaptations occur with a certain time lag, pass-on will be slower. Pass-on is also likely to be slower when the market structure is conducive to tacit collusion(86). If competitors are likely to retaliate against an increase in output by one or more parties to the agreement, the incentive to increase output may be tempered, unless the competitive advantage conferred by the efficiencies is such that the undertakings concerned have an incentive to

break away from the common policy adopted on the market by the members of the oligopoly. In other words, the efficiencies generated by the agreement may turn the undertakings concerned into so-called "mavericks"(87).

98.   The nature of the efficiency gains also plays an important role. According to economic theory undertakings maximise their profits by selling units of output until marginal revenue equals marginal cost. Marginal revenue is the change in total revenue resulting from selling an additional unit of output and marginal cost is the change in total cost resulting from producing that additional unit of output. It follows from this principle that as a general rule output and pricing decisions of a profit maximising undertaking are not determined by its fixed costs (i.e. costs that do not vary with the rate of production) but by its variable costs (i.e. costs that vary with the rate of production). After fixed costs are incurred and capacity is set, pricing and output decisions are determined by variable cost and demand conditions. Take for instance a situation in which two companies each produce two products on two production lines operating only at half their capacities. A specialisation agreement may allow the two undertakings to specialise in producing one of the two products and scrap their second production line for the other product. At the same time the specialisation may allow the companies to reduce variable input and stocking costs. Only the latter savings will have a direct effect on the pricing and output decisions of the undertakings, as they will influence the marginal costs of production. The scrapping by each undertaking of one of their production lines will not reduce their variable costs and will not have an impact on their production costs. It follows that undertakings may have a direct incentive to pass on to consumers in the form of higher output and lower prices efficiencies that reduce marginal costs, whereas they have no such direct incentive with regard to efficiencies that reduce fixed costs. Consumers are therefore more likely to receive a fair share of the cost efficiencies in the case of reductions in variable costs than they are in the case of reductions in fixed costs.

99.   The fact that undertakings may have an incentive to pass on certain types of cost efficiencies does not imply that the pass-on rate will necessarily be 100 %. The actual pass-on rate depends on the extent to which consumers respond to changes in price, i.e. the elasticity of demand. The greater the increase in demand caused by a decrease in price, the greater the pass-on rate. This follows from the fact that the greater the additional sales caused by a price reduction due to an increase in output the more likely it is that these sales will offset the loss of revenue caused by the lower price resulting from the increase in output. In the absence of price discrimination the lowering of prices affects all units sold by the undertaking, in which case marginal revenue is less than the price obtained for the marginal product. If the undertakings concerned are able to charge different prices to different customers, i.e. price discriminate, pass-on will normally only benefit price-sensitive consumers(88).

100.   It must also be taken into account that efficiency gains often do not affect the whole cost structure of the undertakings concerned. In such event the impact on the price to consumers is reduced. If for example an agreement allows the parties to reduce production costs by 6 %, but production costs only make up one third of the costs on the basis of which prices are determined, the impact on the product price is 2 %, assuming that the full amount is passed-on.

101.   Finally, and very importantly, it is necessary to balance the two opposing forces resulting from the restriction of competition and the cost efficiencies. On the one hand, any increase in market power caused by the restrictive agreement gives the undertakings concerned the ability and incentive to raise price. On the other hand, the types of cost efficiencies that are taken into account may give the undertakings concerned an incentive to reduce price, see paragraph 98 above. The effects of these two opposing forces must be balanced

against each other. It is recalled in this regard that the consumer pass-on condition incorporates a sliding scale. When the agreement causes a substantial reduction in the competitive constraint facing the parties, extraordinarily large cost efficiencies are normally required for sufficient pass-on to occur.

3.4.3. Pass-on and balancing of other types of efficiencies

102. Consumer pass-on can also take the form of qualitative efficiencies such as new and improved products, creating sufficient value for consumers to compensate for the anti-competitive effects of the agreement, including a price increase.

103. Any such assessment necessarily requires value judgment. It is difficult to assign precise values to dynamic efficiencies of this nature. However, the fundamental objective of the assessment remains the same, namely to ascertain the overall impact of the agreement on the consumers within the relevant market. Undertakings claiming the benefit of Article 81(3) must substantiate that consumers obtain countervailing benefits (see in this respect paragraphs 57 and 86 above).

104. The availability of new and improved products constitutes an important source of consumer welfare. As long as the increase in value stemming from such improvements exceeds any harm from a maintenance or an increase in price caused by the restrictive agreement, consumers are better off than without the agreement and the consumer pass-on requirement of Article 81(3) is normally fulfilled. In cases where the likely effect of the agreement is to increase prices for consumers within the relevant market it must be carefully assessed whether the claimed efficiencies create real value for consumers in that market so as to compensate for the adverse effects of the restriction of competition.

3.5. Fourth condition of Article 81(3): No elimination of competition

105. According to the fourth condition of Article 81(3) the agreement must not afford the undertakings concerned the possibility of eliminating competition in respect of a substantial part of the products concerned. Ultimately the protection of rivalry and the competitive process is given priority over potentially pro-competitive efficiency gains which could result from restrictive agreements. The last condition of Article 81(3) recognises the fact that rivalry between undertakings is an essential driver of economic efficiency, including dynamic efficiencies in the shape of innovation. In other words, the ultimate aim of Article 81 is to protect the competitive process. When competition is eliminated the competitive process is brought to an end and short-term efficiency gains are outweighed by longer-term losses stemming inter alia from expenditures incurred by the incumbent to maintain its position (rent seeking), misallocation of resources, reduced innovation and higher prices.

106. The concept in Article 81(3) of elimination of competition in respect of a substantial part of the products concerned is an autonomous Community law concept specific to Article 81(3)(89). However, in the application of this concept it is necessary to take account of the relationship between Article 81 and Article 82. According to settled case law the application of Article 81(3) cannot prevent the application of Article 82 of the Treaty(90). Moreover, since Articles 81 and 82 both pursue the aim of maintaining effective competition on the market, consistency requires that Article 81(3) be interpreted as precluding any application of this provision to restrictive agreements that constitute an abuse of a dominant position(91)(92). However, not all restrictive agreements concluded by a dominant undertaking constitute an abuse of a dominant position. This is for instance the case where a dominant undertaking is party to a non-full function joint venture(93), which is found to be restrictive of competition but at the same time involves a substantial integration of assets.

107. Whether competition is being eliminated within the meaning of the last condition of Article 81(3) depends on the degree of competition existing prior to the agreement and on the impact of the restrictive agreement on competition, i.e. the reduction in competition that the agreement brings about. The more competition is already weakened in the market concerned, the slighter the further reduction required for competition to be eliminated within the meaning of Article 81(3). Moreover, the greater the reduction of competition caused by the agreement, the greater the likelihood that competition in respect of a substantial part of the products concerned risks being eliminated.

108. The application of the last condition of Article 81(3) requires a realistic analysis of the various sources of competition in the market, the level of competitive constraint that they impose on the parties to the agreement and the impact of the agreement on this competitive constraint. Both actual and potential competition must be considered.

109. While market shares are relevant, the magnitude of remaining sources of actual competition cannot be assessed exclusively on the basis of market share. More extensive qualitative and quantitative analysis is normally called for. The capacity of actual competitors to compete and their incentive to do so must be examined. If, for example, competitors face capacity constraints or have relatively higher costs of production their competitive response will necessarily be limited.

110. In the assessment of the impact of the agreement on competition it is also relevant to examine its influence on the various parameters of competition. The last condition for exception under Article 81(3) is not fulfilled, if the agreement eliminates competition in one of its most important expressions. This is particularly the case when an agreement eliminates price competition(94) or competition in respect of innovation and development of new products.

111. The actual market conduct of the parties can provide insight into the impact of the agreement. If following the conclusion of the agreement the parties have implemented and maintained substantial price increases or engaged in other conduct indicative of the existence of a considerable degree of market power, it is an indication that the parties are not subject to any real competitive pressure and that competition has been eliminated with regard to a substantial part of the products concerned.

112. Past competitive interaction may also provide an indication of the impact of the agreement on future competitive interaction. An undertaking may be able to eliminate competition within the meaning of Article 81(3) by concluding an agreement with a competitor that in the past has been a "maverick"(95). Such an agreement may change the competitive incentives and capabilities of the competitor and thereby remove an important source of competition in the market.

113. In cases involving differentiated products, i.e. products that differ in the eyes of consumers, the impact of the agreement may depend on the competitive relationship between the products sold by the parties to the agreement. When undertakings offer differentiated products the competitive constraint that individual products impose on each other differs according to the degree of substitutability between them. It must therefore be considered what is the degree of substitutability between the products offered by the parties, i.e. what is the competitive constraint that they impose on each other. The more the products of the parties to the agreement are close substitutes the greater the likely restrictive effect of the agreement. In other words, the more substitutable the products the greater the likely change brought about by the agreement in terms of restriction of competition on the market and the more likely it is that competition in respect of a substantial part of the products concerned risks being eliminated.

114. While sources of actual competition are usually the most important, as they are most easily verified, sources of potential competition must also be taken into account. The assessment of potential competition requires an analysis of barriers to entry facing undertakings that are not already competing within the relevant market. Any assertions by the parties that there are low barriers to market entry must be supported by information identifying the sources of potential competition and the parties must also substantiate why these sources constitute a real competitive pressure on the parties.

115. In the assessment of entry barriers and the real possibility for new entry on a significant scale, it is relevant to examine, inter alia, the following:
    (i)   The regulatory framework with a view to determining its impact on new entry.
    (ii)   The cost of entry including sunk costs. Sunk costs are those that cannot be recovered if the entrant subsequently exits the market. The higher the sunk costs the higher the commercial risk for potential entrants.
    (iii) The minimum efficient scale within the industry, i.e. the rate of output where average costs are minimised. If the minimum efficient scale is large compared to the size of the market, efficient entry is likely to be more costly and risky.
    (iv)   The competitive strengths of potential entrants. Effective entry is particularly likely where potential entrants have access to at least as cost efficient technologies as the incumbents or other competitive advantages that allow them to compete effectively. When potential entrants are on the same or an inferior technological trajectory compared to the incumbents and possess no other significant competitive advantage entry is more risky and less effective.
    (v)   The position of buyers and their ability to bring onto the market new sources of competition. It is irrelevant that certain strong buyers may be able to extract more favourable conditions from the parties to the agreement than their weaker competitors(96). The presence of strong buyers can only serve to counter a prima facie finding of elimination of competition if it is likely that the buyers in question will pave the way for effective new entry.
    (vi)   The likely response of incumbents to attempted new entry. Incumbents may for example through past conduct have acquired a reputation of aggressive behaviour, having an impact on future entry.
    (vii) The economic outlook for the industry may be an indicator of its longer-term attractiveness. Industries that are stagnating or in decline are less attractive candidates for entry than industries characterised by growth.
    (viii) Past entry on a significant scale or the absence thereof.

116. The above principles can be illustrated by the following hypothetical examples, which are not intended to establish thresholds:

Firm A is brewer, holding 70 % of the relevant market, comprising the sale of beer through cafés and other on-trade premises. Over the past 5 years A has increased its market share from 60 %. There are four other competitors in the market, B, C, D and E with market shares of 10 %, 10 %, 5 % and 5 %. No new entry has occurred in the recent past and price changes implemented by A have generally been followed by competitors. A concludes agreements with 20 % of the on-trade premises representing 40 % of sales volumes whereby the contracting parties undertake to purchase beer only from A for a period of 5 years. The agreements raise the costs and reduce the revenues of rivals, which are foreclosed from the most attractive outlets. Given the market position of A, which has been strengthened in recent years, the absence of new entry and the already weak position of competitors it is likely that competition in the market is eliminated within the meaning of Article 81(3).

Shipping firms A, B, C, and D, holding collectively more than 70 % of the relevant market, conclude an agreement whereby they agree to coordinate their schedules and their tariffs. Following the implementation of the agreement prices rise between 30 % and 100 %. There are four other suppliers, the largest holding about 14 % of the relevant market. There has been no new entry in recent years and the parties to the agreement did not lose significant market share following the price increases. The existing competitors brought no significant new capacity to the market and no new entry occurred. In light of the market position of the parties and the absence of competitive response to their joint conduct it can reasonably be concluded that the parties to the agreement are not subject to real competitive pressures and that the agreement affords them the possibility of eliminating competition within the meaning of Article 81(3).

A is a producer of electric appliances for professional users with a market share of 65 % of a relevant national market. B is a competing manufacturer with 5 % market share which has developed a new type of motor that is more powerful while consuming less electricity. A and B conclude an agreement whereby they establish a production joint venture for the production of the new motor. B undertakes to grant an exclusive licence to the joint venture. The joint venture combines the new technology of B with the efficient manufacturing and quality control process of A. There is one other main competitor with 15 % of the market. Another competitor with 5 % market share has recently been acquired by C, a major international producer of competing electric appliances, which itself owns efficient technologies. C has thus far not been active on the market mainly due to the fact that local presence and servicing is desired by customers. Through the acquisition C gains access to the service organisation required to penetrate the market. The entry of C is likely to ensure that competition is not being eliminated.

....

(1) In the following the term "agreement" includes concerted practices and decisions of associations of undertakings.
(2) OJ L 1, 4.1.2003, p. 1.
(3) All existing block exemption regulations and Commission notices are available on the DG Competition web-site: http://www.europa.eu.int/comm/ dgs/competition
(4) See paragraph 36 below.
(5) See Commission Notice on Guidelines on vertical restraints (OJ C 291, 13.10.2000, p. 1), Commission Notice on Guidelines on the application of Article 81 of the Treaty to horizontal cooperation agreements (OJ C 3, 6.1.2001, p. 2), and Commission Notice on Guidelines on the application of Article 81 of the Treaty to technology transfer agreements, not yet published.
(6) The concept of effect on trade between Member States is dealt with in separate guidelines.
(7) In the following the term "restriction" includes the prevention and distortion of competition.
(8) According to Article 81(2) such agreements are automatically void.
(9) Article 81(1) prohibits both actual and potential anti-competitive effects, see e.g. Case C-7/95 P, John Deere, [1998] ECR I-3111, paragraph 77.
(10) See Case T-65/98, Van den Bergh Foods, [2003] ECR II . . ., paragraph 107 and Case T-112/99, Métropole télévision (M6) and others, [2001] ECR II-2459, paragraph 74, where the Court of First Instance held that it is only in the precise framework of Article 81(3) that the pro- and anti-competitive aspects of a restriction may be weighed.
(11) See note above.
(12) See e.g. Case C-49/92 P, Anic Partecipazioni, [1999] ECR I-4125, paragraph 116; and Joined Cases 40/73 to 48/73 and others, Suiker Unie, [1975] ECR page 1663, paragraph 173.
(13) See in this respect paragraph 108 of the judgment in Anic Partecipazioni cited in the previous note and Case C-277/87, Sandoz Prodotti, [1990] ECR I-45.
(14) See in this respect e.g. Case 14/68, Walt Wilhelm, [1969] ECR 1, and more recently Case T-203/01, Michelin (II), [2003] ECR II . . ., paragraph 112.
(15) See Joined Cases T-25/95 and others, Cimenteries CBR, [2000] ECR II-491, paragraphs 1849 and 1852; and Joined Cases T-202/98 and others, British Sugar, [2001] ECR II-2035, paragraphs 58 to 60.
(16) See to that effect Case C-453/99, Courage v Crehan, [2001] ECR I-6297, and paragraph 3444 of the judgment in Cimenteries CBR cited in the previous note.
(17) See in this respect Joined Cases C-2/01 P and C-3/01 P, Bundesverband der Arzneimittel-Importeure, [2004] ECR I . . ., paragraph 102.

(18) See e.g. Joined Cases 25/84 and 26/84, Ford, [1985] ECR 2725.

(19) See in this respect paragraph 141 of the judgment in Bundesverband der Arzneimittel-Importeure cited in note.

(20) See Case 56/65, Société Technique Minière, [1966] ECR 337, and paragraph 76 of the judgment in John Deere, cited in note 9.

(21) See in this respect e.g. Joined Cases 56/64 and 58/66, Consten and Grundig, [1966] ECR 429.

(22) See in this respect e.g. Commission Decision in Elopak/Metal Box – Odin (OJ 1990 L 209, p. 15) and in TPS (OJ 1999 L 90, p. 6).

(23) See in this respect the judgment in Société Technique Minière cited in note 20 and Case 258/78, Nungesser, [1982] ECR 2015.

(24) See rule 10 in paragraph 119 of the Guidelines on vertical restraints cited in note above, according to which inter alia passive sales restrictions – a hardcore restraint – are held to fall outside Article 81(1) for a period of 2 years when the restraint is linked to opening up new product or geographic markets.

(25) See e.g. paragraph 99 of the judgment in Anic Partecipazioni cited in note 12.

(26) See paragraph 46 below.

(27) See Joined Cases 29/83 and 30/83, CRAM and Rheinzink, [1984] ECR 1679, paragraph 26, and Joined Cases 96/82 and others, ANSEAU-NAVEWA, [1983] ECR 3369, paragraphs 23=N25.

(28) See the Guidelines on horizontal cooperation agreements, cited in note, paragraph 25, and Article 5 of Commission Regulation 2658/2000 on the application of Article 81(3) of the Treaty to categories of specialisation agreements (OJ L 304, 5.12.2000, p. 3).

(29) See Article 4 Commission Regulation 2790/1999 on the application of Article 81(3) of the Treaty to categories of vertical agreements and concerted practices (OJ L 336, 29.12.1999, p. 21) and the Guidelines on Vertical Restraints, cited in note, paragraph 46 et seq. See also Case 279/87, Tipp-Ex, [1990] ECR I-261, and Case T-62/98, Volkswagen v Commission, [2000] ECR II-2707, paragraph 178.

(30) See paragraph 77 of the judgment in John Deere cited in note 9.

(31) It is not sufficient in itself that the agreement restricts the freedom of action of one or more of the parties, see paragraphs 76 and 77 of the judgment in Métropole television (M6) cited in note 10. This is in line with the fact that the object of Article 81 is to protect competition on the market for the benefit of consumers.

(32) See e.g. Case 5/69, Völk, [1969] ECR 295, paragraph 7. Guidance on the issue of appreciability can be found in the Commission Notice on agreements of minor importance which do not appreciably restrict competition under Article 81(1) of the Treaty (OJ C 368, 22.12.2001, p. 13) The notice defines appreciability in a negative way. Agreements, which fall outside the scope of the de minimis notice, do not necessarily have appreciable restrictive effects. An individual assessment is required.

(33) See in this respect Joined Cases T-374/94 and others, European Night Services, [1998] ECR II-3141.

(34) See note 32.

(35) See in this respect Commission notice on the definition of the relevant market for the purposes of Community competition law (OJ C 372, 9.12.1997, p. 1).

(36) For the reference in the OJ see note 5.

(37) See paragraph 104 of the judgment in Métropole télévision (M6) and others, cited in note 10.

(38) See e.g. Case C-399/93, Luttikhuis, [1995] ECR I-4515, paragraphs 12 to 14.

(39) See in this respect paragraphs 118 et seq. of the Métropole television judgment cited in note 10.

(40) See paragraph 107 of the judgment in Métropole télévision (M6) judgement cited in note 10.

(41) See e.g. Commission Decision in Elopak/Metal Box – Odin cited in note 22.

(42) See Case 161/84, Pronuptia, [1986] ECR 353.

(43) See note 22. The decision was upheld by the Court of First Instance in the judgment in Métropole télévision (M6) cited in note 10.

(44) Cost savings and other gains to the parties that arise from the mere exercise of market power do not give rise to objective benefits and cannot be taken into account, cf. paragraph 49 below.

(45) See the judgment in Consten and Grundig, cited in note 21.

(46) The fact that an agreement is block exempted does not in itself indicate that the individual agreement is caught by Article 81(1).

(47) See e.g. Case C-234/89, Delimitis, [1991] ECR I-935, paragraph 46.

(48) Article 36(4) of Regulation 1/2003 has, inter alia, repealed Article 5 of Regulation 1017/68 applying rules of competition to transport by rail, road and inland waterway. However, the Commission's case practice adopted under Regulation 1017/68 remains relevant for the purposes of applying Article 81(3) in the inland transport sector.

(49) See paragraph 42 below.

(50) See the judgment in Société Technique Minière cited in note 20.

(51) See in this respect Case 319/82, Kerpen & Kerpen, [1983] ECR 4173, paragraphs 11 and 12.

(52) See e.g. Case T-185/00 and others, Métropole télévision SA (M6), [2002] ECR II-3805, paragraph 86, Case T-17/93, Matra, ECR [1994] II-595, paragraph 85; and Joined Cases 43/82 and 63/82, VBVB and VBBB, [1984] ECR 19, paragraph 61.

(53) See Case T-213/00, CMA CGM and others, [2003] ECR II . . ., paragraph 226.

(54) See to that effect implicitly paragraph 139 of the Matra judgment cited in note 52 and Case 26/76, Metro (I), [1977] ECR 1875, paragraph 43.

(55) As to the concept of consumers see paragraph 84 below where it is stated that consumers are the customers of the parties and subsequent buyers. The parties themselves are not "consumers" for the purposes of Article 81(3).

(56) The test is market specific, see to that effect Case T-131/99, Shaw, [2002] ECR II-2023, paragraph 163, where the Court of First Instance held that the assessment under Article 81(3) had to be made within the same analytical framework as that used for assessing the restrictive effects, and Case C-360/92 P, Publishers Association, [1995] ECR I-23, paragraph 29, where in a case where the relevant market was wider than national the Court of Justice held that in the application of Article 81(3) it was not correct only to consider the effects on the national territory.

(57) In Case T-86/95, Compagnie Générale Maritime and others, [2002] ECR II-1011, paragraphs 343 to 345, the Court of First Instance held that Article 81(3) does not require that the benefits are linked to a specific market and that in appropriate cases regard must be had to benefits "for every other market on which the agreement in question might have beneficial effects, and even, in a more general sense, for any service the quality or efficiency of which might be improved by the existence of that agreement". Importantly, however, in this case the affected group of consumers was the same. The case concerned intermodal transport services encompassing a bundle of, inter alia, inland and maritime transportation provided to shipping companies across the Community. The restrictions related to inland transport services, which were held to constitute a separate market, whereas the benefits were claimed to occur in relation to maritime transport services. Both services were demanded by shippers requiring intermodal transport services between northern Europe and South-East and East Asia. The judgment in CMA CGM, cited in note 53 above, also concerned a situation where the agreement, while covering several distinct services, affected the same group of consumers, namely shippers of containerised cargo between northern Europe and the Far East. Under the agreement the parties fixed charges and surcharges relating to inland transport services, port services and maritime transport services. The Court of First Instance held (cf. paragraphs 226 to 228) that in the circumstances of the case there was no need to define relevant markets for the purpose of applying Article 81(3). The agreement was restrictive of competition by its very object and there were no benefits for consumers.

(58) See paragraphs 126 and 132 of the Guidelines on horizontal co-operation agreements cited in note 5 above.

(59) See the Ford judgment cited in note 18.

(60) See in this respect for example Commission Decision in TPS (OJ L 90, 2.4.1999, p. 6). Similarly, the prohibition of Article 81(1) also only applies as long as the agreement has a restrictive object or restrictive effects.

(61) See paragraph 85 of the Matra judgment cited in note 52.

(62) As to this requirement see paragraph 49 below.

(63) See e.g. Case T-29/92, Vereniging van Samenwerkende Prijsregelende Organisaties in de Bouwnijverheid (SPO), [1995] ECR II-289.

(64) See e.g. Case 258/78, Nungesser, [1982] ECR 2015, paragraph 77, concerning absolute territorial protection.

(65) See in this respect e.g. the judgment in SPO cited in note 63.

(66) National measures must, inter alia, comply with the Treaty rules on free movement of goods, services, persons and capital.

(67) See e.g. the judgment in Consten and Grundig cited in note 21.

(68) See in this respect Commission Decision in Van den Bergh Foods (OJ 1998 L 246, p. 1).

(69) See in this respect Commission Decision in Glaxo Wellcome (OJ 2001 L 302, p. 1).

(70) See e.g. Commission Decision in GEAE/P& W (OJ 2000 L 58, p. 16); in British Interactive Broadcasting/Open (OJ 1999 L 312, p. 1) and in Asahi/Saint Gobain (OJ 1994 L 354, page 87).

(71) See e.g. Commission Decision in Atlas (OJ 1996 L 239, p. 23), and in Phoenix/Global One (OJ 1996 L 239, p. 57).

(72) See e.g. Commission Decision in Uniform Eurocheques (OJ 1985 L 35, p. 43).

(73) See e.g. Commission Decision in Cégétel + 4 (OJ 1999 L 88, p. 26).

(74) As to the former question, which may be relevant in the context of Article 81(1), see paragraph 18 above.

(75) Scale economies are normally exhausted at a certain point. Thereafter average costs will stabilise and eventually rise due to, for example, capacity constraints and bottlenecks.

(76) See in this respect paragraphs 392 to 395 of the judgment in Compagnie Générale Maritime cited in note 57.

(77) See for more detail paragraph 116 of the Guidelines on Vertical Restraints cited in note 5.

(78) See Joined Cases T-374/94 and others, European Night Services, [1998] ECR II-3141, paragraph 230.

(79) See Commission Regulation No 2790/1999 on the application of Article 81(3) of the Treaty on categories of vertical agreements and concerted practices (OJ 1999 L 336, page 21).

(80) See in this respect the judgment in Consten and Grundig cited in note 21, where the Court of Justice held that the improvements within the meaning of the first condition of Article 81(3) must show appreciable objective advantages of such a character as to compensate for the disadvantages which they cause in the field of competition.

(81) It is recalled that positive and negative effects on consumers are in principle balanced within each relevant market (cf. paragraph 43 above).

(82) See in this respect paragraph 48 of the Metro (I) judgment cited in note 54.

(83) See paragraph 163 of the judgment in Shaw cited in note 56.

(84) In the following sections, for convenience the competitive harm is referred to in terms of higher prices; competitive harm could also mean lower quality, less variety or lower innovation than would otherwise have occurred.

(85) In perfectly competitive markets individual undertakings are price-takers. They sell their products at the market price, which is determined by overall supply and demand. The output of the individual undertaking is so small that any individual undertaking's change in output does not affect the market price.

(86) Undertakings collude tacitly when in an oligopolistic market they are able to coordinate their action on the market without resorting to an explicit cartel agreement.

(87) This term refers to undertakings that constrain the pricing behaviour of other undertakings in the market who might otherwise have tacitly colluded.

(88) The restrictive agreement may even allow the undertakings in question to charge a higher price to customers with a low elasticity of demand.

(89) See Joined Cases T-191/98, T-212/98 and T-214/98, Atlantic Container Line (TACA), [2003] ECR II-. . ., paragraph 939, and Case T-395/94, Atlantic Container Line, [2002] ECR II-875, paragraph 330.

(90) See Joined Cases C-395/96 P and C-396/96 P, Compagnie maritime belge, [2000] ECR I-1365, paragraph 130. Similarly, the application of Article 81(3) does not prevent the application of the Treaty rules on the free movement of goods, services, persons and capital. These provisions are in certain circumstances applicable to agreements, decisions and concerted practices within the meaning of Article 81(1), see to that effect Case C-309/99, Wouters, [2002] ECR I-1577, paragraph 120.

(91) See in this respect Case T-51/89, Tetra Pak (I), [1990] ECR II-309, and Joined Cases T-191/98, T-212/98 and T-214/98, Atlantic Container Line (TACA), [2003] ECR II-. . ., paragraph 1456.

(92) This is how paragraph 135 of the Guidelines on vertical restraints and paragraphs 36, 71, 105, 134 and 155 of the Guidelines on horizontal cooperation agreements, cited in note 5, should be understood when they state that in principle restrictive agreements concluded by dominant undertakings cannot be exempted.

(93) Full function joint ventures, i.e. joint ventures that perform on a lasting basis all the functions of an autonomous economic entity, are covered by Council Regulation (EEC) No 4064/89 on the control of concentrations between undertakings (OJ 1990 L 257, p 13).

(94) See paragraph 21 of the judgment in Metro (I) cited in note 54.

(95) See paragraph 97 above.

(96) See in this respect Case T-228/97, Irish Sugar, [1999] ECR II-2969, paragraph 101.

COMMISSION GUIDANCE

on the Commission's enforcement priorities in applying [Article 102 TFEU] to abusive exclusionary conduct by dominant undertakings[1]

OJ C 45, 24.2.2009, P. 7

I. INTRODUCTION

1. Article 82 of the Treaty establishing the European Community ("Article 82") prohibits abuses of a dominant position. In accordance with the case-law, it is not in itself illegal for an undertaking to be in a dominant position and such a dominant undertaking is entitled to compete on the merits. However, the undertaking concerned has a special responsibility not to allow its conduct to impair genuine undistorted competition on the common market. Article 82 is the legal basis for a crucial component of competition policy and its effective enforcement helps markets to work better for the benefit of businesses and consumers. This is particularly important in the context of the wider objective of achieving an integrated internal market.

....

[1] EDITOR'S NOTE: As of 1 May 2012 this Commission Notice has not been reissued following the entry into force of the Treaty of Lisbon. It includes references to the old Treaty article numbers in the text. The title of the Notice has been updated to reflect that fact that Articles 81 and 82 TEC have been replaced by Articles 101 and 102 TFEU. Reference should be made to the Tables of Equivalences accompanying the consolidated Treaties in Part II of this edition for the conversion of old Treaty article numbers to new ones.

II. PURPOSE OF THIS DOCUMENT

2.   This document sets out the enforcement priorities that will guide the Commission's action in applying Article 82 to exclusionary conduct by dominant undertakings. Alongside the Commission's specific enforcement decisions, it is intended to provide greater clarity and predictability as regards the general framework of analysis which the Commission employs in determining whether it should pursue cases concerning various forms of exclusionary conduct and to help undertakings better assess whether certain behaviour is likely to result in intervention by the Commission under Article 82.

3.   This document is not intended to constitute a statement of the law and is without prejudice to the interpretation of Article 82 by the Court of Justice or the Court of First Instance of the European Communities. In addition, the general framework set out in this document applies without prejudice to the possibility for the Commission to reject a complaint when it considers that a case lacks priority on grounds of lack of Community interest.

4.   Article 82 applies to undertakings which hold a dominant position on one or more relevant markets. Such a position may be held by one undertaking (single dominance) or by two or more undertakings (collective dominance). This document only relates to abuses committed by an undertaking holding a single dominant position.

5.   In applying Article 82 to exclusionary conduct by dominant undertakings, the Commission will focus on those types of conduct that are most harmful to consumers. Consumers benefit from competition through lower prices, better quality and a wider choice of new or improved goods and services. The Commission, therefore, will direct its enforcement to ensuring that markets function properly and that consumers benefit from the efficiency and productivity which result from effective competition between undertakings.

6.   The emphasis of the Commission's enforcement activity in relation to exclusionary conduct is on safeguarding the competitive process in the internal market and ensuring that undertakings which hold a dominant position do not exclude their competitors by other means than competing on the merits of the products or services they provide. In doing so the Commission is mindful that what really matters is protecting an effective competitive process and not simply protecting competitors. This may well mean that competitors who deliver less to consumers in terms of price, choice, quality and innovation will leave the market.

7.   Conduct which is directly exploitative of consumers, for example charging excessively high prices or certain behaviour that undermines the efforts to achieve an integrated internal market, is also liable to infringe Article 82. The Commission may decide to intervene in relation to such conduct, in particular where the protection of consumers and the proper functioning of the internal market cannot otherwise be adequately ensured. For the purpose of providing guidance on its enforcement priorities the Commission at this stage limits itself to exclusionary conduct and in, particular, certain specific types of exclusionary conduct which, based on its experience, appear to be the most common.

8.   In applying the general enforcement principles set out in this Communication, the Commission will take into account the specific facts and circumstances of each case. For example, in cases involving regulated markets, the Commission will take into account the specific regulatory environment in conducting its assessment [1]. The Commission may therefore adapt the approach set out in this Communication to the extent that this would appear to be reasonable and appropriate in a given case.

III. GENERAL APPROACH TO EXCLUSIONARY CONDUCT

A. MARKET POWER

9.   The assessment of whether an undertaking is in a dominant position and of the degree of market power it holds is a first step in the application of Article 82. According to the case-law, holding a dominant position confers a special responsibility on the undertaking concerned, the scope of which must be considered in the light of the specific circumstances of each case [2].

10.   Dominance has been defined under Community law as a position of economic strength enjoyed by an undertaking, which enables it to prevent effective competition being maintained on a relevant market, by affording it the power to behave to an appreciable extent independently of its competitors, its customers and ultimately of consumers [3]. This notion of independence is related to the degree of competitive constraint exerted on the undertaking in question. Dominance entails that these competitive constraints are not sufficiently effective and hence that the undertaking in question enjoys substantial market power over a period of time. This means that the undertaking's decisions are largely insensitive to the actions and reactions of competitors, customers and, ultimately, consumers. The Commission may consider that effective competitive constraints are absent even if some actual or potential competition remains [4]. In general, a dominant position derives from a combination of several factors which, taken separately, are not necessarily determinative [5].

11.   The Commission considers that an undertaking which is capable of profitably increasing prices above the competitive level for a significant period of time does not face sufficiently effective competitive constraints and can thus generally be regarded as dominant [6]. In this Communication, the expression "increase prices" includes the power to maintain prices above the competitive level and is used as shorthand for the various ways in which the parameters of competition — such as prices, output, innovation, the variety or quality of goods or services — can be influenced to the advantage of the dominant undertaking and to the detriment of consumers [7].

12.   The assessment of dominance will take into account the competitive structure of the market, and in particular the following factors:
   —   constraints imposed by the existing supplies from, and the position on the market of, actual competitors (the market position of the dominant undertaking and its competitors),
   —   constraints imposed by the credible threat of future expansion by actual competitors or entry by potential competitors (expansion and entry),
   —   constraints imposed by the bargaining strength of the undertaking's customers (countervailing buyer power).

(a) Market position of the dominant undertaking and its competitors
13.   Market shares provide a useful first indication for the Commission of the market structure and of the relative importance of the various undertakings active on the market [8]. However, the Commission will interpret market shares in the light of the relevant market conditions, and in particular of the dynamics of the market and of the extent to which products are differentiated. The trend or development of market shares over time may also be taken into account in volatile or bidding markets.

14.   The Commission considers that low market shares are generally a good proxy for the absence of substantial market power. The Commission's experience suggests that dominance is not likely if the undertaking's market share is below 40 % in the relevant market. However, there may be specific cases below that threshold where competitors are

not in a position to constrain effectively the conduct of a dominant undertaking, for example where they face serious capacity limitations. Such cases may also deserve attention on the part of the Commission.

15.   Experience suggests that the higher the market share and the longer the period of time over which it is held, the more likely it is that it constitutes an important preliminary indication of the existence of a dominant position and, in certain circumstances, of possible serious effects of abusive conduct, justifying an intervention by the Commission under Article 82 [9]. However, as a general rule, the Commission will not come to a final conclusion as to whether or not a case should be pursued without examining all the factors which may be sufficient to constrain the behaviour of the undertaking.

(b) Expansion or entry

16.   Competition is a dynamic process and an assessment of the competitive constraints on an undertaking cannot be based solely on the existing market situation. The potential impact of expansion by actual competitors or entry by potential competitors, including the threat of such expansion or entry, is also relevant. An undertaking can be deterred from increasing prices if expansion or entry is likely, timely and sufficient. For the Commission to consider expansion or entry likely it must be sufficiently profitable for the competitor or entrant, taking into account factors such as the barriers to expansion or entry, the likely reactions of the allegedly dominant undertaking and other competitors, and the risks and costs of failure. For expansion or entry to be considered timely, it must be sufficiently swift to deter or defeat the exercise of substantial market power. For expansion or entry to be considered sufficient, it cannot be simply small-scale entry, for example into some market niche, but must be of such a magnitude as to be able to deter any attempt to increase prices by the putatively dominant undertaking in the relevant market.

17.   Barriers to expansion or entry can take various forms. They may be legal barriers, such as tariffs or quotas, or they may take the form of advantages specifically enjoyed by the dominant undertaking, such as economies of scale and scope, privileged access to essential inputs or natural resources, important technologies [10] or an established distribution and sales network [11]. They may also include costs and other impediments, for instance resulting from network effects, faced by customers in switching to a new supplier. The dominant undertaking's own conduct may also create barriers to entry, for example where it has made significant investments which entrants or competitors would have to match [12], or where it has concluded long-term contracts with its customers that have appreciable foreclosing effects. Persistently high market shares may be indicative of the existence of barriers to entry and expansion.

(c) Countervailing buyer power

18.   Competitive constraints may be exerted not only by actual or potential competitors but also by customers. Even an undertaking with a high market share may not be able to act to an appreciable extent independently of customers with sufficient bargaining strength [13]. Such countervailing buying power may result from the customers' size or their commercial significance for the dominant undertaking, and their ability to switch quickly to competing suppliers, to promote new entry or to vertically integrate, and to credibly threaten to do so. If countervailing power is of a sufficient magnitude, it may deter or defeat an attempt by the undertaking to profitably increase prices. Buyer power may not, however, be considered a sufficiently effective constraint if it only ensures that a particular or limited segment of customers is shielded from the market power of the dominant undertaking.

B. FORECLOSURE LEADING TO CONSUMER HARM ("ANTI-COMPETITIVE FORECLOSURE")

19.   The aim of the Commission's enforcement activity in relation to exclusionary conduct is to ensure that dominant undertakings do not impair effective competition by foreclosing their competitors in an anti-competitive way, thus having an adverse impact on consumer welfare, whether in the form of higher price levels than would have otherwise prevailed or in some other form such as limiting quality or reducing consumer choice. In this document the term "anti-competitive foreclosure" is used to describe a situation where effective access of actual or potential competitors to supplies or markets is hampered or eliminated as a result of the conduct of the dominant undertaking whereby the dominant undertaking is likely to be in a position to profitably increase prices [14] to the detriment of consumers. The identification of likely consumer harm can rely on qualitative and, where possible and appropriate, quantitative evidence. The Commission will address such anti-competitive foreclosure either at the intermediate level or at the level of final consumers, or at both levels [15].

20.   The Commission will normally intervene under Article 82 where, on the basis of cogent and convincing evidence, the allegedly abusive conduct is likely to lead to anti-competitive foreclosure. The Commission considers the following factors to be generally relevant to such an assessment:
—   the position of the dominant undertaking: in general, the stronger the dominant position, the higher the likelihood that conduct protecting that position leads to anti-competitive foreclosure,
—   the conditions on the relevant market: this includes the conditions of entry and expansion, such as the existence of economies of scale and/or scope and network effects. Economies of scale mean that competitors are less likely to enter or stay in the market if the dominant undertaking forecloses a significant part of the relevant market. Similarly, the conduct may allow the dominant undertaking to "tip" a market characterised by network effects in its favour or to further entrench its position on such a market. Likewise, if entry barriers in the upstream and/or downstream market are significant, this means that it may be costly for competitors to overcome possible foreclosure through vertical integration,
—   the position of the dominant undertaking's competitors: this includes the importance of competitors for the maintenance of effective competition. A specific competitor may play a significant competitive role even if it only holds a small market share compared to other competitors. It may, for example, be the closest competitor to the dominant undertaking, be a particularly innovative competitor, or have the reputation of systematically cutting prices. In its assessment, the Commission may also consider in appropriate cases, on the basis of information available, whether there are realistic, effective and timely counterstrategies that competitors would be likely to deploy,
—   the position of the customers or input suppliers: this may include consideration of the possible selectivity of the conduct in question. The dominant undertaking may apply the practice only to selected customers or input suppliers who may be of particular importance for the entry or expansion of competitors, thereby enhancing the likelihood of anti-competitive foreclosure [16]. In the case of customers, they may, for example, be the ones most likely to respond to offers from alternative suppliers, they may represent a particular means of distributing the product that would be suitable for a new entrant, they may be situated in a geographic area well suited to new entry or they may be likely to influence the behaviour of other customers. In the case of input suppliers, those with whom the dominant undertaking has concluded exclusive supply arrangements may be the ones most likely to respond to requests by customers who are competitors of the dominant undertaking in a downstream market, or may

produce a grade of the product — or produce at a location — particularly suitable for a new entrant. Any strategies at the disposal of the customers or input suppliers which could help to counter the conduct of the dominant undertaking will also be considered,

— the extent of the allegedly abusive conduct: in general, the higher the percentage of total sales in the relevant market affected by the conduct, the longer its duration, and the more regularly it has been applied, the greater is the likely foreclosure effect,

— possible evidence of actual foreclosure: if the conduct has been in place for a sufficient period of time, the market performance of the dominant undertaking and its competitors may provide direct evidence of anti-competitive foreclosure. For reasons attributable to the allegedly abusive conduct, the market share of the dominant undertaking may have risen or a decline in market share may have been slowed. For similar reasons, actual competitors may have been marginalised or may have exited, or potential competitors may have tried to enter and failed,

— direct evidence of any exclusionary strategy: this includes internal documents which contain direct evidence of a strategy to exclude competitors, such as a detailed plan to engage in certain conduct in order to exclude a competitor, to prevent entry or to pre-empt the emergence of a market, or evidence of concrete threats of exclusionary action. Such direct evidence may be helpful in interpreting the dominant undertaking's conduct.

21.   When pursuing a case the Commission will develop the analysis of the general factors mentioned in paragraph 20, together with the more specific factors described in the sections dealing with certain types of exclusionary conduct, and any other factors which it may consider to be appropriate. This assessment will usually be made by comparing the actual or likely future situation in the relevant market (with the dominant undertaking's conduct in place) with an appropriate counterfactual, such as the simple absence of the conduct in question or with another realistic alternative scenario, having regard to established business practices.

22.   There may be circumstances where it is not necessary for the Commission to carry out a detailed assessment before concluding that the conduct in question is likely to result in consumer harm. If it appears that the conduct can only raise obstacles to competition and that it creates no efficiencies, its anti-competitive effect may be inferred. This could be the case, for instance, if the dominant undertaking prevents its customers from testing the products of competitors or provides financial incentives to its customers on condition that they do not test such products, or pays a distributor or a customer to delay the introduction of a competitor's product.

C. PRICE-BASED EXCLUSIONARY CONDUCT

23.   The considerations in paragraphs 23 to 27 apply to price-based exclusionary conduct. Vigorous price competition is generally beneficial to consumers. With a view to preventing anti-competitive foreclosure, the Commission will normally only intervene where the conduct concerned has already been or is capable of hampering competition from competitors which are considered to be as efficient as the dominant undertaking [17].

24.   However, the Commission recognises that in certain circumstances a less efficient competitor may also exert a constraint which should be taken into account when considering whether particular price-based conduct leads to anti-competitive foreclosure. The Commission will take a dynamic view of that constraint, given that in the absence of an abusive practice such a competitor may benefit from demand-related advantages, such as network and learning effects, which will tend to enhance its efficiency.

25. In order to determine whether even a hypothetical competitor as efficient as the dominant undertaking would be likely to be foreclosed by the conduct in question, the Commission will examine economic data relating to cost and sales prices, and in particular whether the dominant undertaking is engaging in below-cost pricing. This will require that sufficiently reliable data be available. Where available, the Commission will use information on the costs of the dominant undertaking itself. If reliable information on those costs is not available, the Commission may decide to use the cost data of competitors or other comparable reliable data.

26. The cost benchmarks that the Commission is likely to use are average avoidable cost (AAC) and long-run average incremental cost (LRAIC) [18]. Failure to cover AAC indicates that the dominant undertaking is sacrificing profits in the short term and that an equally efficient competitor cannot serve the targeted customers without incurring a loss. LRAIC is usually above AAC because, in contrast to AAC (which only includes fixed costs if incurred during the period under examination), LRAIC includes product specific fixed costs made before the period in which allegedly abusive conduct took place. Failure to cover LRAIC indicates that the dominant undertaking is not recovering all the (attributable) fixed costs of producing the good or service in question and that an equally efficient competitor could be foreclosed from the market [19].

27. If the data clearly suggest that an equally efficient competitor can compete effectively with the pricing conduct of the dominant undertaking, the Commission will, in principle, infer that the dominant undertaking's pricing conduct is not likely to have an adverse impact on effective competition, and thus on consumers, and will therefore be unlikely to intervene. If, on the contrary, the data suggest that the price charged by the dominant undertaking has the potential to foreclose equally efficient competitors, then the Commission will integrate this in the general assessment of anti-competitive foreclosure (see Section B above), taking into account other relevant quantitative and/or qualitative evidence.

D. OBJECTIVE NECESSITY AND EFFICIENCIES

28. In the enforcement of Article 82, the Commission will also examine claims put forward by a dominant undertaking that its conduct is justified [20]. A dominant undertaking may do so either by demonstrating that its conduct is objectively necessary or by demonstrating that its conduct produces substantial efficiencies which outweigh any anti-competitive effects on consumers. In this context, the Commission will assess whether the conduct in question is indispensable and proportionate to the goal allegedly pursued by the dominant undertaking.

29. The question of whether conduct is objectively necessary and proportionate must be determined on the basis of factors external to the dominant undertaking. Exclusionary conduct may, for example, be considered objectively necessary for health or safety reasons related to the nature of the product in question. However, proof of whether conduct of this kind is objectively necessary must take into account that it is normally the task of public authorities to set and enforce public health and safety standards. It is not the task of a dominant undertaking to take steps on its own initiative to exclude products which it regards, rightly or wrongly, as dangerous or inferior to its own product [21].

30. The Commission considers that a dominant undertaking may also justify conduct leading to foreclosure of competitors on the ground of efficiencies that are sufficient to guarantee that no net harm to consumers is likely to arise. In this context, the dominant undertaking will generally be expected to demonstrate, with a sufficient degree of probability, and on the basis of verifiable evidence, that the following cumulative conditions are fulfilled [22]:

— the efficiencies have been, or are likely to be, realised as a result of the conduct. They may, for example, include technical improvements in the quality of goods, or a reduction in the cost of production or distribution,

— the conduct is indispensable to the realisation of those efficiencies: there must be no less anti-competitive alternatives to the conduct that are capable of producing the same efficiencies,

— the likely efficiencies brought about by the conduct outweigh any likely negative effects on competition and consumer welfare in the affected markets,

— the conduct does not eliminate effective competition, by removing all or most existing sources of actual or potential competition. Rivalry between undertakings is an essential driver of economic efficiency, including dynamic efficiencies in the form of innovation. In its absence the dominant undertaking will lack adequate incentives to continue to create and pass on efficiency gains. Where there is no residual competition and no foreseeable threat of entry, the protection of rivalry and the competitive process outweighs possible efficiency gains. In the Commission's view, exclusionary conduct which maintains, creates or strengthens a market position approaching that of a monopoly can normally not be justified on the grounds that it also creates efficiency gains.

31.   It is incumbent upon the dominant undertaking to provide all the evidence necessary to demonstrate that the conduct concerned is objectively justified. It then falls to the Commission to make the ultimate assessment of whether the conduct concerned is not objectively necessary and, based on a weighing-up of any apparent anti-competitive effects against any advanced and substantiated efficiencies, is likely to result in consumer harm.

IV. SPECIFIC FORMS OF ABUSE

A. EXCLUSIVE DEALING

32.   A dominant undertaking may try to foreclose its competitors by hindering them from selling to customers through use of exclusive purchasing obligations or rebates, together referred to as exclusive dealing [23]. This section sets out the circumstances which are most likely to prompt an intervention by the Commission in respect of exclusive dealing arrangements entered into by dominant undertakings.

(a) Exclusive purchasing

33.   An exclusive purchasing obligation requires a customer on a particular market to purchase exclusively or to a large extent only from the dominant undertaking. Certain other obligations, such as stocking requirements, which appear to fall short of requiring exclusive purchasing, may in practice lead to the same effect [24].

34.   In order to convince customers to accept exclusive purchasing, the dominant undertaking may have to compensate them, in whole or in part, for the loss in competition resulting from the exclusivity. Where such compensation is given, it may be in the individual interest of a customer to enter into an exclusive purchasing obligation with the dominant undertaking. But it would be wrong to conclude automatically from this that all exclusive purchasing obligations, taken together, are beneficial for customers overall, including those currently not purchasing from the dominant undertaking, and the final consumers. The Commission will focus its attention on those cases where it is likely that consumers as a whole will not benefit. This will, in particular, be the case if there are many customers and the exclusive purchasing obligations of the dominant undertaking, taken together, have the effect of preventing the entry or expansion of competing undertakings.

35. In addition to the factors mentioned in paragraph 20, the following factors will generally be of particular relevance in determining whether the Commission will intervene in respect of exclusive purchasing arrangements.

36. The capacity for exclusive purchasing obligations to result in anti-competitive foreclosure arises in particular where, without the obligations, an important competitive constraint is exercised by competitors who either are not yet present in the market at the time the obligations are concluded, or who are not in a position to compete for the full supply of the customers. Competitors may not be able to compete for an individual customer's entire demand because the dominant undertaking is an unavoidable trading partner at least for part of the demand on the market, for instance because its brand is a "must stock item" preferred by many final consumers or because the capacity constraints on the other suppliers are such that a part of demand can only be provided for by the dominant supplier [25]. If competitors can compete on equal terms for each individual customer's entire demand, exclusive purchasing obligations are generally unlikely to hamper effective competition unless the switching of supplier by customers is rendered difficult due to the duration of the exclusive purchasing obligation. In general, the longer the duration of the obligation, the greater the likely foreclosure effect. However, if the dominant undertaking is an unavoidable trading partner for all or most customers, even an exclusive purchasing obligation of short duration can lead to anti-competitive foreclosure.

(b) Conditional rebates

37. Conditional rebates are rebates granted to customers to reward them for a particular form of purchasing behaviour. The usual nature of a conditional rebate is that the customer is given a rebate if its purchases over a defined reference period exceed a certain threshold, the rebate being granted either on all purchases (retroactive rebates) or only on those made in excess of those required to achieve the threshold (incremental rebates). Conditional rebates are not an uncommon practice. Undertakings may offer such rebates in order to attract more demand, and as such they may stimulate demand and benefit consumers. However, such rebates — when granted by a dominant undertaking — can also have actual or potential foreclosure effects similar to exclusive purchasing obligations. Conditional rebates can have such effects without necessarily entailing a sacrifice for the dominant undertaking [26].

38. In addition to the factors already mentioned in paragraph 20, the following factors are of particular importance to the Commission in determining whether a given system of conditional rebates is liable to result in anti-competitive foreclosure and, consequently, will be part of the Commission's enforcement priorities.

39. As with exclusive purchasing obligations, the likelihood of anti-competitive foreclosure is higher where competitors are not able to compete on equal terms for the entire demand of each individual customer. A conditional rebate granted by a dominant undertaking may enable it to use the "non contestable" portion of the demand of each customer (that is to say, the amount that would be purchased by the customer from the dominant undertaking in any event) as leverage to decrease the price to be paid for the "contestable" portion of demand (that is to say, the amount for which the customer may prefer and be able to find substitutes) [27].

40. In general terms, retroactive rebates may foreclose the market significantly, as they may make it less attractive for customers to switch small amounts of demand to an alternative supplier, if this would lead to loss of the retroactive rebates [28]. The potential foreclosing effect of retroactive rebates is in principle strongest on the last purchased unit of the product before the threshold is exceeded. However, what is in the Commission's view relevant for an assessment of the loyalty enhancing effect of a rebate is not simply the

effect on competition to provide the last individual unit, but the foreclosing effect of the rebate system on (actual or potential) competitors of the dominant supplier. The higher the rebate as a percentage of the total price and the higher the threshold, the greater the inducement below the threshold and, therefore, the stronger the likely foreclosure of actual or potential competitors.

41.   When applying the methodology explained in paragraphs 23 to 27, the Commission intends to investigate, to the extent that the data are available and reliable, whether the rebate system is capable of hindering expansion or entry even by competitors that are equally efficient by making it more difficult for them to supply part of the requirements of individual customers. In this context the Commission will estimate what price a competitor would have to offer in order to compensate the customer for the loss of the conditional rebate if the latter would switch part of its demand ("the relevant range") away from the dominant undertaking. The effective price that the competitor will have to match is not the average price of the dominant undertaking, but the normal (list) price less the rebate the customer loses by switching, calculated over the relevant range of sales and in the relevant period of time. The Commission will take into account the margin of error that may be caused by the uncertainties inherent in this kind of analysis.

42.   The relevant range over which to calculate the effective price in a particular case depends on the specific facts of each case and on whether the rebate is incremental or retroactive. For incremental rebates, the relevant range is normally the incremental purchases that are being considered. For retroactive rebates, it will generally be relevant to assess in the specific market context how much of a customer's purchase requirements can realistically be switched to a competitor (the "contestable share" or "contestable portion"). If it is likely that customers would be willing and able to switch large amounts of demand to a (potential) competitor relatively quickly, the relevant range is likely to be relatively large. If, on the other hand, it is likely that customers would only be willing or able to switch small amounts incrementally, then the relevant range will be relatively small. For existing competitors their capacity to expand sales to customers and the fluctuations in those sales over time may also provide an indication of the relevant range. For potential competitors, an assessment of the scale at which a new entrant would realistically be able to enter may be undertaken, where possible. It may be possible to take the historical growth pattern of new entrants in the same or in similar markets as an indication of a realistic market share of a new entrant [29].

43.   The lower the estimated effective price over the relevant range is compared to the average price of the dominant supplier, the stronger the loyalty-enhancing effect. However, as long as the effective price remains consistently above the LRAIC of the dominant undertaking, this would normally allow an equally efficient competitor to compete profitably notwithstanding the rebate. In those circumstances the rebate is normally not capable of foreclosing in an anti-competitive way.

44.   Where the effective price is below AAC, as a general rule the rebate scheme is capable of foreclosing even equally efficient competitors. Where the effective price is between AAC and LRAIC, the Commission will investigate whether other factors point to the conclusion that entry or expansion even by equally efficient competitors is likely to be affected. In this context, the Commission will investigate whether and to what extent competitors have realistic and effective counterstrategies at their disposal, for instance their capacity to also use a "non contestable" portion of their buyers' demand as leverage to decrease the price for the relevant range. Where competitors do not have such counterstrategies at their disposal, the Commission will consider that the rebate scheme is capable of foreclosing equally efficient competitors.

45. As indicated in paragraph 27, this analysis will be integrated in the general assessment, taking into account other relevant quantitative or qualitative evidence. It is normally important to consider whether the rebate system is applied with an individualised or a standardised threshold. An individualised threshold — one based on a percentage of the total requirements of the customer or an individualised volume target — allows the dominant supplier to set the threshold at such a level as to make it difficult for customers to switch suppliers, thereby creating a maximum loyalty enhancing effect [30]. By contrast, a standardised volume threshold — where the threshold is the same for all or a group of customers — may be too high for some smaller customers and/or too low for larger customers to have a loyalty enhancing effect. If, however, it can be established that a standardised volume threshold approximates the requirements of an appreciable proportion of customers, the Commission is likely to consider that such a standardised system of rebates may produce anti-competitive foreclosure effects.

(c) **Efficiencies**
46. Provided that the conditions set out in Section III D are fulfilled, the Commission will consider claims by dominant undertakings that rebate systems achieve cost or other advantages which are passed on to customers [31]. Transaction-related cost advantages are often more likely to be achieved with standardised volume targets than with individualised volume targets. Similarly, incremental rebate schemes are in general more likely to give resellers an incentive to produce and resell a higher volume than retroactive rebate schemes [32]. Under the same conditions, the Commission will consider evidence demonstrating that exclusive dealing arrangements result in advantages to particular customers if those arrangements are necessary for the dominant undertaking to make certain relationship-specific investments in order to be able to supply those customers.

B. TYING AND BUNDLING

47. A dominant undertaking may try to foreclose its competitors by tying or bundling. This section sets out the circumstances which are most likely to prompt an intervention by the Commission when assessing tying and bundling by dominant undertakings.

48. "Tying" usually refers to situations where customers that purchase one product (the tying product) are required also to purchase another product from the dominant undertaking (the tied product). Tying can take place on a technical or contractual basis [33]. "Bundling" usually refers to the way products are offered and priced by the dominant undertaking. In the case of pure bundling the products are only sold jointly in fixed proportions. In the case of mixed bundling, often referred to as a multi-product rebate, the products are also made available separately, but the sum of the prices when sold separately is higher than the bundled price.

49. Tying and bundling are common practices intended to provide customers with better products or offerings in more cost effective ways. However, an undertaking which is dominant in one product market (or more) of a tie or bundle (referred to as the tying market) can harm consumers through tying or bundling by foreclosing the market for the other products that are part of the tie or bundle (referred to as the tied market) and, indirectly, the tying market.

50. The Commission will normally take action under Article 82 where an undertaking is dominant in the tying market [34] and where, in addition, the following conditions are fulfilled: (i) the tying and tied products are distinct products, and (ii) the tying practice is likely to lead to anti-competitive foreclosure [35].

(a) Distinct products
51.   Whether the products will be considered by the Commission to be distinct depends on
      customer demand. Two products are distinct if, in the absence of tying or bundling, a
      substantial number of customers would purchase or would have purchased the tying product
      without also buying the tied product from the same supplier, thereby allowing stand-alone
      production for both the tying and the tied product [36]. Evidence that two products are
      distinct could include direct evidence that, when given a choice, customers purchase the tying
      and the tied products separately from different sources of supply, or indirect evidence, such as
      the presence on the market of undertakings specialised in the manufacture or sale of the tied
      product without the tying product [37] or of each of the products bundled by the dominant
      undertaking, or evidence indicating that undertakings with little market power, particularly in
      competitive markets, tend not to tie or not to bundle such products.

(b) Anti-competitive foreclosure in the tied and/or tying market
52.   Tying or bundling may lead to anti-competitive effects in the tied market, the tying
      market, or both at the same time. However, even when the aim of the tying or bundling is
      to protect the dominant undertaking's position in the tying market, this is done indirectly
      through foreclosing the tied market. In addition to the factors already mentioned in
      paragraph 20, the Commission considers that the following factors are generally of
      particular importance for identifying cases of likely or actual anti-competitive foreclosure.

53.   The risk of anti-competitive foreclosure is expected to be greater where the dominant
      undertaking makes its tying or bundling strategy a lasting one, for example through
      technical tying which is costly to reverse. Technical tying also reduces the opportunities
      for resale of individual components.

54.   In the case of bundling, the undertaking may have a dominant position for more than one
      of the products in the bundle. The greater the number of such products in the bundle, the
      stronger the likely anti-competitive foreclosure. This is particularly true if the bundle is
      difficult for a competitor to replicate, either on its own or in combination with others.

55.   The tying may lead to less competition for customers interested in buying the tied product,
      but not the tying product. If there is not a sufficient number of customers who will buy
      the tied product alone to sustain competitors of the dominant undertaking in the tied
      market, the tying can lead to those customers facing higher prices.

56.   If the tying and the tied product can be used in variable proportions as inputs to a
      production process, customers may react to an increase in price for the tying product by
      increasing their demand for the tied product while decreasing their demand for the tying
      product. By tying the two products the dominant undertaking may seek to avoid this
      substitution and as a result be able to raise its prices.

57.   If the prices the dominant undertaking can charge in the tying market are regulated, tying
      may allow the dominant undertaking to raise prices in the tied market in order to
      compensate for the loss of revenue caused by the regulation in the tying market.

58.   If the tied product is an important complementary product for customers of the tying
      product, a reduction of alternative suppliers of the tied product and hence a reduced
      availability of that product can make entry to the tying market alone more difficult.

(c) Multi-product rebates
59.   A multi-product rebate may be anti-competitive on the tied or the tying market if it is so
      large that equally efficient competitors offering only some of the components cannot
      compete against the discounted bundle.

60.   In theory, it would be ideal if the effect of the rebate could be assessed by examining whether the incremental revenue covers the incremental costs for each product in the dominant undertaking's bundle. However, in practice assessing the incremental revenue is complex. Therefore, in its enforcement practice the Commission will in most situations use the incremental price as a good proxy. If the incremental price that customers pay for each of the dominant undertaking's products in the bundle remains above the LRAIC of the dominant undertaking from including that product in the bundle, the Commission will normally not intervene since an equally efficient competitor with only one product should in principle be able to compete profitably against the bundle. Enforcement action may, however, be warranted if the incremental price is below the LRAIC, because in such a case even an equally efficient competitor may be prevented from expanding or entering [38].

61.   If the evidence suggests that competitors of the dominant undertaking are selling identical bundles, or could do so in a timely way without being deterred by possible additional costs, the Commission will generally regard this as a bundle competing against a bundle, in which case the relevant question is not whether the incremental revenue covers the incremental costs for each product in the bundle, but rather whether the price of the bundle as a whole is predatory.

(d) **Efficiencies**
62.   Provided that the conditions set out in Section III D are fulfilled, the Commission will look into claims by dominant undertakings that their tying and bundling practices may lead to savings in production or distribution that would benefit customers. The Commission may also consider whether such practices reduce transaction costs for customers, who would otherwise be forced to buy the components separately, and enable substantial savings on packaging and distribution costs for suppliers. It may also examine whether combining two independent products into a new, single product might enhance the ability to bring such a product to the market to the benefit of consumers. The Commission may also consider whether tying and bundling practices allow the supplier to pass on efficiencies arising from its production or purchase of large quantities of the tied product.

C. PREDATION

63.   In line with its enforcement priorities, the Commission will generally intervene where there is evidence showing that a dominant undertaking engages in predatory conduct by deliberately incurring losses or foregoing profits in the short term (referred to hereafter as "sacrifice"), so as to foreclose or be likely to foreclose one or more of its actual or potential competitors with a view to strengthening or maintaining its market power, thereby causing consumer harm [39].

(a) **Sacrifice**
64.   Conduct will be viewed by the Commission as entailing a sacrifice if, by charging a lower price for all or a particular part of its output over the relevant time period, or by expanding its output over the relevant time period, the dominant undertaking incurred or is incurring losses that could have been avoided. The Commission will take AAC as the appropriate starting point for assessing whether the dominant undertaking incurred or is incurring avoidable losses. If a dominant undertaking charges a price below AAC for all or part of its output, it is not recovering the costs that could have been avoided by not producing that output: it is incurring a loss that could have been avoided [40]. Pricing below AAC will thus in most cases be viewed by the Commission as a clear indication of sacrifice [41].

65.   However, the concept of sacrifice does not only include pricing below AAC [42]. In order to show a predatory strategy, the Commission may also investigate whether the allegedly predatory conduct led in the short term to net revenues lower than could have been expected from a reasonable alternative conduct, that is to say, whether the dominant undertaking incurred a loss that it could have avoided [43]. The Commission will not compare the actual conduct with hypothetical or theoretical alternatives that might have been more profitable. Only economically rational and practicable alternatives will be considered which, taking into account the market conditions and business realities facing the dominant undertaking, can realistically be expected to be more profitable.

66.   In some cases it will be possible to rely upon direct evidence consisting of documents from the dominant undertaking which clearly show a predatory strategy [44], such as a detailed plan to sacrifice in order to exclude a competitor, to prevent entry or to pre-empt the emergence of a market, or evidence of concrete threats of predatory action [45].

(b) Anti-competitive foreclosure
67.   If sufficient reliable data are available, the Commission will apply the equally efficient competitor analysis, described in paragraphs 25 to 27, to determine whether the conduct is capable of harming consumers. Normally only pricing below LRAIC is capable of foreclosing as efficient competitors from the market.

68.   In addition to the factors already mentioned in paragraph 20, the Commission will generally investigate whether and how the suspected conduct reduces the likelihood that competitors will compete. For instance, if the dominant undertaking is better informed about cost or other market conditions, or can distort market signals about profitability, it may engage in predatory conduct so as to influence the expectations of potential entrants and thereby deter entry. If the conduct and its likely effects are felt on multiple markets and/or in successive periods of possible entry, the dominant undertaking may be shown to be seeking a reputation for predatory conduct. If the targeted competitor is dependent on external financing, substantial price decreases or other predatory conduct by the dominant undertaking could adversely affect the competitor's performance so that its access to further financing may be seriously undermined.

69.   The Commission does not consider that it is necessary to show that competitors have exited the market in order to show that there has been anti-competitive foreclosure. The possibility cannot be excluded that the dominant undertaking may prefer to prevent the competitor from competing vigorously and have it follow the dominant undertaking's pricing, rather than eliminate it from the market altogether. Such disciplining avoids the risk inherent in eliminating competitors, in particular the risk that the assets of the competitor are sold at a low price and stay in the market, creating a new low cost entrant.

70.   Generally speaking, consumers are likely to be harmed if the dominant undertaking can reasonably expect its market power after the predatory conduct comes to an end to be greater than it would have been had the undertaking not engaged in that conduct in the first place, that is to say, if the undertaking is likely to be in a position to benefit from the sacrifice.

71.   This does not mean that the Commission will only intervene if the dominant undertaking would be likely to be able to increase its prices above the level persisting in the market before the conduct. It is sufficient, for instance, that the conduct would be likely to prevent or delay a decline in prices that would otherwise have occurred. Identifying consumer harm is not a mechanical calculation of profits and losses, and proof of overall profits is not required. Likely consumer harm may be demonstrated by assessing the likely

foreclosure effect of the conduct, combined with consideration of other factors, such as entry barriers [46]. In this context, the Commission will also consider possibilities of re-entry.

72.   It may be easier for the dominant undertaking to engage in predatory conduct if it selectively targets specific customers with low prices, as this will limit the losses incurred by the dominant undertaking.

73.   It is less likely that the dominant undertaking engages in predatory conduct if the conduct concerns a low price applied generally for a long period of time.

(c) **Efficiencies**

74.   In general it is considered unlikely that predatory conduct will create efficiencies. However, provided that the conditions set out in Section III D are fulfilled, the Commission will consider claims by a dominant undertaking that the low pricing enables it to achieve economies of scale or efficiencies related to expanding the market.

D. REFUSAL TO SUPPLY AND MARGIN SQUEEZE

75.   When setting its enforcement priorities, the Commission starts from the position that, generally speaking, any undertaking, whether dominant or not, should have the right to choose its trading partners and to dispose freely of its property. The Commission therefore considers that intervention on competition law grounds requires careful consideration where the application of Article 82 would lead to the imposition of an obligation to supply on the dominant undertaking [47]. The existence of such an obligation — even for a fair remuneration — may undermine undertakings' incentives to invest and innovate and, thereby, possibly harm consumers. The knowledge that they may have a duty to supply against their will may lead dominant undertakings — or undertakings who anticipate that they may become dominant — not to invest, or to invest less, in the activity in question. Also, competitors may be tempted to free ride on investments made by the dominant undertaking instead of investing themselves. Neither of these consequences would, in the long run, be in the interest of consumers.

76.   Typically competition problems arise when the dominant undertaking competes on the "downstream" market with the buyer whom it refuses to supply. The term "downstream market" is used to refer to the market for which the refused input is needed in order to manufacture a product or provide a service. This section deals only with this type of refusal.

77.   Other types of possibly unlawful refusal to supply, in which the supply is made conditional upon the purchaser accepting limitations on its conduct, are not dealt with in this section. For instance, halting supplies in order to punish customers for dealing with competitors or refusing to supply customers that do not agree to tying arrangements, will be examined by the Commission in line with the principles set out in the sections on exclusive dealing and tying and bundling. Similarly, refusals to supply aimed at preventing the purchaser from engaging in parallel trade [48] or from lowering its resale price are also not dealt with in this section.

78.   The concept of refusal to supply covers a broad range of practices, such as a refusal to supply products to existing or new customers [49], refusal to license intellectual property rights [50], including when the licence is necessary to provide interface information [51], or refusal to grant access to an essential facility or a network [52].

79.   The Commission does not regard it as necessary for the refused product to have been already traded: it is sufficient that there is demand from potential purchasers and that a

potential market for the input at stake can be identified [53]. Likewise, it is not necessary for there to be actual refusal on the part of a dominant undertaking; "constructive refusal" is sufficient. Constructive refusal could, for example, take the form of unduly delaying or otherwise degrading the supply of the product or involve the imposition of unreasonable conditions in return for the supply.

80.   Finally, instead of refusing to supply, a dominant undertaking may charge a price for the product on the upstream market which, compared to the price it charges on the downstream market [54], does not allow even an equally efficient competitor to trade profitably in the downstream market on a lasting basis (a so-called "margin squeeze"). In margin squeeze cases the benchmark which the Commission will generally rely on to determine the costs of an equally efficient competitor are the LRAIC of the downstream division of the integrated dominant undertaking [55].

81.   The Commission will consider these practices as an enforcement priority if all the following circumstances are present:
—   the refusal relates to a product or service that is objectively necessary to be able to compete effectively on a downstream market,
—   the refusal is likely to lead to the elimination of effective competition on the downstream market, and
—   the refusal is likely to lead to consumer harm.

82.   In certain specific cases, it may be clear that imposing an obligation to supply is manifestly not capable of having negative effects on the input owner's and/or other operators' incentives to invest and innovate upstream, whether ex ante or ex post. The Commission considers that this is particularly likely to be the case where regulation compatible with Community law already imposes an obligation to supply on the dominant undertaking and it is clear, from the considerations underlying such regulation, that the necessary balancing of incentives has already been made by the public authority when imposing such an obligation to supply. This could also be the case where the upstream market position of the dominant undertaking has been developed under the protection of special or exclusive rights or has been financed by state resources. In such specific cases there is no reason for the Commission to deviate from its general enforcement standard of showing likely anti-competitive foreclosure, without considering whether the three circumstances referred to in paragraph 81 are present.

(a) **Objective necessity of the input**
83.   In examining whether a refusal to supply deserves its priority attention, the Commission will consider whether the supply of the refused input is objectively necessary for operators to be able to compete effectively on the market. This does not mean that, without the refused input, no competitor could ever enter or survive on the downstream market [56]. Rather, an input is indispensable where there is no actual or potential substitute on which competitors in the downstream market could rely so as to counter — at least in the long-term — the negative consequences of the refusal [57]. In this regard, the Commission will normally make an assessment of whether competitors could effectively duplicate the input produced by the dominant undertaking in the foreseeable future [58]. The notion of duplication means the creation of an alternative source of efficient supply that is capable of allowing competitors to exert a competitive constraint on the dominant undertaking in the downstream market [59].

84.   The criteria set out in paragraph 81 apply both to cases of disruption of previous supply, and to refusals to supply a good or service which the dominant company has not previously supplied to others (de novo refusals to supply). However, the termination of an existing supply arrangement is more likely to be found to be abusive than a de novo

refusal to supply. For example, if the dominant undertaking had previously been supplying the requesting undertaking, and the latter had made relationship-specific investments in order to use the subsequently refused input, the Commission may be more likely to regard the input in question as indispensable. Similarly, the fact that the owner of the essential input in the past has found it in its interest to supply is an indication that supplying the input does not imply any risk that the owner receives inadequate compensation for the original investment. It would therefore be up to the dominant company to demonstrate why circumstances have actually changed in such a way that the continuation of its existing supply relationship would put in danger its adequate compensation.

(b) Elimination of effective competition

85.   If the requirements set out in paragraphs 83 and 84 are fulfilled, the Commission considers that a dominant undertaking's refusal to supply is generally liable to eliminate, immediately or over time, effective competition in the downstream market. The likelihood of effective competition being eliminated is generally greater the higher the market share of the dominant undertaking in the downstream market. The less capacity-constrained the dominant undertaking is relative to competitors in the downstream market, the closer the substitutability between the dominant undertaking's output and that of its competitors in the downstream market, the greater the proportion of competitors in the downstream market that are affected, and the more likely it is that the demand that could be served by the foreclosed competitors would be diverted away from them to the advantage of the dominant undertaking.

(c) Consumer harm

86.   In examining the likely impact of a refusal to supply on consumer welfare, the Commission will examine whether, for consumers, the likely negative consequences of the refusal to supply in the relevant market outweigh over time the negative consequences of imposing an obligation to supply. If they do, the Commission will normally pursue the case.

87.   The Commission considers that consumer harm may, for instance, arise where the competitors that the dominant undertaking forecloses are, as a result of the refusal, prevented from bringing innovative goods or services to market and/or where follow-on innovation is likely to be stifled [60]. This may be particularly the case if the undertaking which requests supply does not intend to limit itself essentially to duplicating the goods or services already offered by the dominant undertaking on the downstream market, but intends to produce new or improved goods or services for which there is a potential consumer demand or is likely to contribute to technical development [61].

88.   The Commission also considers that a refusal to supply may lead to consumer harm where the price in the upstream input market is regulated, the price in the downstream market is not regulated and the dominant undertaking, by excluding competitors on the downstream market through a refusal to supply, is able to extract more profits in the unregulated downstream market than it would otherwise do.

(d) Efficiencies

89.   The Commission will consider claims by the dominant undertaking that a refusal to supply is necessary to allow the dominant undertaking to realise an adequate return on the investments required to develop its input business, thus generating incentives to continue to invest in the future, taking the risk of failed projects into account. The Commission will also consider claims by the dominant undertaking that its own innovation will be negatively affected by the obligation to supply, or by the structural changes in the market conditions that imposing such an obligation will bring about, including the development of follow-on innovation by competitors.

90.   However, when considering such claims, the Commission will ensure that the conditions set out in Section III D are fulfilled. In particular, it falls on the dominant undertaking to demonstrate any negative impact which an obligation to supply is likely to have on its own level of innovation [62]. If a dominant undertaking has previously supplied the input in question, this can be relevant for the assessment of any claim that the refusal to supply is justified on efficiency grounds.

[1]   See for instance paragraph 82.
[2]   Case 322/81 Nederlandsche Banden Industrie Michelin (Michelin I) v Commission [1983] ECR 3461, paragraph 57; Case T-83/91 Tetra Pak v Commission (Tetra Pak II) [1993] ECR II-755, paragraph 114; Case T-111/96 ITT Promedia v Commission [1998] ECR II-2937, paragraph 139; Case T-228/97 Irish Sugar v Commission [1999] ECR II-2969, paragraph 112; and Case T-203/01 Michelin v Commission (Michelin II) [2003] ECR II-4071, paragraph 97.
[3]   See Case 27/76 United Brands Company and United Brands Continentaal v Commission [1978] ECR 207, paragraph 65; Case 85/76 Hoffmann-La Roche & Co. v Commission [1979] ECR 461, paragraph 38.
[4]   See Case 27/76 United Brands Company and United Brands Continentaal v Commission [1978] ECR 207, paragraphs 113 to 121; Case T-395/94 Atlantic Container Line and Others v Commission [2002] ECR II-875, paragraph 330.
[5]   Case 27/76 United Brands and United Brands Continentaal v Commission [1978] ECR 207, paragraphs 65 and 66; Case C-250/92 Gøttrup-Klim e.a. Grovvareforeninger v Dansk Landbrugs Grovvareselskab [1994] ECR I-5641, paragraph 47; Case T-30/89 Hilti v Commission [1991] ECR II-1439, paragraph 90.
[6]   What is a significant period of time will depend on the product and on the circumstances of the market in question, but normally a period of two years will be sufficient.
[7]   Accounting profitability may be a poor proxy for the exercise of market power. See to that effect Case 27/76 United Brands Company and United Brands Continentaal v Commission [1978] ECR 207, paragraph 126.
[8]   Case 85/76 Hoffmann-La Roche & Co. v Commission [1979] ECR 461, paragraph 39-41; Case C-62/86 AKZO v Commission [1991] ECR I-3359, paragraph 60; Case T-30/89 Hilti v Commission [1991] ECR II-1439, paragraphs 90, 91 and 92; Case T-340/03 France Télécom v Commission [2007] ECR II-107, paragraph 100.
[9]   As to the relationship between the degree of dominance and the finding of abuse, see Joined Cases C-395/96 P and C-396/96 P Compagnie Maritime Belge Transports, Compagnie Maritime Belge and Dafra-Lines v Commission [2000] ECR I-1365, paragraph 119; Case T-228/97 Irish Sugar v Commission [1999] ECR II-2969, paragraph 186.
[10]   Case T-30/89 Hilti v Commission [1991] ECR II-1439, paragraph 19.
[11]   Case 85/76 Hoffmann-La Roche v Commission [1979] ECR 461, paragraph 48.
[12]   Case 27/76 United Brands v Commission [1978] ECR 207, paragraph 91.
[13]   See Case T-228/97 Irish Sugar v Commission [1999] ECR II-2969, paragraphs 97 to 104, in which the Court of First Instance considered whether the alleged lack of independence of the undertaking vis-à-vis its customers should be seen as an exceptional circumstance preventing the finding of a dominant position in spite of the fact that the undertaking was responsible for a very large part of the sales recorded on the industrial sugar market in Ireland.
[14]   For the meaning of the expression "increase price" see paragraph 11.
[15]   The concept of "consumers" encompasses all direct or indirect users of the products affected by the conduct, including intermediate producers that use the products as an input, as well as distributors and final consumers both of the immediate product and of products provided by intermediate producers. Where intermediate users are actual or potential competitors of the dominant undertaking, the assessment focuses on the effects of the conduct on users further downstream.
[16]   Case T-228/97 Irish Sugar v Commission [1999] ECR II-2969, paragraph 188.
[17]   Case 62/86 AKZO Chemie v Commission [1991] ECR I-3359, paragraph 72: in relation to pricing below average total cost (ATC) the Court of Justice stated: "Such prices can drive from the market undertakings which are perhaps as efficient as the dominant undertaking but which, because of their smaller financial resources, are incapable of withstanding the competition waged against them". See also Judgment of 10 April 2008 in Case T-271/03 Deutsche Telekom v Commission not yet reported, paragraph 194.
[18]   Average avoidable cost is the average of the costs that could have been avoided if the company had not produced a discrete amount of (extra) output, in this case the amount allegedly the subject of abusive conduct. In most cases, AAC and the average variable cost (AVC) will be the same, as it is often only variable costs that can be avoided. Long-run average incremental cost is the average of all the (variable and fixed) costs that a company incurs to produce a particular product. LRAIC and average total cost (ATC) are good proxies for each other, and are the same in the case of single product undertakings. If multi-product undertakings have economies of scope, LRAIC would be below ATC for each individual product, as true common costs are not taken into account in LRAIC. In the case of multiple products, any costs that could have been avoided by not producing a particular product or range are not considered to be common costs. In situations where common costs are significant, they may have to be taken into account when assessing the ability to foreclose equally efficient competitors.
[19]   In order to apply these cost benchmarks it may also be necessary to look at revenues and costs of the dominant company and its competitors in a wider context. It may not be sufficient to only assess whether the price or revenue

covers the costs for the product in question, but it may be necessary to look at incremental revenues in case the dominant company's conduct in question negatively affects its revenues in other markets or of other products. Similarly, in the case of two sided markets it may be necessary to look at revenues and costs of both sides at the same time.

[20] See Case 27/76 United Brands v Commission [1978] ECR 207, paragraph 184; Case 311/84 Centre Belge d'études de marché — Télémarketing (CBEM) v Compagnie luxembourgeoise de télédiffusion (CLT) and Information publicité Benelux (IPB) [1985] ECR 3261, paragraph 27; Case T-30/89 Hilti v Commission [1991] ECR II-1439, paragraphs 102 to 119; Case T-83/91 Tetra Pak International v Commission (Tetra Pak II) [1994] ECR II-755, paragraphs 136 and 207; Case C-95/04 P British Airways v Commission [2007] ECR I-2331, paragraphs 69 and 86.

[21] See, for instance, Case T-30/89 Hilti v Commission [1991] ECR II-1439, paragraph 118=N119; Case T-83/91 Tetra Pak International v Commission (Tetra Pak II) [1994] ECR II-755, paragraphs 83 and 84 and 138.

[22] See, in the different context of Article 81, the Communication from the Commission — Notice — Guidelines on the application of Article 81(3) of the Treaty (OJ C 101, 27.4.2004, p. 97).

[23] The notion of exclusive dealing also includes exclusive supply obligations or incentives with the same effect, whereby the dominant undertaking tries to foreclose its competitors by hindering them from purchasing from suppliers. The Commission considers that such input foreclosure is in principle liable to result in anti-competitive foreclosure if the exclusive supply obligation or incentive ties most of the efficient input suppliers and customers competing with the dominant undertaking are unable to find alternative efficient sources of input supply.

[24] Case T-65/98 Van den Bergh Foods v Commission [2003] ECR II-4653. In this case the obligation to use coolers exclusively for the products of the dominant undertaking was considered to lead to outlet exclusivity.

[25] Case T-65/98 Van den Bergh Foods v Commission [2003] ECR II-4653, paragraphs 104 and 156.

[26] In this regard, the assessment of conditional rebates differs from that of predation, which always entails a sacrifice.

[27] See Case T-203/01 Michelin v Commission (Michelin II) [2003] ECR II-4071, paragraphs 162 and 163. See also Case T-219/99 British Airways v Commission [2003] ECR II-5917, paragraphs 277 and 278.

[28] Case 322/81 Nederlandsche Banden Industrie Michelin v Commission (Michelin I) [1983] ECR 3461, paragraphs 70 to 73.

[29] The relevant range will be estimated on the basis of data which may have varying degrees of precision. The Commission will take this into account in drawing any conclusions regarding the dominant undertaking's ability to foreclose equally efficient competitors. It may also be useful to calculate how big a share of customers' requirements on average the entrant should capture as a minimum so that the effective price is at least as high as the LRAIC of the dominant company. In a number of cases the size of this share, when compared with the actual market shares of competitors and their shares of the customers' requirements, may make it clear whether the rebate scheme is capable to have an anti-competitive foreclosure effect.

[30] See Case 85/76 Hoffmann-La Roche & Co. v Commission [1979] ECR 461, paragraphs 89 and 90; Case T-288/97 Irish Sugar v Commission [1999] ECR II-2969, paragraph 213; Case T-219/99 British Airways v Commission [2003] ECR II-5917, paragraphs 7 to 11 and 270 to 273.

[31] For instance, for rebates see Case C-95/04 P British Airways v Commission [2007] ECR I-2331, paragraph 86.

[32] See, to that effect, Case T-203/01 Michelin v Commission (Michelin II) [2003] ECR II-4071, paragraphs 56 to 60, 74 and 75.

[33] Technical tying occurs when the tying product is designed in such a way that it only works properly with the tied product (and not with the alternatives offered by competitors). Contractual tying occurs when the customer who purchases the tying product undertakes also to purchase the tied product (and not the alternatives offered by competitors).

[34] The undertaking should be dominant in the tying market, though not necessarily in the tied market. In bundling cases, the undertaking needs to be dominant in one of the bundled markets. In the special case of tying in after-markets, the condition is that the undertaking is dominant in the tying market and/or the tied after-market.

[35] Case T-201/04 Microsoft v Commission [2007] ECR II-3601, in particular paragraphs 842, 859 to 862, 867 and 869.

[36] Case T-201/04 Microsoft v Commission [2007] ECR II-3601, paragraphs 917, 921 and 922.

[37] Case T-30/89 Hilti v Commission [1991] ECR II-1439, paragraph 67.

[38] In principle, the LRAIC cost benchmark is relevant here as long as competitors are not able to also sell bundles (see paragraphs 23 to 27 and paragraph 61).

[39] The Commission may also pursue predatory practices by dominant undertakings on secondary markets on which they are not yet dominant. In particular, the Commission will be more likely to find such an abuse in sectors where activities are protected by a legal monopoly. While the dominant undertaking does not need to engage in predatory conduct to protect its dominant position in the market protected by legal monopoly, it may use the profits gained in the monopoly market to cross-subsidize its activities in another market and thereby threaten to eliminate effective competition in that other market.

[40] In most cases the average variable cost (AVC) and AAC will be the same, as often only variable costs can be avoided. However, in circumstances where AVC and AAC differ, the latter better reflects possible sacrifice: for example, if the dominant undertaking had to expand capacity in order to be able to predate, then the sunk costs of that extra

capacity should be taken into account in looking at the dominant undertaking's losses. Those costs would be reflected in the AAC, but not the AVC.

[41] In Case 62/86 AKZO Chemie v Commission [1991] ECR I-3359, paragraph 71, the Court held, in relation to pricing below average variable cost (AVC), that: "A dominant undertaking has no interest in applying such prices except that of eliminating competitors so as to enable it subsequently to raise its price by taking advantage of its monopolistic position, since each sale generates a loss . . .".

[42] If the estimate of cost is based on the direct cost of production (as registered in the undertaking's accounts), it may not adequately capture whether or not there has been a sacrifice.

[43] However, undertakings should not be penalised for incurring ex post losses where the ex ante decision to engage in the conduct was taken in good faith, that is to say, if they can provide conclusive evidence that they could reasonably expect that the activity would be profitable.

[44] See Case T-83/91 Tetra Pak International v Commission (Tetra Pak II) [1994] ECR II-755, paragraphs 151 and 171, and Case T-340/03 France Télécom v Commission [2007] ECR II-107, paragraphs 198 to 215.

[45] In Case 62/86 AKZO Chemie v Commission [1991] ECR I-3359, the Court accepted that there was clear evidence of AKZO threatening ECS in two meetings with below cost pricing if it did not withdraw from the organic peroxides market. In addition there was a detailed plan, with figures, describing the measures that AKZO would put into effect if ECS would not withdraw from the market (see paragraphs 76 to 82, 115, and 131 to 140).

[46] This was confirmed in Case T-83/91 Tetra Pak International v Commission (Tetra Pak II) [1994] ECR II-755, upheld on appeal in Case C-333/94 P Tetra Pak International v Commission [1996] ECR I-5951, where the Court of First Instance stated that proof of actual recoupment was not required (paragraph 150 in fine). More in general, as predation may turn out to be more difficult than expected at the start of the conduct, the total costs to the dominant undertaking of predating could outweigh its later profits and thus make actual recoupment impossible while it may still be rational to decide to continue with the predatory strategy that it started some time ago. See also COMP/38.233 Wanadoo Interactive, Commission Decision of 16 July 2003, paragraphs 332 to 367.

[47] Joined Cases C-241/91 P and C-242/91 P Radio Telefis Eireann (RTE) and Independent Television Publications (ITP) v Commission (Magill) [1995] ECR I-743, paragraph 50; Case C-418/01 IMS Health v NDC Health [2004] ECR I-5039, paragraph 35; Case T-201/04 Microsoft v Commission [2007] ECR II-3601, paragraphs 319, 330, 331, 332 and 336.

[48] See Judgment of 16 September 2008 in Joined Cases C-468/06 to C-478/06 Sot. Lélos kai Sia and Others v GlaxoSmithKline, not yet reported.

[49] Joined Cases 6/73 and 7/73 Istituto Chemioterapico Italiano and Commercial Solvents v Commission [1974] ECR 223.

[50] Joined Cases C-241/91 P and C-242/91 P Radio Telefis Eireann (RTE) and Independent Television Publications Ltd (ITP) v Commission (Magill) [1995] ECR 743; Case C-418/01 IMS Health v NDC Health [2004] ECR I-5039. Those judgments show that in exceptional circumstances a refusal to license intellectual property rights is abusive.

[51] See Case T-201/04 Microsoft v Commission [2007] ECR II-3601.

[52] See Commission Decision 94/19/EC of 21 December 1993 in Case IV/34.689 Sea Containers v Stena Sealink — Interim Measures (OJ L 15, 18.1.1994, p. 8) and Commission Decision 92/213/EEC of 26 February 1992 in Case IV/33.544 British Midland v Aer Lingus — (OJ L 96, 10.4.1992, p. 34).

[53] Case C-418/01 IMS Health v NDC Health [2004] ECR I-5039, paragraph 44.

[54] Including a situation in which an integrated undertaking that sells a "system" of complementary products refuses to sell one of the complementary products on an unbundled basis to a competitor that produces the other complementary product.

[55] In some cases, however, the LRAIC of a non-integrated competitor downstream might be used as the benchmark, for example when it is not possible to clearly allocate the dominant undertaking's costs to downstream and upstream operations.

[56] Case T-201/04 Microsoft v Commission [2007] ECR II-3601, paragraphs 428 and 560 to 563.

[57] Joined Cases C-241/91 P and C-242/91 P Radio Telefis Eireann (RTE) and Independent Television Publications LTD (ITP) v Commission (Magill) [1995] ECR 743, paragraphs 52 and 53; Case 7/97 Oscar Bronner v Mediaprint Zeitungs- und Zeitschriftenverlag, Mediaprint Zeitungsvertriebsgesellschaft and Mediaprint Anzeigengesellschaft [1998] ECR I-7791, paragraphs 44 and 45; Case T-201/04 Microsoft v Commission [2007] ECR II-3601, paragraph 421.

[58] In general, an input is likely to be impossible to replicate when it involves a natural monopoly due to scale or scope economies, where there are strong network effects or when it concerns so-called "single source" information. However, in all cases account should be taken of the dynamic nature of the industry and, in particular whether or not market power can rapidly dissipate.

[59] Case 7/97 Oscar Bronner v Mediaprint Zeitungs- und Zeitschriftenverlag, Mediaprint Zeitungsvertriebsgesellschaft and Mediaprint Anzeigengesellschaft [1998] ECR I-7791, paragraph 46, Case C-418/01 IMS Health v NDC Health [2004] ECR I-5039, paragraph 29.

[60] Case T-201/04 Microsoft v Commission [2007] ECR II-3601, paragraphs 643, 647, 648, 649, 652, 653 and 656.

[61] Case C-418/01 IMS Health v NDC Health [2004] ECR I-5039, paragraph 49; Case T-201/04 Microsoft v Commission [2007] ECR II-3601, paragraph 658.

[62] Case T-201/04 Microsoft v Commission [2007] ECR II-3601, paragraph 659.

B) REGULATIONS

COUNCIL REGULATION (EC) NO 659/1999 OF 22 MARCH 1999

laying down detailed rules for the application of [Article 108 TFEU]¹

OJ L 83, 27.3.1999, P. 1*

('State aids Regulation')

(*As amended by Council Regulation (EC) No 1791/2006 of 20 November 2006, OJ L 363, 20.12.2006, p. 1 and the Act concerning the conditions of accession of the Czech Republic, the Republic of Estonia, the Republic of Cyprus, the Republic of Latvia, the Republic of Lithuania, the Republic of Hungary, the Republic of Malta, the Republic of Poland, the Republic of Slovenia and the Slovak Republic and the adjustments to the Treaties on which the European Union is founded, OJ L 236, 23.9.2003, p. 33.)

(footnotes omitted)

THE COUNCIL OF THE EUROPEAN UNION,

Having regard to [Article 109 TFEU],

Having regard to the proposal from the Commission,

Having regard to the opinion of the European Parliament,

Having regard to the opinion of the Economic and Social Committee,

(1) Whereas, without prejudice to special procedural rules laid down in regulations for certain sectors, this Regulation should apply to aid in all sectors; whereas, for the purpose of applying [Articles 93 and 107 TFEU], the Commission has specific competence under [Article 108 TFEU] to decide on the compatibility of State aid with the common market when reviewing existing aid, when taking decisions on new or altered aid and when taking action regarding non-compliance with its decisions or with the requirement as to notification;

(2) Whereas the Commission, in accordance with the case-law of the Court of Justice of the European Communities, has developed and established a consistent practice for the application of [Article 108 TFEU] and has laid down certain procedural rules and principles in a number of communications; whereas it is appropriate, with a view to ensuring effective and efficient procedures pursuant to [Article 108 TFEU], to codify and reinforce this practice by means of a regulation;

(3) Whereas a procedural regulation on the application of [Article 108 TFEU] will increase transparency and legal certainty;

(4) Whereas, in order to ensure legal certainty, it is appropriate to define the circumstances under which aid is to be considered as existing aid; whereas the completion and

---

¹   EDITOR'S NOTE: This Regulation refers to the old EC Treaty article numbers effective prior to the Treaty of Amsterdam, 1999. The replacement article numbers contained in the Treaty on the Functioning of the European Union (TFEU) have been inserted in closed brackets after each Treaty reference for ease of conversion.

enhancement of the internal market is a gradual process, reflected in the permanent development of State aid policy; whereas, following these developments, certain measures, which at the moment they were put into effect did not constitute State aid, may since have become aid;

(5) Whereas, in accordance with [Article 108 TFEU], any plans to grant new aid are to be notified to the Commission and should not be put into effect before the Commission has authorised it;

(6) Whereas, in accordance with [Article 4(3) TEU], Member States are under an obligation to cooperate with the Commission and to provide it with all information required to allow the Commission to carry out its duties under this Regulation;

(7) Whereas the period within which the Commission is to conclude the preliminary examination of notified aid should be set at two months from the receipt of a complete notification or from the receipt of a duly reasoned statement of the Member State concerned that it considers the notification to be complete because the additional information requested by the Commission is not available or has already been provided; whereas, for reasons of legal certainty, that examination should be brought to an end by a decision;

(8) Whereas in all cases where, as a result of the preliminary examination, the Commission cannot find that the aid is compatible with the common market, the formal investigation procedure should be opened in order to enable the Commission to gather all the information it needs to assess the compatibility of the aid and to allow the interested parties to submit their comments; whereas the rights of the interested parties can best be safeguarded within the framework of the formal investigation procedure provided for under [Article 108(2) TFEU];

(9) Whereas, after having considered the comments submitted by the interested parties, the Commission should conclude its examination by means of a final decision as soon as the doubts have been removed; whereas it is appropriate, should this examination not be concluded after a period of 18 months from the opening of the procedure, that the Member State concerned has the opportunity to request a decision, which the Commission should take within two months;

(10) Whereas, in order to ensure that the State aid rules are applied correctly and effectively, the Commission should have the opportunity of revoking a decision which was based on incorrect information;

(11) Whereas, in order to ensure compliance with [Article 108 TFEU], and in particular with the notification obligation and the standstill clause in [Article 108(3) TFEU], the Commission should examine all cases of unlawful aid; whereas, in the interests of transparency and legal certainty, the procedures to be followed in such cases should be laid down; whereas when a Member State has not respected the notification obligation or the standstill clause, the Commission should not be bound by time limits;

(12) Whereas in cases of unlawful aid, the Commission should have the right to obtain all necessary information enabling it to take a decision and to restore immediately, where appropriate, undistorted competition; whereas it is therefore appropriate to enable the Commission to adopt interim measures addressed to the Member State concerned; whereas the interim measures may take the form of information injunctions, suspension injunctions and recovery injunctions; whereas the Commission should be enabled in the event of non-compliance with an information injunction, to decide on the basis of the information available and, in the event of non-compliance with suspension and recovery

injunctions, to refer the matter to the Court of Justice direct, in accordance with the second subparagraph of [Article 108(2) TFEU];

(13) Whereas in cases of unlawful aid which is not compatible with the common market, effective competition should be restored; whereas for this purpose it is necessary that the aid, including interest, be recovered without delay; whereas it is appropriate that recovery be effected in accordance with the procedures of national law; whereas the application of those procedures should not, by preventing the immediate and effective execution of the Commission decision, impede the restoration of effective competition; whereas to achieve this result, Member States should take all necessary measures ensuring the effectiveness of the Commission decision;

(14) Whereas for reasons of legal certainty it is appropriate to establish a period of limitation of 10 years with regard to unlawful aid, after the expiry of which no recovery can be ordered;

(15) Whereas misuse of aid may have effects on the functioning of the internal market which are similar to those of unlawful aid and should thus be treated according to similar procedures; whereas unlike unlawful aid, aid which has possibly been misused is aid which has been previously approved by the Commission; whereas therefore the Commission should not be allowed to use a recovery injunction with regard to misuse of aid;

(16) Whereas it is appropriate to define all the possibilities in which third parties have to defend their interests in State aid procedures;

(17) Whereas in accordance with Article 93(1) of the Treaty, the Commission is under an obligation, in cooperation with Member States, to keep under constant review all systems of existing aid; whereas in the interests of transparency and legal certainty, it is appropriate to specify the scope of cooperation under that Article;

(18) Whereas, in order to ensure compatibility of existing aid schemes with the common market and in accordance with [Article 108(1) TFEU], the Commission should propose appropriate measures where an existing aid scheme is not, or is no longer, compatible with the common market and should initiate the procedure provided for in [Article 108(2) TFEU] if the Member State concerned declines to implement the proposed measures;

(19) Whereas, in order to allow the Commission to monitor effectively compliance with Commission decisions and to facilitate cooperation between the Commission and Member States for the purpose of the constant review of all existing aid schemes in the Member States in accordance with [Article 108(1) TFEU], it is necessary to introduce a general reporting obligation with regard to all existing aid schemes;

(20) Whereas, where the Commission has serious doubts as to whether its decisions are being complied with, it should have at its disposal additional instruments allowing it to obtain the information necessary to verify that its decisions are being effectively complied with; whereas for this purpose on-site monitoring visits are an appropriate and useful instrument, in particular for cases where aid might have been misused; whereas therefore the Commission must be empowered to undertake on-site monitoring visits and must obtain the cooperation of the competent authorities of the Member States where an undertaking opposes such a visit;

(21) Whereas, in the interests of transparency and legal certainty, it is appropriate to give public information on Commission decisions while, at the same time, maintaining the principle that decisions in State aid cases are addressed to the Member State concerned; whereas it is therefore appropriate to publish all decisions which might affect the interests

of interested parties either in full or in a summary form or to make copies of such decisions available to interested parties, where they have not been published or where they have not been published in full; whereas the Commission, when giving public information on its decisions, should respect the rules on professional secrecy, in accordance with [Article 339 TFEU];

(22) Whereas the Commission, in close liaison with the Member States, should be able to adopt implementing provisions laying down detailed rules concerning the procedures under this Regulation; whereas, in order to provide for cooperation between the Commission and the competent authorities of the Member States, it is appropriate to create an Advisory Committee on State aid to be consulted before the Commission adopts provisions pursuant to this Regulation,

HAS ADOPTED THIS REGULATION:

Chapter I GENERAL

Article 1 Definitions
For the purpose of this Regulation:

(a)   'aid' shall mean any measure fulfilling all the criteria laid down in [Article 107(1) TFEU;

(b)   'existing aid' shall mean:
   (i)   without prejudice to Articles 144 and 172 of the Act of Accession of Austria, Finland and Sweden, to Annex IV,point 3 and the Appendix to said Annex of the Act of Accession of the Czech Republic, Estonia, Cyprus, Latvia, Lithuania, Hungary, Malta, Poland, Slovenia and Slovakia, and to Annex V, point 2 and 3(b) and the Appendix to said Annex of the Act of Accession of Bulgaria and Romania, all aid which existed prior to the entry into force of the Treaty in the respective Member States, that is to say, aid schemes and individual aid which were put into effect before, and are still applicable after, the entry into force of the Treaty;
   (ii) authorised aid, that is to say, aid schemes and individual aid which have been authorised by the Commission or by the Council;
   (iii) aid which is deemed to have been authorised pursuant to Article 4(6) of this Regulation or prior to this Regulation but in accordance with this procedure;
   (iv) aid which is deemed to be existing aid pursuant to Article 15;
   (v)   aid which is deemed to be an existing aid because it can be established that at the time it was put into effect it did notconstitute an aid, and subsequently became an aid due to the evolution of the common market and without having been altered by the Member State. Where certain measures become aid following the liberalisation of an activity by Community law, such measures shall not be considered as existing aid after the date fixed for liberalisation;

(c)   'new aid' shall mean all aid, that is to say, aid schemes and individual aid, which is not existing aid, including alterations to existing aid;

(d)   'aid scheme' shall mean any act on the basis of which, without further implementing measures being required, individual aid awards may be made to undertakings defined within the act in a general and abstract manner and any act on the basis of which aid which is not linked to a specific project may be awarded to one or several undertakings for an indefinite period of time and/or for an indefinite amount;

(e)   'individual aid' shall mean aid that is not awarded on the basis of an aid scheme and notifiable awards of aid on the basis of an aid scheme;

(f)   'unlawful aid' shall mean new aid put into effect in contravention of [Article 108(3) TFEU];

(g)   'misuse of aid' shall mean aid used by the beneficiary in contravention of a decision taken pursuant to Article 4(3) or Article 7(3) or (4) of this Regulation;

(h)   'interested party' shall mean any Member State and any person, undertaking or association of undertakings whose interests might be affected by the granting of aid, in particular the beneficiary of the aid, competing undertakings and trade associations.

Chapter II PROCEDURE REGARDING NOTIFIED AID

Article 2 Notification of new aid

1.   Save as otherwise provided in regulations made pursuant to [Article 109 TFEU] or to other relevant provisions thereof, any plans to grant new aid shall be notified to the Commission in sufficient time by the Member State concerned. The Commission shall inform the Member State concerned without delay of the receipt of a notification.

2.   In a notification, the Member State concerned shall provide all necessary information in order to enable the Commission to take a decision pursuant to Articles 4 and 7 (hereinafter referred to as 'complete notification').

Article 3 Standstill clause

Aid notifiable pursuant to Article 2(1) shall not be put into effect before the Commission has taken, or is deemed to have taken, a decision authorising such aid.

Article 4 Preliminary examination of the notification and decisions of the Commission

1.   The Commission shall examine the notification as soon as it is received. Without prejudice to Article 8, the Commission shall take a decision pursuant to paragraphs 2, 3 or 4.

2.   Where the Commission, after a preliminary examination, finds that the notified measure does not constitute aid, it shall record that finding by way of a decision.

3.   Where the Commission, after a preliminary examination, finds that no doubts are raised as to the compatibility with the common market of a notified measure, in so far as it falls within the scope of [Article 107(1) TFEU], it shall decide that the measure is compatible with the common market (hereinafter referred to as a 'decision not to raise objections'). The decision shall specify which exception under the [TFEU] has been applied.

4.   Where the Commission, after a preliminary examination, finds that doubts are raised as to the compatibility with the common market of a notified measure, it shall decide to initiate proceedings pursuant to [Article 108(2) TFEU] (hereinafter referred to as a 'decision to initiate the formal investigation procedure').

5.   The decisions referred to in paragraphs 2, 3 and 4 shall be taken within two months. That period shall begin on the day following the receipt of a complete notification. The notification will be considered as complete if, within two months from its receipt, or from the receipt of any additional information requested, the Commission does not request any further information. The period can be extended with the consent of both the Commission and the Member State concerned. Where appropriate, the Commission may fix shorter time limits.

6.   Where the Commission has not taken a decision in accordance with paragraphs 2, 3 or 4 within the period laid down in paragraph 5, the aid shall be deemed to have been authorised by the Commission. The Member State concerned may thereupon implement the measures in question after giving the Commission prior notice thereof, unless the Commission takes a decision pursuant to this Article within a period of 15 working days following receipt of the notice.

Article 5 Request for information

1. Where the Commission considers that information provided by the Member State concerned with regard to a measure notified pursuant to Article 2 is incomplete, it shall request all necessary additional information. Where a Member State responds to such a request, the Commission shall inform the Member State of the receipt of the response.

2. Where the Member State concerned does not provide the information requested within the period prescribed by the Commission or provides incomplete information, the Commission shall send a reminder, allowing an appropriate additional period within which the information shall be provided.

3. The notification shall be deemed to be withdrawn if the requested information is not provided within the prescribed period, unless before the expiry of that period, either the period has been extended with the consent of both the Commission and the Member State concerned, or the Member State concerned, in a duly reasoned statement, informs the Commission that it considers the notification to be complete because the additional information requested is not available or has already been provided. In that case, the period referred to in Article 4(5) shall begin on the day following receipt of the statement. If the notification is deemed to be withdrawn, the Commission shall inform the Member State thereof.

Article 6 Formal investigation procedure

1. The decision to initiate the formal investigation procedure shall summarise the relevant issues of fact and law, shall include a preliminary assessment of the Commission as to the aid character of the proposed measure and shall set out the doubts as to its compatibility with the common market. The decision shall call upon the Member State concerned and upon other interested parties to submit comments within a prescribed period which shall normally not exceed one month. In duly justified cases, the Commission may extend the prescribed period.

2. The comments received shall be submitted to the Member State concerned. If an interested party so requests, on grounds of potential damage, its identity shall be withheld from the Member State concerned. The Member State concerned may reply to the comments submitted within a prescribed period which shall normally not exceed one month. In duly justified cases, the Commission may extend the prescribed period.

Article 7 Decisions of the Commission to close the formal investigation procedure

1. Without prejudice to Article 8, the formal investigation procedure shall be closed by means of a decision as provided for in paragraphs 2 to 5 of this Article.

2. Where the Commission finds that, where appropriate following modification by the Member State concerned, the notified measure does not constitute aid, it shall record that finding by way of a decision.

3. Where the Commission finds that, where appropriate following modification by the Member State concerned, the doubts as to the compatibility of the notified measure with the common market have been removed, it shall decide that the aid is compatible with the common market (hereinafter referred to as a 'positive decision'). That decision shall specify which exception under the Treaty has been applied.

4. The Commission may attach to a positive decision conditions subject to which an aid may be considered compatible with the common market and may lay down obligations to enable compliance with the decision to be monitored (hereinafter referred to as a 'conditional decision').

5. Where the Commission finds that the notified aid is not compatible with the common market, it shall decide that the aid shall not be put into effect (hereinafter referred to as a 'negative decision').

6.   Decisions taken pursuant to paragraphs 2, 3, 4 and 5 shall be taken as soon as the doubts referred to in Article 4(4) have been removed. The Commission shall as far as possible endeavour to adopt a decision within a period of 18 months from the opening of the procedure. This time limit may be extended by common agreement between the Commission and the Member State concerned.

7.   Once the time limit referred to in paragraph 6 has expired, and should the Member State concerned so request, the Commission shall, within two months, take a decision on the basis of the information available to it. If appropriate, where the information provided is not sufficient to establish compatibility, the Commission shall take a negative decision.

Article 8 Withdrawal of notification

1.   The Member State concerned may withdraw the notification within the meaning of Article 2 in due time before the Commission has taken a decision pursuant to Article 4 or 7.

2.   In cases where the Commission initiated the formal investigation procedure, the Commission shall close that procedure.

Article 9 Revocation of a decision

The Commission may revoke a decision taken pursuant to Article 4(2) or (3), or Article 7(2), (3), (4), after having given the Member State concerned the opportunity to submit its comments, where the decision was based on incorrect information provided during the procedure which was a determining factor for the decision. Before revoking a decision and taking a new decision, the Commission shall open the formal investigation procedure pursuant to Article 4(4). Articles 6, 7 and 10, Article 11(1), Articles 13, 14 and 15 shall apply *mutatismutandis*.

Chapter III PROCEDURE REGARDING UNLAWFUL AID

Article 10 Examination, request for information and information injunction

1.   Where the Commission has in its possession information from whatever source regarding alleged unlawful aid, it shall examine that information without delay.

2.   If necessary, it shall request information from the Member State concerned. Article 2(2) and Article 5(1) and (2) shall apply *mutatismutandis*.

3.   Where, despite a reminder pursuant to Article 5(2), the Member State concerned does not provide the information requested within the period prescribed by the Commission, or where it provides incomplete information, the Commission shall by decision require the information to be provided (hereinafter referred to as an 'information injunction'). The decision shall specify what information is required and prescribe an appropriate period within which it is to be supplied.

Article 11 Injunction to suspend or provisionally recover aid

1.   The Commission may, after giving the Member State concerned the opportunity to submit its comments, adopt a decision requiring the Member State to suspend any unlawful aid until the Commission has taken a decision on the compatibility of the aid with the common market (hereinafter referred to as a 'suspension injunction').

2.   The Commission may, after giving the Member State concerned the opportunity to submit its comments, adopt a decision requiring the Member State provisionally to recover any unlawful aid until the Commission has taken a decision on the compatibility of the aid with the common market (hereinafter referred to as a 'recovery injunction'), if the following criteria are fulfilled:
     —   according to an established practice there are no doubts about the aid character of the measure concerned

and
— there is an urgency to act
and
— there is a serious risk of substantial and irreparable damage to a competitor.
Recovery shall be effected in accordance with the procedure set out in Article 14(2) and (3). After the aid has been effectively recovered, the Commission shall take a decision within the time limits applicable to notified aid. The Commission may authorise the Member State to couple the refunding of the aid with the payment of rescue aid to the firm concerned. The provisions of this paragraph shall be applicable only to unlawful aid implemented after the entry into force of this Regulation.

Article 12 Non-compliance with an injunction decision
If the Member State fails to comply with a suspension injunction or a recovery injunction, the Commission shall be entitled, while carrying out the examination on the substance of the matter on the basis of the information available, to refer the matter to the Court of Justice of the European Communities direct and apply for a declaration that the failure to comply constitutes an infringement of the Treaty.

Article 13 Decisions of the Commission
1.   The examination of possible unlawful aid shall result in a decision pursuant to Article 4(2), (3) or (4). In the case of decisions to initiate the formal investigation procedure, proceedings shall be closed by means of a decision pursuant to Article 7. If a Member State fails to comply with an information injunction, that decision shall be taken on the basis of the information available.

2.   In cases of possible unlawful aid and without prejudice to Article 11(2), the Commission shall not be bound by the time-limit set out in Articles 4(5), 7(6) and 7(7).

3.   Article 9 shall apply *mutatismutandis.*

Article 14 Recovery of aid
1.   Where negative decisions are taken in cases of unlawful aid, the Commission shall decide that the Member State concerned shall take all necessary measures to recover the aid from the beneficiary (hereinafter referred to as a 'recovery decision'). The Commission shall not require recovery of the aid if this would be contrary to a general principle of Community law.

2.   The aid to be recovered pursuant to a recovery decision shall include interest at an appropriate rate fixed by the Commission. Interest shall be payable from the date on which the unlawful aid was at the disposal of the beneficiary until the date of its recovery.

3.   Without prejudice to any order of the Court of Justice of the European Communities pursuant to [Article 278 TFEU], recovery shall be effected without delay and in accordance with the procedures under the national law of the Member State concerned, provided that they allow the immediate and effective execution of the Commission's decision. To this effect and in the event of a procedure before national courts, the Member States concerned shall take all necessary steps which are available in their respective legal systems, including provisional measures, without prejudice to Community law.

Article 15 Limitation period
1.   The powers of the Commission to recover aid shall be subject to a limitation period of ten years.

2.   The limitation period shall begin on the day on which the unlawful aid is awarded to the beneficiary either as individual aid or as aid under an aid scheme. Any action taken by the

Commission or by a Member State, acting at the request of the Commission, with regard to the unlawful aid shall interrupt the limitation period. Each interruption shall start time running afresh. The limitation period shall be suspended for as long as the decision of the Commission is the subject of proceedings pending before the Court of Justice of the European Communities.

3.   Any aid with regard to which the limitation period has expired, shall be deemed to be existing aid.

Chapter IV PROCEDURE REGARDING MISUSE OF AID

Article 16 Misuse of aid
Without prejudice to Article 23, the Commission may in cases of misuse of aid open the formal investigation procedure pursuant to Article 4(4). Articles 6, 7, 9 and 10, Article 11(1), Articles 12, 13,14 and 15 shall apply *mutatismutandis*.

Chapter V PROCEDURE REGARDING EXISTING AID SCHEMES

Article 17 Cooperation pursuant to [Article 108(1) TFEU]
1.   The Commission shall obtain from the Member State concerned all necessary information for the review, in cooperation with the Member State, of existing aid schemes pursuant to [Article 108(1) TFEU].

2.   Where the Commission considers that an existing aid scheme is not, or is no longer, compatible with the common market, it shall inform the Member State concerned of its preliminary view and give the Member State concerned the opportunity to submit its comments within a period of one month. In duly justified cases, the Commission may extend this period.

Article 18 Proposal for appropriate measures
Where the Commission, in the light of the information submitted by the Member State pursuant to Article 17, concludes that the existing aid scheme is not, or is no longer, compatible with the common market, it shall issue a recommendation proposing appropriate measures to the Member State concerned. The recommendation may propose, in particular:

(a)   substantive amendment of the aid scheme,

   or

(b)   introduction of procedural requirements,

   or

(c)   abolition of the aid scheme.

Article 19 Legal consequences of a proposal for appropriate measures
1.   Where the Member State concerned accepts the proposed measures and informs the Commission thereof, the Commission shall record that finding and inform the Member State thereof. The Member State shall be bound by its acceptance to implement the appropriate measures.

2.   Where the Member State concerned does not accept the proposed measures and the Commission, having taken into account the arguments of the Member State concerned, still considers that those measures are necessary, it shall initiate proceedings pursuant to Article 4(4). Articles 6, 7 and 9 shall apply *mutatismutandis*.

Chapter VI INTERESTED PARTIES

Article 20 Rights of interested parties

1.   Any interested party may submit comments pursuant to Article 6 following a Commission decision to initiate the formal investigation procedure. Any interested party which has submitted such comments and any beneficiary of individual aid shall be sent a copy of the decision taken by the Commission pursuant to Article 7.

2.   Any interested party may inform the Commission of any alleged unlawful aid and any alleged misuse of aid. Where the Commission considers that on the basis of the information in its possession there are insufficient grounds for taking a view on the case, it shall inform the interested party thereof. Where the Commission takes a decision on a case concerning the subject matter of the information supplied, it shall send a copy of that decision to the interested party.

3.   At its request, any interested party shall obtain a copy of any decision pursuant to Articles 4 and 7, Article 10(3) and Article 11.

Chapter VII MONITORING

Article 21 Annual reports

1.   Member States shall submit to the Commission annual reports on all existing aid schemes with regard to which no specific reporting obligations have been imposed in a conditional decision pursuant to Article 7(4).

2.   Where, despite a reminder, the Member State concerned fails to submit an annual report, the Commission may proceed in accordance with Article 18 with regard to the aid scheme concerned.

Article 22 On-site monitoring

1.   Where the Commission has serious doubts as to whether decisions not to raise objections, positive decisions or conditional decisions with regard to individual aid are being complied with, the Member State concerned, after having been given the opportunity to submit its comments, shall allow the Commission to undertake on-site monitoring visits.

2.   The officials authorised by the Commission shall be empowered, in order to verify compliance with the decision concerned:
      (a) to enter any premises and land of the undertaking concerned;
      (b) to ask for oral explanations on the spot;
      (c) to examine books and other business records and take, or demand, copies.
      The Commission may be assisted if necessary by independent experts.

3.   The Commission shall inform the Member State concerned, in good time and in writing, of the on-site monitoring visit and of the identities of the authorised officials and experts. If the Member State has duly justified objections to the Commission's choice of experts, the experts shall be appointed in common agreement with the Member State. The officials of the Commission and the experts authorised to carry out the on-site monitoring shall produce an authorisation in writing specifying the subject-matter and purpose of the visit.

4.   Officials authorised by the Member State in whose territory the monitoring visit is to be made may be present at the monitoring visit.

5.   The Commission shall provide the Member State with a copy of any report produced as a result of the monitoring visit.

6.   Where an undertaking opposes a monitoring visit ordered by a Commission decision pursuant to this Article, the Member State concerned shall afford the necessary assistance to

the officials and experts authorised by the Commission to enable them to carry out the monitoring visit. To this end the Member States shall, after consulting the Commission, take the necessary measures within eighteen months after the entry into force of this Regulation.

Article 23 Non-compliance with decisions and judgments

1. Where the Member State concerned does not comply with conditional or negative decisions, in particular in cases referred to in Article 14, the Commission may refer the matter to the Court of Justice of the European Communities direct in accordance with [Article 108(2) TFEU].

2. If the Commission considers that the Member State concerned has not complied with a judgment of the Court of Justice of the European Communities, the Commission may pursue the matter in accordance with [Article 260 TFEU].

Chapter VIII COMMON PROVISIONS

Article 24 Professional secrecy

The Commission and the Member States, their officials and other servants, including independent experts appointed by the Commission, shall not disclose information which they have acquired through the application of this Regulation and which is covered by the obligation of professional secrecy.

Article 25 Addressee of decisions

Decisions taken pursuant to Chapters II, III, IV, V and VII shall be addressed to the Member State concerned. The Commission shall notify them to the Member State concerned without delay and give the latter the opportunity to indicate the Commission which information it considers to be covered by the obligation of professional secrecy.

Article 26 Publication of decisions

1. The Commission shall publish in the *Official Journal of the European Communities* a summary notice of the decisions which it takes pursuant to Article 4(2) and (3) and Article 18 in conjunction with Article 19(1). The summary notice shall state that a copy of the decision may be obtained in the authentic language version or versions.

2. The Commission shall publish in the *Official Journal of the European Communities* the decisions which it takes pursuant to Article 4(4) in their authentic language version. In the Official Journal published in languages other than the authentic language version, the authentic language version will be accompanied by a meaningful summary in the language of that Official Journal.

3. The Commission shall publish in the *Official Journal of the European Communities* the decisions which it takes pursuant to Article 7.

4. In cases where Article 4(6) or Article 8(2) applies, a short notice shall be published in the *Official Journal of the European Communities*.

5. The Council, acting unanimously, may decide to publish decisions pursuant to the third subparagraph of [Article 108(2) TFEU] in the *Official Journal of the European Communities*.

Article 27 Implementing provisions

The Commission, acting in accordance with the procedure laid down in Article 29, shall have the power to adopt implementing provisions concerning the form, content and other details of notifications, the form, content and other details of annual reports, details of time-limits and the calculation of time-limits, and the interest rate referred to in Article 14(2).

Article 28 Advisory Committee on State aid
An Advisory Committee on State aid (hereinafter referred to as the 'Committee') shall be set up. It shall be composed of representatives of the Member States and chaired by the representative of the Commission.

Article 29 Consultation of the Committee
1.   The Commission shall consult the Committee before adopting any implementing provision pursuant to Article 27.

2.   Consultation of the Committee shall take place at a meeting called by the Commission. The drafts and documents to be examined shall be annexed to the notification. The meeting shall take place no earlier than two months after notification has been sent. This period may be reduced in the case of urgency.

3.   The Commission representative shall submit to the Committee a draft of the measures to be taken. The Committee shall deliver an opinion on the draft, within a time-limit which the chairman may lay down according to the urgency of the matter, if necessary by taking a vote.

4.   The opinion shall be recorded in the minutes; in addition, each Member State shall have the right to ask to have its position recorded in the minutes. The Committee may recommend the publication of this opinion in the *Official Journal of the European Communities*.

5.   The Commission shall take the utmost account of the opinion delivered by the Committee. It shall inform the Committee on the manner in which its opinion has been taken into account.

Article 30 Entry into force
This Regulation shall enter into force on the twentieth day following that of its publication in the *Official Journal of the European Communities*. This Regulation shall be binding in its entirety and directly applicable in all Member States.

COUNCIL REGULATION (EC) NO 1/2003 OF 16 DECEMBER 2002
on the implementation of the rules on competition laid down in [Articles 101 and 102 TFEU] * [1]
OJ L 1, 4.1.2003, P. 1

(* As amended by Council Regulation (EC) No 411/2004 of 26 February 2004, L 68, 6.3.2004, p. 1 and Council Regulation (EC) No 1419/2006 of 25 September 2006, L 269, 28.9.2006, p. 1).[2]

THE COUNCIL OF THE EUROPEAN UNION,

Having regard to the Treaty establishing the European Community, and in particular Article 83 thereof,

....

[1]   EDITOR'S NOTE: On 1 May 2004, the date of its implementation, Regulation 1/2003 replaced and repealed the original implementing measure, Council Regulation No 17/62, OJ Special Edition 1962, No. 204/62, p. 87, subject to transitional provisions in Art. 34(2) concerning procedural steps already taken under that Regulation, and Art. 43(1), under which Art. 8(3) of the original Regulation is retained so as to enable the Commission to revoke or amend its decisions or prohibit specified acts by the parties, where those decisions were adopted pursuant to Article 81(3) EC prior to the date of application of Regulation 1/2003 until the date of expiration of those decisions.

[2]   EDITOR'S NOTE: As of 1 May 2012 this Regulation has not been amended following the entry into force of the Treaty of Lisbon. It includes references to the old Treaty article numbers in the text. The title has been amended to reflect the fact that Articles 81 and 82 TEC have been replaced by Articles 101 and 102 TFEU. Reference should be made to the Tables of Equivalences accompanying the consolidated Treaties in Part II of this edition for the conversion of old Treaty article numbers to new ones.

Having regard to the proposal from the Commission(1),

Having regard to the opinion of the European Parliament(2),

Having regard to the opinion of the European Economic and Social Committee(3),

Whereas:
(1)   In order to establish a system which ensures that competition in the common market is not distorted, Articles 81 and 82 of the Treaty must be applied effectively and uniformly in the Community. Council Regulation No 17 of 6 February 1962, First Regulation implementing Articles 81 and 82(4) of the Treaty(5), has allowed a Community competition policy to develop that has helped to disseminate a competition culture within the Community. In the light of experience, however, that Regulation should now be replaced by legislation designed to meet the challenges of an integrated market and a future enlargement of the Community.

(2)   In particular, there is a need to rethink the arrangements for applying the exception from the prohibition on agreements, which restrict competition, laid down in Article 81(3) of the Treaty. Under Article 83(2)(b) of the Treaty, account must be taken in this regard of the need to ensure effective supervision, on the one hand, and to simplify administration to the greatest possible extent, on the other.

(3)   The centralised scheme set up by Regulation No 17 no longer secures a balance between those two objectives. It hampers application of the Community competition rules by the courts and competition authorities of the Member States, and the system of notification it involves prevents the Commission from concentrating its resources on curbing the most serious infringements. It also imposes considerable costs on undertakings.

(4)   The present system should therefore be replaced by a directly applicable exception system in which the competition authorities and courts of the Member States have the power to apply not only Article 81(1) and Article 82 of the Treaty, which have direct applicability by virtue of the case-law of the Court of Justice of the European Communities, but also Article 81(3) of the Treaty.

(5)   In order to ensure an effective enforcement of the Community competition rules and at the same time the respect of fundamental rights of defence, this Regulation should regulate the burden of proof under Articles 81 and 82 of the Treaty. It should be for the party or the authority alleging an infringement of Article 81(1) and Article 82 of the Treaty to prove the existence thereof to the required legal standard. It should be for the undertaking or association of undertakings invoking the benefit of a defence against a finding of an infringement to demonstrate to the required legal standard that the conditions for applying such defence are satisfied. This Regulation affects neither national rules on the standard of proof nor obligations of competition authorities and courts of the Member States to ascertain the relevant facts of a case, provided that such rules and obligations are compatible with general principles of Community law.

(6)   In order to ensure that the Community competition rules are applied effectively, the competition authorities of the Member States should be associated more closely with their application. To this end, they should be empowered to apply Community law.

(7)   National courts have an essential part to play in applying the Community competition rules. When deciding disputes between private individuals, they protect the subjective rights under Community law, for example by awarding damages to the victims of infringements. The role of the national courts here complements that of the competition authorities of the Member States. They should therefore be allowed to apply Articles 81 and 82 of the Treaty in full.

(8)   In order to ensure the effective enforcement of the Community competition rules and the proper functioning of the cooperation mechanisms contained in this Regulation, it is necessary to oblige the competition authorities and courts of the Member States to also apply Articles 81 and 82 of the Treaty where they apply national competition law to agreements and practices which may affect trade between Member States. In order to create a level playing field for agreements, decisions by associations of undertakings and concerted practices within the internal market, it is also necessary to determine pursuant to Article 83(2)(e) of the Treaty the relationship between national laws and Community competition law. To that effect it is necessary to provide that the application of national competition laws to agreements, decisions or concerted practices within the meaning of Article 81(1) of the Treaty may not lead to the prohibition of such agreements, decisions and concerted practices if they are not also prohibited under Community competition law. The notions of agreements, decisions and concerted practices are autonomous concepts of Community competition law covering the coordination of behaviour of undertakings on the market as interpreted by the Community Courts. Member States should not under this Regulation be precluded from adopting and applying on their territory stricter national competition laws which prohibit or impose sanctions on unilateral conduct engaged in by undertakings. These stricter national laws may include provisions which prohibit or impose sanctions on abusive behaviour toward economically dependent undertakings. Furthermore, this Regulation does not apply to national laws which impose criminal sanctions on natural persons except to the extent that such sanctions are the means whereby competition rules applying to undertakings are enforced.

(9)   Articles 81 and 82 of the Treaty have as their objective the protection of competition on the market. This Regulation, which is adopted for the implementation of these Treaty provisions, does not preclude Member States from implementing on their territory national legislation, which protects other legitimate interests provided that such legislation is compatible with general principles and other provisions of Community law. In so far as such national legislation pursues predominantly an objective different from that of protecting competition on the market, the competition authorities and courts of the Member States may apply such legislation on their territory. Accordingly, Member States may under this Regulation implement on their territory national legislation that prohibits or imposes sanctions on acts of unfair trading practice, be they unilateral or contractual. Such legislation pursues a specific objective, irrespective of the actual or presumed effects of such acts on competition on the market. This is particularly the case of legislation which prohibits undertakings from imposing on their trading partners, obtaining or attempting to obtain from them terms and conditions that are unjustified, disproportionate or without consideration.

(10) Regulations such as 19/65/EEC(6), (EEC) No 2821/71(7), (EEC) No 3976/87(8), (EEC) No 1534/91(9), or (EEC) No 479/92(10) empower the Commission to apply Article 81(3) of the Treaty by Regulation to certain categories of agreements, decisions by associations of undertakings and concerted practices. In the areas defined by such Regulations, the Commission has adopted and may continue to adopt so called "block" exemption Regulations by which it declares Article 81(1) of the Treaty inapplicable to categories of agreements, decisions and concerted practices. Where agreements, decisions and concerted practices to which such Regulations apply nonetheless have effects that are incompatible with Article 81(3) of the Treaty, the Commission and the competition authorities of the Member States should have the power to withdraw in a particular case the benefit of the block exemption Regulation.

(11) For it to ensure that the provisions of the Treaty are applied, the Commission should be able to address decisions to undertakings or associations of undertakings for the purpose

of bringing to an end infringements of Articles 81 and 82 of the Treaty. Provided there is a legitimate interest in doing so, the Commission should also be able to adopt decisions which find that an infringement has been committed in the past even if it does not impose a fine. This Regulation should also make explicit provision for the Commission's power to adopt decisions ordering interim measures, which has been acknowledged by the Court of Justice.

(12) This Regulation should make explicit provision for the Commission's power to impose any remedy, whether behavioural or structural, which is necessary to bring the infringement effectively to an end, having regard to the principle of proportionality. Structural remedies should only be imposed either where there is no equally effective behavioural remedy or where any equally effective behavioural remedy would be more burdensome for the undertaking concerned than the structural remedy. Changes to the structure of an undertaking as it existed before the infringement was committed would only be proportionate where there is a substantial risk of a lasting or repeated infringement that derives from the very structure of the undertaking.

(13) Where, in the course of proceedings which might lead to an agreement or practice being prohibited, undertakings offer the Commission commitments such as to meet its concerns, the Commission should be able to adopt decisions which make those commitments binding on the undertakings concerned. Commitment decisions should find that there are no longer grounds for action by the Commission without concluding whether or not there has been or still is an infringement. Commitment decisions are without prejudice to the powers of competition authorities and courts of the Member States to make such a finding and decide upon the case. Commitment decisions are not appropriate in cases where the Commission intends to impose a fine.

(14) In exceptional cases where the public interest of the Community so requires, it may also be expedient for the Commission to adopt a decision of a declaratory nature finding that the prohibition in Article 81 or Article 82 of the Treaty does not apply, with a view to clarifying the law and ensuring its consistent application throughout the Community, in particular with regard to new types of agreements or practices that have not been settled in the existing case-law and administrative practice.

(15) The Commission and the competition authorities of the Member States should form together a network of public authorities applying the Community competition rules in close cooperation. For that purpose it is necessary to set up arrangements for information and consultation. Further modalities for the cooperation within the network will be laid down and revised by the Commission, in close cooperation with the Member States.

(16) Notwithstanding any national provision to the contrary, the exchange of information and the use of such information in evidence should be allowed between the members of the network even where the information is confidential. This information may be used for the application of Articles 81 and 82 of the Treaty as well as for the parallel application of national competition law, provided that the latter application relates to the same case and does not lead to a different outcome. When the information exchanged is used by the receiving authority to impose sanctions on undertakings, there should be no other limit to the use of the information than the obligation to use it for the purpose for which it was collected given the fact that the sanctions imposed on undertakings are of the same type in all systems. The rights of defence enjoyed by undertakings in the various systems can be considered as sufficiently equivalent. However, as regards natural persons, they may be subject to substantially different types of sanctions across the various systems. Where that is the case, it is necessary to ensure that information can only be used if it has been

collected in a way which respects the same level of protection of the rights of defence of natural persons as provided for under the national rules of the receiving authority.

(17) If the competition rules are to be applied consistently and, at the same time, the network is to be managed in the best possible way, it is essential to retain the rule that the competition authorities of the Member States are automatically relieved of their competence if the Commission initiates its own proceedings. Where a competition authority of a Member State is already acting on a case and the Commission intends to initiate proceedings, it should endeavour to do so as soon as possible. Before initiating proceedings, the Commission should consult the national authority concerned.

(18) To ensure that cases are dealt with by the most appropriate authorities within the network, a general provision should be laid down allowing a competition authority to suspend or close a case on the ground that another authority is dealing with it or has already dealt with it, the objective being that each case should be handled by a single authority. This provision should not prevent the Commission from rejecting a complaint for lack of Community interest, as the case-law of the Court of Justice has acknowledged it may do, even if no other competition authority has indicated its intention of dealing with the case.

(19) The Advisory Committee on Restrictive Practices and Dominant Positions set up by Regulation No 17 has functioned in a very satisfactory manner. It will fit well into the new system of decentralised application. It is necessary, therefore, to build upon the rules laid down by Regulation No 17, while improving the effectiveness of the organisational arrangements. To this end, it would be expedient to allow opinions to be delivered by written procedure. The Advisory Committee should also be able to act as a forum for discussing cases that are being handled by the competition authorities of the Member States, so as to help safeguard the consistent application of the Community competition rules.

(20) The Advisory Committee should be composed of representatives of the competition authorities of the Member States. For meetings in which general issues are being discussed, Member States should be able to appoint an additional representative. This is without prejudice to members of the Committee being assisted by other experts from the Member States.

(21) Consistency in the application of the competition rules also requires that arrangements be established for cooperation between the courts of the Member States and the Commission. This is relevant for all courts of the Member States that apply Articles 81 and 82 of the Treaty, whether applying these rules in lawsuits between private parties, acting as public enforcers or as review courts. In particular, national courts should be able to ask the Commission for information or for its opinion on points concerning the application of Community competition law. The Commission and the competition authorities of the Member States should also be able to submit written or oral observations to courts called upon to apply Article 81 or Article 82 of the Treaty. These observations should be submitted within the framework of national procedural rules and practices including those safeguarding the rights of the parties. Steps should therefore be taken to ensure that the Commission and the competition authorities of the Member States are kept sufficiently well informed of proceedings before national courts.

(22) In order to ensure compliance with the principles of legal certainty and the uniform application of the Community competition rules in a system of parallel powers, conflicting decisions must be avoided. It is therefore necessary to clarify, in accordance with the case-law of the Court of Justice, the effects of Commission decisions and proceedings on courts and competition authorities of the Member States. Commitment decisions adopted by the

Commission do not affect the power of the courts and the competition authorities of the Member States to apply Articles 81 and 82 of the Treaty.

(23) The Commission should be empowered throughout the Community to require such information to be supplied as is necessary to detect any agreement, decision or concerted practice prohibited by Article 81 of the Treaty or any abuse of a dominant position prohibited by Article 82 of the Treaty. When complying with a decision of the Commission, undertakings cannot be forced to admit that they have committed an infringement, but they are in any event obliged to answer factual questions and to provide documents, even if this information may be used to establish against them or against another undertaking the existence of an infringement.

(24) The Commission should also be empowered to undertake such inspections as are necessary to detect any agreement, decision or concerted practice prohibited by Article 81 of the Treaty or any abuse of a dominant position prohibited by Article 82 of the Treaty. The competition authorities of the Member States should cooperate actively in the exercise of these powers.

(25) The detection of infringements of the competition rules is growing ever more difficult, and, in order to protect competition effectively, the Commission's powers of investigation need to be supplemented. The Commission should in particular be empowered to interview any persons who may be in possession of useful information and to record the statements made. In the course of an inspection, officials authorised by the Commission should be empowered to affix seals for the period of time necessary for the inspection. Seals should normally not be affixed for more than 72 hours. Officials authorised by the Commission should also be empowered to ask for any information relevant to the subject matter and purpose of the inspection.

(26) Experience has shown that there are cases where business records are kept in the homes of directors or other people working for an undertaking. In order to safeguard the effectiveness of inspections, therefore, officials and other persons authorised by the Commission should be empowered to enter any premises where business records may be kept, including private homes. However, the exercise of this latter power should be subject to the authorisation of the judicial authority.

(27) Without prejudice to the case-law of the Court of Justice, it is useful to set out the scope of the control that the national judicial authority may carry out when it authorises, as foreseen by national law including as a precautionary measure, assistance from law enforcement authorities in order to overcome possible opposition on the part of the undertaking or the execution of the decision to carry out inspections in non-business premises. It results from the case-law that the national judicial authority may in particular ask the Commission for further information which it needs to carry out its control and in the absence of which it could refuse the authorisation. The case-law also confirms the competence of the national courts to control the application of national rules governing the implementation of coercive measures.

(28) In order to help the competition authorities of the Member States to apply Articles 81 and 82 of the Treaty effectively, it is expedient to enable them to assist one another by carrying out inspections and other fact-finding measures.

(29) Compliance with Articles 81 and 82 of the Treaty and the fulfilment of the obligations imposed on undertakings and associations of undertakings under this Regulation should be enforceable by means of fines and periodic penalty payments. To that end, appropriate levels of fine should also be laid down for infringements of the procedural rules.

(30) In order to ensure effective recovery of fines imposed on associations of undertakings for infringements that they have committed, it is necessary to lay down the conditions on which the Commission may require payment of the fine from the members of the association where the association is not solvent. In doing so, the Commission should have regard to the relative size of the undertakings belonging to the association and in particular to the situation of small and medium-sized enterprises. Payment of the fine by one or several members of an association is without prejudice to rules of national law that provide for recovery of the amount paid from other members of the association.

(31) The rules on periods of limitation for the imposition of fines and periodic penalty payments were laid down in Council Regulation (EEC) No 2988/74(11), which also concerns penalties in the field of transport. In a system of parallel powers, the acts, which may interrupt a limitation period, should include procedural steps taken independently by the competition authority of a Member State. To clarify the legal framework, Regulation (EEC) No 2988/74 should therefore be amended to prevent it applying to matters covered by this Regulation, and this Regulation should include provisions on periods of limitation.

(32) The undertakings concerned should be accorded the right to be heard by the Commission, third parties whose interests may be affected by a decision should be given the opportunity of submitting their observations beforehand, and the decisions taken should be widely publicised. While ensuring the rights of defence of the undertakings concerned, in particular, the right of access to the file, it is essential that business secrets be protected. The confidentiality of information exchanged in the network should likewise be safeguarded.

(33) Since all decisions taken by the Commission under this Regulation are subject to review by the Court of Justice in accordance with the Treaty, the Court of Justice should, in accordance with Article 229 thereof be given unlimited jurisdiction in respect of decisions by which the Commission imposes fines or periodic penalty payments.

(34) The principles laid down in Articles 81 and 82 of the Treaty, as they have been applied by Regulation No 17, have given a central role to the Community bodies. This central role should be retained, whilst associating the Member States more closely with the application of the Community competition rules. In accordance with the principles of subsidiarity and proportionality as set out in Article 5 of the Treaty, this Regulation does not go beyond what is necessary in order to achieve its objective, which is to allow the Community competition rules to be applied effectively.

(35) In order to attain a proper enforcement of Community competition law, Member States should designate and empower authorities to apply Articles 81 and 82 of the Treaty as public enforcers. They should be able to designate administrative as well as judicial authorities to carry out the various functions conferred upon competition authorities in this Regulation. This Regulation recognises the wide variation which exists in the public enforcement systems of Member States. The effects of Article 11(6) of this Regulation should apply to all competition authorities. As an exception to this general rule, where a prosecuting authority brings a case before a separate judicial authority, Article 11(6) should apply to the prosecuting authority subject to the conditions in Article 35(4) of this Regulation. Where these conditions are not fulfilled, the general rule should apply. In any case, Article 11(6) should not apply to courts insofar as they are acting as review courts.

(36) As the case-law has made it clear that the competition rules apply to transport, that sector should be made subject to the procedural provisions of this Regulation. Council Regulation No 141 of 26 November 1962 exempting transport from the application of Regulation No 17(12) should therefore be repealed and Regulations (EEC) No

1017/68(13), (EEC) No 4056/86(14) and (EEC) No 3975/87(15) should be amended in order to delete the specific procedural provisions they contain.

(37) This Regulation respects the fundamental rights and observes the principles recognised in particular by the Charter of Fundamental Rights of the European Union. Accordingly, this Regulation should be interpreted and applied with respect to those rights and principles.

(38) Legal certainty for undertakings operating under the Community competition rules contributes to the promotion of innovation and investment. Where cases give rise to genuine uncertainty because they present novel or unresolved questions for the application of these rules, individual undertakings may wish to seek informal guidance from the Commission. This Regulation is without prejudice to the ability of the Commission to issue such informal guidance,

HAS ADOPTED THIS REGULATION:

Chapter I PRINCIPLES

Article 1 Application of Articles 81 and 82 of the Treaty

1. Agreements, decisions and concerted practices caught by Article 81(1) of the Treaty which do not satisfy the conditions of Article 81(3) of the Treaty shall be prohibited, no prior decision to that effect being required.

2. Agreements, decisions and concerted practices caught by Article 81(1) of the Treaty which satisfy the conditions of Article 81(3) of the Treaty shall not be prohibited, no prior decision to that effect being required.

3. The abuse of a dominant position referred to in Article 82 of the Treaty shall be prohibited, no prior decision to that effect being required.

Article 2 Burden of proof

In any national or Community proceedings for the application of Articles 81 and 82 of the Treaty, the burden of proving an infringement of Article 81(1) or of Article 82 of the Treaty shall rest on the party or the authority alleging the infringement. The undertaking or association of undertakings claiming the benefit of Article 81(3) of the Treaty shall bear the burden of proving that the conditions of that paragraph are fulfilled.

Article 3 Relationship between Articles 81 and 82 of the Treaty and national competition laws

1. Where the competition authorities of the Member States or national courts apply national competition law to agreements, decisions by associations of undertakings or concerted practices within the meaning of Article 81(1) of the Treaty which may affect trade between Member States within the meaning of that provision, they shall also apply Article 81 of the Treaty to such agreements, decisions or concerted practices. Where the competition authorities of the Member States or national courts apply national competition law to any abuse prohibited by Article 82 of the Treaty, they shall also apply Article 82 of the Treaty.

2. The application of national competition law may not lead to the prohibition of agreements, decisions by associations of undertakings or concerted practices which may affect trade between Member States but which do not restrict competition within the meaning of Article 81(1) of the Treaty, or which fulfil the conditions of Article 81(3) of the Treaty or which are covered by a Regulation for the application of Article 81(3) of the Treaty. Member States shall not under this Regulation be precluded from adopting and applying on their territory stricter national laws which prohibit or sanction unilateral conduct engaged in by undertakings.

3.   Without prejudice to general principles and other provisions of Community law, paragraphs 1 and 2 do not apply when the competition authorities and the courts of the Member States apply national merger control laws nor do they preclude the application of provisions of national law that predominantly pursue an objective different from that pursued by Articles 81 and 82 of the Treaty.

Chapter II POWERS

Article 4 Powers of the Commission
For the purpose of applying Articles 81 and 82 of the Treaty, the Commission shall have the powers provided for by this Regulation.

Article 5 Powers of the competition authorities of the Member States
The competition authorities of the Member States shall have the power to apply Articles 81 and 82 of the Treaty in individual cases. For this purpose, acting on their own initiative or on a complaint, they may take the following decisions:
—   requiring that an infringement be brought to an end,

—   ordering interim measures,

—   accepting commitments,

—   imposing fines, periodic penalty payments or any other penalty provided for in their national law.

Where on the basis of the information in their possession the conditions for prohibition are not met they may likewise decide that there are no grounds for action on their part.

Article 6 Powers of the national courts
National courts shall have the power to apply Articles 81 and 82 of the Treaty.

Chapter III COMMISSION DECISIONS

Article 7 Finding and termination of infringement
1.   Where the Commission, acting on a complaint or on its own initiative, finds that there is an infringement of Article 81 or of Article 82 of the Treaty, it may by decision require the undertakings and associations of undertakings concerned to bring such infringement to an end. For this purpose, it may impose on them any behavioural or structural remedies which are proportionate to the infringement committed and necessary to bring the infringement effectively to an end. Structural remedies can only be imposed either where there is no equally effective behavioural remedy or where any equally effective behavioural remedy would be more burdensome for the undertaking concerned than the structural remedy. If the Commission has a legitimate interest in doing so, it may also find that an infringement has been committed in the past.

2.   Those entitled to lodge a complaint for the purposes of paragraph 1 are natural or legal persons who can show a legitimate interest and Member States.

Article 8 Interim measures
1.   In cases of urgency due to the risk of serious and irreparable damage to competition, the Commission, acting on its own initiative may by decision, on the basis of a prima facie finding of infringement, order interim measures.

2.   A decision under paragraph 1 shall apply for a specified period of time and may be renewed in so far this is necessary and appropriate.

Article 9 Commitments

1.   Where the Commission intends to adopt a decision requiring that an infringement be brought to an end and the undertakings concerned offer commitments to meet the concerns expressed to them by the Commission in its preliminary assessment, the Commission may by decision make those commitments binding on the undertakings. Such a decision may be adopted for a specified period and shall conclude that there are no longer grounds for action by the Commission.

2.   The Commission may, upon request or on its own initiative, reopen the proceedings:
      (a) where there has been a material change in any of the facts on which the decision was based;
      (b) where the undertakings concerned act contrary to their commitments; or
      (c) where the decision was based on incomplete, incorrect or misleading information provided by the parties.

Article 10 Finding of inapplicability

Where the Community public interest relating to the application of Articles 81 and 82 of the Treaty so requires, the Commission, acting on its own initiative, may by decision find that Article 81 of the Treaty is not applicable to an agreement, a decision by an association of undertakings or a concerted practice, either because the conditions of Article 81(1) of the Treaty are not fulfilled, or because the conditions of Article 81(3) of the Treaty are satisfied.

The Commission may likewise make such a finding with reference to Article 82 of the Treaty.

Chapter IV COOPERATION

Article 11 Cooperation between the Commission and the competition authorities of the Member States

1.   The Commission and the competition authorities of the Member States shall apply the Community competition rules in close cooperation.

2.   The Commission shall transmit to the competition authorities of the Member States copies of the most important documents it has collected with a view to applying Articles 7, 8, 9, 10 and Article 29(1). At the request of the competition authority of a Member State, the Commission shall provide it with a copy of other existing documents necessary for the assessment of the case.

3.   The competition authorities of the Member States shall, when acting under Article 81 or Article 82 of the Treaty, inform the Commission in writing before or without delay after commencing the first formal investigative measure. This information may also be made available to the competition authorities of the other Member States.

4.   No later than 30 days before the adoption of a decision requiring that an infringement be brought to an end, accepting commitments or withdrawing the benefit of a block exemption Regulation, the competition authorities of the Member States shall inform the Commission. To that effect, they shall provide the Commission with a summary of the case, the envisaged decision or, in the absence thereof, any other document indicating the proposed course of action. This information may also be made available to the competition authorities of the other Member States. At the request of the Commission, the acting competition authority shall make available to the Commission other documents it holds which are necessary for the assessment of the case. The information supplied to the Commission may be made available to the competition authorities of the other Member States. National competition authorities may also exchange between themselves information necessary for the assessment of a case that they are dealing with under Article 81 or Article 82 of the Treaty.

5.   The competition authorities of the Member States may consult the Commission on any case involving the application of Community law.

6.   The initiation by the Commission of proceedings for the adoption of a decision under Chapter III shall relieve the competition authorities of the Member States of their competence to apply Articles 81 and 82 of the Treaty. If a competition authority of a Member State is already acting on a case, the Commission shall only initiate proceedings after consulting with that national competition authority.

Article 12 Exchange of information

1.   For the purpose of applying Articles 81 and 82 of the Treaty the Commission and the competition authorities of the Member States shall have the power to provide one another with and use in evidence any matter of fact or of law, including confidential information.

2.   Information exchanged shall only be used in evidence for the purpose of applying Article 81 or Article 82 of the Treaty and in respect of the subject-matter for which it was collected by the transmitting authority. However, where national competition law is applied in the same case and in parallel to Community competition law and does not lead to a different outcome, information exchanged under this Article may also be used for the application of national competition law.

3.   Information exchanged pursuant to paragraph 1 can only be used in evidence to impose sanctions on natural persons where:
       — the law of the transmitting authority foresees sanctions of a similar kind in relation to an infringement of Article 81 or Article 82 of the Treaty or, in the absence thereof,
       — the information has been collected in a way which respects the same level of protection of the rights of defence of natural persons as provided for under the national rules of the receiving authority. However, in this case, the information exchanged cannot be used by the receiving authority to impose custodial sanctions.

Article 13 Suspension or termination of proceedings

1.   Where competition authorities of two or more Member States have received a complaint or are acting on their own initiative under Article 81 or Article 82 of the Treaty against the same agreement, decision of an association or practice, the fact that one authority is dealing with the case shall be sufficient grounds for the others to suspend the proceedings before them or to reject the complaint. The Commission may likewise reject a complaint on the ground that a competition authority of a Member State is dealing with the case.

2.   Where a competition authority of a Member State or the Commission has received a complaint against an agreement, decision of an association or practice which has already been dealt with by another competition authority, it may reject it.

Article 14 Advisory Committee

1.   The Commission shall consult an Advisory Committee on Restrictive Practices and Dominant Positions prior to the taking of any decision under Articles 7, 8, 9, 10, 23, Article 24(2) and Article 29(1).

2.   For the discussion of individual cases, the Advisory Committee shall be composed of representatives of the competition authorities of the Member States. For meetings in which issues other than individual cases are being discussed, an additional Member State representative competent in competition matters may be appointed. Representatives may, if unable to attend, be replaced by other representatives.

3.   The consultation may take place at a meeting convened and chaired by the Commission, held not earlier than 14 days after dispatch of the notice convening it, together with a

summary of the case, an indication of the most important documents and a preliminary draft decision. In respect of decisions pursuant to Article 8, the meeting may be held seven days after the dispatch of the operative part of a draft decision. Where the Commission dispatches a notice convening the meeting which gives a shorter period of notice than those specified above, the meeting may take place on the proposed date in the absence of an objection by any Member State. The Advisory Committee shall deliver a written opinion on the Commission's preliminary draft decision. It may deliver an opinion even if some members are absent and are not represented. At the request of one or several members, the positions stated in the opinion shall be reasoned.

4.   Consultation may also take place by written procedure. However, if any Member State so requests, the Commission shall convene a meeting. In case of written procedure, the Commission shall determine a time-limit of not less than 14 days within which the Member States are to put forward their observations for circulation to all other Member States. In case of decisions to be taken pursuant to Article 8, the time-limit of 14 days is replaced by seven days. Where the Commission determines a time-limit for the written procedure which is shorter than those specified above, the proposed time-limit shall be applicable in the absence of an objection by any Member State.

5.   The Commission shall take the utmost account of the opinion delivered by the Advisory Committee. It shall inform the Committee of the manner in which its opinion has been taken into account.

6.   Where the Advisory Committee delivers a written opinion, this opinion shall be appended to the draft decision. If the Advisory Committee recommends publication of the opinion, the Commission shall carry out such publication taking into account the legitimate interest of undertakings in the protection of their business secrets.

7.   At the request of a competition authority of a Member State, the Commission shall include on the agenda of the Advisory Committee cases that are being dealt with by a competition authority of a Member State under Article 81 or Article 82 of the Treaty. The Commission may also do so on its own initiative. In either case, the Commission shall inform the competition authority concerned.

A request may in particular be made by a competition authority of a Member State in respect of a case where the Commission intends to initiate proceedings with the effect of Article 11(6).

The Advisory Committee shall not issue opinions on cases dealt with by competition authorities of the Member States. The Advisory Committee may also discuss general issues of Community competition law.

Article 15 Cooperation with national courts

1.   In proceedings for the application of Article 81 or Article 82 of the Treaty, courts of the Member States may ask the Commission to transmit to them information in its possession or its opinion on questions concerning the application of the Community competition rules.

2.   Member States shall forward to the Commission a copy of any written judgment of national courts deciding on the application of Article 81 or Article 82 of the Treaty. Such copy shall be forwarded without delay after the full written judgment is notified to the parties.

3.   Competition authorities of the Member States, acting on their own initiative, may submit written observations to the national courts of their Member State on issues relating to the

application of Article 81 or Article 82 of the Treaty. With the permission of the court in question, they may also submit oral observations to the national courts of their Member State. Where the coherent application of Article 81 or Article 82 of the Treaty so requires, the Commission, acting on its own initiative, may submit written observations to courts of the Member States. With the permission of the court in question, it may also make oral observations.

For the purpose of the preparation of their observations only, the competition authorities of the Member States and the Commission may request the relevant court of the Member State to transmit or ensure the transmission to them of any documents necessary for the assessment of the case.

4.   This Article is without prejudice to wider powers to make observations before courts conferred on competition authorities of the Member States under the law of their Member State.

Article 16 Uniform application of Community competition law

1.   When national courts rule on agreements, decisions or practices under Article 81 or Article 82 of the Treaty which are already the subject of a Commission decision, they cannot take decisions running counter to the decision adopted by the Commission. They must also avoid giving decisions which would conflict with a decision contemplated by the Commission in proceedings it has initiated. To that effect, the national court may assess whether it is necessary to stay its proceedings. This obligation is without prejudice to the rights and obligations under Article 234 of the Treaty.

2.   When competition authorities of the Member States rule on agreements, decisions or practices under Article 81 or Article 82 of the Treaty which are already the subject of a Commission decision, they cannot take decisions which would run counter to the decision adopted by the Commission.

Chapter V POWERS OF INVESTIGATION

Article 17 Investigations into sectors of the economy and into types of agreements

1.   Where the trend of trade between Member States, the rigidity of prices or other circumstances suggest that competition may be restricted or distorted within the common market, the Commission may conduct its inquiry into a particular sector of the economy or into a particular type of agreements across various sectors. In the course of that inquiry, the Commission may request the undertakings or associations of undertakings concerned to supply the information necessary for giving effect to Articles 81 and 82 of the Treaty and may carry out any inspections necessary for that purpose.

The Commission may in particular request the undertakings or associations of undertakings concerned to communicate to it all agreements, decisions and concerted practices.

The Commission may publish a report on the results of its inquiry into particular sectors of the economy or particular types of agreements across various sectors and invite comments from interested parties.

2.   Articles 14, 18, 19, 20, 22, 23 and 24 shall apply mutatis mutandis.

Article 18 Requests for information

1.   In order to carry out the duties assigned to it by this Regulation, the Commission may, by simple request or by decision, require undertakings and associations of undertakings to provide all necessary information.

2.   When sending a simple request for information to an undertaking or association of undertakings, the Commission shall state the legal basis and the purpose of the request, specify what information is required and fix the time-limit within which the information is to be provided, and the penalties provided for in Article 23 for supplying incorrect or misleading information.

3.   Where the Commission requires undertakings and associations of undertakings to supply information by decision, it shall state the legal basis and the purpose of the request, specify what information is required and fix the time-limit within which it is to be provided. It shall also indicate the penalties provided for in Article 23 and indicate or impose the penalties provided for in Article 24. It shall further indicate the right to have the decision reviewed by the Court of Justice.

4.   The owners of the undertakings or their representatives and, in the case of legal persons, companies or firms, or associations having no legal personality, the persons authorised to represent them by law or by their constitution shall supply the information requested on behalf of the undertaking or the association of undertakings concerned. Lawyers duly authorised to act may supply the information on behalf of their clients. The latter shall remain fully responsible if the information supplied is incomplete, incorrect or misleading.

5.   The Commission shall without delay forward a copy of the simple request or of the decision to the competition authority of the Member State in whose territory the seat of the undertaking or association of undertakings is situated and the competition authority of the Member State whose territory is affected.

6.   At the request of the Commission the governments and competition authorities of the Member States shall provide the Commission with all necessary information to carry out the duties assigned to it by this Regulation.

Article 19 Power to take statements

1.   In order to carry out the duties assigned to it by this Regulation, the Commission may interview any natural or legal person who consents to be interviewed for the purpose of collecting information relating to the subject-matter of an investigation.

2.   Where an interview pursuant to paragraph 1 is conducted in the premises of an undertaking, the Commission shall inform the competition authority of the Member State in whose territory the interview takes place. If so requested by the competition authority of that Member State, its officials may assist the officials and other accompanying persons authorised by the Commission to conduct the interview.

Article 20 The Commission's powers of inspection

1.   In order to carry out the duties assigned to it by this Regulation, the Commission may conduct all necessary inspections of undertakings and associations of undertakings.

2.   The officials and other accompanying persons authorised by the Commission to conduct an inspection are empowered:
   (a) to enter any premises, land and means of transport of undertakings and associations of undertakings;
   (b) to examine the books and other records related to the business, irrespective of the medium on which they are stored;
   (c) to take or obtain in any form copies of or extracts from such books or records;
   (d) to seal any business premises and books or records for the period and to the extent necessary for the inspection;

(e) to ask any representative or member of staff of the undertaking or association of undertakings for explanations on facts or documents relating to the subject-matter and purpose of the inspection and to record the answers.

3.   The officials and other accompanying persons authorised by the Commission to conduct an inspection shall exercise their powers upon production of a written authorisation specifying the subject matter and purpose of the inspection and the penalties provided for in Article 23 in case the production of the required books or other records related to the business is incomplete or where the answers to questions asked under paragraph 2 of the present Article are incorrect or misleading. In good time before the inspection, the Commission shall give notice of the inspection to the competition authority of the Member State in whose territory it is to be conducted.

4.   Undertakings and associations of undertakings are required to submit to inspections ordered by decision of the Commission. The decision shall specify the subject matter and purpose of the inspection, appoint the date on which it is to begin and indicate the penalties provided for in Articles 23 and 24 and the right to have the decision reviewed by the Court of Justice. The Commission shall take such decisions after consulting the competition authority of the Member State in whose territory the inspection is to be conducted.

5.   Officials of as well as those authorised or appointed by the competition authority of the Member State in whose territory the inspection is to be conducted shall, at the request of that authority or of the Commission, actively assist the officials and other accompanying persons authorised by the Commission. To this end, they shall enjoy the powers specified in paragraph 2.

6.   Where the officials and other accompanying persons authorised by the Commission find that an undertaking opposes an inspection ordered pursuant to this Article, the Member State concerned shall afford them the necessary assistance, requesting where appropriate the assistance of the police or of an equivalent enforcement authority, so as to enable them to conduct their inspection.

7.   If the assistance provided for in paragraph 6 requires authorisation from a judicial authority according to national rules, such authorisation shall be applied for. Such authorisation may also be applied for as a precautionary measure.

8.   Where authorisation as referred to in paragraph 7 is applied for, the national judicial authority shall control that the Commission decision is authentic and that the coercive measures envisaged are neither arbitrary nor excessive having regard to the subject matter of the inspection. In its control of the proportionality of the coercive measures, the national judicial authority may ask the Commission, directly or through the Member State competition authority, for detailed explanations in particular on the grounds the Commission has for suspecting infringement of Articles 81 and 82 of the Treaty, as well as on the seriousness of the suspected infringement and on the nature of the involvement of the undertaking concerned. However, the national judicial authority may not call into question the necessity for the inspection nor demand that it be provided with the information in the Commission's file. The lawfulness of the Commission decision shall be subject to review only by the Court of Justice.

Article 21 Inspection of other premises

1.   If a reasonable suspicion exists that books or other records related to the business and to the subject-matter of the inspection, which may be relevant to prove a serious violation of Article 81 or Article 82 of the Treaty, are being kept in any other premises, land and means of transport, including the homes of directors, managers and other members of staff of the

undertakings and associations of undertakings concerned, the Commission can by decision order an inspection to be conducted in such other premises, land and means of transport.

2.   The decision shall specify the subject matter and purpose of the inspection, appoint the date on which it is to begin and indicate the right to have the decision reviewed by the Court of Justice. It shall in particular state the reasons that have led the Commission to conclude that a suspicion in the sense of paragraph 1 exists. The Commission shall take such decisions after consulting the competition authority of the Member State in whose territory the inspection is to be conducted.

3.   A decision adopted pursuant to paragraph 1 cannot be executed without prior authorisation from the national judicial authority of the Member State concerned. The national judicial authority shall control that the Commission decision is authentic and that the coercive measures envisaged are neither arbitrary nor excessive having regard in particular to the seriousness of the suspected infringement, to the importance of the evidence sought, to the involvement of the undertaking concerned and to the reasonable likelihood that business books and records relating to the subject matter of the inspection are kept in the premises for which the authorisation is requested. The national judicial authority may ask the Commission, directly or through the Member State competition authority, for detailed explanations on those elements which are necessary to allow its control of the proportionality of the coercive measures envisaged.

However, the national judicial authority may not call into question the necessity for the inspection nor demand that it be provided with information in the Commission's file. The lawfulness of the Commission decision shall be subject to review only by the Court of Justice.

4.   The officials and other accompanying persons authorised by the Commission to conduct an inspection ordered in accordance with paragraph 1 of this Article shall have the powers set out in Article 20(2)(a), (b) and (c). Article 20(5) and (6) shall apply mutatis mutandis.

Article 22 Investigations by competition authorities of Member States

1.   The competition authority of a Member State may in its own territory carry out any inspection or other fact-finding measure under its national law on behalf and for the account of the competition authority of another Member State in order to establish whether there has been an infringement of Article 81 or Article 82 of the Treaty. Any exchange and use of the information collected shall be carried out in accordance with Article 12.

2.   At the request of the Commission, the competition authorities of the Member States shall undertake the inspections which the Commission considers to be necessary under Article 20(1) or which it has ordered by decision pursuant to Article 20(4). The officials of the competition authorities of the Member States who are responsible for conducting these inspections as well as those authorised or appointed by them shall exercise their powers in accordance with their national law.

If so requested by the Commission or by the competition authority of the Member State in whose territory the inspection is to be conducted, officials and other accompanying persons authorised by the Commission may assist the officials of the authority concerned.

Chapter VI PENALTIES

Article 23 Fines

1.   The Commission may by decision impose on undertakings and associations of undertakings fines not exceeding 1 % of the total turnover in the preceding business year where, intentionally or negligently:

    (a) they supply incorrect or misleading information in response to a request made pursuant to Article 17 or Article 18(2);

    (b) in response to a request made by decision adopted pursuant to Article 17 or Article 18(3), they supply incorrect, incomplete or misleading information or do not supply information within the required time-limit;

    (c) they produce the required books or other records related to the business in incomplete form during inspections under Article 20 or refuse to submit to inspections ordered by a decision adopted pursuant to Article 20(4);

    (d) in response to a question asked in accordance with Article 20(2)(e),
- they give an incorrect or misleading answer,
- they fail to rectify within a time-limit set by the Commission an incorrect, incomplete or misleading answer given by a member of staff, or
- they fail or refuse to provide a complete answer on facts relating to the subject-matter and purpose of an inspection ordered by a decision adopted pursuant to Article 20(4);

    (e) seals affixed in accordance with Article 20(2)(d) by officials or other accompanying persons authorised by the Commission have been broken.

2.   The Commission may by decision impose fines on undertakings and associations of undertakings where, either intentionally or negligently:

    (a) they infringe Article 81 or Article 82 of the Treaty; or

    (b) they contravene a decision ordering interim measures under Article 8; or

    (c) they fail to comply with a commitment made binding by a decision pursuant to Article 9.

For each undertaking and association of undertakings participating in the infringement, the fine shall not exceed 10% of its total turnover in the preceding business year.

Where the infringement of an association relates to the activities of its members, the fine shall not exceed 10% of the sum of the total turnover of each member active on the market affected by the infringement of the association.

3.   In fixing the amount of the fine, regard shall be had both to the gravity and to the duration of the infringement.

4.   When a fine is imposed on an association of undertakings taking account of the turnover of its members and the association is not solvent, the association is obliged to call for contributions from its members to cover the amount of the fine.

Where such contributions have not been made to the association within a time-limit fixed by the Commission, the Commission may require payment of the fine directly by any of the undertakings whose representatives were members of the decision-making bodies concerned of the association.

After the Commission has required payment under the second subparagraph, where necessary to ensure full payment of the fine, the Commission may require payment of the balance by any of the members of the association which were active on the market on which the infringement occurred.

However, the Commission shall not require payment under the second or the third subparagraph from undertakings which show that they have not implemented the infringing decision of the association and either were not aware of its existence or have actively distanced themselves from it before the Commission started investigating the case.

The financial liability of each undertaking in respect of the payment of the fine shall not exceed 10% of its total turnover in the preceding business year.

5.   Decisions taken pursuant to paragraphs 1 and 2 shall not be of a criminal law nature.

Article 24 Periodic penalty payments

1.   The Commission may, by decision, impose on undertakings or associations of undertakings periodic penalty payments not exceeding 5% of the average daily turnover in the preceding business year per day and calculated from the date appointed by the decision, in order to compel them:
   (a) to put an end to an infringement of Article 81 or Article 82 of the Treaty, in accordance with a decision taken pursuant to Article 7;
   (b) to comply with a decision ordering interim measures taken pursuant to Article 8;
   (c) to comply with a commitment made binding by a decision pursuant to Article 9;
   (d) to supply complete and correct information which it has requested by decision taken pursuant to Article 17 or Article 18(3);
   (e) to submit to an inspection which it has ordered by decision taken pursuant to Article 20(4).

2.   Where the undertakings or associations of undertakings have satisfied the obligation which the periodic penalty payment was intended to enforce, the Commission may fix the definitive amount of the periodic penalty payment at a figure lower than that which would arise under the original decision. Article 23(4) shall apply correspondingly.

Chapter VII LIMITATION PERIODS

Article 25 Limitation periods for the imposition of penalties

1.   The powers conferred on the Commission by Articles 23 and 24 shall be subject to the following limitation periods:
   (a) three years in the case of infringements of provisions concerning requests for information or the conduct of inspections;
   (b) five years in the case of all other infringements.

2.   Time shall begin to run on the day on which the infringement is committed. However, in the case of continuing or repeated infringements, time shall begin to run on the day on which the infringement ceases.

3.   Any action taken by the Commission or by the competition authority of a Member State for the purpose of the investigation or proceedings in respect of an infringement shall interrupt the limitation period for the imposition of fines or periodic penalty payments. The limitation period shall be interrupted with effect from the date on which the action is notified to at least one undertaking or association of undertakings which has participated in the infringement. Actions which interrupt the running of the period shall include in particular the following:
   (a) written requests for information by the Commission or by the competition authority of a Member State;
   (b) written authorisations to conduct inspections issued to its officials by the Commission or by the competition authority of a Member State;
   (c) the initiation of proceedings by the Commission or by the competition authority of a Member State;
   (d) notification of the statement of objections of the Commission or of the competition authority of a Member State.

4.   The interruption of the limitation period shall apply for all the undertakings or associations of undertakings which have participated in the infringement.

5.   Each interruption shall start time running afresh. However, the limitation period shall expire at the latest on the day on which a period equal to twice the limitation period has

elapsed without the Commission having imposed a fine or a periodic penalty payment. That period shall be extended by the time during which limitation is suspended pursuant to paragraph 6.

6.   The limitation period for the imposition of fines or periodic penalty payments shall be suspended for as long as the decision of the Commission is the subject of proceedings pending before the Court of Justice.

Article 26 Limitation period for the enforcement of penalties

1.   The power of the Commission to enforce decisions taken pursuant to Articles 23 and 24 shall be subject to a limitation period of five years.

2.   Time shall begin to run on the day on which the decision becomes final.

3.   The limitation period for the enforcement of penalties shall be interrupted:
      (a) by notification of a decision varying the original amount of the fine or periodic penalty payment or refusing an application for variation;
      (b) by any action of the Commission or of a Member State, acting at the request of the Commission, designed to enforce payment of the fine or periodic penalty payment.

4.   Each interruption shall start time running afresh.

5.   The limitation period for the enforcement of penalties shall be suspended for so long as:
      (a) time to pay is allowed;
      (b) enforcement of payment is suspended pursuant to a decision of the Court of Justice.

Chapter VIII HEARINGS AND PROFESSIONAL SECRECY

Article 27 Hearing of the parties, complainants and others

1.   Before taking decisions as provided for in Articles 7, 8, 23 and Article 24(2), the Commission shall give the undertakings or associations of undertakings which are the subject of the proceedings conducted by the Commission the opportunity of being heard on the matters to which the Commission has taken objection. The Commission shall base its decisions only on objections on which the parties concerned have been able to comment. Complainants shall be associated closely with the proceedings.

2.   The rights of defence of the parties concerned shall be fully respected in the proceedings. They shall be entitled to have access to the Commission's file, subject to the legitimate interest of undertakings in the protection of their business secrets. The right of access to the file shall not extend to confidential information and internal documents of the Commission or the competition authorities of the Member States. In particular, the right of access shall not extend to correspondence between the Commission and the competition authorities of the Member States, or between the latter, including documents drawn up pursuant to Articles 11 and 14. Nothing in this paragraph shall prevent the Commission from disclosing and using information necessary to prove an infringement.

3.   If the Commission considers it necessary, it may also hear other natural or legal persons. Applications to be heard on the part of such persons shall, where they show a sufficient interest, be granted. The competition authorities of the Member States may also ask the Commission to hear other natural or legal persons.

4.   Where the Commission intends to adopt a decision pursuant to Article 9 or Article 10, it shall publish a concise summary of the case and the main content of the commitments or of the proposed course of action. Interested third parties may submit their observations within a time limit which is fixed by the Commission in its publication and which may not

be less than one month. Publication shall have regard to the legitimate interest of undertakings in the protection of their business secrets.

Article 28 Professional secrecy

1. Without prejudice to Articles 12 and 15, information collected pursuant to Articles 17 to 22 shall be used only for the purpose for which it was acquired.

2. Without prejudice to the exchange and to the use of information foreseen in Articles 11, 12, 14, 15 and 27, the Commission and the competition authorities of the Member States, their officials, servants and other persons working under the supervision of these authorities as well as officials and civil servants of other authorities of the Member States shall not disclose information acquired or exchanged by them pursuant to this Regulation and of the kind covered by the obligation of professional secrecy. This obligation also applies to all representatives and experts of Member States attending meetings of the Advisory Committee pursuant to Article 14.

Chapter IX EXEMPTION REGULATIONS

Article 29 Withdrawal in individual cases

1. Where the Commission, empowered by a Council Regulation, such as Regulations 19/65/ EEC, (EEC) No 2821/71, (EEC) No 3976/87, (EEC) No 1534/91 or (EEC) No 479/92, to apply Article 81(3) of the Treaty by regulation, has declared Article 81(1) of the Treaty inapplicable to certain categories of agreements, decisions by associations of undertakings or concerted practices, it may, acting on its own initiative or on a complaint, withdraw the benefit of such an exemption Regulation when it finds that in any particular case an agreement, decision or concerted practice to which the exemption Regulation applies has certain effects which are incompatible with Article 81(3) of the Treaty.

2. Where, in any particular case, agreements, decisions by associations of undertakings or concerted practices to which a Commission Regulation referred to in paragraph 1 applies have effects which are incompatible with Article 81(3) of the Treaty in the territory of a Member State, or in a part thereof, which has all the characteristics of a distinct geographic market, the competition authority of that Member State may withdraw the benefit of the Regulation in question in respect of that territory.

Chapter X GENERAL PROVISIONS

Article 30 Publication of decisions

1. The Commission shall publish the decisions, which it takes pursuant to Articles 7 to 10, 23 and 24.

2. The publication shall state the names of the parties and the main content of the decision, including any penalties imposed. It shall have regard to the legitimate interest of undertakings in the protection of their business secrets.

Article 31 Review by the Court of Justice

The Court of Justice shall have unlimited jurisdiction to review decisions whereby the Commission has fixed a fine or periodic penalty payment. It may cancel, reduce or increase the fine or periodic penalty payment imposed.

Article 32 (*deleted* by Regulation 1419/2006, OJ L269, 28.09.2006, p. 1)

Article 33 Implementing provisions

1. The Commission shall be authorised to take such measures as may be appropriate in order to apply this Regulation. The measures may concern, inter alia:

(a) the form, content and other details of complaints lodged pursuant to Article 7 and the procedure for rejecting complaints;

(b) the practical arrangements for the exchange of information and consultations provided for in Article 11;

(c) the practical arrangements for the hearings provided for in Article 27.

2. Before the adoption of any measures pursuant to paragraph 1, the Commission shall publish a draft thereof and invite all interested parties to submit their comments within the time-limit it lays down, which may not be less than one month. Before publishing a draft measure and before adopting it, the Commission shall consult the Advisory Committee on Restrictive Practices and Dominant Positions.

Chapter XI TRANSITIONAL, AMENDING AND FINAL PROVISIONS

Article 34 Transitional provisions

1. Applications made to the Commission under Article 2 of Regulation No 17, notifications made under Articles 4 and 5 of that Regulation and the corresponding applications and notifications made under Regulations (EEC) No 1017/68, (EEC) No 4056/86 and (EEC) No 3975/87 shall lapse as from the date of application of this Regulation.

2. Procedural steps taken under Regulation No 17 and Regulations (EEC) No 1017/68, (EEC) No 4056/86 and (EEC) No 3975/87 shall continue to have effect for the purposes of applying this Regulation.

Article 35 Designation of competition authorities of Member States

1. The Member States shall designate the competition authority or authorities responsible for the application of Articles 81 and 82 of the Treaty in such a way that the provisions of this regulation are effectively complied with. The measures necessary to empower those authorities to apply those Articles shall be taken before 1 May 2004. The authorities designated may include courts.

2. When enforcement of Community competition law is entrusted to national administrative and judicial authorities, the Member States may allocate different powers and functions to those different national authorities, whether administrative or judicial.

3. The effects of Article 11(6) apply to the authorities designated by the Member States including courts that exercise functions regarding the preparation and the adoption of the types of decisions foreseen in Article 5. The effects of Article 11(6) do not extend to courts insofar as they act as review courts in respect of the types of decisions foreseen in Article 5.

4. Notwithstanding paragraph 3, in the Member States where, for the adoption of certain types of decisions foreseen in Article 5, an authority brings an action before a judicial authority that is separate and different from the prosecuting authority and provided that the terms of this paragraph are complied with, the effects of Article 11(6) shall be limited to the authority prosecuting the case which shall withdraw its claim before the judicial authority when the Commission opens proceedings and this withdrawal shall bring the national proceedings effectively to an end.

Article 36 Amendment of Regulation (EEC) No 1017/68

Regulation (EEC) No 1017/68 is amended as follows:

1. Article 2 is repealed;

2. in Article 3(1), the words "The prohibition laid down in Article 2" are replaced by the words "The prohibition in Article 81(1) of the Treaty";

3.   Article 4 is amended as follows:
      (a) In paragraph 1, the words "The agreements, decisions and concerted practices
           referred to in Article 2" are replaced by the words "Agreements, decisions and
           concerted practices pursuant to Article 81(1) of the Treaty";
      (b) Paragraph 2 is replaced by the following:
           "2. If the implementation of any agreement, decision or concerted practice covered
           by paragraph 1 has, in a given case, effects which are incompatible with the
           requirements of Article 81(3) of the Treaty, undertakings or associations of
           undertakings may be required to make such effects cease."
4.   Articles 5 to 29 are repealed with the exception of Article 13(3) which continues to apply
      to decisions adopted pursuant to Article 5 of Regulation (EEC) No 1017/68 prior to the
      date of application of this Regulation until the date of expiration of those decisions;

5.   in Article 30, paragraphs 2, 3 and 4 are deleted.

Article 37 Amendment of Regulation (EEC) No 2988/74
      In Regulation (EEC) No 2988/74, the following Article is inserted:

      "Article 7a

      Exclusion

This Regulation shall not apply to measures taken under Council Regulation (EC) No 1/2003
of 16 December 2002 on the implementation of the rules on competition laid down in
Articles 81 and 82 of the Treaty(16)."

Article 38 Amendment of Regulation (EEC) No 4056/86
Regulation (EEC) No 4056/86 is amended as follows:

1.   Article 7 is amended as follows:
      (a) Paragraph 1 is replaced by the following:
           "1. Breach of an obligation
               Where the persons concerned are in breach of an obligation which, pursuant to
               Article 5, attaches to the exemption provided for in Article 3, the Commission
               may, in order to put an end to such breach and under the conditions laid down in
               Council Regulation (EC) No 1/2003 of 16 December 2002 on the
               implementation of the rules on competition laid down in Articles 81 and 82 of
               the Treaty(17) adopt a decision that either prohibits them from carrying out or
               requires them to perform certain specific acts, or withdraws the benefit of the
               block exemption which they enjoyed."
      (b) Paragraph 2 is amended as follows:
           (i)   In point (a), the words "under the conditions laid down in Section II" are replaced
                 by the words "under the conditions laid down in Regulation (EC) No 1/2003";
           (ii) The second sentence of the second subparagraph of point (c)(i) is replaced by the
                 following:
                 "At the same time it shall decide, in accordance with Article 9 of Regulation (EC) No
                 1/2003, whether to accept commitments offered by the undertakings concerned with
                 a view, inter alia, to obtaining access to the market for non-conference lines."

2.   Article 8 is amended as follows:
      (a) Paragraph 1 is deleted.
      (b) In paragraph 2 the words "pursuant to Article 10" are replaced by the words
           "pursuant to Regulation (EC) No 1/2003".
      (c) Paragraph 3 is deleted;

3.   Article 9 is amended as follows:
  (a) In paragraph 1, the words "Advisory Committee referred to in Article 15" are
      replaced by the words "Advisory Committee referred to in Article 14 of Regulation
      (EC) No 1/2003";
  (b) In paragraph 2, the words "Advisory Committee as referred to in Article 15" are
      replaced by the words "Advisory Committee referred to in Article 14 of Regulation
      (EC) No 1/2003";

4.   Articles 10 to 25 are repealed with the exception of Article 13(3) which continues to apply
      to decisions adopted pursuant to Article 81(3) of the Treaty prior to the date of
      application of this Regulation until the date of expiration of those decisions;

5.   in Article 26, the words "the form, content and other details of complaints pursuant to
      Article 10, applications pursuant to Article 12 and the hearings provided for in
      Article 23(1) and (2)" are deleted.

Article 39 Amendment of Regulation (EEC) No 3975/87
Articles 3 to 19 of Regulation (EEC) No 3975/87 are repealed with the exception of Article 6(3)
which continues to apply to decisions adopted pursuant to Article 81(3) of the Treaty prior to
the date of application of this Regulation until the date of expiration of those decisions.

**Article 40 Amendment of Regulations No 19/65/EEC, (EEC) No 2821/71 and (EEC) No
1534/91**
Article 7 of Regulation No 19/65/EEC, Article 7 of Regulation (EEC) No 2821/71 and Article 7
of Regulation (EEC) No 1534/91 are repealed.

Article 41 Amendment of Regulation (EEC) No 3976/87
Regulation (EEC) No 3976/87 is amended as follows:
1.   Article 6 is replaced by the following:

      "Article 6

      The Commission shall consult the Advisory Committee referred to in Article 14 of
      Council Regulation (EC) No 1/2003 of 16 December 2002 on the implementation of the
      rules on competition laid down in Articles 81 and 82 of the Treaty(18) before publishing a
      draft Regulation and before adopting a Regulation."

2.   Article 7 is repealed.

Article 42 Amendment of Regulation (EEC) No 479/92
Regulation (EEC) No 479/92 is amended as follows:
1.   Article 5 is replaced by the following:

      "Article 5

      Before publishing the draft Regulation and before adopting the Regulation, the
      Commission shall consult the Advisory Committee referred to in Article 14 of Council
      Regulation (EC) No 1/2003 of 16 December 2002 on the implementation of the rules on
      competition laid down in Articles 81 and 82 of the Treaty(19)."

2.   Article 6 is repealed.

Article 43 Repeal of Regulations No 17 and No 141
1.   Regulation No 17 is repealed with the exception of Article 8(3) which continues to
      apply to decisions adopted pursuant to Article 81(3) of the Treaty prior to the date of
      application of this Regulation until the date of expiration of those decisions.

2.   Regulation No 141 is repealed.

3.   References to the repealed Regulations shall be construed as references to this Regulation.

Article 44 Report on the application of the present Regulation
Five years from the date of application of this Regulation, the Commission shall report to the European Parliament and the Council on the functioning of this Regulation, in particular on the application of Article 11(6) and Article 17.

On the basis of this report, the Commission shall assess whether it is appropriate to propose to the Council a revision of this Regulation.

Article 45 Entry into force
This Regulation shall enter into force on the 20th day following that of its publication in the *Official Journal of the European Communities*.

It shall apply from 1 May 2004.

This Regulation shall be binding in its entirety and directly applicable in all Member States.

(date of signing and signatory omitted)

....

(1) OJ C 365 E, 19.12.2000, p. 284.

(2) OJ C 72 E, 21.3.2002, p. 305.

(3) OJ C 155, 29.5.2001, p. 73.

(4) The title of Regulation No 17 has been adjusted to take account of the renumbering of the Articles of the EC Treaty, in accordance with Article 12 of the Treaty of Amsterdam; the original reference was to Articles 85 and 86 of the Treaty.

(5) OJ 13, 21.2.1962, p. 204/62. Regulation as last amended by Regulation (EC) No 1216/1999 (OJ L 148, 15.6.1999, p. 5).

(6) Council Regulation No 19/65/EEC of 2 March 1965 on the application of Article 81(3) (The titles of the Regulations have been adjusted to take account of the renumbering of the Articles of the EC Treaty, in accordance with Article 12 of the Treaty of Amsterdam; the original reference was to Article 85(3) of the Treaty) of the Treaty to certain categories of agreements and concerted practices (OJ 36, 6.3.1965, p. 533). Regulation as last amended by Regulation (EC) No 1215/1999 (OJ L 148, 15.6.1999, p. 1).

(7) Council Regulation (EEC) No 2821/71 of 20 December 1971 on the application of Article 81(3) (The titles of the Regulations have been adjusted to take account of the renumbering of the Articles of the EC Treaty, in accordance with Article 12 of the Treaty of Amsterdam; the original reference was to Article 85(3) of the Treaty) of the Treaty to categories of agreements, decisions and concerted practices (OJ L 285, 29.12.1971, p. 46). Regulation as last amended by the Act of Accession of 1994.

(8) Council Regulation (EEC) No 3976/87 of 14 December 1987 on the application of Article 81(3) (The titles of the Regulations have been adjusted to take account of the renumbering of the Articles of the EC Treaty, in accordance with Article 12 of the Treaty of Amsterdam; the original reference was to Article 85(3) of the Treaty) of the Treaty to certain categories of agreements and concerted practices in the air transport sector (OJ L 374, 31.12.1987, p. 9). Regulation as last amended by the Act of Accession of 1994.

(9) Council Regulation (EEC) No 1534/91 of 31 May 1991 on the application of Article 81(3) (The titles of the Regulations have been adjusted to take account of the renumbering of the Articles of the EC Treaty, in accordance with Article 12 of the Treaty of Amsterdam; the original reference was to Article 85(3) of the Treaty) of the Treaty to certain categories of agreements, decisions and concerted practices in the insurance sector (OJ L 143, 7.6.1991, p. 1).

(10) Council Regulation (EEC) No 479/92 of 25 February 1992 on the application of Article 81(3) (The titles of the Regulations have been adjusted to take account of the renumbering of the Articles of the EC Treaty, in accordance with Article 12 of the Treaty of Amsterdam; the original reference was to Article 85(3) of the Treaty) of the Treaty to certain categories of agreements, decisions and concerted practices between liner shipping companies (Consortia) (OJ L 55, 29.2.1992, p. 3). Regulation amended by the Act of Accession of 1994.

(11) Council Regulation (EEC) No 2988/74 of 26 November 1974 concerning limitation periods in proceedings and the enforcement of sanctions under the rules of the European Economic Community relating to transport and competition (OJ L 319, 29.11.1974, p. 1).

(12) OJ 124, 28.11.1962, p. 2751/62; Regulation as last amended by Regulation No 1002/67/EEC (OJ 306, 16.12.1967, p. 1).

(13) Council Regulation (EEC) No 1017/68 of 19 July 1968 applying rules of competition to transport by rail, road and inland waterway (OJ L 175, 23.7.1968, p. 1). Regulation as last amended by the Act of Accession of 1994.

(14) Council Regulation (EEC) No 4056/86 of 22 December 1986 laying down detailed rules for the application of Articles 81 and 82 (The title of the Regulation has been adjusted to take account of the renumbering of the Articles of the EC Treaty, in accordance with Article 12 of the Treaty of Amsterdam; the original reference was to Articles 85 and 86 of the Treaty) of the Treaty to maritime transport (OJ L 378, 31.12.1986, p. 4). Regulation as last amended by the Act of Accession of 1994.

(15) Council Regulation (EEC) No 3975/87 of 14 December 1987 laying down the procedure for the application of the rules on competition to undertakings in the air transport sector (OJ L 374, 31.12.1987, p. 1). Regulation as last amended by Regulation (EEC) No 2410/92 (OJ L 240, 24.8.1992, p. 18).

(16) OJ L 1, 4.1.2003, p. 1.

(17) OJ L 1, 4.1.2003, p. 1.

(18) OJ L 1, 4.1.2003, p. 1.

(19) OJ L 1, 4.1.2003, P. 1.

COUNCIL REGULATION (EC) NO 139/2004 OF 20 JANUARY 2004

on the control of concentrations between undertakings
(the EU Merger Regulation)

OJ L 24, 29.1.2004, P. 1[1]

(footnotes omitted)

THE COUNCIL OF THE EUROPEAN UNION,

Having regard to the Treaty establishing the European Community, and in particular Articles 83 and 308 thereof,

Having regard to the proposal from the Commission,

Having regard to the opinion of the European Parliament,

Having regard to the opinion of the European Economic and Social Committee,

Whereas:

(1)   Council Regulation (EEC) No 4064/89 of 21 December 1989 on the control of concentrations between undertakings has been substantially amended. Since further amendments are to be made, it should be recast in the interest of clarity.

(2)   For the achievement of the aims of the Treaty, Article 3(1)(g) gives the Community the objective of instituting a system ensuring that competition in the internal market is not distorted. Article 4(1) of the Treaty provides that the activities of the Member States and the Community are to be conducted in accordance with the principle of an open market economy with free competition. These principles are essential for the further development of the internal market.

(3)   The completion of the internal market and of economic and monetary union, the enlargement of the European Union and the lowering of international barriers to trade

....

[1]   EDITOR'S NOTE: Regulation 139/2004 repeals and replaces the previous Merger Regulation 4064/89 with effect from 1 May 2004. See the Correlation Table in the Annex below to convert article numbers from the previous Regulation. As of 1 May 2012 this Regulation has not been amended following the entry into force of the Treaty of Lisbon. It includes references to the old Treaty article numbers. Reference should be made to the Tables of Equivalences accompanying the consolidated Treaties in Part II of this edition for the conversion of old Treaty article numbers to new ones.

and investment will continue to result in major corporate reorganisations, particularly in the form of concentrations.

(4)   Such reorganisations are to be welcomed to the extent that they are in line with the requirements of dynamic competition and capable of increasing the competitiveness of European industry, improving the conditions of growth and raising the standard of living in the Community.

(5)   However, it should be ensured that the process of reorganisation does not result in lasting damage to competition; Community law must therefore include provisions governing those concentrations which may significantly impede effective competition in the common market or in a substantial part of it.

(6)   A specific legal instrument is therefore necessary to permit effective control of all concentrations in terms of their effect on the structure of competition in the Community and to be the only instrument applicable to such concentrations. Regulation (EEC) No 4064/89 has allowed a Community policy to develop in this field. In the light of experience, however, that Regulation should now be recast into legislation designed to meet the challenges of a more integrated market and the future enlargement of the European Union. In accordance with the principles of subsidiarity and of proportionality as set out in Article 5 of the Treaty, this Regulation does not go beyond what is necessary in order to achieve the objective of ensuring that competition in the common market is not distorted, in accordance with the principle of an open market economy with free competition.

(7)   Articles 81 and 82, while applicable, according to the case-law of the Court of Justice, to certain concentrations, are not sufficient to control all operations which may prove to be incompatible with the system of undistorted competition envisaged in the Treaty. This Regulation should therefore be based not only on Article 83 but, principally, on Article 308 of the Treaty, under which the Community may give itself the additional powers of action necessary for the attainment of its objectives, and also powers of action with regard to concentrations on the markets for agricultural products listed in Annex I to the Treaty.

(8)   The provisions to be adopted in this Regulation should apply to significant structural changes, the impact of which on the market goes beyond the national borders of any one Member State. Such concentrations should, as a general rule, be reviewed exclusively at Community level, in application of a "one-stop shop" system and in compliance with the principle of subsidiarity. Concentrations not covered by this Regulation come, in principle, within the jurisdiction of the Member States.

(9)   The scope of application of this Regulation should be defined according to the geographical area of activity of the undertakings concerned and be limited by quantitative thresholds in order to cover those concentrations which have a Community dimension. The Commission should report to the Council on the implementation of the applicable thresholds and criteria so that the Council, acting in accordance with Article 202 of the Treaty, is in a position to review them regularly, as well as the rules regarding pre-notification referral, in the light of the experience gained; this requires statistical data to be provided by the Member States to the Commission to enable it to prepare such reports and possible proposals for amendments. The Commission's reports and proposals should be based on relevant information regularly provided by the Member States.

(10)   A concentration with a Community dimension should be deemed to exist where the aggregate turnover of the undertakings concerned exceeds given thresholds; that is the case irrespective of whether or not the undertakings effecting the concentration have their

seat or their principal fields of activity in the Community, provided they have substantial operations there.

(11) The rules governing the referral of concentrations from the Commission to Member States and from Member States to the Commission should operate as an effective corrective mechanism in the light of the principle of subsidiarity; these rules protect the competition interests of the Member States in an adequate manner and take due account of legal certainty and the "one-stop shop" principle.

(12) Concentrations may qualify for examination under a number of national merger control systems if they fall below the turnover thresholds referred to in this Regulation. Multiple notification of the same transaction increases legal uncertainty, effort and cost for undertakings and may lead to conflicting assessments. The system whereby concentrations may be referred to the Commission by the Member States concerned should therefore be further developed.

(13) The Commission should act in close and constant liaison with the competent authorities of the Member States from which it obtains comments and information.

(14) The Commission and the competent authorities of the Member States should together form a network of public authorities, applying their respective competences in close cooperation, using efficient arrangements for information-sharing and consultation, with a view to ensuring that a case is dealt with by the most appropriate authority, in the light of the principle of subsidiarity and with a view to ensuring that multiple notifications of a given concentration are avoided to the greatest extent possible. Referrals of concentrations from the Commission to Member States and from Member States to the Commission should be made in an efficient manner avoiding, to the greatest extent possible, situations where a concentration is subject to a referral both before and after its notification.

(15) The Commission should be able to refer to a Member State notified concentrations with a Community dimension which threaten significantly to affect competition in a market within that Member State presenting all the characteristics of a distinct market. Where the concentration affects competition on such a market, which does not constitute a substantial part of the common market, the Commission should be obliged, upon request, to refer the whole or part of the case to the Member State concerned. A Member State should be able to refer to the Commission a concentration which does not have a Community dimension but which affects trade between Member States and threatens to significantly affect competition within its territory. Other Member States which are also competent to review the concentration should be able to join the request. In such a situation, in order to ensure the efficiency and predictability of the system, national time limits should be suspended until a decision has been reached as to the referral of the case. The Commission should have the power to examine and deal with a concentration on behalf of a requesting Member State or requesting Member States.

(16) The undertakings concerned should be granted the possibility of requesting referrals to or from the Commission before a concentration is notified so as to further improve the efficiency of the system for the control of concentrations within the Community. In such situations, the Commission and national competition authorities should decide within short, clearly defined time limits whether a referral to or from the Commission ought to be made, thereby ensuring the efficiency of the system. Upon request by the undertakings concerned, the Commission should be able to refer to a Member State a concentration with a Community dimension which may significantly affect competition in a market within that Member State presenting all the characteristics of a distinct market; the undertakings concerned should not, however, be required to demonstrate that the effects of the concentration would be detrimental to competition. A concentration should not be referred

from the Commission to a Member State which has expressed its disagreement to such a referral. Before notification to national authorities, the undertakings concerned should also be able to request that a concentration without a Community dimension which is capable of being reviewed under the national competition laws of at least three Member States be referred to the Commission. Such requests for pre-notification referrals to the Commission would be particularly pertinent in situations where the concentration would affect competition beyond the territory of one Member State. Where a concentration capable of being reviewed under the competition laws of three or more Member States is referred to the Commission prior to any national notification, and no Member State competent to review the case expresses its disagreement, the Commission should acquire exclusive competence to review the concentration and such a concentration should be deemed to have a Community dimension. Such pre-notification referrals from Member States to the Commission should not, however, be made where at least one Member State competent to review the case has expressed its disagreement with such a referral.

(17) The Commission should be given exclusive competence to apply this Regulation, subject to review by the Court of Justice.

(18) The Member States should not be permitted to apply their national legislation on competition to concentrations with a Community dimension, unless this Regulation makes provision therefor. The relevant powers of national authorities should be limited to cases where, failing intervention by the Commission, effective competition is likely to be significantly impeded within the territory of a Member State and where the competition interests of that Member State cannot be sufficiently protected otherwise by this Regulation. The Member States concerned must act promptly in such cases; this Regulation cannot, because of the diversity of national law, fix a single time limit for the adoption of final decisions under national law.

(19) Furthermore, the exclusive application of this Regulation to concentrations with a Community dimension is without prejudice to Article 296 of the Treaty, and does not prevent the Member States from taking appropriate measures to protect legitimate interests other than those pursued by this Regulation, provided that such measures are compatible with the general principles and other provisions of Community law.

(20) It is expedient to define the concept of concentration in such a manner as to cover operations bringing about a lasting change in the control of the undertakings concerned and therefore in the structure of the market. It is therefore appropriate to include, within the scope of this Regulation, all joint ventures performing on a lasting basis all the functions of an autonomous economic entity. It is moreover appropriate to treat as a single concentration transactions that are closely connected in that they are linked by condition or take the form of a series of transactions in securities taking place within a reasonably short period of time.

(21) This Regulation should also apply where the undertakings concerned accept restrictions directly related to, and necessary for, the implementation of the concentration. Commission decisions declaring concentrations compatible with the common market in application of this Regulation should automatically cover such restrictions, without the Commission having to assess such restrictions in individual cases. At the request of the undertakings concerned, however, the Commission should, in cases presenting novel or unresolved questions giving rise to genuine uncertainty, expressly assess whether or not any restriction is directly related to, and necessary for, the implementation of the concentration. A case presents a novel or unresolved question giving rise to genuine uncertainty if the question is not covered by the relevant Commission notice in force or a published Commission decision.

(22) The arrangements to be introduced for the control of concentrations should, without prejudice to Article 86(2) of the Treaty, respect the principle of non-discrimination between the public and the private sectors. In the public sector, calculation of the turnover of an undertaking concerned in a concentration needs, therefore, to take account of undertakings making up an economic unit with an independent power of decision, irrespective of the way in which their capital is held or of the rules of administrative supervision applicable to them.

(23) It is necessary to establish whether or not concentrations with a Community dimension are compatible with the common market in terms of the need to maintain and develop effective competition in the common market. In so doing, the Commission must place its appraisal within the general framework of the achievement of the fundamental objectives referred to in Article 2 of the Treaty establishing the European Community and Article 2 of the Treaty on European Union.

(24) In order to ensure a system of undistorted competition in the common market, in furtherance of a policy conducted in accordance with the principle of an open market economy with free competition, this Regulation must permit effective control of all concentrations from the point of view of their effect on competition in the Community. Accordingly, Regulation (EEC) No 4064/89 established the principle that a concentration with a Community dimension which creates or strengthens a dominant position as a result of which effective competition in the common market or in a substantial part of it would be significantly impeded should be declared incompatible with the common market.

(25) In view of the consequences that concentrations in oligopolistic market structures may have, it is all the more necessary to maintain effective competition in such markets. Many oligopolistic markets exhibit a healthy degree of competition. However, under certain circumstances, concentrations involving the elimination of important competitive constraints that the merging parties had exerted upon each other, as well as a reduction of competitive pressure on the remaining competitors, may, even in the absence of a likelihood of coordination between the members of the oligopoly, result in a significant impediment to effective competition. The Community courts have, however, not to date expressly interpreted Regulation (EEC) No 4064/89 as requiring concentrations giving rise to such non-coordinated effects to be declared incompatible with the common market. Therefore, in the interests of legal certainty, it should be made clear that this Regulation permits effective control of all such concentrations by providing that any concentration which would significantly impede effective competition, in the common market or in a substantial part of it, should be declared incompatible with the common market. The notion of "significant impediment to effective competition" in Article 2(2) and (3) should be interpreted as extending, beyond the concept of dominance, only to the anti-competitive effects of a concentration resulting from the non-coordinated behaviour of undertakings which would not have a dominant position on the market concerned.

(26) A significant impediment to effective competition generally results from the creation or strengthening of a dominant position. With a view to preserving the guidance that may be drawn from past judgments of the European courts and Commission decisions pursuant to Regulation (EEC) No 4064/89, while at the same time maintaining consistency with the standards of competitive harm which have been applied by the Commission and the Community courts regarding the compatibility of a concentration with the common market, this Regulation should accordingly establish the principle that a concentration with a Community dimension which would significantly impede effective competition, in the common market or in a substantial part thereof, in particular as a result of the creation or strengthening of a dominant position, is to be declared incompatible with the common market.

(27) In addition, the criteria of Article 81(1) and (3) of the Treaty should be applied to joint ventures performing, on a lasting basis, all the functions of autonomous economic entities, to the extent that their creation has as its consequence an appreciable restriction of competition between undertakings that remain independent.

(28) In order to clarify and explain the Commission's appraisal of concentrations under this Regulation, it is appropriate for the Commission to publish guidance which should provide a sound economic framework for the assessment of concentrations with a view to determining whether or not they may be declared compatible with the common market.

(29) In order to determine the impact of a concentration on competition in the common market, it is appropriate to take account of any substantiated and likely efficiencies put forward by the undertakings concerned. It is possible that the efficiencies brought about by the concentration counteract the effects on competition, and in particular the potential harm to consumers, that it might otherwise have and that, as a consequence, the concentration would not significantly impede effective competition, in the common market or in a substantial part of it, in particular as a result of the creation or strengthening of a dominant position. The Commission should publish guidance on the conditions under which it may take efficiencies into account in the assessment of a concentration.

(30) Where the undertakings concerned modify a notified concentration, in particular by offering commitments with a view to rendering the concentration compatible with the common market, the Commission should be able to declare the concentration, as modified, compatible with the common market. Such commitments should be proportionate to the competition problem and entirely eliminate it. It is also appropriate to accept commitments before the initiation of proceedings where the competition problem is readily identifiable and can easily be remedied. It should be expressly provided that the Commission may attach to its decision conditions and obligations in order to ensure that the undertakings concerned comply with their commitments in a timely and effective manner so as to render the concentration compatible with the common market. Transparency and effective consultation of Member States as well as of interested third parties should be ensured throughout the procedure.

(31) The Commission should have at its disposal appropriate instruments to ensure the enforcement of commitments and to deal with situations where they are not fulfilled. In cases of failure to fulfil a condition attached to the decision declaring a concentration compatible with the common market, the situation rendering the concentration compatible with the common market does not materialise and the concentration, as implemented, is therefore not authorised by the Commission. As a consequence, if the concentration is implemented, it should be treated in the same way as a non-notified concentration implemented without authorisation. Furthermore, where the Commission has already found that, in the absence of the condition, the concentration would be incompatible with the common market, it should have the power to directly order the dissolution of the concentration, so as to restore the situation prevailing prior to the implementation of the concentration. Where an obligation attached to a decision declaring the concentration compatible with the common market is not fulfilled, the Commission should be able to revoke its decision. Moreover, the Commission should be able to impose appropriate financial sanctions where conditions or obligations are not fulfilled.

(32) Concentrations which, by reason of the limited market share of the undertakings concerned, are not liable to impede effective competition may be presumed to be compatible with the common market. Without prejudice to Articles 81 and 82 of the Treaty, an indication to this effect exists, in particular, where the market share of the

undertakings concerned does not exceed 25 % either in the common market or in a substantial part of it.

(33) The Commission should have the task of taking all the decisions necessary to establish whether or not concentrations with a Community dimension are compatible with the common market, as well as decisions designed to restore the situation prevailing prior to the implementation of a concentration which has been declared incompatible with the common market.

(34) To ensure effective control, undertakings should be obliged to give prior notification of concentrations with a Community dimension following the conclusion of the agreement, the announcement of the public bid or the acquisition of a controlling interest. Notification should also be possible where the undertakings concerned satisfy the Commission of their intention to enter into an agreement for a proposed concentration and demonstrate to the Commission that their plan for that proposed concentration is sufficiently concrete, for example on the basis of an agreement in principle, a memorandum of understanding, or a letter of intent signed by all undertakings concerned, or, in the case of a public bid, where they have publicly announced an intention to make such a bid, provided that the intended agreement or bid would result in a concentration with a Community dimension. The implementation of concentrations should be suspended until a final decision of the Commission has been taken. However, it should be possible to derogate from this suspension at the request of the undertakings concerned, where appropriate. In deciding whether or not to grant a derogation, the Commission should take account of all pertinent factors, such as the nature and gravity of damage to the undertakings concerned or to third parties, and the threat to competition posed by the concentration. In the interest of legal certainty, the validity of transactions must nevertheless be protected as much as necessary.

(35) A period within which the Commission must initiate proceedings in respect of a notified concentration and a period within which it must take a final decision on the compatibility or incompatibility with the common market of that concentration should be laid down. These periods should be extended whenever the undertakings concerned offer commitments with a view to rendering the concentration compatible with the common market, in order to allow for sufficient time for the analysis and market testing of such commitment offers and for the consultation of Member States as well as interested third parties. A limited extension of the period within which the Commission must take a final decision should also be possible in order to allow sufficient time for the investigation of the case and the verification of the facts and arguments submitted to the Commission.

(36) The Community respects the fundamental rights and observes the principles recognised in particular by the Charter of Fundamental Rights of the European Union. Accordingly, this Regulation should be interpreted and applied with respect to those rights and principles.

(37) The undertakings concerned must be afforded the right to be heard by the Commission when proceedings have been initiated; the members of the management and supervisory bodies and the recognised representatives of the employees of the undertakings concerned, and interested third parties, must also be given the opportunity to be heard.

(38) In order properly to appraise concentrations, the Commission should have the right to request all necessary information and to conduct all necessary inspections throughout the Community. To that end, and with a view to protecting competition effectively, the Commission's powers of investigation need to be expanded. The Commission should, in particular, have the right to interview any persons who may be in possession of useful information and to record the statements made.

(39) In the course of an inspection, officials authorised by the Commission should have the right to ask for any information relevant to the subject matter and purpose of the inspection; they should also have the right to affix seals during inspections, particularly in circumstances where there are reasonable grounds to suspect that a concentration has been implemented without being notified; that incorrect, incomplete or misleading information has been supplied to the Commission; or that the undertakings or persons concerned have failed to comply with a condition or obligation imposed by decision of the Commission. In any event, seals should only be used in exceptional circumstances, for the period of time strictly necessary for the inspection, normally not for more than 48 hours.

(40) Without prejudice to the case-law of the Court of Justice, it is also useful to set out the scope of the control that the national judicial authority may exercise when it authorises, as provided by national law and as a precautionary measure, assistance from law enforcement authorities in order to overcome possible opposition on the part of the undertaking against an inspection, including the affixing of seals, ordered by Commission decision. It results from the case-law that the national judicial authority may in particular ask of the Commission further information which it needs to carry out its control and in the absence of which it could refuse the authorisation. The case-law also confirms the competence of the national courts to control the application of national rules governing the implementation of coercive measures. The competent authorities of the Member States should cooperate actively in the exercise of the Commission's investigative powers.

(41) When complying with decisions of the Commission, the undertakings and persons concerned cannot be forced to admit that they have committed infringements, but they are in any event obliged to answer factual questions and to provide documents, even if this information may be used to establish against themselves or against others the existence of such infringements.

(42) For the sake of transparency, all decisions of the Commission which are not of a merely procedural nature should be widely publicised. While ensuring preservation of the rights of defence of the undertakings concerned, in particular the right of access to the file, it is essential that business secrets be protected. The confidentiality of information exchanged in the network and with the competent authorities of third countries should likewise be safeguarded.

(43) Compliance with this Regulation should be enforceable, as appropriate, by means of fines and periodic penalty payments. The Court of Justice should be given unlimited jurisdiction in that regard pursuant to Article 229 of the Treaty.

(44) The conditions in which concentrations, involving undertakings having their seat or their principal fields of activity in the Community, are carried out in third countries should be observed, and provision should be made for the possibility of the Council giving the Commission an appropriate mandate for negotiation with a view to obtaining non-discriminatory treatment for such undertakings.

(45) This Regulation in no way detracts from the collective rights of employees, as recognised in the undertakings concerned, notably with regard to any obligation to inform or consult their recognised representatives under Community and national law.

(46) The Commission should be able to lay down detailed rules concerning the implementation of this Regulation in accordance with the procedures for the exercise of implementing powers conferred on the Commission. For the adoption of such implementing provisions, the Commission should be assisted by an Advisory Committee composed of the representatives of the Member States as specified in Article 23,

HAS ADOPTED THIS REGULATION:

Article 1 Scope

1.   Without prejudice to Article 4(5) and Article 22, this Regulation shall apply to all concentrations with a Community dimension as defined in this Article.

2.   A concentration has a Community dimension where:
   (a) the combined aggregate worldwide turnover of all the undertakings concerned is more than EUR 5000 million; and
   (b) the aggregate Community-wide turnover of each of at least two of the undertakings concerned is more than EUR 250 million,
   unless each of the undertakings concerned achieves more than two-thirds of its aggregate Community-wide turnover within one and the same Member State.

3.   A concentration that does not meet the thresholds laid down in paragraph 2 has a Community dimension where:
   (a) the combined aggregate worldwide turnover of all the undertakings concerned is more than EUR 2500 million;
   (b) in each of at least three Member States, the combined aggregate turnover of all the undertakings concerned is more than EUR 100 million;
   (c) in each of at least three Member States included for the purpose of point (b), the aggregate turnover of each of at least two of the undertakings concerned is more than EUR 25 million; and
   (d) the aggregate Community-wide turnover of each of at least two of the undertakings concerned is more than EUR 100 million,
   unless each of the undertakings concerned achieves more than two-thirds of its aggregate Community-wide turnover within one and the same Member State.

4.   On the basis of statistical data that may be regularly provided by the Member States, the Commission shall report to the Council on the operation of the thresholds and criteria set out in paragraphs 2 and 3 by 1 July 2009 and may present proposals pursuant to paragraph 5.

5.   Following the report referred to in paragraph 4 and on a proposal from the Commission, the Council, acting by a qualified majority, may revise the thresholds and criteria mentioned in paragraph 3.

Article 2 Appraisal of concentrations

1.   Concentrations within the scope of this Regulation shall be appraised in accordance with the objectives of this Regulation and the following provisions with a view to establishing whether or not they are compatible with the common market.

In making this appraisal, the Commission shall take into account:
   (a) the need to maintain and develop effective competition within the common market in view of, among other things, the structure of all the markets concerned and the actual or potential competition from undertakings located either within or outwith the Community;
   (b) the market position of the undertakings concerned and their economic and financial power, the alternatives available to suppliers and users, their access to supplies or markets, any legal or other barriers to entry, supply and demand trends for the relevant goods and services, the interests of the intermediate and ultimate consumers, and the development of technical and economic progress provided that it is to consumers' advantage and does not form an obstacle to competition.

2.   A concentration which would not significantly impede effective competition in the common market or in a substantial part of it, in particular as a result of the creation or strengthening of a dominant position, shall be declared compatible with the common market.

3.   A concentration which would significantly impede effective competition, in the common market or in a substantial part of it, in particular as a result of the creation or strengthening of a dominant position, shall be declared incompatible with the common market.

4.   To the extent that the creation of a joint venture constituting a concentration pursuant to Article 3 has as its object or effect the coordination of the competitive behaviour of undertakings that remain independent, such coordination shall be appraised in accordance with the criteria of Article 81(1) and (3) of the Treaty, with a view to establishing whether or not the operation is compatible with the common market.

5.   In making this appraisal, the Commission shall take into account in particular:
     —   whether two or more parent companies retain, to a significant extent, activities in the same market as the joint venture or in a market which is downstream or upstream from that of the joint venture or in a neighbouring market closely related to this market,
     —   whether the coordination which is the direct consequence of the creation of the joint venture affords the undertakings concerned the possibility of eliminating competition in respect of a substantial part of the products or services in question.

Article 3 Definition of concentration
1.   A concentration shall be deemed to arise where a change of control on a lasting basis results from:
     (a) the merger of two or more previously independent undertakings or parts of undertakings, or
     (b) the acquisition, by one or more persons already controlling at least one undertaking, or by one or more undertakings, whether by purchase of securities or assets, by contract or by any other means, of direct or indirect control of the whole or parts of one or more other undertakings.

2.   Control shall be constituted by rights, contracts or any other means which, either separately or in combination and having regard to the considerations of fact or law involved, confer the possibility of exercising decisive influence on an undertaking, in particular by:
     (a) ownership or the right to use all or part of the assets of an undertaking;
     (b) rights or contracts which confer decisive influence on the composition, voting or decisions of the organs of an undertaking.

3.   Control is acquired by persons or undertakings which:
     (a) are holders of the rights or entitled to rights under the contracts concerned; or
     (b) while not being holders of such rights or entitled to rights under such contracts, have the power to exercise the rights deriving therefrom.

4.   The creation of a joint venture performing on a lasting basis all the functions of an autonomous economic entity shall constitute a concentration within the meaning of paragraph 1(b).

5.   A concentration shall not be deemed to arise where:
     (a) credit institutions or other financial institutions or insurance companies, the normal activities of which include transactions and dealing in securities for their own account

or for the account of others, hold on a temporary basis securities which they have acquired in an undertaking with a view to reselling them, provided that they do not exercise voting rights in respect of those securities with a view to determining the competitive behaviour of that undertaking or provided that they exercise such voting rights only with a view to preparing the disposal of all or part of that undertaking or of its assets or the disposal of those securities and that any such disposal takes place within one year of the date of acquisition; that period may be extended by the Commission on request where such institutions or companies can show that the disposal was not reasonably possible within the period set;

(b) control is acquired by an office-holder according to the law of a Member State relating to liquidation, winding up, insolvency, cessation of payments, compositions or analogous proceedings;

(c) the operations referred to in paragraph 1(b) are carried out by the financial holding companies referred to in Article 5(3) of Fourth Council Directive 78/660/EEC of 25 July 1978 based on Article 54(3)(g) of the Treaty on the annual accounts of certain types of companies provided however that the voting rights in respect of the holding are exercised, in particular in relation to the appointment of members of the management and supervisory bodies of the undertakings in which they have holdings, only to maintain the full value of those investments and not to determine directly or indirectly the competitive conduct of those undertakings.

Article 4 Prior notification of concentrations and pre-notification referral at the request of the notifying parties

1. Concentrations with a Community dimension defined in this Regulation shall be notified to the Commission prior to their implementation and following the conclusion of the agreement, the announcement of the public bid, or the acquisition of a controlling interest.

    Notification may also be made where the undertakings concerned demonstrate to the Commission a good faith intention to conclude an agreement or, in the case of a public bid, where they have publicly announced an intention to make such a bid, provided that the intended agreement or bid would result in a concentration with a Community dimension.

    For the purposes of this Regulation, the term "notified concentration" shall also cover intended concentrations notified pursuant to the second subparagraph. For the purposes of paragraphs 4 and 5 of this Article, the term "concentration" includes intended concentrations within the meaning of the second subparagraph.

2. A concentration which consists of a merger within the meaning of Article 3(1)(a) or in the acquisition of joint control within the meaning of Article 3(1)(b) shall be notified jointly by the parties to the merger or by those acquiring joint control as the case may be. In all other cases, the notification shall be effected by the person or undertaking acquiring control of the whole or parts of one or more undertakings.

3. Where the Commission finds that a notified concentration falls within the scope of this Regulation, it shall publish the fact of the notification, at the same time indicating the names of the undertakings concerned, their country of origin, the nature of the concentration and the economic sectors involved. The Commission shall take account of the legitimate interest of undertakings in the protection of their business secrets.

4. Prior to the notification of a concentration within the meaning of paragraph 1, the persons or undertakings referred to in paragraph 2 may inform the Commission, by means of a reasoned submission, that the concentration may significantly affect

competition in a market within a Member State which presents all the characteristics of a distinct market and should therefore be examined, in whole or in part, by that Member State.

The Commission shall transmit this submission to all Member States without delay. The Member State referred to in the reasoned submission shall, within 15 working days of receiving the submission, express its agreement or disagreement as regards the request to refer the case. Where that Member State takes no such decision within this period, it shall be deemed to have agreed.

Unless that Member State disagrees, the Commission, where it considers that such a distinct market exists, and that competition in that market may be significantly affected by the concentration, may decide to refer the whole or part of the case to the competent authorities of that Member State with a view to the application of that State's national competition law.

The decision whether or not to refer the case in accordance with the third subparagraph shall be taken within 25 working days starting from the receipt of the reasoned submission by the Commission. The Commission shall inform the other Member States and the persons or undertakings concerned of its decision. If the Commission does not take a decision within this period, it shall be deemed to have adopted a decision to refer the case in accordance with the submission made by the persons or undertakings concerned.

If the Commission decides, or is deemed to have decided, pursuant to the third and fourth subparagraphs, to refer the whole of the case, no notification shall be made pursuant to paragraph 1 and national competition law shall apply. Article 9(6) to (9) shall apply mutatis mutandis.

5.   With regard to a concentration as defined in Article 3 which does not have a Community dimension within the meaning of Article 1 and which is capable of being reviewed under the national competition laws of at least three Member States, the persons or undertakings referred to in paragraph 2 may, before any notification to the competent authorities, inform the Commission by means of a reasoned submission that the concentration should be examined by the Commission.

The Commission shall transmit this submission to all Member States without delay.

Any Member State competent to examine the concentration under its national competition law may, within 15 working days of receiving the reasoned submission, express its disagreement as regards the request to refer the case.

Where at least one such Member State has expressed its disagreement in accordance with the third subparagraph within the period of 15 working days, the case shall not be referred. The Commission shall, without delay, inform all Member States and the persons or undertakings concerned of any such expression of disagreement.

Where no Member State has expressed its disagreement in accordance with the third subparagraph within the period of 15 working days, the concentration shall be deemed to have a Community dimension and shall be notified to the Commission in accordance with paragraphs 1 and 2. In such situations, no Member State shall apply its national competition law to the concentration.

6.   The Commission shall report to the Council on the operation of paragraphs 4 and 5 by 1 July 2009. Following this report and on a proposal from the Commission, the Council, acting by a qualified majority, may revise paragraphs 4 and 5.

Article 5 Calculation of turnover

1.   Aggregate turnover within the meaning of this Regulation shall comprise the amounts derived by the undertakings concerned in the preceding financial year from the sale of products and the provision of services falling within the undertakings' ordinary activities after deduction of sales rebates and of value added tax and other taxes directly related to turnover. The aggregate turnover of an undertaking concerned shall not include the sale of products or the provision of services between any of the undertakings referred to in paragraph 4.

Turnover, in the Community or in a Member State, shall comprise products sold and services provided to undertakings or consumers, in the Community or in that Member State as the case may be.

2.   By way of derogation from paragraph 1, where the concentration consists of the acquisition of parts, whether or not constituted as legal entities, of one or more undertakings, only the turnover relating to the parts which are the subject of the concentration shall be taken into account with regard to the seller or sellers.

However, two or more transactions within the meaning of the first subparagraph which take place within a two-year period between the same persons or undertakings shall be treated as one and the same concentration arising on the date of the last transaction.

3.   In place of turnover the following shall be used:
(a) for credit institutions and other financial institutions, the sum of the following income items as defined in Council Directive 86/635/EEC, after deduction of value added tax and other taxes directly related to those items, where appropriate:
(i)   interest income and similar income;
(ii) income from securities:
— income from shares and other variable yield securities,
— income from participating interests,
— income from shares in affiliated undertakings;
(iii) commissions receivable;
(iv) net profit on financial operations;
(v)   other operating income.
The turnover of a credit or financial institution in the Community or in a Member State shall comprise the income items, as defined above, which are received by the branch or division of that institution established in the Community or in the Member State in question, as the case may be;
(b) for insurance undertakings, the value of gross premiums written which shall comprise all amounts received and receivable in respect of insurance contracts issued by or on behalf of the insurance undertakings, including also outgoing reinsurance premiums, and after deduction of taxes and parafiscal contributions or levies charged by reference to the amounts of individual premiums or the total volume of premiums; as regards Article 1(2)(b) and (3)(b), (c) and (d) and the final part of Article 1(2) and (3), gross premiums received from Community residents and from residents of one Member State respectively shall be taken into account.

4.   Without prejudice to paragraph 2, the aggregate turnover of an undertaking concerned within the meaning of this Regulation shall be calculated by adding together the respective turnovers of the following:
(a) the undertaking concerned;
(b) those undertakings in which the undertaking concerned, directly or indirectly:
(i)   owns more than half the capital or business assets, or
(ii) has the power to exercise more than half the voting rights, or

(iii) has the power to appoint more than half the members of the supervisory board, the administrative board or bodies legally representing the undertakings, or

(iv) has the right to manage the undertakings' affairs;

(c) those undertakings which have in the undertaking concerned the rights or powers listed in (b);

(d) those undertakings in which an undertaking as referred to in (c) has the rights or powers listed in (b);

(e) those undertakings in which two or more undertakings as referred to in (a) to (d) jointly have the rights or powers listed in (b).

5. Where undertakings concerned by the concentration jointly have the rights or powers listed in paragraph 4(b), in calculating the aggregate turnover of the undertakings concerned for the purposes of this Regulation:

(a) no account shall be taken of the turnover resulting from the sale of products or the provision of services between the joint undertaking and each of the undertakings concerned or any other undertaking connected with any one of them, as set out in paragraph 4(b) to (e);

(b) account shall be taken of the turnover resulting from the sale of products and the provision of services between the joint undertaking and any third undertakings. This turnover shall be apportioned equally amongst the undertakings concerned.

Article 6 Examination of the notification and initiation of proceedings

1. The Commission shall examine the notification as soon as it is received.

(a) Where it concludes that the concentration notified does not fall within the scope of this Regulation, it shall record that finding by means of a decision.

(b) Where it finds that the concentration notified, although falling within the scope of this Regulation, does not raise serious doubts as to its compatibility with the common market, it shall decide not to oppose it and shall declare that it is compatible with the common market.

A decision declaring a concentration compatible shall be deemed to cover restrictions directly related and necessary to the implementation of the concentration.

(c) Without prejudice to paragraph 2, where the Commission finds that the concentration notified falls within the scope of this Regulation and raises serious doubts as to its compatibility with the common market, it shall decide to initiate proceedings. Without prejudice to Article 9, such proceedings shall be closed by means of a decision as provided for in Article 8(1) to (4), unless the undertakings concerned have demonstrated to the satisfaction of the Commission that they have abandoned the concentration.

2. Where the Commission finds that, following modification by the undertakings concerned, a notified concentration no longer raises serious doubts within the meaning of paragraph 1(c), it shall declare the concentration compatible with the common market pursuant to paragraph 1(b).

The Commission may attach to its decision under paragraph 1(b) conditions and obligations intended to ensure that the undertakings concerned comply with the commitments they have entered into vis-à-vis the Commission with a view to rendering the concentration compatible with the common market.

3. The Commission may revoke the decision it took pursuant to paragraph 1(a) or (b) where:

(a) the decision is based on incorrect information for which one of the undertakings is responsible or where it has been obtained by deceit,

or

(b) the undertakings concerned commit a breach of an obligation attached to the decision.

4. In the cases referred to in paragraph 3, the Commission may take a decision under paragraph 1, without being bound by the time limits referred to in Article 10(1).

5. The Commission shall notify its decision to the undertakings concerned and the competent authorities of the Member States without delay.

Article 7 Suspension of concentrations

1. A concentration with a Community dimension as defined in Article 1, or which is to be examined by the Commission pursuant to Article 4(5), shall not be implemented either before its notification or until it has been declared compatible with the common market pursuant to a decision under Articles 6(1)(b), 8(1) or 8(2), or on the basis of a presumption according to Article 10(6).

2. Paragraph 1 shall not prevent the implementation of a public bid or of a series of transactions in securities including those convertible into other securities admitted to trading on a market such as a stock exchange, by which control within the meaning of Article 3 is acquired from various sellers, provided that:
   (a) the concentration is notified to the Commission pursuant to Article 4 without delay; and
   (b) the acquirer does not exercise the voting rights attached to the securities in question or does so only to maintain the full value of its investments based on a derogation granted by the Commission under paragraph 3.

3. The Commission may, on request, grant a derogation from the obligations imposed in paragraphs 1 or 2. The request to grant a derogation must be reasoned. In deciding on the request, the Commission shall take into account inter alia the effects of the suspension on one or more undertakings concerned by the concentration or on a third party and the threat to competition posed by the concentration. Such a derogation may be made subject to conditions and obligations in order to ensure conditions of effective competition. A derogation may be applied for and granted at any time, be it before notification or after the transaction.

4. The validity of any transaction carried out in contravention of paragraph 1 shall be dependent on a decision pursuant to Article 6(1)(b) or Article 8(1), (2) or (3) or on a presumption pursuant to Article 10(6).

   This Article shall, however, have no effect on the validity of transactions in securities including those convertible into other securities admitted to trading on a market such as a stock exchange, unless the buyer and seller knew or ought to have known that the transaction was carried out in contravention of paragraph 1.

Article 8 Powers of decision of the Commission

1. Where the Commission finds that a notified concentration fulfils the criterion laid down in Article 2(2) and, in the cases referred to in Article 2(4), the criteria laid down in Article 81(3) of the Treaty, it shall issue a decision declaring the concentration compatible with the common market.

   A decision declaring a concentration compatible shall be deemed to cover restrictions directly related and necessary to the implementation of the concentration.

2. Where the Commission finds that, following modification by the undertakings concerned, a notified concentration fulfils the criterion laid down in Article 2(2) and, in the cases

referred to in Article 2(4), the criteria laid down in Article 81(3) of the Treaty, it shall issue a decision declaring the concentration compatible with the common market.

The Commission may attach to its decision conditions and obligations intended to ensure that the undertakings concerned comply with the commitments they have entered into vis-à-vis the Commission with a view to rendering the concentration compatible with the common market.

A decision declaring a concentration compatible shall be deemed to cover restrictions directly related and necessary to the implementation of the concentration.

3. Where the Commission finds that a concentration fulfils the criterion defined in Article 2(3) or, in the cases referred to in Article 2(4), does not fulfil the criteria laid down in Article 81(3) of the Treaty, it shall issue a decision declaring that the concentration is incompatible with the common market.

4. Where the Commission finds that a concentration:
(a) has already been implemented and that concentration has been declared incompatible with the common market, or
(b) has been implemented in contravention of a condition attached to a decision taken under paragraph 2, which has found that, in the absence of the condition, the concentration would fulfil the criterion laid down in Article 2(3) or, in the cases referred to in Article 2(4), would not fulfil the criteria laid down in Article 81(3) of the Treaty,

the Commission may:

— require the undertakings concerned to dissolve the concentration, in particular through the dissolution of the merger or the disposal of all the shares or assets acquired, so as to restore the situation prevailing prior to the implementation of the concentration; in circumstances where restoration of the situation prevailing before the implementation of the concentration is not possible through dissolution of the concentration, the Commission may take any other measure appropriate to achieve such restoration as far as possible,
— order any other appropriate measure to ensure that the undertakings concerned dissolve the concentration or take other restorative measures as required in its decision.
In cases falling within point (a) of the first subparagraph, the measures referred to in that subparagraph may be imposed either in a decision pursuant to paragraph 3 or by separate decision.

5. The Commission may take interim measures appropriate to restore or maintain conditions of effective competition where a concentration:
(a) has been implemented in contravention of Article 7, and a decision as to the compatibility of the concentration with the common market has not yet been taken;
(b) has been implemented in contravention of a condition attached to a decision under Article 6(1)(b) or paragraph 2 of this Article;
(c) has already been implemented and is declared incompatible with the common market.

6. The Commission may revoke the decision it has taken pursuant to paragraphs 1 or 2 where:
(a) the declaration of compatibility is based on incorrect information for which one of the undertakings is responsible or where it has been obtained by deceit; or
(b) the undertakings concerned commit a breach of an obligation attached to the decision.

7.   The Commission may take a decision pursuant to paragraphs 1 to 3 without being bound by the time limits referred to in Article 10(3), in cases where:

(a) it finds that a concentration has been implemented

   (i)   in contravention of a condition attached to a decision under Article 6(1)(b), or

   (ii) in contravention of a condition attached to a decision taken under paragraph 2 and in accordance with Article 10(2), which has found that, in the absence of the condition, the concentration would raise serious doubts as to its compatibility with the common market; or

(b) a decision has been revoked pursuant to paragraph 6.

8.   The Commission shall notify its decision to the undertakings concerned and the competent authorities of the Member States without delay.

Article 9 Referral to the competent authorities of the Member States

1.   The Commission may, by means of a decision notified without delay to the undertakings concerned and the competent authorities of the other Member States, refer a notified concentration to the competent authorities of the Member State concerned in the following circumstances.

2.   Within 15 working days of the date of receipt of the copy of the notification, a Member State, on its own initiative or upon the invitation of the Commission, may inform the Commission, which shall inform the undertakings concerned, that:

(a) a concentration threatens to affect significantly competition in a market within that Member State, which presents all the characteristics of a distinct market, or

(b) a concentration affects competition in a market within that Member State, which presents all the characteristics of a distinct market and which does not constitute a substantial part of the common market.

3.   If the Commission considers that, having regard to the market for the products or services in question and the geographical reference market within the meaning of paragraph 7, there is such a distinct market and that such a threat exists, either:

(a) it shall itself deal with the case in accordance with this Regulation; or

(b) it shall refer the whole or part of the case to the competent authorities of the Member State concerned with a view to the application of that State's national competition law.

If, however, the Commission considers that such a distinct market or threat does not exist, it shall adopt a decision to that effect which it shall address to the Member State concerned, and shall itself deal with the case in accordance with this Regulation.

In cases where a Member State informs the Commission pursuant to paragraph 2(b) that a concentration affects competition in a distinct market within its territory that does not form a substantial part of the common market, the Commission shall refer the whole or part of the case relating to the distinct market concerned, if it considers that such a distinct market is affected.

4.   A decision to refer or not to refer pursuant to paragraph 3 shall be taken:

(a) as a general rule within the period provided for in Article 10(1), second subparagraph, where the Commission, pursuant to Article 6(1)(b), has not initiated proceedings; or

(b) within 65 working days at most of the notification of the concentration concerned where the Commission has initiated proceedings under Article 6(1)(c), without taking the preparatory steps in order to adopt the necessary measures under Article 8(2), (3) or (4) to maintain or restore effective competition on the market concerned.

5.   If within the 65 working days referred to in paragraph 4(b) the Commission, despite a reminder from the Member State concerned, has not taken a decision on referral in accordance with paragraph 3 nor has taken the preparatory steps referred to in paragraph 4(b), it shall be deemed to have taken a decision to refer the case to the Member State concerned in accordance with paragraph 3(b).

6.   The competent authority of the Member State concerned shall decide upon the case without undue delay.

Within 45 working days after the Commission's referral, the competent authority of the Member State concerned shall inform the undertakings concerned of the result of the preliminary competition assessment and what further action, if any, it proposes to take. The Member State concerned may exceptionally suspend this time limit where necessary information has not been provided to it by the undertakings concerned as provided for by its national competition law.

Where a notification is requested under national law, the period of 45 working days shall begin on the working day following that of the receipt of a complete notification by the competent authority of that Member State.

7.   The geographical reference market shall consist of the area in which the undertakings concerned are involved in the supply and demand of products or services, in which the conditions of competition are sufficiently homogeneous and which can be distinguished from neighbouring areas because, in particular, conditions of competition are appreciably different in those areas. This assessment should take account in particular of the nature and characteristics of the products or services concerned, of the existence of entry barriers or of consumer preferences, of appreciable differences of the undertakings' market shares between the area concerned and neighbouring areas or of substantial price differences.

8.   In applying the provisions of this Article, the Member State concerned may take only the measures strictly necessary to safeguard or restore effective competition on the market concerned.

9.   In accordance with the relevant provisions of the Treaty, any Member State may appeal to the Court of Justice, and in particular request the application of Article 243 of the Treaty, for the purpose of applying its national competition law.

Article 10 Time limits for initiating proceedings and for decisions

1.   Without prejudice to Article 6(4), the decisions referred to in Article 6(1) shall be taken within 25 working days at most. That period shall begin on the working day following that of the receipt of a notification or, if the information to be supplied with the notification is incomplete, on the working day following that of the receipt of the complete information.

That period shall be increased to 35 working days where the Commission receives a request from a Member State in accordance with Article 9(2)or where, the undertakings concerned offer commitments pursuant to Article 6(2) with a view to rendering the concentration compatible with the common market.

2.   Decisions pursuant to Article 8(1) or (2) concerning notified concentrations shall be taken as soon as it appears that the serious doubts referred to in Article 6(1)(c) have been removed, particularly as a result of modifications made by the undertakings concerned, and at the latest by the time limit laid down in paragraph 3.

3.   Without prejudice to Article 8(7), decisions pursuant to Article 8(1) to (3) concerning notified concentrations shall be taken within not more than 90 working days of the date

on which the proceedings are initiated. That period shall be increased to 105 working days where the undertakings concerned offer commitments pursuant to Article 8(2), second subparagraph, with a view to rendering the concentration compatible with the common market, unless these commitments have been offered less than 55 working days after the initiation of proceedings.

The periods set by the first subparagraph shall likewise be extended if the notifying parties make a request to that effect not later than 15 working days after the initiation of proceedings pursuant to Article 6(1)(c). The notifying parties may make only one such request. Likewise, at any time following the initiation of proceedings, the periods set by the first subparagraph may be extended by the Commission with the agreement of the notifying parties. The total duration of any extension or extensions effected pursuant to this subparagraph shall not exceed 20 working days.

4.   The periods set by paragraphs 1 and 3 shall exceptionally be suspended where, owing to circumstances for which one of the undertakings involved in the concentration is responsible, the Commission has had to request information by decision pursuant to Article 11 or to order an inspection by decision pursuant to Article 13.

The first subparagraph shall also apply to the period referred to in Article 9(4)(b).

5.   Where the Court of Justice gives a judgment which annuls the whole or part of a Commission decision which is subject to a time limit set by this Article, the concentration shall be re-examined by the Commission with a view to adopting a decision pursuant to Article 6(1).

The concentration shall be re-examined in the light of current market conditions.

The notifying parties shall submit a new notification or supplement the original notification, without delay, where the original notification becomes incomplete by reason of intervening changes in market conditions or in the information provided. Where there are no such changes, the parties shall certify this fact without delay.

The periods laid down in paragraph 1 shall start on the working day following that of the receipt of complete information in a new notification, a supplemented notification, or a certification within the meaning of the third subparagraph.

The second and third subparagraphs shall also apply in the cases referred to in Article 6(4) and Article 8(7).

6.   Where the Commission has not taken a decision in accordance with Article 6(1)(b), (c), 8(1), (2) or (3) within the time limits set in paragraphs 1 and 3 respectively, the concentration shall be deemed to have been declared compatible with the common market, without prejudice to Article 9.

Article 11 Requests for information
1.   In order to carry out the duties assigned to it by this Regulation, the Commission may, by simple request or by decision, require the persons referred to in Article 3(1)(b), as well as undertakings and associations of undertakings, to provide all necessary information.

2.   When sending a simple request for information to a person, an undertaking or an association of undertakings, the Commission shall state the legal basis and the purpose of the request, specify what information is required and fix the time limit within which the information is to be provided, as well as the penalties provided for in Article 14 for supplying incorrect or misleading information.

3.   Where the Commission requires a person, an undertaking or an association of undertakings to supply information by decision, it shall state the legal basis and the purpose of the request, specify what information is required and fix the time limit within which it is to be provided. It shall also indicate the penalties provided for in Article 14 and indicate or impose the penalties provided for in Article 15. It shall further indicate the right to have the decision reviewed by the Court of Justice.

4.   The owners of the undertakings or their representatives and, in the case of legal persons, companies or firms, or associations having no legal personality, the persons authorised to represent them by law or by their constitution, shall supply the information requested on behalf of the undertaking concerned. Persons duly authorised to act may supply the information on behalf of their clients. The latter shall remain fully responsible if the information supplied is incomplete, incorrect or misleading.

5.   The Commission shall without delay forward a copy of any decision taken pursuant to paragraph 3 to the competent authorities of the Member State in whose territory the residence of the person or the seat of the undertaking or association of undertakings is situated, and to the competent authority of the Member State whose territory is affected. At the specific request of the competent authority of a Member State, the Commission shall also forward to that authority copies of simple requests for information relating to a notified concentration.

6.   At the request of the Commission, the governments and competent authorities of the Member States shall provide the Commission with all necessary information to carry out the duties assigned to it by this Regulation.

7.   In order to carry out the duties assigned to it by this Regulation, the Commission may interview any natural or legal person who consents to be interviewed for the purpose of collecting information relating to the subject matter of an investigation. At the beginning of the interview, which may be conducted by telephone or other electronic means, the Commission shall state the legal basis and the purpose of the interview.

Where an interview is not conducted on the premises of the Commission or by telephone or other electronic means, the Commission shall inform in advance the competent authority of the Member State in whose territory the interview takes place. If the competent authority of that Member State so requests, officials of that authority may assist the officials and other persons authorised by the Commission to conduct the interview.

Article 12 Inspections by the authorities of the Member States
1.   At the request of the Commission, the competent authorities of the Member States shall undertake the inspections which the Commission considers to be necessary under Article 13(1), or which it has ordered by decision pursuant to Article 13(4). The officials of the competent authorities of the Member States who are responsible for conducting these inspections as well as those authorised or appointed by them shall exercise their powers in accordance with their national law.

2.   If so requested by the Commission or by the competent authority of the Member State within whose territory the inspection is to be conducted, officials and other accompanying persons authorised by the Commission may assist the officials of the authority concerned.

Article 13 The Commission's powers of inspection
1.   In order to carry out the duties assigned to it by this Regulation, the Commission may conduct all necessary inspections of undertakings and associations of undertakings.

2. The officials and other accompanying persons authorised by the Commission to conduct an inspection shall have the power:
    (a) to enter any premises, land and means of transport of undertakings and associations of undertakings;
    (b) to examine the books and other records related to the business, irrespective of the medium on which they are stored;
    (c) to take or obtain in any form copies of or extracts from such books or records;
    (d) to seal any business premises and books or records for the period and to the extent necessary for the inspection;
    (e) to ask any representative or member of staff of the undertaking or association of undertakings for explanations on facts or documents relating to the subject matter and purpose of the inspection and to record the answers.

3. Officials and other accompanying persons authorised by the Commission to conduct an inspection shall exercise their powers upon production of a written authorisation specifying the subject matter and purpose of the inspection and the penalties provided for in Article 14, in the production of the required books or other records related to the business which is incomplete or where answers to questions asked under paragraph 2 of this Article are incorrect or misleading. In good time before the inspection, the Commission shall give notice of the inspection to the competent authority of the Member State in whose territory the inspection is to be conducted.

4. Undertakings and associations of undertakings are required to submit to inspections ordered by decision of the Commission. The decision shall specify the subject matter and purpose of the inspection, appoint the date on which it is to begin and indicate the penalties provided for in Articles 14 and 15 and the right to have the decision reviewed by the Court of Justice. The Commission shall take such decisions after consulting the competent authority of the Member State in whose territory the inspection is to be conducted.

5. Officials of, and those authorised or appointed by, the competent authority of the Member State in whose territory the inspection is to be conducted shall, at the request of that authority or of the Commission, actively assist the officials and other accompanying persons authorised by the Commission. To this end, they shall enjoy the powers specified in paragraph 2.

6. Where the officials and other accompanying persons authorised by the Commission find that an undertaking opposes an inspection, including the sealing of business premises, books or records, ordered pursuant to this Article, the Member State concerned shall afford them the necessary assistance, requesting where appropriate the assistance of the police or of an equivalent enforcement authority, so as to enable them to conduct their inspection.

7. If the assistance provided for in paragraph 6 requires authorisation from a judicial authority according to national rules, such authorisation shall be applied for. Such authorisation may also be applied for as a precautionary measure.

8. Where authorisation as referred to in paragraph 7 is applied for, the national judicial authority shall ensure that the Commission decision is authentic and that the coercive measures envisaged are neither arbitrary nor excessive having regard to the subject matter of the inspection. In its control of proportionality of the coercive measures, the national judicial authority may ask the Commission, directly or through the competent authority of that Member State, for detailed explanations relating to the subject matter of the inspection. However, the national judicial authority may not call into question the necessity for the inspection nor demand that it be provided with the information in the

Commission's file. The lawfulness of the Commission's decision shall be subject to review only by the Court of Justice.

Article 14 Fines

1. The Commission may by decision impose on the persons referred to in Article 3(1)b, undertakings or associations of undertakings, fines not exceeding 1 % of the aggregate turnover of the undertaking or association of undertakings concerned within the meaning of Article 5 where, intentionally or negligently:

    (a) they supply incorrect or misleading information in a submission, certification, notification or supplement thereto, pursuant to Article 4, Article 10(5) or Article 22(3);

    (b) they supply incorrect or misleading information in response to a request made pursuant to Article 11(2);

    (c) in response to a request made by decision adopted pursuant to Article 11(3), they supply incorrect, incomplete or misleading information or do not supply information within the required time limit;

    (d) they produce the required books or other records related to the business in incomplete form during inspections under Article 13, or refuse to submit to an inspection ordered by decision taken pursuant to Article 13(4);

    (e) in response to a question asked in accordance with Article 13(2)(e),
    - they give an incorrect or misleading answer,
    - they fail to rectify within a time limit set by the Commission an incorrect, incomplete or misleading answer given by a member of staff, or
    - they fail or refuse to provide a complete answer on facts relating to the subject matter and purpose of an inspection ordered by a decision adopted pursuant to Article 13(4);

    (f) seals affixed by officials or other accompanying persons authorised by the Commission in accordance with Article 13(2)(d) have been broken.

2. The Commission may by decision impose fines not exceeding 10 % of the aggregate turnover of the undertaking concerned within the meaning of Article 5 on the persons referred to in Article 3(1)b or the undertakings concerned where, either intentionally or negligently, they:

    (a) fail to notify a concentration in accordance with Articles 4 or 22(3) prior to its implementation, unless they are expressly authorised to do so by Article 7(2) or by a decision taken pursuant to Article 7(3);

    (b) implement a concentration in breach of Article 7;

    (c) implement a concentration declared incompatible with the common market by decision pursuant to Article 8(3) or do not comply with any measure ordered by decision pursuant to Article 8(4) or (5);

    (d) fail to comply with a condition or an obligation imposed by decision pursuant to Articles 6(1)(b), Article 7(3) or Article 8(2), second subparagraph.

3. In fixing the amount of the fine, regard shall be had to the nature, gravity and duration of the infringement.

4. Decisions taken pursuant to paragraphs 1, 2 and 3 shall not be of a criminal law nature.

Article 15 Periodic penalty payments

1. The Commission may by decision impose on the persons referred to in Article 3(1)b, undertakings or associations of undertakings, periodic penalty payments not exceeding 5 % of the average daily aggregate turnover of the undertaking or association of undertakings concerned within the meaning of Article 5 for each working day of delay, calculated from the date set in the decision, in order to compel them:

(a) to supply complete and correct information which it has requested by decision taken pursuant to Article 11(3);

(b) to submit to an inspection which it has ordered by decision taken pursuant to Article 13(4);

(c) to comply with an obligation imposed by decision pursuant to Article 6(1)(b), Article 7(3) or Article 8(2), second subparagraph; or;

(d) to comply with any measures ordered by decision pursuant to Article 8(4) or (5).

2.   Where the persons referred to in Article 3(1)(b), undertakings or associations of undertakings have satisfied the obligation which the periodic penalty payment was intended to enforce, the Commission may fix the definitive amount of the periodic penalty payments at a figure lower than that which would arise under the original decision.

Article 16 Review by the Court of Justice

The Court of Justice shall have unlimited jurisdiction within the meaning of Article 229 of the Treaty to review decisions whereby the Commission has fixed a fine or periodic penalty payments; it may cancel, reduce or increase the fine or periodic penalty payment imposed.

Article 17 Professional secrecy

1.   Information acquired as a result of the application of this Regulation shall be used only for the purposes of the relevant request, investigation or hearing.

2.   Without prejudice to Article 4(3), Articles 18 and 20, the Commission and the competent authorities of the Member States, their officials and other servants and other persons working under the supervision of these authorities as well as officials and civil servants of other authorities of the Member States shall not disclose information they have acquired through the application of this Regulation of the kind covered by the obligation of professional secrecy.

3.   Paragraphs 1 and 2 shall not prevent publication of general information or of surveys which do not contain information relating to particular undertakings or associations of undertakings.

Article 18 Hearing of the parties and of third persons

1.   Before taking any decision provided for in Article 6(3), Article 7(3), Article 8(2) to (6), and Articles 14 and 15, the Commission shall give the persons, undertakings and associations of undertakings concerned the opportunity, at every stage of the procedure up to the consultation of the Advisory Committee, of making known their views on the objections against them.

2.   By way of derogation from paragraph 1, a decision pursuant to Articles 7(3) and 8(5) may be taken provisionally, without the persons, undertakings or associations of undertakings concerned being given the opportunity to make known their views beforehand, provided that the Commission gives them that opportunity as soon as possible after having taken its decision.

3.   The Commission shall base its decision only on objections on which the parties have been able to submit their observations. The rights of the defence shall be fully respected in the proceedings. Access to the file shall be open at least to the parties directly involved, subject to the legitimate interest of undertakings in the protection of their business secrets.

4.   In so far as the Commission or the competent authorities of the Member States deem it necessary, they may also hear other natural or legal persons. Natural or legal persons showing a sufficient interest and especially members of the administrative or management

bodies of the undertakings concerned or the recognised representatives of their employees shall be entitled, upon application, to be heard.

Article 19 Liaison with the authorities of the Member States

1.   The Commission shall transmit to the competent authorities of the Member States copies of notifications within three working days and, as soon as possible, copies of the most important documents lodged with or issued by the Commission pursuant to this Regulation. Such documents shall include commitments offered by the undertakings concerned vis-à-vis the Commission with a view to rendering the concentration compatible with the common market pursuant to Article 6(2) or Article 8(2), second subparagraph.

2.   The Commission shall carry out the procedures set out in this Regulation in close and constant liaison with the competent authorities of the Member States, which may express their views upon those procedures. For the purposes of Article 9 it shall obtain information from the competent authority of the Member State as referred to in paragraph 2 of that Article and give it the opportunity to make known its views at every stage of the procedure up to the adoption of a decision pursuant to paragraph 3 of that Article; to that end it shall give it access to the file.

3.   An Advisory Committee on concentrations shall be consulted before any decision is taken pursuant to Article 8(1) to (6), Articles 14 or 15 with the exception of provisional decisions taken in accordance with Article 18(2).

4.   The Advisory Committee shall consist of representatives of the competent authorities of the Member States. Each Member State shall appoint one or two representatives; if unable to attend, they may be replaced by other representatives. At least one of the representatives of a Member State shall be competent in matters of restrictive practices and dominant positions.

5.   Consultation shall take place at a joint meeting convened at the invitation of and chaired by the Commission. A summary of the case, together with an indication of the most important documents and a preliminary draft of the decision to be taken for each case considered, shall be sent with the invitation. The meeting shall take place not less than 10 working days after the invitation has been sent. The Commission may in exceptional cases shorten that period as appropriate in order to avoid serious harm to one or more of the undertakings concerned by a concentration.

6.   The Advisory Committee shall deliver an opinion on the Commission's draft decision, if necessary by taking a vote. The Advisory Committee may deliver an opinion even if some members are absent and unrepresented. The opinion shall be delivered in writing and appended to the draft decision. The Commission shall take the utmost account of the opinion delivered by the Committee. It shall inform the Committee of the manner in which its opinion has been taken into account.

7.   The Commission shall communicate the opinion of the Advisory Committee, together with the decision, to the addressees of the decision. It shall make the opinion public together with the decision, having regard to the legitimate interest of undertakings in the protection of their business secrets.

Article 20 Publication of decisions

1.   The Commission shall publish the decisions which it takes pursuant to Article 8(1) to (6), Articles 14 and 15 with the exception of provisional decisions taken in accordance with Article 18(2) together with the opinion of the Advisory Committee in the Official Journal of the European Union.

2.   The publication shall state the names of the parties and the main content of the decision; it shall have regard to the legitimate interest of undertakings in the protection of their business secrets.

Article 21 Application of the Regulation and jurisdiction

1.   This Regulation alone shall apply to concentrations as defined in Article 3, and Council Regulations (EC) No 1/2003, (EEC) No 1017/68, (EEC) No 4056/86 and (EEC) No 3975/87 shall not apply, except in relation to joint ventures that do not have a Community dimension and which have as their object or effect the coordination of the competitive behaviour of undertakings that remain independent.

2.   Subject to review by the Court of Justice, the Commission shall have sole jurisdiction to take the decisions provided for in this Regulation.

3.   No Member State shall apply its national legislation on competition to any concentration that has a Community dimension.

    The first subparagraph shall be without prejudice to any Member State's power to carry out any enquiries necessary for the application of Articles 4(4), 9(2) or after referral, pursuant to Article 9(3), first subparagraph, indent (b), or Article 9(5), to take the measures strictly necessary for the application of Article 9(8).

4.   Notwithstanding paragraphs 2 and 3, Member States may take appropriate measures to protect legitimate interests other than those taken into consideration by this Regulation and compatible with the general principles and other provisions of Community law.

    Public security, plurality of the media and prudential rules shall be regarded as legitimate interests within the meaning of the first subparagraph.

    Any other public interest must be communicated to the Commission by the Member State concerned and shall be recognised by the Commission after an assessment of its compatibility with the general principles and other provisions of Community law before the measures referred to above may be taken. The Commission shall inform the Member State concerned of its decision within 25 working days of that communication.

Article 22 Referral to the Commission

1.   One or more Member States may request the Commission to examine any concentration as defined in Article 3 that does not have a Community dimension within the meaning of Article 1 but affects trade between Member States and threatens to significantly affect competition within the territory of the Member State or States making the request.

    Such a request shall be made at most within 15 working days of the date on which the concentration was notified, or if no notification is required, otherwise made known to the Member State concerned.

2.   The Commission shall inform the competent authorities of the Member States and the undertakings concerned of any request received pursuant to paragraph 1 without delay.

    Any other Member State shall have the right to join the initial request within a period of 15 working days of being informed by the Commission of the initial request.

    All national time limits relating to the concentration shall be suspended until, in accordance with the procedure set out in this Article, it has been decided where the concentration shall be examined. As soon as a Member State has informed the Commission and the undertakings concerned that it does not wish to join the request, the suspension of its national time limits shall end.

3.   The Commission may, at the latest 10 working days after the expiry of the period set in paragraph 2, decide to examine, the concentration where it considers that it affects trade between Member States and threatens to significantly affect competition within the territory of the Member State or States making the request. If the Commission does not take a decision within this period, it shall be deemed to have adopted a decision to examine the concentration in accordance with the request.

The Commission shall inform all Member States and the undertakings concerned of its decision. It may request the submission of a notification pursuant to Article 4.

The Member State or States having made the request shall no longer apply their national legislation on competition to the concentration.

4.   Article 2, Article 4(2) to (3), Articles 5, 6, and 8 to 21 shall apply where the Commission examines a concentration pursuant to paragraph 3. Article 7 shall apply to the extent that the concentration has not been implemented on the date on which the Commission informs the undertakings concerned that a request has been made.

Where a notification pursuant to Article 4 is not required, the period set in Article 10(1) within which proceedings may be initiated shall begin on the working day following that on which the Commission informs the undertakings concerned that it has decided to examine the concentration pursuant to paragraph 3.

5.   The Commission may inform one or several Member States that it considers a concentration fulfils the criteria in paragraph 1. In such cases, the Commission may invite that Member State or those Member States to make a request pursuant to paragraph 1.

Article 23 Implementing provisions

1.   The Commission shall have the power to lay down in accordance with the procedure referred to in paragraph 2:
   (a) implementing provisions concerning the form, content and other details of notifications and submissions pursuant to Article 4;
   (b) implementing provisions concerning time limits pursuant to Article 4(4), (5) Articles 7, 9, 10 and 22;
   (c) the procedure and time limits for the submission and implementation of commitments pursuant to Article 6(2) and Article 8(2);
   (d) implementing provisions concerning hearings pursuant to Article 18.

2.   The Commission shall be assisted by an Advisory Committee, composed of representatives of the Member States.
   (a) Before publishing draft implementing provisions and before adopting such provisions, the Commission shall consult the Advisory Committee.
   (b) Consultation shall take place at a meeting convened at the invitation of and chaired by the Commission. A draft of the implementing provisions to be taken shall be sent with the invitation. The meeting shall take place not less than 10 working days after the invitation has been sent.
   (c) The Advisory Committee shall deliver an opinion on the draft implementing provisions, if necessary by taking a vote. The Commission shall take the utmost account of the opinion delivered by the Committee.

Article 24 Relations with third countries

1.   The Member States shall inform the Commission of any general difficulties encountered by their undertakings with concentrations as defined in Article 3 in a third country.

2.   Initially not more than one year after the entry into force of this Regulation and, thereafter periodically, the Commission shall draw up a report examining the treatment accorded to undertakings having their seat or their principal fields of activity in the Community, in the terms referred to in paragraphs 3 and 4, as regards concentrations in third countries. The Commission shall submit those reports to the Council, together with any recommendations.

3.   Whenever it appears to the Commission, either on the basis of the reports referred to in paragraph 2 or on the basis of other information, that a third country does not grant undertakings having their seat or their principal fields of activity in the Community, treatment comparable to that granted by the Community to undertakings from that country, the Commission may submit proposals to the Council for an appropriate mandate for negotiation with a view to obtaining comparable treatment for undertakings having their seat or their principal fields of activity in the Community.

4.   Measures taken under this Article shall comply with the obligations of the Community or of the Member States, without prejudice to Article 307 of the Treaty, under international agreements, whether bilateral or multilateral.

Article 25 Repeal

1.   Without prejudice to Article 26(2), Regulations (EEC) No 4064/89 and (EC) No 1310/97 shall be repealed with effect from 1 May 2004.

2.   References to the repealed Regulations shall be construed as references to this Regulation and shall be read in accordance with the correlation table in the Annex.

Article 26 Entry into force and transitional provisions

1.   This Regulation shall enter into force on the 20th day following that of its publication in the Official Journal of the European Union.

It shall apply from 1 May 2004.

2.   Regulation (EEC) No 4064/89 shall continue to apply to any concentration which was the subject of an agreement or announcement or where control was acquired within the meaning of Article 4(1) of that Regulation before the date of application of this Regulation, subject, in particular, to the provisions governing applicability set out in Article 25(2) and (3) of Regulation (EEC) No 4064/89 and Article 2 of Regulation (EEC) No 1310/97.

3.   As regards concentrations to which this Regulation applies by virtue of accession, the date of accession shall be substituted for the date of application of this Regulation.

This Regulation shall be binding in its entirety and directly applicable in all Member States.

(date of signing and signatory omitted)

ANNEX

CORRELATION TABLE

Regulation (EEC) No 4064/89	This Regulation
Article 1(1), (2) and (3)	Article 1(1), (2) and (3)
Article 1(4)	Article 1(4)

Regulation (EEC) No 4064/89	This Regulation
Article 1(5)	Article 1(5)
Article 2(1)	Article 2(1)
—	Article 2(2)
Article 2(2)	Article 2(3)
Article 2(3)	Article 2(4)
Article 2(4)	Article 2(5)
Article 3(1)	Article 3(1)
Article 3(2)	Article 3(4)
Article 3(3)	Article 3(2)
Article 3(4)	Article 3(3)
—	Article 3(4)
Article 3(5)	Article 3(5)
Article 4(1) first sentence	Article 4(1) first subpara.
Article 4(1) second sentence	—
—	Article 4(1) second and third subpara.
Article 4(2) and (3)	Article 4(2) and (3)
—	Article 4(4) to (6)
Article 5(1) to (3)	Article 5(1) to (3)
Article 5(4) introductory words	Article 5(4) introductory words
Article 5(4) point (a)	Article 5(4) point (a)
Article 5(4) point (b), introductory words	Article 5(4) point (b), introductory words
Article 5(4) point (b), first indent	Article 5(4) point (b)(i)
Article 5(4) point (b), second indent	Article 5(4) point (b)(ii)
Article 5(4) point (b), third indent	Article 5(4) point (b)(iii)
Article 5(4) point (b), fourth indent	Article 5(4) point (b)(iv)
Article 5(4) points (c), (d) and (e)	Article 5(4) points (c), (d) and (e)
Article 5(5)	Article 5(5)
Article 6(1) introductory words	Article 6(1) introductory words
Article 6(1) points (a) and (b)	Article 6(1) points (a) and (b)
Article 6(1) point (c)	Article 6(1) point (c), first sentence
Article 6(2) to (5)	Article 6(2) to (5)
Article 7(1)	Article 7(1)
Article 7(3)	Article 7(2)
Article 7(4)	Article 7(3)
Article 7(5)	Article 7(4)

Regulation (EEC) No 4064/89	This Regulation
Article 8(1)	Article 6(1) point (c), second sentence
Article 8(2)	Article 8(1) and (2)
Article 8(3)	Article 8(3)
Article 8(4)	Article 8(4)
—	Article 8(5)
Article 8(5)	Article 8(6)
Article 8(6)	Article 8(7)
—	Article 8(8)
Article 9(1) to (9)	Article 9(1) to (9)
Article 9(10)	—
Article 10(1) and (2)	Article 10(1) and (2)
Article 10(3)	Article 10(3) first subpara., first sentence
—	Article 10(3) first subpara., second sentence
—	Article 10(3) second subpara.
Article 10(4)	Article 10(4) first subpara.
—	Article 10(4) second subpara.
Article 10(5)	Article 10(5) first and fourth subparas.
—	Article 10(5) second, third & fifth subparas.
Article 10(6)	Article 10(6)
Article 11(1)	Article 11(1)
Article 11(2)	—
Article 11(3)	Article 11(2)
Article 11(4)	Article 11(4) first sentence
—	Article 11(4) second and third sentences
Article 11(5) first sentence	—
Article 11(5) second sentence	Article 11(3)
Article 11(6)	Article 11(5)
—	Article 11(6) and (7)
Article 12	Article 12
Article 13(1) first subpara.	Article 13(1)
Article 13(1) second subpara. introductory words	Article 13(2) introductory words
Article 13(1) second subpara. point (a)	Article 13(2) point (b)
Article 13(1) second subpara. point (b)	Article 13(2) point (c)
Article 13(1) second subpara. point (c)	Article 13(2) point (e)

Regulation (EEC) No 4064/89	This Regulation
Article 13(1) second subpara. point (d)	Article 13(2) point (a)
—	Article 13(2) point (d)
Article 13(2)	Article 13(3)
Article 13(3)	Article 13(4) first and second sentences
Article 13(4)	Article 13(4) third sentence
Article 13(5)	Article 13(5) first sentence
—	Article 13(5) second sentence
Article 13(6) first sentence	Article 13(6)
Article 13(6) second sentence	—
—	Article 13(7) and (8)
Article 14(1) introductory words	Article 14(1) introductory words
Article 14(1) point (a)	Article 14(2) point (a)
Article 14(1) point (b)	Article 14(1) point (a)
Article 14(1) point (c)	Article 14(1) points (b) and (c)
Article 14(1) point (d)	Article 14(1) point (d)
—	Article 14(1) points (e) and (f)
Article 14(2) introductory words	Article 14(2) introductory words
Article 14(2) point (a)	Article 14(2) point (d)
Article 14(2) points (b) and (c)	Article 14(2) points (b) and (c)
Article 14(3)	Article 14(3)
Article 14(4)	Article 14(4)
Article 15(1) introductory words	Article 15(1) introductory words
Article 15(1) points (a) and (b)	Article 15(1) points (a) and (b)
Article 15(2) introductory words	Article 15(1) introductory words
Article 15(2) point (a)	Article 15(1) point (c)
Article 15(2) point (b)	Article 15(1) point (d)
Article 15(3)	Article 15(2)
Articles 16 to 20	Articles 16 to 20
Article 21(1)	Article 21(2)
Article 21(2)	Article 21(3)
Article 21(3)	Article 21(4)
Article 22(1)	Article 21(1)
Article 22(3)	—
—	Article 22(1) to (3)
Article 22(4)	Article 22(4)

Regulation (EEC) No 4064/89	This Regulation
Article 22(5)	—
—	Article 22(5)
Article 23	Article 23(1)
—	Article 23(2)
Article 24	Article 24
—	Article 25
Article 25(1)	Article 26(1), first subpara.
—	Article 26(1), second subpara.
Article 25(2)	Article 26(2)
Article 25(3)	Article 26(3)
—	Annex

COMMISSION REGULATION (EC) NO 773/2004 OF 7 APRIL 2004

relating to the conduct of proceedings by the Commission pursuant to [Articles 101 and 102 TFEU][1]
OJ L 123, 27.4.2004, P. 18*

(* As amended by Commission Regulation (EC) No 1792/2006 of 23 October 2006, OJ L 362, 20.12.2006, p. 1 and Commission Regulation (EC) No 622/2008 of 30 June 2008, OJ L 171, 1.7.2008, p. 3)

(*footnotes and Annex omitted*)

THE COMMISSION OF THE EUROPEAN COMMUNITIES,

Having regard to the Treaty establishing the European Community,

Having regard to the Agreement on the European Economic Area,

Having regard to Council Regulation (EC) No 1/2003 of 16 December 2002 on the implementation of the rules on competition laid down in Articles 81 and 82 of the Treaty, and in particular Article 33 thereof,

After consulting the Advisory Committee on Restrictive Practices and Dominant Positions,

Whereas:

(1)   Regulation (EC) No 1/2003 empowers the Commission to regulate certain aspects of proceedings for the application of Articles 81 and 82 of the Treaty. It is necessary to lay

---

[1]   EDITOR'S NOTE: As of 1 May 2012 this Regulation has not been amended following the entry into force of the Treaty of Lisbon. It includes references to the old Treaty article numbers in the text. The title has been amended to reflect the fact that Articles 81 and 82 EC have been replaced by Articles 101 and 102 TFEU. Reference should be made to the Tables of Equivalences accompanying the consolidated Treaties in Part II of this edition for the conversion of old Treaty article numbers to new ones.

down rules concerning the initiation of proceedings by the Commission as well as the handling of complaints and the hearing of the parties concerned.

(2)   According to Regulation (EC) No 1/2003, national courts are under an obligation to avoid taking decisions which could run counter to decisions envisaged by the Commission in the same case. According to Article 11(6) of that Regulation, national competition authorities are relieved from their competence once the Commission has initiated proceedings for the adoption of a decision under Chapter III of Regulation (EC) No 1/2003. In this context, it is important that courts and competition authorities of the Member States are aware of the initiation of proceedings by the Commission. The Commission should therefore be able to make public its decisions to initiate proceedings.

(3)   Before taking oral statements from natural or legal persons who consent to be interviewed, the Commission should inform those persons of the legal basis of the interview and its voluntary nature. The persons interviewed should also be informed of the purpose of the interview and of any record which may be made.

In order to enhance the accuracy of the statements, the persons interviewed should also be given an opportunity to correct the statements recorded. Where information gathered from oral statements is exchanged pursuant to Article 12 of Regulation (EC) No 1/2003, that information should only be used in evidence to impose sanctions on natural persons where the conditions set out in that Article are fulfilled.

(4)   Pursuant to Article 23(1)(d) of Regulation (EC) No 1/2003 fines may be imposed on undertakings and associations of undertakings where they fail to rectify within the time limit fixed by the Commission an incorrect, incomplete or misleading answer given by a member of their staff to questions in the course of inspections. It is therefore necessary to provide the undertaking concerned with a record of any explanations given and to establish a procedure enabling it to add any rectification, amendment or supplement to the explanations given by the member of staff who is not or was not authorised to provide explanations on behalf of the undertaking. The explanations given by a member of staff should remain in the Commission file as recorded during the inspection.

(5)   Complaints are an essential source of information for detecting infringements of competition rules. It is important to define clear and efficient procedures for handling complaints lodged with the Commission.

(6)   In order to be admissible for the purposes of Article 7 of Regulation (EC) No 1/2003, a complaint must contain certain specified information.

(7)   In order to assist complainants in submitting the necessary facts to the Commission, a form should be drawn up. The submission of the information listed in that form should be a condition for a complaint to be treated as a complaint as referred to in Article 7 of Regulation (EC) No 1/2003.

(8)   Natural or legal persons having chosen to lodge a complaint should be given the possibility to be associated closely with the proceedings initiated by the Commission with a view to finding an infringement. However, they should not have access to business secrets or other confidential information belonging to other parties involved in the proceedings.

(9)   Complainants should be granted the opportunity of expressing their views if the Commission considers that there are insufficient grounds for acting on the complaint. Where the Commission rejects a complaint on the grounds that a competition authority of a Member State is dealing with it or has already done so, it should inform the complainant of the identity of that authority.

(10) In order to respect the rights of defence of undertakings, the Commission should give the parties concerned the right to be heard before it takes a decision.

(11) Provision should also be made for the hearing of persons who have not submitted a complaint as referred to in Article 7 of Regulation (EC) No 1/2003 and who are not parties to whom a statement of objections has been addressed but who can nevertheless show a sufficient interest. Consumer associations that apply to be heard should generally be regarded as having a sufficient interest, where the proceedings concern products or services used by the end-consumer or products or services that constitute a direct input into such products or services. Where it considers this to be useful for the proceedings, the Commission should also be able to invite other persons to express their views in writing and to attend the oral hearing of the parties to whom a statement of objections has been addressed. Where appropriate, it should also be able to invite such persons to express their views at that oral hearing.

(12) To improve the effectiveness of oral hearings, the Hearing Officer should have the power to allow the parties concerned, complainants, other persons invited to the hearing, the Commission services and the authorities of the Member States to ask questions during the hearing.

(13) When granting access to the file, the Commission should ensure the protection of business secrets and other confidential information. The category of 'other confidential information' includes information other than business secrets, which may be considered as confidential, insofar as its disclosure would significantly harm an undertaking or person. The Commission should be able to request undertakings or associations of undertakings that submit or have submitted documents or statements to identify confidential information.

(14) Where business secrets or other confidential information are necessary to prove an infringement, the Commission should assess for each individual document whether the need to disclose is greater than the harm which might result from disclosure.

(15) In the interest of legal certainty, a minimum time-limit for the various submissions provided for in this Regulation should be laid down.

(16) This Regulation replaces Commission Regulation (EC) No 2842/98 of 22 December 1998 on the hearing of parties in certain proceedings under Articles 85 and 86 of the EC Treaty (1), which should therefore be repealed.

(17) This Regulation aligns the procedural rules in the transport sector with the general rules of procedure in all sectors. Commission Regulation (EC) No 2843/98 of 22 December 1998 on the form, content and other details of applications and notifications provided for in Council Regulations (EEC) No 1017/68, (EEC) No 4056/86 and (EEC) No 3975/87 applying the rules on competition to the transport sector should therefore be repealed.

(18) Regulation (EC) No 1/2003 abolishes the notification and authorisation system. Commission Regulation (EC) No 3385/94 of 21 December 1994 on the form, content and other details of applications and notifications provided for in Council Regulation No 17 should therefore be repealed,

HAS ADOPTED THIS REGULATION:

Chapter I SCOPE

Article 1 Subject-matter and scope
This regulation applies to proceedings conducted by the Commission for the application of Articles 81 and 82 of the Treaty.

Chapter II INITIATION OF PROCEEDINGS

Article 2 Initiation of proceedings

1. The Commission may decide to initiate proceedings with a view to adopting a decision pursuant to Chapter III of Regulation (EC) No 1/2003 at any point in time, but no later than the date on which it issues a preliminary assessment as referred to in Article 9(1) of that Regulation, a statement of objections or a request for the parties to express their interest in engaging in settlement discussions, or the date on which a notice pursuant to Article 27(4) of that Regulation is published, whichever is the earlier.

2. The Commission may make public the initiation of proceedings, in any appropriate way. Before doing so, it shall inform the parties concerned.

3. The Commission may exercise its powers of investigation pursuant to Chapter V of Regulation (EC) No 1/2003 before initiating proceedings.

4. The Commission may reject a complaint pursuant to Article 7 of Regulation (EC) No 1/2003 without initiating proceedings.

Chapter III INVESTIGATIONS BY THE COMMISSION

Article 3 Power to take statements

1. Where the Commission interviews a person with his consent in accordance with Article 19 of Regulation (EC) No 1/2003, it shall, at the beginning of the interview, state the legal basis and the purpose of the interview, and recall its voluntary nature. It shall also inform the person interviewed of its intention to make a record of the interview.

2. The interview may be conducted by any means including by telephone or electronic means.

3. The Commission may record the statements made by the persons interviewed in any form. A copy of any recording shall be made available to the person interviewed for approval. Where necessary, the Commission shall set a time-limit within which the person interviewed may communicate to it any correction to be made to the statement.

Article 4 Oral questions during inspections

1. When, pursuant to Article 20(2)(e) of Regulation (EC) No 1/2003, officials or other accompanying persons authorised by the Commission ask representatives or members of staff of an undertaking or of an association of undertakings for explanations, the explanations given may be recorded in any form.

2. A copy of any recording made pursuant to paragraph 1 shall be made available to the undertaking or association of undertakings concerned after the inspection.

3. In cases where a member of staff of an undertaking or of an association of undertakings who is not or was not authorised by the undertaking or by the association of undertakings to provide explanations on behalf of the undertaking or association of undertakings has been asked for explanations, the Commission shall set a time-limit within which the undertaking or the association of undertakings may communicate to the Commission any rectification, amendment or supplement to the explanations given by such member of staff. The rectification, amendment or supplement shall be added to the explanations as recorded pursuant to paragraph 1.

Chapter IV HANDLING OF COMPLAINTS

Article 5 Admissibility of complaints

1. Natural and legal persons shall show a legitimate interest in order to be entitled to lodge a complaint for the purposes of Article 7 of Regulation (EC) No 1/2003.

   Such complaints shall contain the information required by Form C, as set out in the Annex. The Commission may dispense with this obligation as regards part of the information, including documents, required by Form C.

2. Three paper copies as well as, if possible, an electronic copy of the complaint shall be submitted to the Commission. The complainant shall also submit a non-confidential version of the complaint, if confidentiality is claimed for any part of the complaint.

3. Complaints shall be submitted in one of the official languages of the Community.

Article 6 Participation of complainants in proceedings

1. Where the Commission issues a statement of objections relating to a matter in respect of which it has received a complaint, it shall provide the complainant with a copy of the non-confidential version of the statement of objections, except in cases where the settlement procedure applies, where it shall inform the complainant in writing of the nature and subject matter of the procedure. The Commission shall also set a time limit within which the complainant may make known its views in writing.

2. The Commission may, where appropriate, afford complainants the opportunity of expressing their views at the oral hearing of the parties to which a statement of objections has been issued, if complainants so request in their written comments.

Article 7 Rejection of complaints

1. Where the Commission considers that on the basis of the information in its possession there are insufficient grounds for acting on a complaint, it shall inform the complainant of its reasons and set a time-limit within which the complainant may make known its views in writing. The Commission shall not be obliged to take into account any further written submission received after the expiry of that time-limit.

2. If the complainant makes known its views within the time-limit set by the Commission and the written submissions made by the complainant do not lead to a different assessment of the complaint, the Commission shall reject the complaint by decision.

3. If the complainant fails to make known its views within the time-limit set by the Commission, the complaint shall be deemed to have been withdrawn.

Article 8 Access to information

1. Where the Commission has informed the complainant of its intention to reject a complaint pursuant to Article 7(1) the complainant may request access to the documents on which the Commission bases its provisional assessment. For this purpose, the complainant may however not have access to business secrets and other confidential information belonging to other parties involved in the proceedings.

2. The documents to which the complainant has had access in the context of proceedings conducted by the Commission under Articles 81 and 82 of the Treaty may only be used by the complainant for the purposes of judicial or administrative proceedings for the application of those Treaty provisions.

Article 9 Rejections of complaints pursuant to Article 13 of Regulation (EC) No 1/2003
Where the Commission rejects a complaint pursuant to Article 13 of Regulation (EC) No 1/2003, it shall inform the complainant without delay of the national competition authority which is dealing or has already dealt with the case.

Chapter V EXERCISE OF THE RIGHT TO BE HEARD

Article 10 Statement of objections and reply
1.   The Commission shall inform the parties concerned of the objections raised against them. The statement of objections shall be notified in writing to each of the parties against whom objections are raised.

2.   The Commission shall, when notifying the statement of objections to the parties concerned, set a time-limit within which these parties may inform it in writing of their views. The Commission shall not be obliged to take into account written submissions received after the expiry of that time-limit.

3.   The parties may, in their written submissions, set out all facts known to them which are relevant to their defence against the objections raised by the Commission. They shall attach any relevant documents as proof of the facts set out. They shall provide a paper original as well as an electronic copy or, where they do not provide an electronic copy, 30 paper copies of their submission and of the documents attached to it. They may propose that the Commission hear persons who may corroborate the facts set out in their submission.

Article 10a Settlement procedure in cartel cases
1.   After the initiation of proceedings pursuant to Article 11(6) of Regulation (EC) No 1/2003, the Commission may set a time limit within which the parties may indicate in writing that they are prepared to engage in settlement discussions with a view to possibly introducing settlement submissions. The Commission shall not be obliged to take into account replies received after the expiry of that time limit.

If two or more parties within the same undertaking indicate their willingness to engage in settlement discussions pursuant to the first subparagraph, they shall appoint a joint representation to engage in discussions with the Commission on their behalf. When setting the time limit referred to in the first subparagraph, the Commission shall indicate to the relevant parties that they are identified within the same undertaking, for the sole purpose of enabling them to comply with this provision.

2.   Parties taking part in settlement discussions may be informed by the Commission of:
      (a) the objections it envisages to raise against them;
      (b) the evidence used to determine the envisaged objections;
      (c) non-confidential versions of any specified accessible document listed in the case file at that point in time, in so far as a request by the party is justified for the purpose of enabling the party to ascertain its position regarding a time period or any other particular aspect of the cartel; and
      (d) the range of potential fines.
      This information shall be confidential vis-à-vis third parties, save where the Commission has given a prior explicit authorisation for disclosure.

Should settlement discussions progress, the Commission may set a time limit within which the parties may commit to follow the settlement procedure by introducing settlement submissions reflecting the results of the settlement discussions and acknowledging their participation in an infringement of Article 81 of the Treaty as well as their liability. Before the Commission sets a time limit to introduce their settlement submissions, the parties concerned shall be entitled to have the information specified in Article 10a(2), first subparagraph disclosed to them, upon request, in a timely manner. The Commission shall not be obliged to take into account settlement submissions received after the expiry of that time limit.

3.   When the statement of objections notified to the parties reflects the contents of their settlement submissions, the written reply to the statement of objections by the parties concerned shall, within a time limit set by the Commission, confirm that the statement of objections addressed to them reflects the contents of their settlement submissions.

The Commission may then proceed to the adoption of a Decision pursuant to Article 7 and Article 23 of Regulation (EC) No 1/2003 after consultation of the Advisory Committee on Restrictive Practices and Dominant Positions pursuant to Article 14 of Regulation (EC) No 1/2003.

4.   The Commission may decide at any time during the procedure to discontinue settlement discussions altogether in a specific case or with respect to one or more of the parties involved, if it considers that procedural efficiencies are not likely to be achieved.

Article 11 Right to be heard
1.   The Commission shall give the parties to whom it addresses a statement of objections the opportunity to be heard before consulting the Advisory Committee referred to in Article 14(1) of Regulation (EC) No 1/2003.

2.   The Commission shall, in its decisions, deal only with objections in respect of which the parties referred to in paragraph 1 have been able to comment.

Article 12
1.   The Commission shall give the parties to whom it addresses a statement of objections the opportunity to develop their arguments at an oral hearing, if they so request in their written submissions.

2.   However, when introducing their settlement submissions the parties shall confirm to the Commission that they would only require having the opportunity to develop their arguments at an oral hearing, if the statement of objections does not reflect the contents of their settlement submissions.

Article 13 Hearing of other persons
1.   If natural or legal persons other than those referred to in Articles 5 and 11 apply to be heard and show a sufficient interest, the Commission shall inform them in writing of the nature and subject matter of the procedure and shall set a time-limit within which they may make known their views in writing.

2.   The Commission may, where appropriate, invite persons referred to in paragraph 1 to develop their arguments at the oral hearing of the parties to whom a statement of objections has been addressed, if the persons referred to in paragraph 1 so request in their written comments.

3.   The Commission may invite any other person to express its views in writing and to attend the oral hearing of the parties to whom a statement of objections has been addressed. The Commission may also invite such persons to express their views at that oral hearing.

Article 14 Conduct of oral hearings
1.   Hearings shall be conducted by a Hearing Officer in full independence.

2.   The Commission shall invite the persons to be heard to attend the oral hearing on such date as it shall determine.

3.   The Commission shall invite the competition authorities of the Member States to take part in the oral hearing. It may likewise invite officials and civil servants of other authorities of the Member States.

4.   Persons invited to attend shall either appear in person or be represented by legal representatives or by representatives authorised by their constitution as appropriate. Undertakings and associations of undertakings may also be represented by a duly authorised agent appointed from among their permanent staff.

5.   Persons heard by the Commission may be assisted by their lawyers or other qualified persons admitted by the Hearing Officer.

6.   Oral hearings shall not be public. Each person may be heard separately or in the presence of other persons invited to attend, having regard to the legitimate interest of the undertakings in the protection of their business secrets and other confidential information.

7.   The Hearing Officer may allow the parties to whom a statement of objections has been addressed, the complainants, other persons invited to the hearing, the Commission services and the authorities of the Member States to ask questions during the hearing.

8.   The statements made by each person heard shall be recorded. Upon request, the recording of the hearing shall be made available to the persons who attended the hearing. Regard shall be had to the legitimate interest of the parties in the protection of their business secrets and other confidential information.

Chapter VI ACCESS TO THE FILE AND TREATMENT OF CONFIDENTIAL INFORMATION

Article 15 Access to the file and use of documents
1.   If so requested, the Commission shall grant access to the file to the parties to whom it has addressed a statement of objections. Access shall be granted after the notification of the statement of objections.

1a.   After the initiation of proceedings pursuant to Article 11(6) of Regulation (EC) No 1/2003 and in order to enable the parties willing to introduce settlement submissions to do so, the Commission shall disclose to them the evidence and documents described in Article 10a(2) upon request and subject to the conditions established in the relevant subparagraphs. In view thereof, when introducing their settlement submissions, the parties shall confirm to the Commission that they will only require access to the file after the receipt of the statement of objections, if the statement of objections does not reflect the contents of their settlement submissions.

2.   The right of access to the file shall not extend to business secrets, other confidential information and internal documents of the Commission or of the competition authorities of the Member States.

The right of access to the file shall also not extend to correspondence between the Commission and the competition authorities of the Member States or between the latter where such correspondence is contained in the file of the Commission.

3.   Nothing in this Regulation prevents the Commission from disclosing and using information necessary to prove an infringement of Articles 81 or 82 of the Treaty.

4.   Documents obtained through access to the file pursuant to this Article shall only be used for the purposes of judicial or administrative proceedings for the application of Articles 81 and 82 of the Treaty.

Article 16 Identification and protection of confidential information

1. Information, including documents, shall not be communicated or made accessible by the Commission in so far as it contains business secrets or other confidential information of any person.

2. Any person which makes known its views pursuant to Article 6(1), Article 7(1), Article 10(2) and Article 13(1) and (3) or subsequently submits further information to the Commission in the course of the same procedure, shall clearly identify any material which it considers to be confidential, giving reasons, and provide a separate non-confidential version by the date set by the Commission for making its views known.

3. Without prejudice to paragraph 2 of this Article, the Commission may require undertakings and associations of undertakings which produce documents or statements pursuant to Regulation (EC) No 1/2003 to identify the documents or parts of documents which they consider to contain business secrets or other confidential information belonging to them and to identify the undertakings with regard to which such documents are to be considered confidential. The Commission may likewise require undertakings or associations of undertakings to identify any part of a statement of objections, a case summary drawn up pursuant to Article 27(4) of Regulation (EC) No 1/2003 or a decision adopted by the Commission which in their view contains business secrets.

   The Commission may set a time-limit within which the undertakings and associations of undertakings are to:
   (a) substantiate their claim for confidentiality with regard to each individual document or part of document, statement or part of statement;
   (b) provide the Commission with a non-confidential version of the documents or statements, in which the confidential passages are deleted;
   (c) provide a concise description of each piece of deleted information.

4. If undertakings or associations of undertakings fail to comply with paragraphs 2 and 3, the Commission may assume that the documents or statements concerned do not contain confidential information.

Chapter VII GENERAL AND FINAL PROVISIONS

Article 17 Time-limits

1. In setting the time limits provided for in Article 3(3), Article 4(3), Article 6(1), Article 7(1), Article 10(2), Article 10a(1), Article 10a(2), Article 10a(3) and Article 16(3), the Commission shall have regard both to the time required for preparation of the submission and to the urgency of the case.

2. The time-limits referred to in Article 6(1), Article 7(1) and Article 10(2) shall be at least four weeks. However, for proceedings initiated with a view to adopting interim measures pursuant to Article 8 of Regulation (EC) No 1/2003, the time-limit may be shortened to one week.

3. The time limits referred to in Article 4(3), Article 10a(1), Article 10a(2) and Article 16(3) shall be at least two weeks. The time limit referred to in Article 3(3) shall be at least two weeks, except for settlement submissions, for which corrections shall be made within one week. The time limit referred to in Article 10a(3) shall be at least two weeks.

4. Where appropriate and upon reasoned request made before the expiry of the original time-limit, time-limits may be extended.

Article 18 Repeals
Regulations (EC) No 2842/98, (EC) No 2843/98 and (EC) No 3385/94 are repealed.

References to the repealed regulations shall be construed as references to this regulation.

Article 19 Transitional provisions
Procedural steps taken under Regulations (EC) No 2842/98 and (EC) No 2843/98 shall continue to have effect for the purpose of applying this Regulation.

Article 20 Entry into force
This Regulation shall enter into force on 1 May 2004.

This Regulation shall be binding in its entirety and directly applicable in all Member States.

COMMISSION REGULATION (EU) NO 330/2010 OF 20 APRIL 2010

on the application of Article 101(3) of the Treaty on the Functioning of the European Union to categories of vertical agreements and concerted practices
('Block Exemption Regulation')

OJ L102, 23.4.2010, P. 1

(footnotes omitted)

THE EUROPEAN COMMISSION,

Having regard to the Treaty on the Functioning of the European Union,

Having regard to Regulation No 19/65/EEC of the Council of 2 March 1965 on the application of Article 85(3) of the Treaty to certain categories of agreements and concerted practices, and in particular Article 1 thereof,

Having published a draft of this Regulation,

After consulting the Advisory Committee on Restrictive Practices and Dominant Positions,

Whereas:
(1) Regulation No 19/65/EEC empowers the Commission to apply Article 101(3) of the Treaty on the Functioning of the European Union by regulation to certain categories of vertical agreements and corresponding concerted practices falling within Article 101(1) of the Treaty.

(2) Commission Regulation (EC) No 2790/1999 of 22 December 1999 on the application of Article 81(3) of the Treaty to categories of vertical agreements and concerted practices defines a category of vertical agreements which the Commission regarded as normally satisfying the conditions laid down in Article 101(3) of the Treaty. In view of the overall positive experience with the application of that Regulation, which expires on 31 May 2010, and taking into account further experience acquired since its adoption, it is appropriate to adopt a new block exemption regulation.

(3) The category of agreements which can be regarded as normally satisfying the conditions laid down in Article 101(3) of the Treaty includes vertical agreements for the purchase or sale of goods or services where those agreements are concluded between non-competing undertakings, between certain competitors or by certain associations of retailers of goods.

It also includes vertical agreements containing ancillary provisions on the assignment or use of intellectual property rights. The term 'vertical agreements' should include the corresponding concerted practices.

(4) For the application of Article 101(3) of the Treaty by regulation, it is not necessary to define those vertical agreements which are capable of falling within Article 101(1) of the Treaty. In the individual assessment of agreements under Article 101(1) of the Treaty, account has to be taken of several factors, and in particular the market structure on the supply and purchase side.

(5) The benefit of the block exemption established by this Regulation should be limited to vertical agreements for which it can be assumed with sufficient certainty that they satisfy the conditions of Article 101(3) of the Treaty.

(6) Certain types of vertical agreements can improve economic efficiency within a chain of production or distribution by facilitating better coordination between the participating undertakings. In particular, they can lead to a reduction in the transaction and distribution costs of the parties and to an optimisation of their sales and investment levels.

(7) The likelihood that such efficiency-enhancing effects will outweigh any anti-competitive effects due to restrictions contained in vertical agreements depends on the degree of market power of the parties to the agreement and, therefore, on the extent to which those undertakings face competition from other suppliers of goods or services regarded by their customers as interchangeable or substitutable for one another, by reason of the products' characteristics, their prices and their intended use.

(8) It can be presumed that, where the market share held by each of the undertakings party to the agreement on the relevant market does not exceed 30 %, vertical agreements which do not contain certain types of severe restrictions of competition generally lead to an improvement in production or distribution and allow consumers a fair share of the resulting benefits.

(9) Above the market share threshold of 30 %, there can be no presumption that vertical agreements falling within the scope of Article 101(1) of the Treaty will usually give rise to objective advantages of such a character and size as to compensate for the disadvantages which they create for competition. At the same time, there is no presumption that those vertical agreements are either caught by Article 101(1) of the Treaty or that they fail to satisfy the conditions of Article 101(3) of the Treaty.

(10) This Regulation should not exempt vertical agreements containing restrictions which are likely to restrict competition and harm consumers or which are not indispensable to the attainment of the efficiency-enhancing effects. In particular, vertical agreements containing certain types of severe restrictions of competition such as minimum and fixed resale-prices, as well as certain types of territorial protection, should be excluded from the benefit of the block exemption established by this Regulation irrespective of the market share of the undertakings concerned.

(11) In order to ensure access to or to prevent collusion on the relevant market, certain conditions should be attached to the block exemption. To this end, the exemption of non-compete obligations should be limited to obligations which do not exceed a defined duration. For the same reasons, any direct or indirect obligation causing the members of a selective distribution system not to sell the brands of particular competing suppliers should be excluded from the benefit of this Regulation.

(12) The market-share limitation, the non-exemption of certain vertical agreements and the conditions provided for in this Regulation normally ensure that the agreements to which

the block exemption applies do not enable the participating undertakings to eliminate competition in respect of a substantial part of the products in question.

(13) The Commission may withdraw the benefit of this Regulation, pursuant to Article 29(1) of Council Regulation (EC) No 1/2003 of 16 December 2002 on the implementation of the rules on competition laid down in Articles 81 and 82 of the Treaty, where it finds in a particular case that an agreement to which the exemption provided for in this Regulation applies nevertheless has effects which are incompatible with Article 101(3) of the Treaty.

(14) The competition authority of a Member State may withdraw the benefit of this Regulation pursuant to Article 29(2) of Regulation (EC) No 1/2003 in respect of the territory of that Member State, or a part thereof where, in a particular case, an agreement to which the exemption provided for in this Regulation applies nevertheless has effects which are incompatible with Article 101(3) of the Treaty in the territory of that Member State, or in a part thereof, and where such territory has all the characteristics of a distinct geographic market.

(15) In determining whether the benefit of this Regulation should be withdrawn pursuant to Article 29 of Regulation (EC) No 1/2003, the anti-competitive effects that may derive from the existence of parallel networks of vertical agreements that have similar effects which significantly restrict access to a relevant market or competition therein are of particular importance. Such cumulative effects may for example arise in the case of selective distribution or non compete obligations.

(16) In order to strengthen supervision of parallel networks of vertical agreements which have similar anti-competitive effects and which cover more than 50 % of a given market, the Commission may by regulation declare this Regulation inapplicable to vertical agreements containing specific restraints relating to the market concerned, thereby restoring the full application of Article 101 of the Treaty to such agreements,

HAS ADOPTED THIS REGULATION:

Article 1 Definitions

1. For the purposes of this Regulation, the following definitions shall apply:
    (a) 'vertical agreement' means an agreement or concerted practice entered into between two or more undertakings each of which operates, for the purposes of the agreement or the concerted practice, at a different level of the production or distribution chain, and relating to the conditions under which the parties may purchase, sell or resell certain goods or services;
    (b) 'vertical restraint' means a restriction of competition in a vertical agreement falling within the scope of Article 101(1) of the Treaty;
    (c) 'competing undertaking' means an actual or potential competitor; 'actual competitor' means an undertaking that is active on the same relevant market; 'potential competitor' means an undertaking that, in the absence of the vertical agreement, would, on realistic grounds and not just as a mere theoretical possibility, in case of a small but permanent increase in relative prices be likely to undertake, within a short period of time, the necessary additional investments or other necessary switching costs to enter the relevant market;
    (d) 'non-compete obligation' means any direct or indirect obligation causing the buyer not to manufacture, purchase, sell or resell goods or services which compete with the contract goods or services, or any direct or indirect obligation on the buyer to purchase from the supplier or from another undertaking designated by the supplier more than 80 % of the buyer's total purchases of the contract goods or services and

their substitutes on the relevant market, calculated on the basis of the value or, where such is standard industry practice, the volume of its purchases in the preceding calendar year;

(e) 'selective distribution system' means a distribution system where the supplier undertakes to sell the contract goods or services, either directly or indirectly, only to distributors selected on the basis of specified criteria and where these distributors undertake not to sell such goods or services to unauthorised distributors within the territory reserved by the supplier to operate that system;

(f) 'intellectual property rights' includes industrial property rights, know how, copyright and neighbouring rights;

(g) 'know-how' means a package of non-patented practical information, resulting from experience and testing by the supplier, which is secret, substantial and identified: in this context, 'secret' means that the know-how is not generally known or easily accessible; 'substantial' means that the know-how is significant and useful to the buyer for the use, sale or resale of the contract goods or services; 'identified' means that the know-how is described in a sufficiently comprehensive manner so as to make it possible to verify that it fulfils the criteria of secrecy and substantiality;

(h) 'buyer' includes an undertaking which, under an agreement falling within Article 101(1) of the Treaty, sells goods or services on behalf of another undertaking;

(i) 'customer of the buyer' means an undertaking not party to the agreement which purchases the contract goods or services from a buyer which is party to the agreement.

2. For the purposes of this Regulation, the terms 'undertaking', 'supplier' and 'buyer' shall include their respective connected undertakings.

'Connected undertakings' means:

(a) undertakings in which a party to the agreement, directly or indirectly:
   (i)   has the power to exercise more than half the voting rights, or
   (ii) has the power to appoint more than half the members of the supervisory board, board of management or bodies legally representing the undertaking, or
   (iii) has the right to manage the undertaking's affairs;

(b) undertakings which directly or indirectly have, over a party to the agreement, the rights or powers listed in point (a);

(c) undertakings in which an undertaking referred to in point (b) has, directly or indirectly, the rights or powers listed in point (a);

(d) undertakings in which a party to the agreement together with one or more of the undertakings referred to in points (a), (b) or (c), or in which two or more of the latter undertakings, jointly have the rights or powers listed in point (a);

(e) undertakings in which the rights or the powers listed in point (a) are jointly held by:
   (i) parties to the agreement or their respective connected undertakings referred to in points (a) to (d), or
   (ii) one or more of the parties to the agreement or one or more of their connected undertakings referred to in points (a) to (d) and one or more third parties.

Article 2 Exemption

1. Pursuant to Article 101(3) of the Treaty and subject to the provisions of this Regulation, it is hereby declared that Article 101(1) of the Treaty shall not apply to vertical agreements.

This exemption shall apply to the extent that such agreements contain vertical restraints.

2. The exemption provided for in paragraph 1 shall apply to vertical agreements entered into between an association of undertakings and its members, or between such an association and its suppliers, only if all its members are retailers of goods and if no individual member

of the association, together with its connected undertakings, has a total annual turnover exceeding EUR 50 million. Vertical agreements entered into by such associations shall be covered by this Regulation without prejudice to the application of Article 101 of the Treaty to horizontal agreements concluded between the members of the association or decisions adopted by the association.

3.   The exemption provided for in paragraph 1 shall apply to vertical agreements containing provisions which relate to the assignment to the buyer or use by the buyer of intellectual property rights, provided that those provisions do not constitute the primary object of such agreements and are directly related to the use, sale or resale of goods or services by the buyer or its customers. The exemption applies on condition that, in relation to the contract goods or services, those provisions do not contain restrictions of competition having the same object as vertical restraints which are not exempted under this Regulation.

4.   The exemption provided for in paragraph 1 shall not apply to vertical agreements entered into between competing undertakings. However, it shall apply where competing undertakings enter into a non-reciprocal vertical agreement and:
(a) the supplier is a manufacturer and a distributor of goods, while the buyer is a distributor and not a competing undertaking at the manufacturing level; or
(b) the supplier is a provider of services at several levels of trade, while the buyer provides its goods or services at the retail level and is not a competing undertaking at the level of trade where it purchases the contract services.

5.   This Regulation shall not apply to vertical agreements the subject matter of which falls within the scope of any other block exemption regulation, unless otherwise provided for in such a regulation.

Article 3 Market share threshold

1.   The exemption provided for in Article 2 shall apply on condition that the market share held by the supplier does not exceed 30 % of the relevant market on which it sells the contract goods or services and the market share held by the buyer does not exceed 30 % of the relevant market on which it purchases the contract goods or services.

2.   For the purposes of paragraph 1, where in a multi party agreement an undertaking buys the contract goods or services from one undertaking party to the agreement and sells the contract goods or services to another undertaking party to the agreement, the market share of the first undertaking must respect the market share threshold provided for in that paragraph both as a buyer and a supplier in order for the exemption provided for in Article 2 to apply.

Article 4 Restrictions that remove the benefit of the block exemption — hardcore restrictions

The exemption provided for in Article 2 shall not apply to vertical agreements which, directly or indirectly, in isolation or in combination with other factors under the control of the parties, have as their object:
(a) the restriction of the buyer's ability to determine its sale price, without prejudice to the possibility of the supplier to impose a maximum sale price or recommend a sale price, provided that they do not amount to a fixed or minimum sale price as a result of pressure from, or incentives offered by, any of the parties;

(b) the restriction of the territory into which, or of the customers to whom, a buyer party to the agreement, without prejudice to a restriction on its place of establishment, may sell the contract goods or services, except:

(i) the restriction of active sales into the exclusive territory or to an exclusive customer group reserved to the supplier or allocated by the supplier to another buyer, where such a restriction does not limit sales by the customers of the buyer,

(ii) the restriction of sales to end users by a buyer operating at the wholesale level of trade,

(iii) the restriction of sales by the members of a selective distribution system to unauthorised distributors within the territory reserved by the supplier to operate that system, and

(iv) the restriction of the buyer's ability to sell components, supplied for the purposes of incorporation, to customers who would use them to manufacture the same type of goods as those produced by the supplier;

(c) the restriction of active or passive sales to end users by members of a selective distribution system operating at the retail level of trade, without prejudice to the possibility of prohibiting a member of the system from operating out of an unauthorised place of establishment;

(d) the restriction of cross-supplies between distributors within a selective distribution system, including between distributors operating at different level of trade;

(e) the restriction, agreed between a supplier of components and a buyer who incorporates those components, of the supplier's ability to sell the components as spare parts to end-users or to repairers or other service providers not entrusted by the buyer with the repair or servicing of its goods.

Article 5 Excluded restrictions

1. The exemption provided for in Article 2 shall not apply to the following obligations contained in vertical agreements:
   (a) any direct or indirect non-compete obligation, the duration of which is indefinite or exceeds five years;
   (b) any direct or indirect obligation causing the buyer, after termination of the agreement, not to manufacture, purchase, sell or resell goods or services;
   (c) any direct or indirect obligation causing the members of a selective distribution system not to sell the brands of particular competing suppliers.
   For the purposes of point (a) of the first subparagraph, a non- compete obligation which is tacitly renewable beyond a period of five years shall be deemed to have been concluded for an indefinite duration.

2. By way of derogation from paragraph 1(a), the time limitation of five years shall not apply where the contract goods or services are sold by the buyer from premises and land owned by the supplier or leased by the supplier from third parties not connected with the buyer, provided that the duration of the non-compete obligation does not exceed the period of occupancy of the premises and land by the buyer.

3. By way of derogation from paragraph 1(b), the exemption provided for in Article 2 shall apply to any direct or indirect obligation causing the buyer, after termination of the agreement, not to manufacture, purchase, sell or resell goods or services where the following conditions are fulfilled:
   (a) the obligation relates to goods or services which compete with the contract goods or services;
   (b) the obligation is limited to the premises and land from which the buyer has operated during the contract period;
   (c) the obligation is indispensable to protect know-how transferred by the supplier to the buyer;

(d) the duration of the obligation is limited to a period of one year after termination of the agreement.

Paragraph 1(b) is without prejudice to the possibility of imposing a restriction which is unlimited in time on the use and disclosure of know-how which has not entered the public domain.

Article 6 Non-application of this Regulation

Pursuant to Article 1a of Regulation No 19/65/EEC, the Commission may by regulation declare that, where parallel networks of similar vertical restraints cover more than 50 % of a relevant market, this Regulation shall not apply to vertical agreements containing specific restraints relating to that market.

Article 7 Application of the market share threshold

For the purposes of applying the market share thresholds provided for in Article 3 the following rules shall apply:

(a) the market share of the supplier shall be calculated on the basis of market sales value data and the market share of the buyer shall be calculated on the basis of market purchase value data. If market sales value or market purchase value data are not available, estimates based on other reliable market information, including market sales and purchase volumes, may be used to establish the market share of the undertaking concerned;

(b) the market shares shall be calculated on the basis of data relating to the preceding calendar year;

(c) the market share of the supplier shall include any goods or services supplied to vertically integrated distributors for the purposes of sale;

(d) if a market share is initially not more than 30 % but subsequently rises above that level without exceeding 35 %, the exemption provided for in Article 2 shall continue to apply for a period of two consecutive calendar years following the year in which the 30 % market share threshold was first exceeded;

(e) if a market share is initially not more than 30 % but subsequently rises above 35 %, the exemption provided for in Article 2 shall continue to apply for one calendar year following the year in which the level of 35 % was first exceeded;

(f) the benefit of points (d) and (e) may not be combined so as to exceed a period of two calendar years;

(g) the market share held by the undertakings referred to in point (e) of the second subparagraph of Article 1(2) shall be apportioned equally to each undertaking having the rights or the powers listed in point (a) of the second subparagraph of Article 1(2).

Article 8 Application of the turnover threshold

1. For the purpose of calculating total annual turnover within the meaning of Article 2(2), the turnover achieved during the previous financial year by the relevant party to the vertical agreement and the turnover achieved by its connected undertakings in respect of all goods and services, excluding all taxes and other duties, shall be added together. For this purpose, no account shall be taken of dealings between the party to the vertical agreement and its connected undertakings or between its connected undertakings.

2. The exemption provided for in Article 2 shall remain applicable where, for any period of two consecutive financial years, the total annual turnover threshold is exceeded by no more than 10 %.

Article 9 Transitional period

The prohibition laid down in Article 101(1) of the Treaty shall not apply during the period from 1 June 2010 to 31 May 2011 in respect of agreements already in force on 31 May 2010 which do not satisfy the conditions for exemption provided for in this Regulation but which, on 31 May 2010, satisfied the conditions for exemption provided for in Regulation (EC) No 2790/1999.

Article 10 Period of validity

This Regulation shall enter into force on 1 June 2010.

It shall expire on 31 May 2022.

This Regulation shall be binding in its entirety and directly applicable in all Member States.

(date of signing and signatory omitted)

VII Social Policy

A) EQUALITIES LAW

COUNCIL DIRECTIVE 2000/43/EC OF 29 JUNE 2000
implementing the principle of equal treatment between persons irrespective of racial or ethnic origin

OJ L 180, 19.7.2000, P. 22[1]

(footnotes omitted)

THE COUNCIL OF THE EUROPEAN UNION,

Having regard to the Treaty establishing the European Community and in particular Article 13 thereof,

Having regard to the proposal from the Commission,

Having regard to the opinion of the European Parliament,

Having regard to the opinion of the Economic and Social Committee,

Having regard to the opinion of the Committee of the Regions,

Whereas:

(1) The Treaty on European Union marks a new stage in the process of creating an ever closer union among the peoples of Europe.

(2) In accordance with Article 6 of the Treaty on European Union, the European Union is founded on the principles of liberty, democracy, respect for human rights and fundamental freedoms, and the rule of law, principles which are common to the Member States, and should respect fundamental rights as guaranteed by the European Convention for the protection of Human Rights and Fundamental Freedoms and as they result from the constitutional traditions common to the Member States, as general principles of Community Law.

(3) The right to equality before the law and protection against discrimination for all persons constitutes a universal right recognised by the Universal Declaration of Human Rights, the

---

[1]   EDITOR'S NOTE: As of 1 May 2012 this Directive has not been amended following the entry into force of the Treaty of Lisbon. It includes references to the old Treaty article numbers. Reference should be made to the Tables of Equivalences accompanying the consolidated Treaties in Part II of this edition for the conversion of old Treaty article numbers to new ones.

United Nations Convention on the Elimination of all forms of Discrimination Against Women, the International Convention on the Elimination of all forms of Racial Discrimination and the United Nations Covenants on Civil and Political Rights and on Economic, Social and Cultural Rights and by the European Convention for the Protection of Human Rights and Fundamental Freedoms, to which all Member States are signatories.

(4) It is important to respect such fundamental rights and freedoms, including the right to freedom of association. It is also important, in the context of the access to and provision of goods and services, to respect the protection of private and family life and transactions carried out in this context.

(5) The European Parliament has adopted a number of Resolutions on the fight against racism in the European Union.

(6) The European Union rejects theories which attempt to determine the existence of separate human races. The use of the term "racial origin" in this Directive does not imply an acceptance of such theories.

(7) The European Council in Tampere, on 15 and 16 October 1999, invited the Commission to come forward as soon as possible with proposals implementing Article 13 of the EC Treaty as regards the fight against racism and xenophobia.

(8) The Employment Guidelines 2000 agreed by the European Council in Helsinki, on 10 and 11 December 1999, stress the need to foster conditions for a socially inclusive labour market by formulating a coherent set of policies aimed at combating discrimination against groups such as ethnic minorities.

(9) Discrimination based on racial or ethnic origin may undermine the achievement of the objectives of the EC Treaty, in particular the attainment of a high level of employment and of social protection, the raising of the standard of living and quality of life, economic and social cohesion and solidarity. It may also undermine the objective of developing the European Union as an area of freedom, security and justice.

(10) The Commission presented a communication on racism, xenophobia and anti-Semitism in December 1995.

(11) The Council adopted on 15 July 1996 Joint Action (96/443/JHA) concerning action to combat racism and xenophobia under which the Member States undertake to ensure effective judicial cooperation in respect of offences based on racist or xenophobic behaviour.

(12) To ensure the development of democratic and tolerant societies which allow the participation of all persons irrespective of racial or ethnic origin, specific action in the field of discrimination based on racial or ethnic origin should go beyond access to employed and self-employed activities and cover areas such as education, social protection including social security and healthcare, social advantages and access to and supply of goods and services.

(13) To this end, any direct or indirect discrimination based on racial or ethnic origin as regards the areas covered by this Directive should be prohibited throughout the Community. This prohibition of discrimination should also apply to nationals of third countries, but does not cover differences of treatment based on nationality and is without prejudice to provisions governing the entry and residence of third-country nationals and their access to employment and to occupation.

(14) In implementing the principle of equal treatment irrespective of racial or ethnic origin, the Community should, in accordance with Article 3(2) of the EC Treaty, aim to eliminate

inequalities, and to promote equality between men and women, especially since women are often the victims of multiple discrimination.

(15) The appreciation of the facts from which it may be inferred that there has been direct or indirect discrimination is a matter for national judicial or other competent bodies, in accordance with rules of national law or practice. Such rules may provide in particular for indirect discrimination to be established by any means including on the basis of statistical evidence.

(16) It is important to protect all natural persons against discrimination on grounds of racial or ethnic origin. Member States should also provide, where appropriate and in accordance with their national traditions and practice, protection for legal persons where they suffer discrimination on grounds of the racial or ethnic origin of their members.

(17) The prohibition of discrimination should be without prejudice to the maintenance or adoption of measures intended to prevent or compensate for disadvantages suffered by a group of persons of a particular racial or ethnic origin, and such measures may permit organisations of persons of a particular racial or ethnic origin where their main object is the promotion of the special needs of those persons.

(18) In very limited circumstances, a difference of treatment may be justified where a characteristic related to racial or ethnic origin constitutes a genuine and determining occupational requirement, when the objective is legitimate and the requirement is proportionate. Such circumstances should be included in the information provided by the Member States to the Commission.

(19) Persons who have been subject to discrimination based on racial and ethnic origin should have adequate means of legal protection. To provide a more effective level of protection, associations or legal entities should also be empowered to engage, as the Member States so determine, either on behalf or in support of any victim, in proceedings, without prejudice to national rules of procedure concerning representation and defence before the courts.

(20) The effective implementation of the principle of equality requires adequate judicial protection against victimisation.

(21) The rules on the burden of proof must be adapted when there is a prima facie case of discrimination and, for the principle of equal treatment to be applied effectively, the burden of proof must shift back to the respondent when evidence of such discrimination is brought.

(22) Member States need not apply the rules on the burden of proof to proceedings in which it is for the court or other competent body to investigate the facts of the case. The procedures thus referred to are those in which the plaintiff is not required to prove the facts, which it is for the court or competent body to investigate.

(23) Member States should promote dialogue between the social partners and with non-governmental organisations to address different forms of discrimination and to combat them.

(24) Protection against discrimination based on racial or ethnic origin would itself be strengthened by the existence of a body or bodies in each Member State, with competence to analyse the problems involved, to study possible solutions and to provide concrete assistance for the victims.

(25) This Directive lays down minimum requirements, thus giving the Member States the option of introducing or maintaining more favourable provisions. The implementation of

this Directive should not serve to justify any regression in relation to the situation which already prevails in each Member State.

(26) Member States should provide for effective, proportionate and dissuasive sanctions in case of breaches of the obligations under this Directive.

(27) The Member States may entrust management and labour, at their joint request, with the implementation of this Directive as regards provisions falling within the scope of collective agreements, provided that the Member States take all the necessary steps to ensure that they can at all times guarantee the results imposed by this Directive.

(28) In accordance with the principles of subsidiarity and proportionality as set out in Article 5 of the EC Treaty, the objective of this Directive, namely ensuring a common high level of protection against discrimination in all the Member States, cannot be sufficiently achieved by the Member States and can therefore, by reason of the scale and impact of the proposed action, be better achieved by the Community. This Directive does not go beyond what is necessary in order to achieve those objectives,

HAS ADOPTED THIS DIRECTIVE:

Chapter I GENERAL PROVISIONS

Article 1 Purpose
The purpose of this Directive is to lay down a framework for combating discrimination on the grounds of racial or ethnic origin, with a view to putting into effect in the Member States the principle of equal treatment.

Article 2 Concept of discrimination
1. For the purposes of this Directive, the principle of equal treatment shall mean that there shall be no direct or indirect discrimination based on racial or ethnic origin.

2. For the purposes of paragraph 1:
    (a) direct discrimination shall be taken to occur where one person is treated less favourably than another is, has been or would be treated in a comparable situation on grounds of racial or ethnic origin;
    (b) indirect discrimination shall be taken to occur where an apparently neutral provision, criterion or practice would put persons of a racial or ethnic origin at a particular disadvantage compared with other persons, unless that provision, criterion or practice is objectively justified by a legitimate aim and the means of achieving that aim are appropriate and necessary.

3. Harassment shall be deemed to be discrimination within the meaning of paragraph 1, when an unwanted conduct related to racial or ethnic origin takes place with the purpose or effect of violating the dignity of a person and of creating an intimidating, hostile, degrading, humiliating or offensive environment. In this context, the concept of harassment may be defined in accordance with the national laws and practice of the Member States.

4. An instruction to discriminate against persons on grounds of racial or ethnic origin shall be deemed to be discrimination within the meaning of paragraph 1.

Article 3 Scope
1. Within the limits of the powers conferred upon the Community, this Directive shall apply to all persons, as regards both the public and private sectors, including public bodies, in relation to:

(a) conditions for access to employment, to self-employment and to occupation, including selection criteria and recruitment conditions, whatever the branch of activity and at all levels of the professional hierarchy, including promotion;

(b) access to all types and to all levels of vocational guidance, vocational training, advanced vocational training and retraining, including practical work experience;

(c) employment and working conditions, including dismissals and pay;

(d) membership of and involvement in an organisation of workers or employers, or any organisation whose members carry on a particular profession, including the benefits provided for by such organisations;

(e) social protection, including social security and healthcare;

(f) social advantages;

(g) education;

(h) access to and supply of goods and services which are available to the public, including housing.

2.   This Directive does not cover difference of treatment based on nationality and is without prejudice to provisions and conditions relating to the entry into and residence of third-country nationals and stateless persons on the territory of Member States, and to any treatment which arises from the legal status of the third-country nationals and stateless persons concerned.

Article 4 Genuine and determining occupational requirements

Notwithstanding Article 2(1) and (2), Member States may provide that a difference of treatment which is based on a characteristic related to racial or ethnic origin shall not constitute discrimination where, by reason of the nature of the particular occupational activities concerned or of the context in which they are carried out, such a characteristic constitutes a genuine and determining occupational requirement, provided that the objective is legitimate and the requirement is proportionate.

Article 5 Positive action

With a view to ensuring full equality in practice, the principle of equal treatment shall not prevent any Member State from maintaining or adopting specific measures to prevent or compensate for disadvantages linked to racial or ethnic origin.

Article 6 Minimum requirements

1.   Member States may introduce or maintain provisions which are more favourable to the protection of the principle of equal treatment than those laid down in this Directive.

2.   The implementation of this Directive shall under no circumstances constitute grounds for a reduction in the level of protection against discrimination already afforded by Member States in the fields covered by this Directive.

Chapter II REMEDIES AND ENFORCEMENT

Article 7 Defence of rights

1.   Member States shall ensure that judicial and/or administrative procedures, including where they deem it appropriate conciliation procedures, for the enforcement of obligations under this Directive are available to all persons who consider themselves wronged by failure to apply the principle of equal treatment to them, even after the relationship in which the discrimination is alleged to have occurred has ended.

2.   Member States shall ensure that associations, organisations or other legal entities, which have, in accordance with the criteria laid down by their national law, a legitimate interest in ensuring that the provisions of this Directive are complied with, may engage, either on

behalf or in support of the complainant, with his or her approval, in any judicial and/or administrative procedure provided for the enforcement of obligations under this Directive.

3.   Paragraphs 1 and 2 are without prejudice to national rules relating to time limits for bringing actions as regards the principle of equality of treatment.

Article 8 Burden of proof
1.   Member States shall take such measures as are necessary, in accordance with their national judicial systems, to ensure that, when persons who consider themselves wronged because the principle of equal treatment has not been applied to them establish, before a court or other competent authority, facts from which it may be presumed that there has been direct or indirect discrimination, it shall be for the respondent to prove that there has been no breach of the principle of equal treatment.

2.   Paragraph 1 shall not prevent Member States from introducing rules of evidence which are more favourable to plaintiffs.

3.   Paragraph 1 shall not apply to criminal procedures.

4.   Paragraphs 1, 2 and 3 shall also apply to any proceedings brought in accordance with Article 7(2).

5.   Member States need not apply paragraph 1 to proceedings in which it is for the court or competent body to investigate the facts of the case.

Article 9 Victimisation
Member States shall introduce into their national legal systems such measures as are necessary to protect individuals from any adverse treatment or adverse consequence as a reaction to a complaint or to proceedings aimed at enforcing compliance with the principle of equal treatment.

Article 10 Dissemination of information
Member States shall take care that the provisions adopted pursuant to this Directive, together with the relevant provisions already in force, are brought to the attention of the persons concerned by all appropriate means throughout their territory.

Article 11 Social dialogue
1.   Member States shall, in accordance with national traditions and practice, take adequate measures to promote the social dialogue between the two sides of industry with a view to fostering equal treatment, including through the monitoring of workplace practices, collective agreements, codes of conduct, research or exchange of experiences and good practices.

2.   Where consistent with national traditions and practice, Member States shall encourage the two sides of the industry without prejudice to their autonomy to conclude, at the appropriate level, agreements laying down anti-discrimination rules in the fields referred to in Article 3 which fall within the scope of collective bargaining. These agreements shall respect the minimum requirements laid down by this Directive and the relevant national implementing measures.

Article 12 Dialogue with non-governmental organisations
Member States shall encourage dialogue with appropriate non-governmental organisations which have, in accordance with their national law and practice, a legitimate interest in

contributing to the fight against discrimination on grounds of racial and ethnic origin with a view to promoting the principle of equal treatment.

Chapter III BODIES FOR THE PROMOTION OF EQUAL TREATMENT

Article 13

1. Member States shall designate a body or bodies for the promotion of equal treatment of all persons without discrimination on the grounds of racial or ethnic origin. These bodies may form part of agencies charged at national level with the defence of human rights or the safeguard of individuals' rights.

2. Member States shall ensure that the competences of these bodies include:
    — without prejudice to the right of victims and of associations, organisations or other legal entities referred to in Article 7(2), providing independent assistance to victims of discrimination in pursuing their complaints about discrimination,
    — conducting independent surveys concerning discrimination,
    — publishing independent reports and making recommendations on any issue relating to such discrimination.

Chapter IV FINAL PROVISIONS

Article 14 Compliance

Member States shall take the necessary measures to ensure that:

(a) any laws, regulations and administrative provisions contrary to the principle of equal treatment are abolished;

(b) any provisions contrary to the principle of equal treatment which are included in individual or collective contracts or agreements, internal rules of undertakings, rules governing profit-making or non-profit-making associations, and rules governing the independent professions and workers' and employers' organisations, are or may be declared, null and void or are amended.

Article 15 Sanctions

Member States shall lay down the rules on sanctions applicable to infringements of the national provisions adopted pursuant to this Directive and shall take all measures necessary to ensure that they are applied. The sanctions, which may comprise the payment of compensation to the victim, must be effective, proportionate and dissuasive. The Member States shall notify those provisions to the Commission by 19 July 2003 at the latest and shall notify it without delay of any subsequent amendment affecting them.

Article 16 Implementation

Member States shall adopt the laws, regulations and administrative provisions necessary to comply with this Directive by 19 July 2003 or may entrust management and labour, at their joint request, with the implementation of this Directive as regards provisions falling within the scope of collective agreements. In such cases, Member States shall ensure that by 19 July 2003, management and labour introduce the necessary measures by agreement, Member States being required to take any necessary measures to enable them at any time to be in a position to guarantee the results imposed by this Directive. They shall forthwith inform the Commission thereof.

When Member States adopt these measures, they shall contain a reference to this Directive or be accompanied by such a reference on the occasion of their official publication. The methods of making such a reference shall be laid down by the Member States.

Article 17 Report

1. Member States shall communicate to the Commission by 19 July 2005, and every five years thereafter, all the information necessary for the Commission to draw up a report to the European Parliament and the Council on the application of this Directive.

2. The Commission's report shall take into account, as appropriate, the views of the European Monitoring Centre on Racism and Xenophobia, as well as the viewpoints of the social partners and relevant non-governmental organisations. In accordance with the principle of gender mainstreaming, this report shall, inter alia, provide an assessment of the impact of the measures taken on women and men. In the light of the information received, this report shall include, if necessary, proposals to revise and update this Directive.

Article 18 Entry into force

This Directive shall enter into force on the day of its publication in the *Official Journal of the European Communities*.

Article 19 Addressees

This Directive is addressed to the Member States.

(*date of signing and signatory omitted*)

COUNCIL DIRECTIVE 2000/78/EC OF 27 NOVEMBER 2000

establishing a general framework for equal treatment in employment and occupation

OJ L 303, 2.12.2000, P. 16[1]

(*footnotes omitted*)

THE COUNCIL OF THE EUROPEAN UNION,

Having regard to the Treaty establishing the European Community, and in particular Article 13 thereof,

Having regard to the proposal from the Commission,

Having regard to the Opinion of the European Parliament,

Having regard to the Opinion of the Economic and Social Committee,

Having regard to the Opinion of the Committee of the Regions,

Whereas:

(1) In accordance with Article 6 of the Treaty on European Union, the European Union is founded on the principles of liberty, democracy, respect for human rights and fundamental freedoms, and the rule of law, principles which are common to all Member States and it respects fundamental rights, as guaranteed by the European Convention for the Protection

---

[1]   EDITOR'S NOTE: As of 1 May 2012 this Directive has not been amended following the entry into force of the Treaty of Lisbon. It includes references to the old Treaty article numbers. Reference should be made to the Tables of Equivalences accompanying the consolidated Treaties in Part II of this edition for the conversion of old Treaty article numbers to new ones.

of Human Rights and Fundamental Freedoms and as they result from the constitutional traditions common to the Member States, as general principles of Community law.

(2)   The principle of equal treatment between women and men is well established by an important body of Community law, in particular in Council Directive 76/207/EEC of 9 February 1976 on the implementation of the principle of equal treatment for men and women as regards access to employment, vocational training and promotion, and working conditions.

(3)   In implementing the principle of equal treatment, the Community should, in accordance with Article 3(2) of the EC Treaty, aim to eliminate inequalities, and to promote equality between men and women, especially since women are often the victims of multiple discrimination.

(4)   The right of all persons to equality before the law and protection against discrimination constitutes a universal right recognised by the Universal Declaration of Human Rights, the United Nations Convention on the Elimination of All Forms of Discrimination against Women, United Nations Covenants on Civil and Political Rights and on Economic, Social and Cultural Rights and by the European Convention for the Protection of Human Rights and Fundamental Freedoms, to which all Member States are signatories. Convention No 111 of the International Labour Organisation (ILO) prohibits discrimination in the field of employment and occupation.

(5)   It is important to respect such fundamental rights and freedoms. This Directive does not prejudice freedom of association, including the right to establish unions with others and to join unions to defend one's interests.

(6)   The Community Charter of the Fundamental Social Rights of Workers recognises the importance of combating every form of discrimination, including the need to take appropriate action for the social and economic integration of elderly and disabled people.

(7)   The EC Treaty includes among its objectives the promotion of coordination between employment policies of the Member States. To this end, a new employment chapter was incorporated in the EC Treaty as a means of developing a coordinated European strategy for employment to promote a skilled, trained and adaptable workforce.

(8)   The Employment Guidelines for 2000 agreed by the European Council at Helsinki on 10 and 11 December 1999 stress the need to foster a labour market favourable to social integration by formulating a coherent set of policies aimed at combating discrimination against groups such as persons with disability. They also emphasise the need to pay particular attention to supporting older workers, in order to increase their participation in the labour force.

(9)   Employment and occupation are key elements in guaranteeing equal opportunities for all and contribute strongly to the full participation of citizens in economic, cultural and social life and to realising their potential.

(10)   On 29 June 2000 the Council adopted Directive 2000/43/EC implementing the principle of equal treatment between persons irrespective of racial or ethnic origin. That Directive already provides protection against such discrimination in the field of employment and occupation.

(11)   Discrimination based on religion or belief, disability, age or sexual orientation may undermine the achievement of the objectives of the EC Treaty, in particular the attainment of a high level of employment and social protection, raising the standard of living and the

quality of life, economic and social cohesion and solidarity, and the free movement of persons.

(12) To this end, any direct or indirect discrimination based on religion or belief, disability, age or sexual orientation as regards the areas covered by this Directive should be prohibited throughout the Community. This prohibition of discrimination should also apply to nationals of third countries but does not cover differences of treatment based on nationality and is without prejudice to provisions governing the entry and residence of third-country nationals and their access to employment and occupation.

(13) This Directive does not apply to social security and social protection schemes whose benefits are not treated as income within the meaning given to that term for the purpose of applying Article 141 of the EC Treaty, nor to any kind of payment by the State aimed at providing access to employment or maintaining employment.

(14) This Directive shall be without prejudice to national provisions laying down retirement ages.

(15) The appreciation of the facts from which it may be inferred that there has been direct or indirect discrimination is a matter for national judicial or other competent bodies, in accordance with rules of national law or practice. Such rules may provide, in particular, for indirect discrimination to be established by any means including on the basis of statistical evidence.

(16) The provision of measures to accommodate the needs of disabled people at the workplace plays an important role in combating discrimination on grounds of disability.

(17) This Directive does not require the recruitment, promotion, maintenance in employment or training of an individual who is not competent, capable and available to perform the essential functions of the post concerned or to undergo the relevant training, without prejudice to the obligation to provide reasonable accommodation for people with disabilities.

(18) This Directive does not require, in particular, the armed forces and the police, prison or emergency services to recruit or maintain in employment persons who do not have the required capacity to carry out the range of functions that they may be called upon to perform with regard to the legitimate objective of preserving the operational capacity of those services.

(19) Moreover, in order that the Member States may continue to safeguard the combat effectiveness of their armed forces, they may choose not to apply the provisions of this Directive concerning disability and age to all or part of their armed forces. The Member States which make that choice must define the scope of that derogation.

(20) Appropriate measures should be provided, i.e. effective and practical measures to adapt the workplace to the disability, for example adapting premises and equipment, patterns of working time, the distribution of tasks or the provision of training or integration resources.

(21) To determine whether the measures in question give rise to a disproportionate burden, account should be taken in particular of the financial and other costs entailed, the scale and financial resources of the organisation or undertaking and the possibility of obtaining public funding or any other assistance.

(22) This Directive is without prejudice to national laws on marital status and the benefits dependent thereon.

(23) In very limited circumstances, a difference of treatment may be justified where a characteristic related to religion or belief, disability, age or sexual orientation constitutes a genuine and determining occupational requirement, when the objective is legitimate and the requirement is proportionate. Such circumstances should be included in the information provided by the Member States to the Commission.

(24) The European Union in its Declaration No 11 on the status of churches and non-confessional organisations, annexed to the Final Act of the Amsterdam Treaty, has explicitly recognised that it respects and does not prejudice the status under national law of churches and religious associations or communities in the Member States and that it equally respects the status of philosophical and non-confessional organisations. With this in view, Member States may maintain or lay down specific provisions on genuine, legitimate and justified occupational requirements which might be required for carrying out an occupational activity.

(25) The prohibition of age discrimination is an essential part of meeting the aims set out in the Employment Guidelines and encouraging diversity in the workforce. However, differences in treatment in connection with age may be justified under certain circumstances and therefore require specific provisions which may vary in accordance with the situation in Member States. It is therefore essential to distinguish between differences in treatment which are justified, in particular by legitimate employment policy, labour market and vocational training objectives, and discrimination which must be prohibited.

(26) The prohibition of discrimination should be without prejudice to the maintenance or adoption of measures intended to prevent or compensate for disadvantages suffered by a group of persons of a particular religion or belief, disability, age or sexual orientation, and such measures may permit organisations of persons of a particular religion or belief, disability, age or sexual orientation where their main object is the promotion of the special needs of those persons.

(27) In its Recommendation 86/379/EEC of 24 July 1986 on the employment of disabled people in the Community, the Council established a guideline framework setting out examples of positive action to promote the employment and training of disabled people, and in its Resolution of 17 June 1999 on equal employment opportunities for people with disabilities, affirmed the importance of giving specific attention inter alia to recruitment, retention, training and lifelong learning with regard to disabled persons.

(28) This Directive lays down minimum requirements, thus giving the Member States the option of introducing or maintaining more favourable provisions. The implementation of this Directive should not serve to justify any regression in relation to the situation which already prevails in each Member State.

(29) Persons who have been subject to discrimination based on religion or belief, disability, age or sexual orientation should have adequate means of legal protection. To provide a more effective level of protection, associations or legal entities should also be empowered to engage in proceedings, as the Member States so determine, either on behalf or in support of any victim, without prejudice to national rules of procedure concerning representation and defence before the courts.

(30) The effective implementation of the principle of equality requires adequate judicial protection against victimisation.

(31) The rules on the burden of proof must be adapted when there is a prima facie case of discrimination and, for the principle of equal treatment to be applied effectively, the burden of proof must shift back to the respondent when evidence of such discrimination is brought. However, it is not for the respondent to prove that the plaintiff adheres to a particular religion or belief, has a particular disability, is of a particular age or has a particular sexual orientation.

(32) Member States need not apply the rules on the burden of proof to proceedings in which it is for the court or other competent body to investigate the facts of the case. The procedures thus referred to are those in which the plaintiff is not required to prove the facts, which it is for the court or competent body to investigate.

(33) Member States should promote dialogue between the social partners and, within the framework of national practice, with non-governmental organisations to address different forms of discrimination at the workplace and to combat them.

(34) The need to promote peace and reconciliation between the major communities in Northern Ireland necessitates the incorporation of particular provisions into this Directive.

(35) Member States should provide for effective, proportionate and dissuasive sanctions in case of breaches of the obligations under this Directive.

(36) Member States may entrust the social partners, at their joint request, with the implementation of this Directive, as regards the provisions concerning collective agreements, provided they take any necessary steps to ensure that they are at all times able to guarantee the results required by this Directive.

(37) In accordance with the principle of subsidiarity set out in Article 5 of the EC Treaty, the objective of this Directive, namely the creation within the Community of a level playing-field as regards equality in employment and occupation, cannot be sufficiently achieved by the Member States and can therefore, by reason of the scale and impact of the action, be better achieved at Community level. In accordance with the principle of proportionality, as set out in that Article, this Directive does not go beyond what is necessary in order to achieve that objective,

HAS ADOPTED THIS DIRECTIVE:

Chapter I GENERAL PROVISIONS

Article 1 Purpose
The purpose of this Directive is to lay down a general framework for combating discrimination on the grounds of religion or belief, disability, age or sexual orientation as regards employment and occupation, with a view to putting into effect in the Member States the principle of equal treatment.

Article 2 Concept of discrimination
1.   For the purposes of this Directive, the "principle of equal treatment" shall mean that there shall be no direct or indirect discrimination whatsoever on any of the grounds referred to in Article 1.

2.   For the purposes of paragraph 1:
      (a) direct discrimination shall be taken to occur where one person is treated less favourably than another is, has been or would be treated in a comparable situation, on any of the grounds referred to in Article 1;
      (b) indirect discrimination shall be taken to occur where an apparently neutral provision, criterion or practice would put persons having a particular religion or belief, a

particular disability, a particular age, or a particular sexual orientation at a particular disadvantage compared with other persons unless:

(i)   that provision, criterion or practice is objectively justified by a legitimate aim and the means of achieving that aim are appropriate and necessary, or

(ii) as regards persons with a particular disability, the employer or any person or organisation to whom this Directive applies, is obliged, under national legislation, to take appropriate measures in line with the principles contained in Article 5 in order to eliminate disadvantages entailed by such provision, criterion or practice.

3.   Harassment shall be deemed to be a form of discrimination within the meaning of paragraph 1, when unwanted conduct related to any of the grounds referred to in Article 1 takes place with the purpose or effect of violating the dignity of a person and of creating an intimidating, hostile, degrading, humiliating or offensive environment. In this context, the concept of harassment may be defined in accordance with the national laws and practice of the Member States.

4.   An instruction to discriminate against persons on any of the grounds referred to in Article 1 shall be deemed to be discrimination within the meaning of paragraph 1.

5.   This Directive shall be without prejudice to measures laid down by national law which, in a democratic society, are necessary for public security, for the maintenance of public order and the prevention of criminal offences, for the protection of health and for the protection of the rights and freedoms of others.

Article 3 Scope

1.   Within the limits of the areas of competence conferred on the Community, this Directive shall apply to all persons, as regards both the public and private sectors, including public bodies, in relation to:

(a) conditions for access to employment, to self-employment or to occupation, including selection criteria and recruitment conditions, whatever the branch of activity and at all levels of the professional hierarchy, including promotion;

(b) access to all types and to all levels of vocational guidance, vocational training, advanced vocational training and retraining, including practical work experience;

(c) employment and working conditions, including dismissals and pay;

(d) membership of, and involvement in, an organisation of workers or employers, or any organisation whose members carry on a particular profession, including the benefits provided for by such organisations.

2.   This Directive does not cover differences of treatment based on nationality and is without prejudice to provisions and conditions relating to the entry into and residence of third-country nationals and stateless persons in the territory of Member States, and to any treatment which arises from the legal status of the third-country nationals and stateless persons concerned.

3.   This Directive does not apply to payments of any kind made by state schemes or similar, including state social security or social protection schemes.

4.   Member States may provide that this Directive, in so far as it relates to discrimination on the grounds of disability and age, shall not apply to the armed forces.

Article 4 Occupational requirements

1.   Notwithstanding Article 2(1) and (2), Member States may provide that a difference of treatment which is based on a characteristic related to any of the grounds referred to in Article 1 shall not constitute discrimination where, by reason of the nature of the

particular occupational activities concerned or of the context in which they are carried out, such a characteristic constitutes a genuine and determining occupational requirement, provided that the objective is legitimate and the requirement is proportionate.

2. Member States may maintain national legislation in force at the date of adoption of this Directive or provide for future legislation incorporating national practices existing at the date of adoption of this Directive pursuant to which, in the case of occupational activities within churches and other public or private organisations the ethos of which is based on religion or belief, a difference of treatment based on a person's religion or belief shall not constitute discrimination where, by reason of the nature of these activities or of the context in which they are carried out, a person's religion or belief constitute a genuine, legitimate and justified occupational requirement, having regard to the organisation's ethos. This difference of treatment shall be implemented taking account of Member States' constitutional provisions and principles, as well as the general principles of Community law, and should not justify discrimination on another ground.

Provided that its provisions are otherwise complied with, this Directive shall thus not prejudice the right of churches and other public or private organisations, the ethos of which is based on religion or belief, acting in conformity with national constitutions and laws, to require individuals working for them to act in good faith and with loyalty to the organisation's ethos.

Article 5 Reasonable accommodation for disabled persons
In order to guarantee compliance with the principle of equal treatment in relation to persons with disabilities, reasonable accommodation shall be provided. This means that employers shall take appropriate measures, where needed in a particular case, to enable a person with a disability to have access to, participate in, or advance in employment, or to undergo training, unless such measures would impose a disproportionate burden on the employer. This burden shall not be disproportionate when it is sufficiently remedied by measures existing within the framework of the disability policy of the Member State concerned.

Article 6 Justification of differences of treatment on grounds of age
1. Notwithstanding Article 2(2), Member States may provide that differences of treatment on grounds of age shall not constitute discrimination, if, within the context of national law, they are objectively and reasonably justified by a legitimate aim, including legitimate employment policy, labour market and vocational training objectives, and if the means of achieving that aim are appropriate and necessary.

Such differences of treatment may include, among others:

(a) the setting of special conditions on access to employment and vocational training, employment and occupation, including dismissal and remuneration conditions, for young people, older workers and persons with caring responsibilities in order to promote their vocational integration or ensure their protection;

(b) the fixing of minimum conditions of age, professional experience or seniority in service for access to employment or to certain advantages linked to employment;

(c) the fixing of a maximum age for recruitment which is based on the training requirements of the post in question or the need for a reasonable period of employment before retirement.

2. Notwithstanding Article 2(2), Member States may provide that the fixing for occupational social security schemes of ages for admission or entitlement to retirement or invalidity benefits, including the fixing under those schemes of different ages for employees or groups or categories of employees, and the use, in the context of such schemes, of age

criteria in actuarial calculations, does not constitute discrimination on the grounds of age, provided this does not result in discrimination on the grounds of sex.

Article 7 Positive action

1.   With a view to ensuring full equality in practice, the principle of equal treatment shall not prevent any Member State from maintaining or adopting specific measures to prevent or compensate for disadvantages linked to any of the grounds referred to in Article 1.

2.   With regard to disabled persons, the principle of equal treatment shall be without prejudice to the right of Member States to maintain or adopt provisions on the protection of health and safety at work or to measures aimed at creating or maintaining provisions or facilities for safeguarding or promoting their integration into the working environment.

Article 8 Minimum requirements

1.   Member States may introduce or maintain provisions which are more favourable to the protection of the principle of equal treatment than those laid down in this Directive.

2.   The implementation of this Directive shall under no circumstances constitute grounds for a reduction in the level of protection against discrimination already afforded by Member States in the fields covered by this Directive.

Chapter II REMEDIES AND ENFORCEMENT

Article 9 Defence of rights

1.   Member States shall ensure that judicial and/or administrative procedures, including where they deem it appropriate conciliation procedures, for the enforcement of obligations under this Directive are available to all persons who consider themselves wronged by failure to apply the principle of equal treatment to them, even after the relationship in which the discrimination is alleged to have occurred has ended.

2.   Member States shall ensure that associations, organisations or other legal entities which have, in accordance with the criteria laid down by their national law, a legitimate interest in ensuring that the provisions of this Directive are complied with, may engage, either on behalf or in support of the complainant, with his or her approval, in any judicial and/or administrative procedure provided for the enforcement of obligations under this Directive.

3.   Paragraphs 1 and 2 are without prejudice to national rules relating to time limits for bringing actions as regards the principle of equality of treatment.

Article 10 Burden of proof

1.   Member States shall take such measures as are necessary, in accordance with their national judicial systems, to ensure that, when persons who consider themselves wronged because the principle of equal treatment has not been applied to them establish, before a court or other competent authority, facts from which it may be presumed that there has been direct or indirect discrimination, it shall be for the respondent to prove that there has been no breach of the principle of equal treatment.

2.   Paragraph 1 shall not prevent Member States from introducing rules of evidence which are more favourable to plaintiffs.

3.   Paragraph 1 shall not apply to criminal procedures.

4.   Paragraphs 1, 2 and 3 shall also apply to any legal proceedings commenced in accordance with Article 9(2).

5.   Member States need not apply paragraph 1 to proceedings in which it is for the court or competent body to investigate the facts of the case.

Article 11 Victimisation
Member States shall introduce into their national legal systems such measures as are necessary to protect employees against dismissal or other adverse treatment by the employer as a reaction to a complaint within the undertaking or to any legal proceedings aimed at enforcing compliance with the principle of equal treatment.

Article 12 Dissemination of information
Member States shall take care that the provisions adopted pursuant to this Directive, together with the relevant provisions already in force in this field, are brought to the attention of the persons concerned by all appropriate means, for example at the workplace, throughout their territory.

Article 13 Social dialogue
1.   Member States shall, in accordance with their national traditions and practice, take adequate measures to promote dialogue between the social partners with a view to fostering equal treatment, including through the monitoring of workplace practices, collective agreements, codes of conduct and through research or exchange of experiences and good practices.

2.   Where consistent with their national traditions and practice, Member States shall encourage the social partners, without prejudice to their autonomy, to conclude at the appropriate level agreements laying down anti-discrimination rules in the fields referred to in Article 3 which fall within the scope of collective bargaining. These agreements shall respect the minimum requirements laid down by this Directive and by the relevant national implementing measures.

Article 14 Dialogue with non-governmental organisations
Member States shall encourage dialogue with appropriate non-governmental organisations which have, in accordance with their national law and practice, a legitimate interest in contributing to the fight against discrimination on any of the grounds referred to in Article 1 with a view to promoting the principle of equal treatment.

Chapter III PARTICULAR PROVISIONS

Article 15 Northern Ireland
1.   In order to tackle the under-representation of one of the major religious communities in the police service of Northern Ireland, differences in treatment regarding recruitment into that service, including its support staff, shall not constitute discrimination insofar as those differences in treatment are expressly authorised by national legislation.

2.   In order to maintain a balance of opportunity in employment for teachers in Northern Ireland while furthering the reconciliation of historical divisions between the major religious communities there, the provisions on religion or belief in this Directive shall not apply to the recruitment of teachers in schools in Northern Ireland in so far as this is expressly authorised by national legislation.

Chapter IV FINAL PROVISIONS

Article 16 Compliance
Member States shall take the necessary measures to ensure that:
(a)   any laws, regulations and administrative provisions contrary to the principle of equal treatment are abolished;

(b)   any provisions contrary to the principle of equal treatment which are included in contracts or collective agreements, internal rules of undertakings or rules governing the independent occupations and professions and workers' and employers' organisations are, or may be, declared null and void or are amended.

Article 17 Sanctions

Member States shall lay down the rules on sanctions applicable to infringements of the national provisions adopted pursuant to this Directive and shall take all measures necessary to ensure that they are applied. The sanctions, which may comprise the payment of compensation to the victim, must be effective, proportionate and dissuasive. Member States shall notify those provisions to the Commission by 2 December 2003 at the latest and shall notify it without delay of any subsequent amendment affecting them.

Article 18 Implementation

Member States shall adopt the laws, regulations and administrative provisions necessary to comply with this Directive by 2 December 2003 at the latest or may entrust the social partners, at their joint request, with the implementation of this Directive as regards provisions concerning collective agreements. In such cases, Member States shall ensure that, no later than 2 December 2003, the social partners introduce the necessary measures by agreement, the Member States concerned being required to take any necessary measures to enable them at any time to be in a position to guarantee the results imposed by this Directive. They shall forthwith inform the Commission thereof.

In order to take account of particular conditions, Member States may, if necessary, have an additional period of 3 years from 2 December 2003, that is to say a total of 6 years, to implement the provisions of this Directive on age and disability discrimination. In that event they shall inform the Commission forthwith. Any Member State which chooses to use this additional period shall report annually to the Commission on the steps it is taking to tackle age and disability discrimination and on the progress it is making towards implementation. The Commission shall report annually to the Council.

When Member States adopt these measures, they shall contain a reference to this Directive or be accompanied by such reference on the occasion of their official publication. The methods of making such reference shall be laid down by Member States.

Article 19 Report

1.   Member States shall communicate to the Commission, by 2 December 2005 at the latest and every five years thereafter, all the information necessary for the Commission to draw up a report to the European Parliament and the Council on the application of this Directive.

2.   The Commission's report shall take into account, as appropriate, the viewpoints of the social partners and relevant non-governmental organisations. In accordance with the principle of gender mainstreaming, this report shall, inter alia, provide an assessment of the impact of the measures taken on women and men. In the light of the information received, this report shall include, if necessary, proposals to revise and update this Directive.

Article 20 Entry into force

This Directive shall enter into force on the day of its publication in the *Official Journal of the European Communities*.

Article 21 Addressees
This Directive is addressed to the Member States.

(*date of signing and signatory omitted*)

COUNCIL DIRECTIVE 2004/113/EC OF
13 DECEMBER 2004
implementing the principle of equal treatment between men and women in the access to and supply of goods and services
OJ L 373, 21.12.2004, P. 37[1]

(*footnotes and preamble omitted*)

Chapter I GENERAL PROVISIONS

Article 1 Purpose
The purpose of this Directive is to lay down a framework for combating discrimination based on sex in access to and supply of goods and services, with a view to putting into effect in the Member States the principle of equal treatment between men and women.

Article 2 Definitions
For the purposes of this Directive, the following definitions shall apply:
(a)   direct discrimination: where one person is treated less favourably, on grounds of sex, than another is, has been or would be treated in a comparable situation;

(b)   indirect discrimination: where an apparently neutral provision, criterion or practice would put persons of one sex at a particular disadvantage compared with persons of the other sex, unless that provision, criterion or practice is objectively justified by a legitimate aim and the means of achieving that aim are appropriate and necessary;

(c)   harassment: where an unwanted conduct related to the sex of a person occurs with the purpose or effect of violating the dignity of a person and of creating an intimidating, hostile, degrading, humiliating or offensive environment;

(d)   sexual harassment: where any form of unwanted physical, verbal, non-verbal or physical conduct of a sexual nature occurs, with the purpose or effect of violating the dignity of a person, in particular when creating an intimidating, hostile, degrading, humiliating or offensive environment.

Article 3 Scope
1.   Within the limits of the powers conferred upon the Community, this Directive shall apply to all persons who provide goods and services, which are available to the public irrespective of the person concerned as regards both the public and private sectors, including public bodies, and which are offered outside the area of private and family life and the transactions carried out in this context.

2.   This Directive does not prejudice the individual's freedom to choose a contractual partner as long as an individual's choice of contractual partner is not based on that person's sex.

---

[1]   EDITOR'S NOTE: As of 1 May 2012 this Directive has not been amended following the entry into force of the Treaty of Lisbon (but see note 2 below). It includes references to the old Treaty article numbers. Reference should be made to the Tables of Equivalences accompanying the consolidated Treaties in Part II of this edition for the conversion of old Treaty article numbers to new ones.

3. This Directive shall not apply to the content of media and advertising nor to education.

4. This Directive shall not apply to matters of employment and occupation. This Directive shall not apply to matters of selfemployment, insofar as these matters are covered by other Community legislative acts.

Article 4 Principle of equal treatment

1. For the purposes of this Directive, the principle of equal treatment between men and women shall mean that
    (a) there shall be no direct discrimination based on sex, including less favourable treatment of women for reasons of pregnancy and maternity;
    (b) there shall be no indirect discrimination based on sex.

2. This Directive shall be without prejudice to more favourable provisions concerning the protection of women as regards pregnancy and maternity.

3. Harassment and sexual harassment within the meaning of this Directive shall be deemed to be discrimination on the grounds of sex and therefore prohibited. A person's rejection of, or submission to, such conduct may not be used as a basis for a decision affecting that person.

4. Instruction to direct or indirect discrimination on the grounds of sex shall be deemed to be discrimination within the meaning of this Directive.

5. This Directive shall not preclude differences in treatment, if the provision of the goods and services exclusively or primarily to members of one sex is justified by a legitimate aim and the means of achieving that aim are appropriate and necessary.

Article 5 Actuarial factors[1]

1. Member States shall ensure that in all new contracts concluded after 21 December 2007 at the latest, the use of sex as a factor in the calculation of premiums and benefits for the purposes of insurance and related financial services shall not result in differences in individuals' premiums and benefits.

2. Notwithstanding paragraph 1, Member States may decide before 21 December 2007 to permit proportionate differences in individuals' premiums and benefits where the use of sex is a determining factor in the assessment of risk based on relevant and accurate actuarial and statistical data. The Member States concerned shall inform the Commission and ensure that accurate data relevant to the use of sex as a determining actuarial factor are compiled, published and regularly updated. These Member States shall review their decision five years after 21 December 2007, taking into account the Commission report referred to in Article 16, and shall forward the results of this review to the Commission.

3. In any event, costs related to pregnancy and maternity shall not result in differences in individuals' premiums and benefits. Member States may defer implementation of the measures necessary to comply with this paragraph until two years after 21 December 2007 at the latest. In that case the Member States concerned shall immediately inform the Commission.

---

[1] In Case C-236/09 *Association Belge des Consommateurs Test-Achats ASBL and Others* v. *Conseil des ministres* (1 March 2011), the Court of Justice of the European Union has ruled that Article 5(2) of the Directive is invalid with effect from 21 December 2012.

Article 6 Positive action
With a view to ensuring full equality in practice between men and women, the principle of equal treatment shall not prevent any Member State from maintaining or adopting specific measures to prevent or compensate for disadvantages linked to sex.

Article 7 Minimum requirements
1.   Member States may introduce or maintain provisions which are more favourable to the protection of the principle of equal treatment between men and women than those laid down in this Directive.

2.   The implementation of this Directive shall in no circumstances constitute grounds for a reduction in the level of protection against discrimination already afforded by Member States in the fields covered by this Directive.

Chapter II REMEDIES AND ENFORCEMENT

Article 8 Defence of rights
1.   Member States shall ensure that judicial and/or administrative procedures, including where they deem it appropriate conciliation procedures, for the enforcement of the obligations under this Directive are available to all persons who consider themselves wronged by failure to apply the principle of equal treatment to them, even after the relationship in which the discrimination is alleged to have occurred has ended.

2.   Member States shall introduce into their national legal systems such measures as are necessary to ensure real and effective compensation or reparation, as the Member States so determine, for the loss and damage sustained by a person injured as a result of discrimination within the meaning of this Directive, in a way which is dissuasive and proportionate to the damage suffered. The fixing of a prior upper limit shall not restrict such compensation or reparation.

3.   Member States shall ensure that associations, organisations or other legal entities, which have, in accordance with the criteria laid down by their national law, a legitimate interest in ensuring that the provisions of this Directive are complied with, may engage, on behalf or in support of the complainant, with his or her approval, in any judicial and/or administrative procedure provided for the enforcement of obligations under this Directive.

4.   Paragraphs 1 and 3 shall be without prejudice to national rules on time limits for bringing actions relating to the principle of equal treatment.

Article 9 Burden of proof
1.   Member States shall take such measures as are necessary, in accordance with their national judicial systems, to ensure that, when persons who consider themselves wronged because the principle of equal treatment has not been applied to them establish, before a court or other competent authority, facts from which it may be presumed that there has been direct or indirect discrimination, it shall be for the respondent to prove that there has been no breach of the principle of equal treatment.

2.   Paragraph 1 shall not prevent Member States from introducing rules of evidence, which are more favourable to plaintiffs.

3.   Paragraph 1 shall not apply to criminal procedures.

4.   Paragraphs 1, 2 and 3 shall also apply to any proceedings brought in accordance with Article 8(3).

5.   Member States need not apply paragraph 1 to proceedings in which it is for the court or other competent authority to investigate the facts of the case.

Article 10 Victimisation

Member States shall introduce into their national legal systems such measures as are necessary to protect persons from any adverse treatment or adverse consequence as a reaction to a complaint or to legal proceedings aimed at enforcing compliance with the principle of equal treatment.

Article 11 Dialogue with relevant stakeholders

With a view to promoting the principle of equal treatment, Member States shall encourage dialogue with relevant stakeholders which have, in accordance with national law and practice, a legitimate interest in contributing to the fight against discrimination on grounds of sex in the area of access to and supply of goods and services.

Chapter III BODIES FOR THE PROMOTION OF EQUAL TREATMENT

Article 12

1.   Member States shall designate and make the necessary arrangements for a body or bodies for the promotion, analysis, monitoring and support of equal treatment of all persons without discrimination on the grounds of sex. These bodies may form part of agencies charged at national level with the defence of human rights or the safeguard of individuals' rights, or the implementation of the principle of equal treatment.

2.   Member States shall ensure that the competencies of the bodies referred to in paragraph 1 include:
    (a) without prejudice to the rights of victims and of associations, organisations or other legal entities referred to in Article 8(3), providing independent assistance to victims of discrimination in pursuing their complaints about discrimination;
    (b) conducting independent surveys concerning discrimination;
    (c) publishing independent reports and making recommendations on any issue relating to such discrimination.

Chapter IV FINAL PROVISIONS

Article 13 Compliance

Member States shall take the necessary measures to ensure that the principle of equal treatment is respected in relation to the access to and supply of goods and services within the scope of this Directive, and in particular that:
(a)   any laws, regulations and administrative provisions contrary to the principle of equal treatment are abolished;

(b)   any contractual provisions, internal rules of undertakings, and rules governing profit-making or non-profit-making associations contrary to the principle of equal treatment are, or may be, declared null and void or are amended.

Article 14 Penalties

Member States shall lay down the rules on penalties applicable to infringements of the national provisions adopted pursuant to this Directive and shall take all measures necessary to ensure that they are applied. The penalties, which may comprise the payment of compensation to the victim, shall be effective, proportionate and dissuasive. Member States shall notify those provisions to the Commission by 21 December 2007 at the latest and shall notify it without delay of any subsequent amendment affecting them.

Article 15 Dissemination of information

Member States shall take care that the provisions adopted pursuant to this Directive, together with the relevant provisions already in force, are brought to the attention of the persons concerned by all appropriate means throughout their territory.

Article 16 Reports

1.   Member States shall communicate all available information concerning the application of this Directive to the Commission, by 21 December 2009, and every five years thereafter.

The Commission shall draw up a summary report, which shall include a review of the current practices of Member States in relation to Article 5 with regard to the use of sex as a factor in the calculation of premiums and benefits. It shall submit this report to the European Parliament and to the Council no later 21 December 2010. Where appropriate, the Commission shall accompany its report with proposals to modify the Directive.

2.   The Commission's report shall take into account the viewpoints of relevant stakeholders.

Article 17 Transposition

1.   Member States shall bring into force the laws, regulations and administrative provisions necessary to comply with this Directive by 21 December 2007 at the latest. They shall forthwith communicate to the Commission the text of those provisions.

When Member States adopt these measures, they shall contain a reference to this Directive or be accompanied by such a reference on the occasion of their official publication. The methods of making such publication of reference shall be laid down by the Member States.

2.   Member States shall communicate to the Commission the text of the main provisions of national law which they adopt in the field covered by this Directive.

Article 18 Entry into force

This Directive shall enter into force on the day of its publication in the *Official Journal of the European Union*.

Article 19 Addressees

This Directive is addressed to the Member States.

(*date of signing and signatory omitted*)

DIRECTIVE 2006/54/EC OF THE EUROPEAN PARLIAMENT AND OF THE COUNCIL OF 5 JULY 2006

on the implementation of the principle of equal opportunities and equal treatment of men and women in matters of employment and occupation (recast)[1]

OJ L 204, 26.7.2006, P. 23[2]

THE EUROPEAN PARLIAMENT AND THE COUNCIL OF THE EUROPEAN UNION,

Having regard to the Treaty establishing the European Community, and in particular Article 141(3) thereof,

Having regard to the proposal from the Commission,

....

[1]   EDITOR'S NOTE: Directive 2006/54 repeals and replaces the following directives on gender equality: Directives 75/117/EEC; 76/207/EEC; 86/378/EEC; and 97/80/EC, with effect from 15 August 2009. See the Correlation Table in Annex II below to convert article numbers from the previous directives.

[2]   EDITOR'S NOTE: As of 1 May 2012 this Directive has not been amended following the entry into force of the Treaty of Lisbon. It includes references to the old Treaty article numbers. Reference should be made to the Tables of Equivalences accompanying the consolidated Treaties in Part II of this edition for the conversion of old Treaty article numbers to new ones.

Having regard to the opinion of the European Economic and Social Committee [1],

Acting in accordance with the procedure laid down in Article 251 of the Treaty [2],

Whereas:

(1)   Council Directive 76/207/EEC of 9 February 1976 on the implementation of the principle of equal treatment for men and women as regards access to employment, vocational training and promotion, and working conditions [3] and Council Directive 86/378/EEC of 24 July 1986 on the implementation of the principle of equal treatment for men and women in occupational social security schemes [4] have been significantly amended [5]. Council Directive 75/117/EEC of 10 February 1975 on the approximation of the laws of the Member States relating to the application of the principle of equal pay for men and women [6] and Council Directive 97/80/EC of 15 December 1997 on the burden of proof in cases of discrimination based on sex [7] also contain provisions which have as their purpose the implementation of the principle of equal treatment between men and women. Now that new amendments are being made to the said Directives, it is desirable, for reasons of clarity, that the provisions in question should be recast by bringing together in a single text the main provisions existing in this field as well as certain developments arising out of the case-law of the Court of Justice of the European Communities (hereinafter referred to as the Court of Justice).

(2)   Equality between men and women is a fundamental principle of Community law under Article 2 and Article 3(2) of the Treaty and the case-law of the Court of Justice. Those Treaty provisions proclaim equality between men and women as a "task" and an "aim" of the Community and impose a positive obligation to promote it in all its activities.

(3)   The Court of Justice has held that the scope of the principle of equal treatment for men and women cannot be confined to the prohibition of discrimination based on the fact that a person is of one or other sex. In view of its purpose and the nature of the rights which it seeks to safeguard, it also applies to discrimination arising from the gender reassignment of a person.

(4)   Article 141(3) of the Treaty now provides a specific legal basis for the adoption of Community measures to ensure the application of the principle of equal opportunities and equal treatment in matters of employment and occupation, including the principle of equal pay for equal work or work of equal value.

(5)   Articles 21 and 23 of the Charter of Fundamental Rights of the European Union also prohibit any discrimination on grounds of sex and enshrine the right to equal treatment between men and women in all areas, including employment, work and pay.

(6)   Harassment and sexual harassment are contrary to the principle of equal treatment between men and women and constitute discrimination on grounds of sex for the purposes of this Directive. These forms of discrimination occur not only in the workplace, but also in the context of access to employment, vocational training and promotion. They should therefore be prohibited and should be subject to effective, proportionate and dissuasive penalties.

(7)   In this context, employers and those responsible for vocational training should be encouraged to take measures to combat all forms of discrimination on grounds of sex and, in particular, to take preventive measures against harassment and sexual harassment in the workplace and in access to employment, vocational training and promotion, in accordance with national law and practice.

(8)   The principle of equal pay for equal work or work of equal value as laid down by Article 141 of the Treaty and consistently upheld in the case-law of the Court of Justice constitutes an important aspect of the principle of equal treatment between men and women and an essential and indispensable part of the *acquis communautaire*, including the case-law of the Court concerning sex discrimination. It is therefore appropriate to make further provision for its implementation.

(9)   In accordance with settled case-law of the Court of Justice, in order to assess whether workers are performing the same work or work of equal value, it should be determined whether, having regard to a range of factors including the nature of the work and training and working conditions, those workers may be considered to be in a comparable situation.

(10)   The Court of Justice has established that, in certain circumstances, the principle of equal pay is not limited to situations in which men and women work for the same employer.

(11)   The Member States, in collaboration with the social partners, should continue to address the problem of the continuing gender-based wage differentials and marked gender segregation on the labour market by means such as flexible working time arrangements which enable both men and women to combine family and work commitments more successfully. This could also include appropriate parental leave arrangements which could be taken up by either parent as well as the provision of accessible and affordable child-care facilities and care for dependent persons.

(12)   Specific measures should be adopted to ensure the implementation of the principle of equal treatment in occupational social security schemes and to define its scope more clearly.

(13)   In its judgment of 17 May 1990 in Case C-262/88 [8], the Court of Justice determined that all forms of occupational pension constitute an element of pay within the meaning of Article 141 of the Treaty.

(14)   Although the concept of pay within the meaning of Article 141 of the Treaty does not encompass social security benefits, it is now clearly established that a pension scheme for public servants falls within the scope of the principle of equal pay if the benefits payable under the scheme are paid to the worker by reason of his/her employment relationship with the public employer, notwithstanding the fact that such scheme forms part of a general statutory scheme. According to the judgments of the Court of Justice in Cases C-7/93 [9] and C-351/00 [10], that condition will be satisfied if the pension scheme concerns a particular category of workers and its benefits are directly related to the period of service and calculated by reference to the public servant's final salary. For reasons of clarity, it is therefore appropriate to make specific provision to that effect.

(15)   The Court of Justice has confirmed that whilst the contributions of male and female workers to a defined-benefit pension scheme are covered by Article 141 of the Treaty, any inequality in employers' contributions paid under funded defined-benefit schemes which is due to the use of actuarial factors differing according to sex is not to be assessed in the light of that same provision.

(16)   By way of example, in the case of funded defined-benefit schemes, certain elements, such as conversion into a capital sum of part of a periodic pension, transfer of pension rights, a reversionary pension payable to a dependant in return for the surrender of part of a pension or a reduced pension where the worker opts to take earlier retirement, may be unequal where the inequality of the amounts results from the effects of the use of actuarial factors differing according to sex at the time when the scheme's funding is implemented.

(17) It is well established that benefits payable under occupational social security schemes are not to be considered as remuneration insofar as they are attributable to periods of employment prior to 17 May 1990, except in the case of workers or those claiming under them who initiated legal proceedings or brought an equivalent claim under the applicable national law before that date. It is therefore necessary to limit the implementation of the principle of equal treatment accordingly.

(18) The Court of Justice has consistently held that the Barber Protocol [11] does not affect the right to join an occupational pension scheme and that the limitation of the effects in time of the judgment in Case C-262/88 does not apply to the right to join an occupational pension scheme. The Court of Justice also ruled that the national rules relating to time limits for bringing actions under national law may be relied on against workers who assert their right to join an occupational pension scheme, provided that they are not less favourable for that type of action than for similar actions of a domestic nature and that they do not render the exercise of rights conferred by Community law impossible in practice. The Court of Justice has also pointed out that the fact that a worker can claim retroactively to join an occupational pension scheme does not allow the worker to avoid paying the contributions relating to the period of membership concerned.

(19) Ensuring equal access to employment and the vocational training leading thereto is fundamental to the application of the principle of equal treatment of men and women in matters of employment and occupation. Any exception to this principle should therefore be limited to those occupational activities which necessitate the employment of a person of a particular sex by reason of their nature or the context in which they are carried out, provided that the objective sought is legitimate and complies with the principle of proportionality.

(20) This Directive does not prejudice freedom of association, including the right to establish unions with others and to join unions to defend one's interests. Measures within the meaning of Article 141(4) of the Treaty may include membership or the continuation of the activity of organisations or unions whose main objective is the promotion, in practice, of the principle of equal treatment between men and women.

(21) The prohibition of discrimination should be without prejudice to the maintenance or adoption of measures intended to prevent or compensate for disadvantages suffered by a group of persons of one sex. Such measures permit organisations of persons of one sex where their main object is the promotion of the special needs of those persons and the promotion of equality between men and women.

(22) In accordance with Article 141(4) of the Treaty, with a view to ensuring full equality in practice between men and women in working life, the principle of equal treatment does not prevent Member States from maintaining or adopting measures providing for specific advantages in order to make it easier for the under-represented sex to pursue a vocational activity or to prevent or compensate for disadvantages in professional careers. Given the current situation and bearing in mind Declaration No 28 to the Amsterdam Treaty, Member States should, in the first instance, aim at improving the situation of women in working life.

(23) It is clear from the case-law of the Court of Justice that unfavourable treatment of a woman related to pregnancy or maternity constitutes direct discrimination on grounds of sex. Such treatment should therefore be expressly covered by this Directive.

(24) The Court of Justice has consistently recognised the legitimacy, as regards the principle of equal treatment, of protecting a woman's biological condition during pregnancy and maternity and of introducing maternity protection measures as a means to achieve

substantive equality. This Directive should therefore be without prejudice to Council Directive 92/85/EEC of 19 October 1992 on the introduction of measures to encourage improvements in the safety and health at work of pregnant workers and workers who have recently given birth or are breastfeeding [12]. This Directive should further be without prejudice to Council Directive 96/34/EC of 3 June 1996 on the framework agreement on parental leave concluded by UNICE, CEEP and the ETUC [13].

(25) For reasons of clarity, it is also appropriate to make express provision for the protection of the employment rights of women on maternity leave and in particular their right to return to the same or an equivalent post, to suffer no detriment in their terms and conditions as a result of taking such leave and to benefit from any improvement in working conditions to which they would have been entitled during their absence.

(26) In the Resolution of the Council and of the Ministers for Employment and Social Policy, meeting within the Council, of 29 June 2000 on the balanced participation of women and men in family and working life [14], Member States were encouraged to consider examining the scope for their respective legal systems to grant working men an individual and non-transferable right to paternity leave, while maintaining their rights relating to employment.

(27) Similar considerations apply to the granting by Member States to men and women of an individual and non-transferable right to leave subsequent to the adoption of a child. It is for the Member States to determine whether or not to grant such a right to paternity and/ or adoption leave and also to determine any conditions, other than dismissal and return to work, which are outside the scope of this Directive.

(28) The effective implementation of the principle of equal treatment requires appropriate procedures to be put in place by the Member States.

(29) The provision of adequate judicial or administrative procedures for the enforcement of the obligations imposed by this Directive is essential to the effective implementation of the principle of equal treatment.

(30) The adoption of rules on the burden of proof plays a significant role in ensuring that the principle of equal treatment can be effectively enforced. As the Court of Justice has held, provision should therefore be made to ensure that the burden of proof shifts to the respondent when there is a prima facie case of discrimination, except in relation to proceedings in which it is for the court or other competent national body to investigate the facts. It is however necessary to clarify that the appreciation of the facts from which it may be presumed that there has been direct or indirect discrimination remains a matter for the relevant national body in accordance with national law or practice. Further, it is for the Member States to introduce, at any appropriate stage of the proceedings, rules of evidence which are more favourable to plaintiffs.

(31) With a view to further improving the level of protection offered by this Directive, associations, organisations and other legal entities should also be empowered to engage in proceedings, as the Member States so determine, either on behalf or in support of a complainant, without prejudice to national rules of procedure concerning representation and defence.

(32) Having regard to the fundamental nature of the right to effective legal protection, it is appropriate to ensure that workers continue to enjoy such protection even after the relationship giving rise to an alleged breach of the principle of equal treatment has ended. An employee defending or giving evidence on behalf of a person protected under this Directive should be entitled to the same protection.

(33) It has been clearly established by the Court of Justice that in order to be effective, the principle of equal treatment implies that the compensation awarded for any breach must be adequate in relation to the damage sustained. It is therefore appropriate to exclude the fixing of any prior upper limit for such compensation, except where the employer can prove that the only damage suffered by an applicant as a result of discrimination within the meaning of this Directive was the refusal to take his/her job application into consideration.

(34) In order to enhance the effective implementation of the principle of equal treatment, Member States should promote dialogue between the social partners and, within the framework of national practice, with non-governmental organisations.

(35) Member States should provide for effective, proportionate and dissuasive penalties for breaches of the obligations under this Directive.

(36) Since the objectives of this Directive cannot be sufficiently achieved by the Member States and can therefore be better achieved at Community level, the Community may adopt measures in accordance with the principle of subsidiarity as set out in Article 5 of the Treaty. In accordance with the principle of proportionality, as set out in that Article, this Directive does not go beyond what is necessary in order to achieve those objectives.

(37) For the sake of a better understanding of the different treatment of men and women in matters of employment and occupation, comparable statistics disaggregated by sex should continue to be developed, analysed and made available at the appropriate levels.

(38) Equal treatment of men and women in matters of employment and occupation cannot be restricted to legislative measures. Instead, the European Union and the Member States should continue to promote the raising of public awareness of wage discrimination and the changing of public attitudes, involving all parties concerned at public and private level to the greatest possible extent. The dialogue between the social partners could play an important role in this process.

(39) The obligation to transpose this Directive into national law should be confined to those provisions which represent a substantive change as compared with the earlier Directives. The obligation to transpose the provisions which are substantially unchanged arises under the earlier Directives.

(40) This Directive should be without prejudice to the obligations of the Member States relating to the time limits for transposition into national law and application of the Directives set out in Annex I, Part B.

(41) In accordance with paragraph 34 of the Interinstitutional agreement on better law-making [15], Member States are encouraged to draw up, for themselves and in the interest of the Community, their own tables, which will, as far as possible, illustrate the correlation between this Directive and the transposition measures and to make them public,

HAVE ADOPTED THIS DIRECTIVE:

TITLE I
GENERAL PROVISIONS

Article 1 Purpose
The purpose of this Directive is to ensure the implementation of the principle of equal opportunities and equal treatment of men and women in matters of employment and occupation.

To that end, it contains provisions to implement the principle of equal treatment in relation to:

(a)   access to employment, including promotion, and to vocational training;

(b)   working conditions, including pay;

(c)   occupational social security schemes.

It also contains provisions to ensure that such implementation is made more effective by the establishment of appropriate procedures.

Article 2 Definitions

1.   For the purposes of this Directive, the following definitions shall apply:

    (a)   "direct discrimination": where one person is treated less favourably on grounds of sex than another is, has been or would be treated in a comparable situation;

    (b)   "indirect discrimination": where an apparently neutral provision, criterion or practice would put persons of one sex at a particular disadvantage compared with persons of the other sex, unless that provision, criterion or practice is objectively justified by a legitimate aim, and the means of achieving that aim are appropriate and necessary;

    (c)   "harassment": where unwanted conduct related to the sex of a person occurs with the purpose or effect of violating the dignity of a person, and of creating an intimidating, hostile, degrading, humiliating or offensive environment;

    (d)   "sexual harassment": where any form of unwanted verbal, non-verbal or physical conduct of a sexual nature occurs, with the purpose or effect of violating the dignity of a person, in particular when creating an intimidating, hostile, degrading, humiliating or offensive environment;

    (e)   "pay": the ordinary basic or minimum wage or salary and any other consideration, whether in cash or in kind, which the worker receives directly or indirectly, in respect of his/her employment from his/her employer;

    (f)   "occupational social security schemes": schemes not governed by Council Directive 79/7/EEC of 19 December 1978 on the progressive implementation of the principle of equal treatment for men and women in matters of social security [16] whose purpose is to provide workers, whether employees or self-employed, in an undertaking or group of undertakings, area of economic activity, occupational sector or group of sectors with benefits intended to supplement the benefits provided by statutory social security schemes or to replace them, whether membership of such schemes is compulsory or optional.

2.   For the purposes of this Directive, discrimination includes:

    (a)   harassment and sexual harassment, as well as any less favourable treatment based on a person's rejection of or submission to such conduct;

    (b)   instruction to discriminate against persons on grounds of sex;

    (c)   any less favourable treatment of a woman related to pregnancy or maternity leave within the meaning of Directive 92/85/EEC.

Article 3 Positive action

Member States may maintain or adopt measures within the meaning of Article 141(4) of the Treaty with a view to ensuring full equality in practice between men and women in working life.

TITLE II
SPECIFIC PROVISIONS

Chapter 1 EQUAL PAY

Article 4 Prohibition of discrimination

For the same work or for work to which equal value is attributed, direct and indirect discrimination on grounds of sex with regard to all aspects and conditions of remuneration shall be eliminated.

In particular, where a job classification system is used for determining pay, it shall be based on the same criteria for both men and women and so drawn up as to exclude any discrimination on grounds of sex.

Chapter 2 EQUAL TREATMENT IN OCCUPATIONAL SOCIAL SECURITY SCHEMES

Article 5 Prohibition of discrimination
Without prejudice to Article 4, there shall be no direct or indirect discrimination on grounds of sex in occupational social security schemes, in particular as regards:
(a)   the scope of such schemes and the conditions of access to them;

(b)   the obligation to contribute and the calculation of contributions;

(c)   the calculation of benefits, including supplementary benefits due in respect of a spouse or dependants, and the conditions governing the duration and retention of entitlement to benefits.

Article 6 Personal scope
This Chapter shall apply to members of the working population, including self-employed persons, persons whose activity is interrupted by illness, maternity, accident or involuntary unemployment and persons seeking employment and to retired and disabled workers, and to those claiming under them, in accordance with national law and/or practice.

Article 7 Material scope
1.   This Chapter applies to:
   (a) occupational social security schemes which provide protection against the following risks:
      (i)   sickness,
      (ii) invalidity,
      (iii) old age, including early retirement,
      (iv) industrial accidents and occupational diseases,
      (v)   unemployment;
   (b) occupational social security schemes which provide for other social benefits, in cash or in kind, and in particular survivors' benefits and family allowances, if such benefits constitute a consideration paid by the employer to the worker by reason of the latter's employment.

2.   This Chapter also applies to pension schemes for a particular category of worker such as that of public servants if the benefits payable under the scheme are paid by reason of the employment relationship with the public employer. The fact that such a scheme forms part of a general statutory scheme shall be without prejudice in that respect.

Article 8 Exclusions from the material scope
1.   This Chapter does not apply to:
   (a) individual contracts for self-employed persons;
   (b) single-member schemes for self-employed persons;
   (c) insurance contracts to which the employer is not a party, in the case of workers;
   (d) optional provisions of occupational social security schemes offered to participants individually to guarantee them:
      (i)   either additional benefits,
      (ii) or a choice of date on which the normal benefits for self-employed persons will start, or a choice between several benefits;
   (e) occupational social security schemes in so far as benefits are financed by contributions paid by workers on a voluntary basis.

2.   This Chapter does not preclude an employer granting to persons who have already reached the retirement age for the purposes of granting a pension by virtue of an occupational social security scheme, but who have not yet reached the retirement age for the purposes of granting a statutory retirement pension, a pension supplement, the aim of which is to make equal or more nearly equal the overall amount of benefit paid to these persons in relation to the amount paid to persons of the other sex in the same situation who have already reached the statutory retirement age, until the persons benefiting from the supplement reach the statutory retirement age.

Article 9 Examples of discrimination

1.   Provisions contrary to the principle of equal treatment shall include those based on sex, either directly or indirectly, for:

(a) determining the persons who may participate in an occupational social security scheme;

(b) fixing the compulsory or optional nature of participation in an occupational social security scheme;

(c) laying down different rules as regards the age of entry into the scheme or the minimum period of employment or membership of the scheme required to obtain the benefits thereof;

(d) laying down different rules, except as provided for in points (h) and (j), for the reimbursement of contributions when a worker leaves a scheme without having fulfilled the conditions guaranteeing a deferred right to long-term benefits;

(e) setting different conditions for the granting of benefits or restricting such benefits to workers of one or other of the sexes;

(f) fixing different retirement ages;

(g) suspending the retention or acquisition of rights during periods of maternity leave or leave for family reasons which are granted by law or agreement and are paid by the employer;

(h) setting different levels of benefit, except in so far as may be necessary to take account of actuarial calculation factors which differ according to sex in the case of defined-contribution schemes; in the case of funded defined-benefit schemes, certain elements may be unequal where the inequality of the amounts results from the effects of the use of actuarial factors differing according to sex at the time when the scheme's funding is implemented;

(i) setting different levels for workers' contributions;

(j) setting different levels for employers' contributions, except:

(i)   in the case of defined-contribution schemes if the aim is to equalise the amount of the final benefits or to make them more nearly equal for both sexes,

(ii) in the case of funded defined-benefit schemes where the employer's contributions are intended to ensure the adequacy of the funds necessary to cover the cost of the benefits defined;

(k) laying down different standards or standards applicable only to workers of a specified sex, except as provided for in points (h) and (j), as regards the guarantee or retention of entitlement to deferred benefits when a worker leaves a scheme.

2.   Where the granting of benefits within the scope of this Chapter is left to the discretion of the scheme's management bodies, the latter shall comply with the principle of equal treatment.

Article 10 Implementation as regards self-employed persons

1.   Member States shall take the necessary steps to ensure that the provisions of occupational social security schemes for self-employed persons contrary to the principle of equal treatment are revised with effect from 1 January 1993 at the latest or for Member States

whose accession took place after that date, at the date that Directive 86/378/EEC became applicable in their territory.

2.   This Chapter shall not preclude rights and obligations relating to a period of membership of an occupational social security scheme for self-employed persons prior to revision of that scheme from remaining subject to the provisions of the scheme in force during that period.

Article 11 Possibility of deferral as regards self-employed persons
As regards occupational social security schemes for self-employed persons, Member States may defer compulsory application of the principle of equal treatment with regard to:
(a)   determination of pensionable age for the granting of old-age or retirement pensions, and the possible implications for other benefits:
    (i)   either until the date on which such equality is achieved in statutory schemes,
    (ii) or, at the latest, until such equality is prescribed by a directive;
(b)   survivors' pensions until Community law establishes the principle of equal treatment in statutory social security schemes in that regard;

(c)   the application of Article 9(1)(i) in relation to the use of actuarial calculation factors, until 1 January 1999 or for Member States whose accession took place after that date until the date that Directive 86/378/EEC became applicable in their territory.

Article 12 Retroactive effect
1.   Any measure implementing this Chapter, as regards workers, shall cover all benefits under occupational social security schemes derived from periods of employment subsequent to 17 May 1990 and shall apply retroactively to that date, without prejudice to workers or those claiming under them who have, before that date, initiated legal proceedings or raised an equivalent claim under national law. In that event, the implementation measures shall apply retroactively to 8 April 1976 and shall cover all the benefits derived from periods of employment after that date. For Member States which acceded to the Community after 8 April 1976, and before 17 May 1990, that date shall be replaced by the date on which Article 141 of the Treaty became applicable in their territory.

2.   The second sentence of paragraph 1 shall not prevent national rules relating to time limits for bringing actions under national law from being relied on against workers or those claiming under them who initiated legal proceedings or raised an equivalent claim under national law before 17 May 1990, provided that they are not less favourable for that type of action than for similar actions of a domestic nature and that they do not render the exercise of rights conferred by Community law impossible in practice.

3.   For Member States whose accession took place after 17 May 1990 and which were on 1 January 1994 Contracting Parties to the Agreement on the European Economic Area, the date of 17 May 1990 in the first sentence of paragraph 1 shall be replaced by 1 January 1994.

4.   For other Member States whose accession took place after 17 May 1990, the date of 17 May 1990 in paragraphs 1 and 2 shall be replaced by the date on which Article 141 of the Treaty became applicable in their territory.

Article 13 Flexible pensionable age
Where men and women may claim a flexible pensionable age under the same conditions, this shall not be deemed to be incompatible with this Chapter.

Chapter 3 EQUAL TREATMENT AS REGARDS ACCESS TO EMPLOYMENT, - VOCATIONAL TRAINING AND PROMOTION AND WORKING CONDITIONS

Article 14 Prohibition of discrimination

1.   There shall be no direct or indirect discrimination on grounds of sex in the public or private sectors, including public bodies, in relation to:

   (a) conditions for access to employment, to self-employment or to occupation, including selection criteria and recruitment conditions, whatever the branch of activity and at all levels of the professional hierarchy, including promotion;

   (b) access to all types and to all levels of vocational guidance, vocational training, advanced vocational training and retraining, including practical work experience;

   (c) employment and working conditions, including dismissals, as well as pay as provided for in Article 141 of the Treaty;

   (d) membership of, and involvement in, an organisation of workers or employers, or any organisation whose members carry on a particular profession, including the benefits provided for by such organisations.

2.   Member States may provide, as regards access to employment including the training leading thereto, that a difference of treatment which is based on a characteristic related to sex shall not constitute discrimination where, by reason of the nature of the particular occupational activities concerned or of the context in which they are carried out, such a characteristic constitutes a genuine and determining occupational requirement, provided that its objective is legitimate and the requirement is proportionate.

Article 15 Return from maternity leave

A woman on maternity leave shall be entitled, after the end of her period of maternity leave, to return to her job or to an equivalent post on terms and conditions which are no less favourable to her and to benefit from any improvement in working conditions to which she would have been entitled during her absence.

Article 16 Paternity and adoption leave

This Directive is without prejudice to the right of Member States to recognise distinct rights to paternity and/or adoption leave. Those Member States which recognise such rights shall take the necessary measures to protect working men and women against dismissal due to exercising those rights and ensure that, at the end of such leave, they are entitled to return to their jobs or to equivalent posts on terms and conditions which are no less favourable to them, and to benefit from any improvement in working conditions to which they would have been entitled during their absence.

TITLE III

HORIZONTAL PROVISIONS

Chapter 1 REMEDIES AND ENFORCEMENT

SECTION 1 REMEDIES

Article 17 Defence of rights

1.   Member States shall ensure that, after possible recourse to other competent authorities including where they deem it appropriate conciliation procedures, judicial procedures for the enforcement of obligations under this Directive are available to all persons who consider themselves wronged by failure to apply the principle of equal treatment to them, even after the relationship in which the discrimination is alleged to have occurred has ended.

2.   Member States shall ensure that associations, organisations or other legal entities which have, in accordance with the criteria laid down by their national law, a legitimate interest

in ensuring that the provisions of this Directive are complied with, may engage, either on behalf or in support of the complainant, with his/her approval, in any judicial and/or administrative procedure provided for the enforcement of obligations under this Directive.

3.   Paragraphs 1 and 2 are without prejudice to national rules relating to time limits for bringing actions as regards the principle of equal treatment.

Article 18 Compensation or reparation

Member States shall introduce into their national legal systems such measures as are necessary to ensure real and effective compensation or reparation as the Member States so determine for the loss and damage sustained by a person injured as a result of discrimination on grounds of sex, in a way which is dissuasive and proportionate to the damage suffered. Such compensation or reparation may not be restricted by the fixing of a prior upper limit, except in cases where the employer can prove that the only damage suffered by an applicant as a result of discrimination within the meaning of this Directive is the refusal to take his/her job application into consideration.

SECTION 2 BURDEN OF PROOF

Article 19 Burden of proof

1.   Member States shall take such measures as are necessary, in accordance with their national judicial systems, to ensure that, when persons who consider themselves wronged because the principle of equal treatment has not been applied to them establish, before a court or other competent authority, facts from which it may be presumed that there has been direct or indirect discrimination, it shall be for the respondent to prove that there has been no breach of the principle of equal treatment.

2.   Paragraph 1 shall not prevent Member States from introducing rules of evidence which are more favourable to plaintiffs.

3.   Member States need not apply paragraph 1 to proceedings in which it is for the court or competent body to investigate the facts of the case.

4.   Paragraphs 1, 2 and 3 shall also apply to:
   (a) the situations covered by Article 141 of the Treaty and, insofar as discrimination based on sex is concerned, by Directives 92/85/EEC and 96/34/EC;
   (b) any civil or administrative procedure concerning the public or private sector which provides for means of redress under national law pursuant to the measures referred to in (a) with the exception of out-of-court procedures of a voluntary nature or provided for in national law.

5.   This Article shall not apply to criminal procedures, unless otherwise provided by the Member States.

Chapter 2 PROMOTION OF EQUAL TREATMENT — DIALOGUE

Article 20 Equality bodies

1.   Member States shall designate and make the necessary arrangements for a body or bodies for the promotion, analysis, monitoring and support of equal treatment of all persons without discrimination on grounds of sex. These bodies may form part of agencies with responsibility at national level for the defence of human rights or the safeguard of individuals' rights.

2.   Member States shall ensure that the competences of these bodies include:
   (a) without prejudice to the right of victims and of associations, organisations or other legal entities referred to in Article 17(2), providing independent assistance to victims of discrimination in pursuing their complaints about discrimination;

(b) conducting independent surveys concerning discrimination;

(c) publishing independent reports and making recommendations on any issue relating to such discrimination;

(d) at the appropriate level exchanging available information with corresponding European bodies such as any future European Institute for Gender Equality.

Article 21 Social dialogue

1. Member States shall, in accordance with national traditions and practice, take adequate measures to promote social dialogue between the social partners with a view to fostering equal treatment, including, for example, through the monitoring of practices in the workplace, in access to employment, vocational training and promotion, as well as through the monitoring of collective agreements, codes of conduct, research or exchange of experience and good practice.

2. Where consistent with national traditions and practice, Member States shall encourage the social partners, without prejudice to their autonomy, to promote equality between men and women, and flexible working arrangements, with the aim of facilitating the reconciliation of work and private life, and to conclude, at the appropriate level, agreements laying down anti-discrimination rules in the fields referred to in Article 1 which fall within the scope of collective bargaining. These agreements shall respect the provisions of this Directive and the relevant national implementing measures.

3. Member States shall, in accordance with national law, collective agreements or practice, encourage employers to promote equal treatment for men and women in a planned and systematic way in the workplace, in access to employment, vocational training and promotion.

4. To this end, employers shall be encouraged to provide at appropriate regular intervals employees and/or their representatives with appropriate information on equal treatment for men and women in the undertaking.

Such information may include an overview of the proportions of men and women at different levels of the organisation; their pay and pay differentials; and possible measures to improve the situation in cooperation with employees' representatives.

Article 22 Dialogue with non-governmental organisations

Member States shall encourage dialogue with appropriate non-governmental organisations which have, in accordance with their national law and practice, a legitimate interest in contributing to the fight against discrimination on grounds of sex with a view to promoting the principle of equal treatment.

Chapter 3 GENERAL HORIZONTAL PROVISIONS

Article 23 Compliance

Member States shall take all necessary measures to ensure that:

(a) any laws, regulations and administrative provisions contrary to the principle of equal treatment are abolished;

(b) provisions contrary to the principle of equal treatment in individual or collective contracts or agreements, internal rules of undertakings or rules governing the independent occupations and professions and workers' and employers' organisations or any other arrangements shall be, or may be, declared null and void or are amended;

(c) occupational social security schemes containing such provisions may not be approved or extended by administrative measures.

Article 24 Victimisation
Member States shall introduce into their national legal systems such measures as are necessary to protect employees, including those who are employees' representatives provided for by national laws and/or practices, against dismissal or other adverse treatment by the employer as a reaction to a complaint within the undertaking or to any legal proceedings aimed at enforcing compliance with the principle of equal treatment.

Article 25 Penalties
Member States shall lay down the rules on penalties applicable to infringements of the national provisions adopted pursuant to this Directive, and shall take all measures necessary to ensure that they are applied. The penalties, which may comprise the payment of compensation to the victim, must be effective, proportionate and dissuasive. The Member States shall notify those provisions to the Commission by 5 October 2005 at the latest and shall notify it without delay of any subsequent amendment affecting them.

Article 26 Prevention of discrimination
Member States shall encourage, in accordance with national law, collective agreements or practice, employers and those responsible for access to vocational training to take effective measures to prevent all forms of discrimination on grounds of sex, in particular harassment and sexual harassment in the workplace, in access to employment, vocational training and promotion.

Article 27 Minimum requirements
1.   Member States may introduce or maintain provisions which are more favourable to the protection of the principle of equal treatment than those laid down in this Directive.

2.   Implementation of this Directive shall under no circumstances be sufficient grounds for a reduction in the level of protection of workers in the areas to which it applies, without prejudice to the Member States' right to respond to changes in the situation by introducing laws, regulations and administrative provisions which differ from those in force on the notification of this Directive, provided that the provisions of this Directive are complied with.

Article 28 Relationship to Community and national provisions
1.   This Directive shall be without prejudice to provisions concerning the protection of women, particularly as regards pregnancy and maternity.

2.   This Directive shall be without prejudice to the provisions of Directive 96/34/EC and Directive 92/85/EEC.

Article 29 Gender mainstreaming
Member States shall actively take into account the objective of equality between men and women when formulating and implementing laws, regulations, administrative provisions, policies and activities in the areas referred to in this Directive.

Article 30 Dissemination of information
Member States shall ensure that measures taken pursuant to this Directive, together with the provisions already in force, are brought to the attention of all the persons concerned by all suitable means and, where appropriate, at the workplace.

TITLE IV
FINAL PROVISIONS

Article 31 Reports

1. By 15 February 2011, the Member States shall communicate to the Commission all the information necessary for the Commission to draw up a report to the European Parliament and the Council on the application of this Directive.

2. Without prejudice to paragraph 1, Member States shall communicate to the Commission, every four years, the texts of any measures adopted pursuant to Article 141(4) of the Treaty, as well as reports on these measures and their implementation. On the basis of that information, the Commission will adopt and publish every four years a report establishing a comparative assessment of any measures in the light of Declaration No 28 annexed to the Final Act of the Treaty of Amsterdam.

3. Member States shall assess the occupational activities referred to in Article 14(2), in order to decide, in the light of social developments, whether there is justification for maintaining the exclusions concerned. They shall notify the Commission of the results of this assessment periodically, but at least every 8 years.

Article 32 Review

By 15 February 2011 at the latest, the Commission shall review the operation of this Directive and if appropriate, propose any amendments it deems necessary.

Article 33 Implementation

Member States shall bring into force the laws, regulations and administrative provisions necessary to comply with this Directive by 15 August 2008 at the latest or shall ensure, by that date, that management and labour introduce the requisite provisions by way of agreement. Member States may, if necessary to take account of particular difficulties, have up to one additional year to comply with this Directive. Member States shall take all necessary steps to be able to guarantee the results imposed by this Directive. They shall forthwith communicate to the Commission the texts of those measures.

When Member States adopt these measures, they shall contain a reference to this Directive or be accompanied by such reference on the occasion of their official publication. They shall also include a statement that references in existing laws, regulations and administrative provisions to the Directives repealed by this Directive shall be construed as references to this Directive. Member States shall determine how such reference is to be made and how that statement is to be formulated.

The obligation to transpose this Directive into national law shall be confined to those provisions which represent a substantive change as compared with the earlier Directives. The obligation to transpose the provisions which are substantially unchanged arises under the earlier Directives.

Member States shall communicate to the Commission the text of the main provisions of national law which they adopt in the field covered by this Directive.

Article 34 Repeal

1. With effect from 15 August 2009 Directives 75/117/EEC, 76/207/EEC, 86/378/EEC and 97/80/EC shall be repealed without prejudice to the obligations of the Member States relating to the time-limits for transposition into national law and application of the Directives set out in Annex I, Part B.

2. References made to the repealed Directives shall be construed as being made to this Directive and should be read in accordance with the correlation table in Annex II.

Article 35 Entry into force
This Directive shall enter into force on the 20th day following its publication in the *Official Journal of the European Union.*

Article 36 Addressees
This Directive is addressed to the Member States.

(date of signing and signatories omitted)

[1] OJ C 157, 28.6.2005, p. 83.
[2] Opinion of the European Parliament of 6 July 2005 (not yet published in the *Official Journal*), Council Common Position of 10 March 2006 (OJ C 126 E, 30.5.2006, p. 33) and Position of the European Parliament of 1 June 2006 (not yet published in the *Official Journal*).
[3] OJ L 39, 14.2.1976, p. 40. Directive as amended by Directive 2002/73/EC of the European Parliament and of the Council (OJ L 269, 5.10.2002, p. 15).
[4] OJ L 225, 12.8.1986, p. 40. Directive as amended by Directive 96/97/EC (OJ L 46, 17.2.1997, p. 20).
[5] See Annex I Part A.
[6] OJ L 45, 19.2.1975, p. 19.
[7] OJ L 14, 20.1.1998, p. 6. Directive as amended by Directive 98/52/EC (OJ L 205, 22.7.1998, p. 66).
[8] C-262/88: Barber v Guardian Royal Exchange Assurance Group (1990 ECR I-1889).
[9] C-7/93: Bestuur van het Algemeen Burgerlijk Pensioenfonds v G. A. Beune (1994 ECR I-4471).
[10] C-351/00: Pirkko Niemi (2002 ECR I-7007).
[11] Protocol 17 concerning Article 141 of the Treaty establishing the European Community (1992).
[12] OJ L 348, 28.11.1992, p. 1.
[13] OJ L 145, 19.6.1996, p. 4. Directive as amended by Directive 97/75/EC (OJ L 10, 16.1.1998, p. 24).
[14] OJ C 218, 31.7.2000, p. 5.
[15] OJ C 321, 31.12.2003, p. 1.
[16] OJ L 6, 10.1.1979, p. 24.

ANNEX I *(omitted)*

ANNEX II CORRELATION TABLE

Dir. 75/117	Dir. 76/207	Dir. 86/378	Dir. 97/80	This Directive
—	Art. 1(1)	Art. 1	Art. 1	Art. 1
—	Art. 1(2)	—	—	—
—	Art. 2(2), first indent	—	Art. 2(1), (a)	—
—	Art. 2(2), second indent	—	Art. 2(2)	Art. 2(1),(b)
—	Art. 2(2), third and fourth indents	—	—	Art. 2(1),(c) & (d)
—	—	—	—	Art. 2(1), (e)
—	—	Art. 2(1)	—	Art. 2(1), (f)
—	Art. 2(3),(4) & (7) third subpara.	—	—	Art. 2(2)
—	Art. 2(8)	—	—	Art. 3
Art. 1	—	—	—	Art. 4
—	—	Art. 5(1)	—	Art. 5
—	—	Art. 3	—	Art. 6
—	—	Art. 4	—	Art. 7(1)
—	—	—	—	Art. 7(2)
		Art. 2(2)		Art. 8(1)

Dir. 75/117	Dir. 76/207	Dir. 86/378	Dir. 97/80	This Directive
—	—	Art. 2(3)	—	Art. 8(2)
—	—	Art. 6	—	Art. 9
—	—	Art. 8	—	Art. 10
—	—	Art. 9	—	Art. 11
—	—	(Art. 2 of Dir. 96/97)	—	Art. 12
—	—	Art. 9a	—	Art. 13
—	Arts. 2(1) & 3(1)	—	Art. 2(1)	Art. 14(1)
—	Art. 2(6)	—	—	Art. 14(2)
—	Art. 2(7), second subpara.	—	—	Art. 15
—	Art. 2(7), fourth subpara., second & third sentence	—	—	Art. 16
Art. 2	Art. 6(1)	Art. 10	—	Art. 17(1)
—	Art. 6(3)	—	—	Art. 17(2)
—	Art. 6(4)	—	—	Art. 17(3)
—	Art. 6(2)	—	—	Art. 18
—	—	—	Arts. 3 & 4	Art. 19
—	Art. 8a	—	—	Art. 20
—	Art. 8b	—	—	Art. 21
—	Art. 8c	—	—	Art. 22
Arts. 3 & 6	Art. 3 (2)(a)	—	—	Art. 23(a)
Art. 4	Art. 3(2)(b)	Art. 7(a)	—	Art. 23(b)
—	—	Art. 7(b)	—	Art. 23(c)
Art. 5	Art. 7	Art. 11	—	Art. 24
Art. 6	—	—	—	—
—	Art. 8d	—	—	Art. 25
	Art. 2(5)			Art. 26
—	Art. 8e(1)	—	Art. 4(2)	Art. 27(1)
—	Art. 8e(2)	—	Art. 6	Art. 27(2)
—	Art. 2(7) first subpara.	Art. 5(2)	—	Art. 28(1)
—	Art. 2(7) fourth subpara. first sentence			Art. 28(2)
—	Art. 1(1a)			Art. 29
Art. 7	Art. 8	—	Art. 5	Art. 30
Art. 9	Art. 10	Art. 12(2)	Art. 7, fourth Subpara.	Art. 31(1) & (2)

—	Art. 9(2)	—	—	Art. 31(3)
—	—	—	—	Art. 32
Art. 8	Art. 9(1), first subpara. & 9 (2) & (3)	Art. 12(1)	Art. 7, first, second & third subparas.	Art. 33
—	Art. 9(1), second subpara.	—	—	—
—	—	—	—	Art. 34
—	—	—	—	Art. 35
—	—	—	—	Art. 36
—	—	Annex	—	—

B) WORKING CONDITIONS

COUNCIL DIRECTIVE 92/85/EEC OF 19 OCTOBER 1992

on the introduction of measures to encourage improvements in the safety and health at work of pregnant workers and workers who have recently given birth or are breastfeeding (tenth individual Directive within the meaning of Article 16 (1) of Directive 89/391/EEC)*

OJ L 348, 28.11.1992, P. 1

(* As amended by Directive 2007/30/EC of the European Parliament and of the Council of 20 June 2007, OJ L 165, 27.6.2007, p. 21)[1]

> FORTHCOMING AMENDMENTS: The European Commission has proposed amendments to this directive in a Communication published on 3 October 2008, COM(2008) 637, available on EUR-Lex: http://eur-lex.europa.eu/en/index.htm

(footnotes omitted)

THE COUNCIL OF THE EUROPEAN COMMUNITIES,

Having regard to the Treaty establishing the European Economic Community, and in particular Article 118a thereof [Article 153 TFEU],

Having regard to the proposal from the Commission, drawn up after consultation with the Advisory Committee on Safety, Hygiene and Health Protection at work,

In cooperation with the European Parliament,

Having regard to the opinion of the Economic and Social Committee,

[1]   EDITOR'S NOTE: This Directive refers to the original European Economic Community (EEC) Treaty numbers in force at the time of its publication. In this edition the replacement article numbers contained in the Treaty on the Functioning of the European Union (TFEU) have been inserted in closed brackets after each Treaty reference for ease of conversion.

Whereas Article 118a of the Treaty [Article 153 TFEU] provides that the Council shall adopt, by means of directives, minimum requirements for encouraging improvements, especially in the working environment, to protect the safety and health of workers;

Whereas this Directive does not justify any reduction in levels of protection already achieved in individual Member States, the Member States being committed, under the Treaty, to encouraging improvements in conditions in this area and to harmonizing conditions while maintaining the improvements made;

Whereas, under the terms of Article 118a of the Treaty [Article 153 TFEU], the said directives are to avoid imposing administrative, financial and legal constraints in a way which would hold back the creation and development of small and medium-sized undertakings;

Whereas, pursuant to Decision 74/325/EEC, as last amended by the 1985 Act of Accession, the Advisory Committee on Safety, Hygiene and Health protection at Work is consulted by the Commission on the drafting of proposals in this field;

Whereas the Community Charter of the fundamental social rights of workers, adopted at the Strasbourg European Council on 9 December 1989 by the Heads of State or Government of 11 Member States, lays down, in paragraph 19 in particular, that:

'Every worker must enjoy satisfactory health and safety conditions in his working environment. Appropriate measures must be taken in order to achieve further harmonization of conditions in this area while maintaining the improvements made';

Whereas the Commission, in its action programme for the implementation of the Community Charter of the fundamental social rights of workers, has included among its aims the adoption by the Council of a Directive on the protection of pregnant women at work;

Whereas Article 15 of Council Directive 89/391/EEC of 12 June 1989 on the introduction of measures to encourage improvements in the safety and health of workers at work provides that particularly sensitive risk groups must be protected against the dangers which specifically affect them;

Whereas pregnant workers, workers who have recently given birth or who are breastfeeding must be considered a specific risk group in many respects, and measures must be taken with regard to their safety and health;

Whereas the protection of the safety and health of pregnant workers, workers who have recently given birth or workers who are breastfeeding should not treat women on the labour market unfavourably nor work to the detriment of directives concerning equal treatment for men and women;

Whereas some types of activities may pose a specific risk, for pregnant workers, workers who have recently given birth or workers who are breastfeeding, of exposure to dangerous agents, processes or working conditions; whereas such risks must therefore be assessed and the result of such assessment communicated to female workers and/or their representatives;

Whereas, further, should the result of this assessment reveal the existence of a risk to the safety or health of the female worker, provision must be made for such worker to be protected;

Whereas pregnant workers and workers who are breastfeeding must not engage in activities which have been assessed as revealing a risk of exposure, jeopardizing safety and health, to certain particularly dangerous agents or working conditions;

Whereas provision should be made for pregnant workers, workers who have recently given birth or workers who are breastfeeding not to be required to work at night where such provision is necessary from the point of view of their safety and health;

Whereas the vulnerability of pregnant workers, workers who have recently given birth or who are breastfeeding makes it necessary for them to be granted the right to maternity leave of at least 14 continuous weeks, allocated before and/or after confinement, and renders necessary the compulsory nature of maternity leave of at least two weeks, allocated before and/or after confinement;

Whereas the risk of dismissal for reasons associated with their condition may have harmful effects on the physical and mental state of pregnant workers, workers who have recently given birth or who are breastfeeding; whereas provision should be made for such dismissal to be prohibited;

Whereas measures for the organization of work concerning the protection of the health of pregnant workers, workers who have recently given birth or workers who are breastfeeding would serve no purpose unless accompanied by the maintenance of rights linked to the employment contract, including maintenance of payment and/or entitlement to an adequate allowance;

Whereas, moreover, provision concerning maternity leave would also serve no purpose unless accompanied by the maintenance of rights linked to the employment contract and or entitlement to an adequate allowance;

Whereas the concept of an adequate allowance in the case of maternity leave must be regarded as a technical point of reference with a view to fixing the minimum level of protection and should in no circumstances be interpreted as suggesting an analogy between pregnancy and illness,

HAS ADOPTED THIS DIRECTIVE

SECTION I PURPOSE AND DEFINITIONS

Article 1 Purpose

1. The purpose of this Directive, which is the tenth individual Directive within the meaning of Article 16 (1) of Directive 89/391/EEC, is to implement measures to encourage improvements in the safety and health at work of pregnant workers and workers who have recently given birth or who are breastfeeding.

2. The provisions of Directive 89/391/EEC, except for Article 2 (2) thereof, shall apply in full to the whole area covered by paragraph 1, without prejudice to any more stringent and/or specific provisions contained in this Directive.

3. This Directive may not have the effect of reducing the level of protection afforded to pregnant workers, workers who have recently given birth or who are breastfeeding as compared with the situation which exists in each Member State on the date on which this Directive is adopted.

Article 2 Definitions

For the purposes of this Directive:

(a) pregnant worker shall mean a pregnant worker who informs her employer of her condition, in accordance with national legislation and/or national practice;

(b) worker who has recently given birth shall mean a worker who has recently given birth within the meaning of national legislation and/or national practice and who informs her employer of her condition, in accordance with that legislation and/or practice;

(c) worker who is breastfeeding shall mean a worker who is breastfeeding within the meaning of national legislation and/or national practice and who informs her employer of her condition, in accordance with that legislation and/or practice.

SECTION II GENERAL PROVISIONS

Article 3 Guidelines

1.   In consultation with the Member States and assisted by the Advisory Committee on Safety, Hygiene and Health Protection at Work, the Commission shall draw up guidelines on the assessment of the chemical, physical and biological agents and industrial processes considered hazardous for the safety or health of workers within the meaning of Article 2.

   The guidelines referred to in the first subparagraph shall also cover movements and postures, mental and physical fatigue and other types of physical and mental stress connected with the work done by workers within the meaning of Article 2.

2.   The purpose of the guidelines referred to in paragraph 1 is to serve as a basis for the assessment referred to in Article 4 (1).

   To this end, Member States shall bring these guidelines to the attention of all employers and all female workers and/or their representatives in the respective Member State.

Article 4 Assessment and information

1.   For all activities liable to involve a specific risk of exposure to the agents, processes or working conditions of which a non-exhaustive list is given in Annex I, the employer shall assess the nature, degree and duration of exposure, in the undertaking and/or establishment concerned, of workers within the meaning of Article 2, either directly or by way of the protective and preventive services referred to in Article 7 of Directive 89/391/EEC, in order to:
   —   assess any risks to the safety or health and any possible effect on the pregnancy or breastfeeding of workers within the meaning of Article 2,
   —   decide what measures should be taken.

2.   Without prejudice to Article 10 of Directive 89/391/EEC, workers within the meaning of Article 2 and workers likely to be in one of the situations referred to in Article 2 in the undertaking and/or establishment concerned and/or their representatives shall be informed of the results of the assessment referred to in paragraph 1 and of all measures to be taken concerning health and safety at work.

Article 5 Action further to the results of the assessment

1.   Without prejudice to Article 6 of Directive 89/391/EEC, if the results of the assessment referred to in Article 4 (1) reveal a risk to the safety or health or an effect on the pregnancy or breastfeeding of a worker within the meaning of Article 2, the employer shall take the necessary measures to ensure that, by temporarily adjusting the working conditions and/or the working hours of the worker concerned, the exposure of that worker to such risks is avoided.

2.   If the adjustment of her working conditions and/or working hours is not technically and/or objectively feasible, or cannot reasonably be required on duly substantiated grounds, the employer shall take the necessary measures to move the worker concerned to another job.

3.   If moving her to another job is not technically and/or objectively feasible or cannot reasonably be required on duly substantiated grounds, the worker concerned shall be granted leave in accordance with national legislation and/or national practice for the whole of the period necessary to protect her safety or health.

4.   The provisions of this Article shall apply mutatis mutandis to the case where a worker pursuing an activity which is forbidden pursuant to Article 6 becomes pregnant or starts breastfeeding and informs her employer thereof.

Article 6 Cases in which exposure is prohibited

In addition to the general provisions concerning the protection of workers, in particular those relating to the limit values for occupational exposure:

1. pregnant workers within the meaning of Article 2 (a) may under no circumstances be obliged to perform duties for which the assessment has revealed a risk of exposure, which would jeopardize safety or health, to the agents and working conditions listed in Annex II, Section A;

2. workers who are breastfeeding, within the meaning of Article 2 (c), may under no circumstances be obliged to perform duties for which the assessment has revealed a risk of exposure, which would jeopardize safety or health, to the agents and working conditions listed in Annex II, Section B.

Article 7 Night work

1. Member States shall take the necessary measures to ensure that workers referred to in Article 2 are not obliged to perform night work during their pregnancy and for a period following childbirth which shall be determined by the national authority competent for safety and health, subject to submission, in accordance with the procedures laid down by the Member States, of a medical certificate stating that this is necessary for the safety or health of the worker concerned.

2. The measures referred to in paragraph 1 must entail the possibility, in accordance with national legislation and/or national practice, of:
   (a) transfer to daytime work; or
   (b) leave from work or extension of maternity leave where such a transfer is not technically and/or objectively feasible or cannot reasonably by required on duly substantiated grounds.

Article 8 Maternity leave

1. Member States shall take the necessary measures to ensure that workers within the meaning of Article 2 are entitled to a continuous period of maternity leave of a least 14 weeks allocated before and/or after confinement in accordance with national legislation and/or practice.

2. The maternity leave stipulated in paragraph 1 must include compulsory maternity leave of at least two weeks allocated before and/or after confinement in accordance with national legislation and/or practice.

Article 9 Time off for ante-natal examinations

Member States shall take the necessary measures to ensure that pregnant workers within the meaning of Article 2 (a) are entitled to, in accordance with national legislation and/or practice, time off, without loss of pay, in order to attend ante-natal examinations, if such examinations have to take place during working hours.

Article 10 Prohibition of dismissal

In order to guarantee workers, within the meaning of Article 2, the exercise of their health and safety protection rights as recognized under this Article, it shall be provided that:

1. Member States shall take the necessary measures to prohibit the dismissal of workers, within the meaning of Article 2, during the period from the beginning of their pregnancy to the end of the maternity leave referred to in Article 8 (1), save in exceptional cases not connected with their condition which are permitted under national legislation and/or practice and, where applicable, provided that the competent authority has given its consent;

2. if a worker, within the meaning of Article 2, is dismissed during the period referred to in point 1, the employer must cite duly substantiated grounds for her dismissal in writing;

3. Member States shall take the necessary measures to protect workers, within the meaning of Article 2, from consequences of dismissal which is unlawful by virtue of point 1.

Article 11 Employment rights

In order to guarantee workers within the meaning of Article 2 the exercise of their health and safety protection rights as recognized in this Article, it shall be provided that:

1.   in the cases referred to in Articles 5, 6 and 7, the employment rights relating to the employment contract, including the maintenance of a payment to, and/or entitlement to an adequate allowance for, workers within the meaning of Article 2, must be ensured in accordance with national legislation and/or national practice;

2.   in the case referred to in Article 8, the following must be ensured:
      (a) the rights connected with the employment contract of workers within the meaning of Article 2, other than those referred to in point (b) below;
      (b) maintenance of a payment to, and/or entitlement to an adequate allowance for, workers within the meaning of Article 2;

3.   the allowance referred to in point 2 (b) shall be deemed adequate if it guarantees income at least equivalent to that which the worker concerned would receive in the event of a break in her activities on grounds connected with her state of health, subject to any ceiling laid down under national legislation;

4.   Member States may make entitlement to pay or the allowance referred to in points 1 and 2 (b) conditional upon the worker concerned fulfilling the conditions of eligibility for such benefits laid down under national legislation.

      These conditions may under no circumstances provide for periods of previous employment in excess of 12 months immediately prior to the presumed date of confinement.

Article 12 Defence of rights

Member States shall introduce into their national legal systems such measures as are necessary to enable all workers who should themselves wronged by failure to comply with the obligations arising from this Directive to pursue their claims by judicial process (and/or, in accordance with national laws and/or practices) by recourse to other competent authorities.

Article 13 Amendments to the Annexes

1.   Strictly technical adjustments to Annex I as a result of technical progress, changes in international regulations or specifications and new findings in the area covered by this Directive shall be adopted in accordance with the procedure laid down in Article 17 of Directive 89/391/EEC.

2.   Annex II may be amended only in accordance with the procedure laid down in Article 118a of the Treaty [Article 153 TFEU].

Article 14 Final provisions

1.   Member States shall bring into force the laws, regulations and administrative provisions necessary to comply with this Directive not later than two years after the adoption thereof or ensure, at the latest two years after adoption of this Directive, that the two sides of industry introduce the requisite provisions by means of collective agreements, with Member States being required to make all the necessary provisions to enable them at all times to guarantee the results laid down by this Directive. They shall forthwith inform the Commission thereof.

2.   When Member States adopt the measures referred to in paragraph 1, they shall contain a reference of this Directive or shall be accompanied by such reference on the occasion of their official publication. The methods of making such a reference shall be laid down by the Member States.

3.   Member States shall communicate to the Commission the texts of the essential provisions of national law which they have already adopted or adopt in the field governed by this Directive.

Article 15
This Directive is addressed to the Member States.

(date of signing and signatory omitted)

ANNEXES *(omitted)*

DIRECTIVE 2003/88/EC OF THE EUROPEAN PARLIAMENT AND OF THE COUNCIL OF 4 NOVEMBER 2003

concerning certain aspects of the organisation of working time
OJ L 299, 18.11.2003, P. 9[1]

FORTHCOMING AMENDMENTS: The European Commission proposed amendments to this directive in a Communication published in 2004, COM(2004) 607, and a revised proposal in COM(2005) 246. Following political deadlock the Commission launched consulations in 2010 – see COM(2010) 106 and COM(2010) 802. In November 2011 the social partners indicated a willingness to attempt to negotiate a revised text over a maximum nine-month period. See further, the European industrial relations observatory on-line < http://www.eurofound.europa. eu/eiro/2011/11/articles/eu1111051i.htm> accessed 20 May 2012.

(footnotes omitted)

THE EUROPEAN PARLIAMENT AND THE COUNCIL OF THE EUROPEAN UNION,

Having regard to the Treaty establishing the European Community, and in particular Article 137(2) thereof,

Having regard to the proposal from the Commission,

Having regard to the opinion of the European Economic and Social Committee,

Having consulted the Committee of the Regions,

Acting in accordance with the procedure referred to in Article 251 of the Treaty,

Whereas:
(1)   Council Directive 93/104/EC of 23 November 1993, concerning certain aspects of the organisation of working time, which lays down minimum safety and health requirements for the organisation of working time, in respect of periods of daily rest, breaks, weekly rest, maximum weekly working time, annual leave and aspects of night work, shift work and patterns of work, has been significantly amended. In order to clarify matters, a codification of the provisions in question should be drawn up.

....

[1]   EDITOR'S NOTE: Directive 2003/88 repealed and replaced Directive 93/104/EC and its amendment, Directive 2000/34/EC. See the Correlation Table in Annex II below to convert article numbers from the original Directive. For conversion of the Treaty numbers from the EC Treaty to the Treaty on the Functioning of the European Union (TFEU) refer to the Table of Equivalences for the TFEU in Part II of this edition.

(2)   Article 137 of the Treaty provides that the Community is to support and complement the activities of the Member States with a view to improving the working environment to protect workers' health and safety. Directives adopted on the basis of that Article are to avoid imposing administrative, financial and legal constraints in a way which would hold back the creation and development of small and medium-sized undertakings.

(3)   The provisions of Council Directive 89/391/EEC of 12 June 1989 on the introduction of measures to encourage improvements in the safety and health of workers at work remain fully applicable to the areas covered by this Directive without prejudice to more stringent and/or specific provisions contained herein.

(4)   The improvement of workers' safety, hygiene and health at work is an objective which should not be subordinated to purely economic considerations.

(5)   All workers should have adequate rest periods. The concept of "rest" must be expressed in units of time, i.e. in days, hours and/or fractions thereof. Community workers must be granted minimum daily, weekly and annual periods of rest and adequate breaks. It is also necessary in this context to place a maximum limit on weekly working hours.

(6)   Account should be taken of the principles of the International Labour Organisation with regard to the organisation of working time, including those relating to night work.

(7)   Research has shown that the human body is more sensitive at night to environmental disturbances and also to certain burdensome forms of work organisation and that long periods of night work can be detrimental to the health of workers and can endanger safety at the workplace.

(8)   There is a need to limit the duration of periods of night work, including overtime, and to provide for employers who regularly use night workers to bring this information to the attention of the competent authorities if they so request.

(9)   It is important that night workers should be entitled to a free health assessment prior to their assignment and thereafter at regular intervals and that whenever possible they should be transferred to day work for which they are suited if they suffer from health problems.

(10)   The situation of night and shift workers requires that the level of safety and health protection should be adapted to the nature of their work and that the organisation and functioning of protection and prevention services and resources should be efficient.

(11)   Specific working conditions may have detrimental effects on the safety and health of workers. The organisation of work according to a certain pattern must take account of the general principle of adapting work to the worker.

(12)   A European Agreement in respect of the working time of seafarers has been put into effect by means of Council Directive 1999/63/EC of 21 June 1999 concerning the Agreement on the organisation of working time of seafarers concluded by the European Community Shipowners' Association (ECSA) and the Federation of Transport Workers' Unions in the European Union (FST) based on Article 139(2) of the Treaty. Accordingly, the provisions of this Directive should not apply to seafarers.

(13)   In the case of those "share-fishermen" who are employees, it is for the Member States to determine, pursuant to this Directive, the conditions for entitlement to, and granting of, annual leave, including the arrangements for payments.

(14)   Specific standards laid down in other Community instruments relating, for example, to rest periods, working time, annual leave and night work for certain categories of workers should take precedence over the provisions of this Directive.

(15) In view of the question likely to be raised by the organisation of working time within an undertaking, it appears desirable to provide for flexibility in the application of certain provisions of this Directive, whilst ensuring compliance with the principles of protecting the safety and health of workers.

(16) It is necessary to provide that certain provisions may be subject to derogations implemented, according to the case, by the Member States or the two sides of industry. As a general rule, in the event of a derogation, the workers concerned must be given equivalent compensatory rest periods.

(17) This Directive should not affect the obligations of the Member States concerning the deadlines for transposition of the Directives set out in Annex I, part B,

HAVE ADOPTED THIS DIRECTIVE:

Chapter 1 SCOPE AND DEFINITIONS

Article 1 Purpose and scope

1.   This Directive lays down minimum safety and health requirements for the organisation of working time.

2.   This Directive applies to:
   (a) minimum periods of daily rest, weekly rest and annual leave, to breaks and maximum weekly working time; and
   (b) certain aspects of night work, shift work and patterns of work.

3.   This Directive shall apply to all sectors of activity, both public and private, within the meaning of Article 2 of Directive 89/391/EEC, without prejudice to Articles 14, 17, 18 and 19 of this Directive.

   This Directive shall not apply to seafarers, as defined in Directive 1999/63/EC without prejudice to Article 2(8) of this Directive.

4.   The provisions of Directive 89/391/EEC are fully applicable to the matters referred to in paragraph 2, without prejudice to more stringent and/or specific provisions contained in this Directive.

Article 2 Definitions

For the purposes of this Directive, the following definitions shall apply:

1.   "working time" means any period during which the worker is working, at the employer's disposal and carrying out his activity or duties, in accordance with national laws and/or practice;

2.   "rest period" means any period which is not working time;

3.   "night time" means any period of not less than seven hours, as defined by national law, and which must include, in any case, the period between midnight and 5.00;

4.   "night worker" means:
   (a) on the one hand, any worker, who, during night time, works at least three hours of his daily working time as a normal course; and
   (b) on the other hand, any worker who is likely during night time to work a certain proportion of his annual working time, as defined at the choice of the Member State concerned:
      (i)   by national legislation, following consultation with the two sides of industry; or
      (ii) by collective agreements or agreements concluded between the two sides of industry at national or regional level;

5.   "shift work" means any method of organising work in shifts whereby workers succeed each other at the same work stations according to a certain pattern, including a rotating pattern, and which may be continuous or discontinuous, entailing the need for workers to work at different times over a given period of days or weeks;

6.   "shift worker" means any worker whose work schedule is part of shift work;

7.   "mobile worker" means any worker employed as a member of travelling or flying personnel by an undertaking which operates transport services for passengers or goods by road, air or inland waterway;

8.   "offshore work" means work performed mainly on or from offshore installations (including drilling rigs), directly or indirectly in connection with the exploration, extraction or exploitation of mineral resources, including hydrocarbons, and diving in connection with such activities, whether performed from an offshore installation or a vessel;

9.   "adequate rest" means that workers have regular rest periods, the duration of which is expressed in units of time and which are sufficiently long and continuous to ensure that, as a result of fatigue or other irregular working patterns, they do not cause injury to themselves, to fellow workers or to others and that they do not damage their health, either in the short term or in the longer term.

Chapter 2 MINIMUM REST PERIODS – OTHER ASPECTS OF THE ORGANISATION OF WORKING TIME

Article 3 Daily rest
Member States shall take the measures necessary to ensure that every worker is entitled to a minimum daily rest period of 11 consecutive hours per 24-hour period.

Article 4 Breaks
Member States shall take the measures necessary to ensure that, where the working day is longer than six hours, every worker is entitled to a rest break, the details of which, including duration and the terms on which it is granted, shall be laid down in collective agreements or agreements between the two sides of industry or, failing that, by national legislation.

Article 5 Weekly rest period
Member States shall take the measures necessary to ensure that, per each seven-day period, every worker is entitled to a minimum uninterrupted rest period of 24 hours plus the 11 hours' daily rest referred to in Article 3.

If objective, technical or work organisation conditions so justify, a minimum rest period of 24 hours may be applied.

Article 6 Maximum weekly working time
Member States shall take the measures necessary to ensure that, in keeping with the need to protect the safety and health of workers:
(a)   the period of weekly working time is limited by means of laws, regulations or administrative provisions or by collective agreements or agreements between the two sides of industry;

(b)   the average working time for each seven-day period, including overtime, does not exceed 48 hours.

Article 7 Annual leave
1.   Member States shall take the measures necessary to ensure that every worker is entitled to paid annual leave of at least four weeks in accordance with the conditions for entitlement to, and granting of, such leave laid down by national legislation and/or practice.

2.   The minimum period of paid annual leave may not be replaced by an allowance in lieu, except where the employment relationship is terminated.

Chapter 3 NIGHT WORK – SHIFT WORK – PATTERNS OF WORK

Article 8 Length of night work
Member States shall take the measures necessary to ensure that:
(a)   normal hours of work for night workers do not exceed an average of eight hours in any 24-hour period;

(b)   night workers whose work involves special hazards or heavy physical or mental strain do not work more than eight hours in any period of 24 hours during which they perform night work.

For the purposes of point (b), work involving special hazards or heavy physical or mental strain shall be defined by national legislation and/or practice or by collective agreements or agreements concluded between the two sides of industry, taking account of the specific effects and hazards of night work.

Article 9 Health assessment and transfer of night workers to day work
1.   Member States shall take the measures necessary to ensure that:
(a)   night workers are entitled to a free health assessment before their assignment and thereafter at regular intervals;
(b)   night workers suffering from health problems recognised as being connected with the fact that they perform night work are transferred whenever possible to day work to which they are suited.

2.   The free health assessment referred to in paragraph 1(a) must comply with medical confidentiality.

3.   The free health assessment referred to in paragraph 1(a) may be conducted within the national health system.

Article 10 Guarantees for night-time working
Member States may make the work of certain categories of night workers subject to certain guarantees, under conditions laid down by national legislation and/or practice, in the case of workers who incur risks to their safety or health linked to night-time working.

Article 11 Notification of regular use of night workers
Member States shall take the measures necessary to ensure that an employer who regularly uses night workers brings this information to the attention of the competent authorities if they so request.

Article 12 Safety and health protection
Member States shall take the measures necessary to ensure that:
(a)   night workers and shift workers have safety and health protection appropriate to the nature of their work;

(b)   appropriate protection and prevention services or facilities with regard to the safety and health of night workers and shift workers are equivalent to those applicable to other workers and are available at all times.

Article 13 Pattern of work
Member States shall take the measures necessary to ensure that an employer who intends to organise work according to a certain pattern takes account of the general principle of adapting work to the worker, with a view, in particular, to alleviating monotonous work and work at a predetermined work-rate, depending on the type of activity, and of safety and health requirements, especially as regards breaks during working time.

Chapter 4 MISCELLANEOUS PROVISIONS

Article 14 More specific Community provisions
This Directive shall not apply where other Community instruments contain more specific requirements relating to the organisation of working time for certain occupations or occupational activities.

Article 15 More favourable provisions
This Directive shall not affect Member States' right to apply or introduce laws, regulations or administrative provisions more favourable to the protection of the safety and health of workers or to facilitate or permit the application of collective agreements or agreements concluded between the two sides of industry which are more favourable to the protection of the safety and health of workers.

Article 16 Reference periods
Member States may lay down:

(a)   for the application of Article 5 (weekly rest period), a reference period not exceeding 14 days;

(b)   for the application of Article 6 (maximum weekly working time), a reference period not exceeding four months.

The periods of paid annual leave, granted in accordance with Article 7, and the periods of sick leave shall not be included or shall be neutral in the calculation of the average;

(c)   for the application of Article 8 (length of night work), a reference period defined after consultation of the two sides of industry or by collective agreements or agreements concluded between the two sides of industry at national or regional level.

If the minimum weekly rest period of 24 hours required by Article 5 falls within that reference period, it shall not be included in the calculation of the average.

Chapter 5 DEROGATIONS AND EXCEPTIONS

Article 17 Derogations
1.   With due regard for the general principles of the protection of the safety and health of workers, Member States may derogate from Articles 3 to 6, 8 and 16 when, on account of the specific characteristics of the activity concerned, the duration of the working time is not measured and/or predetermined or can be determined by the workers themselves, and particularly in the case of:
(a) managing executives or other persons with autonomous decision-taking powers;
(b) family workers; or
(c) workers officiating at religious ceremonies in churches and religious communities.

2.   Derogations provided for in paragraphs 3, 4 and 5 may be adopted by means of laws, regulations or administrative provisions or by means of collective agreements or agreements between the two sides of industry provided that the workers concerned are afforded equivalent periods of compensatory rest or that, in exceptional cases in which it is not possible, for objective reasons, to grant such equivalent periods of compensatory rest, the workers concerned are afforded appropriate protection.

3.   In accordance with paragraph 2 of this Article derogations may be made from Articles 3, 4, 5, 8 and 16:
(a) in the case of activities where the worker's place of work and his place of residence are distant from one another, including offshore work, or where the worker's different places of work are distant from one another;

(b) in the case of security and surveillance activities requiring a permanent presence in order to protect property and persons, particularly security guards and caretakers or security firms;

(c) in the case of activities involving the need for continuity of service or production, particularly:

   (i) services relating to the reception, treatment and/or care provided by hospitals or similar establishments, including the activities of doctors in training, residential institutions and prisons;

   (ii) dock or airport workers;

   (iii) press, radio, television, cinematographic production, postal and telecommunications services, ambulance, fire and civil protection services;

   (iv) gas, water and electricity production, transmission and distribution, household refuse collection and incineration plants;

   (v) industries in which work cannot be interrupted on technical grounds;

   (vi) research and development activities;

   (vii) agriculture;

   (viii) workers concerned with the carriage of passengers on regular urban transport services;

(d) where there is a foreseeable surge of activity, particularly in:

   (i) agriculture;

   (ii) tourism;

   (iii) postal services;

(e) in the case of persons working in railway transport:

   (i) whose activities are intermittent;

   (ii) who spend their working time on board trains; or

   (iii) whose activities are linked to transport timetables and to ensuring the continuity and regularity of traffic;

(f) in the circumstances described in Article 5(4) of Directive 89/391/EEC;

(g) in cases of accident or imminent risk of accident.

4. In accordance with paragraph 2 of this Article derogations may be made from Articles 3 and 5:

(a) in the case of shift work activities, each time the worker changes shift and cannot take daily and/or weekly rest periods between the end of one shift and the start of the next one;

(b) in the case of activities involving periods of work split up over the day, particularly those of cleaning staff.

5. In accordance with paragraph 2 of this Article, derogations may be made from Article 6 and Article 16(b), in the case of doctors in training, in accordance with the provisions set out in the second to the seventh subparagraphs of this paragraph.

With respect to Article 6 derogations referred to in the first subparagraph shall be permitted for a transitional period of five years from 1 August 2004.

Member States may have up to two more years, if necessary, to take account of difficulties in meeting the working time provisions with respect to their responsibilities for the organisation and delivery of health services and medical care. At least six months before the end of the transitional period, the Member State concerned shall inform the Commission giving its reasons, so that the Commission can give an opinion, after appropriate consultations, within the three months following receipt of such information. If the Member State does not follow the opinion of the Commission, it will justify its decision. The notification and justification of the Member State and the opinion of the

Commission shall be published in the *Official Journal of the European Union* and forwarded to the European Parliament.

Member States may have an additional period of up to one year, if necessary, to take account of special difficulties in meeting the responsibilities referred to in the third subparagraph. They shall follow the procedure set out in that subparagraph.

Member States shall ensure that in no case will the number of weekly working hours exceed an average of 58 during the first three years of the transitional period, an average of 56 for the following two years and an average of 52 for any remaining period.

The employer shall consult the representatives of the employees in good time with a view to reaching an agreement, wherever possible, on the arrangements applying to the transitional period. Within the limits set out in the fifth subparagraph, such an agreement may cover:
(a) the average number of weekly hours of work during the transitional period; and
(b) the measures to be adopted to reduce weekly working hours to an average of 48 by the end of the transitional period.

With respect to Article 16(b) derogations referred to in the first subparagraph shall be permitted provided that the reference period does not exceed 12 months, during the first part of the transitional period specified in the fifth subparagraph, and six months thereafter.

Article 18 Derogations by collective agreements

Derogations may be made from Articles 3, 4, 5, 8 and 16 by means of collective agreements or agreements concluded between the two sides of industry at national or regional level or, in conformity with the rules laid down by them, by means of collective agreements or agreements concluded between the two sides of industry at a lower level.

Member States in which there is no statutory system ensuring the conclusion of collective agreements or agreements concluded between the two sides of industry at national or regional level, on the matters covered by this Directive, or those Member States in which there is a specific legislative framework for this purpose and within the limits thereof, may, in accordance with national legislation and/or practice, allow derogations from Articles 3, 4, 5, 8 and 16 by way of collective agreements or agreements concluded between the two sides of industry at the appropriate collective level.

The derogations provided for in the first and second subparagraphs shall be allowed on condition that equivalent compensating rest periods are granted to the workers concerned or, in exceptional cases where it is not possible for objective reasons to grant such periods, the workers concerned are afforded appropriate protection.

Member States may lay down rules:
(a)   for the application of this Article by the two sides of industry; and

(b)   for the extension of the provisions of collective agreements or agreements concluded in conformity with this Article to other workers in accordance with national legislation and/or practice.

Article 19 Limitations to derogations from reference periods

The option to derogate from Article 16(b), provided for in Article 17(3) and in Article 18, may not result in the establishment of a reference period exceeding six months.

However, Member States shall have the option, subject to compliance with the general principles relating to the protection of the safety and health of workers, of allowing, for objective or technical reasons or reasons concerning the organisation of work, collective agreements or agreements concluded between the two sides of industry to set reference periods in no event exceeding 12 months.

Before 23 November 2003, the Council shall, on the basis of a Commission proposal accompanied by an appraisal report, re-examine the provisions of this Article and decide what action to take.

Article 20 Mobile workers and offshore work
1.   Articles 3, 4, 5 and 8 shall not apply to mobile workers.

Member States shall, however, take the necessary measures to ensure that such mobile workers are entitled to adequate rest, except in the circumstances laid down in Article 17(3)(f) and (g).

2.   Subject to compliance with the general principles relating to the protection of the safety and health of workers, and provided that there is consultation of representatives of the employer and employees concerned and efforts to encourage all relevant forms of social dialogue, including negotiation if the parties so wish, Member States may, for objective or technical reasons or reasons concerning the organisation of work, extend the reference period referred to in Article 16(b) to 12 months in respect of workers who mainly perform offshore work.

3.   Not later than 1 August 2005 the Commission shall, after consulting the Member States and management and labour at European level, review the operation of the provisions with regard to offshore workers from a health and safety perspective with a view to presenting, if need be, the appropriate modifications.

Article 21 Workers on board seagoing fishing vessels
1.   Articles 3 to 6 and 8 shall not apply to any worker on board a seagoing fishing vessel flying the flag of a Member State.

Member States shall, however, take the necessary measures to ensure that any worker on board a seagoing fishing vessel flying the flag of a Member State is entitled to adequate rest and to limit the number of hours of work to 48 hours a week on average calculated over a reference period not exceeding 12 months.

2.   Within the limits set out in paragraph 1, second subparagraph, and paragraphs 3 and 4 Member States shall take the necessary measures to ensure that, in keeping with the need to protect the safety and health of such workers:
(a) the working hours are limited to a maximum number of hours which shall not be exceeded in a given period of time; or
(b) a minimum number of hours of rest are provided within a given period of time.

The maximum number of hours of work or minimum number of hours of rest shall be specified by law, regulations, administrative provisions or by collective agreements or agreements between the two sides of the industry.

3.   The limits on hours of work or rest shall be either:
(a) maximum hours of work which shall not exceed:
   (i)   14 hours in any 24-hour period; and
   (ii) 72 hours in any seven-day period; or
(b) minimum hours of rest which shall not be less than:
   (i)   10 hours in any 24-hour period; and
   (ii) 77 hours in any seven-day period.

4.   Hours of rest may be divided into no more than two periods, one of which shall be at least six hours in length, and the interval between consecutive periods of rest shall not exceed 14 hours.

5.   In accordance with the general principles of the protection of the health and safety of workers, and for objective or technical reasons or reasons concerning the organisation of work, Member States may allow exceptions, including the establishment of reference periods, to the limits laid down in paragraph 1, second subparagraph, and paragraphs 3 and 4. Such exceptions shall, as far as possible, comply with the standards laid down but may take account of more frequent or longer leave periods or the granting of compensatory leave for the workers. These exceptions may be laid down by means of:
   (a) laws, regulations or administrative provisions provided there is consultation, where possible, of the representatives of the employers and workers concerned and efforts are made to encourage all relevant forms of social dialogue; or
   (b) collective agreements or agreements between the two sides of industry.

6.   The master of a seagoing fishing vessel shall have the right to require workers on board to perform any hours of work necessary for the immediate safety of the vessel, persons on board or cargo, or for the purpose of giving assistance to other vessels or persons in distress at sea.

7.   Member States may provide that workers on board seagoing fishing vessels for which national legislation or practice determines that these vessels are not allowed to operate in a specific period of the calendar yearexceeding one month, shall take annual leave in accordance with Article 7 within that period.

Article 22 Miscellaneous provisions

1.   A Member State shall have the option not to apply Article 6, while respecting the general principles of the protection of the safety and health of workers, and provided it takes the necessary measures to ensure that:
   (a) no employer requires a worker to work more than 48 hours over a seven-day period, calculated as an average for the reference period referred to in Article 16(b), unless he has first obtained the worker's agreement to perform such work;
   (b) no worker is subjected to any detriment by his employer because he is not willing to give his agreement to perform such work;
   (c) the employer keeps up-to-date records of all workers who carry out such work;
   (d) the records are placed at the disposal of the competent authorities, which may, for reasons connected with the safety and/or health of workers, prohibit or restrict the possibility of exceeding the maximum weekly working hours;
   (e) the employer provides the competent authorities at their request with information on cases in which agreement has been given by workers to perform work exceeding 48 hours over a period of seven days, calculated as an average for the reference period referred to in Article 16(b).
Before 23 November 2003, the Council shall, on the basis of a Commission proposal accompanied by an appraisal report, re-examine the provisions of this paragraph and decide on what action to take.

2.   Member States shall have the option, as regards the application of Article 7, of making use of a transitional period of not more than three years from 23 November 1996, provided that during that transitional period:
   (a) every worker receives three weeks' paid annual leave in accordance with the conditions for the entitlement to, and granting of, such leave laid down by national legislation and/or practice; and

(b) the three-week period of paid annual leave may not be replaced by an allowance in lieu, except where the employment relationship is terminated.

3.   If Member States avail themselves of the options provided for in this Article, they shall forthwith inform the Commission thereof.

Chapter 6 FINAL PROVISIONS

Article 23 Level of Protection

Without prejudice to the right of Member States to develop, in the light of changing circumstances, different legislative, regulatory or contractual provisions in the field of working time, as long as the minimum requirements provided for in this Directive are complied with, implementation of this Directive shall not constitute valid grounds for reducing the general level of protection afforded to workers.

Article 24 Reports

1.   Member States shall communicate to the Commission the texts of the provisions of national law already adopted or being adopted in the field governed by this Directive.

2.   Member States shall report to the Commission every five years on the practical implementation of the provisions of this Directive, indicating the viewpoints of the two sides of industry.

The Commission shall inform the European Parliament, the Council, the European Economic and Social Committee and the Advisory Committee on Safety, Hygiene and Health Protection at Work thereof.

3.   Every five years from 23 November 1996 the Commission shall submit to the European Parliament, the Council and the European Economic and Social Committee a report on the application of this Directive taking into account Articles 22 and 23 and paragraphs 1 and 2 of this Article.

Article 25 Review of the operation of the provisions with regard to workers on board seagoing fishing vessels

Not later than 1 August 2009 the Commission shall, after consulting the Member States and management and labour at European level, review the operation of the provisions with regard to workers on board seagoing fishing vessels, and, in particular examine whether these provisions remain appropriate, in particular, as far as health and safety are concerned with a view to proposing suitable amendments, if necessary.

Article 26 Review of the operation of the provisions with regard to workers concerned with the carriage of passengers

Not later than 1 August 2005 the Commission shall, after consulting the Member States and management and labour at European level, review the operation of the provisions with regard to workers concerned with the carriage of passengers on regular urban transport services, with a view to presenting, if need be, the appropriate modifications to ensure a coherent and suitable approach in the sector.

Article 27 Repeal

1.   Directive 93/104/EC, as amended by the Directive referred to in Annex I, part A, shall be repealed, without prejudice to the obligations of the Member States in respect of the deadlines for transposition laid down in Annex I, part B.

2.   The references made to the said repealed Directive shall be construed as references to this Directive and shall be read in accordance with the correlation table set out in Annex II.

Article 28 Entry into force
This Directive shall enter into force on 2 August 2004.

Article 29 Addressees
This Directive is addressed to the Member States.

(Date of signing and signatories omitted)

ANNEX I (*omitted*)

ANNEX II CORRELATION TABLE

Directive 93/104/EC	This Directive
Articles 1 to 5	Articles 1 to 5
Article 6, introductory words	Article 6, introductory words
Article 6(1)	Article 6(a)
Article 6(2)	Article 6(b)
Article 7	Article 7
Article 8, introductory words	Article 8, introductory words
Article 8(1)	Article 8(a)
Article 8(2)	Article 8(b)
Articles 9, 10 and 11	Articles 9, 10 and 11
Article 12, introductory words	Article 12, introductory words
Article 12(1)	Article 12(a)
Article 12(2)	Article 12(b)
Articles 13, 14 and 15	Articles 13, 14 and 15
Article 16, introductory words	Article 16, introductory words
Article 16(1)	Article 16(a)
Article 16(2)	Article 16(b)
Article 16(3)	Article 16(c)
Article 17(1)	Article 17(1)
Article 17(2), introductory words	Article 17(2)
Article 17(2)(1)	Article 17(3)(a) to (e)
Article 17(2)(2)	Article 17(3)(f) to (g)
Article 17(2)(3)	Article 17(4)
Article 17(2)(4)	Article 17(5)
Article 17(3)	Article 18
Article 17(4)	Article 19
Article 17a(1)	Article 20(1), first subpara.
Article 17a(2)	Article 20(1), second subpara.
Article 17a(3)	Article 20(2)

Directive 93/104/EC	This Directive
Article 17a(4)	Article 20(3)
Article 17b(1)	Article 21(1), first subparagraph
Article 17b(2)	Article 21(1), second subparagraph
Article 17b(3)	Article 21(2)
Article 17b(4)	Article 21(3)
Article 17b(5)	Article 21(4)
Article 17b(6)	Article 21(5)
Article 17b(7)	Article 21(6)
Article 17b(8)	Article 21(7)
Article 18(1)(a)	—
Article 18(1)(b)(i)	Article 22(1)
Article 18(1)(b)(ii)	Article 22(2)
Article 18(1)(c)	Article 22(3)
Article 18(2)	—
Article 18(3)	Article 23
Article 18(4)	Article 24(1)
Article 18(5)	Article 24(2)
Article 18(6)	Article 24(3)
—	Article 25 (1)
—	Article 26 (2)
—	Article 27
—	Article 28
Article 19	Article 29
—	Annex I
—	Annex II

COUNCIL DIRECTIVE 2010/18/EU OF 8 MARCH 2010
implementing the revised Framework Agreement on parental leave concluded by
BUSINESSEUROPE, UEAPME, CEEP and ETUC and repealing Directive 96/34/EC

OJ L 68, 18.3.2010, P. 13

(footnotes and preamble omitted)

Article 1
This Directive puts into effect the revised Framework Agreement on parental leave concluded
on 18 June 2009 by the European cross-industry social partner organisations
(BUSINESSEUROPE, UEAPME, CEEP and ETUC), as set out in the Annex.

Article 2

Member States shall determine what penalties are applicable when national provisions enacted pursuant to this Directive are infringed. The penalties shall be effective, proportionate and dissuasive.

Article 3

1.   Member States shall bring into force the laws, regulations and administrative provisions necessary to comply with this Directive or shall ensure that the social partners have introduced the necessary measures by agreement by 8 March 2012 at the latest. They shall forthwith inform the Commission thereof.

When those provisions are adopted by Member States, they shall contain a reference to this Directive or shall be accompanied by such reference on the occasion of their official publication. The methods of making such reference shall be laid down by Member States.

2.   Member States may have a maximum additional period of one year to comply with this Directive, if this is necessary to take account of particular difficulties or implementation by collective agreement. They shall inform the Commission thereof by 8 March 2012 at the latest, stating the reasons for which an additional period is required.

3.   Member States shall communicate to the Commission the text of the main provisions of national law which they adopt in the field covered by this Directive.

Article 4

Directive 96/34/EC shall be repealed with effect from 8 March 2012. References to Directive 96/34/EC shall be construed as references to this Directive.

Article 5

This Directive shall enter into force on the 20th day following its publication in the Official Journal of the European Union.

Article 6

This Directive is addressed to the Member States.

(Date and place of signing and signatories omitted)

ANNEX

FRAMEWORK AGREEMENT ON PARENTAL LEAVE (REVISED)

18 June 2009

PREAMBLE

This framework agreement between the European social partners, BUSINESSEUROPE, UEAPME, CEEP and ETUC (and the liaison committee Eurocadres/CEC) revises the framework agreement on parental leave, concluded on 14 December 1995, setting out the minimum requirements on parental leave, as an important means of reconciling professional and family responsibilities and promoting equal opportunities and treatment between men and women.

The European social partners request the Commission to submit this framework agreement to the Council for a Council decision making these requirements binding in the Member States of the European Union.

I. GENERAL CONSIDERATIONS

1.   Having regard to the EC Treaty and in particular Articles 138 and 139 thereof[*];

2.   Having regard to Articles 137(1)(c) and 141 of the EC Treaty [**] and the principle of equal treatment (Articles 2, 3 and 13 of the EC Treaty [***]) and the secondary legislation based on this, in particular Council Directive 75/117/EEC on the approximation of the laws of the Member States relating to the application of the principle of equal pay for men and women; Council Directive 92/85/EEC on the introduction of measures to encourage improvements in the safety and health at work of pregnant workers and workers who have recently given birth or are breastfeeding; Council Directive 96/97/EC amending Directive 86/378/EEC on the implementation of the principle of equal treatment for men and women in occupational social security schemes; and Directive 2006/54/EC on the implementation of the principle of equal opportunities and equal treatment of men and women in matters of employment and occupation (recast);

3.   Having regard to the Charter of Fundamental Rights of the European Union of 7 December 2000 and Articles 23 and 33 thereof relating to equality between men and women and reconciliation of professional, private and family life;

4.   Having regard to the 2003 Report from the Commission on the Implementation of Council Directive 96/34/EC of 3 June 1996 on the framework agreement on parental leave concluded by UNICE, CEEP and the ETUC;

5.   Having regard to the objective of the Lisbon strategy on growth and jobs of increasing overall employment rates to 70 %, women's employment rates to 60 % and the employment rates of older workers to 50 %; to the Barcelona targets on the provision of childcare facilities; and to the contribution of policies to improve reconciliation of professional, private and family life in achieving these targets;

6.   Having regard to the European social partners' Framework of Actions on Gender Equality of 22 March 2005 in which supporting work-life balance is addressed as a priority area for action, while recognising that, in order to continue to make progress on the issue of reconciliation, a balanced, integrated and coherent policy mix must be put in place, comprising of leave arrangements, working arrangements and care infrastructures;

7.   Whereas measures to improve reconciliation are part of a broader policy agenda to address the needs of employers and workers and improve adaptability and employability, as part of a flexicurity approach;

8.   Whereas family policies should contribute to the achievement of gender equality and be looked at in the context of demographic changes, the effects of an ageing population, closing the generation gap, promoting women's participation in the labour force and the sharing of care responsibilities between women and men;

9.   Whereas the Commission has consulted the European social partners in 2006 and 2007 in a first and second stage consultation on reconciliation of professional, private and family life, and, among other things, has addressed the issue of updating the regulatory framework at Community level, and has encouraged the European social partners to assess the provisions of their framework agreement on parental leave with a view to its review;

10.   Whereas the Framework agreement of the European social partners of 1995 on parental leave has been a catalyst for positive change, ensured common ground on work life balance in the Member States and played a significant role in helping working parents in Europe to achieve better reconciliation; however, on the basis of a joint evaluation, the

European social partners consider that certain elements of the agreement need to be adapted or revised in order to better achieve its aims;

11. Whereas certain aspects need to be adapted, taking into account the growing diversity of the labour force and societal developments including the increasing diversity of family structures, while respecting national law, collective agreements and/or practice;

12. Whereas in many Member States encouraging men to assume an equal share of family responsibilities has not led to sufficient results; therefore, more effective measures should be taken to encourage a more equal sharing of family responsibilities between men and women;

13. Whereas many Member States already have a wide variety of policy measures and practices relating to leave facilities, childcare and flexible working arrangements, tailored to the needs of workers and employers and aiming to support parents in reconciling their professional, private and family life; these should be taken into account when implementing this agreement;

14. Whereas this framework agreement provides one element of European social partners' actions in the field of reconciliation;

15. Whereas this agreement is a framework agreement setting out minimum requirements and provisions for parental leave, distinct from maternity leave, and for time off from work on grounds of force majeure, and refers back to Member States and social partners for the establishment of conditions for access and modalities of application in order to take account of the situation in each Member State;

16. Whereas the right of parental leave in this agreement is an individual right and in principle non-transferable, and Member States are allowed to make it transferable. Experience shows that making the leave non-transferable can act as a positive incentive for the take up by fathers, the European social partners therefore agree to make a part of the leave non-transferable;

17. Whereas it is important to take into account the special needs of parents with children with disabilities or long term illness;

18. Whereas Member States should provide for the maintenance of entitlements to benefits in kind under sickness insurance during the minimum period of parental leave;

19. Whereas Member States should also, where appropriate under national conditions and taking into account the budgetary situation, consider the maintenance of entitlements to relevant social security benefits as they stand during the minimum period of parental leave as well as the role of income among other factors in the take-up of parental leave when implementing this agreement;

20. Whereas experiences in Member States have shown that the level of income during parental leave is one factor that influences the take up by parents, especially fathers;

21. Whereas the access to flexible working arrangements makes it easier for parents to combine work and parental responsibilities and facilitates the reintegration into work, especially after returning from parental leave;

22. Whereas parental leave arrangements are meant to support working parents during a specific period of time, aimed at maintaining and promoting their continued labour market participation; therefore, greater attention should be paid to keeping in contact with the employer during the leave or by making arrangements for return to work;

23. Whereas this agreement takes into consideration the need to improve social policy requirements, to enhance the competitiveness of the European Union economy and to avoid imposing administrative, financial and legal constraints in a way which would hold back the creation and development of small and medium sized undertakings;

24. Whereas the social partners are best placed to find solutions that correspond to the needs of both employers and workers and shall therefore play a special role in the implementation, application, monitoring and evaluation of this agreement, in the broader context of other measures to improve the reconciliation of professional and family responsibilities and to promote equal opportunities and treatment between men and women.

THE SIGNATORY PARTIES HAVE AGREED THE FOLLOWING:

II. CONTENT

Clause 1: Purpose and scope

1. This agreement lays down minimum requirements designed to facilitate the reconciliation of parental and professional responsibilities for working parents, taking into account the increasing diversity of family structures while respecting national law, collective agreements and/or practice.

2. This agreement applies to all workers, men and women, who have an employment contract or employment relationship as defined by the law, collective agreements and/or practice in force in each Member State.

3. Member States and/or social partners shall not exclude from the scope and application of this agreement workers, contracts of employment or employment relationships solely because they relate to part-time workers, fixed-term contract workers or persons with a contract of employment or employment relationship with a temporary agency.

Clause 2: Parental leave

1. This agreement entitles men and women workers to an individual right to parental leave on the grounds of the birth or adoption of a child to take care of that child until a given age up to eight years to be defined by Member States and/or social partners.

2. The leave shall be granted for at least a period of four months and, to promote equal opportunities and equal treatment between men and women, should, in principle, be provided on a non-transferable basis. To encourage a more equal take-up of leave by both parents, at least one of the four months shall be provided on a non-transferable basis. The modalities of application of the non-transferable period shall be set down at national level through legislation and/or collective agreements taking into account existing leave arrangements in the Member States.

Clause 3: Modalities of application

1. The conditions of access and detailed rules for applying parental leave shall be defined by law and/or collective agreements in the Member States, as long as the minimum requirements of this agreement are respected. Member States and/or social partners may, in particular:
   (a) decide whether parental leave is granted on a full-time or part-time basis, in a piecemeal way or in the form of a time-credit system, taking into account the needs of both employers and workers;

(b) make entitlement to parental leave subject to a period of work qualification and/or a length of service qualification which shall not exceed one year; Member States and/or social partners shall ensure, when making use of this provision, that in case of successive fixed term contracts, as defined in Council Directive 1999/70/EC on fixed-term work, with the same employer the sum of these contracts shall be taken into account for the purpose of calculating the qualifying period;

(c) define the circumstances in which an employer, following consultation in accordance with national law, collective agreements and/or practice, is allowed to postpone the granting of parental leave for justifiable reasons related to the operation of the organisation. Any problem arising from the application of this provision should be dealt with in accordance with national law, collective agreements and/or practice;

(d) in addition to (c), authorise special arrangements to meet the operational and organisational requirements of small undertakings.

2.   Member States and/or social partners shall establish notice periods to be given by the worker to the employer when exercising the right to parental leave, specifying the beginning and the end of the period of leave. Member States and/or social partners shall have regard to the interests of workers and of employers in specifying the length of such notice periods.

3.   Member States and/or social partners should assess the need to adjust the conditions for access and modalities of application of parental leave to the needs of parents of children with a disability or a long-term illness.

Clause 4: Adoption

1.   Member States and/or social partners shall assess the need for additional measures to address the specific needs of adoptive parents.

Clause 5: Employment rights and non-discrimination

1.   At the end of parental leave, workers shall have the right to return to the same job or, if that is not possible, to an equivalent or similar job consistent with their employment contract or employment relationship.

2.   Rights acquired or in the process of being acquired by the worker on the date on which parental leave starts shall be maintained as they stand until the end of parental leave. At the end of parental leave, these rights, including any changes arising from national law, collective agreements and/or practice, shall apply.

3.   Member States and/or social partners shall define the status of the employment contract or employment relationship for the period of parental leave.

4.   In order to ensure that workers can exercise their right to parental leave, Member States and/or social partners shall take the necessary measures to protect workers against less favourable treatment or dismissal on the grounds of an application for, or the taking of, parental leave in accordance with national law, collective agreements and/or practice.

5.   All matters regarding social security in relation to this agreement are for consideration and determination by Member States and/or social partners according to national law and/or collective agreements, taking into account the importance of the continuity of the entitlements to social security cover under the different schemes, in particular health care.

All matters regarding income in relation to this agreement are for consideration and determination by Member States and/or social partners according to national law, collective agreements and/or practice, taking into account the role of income – among other factors – in the take-up of parental leave.

Clause 6: Return to work

1. In order to promote better reconciliation, Member States and/or social partners shall take the necessary measures to ensure that workers, when returning from parental leave, may request changes to their working hours and/or patterns for a set period of time. Employers shall consider and respond to such requests, taking into account both employers' and workers' needs.

   The modalities of this paragraph shall be determined in accordance with national law, collective agreements and/or practice.

2. In order to facilitate the return to work following parental leave, workers and employers are encouraged to maintain contact during the period of leave and may make arrangements for any appropriate reintegration measures, to be decided between the parties concerned, taking into account national law, collective agreements and/or practice.

Clause 7: Time off from work on grounds of force majeure

1. Member States and/or social partners shall take the necessary measures to entitle workers to time off from work, in accordance with national legislation, collective agreements and/or practice, on grounds of force majeure for urgent family reasons in cases of sickness or accident making the immediate presence of the worker indispensable.

2. Member States and/or social partners may specify the conditions of access and detailed rules for applying clause 7.1 and limit this entitlement to a certain amount of time per year and/or per case.

Clause 8: Final provisions

1. Member States may apply or introduce more favourable provisions than those set out in this agreement.

2. Implementation of the provisions of this agreement shall not constitute valid grounds for reducing the general level of protection afforded to workers in the field covered by this agreement. This shall not prejudice the right of Member States and/or social partners to develop different legislative, regulatory or contractual provisions, in the light of changing circumstances (including the introduction of non-transferability), as long as the minimum requirements provided for in the present agreement are complied with.

3. This agreement shall not prejudice the right of social partners to conclude, at the appropriate level including European level, agreements adapting and/or complementing the provisions of this agreement in order to take into account particular circumstances.

4. Member States shall adopt the laws, regulations and administrative provisions necessary to comply with the Council decision within a period of two years from its adoption or shall ensure that social partners introduce the necessary measures by way of agreement by the end of this period. Member States may, if necessary to take account of particular difficulties or implementation by collective agreements, have up to a maximum of one additional year to comply with this decision.

5. The prevention and settlement of disputes and grievances arising from the application of this agreement shall be dealt with in accordance with national law, collective agreements and/or practice.

6.   Without prejudice to the respective role of the Commission, national courts and the European Court of Justice, any matter relating to the interpretation of this agreement at European level should, in the first instance, be referred by the Commission to the signatory parties who will give an opinion.

7.   The signatory parties shall review the application of this agreement five years after the date of the Council decision if requested by one of the parties to this agreement.

(Date, place of signing and names of signatories omitted)

---

[*]   Renumbered: Articles 154 and 155 of the TFEU.
[**]   Renumbered: Articles 153(1)c and 157 of the TFEU.
[***]   Article 2 of the EC Treaty is repealed and replaced, in substance, by Article 3 of the Treaty on the European Union. Article 3(1) of the EC Treaty is repealed and replaced, in substance, by Articles 3 to 6 of the TFEU. Article 3(2) of the EC Treaty is renumbered as Article 8 of the TFEU. Article 13 of the EC Treaty is renumbered as Article 19 of the TFEU.

Thematic Index